Chambers
primary
dictionary

Chambers

CHAMBERS

An imprint of Chambers Harrap Publishers Ltd
7 Hopetoun Crescent
Edinburgh, EH7 4AY

Previous edition published 2002
This edition published by Chambers Harrap Publishers Ltd 2008

A CIP catalogue record for this book is available from the British Library.

ISBN 978 0550 10319 2

Designed and typeset by Chambers Harrap Publishers Ltd, Edinburgh
Printed in Italy by L.E.G.O. S.p.A., Lavis (TN)

Contents

Contributors

Project Editor
Mary O'Neill

Editors
Lucy Hollingworth
Howard Sargeant

Data Management
Patrick Gaherty

Prepress
Becky Pickard

The editors would like to acknowledge with thanks the assistance and advice of the following:

Briar Hill Lower School, Northampton
Chirnside Primary School, Chirnside, Scottish Borders
Hatherleigh Community Primary School, Hatherleigh, Devon
Ide First School, Ide, Exeter
St Patrick's Primary School, Coatbridge, Lanarkshire
Woodlands Junior School, Tonbridge, Kent

Preface

Chambers Primary Dictionary has been specially written for use by primary school pupils aged 7–11, and this edition complements the renewed Primary Framework in England and Wales, the revised Key Stage 2 Curriculum in Northern Ireland and National Guidelines in Scotland. It has been compiled with the benefit of advice from a number of primary school teachers, ensuring that the book provides all the information a pupil at this level needs in the most straightforward terms.

Over 10,000 look-up words give wide coverage, including definitions of words used in subjects such as mathematics and science at Key Stage 2. Labelled pictures have been chosen not just to lend attractiveness to the page, but to illustrate, for example, the parts of a flower and the planets in the solar system.

To encourage young dictionary users, definitions are worded so that all children can easily understand them, and examples have been carefully selected to make the meaning and use of the words even more clear. In many cases, these examples have been taken directly from our corpus of children's literature, a resource which has helped the editors to make informed decisions about the words a child is likely to meet in his or her reading.

Further assistance with language is provided by clear, coloured word class labels (noun, verb, etc). The inclusion of full-out forms such as the plurals of nouns and past tenses of verbs makes such forms easy to identify and spell. Extra pieces of important and interesting information, such as homophones that can be confused and word histories, are included in short, eye-catching boxes. It is all these features that make *Chambers Primary Dictionary* an invaluable resource for primary school pupils, in dictionary work and for everyday reference.

www

For lots of free online resources that can be used in conjunction with the dictionary, visit our website at

www.chamberslearning.com

Illustrations in this book

There are some pictures in this dictionary. These give you lots more information about things like **cars** and **flowers** by showing you what the different parts of them are called.

Some of the pictures, such as **angles**, show you examples of something.

Here is a list of the pictures in the book and the pages where you will find them.

How do I use my Primary Dictionary?

A **dictionary** is a book that contains lists of words and their meanings, in alphabetical order.

You can use a dictionary to find out what a word means, but there are other things you can use it for. For example, you can use a dictionary to check that you have spelt a word correctly or said it properly.

How do I find a word?

Imagine that you want to look up the word **balloon**.

❶ The alphabet down the side of the page shows you the letter that the words on that page begin with, so you look for the pages where **Bb** is marked.

Aa

Bb

Cc

Dd

❷ The blue words at the top of the page show you which words appear in alphabetical order on that page, for example on page 38:

ball → bangle

Because the word **balloon** comes between these two words in alphabetical order, you know to look for it on that page.

❸ The words that you look up are in alphabetical order. These words are large and coloured blue so it is easy to find them.

ballet
balloon

The look-up word and the block of information below it is called a dictionary **entry**.

❹ You might find the word you want marked with a blue arrow like this ▸. A word in **blue** after a blue arrow is part of the **word family** of the main word. It will be in alphabetical order after the look-up word.

> **absolute** ADJECTIVE complete: *absolute rubbish*
> ▸ **absolutely** ADVERB **1** completely: *absolutely ridiculous* **2** yes, certainly: *'Please can I have one of those?' 'Absolutely.'*

❺ What if the word you are looking for is part of a **phrase**? A phrase is a group of words that always appear together and have a single meaning. For example, *better off* and *keep count* are phrases.
Some of these phrases are **idioms**. These are phrases with a very special meaning that you cannot work out from the meanings of the words themselves. For example, *bury the hatchet* and *let the cat out of the bag* are idioms.
Phrases and idioms like these come after a blue dot •. All you need to do is look up the main word in the phrase, and if the phrase is there you will spot it right away and find the meaning.

> **cat** NOUN **cats 1** an animal, often kept as a pet, that has soft fur and claws **2** any animal that belongs to the family of animals that includes cats, lions, leopards and tigers
> • **let the cat out of the bag** if you let the cat out of the bag, you tell people something that they aren't supposed to know

What will my dictionary tell me?

❶ If it is hard to guess how to say the word from its spelling, the dictionary will tell you how to say it.

> **bouquet** (pronounced **book**-ay)

The word is shown in sounds you will recognize from the spelling.

ai	is the sound your hear in the words	p<u>ai</u>n, tr<u>ai</u>n
ay	is the sound your hear in the words	d<u>ay</u>, pl<u>ay</u>
ie	is the sound your hear in the words	l<u>ie</u>, t<u>ie</u>
o	is the sound your hear in the words	c<u>o</u>t, st<u>o</u>p
oa	is the sound your hear in the words	l<u>oa</u>n, m<u>oa</u>t
oe	is the sound your hear in the words	n<u>o</u>, t<u>oe</u>
oi	is the sound your hear in the words	b<u>oy</u>, s<u>oil</u>
ow	is the sound your hear in the words	n<u>ow</u>, pl<u>ough</u>
u	is the sound your hear in the words	b<u>u</u>s, t<u>u</u>b

❷ The **BLUE** word in capital letters tells you the **word class** the look-up word belongs to. This simply tells you the job that it does.
These are the word classes we divide words into.

NOUN	A noun names a person, thing or place: *rice*, ***the doctor***, ***Europe***
VERB	A verb is used to tell what people are doing or what is happening: *Tom **knows** Sanjay.*
ADJECTIVE	An adjective describes people or things: *The **old** teacher wore a **red** hat.*
ADVERB	An adverb describes the way something is done: *They went **outside** and looked **up**.*
PRONOUN	A pronoun is used to replace a noun so that you do not repeat the noun over and over again: *The boy bought an ice cream, then **he** ate **it**.*
PREPOSITION	A preposition is placed before a noun to tell you where something is or where it is moving to: *The cat ran **out of** the house and sat **on** the wall.*
CONJUNCTION	A conjunction joins two words or two parts of a sentence together: *Jane dashed down the road **but** didn't look ahead.*
INTERJECTION	An interjection expresses a feeling such as surprise or anger: ***Hello!**, **Oh no!***
PREFIX	A prefix is added to the beginning of a word to make a new word: ***anti**clockwise*, ***un**happy*

❸ A word in **black** after NOUN is the **plural** of the noun. This is the word you use when you are talking about more than one of something.

apple NOUN **apples**

Would you like an *apple*?
Do you like *apples*?

❹ Words in **black** after VERB show you how to spell the different **forms** of the verb. The one you use depends on who did the action or when it happened.

drag VERB **drags, dragging, dragged**

He *drags* himself out of bed every day.
I *dragged* myself out of bed yesterday.

❺ Words in **black** after ADJECTIVE are the ones you use when you are making a comparison and you want to say something is *more* or *the most*.

old ADJECTIVE **older, oldest**

I am *older* than Leo.
I am the *oldest* of my brothers and sisters.

❻ If you see a word in brackets, it might tell you which **subject** the word comes from.

atom NOUN **atoms** (*science*) the tiniest possible part of a substance.

It might tell you if a word is **formal** or **informal**. If it is informal, you could use it when talking to your friends. You might not use it when you are speaking to your teacher and you should not use it in your school work.

nab VERB **nabs, nabbing, nabbed**
(*informal*) **1** to nab something is to grab or take it: *Someone's nabbed all the best sandwiches already.*

If a word is formal, it is not likely that you will use it when you are talking to your friends. You might use it when you are being very polite!

> **refrain** VERB **refrains, refraining, refrained** (*formal*) to stop yourself doing something: *Please refrain from talking in the library.*

❼ Numbers show you that there are different meanings of the word. Each meaning has a different number.

> **bed** NOUN **beds 1** a piece of furniture to sleep on, or any place for sleeping: *Time to get ready for bed.* • *Each night, chimpanzees make beds of twigs high up in the trees.* **2** (*geography*) the bottom of a river, a lake or the sea **3** an area in a garden that contains flowers and other plants: *a bed of lilies*

❽ The meaning of the word is explained after this. This is called the **definition** of the word.

❾ The phrases or sentences in *italic* after some of the meanings are **examples** to show you how you might use the main word. The examples also help explain the meaning even more.

> **bedraggled** ADJECTIVE untidy and dirty: *The kitten had been caught in the rain and its fur was all bedraggled.*

❿ Sometimes you will see a **blue** box.
These boxes might tell you how to spell or use a word properly, for example by not getting the word mixed up with another one that sounds the same.

> ✦ You have to be careful not to confuse **affect**, which is a verb, with **effect**, which is a noun.
> *One thing **affects** another.*
> *One thing has an **effect** on another.*

They might tell you where the word comes from, and other words linked to it.

> ✦**Astron** is the Greek word for *star*.
> If a word starts with **astro**, you can guess that it has something to do with the stars or space.
> Other examples are **astronaut** and **astronomy**.

Aa

a *or* **an** ADJECTIVE **1** one: *a hundred miles* **2** any: *I need a pen.* **3** each: *Tommy gets £5 pocket money a week.*

✦ You use **a** before words that begin with a consonant, for example *a horse.*

You also use **a** before words that begin with **u** if they are pronounced like 'you', for example *a uniform.*

You use **an** before words that begin with a vowel (**a, e, i, o, u**), for example *an eye.* You also use **an** when it is not pronounced, for example *an eye, an hour.*

aback ADVERB
• **taken aback** if someone is taken aback, they are rather shocked: *I was taken aback by the change in Dad.*

abacus NOUN **abacuses** a frame with rows of beads that can be used for counting and doing sums

abandon VERB **abandons, abandoning, abandoned 1** to go away, leaving something or someone behind on purpose: *He abandoned the stolen car in a ditch.* **2** to give up something such as an idea or plan: *If it rains, we'll have to abandon the trip.*

abbey NOUN **abbeys 1** the home of a group of Christian monks or nuns **2** a church built for monks or nuns to use

abbot NOUN **abbots** a monk who is in charge of an abbey

abbreviate VERB **abbreviates, abbreviating, abbreviated** to abbreviate a word or phrase is to make it shorter: *Everyone abbreviates John Paul's name to JP.*
▶ **abbreviation** NOUN **abbreviations** a short form of a word or phrase. For example, **UK** is an abbreviation of *United Kingdom*

abdomen NOUN **abdomens 1** the part of a human's or an animal's body that contains the stomach **2** the back part of an insect's body
▶ **abdominal** ADJECTIVE in the area of the stomach

abduct VERB **abducts, abducting, abducted** to take someone away by using force: *Two people were abducted from the street.*
▶ **abduction** NOUN **abductions** taking someone away using force

abide VERB **abides, abiding, abode** *or* **abided 1** if you cannot abide something or someone, you cannot put up with them: *I can't abide cabbage.* **2** to abide by a rule, decision or promise is to keep to it

ability NOUN **abilities 1** the skill or power to do something: *Not everyone has the ability to keep a secret.* **2** talent: *a pupil with great ability*

ablaze ADJECTIVE AND ADVERB if a building is ablaze, it is on fire

able ADJECTIVE **abler, ablest 1** if you are able to do something, you can do it: *He wasn't able to run fast enough.* • *Will you be able to help me?* **2** an able person is good at doing something: *a very able singer*

ably ADVERB if you do something ably, you do it well

abnormal ADJECTIVE not normal, especially in a worrying way: *abnormal behaviour for a five-year-old*
▶ **abnormality** NOUN **abnormalities** something that is not normal
▶ **abnormally** ADVERB unusually: *an abnormally fast heartbeat*

aboard PREPOSITION AND ADVERB on a bus, train, ship or aeroplane: *the team aboard the space shuttle* • *Everyone should go aboard now.*

abode NOUN an old word for the place where someone lives: *What brings you to my humble abode?*

abolish VERB **abolishes, abolishing, abolished** to abolish a rule or a way of doing something is to get rid of it: *a plan to abolish smoking in public places*

▶ **abolition** NOUN getting rid of something such as a law or system of doing something

abominable ADJECTIVE very bad

Aborigine (pronounced ab-o-**rij**-in-i) NOUN one of the people who lived in Australia before anyone arrived from other countries

▶ **Aboriginal** ADJECTIVE to do with Australian Aborigines

> ✦ If you are talking about Aboriginal people, you should use **Aborigine** when you are talking about one person, and **Aboriginals** for more than one.

> ✦ This word comes from the Latin words **ab**, which means *from*, and **origo**, which means *the beginning*.
> The word **origin** is also linked to the Latin word **origo**.

abort VERB **aborts, aborting, aborted** to abort a plan or process is to stop it after it has already started: *We were spotted by a guard and decided to abort the whole mission.*

abound VERB **abounds, abounding, abounded** if things abound, there are a lot of them: *Stories abound of boys running away to sea to seek their fortunes.*

about PREPOSITION **1** to do with: *a book about bats* **2** not exactly but nearly the number given: *about five years ago* • *about four centimetres* **3** around: *books scattered about the room*
ADVERB **1** in or to one place and then another: *move things about* • *running about all day* **2** in the opposite direction: *He turned about and walked away.*
• **about to** just going to: *I was about to leave when the phone rang.* • *I think it's about to rain.*

above PREPOSITION **1** in a higher position: *the shelf above the sink* • *two degrees above zero* • *in the class above me* **2** if someone feels they are above a feeling or action, they think it is not

worth their time: *James was above asking for his ten pence back.*
ADVERB **1** higher up: *clouds in the sky above* **2** earlier in a piece of writing: *See instruction 5 above.*
• **above all** more than anything else: *We were, above all, hungry.*

abrasion NOUN **abrasions** a graze on the skin

abrasive ADJECTIVE scratchy: *Rub the dirt off with abrasive paper.*

abreast ADVERB side by side: *walking three abreast*
ADJECTIVE if someone is abreast of the news or some other subject, they know all the most recent facts about it

abroad ADVERB in or to a foreign country: *My grandparents went to live abroad.*

abrupt ADJECTIVE **1** sudden: *an abrupt change of direction* **2** an abrupt person speaks sharply **3** an abrupt statement or question is sudden and short

▶ **abruptly** ADVERB **1** suddenly: *He abruptly stopped speaking and left.* **2** if someone speaks abruptly, they say something sharply

abscess NOUN **abscesses** a lump inside the body that is painful and filled with liquid

abseil VERB **abseils, abseiling, abseiled** if you abseil down a wall or cliff, you let yourself down using a rope with your feet against the wall or cliff

absence NOUN **absences** being away from a place: *Your absence from school was noticed.*

absent ADJECTIVE away for a short time: *Is anyone absent today?* • *Two people were absent from the rehearsal.*

▶ **absentee** NOUN **absentees** someone who is not present, for example at school

absent-minded ADJECTIVE an absent-minded person often forgets things and does not notice what is going on around them

▶ **absent-mindedly** ADVERB in an absent-minded way: *Tanya absent-mindedly picked at her food as she replied.*

absolute ADJECTIVE complete: *absolute rubbish*

▸ **absolutely** ADVERB **1** completely: *absolutely ridiculous* **2** yes, certainly: *'Please can I have one of those?' 'Absolutely.'*

absorb VERB **absorbs, absorbing, absorbed 1** to soak up liquid: *The bath mat will absorb the splashes.* **2** if you are absorbed in something, you are giving it all your attention: *We were so absorbed in our game, we didn't hear the bell.*

▸ **absorbing** ADJECTIVE very interesting and taking all your attention: *an absorbing puzzle*

absorbent ADJECTIVE able to soak up liquid: *absorbent kitchen cloths*

▸ **absorbency** NOUN **absorbencies** how absorbent something is

abstract ADJECTIVE **1** something that is abstract cannot be seen or touched, for example *honesty* and *an argument*. The opposite is **concrete 2** (*art*) an abstract picture does not show things as they really look, but presents ideas in shapes and designs

absurd ADJECTIVE ridiculous: *What an absurd idea!*

▸ **absurdity** NOUN **absurdities** something that is ridiculous

▸ **absurdly** ADVERB in a ridiculous way: *That was an absurdly easy question.*

abundance NOUN **1** an abundance of something is a lot of it: *the abundance of trees in the forest* **2** if something is in abundance, there is plenty of it: *There was food in abundance at the party.*

▸ **abundant** ADJECTIVE existing in large amounts: *an abundant harvest • abundant hair*

▸ **abundantly** ADVERB **1** in large amounts: *Fruit is abundantly available in the market.* **2** very: *It is abundantly clear that you're not happy.*

abuse NOUN (pronounced a-**byoos**) **abuses 1** bad or cruel treatment: *child abuse* **2** using something the wrong way on purpose: *alcohol abuse* **3** insults: *shouting abuse at the referee*
VERB (pronounced a-**byooz**) **abuses, abusing, abused 1** to use something

the wrong way on purpose **2** to treat someone or something badly: *people who abuse animals*

▸ **abusive** ADJECTIVE rude or insulting

abysmal ADJECTIVE very bad: *abysmal exam results*

▸ **abysmally** ADVERB very badly: *The team played abysmally.*

academic ADJECTIVE to do with studying and education: *academic qualifications*

▸ **academically** ADVERB to do with studying and learning: *an academically bright pupil*

academy NOUN **academies** a school or college

accelerate VERB **accelerates, accelerating, accelerated** to go faster

▸ **acceleration** NOUN acceleration is increasing speed: *You'll be pushed back into your seat during acceleration.*

▸ **accelerator** NOUN **accelerators** the pedal or lever that makes a vehicle go faster

accent NOUN **accents 1** the way people from a certain area pronounce words: *I have a Scottish accent.* **2** a mark over a letter in a foreign language that shows how to pronounce it, for example over *e* in the word *café* **3** a stress on one part of a word or a sentence, or one note in music, that makes it stand out more than the others: *Put the accent on the third syllable in the word 'preparation'.*

accept VERB **accepts, accepting, accepted 1** to accept something is to take it when someone offers it to you **2** you accept an invitation when you say 'yes' to it **3** you accept something like an idea if you agree that it is true: *I accept that I was wrong and I'm sorry.*

▸ **acceptable** ADJECTIVE good enough: *This kind of behaviour is just not acceptable!*

▸ **acceptance** NOUN taking something that is given to you

access NOUN **accesses** a way of getting to or into a place: *The builders will need access to the house while you're out.*
VERB **accesses, accessing, accessed** (*ICT*) to get and be able to use

Aa
Bb
Cc
Dd
Ee
Ff
Gg
Hh
Ii
Jj
Kk
Ll
Mm
Nn
Oo
Pp
Qq
Rr
Ss
Tt
Uu
Vv
Ww
Xx
Yy
Zz

Aa
Bb
Cc
Dd
Ee
Ff
Gg
Hh
Ii
Jj
Kk
Ll
Mm
Nn
Oo
Pp
Qq
Rr
Ss
Tt
Uu
Vv
Ww
Xx
Yy
Zz

information on a computer: *This file was last accessed yesterday.*

▶ **accessible** ADJECTIVE easy to get to: *The house is not very accessible.*

accessory NOUN **accessories 1** an extra part that can be used with something bigger: *a hairdrier with lots of accessories* **2** something like a bag, a scarf or jewellery, that goes with your clothes

accident NOUN **accidents 1** a bad thing that happens by chance: *We had an accident with the glue and now it's everywhere.* **2** a road accident is when a vehicle crashes into something on a road

• **by accident** by chance: *I dropped the glass by accident and it smashed.*

▶ **accidental** ADJECTIVE if something is accidental, it happens by mistake

▶ **accidentally** ADVERB by accident: *I accidentally shut the door on my brother's hand.*

acclaim NOUN praise

▶ **acclaimed** ADJECTIVE if something is acclaimed, it has had a lot of praise: *an acclaimed television show*

accommodate VERB **accommodates, accommodating, accommodated 1** to accommodate someone or something is to find space for them: *The whole class can be accommodated in this room.* **2** to accommodate someone is to do what you can to help them

▶ **accommodation** NOUN somewhere to stay or live: *We'll look for accommodation as soon as we arrive.*

accompaniment NOUN **accompaniments** the music that someone sings to: *a love song with a guitar accompaniment*

accompany VERB **accompanies, accompanying, accompanied 1** to accompany someone is to go with them: *Would you mind accompanying me to the police station, sir?* **2** to play an instrument while someone else sings a song: *Her sister usually accompanies her on the piano.*

accomplish VERB **accomplishes, accomplishing, accomplished** to accomplish something is to do it

successfully: *Most children accomplished the task in a few minutes.*

▶ **accomplished** ADJECTIVE talented at doing something: *an accomplished goalkeeper*

▶ **accomplishment** NOUN **accomplishments** something you are very good at: *Cooking is just one of her accomplishments.*

accord NOUN

• **of your own accord** if you do something of your own accord, you do it without being asked or told: *I was surprised when my little sister thanked me of her own accord.*

according to PREPOSITION **1** if you say some information is according to someone, that is where the information comes from: *Hannah's ill, according to Lucy.* **2** if you measure one thing according to another, you compare those things with each other: *The animals were sorted according to their size.* • *Did everything go according to plan?*

▶ **accordingly** ADVERB in a way that suits what has just been said or what is happening: *The sun was shining and Jake dressed accordingly.*

accordion NOUN **accordions** a musical instrument with a small keyboard like a piano on the side of a big folding box that you squeeze in and out

account NOUN **accounts 1** a description of something that happened: *His account of the journey made us laugh.* **2** money that someone keeps in a bank **3** a bill showing how much someone has paid and how much they must still pay

• **on account of** because of: *I can't run very well on account of my bad leg.*

• **on no account** definitely not: *You are on no account to stay out late.*

• **take something into account** to take something into account is to consider it: *Will they take my age into account when they decide who can go?*

VERB **accounts, accounting, accounted** to account for something is to explain it: *It's her birthday, which* accounts for all the visitors she's had today.

accountant NOUN **accountants** someone whose job is to record a person's or company's money accounts and keep them in order

▸ **accountancy** NOUN the job of organizing and keeping records of a person's or a company's money

accumulate VERB **accumulates, accumulating, accumulated 1** to accumulate things is to collect a lot of them **2** things accumulate when they pile up: *A pile of books had accumulated on my desk.*

accuracy NOUN being exactly right: *Please check the accuracy of this measurement.*

accurate ADJECTIVE exactly right: *an accurate guess*

▸ **accurately** ADVERB exactly: *Copy the shape as accurately as possible.*

accusation NOUN **accusations** a statement saying that a person has done something wrong: *Jude has made a very serious accusation against you.*

accuse VERB **accuses, accusing, accused** to accuse someone is to say they have done something wrong: *Are you accusing me of lying?*

accustomed ADJECTIVE if you are accustomed to something, you are used to it: *We've all become accustomed to his strange way of talking.*

ace NOUN **aces 1** a playing-card with one symbol on it and an **A** in the corner: *the ace of spades* **2** an expert: *a Brazilian football ace* **3** in tennis, an ace is a serve that the other player cannot reach
ADJECTIVE (*informal*) very good: *The food was ace.* • *an ace detective*

ache NOUN **aches** a pain that goes on and on: *an ache behind my eyes*
VERB **aches, aching, ached** if part of your body aches, it hurts for a long time, especially in a dull, heavy sort of way: *My arm aches from playing too much tennis.*

achieve VERB **achieves, achieving, achieved** to achieve something is to succeed in doing it or getting it: *We*

have achieved everything we set out to do.* • *She could achieve a very good mark.*

▸ **achievement** NOUN **achievements 1** an achievement is a success or good result: *a list of his achievements so far* **2** achievement is having success: *This school has a high level of achievement*

acid NOUN **acids** a type of chemical that contains hydrogen and that can dissolve certain metals. Acids can be cancelled out by substances called alkalis

▸ **acidic** ADJECTIVE **1** containing acid **2** with a sharp, sour taste

▸ **acidity** NOUN how acidic something is

acid rain NOUN rain that contains chemicals that factories and towns have released into the air

acknowledge VERB **acknowledges, acknowledging, acknowledged 1** to admit that something is true **2** to tell someone that you have received something they sent you: *They never acknowledge my letters.*

▸ **acknowledgement** NOUN **acknowledgements** a note to tell someone that you have received something: *I sent two letters but only got one acknowledgement.*

acne NOUN a skin problem that causes spots, usually on someone's face

acorn NOUN **acorns** the fruit of the oak tree

acoustic (pronounced a-**koos**-tik) ADJECTIVE **1** to do with sound and hearing **2** an acoustic musical instrument does not need electrical equipment to work

▸ **acoustics** PLURAL NOUN the way a room can make music or speech sound better or worse: *The hall has wonderful acoustics.*

acquaint VERB **acquaints, acquainting, acquainted** (*formal*) **1** to acquaint someone with something is to tell them about it: *Let me acquaint you with the facts.* **2** if you are acquainted with something or someone, you have met them and know them slightly

▸ **acquaintance** NOUN **acquaintances** someone you have met and you know slightly

Aa
Bb
Cc
Dd
Ee
Ff
Gg
Hh
Ii
Jj
Kk
Ll
Mm
Nn
Oo
Pp
Qq
Rr
Ss
Tt
Uu
Vv
Ww
Xx
Yy
Zz

Aa
Bb
Cc
Dd
Ee
Ff
Gg
Hh
Ii
Jj
Kk
Ll
Mm
Nn
Oo
Pp
Qq
Rr
Ss
Tt
Uu
Vv
Ww
Xx
Yy
Zz

• **make someone's acquaintance** to meet someone for the first time and get to know them

acquire VERB **acquires, acquiring, acquired** to acquire something is to get it

acquit VERB **acquits, acquitting, acquitted** to acquit someone of a crime is to decide in a court that they did not do it

• **acquit yourself well** to do something well

acre NOUN **acres** an area of land of about 4047 square metres

acrobat NOUN **acrobats** someone who performs gymnastic tricks like somersaults and tightrope-walking

▸ **acrobatic** ADJECTIVE to do with gymnastic movements, especially jumping

▸ **acrobatics** PLURAL NOUN clever physical movements like skilful jumping and balancing

acronym (pronounced **ak**-ron-im) NOUN **acronyms** a word made from the first letters of other words. For example, the second part of *CD-ROM* is an acronym for *Read Only Memory*

across ADVERB **1** from one side of something to the other: *Don't run, but walk across quickly.* • *clouds moving across the sky* **2** on or to the other side: *I ran across the road.*

PREPOSITION **1** on the other side: *Their house is across the river from ours.* **2** from one side of something to the other: *a bridge across the river*

acrylic (pronounced a-**kril**-ik) NOUN a chemical substance used for making some paints, fabrics and different kinds of plastic materials

ADJECTIVE made with acrylic

act VERB **acts, acting, acted 1** to perform in a play or film **2** to behave in a certain way: *Stop acting like a baby.* **3** to do something: *We must act now to save the planet!*

• **act up** to behave badly

NOUN **acts**

1 something that someone does: *a brave act*

2 a piece of entertainment in a show: *a comedy act*

3 a law made by the government

4 a section of a play

action NOUN **actions**

1 an action is a movement someone or something makes: *Hit the ball with a swinging action.*

2 action is moving or doing something: *Let's see some action around here!*

3 the action of a film, book or play is what happens in the story: *Most of the action takes place in America.*

4 action is fighting in a war: *a soldier killed in action*

• **out of action** not working

activate VERB **activates, activating, activated** to make something start working

active ADJECTIVE **1** busy doing a lot of things: *Her sister is active in the drama club.* **2** working: *an active machine* **3** (*grammar*) an active verb is one that the subject of the sentence performs, for example in the sentence *The cat chased the mouse*

▸ **actively** ADVERB in a way that involves doing a lot of things: *actively helping people with problems*

▸ **activity** NOUN **activities 1** an activity is something you do, especially something you do for fun, in an organized way: *a variety of sporting activities* **2** activity is doing something, especially in a busy way

actor NOUN **actors** a person who performs in plays or films

actress NOUN **actresses** a woman who performs in plays or films

actual ADJECTIVE real: *We guessed there were about 100 people but the actual number was 110.*

▸ **actually** ADVERB in fact: *Actually, there are a lot of things you don't know.*

acute ADJECTIVE **1** an acute problem, especially a pain or illness, is very bad **2** quick to realize or understand something: *an acute mind* **3** an acute accent is a line that slopes up over a letter in some languages, for example over *e* in the French word *café*, to show how it is pronounced

acute angle NOUN **acute angles** an angle that is less than 90 degrees

ad NOUN **ads** (*informal*) an advertisement

AD ABBREVIATION short for **Anno Domini**, which is Latin for 'in the year of our Lord'. AD is added after a date to show that the date was after the birth of Jesus Christ, for example *2000 AD*

✦ **BC** is the abbreviation used with dates before the birth of Christ.

Adam's apple NOUN **Adam's apples** the lump you can see at the front of a man's neck

adamant ADJECTIVE very firm and not likely to give in: *Her father was adamant about going home immediately.*

adapt VERB **adapts, adapting, adapted 1** to change something to make it more suitable: *Can you adapt this dress to fit me?* **2** if you adapt to something, you get used to it: *It didn't take long to adapt to the heat.*

▸ **adaptable** ADJECTIVE an adaptable person can easily fit in with new or different situations

▸ **adaptation** NOUN **adaptations** an old story that is told in a new way: *a television adaptation of Roald Dahl's novel*

▸ **adaptor** NOUN **adaptors** a kind of plug you can use to connect up electrical equipment

add VERB **1** to put things together: *Add two and two.* • *Add the milk and sugar to the mixture.* **2** to say or write something else: *'If you don't mind?' he added.*

• **add up 1** to find the total of numbers put together: *Can you add these numbers up in your head?* **2** if things add up, they grow into a large amount: *£1 a week soon adds up.*

adder NOUN **adders** a poisonous snake with a black zigzag pattern on its back

addict NOUN **addicts** someone who cannot stop taking something: *a drug addict*

▸ **addicted** ADJECTIVE if you are addicted to something, you cannot manage without it

▸ **addiction** NOUN **addictions** not being able to stop taking something

▸ **addictive** ADJECTIVE if something is addictive, it makes you want to do it more and more

addition NOUN **additions 1** addition is adding up numbers **2** an addition is something that has been added: *a new addition to the collection*

▸ **additional** ADJECTIVE extra: *We're having three additional classrooms built.*

▸ **additionally** ADVERB as well as that: *Additionally, you have to pay to get in.*

• **in addition** as well

address NOUN **addresses**
1 your address is the name or number of the house, street and town where you live
2 a speech
3 (*ICT*) a place where you can find a piece of information in a computer's memory
4 (*ICT*) a group of letters and numbers that you can send emails to: *I have a new email address.*
VERB **addresses, addressing, addressed 1** (*formal*) to speak to someone: *Were you addressing me?* **2** to write an address on something like an envelope

address book NOUN **address books**
1 a book where you keep the addresses of people you know **2** (*ICT*) a place in a computer's memory where you can keep email addresses

adequate ADJECTIVE enough: *Three rooms should be adequate.*

adhesive NOUN **adhesives** glue
ADJECTIVE sticky: *adhesive tape*

Adi-Granth (pronounced u-dee-**grunt**) NOUN the Guru Granth Sahib, the holy book of the Sikh religion

adjacent ADJECTIVE next to: *The school is adjacent to the hospital.* • *A policeman was in the adjacent room.*

adjective WORD CLASS **adjectives** (*grammar*) a word that tells you something about a noun. For example, *difficult, good* and *stupid* are adjectives

Aa
Bb
Cc
Dd
Ee
Ff
Gg
Hh
Ii
Jj
Kk
Ll
Mm
Nn
Oo
Pp
Qq
Rr
Ss
Tt
Uu
Vv
Ww
Xx
Yy
Zz

Aa
Bb
Cc
Dd
Ee
Ff
Gg
Hh
Ii
Jj
Kk
Ll
Mm
Nn
Oo
Pp
Qq
Rr
Ss
Tt
Uu
Vv
Ww
Xx
Yy
Zz

adjust VERB **adjusts, adjusting, adjusted 1** to change something a little bit: *I adjusted the clock by two minutes.* **2** to get used to something: *It was difficult to adjust to living in a flat.*

▶ **adjustable** ADJECTIVE something adjustable can be changed to fit: *adjustable seat belts*

▶ **adjustment** NOUN **adjustments 1** an adjustment is a slight change: *We've made a few adjustments to lessons this week.* **2** adjustment is making changes to suit a new situation

administer VERB **administers, administering, administered** to administer a medicine is to give it to someone

administrate VERB **administrates, administrating, administrated** to run an organization

▶ **administration** NOUN **administrations 1** administration is running an organization **2** in the USA, the administration is the government

▶ **administrative** ADJECTIVE to do with running a business or country: *an administrative job*

▶ **administrator** NOUN **administrators** a person who runs or helps to run an organization

admirable ADJECTIVE if something is admirable, a lot of people think it is very good: *The way he behaved was admirable.*

▶ **admirably** ADVERB very well: *I thought you spoke admirably.*

admiral NOUN **admirals** one of the most important officers in the navy

admire VERB **admires, admiring, admired 1** to like someone or something very much **2** to enjoy looking at something: *I've been admiring your new bike.*

▶ **admiration** NOUN a feeling of liking someone or something very much because you think they are good: *He looked at the boy with admiration.*

▶ **admirer** NOUN **admirers** a person who likes someone or something very much

admission NOUN **admissions 1** being allowed into a place: *A sign on the door said 'No admission'.* **2** the cost of getting in: *We don't charge admission here.* **3** an admission is when you agree that something bad is true: *We were surprised by his admission that he had done it.*

admit VERB **admits, admitting, admitted 1** to agree that you have done something bad: *I admit that I should have told you sooner.* **2** to agree that something is true: *I admit that this is a difficult exercise, but do your best.* **3** to let someone in: *They won't admit anyone not wearing trainers.*

▶ **admittance** NOUN being allowed to go in somewhere: *No admittance for anyone under 18.*

ado NOUN
• **without further ado** without any more fuss

adolescence NOUN the time between childhood and being an adult

▶ **adolescent** NOUN **adolescents** someone older than a child, but not yet an adult

adopt VERB **adopts, adopting, adopted 1** to adopt a child is to take them into your own family and legally become their parent **2** to adopt a way of doing something is to start to do it that way

▶ **adoption** NOUN **1** taking a child into a new family: *Adoption can take a long time.* **2** taking on something new: *the adoption of a new homework timetable*

▶ **adoptive** ADJECTIVE adoptive parents are the new parents of a child who goes into a new family

adorable ADJECTIVE a thing or person is adorable if you cannot help liking them very much

adore VERB **adores, adoring, adored** to think something or someone is wonderful: *She just adores her father.*

▶ **adoration** NOUN loving very much: *a look of adoration*

adorn VERB **adorns, adorning, adorned** to decorate: *Their hair was adorned with flowers.*

adrenalin or **adrenaline** NOUN a

chemical in your body that is produced when you are afraid, angry or excited

adrift ADJECTIVE a boat that is adrift is not tied up and is probably moving in the wind

ADVERB if a boat goes adrift it floats too far from the shore

adult NOUN **adults** a grown-up

ADJECTIVE to do with or for grown-ups: *adult sizes*

▶ **adulthood** NOUN the period of time in your life when you are an adult

advance VERB **advances, advancing, advanced** to move forwards: *a crowd advancing towards us*

ADJECTIVE happening before an event: *an advance booking for the show*

NOUN **advances 1** advance is movement forward **2** an advance is a payment made before it is due

• **in advance** earlier: *I arrived in advance to make sure everything was ready.*

▶ **advanced** ADJECTIVE at a high level: *an advanced Spanish course*

advantage NOUN **advantages** if you have an advantage over someone else, things are better for you for some reason: *Her long legs give her an advantage in the high jump.*

• **take advantage of 1** to take advantage of a situation is to use it well: *We took advantage of the sunshine to get the clothes dry.* **2** to take advantage of a person is to use them because you know they are kind or because they will not complain

advent NOUN **1** the arrival of something: *the advent of the steam engine* **2** Advent is the four weeks before Christmas

adventure NOUN **adventures** something exciting that you do: *Going into space would be a real adventure.*

▶ **adventurous** ADJECTIVE an adventurous person likes to do exciting new things

adverb WORD CLASS **adverbs** (*grammar*) a word that you use to describe verbs, adjectives or other adverbs. For example, *really*, *badly*, *abroad* and *often*

are adverbs

adversary NOUN **adversaries** an enemy or somebody who is against you in a competition

adverse ADJECTIVE harmful or bad: *adverse weather for sailing*

▶ **adversity** NOUN problems

advert NOUN **adverts** an advertisement

advertise VERB **advertises, advertising, advertised 1** a company advertises a new product when it presents it on television or radio, or in a magazine or newspaper, so that people know about it and buy it **2** to tell as many people as possible about something: *Nobody will come unless we advertise the concert.*

▶ **advertisement** NOUN **advertisements** a notice or short film about something that somebody is trying to sell: *I saw an advertisement for a new chocolate bar.*

advice NOUN someone who gives you advice tells you what they think you should do: *If I follow her advice, I won't have any money left!*

✦ Remember that **advice** with a **c** is a noun: *Can you give me some advice?*
Advise with an **s** is a verb: *Can you advise me?*

advisable ADJECTIVE something that is advisable is probably a sensible thing to do

advise VERB **advises, advising, advised** to tell someone what you think they should do

▶ **adviser** *or* **advisor** NOUN **advisers** *or* **advisors** a person who tries to tell people the best thing to do

▶ **advisory** ADJECTIVE telling people the best thing to do

advocate VERB **advocates, advocating, advocated** to say that you support an idea: *Many people advocate recycling.*

NOUN **advocates** a person who supports an idea

aeon NOUN **aeons** another spelling of **eon**

aerial NOUN **aerials** a rod made of

Aa
Bb
Cc
Dd
Ee
Ff
Gg
Hh
Ii
Jj
Kk
Ll
Mm
Nn
Oo
Pp
Qq
Rr
Ss
Tt
Uu
Vv
Ww
Xx
Yy
Zz

an aeroplane

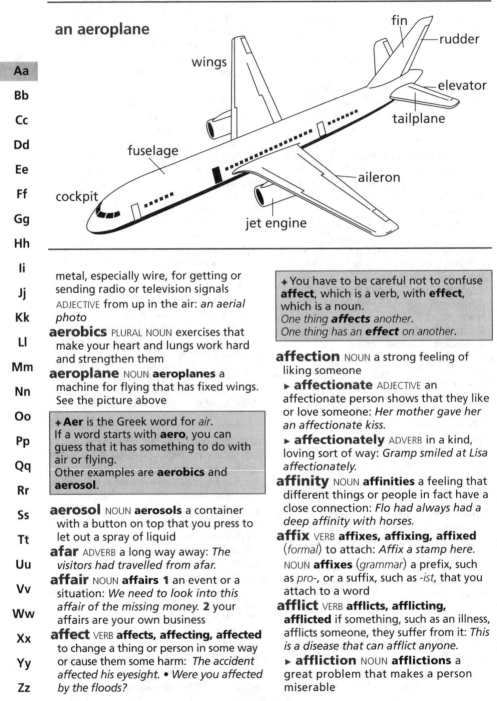

Labels: fin, rudder, wings, elevator, tailplane, fuselage, aileron, cockpit, jet engine

metal, especially wire, for getting or sending radio or television signals
ADJECTIVE from up in the air: *an aerial photo*

aerobics PLURAL NOUN exercises that make your heart and lungs work hard and strengthen them

aeroplane NOUN **aeroplanes** a machine for flying that has fixed wings. See the picture above

✦**Aer** is the Greek word for *air*. If a word starts with **aero**, you can guess that it has something to do with air or flying.
Other examples are **aerobics** and **aerosol**.

aerosol NOUN **aerosols** a container with a button on top that you press to let out a spray of liquid

afar ADVERB a long way away: *The visitors had travelled from afar.*

affair NOUN **affairs 1** an event or a situation: *We need to look into this affair of the missing money.* **2** your affairs are your own business

affect VERB **affects, affecting, affected** to change a thing or person in some way or cause them some harm: *The accident affected his eyesight.* • *Were you affected by the floods?*

✦ You have to be careful not to confuse **affect**, which is a verb, with **effect**, which is a noun.
*One thing **affects** another.*
*One thing has an **effect** on another.*

affection NOUN a strong feeling of liking someone
▸ **affectionate** ADJECTIVE an affectionate person shows that they like or love someone: *Her mother gave her an affectionate kiss.*
▸ **affectionately** ADVERB in a kind, loving sort of way: *Gramp smiled at Lisa affectionately.*

affinity NOUN **affinities** a feeling that different things or people in fact have a close connection: *Flo had always had a deep affinity with horses.*

affix VERB **affixes, affixing, affixed** (*formal*) to attach: *Affix a stamp here.*
NOUN **affixes** (*grammar*) a prefix, such as *pro-*, or a suffix, such as *-ist*, that you attach to a word

afflict VERB **afflicts, afflicting, afflicted** if something, such as an illness, afflicts someone, they suffer from it: *This is a disease that can afflict anyone.*
▸ **affliction** NOUN **afflictions** a great problem that makes a person miserable

affluent ADJECTIVE having a lot of money and possessions
▶ **affluence** NOUN having lots of money to spend: *There was greater affluence in this country after the war.*

afford VERB **affords, affording, afforded 1** to have enough money to pay for something: *We can't afford to go on holiday.* **2** to have enough time to do something: *I can't afford to stay any longer or I'll be late.*
▶ **affordable** ADJECTIVE at a low enough price to buy

afloat ADVERB floating: *Donny held on to a piece of wood to stay afloat.*

afoot ADJECTIVE if something is afoot, it is happening

afraid ADJECTIVE frightened: *There's no need to be afraid.* • *Small children are often afraid of dogs.*
• **I'm afraid** if you say 'I'm afraid' you mean you are sorry: *I'm afraid I don't know the answer.*

after PREPOSITION **1** following: *I'll do it after dinner.* • *Your name's after mine on the list.* **2** if you were named after someone, you were given their name: *Gordon was named after his uncle.* **3** to ask after someone is to ask how they are: *Mrs Young was asking after you.*
• **after all** anyway: *I went after all.*
ADVERB later: *Can you come the week after?*
CONJUNCTION following in time: *Mrs Shaw died after we moved.* • *After we'd said goodbye, we felt awfully sad.*

afternoon NOUN **afternoons** the time between midday and the evening

afterwards ADVERB later on: *He's busy now but I'll speak to him afterwards.*

again ADVERB **1** once more: *Do it again!* **2** to the place you started from or the way you were before: *Can we go home again now?* • *Grandad would like to be young again.*
• **again and again** lots of times

against PREPOSITION **1** leaning on, touching or hitting something: *throwing the ball against the wall* • *sitting against a tree* **2** competing with someone: *We're playing against you next.* **3** if you are

against something, you do not like or want it: *We're against starting any earlier than 8.30.*

age NOUN **ages 1** a person's age is how old they are **2** (*informal*) an age is a very long time: *We had to wait an age for him to come out.* **3** a time in history: *the Stone Age*
• **ages** (*informal*) a long time: *You took ages to finish.*
• **come of age** to become an adult
• **under age** too young to legally do something: *You can't get married – you're under age.*
VERB **ages, aging** or **ageing, aged 1** to get older **2** to look older: *She's aged a lot recently.*
▶ **aged** ADJECTIVE **1** (pronounced aijd) having the age of: *a boy aged 10* **2** (pronounced **aij**-id) old

agency NOUN **agencies** an office or business that organizes something: *a travel agency*

agenda NOUN **agendas** a list of things that have to be done or talked about: *What's on the agenda for the meeting?*

agent NOUN **agents 1** a person whose job is arranging things for someone else: *The travel agent will send you the tickets before you leave.* **2** a spy: *a secret agent*

aggravate VERB **aggravates, aggravating, aggravated 1** to make something worse: *Don't scratch or you'll aggravate the infection.* **2** (*informal*) to aggravate someone or something is to annoy them: *Don't aggravate the dog or it will bite.*
▶ **aggravation** NOUN **1** making something worse **2** (*informal*) irritating kind of trouble

aggression NOUN a way of behaving that is angry and threatening

aggressive ADJECTIVE angry and ready to attack

aghast ADJECTIVE horrified

agile ADJECTIVE good at moving about quickly and easily: *These children were as agile as monkeys.*
▶ **agility** NOUN being able to move about and change direction quickly

Aa
Bb
Cc
Dd
Ee
Ff
Gg
Hh
Ii
Jj
Kk
Ll
Mm
Nn
Oo
Pp
Qq
Rr
Ss
Tt
Uu
Vv
Ww
Xx
Yy
Zz

Aa
Bb
Cc
Dd
Ee
Ff
Gg
Hh
Ii
Jj
Kk
Ll
Mm
Nn
Oo
Pp
Qq
Rr
Ss
Tt
Uu
Vv
Ww
Xx
Yy
Zz

agitate VERB **agitates, agitating, agitated 1** something agitates you if it makes you nervous and worried: *That news will agitate her.* **2** to agitate for something is to stir up people so that they make it happen: *We must agitate for a change in the law.*

▸ **agitation** NOUN getting nervous and upset: *She tried to hide her agitation.*

agnostic NOUN **agnostics** a person who believes you cannot tell if God exists or not

ago ADVERB in the past: *Lily was born ten years ago.*

agony NOUN very great pain

agoraphobia NOUN people who have agoraphobia may be afraid of being in open spaces or of going outside at all

▸ **agoraphobic** ADJECTIVE afraid of leaving a place that feels safe

> ✦ The word **agoraphobia** comes from the Greek words **agora**, which means *market place*, and **phobia**, which means *fear*.
> Another **phobia** is **claustrophobia**, a fear of being closed in.

agree VERB **agrees, agreeing, agreed 1** to agree with someone is to think the same as them about something: *Don't you agree?* • *I agree with everything you've said.* **2** to agree to do what someone has asked you to is to say that you will do it : *I only agreed to come if you came too.* **3** if some food or drink does not agree with you, it upsets your stomach

▸ **agreeable** ADJECTIVE **1** something that is agreeable is pleasant or enjoyable **2** someone who is agreeable is willing to do something: *If you're agreeable, we'll leave at about 3 o'clock.*

▸ **agreement** NOUN **agreements 1** an agreement is something that people have decided together that they will do: *These countries have made an agreement not to fight.* **2** agreement is when things such as opinions or answers are the same: *We are in complete agreement about this.*

agriculture NOUN growing crops

▸ **agricultural** ADJECTIVE to do with growing crops

ahead ADVERB in front: *Run on ahead and tell them we're coming.* • *Our house is straight ahead.* • *We've got a long journey ahead of us.*

aid NOUN **1** help: *He can walk with the aid of a stick.* • *Mr Oliver came to our aid.* **2** money and food sent to help people in need

• **in aid of** in order to help: *a collection in aid of the flood victims*

VERB **aids, aiding, aided** to help someone

AIDS NOUN a condition that makes every illness very dangerous to the person that has it. AIDS stands for Acquired Immune Deficiency Syndrome

ailment NOUN **ailments** something wrong with you, like an illness

aim VERB **aims, aiming, aimed 1** to aim something like a gun is to point it at something: *Paul was aiming at the target but missed it.* **2** to aim to do something is to intend to do it: *We aim to help all our customers.*

NOUN **aims 1** an aim is something that you are trying to do: *Here's a list of our aims for the year.* **2** if you take aim, you point something at a target **3** if you have good aim, you can hit a target well

aimless ADJECTIVE having no goal or purpose: *an aimless stroll*

▸ **aimlessly** ADVERB without a reason: *walking aimlessly around the house*

air NOUN **1** air is the gases around us that we breathe in: *Kelly left the room to get some air.* • *The air carries the seeds for miles.* **2** an air of secrecy or mystery is a feeling that there is a secret or mystery **3** an air is a tune

3 to air your views or opinions is to tell people what you think

• **by air** in an aeroplane or helicopter

• **on the air** broadcasting a radio or television programme

• **up in the air** not yet definite or decided: *Our holiday plans are still up in the air.*

VERB **airs, airing, aired 1** to air washing is to make it completely dry **2** to air a room is to let some fresh air into it

airborne ADJECTIVE moving in the air: *airborne seeds*

air conditioning NOUN a system that keeps a room or building at a certain temperature

aircraft NOUN **aircraft** a vehicle that you can fly in

air force NOUN **air forces** the part of an army that uses aircraft

airgun NOUN **airguns** a gun that fires using the power of compressed air

airline NOUN **airlines** a company that takes people to places by aeroplane: *an airline ticket*

airlock NOUN **airlocks 1** a bubble in a pipe that stops liquid flowing through it **2** a compartment with two doors for getting in and out of a spaceship or submarine

airport NOUN **airports** a place where passengers can get on and off aircraft

air raid NOUN **air raids** an attack by weapons fired from aircraft

airship NOUN **airships** a large balloon with engines for carrying things or people

airtight ADJECTIVE if something is airtight, air cannot pass in or out of it

airy ADJECTIVE **airier, airiest 1** with lots of fresh air **2** not very serious: *an airy way of talking*

aisle (rhymes with **mile**) NOUN **aisles** the space that you can walk along between rows of seats or shelves

ajar ADVERB slightly open: *David left the door ajar on purpose.*

alarm NOUN **alarms 1** an alarm is a signal to warn people: *The ringing sound is the fire alarm.* **2** alarm is a sudden feeling of fear: *Freddie jumped back in alarm.*
VERB **alarms, alarming, alarmed** to frighten someone, especially suddenly
▸ **alarming** ADJECTIVE frightening: *an alarming sight*

alas INTERJECTION an old word that a person said when they were sad

albatross NOUN **albatrosses** a large white sea bird

album NOUN **albums 1** a book for keeping a collection of something like photos or autographs **2** a collection of songs or pieces of music put on a CD, tape or record

alcohol NOUN **1** a kind of chemical that burns easily and is contained in substances such as paint and perfume **2** a kind of chemical that is contained in some drinks. It can change the way you behave, and make you ill if you drink too much **3** alcohol is drinks containing this chemical, for example beer, wine and whisky
▸ **alcoholic** ADJECTIVE containing alcohol: *alcoholic drinks*
NOUN **alcoholics** a person who cannot stop drinking alcohol

alcove NOUN **alcoves** a space where part of a wall is further back than the rest

ale NOUN **ales** a kind of beer

alert ADJECTIVE wide awake and ready for action
VERB **alerts, alerting, alerted** to alert someone to a problem or a danger is to warn them about it
NOUN **alerts** an alarm
• **on the alert** ready to deal with possible problems

algae (pronounced al-gi) PLURAL NOUN a group of plants that grow near or in water and which do not have stems, leaves or flowers, for example seaweed

algebra (pronounced al-ji-bra) NOUN a type of mathematics that uses letters and signs as well as numbers

alias ADVERB also known as: *Peter Parker, alias Spiderman*
NOUN **aliases** another name that a person uses

alibi (pronounced al-i-bie) NOUN **alibis** proof that a person could not have committed a particular crime, because they were somewhere else: *Taylor has a great alibi – he was in prison when the robbery took place.*

alien NOUN **1** a person from another country **2** a creature from another planet
ADJECTIVE **1** from another country **2** something that is alien is not in keeping

Aa
Bb
Cc
Dd
Ee
Ff
Gg
Hh
Ii
Jj
Kk
Ll
Mm
Nn
Oo
Pp
Qq
Rr
Ss
Tt
Uu
Vv
Ww
Xx
Yy
Zz

with other things: *Being unkind is alien to her nature.*

alight ADJECTIVE AND ADVERB on fire

VERB **alights, alighting, alighted 1** to get off a train or bus **2** to settle or land: *A seagull alighted on the wall.*

align VERB to align things is to bring things into line with each other, or with something else: *Align the words down the left side of the page.* • *Align the buttons with the holes before you do them up.*

▶ **alignment** NOUN the arrangement of things in a straight line: *The wheels need to be in alignment to work properly.*

alike ADJECTIVE like one another: *The twins aren't alike.*

ADVERB the same way: *He treats us both alike.*

alive ADJECTIVE **1** living: *the greatest ballerina alive* **2** lively: *The town comes alive at night.*

alkali (pronounced al-ka-lie) NOUN **alkalis** (*science*) a type of chemical that behaves in the opposite way to acids and can cancel them out. It is used in substances such as soap and dye

▶ **alkaline** ADJECTIVE containing an alkali

all ADJECTIVE **1** every one: *All the children stood up.* **2** every part: *We ate all the cake.*

• **all in** (*informal*) tired out: *We were all in after the race.*

ADVERB completely: *all dirty*

PRONOUN **1** every one: *I want to see them all.* **2** every part of something: *Don't spend it all.*

Allah NOUN the Muslim name for the creator of the world

allegation NOUN **allegations** to make an allegation against someone is to claim that they have done something wrong

allege VERB **alleges, alleging, alleged** to say that a person has done something wrong: *The boys allege that they are being bullied.*

▶ **allegedly** ADVERB something that is allegedly true is only what people say,

without any proof: *He allegedly stole money out of the till but he still works there.*

allegiance NOUN loyalty: *The soldiers all swear allegiance to their country.*

allegory NOUN **allegories** a story, play, poem or picture where the characters stand for real people in real situations

allergy NOUN **allergies** a condition where your body reacts badly to something you touch, breathe in, eat or drink: *a peanut allergy*

▶ **allergic** ADJECTIVE if you are allergic to something, you become uncomfortable or ill when you eat it or have contact with it: *I'm allergic to citrus fruit.*

alley NOUN **alleys 1** a narrow passage in between buildings **2** a place where you can play games like skittles: *a bowling alley*

alliance NOUN **alliances** an agreement between people or countries to be on the same side if there is an argument

alligator NOUN **alligators** a large reptile like a crocodile, with thick skin, a long tail and large jaws

alliteration NOUN using the same sound to begin two or more words that are close together, for example *sing a song of sixpence*

▶ **alliterative** ADJECTIVE with the same sound at the beginning of words that are close together

allocate VERB **allocates, allocating, allocated** to allocate something is to give someone their part of it: *We'll allocate the rooms you will be staying in.*

▶ **allocation** NOUN **1** allocation is giving or sharing something out **2** an allocation is something that has been given out: *Both teams have the same allocation of tickets for the cup final.*

allot VERB **allots, allotting, allotted** to allot something is to share it out: *The prize money was allotted to the winners.*

▶ **allotment** NOUN **allotments 1** allotment is giving out shares of something **2** an allotment is a share of something **3** an allotment is a small piece of land for growing plants

allow VERB **allows, allowing, allowed 1** to allow someone to do something is to let them do it: *Will you allow me to come in now?* **2** to allow something is to let it happen: *We do not allow smoking in the house.* **3** to allow someone something is to give it to them: *Jack was allowed money to go the cinmea.*

▸ **allowance** NOUN **allowances 1** an amount of money that someone is given regularly: *My parents have promised to give me an allowance when I'm a teenager.* **2** the amount that you are allowed to have of something: *There's a baggage allowance on the plane.*

• **make allowances for** to make allowances for something is to consider it: *He lost the race, but we'll make allowances for the fact that he's tired.*

alloy NOUN **alloys** a mixture of two or more metals

all right ADVERB **1** reasonably good: *The party was all right I suppose.* **2** safe: *I'm glad you're all right – we heard there had been an accident.* **3** satisfactory: *Is it all right if I go out tonight?*

INTERJECTION you can say 'all right' when you agree to something: *All right, I'll go then.*

✦Some people think it is wrong to use the spelling *alright*, so it is best to write it as two words: **all right**.

---

ally NOUN **allies** a country, business or person that is joined to or supports another

VERB **allies, allying, allied** if a country or business is allied to another, they are joined as partners

almighty ADJECTIVE **1** very powerful **2** very big: *There was an almighty row.*

almond (pronounced **a**-mond) NOUN **almonds** a type of long narrow nut

almost ADVERB very nearly but not quite: *She is almost ten years old.*

aloft ADVERB high up: *banners waving aloft*

alone ADJECTIVE without anyone else: *I was alone in the house.*

ADVERB **1** not with others: *I live alone.* **2** without other things: *The ticket alone will use up all my money.*

along PREPOSITION **1** from one end to the other: *Shona walked along the street.* **2** on the length of: *Harry's house is somewhere along this street.*

ADVERB **1** onwards: *Move along please.* **2** to a particular place: *I'll come along later.*

• **along with** together with: *We'd packed drinks along with the sandwiches.*

alongside PREPOSITION beside: *The hat was alongside the coat on the bench.*

aloof ADJECTIVE staying apart from other people and not being interested in them

aloud ADVERB if you do something aloud, you do it so that someone can hear you: *It's much slower to count aloud.*

alphabet NOUN **alphabets** all the letters of a language arranged in a particular order

▸ **alphabetical** ADJECTIVE **1** to do with the alphabet **2** arranged in the order of an alphabet: *an alphabetical index*

• **alphabetical order** something that is arranged in alphabetical order is arranged so that words beginning with **a** come first, then **b** and so on: *This dictionary is in alphabetical order.*

▸ **alphabetically** ADVERB with the letters in the order of the alphabet: *The list has been arranged alphabetically.*

✦**Alphabet** comes from the Greek word **alphabetos**, which is made up of the first two Greek letters – these are **alpha** (a) and **beta** (b).

---

alps PLURAL NOUN high mountains

▸ **alpine** ADJECTIVE to do with high parts of mountains: *alpine meadow*

already ADVERB **1** before a particular time: *I had already gone when Bob arrived.* **2** now, before the expected time: *Is he here already?*

Aa
Bb
Cc
Dd
Ee
Ff
Gg
Hh
Ii
Jj
Kk
Ll
Mm
Nn
Oo
Pp
Qq
Rr
Ss
Tt
Uu
Vv
Ww
Xx
Yy
Zz

> ✦ If you write *all ready* as two words, then it means 'completely prepared'. For example: *Are you all ready to go?*

alsatian NOUN **alsatians** a large breed of dog with a short brown and black coat. An alsatian can also be called a **German shepherd**

also ADVERB in addition: *Bernie speaks French and also some Italian.* • *My sister also attends this school.*

altar NOUN **altars** a raised place or table, used in religious services to make offerings to a god

alter VERB **alters, altering, altered 1** to alter something is to change it: *Can you alter this skirt to fit me?* **2** to alter is to change: *The town has altered a lot recently.*

▶ **alteration** NOUN **alterations 1** an alteration is a change **2** alteration is change

alternate (pronounced **ol**-ter-nait) VERB **alternates, alternating, alternated** to do or happen in turn: *Rain and sun alternated throughout the day.*

ADJECTIVE (pronounced ol-**ter**-nat) **1** every second one : *We meet on alternate Mondays.* **2** alternate things are in turn, first one then the other: *a fence with alternate stripes of red and green*

alternative (pronounced ol-**ter**-na-tiv) ADJECTIVE giving you another choice or possibility: *If you cannot come on Tuesday you can come on an alternative day.*

NOUN **alternatives** another possibility: *Is there an alternative to chips on the menu?*

alternator (pronounced **ol**-ter-nay-ter) NOUN **alternators** an electricity generator that produces an electric current that keeps changing its direction

although CONJUNCTION in spite of the fact that: *He was late for school although he'd hurried.*

altitude NOUN **altitudes** the altitude something has is its height above the level of the sea: *We are flying at an altitude of 20000 metres.*

alto NOUN **altos** (*music*) **1** the lowest singing voice for a woman **2** the highest singing voice for a man

altogether ADVERB **1** completely: *I'm not altogether happy.* **2** in total: *We raised £100 altogether.*

> ✦ If you write *all together* as two words, then it means 'together in a group'. For example: *It's good that we're all together again.*

aluminium NOUN a very light, silver-coloured metal

always ADVERB **1** at all times: *I always work hard.* **2** continually or often: *I'm always getting this wrong.* **3** forever: *I'll always remember that day.*

am¹ VERB **1** the form of the verb **be** that you use with **I**: *I am happy.* **2 am** is also used as a helping verb along with a main verb: *I am going out.*

am² or **a.m.** ABBREVIATION short for **ante meridiem**, which is Latin for 'before midday'. **am** is added after the time to show that the time is in the morning, for example *7am*. Look up and compare **pm**

amalgamate VERB **amalgamates, amalgamating, amalgamated** to join with something else: *The two firms amalgamated last year.*

▶ **amalgamation** NOUN **1** amalgamation is the joining of two or more things, especially organizations **2** an amalgamation is two or more things joined together

amateur (pronounced **am**-a-ter) NOUN someone who does something because they enjoy it, not because they are paid for it: *Holly's a good actress even though she's an amateur.*

ADJECTIVE performed by people who are not paid: *amateur athletics*

amaze VERB **amazes, amazing, amazed** to surprise someone very much: *It amazes me how stupid you can be.*

▶ **amazement** NOUN great surprise: *To my amazement, Dad agreed with me.*

▶ **amazing** ADJECTIVE very surprising: *an amazing sight*

ambassador NOUN **ambassadors** someone who represents their own government in a foreign country

amber NOUN a clear yellowish-brown

liquid that has gone hard, and that may contain fossils. Amber is sometimes used to make jewellery

ambiguous ADJECTIVE with two possible meanings: *This question is ambiguous.*

▶ **ambiguity** NOUN **ambiguities 1** an ambiguity is something with more than one meaning **2** ambiguity is uncertainty

ambition NOUN **ambitions 1** an ambition is something that you have wanted to do for a long time: *I have an ambition to see the pyramids.* **2** ambition is wanting to be very successful

▶ **ambitious** ADJECTIVE **1** an ambitious person wants to be very successful in life **2** an ambitious project is one that you know will be difficult for you

amble VERB **ambles, ambling, ambled** to walk slowly in a relaxed way

ambulance NOUN **ambulances** a vehicle for taking sick or injured people to hospital

ambush NOUN **ambushes** an ambush is when a person hides so that they can make a surprise attack on someone VERB **ambushes, ambushing, ambushed** to attack someone from a hiding place

amend VERB **amends, amending, amended** to improve something you have said or written by making small changes

▶ **amendment** NOUN **amendments** a slight change to something like a law

amenity NOUN **amenities** something such as a shop or park that makes life easier or more pleasant for people in that area

amethyst NOUN a purple precious stone

amiable ADJECTIVE friendly and relaxed

▶ **amiability** NOUN friendliness

▶ **amiably** ADVERB in an easy-going, friendly way

amicable ADJECTIVE you reach an amicable agreement without any argument

▶ **amicably** ADVERB in a friendly way

amid or **amidst** ADVERB in the middle of: *a moment of calm amid great excitement*

ammonia NOUN a substance that can be a gas or a liquid and has a very strong smell

ammunition NOUN something, like bullets or bombs, that you can fire from a weapon

amnesia NOUN amnesia is losing your memory

amnesty NOUN a period of time when criminals are pardoned, or the usual punishments for crimes do not apply: *an amnesty for people who owe parking fines*

amoeba (pronounced a-**mee**-ba) NOUN **amoebas** or **amoebae** a microscopic creature that is made up of only one cell and usually lives in water

amok ADVERB
• **run amok** to go mad and do a lot of damage

among or **amongst** PREPOSITION **1** surrounded by or in the middle of: *You are among your friends.* **2** one of a group of: *Among all my books, this is my favourite.* **3** between: *Divide the chocolate among yourselves.*

✦ If you are talking about more than two people, you use **among** or **amongst**. For example: *The work was divided among the pupils.*

If you are talking about two people, you use **between**. For example: *Carl and Sue divided the sweets between them.*

amount NOUN **amounts** a quantity: *a small amount of money* • *large amounts of land*
VERB **amounts, amounting, amounted** to amount to a particular number is to add up to that much: *What I've spent amounts to exactly £10.*

amp NOUN **amps 1** amps are used to measure how strong an electric current is. Amp is short for **ampere 2** a short form of the word **amplifier**

ampersand NOUN **ampersands** the sign &, which means 'and'

Aa
Bb
Cc
Dd
Ee
Ff
Gg
Hh
Ii
Jj
Kk
Ll
Mm
Nn
Oo
Pp
Qq
Rr
Ss
Tt
Uu
Vv
Ww
Xx
Yy
Zz

Aa
Bb
Cc
Dd
Ee
Ff
Gg
Hh
Ii
Jj
Kk
Ll
Mm
Nn
Oo
Pp
Qq
Rr
Ss
Tt
Uu
Vv
Ww
Xx
Yy
Zz

amphibian NOUN **amphibians 1** an animal that can live on land and in water **2** a vehicle that can travel on land and on water

▶ **amphibious** ADJECTIVE able to go or live on land and in water

amphitheatre NOUN **amphitheatres** a theatre that has seats in a circle around an area in the centre

ample ADJECTIVE plenty or more than enough: *You had ample time to finish the test.*

▶ **amply** ADVERB very well or even more than necessary: *We were amply rewarded with tea and chocolate cake.*

amplifier NOUN **amplifiers** a machine that makes sounds louder

amplify VERB **amplifies, amplifying, amplified** to amplify a sound is to make it louder

▶ **amplification** NOUN making sounds louder: *It was impossible to hear the singer without amplification.*

amputate VERB **amputates, amputating, amputated** to amputate a part of the body is to cut it off

▶ **amputation** NOUN **amputations 1** amputation is cutting off part of the body **2** an amputation is an operation to cut off part of the body

amrit NOUN a Sikh ceremony where someone drinks amrit, a special mixture of water and sugar, as a sign that they are joining the body of Sikhs

amuse VERB **amuses, amusing, amused 1** to make someone laugh **2** to keep someone happy for a while: *Would you amuse the children for half an hour?*

▶ **amusement** NOUN **amusements 1** amusement is the feeling that makes you laugh **2** amusement is entertainment: *What did you do for amusement on holiday?* **3** amusements are machines or activities that you can play: *There were amusements and food stalls at the fair.*

an ADJECTIVE you use **an** instead of **a** before words beginning with a vowel or before the letter 'h' when it is not pronounced: *an honest person*

anaemia (pronounced an-**ee**-mi-a) NOUN a condition where someone does not have enough red blood cells and looks pale

▶ **anaemic** ADJECTIVE **1** suffering from anaemia **2** looking pale or ill

anaesthesia (pronounced an-is-**thee**-zi-a) NOUN giving someone a drug to stop them feeling any pain

anaesthetic (pronounced an-is-**thet**-ik) NOUN **anaesthetic** a drug that stops you feeling pain

▶ **anaesthetist** NOUN **anaesthetists** a doctor whose job is to help control the pain of people in hospital

anagram NOUN **anagrams** a word or sentence that has the same letters as another word or sentence, but in a different order. For example, *live* is an anagram of *evil*

analogue ADJECTIVE an analogue watch or clock has hands that move around a dial to show the time. Look up and compare **digital**

analogy NOUN **analogies** comparing two things that are similar to help explain one of them: *You can make an analogy between a computer and a brain.*

analyse VERB **analyses, analysing, analysed** to examine the different parts of something: *He analysed the evidence and worked out what had happened.*

▶ **analysis** NOUN **analyses** an examination of the different parts of something

▶ **analyst** NOUN **analysts** a person who examines something and works out how to improve it

anatomy NOUN **1** the study of the parts of the body **2** all the parts of the body: *A human's anatomy is very complex.*

ancestor NOUN **ancestors** your ancestors are all the past members of your family

▶ **ancestral** ADJECTIVE belonging to a person's family in the past: *the Duke's ancestral home*

▶ **ancestry** NOUN your ancestry is your family's past

anchor NOUN **anchors** a heavy piece of metal on a rope or chain that is

angles

acute angle
right angle
reflex angle
obtuse angle

Aa
Bb
Cc
Dd
Ee
Ff
Gg
Hh
Ii
Jj
Kk
Ll
Mm
Nn
Oo
Pp
Qq
Rr
Ss
Tt
Uu
Vv
Ww
Xx
Yy
Zz

attached to a boat, and that can be dropped to the bottom of the water to stop the boat from moving away
VERB **anchors, anchoring, anchored 1** to drop the anchor of a boat or ship to stop it moving away **2** to fix something firmly to the spot
▶ **anchorage** NOUN **anchorages** a place where ships can stop
anchovy NOUN **anchovies** a type of small fish with a very salty taste
ancient ADJECTIVE **1** belonging to a very long time ago: *the ancient people who once lived here* **2** very old
and CONJUNCTION **1** a word that is used to join parts of sentences: *We'll have bread and butter.* • *red and green striped paper* • *Go and get ready.* **2** plus: *Two and two make four.*
anemone (pronounced a-**nem**-on-i) NOUN **anemones** a kind of flower that often grows in woodland
angel NOUN **angels 1** a messenger from God **2** a very good person
▶ **angelic** ADJECTIVE very beautiful and good

◆**Angel** comes from the Greek word **angelos**, which means *messenger*.

anger NOUN the bad feeling you get about someone or something that annoys you

VERB **angers, angering, angered** to make someone feel angry
angle NOUN **angles 1** the shape that is made at the point where two straight lines meet. See the examples above **2** a point of view. *What's your angle on this?*
VERB **angles, angling, angled 1** to put something at a slope: *Did you hear her angling to borrow my new coat?* **2** if you angle a story, you tell it with your point of view
angler NOUN **anglers** a person who fishes, using a fishing rod
Anglican ADJECTIVE to do with or belonging to the Church of England
NOUN **Anglicans** a member of the Church of England
angling NOUN the sport of fishing with a fishing rod
Anglo-Saxon NOUN **1** the peoples who came to live in England and parts of Scotland in the 5th century **2** Old English, the English language before about 1150
ADJECTIVE belonging to or to do with the Anglo-Saxon people or their language, Old English
angry ADJECTIVE **angrier, angriest** cross or very cross: *Mum got very angry.* • *an angry crowd*
▶ **angrily** ADVERB in a very cross way: *A young girl came in, crying angrily.*

anguish NOUN a terrible feeling of unhappiness and suffering

▶ **anguished** ADJECTIVE miserable and suffering: *an anguished look*

angular ADJECTIVE an angular body or face is thin and pointed

animal NOUN **animals** a living being that can feel and move

✦ This word comes from the Latin word **anima**, which means *life*. The word **animation** is also linked to the Latin word **anima**.

animated ADJECTIVE **1** in an animated film, still drawings or objects are shown very quickly, one after the other, so that things in them appear to move **2** moving in a lively way

▶ **animatedly** ADVERB in a lively way

animation NOUN **animations 1** an animation is a film where pictures or objects appear to move by themselves **2** animation is energy and liveliness

aniseed NOUN a seed that tastes like liquorice and is used in making sweets, drinks and medicines

ankle NOUN **ankles** the place where your foot joins your leg

annex *or* **annexe** NOUN **annexes** an extra part of a building that may be added on to it or in a separate place

VERB **annexes, annexing, annexed** to annex something such as land is to take it and use it like your own

✦ The spelling **annexe**, with an **e** at the end, can only be used for the noun. The verb is 'to **annex**'.

annihilate (pronounced a-**nie**-il-ait) VERB **annihilates, annihilating, annihilated** to destroy somebody or something completely

▶ **annihilation** NOUN destroying somebody or something completely

anniversary NOUN **anniversaries** a day that is the same date as an event in the past: *a wedding anniversary • Today is the anniversary of the King's death.*

announce VERB **announces, announcing, announced** to tell everyone something: *Have they announced their engagement yet?*

▶ **announcement** NOUN **announcements** something that everybody is told, either in a special speech or on a notice: *Listen everyone; I want to make an announcement.*

▶ **announcer** NOUN **announcers** a person who introduces programmes on television or the radio

annoy VERB **annoys, annoying, annoyed** to annoy someone is to make them feel rather angry: *The way she never listens to me really annoys me.*

▶ **annoyance** NOUN **annoyances 1** annoyance is a feeling of irritation: *a look of annoyance* **2** an annoyance is something that irritates you

▶ **annoyed** ADJECTIVE rather angry

annual ADJECTIVE an annual event happens once every year: *an annual meeting of head teachers*

NOUN **annuals 1** a book that is published every year **2** a plant that lives for only one year

▶ **annually** ADVERB happening once every year

anon ABBREVIATION a short form of the word **anonymous**

anonymous ADJECTIVE **1** an anonymous letter or book is written by an unknown writer **2** an anonymous telephone call is made by someone who does not give their name

▶ **anonymously** ADVERB by a person who does not give their name: *The money has been given anonymously.*

anorak NOUN **anoraks** a waterproof jacket, usually with a hood

anorexia NOUN an illness that makes a person very thin because they do not want to eat

▶ **anorexic** ADJECTIVE suffering from anorexia and perhaps very thin

another ADJECTIVE **1** one more: *Have another piece of chocolate.* **2** a different one: *Another day we'll walk further.*

PRONOUN **1** one more: *He had two gold medals and now he has another.* **2** a different one: *If that pencil is broken, use another.*

answer NOUN **answers 1** an answer is what you reply when someone asks you a question **2** the answer to a problem is the thing that solves it
VERB **answers, answering, answered 1** to reply when someone asks you a question **2** to answer the telephone is to speak to the person calling when it rings **3** to open the door when someone rings or knocks: *Would you answer the door please?*
• **answer back** to be cheeky or rude to someone who has told you off

ant NOUN **ants** a tiny insect

antagonism NOUN a feeling of wanting to fight against someone or an idea
▸ **antagonistic** ADJECTIVE wanting to fight with someone or something

ante- PREFIX if a word starts with **ante-**, it often means 'before something'. For example, an *anteroom* is a room you go into before you enter a larger room

anteater NOUN **anteaters** an animal with a long nose and no teeth, that mainly eats ants

antelope NOUN **antelope** *or* **antelopes** an animal like a deer, that has long horns and runs very fast

antenna NOUN **antennae** *or* **antennas 1** a long thin feeler on the head of an insect or shellfish **2** an aerial, for example for a television

✦ The plural of **antenna** when it means 'a feeler' is **antennae**.
The plural when it means 'an aerial' is **antennas**.

anthem NOUN **anthems** a song that praises someone or something, for example a national anthem, which praises a country or its ruler

anthill NOUN **anthills** a pile of earth that ants build up over their nest

anthology NOUN **anthologies** a book of stories, poems or songs

anti- PREFIX if a word starts with **anti-**, it means 'against'. For example, *anti-aircraft* weapons are used to fight enemy aircraft

antibiotic NOUN **antibiotics** a medicine that fights bacteria that can cause infections: *Penicillin is an antibiotic.*

antibody NOUN **antibodies** a substance that the body produces in the blood to fight harmful bacteria

anticipate VERB **anticipates, anticipating, anticipated** to anticipate something is to expect it to happen and to do something about it: *A couple of prison officers had anticipated his escape.*
▸ **anticipation** NOUN excitement about something that is going to happen

anticlockwise ADVERB going in the opposite direction to the hands of a clock
ADJECTIVE in the opposite direction to the hands of a clock

antics PLURAL NOUN someone's antics are the funny things that they do

antidote NOUN **antidotes** a medicine that stops a poison being harmful

antifreeze NOUN a chemical that you can add to a liquid to stop it from freezing, especially the water in a car radiator

antiquated ADJECTIVE old-fashioned

antique NOUN **antiques** an object that is old and valuable: *a collector of antiques*
ADJECTIVE old and valuable

antiseptic NOUN **antiseptics** a substance that kills germs

antler NOUN **antlers** a horn that divides like branches and grows on the head of a deer

antonym NOUN **antonyms** a word that means the opposite of another word. For example, *big* is an antonym of *small*. Look up and compare **synonym**

anus NOUN the opening in a bottom that lets out the solid matter that the body does not need

anvil NOUN **anvils** a heavy metal block that a blacksmith holds hot metal against when it is being hammered into shape

anxiety NOUN **anxieties 1** anxiety is worrying, especially about what may

Aa
Bb
Cc
Dd
Ee
Ff
Gg
Hh
Ii
Jj
Kk
Ll
Mm
Nn
Oo
Pp
Qq
Rr
Ss
Tt
Uu
Vv
Ww
Xx
Yy
Zz

happen **2** an anxiety is something you are worried about

anxious ADJECTIVE **1** worried: *an anxious look on his face* **2** nervous and uncomfortable: *an anxious time for the family* **3** keen: *I'm anxious to get there on time to get a good seat.*

▸ **anxiously** ADVERB in a worried way: *He looked anxiously at his watch.*

any ADJECTIVE **1** every: *Any child would know that answer.* **2** one, but not a particular one: *It'll be here any day now.* **3** some: *Have we got any sweets?* ADVERB at all: *I can't go on any longer.* PRONOUN **1** one: *Ask any of them.* **2** some: *We haven't got any left.*

anybody PRONOUN any person at all: *Anybody is allowed to enter.*

anyhow ADVERB **1** anyway: *I missed lunch but I wasn't hungry anyhow.* **2** in an untidy, careless way: *The books had been left anyhow all over the floor.*

anyone PRONOUN any person at all: *There isn't anyone left.*

anything PRONOUN something of any kind: *He hasn't eaten anything.* • *Has anything happened?*

anyway ADVERB **1** in any case: *Leon couldn't go with me but I enjoyed the party anyway.* **2** a word you use to change the subject in a conversation: *Anyway, how have you been?*

anywhere ADVERB in or to any place: *I'm not going anywhere.* • *I can't find my keys anywhere.* PRONOUN any place: *Anywhere would be better than this.*

apart ADVERB **1** separated by distance or time: *Stand with your feet apart.* • *two classes, a week apart* **2** into pieces: *My brother took my doll apart.* PREPOSITION except for: *Apart from us, nobody's interested.*

apartment NOUN **apartments 1** a set of rooms on one level of a building **2** a room in a building: *a three-apartment house*

ape NOUN **apes** a kind of monkey that is large and has no tail VERB **apes, aping, aped** to ape someone is to copy what they do

apex NOUN **apexes** or **apices** the top point of something, especially a triangle

aphid (pronounced ay-fid) NOUN **aphids** a small insect, for example a greenfly, that feeds on plants

apologetic ADJECTIVE if you are apologetic, you show that you are sorry for something you have done

▸ **apologetically** ADVERB showing that you are sorry

apologize or **apologise** VERB **apologizes, apologizing, apologized** to say sorry for doing something wrong: *I had to apologize to the rest of the family for being so rude.*

▸ **apology** NOUN **apologies** an apology is when you say you are sorry for something you have done: *The head teacher sat waiting for our apology.*

apostle NOUN **apostles** in Christianity, an apostle was one of the first twelve followers of Jesus Christ

apostrophe (pronounced a-**pos**-tri-fi) NOUN **apostrophes** the punctuation mark that looks like a very short line at the top of a word. You use it to show where a letter or letters have been missed out, for example *don't* or *he's*. It also shows who owns something when it is used with *s*, for example *Nicky's desk*

appal VERB **appals, appalling, appalled** if something appals you, you are shocked because it is so bad: *I was appalled by her language.*

▸ **appalling** ADJECTIVE **1** shocking: *an appalling accident* **2** very bad: *appalling weather*

apparatus NOUN the equipment that you need for a particular task: *breathing apparatus for the divers*

apparent ADJECTIVE **1** easy to see: *Then, for no apparent reason, he began to cry.* **2** appearing to be true: *His apparent magical powers were false.*

▸ **apparently** ADVERB it appears or seems: *David is apparently off sick today.*

appeal VERB **appeals, appealing, appealed 1** to appeal for something is to ask everyone for what you badly need: *The police have appealed to the public for more information.* **2** to appeal to someone is to be attractive to them: *Horse riding doesn't appeal to me one bit.* **3** to appeal against a decision is to ask someone to change their mind

NOUN **appeals 1** an appeal is a request for something you want very much **2** appeal is what makes a thing or person attractive and interesting: *I don't understand the appeal of stamp collecting.* **3** an appeal is asking someone to change a decision, especially in a court of law

appear VERB **appears, appearing, appeared**

1 a thing or person appears when you can suddenly see them: *Then Greta appeared round the corner. • A black mark has appeared on the wall.*

2 to seem: *Jill appeared to be getting very cross. • You don't appear to be ready yet.*

3 to appear in a play or film is to perform in it: *Tom is appearing as Hamlet at the Globe Theatre.*

4 to appear in a court of law is to be tried there for a crime

▶ **appearance** NOUN **appearances**

1 arriving: *Until Linda's appearance, we had been really bored.*

2 the way a thing or person looks: *Change your appearance with a new hairstyle.*

3 a performance in a play or film: *This is Mel's second appearance in a comedy.*

4 someone makes an appearance in a law court when they have been charged with a crime and have to be found guilty or not guilty

5 appearances are the way things seem to be, but possibly not the way they really are

appease VERB **appeases, appeasing, appeased** to make someone feel better by giving them what they want

appendicitis NOUN an illness where the appendix is painful and usually has to be removed

appendix NOUN **appendixes** or **appendices 1** a small tube on the right side of the body that is a part of the human intestines **2** an extra section at the end of a book or document that gives more details about something

✦ The plural of **appendix** when it is a part of the body is **appendixes**: *The doctor removed two appendixes that day.* The plural when it is part of a book is **appendices**: *The appendices begin on page 400.*

appetite NOUN **appetites** your appetite, usually for food, is how much you want any: *Elly has lost her appetite since she's been ill.*

▶ **appetizer** or **appetiser** NOUN **appetizers** something small to eat or drink before a meal

▶ **appetizing** or **appetising** ADJECTIVE making you want to eat: *an appetizing smell*

applaud VERB **applauds, applauding, applauded** to praise someone, especially by clapping: *The audience applauded Nancy loudly.*

▶ **applause** NOUN clapping

apple NOUN **apples** a hard, round fruit with red, green or yellow skin

appliance NOUN **appliances** a piece of equipment: *kitchen appliances*

applicant NOUN **applicants** a person who applies to get something, for example a job

application NOUN **applications**

1 an application is a letter or a form asking for something like a job

2 application is an effort to do something well: *He could pass the test with a little more application.*

3 an application is when you put something such as paint or cream on a surface: *Let the paint dry between applications.*

4 (*ICT*) an application is a computer program that does a particular kind of job, for example a word processing program

applied ADJECTIVE an applied science is one that has a practical use

apply VERB **applies, applying, applied**

1 to ask for something like a job, usually by writing a letter or filling in a form: *Martin's applying to go to university this year.*

Aa
Bb
Cc
Dd
Ee
Ff
Gg
Hh
Ii
Jj
Kk
Ll
Mm
Nn
Oo
Pp
Qq
Rr
Ss
Tt
Uu
Vv
Ww
Xx
Yy
Zz

Aa
Bb
Cc
Dd
Ee
Ff
Gg
Hh
Ii
Jj
Kk
Ll
Mm
Nn
Oo
Pp
Qq
Rr
Ss
Tt
Uu
Vv
Ww
Xx
Yy
Zz

2 to apply something to a surface is to put or spread it on: *Apply the cream to your skin three times a day.*
3 if something applies to you, it affects you: *Do these rules apply to all of us?*
4 to apply yourself is to work hard at something

appoint VERB **appoints, appointing, appointed 1** to appoint someone is to give them a job: *Who will be appointed as the new manager of Wales?* **2** to appoint a time or place for something is to arrange it in advance
▸ **appointment** NOUN **appointments 1** an appointment is a time and place that you must meet someone: *I have a dentist's appointment at 2 o'clock tomorrow.* **2** an appointment is a job **3** appointment is giving someone a job: *the appointment of a new music teacher*

appreciate VERB **appreciates, appreciating, appreciated 1** to appreciate someone or something is to think they are valuable, useful, important or kind: *Rosie appreciated the card we sent her.* **2** if you appreciate something, you understand it: *Hasim appreciates that he won't live forever.* **3** if something appreciates, it becomes more valuable
▸ **appreciation** NOUN **1** understanding and awareness: *the appreciation of music* **2** showing you are grateful for or pleased by something: *a gift in appreciation of your help* **3** increasing value
▸ **appreciative** ADJECTIVE an appreciative person shows that they are grateful or pleased by something: *an appreciative audience for the show*

apprehension NOUN worry about what will happen in future
▸ **apprehensive** ADJECTIVE nervous and afraid: *Are you apprehensive about the future?*

apprentice NOUN **apprentices** a person who is learning how to do a skilled job from someone who can already do it
▸ **apprenticeship** NOUN the time when someone is learning their job

approach VERB **approaches,**

approaching, approached 1 to come towards a place, person or thing: *approach the animals very slowly* • *a plane approaching Paris from the south* **2** to go to a person with a suggestion: *If you are worried about something, you can approach your teacher.*
NOUN **approaches 1** coming near: *the approach of summer* **2** the way up to a building: *a tree-lined approach to the castle* **3** a way of trying to deal with something: *a clever approach to the problem*
▸ **approachable** ADJECTIVE an approachable person is easy to talk to

appropriate ADJECTIVE suitable: *Please wear appropriate clothing on the school trip.*

approve VERB **approves, approving, approved 1** to approve of something is to think it is good: *He did not approve of children daydreaming in class.* **2** to approve something is to agree to it
▸ **approval** NOUN approval is when someone thinks something is good or satisfactory

approximate ADJECTIVE not exact: *What is the approximate number of chairs we need?*
▸ **approximately** ADVERB more or less: *approximately one thousand people*

apricot NOUN **apricots 1** a small orange-coloured fruit with a soft skin and a stone inside **2** a soft orange colour

April NOUN the fourth month of the year, after March and before May

✦**April** comes from the Latin word **aperire**, which means *to open*, because the spring flowers start to open around this time.

apron NOUN **aprons** a piece of cloth you wear over the front of your clothes to keep them clean or dry

apt ADJECTIVE **1** likely to: *She is apt to fly into a temper.* **2** suitable: *an apt description*
▸ **aptly** ADVERB suitably: *a house by the*

river, aptly named 'River's Edge'

aptitude NOUN talent: *Hayley shows an aptitude for maths.*

aquarium NOUN **aquariums** *or* **aquaria** a glass tank or a building, for example in a zoo, for keeping fish or water animals in

✦ **Aqua** is the Latin word for *water*. If a word starts with **aqua**, you can guess that it has something to do with water.

aquatic ADJECTIVE to do with water: *aquatic sports • Aquatic plants live in water.*

aqueduct NOUN **aqueducts** a bridge that carries a river or canal across a valley

arable ADJECTIVE arable land is farming land where crops grow

arc NOUN **arcs 1** (*maths*) part of the circumference of a circle **2** a curve

arcade NOUN **arcades** a covered walk, especially with shops along the side

arch NOUN **arches 1** the curved top of a doorway or between the supports of a bridge **2** the curved underneath part of your foot

VERB **arches, arching, arched** to curve over: *a cat arching its back*

arch- PREFIX if a word starts with **arch-**, it means 'most important'. For example, your *arch-enemy* is your main enemy

archaeology NOUN the study of things that people from the past have left behind, often things that have been dug out from under the ground

▸ **archaeological** ADJECTIVE to do with studying the things left by people in the past

▸ **archaeologist** NOUN **archaeologists** a person who studies things left by people in the past

archbishop NOUN **archbishops** a chief bishop

archery NOUN the sport of shooting with a bow and arrow

▸ **archer** NOUN **archers** a person who shoots with a bow and arrow

architect (pronounced **ar**-ki-tekt) NOUN **architects** a person whose job is to design buildings

▸ **architecture** NOUN **1** the job of designing buidings **2** a style of building: *Roman architecture*

archives (pronounced **ar**-kievz) PLURAL NOUN the historical records of a place or organization

are VERB **1** the form of the verb **be** in the present tense that is used with **you, we, they** and plural nouns: *We are all here today. • Where are the best places to visit?* **2** **are** is also used as a helping verb along with a main verb: *We are leaving tomorrow.*

area NOUN **areas 1** a part or region: *a children's play area • There are a lot of farms in this area.* **2** the size of a surface, that you measure in **square** units: *A floor that is 5 metres by 5 metres has an area of 25 square metres.*

aren't a short way to say and write **are not**: *These aren't my boots.*

arena NOUN **arenas** a large space for sports or other entertainments with seats all around it

✦ **Arena** means *sand* in Latin. In ancient times an arena would have been the part of a theatre covered with sand.

argue VERB **argues, arguing, argued 1** to quarrel: *The children never stop arguing with each other.* **2** to argue with someone is to tell them you disagree with what they have said **3** to argue something is to give reasons for it: *The manager argued that the shop would have to close.*

argument NOUN **arguments 1** a discussion where people do not agree with each other: *There was a loud argument going on next door.* **2** the reasons for having or doing something: *My argument against the trip is that we don't have enough money.*

arid ADJECTIVE very dry: *the arid deserts of Arizona*

arise VERB **arises, arising, arose, arisen 1** to happen: *A small problem has arisen.* **2** to move upwards: *A*

Aa
Bb
Cc
Dd
Ee
Ff
Gg
Hh
Ii
Jj
Kk
Ll
Mm
Nn
Oo
Pp
Qq
Rr
Ss
Tt
Uu
Vv
Ww
Xx
Yy
Zz

Aa
Bb
Cc
Dd
Ee
Ff
Gg
Hh
Ii
Jj
Kk
Ll
Mm
Nn
Oo
Pp
Qq
Rr
Ss
Tt
Uu
Vv
Ww
Xx
Yy
Zz

wonderful smell arose from the basement. **3** an old word meaning to get up or stand up: *He arose early to walk the dog.*

aristocracy NOUN people from families that were often close to the royal families of the past

▶ **aristocrat** NOUN **aristocrats** a person from an upper-class family who often has a title like *Lord* or *Lady*

▶ **aristocratic** ADJECTIVE belonging to a country's upper class

arithmetic NOUN adding, subtracting, dividing and multiplying numbers

▶ **arithmetical** ADJECTIVE to do with calculating numbers

ark NOUN **arks** the boat that carried Noah, his family and two of every animal during the flood in the Bible story

arm¹ NOUN **arms 1** the part of your body between your shoulder and your hand **2** the arm of a piece of clothing is a sleeve **3** a part of something that sticks out of its side, usually with a bend or angle in it: *the arm of a chair*

arm² VERB **arms, arming, armed** to arm someone is to give them a weapon to fight with

▶ **armed** ADJECTIVE someone who is armed has a weapon with them

armada NOUN a fleet of ships going to war

armadillo NOUN **armadillos** a small animal from America that has a kind of protective shell made of small pieces of bone

armaments PLURAL NOUN weapons and other war equipment

armchair NOUN **armchairs** a chair with sides for resting your arms on

armistice NOUN a time when enemies agree to stop fighting for a while, especially to talk about stopping for ever

armour NOUN a hard cover, usually made from metal, that protects someone or something in a battle: *a knight wearing a suit of armour*

▶ **armoured** ADJECTIVE protected by a hard layer of something such as metal: *an armoured vehicle*

armpit NOUN **armpits** the angle where your arm joins your body under your shoulder

arms PLURAL NOUN weapons

army NOUN **armies** an organization of many soldiers, who will fight against an enemy

aroma NOUN **aromas** a nice smell, especially of food

▶ **aromatic** ADJECTIVE having a good smell: *aromatic plants*

arose VERB a way of changing the verb **arise** to make a past tense: *The people arose when the judge entered the court.*

around PREPOSITION
1 on all sides: *sitting around the table*
2 in a circle: *hold hands around the tree*
3 at or to different parts of a place: *walking around the city*
4 about: *at around 4 o'clock* • *She lives somewhere around here.*
ADVERB all about in different places: *clothes lying all around* • *children running around*

arouse VERB **arouses, arousing, aroused 1** to arouse someone is to wake them up **2** to arouse a feeling in someone is to make them have that feeling

arrange VERB **arranges, arranging, arranged 1** to set things out carefully: *Arrange the bowls on the table.* **2** to make plans so that something happens: *Who is arranging the wedding?*

▶ **arrangement** NOUN **arrangements 1** an arrangement is the position that things are put in: *a flower arrangement* **2** an arrangement is a plan or set of plans that you make with someone else: *The arrangement was that we should meet back at the car.*

array NOUN **arrays** a lot of things set out for people to see: *The table had an array of different foods.*

arrest VERB **arrests, arresting, arrested 1** to arrest someone is to catch them and take them to be charged with a crime **2** to arrest something is to stop it from continuing: *to arrest the progress of the illness*
NOUN **arrests** an arrest is when the

police take a person to be charged with a crime

• **under arrest** a person is under arrest when the police hold them before charging them with a crime

arrival NOUN **arrivals 1** an arrival is when someone reaches a place: *We are all looking forward to Alice's arrival.* **2** an arrival is a person or thing that has come to a place: *Come and meet the new arrivals to the school.*

arrive VERB **arrives, arriving, arrived 1** to arrive is to reach a place: *Please arrive at the station by 5.30.* • *If they don't arrive soon, we'll have to go without them.* **2** when a time or event arrives, it happens: *Would her birthday ever arrive?* **3** to arrive at a decision is to finally make a decision

arrogant ADJECTIVE an arrogant person thinks they are better than other people
▸ **arrogance** NOUN a feeling of being more important or better than other people

arrow NOUN **arrows 1** a pointed stick that you can shoot from a bow **2** a pointed shape that shows a particular direction

arsenal NOUN **arsenals** a weapons store

arsenic NOUN a strong poison

arson NOUN the crime of setting fire to a building on purpose
▸ **arsonist** NOUN **arsonists** a person who sets fire to a building on purpose

art NOUN **arts 1** art is the beautiful things that people do and invent in painting, sculpture, music and literature **2** an art is a skill that you use to do or make something beautiful **3** arts are subjects that you can study that are not sciences

artefact NOUN **artefacts** any object that a human being has made

artery NOUN **arteries** a tube that takes blood around the body from the heart

artful ADJECTIVE clever in a sneaky, dishonest way
▸ **artfully** ADVERB in a way that gets you what you want, but not obviously

arthritis NOUN swollen joints that are painful and make moving difficult
▸ **arthritic** ADJECTIVE swollen and painful because of arthritis

artichoke NOUN **artichokes** a vegetable that grows on a long stem and looks a bit like a pineapple

article NOUN **articles 1** a thing or item: *articles of clothing* **2** a piece of writing in a magazine or newspaper: *an article about bullies in the school paper* **3** (*grammar*) the word **a** or the word **the**

articulate VERB **articulates, articulating, articulated** (pronounced ar-**tik**-yoo-lait) to articulate something is to say it clearly
ADJECTIVE (pronounced ar-**tik**-yoo-lit) an articulate person speaks clearly
▸ **articulation** NOUN your articulation is the way you speak

articulated ADJECTIVE an articulated lorry has a joint between the cab and the trailer that makes turning easier

artificial ADJECTIVE looking natural, but actually made by humans or by a machine: *artificial fur*
▸ **artificially** ADVERB not naturally

artillery NOUN big guns that an army uses

artist NOUN **artists 1** a person who paints, draws or makes sculptures **2** a person who does something very skilfully, especially some kind of performing
▸ **artistic** ADJECTIVE **1** an artistic person is creative and enjoys art **2** something artistic is creative and skilful: *a very artistic use of colours*

as CONJUNCTION

1 a word you use when you compare things or people: *Are you as tall as me?*
2 while: *As we climbed, the air got colder.*
3 because: *I went first as I was the youngest.*
4 like: *As I thought, most people had already left.*

ascend VERB **ascends, ascending, ascended 1** to ascend is to go upwards: *a bird ascending into the sky* **2** to ascend something like a hill is to climb it

Aa
Bb
Cc
Dd
Ee
Ff
Gg
Hh
Ii
Jj
Kk
Ll
Mm
Nn
Oo
Pp
Qq
Rr
Ss
Tt
Uu
Vv
Ww
Xx
Yy
Zz

▶ **ascent** NOUN **ascents** an upward movement or climb: *The plane will now begin its ascent.*

ash¹ NOUN **ashes** the white powder that remains after something is burnt

ash² NOUN **ashes** a tree with a silvery-grey bark

ashamed ADJECTIVE **1** to be ashamed of yourself or something you have done is to feel bad about the thing that you have done: *I'm ashamed of my behaviour today.* **2** to be ashamed of a thing or person is to feel bad because they are not good enough: *I'm ashamed of my Dad's rotten old car but he likes it.*

ashore ADVERB on or on to dry land: *We went ashore for dinner and returned to the ship later.*

ashtray NOUN **ashtrays** a small dish for the ash from people's cigarettes

aside ADVERB to or on one side: *Please stand aside and let us through.*

NOUN **asides** an aside is a remark that someone makes that not everyone present is supposed to hear

ask VERB **asks, asking, asked 1** to say a question so that you get information from someone: *They asked me about my family.* **2** to ask someone for something is to tell them that you would like them to give it to you: *Ask your brother for a sweet.* **3** to ask someone to an event like a party is to invite them: *We've asked twenty people but they won't all turn up.*

• **ask for it** to do something that will definitely get you into trouble

• **ask for trouble** to do something stupid that will probably end badly

asleep ADJECTIVE sleeping: *Don't wake her if she's asleep.*

ADVERB into sleep: *I fell asleep after a while.*

asp NOUN **asps** a small, poisonous snake

asparagus NOUN a plant with fat, pale green stems that can be cooked and eaten as a vegetable

aspect NOUN **aspects 1** a part of a situation or problem: *Many aspects of this plan bother me.* **2** the direction a building faces: *a house with a northern aspect*

asphalt NOUN a surface for roads and paths that looks like gravel mixed with tar

aspirin NOUN **aspirins** a medicine for stopping pain, usually made into tablets

ass NOUN **asses 1** a donkey **2** (*informal*) a stupid person

assassin NOUN **assassins** a person who deliberately kills someone, especially a politician or other leader

▶ **assassinate** VERB **assassinates, assassinating, assassinated** to kill someone, especially a politician or leader

▶ **assassination** NOUN **assassinations** a planned killing

assault NOUN **assaults** an attack

VERB **assaults, assaulting, assaulted** to attack someone

assemble VERB **assembles, assembling, assembled 1** to get several things or people together: *We assembled a cast for the school play.* **2** to put something together from several parts: *instructions for assembling the bookcase* **3** to come together in a group: *Please assemble in the hall.*

▶ **assembly** NOUN **assemblies 1** putting something together from different parts: *assembly instructions* **2** coming together to form a group: *the morning assembly at school* **3** an assembly is a group of important people such as politicians, who make decisions for other people: *the General Assembly of the United Nations*

assent VERB **assents, assenting, assented** to agree

NOUN agreement or permission

assess VERB **assesses, assessing, assessed** to consider and decide how good, important or expensive something is: *Now we'll have to assess how much damage has been done.*

▶ **assessment** NOUN **assessments** an opinion about something from someone who has considered it carefully: *What is your assessment of the situation?*

asset NOUN **assets** something you have that is useful or valuable

assign VERB **assigns, assigning, assigned** to assign a job or task to someone is to give it to them to do

▶ **assignment** NOUN **assignments** a job or task to do

assist VERB **assists, assisting, assisted** to help someone to do something

▶ **assistance** NOUN help for someone who is trying to do something

▶ **assistant** NOUN **assistants 1** a person whose job is to help someone else **2** a person whose job is to serve customers in a shop

associate VERB **associates, associating, associated 1** to associate with someone is to spend time with them: *Frank associates with a lot of very important people.* **2** to associate things is to make connections between them in your mind: *I always associate spring with rain.*

NOUN **associates** your associates are the people you mix with

association NOUN **associations 1** an association is a club or society **2** association is putting things or people together: *a word association game*

association football NOUN a game in which two teams of eleven players try to kick a ball into a goal, without handling the ball while it is in play. It is also called **soccer**

assorted ADJECTIVE mixed: *assorted flavours*

▶ **assortment** NOUN **assortments** a mixture: *a strange assortment of people*

assume VERB **assumes, assuming, assumed 1** to suppose something: *I just assumed that you had met each other before.* **2** to assume something like a look or attitude is to begin to have it: *He assumed a puzzled look but of course he knew the answer.* **3** to assume a new name is to change your name

▶ **assumption** NOUN **assumptions** something you suppose

assurance NOUN **assurances 1** assurance is being confident: *Andy plays tennis with complete assurance.* **2** assurance is being certain about something **3** an assurance is similar to a promise

assure VERB **assures, assuring, assured** to try to make someone feel certain about what you are telling them: *Mr Harris has assured us that the weather will be good tomorrow.*

asterisk NOUN **asterisks** a star (*) put beside something in a piece of writing, usually to tell you there is a note about it at the bottom of the page

asteroid NOUN **asteroids** one of the rocky objects that circle the sun, mostly between Jupiter and Mars

asthma NOUN an illness that people may suffer from for a long time and that makes breathing difficult

▶ **asthmatic** ADJECTIVE a person who is asthmatic sometimes finds it very difficult to breathe

NOUN **asthmatics** a person who has trouble breathing because they suffer from asthma

astonish VERB **astonishes, astonishing, astonished** to astonish someone is to surprise them very much

▶ **astonishment** NOUN great surprise: *We stared at our friend in astonishment.*

astound VERB **astounds, astounding, astounded** to astound someone is to surprise or shock them very much: *The news astounded us all.*

▶ **astounding** ADJECTIVE amazing

astray ADVERB to go astray is to go to the wrong place or in the wrong direction

astride PREPOSITION with one leg on each side: *sitting astride a horse*

astrology NOUN the study of how the stars and the way they move may affect our lives

▶ **astrologer** NOUN **astrologers** a person who studies astrology

✦ **Astron** is the Greek word for *star*. If a word starts with **astro**, you can guess that it has something to do with the stars or space. Other examples are **astronaut** and **astronomy**.

astronaut NOUN **astronauts** a member of the crew of a spacecraft

astronomical ADJECTIVE **1** to do with the stars: *the American Astronomical Society* **2** very large: *an astronomical number*

Aa
Bb
Cc
Dd
Ee
Ff
Gg
Hh
Ii
Jj
Kk
Ll
Mm
Nn
Oo
Pp
Qq
Rr
Ss
Tt
Uu
Vv
Ww
Xx
Yy
Zz

▶ **astronomically** ADVERB very much: *Prices have risen astronomically.*

astronomy NOUN the study of the stars and the way they move

▶ **astronomer** NOUN **astronomers** a person who studies the stars

asylum NOUN **1** asylum is safety and protection, especially for people who do not feel safe in their own country: *people who seek asylum in this country* **2** an old-fashioned word for a home for people with mental illnesses

asymmetry NOUN asymmetry is where a single thing has two parts or halves that have different shapes. The opposite of asymmetry is **symmetry**

▶ **asymmetrical** ADJECTIVE something asymmetrical has two sides of different shapes

at PREPOSITION **1** showing where or when you mean: *Look at me!* • *Meet at the station.* • *School finishes at 4 o'clock.* **2** costing: *four bottles at 75p each*

ate VERB a way of changing the verb **eat** to make a past tense: *The dog ate most of my dinner last night.*

atheist NOUN **atheists** a person who does not believe in a god

▶ **atheism** NOUN the belief that there is no god

athlete NOUN **athletes** a person who is very fit and good at sport

▶ **athletic** ADJECTIVE **1** fit and strong **2** to do with the sports of running, jumping and throwing

▶ **athletics** PLURAL NOUN the group of sports that include running, jumping and throwing

atlas NOUN **atlases** a book of maps

✦ This word comes from the name of a character in Greek mythology, **Atlas**. He was forced by the Greek gods to carry the universe on his shoulders as a punishment.

atmosphere NOUN **atmospheres**
1 the air around a planet: *the Earth's atmosphere* **2** a feeling around where you are: *There was an atmosphere of excitement in the town.*

▶ **atmospheric** ADJECTIVE **1** to do with the air **2** with a very strong feeling in the air: *a very atmospheric experience*

atoll NOUN **atolls** an island made of coral

atom NOUN **atoms** (*science*) the tiniest possible part of a substance. More than one atom can make up a **molecule**

▶ **atomic** ADJECTIVE using the power that is created when atoms are broken: *atomic weapons*

atrocious ADJECTIVE very bad

▶ **atrocity** NOUN **atrocities** a terrible, violent crime

attach VERB **attaches, attaching, attached** to attach one thing to another is to fix it there: *attached to the wall with a nail*

▶ **attached** ADJECTIVE if you are attached to someone, you are very fond of them

▶ **attachment** NOUN **attachments**
1 a friendship **2** an extra part that you can add to a machine to make it do something different: *a cutting attachment on the food mixer* **3** (*ICT*) something like a document or picture that you send with an email message

attack VERB **attacks, attacking, attacked 1** to attack a person is to suddenly try to hurt them: *A man was attacked and robbed on Friday.* **2** to attack a person or thing is to say bad things about them: *The newspapers attacked the prime minister's speech.* **3** to attack a place is to fire at it or drop bombs on it: *The airfield is being attacked by enemy bombers.*

NOUN **attacks 1** a violent act against a place or person: *an attack on the west of the city* **2** an attempt to hurt someone by writing or saying bad things about them: *an attack in the newspapers* **3** a sudden pain or illness: *an attack of hay fever*

▶ **attacker** NOUN **attackers** a person who tries to hurt someone violently

attain VERB **attains, attaining, attained** to attain something is to achieve it: *Penny has attained Level D this term.*

▶ **attainment** NOUN **attainments**
1 attainment is how much you have

achieved: *an attainment test* **2** an attainment is something you have achieved

attempt VERB **attempt, attempting, attempted** to attempt something or to attempt to do something is to try to do it: *We are attempting a very steep climb to the top.* • *Nobody has ever attempted to do this before.*
NOUN **attempts** when you make an attempt, you try to do something: *an attempt to break the world record*

attend VERB **attends, attending, attended**
1 to attend an event is to go to it: *Thousands of people attended the concert in the park.*
2 to attend school is to go there
3 to attend to a thing is to deal with it: *I've got a lot of work to attend to this morning.*
4 to attend to a person is to do what they need you to do for them: *The doctor will attend to the children first.*
▶ **attendance** NOUN **1** being present somewhere: *the school attendance register* **2** the number of people who are present somewhere: *a poor attendance at the match*
▶ **attendant** NOUN **attendants** a person whose job is to help

attention NOUN **1** you pay attention to something when you think about it, listen to it or look at it **2** attention is care or concentration: *He needs medical attention.* • *I found it difficult to hold the audience's attention.*
• **stand to attention** to stand up straight like a soldier

attentive ADJECTIVE an attentive person gives careful attention to someone or something: *You have to be attentive in class.* • *My sister was very attentive when I was ill.*
▶ **attentively** ADVERB with thought and care: *Listen attentively to this story.*

attic NOUN **attics** the space in the roof of a house

attitude NOUN **attitudes 1** the way a person thinks about something: *John's*

attitude to school is not good. **2** if someone has attitude, they are very confident, sometimes in a rude way

attract VERB **attracts, attracting, attracted 1** to be attracted to someone or something is to be interested in them and to like them: *The children are always attracted to the big dipper first.* **2** to attract someone's attention is to get them to look or listen **3** things are attracted to each other when they move towards each other without any help: *The dust is attracted to the shiny surfaces first.*
▶ **attraction** NOUN **attractions 1** being attracted to something **2** an attraction is something that you want to see or do: *What do you think are the main attractions here?* **3** (*science*) attraction is the way things seem to pull together without any help

attractive ADJECTIVE **1** an attractive thing or person looks nice **2** an attractive idea sounds interesting or pleasant

aubergine (pronounced oh-ber-jeen) NOUN **aubergines** an oval vegetable with a smooth, shiny, dark purple skin

auburn ADJECTIVE auburn hair is reddish-brown

auction NOUN **auctions** a sale where the person who offers the highest price for something is able to buy it
VERB **auctions, auctioning, auctioned** to auction something is to sell it to the person who offers the most money for it
▶ **auctioneer** NOUN **auctioneers** a person whose job is to sell things to the person who offers the most money for them

audible ADJECTIVE an audible sound can be heard easily
▶ **audibly** ADVERB in a way that people can hear: *Douglas giggled audibly.*

audience NOUN **audiences 1** the people who listen to or watch a performance **2** an interview with an important person: *an audience with the Queen*

audio ADJECTIVE to do with hearing: *an audio cassette*

Aa
Bb
Cc
Dd
Ee
Ff
Gg
Hh
Ii
Jj
Kk
Ll
Mm
Nn
Oo
Pp
Qq
Rr
Ss
Tt
Uu
Vv
Ww
Xx
Yy
Zz

✦ **Audio** is Latin for *I hear*. If a word starts with **audio** or **audi**, you can guess that it has something to do with hearing or listening. Other examples are **audiovisual** and **auditorium**.

audiovisual ADJECTIVE something that uses both sound and pictures: *an audiovisual presentation to the class*

audition NOUN **auditions** a short performance in front of one or more people to show what you can do: *There are auditions to choose the best dancers to go to ballet school.* VERB **auditions, auditioning, auditioned 1** to try to get a place in a show or a musical group by showing how well you can do **2** to listen to performers and try to choose the best ones for something like a choir or play

auditorium NOUN **auditoriums** the part of a theatre where the audience sits

August NOUN the eighth month of the year, after July and before September

✦ **August** comes from the Latin word for this month, **Augustus**, which was named after the Roman emperor *Augustus Caesar*.

aunt NOUN **aunts 1** the sister of one of your parents **2** your uncle's wife

au pair (pronounced oh **pair**) NOUN **au pairs** a person, usually a young woman, who lives with a family in another country and works for them in return for some money

aural ADJECTIVE to do with your ears or hearing: *We're going to have an aural comprehension test.*

austere ADJECTIVE **1** something that is austere looks plain, hard and dull: *an austere waiting room* **2** a person who is austere is hard and unfriendly
▸ **austerity** NOUN **1** a plain, hard appearance **2** strictness

authentic ADJECTIVE real: *an authentic wartime uniform*
▸ **authenticity** NOUN how real or true something is: *It's difficult to prove the authenticity of the story.*

author NOUN **authors** a writer of something such as a book

authority NOUN **authorities 1** authority is power and control: *You have no authority in this building.* **2** an authority is the group of people who control an activity or area: *The local authority gives funds to schools in the area.* **3** an authority on a subject is an expert on it: *She's a world authority on butterflies.*

authorize or **authorise** VERB **authorizes, authorizing, authorized 1** to give someone permission to do something **2** to officially allow something to happen
▸ **authorization** or **authorisation** NOUN official permission for someone to do something

autism NOUN a condition where someone finds it very difficult to communicate and mix with other people and the world outside themselves
▸ **autistic** ADJECTIVE an autistic person suffers from autism

autobiography NOUN **autobiographies** the story of a person's own life
▸ **autobiographical** ADJECTIVE to do with a person's own life: *Many of the events in Barrie's story are autobiographical.*

✦ **Autos** is a Greek word that means *self*. If a word starts with **auto**, you can guess that it has something to do with yourself, or doing something yourself. Other examples are **autograph** and **automatic**.

autograph NOUN **autographs** the signature of someone famous: *He collects pop stars' autographs.* VERB **autographs, autographing, autographed** to sign your name on something like your photograph or a book that you have written

automate VERB **automates, automating, automated** to automate a process is to get machines to do it rather than people

▶ **automation** NOUN using machines to do things instead of people

automatic ADJECTIVE an automatic machine only needs to be switched on and then it works by itself

NOUN **automatics** a machine such as a car or a rifle, that does certain things by itself

▶ **automatically** ADVERB **1** working or happening without being controlled all the time **2** if you do something automatically, you do it without thinking: *When I saw the stone coming I automatically ducked.*

automobile NOUN **automobiles** the American word for a car

autumn NOUN **autumns** the season of the year between summer and winter when the leaves change colour and fall, and it gets dark earlier

▶ **autumnal** ADJECTIVE happening after summer and before winter: *trees in their autumnal colours*

auxiliary NOUN **auxiliaries** a helper: *He's a hospital auxiliary.*

ADJECTIVE helping, additional: *an auxiliary worker*

auxiliary verb WORD CLASS **auxiliary verbs** (*grammar*) a short verb like *should*, *will* or *can* that you use with a main verb to make slight differences of meaning, for example a past tense in *Have you finished?* These words are sometimes called **helping verbs**

available ADJECTIVE **1** if something is available, you can get it, usually by buying it **2** if someone is available, they are free to do something: *I'm sorry, Mr Wright isn't available just now.*

▶ **availability** NOUN how possible it is to get something

avalanche (pronounced **av**-a-lansh) NOUN **avalanches** a huge amount of snow and ice sliding down the side of a mountain

avarice NOUN greed

avenge VERB **avenges, avenging, avenged** if you avenge something bad that has been done to you or to someone you care about, you punish the person who did it

avenue NOUN **avenues** a street, usually with trees on both sides

average NOUN **averages** **1** the number you get if you add amounts together and then divide that total by the number of amounts: *The average of 4, 6 and 8 is 6.* **2** the normal level or standard: *We spend an average of £100 a week on food.*

ADJECTIVE usual or ordinary: *What do you do in an average day?*

avert VERB **averts, averting, averted** **1** to turn away: *Avert your eyes for a moment please.* **2** to manage to stop something happening: *The countries are trying to avert war.*

aviary NOUN **aviaries** a large cage or building for keeping birds

aviation NOUN flying in aircraft

avid ADJECTIVE keen: *an avid reader*

avocado NOUN **avocados** or **avocadoes** **1** a pear-shaped fruit with dark green skin and a large stone in the middle **2** a light green colour

avoid VERB **avoids, avoiding, avoided** **1** to keep out of the way of a thing or person: *Have you been avoiding me for some reason?* **2** to avoid something is to find a way not to do it: *Try to avoid being seen.*

await VERB **awaits, awaiting, awaited** to wait for a thing or person: *Stay there and await my instructions.*

awake ADJECTIVE not sleeping: *Are you still awake?*

VERB **awakes, awaking, awoke, awoken** to wake up: *Gloria awoke early.* • *Grandma awoke the whole family in the night.*

▶ **awaken** VERB **awakens, awakening, awakened** to wake up: *We were awakened by the bombs.*

award NOUN **awards** a prize: *Joe has won an award for being so good at basketball.*

VERB **awards, awarding, awarded** to award someone something is to give it to them because they deserve it: *We have been awarded the title of 'School of the Year'.*

aware ADJECTIVE if you are aware of something, you know about it or know that it exists: *Derek became aware of someone else in the room.*

▶ **awareness** NOUN knowing about and understanding something: *road safety awareness*

away ADVERB **1** somewhere else: *Go away!* • *Throw that away.* **2** at a distance: *How far away is the school?* • *only a week away* **3** in the opposite direction: *Peter turned away.* • *Remember to put all the toys away again.*

ADJECTIVE an away game or match is one that is played on an opponent's ground and that a team has to travel to

awe NOUN a feeling that a thing or person is wonderful but a little frightening: *Freddie and Bob looked at their hero in awe.*

▶ **awesome** ADJECTIVE **1** (*informal*) very good or impressive **2** making you feel very small and scared: *the awesome thought of war*

awful ADJECTIVE **1** very bad: *an awful headache* **2** very great: *That won't make an awful lot of difference.*

▶ **awfully** ADVERB **1** very: *It's an awfully long way.* **2** very badly: *We played awfully.*

awkward ADJECTIVE **1** difficult to manage or use: *That's an awkward question.* • *This keyboard is a bit awkward.* **2** someone who is being

awkward is not being helpful deliberately: *Just stop being awkward and say you'll come.* **3** if you feel awkward, you feel uncomfortable or embarrassed: *I began to feel awkward when they started to talk about me.*

▶ **awkwardly** ADVERB in a difficult or uncomfortable way

awoke VERB a way of changing the verb **awake** to make a past tense: *I awoke to the sound of birds singing.*

awoken VERB a way of changing the verb **awake** that is used with a helping verb to show that something happened in the past: *I was awoken by someone banging on the door.*

axe NOUN **axes** a tool for chopping wood
VERB **axes, axing, axed** (*informal*) to axe something is to get rid of it

axis NOUN **axes 1** the line through the middle of something, for example a planet, that it seems to spin around **2** (*maths*) in a graph, an axis is the line up the side or the one along the bottom that you measure against

axle NOUN **axles** a rod fixed to the centre of a wheel, and which the wheel turns around

aye INTERJECTION an old-fashioned word for **yes**. It is also used in some dialects

azure NOUN the bright blue colour of the sky

Aa
Bb
Cc
Dd
Ee
Ff
Gg
Hh
Ii
Jj
Kk
Ll
Mm
Nn
Oo
Pp
Qq
Rr
Ss
Tt
Uu
Vv
Ww
Xx
Yy
Zz

Bb

babble VERB **babbles, babbling, babbled 1** to talk or say something quickly without making very much sense **2** running water babbles when it makes a pleasant bubbling sound

baboon NOUN **baboons** a type of large monkey with a long pointed nose and long teeth, found in Africa and parts of Asia

baby NOUN **babies 1** a very young child **2** a young animal: *a baby elephant*
▶ **babyish** ADJECTIVE **1** like a baby: *He had a smooth babyish face.* **2** suitable for babies or younger children: *This game is probably too babyish for ten-year-olds.*

babysit VERB **babysits, babysitting, babysat** to look after a baby or a child when its parents are out: *My brother is babysitting for a neighbour.* • *Would you babysit the boys next Saturday?*
▶ **babysitter** NOUN **babysitters** someone who looks after a baby or a child when its parents are out

bachelor NOUN **bachelors** a man who has never married

✦Remember there is no **t** before the **c** in **bachelor**.

back NOUN **backs 1** the back of something is the side that is opposite to or furthest away from its front: *The socks were at the back of the drawer.* **2** the part of your body that stretches from the back of your neck to your bottom: *I always sleep on my back.*
• **back to front** with the back part wrongly at the front: *Your T-shirt's on back to front.*
ADJECTIVE behind or opposite the front: *He's had one of his back teeth out.*
ADVERB **1** farther away in distance: *Stand back while Dad lights the fireworks.* **2** to the place, person or state from which someone or something came: *I'm taking*

these books back to the library. **3** in or to an earlier time: *Think back and try to remember exactly what happened.*
VERB **backs, backing, backed 1** to move backwards: *The dog growled and the boys backed away in fear.* **2** to back someone is to give them support or help, often money: *A local shopkeeper has offered to back our football team.*
• **back down** someone backs down when they admit they are beaten or have lost an argument
• **back up** (*ICT*) to back up computer information is to make a separate copy of it so that the information is not lost if the computer breaks down
• **back someone up** to back someone up is to support them

backbone NOUN **backbones** the row of bones down the middle of your back that forms your spine

backfire VERB **backfires, backfiring, backfired 1** if a plan backfires, it goes wrong **2** if a motor vehicle backfires, its fuel burns too soon and causes a loud bang in its exhaust pipe

backgammon NOUN a game where you throw dice and move round pieces on a patterned board

background NOUN **backgrounds 1** the part of a picture behind the main figures: *Here's a photo of us with Ben Nevis in the background.* **2** a person's background is their family, the kind of life they have had, and the things they have done in the past: *children from poorer backgrounds* **3** the background to an event is anything that happened before that helps to explain how the event came about: *the background to the English Civil War*

backhand NOUN in games like tennis and squash, a way of hitting the ball by holding the racket across the front of your body with the back of your hand facing towards the ball

Aa **Bb** Cc Dd Ee Ff Gg Hh Ii Jj Kk Ll Mm Nn Oo Pp Qq Rr Ss Tt Uu Vv Ww Xx Yy Zz

35

Aa

Bb

Cc

Dd

Ee

Ff

Gg

Hh

Ii

Jj

Kk

Ll

Mm

Nn

Oo

Pp

Qq

Rr

Ss

Tt

Uu

Vv

Ww

Xx

Yy

Zz

backspace NOUN **backspaces** (*ICT*) a key on a computer keyboard that you press to move the cursor back by one space

VERB **backspaces, backspacing, backspaced** to move the cursor on a computer screen back one space

backstroke NOUN a way of swimming where you lie on your back, kick your legs and swing your arms backwards over your shoulders

backup NOUN **backups** 1 backup is help or support 2 (*ICT*) a backup of a computer file is a copy you have made so the information is not lost if the computer breaks down

backward ADJECTIVE 1 facing or aimed towards the back: *a backward look* 2 slow to learn or develop

ADVERB backwards: *She was looking backward over her shoulder.*

backwards ADVERB 1 in the direction opposite to the one you are facing: *He stepped backwards without looking and fell down the stairs.* 2 towards the past: *If we move further backwards in time, we come to the age of the dinosaurs.* 3 in the opposite way to the usual way: *He can say the alphabet backwards.*

bacon NOUN salted meat from a pig, usually eaten in thin strips called rashers

bacteria PLURAL NOUN very small creatures living in air, water, living animals and plants, and in dead and decaying things. Some types of bacteria can cause diseases or illness in humans and animals

bad ADJECTIVE **worse, worst**

1 wicked or naughty: *Tony and Harry have been very bad boys today.* • *Don't jump up on me, you bad dog!*

2 not of a good standard: *His handwriting is bad, and his spelling is worse.*

3 nasty or upsetting: *a bad storm* • *very bad news*

4 harmful to your health: *Eating too many fatty foods can be bad for you.*

5 if someone is bad at doing something they do not do it well: *I'm very bad at maths.*

6 something is bad or has gone bad if it is rotten or decaying: *Don't eat that pear – it's bad.* • *Your teeth will go bad if you don't brush them regularly.*

• **not bad** or **not too bad** you say 'not bad' or 'not too bad' to mean quite good: *'How are you feeling today?' 'Not too bad, thanks.'*

✦ Comparing how **bad** things are: *The weather was **bad** yesterday, it was **worse** the day before and last Friday was **worst** of all.*

badge NOUN **badges** a small object with words or pictures printed on it that you pin or sew on to your clothing to show, for example, that you are a member of a group or club

badger NOUN **badgers** an animal with a pointed black-and-white striped face and grey fur on the rest of its body. Badgers live underground and come out at night to feed

badly ADVERB 1 not well: *The work was done very badly.* 2 seriously: *The car was badly damaged in the crash.* 3 very much: *I badly wanted a new pair of trainers.*

badminton NOUN a game in which two or four players use rackets to hit a light object called a shuttlecock across a net

bad-tempered ADJECTIVE speaking or behaving angrily or rudely: *She gets bad-tempered when she's tired.*

baffle VERB **baffles, baffling, baffled** if a problem baffles you, you cannot work out what it is about or how to solve it: *The first question in the test baffled everyone.*

▶ **baffling** ADJECTIVE puzzling

bag NOUN **bags** an object used for carrying things in, made of paper, plastic, cloth or leather

• **bags of** (*informal*) lots of: *We've got bags of time before the bus comes.*

VERB **bags, bagging, bagged** 1 (*informal*) to claim something as your own: *I bagged the best seat.* 2 to put things into a bag or bags: *We helped Dad bag all the garden rubbish.*

bagful NOUN **bagfuls** the amount that a bag holds: *He's eaten four or five bagfuls of crisps.*

baggage NOUN the cases and bags that a person takes with them when they travel

baggy ADJECTIVE **baggier, baggiest** baggy clothes are too big for the person wearing them and hang loosely from their body

bagpipes PLURAL NOUN bagpipes are a musical instrument made up of a cloth or leather bag with pipes attached to it

baguette (pronounced bag-**et**) NOUN **baguettes** a long narrow loaf of French bread, also called a **French stick**

bail¹ NOUN money that has to be paid to a court so that someone who has been arrested for a crime can be let out of prison until their trial

VERB **bails, bailing, bailed**

• **bail out** a prisoner is bailed or bailed out when a sum of money is paid to the court and they are set free until their trial

✦ Be careful not to confuse the spellings or meanings of **bail** and **bale**.

bail² NOUN **bails** on a cricket wicket, the bails are the short pieces of wood that lie across the top of the stumps

Baisakhi (pronounced bie-**sak**-i) NOUN **1** a Sikh festival celebrating the new year **2** a Hindu festival to celebrate the new year or the harvest, or to honour a god

bait NOUN food put on a hook to catch fish or put in a trap to catch animals

VERB **baits, baiting, baited** to bait a hook or trap is to put food on it to attract and catch fish or animals

✦ Be careful not to confuse the spellings of **baited**, the past tense of bait, and **bated**, which is used in the phrase **with bated breath**.

bake VERB **bakes, baking, baked 1** to cook something such as bread or a cake in an oven: *Mum does a lot of cooking but she doesn't bake very often.* **2** to bake food is to cook it in an oven: *Bake*

the lasagne in the oven until it is golden brown. **3** to bake things that are soft is to harden them in the sun or in an oven: *The clay hardens when it is baked in a kiln.*

baker NOUN **bakers 1** someone who bakes bread and cakes: *My grandma is a brilliant baker.* **2** a baker's is a shop selling freshly baked bread and cakes

bakery NOUN **bakeries** a shop or factory where bread and cakes are made

balance NOUN **1** if you keep your balance, you are steady enough not to fall over: *I lost my balance and fell in the stream.* **2** the balance of a bank or building society account is the amount of money in it

VERB **balances, balancing, balanced** to balance something is to make or keep it steady: *The women balance huge pots on their heads.*

balcony NOUN **balconies 1** a platform built out from the wall of a building, usually with a railing around it **2** the balcony in a theatre or cinema is an area upstairs where the seats are above the rest of the audience

bald ADJECTIVE **balder, baldest 1** someone who is bald has very little or no hair: *His uncle is completely bald.* **2** something that is bald has very little covering: *There are a few bald patches in the carpet.*

▸ **baldness** NOUN having very little hair or covering

bale¹ NOUN **bales** a bundle of hay, cloth or paper that has been tied up tightly

VERB **bales, baling, baled** to bale hay, cloth or paper is to tie it tightly in bundles

✦ Be careful not to confuse the spellings or meanings of **bale** and **bail**.

bale² VERB **bales, baling, baled**

• **bale out** to escape from a dangerous place or an emergency situation: *As the plane was going down, they saw the pilot bale out.*

ball¹ NOUN **balls 1** a round object that you use for playing games like football, hockey, cricket and tennis **2** anything

ball → bangle

that has a round shape: *a ball of string* • *The hedgehog had rolled itself into a tight ball.*

✦ The words **ball** and **bawl** sound the same, but remember that they have different spellings. To **bawl** is to cry out.

ball² NOUN **balls** a big formal party where people dance: *Cinderella couldn't go to the ball.*

ballad NOUN **ballads** a poem or song that tells a story, often about love

ballerina NOUN **ballerinas** a female ballet dancer

ballet NOUN **ballets** 1 a type of dancing that uses graceful steps and movements: *Emily prefers ballet to tap dancing.* 2 a ballet is a story told using dance: *My favourite ballets are The Nutcracker and Swan Lake.*

balloon NOUN **balloons** a very light object made of thin rubber that expands and floats when it is filled with air or gas

VERB **balloons, ballooning, ballooned** to balloon is to expand or swell like a balloon does when it is filled with air or gas: *The sail ballooned out in the breeze.*

ballot NOUN **ballots** a way of voting in secret by marking a paper and putting it into a special box

VERB **ballots, balloting, balloted** to ballot a group of people is to get votes from them by ballot: *The workers were balloted and voted to strike.*

ballpoint *or* **ballpoint pen** NOUN **ballpoints** *or* **ballpoint pens** a pen with a small circular metal tip

balsa *or* **balsa wood** NOUN a very light wood that is often used to make model boats and aircraft

bamboo NOUN **bamboos** a type of Asian grass that can grow very tall and has hard round hollow stems

ban VERB **bans, banning, banned** to ban something is to not allow it: *Cycling is banned in the park.*

NOUN **bans** an order that something is not allowed: *a ban on smoking.*

banana NOUN **bananas** a long, yellow, very soft fruit that you peel to eat and that grows in hot countries

band NOUN **bands**
1 a group of musicians who play together: *My big brother has formed a rock band with some of his school friends.*
2 a group: *a band of robbers*
3 a strip of material to put round something: *a rubber band* • *a headband*
4 a stripe: *a broad band of colour*

VERB **bands, banding, banded**
• **band together** to band together is to join together to do something as a group: *All the parents banded together to campaign for a new school crossing.*

bandage NOUN **bandages** a strip of cloth for wrapping round a part of your body that has been cut or hurt

VERB **bandages, bandaging, bandaged** to bandage a part of the body is to wrap it in a bandage

bandit NOUN **bandits** an armed criminal who attacks and robs travellers

bandwagon NOUN
• **jump** *or* **climb on the bandwagon** join something only because it is fashionable or successful, not because it is right or worthwhile

bandy ADJECTIVE **bandier, bandiest** bandy legs curve outwards at the knees

bang NOUN **bangs** 1 a sudden loud noise: *There was a loud bang and all the lights went out.* 2 a hard knock: *She's had a bang on the head and is feeling a bit dizzy.*

VERB **bangs, banging, banged** 1 a door or window bangs when it closes or is shut roughly so that it makes a loud noise: *The door banged shut in the wind.* 2 to bang something is to knock it hard against something else: *Neil banged his books down on the table.*

banger NOUN **bangers** 1 a type of firework that makes loud banging noises when it is set off 2 (*informal*) a sausage: *bangers and mash* 3 (*informal*) a rusty car that is falling to pieces

bangle NOUN **bangles** a ring of metal, wood or plastic that you wear on your wrist

Aa **Bb** Cc Dd Ee Ff Gg Hh Ii Jj Kk Ll Mm Nn Oo Pp Qq Rr Ss Tt Uu Vv Ww Xx Yy Zz

banish VERB **banishes, banishing, banished 1** to banish someone is to make them leave the country or their home as a punishment **2** to banish a feeling is to make it go away

► **banishment** NOUN being banished

banisters PLURAL NOUN the rail and its supports that you hold on to as you go up and down stairs

banjo NOUN **banjos** or **banjoes** a musical instrument with a round body and a long neck which you play by plucking the strings

bank NOUN **banks**
1 a business that looks after and lends money: *He puts his pocket money in the bank every month.*
2 a place where a particular thing is stored so that it can be used later: *a blood bank*
3 the banks of a river or a lake are the areas of ground beside it: *We camped on the banks of Loch Lomond.*
4 a sloping area of ground
VERB **banks, banking, banked 1** to bank money is to put it in a bank **2** an aeroplane banks when it tips over to one side as it changes direction
• **bank on something** to depend on something happening: *You can't bank on the weather staying dry, so take an umbrella.*

bank holiday NOUN **bank holidays** a public holiday when the banks and many shops are closed

banknote NOUN **banknotes** a piece of paper money

bankrupt ADJECTIVE a person or a business is bankrupt or goes bankrupt if they are not able to pay the money they owe

► **bankruptcy** NOUN **bankruptcies** being bankrupt: *The business is facing bankruptcy.* • *The number of bankruptcies went up last year.*

banner NOUN **banners** a large piece of cloth with printing or writing on it which is carried on poles

banquet (pronounced **bank**-wit) NOUN **banquets** a formal dinner that is attended by a lot of people and where guests often make speeches and toasts

> ✦ **Banquet** is a French word, which in turn comes from an Italian word that means a *little bench*. This is because of the benches that people put around a table when they were eating a meal.

banter NOUN banter is friendly talk where people tease each other or make funny remarks to each other

baptism NOUN **baptisms** a Christian ceremony where someone has water sprinkled on their head to show they have become a Christian

baptize or **baptise** VERB **baptizes, baptizing, baptized** to baptize someone is to make them part of the Christian Church by the ceremony of sprinkling water on their head

bar NOUN **bars**
1 a piece of hard material: *an iron bar*
2 a bar of something is a solid piece of it: *a bar of soap*
3 a broad line or band: *a brown bird with black bars on its wings*
4 a room or counter serving drinks or food: *a burger bar*
5 one of the sections of equal time into which a piece of music is divided: *four beats to the bar*
VERB **bars, barring, barred 1** to bar a door, a window or a gate is to put metal or wooden bars across it so that no one can get in or out **2** if people are barred from a place or from doing something, they are not allowed in or are not allowed to do it: *Anyone over the age of 12 is barred from the competition.*

barb NOUN **barbs** a point on a head of an arrow, or on a fish hook, that faces backwards and makes the arrow or hook stick firmly

barbarian NOUN **barbarians** a savage or uncivilized person

barbaric ADJECTIVE cruel or uncivilized: *a barbaric custom*

barbecue NOUN **barbecues 1** a grill used for cooking food outdoors **2** an outdoor party where food is grilled on a barbecue

Aa
Bb
Cc
Dd
Ee
Ff
Gg
Hh
Ii
Jj
Kk
Ll
Mm
Nn
Oo
Pp
Qq
Rr
Ss
Tt
Uu
Vv
Ww
Xx
Yy
Zz

VERB **barbecues, barbecuing, barbecued** to barbecue food is to grill it on a barbecue

barbed wire NOUN wire that has sharp spikes twisted round it. Barbed wire is used on walls and fences to stop people and animals climbing over

barber NOUN **barbers 1** a man who cuts men's hair **2** a barber's is a shop where men have their hair cut: *Dad's just been to the barber's.*

bar chart NOUN **bar charts** a diagram in which various amounts are shown using coloured or shaded blocks of different heights

bar code NOUN **bar codes** a code made up of lines and spaces which is printed on an item for sale so that it can be identified by a computer

bard NOUN **bards** a poet or travelling singer

bare ADJECTIVE **barer, barest** naked or without any covering: *It's a bit too cold to be going out with bare legs.* • *Without the posters on the walls the bedroom looks really bare.*

barefaced ADJECTIVE something that is barefaced is done without feeling any guilt or embarrassment: *a barefaced lie*

barely ADVERB hardly or almost not: *They had barely arrived when they had to leave again.* • *The truck skidded and barely avoided hitting a wall.*

bargain NOUN **bargains 1** if something is a bargain, it is cheap or cheaper than usual: *These jeans were a real bargain.* **2** an agreement people make between themselves
• **into the bargain** as well or besides: *It's a good warm jacket and waterproof into the bargain.*
VERB **bargains, bargaining, bargained** to bargain is to argue about the price you will pay for something
• **get more than you bargain for** get something extra, usually something bad, that you didn't expect

barge NOUN **barges** a flat-bottomed boat used on canals and rivers
VERB **barges, barging, barged 1** to barge into a place is to rush in noisily

or clumsily and interrupt people: *He barged into my room while I was sleeping.* **2** to push people roughly and rudely: *He barged right past us to the front of the queue.*

baritone NOUN **baritones** (*music*) **1** a male singing voice between the lowest and highest pitch **2** a man with this singing voice

bark[1] NOUN **barks** the short loud sound that a dog or fox makes
VERB **barks, barking, barked 1** animals bark when they make this sound **2** if a person barks they speak loudly and sharply: *'Hurry up, you lot!' he barked.*

bark[2] NOUN the bark of a tree is the rough outer covering of its trunk and branches

barley NOUN a grain used for food and for making beer

bar mitzvah NOUN **bar mitzvahs** a religious ceremony for Jewish boys to mark the time, at about age 13, when they are expected to take some of the responsibilities of an adult

barn NOUN **barns** a large building on a farm for storing grain or hay

barnacle NOUN **barnacles** a type of small shellfish that fastens itself on to rocks and the bottoms of boats

barometer NOUN **barometers** an instrument for measuring the pressure of air and showing changes in the weather

baron NOUN **barons** a type of nobleman

baroness NOUN **baronesses** a female baron or a baron's wife: *Baroness Thatcher*

barracks NOUN **barracks** a place where soldiers live or are based

barrage NOUN **barrages 1** heavy and continuous gunfire **2** a large number: *a barrage of warnings*

barrel NOUN **barrels 1** a wooden or metal container with curved sides used for holding liquids like beer and wine **2** the barrel of a gun is the metal tube through which the bullet is fired

barren ADJECTIVE a barren landscape has very little or nothing growing on it

barricade NOUN **barricades** a barrier put up in a street to stop people passing through

VERB **barricades, barricading, barricaded** to barricade a place is to put up a barrier to stop people getting in or passing through

barrier NOUN **barriers 1** a gate or fence used for stopping people from getting past **2** a barrier is anything that stops you doing something: *Nowadays, being a girl isn't a barrier to a career in the navy.*

barrister NOUN **barristers** a lawyer who presents people's cases in court

barrow NOUN **barrows** a type of small cart

barter VERB **barters, bartering, bartered** to give one thing in exchange for another, without using any money

base NOUN **bases 1** the surface or part on which a thing rests: *a bronze statue on a black marble base* **2** the lowest part of something: *the base of the tree* **3** a place where people work, or where an activity happens: *an army base*

VERB **bases, basing, based** to base one thing on another is to create it using the other thing: *a film based on a Roald Dahl book*

✦The words **base** and **bass** sound the same but remember that they have different spellings. **Bass** is the lowest range of musical notes.

baseball NOUN **baseballs 1** a game played with a long rounded bat and a ball by two teams of nine players **2** a baseball is a small ball used in the game of baseball

basement NOUN **basements** the lowest floor in a building, usually below the level of the ground

bases NOUN the plural form of **basis** and **base**

bash VERB **bashes, bashing, bashed** to bash something is to hit it hard: *The door closed suddenly and bashed me on the nose.*

NOUN **bashes** a hard hit: *He gave the nail a couple of good bashes.*

• **have a bash** to try: *I don't know exactly how to do it, but I'll have a bash at it anyway.*

bashful ADJECTIVE shy

basic ADJECTIVE **1** basic describes things that are at the most essential or simple level: *basic driving skills* **2** something is basic if it does not include anything unnecessary or too fancy: *The cottage was pretty basic – it didn't even have a proper bath.*

basically ADVERB in the most important or essential way: *He's basically a good person.*

basil NOUN a herb with sweet-smelling leaves that are used in cookery

basin NOUN **basins 1** a sink for washing your hands and face in **2** a bowl used in the kitchen for holding liquids or food: *a pudding basin* **3** (*geography*) an area of land from which water flows into a river: *the Amazon basin*

basis NOUN **bases** the basis of something is what it is built on or what it is based on: *They've always been on a very friendly basis until now.*

bask VERB **basks, basking, basked 1** to bask is to sit or lie enjoying warmth: *We basked in the warm sunshine.* **2** to bask in other people's praise or attention is to enjoy it

basket NOUN **baskets** a container made of strips of wood or canes woven together

basketball NOUN **basketballs 1** a game played by two teams who try to score points by throwing a ball through a hoop fixed high above the ground on a post **2** a basketball is a large ball used to play basketball

bass (rhymes with **face**) NOUN **basses** (*music*) **1** the lowest range of musical notes **2** a musical instrument with a low tone, such as a bass guitar or double bass **3** a man with the deepest kind of singing or speaking voice

ADJECTIVE of or making the lowest range of musical notes: *singing the bass part*

bass clef NOUN **bass clefs** a musical sign that shows you that the pitch of the following notes should be bass

Aa
Bb
Cc
Dd
Ee
Ff
Gg
Hh
Ii
Jj
Kk
Ll
Mm
Nn
Oo
Pp
Qq
Rr
Ss
Tt
Uu
Vv
Ww
Xx
Yy
Zz

bassoon NOUN **bassoons** a long wooden instrument that makes a low sound when it is blown into

bat¹ NOUN **bats** a shaped piece of wood that you use to hit the ball in games like cricket and baseball
• **off your own bat** if you do something off your own bat, you do it without anyone telling you that you have to do it
VERB **bats, batting, batted** to use the bat in games like cricket and rounders: *It's Gary's turn to bat next.*

bat² NOUN **bats** a flying animal that comes out at night to feed

batch NOUN **batches 1** a number of things, especially pieces of food, all made at one time: *a batch of scones* **2** a group of people or things that arrive at one time: *this year's batch of students*

bated ADJECTIVE
• **with bated breath** if you are waiting with bated breath, you are excited or anxious to find out what will happen next

bath NOUN **baths 1** a bath is a large container that you sit in to wash yourself **2** a bath is a wash in this kind of container: *You're filthy! When did you last have a bath?* **3** baths are a building which contains a public swimming pool: *I learnt to swim in the local baths.*
VERB **baths, bathing, bathed** to bath someone is to wash them in a bath: *Dad is bathing my baby brother.*

bathe VERB **bathes, bathing, bathed 1** you bathe a sore part of your body when you wash it gently **2** to swim in water: *They always bathe in the sea before breakfast.* **3** to wash yourself in a bath

bathroom NOUN **bathrooms** a room for washing yourself in, usually containing a bath or a shower, a washbasin and a lavatory

bat mitzvah NOUN **bat mitzvahs** a religious ceremony for Jewish girls to mark the time, at about age 12, when they are expected to start taking some of the responsibilites of an adult

baton NOUN **batons** a short stick used, for example, by someone who is conducting music or by runners in a relay race

batsman NOUN **batsmen** a man who bats in cricket

battalion NOUN **battalions** a large group of soldiers that are part of a regiment

batten VERB **battens, battening, battened**
• **batten something down** to fasten something down firmly and make it secure: *He battened down the edges of the tent.*

batter VERB **batters, battering, battered** to hit something hard over and over again: *The rain battered down on the metal roof.*
NOUN batter is a mixture of flour, milk and eggs used to coat fish and other food before it is fried in oil

battering ram NOUN **battering rams** a large heavy log hit against a door or gate to break it down

battery NOUN **batteries 1** a device used to supply electrical power to things like watches, cameras and car engines **2** a set of cages that hens are kept in so that their eggs can be collected easily

battle NOUN **battles 1** a fight between two armies: *the Battle of Hastings* **2** any fight or struggle: *It's always been a bit of a battle to get him to do his homework.*
VERB **battles, battling, battled** to battle is to fight or struggle: *The ship battled bravely through the storm.*

battlements PLURAL NOUN a wall around the top of a castle or fort that has spaces cut in it for the people inside to shoot at people outside

battleship NOUN **battleships** a very large ship that has big guns and is used in naval battles

bauble NOUN **baubles** a shiny or glittery decoration

bawl VERB **bawls, bawling, bawled** to cry or shout very loudly: *You'll have to bawl at him to make him hear you.*

bay NOUN **bays 1** a piece of land on

Aa
Bb
Cc
Dd
Ee
Ff
Gg
Hh
Ii
Jj
Kk
Ll
Mm
Nn
Oo
Pp
Qq
Rr
Ss
Tt
Uu
Vv
Ww
Xx
Yy
Zz

the coast or on the shore of a lake that bends inwards: *the Bay of Biscay* **2** an area that is marked out for a particular use: *a loading bay*

• **at bay** if you keep something at bay, you do not let it come near you or harm you: *Vitamin C helps to keep colds at bay.*

bayonet NOUN **bayonets** a long sharp blade that can be fixed on to the end of a soldier's rifle

bazaar NOUN **bazaars** **1** an event when goods are sold to raise money, especially for a good cause **2** a type of Middle Eastern market, usually with small shops or stalls selling different goods

✦This word comes from the Persian word **bazar**, which means *market*.

BC ABBREVIATION short for **before Christ**. BC is added after a date to show that the date was before the birth of Jesus Christ, for example *450 BC*

✦**AD** is the abbreviation used with dates after the birth of Christ.

be VERB **1** to be is to exist: *There may be a very good reason for it.* **2** to be something is to have that position or to do that job: *What do you want to be when you grow up?* **3** to be a particular thing is to have that feeling or quality: *Try to be happy.* • *We can't all be as clever as you.*

✦There are many different forms of the verb **be**.
If you are talking about something that is happening at this very time, you use the present tense forms.
These are *I* **am**; *you* or *they* **are**; *he, she* or *it* **is**.
You can also say *I* **am being**; *you we* or *they* **are being**; *he, she* or *it* **is being**.
If you are talking about something that was the case in the past, you use the past tense forms.
These are *I, he, she* or *it* **was**; *you, we* or *they* **were**.
You can also say *I, you, we* or *they* **have been**; *he, she* or *it* **has been**.

beach NOUN **beaches** an area of sand or pebbles at the edge of the sea

beacon NOUN **beacons** a light or a fire that can be seen from a long distance away and acts as a warning or a signal

bead NOUN **beads** **1** a small round piece of glass, plastic or wood with a hole through the middle, used to make necklaces or sewn on to clothes as decoration **2** a round drop of liquid: *There were beads of sweat on his forehead.*

beady ADJECTIVE **beadier, beadiest** beady eyes are round and shiny

beagle NOUN **beagles** a type of dog with a black, white and brown coat and long ears

beak NOUN **beaks** a bird's beak is the hard, pointed part of its mouth that it uses to pick up food

beaker NOUN **beakers** **1** a straight glass or plastic container, used in laboratories **2** a type of drinking cup, usually without a handle

beam NOUN **beams** **1** a long thick piece of wood or metal used to support a building or bridge **2** a line of light
VERB **beams, beaming, beamed** **1** to shine: *The sun beamed down all day.* **2** if someone beams, they smile broadly

bean NOUN **beans** a type of seed that grows in a pod and is eaten as a vegetable

• **full of beans** if someone is full of beans, they have lots of energy

bear¹ NOUN **bears** a large heavy animal with a thick coat and hooked claws

bear² VERB **bears, bearing, bore, born** *or* **borne** **1** to bear something is to put up with it: *She couldn't bear the cold winters.* **2** to bear something is to carry it or have it: *Three men arrived, bearing gifts.* • *The door bore the family's name.* **3** women bear children and animals bear young when they give birth to them

• **bear in mind** if you bear something in mind, you remember that it is important: *Please bear in mind that you only have an hour to write your essay.*

▶ **bearable** ADJECTIVE if something is bearable, you are able to put up with it: *'Is the pain bad?' 'It's bearable.'*

+ If you are talking about the birth of a child or young animal, you use the spelling **born**: *He was born at midnight on New Year's Eve.* If you mean that something is carried, or someone has put up with something, or a woman has given birth to a child, you use the spelling **borne**: *She had borne five children.* • *The seeds are borne on the wind.*

beard NOUN **beards** the hair that grows on a man's chin and cheeks: *He'd shaved off his beard.*
▶ **bearded** ADJECTIVE having a beard: *a tall bearded man*

bearing NOUN **bearings 1** something that has a bearing on a situation affects it in some way: *His age will have a bearing on how quickly he recovers from his illness.* **2** a person's bearing is the way they behave, especially the way they stand and walk: *an old gentleman with a dignified bearing*
• **lose your bearings** to lose your way and not know where you are

beast NOUN **beasts 1** a four-footed animal: *the beasts of the field* **2** a cruel or nasty person: *Don't do that, you beast!*
▶ **beastly** ADJECTIVE **beastlier, beastliest** horrible or nasty: *Stop being so beastly to your little brother.*

beat VERB **beats, beating, beat, beaten**
1 to hit over and over again: *He beat his fists on the table.*
2 to beat someone is to defeat them or win against them: *Do you think Manchester United can beat Real Madrid?*
3 to make a regular sound or movement: *He could hear his heart beating.*
4 to beat food is to stir or mix it by making quick regular movements through it with a spoon, fork or whisk
• **beat someone up** to injure someone by hitting them over and over again
NOUN **beats 1** a beat is a regular sound

or movement like that made by your heart or your pulse **2** (*music*) a regular rhythm **3** a police officer's beat is the regular route he or she takes around an area

beautiful ADJECTIVE **1** a beautiful person is very pretty or handsome **2** very pleasant to see, hear or smell: *a beautiful sunset* • *a beautiful voice* • *a rose with a beautiful scent* **3** the weather is beautiful when it is very pleasant, especially if it is bright, dry and sunny: *It's a beautiful morning.*
▶ **beautifully** ADVERB in a pleasant or attractive way: *She is always beautifully dressed.* • *He sings beautifully.*

beauty NOUN **beauties 1** beauty is the quality of being very attractive, and pleasant to see or hear: *the beauty of the alpine scenery* **2** a person who is beautiful to look at: *Her grandmother was a famous beauty.* **3** something you think is excellent: *Just look at the fish he caught. Isn't it a beauty?*

beaver NOUN **beavers 1** an animal with a soft brown coat and a large flat tail, which lives in dams built across rivers using tree branches **2** a member of the most junior branch of the Scout Association

became VERB a way of changing the verb **become** to make a past tense

because CONJUNCTION for the reason that: *You can't borrow my bike because there's something wrong with the brakes.* • *Just because it's raining, it doesn't mean you should do nothing all day.*
• **because of** as a result of: *Because of the school holidays, the return match will be delayed for a fortnight.*

beckon VERB **beckons, beckoning, beckoned** to beckon to someone is to make a sign with your hand to show them that you want them to come nearer: *The teacher beckoned to Michael to come over to her desk.*

become VERB **becomes, becoming, became 1** to come to be: *She'd become old and frail.* • *Tony Blair became prime minister in 1997.* **2** if something becomes you it suits you

Aa
Bb
Cc
Dd
Ee
Ff
Gg
Hh
Ii
Jj
Kk
Ll
Mm
Nn
Oo
Pp
Qq
Rr
Ss
Tt
Uu
Vv
Ww
Xx
Yy
Zz

▶ **becoming** ADJECTIVE something that is becoming looks nice on the person wearing it

bed NOUN **beds 1** a piece of furniture to sleep on, or any place for sleeping: *Time to get ready for bed.* • *Each night, chimpanzees make beds of twigs high up in the trees.* **2** (*geography*) the bottom of a river, a lake or the sea **3** an area in a garden that contains flowers and other plants: *a bed of lilies*

bedclothes PLURAL NOUN things like sheets, blankets or a quilt used to cover a bed

bedding NOUN anything used to make a bed with, for example a mattress, sheets and pillows, or for animals, straw or hay

bedlam NOUN a place full of confusion and noise: *The railway station was bedlam with thousands of people stranded.*

bedraggled ADJECTIVE untidy and dirty: *The kitten had been caught in the rain and its fur was all bedraggled.*

bedroom NOUN **bedrooms** a room with a bed or beds used for sleeping in

bedspread NOUN **bedspreads** a cover that goes over the top of the other bedclothes on a bed

bedstead NOUN **bedsteads** the metal or wooden framework of a bed

bee NOUN **bees** a small winged insect that can sting you. Bees fly from flower to flower collecting nectar to make honey

beech NOUN **beeches** a tree with grey smooth bark and rounded leaves

beef NOUN meat from a cow

beefburger NOUN **beefburgers** a hamburger

beefeater NOUN **beefeaters** one of the guards at the Tower of London, who wear an old-fashioned red uniform

beehive NOUN **beehives** a box or container where bees are kept so that the honey they make can be collected

beeline NOUN
• **make a beeline for something** if you make a beeline for something, you go straight towards it: *As soon as the* cinema opened we made a beeline for the best seats.

been VERB a form of the verb **be** that is used with a helping verb to show that something happened in the past: *My brother has been very good today.*

beer NOUN **beers** an alcoholic drink made from barley and often flavoured with hops

beetle NOUN **beetles** an insect with two pairs of wings. Its front wings are hard and cover its back wings when the beetle is not flying

beetroot NOUN **beetroots** a small, round, dark red vegetable that grows under the ground

before PREPOSITION earlier than something: *Let's go for a walk before lunch.* • *I sent the letter the day before yesterday.*
ADVERB at an earlier time: *I don't think we've met before.* • *We had all been to the beach the day before.*
CONJUNCTION **1** earlier than the time when something will happen: *Wash your hands before you come to the table.* **2** rather than: *Ali would die before he would admit he was wrong.*

beforehand ADVERB before the time when something else happens: *If you're coming to the party next week, would you let me know beforehand.*

befriend VERB **befriends, befriending, befriended** to befriend someone is to become friends with them

beg VERB **begs, begging, begged 1** if someone begs, they ask other people to give them money or food because they are poor: *children begging in the streets* **2** if you beg for something, you ask someone very eagerly for it because you want it very much: *Kiera begged her father to buy her the shoes.*

began VERB a way of changing the verb **begin** to make a past tense: *It began to rain and we stayed in.*

beggar NOUN **beggars** someone who lives by begging for money or food from people who pass by

begin VERB **begins, beginning, began, begun** to start: *The concert*

Aa **Bb** Cc Dd Ee Ff Gg Hh Ii Jj Kk Ll Mm Nn Oo Pp Qq Rr Ss Tt Uu Vv Ww Xx Yy Zz began at 7.30 and finished at about 9.30. • *Marie had begun to enjoy being at the new school.*

▸ **beginner** NOUN **beginners** someone who has only just started to do or to learn something: *a guitar class for beginners*

▸ **beginning** NOUN **beginnings 1** the start of something: *He led from the beginning of the race.* **2** the early part of a period of time: *In the beginning, I didn't like her much.* • *My birthday is at the beginning of July.*

begun VERB a form of the verb **begin** that is used with a helping verb to show that something happened in the past: *I had just begun my homework when James phoned.*

behalf NOUN to do something on someone's behalf is to do it for them: *Please don't go to any trouble on my behalf.* • *I'll speak to the teacher on your behalf.*

behave VERB **behaves, behaving, behaved 1** to behave in a certain way is to act in that way: *If you behave badly today, you won't get sweets.* **2** if you behave, or behave yourself, you are good and don't do anything that you shouldn't

behaviour NOUN **1** the way you behave: *Gold stars are awarded for good behaviour.* **2** the way an animal or other living thing normally behaves: *He wants to study the behaviour of gorillas.*

behead VERB **beheads, beheading, beheaded** to behead someone is to cut their head off: *King Charles I was beheaded in 1649.*

behind PREPOSITION

1 at or to the back of something: *Look behind the sofa.* • *Shut the door behind you, please.*

2 staying after someone or something: *When you leave the camp, don't leave litter behind you.*

3 not as far ahead as other people: *He's fallen behind the rest of the class.*

4 helping or encouraging someone or something: *The crowd really got behind their team.*

5 responsible for something: *The school didn't know who was behind the break-in.*

6 an experience is behind you when it happened in the past: *His problems are all behind him now.*

• **behind someone's back** if something is done behind your back, it is done without you knowing about it: *I don't like people talking about me behind my back.*

ADVERB **1** at or to the back: *a mother hen with six chicks running behind* **2** late or not up to date: *She's fallen behind with her work.* **3** if you stay behind, you do not leave when other people leave: *I stayed behind to help with the tidying up.*

NOUN **behinds** (*informal*) your bottom: *Get up off your behind and do some work!*

behold VERB **beholds, beholding, beheld** (*old-fashioned*) to behold something is to see it: *He beheld a huge, tawny lion, with great glistening white teeth.*

beige (pronounced **baij**) NOUN a very light pinkish brown colour, like the colour of milky coffee or tea

being VERB the form of the verb **be** that is used to make certain tenses: *I am being good today.* • *He was just being kind.*

NOUN **beings** a being is something that lives or exists: *a science fiction story about beings from other planets*

belated ADJECTIVE arriving late: *a belated birthday present*

belch VERB **belches, belching, belched** to belch is to let air from your stomach come out of your mouth with a loud noise

belfry NOUN **belfries** a tower, especially on a church, where a bell is hung

belief NOUN **beliefs** something you believe, especially something that you think is true or exists

believe VERB **believes, believing, believed 1** to be sure that something is true or real: *I believed his story.* • *Do you believe in ghosts?* **2** to think that something is true though you are not completely sure: *I believe he was once a famous film star.*

• **make believe** if you make believe, you pretend something is real when it isn't

▸ **believable** ADJECTIVE if something is believable, it can be believed: *a believable excuse*

▸ **believer** NOUN **believers** someone who believes something, especially someone who believes in a particular religion

bell NOUN **bells 1** a hollow metal object with a long piece of metal inside that swings and hits the sides of the bell making a ringing sound **2** any device that makes a ringing sound: *a doorbell • a bicycle bell*

bellow VERB **bellows, bellowing, bellowed** to bellow is to roar like a bull: *He bellowed at us to stop what we were doing.*

belly NOUN **bellies 1** the front part of your body between your chest and the tops of your legs **2** your stomach **3** the part underneath an animal's body between its front legs and its back legs

belong VERB **belongs, belonging, belonged**

1 if something belongs to you, you own it: *Who does this suitcase belong to?*

2 you belong to the place where you feel at home: *She felt as if she didn't belong there.*

3 if you belong to a club or organization, you are a member: *Peter belongs to the local tennis club.*

4 something belongs in a particular place if that is where it is usually kept: *That big chair belongs over there by the fireplace.*

5 people or things that belong with each other match each other, fit together or make a pair: *These socks don't belong together.*

▸ **belongings** PLURAL NOUN your belongings are the things you own: *He just packed up all his belongings and moved out.*

beloved (pronounced bi-**luv**-id) ADJECTIVE loved very much: *a photo of her beloved*

grandfather

below PREPOSITION lower than or under something: *the cupboard below the stairs • Simon was below me in school.*

ADVERB at or in a lower place: *From the top of the hill, we looked down on the valley below. • Write your name in the box below.*

belt NOUN **belts 1** a band of leather, cloth or plastic that you wear around your waist **2** a loop of material in a machine that moves round and round: *a conveyor belt • a fan belt*

VERB **belts, belting, belted 1** to belt someone is to hit them hard: *The branch sprang back and belted him on the nose.* **2** (*informal*) to belt is to go very fast: *The boys came belting down the hill on their bikes.*

bench NOUN **benches 1** a long seat: *We sat on a wooden bench in the park.* **2** a table used to make things on: *a carpenter's bench*

bend VERB **bends, bending, bent 1** you bend or bend down when you lower your body by making your back curve: *She bent down to look more closely at the tiny insects.* **2** to bend is to curve: *He bent the wire around the post.*

NOUN **bends** a curve: *a bend in the road*

• **bend the rules** to break the rules in a way that will not be noticed or is not very important

▸ **bendy** ADJECTIVE **bendier, bendiest 1** with bends in it: *bendy knees* **2** able to bend easily: *a bendy piece of rubber*

beneath PREPOSITION below or under: *Atlantis, the lost city beneath the sea*

ADVERB (*formal*) below or under something: *the sky above and the earth beneath*

benefit NOUN **benefits 1** a benefit is something that helps you: *Having a mobile phone can be a real benefit in an emergency.* **2** people on benefit get money from the government to help them with their living expenses

VERB **benefits, benefiting** or **benefitting, benefited** or **benefitted** if you benefit from something, or if something benefits you, it helps you:

I think you'll benefit from the extra lessons.

bent VERB a way of changing the verb **bend** to make a past tense, either with or without a helping verb: *The striker bent the ball round the defenders.* • *I have bent this fork.*

ADJECTIVE not straight: *a bent pin*

bereaved ADJECTIVE someone is bereaved if one of their close relatives or friends has died: *the bereaved families of the accident victims*

▶ **bereavement** NOUN **bereavements** someone suffers a bereavement when a relative or close friend dies

beret (pronounced **ber**-ay) NOUN **berets** a flat round hat made of felt or some other kind of soft fabric

berry NOUN **berries** a small fruit containing lots of seeds that grows on certain types of plant: *Holly has red berries.*

✦ Do not confuse the spellings of **berry**, **beret** and **bury**, which can sound the same.

berserk ADJECTIVE to go berserk is to become very angry or violent: *My sister will go berserk if she finds out I've been wearing her T-shirt.*

berth NOUN **berths** **1** a bed on a boat or a train **2** a place in a harbour where a boat or ship can tie up or anchor

VERB **berths, berthing, berthed** a ship berths when it reaches the end of a journey and ties up or anchors in a harbour

beside PREPOSITION **1** next to or at the side of someone or something: *We do like to be beside the sea.* • *Go and stand beside Billy.* **2** compared with: *Beside that tiny kitten the dog looks enormous.*

• **beside the point** if something is beside the point, it has nothing to do with the thing being talked about or dealt with

• **beside yourself** terribly upset: *She's beside herself with grief.*

besides PREPOSITION as well as: *He isn't really interested in anything besides football.*

ADVERB also: *It's too wet to go out. Besides, I have a lot of homework to do.*

besiege VERB **besieges, besieging, besieged** to surround a place so that no one or nothing can get out easily: *Their house was besieged by photographers.*

best ADJECTIVE better than all the rest: *the best film they'd ever seen*

ADVERB in the most suitable or pleasing way: *I know it's difficult but just do it as best you can.* • *The city is best seen at night when all the skyscrapers are lit up.*

NOUN the most excellent things: *Parents want the best for their children.*

• **do your best** to do as well as you can

• **make the best of something** to enjoy something, or do as well as you can with it, even if it is not very good: *Although it was raining, we made the best of our trip to the seaside.*

best man NOUN the best man at a wedding is the man who helps the bridegroom and stands beside him during the ceremony

bet NOUN **bets** a bet is money that you risk on the result of something before the result is known. If the result is what you guessed, you win more money, but if the result is different, you lose the money you bet

VERB **bets, betting, bet** or **betted** **1** to make a bet **2** to bet is to say that something will happen because you are pretty sure that it will: *I bet that Jackie will be late again.*

betray VERB **betrays, betraying, betrayed** to betray someone who trusts you is to do something to harm them: *He betrayed his country by selling secrets to the enemy.*

▶ **betrayal** NOUN **betrayals** betrayal is harm done to a person who trusts you

better ADJECTIVE **1** of a higher standard or more excellent: *This is a better way to do it.* **2** not as bad or as ill as before: *My cold's much better today.* • *Don't go back to school until you're better.*

ADVERB in a more pleasing or more suitable way: *Which do you like better, the green one or the blue one?* • *Try to do better next time.*

• **better off** in a better position: *We'd be better off taking the plane. We'd get there quicker.*

• **had better do something** if you say you had better do something, you mean that you ought to do it: *I had better hurry, or I'll be late.*

NOUN something of a higher standard than others: *Of the two players, Federer is definitely the better.*

• **get the better of someone** to defeat someone: *You'll never get the better of him, no matter how long you argue.*

between PREPOSITION

1 in the area or space that divides two people, things or places: *What letter comes between Q and S in the alphabet?* • *the road between San Francisco and Los Angeles*

2 giving each a part or a piece: *Colin and Russell divided the work between them.*

3 including or involving each one: *They'll have to sort it out between them. We're not getting mixed up in it.*

4 one and not the other: *I had to decide between going to the concert or staying to watch the fireworks.*

ADVERB things between or in between are in the middle: *He'd had a big breakfast, an enormous lunch and lots of snacks in between.*

beverage NOUN **beverages** a drink

beware VERB to tell someone to beware or beware of something is to warn them that there is danger: *The sign on the gate said 'Beware of the dog'.*

bewildered ADJECTIVE confused
▶ **bewildering** ADJECTIVE confusing

bewitch VERB **bewitches, bewitching, bewitched 1** to bewitch someone is to put a magic spell on them **2** if you are bewitched by something, it is so attractive that you feel as if you are under a magic spell: *a bewitching smile*

beyond PREPOSITION **1** on the far side of something: *Turn right just beyond the bridge.* **2** more than or greater than something: *The noise level was beyond*

anything I'd ever experienced before. **3** if something is beyond someone, it is too difficult or confusing for them to understand: *It's beyond me why he didn't grab the opportunity when he had it.*

ADVERB further away: *We could see right across the valley to the mountains beyond.*

bi- PREFIX **1** if a word starts with **bi-**, it sometimes means *two*. For example, a *bicycle* is so called because it has two wheels **2** if a word starts with **bi-**, it sometimes means *twice*. For example, *bimonthly* means twice a month

✦This comes from **bis**, a Latin word which means *twice* or *two of*.

bias NOUN **biases** to have a bias towards a person, thing or point of view is to prefer them, often without thinking about whether someone or something else may be just as good or right: *There is a bias against girls when it comes to choosing the school football team.*
▶ **biased** or **biassed** ADJECTIVE favouring one person or thing unfairly: *a biased point of view*

bib NOUN **bibs** a piece of cloth or plastic tied under a baby's chin to protect its clothes while it is eating

Bible NOUN **Bibles** the holy book of the Christian and Jewish religions
▶ **biblical** ADJECTIVE to do with or in the Bible: *a biblical character*

bibliography NOUN **bibliographies** a list of books, for example ones that you have looked at for a piece of school work, or books by a particular writer

✦**Biblion** is the Greek word for *book*. If a word starts with **bibli**, you can guess that it has something to do with books.
The word **Bible** is also linked to the word **biblion**.

bicker VERB **bickers, bickering, bickered** to bicker is to argue about things that are not very important

bicycle NOUN **bicycles** a machine you ride on, made up of a metal frame

Aa
Bb
Cc
Dd
Ee
Ff
Gg
Hh
Ii
Jj
Kk
Ll
Mm
Nn
Oo
Pp
Qq
Rr
Ss
Tt
Uu
Vv
Ww
Xx
Yy
Zz

a bicycle

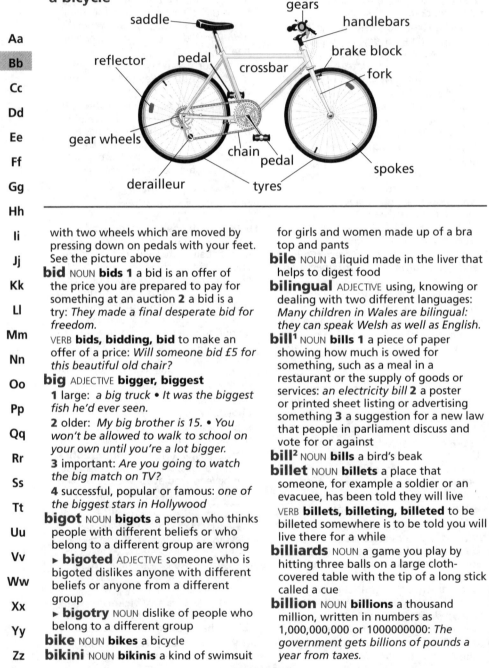

Aa
Bb
Cc
Dd
Ee
Ff
Gg
Hh
Ii
Jj
Kk
Ll
Mm
Nn
Oo
Pp
Qq
Rr
Ss
Tt
Uu
Vv
Ww
Xx
Yy
Zz

with two wheels which are moved by pressing down on pedals with your feet. See the picture above

bid NOUN **bids 1** a bid is an offer of the price you are prepared to pay for something at an auction **2** a bid is a try: *They made a final desperate bid for freedom.*
VERB **bids, bidding, bid** to make an offer of a price: *Will someone bid £5 for this beautiful old chair?*

big ADJECTIVE **bigger, biggest**
1 large: *a big truck* • *It was the biggest fish he'd ever seen.*
2 older: *My big brother is 15.* • *You won't be allowed to walk to school on your own until you're a lot bigger.*
3 important: *Are you going to watch the big match on TV?*
4 successful, popular or famous: *one of the biggest stars in Hollywood*

bigot NOUN **bigots** a person who thinks people with different beliefs or who belong to a different group are wrong
▶ **bigoted** ADJECTIVE someone who is bigoted dislikes anyone with different beliefs or anyone from a different group
▶ **bigotry** NOUN dislike of people who belong to a different group

bike NOUN **bikes** a bicycle

bikini NOUN **bikinis** a kind of swimsuit

for girls and women made up of a bra top and pants

bile NOUN a liquid made in the liver that helps to digest food

bilingual ADJECTIVE using, knowing or dealing with two different languages: *Many children in Wales are bilingual: they can speak Welsh as well as English.*

bill¹ NOUN **bills 1** a piece of paper showing how much is owed for something, such as a meal in a restaurant or the supply of goods or services: *an electricity bill* **2** a poster or printed sheet listing or advertising something **3** a suggestion for a new law that people in parliament discuss and vote for or against

bill² NOUN **bills** a bird's beak

billet NOUN **billets** a place that someone, for example a soldier or an evacuee, has been told they will live
VERB **billets, billeting, billeted** to be billeted somewhere is to be told you will live there for a while

billiards NOUN a game you play by hitting three balls on a large cloth-covered table with the tip of a long stick called a cue

billion NOUN **billions** a thousand million, written in numbers as 1,000,000,000 or 1000000000: *The government gets billions of pounds a year from taxes.*

billow VERB **billows, billowing, billowed** to billow is to rise in curving shapes like waves: *storm clouds billowing in from the west*

billy-goat NOUN **billy-goats** a male goat

bin NOUN **bins 1** a container for putting rubbish in **2** a container for storing something: *a bread bin*

binary ADJECTIVE made up of two parts: *a binary star*

binary number NOUN **binary numbers** a number that is made up of the digits 0 and 1 only, used to stand for the amount of units, twos, fours and so on in the number. Computers use these numbers to operate

bind VERB **binds, binding, bound** to tie or fasten together: *They bound his hands and feet with tape.*

binge VERB **binges, bingeing** or **binging, binged** to eat or drink too much, especially in a short time
NOUN **binges** a spell of eating or drinking too much

bingo NOUN a gambling game where people match the numbers on their card against numbers picked out at random and called out

binoculars PLURAL NOUN an instrument that is like a telescope but has a lens for each eye: *a pair of binoculars*

> ✦**Binoculars** comes from the Latin words **bini**, which means *two by two*, and **oculus**, which means *an eye*, because both eyes are used at the same time to look through binoculars.

bio- PREFIX if a word starts with **bio-**, it has something to do with life or living things. For example, *biology* is the study of living things

biodegradable ADJECTIVE (*science*) a biodegradable substance can be broken down by bacteria or in other natural ways

biographical ADJECTIVE about a person's life: *biographical details* • *a biographical film*

biography NOUN **biographies** a story about a real person's life

> ✦**Bios** is a Greek word that means *life*. If a word starts with **bio**, you can guess that it has something to do with life or living things. Other examples are **biology** and **bionic**.

biology NOUN the study of living things
> ▸ **biological** ADJECTIVE to do with living things and the way they grow and behave: *a biological process*
> ▸ **biologist** NOUN **biologists** a person who studies living things and their behaviour

bionic ADJECTIVE (*technology*) something that is bionic acts like a living thing, but works electronically

biosphere NOUN (*geography*) the area on and above the Earth where living things exist

birch NOUN **birches** a kind of tree with grey or silvery bark and small leaves

bird NOUN **birds** a creature with feathers growing on its body and which lays eggs: *Penguins are flightless birds.* See the picture on the next page

bird's eye view NOUN (*art*) how something looks when you look down on it from above, as if you were a bird in the air

bird of prey NOUN **birds of prey** a bird which kills and eats small animals or birds

birdwatching NOUN the hobby of looking at birds in their natural surroundings

Biro NOUN **Biros** (*trademark*) a kind of ballpoint pen

birth NOUN **births 1** birth is the process of being born: *Life is the time between birth and death.* • *the birth of nations* **2** a birth is the time when a particular person or animal is born

birthday NOUN **birthdays** your birthday is the anniversary of the date when you were born

birthmark NOUN **birthmarks** a mark on someone's body which they have had since they were born

biscuit NOUN **biscuits** a kind of hard, baked cake made from dough

Aa
Bb
Cc
Dd
Ee
Ff
Gg
Hh
Ii
Jj
Kk
Ll
Mm
Nn
Oo
Pp
Qq
Rr
Ss
Tt
Uu
Vv
Ww
Xx
Yy
Zz

a bird

crown

flight feathers

beak or bill

wings

breast

talons or claws

tail feathers

Aa
Bb
Cc
Dd
Ee
Ff
Gg
Hh
Ii
Jj
Kk
Ll
Mm
Nn
Oo
Pp
Qq
Rr
Ss
Tt
Uu
Vv
Ww
Xx
Yy
Zz

bisect VERB **bisects, bisecting, bisected** (*maths*) a line bisects another line when it cuts it into two parts

bishop NOUN **bishops 1** in some Christian churches such as the Catholic Church and the Church of England, a bishop is a member of the clergy in charge of a district **2** in the game of chess, a bishop is a piece which has a bishop's hat

bison NOUN **bison** or **bisons** a kind of wild ox with a long shaggy coat

bit¹ NOUN **bits**

1 a piece or a part: *There was one bit of the book that I really enjoyed.* • *The toy came to bits in my hand.*

2 a small amount: *I need a bit of help with this sum.*

3 a short time: *Let's wait a bit longer.*

4 a metal bar on a horse's bridle that the horse holds in its mouth

5 (*ICT*) the smallest piece of computer information

• **bit by bit** gradually

bit² VERB a way of changing the verb **bite** to make a past tense

bitch NOUN **bitches** a female dog

▸ **bitchy** ADJECTIVE **bitchier, bitchiest** nasty or spiteful: *a bitchy remark* • *Don't be bitchy.*

bite VERB **bites, biting, bit, bitten**
1 you bite something when you cut through it by bringing your top and bottom teeth together: *He stumbled and bit his tongue.* **2** if an animal bites, it uses its teeth to attack or injure: *Be careful! The cat sometimes bites.*

NOUN **bites** a cut or injury made with the teeth, or the part cut off by biting: *The dog gave the postman a nasty bite.* • *Can I have a bite of your apple?*

✦ Be careful not to confuse the spelling of **bite** with **byte**, a unit of computer memory.

bitmap NOUN **bitmaps** (*ICT*) a bitmap is a way of displaying an image on a computer. The image is broken up into small pieces of information called pixels that can be stored as units in computer memory

VERB **bitmaps, bitmapping, bitmapped** (*ICT*) to create or display an image on a computer in this way

bitter ADJECTIVE **1** bitter things have a sour rather than a sweet taste: *Lemon juice is bitter.* **2** if the weather is bitter, it is uncomfortably cold: *a bitter winter's night* **3** to be bitter is to be angry and resentful because of disappointment: *He turned into a bitter old man who hated the world.*

bizarre ADJECTIVE very odd or strange

black NOUN the darkest colour, the colour of coal or a dark night ADJECTIVE of the colour black VERB **blacks, blacking, blacked**
• **black out** if someone blacks out, they become unconscious for a short time
▶ **blackish** ADJECTIVE quite black, but not completely black in colour

blackberry NOUN **blackberries** a small, very dark purple or black fruit that grows on a plant with prickly stems

blackbird NOUN **blackbirds** a bird with black feathers and an orange beak. Female blackbirds are dark brown

blackboard NOUN **blackboards** a dark board for writing on with chalk

blacken VERB **blackens, blackening, blackened** to make something black or dark: *The soldiers blackened their faces so that they wouldn't be seen.*

black eye NOUN **black eyes** an injury that has bruised the skin around the eye

black hole NOUN **black holes** an area in outer space that draws everything into it by gravity. Nothing can escape from a black hole

black ice NOUN clear ice on roads that is difficult to see and so is dangerous for drivers

blacklist NOUN **blacklists** a list of people who are not to be given something, such as jobs VERB **blacklists, blacklisting, blacklisted** to blacklist someone is to put their name on a blacklist, so that they are not given something

blackmail VERB **blackmails, blackmailing, blackmailed** to blackmail someone is to threaten them with something bad, such as hurting one of their friends or relatives or telling one of their secrets, if they do not pay money NOUN the crime of blackmailing someone

black market NOUN something bought or sold on the black market is bought or sold illegally or dishonestly

blackout NOUN **blackouts 1** if there is a blackout somewhere, the place is in total darkness because there are no lights on **2** if someone has a blackout, they become unconscious for a short time and don't remember anything from that time

blacksmith NOUN **blacksmiths** someone who makes and repairs things made of iron, especially horseshoes

bladder NOUN **bladders** the organ in your body where urine is collected

blade NOUN **blades 1** the cutting part of a knife, sword or razor that has a thin sharp edge **2** a long thin leaf of grass

blame VERB **blames, blaming, blamed 1** to blame someone is to say that something is their fault: *I was nowhere near the window, so don't try to blame me.* **2** if you say that you do not blame someone, you mean you understand their reasons for doing something: *We shouldn't blame him for being angry.* NOUN **1** blame is responsibility for something bad that has happened: *They were made to take the blame.* **2** you are to blame for something bad if you have caused it: *Who is to blame for this mess?*

blancmange (pronounced bla-**monj**) NOUN **blancmanges** a soft jelly-like pudding made with milk

✦ This word comes from the French words **blanc**, which means *white*, and **manger**, which means *to eat*. In the past, blancmange was always white. The word **manger**, a box that animals feed from, is also linked to the word **manger**.

bland ADJECTIVE **blander, blandest 1** bland food is mild and doesn't have any strong flavours or spices **2** not causing any offence, but not very interesting or exciting either: *a pretty bland film*

blank ADJECTIVE **blanker, blankest 1** if something such as a sheet of paper is blank, it has nothing marked or written on it **2** if someone's face is blank, their face or eyes do not show any feeling: *He gave me a blank stare.*

Aa
Bb
Cc
Dd
Ee
Ff
Gg
Hh
Ii
Jj
Kk
Ll
Mm
Nn
Oo
Pp
Qq
Rr
Ss
Tt
Uu
Vv
Ww
Xx
Yy
Zz

Aa
Bb
Cc
Dd
Ee
Ff
Gg
Hh
Ii
Jj
Kk
Ll
Mm
Nn
Oo
Pp
Qq
Rr
Ss
Tt
Uu
Vv
Ww
Xx
Yy
Zz

NOUN **blanks 1** an empty space: *Fill in the blanks in the sentences below.* **2** a cartridge for a gun that contains an explosive but no bullet: *The actors use blanks.*

blanket NOUN **blankets 1** a covering for a bed, usually made of wool or some other warm fabric **2** a layer that covers everything: *a blanket of snow*

blare VERB **blares, blaring, blared** to sound loudly: *Music was blaring from his car.*

blasphemy NOUN blasphemy is speaking about religious things in a rude or disrespectful way

▸ **blasphemous** ADJECTIVE disrespectful or rude about religious things

blast NOUN **blasts 1** a loud violent explosion: *The bomb went off and many people were injured in the blast.* **2** a strong wind or gust of wind: *They stood shivering in the icy blast.* **3** a loud sound from a trumpet or horn: *The driver gave a couple of blasts on his horn.*

VERB **blasts, blasting, blasted 1** to explode and damage something: *The bomb blasted the windows out of the building.* **2** to make a loud noise: *music blasting out of the open windows* **3** to blast something is to strongly criticize it: *He made a speech blasting all his opponents.*

blast-off NOUN **blast-offs** the moment when a rocket is launched

blatant ADJECTIVE bad behaviour is blatant when it is very obvious and the person doing it doesn't seem to care that it is obvious: *It was a blatant lie.*

blaze NOUN **blazes 1** a large and dangerous fire: *The firefighters put out the blaze.* **2** something that is very bright: *The garden is a blaze of colour.*

VERB **blazes, blazing, blazed** to glow brightly with, or as if with, flames: *She was blazing with anger.*

blazer NOUN **blazers** a kind of jacket worn as part of a school uniform or by members of a club

bleach NOUN a chemical used to whiten or lighten fabrics or as a household cleaner

VERB **bleaches, bleaching, bleached 1** if something such as your hair is bleached by the sun, the sun makes it a lighter colour **2** to make something white or light using bleach

bleak ADJECTIVE **bleaker, bleakest 1** cold, bare and miserable: *a bleak winter landscape* **2** hopeless and miserable: *Our chances of winning the match looked bleak.*

▸ **bleakly** ADVERB in a cold or miserable way: *He smiled bleakly.*

▸ **bleakness** NOUN being bleak: *the bleakness of the dark hills • The bleakness did not leave his eyes.*

bleary ADJECTIVE **blearier, bleariest** if your eyes are bleary, they are tired and you aren't able to see clearly

▸ **blearily** ADVERB in a tired and sleepy way: *She sat up blearily, blinking in the light.*

bleat VERB **bleats, bleating, bleated 1** a sheep or goat bleats when it makes its usual sound **2** to speak in an annoying complaining way: *She was bleating on about how unfair it all was.*

NOUN **bleats** the sound a sheep or goat makes

bleed VERB **bleeds, bleeding, bled** you bleed when you lose blood, especially from a cut or injury

bleep NOUN **bleeps** a short high-pitched sound made by an electronic device as a signal

VERB **bleeps, bleeping, bleeped 1** an device bleeps when it makes a short high-pitched sound **2** to signal to someone using an electronic device: *The nurse said she would bleep one of the doctors.*

blemish NOUN **blemishes 1** a mark that spoils something's appearance: *an apple covered with blemishes* **2** something that spoils someone's good reputation: *a blemish on his character*

blend VERB **blends, blending, blended** to put things together so that they are mixed in with each other: *Blend the butter and the sugar.*

• **blend in** if people or things blend

in somewhere, they fit in well with the people or things around them

NOUN blends a mixture of two or more things: *Banana milkshake is a blend of milk, banana and ice cream.*

▸ **blender** NOUN **blenders** a machine with a blade that turns quickly, used for mixing foods or liquids together

bless VERB **blesses, blessing, blessed 1** if someone is blessed, they are made happy or they have good luck: *They've been blessed with two beautiful children.* **2** to bless someone or something is to ask God to help or protect them: *The cardinal blessed the poor.*

▸ **blessing** NOUN **blessings 1** a wish for happiness: *He gave the young couple his blessing.* **2** something that brings happiness or relief: *In this dry, hot country, rain is a blessing.*

blew VERB a way of changing the verb **blow** to make a past tense

blind ADJECTIVE not able to see: *Newborn kittens are blind.*

VERB **blinds, blinding, blinded** to make someone blind: *He was blinded in the war.* • *The light blinded me for a moment.*

NOUN **blinds** a covering for a window, used instead of curtains or to keep out strong sunlight: *I'll pull down the blinds.*

blindfold NOUN **blindfolds** a cover put over someone's eyes to stop them seeing

VERB **blindfolds, blindfolding, blindfolded** to put a blindfold on someone

blindman's buff NOUN a game where one of the players is blindfolded and tries to catch the other players

blink VERB **blinks, blinking, blinked** to close and open your eyes very quickly: *She blinked in the strong sunlight.*

bliss NOUN bliss is a feeling of very great happiness: *It was bliss not to have to go to school for a couple of days.*

▸ **blissful** ADJECTIVE lovely: *We spent a blissful day at the seaside.*

▸ **blissfully** ADVERB happily: *He was blissfully unaware of the trouble he had caused.*

blister NOUN **blisters** a thin bubble on the skin that is caused by burning or rubbing the skin

VERB **blisters, blistering, blistered** to form blisters

blitz NOUN **blitzes 1** an attack made by many military aircraft dropping bombs **2** a quick attack, for example, to get through tidying or other work that needs to be done

blizzard NOUN **blizzards** a storm with wind and heavy snow

bloated ADJECTIVE swollen: *His stomach felt bloated after the huge meal.*

blob NOUN **blobs** a round lump of something soft or liquid: *blobs of paint*

block NOUN **blocks 1** a solid lump of something: *Cut the wood into blocks.* • *a block of ice cream* **2** a group of buildings or houses that are joined together: *a block of flats* **3** a barrier or obstacle that stops people or things getting through: *a road block*

VERB **blocks, blocking, blocked 1** to block something which things usually pass through, like a road or a pipe, is to make a barrier on or in it so that nothing can get through: *The fallen leaves had blocked the drain.* **2** to block something is to get in its way: *There were lots of taller people in front blocking our view.*

▸ **blockage** NOUN **blockages** something that stops people or things getting through: *The tree caused a blockage in the road.*

blockade NOUN **blockades** the surrounding of a place by soldiers or ships to stop people or things getting in and out: *a blockade of French ports*

VERB **blockades, blockading, blockaded** to surround a place to stop people or things getting in and out

block capitals PLURAL NOUN you use block capitals when you use capital letters to write every letter in every word, LIKE THIS

block graph NOUN **block graphs** a graph with piles of blocks that show the number of things in different groups

blog NOUN **blogs** a personal record that

Aa

Bb

Cc

Dd

Ee

Ff

Gg

Hh

Ii

Jj

Kk

Ll

Mm

Nn

Oo

Pp

Qq

Rr

Ss

Tt

Uu

Vv

Ww

Xx

Yy

Zz

someone puts on their own website, saying what has happened to them and what they think about things

VERB **blogs, blogging, blogged** to write a personal journal on a website

▸ **blogger** NOUN **bloggers** someone who writes a blog

blond *or* **blonde** ADJECTIVE **blonder, blondest** fair-haired

NOUN **blonds** *or* **blondes** a person with fair hair

✦ The spelling **blonde**, with an **e**, is used for girls and women. The spelling **blond**, without an **e**, is used for boys and men.

blood NOUN the red liquid that carries nutrients, oxygen and other substances round your body in veins

bloodhound NOUN **bloodhounds** a kind of hunting dog with long ears, a wrinkled face and a very good sense of smell

bloodshed NOUN bloodshed is violence in which people are injured or killed

bloodshot ADJECTIVE if your eyes are bloodshot the white parts are red

bloodstream NOUN your bloodstream is the blood moving round your body inside a system of veins: *If the infection gets into the bloodstream it is carried quickly round the body.*

bloodthirsty ADJECTIVE **bloodthirstier, bloodthirstiest** a bloodthirsty person is eager to kill or enjoys seeing people or animals being killed

blood vessel NOUN **blood vessels** a tube, such as an artery or vein, that carries blood around the body

bloody ADJECTIVE **bloodier, bloodiest** **1** covered in blood: *a bloody nose* **2** involving a lot of violence or killing: *a bloody conflict*

bloom VERB **blooms, blooming, bloomed** to flower: *Many plants in the garden have bloomed early this year.*

NOUN **blooms** a flower: *a rose bush with many blooms*

blossom NOUN **blossoms** the flowers that appear on a fruit tree before the fruit

VERB **blossoms, blossoming, blossomed** **1** a tree or bush blossoms when it flowers before producing fruit **2** a person blossoms when they become more successful or attractive: *Under the teacher's guidance, his musical talent blossomed.*

blot NOUN **blots** an inky stain

VERB **blots, blotting, blotted** to remove liquid from a surface by dabbing it with paper or a cloth

• **blot something out** if you blot out an unpleasant thought or memory, you put it out of your mind completely: *Jackson had blotted the accident out of his mind.*

blotch NOUN **blotches** a spot or patch of a different colour: *The illness causes red blotches to appear on your face.*

▸ **blotchy** ADJECTIVE **blotchier, blotchiest** marked with blotches

blouse NOUN **blouses** a shirt for girls or women

blow VERB **blows, blowing, blew, blown** **1** wind blows when it moves around: *a breeze blowing from the west* **2** to blow something is to force air on to it or into it: *She managed to blow all the candles out in one go.* • *You'd have to blow hard to inflate a balloon that big.* **3** to blow a musical instrument is to breathe into it to make a sound

• **blow over** when something unpleasant blows over, it passes and is forgotten

• **blow something up 1** to blow something up is to destroy it with an explosion: *Guy Fawkes plotted to blow up the Houses of Parliament.* **2** to inflate something such as a balloon by blowing air into it: *We got Dad to blow up the balloons.*

NOUN **blows 1** a hard knock: *a blow to the face* **2** a sudden piece of bad luck: *Missing the train was a bit of a blow.*

blowtorch NOUN **blowtorches** a tool for aiming a very hot flame at something to heat it up and melt it

blubber NOUN the fat from whales and other sea animals

blue NOUN **blues** the colour of the sky in the day time if there are no clouds

• **out of the blue** if something comes out of the blue, it happens without anyone expecting it

ADJECTIVE of the colour blue

▶ **bluish** ADJECTIVE quite blue, but not completely blue in colour

bluebell NOUN **bluebells** a flower with blue bell-shaped flowers

bluebottle NOUN **bluebottles** a large fly with a shiny blue body

blueprint NOUN **blueprints** a plan of work that is to be done, especially of something that is to be built

bluff VERB **bluffs, bluffing, bluffed** to bluff is to make people think that you know something when you don't, or that you are going to do something that you have no intention of doing

NOUN **bluffs** a trick or deception: *They weren't going to attack. It was only a bluff.*

blunder NOUN **blunders** a bad or embarrassing mistake

blunt ADJECTIVE **blunter, bluntest 1** with an edge or point that is not sharp: *This knife is blunt.* **2** saying what you think without trying to be polite: *He is always blunt and to the point.*

▶ **bluntly** ADVERB without trying to be polite: *'I hate it,' she said bluntly.*

blur NOUN **blurs 1** a shape with edges that can't be seen clearly: *a blur of faces* **2** something that you can't remember clearly: *I don't really know what happened. It was all a blur.*

VERB **blurs, blurring, blurred** to become unclear: *When I take my glasses off, the sign just blurs.*

blurt VERB **blurts, blurting, blurted**

• **blurt something out** to say something suddenly without thinking, especially something that gives away a secret or hurts someone's feelings

blush VERB **blushes, blushing, blushed** to go pink in the face with embarrassment: *Everyone turned to look at Philip, who blushed.*

blustery ADJECTIVE if the weather is blustery, the wind is blowing in strong gusts

boar NOUN **boars 1** a male pig **2** a wild pig

board NOUN **boards 1** a flat piece of cut wood **2** a flat piece of material with a pattern or divisions marked on it, used to play a game: *a backgammon board* **3** a group of people who manage a business company or other organization: *She's on the school's board of governors.*

• **on board** on a ship or aircraft

VERB **boards, boarding, boarded 1** to board a ship or an aircraft is to get on it to make a journey: *More passengers boarded at Carlisle.* **2** if someone boards they are provided with their meals and lodging somewhere: *The boys will board during term time while their parents are away.*

▶ **boarder** NOUN **boarders 1** someone who stays in a boarding house **2** a pupil who stays at a boarding school

boarding house NOUN **boarding houses** a house where guests pay a fixed price for meals and their room

boarding school NOUN **boarding schools** a school where pupils stay during term time and are given food and lodging

boast VERB **boasts, boasting, boasted** to talk proudly about things you own or things you have done, in a way that other people find annoying: *He's always boasting about his expensive trainers.*

NOUN **boasts** something you say when you boast: *It was her proud boast that she always got the highest mark in her class.*

▶ **boastful** ADJECTIVE a boastful person is in the habit of talking proudly about what they own or what they have done

boat NOUN **boats** a vehicle for travelling over the surface of water. A boat is smaller than a ship

• **in the same boat** if two or more people are in the same boat, they have the same problems or difficulties

bob VERB **bobs, bobbing, bobbed** to bob is to move up and down

Aa
Bb
Cc
Dd
Ee
Ff
Gg
Hh
Ii
Jj
Kk
Ll
Mm
Nn
Oo
Pp
Qq
Rr
Ss
Tt
Uu
Vv
Ww
Xx
Yy
Zz

quickly above the surface or top of something: *little boats bobbing on the lake • I saw their heads bob up from behind the hedge.*

bobble NOUN **bobbles 1** a small, round piece of soft material used for decoration on clothing, especially on hats **2** a small band used to tie up or decorate hair

bobsleigh NOUN **bobsleighs** a long sledge which has a compartment for the riders and is used for racing down ice slopes

bode VERB **bodes** if something bodes well, or bodes ill, it shows that something good, or something bad, is likely to happen

bodice NOUN **bodices** the part of a dress that fits tightly on the body above the waist

bodily ADJECTIVE bodily means of the body: *Blood and saliva are bodily fluids.*
ADVERB entirely: *He was carried bodily down the river by the current.*

body NOUN **bodies 1** the whole of a human being or an animal: *I had a rash all over my body.* **2** a dead person or animal: *They found the bodies of hundreds of dead birds on the shore.*

bodyguard NOUN **bodyguards** someone whose job is to protect an important or famous person

bog NOUN **bogs** an area of land that is very wet and where the ground is very soft
VERB **bogs, bogging, bogged**
• **bog down** you get bogged down if something stops you making good progress: *She got bogged down in one question and didn't finish the test.*
▶**boggy** ADJECTIVE **boggier, boggiest** boggy ground is wet and sinks under you when you step on it

✦This word comes from the Gaelic word **bogach**, which means *swamp*.

bogus ADJECTIVE **1** pretending to be something they are not: *He was tricked out of his money by a bogus salesmen.* **2** false: *The documents turned out to be bogus.*

boil¹ VERB **boils, boiling, boiled 1** something boils when it is heated until it bubbles and turns into gas or vapour: *Is the water boiling yet?* **2** to boil a liquid is to heat it until it bubbles: *Boil some water in a saucepan and add the pasta.* **3** to boil food is to cook it in boiling water: *Are you going to boil or fry the potatoes?*
NOUN a state of boiling: *Bring the water to the boil.*

boil² NOUN **boils** a boil is a red painful swelling on the skin caused by an infection

boiler NOUN **boilers** a container in which water is heated or steam is made. It might be used in a central heating system, for example

boiling ADJECTIVE very hot: *It's boiling in here.*

boiling point NOUN **boiling points** the temperature at which a particular liquid boils: *The boiling point of water is 100 degrees Celsius.*

boisterous ADJECTIVE very active and full of energy, especially playing roughly and noisily: *The children are excited and are very boisterous.*

bold ADJECTIVE **bolder, boldest 1** daring or fearless: *a bold leader • It was rather bold of him to ask that question.* **2** standing out clearly: *a bold swirly pattern* **3** printed in thick letters, like this **bold print**
▶ **boldly** ADVERB **1** fearlessly: *He walked boldly into the room, which was full of strangers.* **2** clearly: *The bright red flowers stood out boldly against the green leaves.*

✦Be careful not to confuse the spellings of **bolder** meaning 'more bold' and **boulder** meaning 'a large rock'.

bollard NOUN **bollards** a short post placed on a road to stop cars from driving into or on an area

bolster VERB **bolsters, bolstering, bolstered** to bolster something, or to bolster it up, is to do something to support or strengthen it: *A local supermarket donated money to bolster our charity fund.*

bolt NOUN **bolts 1** a metal bar that slides across to fasten a door **2** a kind of heavy screw that is held in place by a nut **3** a streak of lightning
VERB **bolts, bolting, bolted 1** to bolt a door is to fasten it securely with a bolt **2** to bolt is to run away very fast: *There was a loud bang and Beth's pony bolted.*

bomb NOUN **bombs** an object that is designed to explode and cause damage or injuries
VERB **bombs, bombing, bombed** to bomb a place is to drop bombs on it or explode a bomb in it

bombard VERB **bombard, bombarding, bombarded 1** an army bombards a place when it attacks it with lots of missiles **2** if you are bombarded with things they come at you very quickly all together or one after the other: *His parents bombarded him with questions.*

bomber NOUN **bombers 1** an aeroplane that carries and drops bombs **2** someone who sets off a bomb

bombshell NOUN **bombshells** (*informal*) a piece of news that takes you completely by surprise

bond NOUN **bonds 1** something that brings or keeps people together: *a bond of friendship* **2** something used for tying someone up or taking away their freedom: *He struggled against his bonds but he couldn't break them without a knife.* **3** (*science*) a bond is the strong force that holds two atoms together: *a chemical bond*
VERB **bonds, bonding, bonded 1** to bond one thing to another is to make the first thing stick firmly to the second thing: *Use glue to bond the two pieces together.* **2** if two people bond, they feel close to each other, usually because they have something in common

bone NOUN **bones 1** bone is the hard substance that forms a skeleton and supports the flesh and muscle in the body **2** a bone is one of the pieces of a skeleton: *He broke a bone in his arm.*

bonfire NOUN **bonfires** a large fire built outside

bonnet NOUN **bonnets 1** the piece at the front of a car that covers the engine **2** a hat that ties under the chin

bonny ADJECTIVE **bonnier, bonniest** pretty: *a bonny baby*

bonus NOUN **bonuses** something extra that is good to get: *The campsite was great and the hot weather was a real bonus.*

bony ADJECTIVE **bonier, boniest 1** so thin that the shape of the bones can be seen through the skin: *long bony fingers* **2** full of bones: *a bony piece of fish*

boo VERB **boos, booing, booed** people in an audience boo when they make loud rude noises because they don't like what they have seen or heard: *He was booed off the stage.*
NOUN **boos** a word that people in an audience shout when they are not pleased

booby prize NOUN **booby prizes** a prize sometimes given to the person who has come last

booby trap NOUN **booby traps** a trap or bomb that people don't know is there until it is too late

book NOUN **books** pages joined together and given a cover
VERB **books, booking, booked** if you book something such as tickets for an event or a table in a restaurant, you tell the company that you want it and will pay for it: *Mum is booking our holiday today.*

booklet NOUN **booklets** a small book, usually with only a few pages, that gives information about something

bookmark NOUN **bookmarks 1** a strip of paper or other material that you put between the pages of a book so that you can go back later to the place where you had stopped reading **2** (*ICT*) a record on a computer of where you can find one of your favourite websites
VERB **bookmarks, bookmarking, bookmarked** (*ICT*) to bookmark a website is to make a record on the computer of where you can find it

bookworm NOUN **bookworms** someone who likes reading lots of books

Aa
Bb
Cc
Dd
Ee
Ff
Gg
Hh
Ii
Jj
Kk
Ll
Mm
Nn
Oo
Pp
Qq
Rr
Ss
Tt
Uu
Vv
Ww
Xx
Yy
Zz

boom NOUN **booms 1** a boom is a loud noise like the sound a big drum makes: *We could hear the boom of thunder in the distance.* **2** if there is a boom in business or in a country, a lot more things are bought and sold, and more money is made

VERB **booms, booming, boomed 1** to boom is to make a loud sound **2** business booms when a lot more things are sold

boomerang NOUN **boomerangs** a boomerang is a curved piece of wood that flies back to you when you throw it in the air

boon NOUN **boons** a boon is something good that happens that you are grateful for: *It would be a real boon if we got hot weather for the barbecue next Saturday.*

boost NOUN **boosts** something that helps to improve something or raise it to a higher or better level: *The school funds got a boost from the money raised at the summer fair.*

VERB **boosts, boosting, boosted** to boost something is to help raise it to a higher or better level: *Playing in the school concert will boost her confidence.*

boot NOUN **boots 1** a kind of shoe that covers the ankle and often part of the leg **2** the part at the back of a car where you carry things

VERB **boots, booting, booted** to boot something is to kick it: *Georgie booted the ball right over the bar.*

• **boot up** (*ICT*) to boot up a computer is to start its operating system, the program that controls all the other programs

booth NOUN **booths** a small enclosed place, for example a place where a machine takes your photo

booty NOUN booty is the things that thieves, pirates or invading soldiers steal or take by force and keep for themselves

border NOUN **borders 1** the border between two countries or areas is the line on the map which separates them: *They settled near the Canadian and*

United States border. **2** an edge of something or a strip round its edge: *a pillowcase with a lace border*

VERB **borders, bordering, bordered**

• **border on** one thing borders on another when the first thing is very close to the second thing: *Jumping off that wall borders on stupidity.*

borderline NOUN **borderlines** a line that separates two places or things

ADJECTIVE something that is borderline is so close to two different things that it is difficult to decide which it is: *Your work is borderline. You might get a pass or a fail.*

bore¹ VERB **bores, boring, bored** if something bores you, it makes you feel tired and fed up because it doesn't interest you: *The speech bored him.*

NOUN **bores** someone or something that makes you feel tired and fed-up: *It was a real bore having to sort all the papers.*

✦ Be careful not to confuse the spelling of **bore** with **boar**, which means a male pig.

---

bore² VERB **bores, boring, bored** to bore something is to use a drill, or something that works like a drill, to make a hole in or through that thing: *The insect bores a tiny hole in the fruit.*

bore³ VERB a way of changing the verb **bear** to make a past tense

bored ADJECTIVE if you are bored, you feel tired and fed-up because you are doing something that isn't interesting, or because you have nothing to do: *I'm bored. Let's go out and play.*

boredom NOUN the feeling of being fed up and not interested in anything

boring ADJECTIVE not at all interesting: *a long boring journey*

born VERB **1** a form of the verb **bear** that you use if you are talking about the birth of a baby or animal: *My sister was born three years ago.* **2** to be born is to come into existence: *A new star was born.*

ADJECTIVE having a talent you seem to have been born with: *She's a born entertainer.*

Aa
Bb
Cc
Dd
Ee
Ff
Gg
Hh
Ii
Jj
Kk
Ll
Mm
Nn
Oo
Pp
Qq
Rr
Ss
Tt
Uu
Vv
Ww
Xx
Yy
Zz

borne VERB a form of the verb **bear** that is used with a helping verb to show that something happened in the past: *He had borne the hardships of his life without complaining.*

borough NOUN **boroughs** a town or area with a local council

borrow VERB **borrows, borrowing, borrowed** to borrow something is to take it with the owner's permission and give it back to them later: *Can I borrow your pencil for a minute, please?*
▶ **borrower** NOUN **borrowers** a person who borrows something

✦ Try not to confuse **borrowing** and **lending**. If you **borrow** something *from* someone you get it from them and if you **lend** something *to* someone, you give it to them.

bosom (pronounced **booz**-im) NOUN **bosoms 1** a woman's breasts **2** your chest

boss NOUN **bosses 1** a manager in a workplace who is in charge of other people working there: *Her boss gave her a pay rise.* **2** the most important person in a group, who orders the others about: *I'm the boss, so you've got to do what I tell you.*
VERB **bosses, bossing, bossed**
• **boss someone around** if someone bosses you around, they keep telling you what to do because they think they are more important than you

bossy ADJECTIVE **bossier, bossiest** someone who is bossy likes telling other people what to do: *Stop being so bossy. You're not in charge here.*

botany NOUN the study of plants
▶ **botanic** or **botanical** ADJECTIVE to do with plants or the study of plants: *We visited the city's botanic gardens.* • *a botanical specimen*
▶ **botanist** NOUN **botanists** someone who studies plants

botch VERB **botches, botching, botched** (*informal*) to botch something is to make a mess of it or to do it wrongly

both ADJECTIVE you use 'both' to refer to two people or things when you mean the one and also the other: *She ate both cakes, and I didn't get one.* • *Both the boys are good at tennis.*
PRONOUN two people or things together: *John and Andrew are nice boys – I like them both.* • *Both of these chairs are broken.*

bother VERB **bothers, bothering, bothered 1** if you bother someone, you do something that annoys them or interrupts them: *Stop bothering me, I'm busy.* **2** if something bothers you, it makes you feel unhappy or worried: *It doesn't bother me that I lost the game.* **3** to bother to do something is to take the time or trouble to do it: *Don't bother tidying up yet.*
NOUN nuisance or trouble: *The address book saves you the bother of having to remember email addresses.* • *It was no bother to help you out.*

bottle NOUN **bottles** a container with a narrow neck used for holding liquids like milk, lemonade or wine
VERB **bottles, bottling, bottled** to bottle a liquid is to put it in a bottle
• **bottle something up** if someone bottles up unpleasant feelings, they avoid talking about them, even though this might make them feel better

bottle bank NOUN **bottle banks** a container where you put empty glass bottles to be recycled

bottleneck NOUN **bottlenecks** a place where traffic moves slowly, for example because the road is too narrow

bottom NOUN **bottoms 1** the lowest part of something: *the bottom of the stairs* • *the bottom of the sea* **2** the part of your body that you sit on **3** the lowest position: *the team at the bottom of the league*
ADJECTIVE in the lowest position, with other things above: *the bottom shelf*
▶ **bottomless** ADJECTIVE very deep, as if having no bottom: *a bottomless pit*

bough (rhymes with **cow**) NOUN **boughs** one of the bigger branches that grows from the trunk of a tree

bought VERB a way of changing

the verb **buy** to make a past tense. It can be used with or without a helping verb: *She bought me an ice cream.* • *Mum has bought a new car.*

boulder NOUN **boulders** a big piece of stone or rock

bounce VERB **bounces, bouncing, bounced 1** to bounce is to jump up and down quickly on a springy surface: *We bounced on the trampoline.* **2** a ball bounces when it hits something hard and moves away again in another direction

▸ **bouncy** ADJECTIVE **bouncier, bounciest** springy and able to move up and down

bound¹ VERB **bounds, bounding, bounded** to run with jumping movements: *The dogs bounded into the room, barking excitedly.*

NOUN **bounds** a leap or jumping movement: *The deer was over the fence in a single bound.*

bound² VERB **bounds, bounding, bounded** the place where one area bounds another is the place which marks the boundary between them: *The farm is bounded in the east by a forest and in the west by a large lake.*

• **out of bounds** if a place is out of bounds, you are not allowed to go there: *The riverbank is out of bounds for the younger children.*

bound³ ADJECTIVE **1** to be bound to do something is to be certain or very likely to do it: *The plants are bound to grow if you keep them well watered.* **2** going in a particular direction: *We were homeward bound.* **3** to be bound for a place is to be on your way there or planning to go there: *ships bound for the Far East*

bound⁴ VERB a way of changing the verb **bind** to make a past tense. It can be used with or without a helping verb: *He has bound the ropes tight.*

boundary NOUN **boundaries** a line that divides a place or thing from what is next to it: *the boundary between the city and the countryside*

bouquet (pronounced **book**-ay) NOUN **bouquets** a bunch of flowers

bout NOUN **bouts 1** a period of illness: *a bout of flu* **2** a boxing match or wrestling match

boutique (pronounced boo-**teek**) NOUN **boutiques** a small shop selling fashionable clothes

bow¹ (rhymes with **cow**) VERB **bows, bowing, bowed 1** if you bow to someone, you bend your head or the top half of your body forward to greet them or show them respect: *Everyone bowed to the king and queen.* **2** if you bow your head, you look at the ground because you are ashamed

• **bow to** if someone bows to something, they give in to it: *The government bowed to pressure and changed the law.*

NOUN **bows** a bending of the head or body: *The pianist took a bow when the audience clapped.*

bow² (rhymes with **no**) NOUN **bows 1** a weapon for shooting arrows, made from a curved piece of wood with a string stretched between its two ends **2** a wooden rod with a string stretched along it, used for playing a musical instrument such as a violin or cello **3** a knot made with loops on either side: *She wore bows in her hair.*

VERB **bows, bowing, bowed 1** to use a bow to play a stringed musical instrument **2** to bend into a curved shape: *The shelf bowed under the weight of the books.*

ADJECTIVE in a curved shape: *bow legs* • *bow-legged*

bow³ (rhymes with **cow**) NOUN **bows** the pointed front part of a ship or boat

bowels PLURAL NOUN a long tube inside the lower part of your body that food goes through after leaving your stomach

bowl NOUN **bowls 1** a wide container open at the top and used for holding various things: *a soup bowl* **2** anything round and hollow that is shaped like this kind of container, such as a sports stadium **3** a heavy ball used in games like bowls and skittles

VERB **bowls, bowling, bowled 1** to

bowl is to throw the ball towards the person batting in cricket and rounders **2** to bowl is to play the game of bowls

bowler¹ NOUN **bowlers 1** someone who bowls in cricket and rounders **2** someone who plays the game of bowls

bowler² *or* **bowler hat** NOUN **bowlers** *or* **bowler hats** a smart hat with a rounded top, worn by businessmen in the past

bowling NOUN **1** the game of tenpin bowling, played with skittles **2** the game of bowls, played on a bowling green

bowls NOUN a game in which heavy balls are rolled along a special flat surface called a bowling green

bow tie NOUN **bow ties** a tie that is shaped like a small bow and is worn by men

box NOUN **boxes** a container, sometimes with a lid, used for holding or storing things

VERB **boxes, boxing, boxed 1** to box something is to put it in a box or boxes **2** people box when they hit each other with their fists

▶ **boxer** NOUN **boxers** someone who does the sport of boxing

▶ **boxing** NOUN a sport in which two people hit each other with their fists, usually while wearing heavy leather gloves

Boxing Day NOUN the day after Christmas Day

box office NOUN a theatre box office is the place where you can buy tickets for shows

boy NOUN **boys** a male child

✦ Be careful not to confuse the spelling of **boy** with **buoy**, a floating object on the sea.

boycott VERB **boycotts, boycotting, boycotted** to boycott something is to refuse to take part in it or buy it, as a protest

NOUN **boycotts** a refusal to take part in something or buy it, as a protest

boyfriend NOUN **boyfriends** a male

friend, especially someone you are having a special relationship with

boyhood NOUN the period of time in your life when you are a boy

boyish ADJECTIVE **1** behaving like a boy: *She's always been boyish and full of mischief.* **2** looking like a young boy: *He has a charming boyish grin.*

bra NOUN **bras** a piece of underwear that women wear to support their breasts

brace NOUN **braces 1** a piece of wire put on teeth to straighten them **2** a device that forces or holds two things together tightly

bracelet NOUN **bracelets** a piece of jewellery that you wear around your wrist

braces PLURAL NOUN **1** two sets of wires used to straighten the top and bottom teeth **2** two stretchy straps that hold a man's trousers up, worn over the shoulders

bracing ADJECTIVE healthy and fresh: *a bracing walk by the sea*

bracken NOUN a wild plant like a fern that grows in clumps in woods and on hillsides

bracket NOUN **brackets 1** a punctuation mark that looks like a curved line. You use them in pairs to show that the words, letters or numbers inside them are separated from the writing coming before or after, for example *Tomorrow (April 30), the new term begins.* **2** a grouping or category: *Caribbean holidays are in the highest price bracket.* **3** a piece of metal used to attach things to walls

brag VERB **brags, bragging, bragged** to brag is to boast: *She's always bragging about her fashionable clothes.*

Brahma NOUN in Hinduism, Brahma is the god who created the world

braid NOUN **braids 1** braid is a thick kind of fancy ribbon used to trim things with **2** a plait of hair

VERB **braids, braiding, braided** to plait hair

braille NOUN a writing system for blind people, which instead of printed letters

Aa
Bb
Cc
Dd
Ee
Ff
Gg
Hh
Ii
Jj
Kk
Ll
Mm
Nn
Oo
Pp
Qq
Rr
Ss
Tt
Uu
Vv
Ww
Xx
Yy
Zz

has groups of raised dots which can be read by touching them

> **◆Braille** was named after the man who invented it, Louis *Braille*, who was a teacher in France.

brain NOUN **brains** the organ inside your skull that controls all the other parts of your body and with which you think

brainstorm NOUN **brainstorms** a discussion in which everyone in a group gives their ideas

VERB **brainstorms, brainstorming, brainstormed** to brainstorm, or brainstorm something, is to discuss something with a group of people so you get lots of different ideas about it

brainwash VERB **brainwashes, brainwashing, brainwashed** to brainwash someone is to make them believe something by telling them over and over again that it is true

brainwave NOUN **brainwaves** if you have a brainwave, you suddenly have a very good idea

brainy ADJECTIVE **brainier, brainiest** (*informal*) clever: *Caitlin is definitely brainy enough to be a doctor.*

brake NOUN **brakes** a device or system in a vehicle that is used for stopping or slowing down: *Always check your brakes before you go out on a long bike ride.*

VERB **brakes, braking, braked** to use a brake to slow down or stop: *He braked suddenly and we were all thrown forward.*

> **◆The words brake** and **break** sound the same but remember that they have different spellings. To **break** is to fall to pieces, or to damage something.

bramble NOUN **brambles** a blackberry plant

bran NOUN the brown parts that cover wheat grains

branch NOUN **branches 1** any of the parts of a tree that grow out from the trunk: *Rooks build their nests high in the branches of trees.* **2** one of the shops or businesses that belong to a larger organization: *the local branch of the bank* **3** (*ICT*) a point in a computer program that leads to a different part of the program

VERB **branches, branching, branched** to form branches or to separate into different parts like the branches of a tree: *The road branches to the north and west.*

• **branch out** to branch out is to start to be involved in something new: *Dad's company is branching out into selling on the Internet.*

brand NOUN **brands** a name given to a particular product by the company that makes it: *This shampoo is better than that more expensive brand.*

brandish VERB **brandishes, brandishing, brandished** to brandish a weapon is to wave it about in a threatening way: *The robbers burst in brandishing guns.*

brand-new ADJECTIVE completely new: *a brand-new bike*

brandy NOUN **brandies** a kind of very strong alcoholic drink

brash ADJECTIVE **brasher, brashest 1** something that is brash is too bright and showy **2** someone who is brash is very forward and rude

brass NOUN **1** a metal made by mixing copper and zinc **2** musical instruments made of brass, like trumpets and tubas, that form part of a bigger orchestra or are used in a brass band

ADJECTIVE made of brass: *a brass name plate*

brass band NOUN **brass bands** a musical group in which wind instruments made of brass are played

brassy ADJECTIVE **brassier, brassiest 1** yellowish in colour like brass: *brassy blonde hair* **2** having a loud harsh sound like a musical instrument made of brass: *a brassy voice*

brave ADJECTIVE **braver, bravest** able to face danger without fear, or able to suffer pain without complaining: *It was brave of you to chase away that bull.*

▸ **bravely** ADVERB courageously: *She smiled bravely, though she was in pain.*

Aa
Bb
Cc
Dd
Ee
Ff
Gg
Hh
Ii
Jj
Kk
Ll
Mm
Nn
Oo
Pp
Qq
Rr
Ss
Tt
Uu
Vv
Ww
Xx
Yy
Zz

▶ **bravery** NOUN courage: *an award for bravery*

bravo INTERJECTION a word that means 'well done!'

brawl NOUN **brawls** a noisy fight or quarrel, especially in a public place VERB **brawls, brawling, brawled** to brawl is to fight or quarrel noisily, especially in a public place

brawny ADJECTIVE **brawnier, brawniest** a brawny person has strong muscles

bray VERB **brays, braying, brayed** a donkey brays when it makes its usual loud harsh sound

brazen ADJECTIVE showing no respect or shame

▶ **brazenly** ADVERB in a way that shows no respect or shame

breach NOUN **breaches 1** a breaking of an agreement or a relationship: *a breach of the peace agreement* **2** a gap or hole made in something solid like a wall VERB **breaches, breaching, breached** to make a hole in something solid like a wall: *The explosion breached the castle wall.*

bread NOUN a food whose main ingredient is flour. Bread is baked in an oven and is often cut into slices for making sandwiches and toast

breadth NOUN **breadths** the size of something measured from one side to the other: *Measure the length and the breadth and multiply the two to get the area.*

breadwinner NOUN **breadwinners** the person in a family who earns the money

break VERB **breaks, breaking, broke, broken**
1 something breaks when it falls to pieces: *The vase fell over and broke.*
2 to break something is to cause it to fall to pieces, usually by dropping it or hitting it against something: *Careful, or you'll break that glass.*
3 to break a law is to do something that law forbids
4 to break news is to tell it: *I didn't want to break the bad news to them before they had finished their holiday.*
5 to break a record is to improve on what the previous record holder has done
6 (*science*) to break an electrical circuit is to stop the flow of electricity through it
7 a boy's voice breaks when it gets deeper and becomes like a man's
• **break down** if a machine breaks down it stops working
• **break in** if someone breaks in to a locked building, they force their way in
• **break off** if you break off what you are doing, you stop doing it for a while
• **break out** fire, fighting or a disease breaks out when it starts suddenly
• **break up** school breaks up when the term finishes and the teachers and pupils go on holiday
NOUN **breaks 1** a opening or crack in something: *a break in the clouds* • *Colin had a bad break in his leg.* **2** a pause: *a break in her studies* **3** a piece of good luck: *It was a lucky break finding someone to buy your old bike.*

▶ **breakable** ADJECTIVE something breakable can be broken if you don't handle it carefully

✦ The words **break** and **brake** sound the same but remember that they have different spellings. To **brake** is to slow down or stop.

breakdown NOUN **breakdowns**
1 a breakdown happens when a machine breaks or stops working: *We had a breakdown on the motorway.*
2 someone has a breakdown if they become depressed and anxious and can't cope with everyday life

breaker NOUN **breakers** a large wave that breaks on the shore

breakfast NOUN **breakfasts** a meal people eat in the morning soon after getting out of bed

breakwater NOUN **breakwaters** a barrier built in or near the sea that stops the force of the waves

breast NOUN **breasts 1** a woman's breasts are the two organs on her chest

Aa
Bb
Cc
Dd
Ee
Ff
Gg
Hh
Ii
Jj
Kk
Ll
Mm
Nn
Oo
Pp
Qq
Rr
Ss
Tt
Uu
Vv
Ww
Xx
Yy
Zz

Aa
Bb
Cc
Dd
Ee
Ff
Gg
Hh
Ii
Jj
Kk
Ll
Mm
Nn
Oo
Pp
Qq
Rr
Ss
Tt
Uu
Vv
Ww
Xx
Yy
Zz

that produce milk for feeding a baby **2** your breast is your chest

breaststroke NOUN a way of swimming where you hold your hands together in front of you and then push forwards and sideways with your arms, while moving your legs like a frog

breath NOUN **breaths 1** you take a breath when you fill your lungs with air and then let the air out again: *Take a few deep breaths.* **2** your breath is the air that comes out of your mouth: *We could see our breath in the freezing air.*

✦Remember that the verb **breathe** has an **e** at the end, and the noun **breath** does not.
Be careful not to confuse the spelling of the verb **breathes** with **breaths**, which means more than one breath.

breathe VERB **breathes, breathing, breathed** to take in air through your mouth or nose, and blow air back out through your mouth or nose: *I found it hard to breathe.*

breathless ADJECTIVE if you are breathless, you are finding it difficult to breathe, usually because of hard exercise or an illness like asthma

breathtaking ADJECTIVE very impressive, surprising or exciting: *The scenery was breathtaking.*

breeches PLURAL NOUN breeches are short trousers that fit or are tied tightly around the knees

breed VERB **breeds, breeding, bred 1** animals breed when they mate and have babies or young **2** to breed animals is to allow them to mate and have young: *a farmer who breeds rare types of cattle*
NOUN **breeds** a particular type of animal: *The Aberdeen Angus is a famous Scottish breed of cattle.*

▶ **breeder** NOUN **breeders** someone who breeds animals: *a dog breeder*

breeze NOUN **breezes** a light wind

▶ **breezy** ADJECTIVE **breezier, breeziest 1** if the weather is breezy there is a light wind blowing **2** someone who is breezy is cheerful

brethren PLURAL NOUN an old-fashioned word meaning 'brothers'

brew VERB **brews, brewing, brewed 1** to make beer **2** to make tea by letting tea leaves soak in boiling water **3** if there is a storm or trouble brewing, then it is just about to begin

▶ **brewer** NOUN **brewers** a person or business that makes beer

▶ **brewery** NOUN **breweries** a factory where beer is made

briar NOUN **briars** a wild rose bush with prickly stems

bribe NOUN **bribes** a bribe is money or a gift offered to someone to get them to do something wrong or dishonest: *Some police officers were accused of taking bribes.*
VERB **bribes, bribing, bribed** to bribe someone is to offer them money or a gift to get them to do something wrong or dishonest: *They tried to bribe the competition judges.*

▶ **bribery** NOUN offering or taking bribes

bric-a-brac NOUN small ornaments that are attractive but not worth very much

brick NOUN **bricks** a block of baked clay used for building: *a pile of bricks • a wall made of brick, not stone*

bricklayer NOUN **bricklayers** a worker whose job is to build things with bricks, especially walls

bridal ADJECTIVE used by a bride or having to do with brides: *a bridal bouquet • a white bridal car*

bride NOUN **brides** a bride is a woman on her wedding day

bridegroom NOUN **bridegrooms** a bridegroom is a man on his wedding day

bridesmaid NOUN **bridesmaids** a bridesmaid is a girl or unmarried woman who helps a bride on her wedding day

bridge NOUN **bridges 1** a structure built over a river, road or valley, to allow people or vehicles to cross from one side to the other **2** a platform on a ship where the captain usually stands **3** the bridge of your nose is the bony part

bridle NOUN **bridles** a horse's bridle is the part of its harness that goes around its head

bridlepath *or* **bridleway** NOUN **bridlepaths** *or* **bridleways** a path for people to ride horses on

brief ADJECTIVE **briefer, briefest** short: *a brief explanation* • *The visit was brief.*

VERB **briefs, briefing, briefed** to brief someone is to give them information or instructions about something: *Our coach briefed us on the other team's strengths.*

NOUN **briefs** a set of instructions on how to do a particular job

▶ **briefly** ADVERB in a short form or for a short time: *Tell us briefly what you want us to do.* • *They stopped briefly to get more petrol.*

briefcase NOUN **briefcases** a flat case for carrying business papers in

briefs PLURAL NOUN briefs are short underpants

brier NOUN **briers** another spelling of **briar**

brigade NOUN **brigades 1** a group of soldiers that form part of an army division **2** a group of people who do a special job: *the fire brigade*

brigadier NOUN **brigadiers** a senior army officer in command of a brigade

bright ADJECTIVE **brighter, brightest**
1 giving out a lot of light or having a lot of light: *the bright lights of the city* • *a nice bright bedroom*
2 a bright colour is strong and clear: *His eyes were bright blue.*
3 cheerful, happy and interested in what is going on around you: *Grandad was a lot brighter this morning.*
4 a bright person is clever: *She's bright but she's a bit lazy.*

▶ **brighten** VERB **brightens, brightening, brightened 1** to become sunnier: *The weather had brightened, so we went out for a walk* **2** to make someone more cheerful and happy: *This good news brightened everyone up.*

▶ **brightly** ADVERB in a bright way: *The sun shone brightly.*

▶ **brightness** NOUN being bright

brilliance NOUN **1** impressiveness or cleverness: *her brilliance as an actress* **2** being very bright or giving out strong light: *the brilliance of the diamonds*

brilliant ADJECTIVE **1** very clever or impressive: *Fiona gave a brilliant speech.* **2** very bright or giving out strong light: *brilliant sunshine*

brim NOUN **brims 1** the edge of a container: *His glass was filled right up to the brim.* **2** the lower part of a hat that sticks out: *a big felt hat with a wide brim*

▶ **brimming** ADJECTIVE **1** full of liquid: *a brimming mug of hot soup* **2** full of a particular quality: *a student brimming with confidence*

brine NOUN water with salt in it, often used to keep food in

bring VERB **brings, bringing, brought**
1 to bring is to take, lead or carry a person or thing with you: *You can bring all your friends to the party.* • *He'd brought a couple of jigsaws out of the cupboard.* **2** if one thing brings another the first thing causes the second to come: *The drought brought famine to the area.* • *Dad's job brings him into contact with a lot of famous people.*

• **bring about** if one event brings about another, the first causes the second: *Scientists say that changes in climate are brought about by global warming.*

• **bring something off** if someone brings something off, they manage to do it successfully

• **bring someone round 1** if you bring someone round, you persuade them to change their opinion and agree with you: *We have to bring him round to our point of view.* **2** to bring someone round when they are unconscious is to make them wake up

• **bring up 1** to bring up a subject is to mention it: *You shouldn't have brought up the subject of money.* **2** to bring up children or young animals is to look after them until they are old enough to look after themselves: *Oliver Twist was brought up in an orphanage.* **3** if someone brings up their food, they vomit

brink NOUN **1** if you are on the brink

Aa
Bb
Cc
Dd
Ee
Ff
Gg
Hh
Ii
Jj
Kk
Ll
Mm
Nn
Oo
Pp
Qq
Rr
Ss
Tt
Uu
Vv
Ww
Xx
Yy
Zz

of something, it is about to happen: *We could see that Noreen was on the brink of tears.* **2** the edge of something high or deep, like a cliff or river: *The boat stopped right on the brink of a waterfall.*

brisk ADJECTIVE **brisker, briskest** quick and lively: *walking at a brisk pace*
▶ **briskly** ADVERB quickly

bristle NOUN **bristles** a short stiff hair: *This brush is losing its bristles.*
▶ **bristly** ADJECTIVE **bristlier, bristliest** having or covered with bristles: *Dad had a bristly chin because he hadn't shaved.*

brittle ADJECTIVE hard but easily broken: *Eggshells are brittle.*

broad ADJECTIVE **broader, broadest**
1 wide: *a broad avenue* • *My feet are small but broad.* **2** a broad accent or dialect is strong or noticeable: *He wrote poetry in broad Scots.*
▶ **broaden** VERB **broadens, broadening, broadened** to make something wider: *They'd broadened the road and made two lanes.*
▶ **broadly** ADVERB **1** widely: *Jack was smiling broadly.* **2** generally: *Your answer is broadly right but a few of the details are incorrect.*

broadband NOUN a type of connection to the Internet that is very fast, as it can send and receive a lot of information every second

broadcast VERB **broadcasts, broadcasting, broadcast 1** a TV or radio station broadcasts when it sends out programmes which people can receive on their televisions or radios **2** to broadcast something is to tell it to a lot of people: *Someone's been broadcasting lies about him.*
NOUN **broadcasts** a programme sent out by a TV or radio station
▶ **broadcaster** NOUN **broadcasters** someone whose job is presenting programmes on TV or radio

broccoli NOUN a vegetable with lots of tiny, tightly-packed, green or purple flowerheads growing from a thick stalk

brochure NOUN **brochures** a booklet with information about a particular

range of products, often with pictures: *a holiday brochure*

brogue[1] NOUN **brogues** brogues are leather shoes with laces and patterns of small holes in the leather

brogue[2] NOUN **brogues** a strong accent: *an Irish brogue*

broke[1] VERB a way of changing the verb **break** to make a past tense: *She always broke their toys, but she didn't mean to.*

broke[2] ADJECTIVE having no money: *I can't afford a new game – I'm completely broke.*

broken VERB a form of the verb **break** that is used with a helping verb to show that something happened in the past: *Did you know Alan has broken his leg?*
ADJECTIVE with a break or breaks: *a broken window*

bronchitis NOUN a lung disease which makes breathing difficult

bronze NOUN **1** a metal that is a mixture of copper and tin: *The statue was cast in bronze.* **2** a yellowish-brown colour like this metal
ADJECTIVE made of, or the colour of, bronze: *a bronze medal*
▶ **bronzed** ADJECTIVE very tanned: *his bronzed face*

bronze medal NOUN **bronze medals** a medal made of bronze awarded to the person who comes third in sporting events

brooch (rhymes with **coach**) NOUN **brooches** a piece of woman's jewellery that is pinned onto a jacket or dress

brood NOUN **broods** a brood is a group of young birds that hatch out of their eggs at the same time
VERB **broods, brooding, brooded 1** a female bird broods when it sits on its eggs to hatch them **2** to brood, or brood over or about something, is to worry about something for a long time: *There's no point brooding over little mistakes like that.*
▶ **broody** ADJECTIVE **1** a broody hen is sitting on eggs to hatch them **2** if someone is broody they are worrying about something

brook NOUN **brooks** a small stream

broom NOUN **brooms** a brush with a long handle, used for sweeping floors

broomstick NOUN **broomsticks** a long handle with thin sticks tied to one end that witches are supposed to ride on

broth NOUN **broths** a kind of soup made with vegetables and sometimes meat

brother NOUN **brothers** your brother is a boy or man who has the same parents as you do

▸ **brotherhood** NOUN **brotherhoods** **1** brotherhood is a feeling of friendship among boys and men **2** a brotherhood is a group or society for men

brother-in-law NOUN **brothers-in-law** the husband of someone's sister, or the brother of someone's wife or husband

brought VERB a way of changing the verb **bring** to make a past tense. It can be used with or without a helping verb: *Jeremy brought me a cup of hot tea.* • *I have brought a box of chocolates for you.*

brow NOUN **brows** **1** your brow is your forehead **2** your brows are your eyebrows **3** the brow of a hill is the point at the top from where it slopes down

brown NOUN the colour of soil and most kinds of wood, made by mixing red, yellow and blue
ADJECTIVE of the colour brown

▸ **brownish** ADJECTIVE quite brown, but not completely brown in colour

brownie NOUN **brownies** **1** a Brownie is a member of the Brownie Guides, the junior branch of the Guide Association **2** a brownie is a helpful fairy in stories

browse VERB **browses, browsing, browsed** **1** to browse is to look quickly through a range of things to see if there is anything you want or like **2** (*ICT*) to look through information on a computer screen until you find the particular thing you are looking for

▸ **browser** NOUN **browsers** (*ICT*) a browser is a computer program that lets you search for things on the Internet

bruise NOUN **bruises** a mark on the skin caused by a knock or blow: *He's got a big bruise just under his eye.*
VERB **bruises, bruising, bruised** to make a bruise on skin, or to become marked by a bruise: *Daniel bruised his knees when he fell.* • *These ripe peaches will bruise easily.*

brunette ADJECTIVE having brown hair
NOUN **brunettes** a woman with brown hair

brush NOUN **brushes** **1** a device with tufts of bristles used to smooth hair, paint with, or clean dirt or dust away **2** a brush with something unpleasant is an occasion when you experience it: *It was Kamal's first brush with racism.*
VERB **brushes, brushing, brushed** **1** to make something tidy or clean using a brush: *Have you brushed your hair?* **2** to touch something lightly with part of your body: *I brushed against the desk on my way past.*

Brussels sprout NOUN **Brussels sprouts** a vegetable that looks like a tiny cabbage

brutal ADJECTIVE very cruel: *a brutal murder*

▸ **brutality** NOUN violent cruelty

▸ **brutally** ADVERB cruelly, savagely: *The poor horses had been brutally beaten.*

brute NOUN **brutes** **1** a very cruel or savage man **2** an animal, especially a big strong animal like a bull or a horse

bubble NOUN **bubbles** **1** a very thin, light ball of liquid filled with air: *soap bubbles* **2** a small ball of air inside a liquid: *We could see the air bubbles in the water.*
VERB **bubbles, bubbling, bubbled** **1** something bubbles when small balls of air form in it: *A big pot of soup was bubbling away in the kitchen.* **2** if something bubbles up, it is forced up to the surface like bubbles rising in a liquid: *Excitement was bubbling up inside her.*

▸ **bubbly** ADJECTIVE **bubblier, bubbliest** **1** full of bubbles: *The paint had gone all bubbly in the heat of the sun.* **2** full of energy and life: *She has a bubbly personality.*

Aa
Bb
Cc
Dd
Ee
Ff
Gg
Hh
Ii
Jj
Kk
Ll
Mm
Nn
Oo
Pp
Qq
Rr
Ss
Tt
Uu
Vv
Ww
Xx
Yy
Zz

buccaneer NOUN **buccaneers** someone who attacks ships while they are at sea and steals things from them: *an adventure story about pirates and buccaneers*

buck NOUN **bucks 1** a male rabbit, hare or deer **2** (*informal*) an American dollar: *It cost twenty bucks.*

VERB **bucks, bucking, bucked** a horse bucks when it jumps into the air kicking its back legs outwards

bucket NOUN **buckets 1** a container, usually with a handle, used for carrying water or things like earth, sand or cement **2** the amount that a bucket will hold: *four buckets of water*

bucketful NOUN **bucketfuls** the amount that a bucket will hold: *We'll need a couple more bucketfuls of sand to finish the castle.*

buckle NOUN **buckles** a clip for fastening a belt or a strap

VERB **buckles, buckling, buckled 1** to buckle something is to fasten it with a buckle **2** if metal buckles, it becomes bent out of shape: *The car hit a wall and its bonnet buckled.*

• **buckle down** to buckle down is to start working hard or with determination

bud NOUN **buds** the part of a plant from which a leaf or flower develops

VERB **buds, budding, budded** a plant buds when its buds start to show

Buddhism NOUN a religion, practised in many parts of the world, that follows the teachings of Buddha

▶ **Buddhist** NOUN **Buddhists** someone who follows the teachings of Buddha ADJECTIVE to do with Buddhism or Buddhists

budding ADJECTIVE in the early stages of becoming something: *Henry's a budding scientist.*

budge VERB **budges, budging, budged** to budge means to move slightly: *We all tried to turn the key in the lock, but it wouldn't budge.*

budgerigar NOUN **budgerigars** a small bird with brightly coloured feathers that is often kept as a pet

budget NOUN **budgets 1** an amount of money that is available to spend: *I have a weekly budget of £10 for school meals and sweets.* **2** a plan for spending money during a certain period: *The Chancellor announces his budget next week.*

VERB **budgets, budgeting, budgeted** to budget is to make careful plans about how you spend your money: *You'll have to budget carefully if you're saving for your holidays.*

budgie NOUN **budgies** a budgerigar: *We've taught our budgie to talk.*

buff NOUN **1** a light yellowish-brown colour: *buff envelopes* **2** someone who is interested in a particular subject and knows a lot about it: *a film buff • a computer buff*

VERB **buffs, buffing, buffed** to buff a surface, or to buff it up, is to rub it with a soft dry cloth to make it shiny

buffalo NOUN **buffalos** or **buffaloes 1** a large ox with big curved horns, found in Asia and Africa **2** a bison

buffer NOUN **buffers** something designed to reduce the force of a collision, especially the metal posts on a railway barrier that help bring a moving train to a stop

buffet¹ (pronounced **boof**-ay) NOUN **buffets 1** a meal at which various types of food are set out on a table for people to help themselves **2** a compartment on a train where food and drinks are served

buffet² (pronounced **buf**-it) VERB **buffets, buffeting, buffeted** to buffet something is to knock it about roughly: *The little boat was buffeted by the storm.*

bug NOUN **bugs**
1 a small insect, especially one that bites
2 a germ that causes illness: *She had a tummy bug.*
3 a tiny hidden microphone used to record secretly what people say
4 (*ICT*) a fault in a computer program that stops it working properly

VERB **bugs, bugging, bugged 1** (*slang*) to bug someone is to annoy them **2** to bug a room or a telephone is to put a hidden microphone in it to record what people say

buggy NOUN **buggies** a baby's pushchair

bugle NOUN **bugles** an instrument like a small trumpet, used for military signals

build VERB **builds, building, built 1** to create something is to put together its parts bit by bit: *He's building a wall.* • *Milk builds healthy teeth and bones.* **2** to create something by working on it: *You build close friendships through trust.*
• **build up 1** if something builds up, it increases: *If you heat the container, the air pressure builds up inside.* **2** if something builds you up, it makes you stronger
NOUN your build is the shape of your body: *He's got a strong, muscular build.*

builder NOUN **builders** someone who builds and repairs houses

building NOUN **buildings 1** building is the trade or action of making houses and other structures: *There is a lot of building going on in this street.* **2** a building is a house or other structure: *New York has lots of tall buildings.*

building society NOUN **building societies** an organization, rather like a bank, whose main business is lending money so that people can buy houses

bulb NOUN **bulbs 1** a glass globe with an electrical part inside that gives out light: *The bulb's gone in my bedside lamp.* **2** the rounded part of plants like onions or tulips that the rest grows out of: *daffodil bulbs*

bulge NOUN **bulges** a swelling or lump: *I knew the cat was in the bed when I saw the bulge in the duvet.*
VERB **bulges, bulging, bulged** to stick out: *His eyes bulged in horror.*
▶ **bulging** very full: *pockets bulging with sweets*

bulk NOUN **1** something's bulk is its size, especially if it is large and heavy: *Wrestlers use their bulk to throw their opponents.* **2** the bulk of something is most of it: *The bulk of his pocket money was spent on computer games.* **3** if you buy in bulk, you buy large quantities at one time: *It's much*

cheaper to buy household goods in bulk.

▶ **bulky** ADJECTIVE **bulkier, bulkiest** large or taking up a lot of space: *a bulky package*

bull NOUN **bulls 1** a male cow **2** a male elephant or a male whale

bull's-eye NOUN **bull's-eyes** the mark in the centre of an archery target or dartboard that scores very high points if you hit it

bulldog NOUN **bulldogs** a kind of dog with short legs, a strong body and a wrinkled face

bulldozer NOUN **bulldozers** a large machine with a heavy triangular metal device at the front used to move big amounts of earth and stones

bullet NOUN **bullets** a piece of shaped metal fired from a gun

bulletin NOUN **bulletins** a report of the latest news: *The next bulletin will be at 6 p.m.*

bullet-proof ADJECTIVE specially strengthened so that bullets cannot go through: *a bullet-proof vest*

bullfight NOUN **bullfights** a kind of entertainment held in Spain and some other countries, in which a bull charges at men on horseback or on foot, and is usually killed with a sword by a man called a matador
▶ **bullfighter** NOUN **bullfighters** someone who fights bulls as part of this entertainment

bullion NOUN brick-shaped bars of gold or silver

bullock NOUN **bullocks** a young bull

bully NOUN **bullies** a person who is cruel to people smaller or weaker than they are
VERB **bullies, bullying, bullied** to be cruel to smaller or weaker people
▶ **bullying** NOUN what bullies do to people smaller or weaker than they are

bum NOUN **bums** (*informal*) your bottom

bumblebee NOUN **bumblebees** a kind of bee with a fat yellow and black striped body

bump NOUN **bumps 1** a knock or blow: *He got a bump on the head and*

Aa
Bb
Cc
Dd
Ee
Ff
Gg
Hh
Ii
Jj
Kk
Ll
Mm
Nn
Oo
Pp
Qq
Rr
Ss
Tt
Uu
Vv
Ww
Xx
Yy
Zz

was knocked unconscious. **2** a raised or swollen part on the surface of something: *a road with speed bumps to slow the traffic down*

VERB **bumps, bumping, bumped** to bump something is to knock it by accident: *Try not to bump my arm when I'm writing.* • *The baby bumped her head on the table.*

• **bump into** if you bump into someone, you meet them by chance: *I bumped into Helen in the street yesterday.*

bumper NOUN **bumpers** a car's bumper is the piece of metal or plastic around the front or back that protects it from knocks

ADJECTIVE a bumper crop or a bumper harvest is bigger than usual

bumpy ADJECTIVE **bumpier, bumpiest** full of bumps: *a very bumpy ride across the fields*

bun NOUN **buns** a kind of cake made with sweet dough: *a currant bun*

bunch NOUN **bunches 1** a group of things tied or growing together: *a bunch of grapes* • *He carried a big bunch of keys.* **2** (*informal*) a group of people: *Josh's friends are a nice bunch.*

VERB **bunches, bunching, bunched**

• **bunch together** or **bunch up** to bunch together, or to bunch up, is to be or move close together: *Don't all bunch together – keep to your positions on the pitch.*

bundle NOUN **bundles** a number of things fastened or tied up together: *a bundle of newspapers*

VERB **bundles, bundling, bundled 1** to bundle things is to tie them up in a bundle **2** to bundle someone into something is to push them roughly into it: *The star was bundled into a car and away from photographers.*

bung NOUN **bungs** something used to block a hole so that liquid does not get in or out

VERB **bungs, bunging, bunged**

• **bung something up** to bung something up is to block it: *His voice sounded funny because his nose was all bunged up.*

bungalow NOUN **bungalows** a house with only one storey

bungle VERB **bungles, bungling, bungled** to bungle something is to do it badly or clumsily

bunk NOUN **bunks** a narrow bed fitted against a wall like the bed in a ship's cabin

bunk bed NOUN **bunk beds** two or more beds built one above the other

bunker NOUN **bunkers 1** a sandpit on a golf course that players try to avoid because it is difficult to hit the ball out of **2** an underground shelter used to escape from bombs during a war

bunny NOUN **bunnies** a rabbit

Bunsen burner NOUN **Bunsen burners** a gas burner with an open flame used to heat things up in science laboratories

bunting NOUN a row of little flags tied to a length of rope and used to decorate ships or streets during celebrations

buoy NOUN **buoys** a large floating object anchored to the seabed and used to mark a shipping channel or to warn ships that there is shallow water

✦Remember the **u** comes before the **o**, not after it.

buoyant ADJECTIVE able to float

bur NOUN **burs** the small, prickly case full of seeds that some plants have

burden NOUN **burdens 1** a difficult job or responsibility that someone has to deal with **2** something heavy that has to be carried

VERB **burdens, burdening, burdened 1** to give someone a difficult job or responsibility: *Many students will be burdened with debt.* **2** to burden someone is to give them a load to carry: *Dad was burdened with all the suitcases.*

bureau NOUN **bureaux 1** an office where you can get information: *a travel bureau* **2** a writing desk with drawers

burger NOUN **burgers** a hamburger

burglar NOUN **burglars** a criminal who breaks into a house or other building to steal things

Aa
Bb
Cc
Dd
Ee
Ff
Gg
Hh
Ii
Jj
Kk
Ll
Mm
Nn
Oo
Pp
Qq
Rr
Ss
Tt
Uu
Vv
Ww
Xx
Yy
Zz

▶ **burglary** NOUN **burglaries** the crime of breaking into houses to steal things

burgle VERB **burgles, burgling, burgled 1** to burgle is to break into a building and steal things from it **2** to burgle someone is to break into their home and steal things

burial NOUN **burials** putting a dead person in the ground

burly ADJECTIVE **burlier, burliest** a burly person is big, strong and heavy

burn VERB **burns, burning, burnt 1** to burn something is to set fire to it: *Be careful with that wok or you'll burn the house down.* **2** to burn is to be on fire: *We could see the grass burning from miles away.* **3** if something burns you, it injures you by burning or being very hot: *The soup burnt his tongue.*
NOUN **burns** an injury or mark left after touching fire or something very hot

burp VERB **burps, burping, burped** to burp is to make a rude sound by letting air come out of your stomach through your mouth
NOUN **burps** this sound

burrow NOUN **burrows** a hole in the ground made by a rabbit or other animal
VERB **burrows, burrowing, burrowed** to burrow is to make a hole in the ground

burst VERB **bursts, bursting, burst** to break or tear, especially from being put under too much pressure: *He blew and blew until the balloon burst.*
• **burst in** to burst in is to come in suddenly and noisily: *He burst in just as I was falling asleep.*
ADJECTIVE broken or torn: *a burst tyre*
NOUN a short time when you do or feel something a lot: *After that burst of energy, I feel tired now.*

bury VERB **buries, burying, buried 1** to bury a dead person is to put their body in the ground **2** to bury something is to cover or hide it: *She buried her face in her hands.*

bus NOUN **buses** a large vehicle with lots of seats for passengers

bush NOUN **bushes 1** a plant that has many leaves and is smaller than a tree: *a rose bush* **2** (*geography*) the bush is wild areas in hot countries, where nobody lives and where only wild plants grow: *walking in the Australian bush*

▶ **bushy** ADJECTIVE **bushier, bushiest 1** covered with bushes **2** growing thickly: *a long bushy tail*

busily ADVERB in a busy, hard-working way: *He was busily trying to persuade all his friends to join the club.*

business NOUN **businesses**
1 business is buying and selling, and the work of producing things that people want to buy: *Dad has gone into business with Uncle Frank.*
2 a business is any company that makes and sells goods, or that sells services
3 someone's business is their work or trade: *What business is Tom's mother in?*
4 your business is the things that involve you only, which other people should not ask about or become involved in: *It's none of your business what I spend my pocket money on!*
• **go out of business** a company goes out of business when it stops trading

businessman or **businesswoman** NOUN **businessmen** or **businesswomen** a man or woman who does important work in companies that buy and sell

bus stop NOUN **bus stops** a place where a bus stops on its route to let passengers get on and off

bust NOUN **busts 1** a woman's bust is her breasts **2** a bust is a sculpture of a person's head and shoulders
ADJECTIVE (*informal*) **1** broken: *The DVD player's bust.* **2** bankrupt: *The business is almost bust.*

bustle VERB **bustles, bustling, bustled** to bustle is to hurry or make yourself busy: *She was bustling around trying to make lunch.*
NOUN busy activity: *the bustle of a school at playtime*

busy ADJECTIVE **busier, busiest 1** someone is busy when they have a lot to do: *Dad's busy making lunch in the kitchen.* **2** if a place or a road is busy

Aa
Bb
Cc
Dd
Ee
Ff
Gg
Hh
Ii
Jj
Kk
Ll
Mm
Nn
Oo
Pp
Qq
Rr
Ss
Tt
Uu
Vv
Ww
Xx
Yy
Zz

there are lots of people or a lot of traffic in it: *London's busy streets*

busybody NOUN **busybodies** a nosey person who tries to find out everyone else's business

but CONJUNCTION **1 but** is used between parts of a sentence to show that there is a difference between the first part and the second part: *I can write stories but I can't draw very well.* • *I'd like to go to the cinema but I don't have any money.* **2 but** is also used between parts of a sentence to mean 'except': *You are nothing but a liar.*

PREPOSITION except: *No one but me turned up.*

butcher NOUN **butchers 1** someone whose job is to carve up raw meat **2** a butcher's is a shop that sells meat

butler NOUN **butlers** a male servant who looks after a rich person or who is in charge of the other servants in a rich person's house

butt NOUN **butts 1** the butt of a gun or rifle is the thick part furthest away from the barrel **2** if you are the butt of other people's jokes, they all make jokes about you or laugh at you **3** (*slang*) someone's butt is their bottom

VERB **butts, butting, butted** to butt something is to hit it using the head: *The goat butted me when I tried to stroke it.*

• **butt in** to butt in is to interrupt other people while they are talking together

butter NOUN a yellow fatty food made from milk and used to spread on bread or for cooking

VERB **butters, buttering, buttered** to spread butter on bread or toast: *Mum buttered and filled about two hundred sandwiches for the party.*

buttercup NOUN **buttercups** a common wild flower with yellow petals

butterfly NOUN **butterflies** a kind of insect with brightly coloured patterned wings

buttermilk NOUN the part of milk that is left after making butter

butterscotch NOUN a type of hard toffee made with butter

buttocks PLURAL NOUN your buttocks are your bottom

button NOUN **buttons 1** a round object used to fasten clothes **2** something you press to make a machine work **3** (*ICT*) a small shape on a computer screen that you click on with the mouse or the keyboard to make something happen

VERB **buttons, buttoning, buttoned** to fasten with buttons

buttonhole NOUN **buttonholes** a hole that you push a button through to fasten your clothes

buttress NOUN **buttresses** a support built against a wall

buy VERB **buys, buying, bought** to buy something is to give money so that it becomes yours: *I've bought all their albums.*

▶ **buyer** NOUN **buyers** someone who buys something: *We couldn't find a buyer for our old computer.*

buzz VERB **buzzes, buzzing, buzzed** to make a sound like a bee: *Flies buzzed round our heads.*

NOUN **buzzes**

1 the sound a bee makes when it is flying

2 a murmuring sound made by lots of people talking at once: *a buzz of excitement*

3 (*informal*) a pleasant feeling you get when you do something exciting or successful: *I always get a buzz out of performing on stage.*

4 (*informal*) a call using the telephone: *Give me a buzz tomorrow.*

buzzard NOUN **buzzards** a large bird which kills and eats small animals

buzzer NOUN **buzzers** a device that makes a buzzing noise

by PREPOSITION

1 near to or next to something: *the big house by the station*

2 past someone or something: *He ran by me.*

3 through, along or across something: *We came by the north road.*

4 something is by someone when they

are the person who has created it: *a painting by Lowry*

5 something happens or is done by a certain time when it happens or is done no later than that time: *I'll be home by 7.30.*

6 by means of something: *go by train*

7 to the extent of something: *He won by a couple of metres.*

8 by is used when giving measurements of length and width: *The room is 5 metres by 3 metres.*

9 by is used to say how much or how often: *Will he be paid by the week or by the month?*

ADVERB **1** near: *They all stood by, watching but doing nothing to help.* **2** past: *The cars went whizzing by.* **3** aside: *Try to put some money by for an emergency.*

• **by the way** something you say when you want to add something to what you have just said: *I've done my homework and fed the cat. By the way, there's no milk left.*

by- PREFIX **by-** is put in front of some words where it adds the meaning 'at or to the side': *bystander • bypass*

bye NOUN **byes 1** a short way of saying **goodbye 2** in competitions, you get a bye if you have no opponent in a round and automatically go into the next round

bye-bye INTERJECTION a more informal way of saying **goodbye**

by-election NOUN **by-elections** an election to vote in a new member of parliament that happens between general elections

by-law NOUN **by-laws** a law made by a local council rather than by a national parliament

bypass NOUN **bypasses** a road built around a town or city so that traffic does not need to pass through it

VERB **bypasses, bypassing, bypassed** to go round something rather than through it

by-product NOUN **by-products** something useful that is produced when making something else

bystander NOUN **bystanders** someone who watches something happening but isn't involved in it

byte NOUN **bytes** (*ICT*) a unit used to measure computer memory or data

✦ Remember that a computer **byte** is spelt with a **y**.

Aa
Bb
Cc
Dd
Ee
Ff
Gg
Hh
Ii
Jj
Kk
Ll
Mm
Nn
Oo
Pp
Qq
Rr
Ss
Tt
Uu
Vv
Ww
Xx
Yy
Zz

Cc

Aa
Bb
Cc
Dd
Ee
Ff
Gg
Hh
Ii
Jj
Kk
Ll
Mm
Nn
Oo
Pp
Qq
Rr
Ss
Tt
Uu
Vv
Ww
Xx
Yy
Zz

C ABBREVIATION short for **Celsius**

cab NOUN **cabs 1** a taxi: *We took a cab to the airport.* **2** a compartment at the front of a lorry or bus where the driver sits

cabbage NOUN **cabbages** a large, round, green vegetable with layers of leaves very close together

cabin NOUN **cabins 1** a wooden hut or house: *a log cabin* **2** one of the small rooms in a ship used for sleeping in **3** the part of an aeroplane where the passengers sit

cabinet NOUN **cabinets 1** a cupboard with shelves and doors used for storing things: *a bathroom cabinet* **2** a group of government members who decide what the government will do

cable NOUN **cables 1** strong metal rope used for tying up ships or for supporting heavy loads **2** a tube with wires inside that carry electronic signals or electric current: *a telephone cable* **3** cable television: *We can't get cable or satellite here.*

cable car NOUN **cable cars** a vehicle that hangs from a moving cable, used to carry people up mountains

cable television NOUN a television service in which programmes are transmitted along underground cables to people's houses

cackle NOUN **cackles 1** a loud sound made by a hen or a goose **2** a loud harsh-sounding laugh
VERB **cackles, cackling, cackled 1** a hen or goose cackles when it makes this sound **2** if someone cackles they laugh loudly and harshly

cactus NOUN **cactuses** or **cacti** a prickly plant that grows in deserts and stores water in its thick leaves

CAD ABBREVIATION short for **computer-aided design**, where computers are used to help draw plans for things like buildings or machines: *a new CAD program*

caddie NOUN **caddies** someone whose job is to carry a golfer's clubs around the golf course

caddy NOUN **caddies** a box for keeping tea in

cadet NOUN **cadets 1** a young person training to be an officer in the armed forces or the police **2** a school pupil who is doing military training

Caesarean section or **Caesarean** NOUN **Caesarean sections** or **Caesareans** a surgical operation in which a pregnant woman's stomach is cut so that the baby inside her womb can be taken out

> ✦ The word **Caesarean** is used because the Roman emperor Julius *Caesar* was supposed to have been born this way.

café NOUN **cafés** a small restaurant that serves drinks and snacks

cafeteria NOUN **cafeterias** a restaurant where the customers serve themselves from a counter

caffeine NOUN a substance in some drinks that makes you feel more alert and active

cage NOUN **cages** a box or enclosure with bars where a bird or animal is kept so that it can't escape
VERB **cages, caging, caged** to cage an animal or bird is to put it in a cage
▶ **caged** ADJECTIVE kept in a cage: *caged birds*

cagoule NOUN **cagoules** a waterproof jacket with a hood

cake NOUN **cakes** a food made from flour, eggs, sugar and other ingredients mixed together and baked in an oven until they are firm: *Do you like cake?* • *a Christmas cake*

calamine NOUN a pink powder used in a lotion that soothes burns or sore skin

calamity NOUN **calamities** something terrible that happens, a disaster

calcium NOUN a chemical found in chalk and lime and in bones and teeth

calculate VERB **calculates, calculating, calculated 1** to calculate something is to count it up or work it out using numbers or mathematics: *Calculate the area of this triangle.* **2** if you calculate something, you make a guess about it using all the facts that you have: *The robbers calculated that the house would be empty at that time.*

▸ **calculating** ADJECTIVE a calculating person works out what is going to benefit them

▸ **calculation** NOUN **calculations** something you work out, either using numbers or what you know: *By my calculation, we should be finished by Tuesday.*

▸ **calculator** NOUN **calculators** an electronic machine that you use to do mathematical calculations quickly

calendar NOUN **calendars** a table or list that shows the days of the year with their dates, divided into weeks and months

calf¹ NOUN **calves 1** a young cow **2** a young elephant, whale or deer

calf² NOUN **calves** the back part of your leg just below the knee where there is a big muscle

call VERB **calls, calling, called**
1 to call is to shout: *I heard him calling my name.*
2 to call someone is to ask them to come to you: *Mum called us in from the garden.*
3 to call someone is to speak to them on the telephone: *I'll call you later.*
4 to call someone something is to give them that name: *He's called Jonathan James.* • *How dare you call me a liar.*
5 to call at a place is to stop there for a short time: *We'll call at the shop on the way home.*
NOUN **calls 1** a shout: *calls for help* **2** a telephone conversation: *I had a call from David yesterday.* **3** a short visit: *I've got a couple of calls to make on the way home.*

callous ADJECTIVE cruel or unkind to other people: *a callous murderer*

✦ Be careful not to confuse the spellings of **callous** and **callus**.

callus NOUN **calluses** an area of hard skin on the hands or feet, caused by constant rubbing

calm ADJECTIVE **calmer, calmest 1** still and quiet: *a calm sea* **2** not worried, excited or upset
VERB **calms, calming, calmed**
• **calm down** to calm, or to calm down, is to become quiet and still again after being noisy or disturbed: *The boats can sail when the weather calms down.*
• **calm someone down** to calm someone down is to stop them being so excited or upset: *She took a couple of deep breaths to calm herself down.*

▸ **calmly** ADVERB without feeling worried or excited: *Grace walked calmly on to the stage.*

▸ **calmness** NOUN being calm: *We were impressed by his calmness under pressure.*

calorie NOUN **calories** a unit of heat used to measure how much energy a food gives

calypso (pronounced ka-**lip**-soh) NOUN **calypsos** (*music*) a type of West Indian popular song, usually with words that are made up as it is sung

camcorder NOUN **camcorders** a video camera that also records sound

came VERB a way of changing the verb **come** to make a past tense: *They came downstairs, laughing and shouting.*

camel NOUN **camels** a desert animal with a long neck and one or two humps on its back for storing water

camera NOUN **cameras** a device for taking photographs, or for making television programmes or films

camouflage NOUN **camouflages** a way of disguising things so that they are not easily seen, especially by making them blend in with their background
VERB **camouflages, camouflaging, camouflaged** to camouflage

Aa
Bb
Cc
Dd
Ee
Ff
Gg
Hh
Ii
Jj
Kk
Ll
Mm
Nn
Oo
Pp
Qq
Rr
Ss
Tt
Uu
Vv
Ww
Xx
Yy
Zz

Aa
Bb
Cc
Dd
Ee
Ff
Gg
Hh
Ii
Jj
Kk
Ll
Mm
Nn
Oo
Pp
Qq
Rr
Ss
Tt
Uu
Vv
Ww
Xx
Yy
Zz

something is to disguise it so that it will not be noticed easily: *The stick insect camouflages itself by sitting on a twig.*

camp NOUN **camps** a place where people live in tents, huts or caravans, usually for a short time: *a refugee camp* VERB **camps, camping, camped** to camp is to stay somewhere for a short time in a tent, hut or caravan: *We camped in a clearing in the woods.*

▶ **camper** NOUN **campers** someone who stays in a tent or hut, usually while they are on holiday

▶ **camping** NOUN if you go camping you go somewhere where you stay in a shelter like a tent, hut or caravan

campaign NOUN **campaigns** a series of activities that people do to achieve something or make people aware of something

VERB **campaigns, campaigning, campaigned** to campaign for something is to organize support for it: *They've been campaigning to have a new school built.*

▶ **campaigner** NOUN **campaigners** someone who organizes support for something

campsite NOUN **campsites** a place where people camp in tents

can¹ VERB **1** to be able to: *Can you swim? Yes, I can.* **2** to be allowed to: *Can I go swimming? Yes, you can.*

can² NOUN **cans** a metal container that food or drink is sold in

canal NOUN **canals** a long channel filled with water and built so that boats can travel across an area of land: *the Panama Canal*

canary NOUN **canaries** a small singing bird with yellow feathers, often kept as a pet

cancel VERB **cancels, cancelling, cancelled 1** to cancel an arrangement is to say that it will not happen: *The match was cancelled because of the snow.* **2** to cancel a cheque or a payment is to stop it being paid

▶ **cancellation** NOUN **cancellations** a cancellation is something that had been booked in advance and has then been cancelled: *You'll get a seat on the flight if there are any last-minute cancellations.*

cancer NOUN **cancers** a serious disease in which some cells in the body start to grow very quickly and form lumps

candidate NOUN **candidates 1** someone who is taking an exam **2** someone who is being interviewed for a job

candle NOUN **candles** a stick of wax that you burn to give out light

candlestick NOUN **candlesticks** a holder for keeping a candle upright

candy NOUN **candies 1** candy is sugar that has been boiled and then become solid **2** a candy is a sweet

candyfloss NOUN candyfloss is sugar that has been heated and spun into fluff which you eat off a stick

cane NOUN **canes 1** the hollow woody stem of bamboo and some other plants **2** a walking stick VERB **canes, caning, caned** to cane someone is to hit them with a long stick as a punishment

canine ADJECTIVE **1** to do with dogs or like a dog: *canine behaviour* **2** canine teeth are sharp and pointed. Humans have four canine teeth

canister NOUN **canisters** a container, often made of metal, used for storing things: *a canister of tea*

cannibal NOUN **cannibals** a person who eats other people, or an animal that eats animals of the same species

▶ **cannibalism** NOUN eating other people, or eating other animals of the same species

cannon NOUN **cannons** a type of large gun that fires cannonballs or heavy shells

cannonball NOUN **cannonballs** a heavy ball of metal or stone fired from a cannon

cannot VERB **1** cannot is used with another verb to say that you are not able to do something: *I cannot read your writing.* **2** cannot is used with another verb when you are not giving permission for something: *No, you* *cannot have another slice of cake.*

canoe NOUN **canoes** a light boat that is pointed at both ends and that you move through the water using a paddle

VERB **canoes, canoeing, canoed** to canoe is to paddle, or to travel in, a canoe

canopy NOUN **canopies** a covering that is hung above something: *a canopy over a bed*

can't a short way to say and write *cannot*: *I can't hear you.*

canteen NOUN **canteens** a restaurant in a school, office or factory where pupils or workers can get meals and snacks

canter NOUN **canters** a gentle running pace of a horse that is faster than a trot and slower than a gallop

VERB **canters, cantering, cantered** to canter is to go at a pace between a trot and a gallop

canvas NOUN **canvases 1** canvas is a strong cloth used to make tents and sails **2** a canvas is a piece of this cloth stretched and used for painting on

✦ Be careful not to confuse the spellings of **canvas** and **canvass**.

canvass VERB **canvasses, canvassing, canvassed** to canvass opinion or support is to go round asking people for it: *He's canvassing for the Green Party.*

canyon NOUN **canyons** (*geography*) a deep valley with a river running through it

cap NOUN **caps 1** a soft hat that often has a peak at the front **2** a small top for a bottle, tube or pen

VERB **caps, capping, capped 1** to cap something is to put a covering or lid on it: *mountains capped with snow* **2** a sportsman is capped when he or she is chosen to play in the team representing their country

capable ADJECTIVE **1** if you are capable of something, you are able to do it or achieve it: *The old lady isn't capable of looking after herself any more.* **2** a capable person is able to deal with problems or difficulties without help

▸ **capably** ADVERB to do something capably is to deal with it well or efficiently

capacity NOUN **capacities 1** the capacity of a container or building is the total amount that it will hold: *a barrel with a capacity of 100 litres* **2** someone's capacity to do something is their ability to do it: *He has the capacity to be a great leader.* **3** to do something in your capacity as something is to do it as part of a job you have: *Mrs Jones came to the meeting in her capacity as head teacher.*

cape[1] NOUN **capes** a kind of coat with no sleeves which is tied at the neck

cape[2] NOUN **capes** a piece of land that sticks out into the sea: *The boat sailed round the Cape of Good Hope.*

caper NOUN **capers** (*informal*) an adventure or an amusing activity: *Dad's off on one of his climbing capers.*

capital NOUN **capitals 1** the capital of a country or state is the city where its government is based: *What's the capital of Sweden?* **2** a capital is a capital letter: *Write your name in capitals.* **3** capital is money that can be invested, for example in a business or a savings account, to make more money

ADJECTIVE **1** most important: *a capital city* **2** punishable by death: *Murder is still a capital crime in some states in the US.*

capitalism NOUN a system in which businesses are owned and run by individuals rather than being controlled by the government of a country

▸ **capitalist** NOUN **capitalists** someone who believes in capitalism

ADJECTIVE having a system of capitalism: *capitalist countries*

capitalize or **capitalise** VERB **capitalizes, capitalizing, capitalized** • **capitalize on something** to use something in a way that gives you some benefit: *Try to capitalize on your opponent's mistakes.*

capital letter NOUN **capital letters** a letter like THESE LETTERS

capital punishment NOUN capital punishment is being killed

Aa
Bb
Cc
Dd
Ee
Ff
Gg
Hh
Ii
Jj
Kk
Ll
Mm
Nn
Oo
Pp
Qq
Rr
Ss
Tt
Uu
Vv
Ww
Xx
Yy
Zz

a car

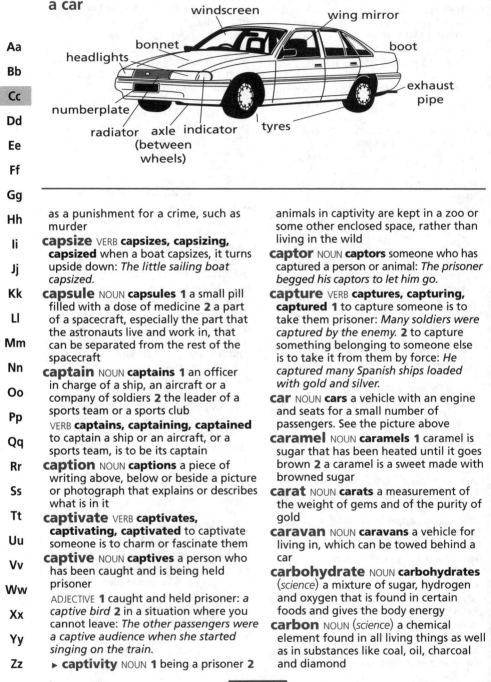

windscreen

wing mirror

bonnet

boot

headlights

exhaust pipe

numberplate

radiator   axle indicator   tyres
           (between
           wheels)

Aa
Bb
Cc
Dd
Ee
Ff
Gg
Hh
Ii
Jj
Kk
Ll
Mm
Nn
Oo
Pp
Qq
Rr
Ss
Tt
Uu
Vv
Ww
Xx
Yy
Zz

as a punishment for a crime, such as murder

capsize VERB **capsizes, capsizing, capsized** when a boat capsizes, it turns upside down: *The little sailing boat capsized.*

capsule NOUN **capsules 1** a small pill filled with a dose of medicine **2** a part of a spacecraft, especially the part that the astronauts live and work in, that can be separated from the rest of the spacecraft

captain NOUN **captains 1** an officer in charge of a ship, an aircraft or a company of soldiers **2** the leader of a sports team or a sports club
VERB **captains, captaining, captained** to captain a ship or an aircraft, or a sports team, is to be its captain

caption NOUN **captions** a piece of writing above, below or beside a picture or photograph that explains or describes what is in it

captivate VERB **captivates, captivating, captivated** to captivate someone is to charm or fascinate them

captive NOUN **captives** a person who has been caught and is being held prisoner
ADJECTIVE **1** caught and held prisoner: *a captive bird* **2** in a situation where you cannot leave: *The other passengers were a captive audience when she started singing on the train.*

► **captivity** NOUN **1** being a prisoner **2**

animals in captivity are kept in a zoo or some other enclosed space, rather than living in the wild

captor NOUN **captors** someone who has captured a person or animal: *The prisoner begged his captors to let him go.*

capture VERB **captures, capturing, captured 1** to capture someone is to take them prisoner: *Many soldiers were captured by the enemy.* **2** to capture something belonging to someone else is to take it from them by force: *He captured many Spanish ships loaded with gold and silver.*

car NOUN **cars** a vehicle with an engine and seats for a small number of passengers. See the picture above

caramel NOUN **caramels 1** caramel is sugar that has been heated until it goes brown **2** a caramel is a sweet made with browned sugar

carat NOUN **carats** a measurement of the weight of gems and of the purity of gold

caravan NOUN **caravans** a vehicle for living in, which can be towed behind a car

carbohydrate NOUN **carbohydrates** (*science*) a mixture of sugar, hydrogen and oxygen that is found in certain foods and gives the body energy

carbon NOUN (*science*) a chemical element found in all living things as well as in substances like coal, oil, charcoal and diamond

▶ **carbonated** ADJECTIVE a carbonated drink has carbon dioxide gas added to it to make it fizzy

carbon dioxide NOUN (*science*) a gas found in air and breathed out by humans and animals

carbon monoxide NOUN (*science*) a poisonous gas with no smell, which is made when carbon is burned

carburettor NOUN **carburettors** the part inside an engine where air and the fuel are mixed to produce a gas that will burn to give power to the engine

carcass NOUN **carcasses** a dead body of an animal

card NOUN **cards**
1 card is thick, stiff paper
2 a card is a piece of thick, stiff paper used to give a greeting or information to someone: *a birthday card • a business card*
3 cards, or playing cards, are a set of pieces of card used for playing games. They have numbers and symbols printed on one side
4 if you play cards, you play games like snap or rummy with a set of playing cards
• **on the cards** something that is on the cards is likely to happen

cardboard NOUN cardboard is very thick paper used to make boxes and packaging

cardiac ADJECTIVE to do with the heart: *a cardiac surgeon*

cardigan NOUN **cardigans** a piece of knitted clothing worn on the top of the body, which has buttons down the front

✦ Cardigans were named after the Earl of *Cardigan*, whose soldiers in the 19th century wore woollen jackets with buttons.

cardinal NOUN **cardinals 1** a high ranking priest in the Roman Catholic Church **2** (*maths*) a cardinal number

cardinal number NOUN **cardinal numbers** (*maths*) a cardinal number is any number used to represent a number or quantity, such as 1, 2, 3, 9, 16, 47, 102. Look up and compare **ordinal number**

care NOUN **cares 1** care is the effort you make to do something well, or to avoid accidents: *Meg does her school work with great care. • Handle these glasses with care.* **2** a care is something you worry about: *She doesn't have a care in the world.* **3** care is worried feelings: *We all want a life with as little care and trouble as possible.*

VERB **cares, caring, cared 1** to care is to be concerned or interested: *He said he didn't care what happened.* **2** to care for a child or an ill person is to look after them: *She wants to be a vet so that she can care for sick animals.* **3** if you say you care for something, it is a way of saying that you like it or want it: *I don't care much for fish.*

▶ **carer** NOUN **carers 1** someone who looks after an old or ill person, especially in their home **2** someone who brings up a child but is not the child's parent, for example a grandparent

career NOUN **careers** a job or profession that someone has trained for and can get more senior positions in as they get more experience: *He wants a career in the police force.*

VERB **careers, careering, careered** to career is to move very quickly and without proper control: *The car careered into a wall.*

carefree ADJECTIVE having no worries: *a carefree life*

careful ADJECTIVE making sure that you do something properly without making a mistake or causing an accident: *Dad is always careful to lock all the doors. • Be careful when you cross the road.*

▶ **carefully** ADVERB without making mistakes or causing damage: *She wrapped up the ornament carefully in tissue paper.*

careless ADJECTIVE not being careful or not paying close attention: *a careless mistake • He is a bit careless with his money.*

▶ **carelessly** ADVERB in a careless or clumsy way

▶ **carelessness** NOUN being careless and not paying attention

Aa
Bb
Cc
Dd
Ee
Ff
Gg
Hh
Ii
Jj
Kk
Ll
Mm
Nn
Oo
Pp
Qq
Rr
Ss
Tt
Uu
Vv
Ww
Xx
Yy
Zz

caress VERB **caresses, caressing, caressed** to caress something is to touch it or stroke it lovingly: *A gentle breeze caressed her face.*

caretaker NOUN **caretakers** someone whose job is to look after a building

cargo NOUN **cargoes** the things carried by a ship or aeroplane: *a cargo of iron ore*

caricature NOUN **caricatures** a caricature of a person is a drawing of them that makes their features look funny or ridiculous

carnage NOUN carnage is the death or injuring of many people, for example in a major accident

carnation NOUN **carnations** a garden plant that has long stems and brightly coloured pink, red or white flowers with lots of petals

carnival NOUN **carnivals** carnival or a carnival is a celebration for which people get dressed up in costumes and sing and dance outdoors

carnivore NOUN **carnivores** any animal that eats meat. Look up and compare **herbivore** and **omnivore**
▸ **carnivorous** ADJECTIVE eating meat: *Tyrannosaurus rex was a huge carnivorous dinosaur.*

carol NOUN **carols** a song sung at Christmas time
▸ **caroller** NOUN **carollers** someone, often part of a group, who sings carols at Christmas time
▸ **carolling** NOUN singing carols at Christmas time, usually going from one house to another

carp NOUN **carp** or **carps** a kind of fish with a wide body, often kept in ponds

car park NOUN **car parks** a place where cars can be left for a short time

carpenter NOUN **carpenters** someone who works at making things from wood
▸ **carpentry** NOUN making things from wood

carpet NOUN **carpets 1** a covering for a floor made of wool or some other soft strong fabric **2** anything that forms a covering on the ground: *a carpet of primroses and bluebells*

VERB **carpets, carpeting, carpeted** to carpet a floor is to cover it with a carpet

carriage NOUN **carriages 1** one of the long sections of a train where passengers sit or sleep **2** a vehicle that can carry passengers and is pulled by horses **3** carriage is the process or the cost of delivering something in a vehicle

Carroll diagram NOUN **Carroll diagrams** (*maths*) a diagram made up of a square or rectangle divided into sections, used to show which members of one set are also members of another set

carrot NOUN **carrots** a long orange vegetable that grows under the ground

✦ The words **carrot** and **carat** sound the same but remember that they have different spellings. A **carat** measures gold and precious stones.

carry VERB **carries, carrying, carried 1** if you carry something, you pick it up and take it somewhere: *This bag is too heavy for me to carry.* **2** when sound carries, it travels over a long distance: *He has the sort of voice that carries.*
• **carry on 1** to carry on is to continue: *Carry on with your work while I go and see the headmaster.* **2** to carry on is to behave badly: *Will you two stop carrying on like babies, please.*
• **carry something out** to carry something out is to do it: *The surgeon will carry out the operation tomorrow morning.*
• **get carried away** if someone gets carried away, they get too excited by something: *He got a bit carried away by the music and started jumping up and down.*

cart NOUN **carts 1** a vehicle pulled by a horse and used for carrying loads **2** a small vehicle with wheels that is pushed by hand

cartilage NOUN **cartilages** cartilage is a strong stretchy type of body tissue found between certain bones and in the nose and ears

carton NOUN **cartons** a cardboard container that drinks are sometimes sold in

Aa
Bb
Cc
Dd
Ee
Ff
Gg
Hh
Ii
Jj
Kk
Ll
Mm
Nn
Oo
Pp
Qq
Rr
Ss
Tt
Uu
Vv
Ww
Xx
Yy
Zz

cartoon NOUN **cartoons 1** a drawing or a series of drawings printed in a newspaper or magazine, often making fun of someone famous **2** a film made by drawing the characters and action

▶ **cartoonist** NOUN **cartoonists** someone who draws cartoons

cartridge NOUN **cartridges** a small case holding, for example, film for a camera, ink for a pen or the bullet for a gun. A cartridge can be removed and replaced easily

cartwheel NOUN **cartwheels** a movement in which you take your weight on your hands and turn your whole body sideways in a circle through the air to land on your feet

carve VERB **carves, carving, carved 1** to carve something is to make it by cutting stone or wood: *He carved his name in the trunk of the tree.* **2** to carve meat is to cut it into slices or pieces using a sharp knife

cascade VERB **cascades, cascading, cascaded** to cascade is to tumble downwards like water in a waterfall NOUN **cascades** a waterfall

case¹ NOUN **cases 1** a suitcase: *Have you unpacked your cases yet?* **2** a container or covering: *The jewels are kept in a glass case.*

case² NOUN **cases 1** a particular example of something happening: *It was a case of having to wait until the train arrived.* **2** a problem that is dealt with by a lawyer, a doctor or the police: *a court case • There had been no cases of smallpox for many years.*
• **in case** because a certain thing might happen: *Take an umbrella in case it rains.*

cash NOUN cash is banknotes and coins: *I didn't have enough cash to pay the fare, so I had to go to the bank.*
VERB **cashes, cashing, cashed** to cash a cheque is to change it for banknotes or coins
• **cash in on** to cash in on something is to profit from it

cashew NOUN **cashews** a curved nut with a buttery taste

cashier NOUN **cashiers** someone whose job is to take in and pay out money, for example in a bank

cash machine *or* **cash dispenser** NOUN **cash machines** *or* **cash dispensers** a machine in or outside a bank, which gives out cash to customers when they insert a special card

casino NOUN **casinos** a building where people can gamble

cask NOUN **casks** a barrel for holding wine or beer

casket NOUN **caskets 1** a wooden or metal box for keeping things in, especially jewels **2** a coffin

casserole NOUN **casseroles 1** a dish with a cover for cooking and serving food **2** the food cooked in a casserole: *a beef casserole*

cassette NOUN **cassettes** a small plastic case containing tape for recording sound or pictures

cast VERB **casts, casting, cast**
1 to cause light or a shadow to appear in a particular place: *The green bulb cast an eery light on his face.*
2 to cast something is to throw it somewhere: *Her clothes had been cast on a chair.*
3 to cast an object in metal or plaster is to shape it in a mould
4 to cast a play or a film is to choose the actors who will be in it
NOUN **casts 1** the cast of a play or film are the actors in it **2** an object formed in a mould: *Police officers made a plaster cast of the footprints.*

castanets PLURAL NOUN castanets are two shells made of hard wood that are held in the hand and hit together to make a loud clicking sound

✦ This word comes from a Spanish word for *chestnuts*, because they have a rounded shape.

castaway NOUN **castaways** someone who has been left in a lonely place, such as a desert island, usually after a shipwreck

caste NOUN **castes** one of several classes that people are divided into in Hindu society

Aa
Bb
Cc
Dd
Ee
Ff
Gg
Hh
Ii
Jj
Kk
Ll
Mm
Nn
Oo
Pp
Qq
Rr
Ss
Tt
Uu
Vv
Ww
Xx
Yy
Zz

castle NOUN **castles** a type of large house with thick high walls and usually towers and battlements, which was built to protect the people inside from attack

castor or **caster** NOUN **castors** or **casters** one of a set of small wheels attached to the legs of a piece of furniture so that it can be moved about easily

castor oil NOUN a yellowish oil from a kind of palm that is used as medicine

castor sugar NOUN a kind of sugar in the form of very fine granules that is used in cooking and baking

casual ADJECTIVE **1** not suitable for formal occasions: *casual clothes* **2** not serious, not caring or not taking much interest: *She's a bit too casual in her attitude to her schoolwork.*

▶ **casually** ADVERB in a casual way: *casually dressed*

casualty NOUN **casualties 1** a casualty is someone who has been injured or killed: *ambulances ferrying the casualties to hospital* **2** casualty is a hospital department that deals with people who have been injured and need medical attention

cat NOUN **cats 1** an animal, often kept as a pet, that has soft fur and claws **2** any animal that belongs to the family of animals that includes cats, lions, leopards and tigers

• **let the cat out of the bag** if you let the cat out of the bag, you tell people something that they aren't supposed to know

catalogue NOUN **catalogues 1** a book showing pictures of a company's products **2** a list of all the books available in a library

VERB **catalogues, cataloguing, catalogued** to catalogue things is to put details about them in a list

catalyst (pronounced **ka**-ti-list) NOUN **catalysts 1** (*science*) a substance which starts a chemical reaction but which does not itself react or change **2** something that makes a change happen

catamaran NOUN **catamarans** a type of sailing boat with two hulls beside each other

catapult NOUN **catapults** a small weapon used for firing small stones, made of a Y-shaped stick with elastic stretched on it

VERB **catapults, catapulting, catapulted** to be catapulted is to be thrown forward forcefully: *The bike hit a rock and he was catapulted over the handlebars.*

cataract NOUN **cataracts** an eye disease in which the lens at the front of the eye becomes gradually thicker so that it becomes more and more difficult to see

catastrophe (pronounced kat-**as**-tri-fi) NOUN **catastrophes** a sudden terrible disaster

▶ **catastrophic** (pronounced kat-as-**strof**-ik) ADJECTIVE absolutely terrible: *the catastrophic effects of the earthquake*

catch VERB **catches, catching, caught**
1 to catch something is to hold it and stop it from escaping: *Throw the ball and I'll try to catch it.* • *He caught a fish but let it go again.*
2 to catch an illness is to get it: *Be careful not to catch a cold.*
3 to catch a bus or train is to be in time to get on to it: *Dad left early so that he would catch the 8.30 bus.*
4 to catch someone doing something bad is to discover them while they are doing it: *My sister caught me making faces at her.*
5 if you catch part of your body or your clothing you injure or damage it on something: *I caught my sleeve on the barbed wire.*
• **catch fire** to start to burn and produce flames
• **catch up** to catch up, or catch up with people who are ahead of you, is to reach the place where they are
NOUN **catches 1** a fastening: *The catch on my bracelet has broken.* **2** a fisherman's catch is the number of fish he has caught **3** something that seems good at first has a catch if it has a disadvantage that you didn't know

about: *The holiday was supposed to be free, but there was a catch, of course.*

▶ **catching** ADJECTIVE if an illness or disease is catching, it is infectious: *I hope that sore throat you have isn't catching.*

catchment area NOUN **catchment areas 1** an area from which a particular school gets its pupils **2** an area from which water drains into a particular river

catchphrase NOUN **catchphrases** a phrase that is used a lot by an entertainer, so people remember it

catchy ADJECTIVE **catchier, catchiest** a catchy tune is one that you remember easily

categorize *or* **categorise** VERB **categorizes, categorizing, categorized** to categorize people or things is to group them together according to what type, size or age they are

category NOUN **categories** a grouping of people or things of the same type: *different categories of trees*

cater VERB **caters, catering, catered** to cater for something or someone is to provide what is wanted or needed: *an exhibition that caters for every type of gardener*

▶ **caterer** NOUN **caterers** a person or business whose job is to prepare and provide food for people, for example at a conference or wedding

caterpillar NOUN **caterpillars** a small creature with a soft body that feeds on plants and leaves and which turns into a moth or butterfly

caterwaul VERB **caterwauls, caterwauling, caterwauled** to caterwaul is to make a horrible howling or screeching noise like a cat

cat flap NOUN **cat flaps** a small door cut in a door through which a pet cat can come in or go out

cathedral NOUN **cathedrals 1** a church where a bishop preaches **2** the main church in an area

catherine wheel NOUN **catherine wheels** a firework that spins round and round as it burns

catholic ADJECTIVE covering a wide range: *His musical taste is catholic; he likes all kinds.*

▶ **Catholic** ADJECTIVE having to do with, or belonging to, the Roman Catholic Church NOUN **Catholics** a Roman Catholic

catkin NOUN **catkins** a long flower that hangs from some trees, for example willow and hazel

catseye NOUN **catseyes** (*trademark*) catseyes are small objects fixed in a road surface, which reflect light and guide drivers at night

cattle PLURAL NOUN cows, bulls and any other grass-eating animals of this family

caught VERB a way of changing the verb **catch** to make a past tense. It can be used with or without a helping verb: *Emily caught a cold.* • *She must have caught it from Sophie.*

cauldron NOUN **cauldrons** a big pot heated over a fire and used to cook things in

cauliflower NOUN **cauliflowers** a large, round vegetable with a hard, white middle part made up of pieces that look like small trees

cause VERB **causes, causing, caused** to cause something is to make it happen: *The leak in the roof caused damp in the bedroom.*
NOUN **causes 1** a cause of something is what makes it happen: *the causes of poverty* **2** a cause is something that people support because they believe it is right: *She supports many good causes.*

causeway NOUN **causeways** a causeway is a raised road over shallow water or wet ground

cauterize *or* **cauterise** VERB **cauterizes, cauterizing, cauterized** to cauterize a wound is to burn it with hot metal so that it heals well

caution NOUN **cautions 1** caution is taking care to avoid danger or risk: *Please drive with caution.* **2** a caution is a warning

▶ **cautionary** ADJECTIVE a cautionary story or tale is one that gives a warning

▶ **cautious** ADJECTIVE to be cautious is to be very careful to avoid danger or risk

Aa
Bb
Cc
Dd
Ee
Ff
Gg
Hh
Ii
Jj
Kk
Ll
Mm
Nn
Oo
Pp
Qq
Rr
Ss
Tt
Uu
Vv
Ww
Xx
Yy
Zz

cavalcade NOUN **cavalcades** a long line of people on horseback or in vehicles moving along a route to celebrate something

Cavalier NOUN **Cavaliers** one of the King's supporters in the English Civil War

cavalry NOUN cavalry or the cavalry are soldiers on horseback: *He joined the cavalry.*

cave NOUN **caves** a large hole in the side of a hill, cliff or mountain or under the ground

caveman or **cavewoman** NOUN **cavemen** or **cavewomen** a human from prehistoric times who lived in a cave

cavern NOUN **caverns** a large cave

▶ **cavernous** ADJECTIVE deep and wide, like a cavern: *inside the whale's cavernous mouth*

cavity NOUN **cavities 1** a hollow space or hole **2** a hollow in a tooth caused by decay

caw VERB **caws, cawing, cawed** a crow caws when it makes a loud harsh sound NOUN **caws** the sound a crow makes

CD ABBREVIATION **CD's** or **CDs** a compact disc

CD-ROM ABBREVIATION **CD-ROMs** a type of CD that contains computer information you can look at but cannot change

cease VERB **ceases, ceasing, ceased** to cease is to stop

ceasefire NOUN **ceasefires** an agreement made between two armies or fighting groups to stop fighting for a time

ceaseless ADJECTIVE not stopping: *a ceaseless thump, thump, thump*

cedar NOUN **cedars** a kind of tall evergreen tree

ceiling NOUN **ceilings 1** the inner roof of a room **2** an upper limit: *The teachers set a ceiling of £10 on spending money for the school trip.*

celebrate VERB **celebrates, celebrating, celebrated** to celebrate something is to have a party or do something special because of it: *Everyone was celebrating the New Year.*

▶ **celebrated** ADJECTIVE a celebrated person or event is famous

▶ **celebration** NOUN **celebrations** celebration or a celebration is something done to celebrate an event: *They've won money on the lottery and are having a celebration.*

celebrity NOUN **celebrities 1** a celebrity is someone who has become famous **2** celebrity is fame

celery NOUN a vegetable with thick, crunchy stalks that you eat raw in salads

cell NOUN **cells 1** (*science*) the smallest part of a living thing. The cells in most living things divide so that the animal or plant can grow or repair any part that has been damaged or injured **2** a small room that a prisoner is kept in **3** (*science*) a device in a battery that produces electrical energy using chemicals

cellar NOUN **cellars** an underground room used for storing things

cello (pronounced **chel**-oh) NOUN **cellos** an instrument like a large violin that is held upright on the floor and played with a bow

▶ **cellist** NOUN **cellists** someone who plays the cello

cellophane NOUN (*trademark*) cellophane is a thin transparent material used for wrapping things in

cellular ADJECTIVE (*science*) made up of or having cells: *the cellular structure of a honeycomb*

cellulose NOUN (*science*) a substance that makes up the cell walls of plants and is used to make paper and textiles

Celsius ADJECTIVE of the temperature scale at which water freezes at 0 degrees and boils at 100 degrees, or measured using this scale: *57 degrees Celsius*

Celtic ADJECTIVE of or having to do with the ancient European people, the Celts, whose modern descendants live in Ireland, Scotland, Wales and parts of Cornwall and northern France

cement NOUN **1** a grey powder that is mixed with sand and water and used to stick bricks together in a wall or to make

Aa
Bb
Cc
Dd
Ee
Ff
Gg
Hh
Ii
Jj
Kk
Ll
Mm
Nn
Oo
Pp
Qq
Rr
Ss
Tt
Uu
Vv
Ww
Xx
Yy
Zz

concrete **2** any type of strong glue that bonds things together firmly: *plastic cement*

VERB **cements, cementing, cemented 1** to cement things is to join or bond them with cement **2** to cement something is to fix it or bond it firmly: *an exchange of gifts to cement their new friendship*

cemetery NOUN **cemeteries** a place where dead people are buried

censor NOUN **censors** someone whose job is to cut any unsuitable parts out of books and films before they are seen by the public

VERB **censors, censoring, censored** to censor something is stop it being sold or shown to the public

census NOUN **censuses** an official survey carried out every few years to find out how many people are living in a particular country

cent NOUN **cents** a unit of money worth one hundredth of a dollar or a euro

cent- *or* **centi-** PREFIX if a word starts with **cent-** or **centi-**, it means a hundred or a hundredth part of: *centimetre • century*

centaur NOUN **centaurs** a creature from old stories or myths which was half man and half horse

centenary NOUN **centenaries** the hundredth anniversary of an event: *2007 was the centenary of the Scout movement.*

centennial ADJECTIVE **1** having lasted for a hundred years **2** happening every hundred years

NOUN **centennials** a centenary

centigrade ADJECTIVE **1** of temperature or a temperature scale that is measured in or made up of a hundred degrees **2** Celsius

centigram *or* **centigramme** NOUN **centigrams** *or* **centigrammes** a metric unit for measuring weight, equal to one hundredth of a gram. This is often shortened to **cg**

centilitre NOUN **centilitres** a metric unit for measuring the volume of a liquid, equal to one hundredth of a litre.

This is often shortened to **cl**

centimetre NOUN **centimetres** a metric unit for measuring length, equal to one hundredth of a metre. This is often shortened to **cm**

centipede NOUN **centipedes** a crawling insect with a long body and lots of pairs of legs

central ADJECTIVE **1** near or at the centre: *an office in central London* **2** very important: *These players are central to the team's success.*

central heating NOUN a system used for heating houses where water is heated in a boiler and sent through pipes to radiators in each room

centre NOUN **centres 1** the centre of something is its middle point or part: *the centre of a circle • chocolates with soft centres* **2** a centre is a building or group of buildings used for a particular activity: *a sports centre*

VERB **centres, centring, centred** to centre something is to put it or place it in the centre

centurion NOUN **centurions** (*history*) a soldier in the ancient Roman army who was in command of a hundred soldiers

century NOUN **centuries 1** a hundred years **2** if a cricketer scores a century, he or she scores a hundred runs in a match

ceramic ADJECTIVE made of clay that is baked until hard in a very hot oven called a kiln: *a ceramic dish*

▶ **ceramics** NOUN ceramics is the art or craft of making things with clay which are then baked in a kiln

cereal NOUN **cereals 1** a cereal is a grain that is used as food, for example wheat, maize, oats, barley and rice **2** cereal or a cereal is this food, especially one that is eaten for breakfast

---

✦ The words **cereal** and **serial** sound the same, but remember that they have different spellings. A **serial** is a story in parts.

---

ceremonial ADJECTIVE to do with ceremony or a particular ceremony: *the Queen's ceremonial duties*

ceremonious ADJECTIVE ceremonious

Aa
Bb
Cc
Dd
Ee
Ff
Gg
Hh
Ii
Jj
Kk
Ll
Mm
Nn
Oo
Pp
Qq
Rr
Ss
Tt
Uu
Vv
Ww
Xx
Yy
Zz

Aa
Bb
Cc
Dd
Ee
Ff
Gg
Hh
Ii
Jj
Kk
Ll
Mm
Nn
Oo
Pp
Qq
Rr
Ss
Tt
Uu
Vv
Ww
Xx
Yy
Zz

behaviour is very correct and polite: *He gave a ceremonious bow.*

▶ **ceremoniously** ADVERB with grand gestures or actions: *A huge cake was placed ceremoniously in the centre of the table.*

ceremony NOUN **ceremonies 1** a ceremony is an event where special forms or customs are used: *a wedding ceremony* **2** ceremony is formal behaviour at a grand or important occasion: *all the ceremony of a coronation*

certain ADJECTIVE **1** if something is certain, it will definitely happen or be the case: *The concert is certain to be an exciting event.* **2** if you are certain about something, you are sure about it: *I'm certain I put the money in my pocket.*

• **for certain** for certain means definitely or surely: *How can you say for certain that this is a dinosaur bone?*

• **make certain** to make certain is to make sure: *Make certain that rope is tied tightly.*

▶ **certainly** ADVERB definitely: *Joe certainly impressed us with his acting.*

▶ **certainty** NOUN **certainties 1** certainty is being or feeling definite **2** a certainty is something that will definitely happen

certificate NOUN **certificates** an official piece of paper that gives written details of something, such as a person's birth or death, or an exam they have passed: *Peter got first prize for English and Sheila got a certificate of merit.*

▶ **certify** VERB **certifies, certifying, certified** to certify something is to put it down in writing as an official statement or promise

CFC ABBREVIATION **CFCs** short for **chlorofluorocarbon**, a chemical that can damage the Earth's ozone layer and which was used in the past in fridges

cg ABBREVIATION short for **centigram** or **centigrams**

chafe VERB **chafes, chafing, chafed** if something chafes, or chafes you, it rubs your skin and makes it sore: *These wellies chafe my legs.* • *If your shorts are too tight, they'll chafe.*

chaffinch NOUN **chaffinches** a small singing bird with black, white and brown stripes on its wings

chain NOUN **chains 1** chain, or a chain, is several rings that are linked together **2** a chain of things is several things that are linked or connected: *a chain of events* **3** a chain of shops is several similar shops owned by the same person or company

chain letter NOUN **chain letters** a letter that asks the person receiving it to send a copy to several other people

chain reaction NOUN **chain reactions** a chain reaction happens when one event causes another event to happen and so on

chain saw NOUN **chain saws** a motorized saw that has cutting teeth on the edge of a chain which rotates very quickly

chair NOUN **chairs** a chair is a piece of furniture with a back on which one person sits

VERB **chairs, chairing, chaired** someone chairs a meeting when they act as its chairperson

chairman, chairwoman or **chairperson** NOUN **chairmen, chairwomen** or **chairpersons** a person who is in charge of a meeting

chalet (pronounced **shal**-ay) NOUN **chalets** a small wooden house

chalk NOUN **chalks 1** chalk is a kind of soft white limestone **2** a chalk is a piece of this, often with a colour mixed through it, that is used to draw with

▶ **chalky** ADJECTIVE **chalkier, chalkiest 1** tasting or feeling like chalk **2** pale or white like chalk: *unhealthy-looking chalky skin*

challenge VERB **challenges, challenging, challenged 1** to challenge someone is to ask them to compete or fight: *He challenged his enemy to a duel.* **2** if something challenges you, you have to work hard or use all your abilities to get it done: *This exam will challenge even the most* *able pupil.* **3** to challenge a person or their actions is to question whether they are right: *We were challenged at the border by soldiers.*

NOUN **challenges 1** a challenge is something that needs all your ability to do it **2** a challenge is an invitation to fight or compete with someone

▶ **challenger** NOUN **challengers** someone who is competing against a champion

▶ **challenging** ADJECTIVE something challenging is difficult to do

chamber NOUN **chambers 1** a large room for meetings: *the debating chamber of the Scottish parliament* **2** an enclosed space: *Divers spend a few minutes in the decompression chamber.* **3** an old-fashioned word for a bedroom: *in my lady's chamber*

chamber music NOUN *(music)* classical music of a kind played by a small group of musicians, rather than by an orchestra

chameleon (pronounced ka-**mee**-li-on) NOUN **chameleons** a small lizard that can change its colour to match its surroundings

champagne NOUN a type of sparkling wine produced in the Champagne area of France

champion NOUN **champions 1** someone who has beaten all the others in a contest or competition: *the world boxing champion* **2** someone who is a champion of a cause is a strong supporter of that cause: *Mrs Pankhurst, the champion of women's right to vote*

VERB **champions, championing, championed** to champion something is to support it strongly

▶ **championship** NOUN **championships** a competition or contest to decide the champion

chance NOUN **chances 1** a possibility: *Is there any chance that I'll be picked for the school team?* **2** an opportunity: *You didn't give me a chance to answer.*

• **by chance** something that happens by chance happens when you have not planned it: *I met Alan by chance, when I*

was playing football in the park.

• **take a chance** to take a chance is to take a risk: *We didn't phone – we just took a chance that she'd be in.*

chancellor NOUN **chancellors 1** a high-ranking government official or minister: *the Chancellor of the Exchequer* **2** the title given to the prime minister in some European countries: *the German chancellor*

change VERB **changes, changing, changed**

1 to change is to become different: *The leaves changed from green to golden brown.*

2 to change something is to make it different: *We've changed the garage into an extra bedroom.*

3 if you change, you put on different clothes

4 if you change schools, jobs or houses, you leave one and go to another

5 to change money is to exchange one type of money for another

6 if you change your mind, your opinion changes

NOUN **changes**

1 a change is a difference

2 a change of clothes is a different set of clothes

3 change is money in the form of coins

4 change is the money that a customer gets back because they gave too much money when they paid for something

changeable ADJECTIVE the weather is changeable when it changes often or is likely to change

channel NOUN **channels**

1 a television or radio station that is broadcast on a particular frequency: *Let's turn over to the other channel.*

2 a groove or passage that water can travel along: *a drainage channel*

3 a narrow sea or part of a sea: *the English Channel*

4 a part of a sea or river that is deep enough for ships to travel along: *a shipping channel*

VERB **channels, channelling, channelled** to channel something is to make it go in a particular direction: *They should channel their energies into something more useful.*

chant VERB **chants, chanting, chanted** to chant something is to say it or repeat it as if you were singing

NOUN **chants** a chant is something that is repeated again and again in a singing voice

Chanukah NOUN another spelling of **Hanukkah**, a Jewish festival

chaos (pronounced **kay**-os) NOUN great disorder and confusion

▸ **chaotic** ADJECTIVE completely disorganized: *The traffic was chaotic.*

chap NOUN **chaps** (*informal*) a man

chapatti NOUN **chapattis** a kind of flat Indian bread

chapel NOUN **chapels 1** a small church or a small part of a larger church **2** a room inside a building that is used for worship

chaplain NOUN **chaplains** someone, often a priest or minister of the church, who conducts religious services in an organization such as the army, a hospital or a school

chapped ADJECTIVE chapped skin is dry, red and sore

chapter NOUN **chapters** one of the sections of a book: *Turn to chapter three in your history books.*

char VERB **chars, charring, charred** if something chars or is charred it is burnt black

character NOUN **characters 1** your character is the type of nature you have or the good and bad points that make you the way you are **2** a person that a writer creates for a story, film or play: *Sam Weller, Mr Micawber and other Dickens characters*

characteristic NOUN **characteristics** a person's or thing's characteristics are the features or qualities that you notice or that make them what they are

ADJECTIVE a characteristic feature or quality is one that is typical of a particular person or thing

characterize *or* **characterise** VERB **characterizes, characterizing, characterized 1** a quality or feature that characterizes someone or something is the one that is typical of them or by which they can be recognized **2** to characterize someone in a certain way is to describe them in that way: *He'd been characterized as a villain.*

▸ **characterization** *or* **characterisation** NOUN characterization is the creation of different characters by a writer and the way the writer makes these characters change and develop during the story

charades PLURAL NOUN a game in which one player acts out the title of a book, film or television programme and the others have to guess what it is

charcoal NOUN charcoal is wood that has been burnt until it is black. Charcoal is used to draw with and as fuel

charge VERB **charges, charging, charged 1** to charge a certain price for something is to ask that amount of money for it: *The shopkeeper charged me 50 pence too much.* **2** to charge someone with a crime is to accuse them of it: *He was charged with murder.* **3** to charge is to move forward in a sudden rush

NOUN **charges**
1 a price or fee: *There will be a small extra charge for postage and packing.*
2 an accusation: *He was arrested on a charge of robbery.*
3 a sudden rush to attack
4 (*science*) an amount of electricity in something
• **in charge** to be in charge is to be the person controlling or managing something: *Miss Handy is in charge of the younger children.*

chariot NOUN **chariots** a type of two-wheeled open carriage pulled by horses, used in ancient Egypt, Greece and Rome

charisma (pronounced ka-**riz**-ma) NOUN charisma is a personal quality that charms and impresses people: *a leader with lots of charisma*

▸ **charismatic** (pronounced ka-riz-ma-tik) ADJECTIVE a charismatic person attracts or impresses people by the way they speak or act

Aa
Bb
Cc
Dd
Ee
Ff
Gg
Hh
Ii
Jj
Kk
Ll
Mm
Nn
Oo
Pp
Qq
Rr
Ss
Tt
Uu
Vv
Ww
Xx
Yy
Zz

charitable ADJECTIVE **1** a charitable person or a charitable act is kind and generous without asking anything in return **2** a charitable organization is a charity

charity NOUN **charities 1** a charity is an organization that raises money to improve life for particular people, for example people with a disability **2** charity is kindness, especially in the form of money given to people who need it

charm NOUN **charms 1** charm is a quality some people have that attracts and delights other people **2** a charm is a magic spell or something that is believed to have magical powers

VERB **charms, charming, charmed 1** if someone or something charms you, they have qualities that make you like them a lot **2** to charm someone or something is to put a magic spell on them: *The Pied Piper charmed the rats with his playing.*

▶ **charming** ADJECTIVE with pleasant and attractive qualities: *a charming little village by the sea*

chart NOUN **charts 1** a table or diagram showing various measurements: *a temperature chart* **2** a map of the sea used by sailors **3** a list of the most popular CDs

charter NOUN **charters** an official document listing rights that people have

VERB **charters, chartering, chartered** to charter a boat or an aeroplane is to hire it

chase VERB **chases, chasing, chased** to chase someone or something is to run after them

NOUN **chases** a chase is a hunt or pursuit

chasm (pronounced ka-zim) NOUN **chasms** a deep narrow opening between rocks

chassis (pronounced shas-i) NOUN **chassis** a vehicle's chassis is the frame and wheels that support its body

chat VERB **chats, chatting, chatted** people chat when they talk to each other in a friendly way about everyday things

NOUN **chats** a friendly talk

chateau (pronounced **sha**-toh) NOUN **chateaux** a castle or large house in France

chatroom NOUN **chatrooms** a place on the Internet where people can swap messages

chatter VERB **chatters, chattering, chattered 1** if animals or birds chatter, they make loud cries quickly one after the other: *monkeys chattering in the treetops* **2** to chatter is to talk about silly or unimportant things: *Stop chattering, you two, and get on with your work.* **3** if your teeth chatter, they rattle against each other, usually because you are cold or frightened

chatty ADJECTIVE **chattier, chattiest** if someone is chatty, they like to talk or chat to other people: *At first she was shy, but now she's become quite chatty.*

chauffeur (pronounced **shoh**-fer) NOUN **chauffeurs** someone whose job is to drive a car, especially a big expensive car belonging to a rich person

chauvinism (pronounced **shoh**-vin-izm) NOUN chauvinism is a belief that your own country or your own sex is the best or the most important

▶ **chauvinist** NOUN **chauvinists** someone who believes that their own sex or their own country is superior

ADJECTIVE showing chauvinism: *a chauvinist attitude*

✦**Chauvinism** is named after Nicholas Chauvin, a French soldier who was very proud of his country.

cheap ADJECTIVE **cheaper, cheapest 1** something cheap does not cost a lot: *a cheap fare* **2** something that is cheap is of little value: *a cheap imitation diamond*

▶ **cheapen** VERB **cheapens, cheapening, cheapened** to cheapen something is to make it be or appear shoddy or worthless

▶ **cheaply** ADVERB inexpensively: *You can eat quite cheaply at these cafés.*

cheat VERB **cheats, cheating, cheated 1** to cheat someone is to deceive them: *The man cheated the old lady out of*

Aa
Bb
Cc
Dd
Ee
Ff
Gg
Hh
Ii
Jj
Kk
Ll
Mm
Nn
Oo
Pp
Qq
Rr
Ss
Tt
Uu
Vv
Ww
Xx
Yy
Zz

all her savings. **2** to cheat in a game or exam is to act dishonestly so that you gain an advantage: *It's cheating to look at someone else's cards.*
NOUN **cheats** a cheat is someone who deceives people or tries to gain an advantage by behaving dishonestly

check¹ VERB **checks, checking, checked 1** to check something is to make sure that it is correct or that it is working properly: *Can you check these sums, please.* **2** to check something is to make sure that it is safe, or that it has definitely been done: *I'll just check that the back door is locked.* • *Check the soup to make sure it isn't boiling.* **3** to check something is to stop it: *He tried to check the bleeding by tying a handkerchief round his leg.*
• **check something out** if you check something out, you find out about it: *Can you check out the times of the trains for me, please?*
NOUN **checks** a test to see that something is correct or is working properly: *a health check*

check² NOUN **checks** a pattern of squares: *trousers with a bold check*
▸ **checked** ADJECTIVE having a pattern of squares: *a checked skirt*

checkmate NOUN checkmate is a position in chess from which the king cannot escape

checkout NOUN **checkouts** a checkout is the place where you pay at a supermarket or self-service shop

cheek NOUN **cheeks 1** your cheeks are the two areas of your face that stretch from below your eyes to your chin **2** cheek, or a cheek, is behaviour that people think is rude or offensive: *He didn't even thank me for the present. What a cheek!*
▸ **cheekily** ADVERB rudely and disrespectfully
▸ **cheeky** ADJECTIVE **cheekier, cheekiest** rude and showing lack of respect: *Don't be cheeky to your father!*

cheer NOUN **cheers 1** a cheer is a loud shout to someone to give them encouragement or to show that you

think they are doing well **2** (*formal*) cheer is happiness and fun
VERB **cheers, cheering, cheered 1** to cheer is to shout encouragement or approval: *They cheered each runner as he ran into the stadium.* **2** to cheer someone is to make them feel happier or more hopeful
• **cheer up** to cheer up is to feel happier
• **cheer someone up** to cheer someone up is to make them feel happier

cheerful ADJECTIVE **1** a cheerful person behaves in a happy way **2** if a place is cheerful it is bright and pleasant and makes you feel comfortable or happy
▸ **cheerfully** ADVERB in a happy or bright way

cheerio INTERJECTION a word people use instead of 'goodbye' when they want to sound informal or friendly: *Cheerio, see you tomorrow.*

cheers INTERJECTION **1** a word people use as a toast: *Cheers, everyone. Happy New Year!* **2** (*informal*) a word people use when they want to say 'thank you': *'Here's your book back.' 'Cheers.'*

cheery ADJECTIVE **cheerier, cheeriest** a cheery person or thing is bright and merry: *He gave me a cheery smile as he drove away.*

cheese NOUN **cheeses** a white or yellow food made from milk, which can be solid or soft
ADJECTIVE made with or containing cheese: *a cheese sandwich*

cheesecake NOUN **cheesecakes** a dessert that has a crisp biscuit base with a sweet mixture containing cream cheese on top

cheetah NOUN **cheetahs** a spotted African animal, related to the cat, that can run very fast over short distances

chef (pronounced **shef**) NOUN **chefs** a person with special training who cooks in the kitchen of a restaurant or hotel

chemical NOUN **chemicals** a chemical is a substance formed by or connected with chemistry
ADJECTIVE formed by, using, or containing a chemical or chemicals: *a chemical reaction*

chemist NOUN **chemists 1** someone who studies chemistry **2** someone who makes up medicines and medical prescriptions **3** a chemist's is a shop where medicines and toiletries are sold

chemistry NOUN **1** (*science*) chemistry is the study of chemical elements and the way they combine and react with each other **2** the chemistry between people is the way they act or react to each other

cheque NOUN **cheques** a piece of printed paper used to pay for things with money from a bank account

chequered ADJECTIVE having a pattern of different coloured squares, like a chessboard

chequers PLURAL NOUN **1** black and white squares like those on a chessboard **2** another name for the game of **draughts**

cherish VERB **cherishes, cherishing, cherished** to cherish someone or something is to care for and look after them

cherry NOUN **cherries 1** a kind of small, round, red fruit with a large stone inside **2** the tree that this fruit grows on

cherub NOUN **cherubs** *or* **cherubim** an angel that looks like a plump baby with wings

chess NOUN a game played on a chequered board, called a **chessboard**, by two players. Each player has a set of chess pieces, or **chessmen**, which are moved in various ways to capture the other player's pieces

chest NOUN **chests 1** your chest is the area of your body from the bottom of your neck to your stomach **2** a large box for storing or carrying things: *a treasure chest*

chestnut NOUN **chestnuts 1** a shiny reddish-brown nut that grows inside a prickly skin **2** a tree that chestnuts grow on **3** a reddish-brown colour

chew VERB **chews, chewing, chewed** to chew is to break up food with the teeth before swallowing it

• **chew something over** to think about something carefully for a while

▶ **chewy** ADJECTIVE **chewier, chewiest** soft and sticky, or needing to be chewed

chick NOUN **chicks** a baby bird

chicken NOUN **chickens 1** a chicken is a hen, especially a young hen **2** chicken is the meat from a hen: *roast chicken* **3** (*informal*) a coward: *Jump! Don't be such a chicken.*

chickenpox NOUN an infectious disease, which causes large itchy spots to appear on your skin

chickpea NOUN **chickpeas** a type of light brown pea that can be boiled and eaten in sauces or salads

chief NOUN **chiefs 1** a ruler or leader: *the chief of an African tribe* **2** a boss: *the chiefs of industry*

ADJECTIVE main or most important: *the chief city of the region*

▶ **chiefly** ADVERB mainly: *They ate some meat but chiefly their diet consisted of roots and berries.*

chieftain NOUN **chieftains** a leader or ruler of a tribe or clan: *a Scottish Highland chieftain*

chiffon (pronounced **shif**-on) NOUN a thin see-through material made of silk or nylon

chihuahua (pronounced chi-**wa**-wa) NOUN **chihuahuas** a tiny breed of dog, originally from Mexico

child NOUN **children 1** a young human being: *a child's view of the world* **2** a son or daughter: *Their children are grown up.*

▶ **childhood** NOUN the period of time in your life when you are a child: *memories of childhood*

childish ADJECTIVE silly, and not grown-up: *childish behaviour*

▶ **childishly** ADVERB in a silly way, not like a grown-up

childminder NOUN **childminders** someone who looks after a child or children when their parents are at work

children NOUN the plural of **child**: *One child was late and the rest of the children had to wait.*

chill NOUN **chills 1** if there is a chill in the air, it feels cold **2** if you get a chill, you suffer from a fever and shivering

Aa
Bb
Cc
Dd
Ee
Ff
Gg
Hh
Ii
Jj
Kk
Ll
Mm
Nn
Oo
Pp
Qq
Rr
Ss
Tt
Uu
Vv
Ww
Xx
Yy
Zz

ADJECTIVE cold: *a chill wind blowing from the mountains*
VERB **chills, chilling, chilled** to chill something is to make it cold

chilli NOUN **chillis** a pod from a type of pepper that has a hot, fiery taste and is used in cooking

chilly ADJECTIVE **chillier, chilliest** cold: *Shut the window. It's a bit chilly in here.*

chime NOUN **chimes** a chime is the sound of a bell or bells ringing
VERB **chimes, chiming, chimed 1** bells chime when they make ringing sounds **2** a clock chimes when it makes a ringing sound as it strikes the hour

chimney NOUN **chimneys** a passage above a fire that allows smoke to escape

chimneysweep NOUN **chimneysweeps** someone who sweeps the soot out of chimneys

chimpanzee NOUN **chimpanzees** a small African ape with black fur, a flat face and large brown eyes

chin NOUN **chins** your chin is the part of your face that sticks out below your mouth

china NOUN china is porcelain, a high quality material used to make things like cups, plates and ornaments

chink NOUN **chinks 1** a small gap: *a shaft of sunlight coming through a chink in the curtains* **2** a sound made when coins or other small metal objects hit each other

chip VERB **chips, chipping, chipped** to chip something is to break a small piece off it: *Roy chipped one of his teeth playing rugby.*
• **chip in** if someone chips in, they contribute to a discussion, usually with a suggestion or comment
NOUN **chips 1** chips are potatoes cut into strips and fried: *fish and chips* **2** a small piece broken off a hard object, or the place where a small piece has been broken off

chipmunk NOUN **chipmunks** a small North American animal with a long bushy tail and stripes on its back

chiropodist (pronounced ki-**rop**-o-dist) NOUN **chiropodists** someone who treats

problems and diseases of the feet
▸ **chiropody** NOUN the care and treatment of people's feet, especially problems like corns and verrucas

chirp or **chirrup** VERB **chirps, chirping, chirped** or **chirrups, chirruping, chirruped** to chirp is to make a short shrill sound or sounds: *sparrows chirping*
NOUN **chirps** or **chirrups** a short shrill sound: *the chirp of baby birds*
▸ **chirpy** ADJECTIVE **chirpier, chirpiest** happy and cheerful: *You sound very chirpy this morning.*

chisel NOUN **chisels** a very sharp tool used for cutting pieces off wood, stone or metal
VERB **chisels, chiselling, chiselled** to chisel something is to cut it using a chisel: *He chiselled his name in the stone.*

chive NOUN **chives** a herb with long thin hollow shoots that have a flavour like a mild-tasting onion

chlorine NOUN (*science*) a yellowish-green gas with a harsh smell which is used as a bleach and disinfectant

chlorophyll (pronounced **klor**-o-fil) NOUN (*science*) the green substance in the leaves of a plant that allows the plant to use energy from the sun in a process called photosynthesis

chocolate NOUN **chocolates 1** chocolate is a sweet food made from the beans of the cacao tree: *a bar of chocolate* **2** a chocolate is a sweet made with chocolate

choice NOUN **choices** there is choice, or a choice, when you are able to decide which thing you will have because there is more than one thing available or on offer: *We were given a choice of meat or fish.* • *He had to do it; he had no choice in the matter.*
ADJECTIVE **choicer, choicest** choice things are of the best quality available: *the choicest vegetables*

choir (pronounced kwire) NOUN **choirs 1** a group of singers: *He sings in the church choir.* **2** part of a church where the choir sings

choke VERB **chokes, choking, choked**
1 to choke on something is to have your breathing tubes blocked, especially by a piece of food that has got stuck in your throat: *She choked on a fish bone.* **2** if something chokes you, you can't breathe properly because of it: *This collar's far too tight; it's choking me.* **3** if a drain or something similar is choked, it is blocked up with things: *gutters choked with leaves*

cholesterol (pronounced ko-**les**-trol) NOUN (*science*) a substance found in the body that helps to carry fats in the blood to the body tissues

chomp VERB **chomps, chomping, chomped** to chomp is to chew noisily

choose VERB **chooses, choosing, chose, chosen** to choose a person or thing from a group of people or things is to decide that you want that particular person or thing: *If you could have only one of them, which would you choose?*

chop VERB **chops, chopping, chopped**
1 to chop something is to cut it with an axe or a sharp tool like an axe: *Mr Willis was busy chopping a tree down.* **2** to chop something up is to cut it into small pieces: *He chopped the wood up to put on the fire.*
NOUN **chops** a chop is a piece of meat, usually with a bit of bone, that has been cut off a larger piece of meat

chopper NOUN **choppers** (*informal*) a helicopter

choppy ADJECTIVE **choppier, choppiest** if the sea is choppy, it is rough with lots of little waves

chopsticks PLURAL NOUN chopsticks are two thin pieces of wood or plastic held in one hand and used to pick up food and put it in your mouth. Chopsticks are used in the Far East, in places like China and Japan

choral ADJECTIVE sung by or written for a choir: *choral music*

chord NOUN **chords 1** a musical sound made by playing several notes together: *Andy can play a few chords on the guitar.* **2** (*maths*) a straight line joining two points on a curve

chore NOUN **chores** a job, often one that is difficult or boring and has to be done regularly

choreographer NOUN **choreographers** someone who designs and arranges dances and dance steps, especially for a ballet or musical
▸ **choreography** NOUN the design and arrangement of dances and dance steps

chortle VERB **chortles, chortling, chortled** to chortle is to laugh or chuckle happily

chorus NOUN **choruses**
1 the part of a song that is repeated after every verse
2 the chorus in a play or musical is a group of singers that perform together on the stage
3 a choir
4 lots of people speaking or shouting together: *a chorus of protest*
VERB **choruses, chorusing, chorused** to chorus is to speak or sing all together: *'Happy birthday to you,' they chorused.*

chose VERB a way of changing the verb **choose** to make a past tense: *I wasn't made to do it; I chose to do it.*

chosen VERB a form of the verb **choose** that is used with a helping verb to show that something happened in the past: *John has been chosen for the football team.*
ADJECTIVE being your choice: *your chosen career*

christen VERB **christens, christening, christened** to christen a child is to baptize it and give it a name
▸ **christening** NOUN **christenings** a ceremony at which a child is baptized

Christian NOUN **Christians** someone who is a believer in Christianity and follows the teachings of Jesus Christ
ADJECTIVE to do with Christianity or Christians
▸ **Christianity** NOUN a religion, practised in many parts of the world, that follows the teachings of Jesus Christ

Christian name NOUN **Christian names** a first name or personal name. Look up and compare **surname**

Aa
Bb
Cc
Dd
Ee
Ff
Gg
Hh
Ii
Jj
Kk
Ll
Mm
Nn
Oo
Pp
Qq
Rr
Ss
Tt
Uu
Vv
Ww
Xx
Yy
Zz

Christmas NOUN a Christian festival celebrating the birth of Christ and held on 25 December each year

Christmas Eve NOUN 24 December, the day before Christmas Day

chromosome NOUN **chromosomes** (*science*) a rod-shaped part found in every body cell of living things. Chromosomes contain the special chemical patterns, or genes, that control what an individual living thing is like

chronic ADJECTIVE **1** a chronic disease is one that goes on for a long time **2** a chronic problem is very bad and has existed for a long time: *a chronic shortage of clean water in some of the villages*

chronicle NOUN **chronicles** a record of things in the order that they happened VERB **chronicles, chronicling, chronicled** to chronicle events is to write them down in the order that they happen

chronological ADJECTIVE if a record of events is chronological, or in chronological order, it is arranged in the order in which the events happened

chrysalis (pronounced **kris**-al-is) NOUN **chrysalises** (*science*) an insect, for example a moth or butterfly, at the stage of its life when it covers itself with a case

chrysanthemum NOUN **chrysanthemums** a garden plant with flowers that have lots of petals

chubby ADJECTIVE **chubbier, chubbiest** rather fat, but in an attractive way: *the baby's chubby little legs*

chuck VERB **chucks, chucking, chucked** (*informal*) to chuck something is to throw it or toss it: *He'd chucked his schoolbag down on the floor.*

chuckle VERB **chuckles, chuckling, chuckled** to chuckle is to laugh softly: *The story made me chuckle to myself.* NOUN **chuckles** a low or quiet laugh

chug VERB **chugs, chugging, chugged** to chug is to make a noise like a slowly moving engine, or to move along slowly: *The little steam train came chugging up the hill.*

chum NOUN **chums** an old-fashioned word meaning a friend

chunk NOUN **chunks** **1** a thick or uneven lump of something: *a chunk of cheese • pineapple chunks* **2** a large part of something: *He use quite a chunk of his pocket money to buy the boots.*
▶ **chunky** ADJECTIVE **chunkier, chunkiest 1** thick and heavy: *a warm chunky sweater* **2** broad and heavy: *a chunky body*

church NOUN **churches** a building where people, especially Christians, go to worship

churchyard NOUN **churchyards** the area of land around a church where people are buried

churn NOUN **churns** a special container for making butter from milk. The milk inside is moved about quickly by paddles until the fat separates VERB **churns, churning, churned 1** to churn milk is to make it into butter inside a churn **2** if your stomach churns, you have an unpleasant feeling in it because you are nervous

chute NOUN **chutes 1** a long sloping channel that water, objects or people slide down **2** a piece of playground equipment with a sloping part that children can slide down **3** a short form of the word **parachute**

chutney NOUN chutney is a thick sauce made from fruit or vegetables, vinegar and spices. You eat it cold with meat or cheese

cider NOUN an alcoholic drink made from apples

cigar NOUN **cigars** a thick tube made from tobacco leaves that people smoke

cigarette NOUN **cigarettes** a tube of thin paper filled with chopped tobacco that people smoke

cinder NOUN **cinders** a small piece of burnt coal or wood that is left at the bottom of a fire

cinema NOUN **cinemas 1** a cinema is a place where films are shown on a big screen **2** cinema is films as an industry or an art form: *a career in cinema*

cinnamon NOUN a yellowish-brown

Aa
Bb
Cc
Dd
Ee
Ff
Gg
Hh
Ii
Jj
Kk
Ll
Mm
Nn
Oo
Pp
Qq
Rr
Ss
Tt
Uu
Vv
Ww
Xx
Yy
Zz

sweet-tasting spice used in puddings and cakes

circa PREPOSITION if circa is used before a date, it means 'about' or 'approximately': *circa 1850*

circle NOUN **circles 1** a shape whose outside edge is an endless curving line, which is always the same distance away from a central point: *Draw one circle for the head and another for the body.* **2** a circle of people is a group of people who know each other, have something in common or do a particular thing together: *He's not part of my circle of friends.* **3** the circle in a theatre is the set of seats in one of the upper floors
• **come full circle** if something comes full circle it returns to the point where it began
VERB **circles, circling, circled 1** to circle is to go round and round: *vultures circling overhead* **2** to circle something is to draw a circle round it: *She circled the area on the map with a red marker.*

circuit NOUN **circuits**
1 if you do a circuit of something you go right round it, often arriving back at or near the place where you started
2 a racing circuit is a track that racing cars and motorbikes race round
3 an electrical circuit is the path that electricity follows between two points
4 a connected group of events, especially of a particular sport: *the international golf circuit*

circular ADJECTIVE round, in the shape of a circle: *a circular window*
NOUN **circulars** a letter or notice that is sent round to a lot of different people

circulate VERB **circulates, circulating, circulated 1** to circulate is to move round or through: *water circulating in the central heating system* **2** to circulate something is to send it round: *Details of the sports day will be circulated to all teachers.*

▶ **circulation** NOUN **1** circulation is movement round or through something **2** your circulation is the movement of blood round your body, pumped by your heart through your veins and arteries **3** a particular newspaper's or magazine's circulation is the number of copies that are sold

circumference NOUN **circumferences** (*maths*) **1** the length of the outside edge of a circle: *What's the circumference of this coin?* **2** the outside edge of a circle: *Mark a point on the circumference of the circle and draw a line through it.*

circumstance NOUN **circumstances 1** circumstances are the events that make a situation the way it is: *In different circumstances, I might not have been angry about what Jack said.* **2** your circumstances are the condition of your life, especially how much money or wealth you have

circus NOUN **circuses** a type of travelling entertainment that usually includes clowns, acrobats, trapeze artistes, and often performing animals

✦ **Circus** is the Latin word for a *circle* or *ring*, so a circus is so called because it takes place inside a ring.

cistern NOUN **cisterns** a tank for storing water

citadel NOUN **citadels** a fort inside a city where the people from the city can go if they are attacked

citizen NOUN **citizens 1** someone who lives in a particular town, state or country: *citizens of Paris* **2** someone who belongs officially to a particular country: *He lives in Singapore but he's an Australian citizen.*

▶ **citizenship** NOUN **1** to have citizenship of a country is to belong officially to that country: *He's applied for Canadian citizenship.* **2** citizenship is the responsibilities and duties you have by being a citizen of a particular state or country: *Children should be taught good citizenship.*

citrus fruit NOUN **citrus fruits** fruits with a thick skin and a sharp flavour, such as oranges, lemons, limes and grapefruit

city NOUN **cities** a large important town: *What's the biggest city in Europe?*

Aa
Bb
Cc
Dd
Ee
Ff
Gg
Hh
Ii
Jj
Kk
Ll
Mm
Nn
Oo
Pp
Qq
Rr
Ss
Tt
Uu
Vv
Ww
Xx
Yy
Zz

civic ADJECTIVE to do with a city or citizens: *civic pride* • *a civic centre*

civil ADJECTIVE **1** if a person is civil, they talk or behave in a polite way **2** civil means involving or having to do with the citizens of a country: *a civil war* **3** civil means having to do with ordinary people or civilians, not the military or the church: *civil life* • *a civil marriage ceremony*

civil engineer NOUN **civil engineers** someone whose job is to plan and build public buildings and things like roads and bridges

civilian NOUN **civilians** a person who is not in the armed forces

civilization *or* **civilisation** NOUN **civilizations** *or* **civilisations** **1** a civilization is a particular society or culture at a particular period in time: *the ancient civilizations of South America* **2** civilization is being or becoming civilized

civilize *or* **civilise** VERB **civilizes, civilizing, civilized 1** to civilize people is to teach them how things are done in more advanced cultures or societies, so that their society becomes more developed **2** to civilize someone is to teach them good behaviour

▸ **civilized** *or* **civilised** ADJECTIVE behaving well or politely, without arguing or being aggressive: *Let's try and have a civilized discussion instead of all shouting at once.*

civil rights PLURAL NOUN civil rights are your rights to be treated fairly in society no matter what sex, colour or religion you are

civil war NOUN **civil wars** a war between two groups within the same country

cl ABBREVIATION short for **centilitre** or **centilitres**

clad ADJECTIVE **1** covered: *snow-clad mountains* **2** an old-fashioned word that means wearing particular clothes: *nurses clad in crisp white uniforms*

claim VERB **claims, claiming, claimed 1** to claim that something is true is to state that it is a fact, even though there

is no real proof: *He claims he saw a flying saucer.* **2** to claim something is to demand it as your right or to state that it is yours: *To claim your free gift, just send in the form below.*

NOUN **claims 1** a statement that something is a fact: *No one listened to his repeated claims that he was innocent.* **2** a demand or request for something that you have a right to or that you say you own: *an insurance claim*

▸ **claimant** NOUN **claimants** someone who makes a claim

clairvoyant NOUN **clairvoyants** someone who claims that they can see things that will happen in the future

clam NOUN **clams** a large shellfish with two shells that are joined at one side and which can be closed tightly for protection

VERB **clams, clamming, clammed**
• **clam up** (*informal*) if someone clams up, they stop talking or won't give any more information

clamber VERB **clambers, clambering, clambered** to clamber is to climb up or over things using your hands and feet: *They tried to clamber up the steep and slippery slope.*

clammy ADJECTIVE **clammier, clammiest** damp in a sticky unpleasant way: *clammy hands*

clamour VERB **clamours, clamouring, clamoured** if people clamour for something, they all say they want it: *twenty children clamouring for a chance to play in the team*

NOUN clamour, or a clamour, is noisy shouts or demands

clamp NOUN **clamps** a device for holding things together tightly or a device attached tightly to something to stop it moving: *a wheel clamp*

VERB **clamps, clamping, clamped** to clamp something is to put a clamp on it: *Clamp the two pieces of wood together until the glue dries.*

• **clamp down** to clamp down on something is to stop it happening by controlling it more strictly: *The council*

clan ➜ classics

will have to clamp down on litter if they want to clean up the city.

clan NOUN **clans** a group of families all descended from the same family and usually all having the same name

> ✦This word comes from the Scottish Gaelic word **clann**, which means *children* or *family*.

clang VERB **clangs, clanging, clanged** to clang is to make a loud ringing sound, like a heavy piece of metal hitting against a hard material: *The prison gate clanged shut behind them.*
NOUN **clangs** a loud ringing sound

clank VERB **clanks, clanking, clanked** to make a loud dull sound, like metal hitting metal: *Strange machines were clanking in the gloomy shed.*
NOUN **clanks** a loud dull sound: *the clank of heavy chains*

clap VERB **claps, clapping, clapped** you clap when you hit the palms of your hands together making a slapping sound: *The audience clapped and cheered.*
NOUN **claps 1** if you give someone a clap, you clap your hands to show you like what they have done **2** a sudden very loud sound made by thunder

clarify VERB **clarifies, clarifying, clarified** to clarify something is to make it clearer or easier to understand

clarinet NOUN **clarinets** an instrument made of wood that you play by blowing through it and pressing keys with your fingers
▸ **clarinettist** NOUN **clarinettists** someone who plays the clarinet

clarity NOUN clearness: *the clarity of the image*

clash VERB **clashes, clashing, clashed 1** if two people clash, they disagree or argue angrily with each other **2** if two colours clash, they do not go well together: *The purple clashes with the red.* **3** if two pieces of hard material clash, they make a loud sound as they hit each other: *cymbals clashing*
NOUN **clashes 1** an angry disagreement between people: *They've had a few*

clashes over the years. **2** a sound made when two things hit against each other: *the clash of cymbals*

clasp VERB **clasps, clasping, clasped** to clasp something is to hold it tightly or closely: *She was clasping a little child in her arms.*
NOUN **clasps 1** a hook or pin for holding things together: *a hair clasp* **2** a tight way of holding something

class NOUN **classes**
1 a group of schoolchildren or students who are taught together, or a period of time during which a particular subject is taught: *It was Megan's first day in Miss Smith's class.* • *Mum is going to her aerobics class tonight.*
2 a grouping of people who have similar backgrounds or who belong to the same rank in society: *the working class*
3 a division of things according to how good they are: *He's a first-class student.*
4 a grouping of animals or plants that are related to each other or have something in common
VERB **classes, classing, classed** to class people or things is to put them in a grouping with others of the same type or rank: *Anyone under 16 is classed as a junior member.*

classic NOUN **classics** a great book or other work of art that goes on being admired long after it was written or made
ADJECTIVE **1** recognized as great for all time: *classic children's stories* **2** a classic example of something is typical: *He made the classic mistake of thinking that he could do all his studying in the week before the exam.*
▸ **classical** ADJECTIVE **1** belonging to the style or culture of ancient Greece or Rome: *classical architecture* **2** traditional: *classical ballet*

classical music NOUN high quality or serious music that goes on being played or listened to for a long time after it has been composed

classics NOUN the study of the ancient Greek and Latin languages, and the work of ancient Greek and Roman writers

Aa Bb Cc Dd Ee Ff Gg Hh Ii Jj Kk Ll Mm Nn Oo Pp Qq Rr Ss Tt Uu Vv Ww Xx Yy Zz

Aa
Bb
Cc
Dd
Ee
Ff
Gg
Hh
Ii
Jj
Kk
Ll
Mm
Nn
Oo
Pp
Qq
Rr
Ss
Tt
Uu
Vv
Ww
Xx
Yy
Zz

classify VERB **classifies, classifying, classified** to classify people or things is to put them into groups or classes according to what type they are

▸ **classification** NOUN **classifications** 1 a classification is a group that includes people or things of the same type 2 classification is putting things into groups of different types

▸ **classified** ADJECTIVE classified information is information that the government keeps secret from the public

classmate NOUN **classmates** your classmates are the people in your class at school

classroom NOUN **classrooms** a room where lessons are given in a school or college

classy ADJECTIVE **classier, classiest** stylish and expensive: *He's always worn classy clothes.*

clatter VERB **clatters, clattering, clattered** to clatter is to make a loud noise like hard objects falling or hitting each other: *He came clattering downstairs in his ski boots.*
NOUN a sound made when hard objects fall or hit against each other: *the clatter of dishes being washed*

clause NOUN **clauses** 1 a group of words that make up a sentence or part of a sentence 2 a part of an official document or contract

claustrophobia NOUN people who have claustrophobia are afraid of small, enclosed or crowded spaces

▸ **claustrophobic** ADJECTIVE 1 a claustrophobic person is afraid of small, enclosed or crowded spaces 2 a claustrophobic place is so small that it makes you feel nervous or afraid to be in it

claw NOUN **claws** 1 one of the long pointed nails on some animals' paws 2 a part on the end of a crab's or lobster's leg that it uses for gripping things
VERB **claws, clawing, clawed** to claw something is to scratch it with claws or fingernails

clay NOUN soft sticky material found in the ground and used for making pottery

clean ADJECTIVE **cleaner, cleanest** 1 if something is clean, it has no dirt or germs on or in it: *a clean face and hands* • *There was no clean water to drink.*
2 straight, without any jagged or rough edges: *It is a clean break so the bone should heal well.*
3 unused: *Take a clean sheet of paper and start again.*
4 fair and honest: *a clean game of football*
ADVERB completely: *It went clean through and out the other side.* • *He's gone clean mad.*
• **come clean** if someone comes clean they tell the truth
VERB **cleans, cleaning, cleaned** to clean something is to remove the dirt from it
• **clean up** to clean up is to tidy a place, removing any dirt and rubbish

▸ **cleaner** NOUN **cleaners** 1 a person whose job is to clean houses, offices or other buildings 2 a product for cleaning things: *lavatory cleaner*

▸ **cleanliness** NOUN cleanliness is keeping things clean and pure: *Cleanliness helps prevent germs spreading.*

cleanse VERB **cleanses, cleansing, cleansed** to cleanse something is to make it clean: *cleanse the wound with an antiseptic*

▸ **cleanser** NOUN **cleansers** a product that cleanses something, especially your skin

clear ADJECTIVE **clearer, clearest** 1 easy to see, hear or understand: *a clear view* • *She spoke in a clear voice.* • *His explanation wasn't very clear.*
2 see-through: *clear glass*
3 not blocked or marked by anything: *a clear sky* • *The road was clear.*
4 without meeting any difficulties or obstacles: *The way is clear for him to win the title.*
ADVERB not near something and not touching it: *Stand clear of the gates.*
VERB **clears, clearing, cleared**

1 to clear is to become clear: *The sky cleared and the sun came out.*
2 to clear things is to move them or tidy them away: *Whose turn is it to clear the dirty supper dishes?*
3 if someone is cleared of something, they are found to be not guilty or not to blame
4 to clear something is to jump over it without touching it: *Janey's pony cleared all the fences.*
• **clear off** (*informal*) to clear off is to go right away from somewhere: *We had wandered on to his land and he told us to clear off.*
• **clear up** if something such as a rash clears up, it goes away
▶ **clearly** ADVERB **1** in a way that is easy to understand or see: *The rules are clearly explained.* **2** without any difficulty : *I can't see it very clearly.* **3** obviously: *Clearly, we couldn't continue without proper equipment.*
▶ **clearness** NOUN being clear
clearance NOUN **clearances 1** clearing something away: *the clearance of the land to make room for housing* **2** the amount of space between one thing and another passing beside it or under it: *There isn't enough clearance for the lorry to go through that gap.* **3** if someone or something has clearance to do something, they have permission to do it: *Air traffic controllers give aeroplanes clearance to land.*
clearing NOUN **clearings** a gap in a forest where there are no trees
cleave VERB **cleaves, cleaving, clove** or **cleft** or **cleaved, cloven** or **cleft** or **cleaved** to cleave something is to split it
▶ **cleaver** NOUN **cleavers** a cutting tool with a large square blade fitted to a handle
clef NOUN **clefs** (*music*) a symbol used at the beginning of a piece of music to show how high or low the notes should be
cleft NOUN **clefts** a split or opening: *A jagged cleft had opened up in the rocks.* ADJECTIVE split: *a cleft stick*
cleft palate NOUN **cleft palates** a split in the roof of the mouth that some

people have when they are born
clench VERB **clenches, clenching, clenched** to clench something is to hold it tightly or press it tightly together: *Clenching his teeth, he jumped out of the plane.*
clergy PLURAL NOUN the clergy are priests or ministers in the Christian church
clergyman or **clergywoman** NOUN **clergymen** or **clergywomen** a man who is a priest or minister of the church
cleric NOUN **clerics** a member of the clergy
▶ **clerical** ADJECTIVE **1** to do with office work: *a clerical assistant* **2** to do with priests or ministers of the church: *a clerical collar*
clerk NOUN **clerks** an office worker whose job is to write letters, do filing, or keep accounts
clever ADJECTIVE **cleverer, cleverest 1** quick to learn and understand things: *He's the cleverest boy in his class.* **2** skilful: *He's clever with his hands.*
cliché (pronounced **klee**-shay) NOUN **clichés** a phrase that has been used so often it no longer has the effect it once had
click NOUN **clicks** a short sharp sound like the sound made when a door lock is closed gently
VERB **clicks, clicking, clicked** to make this sound: *We could hear her heels clicking on the stone floor.*
• **click on something** (*ICT*) if you click on something that appears on a computer screen, you choose it by pressing the button on the mouse
client NOUN **clients 1** someone who uses the services of a person like a lawyer or accountant **2** a customer
cliff NOUN **cliffs** a high steep rocky slope, usually facing the sea
cliffhanger NOUN **cliffhangers** a situation or story that is exciting because you don't know how it will turn out until the very end
climate NOUN **climates** (*geography*) the usual sort of weather there is in a

Aa Bb Cc Dd Ee Ff Gg Hh Ii Jj Kk Ll Mm Nn Oo Pp Qq Rr Ss Tt Uu Vv Ww Xx Yy Zz

region or area: *The Earth's climate is getting warmer.* • *plants that only grow in warmer climates*

climax NOUN **climaxes** the most important, most exciting or most interesting point in a story or situation

climb VERB **climbs, climbing, climbed** to climb, or climb something, is to go up, or to go towards the top: *He likes to climb mountains.* • *We carried on climbing until we reached the top of the mountain.*

• **climb down** if someone involved in an argument or disagreement climbs down, they eventually admit that they were wrong

NOUN **climbs** an act of climbing: *We had a steep climb to the top.*

▶ **climber** NOUN **climbers 1** someone who climbs, often as a pastime or sport **2** a plant that climbs up things like walls and fences

clinch VERB **clinches, clinching, clinched** to clinch a bargain or argument is to settle it

cling VERB **clings, clinging, clung** to cling to something is to stick to it or hang on to it tightly: *shellfish clinging to the rocks*

clingfilm NOUN clingfilm is a very thin sheet of plastic that is used to cover food

clinic NOUN **clinics** a place where people can be seen by doctors to get treatment and advice: *an eye clinic*

clink NOUN **clinks** a sharp ringing sound like the sound made when glasses or coins are hit together

VERB **clinks, clinking, clinked** to clink is to make this sound

clip VERB **clips, clipping, clipped 1** to clip something is to cut small or short parts off it: *clipping the hedge with shears* **2** to clip something is to fasten it with a clip: *a badge clipped on to his lapel*

NOUN **clips** a small fastening device: *a paper clip*

clip art NOUN (*ICT*) pictures that you can copy from the Internet or from a disk into documents on your computer

clique (pronounced **kleek**) NOUN **cliques** a small group of people who are friendly to each other but keep other people out of the group

cloak NOUN **cloaks 1** a piece of clothing without sleeves that is worn over other clothing and hangs down loosely from the shoulders **2** anything that covers or hides: *the cloak of darkness*

VERB **cloaks, cloaking, cloaked** to cloak something is to cover or hide it: *hills cloaked in mist*

cloakroom NOUN **cloakrooms** a room or area in a building where visitors can leave their coats, hats and bags

clobber VERB **clobbers, clobbering, clobbered** (*informal*) to clobber someone is to hit them hard

clock NOUN **clocks** a machine for measuring time

clockwise ADJECTIVE turning or moving in the same direction as the hands of a clock

clockwork NOUN the machinery of an old-fashioned clock with a spring that you wind up

• **like clockwork** if something goes or works like clockwork, it goes or works smoothly without any problems

clod NOUN **clods** a solid lump of earth

clog NOUN **clogs** a shoe with a wooden sole

VERB **clogs, clogging, clogged** to clog something, or to clog it up, is to block it: *The drains are clogged up with leaves and litter.*

cloister NOUN **cloisters** a covered passageway that is open on one side and goes round a courtyard in a monastery, cathedral or college

clone NOUN **clones** (*science*) an exact copy of a plant or animal, made artificially by taking cells from it

VERB **clones, cloning, cloned** to make an exact copy of a plant or animal in this way

close¹ (pronounced **kloas**) ADJECTIVE **closer, closest**

1 near in distance or time: *They are quite close in age.*

2 very dear or affectionate: *a close friendship*

3 tight, with little space: *a close fit* **4** thorough or careful: *Pay close attention.* **5** with no fresh air: *a close atmosphere* ADVERB **closer, closest** near: *He came close to winning.* • *She stood close by.*

▶ **closely** ADVERB **1** at a close distance: *He came into the room, closely followed by his two friends.* **2** tightly: *closely packed sardines*

close² (pronounced **kloaz**) VERB **closes, closing, closed 1** to shut, or shut something: *I didn't hear the door closing.* • *Will you close the window, please?* **2** to finish, or finish something: *They closed the concert by singing the national anthem.* • *Sports day closed with the boys' race.* NOUN **closes 1** the end of something: *at the close of day* **2** (pronounced **kloas**) a street that is blocked at one end

closet NOUN **closets** a cupboard

close-up NOUN **close-ups** a photograph or a shot in a film that has been taken very close to something so that all the details can be seen

closure NOUN **closures** an occasion when something closes: *the closure of the old school*

clot NOUN **clots** a lump that forms in liquids, especially in cream or blood VERB **clots, clotting, clotted** if a liquid clots, clots form in it

cloth NOUN **cloths 1** cloth is material made by weaving threads of wool, silk, cotton or some other fibre **2** a cloth is a piece of fabric

clothe VERB **clothes, clothing, clothed** to put clothes on someone, or to provide someone with clothes: *They need money to feed and clothe themselves.*

▶ **clothes** PLURAL NOUN clothes are the things people wear to cover their bodies

▶ **clothing** NOUN clothing is clothes

cloud NOUN **clouds 1** clouds are masses of tiny water drops floating in the sky **2** a cloud of something is a mass of it in the air: *a cloud of dust* VERB **clouds, clouding, clouded** to become cloudy: *The sky clouded over and it started to rain.*

cloudburst NOUN **cloudbursts** a sudden spell of very heavy rain

cloudy ADJECTIVE **cloudier, cloudiest 1** filled with clouds: *a cloudy sky* **2** not clear: *a cloudy liquid*

clout NOUN **clouts** (*informal*) a blow with the hand VERB **clouts, clouting, clouted** to hit with the hand

clove¹ NOUN **cloves** a small dried bud of a tropical plant, used in cooking as a spice

clove² NOUN **cloves** one of the sections into which a plant bulb splits: *a clove of garlic*

clover NOUN a small flowering plant that grows amongst grass

clown NOUN **clowns** someone who works in a circus and does funny acts dressed up in ridiculous clothes VERB **clowns, clowning, clowned** • **clown around** to clown or clown around is to act in a funny or silly way

club NOUN **clubs 1** an organized group of people who meet regularly to take part in an activity, or the place where they meet **2** one of the metal sticks used in golf to hit the ball **3** clubs is one of the four suits of playing cards, which have the symbol ♣ printed on them **4** a place where adults go in the evening to dance and drink **5** a heavy piece of wood or metal used as a weapon VERB **clubs, clubbing, clubbed** • **club together** if people club together, they each put some money in to buy something

cluck VERB **clucks, clucking, clucked** when a hen clucks, it makes its normal sound NOUN **clucks** a sound made by a hen

clue NOUN **clues 1** a piece of evidence that helps solve a crime or mystery **2** if someone doesn't have a clue, they don't know anything or they don't know how to do something

clump NOUN **clumps** a group of plants

Aa Bb Cc Dd Ee Ff Gg Hh Ii Jj Kk Ll Mm Nn Oo Pp Qq Rr Ss Tt Uu Vv Ww Xx Yy Zz

Aa

Bb

Cc

Dd

Ee

Ff

Gg

Hh

Ii

Jj

Kk

Ll

Mm

Nn

Oo

Pp

Qq

Rr

Ss

Tt

Uu

Vv

Ww

Xx

Yy

Zz

growing close together: *a clump of bluebells*

clumsy ADJECTIVE **clumsier, clumsiest** a clumsy person often has accidents because they are careless or because they move in an awkward way

clung VERB a way of changing the verb **cling** to make a past tense. It can be used with or without a helping verb: *We clung to the edge of the cliff.* • *She had clung on to her teddy bear all day.*

cluster NOUN **clusters** several things placed or growing very close together: *roses growing in clusters*

VERB **clusters, clustering, clustered** to cluster is to move or be very close together: *The children clustered round the teacher.*

clutch VERB **clutches, clutching, clutched 1** to clutch something is to hold it tightly in your hand or hands **2** to clutch at something is to try to get hold of it

• **clutch at straws** if you are clutching at straws, the way you are trying to do something has very little chance of being successful

NOUN **clutches 1** to be in someone's clutches is to be in their grasp, especially if they have control or power over you **2** the part of a car's engine that you operate with a pedal to control the gears

clutter NOUN clutter is lots of things that cover or fill a space so that it looks untidy or disorganized

VERB **clutters, cluttering, cluttered** to clutter a place, or to clutter it up, is to fill it with lots of things and make it untidy: *Books cluttered up the shelves.*

cm ABBREVIATION short for **centimetre** or **centimetres**

co- PREFIX if a word starts with **co-**, it adds the meaning 'together with'. For example, a *co-author* is someone who has written a book with another writer

Co. ABBREVIATION short for **Company** or **County**: *Reginald Bloggs & Co., Ironmongers* • *Co. Clare, Ireland*

coach NOUN **coaches**

1 a single-decker bus used to carry passengers over long distances

2 a person who trains someone in a particular skill or prepares them for a competition or performance: *a rugby coach* • *a singing coach*

3 a railway carriage for passengers

4 a type of large four-wheeled carriage pulled by horses and used to carry passengers

VERB **coaches, coaching, coached** to coach someone is to prepare them for a competition or performance

coal NOUN a hard black substance containing carbon that is dug out of the ground and burnt as fuel

coarse ADJECTIVE **coarser, coarsest 1** feeling rough or harsh: *coarse cloth* **2** vulgar: *coarse language*

✦The words **coarse** and **course** sound the same but remember that they have different spellings.

coast NOUN **coasts** (*geography*) the coast is the area of land next to the sea

• **the coast is clear** if the coast is clear there is no one around to see you or stop you doing something

VERB **coasts, coasting, coasted**

• **coast along** to coast, or to coast along, is to go along without making much effort

▸ **coastal** ADJECTIVE beside the sea

coastguard NOUN **coastguards** someone whose job is to guard the coast of a country against smugglers and to help ships in danger

coat NOUN **coats 1** a piece of clothing with sleeves that usually reaches to your knees and that you wear over your other clothes **2** a layer: *three coats of paint*

VERB **coats, coating, coated** to coat something is to cover it with a layer of something: *They'd coated their bodies with mud.*

coat of arms NOUN **coats of arms** a coat of arms is the badge or crest used by a particular family

coax VERB **coaxes, coaxing, coaxed** to coax someone to do something is to persuade them gently to do it

cob NOUN **cobs** a long round solid part of a corn plant that the seeds grow on

cobble NOUN **cobbles** cobbles are rounded stones that form the surface of some old roads. They are sometimes called **cobblestones**

▸ **cobbled** ADJECTIVE covered with cobbles

cobbler NOUN **cobblers** someone whose job is making and repairing shoes

cobra NOUN **cobras** a type of poisonous snake that raises itself up before it bites

cobweb NOUN **cobwebs** a criss-cross pattern of thin threads that a spider makes to catch insects

cock NOUN **cocks** a male bird
VERB **cocks, cocking, cocked 1** an animal cocks its ears when it makes its ears stand upright so that it can hear better **2** you cock your head when you tilt it to one side

cockatoo NOUN **cockatoos** a type of large parrot with a crest on top of its head that it can raise and lower

cockerel NOUN **cockerels** a male chicken

cocker spaniel NOUN **cocker spaniels** a breed of small dog with a long silky coat and ears that hang down

cockle NOUN **cockles** a type of small round edible shellfish that lives in the sea

cockney NOUN **cockneys 1** someone who comes from the east end of London **2** the accent or way of speaking of people who come from around the east end of London

cockpit NOUN **cockpits** the space in an aeroplane where the pilot sits

cockroach NOUN **cockroaches** a large crawling insect usually found in damp or dirty places

cocky ADJECTIVE **cockier, cockiest** a cocky person is very confident in a way that is annoying

cocoa NOUN a hot drink made with the powdered seeds of the cacao plant, which are also used to make chocolate

coconut NOUN **coconuts** a large hairy nut from a tropical palm tree that has white firm flesh and a thin liquid called coconut milk inside

cocoon NOUN **cocoons** a case made by a caterpillar inside which it changes into an adult moth or butterfly

cod NOUN **cod** a large sea fish found in northern seas of the world and caught for food

code NOUN **codes 1** code, or a code, is a set of signs or letters used for signalling or writing: *a message written in secret code* **2** a set of rules or laws: *a code of honour*
VERB **codes, coding, coded** to code something is to put it in a particular code of letters or signs: *All messages were coded before being sent.*

coeducation NOUN the teaching of boys and girls in the same school or college

▸ **coeducational** ADJECTIVE teaching both male and female students: *a coeducational school*

coffee NOUN **coffees 1** coffee is a drink made from the roasted and ground-up beans of a tropical plant **2** a coffee is a cup of this drink

coffin NOUN **coffins** a long wooden box that a dead body is put into

cog NOUN **cogs** a metal wheel with tooth-shaped parts round the edge that fits into another wheel and turns it to make a machine or engine work

coherent ADJECTIVE **1** coherent speech is clear and easy to understand **2** coherent thoughts or ideas are connected in a sensible way

▸ **coherence** NOUN sensible connection between things, especially thoughts or ideas

▸ **coherently** ADVERB clearly and in a sensible way

cohesion NOUN sticking together

▸ **cohesive** ADJECTIVE closely linked or connected

cohort NOUN **cohorts 1** (*history*) in the ancient Roman army, a cohort was a tenth part of a legion **2** someone who keeps company with or follows someone else: *The president arrived with all his cohorts.*

coil VERB **coils, coiling, coiled** to coil is to twist or wind to form rings or loops:

Aa
Bb
Cc
Dd
Ee
Ff
Gg
Hh
Ii
Jj
Kk
Ll
Mm
Nn
Oo
Pp
Qq
Rr
Ss
Tt
Uu
Vv
Ww
Xx
Yy
Zz

The huge snake coiled itself round the branch.

NOUN **coils** a loop or series of loops in something long, such as rope or hair: *a coil of thin wire*

coin NOUN **coins** a piece of metal money VERB **coins, coining, coined** to coin a new word or phrase is to invent it

coinage NOUN **coinages 1** a country's coinage is all the coins used in its particular money system **2** a coinage is a newly invented word or phrase

coincide VERB **coincides, coinciding, coincided** events coincide with each other when they happen at the same time: *The carnival will coincide with the beginning of the school holidays.*

coincidence NOUN **coincidences** a coincidence is when two things happen at the same time, without being planned: *Both families booked holidays at the same resort by sheer coincidence.*

▸ **coincidental** ADJECTIVE happening at the same time by chance

coke NOUN a type of fuel made from coal

cola NOUN **colas** a dark brown fizzy drink

colander NOUN **colanders** a container with holes in the bottom used to drain water from food

cold ADJECTIVE **colder, coldest 1** low in temperature: *a cold drink* • *It's too cold to go outside.* **2** unfriendly: *a cold stare* NOUN **colds 1** cold weather: *I don't like the cold.* **2** an illness caused by a virus which makes you sneeze and cough, and makes your nose run

▸ **coldly** ADVERB in an unfriendly way: *She treated them coldly.*

▸ **coldness** NOUN being cold

cold-blooded ADJECTIVE **1** (*science*) a cold-blooded animal is not able to store heat in its body. Reptiles and snakes are cold-blooded **2** a cold-blooded person is unfeeling and cruel

cold sore NOUN **cold sores** a blister, usually somewhere on the lip or mouth, caused by a virus

coleslaw NOUN a salad made from sliced raw cabbage mixed with mayonnaise

colic NOUN a sudden and severe pain in the stomach

collaborate VERB **collaborates, collaborating, collaborated 1** if two or more people collaborate, they help each other by sharing information and ideas **2** if someone collaborates, they give an enemy information or help

▸ **collaboration** NOUN sharing information or ideas

▸ **collaborator** NOUN **collaborators** someone who shares information with another person

collage (pronounced kol-**aj**) NOUN **collages** (*art*) a picture or design made by sticking different materials, for example paper, photographs or small objects, on to a sheet of card or wood

collapse VERB **collapses, collapsing, collapsed** to fall down from being under too much weight or because of lack of strength: *The bridge collapsed under the lorry's weight.* • *The runner collapsed, exhausted, just before the finish line.*

NOUN **collapses** an occasion when something falls down or caves in

▸ **collapsible** ADJECTIVE collapsible furniture or equipment can be folded or broken down so that it fits into a smaller space

collar NOUN **collars 1** a band of material on a shirt or other piece of clothing that fits round your neck **2** a band of leather or other material fastened round an animal's neck VERB **collars, collaring, collared** to collar someone or something is to get hold of them

collarbone NOUN **collarbones** one of two bones in your body that stretch from your shoulder to just under the front of your neck

collate VERB **collates, collating, collated** to collate different pieces of information or pieces of paper is to bring them together and arrange them in order

colleague NOUN **colleagues** a person's colleagues are the people they work with

collect → colouring

collect VERB **collects, collecting, collected 1** to collect things is to find them and gather them together: *He collects unusual postcards.* **2** to collect someone or something from a place is to go there and pick them up: *George's dad usually collects him from school.*
▶ **collection** NOUN **collections** a number of things that have been gathered together by one person or in one place: *a stamp collection*
▶ **collective** ADJECTIVE done by several people or groups, not just one: *a collective decision*
collective noun NOUN **collective nouns** *(grammar)* a collective noun is a word used to refer to a group or collection of people or things. The words *family, team, staff, government, police, herd, flock, cattle, luggage* and *furniture* are examples of collective nouns
collector NOUN **collectors** someone who finds and gathers several things of the same type to make a collection: *a collector of antiques*
college NOUN **colleges** a place where people go to learn or be trained after leaving school: *He's going to engineering college.*
collide VERB **collides, colliding, collided** moving objects collide when they hit each other
collie NOUN **collies** a kind of sheepdog
collision NOUN **collisions** a crash between moving vehicles or objects: *a collision between two lorries on the motorway*
colloquial ADJECTIVE colloquial language is used in everyday speech but not in formal speaking or writing. For example, *ta-ta* is a colloquial expression for 'goodbye'
▶ **colloquially** ADVERB informally
colon¹ NOUN **colons** the punctuation mark that looks like one full stop on top of another. You use it to separate parts of a sentence or before a list, for example *There are three things you will need: paper, scissors, and glue.*
colon² NOUN **colons** your colon is part of your bowels

colonel (pronounced **kur**-nel) NOUN **colonels** a high-ranking officer in the army or air force
colonial ADJECTIVE to do with a country's colonies abroad
colonize *or* **colonise** VERB **colonizes, colonizing, colonized 1** people, animals or plants colonize an area when they move into it and begin to live or grow there **2** if a country colonizes another part of the world it takes it over and controls it
▶ **colonist** NOUN **colonists** someone who goes to another country to set up a colony
colony NOUN **colonies 1** a group of people who have settled in another part of the world, or the new settlement they have made: *The Pilgrim Fathers set up colonies on the east coast of America.* **2** a group of people, animals or plants of the same type living together: *a colony of ants* **3** a country's foreign colonies were the parts of the world that it controlled: *Hong Kong used to be a British colony.*
colossal ADJECTIVE enormous: *a colossal appetite*
colour NOUN **colours 1** colour, or a colour, is a quality that shows up when light hits an object, for example, redness, blueness, yellowness, and so on: *What colour are your eyes?* • *The sea was a lovely greenish-blue colour.* **2** a person's colour is the shade of their skin
VERB **colours, colouring, coloured** to colour a picture is to add colours to it with paints or crayons
▶ **coloured** ADJECTIVE having colour: *a brightly coloured scarf*
colour blind ADJECTIVE not able to tell the difference between certain colours, especially red and green
colourful ADJECTIVE **1** having lots of bright colours: *colourful clothing* **2** interesting or exciting: *He's a colourful character.*
colouring NOUN **colourings 1** colouring is a substance used to give something a colour: *red food colouring*

Aa Bb Cc Dd Ee Ff Gg Hh Ii Jj Kk Ll Mm Nn Oo Pp Qq Rr Ss Tt Uu Vv Ww Xx Yy Zz

107

Aa
Bb
Cc
Dd
Ee
Ff
Gg
Hh
Ii
Jj
Kk
Ll
Mm
Nn
Oo
Pp
Qq
Rr
Ss
Tt
Uu
Vv
Ww
Xx
Yy
Zz

2 someone's colouring is the colour of their skin and hair: *That shade of green suits her dark colouring.*

colourless ADJECTIVE having no colour: *Water is a colourless liquid.*

colt NOUN **colts** a young horse

column NOUN **columns**
1 a stone or wooden pillar
2 something with a long or tall narrow shape: *Columns of smoke and dust rose from the erupting volcano.*
3 a long line of people one behind the other or things one below the other: *a column of marching soldiers • a column of figures*
4 a part in a newspaper that appears regularly and is usually written by the same person

▶ **columnist** NOUN **columnists** a person who writes an article in a newspaper

coma NOUN **comas** if someone is in a coma they are unconscious for a long period of time

▶ **comatose** ADJECTIVE in a coma or seeming to be in a coma

comb NOUN **combs 1** an object with a row of teeth along one side that you use to make your hair tidy **2** a part that sticks up on the top of some birds' heads

VERB **combs, combing, combed 1** to comb hair is to make it tidy using a comb **2** to comb a place is to search it carefully and thoroughly: *Detectives were combing the area for clues.*

combat NOUN combat is fighting: *soldiers in combat*

VERB **combats, combatting, combatted** to combat something is to fight or struggle against it: *a superhero who combats crime*

combination NOUN **combinations 1** combination is the joining or mixing of two or more things **2** a combination is several things that have been joined or mixed

combine VERB **combines, combining, combined** to combine things is to join or mix them together: *Combine all the ingredients in a mixing bowl.*

combine harvester NOUN **combine harvesters** a large farm machine that both cuts and threshes crops

combustible ADJECTIVE a combustible substance will burn or catch fire: *a highly combustible gas found in coal mines*

combustion NOUN burning: *the combustion of gases*

come VERB **comes, coming, came, come 1** to move towards the person speaking or to move to the place where they are: *Are you coming with us or not? • They came by boat and train.*
2 to arrive or happen: *Has my parcel come yet? • The mountains came into view. • People come in all shapes and sizes.*

• **come about** to come about is to happen: *How did this disagreement come about?*

• **come across someone** or **something** to come across a person or thing is to meet or find them by accident: *I came across a letter my great-grandmother had written in 1944.*

• **come by something** to come by something is to get it: *Work was becoming harder and harder to come by.*

• **come round** or **come to** someone who has been unconscious or has fainted comes round or comes to when they wake up

comedian NOUN **comedians** a performer who tells jokes and funny stories or who acts in comedies

comedy NOUN **comedies 1** comedy is the art of making people laugh **2** a comedy is a funny play or film

✦ This comes from a French word, **comedie**. The French word comes from the Greek word **komos**, which means *merrymaking*.

comet NOUN **comets** a kind of star that travels across the sky trailing a tail of light behind it

comfort NOUN **comforts 1** comfort is a pleasant feeling you get if you are relaxed, happy, warm or secure

comfortable → comment

2 comforts are luxuries or pleasant surroundings: *a hotel with all the comforts of home*
VERB **comforts, comforting, comforted** to comfort someone who is sad or upset is to make them feel happier by saying or doing nice things

comfortable ADJECTIVE **1** something which is comfortable is pleasant to wear, sit in or be in: *a comfortable chair* • *a comfortable hotel* **2** someone who is comfortable has no pain, worry or trouble
▶ **comfortably** ADVERB in a way that feels pleasant, without any pain or trouble: *Are you all sitting comfortably?*

comfy ADJECTIVE **comfier, comfiest** an informal word for **comfortable**: *a comfy chair*

comic ADJECTIVE **1** to do with or involved in comedy: *a comic actor* **2** funny, amusing: *His face had a really comic expression.*
NOUN **comics 1** a magazine, especially for children, that has funny stories told in pictures **2** someone who is funny, especially a comedian
▶ **comical** ADJECTIVE funny: *He looked comical in his orange hat.*

comic strip NOUN **comic strips** a series of drawings that tell a funny story

comma NOUN **commas** the punctuation mark that looks like a small dot with a tail. You use it to separate parts of a sentence and make it easier to read, for example *Max put on his hat, his gloves, his coat and his scarf.*

command VERB **commands, commanding, commanded 1** to command someone to do something is to order them to do it: *'I command you to kneel before me,' shouted the king.* **2** to command something is to be in control or in charge of it: *He commanded the Roman legions.*
NOUN **commands 1** an order **2** (*ICT*) an order that you give to a computer to carry out an action **3** to be in command is to be in charge or in control: *Who's the officer in command?*
▶ **commander** NOUN **commanders** someone who commands or is in

command, especially an officer in the police or navy
▶ **commandment** NOUN **commandments** a command or order, especially one of the ten commandments given to Moses by God

commando NOUN **commandos** or **commandoes** a soldier who works with others in a small group and is specially trained to do difficult or dangerous tasks

commemorate VERB **commemorates, commemorating, commemorated** to commemorate something, such as a battle or some other famous event, is to remember it by holding a ceremony or putting up a monument
▶ **commemoration** NOUN **commemorations** a commemoration of a person or event is something that is done to remember and celebrate that person or event

commence VERB **commences, commencing, commenced** (*formal*) to begin: *The meeting will commence at 3 o'clock precisely.*
▶ **commencement** NOUN the beginning of something

commend VERB **commends, commending, commended** to commend someone or something is to praise them or to say that they deserve praise
▶ **commendable** ADJECTIVE commendable behaviour or personal qualities deserve praise: *He has shown commendable honesty.*
▶ **commendation** NOUN **commendations** an honour or praise given to someone who has done something well

comment NOUN **comments** a remark or opinion about someone or something: *The school would welcome any comments from parents about the revised timetable.*
VERB **comments, commenting, commented** to comment, or comment on something, is to make a remark or give your opinion about it: *The teacher commented on what I've written so far.*

Aa
Bb
Cc
Dd
Ee
Ff
Gg
Hh
Ii
Jj
Kk
Ll
Mm
Nn
Oo
Pp
Qq
Rr
Ss
Tt
Uu
Vv
Ww
Xx
Yy
Zz

▶ **commentary** NOUN **commentaries** a description or explanation of an event as it happens by someone who is there

▶ **commentator** NOUN **commentators** someone who gives a commentary: *a cricket commentator*

commerce NOUN commerce is the buying and selling of goods and services: *international commerce*

▶ **commercial** ADJECTIVE **1** to do with trade or making money by selling goods and services **2** paid for by selling advertising space or time: *commercial TV* NOUN **commercials** an advertisement for a product on TV or radio

commiserate VERB **commiserates, commiserating, commiserated** to commiserate with someone is to sympathize with them about something that is making them unhappy

▶ **commiserations** PLURAL NOUN when you offer someone your commiserations, you let them know you are sorry about a disappointment or upset they have suffered

commission NOUN **commissions 1** a commission is when someone pays another person to design, do or make something for them **2** a commission is a group of people who investigate something or have authority over something: *the Commission for Racial Equality* **3** someone who is paid commission is paid a fee for each thing they sell

VERB **commissions, commissioning, commissioned** to commission something, or to commission someone to do something, is to pay a person to design, do or make something for you: *He was commissioned to write a book.*

commit VERB **commits, committing, committed 1** to commit a crime is to do something that breaks the law **2** to commit yourself to something is to say, promise or decide that you will do it

▶ **commitment** NOUN **commitments 1** a commitment is a promise to do something: *made a definite commitment to be there* **2** commitment is willingness to work hard and give a lot of time to something: *Being a top*

athlete requires a lot of commitment.

▶ **committed** ADJECTIVE having strong beliefs: *a committed Christian*

committee NOUN **committees** a group of people who have been chosen to deal with something and make decisions: *the organizing committee for the school show*

commodity NOUN **commodities** anything that can be bought and sold

common ADJECTIVE **commoner, commonest 1** seen or happening often and in many places: *Traffic jams are a common occurrence in cities.* • *one of the commonest childhood diseases* **2** ordinary: *the common people* **3** shared by many: *Their common goal was to make the Games a success.*

NOUN **commons** a common is a piece of land that all the people in a town can use: *Wimbledon Common*

• **have something in common** if people or things have something in common, they are similar in some way

common noun NOUN **common nouns** (*grammar*) a general name for a thing. Common nouns do not usually begin with a capital letter, for example *cat, river, day* and *thought*

commonplace ADJECTIVE not at all unusual

common sense NOUN the ability to think and behave sensibly

commonwealth NOUN a group of countries or states that cooperate with each other, especially in trade

commotion NOUN a noisy disturbance

communal ADJECTIVE shared by several people: *a communal garden*

commune NOUN **communes** a group of people who live together and share work, possessions and expenses

communicate VERB **communicates, communicating, communicated 1** to communicate is to give information to others, for example by making sounds or by writing: *The monkeys communicate with loud barking calls.* **2** to communicate with someone is to get in touch with them: *We communicate mainly by telephone and email.*

▸ **communication** NOUN **communcations 1** communication is conveying information: *Text messaging is a common form of communication.* **2** (*formal*) a communication is a message: *They received an urgent communication from head office.*

▸ **communicative** ADJECTIVE a communicative person is willing to talk to others and give them information

Communion NOUN in the Christian Church, Communion is the ceremony celebrating the Last Supper of Jesus and his disciples

communism NOUN communism is the belief that all the wealth created by industry should be shared by everyone in society

▸ **communist** NOUN **communists** someone who believes in communism ADJECTIVE believing in communism or to do with communists: *a communist country*

community NOUN **communities 1** a group living in a particular area or a group sharing the same background: *a school serving the local community* **2** the community is all of society or all the people of the world

commute VERB **commutes, commuting, commuted** to travel regularly between two places, especially between home and the place where you work

▸ **commuter** NOUN **commuters** someone who commutes

compact ADJECTIVE with all its parts fitted tightly or closely together so that they take up very little space: *a compact little garden*

compact disc NOUN **compact discs** a small metal and plastic disc on which sound and images are recorded in digital form. The disc is read by a laser beam in a compact disc player or computer

companion NOUN **companions** someone who spends a lot of time with another person

▸ **companionship** NOUN being with each other and having a friendly relationship

company NOUN **companies 1** a company is a business firm: *They've formed a company to design video games.* **2** company is being with someone else: *He's very good company.*
- **get into bad company** to start spending time with people that other people disapprove of: *She got into bad company and started going out late.*
- **keep someone company** if you keep someone company you stay with them or go somewhere with them
- **part company** if two people part company they leave each other

comparable ADJECTIVE similar: *The two games are comparable in difficulty.*

comparative ADJECTIVE judged by comparing with something else: *He had not lived here as long as the rest of us and was a comparative stranger.* NOUN **comparatives** (*grammar*) a comparative of an adjective or adverb is the form that usually ends with -*er* or is used with *more*. For example *better, worse, luckier, braver* and *more dangerous* are comparative

▸ **comparatively** ADVERB compared with something else: *The house was noisy, and the garden was comparatively quiet.*

compare VERB **compares, comparing, compared 1** to put two or more things together to show how they are similar or different, or which is better: *The weather today is lovely compared to last week.* **2** to describe someone or something as like another person or thing: *She compared him to a mad dog.*

▸ **comparison** NOUN **comparisons** putting two or more things together to show how they are similar or different

compartment NOUN **compartments** a separate enclosed part within a larger thing: *a secret compartment at the back of the desk*

compass NOUN **compasses** an instrument that shows the direction of north with a magnet and which you can use to find your way

compasses PLURAL NOUN compasses, or a pair of compasses, are an instrument

Aa
Bb
Cc
Dd
Ee
Ff
Gg
Hh
Ii
Jj
Kk
Ll
Mm
Nn
Oo
Pp
Qq
Rr
Ss
Tt
Uu
Vv
Ww
Xx
Yy
Zz

Aa
Bb
Cc
Dd
Ee
Ff
Gg
Hh
Ii
Jj
Kk
Ll
Mm
Nn
Oo
Pp
Qq
Rr
Ss
Tt
Uu
Vv
Ww
Xx
Yy
Zz

with two hinged prongs used to draw circles or to measure out distances between two points

compassion NOUN if you have or show compassion for people, you feel pity because they are suffering

▸ **compassionate** ADJECTIVE showing pity or mercy for people who are suffering or in trouble

compatible NOUN able to exist or work well together: *The two computer programs weren't compatible.*

compel VERB **compels, compelling, compelled** to compel someone to do something is to force them to do it

▸ **compelling** ADJECTIVE **1** so interesting or exciting that you are forced to go on reading, watching or listening **2** a compelling argument is so strong that you cannot disagree with it

compendium NOUN **compendiums** or **compendia 1** a book in which lots of different information about a particular subject is brought together **2** a box that contains several different board games

compensate VERB **compensates, compensating, compensated 1** to compensate someone is to give them something, especially money, because they have suffered an injury, damage or loss **2** if one thing compensates for another, it makes up for it: *His sunny personality compensates for his lack of learning.*

▸ **compensation** NOUN compensation is something, especially money, given to make up for loss or damage

compete VERB **competes, competing, competed** to compete is to try to beat or be more successful than others: *athletes competing in the Olympics*

competence NOUN the ability or skill to do something properly or well

▸ **competent** ADJECTIVE capable, efficient or skilled: *a very competent pianist*

▸ **competently** ADVERB efficiently or skilfully

competition NOUN **competitions** a contest between people who are each trying to win or be better than the others

▸ **competitive** ADJECTIVE a competitive person likes to compete and win against other people

▸ **competitor** NOUN **competitors** someone taking part in a competition

compilation NOUN **compilations 1** compilation is the process of compiling something **2** a compilation is a collection of pieces of writing, music or information: *The album is a compilation of the band's greatest hits.*

compile VERB **compiles, compiling, compiled** to compile something, such as an encyclopedia, is to make it using information that has been collected together

▸ **compiler** NOUN **compilers** a person or machine that compiles

complacency NOUN an attitude in which you become lazy because you think you have done all that you need to

▸ **complacent** ADJECTIVE too satisfied with what you do

complain VERB **complains, complaining, complained** to say or write that you are not happy or satisfied: *He complained that it was too hot and that he hated the food.*

▸ **complaint** NOUN **complaints 1** a statement that lets people know that you are not happy or satisfied **2** an illness

complement NOUN **complements 1** something that is added to make something complete **2** the number needed to make something complete **3** something that goes very well with another thing: *The sauce is a lovely complement to the meal.*

VERB **complements, complementing, complemented** if two things complement each other, they go very well together

▸ **complementary** ADJECTIVE **1** going well together **2** together making up a whole

✦ The words **complement** and **compliment** sound the same but they have different spellings. A **compliment** is something you say to praise someone.

complementary angle NOUN
complementary angles (*maths*) an angle that must be added to one that is less than 90 degrees to make a right angle

complete VERB **completes, completing, completed** to complete something is to finish it or make it whole: *He completed the test in time.* ADJECTIVE **1** with nothing missing: *a complete set of golf clubs* **2** finished: *When the dam is complete it will be over 150 metres high.* **3** total: *I felt a complete fool.*
▶ **completely** ADVERB totally: *I agree completely.*
▶ **completeness** NOUN wholeness
▶ **completion** NOUN the process of finishing something, or the state of being finished: *The filming is nearing completion.*

complex ADJECTIVE **1** made up of many parts: *a complex network of streets* **2** difficult to understand or work out: *a complex problem*
NOUN **complexes 1** a group of buildings all with the same use: *a sports complex* **2** if someone has a complex, there is something that they are very sensitive about
▶ **complexity** NOUN **complexities** complexity is being complicated or difficult

complexion NOUN **complexions** your complexion is the colouring of your skin: *a rosy complexion*

complicate VERB **complicates, complicating, complicated** to complicate something is to make it more difficult
▶ **complicated** ADJECTIVE difficult to work out or understand: *a complicated sum*
▶ **complication** NOUN **complications** something that creates a problem or difficulty

compliment NOUN **compliments** something that you say that praises someone: *He paid me a compliment.*
VERB **compliments, complimenting, complimented** to compliment

someone is to praise them: *He complimented her on her good taste.*
▶ **complimentary** ADJECTIVE **1** flattering or praising: *The article she wrote was very complimentary.* **2** given free: *a complimentary ticket for the show*
▶ **compliments** PLURAL NOUN to give your compliments to someone is to give them your good wishes

> ✦ The words **compliment** and **complement** sound the same but they have different spellings. A **complement** is something that makes another thing complete.

comply VERB **complies, complying, complied** to comply is to obey or agree to do something: *It is impossible to comply with such demands.*

component NOUN **components** one of the parts that are put together to make a whole, for example one of the different parts that make up a machine

compose VERB **composes, composing, composed 1** to compose something is to create it by putting together various things, such as the notes to make a piece of music **2** to compose yourself is to become calm
▶ **composed** ADJECTIVE in control of your feelings
▶ **composer** NOUN **composers** someone who writes music
▶ **composition** NOUN **compositions 1** composition is creating something, such as a piece of writing: *a lesson in spelling and composition* **2** a composition is something made up, such as a piece of writing or music **3** (*art*) the way the different parts of a picture are arranged

compost NOUN compost is a mixture made up of decayed plants and manure that is spread on soil

composure NOUN being in control of your feelings so that you are calm

compound NOUN (pronounced **kom-pownd**) **compounds 1** something formed from two or more parts: *a chemical compound* **2** an area enclosed

Aa
Bb
Cc
Dd
Ee
Ff
Gg
Hh
Ii
Jj
Kk
Ll
Mm
Nn
Oo
Pp
Qq
Rr
Ss
Tt
Uu
Vv
Ww
Xx
Yy
Zz

a computer

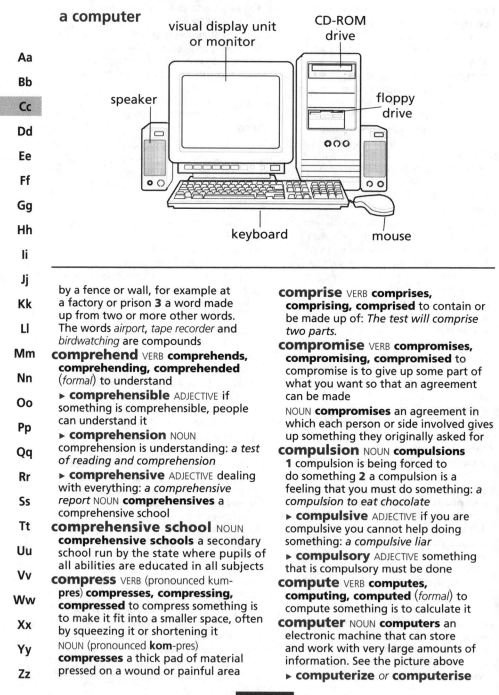

visual display unit or monitor

CD-ROM drive

speaker

floppy drive

keyboard

mouse

by a fence or wall, for example at a factory or prison **3** a word made up from two or more other words. The words *airport*, *tape recorder* and *birdwatching* are compounds

comprehend VERB **comprehends, comprehending, comprehended** (*formal*) to understand

▶ **comprehensible** ADJECTIVE if something is comprehensible, people can understand it

▶ **comprehension** NOUN comprehension is understanding: *a test of reading and comprehension*

▶ **comprehensive** ADJECTIVE dealing with everything: *a comprehensive report* NOUN **comprehensives** a comprehensive school

comprehensive school NOUN **comprehensive schools** a secondary school run by the state where pupils of all abilities are educated in all subjects

compress VERB (pronounced kum-pres) **compresses, compressing, compressed** to compress something is to make it fit into a smaller space, often by squeezing or shortening it

NOUN (pronounced **kom**-pres) **compresses** a thick pad of material pressed on a wound or painful area

comprise VERB **comprises, comprising, comprised** to contain or be made up of: *The test will comprise two parts.*

compromise VERB **compromises, compromising, compromised** to compromise is to give up some part of what you want so that an agreement can be made

NOUN **compromises** an agreement in which each person or side involved gives up something they originally asked for

compulsion NOUN **compulsions 1** compulsion is being forced to do something **2** a compulsion is a feeling that you must do something: *a compulsion to eat chocolate*

▶ **compulsive** ADJECTIVE if you are compulsive you cannot help doing something: *a compulsive liar*

▶ **compulsory** ADJECTIVE something that is compulsory must be done

compute VERB **computes, computing, computed** (*formal*) to compute something is to calculate it

computer NOUN **computers** an electronic machine that can store and work with very large amounts of information. See the picture above

▶ **computerize** *or* **computerise**

VERB **computerizes, computerizing, computerized** to computerize a system or a set of information is to organize it so that it can be held in a computer's memory

▶ **computerized** *or* **computerised** ADJECTIVE stored in or dealt with by a computer: *computerized records of fingerprints*

▶ **computing** NOUN the operation of computers or the skill of working with computers

comrade NOUN **comrades** a friend or close companion, for example soldiers who are in the same army in a war

con VERB **cons, conning, conned** to con someone is to trick them into doing something or thinking something is true

NOUN **cons** a trick used to deceive someone

concave ADJECTIVE curving inwards or downwards. Look up and compare **convex**

conceal VERB **conceals, concealing, concealed** to conceal someone or something is to hide them: *She concealed herself behind a bush.* • *He couldn't conceal his disappointment.*

▶ **concealment** NOUN concealment is the careful hiding of something: *concealment of his true feelings*

concede VERB **concedes, conceding, conceded 1** to concede something is to admit that it is true: *'It may be possible,' he conceded.* **2** to concede defeat is to accept that you have lost

conceit NOUN conceit is thinking that you are very good, clever, attractive etc in a way that annoys other people

▶ **conceited** ADJECTIVE thinking that you are very good, clever, attractive etc in a way that annoys other people

conceivable ADJECTIVE something that is conceivable is possible to imagine or believe

▶ **conceivably** ADVERB possibly

conceive VERB **conceives, conceiving, conceived 1** to conceive something is to form an idea of it in your mind **2** if a woman conceives, she becomes pregnant

concentrate VERB **concentrates, concentrating, concentrated 1** if you concentrate, or concentrate on something, you give all your attention to it: *Try to concentrate on one thing at a time.* **2** if things are concentrated in one place, they are all together in that place

▶ **concentrated** ADJECTIVE a concentrated liquid is stronger and thicker because some of the water in it has been taken out

▶ **concentration** NOUN concentration is giving all your attention to something

concentration camp NOUN **concentration camps** a camp where certain types of people are kept prisoner

concentric ADJECTIVE (*maths*) concentric circles are inside each other and have the same centre

concept NOUN **concepts** an idea or picture in your mind: *He doesn't seem to have any concept of right and wrong.*

▶ **conception** NOUN **conceptions 1** conception is the forming of ideas or pictures in your mind **2** conception happens when a woman becomes pregnant

concern VERB **concerns, concerning, concerned 1** if something concerns you, it worries you or is important to you: *His disappearance was beginning to concern us.* **2** if something concerns you, it affects or involves you: *Don't interfere in things that don't concern you.*

NOUN **concerns 1** concern is caring about something: *They showed no concern for the law.* **2** a concern is a worry or doubt: *If you have any concerns about the exam, you should speak to your class teacher.* **3** a concern is a business: *The garage has always been a family concern.*

▶ **concerned** ADJECTIVE worried or caring about someone or something: *concerned parents*

▶ **concerning** PREPOSITION about or involving someone or something: *a matter concerning the older pupils*

concert NOUN **concerts** a performance by musicians or singers

Aa
Bb
Cc
Dd
Ee
Ff
Gg
Hh
Ii
Jj
Kk
Ll
Mm
Nn
Oo
Pp
Qq
Rr
Ss
Tt
Uu
Vv
Ww
Xx
Yy
Zz

Aa
Bb
Cc
Dd
Ee
Ff
Gg
Hh
Ii
Jj
Kk
Ll
Mm
Nn
Oo
Pp
Qq
Rr
Ss
Tt
Uu
Vv
Ww
Xx
Yy
Zz

concerted ADJECTIVE done together: *We must make a concerted effort to win this match.*

concertina NOUN **concertinas** a musical instrument that you hold in both hands and play by squeezing it inwards while pressing buttons to make the notes

concerto NOUN **concertos** (*music*) a piece of music for a solo instrument and an orchestra: *a piano concerto*

concession NOUN **concessions** something that you allow someone to have so that an argument or protest can be ended: *The company refused to make any concessions and the strike continued.*

concise ADJECTIVE short and containing all the information without unnecessary details

conclude VERB **concludes, concluding, concluded 1** to end: *That concludes today's lesson.* • *He concluded by asking if anyone had any questions.* **2** to decide something because of what you have seen or heard: *He concluded she was lying.*

▸ **conclusion** NOUN **conclusions** a decision you make after thinking about something: *I've come to the conclusion that she just doesn't care.*

concoct VERB **concocts, concocting, concocted 1** to concoct something is to make it by mixing different things together **2** to concoct a story or plan is to make it up

▸ **concoction** NOUN **concoctions** something made by mixing different things together: *The drink is a concoction of fruit juices.*

concourse NOUN **concourses** a large hall where people can gather, for example at an airport or station building

concrete NOUN concrete is a strong hard building material made by mixing sand, cement, tiny stones and water
ADJECTIVE **1** made of concrete: *a concrete floor* **2** something that is concrete can be seen or touched. The opposite is **abstract 3** something that is concrete is definite: *We don't have any concrete plans yet.*

concussion NOUN injury to the brain that makes a person feel dizzy or become unconscious for a while, caused by a blow to the head

condemn VERB **condemns, condemning, condemned 1** to condemn someone or something is to say that they are wrong or bad **2** someone condemned to a punishment is sentenced by a court to that punishment: *Mary Queen of Scots was condemned to death.*

▸ **condemnation** NOUN **condemnations** saying that something is wrong or bad

condense VERB **condenses, condensing, condensed 1** when a gas condenses it becomes a liquid **2** to condense something is to make it shorter

▸ **condensation** NOUN condensation happens when moisture in the air cools and becomes liquid, for example when water in the air in a warm room cools and forms drops on the cooler surface of a window

condescending ADJECTIVE if you are condescending, you act like you are better than other people

condition NOUN **conditions 1** the state or circumstances a person or thing is in: *The building is in a dangerous condition.* **2** something that has to happen before something else does: *I'll go on the condition that you come too.*

▸ **conditional** ADJECTIVE depending on something else happening

▸ **conditionally** ADVERB only if something else happens

▸ **conditioner** NOUN **conditioners** conditioner is a liquid that improves the texture and condition of your hair or of things washed in a machine

condolences PLURAL NOUN you give or send your condolences to someone to show your sympathy when someone close to them has died

condone VERB **condones, condoning, condoned** to condone bad behaviour is to allow it to happen without saying that it is wrong

conduct VERB (pronounced kon-**dukt**) **conducts, conducting, conducted** **1** to conduct someone or something is to guide, manage or control them: *He conducted me into his office.* • *Mrs Hobbs, the music teacher, conducted the school orchestra.* **2** (*formal*) if you conduct yourself in a certain way, you behave in that way: *We expect you to conduct yourselves well on the school trip.* **3** (*science*) if a material conducts electricity or heat, it allows electricity or heat to flow through it or be transferred from one place to another NOUN (pronounced **kon**-dukt) your conduct is the way you behave
▶ **conduction** NOUN (*science*) conduction is the transfer of electricity or heat through something
▶ **conductor** NOUN **conductors 1** someone who leads the musicians in an orchestra **2** (*science*) an object or a material that allows electricity through it: *a lightning conductor*

cone NOUN **cones 1** a solid shape with a round base and sides that slope up to a point at the top **2** a container of this shape made of wafer and used to hold ice cream **3** a fruit of a pine or fir tree containing its seeds

confectioner NOUN **confectioners 1** someone who makes cakes and sweets **2** a confectioner's is a shop selling cakes and sweets
▶ **confectionery** NOUN cakes and sweets

confer VERB **confers, conferring, conferred** people confer when they discuss something together
▶ **conference** NOUN **conferences** a meeting of people to discuss a particular subject

confess VERB **confesses, confessing, confessed 1** to admit to someone such as a police officer or judge that you have done something illegal: *He confessed to the murder.* **2** to admit something to other people which you are slightly embarrassed about: *I don't mind confessing that I was terrified.*
▶ **confession** NOUN **confessions** confession is admitting you are guilty

of a crime or some other bad thing: *He made a full confession to the police.*

confetti NOUN tiny pieces of coloured paper that people throw over a married couple after the wedding ceremony

confide VERB **confides, confiding, confided** to confide in someone is to tell them your secrets

confidence NOUN **confidences 1** confidence is being sure of yourself **2** if you have confidence in someone, you trust them
• **in confidence** if you tell someone something in confidence, you expect them not to tell it to anyone else

confidence trick NOUN **confidence tricks** a trick that is meant to deceive people, especially in order to get their money

confident ADJECTIVE **1** sure of yourself or of your ability to do something: *She's a very confident swimmer.* **2** sure that something will happen the way you expect it to: *I'm confident we'll find the lost children safe and well.*

confidential ADJECTIVE confidential information should not be told to other people
▶ **confidentially** ADVERB in confidence

confine VERB **confines, confining, confined 1** to confine someone to a place is to make them stay there: *The soldiers were confined to barracks.* **2** to limit yourself or your activities to just one thing: *an author who confined herself to writing for children*
▶ **confined** ADJECTIVE a confined space is very small and restricted
▶ **confinement** NOUN being locked up or confined

confirm VERB **confirms, confirming, confirmed** to confirm something is to say or make sure that it is correct or true: *Please confirm that you will be able to come to the party.*
▶ **confirmation** NOUN something that confirms: *Have you had confirmation of your marks yet?*

confiscate VERB **confiscates, confiscating, confiscated** to

Aa Bb Cc Dd Ee Ff Gg Hh Ii Jj Kk Ll Mm Nn Oo Pp Qq Rr Ss Tt Uu Vv Ww Xx Yy Zz

confiscate something is to take it away from someone as a punishment

▶ **confiscation** NOUN taking something away as a punishment

conflict NOUN **conflicts 1** conflict is argument or disagreement **2** a conflict is a battle or war **3** if there is a conflict between two things, they cannot work together: *a conflict of ideas*

▶ **conflicting** ADJECTIVE two conflicting things contradict each other or compete with each other

conform VERB **conforms, conforming, conformed** to conform is to behave in a way that obeys the rules or laws that most other people obey

confound VERB **confounds, confounding, confounded** if something confounds you, it puzzles you

confront VERB **confronts, confronting, confronted 1** if a problem or difficult situation confronts someone, they experience it and have to deal with it: *the problems which confront pupils in school* **2** to confront something unpleasant is to deal with it in a determined way: *You must confront your fears and doubts.* **3** to confront a person is to meet them as an enemy or to accuse them of something: *He turned and confronted his attackers.* • *You should confront her and ask her about the missing money.*

▶ **confrontation** NOUN **confrontations** a face-to-face argument or fight between two people or sides

confuse VERB **confuses, confusing, confused 1** to confuse things is to mix them up so that you think one thing is the other **2** if something confuses you, you aren't able to think clearly and don't know what to do or say next

▶ **confusing** ADJECTIVE difficult to follow or understand

▶ **confusion** NOUN being confused or mixed up

congeal VERB **congeals, congealing, congealed** if a liquid congeals, it forms a thick jelly-like mass

congested ADJECTIVE a congested road or passageway is crowded or blocked up so people or things can't move through easily

▶ **congestion** NOUN crowding or blocking

congratulate VERB **congratulates, congratulating, congratulated** to congratulate someone is to tell them you are happy about something they have achieved: *I congratulated her on her exam results.*

▶ **congratulations** PLURAL NOUN you say 'congratulations' to someone when you want to show them that you are happy at their success

congregate VERB **congregates, congregating, congregated** to congregate is to gather together somewhere in a group or crowd

▶ **congregation** NOUN **congregations** a church congregation is all the people who have come to a church for a service

congress NOUN **congresses 1** a meeting of many different people: *an international congress to discuss refugees* **2** Congress is the parliament of the United States, made up of the Senate and the House of Representatives

congruent ADJECTIVE (*maths*) congruent things are the same shape or size: *congruent triangles*

conic ADJECTIVE to do with a cone or forming part of a cone

▶ **conical** ADJECTIVE shaped like a cone

conifer NOUN **conifers** a type of tree with long thin leaves shaped like needles and seeds inside cones

▶ **coniferous** ADJECTIVE coniferous trees grow cones

conjoined twins PLURAL NOUN twins who are joined together at some part of their body when they are born

conjunction NOUN
• **in conjunction with someone or something** something that happens or is done in conjunction with something else happens or is done at the same time
WORD CLASS **conjunctions** (*grammar*) a

conjunction is a word that links other words or parts of a sentence. For example, the words *and, but* and *or* are conjunctions

conjure VERB **conjures, conjuring, conjured** to conjure is to do magic tricks that seem to make things appear or disappear
• **conjure something up** if something conjures something up, it makes it appear in your mind: *The smell of new hay conjured up a picture of the countryside.*
▶ **conjuror** NOUN **conjurors** someone who does tricks that make things seem to appear or disappear by magic

conker NOUN **conkers** a large brown seed of the horse chestnut tree
▶ **conkers** NOUN a game played with conkers tied to pieces of string. Each player takes a turn to hit the other player's conker until one conker breaks

conman NOUN **conmen** someone who tricks or deceives other people, usually to get money

connect VERB **connects, connecting, connected** to connect things is to join them: *How do you connect the PC to the Internet? • The detective hadn't connected the two events in his mind.*
▶ **connection** NOUN **connections** **1** something that joins two things together **2** a train, bus or plane that you need to catch so that you can continue a journey: *We missed our connection to Dover because the train was late.*
• **in connection with** to do with: *He is wanted by the police in connection with a theft.*

connotation NOUN **connotations** what is suggested by a word as well as its obvious meaning

conquer VERB **conquers, conquering, conquered** **1** to conquer a place is to get control of it by fighting: *Napoleon tried to conquer Egypt.* **2** to conquer a problem or strong feeling is to succeed in controlling it: *She struggled to conquer her shyness.*
▶ **conqueror** NOUN **conquerors** someone who conquers a country
▶ **conquest** NOUN **conquests**

something that is won by great effort or force

conscience NOUN **consciences** your conscience is your sense of right and wrong
▶ **conscientious** ADJECTIVE a conscientious person works hard and carefully to get things right
▶ **conscientiously** ADVERB carefully and diligently

✦ Be careful how you spell this word. Remember it is spelt **con** + the word **science**.

conscious ADJECTIVE **1** you are conscious when you are awake and aware of your surroundings **2** you are conscious of something happening when you are aware of it **3** a conscious act or decision is one that you have thought about
▶ **consciously** ADVERB deliberately or being aware of what you are doing
▶ **consciousness** NOUN the state of being aware of yourself and what is going on around you: *She lost consciousness and woke up in hospital.*

conscript VERB (pronounced kun-**skript**) **conscripts, conscripting, conscripted** to force someone by law to join the armed forces: *The government conscripted young men.*
NOUN (pronounced **kon**-skript) **conscripts** someone who is forced by law to join the armed forces
▶ **conscription** NOUN forcing people to join the armed forces

consecrate VERB **consecrates, consecrating, consecrated** to consecrate something is to have a religious ceremony to make it holy
▶ **consecration** NOUN consecrating something

consecutive ADJECTIVE one after the other: *It snowed on three consecutive days.*

consent VERB **consents, consenting, consented** someone consents to something when they agree to it
NOUN to give consent for something is to allow it

Aa
Bb
Cc
Dd
Ee
Ff
Gg
Hh
Ii
Jj
Kk
Ll
Mm
Nn
Oo
Pp
Qq
Rr
Ss
Tt
Uu
Vv
Ww
Xx
Yy
Zz

consequence NOUN **consequences**
1 a consequence is something that happens as a result of something else: *He did no work and the consequence was that he failed all his exams.* **2** (*formal*) consequence is importance: *It was of no consequence.*
▸ **consequent** ADJECTIVE following as a result
▸ **consequently** ADVERB as a result

conservation NOUN **1** looking after things, such as old buildings, works of art, or the environment, and working to prevent them being damaged or destroyed **2** keeping the same amount
▸ **conservationist** NOUN **conservationists** a conservationist is someone who works to stop things being ruined

conservative ADJECTIVE **1** a conservative person does not like changes or new fashions: *He's a very conservative dresser.* **2** a conservative estimate or guess is cautious and is usually less than the actual amount

conservatory NOUN **conservatories** a room or building which has walls and a roof made of glass

conserve VERB **conserves, conserving, conserved** to conserve things is to keep them from being wasted or lost: *Close the windows to conserve heat.*

consider VERB **considers, considering, considered 1** to consider something is to think about it carefully: *I'll consider your idea.* **2** to consider someone or something as being something is to think of them like that: *I consider him to be a true friend.* **3** to consider other people is to think about what they want or need

considerable ADJECTIVE quite big: *a considerable distance*
▸ **considerably** ADVERB quite a lot: *This test was considerably harder than the last one.*

considerate ADJECTIVE thinking of other people and what they want: *It was considerate of you to help me.*

consideration NOUN **considerations**
1 consideration is thinking carefully about things **2** a consideration is something that you take into account when you are making a decision
• **take something into consideration** to take something into consideration is to think about it while you are making a decision

considering PREPOSITION taking into account: *Considering how clever you are, I think you should have got a better mark.*

consist VERB **consists, consisting, consisted** to be made up of: *a simple meal consisting of a small loaf and cheese*

consistency NOUN **consistencies 1** consistency is being always the same **2** something's consistency is its thickness or firmness: *a sauce with the consistency of cream*
▸ **consistent** ADJECTIVE staying the same all the way through: *Keep the style of your essay consistent.*
▸ **consistently** ADVERB without changing: *He consistently spells the word wrong.*

consolation NOUN **consolations** something that makes a disappointment seem less bad

consolation prize NOUN **consolation prizes** a prize given to someone who has come second in a competition

console[1] (pronounced kon-**soal**) VERB **consoles, consoling, consoled** to console someone is to comfort them

console[2] (pronounced **kon**-soal) NOUN **consoles** a console is a board or box with the controls for a machine arranged on it

consonant NOUN **consonants** a consonant is any letter of the alphabet except *a, e, i, o* or *u*

consort VERB (pronounced kun-**sort**) **consorts, consorting, consorted** (*formal*) to consort with someone that other people do not approve of is to spend time with them
NOUN (pronounced **kon**-sort) **consorts**

the husband of a queen or the wife of a king

conspicuous ADJECTIVE very obvious or easily seen

conspiracy NOUN **conspiracies** a secret plot between several people to commit a crime together

▶ **conspirator** NOUN **conspirators** someone who plots with others to commit a crime

conspire VERB **conspires, conspiring, conspired 1** to conspire is to plot with other people to commit a crime **2** if things conspire against you, they come together to stop you doing something you want to do

constable NOUN **constables** an ordinary police officer

▶ **constabulary** NOUN the constabulary are the police

constant ADJECTIVE **1** never stopping: *constant sunshine* **2** faithful: *His little dog was his constant companion.*

▶ **constancy** NOUN being faithful or never changing or stopping

▶ **constantly** ADVERB all the time: *It rained constantly for a week.*

constellation NOUN **constellations** a large group of stars that you can see in the sky at night

constipated ADJECTIVE someone is constipated when their bowels don't work well and they can't get rid of the waste from their body

▶ **constipation** NOUN being constipated

constituency NOUN **constituencies** a district of the country that has a member of parliament

▶ **constituent** NOUN **constituents 1** something that is a part of a larger thing: *The main constituent of the human body is water.* **2** a voter in a constituency

constitute VERB **constitutes, constituting, constituted** to constitute something is to be or to form it: *Global warming constitutes a risk to the environment.*

constitution NOUN **constitutions 1** a constitution is a set of rules or laws

by which a country or organization is governed **2** your constitution is the health and strength of your body, especially its ability to fight off illness or injury

▶ **constitutional** ADJECTIVE to do with a constitution

constrict VERB **constricts, constricting, constricted** to constrict something is to squeeze it tightly

construct VERB **constructs, constructing, constructed** to construct something is to build it up from several parts: *construct a model*

▶ **construction** NOUN **constructions 1** construction is building **2** a construction is something built up from several parts

▶ **constructive** ADJECTIVE helpful: *a constructive comment*

consul NOUN **consuls** a person who represents his or her country in a foreign country and helps people from his or her own country who are there

▶ **consulate** NOUN **consulates** the office of a consul

consult VERB **consults, consulting, consulted** to consult someone or something is to ask advice or get information from them: *He consulted the road map to find out where he was.*

▶ **consultant** NOUN **consultants 1** someone whose job is to give advice on a subject that they know a lot about **2** a hospital doctor who is an expert in a particular type of illness

▶ **consultation** NOUN **consultations** a meeting with an expert who can give you advice and information

consume VERB **consumes, consuming, consumed 1** to consume something is to use it up **2** to consume food is to eat it **3** to consume something is to destroy it: *The fire consumed the forest.*

▶ **consumer** NOUN **consumers** someone who buys and uses things

▶ **consumption** NOUN consuming or the amount that is consumed: *the world's consumption of oil*

contact VERB **contacts, contacting, contacted 1** to contact someone is to get in touch with them **2** things contact each other when they touch or come together

NOUN **contacts 1** contact is being in touch or touching **2** your contacts are the people you keep in touch with

contact lens NOUN **contact lenses** a thin piece of plastic worn on the front of the eye to help you see better

contagious ADJECTIVE a contagious disease is one that you can catch from other people

contain VERB **contains, containing, contained 1** to contain something is to have it inside: *How much does this bucket contain?* **2** to contain yourself is to hold back your feelings: *She couldn't contain her excitement.*

▶ **container** NOUN **containers** something for putting things in, such as a box or jar

contaminate VERB **contaminates, contaminating, contaminated** to contaminate something clean or pure is to make it dirty or poisonous by putting something in it

▶ **contaminated** ADJECTIVE not clean or pure because something dirty or dangerous has been added

▶ **contamination** NOUN making impure or poisonous

contemplate VERB **contemplates, contemplating, contemplated** to contemplate something is to think about it: *The possibility is just too horrible to contemplate.*

▶ **contemplation** NOUN **contemplations** thinking in a quiet, serious way

▶ **contemplative** ADJECTIVE spending time thinking

contemporary ADJECTIVE **1** belonging to the time now: *contemporary art* **2** if one thing is contemporary with another, they exist at the same time

NOUN **contemporaries** your contemporaries are people who are living at the same time as you

contempt NOUN if you have contempt for someone or something, you have a very low opinion of them

and don't think they deserve any respect

contend VERB **contends, contending, contended** to contend with something is to struggle with it: *He has enough to contend with, studying for all these exams.*

▶ **contender** NOUN **contenders** someone who has entered a competition

▶ **contention** NOUN **contentions** contention is disagreement between people

content¹ (pronounced kon-**tent**) ADJECTIVE to be content is to be happy and satisfied

▶ **contented** ADJECTIVE a contented person is happy and satisfied

▶ **contentment** NOUN being happy with what you have

content² (pronounced **kon**-tent) NOUN **contents** the content or contents of something are the things that it contains

contest NOUN **contests** a competition: *a contest of strength*

▶ **contestant** NOUN **contestants** someone involved in a contest

context NOUN **contexts** the context of a word or sentence is what is said or written before and after it and which makes its meaning clear

continent NOUN **continents** one of the large areas that the Earth's land is divided into. The continents are Africa, Antarctica, North America, South America, Asia, Australia and Europe

• **the Continent** the Continent is a British name for the European mainland: *They always go to the Continent on holiday.*

▶ **continental** ADJECTIVE to do with a continent, especially the European continent seen from the point of view of people living in Britain

continual ADJECTIVE **1** going on without stopping: *the continual noise of traffic* **2** happening again and again: *I'm tired of your continual bad behaviour.*

▶ **continually** ADVERB all the time or again and again: *Matt is continually late for school.*

continue VERB **continues, continuing, continued 1** to continue is to go on in the same way or in the same direction as before **2** to continue with something is to go on with it

▶ **continuity** NOUN being without breaks or stops

▶ **continuous** ADJECTIVE going on without a break or stop: *a continuous line from north to south*

contorted ADJECTIVE twisted in an unnatural way

▶ **contortion** NOUN **contortions** a twist

contour NOUN **contours 1** the contour of something is its shape seen in outline: *a car with sleek contours* **2** a line on a map which links points of the same height and shows the shape of a hill or mountain

contra- PREFIX if a word starts with **contra-**, it adds the meaning 'against' or 'opposite to' to the rest of the word. For example, a *contraflow* is a flow in the opposite direction

contract NOUN (pronounced **kon**-trakt) **contracts** a contract is a written agreement

VERB (prounounced kon-**trakt**) **contracts, contracting, contracted 1** to contract is to get smaller: *As the muscle contracts, your arm is raised.* **2** to contract a disease is to catch it: *People who contracted polio were often left crippled.* **3** to contract someone to do something is to make an agreement with them that they will do the work

▶ **contraction** NOUN contraction is getting smaller or shorter

▶ **contractor** NOUN **contractors** someone who is given a contract to do a particular job: *a building contractor*

contradict VERB **contradicts, contradicting, contradicted** to contradict someone is to say that what they have just said is not correct

▶ **contradiction** NOUN **contradictions** something that makes a statement or fact seem untrue because it shows the opposite

▶ **contradictory** ADJECTIVE a contradictory statement is one that states the opposite of what has just been said

contraflow NOUN **contraflows** a contraflow is when cars going in both directions use one side of a road like a motorway, because repairs are being done

contraption NOUN **contraptions** a contraption is an odd-looking machine or instrument

contrary ADJECTIVE opposite or opposed to each other: *They have contrary views on the subject.*

NOUN

• **on the contrary** you say 'on the contrary' when you want to say that the opposite is true

contrast NOUN (pronounced **kon**-trast) **contrasts** if there is a contrast between things, they are different in some way

VERB (pronounced kon-**trast**) **contrasts, contrasting, contrasted** to contrast one thing with another is to show the differences between them

contribute VERB **contributes, contributing, contributed 1** to contribute money or time is to give it: *We each had to contribute towards Gran's present.* **2** if one thing contributes to another, it is one of its causes: *People driving too close to the car in front contributed to the accident.*

▶ **contribution** NOUN **contributions** something such as money or time that you give towards something

▶ **contributor** NOUN **contributors** someone who makes a contribution

contrive VERB **contrives, contriving, contrived 1** to contrive something is to make it, especially from things that are available: *He'd contrived a sort of ladder out of pieces of wood.* **2** to contrive to do something is to try to do it: *She contrived to hide her disappointment.*

control NOUN **controls 1** control is the power someone has to rule or make decisions **2** if you have control over someone or something, you are able to make them behave in the way you want: *She keeps tight control over her class.*

Aa
Bb
Cc
Dd
Ee
Ff
Gg
Hh
Ii
Jj
Kk
Ll
Mm
Nn
Oo
Pp
Qq
Rr
Ss
Tt
Uu
Vv
Ww
Xx
Yy
Zz

• **in control** to be in control is to be in charge

• **out of control** behaving or working in a way that can't be controlled

VERB **controls, controlling, controlled** **1** to control something is to have power over it or to run it **2** to control yourself is to stay calm and not show your feelings

▶ **controller** NOUN **controllers** a person or thing that controls or directs something

▶ **controls** PLURAL NOUN the controls of a vehicle or other machine are the buttons, levers and pedals that make it go or work

control tower NOUN **control towers** a tall building at an airport where air traffic controllers direct the planes that are taking off and landing

controversial ADJECTIVE if something is controversial, it causes arguments because some people don't agree with it

▶ **controversy** NOUN **controversies** something that causes arguments or discussions because some people agree with it and some people don't

conundrum NOUN **conundrums** a puzzling question or riddle

convalesce VERB **convalesces, convalescing, convalesced** someone who has been ill convalesces when they rest and recover their health

▶ **convalescence** NOUN the time taken by someone to recover their health and strength after an illness

▶ **convalescent** NOUN **convalescents** someone recovering from an illness

convection NOUN (*science*) convection is the spreading of heat through air or water

▶ **convector** NOUN **convectors** a heater that works by convection

convenience NOUN **conveniences** **1** convenience is being easy to use, reach or do, or being suitable: *I like the convenience of living so close to the shops.* • *For everyone's convenience, we will meet after school.* **2** a convenience is something that makes people's lives easy or comfortable: *The hotel has*

every modern convenience. **3** (*formal*) a convenience is a public toilet

• **at your convenience** to do something at your convenience is to do it when it suits you

▶ **convenient** ADJECTIVE handy or suitable: *If it isn't convenient just now, I can call round later.*

▶ **conveniently** ADVERB in a way that is useful or suitable: *The house is conveniently close to the bus stop.*

convent NOUN **convents** a building where a group of nuns lives

convention NOUN **conventions 1** convention, or a convention, is a way of behaving that has become normal because people have been doing it for a long time **2** a convention is a meeting of people, usually to discuss a particular subject

▶ **conventional** ADJECTIVE if something is conventional it is traditional and not at all unusual

▶ **conventionally** ADVERB by custom or tradition

converge VERB **converges, converging, converged** to converge is to come together at a certain point: *The two roads converge just beyond the bridge.*

conversation NOUN **conversations** talk or a talk between people: *He's not very good at making conversation.* • *We had a long conversation about music.*

▶ **conversational** ADJECTIVE to do with conversation: *written in a conversational tone*

converse¹ (pronounced kon-**vers**) VERB **converses, conversing, conversed** (*formal*) when people converse they talk to each other

converse² (pronounced **kon**-vers) NOUN the converse of something is its opposite

▶ **conversely** ADVERB in the opposite way or from the opposite point of view

conversion NOUN conversion is changing from one thing to another

convert VERB (pronounced kon-**vert**) **converts, converting, converted** to convert something is to change it into something else: *Convert this money from pounds into dollars.*

NOUN (pronounced **kon**-vert) **converts** a convert is someone who has changed one set of opinions or beliefs for another set of opinions or beliefs

▶ **convertible** ADJECTIVE able to be changed from one thing to another

convex ADJECTIVE curving outwards or upwards. Look up and compare **concave**

convey VERB **conveys, conveying, conveyed 1** (*formal*) to convey something or someone is to carry or transport them: *A bus conveyed us to school.* **2** to convey a meaning is to pass it on to other people: *What are you trying to convey in this poem?*

conveyor belt NOUN **conveyor belts** a moving surface used to carry things from one place to another, especially in a factory or at a supermarket checkout

convict VERB (pronounced kun-**vikt**) **convicts, convicting, convicted** to convict someone is to say in a court of law that they are guilty of a crime

NOUN (pronounced **kon**-vikt) **convicts** someone who has been found guilty of a crime and sent to prison

▶ **conviction** NOUN **convictions 1** conviction is strong belief **2** a conviction is a decision in a court of law that someone is guilty of a crime: *He's had many convictions for theft.*

convince VERB **convinces, convincing, convinced** to convince someone of something is to make them believe that it is true or real: *Stephanie hoped to convince her parents that she was too ill to go to school.*

▶ **convinced** ADJECTIVE certain that something is true or real: *He's convinced that he saw a ghost.*

convoy NOUN **convoys** a number of ships, lorries or other vehicles travelling along together in a line

convulse VERB **convulses, convulsing, convulsed** to convulse is to twist or shake violently: *We were convulsed with laughter.*

▶ **convulsion** NOUN **convulsions** a sudden jerking, twisting or shaking, especially caused by muscle movements that you can't control

coo NOUN **coos** a soft gentle sound made by a dove or a pigeon

VERB **coos, cooing, cooed** to make this sound

cook VERB **cooks, cooking, cooked 1** to cook food is to heat it by baking, frying, roasting or boiling **2** food cooks when it heats up and becomes ready to eat

NOUN **cooks** a cook is someone who prepares and cooks food

▶ **cooker** NOUN **cookers** a device in kitchens, used for cooking food

▶ **cookery** NOUN the skill or activity of cooking food

cookie NOUN **cookies** a biscuit

cool ADJECTIVE **cooler, coolest**

1 slightly cold: *a cool drink*

2 calm and controlled: *If you find yourself in a dangerous situation, try to stay cool.*

3 not friendly: *He gave a cool reply.*

4 (*informal*) a way of describing someone or something you think is great: *He has a really cool haircut.*

▶ **coolly** ADVERB **1** calmly **2** in an unfriendly way

▶ **coolness** NOUN being cool

coop NOUN **coops** a cage where chickens are kept

VERB **coops, cooping, cooped**

• **cooped up** if you are cooped up somewhere, you are inside or in a small space that you would like to escape from

cooperate VERB **cooperates, cooperating, cooperated 1** people cooperate when they work together to do or achieve something **2** to cooperate with someone is to do what they want you to do

▶ **cooperation** NOUN **1** working with others so that something can be done or achieved **2** doing what someone asks or tells you to do

▶ **cooperative** ADJECTIVE **1** willing to do something someone asks you or tells

Aa
Bb
Cc
Dd
Ee
Ff
Gg
Hh
Ii
Jj
Kk
Ll
Mm
Nn
Oo
Pp
Qq
Rr
Ss
Tt
Uu
Vv
Ww
Xx
Yy
Zz

you to do **2** a cooperative business or organization is one that is managed or owned by everyone who works in it or uses it

coordinate VERB **coordinates, coordinating, coordinated** to coordinate movements or actions is to make them fit in with each other or work smoothly together

▶ **coordinates** PLURAL NOUN two sets of numbers or letters used to show a position on a graph or find a place on a map

▶ **coordination** NOUN **1** the organization of different people or things so that they work together smoothly or well **2** the ability to control your body so that different parts work well together: *hand and eye coordination*

cop¹ VERB **cops, copping, copped**
• **cop out** to cop out of something that is your responsibility is to avoid doing it

cop² NOUN **cops** (*informal*) a police officer

cope VERB **copes, coping, coped** to cope with something is to manage to deal with it: *She said she couldn't cope with any more work.*

copious ADJECTIVE in large quantities: *He made copious notes during the lecture.*

copper NOUN **1** copper is a reddish brown metal **2** a reddish brown colour **3** a coin that is made of copper and which usually has a low value: *He gave the beggar a few coppers.*

copse or **coppice** NOUN **copses** or **coppices** a wood made up of small or low-growing trees

copy VERB **copies, copying, copied**
1 to copy something is to make another thing that looks exactly the same or nearly the same
2 (*ICT*) to copy a piece of information or a file on the computer is to make one that is exactly the same, so you can put it into another place as well
3 to copy something down is to write it down
4 to copy someone is to do the same

thing that they do: *He copies everything his big brother does.*
NOUN **copies 1** a copy is something that has been copied from something else **2** a copy of a book, magazine or newspaper is one of several that have been printed

copy and paste NOUN (*ICT*) to copy something from one file into another, or to copy a whole file into another place

copyright NOUN copyright is the right a person or organization has to copy or publish a book, a piece of music, a film or a video game

coral NOUN a hard material made up of the skeletons of tiny sea creatures
ADJECTIVE made of coral: *a coral island*

cord NOUN **cords 1** cord is thin rope or thick string: *His hands were tied with cord.* **2** a cord is a thin rope: *a window cord* **3** an electric cable or flex

✦ The words **cord** and **chord** sound the same but remember that they have different spellings. A **chord** is a musical sound made of several notes.

cordial ADJECTIVE polite and friendly in a formal way: *Their discussions were perfectly cordial.*
NOUN **cordials** a fruit juice that you drink diluted with water: *lime cordial*

cordon NOUN **cordons** a line of police, soldiers or guards around an area to keep people back

corduroy NOUN a cotton cloth with rows of soft velvety ridges on the outer surface

core NOUN **cores** the inner part of something, such as a fruit or the earth
VERB **cores, coring, cored** to core an apple is to take out the inner part that you don't normally eat

corgi NOUN **corgis** a breed of dog with short legs and upright ears

cork NOUN **corks 1** a light substance that floats, which comes from the bark of a type of oak tree **2** a piece of this used as a stopper for a bottle

corkscrew NOUN **corkscrews** a device with a twisted metal spike used to pull corks from wine bottles

cormorant NOUN **cormorants** a type of large black sea bird with a long curved beak

corn[1] NOUN **1** wheat or a similar crop **2** maize

corn[2] NOUN **corns** a sore hard lump on your toe caused by your shoe rubbing the skin

cornea NOUN **corneas** the see-through covering at the front of your eyeball

corned beef NOUN beef that has been salted and packed into tins

corner NOUN **corners 1** a point where two roads, walls, edges or lines meet: *I'll meet you at the corner of George Street and Alexander Road.* **2** a place away from the main part or far away: *a secluded corner in the garden* • *travelling to the far corners of the world* **3** in soccer and hockey, a kick or hit that you take from one of the corners at the opposing team's end of the pitch

VERB **corners, cornering, cornered** to force a person or animal into a position from which they can't escape

cornet NOUN **cornets 1** a musical instrument that looks like a small trumpet **2** a cone-shaped wafer that you put ice cream in

cornflour NOUN a white powder made from ground maize and used in cooking, for example to thicken sauces

cornflower NOUN **cornflowers** a plant with bright blue flowers that grows wild in fields

corny ADJECTIVE **cornier, corniest 1** corny jokes or phrases are silly, weak, or have been heard many times before **2** having too much emotion so it doesn't sound sincere: *a corny love song*

corona NOUN **coronas** the sun's corona is the spiky circle of light shaped rather like a crown that you see when the moon passes in front of the sun

coronation NOUN **coronations** the crowning of a king, queen or emperor

coronet NOUN **coronets** a small crown, especially one worn by a duke

corporal[1] NOUN **corporals** a soldier with a rank between private and sergeant

corporal[2] ADJECTIVE to do with the body

corporal punishment NOUN punishment that involves hitting someone

corporation NOUN **corporations** a corporation is a large business or a group of businesses

corps (pronounced **koar**) NOUN **corps** a division of the army, especially one that does a special job: *the Army Medical Corps*

corpse NOUN **corpses** a dead body

corral (pronounced **ko-ral**) NOUN **corrals** an enclosure where animals such as cattle and horses are kept, especially in the USA

correct ADJECTIVE **1** right, not wrong: *The correct answer is 15.* **2** correct behaviour is the sort of behaviour that people find acceptable

VERB **corrects, correcting, corrected 1** to correct something is to mark or change any mistakes or faults in it: *The teacher corrects our homework books.* **2** to correct someone is to tell them that what they have said or done is wrong

▶ **correction** NOUN **corrections 1** a correction is a mark or change made to correct a mistake **2** correction is checking and altering something to make it better or more accurate: *Hand in your exercise books for correction.*

correspond VERB **corresponds, corresponding, corresponded 1** if two things correspond, they are the same **2** people correspond when they write to each other

▶ **correspondence** NOUN **1** letters **2** likeness or similarity: *There was no correspondence between their two stories.*

▶ **correspondent** NOUN **correspondents** a journalist who writes news reports about a particular subject: *a war correspondent*

corridor NOUN **corridors** a corridor is a passageway in a building or train

corrie NOUN **corries** (*geography*) a large bowl-shaped hollow high on a mountain and sometimes filled with water

Aa
Bb
Cc
Dd
Ee
Ff
Gg
Hh
Ii
Jj
Kk
Ll
Mm
Nn
Oo
Pp
Qq
Rr
Ss
Tt
Uu
Vv
Ww
Xx
Yy
Zz

Aa
Bb
Cc
Dd
Ee
Ff
Gg
Hh
Ii
Jj
Kk
Ll
Mm
Nn
Oo
Pp
Qq
Rr
Ss
Tt
Uu
Vv
Ww
Xx
Yy
Zz

corrode VERB **corrodes, corroding, corroded** metal corrodes when it rusts or is eaten away by a chemical
▶ **corrosion** NOUN corroding
▶ **corrosive** ADJECTIVE able to destroy or wear away metal: *a corrosive acid*

corrugated ADJECTIVE folded or shaped into a series of ridges: *a corrugated iron roof*

corrupt VERB **corrupts, corrupting, corrupted** to corrupt someone is to make them dishonest or evil
ADJECTIVE someone who is corrupt behaves dishonestly, usually by taking bribes
▶ **corruption** NOUN dishonest behaviour, especially when people in important jobs take bribes: *accusations of widespread corruption in the government*

corset NOUN **corsets** a stiff garment that fits tightly around the middle part of the body and is worn under other clothes to support your back or give your body a better shape

cosh NOUN **coshes** a short heavy stick used for hitting people

cosmetic NOUN **cosmetics** cosmetics are things like lipstick, powder and face cream that people use to improve their looks

cosmic ADJECTIVE to do with the universe and outer space

cosmonaut NOUN **cosmonauts** a Russian astronaut

cosmopolitan ADJECTIVE including people or ideas from many parts of the world: *cosmopolitan cities like London and New York*

cosmos NOUN the cosmos is the universe

cost VERB **costs, costing, cost 1** if something costs a certain amount of money, that is the amount you have to pay for it: *How much does a litre of milk cost?* **2** to cost someone something is to make them lose that thing: *His heroism cost him his life.*
NOUN **costs 1** the cost of something is the amount of money that has to be spent to buy it or make it **2** the cost of

something is what has to be suffered to do it or get it
● **at all costs** no matter what cost or suffering may be involved
▶ **costly** ADVERB **costlier, costliest** costing a lot: *a costly item of jewellery*

costume NOUN **costumes 1** a special set of clothes worn by an actor in a play or film **2** the clothes worn by the people of a particular country or in a particular period of history: *The children were dressed in national costume for the parade.* **3** fancy dress

cosy ADJECTIVE **cosier, cosiest** warm and comfortable: *a cosy little bedroom* ● *I'm nice and cosy sitting here by the fire.*

cot NOUN **cots** a bed with high sides for a baby or young child to sleep in

✦ This word comes from the Hindi language of India. It comes from the word **khat**, which means *bedstead*.

cot death NOUN **cot deaths** the death of a baby while it is asleep in its cot

cottage NOUN **cottages** a small house in the country or in a village

cotton NOUN a type of cloth made from the fibres inside the seeds of a plant, that is grown in warm climates

cotton wool NOUN a mass of soft loose fibres of cotton used to clean wounds or take off make-up

couch NOUN **couches** a sofa

couch potato NOUN **couch potatoes** a person who is not active enough, especially someone who sits watching TV a lot

cough VERB **coughs, coughing, coughed** you cough when you make a loud rough sound in your throat as you force air out of your lungs
NOUN **coughs 1** the noise you make when you cough **2** an illness that causes you to cough

could VERB **1** you use **could** with another verb to say that something is or might be possible, or to ask politely if something is possible: *He could do it if he tried hard enough.* ● *Could I have a drink of water, please?* **2 could** is the past tense form of the verb **can**: *He could run fast when he was young.*

couldn't a short way to say and write **could not**

council NOUN **councils** a group of people who are elected to discuss and manage the affairs of a town or city

▸ **councillor** NOUN **councillors** someone elected to a town or city council

✦ The words **councillor** and **counsellor** sound the same but remember that they have ifferent spellings. A **counsellor** gives advice, or **counsel**.

counsel VERB **counsels, counselling, counselled** to counsel someone is to give them advice

NOUN **counsels** 1 advice 2 a lawyer who presents evidence at a trial: *the counsel for the defence*

▸ **counsellor** NOUN **counsellors** someone whose job is to give advice

count¹ VERB **counts, counting, counted** 1 to count is to say numbers in order: *Can you count backwards from 10?* 2 to count something or to count something up is to work out the total: *He was busy counting his money.* 3 if something counts, it is important or has value: *Every school day counts.*

• **count on someone or something** if you can count on someone or something, you can rely on them

NOUN **counts** a count is a number of things to be counted: *The teacher did a head count before we left.*

• **keep count** to keep count is to know how many things there are or have been

• **lose count** to lose count is to forget how many you have already counted

count² NOUN **counts** a nobleman in certain countries

countdown NOUN a countdown is counting backwards to the exact time when a spacecraft or rocket will be launched

counter- PREFIX if **counter-** is put at the beginning of a word, it adds the meaning 'opposite' to the rest of the word. For example, in American English, *counterclockwise* means going round in the opposite direction to clockwise

counter¹ VERB **counters, countering, countered** to counter something is to respond to it by fighting back or saying or doing the opposite

ADVERB against or in the opposite direction: *Counter to our advice, he wants to be a racing driver.*

counter² NOUN **counters** 1 a table or surface across which customers are served, for example in a shop, a bank or a café 2 a small plastic or metal disc used in some board games

counterattack NOUN **counterattacks** a counterattack is an attack made against an enemy who has attacked first

counterfeit ADJECTIVE not real or genuine: *a counterfeit stamp*

NOUN **counterfeits** a counterfeit is a copy made to look like the real thing

counterpart NOUN **counterparts** someone's counterpart is a person who has a similar job in a different place: *The British Prime Minister will be meeting his European counterparts.*

countess NOUN **countesses** 1 a woman with the same rank as a count or earl 2 the wife of a count

countless ADJECTIVE too many to count: *I've done this countless times.*

country NOUN **countries** 1 a nation or one of the areas of the world controlled by its own government 2 the land where certain people or animals live: *This is grizzly bear country.* 3 an area: *the West Country* 4 the country is the parts of the land away from towns and cities: *They live in the country.*

countryman or **countrywoman** NOUN **countrymen** or **countrywomen** 1 a man or woman who lives and works in the countryside 2 your countrymen are people who come from the same country as you do

countryside NOUN the countryside is land away from towns and cities

county NOUN **counties** a county is one of the areas that some countries or states are divided into, which each have their own local government

coup (pronounced **koo**) NOUN **coups** a sudden change of government in which new people take power without an election being held

couple NOUN **couples 1** two or approximately two: *I hadn't seen him for a couple of months.* **2** a husband and wife or two people who have a similar close relationship: *an elderly couple* VERB **couples, coupling, coupled** to couple things is to join one to the other

coupon NOUN **coupons** a coupon is a piece of paper that you can use to claim a free gift or get money off something

courage NOUN courage is the quality some people have that allows them to do dangerous or frightening things
▶ **courageous** ADJECTIVE brave

courgette (pronounced koor-**jet**) NOUN **courgettes** a type of vegetable that looks like a small cucumber

courier NOUN **couriers** someone who carries messages or packages from one place to another
VERB **couriers, couriering, couriered** to courier something is to send it using a courier

course NOUN **courses**
1 a number of lessons on a particular subject: *a French course*
2 a course of treatment is medical treatment given in stages or over a period of time
3 a course is the ground that a race is run over or a game is played on: *a racecourse* • *a golf course*
4 one of the parts of a meal: *We had soup for the first course.*
5 the route or direction that something moves or travels along: *following the river's course for several miles*
• **in due course** after a while or at its proper time
• **in the course of** during
• **of course** you say 'of course' when you want to agree to a request someone has made in a polite way or when you want to show that something was

expected: *'Can I borrow that book for a few days?' 'Of course you can.'* • We went on holiday and of course it rained the whole time.

✦ The words **course** and **coarse** sound the same, but remember that they have different spellings. **Coarse** means rough.

court NOUN **courts 1** a building or room where trials are held, or where judges make decisions on matters to do with the law. This is also called a **lawcourt** **2** the place where a king or queen and the people who attend to them have their official home **3** an area marked out with lines where a game, such as tennis, basketball or squash, is played
VERB **courts, courting, courted** to court someone is to try to win their love or friendship

courteous (pronounced **ker**-tee-us) ADJECTIVE polite and respectful towards other people
▶ **courtesy** NOUN **courtesies 1** courtesy is polite behaviour towards other people **2** a courtesy is a polite action

courtier NOUN **courtiers** someone who attends a king or queen at their official home

court-martial NOUN **court-martials** or **courts-martial** a military trial
VERB **court-martials, court-martialling, court-martialled** to court-martial someone in the armed forces is to put them on trial for breaking military law

courtyard NOUN **courtyards** an open area inside a building surrounded on all sides by walls

cousin NOUN **cousins** the son or daughter of your aunt or uncle

cove NOUN **coves** a small bay on the sea coast

coven NOUN **covens** a group of witches

covenant NOUN **covenants** a solemn agreement that people make to do or not to do something

cover VERB **covers, covering, covered**
1 to cover something or cover something

up is to put or spread something else on or over it so that it is hidden : *She'd covered the table with a clean cloth.* **2** to cover a distance or period of time is to travel over that distance or stretch over that period of time: *We covered ten miles in three hours.* • *The history book covers the whole of Queen Victoria's reign.* **3** to cover something is to deal with it: *The local newspaper covered the story.* • *We'll need some cash to cover our expenses.*

• **cover something up** to cover something up is to stop people from discovering the truth about it: *His actions since then had been merely to cover up the crime.*

NOUN **covers** something that covers, hides or protects something else: *a bed cover*

▶ **coverage** NOUN coverage is the amount of space or time given to an item of news in a newspaper or on a TV or radio programme

covert ADJECTIVE covert actions are done in secret

covet VERB **covets, coveting, coveted** to covet something is to want it for yourself

cow NOUN **cows 1** a large animal kept on farms for its milk: *a dairy cow* **2** a female animal of the ox family or a female elephant or whale

coward NOUN **cowards** someone who lacks courage

▶ **cowardice** NOUN a lack of courage
▶ **cowardly** ADJECTIVE behaving like a coward

cowboy NOUN **cowboys** a man who herds cattle while on horseback, especially in the western United States

cowed ADJECTIVE behaving in a timid way

cower VERB **cowers, cowering, cowered** to bend low and move back because you are frightened

cox NOUN **coxes** the cox of a rowing boat or a lifeboat is the person whose job it is to steer. Cox is a shortened form of **coxswain**

VERB **coxes, coxing, coxed** to cox a boat is to steer it

coxswain (pronounced **kok**-sun) NOUN **coxswains 1** someone who steers a boat **2** someone who is in charge of the crew on a ship

coy ADJECTIVE **coyer, coyest** pretending to be shy: *a coy smile*

coyote NOUN **coyotes** a type of wild dog that lives in North America

crab NOUN **crabs** a sea animal with a broad shell and five pairs of legs. A crab has claws on its front pair of legs

crab apple NOUN **crab apples** a type of small bitter apple that grows wild

crack NOUN **cracks 1** a narrow break or split **2** a sudden sharp sound: *the crack of a whip*

• **have a crack at something** to try to do something

VERB **cracks, cracking, cracked 1** to crack is to split or break so that a small gap appears: *The ice had started to crack.* **2** to crack something is to split or break it so that a small gap appears: *She cracked an egg.* **3** to crack a joke is to make a joke

▶ **cracker** NOUN **crackers** a Christmas toy made of a paper tube, which two people pull and which makes a bang or crack when it comes apart

crackle VERB **crackles, crackling, crackled** to make a series of short cracking noises: *Thunder roared and lightning crackled.*

NOUN short cracking noises: *the crackle of twigs underfoot*

cradle NOUN **cradles** a baby's bed, especially one that can be rocked from side to side

VERB **cradles, cradling, cradled** to cradle something is to hold it gently: *She cradled his head in her arms.*

craft NOUN **crafts 1** a skill, like pottery or wood carving, in which you make something with your hands **2** a boat, ship, aeroplane or spaceship

craftsman or **craftswoman** NOUN **craftsmen** or **craftswomen** someone who is skilled at making things with their hands

crafty ADJECTIVE **craftier, craftiest** a crafty person is clever at getting things

Aa
Bb
Cc
Dd
Ee
Ff
Gg
Hh
Ii
Jj
Kk
Ll
Mm
Nn
Oo
Pp
Qq
Rr
Ss
Tt
Uu
Vv
Ww
Xx
Yy
Zz

done in the way they want, often by tricking or deceiving people

▸ **craftily** ADVERB in a clever way that gets you what you want

▸ **craftiness** NOUN cleverness at getting what you want

crag NOUN **crags** a high steep rock or rough mass of rocks

▸ **craggy** ADJECTIVE **craggier, craggiest 1** steep and rough: *a great craggy mountain* **2** someone with craggy features has lots of lines on their face

cram VERB **crams, cramming, crammed 1** to cram things somewhere is to push or force them into a space that is too small: *Elizabeth tried to cram even more crisps into her mouth.* **2** if a place or container is crammed with things, it is filled very full: *All the shelves were crammed with books of every size.* **3** to cram for an exam is to learn as much as possible in the short time before you have to sit the exam

cramp NOUN **cramps 1** cramp is pain somewhere in your body caused when a muscle suddenly tightens **2** cramps are pains in a muscle or muscles, especially in your stomach

VERB **cramps, cramping, cramped** muscles cramp when they tighten up suddenly causing pain

▸ **cramped** ADJECTIVE a cramped space is uncomfortable because it is too small to move about in or because it is crowded with people or things

cranberry NOUN **cranberries** cranberries are small red fruits with a sour taste, used to make sauces and drinks

crane NOUN **cranes 1** a tall machine used to lift heavy weights, such as pieces of cargo that have to be taken off a ship **2** a type of large bird with a long neck and long thin legs

VERB **cranes, craning, craned** if you crane your neck, you stretch your neck as far as possible so that you can get a better view of something

crane fly NOUN **crane flies** an insect with a thin body and very long legs.

Another name for a crane fly is a **daddy-long-legs**

crank NOUN **cranks 1** a crank is a lever that you turn to make an engine or a piece of machinery move or work **2** a crank is someone who has strange ideas or behaves in an odd way

VERB **cranks, cranking, cranked** to crank an engine or a piece of machinery, or to crank it up, is to turn a lever over and over again to make it move or work

▸ **cranky** ADJECTIVE **crankier, crankiest 1** a cranky person has strange ideas or behaves in an odd way **2** if someone is cranky they are bad-tempered

cranny NOUN **crannies** a narrow opening or crack, especially in a room or rock

crash NOUN **crashes 1** a loud noise, especially one made when something hard hits another hard thing causing damage **2** a car crash is an accident in which a car hits something else **3** a computer crash is when a computer suddenly stops working properly while you are using it, for example because it can't process the information

VERB **crashes, crashing, crashed 1** to crash is to make a loud noise **2** to crash is to be involved in a car crash **3** if a computer crashes it suddenly stops working properly while you are using it, for example because it can't process the information

crash helmet NOUN **crash helmets** a hard helmet worn by motorcyclists or racing drivers to protect their head

crash-land VERB **crash-lands, crash-landing, crash-landed** if an aeroplane crash-lands it hits the ground hard, either because it is out of control or because the pilot has to land in an emergency

crate NOUN **crates** a wooden or plastic box used for carrying things, especially breakable things like bottles

crater NOUN **craters 1** a bowl-shaped hole in the ground where a bomb has exploded or a meteor has landed **2** a bowl-shaped hollow at the top of a volcano where it has erupted

crave VERB **craves, craving, craved** to crave something is to want it very much

▶ **craving** NOUN **cravings** if you have a craving for something, you have a strong urge to have it

crawl VERB **crawls, crawling, crawled 1** if a person crawls, they move forwards on their hands and knees: *Pat had to crawl under the desk to get the pen she'd dropped.* **2** insects or reptiles crawl when they move about on their legs: *Look! There's a spider crawling up the wall behind you.* **3** to move at a very slow pace: *The traffic was crawling along at about 2 miles an hour.*
NOUN **1** a very slow pace: *We were moving forward at a crawl.* **2** the crawl is a way of swimming where you kick your legs and swing first one arm and then the other into the water ahead of you

crayon NOUN **crayons** a stick of coloured wax or a coloured pencil for drawing with

craze NOUN **crazes** a fashion or pastime that is very popular for a short time

crazy ADJECTIVE **crazier, craziest 1** mad: *a crazy idea • I think he's gone crazy.* **2** if you are crazy about someone or something, you love them or like them very much

creak VERB **creaks, creaking, creaked** if something creaks, it makes a squeaking or grating noise: *The floorboards creaked as he tried to tiptoe along the corridor.*
NOUN **creaks** a squeaking or grating noise
▶ **creaky** ADJECTIVE **creakier, creakiest** something that is creaky makes squeaking or grating noises: *a creaky old bed*

cream NOUN **creams 1** a thick yellowish-white liquid that is separated from milk **2** a yellowish-white colour **3** a thick liquid that you put on your skin or hair: *suntan cream*
▶ **creamy** ADJECTIVE **creamier, creamiest** containing cream or thick like cream: *creamy milk*

crease NOUN **creases 1** a wrinkle, line or fold made by bending or crushing fabric or paper: *Always fold your trousers along the creases before you*

hang them up. **2** in cricket, a crease is one of the lines where either the batsman or the bowler should stand
VERB **creases, creasing, creased 1** material that creases will crush easily so that lines or wrinkles form in it **2** to crease material is to press it or bend it into lines or folds

create VERB **creates, creating, created** to create something is to make it or invent it, or to make it happen or exist: *They created a big fuss until they got what they wanted.*
▶ **creation** NOUN **creations 1** the creation of something is making it: *the creation of the universe* **2** a creation is something new that has been made: *one of the designer's latest creations*
▶ **creative** ADJECTIVE a creative person has the skill and imagination to make new things, especially works of art
▶ **creativity** NOUN creativity is the talent or imagination to make or invent things
▶ **creator** NOUN **creators** someone who makes something new

creature NOUN **creatures** a living thing that is able to move about. Animals are creatures, but plants are not

crèche (pronounced **kresh**) NOUN **crèches** a place where young children are looked after while their parents are elsewhere

credible ADJECTIVE if someone or something is credible, you can believe them: *a credible explanation*

credit NOUN **credits 1** if people give you credit for something good, they give you praise or approval because of it **2** credit is a system used in shops and businesses where customers can get things now and pay for them later **3** your bank account is in credit when you have money in it
VERB **credits, crediting, credited 1** to credit someone with an achievement or a good quality is to say that they have done it or have it **2** to credit something is to believe it: *You wouldn't credit how many times we had to go back over the same thing.*

Aa Bb **Cc** Dd Ee Ff Gg Hh Ii Jj Kk Ll Mm Nn Oo Pp Qq Rr Ss Tt Uu Vv Ww Xx Yy Zz

credit card ➜ crick

▶ **creditable** ADJECTIVE good enough to deserve praise or respect: *a very creditable performance*

credit card NOUN **credit cards** a small plastic card that allows you to buy things when you want them and to pay for them later

creed NOUN **creeds** something that you believe in, especially the religious beliefs that you have

creek NOUN **creeks** a short or narrow river, especially one that flows into the sea or a lake

creep VERB **creeps, creeping, crept 1** to move somewhere slowly and quietly: *He crept downstairs in the middle of the night.* **2** animals that creep move slowly with their bodies close to the ground

NOUN **creeps** someone who is unpleasant or weird

• **give someone the creeps** if someone or something gives you the creeps, they make you shiver with disgust or fear

▶ **creeper** NOUN **creepers** a plant that grows over the ground or up a wall

▶ **creepy** ADJECTIVE **creepier, creepiest** a creepy place or person makes you shiver with fear or disgust

cremate VERB **cremates, cremating, cremated** to cremate a dead person is to burn their body rather than bury it

▶ **cremation** NOUN **cremations** the burning of a dead body or dead bodies

crematorium NOUN **crematoriums** or **crematoria** a building where dead people's bodies are burned

crêpe NOUN **1** a thin fabric with a wrinkled surface: *a crêpe bandage* **2** a type of very thin wrinkled paper used for decoration or for wrapping things in

crept VERB a way of changing the verb **creep** to make a past tense. It can be used with or without a helping verb: *We had crept in unnoticed.* • *They crept up on him and said 'Boo!'.*

crescendo (pronounced kri-**shen**-doh) NOUN **crescendos 1** a sound that gets louder and louder **2** (*music*) a place in

a piece of music where the music gets gradually louder

crescent NOUN **crescents** a curved shape, which comes to a point at each end and is wider in the middle, like the shape of the moon at certain times of the month

✦The word **crescent** comes from the Latin word **crescere**, which means *to grow*. This is because the moon is in a crescent shape when it is growing into a full moon.
The word **increase**, which means to grow bigger, is also linked to the word **crescere**.

cress NOUN a small green plant with peppery-tasting leaves which are used in salads and sandwiches

crest NOUN **crests 1** the crest of a wave or hill is its highest point **2** the feathers that stick up on the top of some birds' heads **3** a family's or organization's badge or emblem

crestfallen ADJECTIVE if someone is crestfallen, they look sad and disappointed because something they had hoped for or had being trying to do has not turned out well

crevasse NOUN **crevasses** a deep crack in ice

crevice NOUN **crevices** a thin crack or opening in rock

crew[1] NOUN **crews** a group of people who work together, especially on a ship or aeroplane: *The lifeboat has a crew of five.* • *The film crew were busy setting up lights and cameras.*

VERB **crews, crewing, crewed** to crew a boat or ship is to work as a member of its crew

crew[2] VERB a way of changing the verb **crow** to make a past tense: *The cock crew.*

crib NOUN **cribs** a small cot for a baby
VERB **cribs, cribbing, cribbed** to crib is to copy someone else's work and pretend it is your own

crick NOUN **cricks** if you have a crick in your neck, your neck feels stiff and painful because the muscles have tightened up

cricket¹ NOUN a game played outdoors between two sides of eleven players with a wooden bat and ball
▶ **cricketer** NOUN **cricketers** someone who plays cricket

cricket² NOUN **crickets** a small insect that lives in grass. A cricket makes a high-pitched whirring sound by rubbing its wings together

cried VERB a way of changing the verb **cry** to make a past tense. It can be used with or without a helping verb: *The baby cried and cried.* • *He had cried all day.*

cries NOUN the plural of the noun **cry**: *No one heard their cries for help.*
VERB the form of the verb **cry** in the present tense that you use with **he, she** or **it**: *She always cries when she watches sad films.*

crime NOUN **crimes 1** a crime is an illegal activity, such as robbery, murder, assault or dangerous driving. Someone who has committed a crime can be punished by law **2** crime is all these activities
▶ **criminal** NOUN **criminals** someone who has committed a crime ADJECTIVE **1** to do with crime or criminals: *a criminal court* **2** against the law or very wrong: *a criminal act*

crimson NOUN a bright red colour

cringe VERB **cringes, cringing, cringed 1** to cringe is to crouch or back away from something in fear: *The dog cringed and showed its teeth.* **2** if something you or someone else has done makes you cringe, it makes you feel very embarrassed

crinkle NOUN **crinkles** a small crease or wrinkle
VERB **crinkles, crinkling, crinkled** to crinkle something is to form small creases or wrinkles in it
▶ **crinkly** ADJECTIVE **crinklier, crinkliest** having lots of small creases or wrinkles

cripple VERB **cripples, crippling, crippled 1** an injury or disease cripples someone if it causes damage to their body, or part of their body, which stops them moving about normally **2** to

cripple something is to damage it so that it cannot function properly
▶ **crippled** ADJECTIVE **1** unable to move about normally: *a crippled bird with a broken wing* **2** so badly damaged it cannot work normally: *The crippled warship limped back into port.*

crisis NOUN **crises** a very difficult or dangerous time or event that causes suffering or worry

crisp ADJECTIVE **crisper, crispest 1** stiff or hard and easily broken: *nice crisp salad leaves* **2** crisp weather is frosty and dry
NOUN **crisps** a thin slice of potato that has been fried in oil until it is crisp: *a bag of crisps*
▶ **crispness** NOUN being crisp
▶ **crispy** ADJECTIVE **crispier, crispiest** hard or firm enough to break easily: *a crispy sugar topping*

criss-cross VERB **criss-crosses, criss-crossing, criss-crossed** things criss-cross when they cross each other again and again to form a pattern of crossed lines

critic NOUN **critics 1** someone who thinks there are faults in something: *a critic of the government* **2** someone who writes about new books, films, music or shows and says what is good or bad about them
▶ **critical** ADJECTIVE to be critical of something is to say what you think its faults are

criticize or **criticise** VERB **criticizes, criticizing, criticized** to criticize something is to say what you think its faults are: *It always hurts when you criticize me.*
▶ **criticism** NOUN **criticisms 1** criticism is pointing out faults: *Try not to be hurt by criticism.* **2** a criticism is a statement about a fault you think someone or something has: *My only criticism is the story is too long.*

croak VERB **croaks, croaking, croaked 1** to croak is to speak in a hoarse voice because your throat is sore or dry **2** a frog croaks when it makes its deep harsh sound
NOUN **croaks 1** the sound made by a frog or toad **2** a low hoarse voice

Aa
Bb
Cc
Dd
Ee
Ff
Gg
Hh
Ii
Jj
Kk
Ll
Mm
Nn
Oo
Pp
Qq
Rr
Ss
Tt
Uu
Vv
Ww
Xx
Yy
Zz

crochet → crossbow

► croaky ADJECTIVE **croakier, croakiest** a croaky voice is deep and hoarse

crochet (pronounced **kroh**-shay) NOUN crochet is a type of knitting in which stitches are made by twisting thread or wool around a single needle VERB **crochets, crocheting, crocheted** to crochet is to make something out of wool or thread using a single needle to make the stitches

crock NOUN **crocks 1** a pot or jar made out of clay **2** a crock is an old broken-down person or machine

crockery NOUN crockery is plates, bowls and cups used for eating food

crocodile NOUN **crocodiles** a large reptile with thick skin, a long tail and big jaws. Crocodiles are found mainly in Africa and Australia and live in rivers and lakes

crocodile tears PLURAL NOUN sorrow that is not sincere

crocus NOUN **crocuses** a small plant that grows from a bulb and has white, purple or yellow flowers that come out in the spring

croft NOUN **crofts** a small farm in the Scottish Highlands with a cottage and a small amount of land

► crofter NOUN **crofters** someone who lives and works on a croft

crook NOUN **crooks 1** a stick carried by a shepherd, which has a curved top that the shepherd uses for catching sheep by their necks **2** the crook of your arm or leg is the part at the inside of your elbow or the back of your knee that curves inwards **3** a crook is a criminal or someone who behaves dishonestly VERB **crooks, crooking, crooked** to crook something is to bend it or form it into a curve: *He crooked one eyebrow and looked at me.*

► crooked (pronounced **krook**-id) ADJECTIVE bent or forming a curve

croon VERB **croons, crooning, crooned** to croon is to sing in a low loving voice

crop NOUN **crops 1** crops are plants that are gathered or harvested for food from fields, trees or bushes **2** a crop is a particular kind of plant or fruit that

grows and is harvested at one time: *We'll get a good crop of apples this year.* **3** a riding crop is a short whip used by jockeys and horse riders VERB **crops, cropping, cropped** to crop something is to cut it short

• crop up when something crops up, it happens without being expected or planned

croquet (pronounced **kroh**-kay) NOUN a game played on a lawn with wooden balls that the players hit through metal hoops using long wooden hammers called mallets

cross NOUN **crosses 1** a shape made when two straight lines go over each other at a point in the middle, ✖ or + **2** a symbol used in the Christian religion to stand for the cross on which Christ was crucified **3** a mixture of two things, especially an animal or plant that has been bred from two different animals or plants: *A mule is a cross between a donkey and a horse.* VERB **crosses, crossing, crossed 1** to cross something is to go over it from one side to the other: *cross a bridge* **2** if one thing crosses another, they meet at a certain point and go on beyond it: *at the place where the road crosses the railway line* **3** to cross things is to put one across and on top of the other: *cross your fingers*

• cross something out to cross something out is to draw a line or lines through it because you want to get rid of it or to replace it with something else: *He crossed out John's name and wrote in his own.* ADJECTIVE **crosser, crossest** annoyed or angry: *I got very cross when he didn't turn up.*

► crossly ADVERB angrily

crossbar NOUN **crossbars 1** the crossbar on a man's bike is the horizontal piece of metal between the saddle and the handlebars **2** the crossbar on a goal is the horizontal piece of wood between the uprights

crossbow NOUN **crossbows** a weapon for shooting arrows with a bow string stretched horizontally on a cross-shaped frame

cross-country ADJECTIVE a cross-country race is one where the runners go across the countryside rather than along a road or track

cross-examine VERB **cross-examines, cross-examining, cross-examined** to cross-examine someone is to ask them questions so that their answers can be compared with answers they had given earlier

▶ **cross-examination** NOUN **cross-examinations** a series of questions asked to check whether earlier answers are the same

cross-eyed ADJECTIVE a cross-eyed person has eyes that look towards their nose instead of straight ahead

crossfire NOUN crossfire is gunfire coming from different directions

crossing NOUN **crossings 1** a place where a road or river can be crossed **2** a journey made by a ship between two pieces of land: *a short ferry crossing from Mull to Iona*

crossroads NOUN a place where two or more roads meet

cross-section NOUN **cross-sections 1** a cut made through a solid object so that you can see the structure inside, or a picture of this **2** a cross-section of a group of people or things is a sample that includes all the different types of people or things: *a cross-section of the public*

crossword NOUN **crosswords** a word game where you fill in words or letters on a grid by solving clues

crotchet NOUN **crotchets** (*music*) a musical note equal to a quarter of a semibreve. The symbol for a crotchet is ♩

crouch VERB **crouches, crouching, crouched** you crouch when you bend your legs and back so that your body is close to the ground

crow's-nest NOUN **crow's nests** the place at the top of a ship's mast where a sailor goes to get a view of things far away

crow[1] NOUN **crows** a large black bird that makes a loud harsh sound

crow[2] VERB **crows, crowing, crowed** or **crew 1** when a cock crows it makes a loud sound, especially early in the morning **2** to talk in a boastful way: *He was crowing about his success.*

crowbar NOUN **crowbars** a heavy metal bar curved at one end that is used as a lever

crowd NOUN **crowds** a large number of people or things gathered in one place: *a football crowd • crowds of shoppers*

VERB **crowds, crowding, crowded** if people or things crowd in or into a place, they fill it up so that there is hardly any space left

▶ **crowded** ADJECTIVE full of people or things: *a crowded street*

crown NOUN **crowns 1** an ornament, often made of gold and studded with jewels, worn by a king or queen on their head during formal occasions **2** the top of something, such as your head or a hill

VERB **crowns, crowning, crowned 1** a king or queen is crowned when they are made the monarch of a country in a ceremony where a crown is put on their head **2** to crown something is to add something on top: *We had a very long tiring journey, and to crown it all, our luggage was lost at the airport.*

crucial ADJECTIVE extremely important: *a crucial exam*

crucify VERB **crucifies, crucifying, crucified** to crucify someone is to nail their hands and feet to a large wooden cross and leave them to die

▶ **crucifixion** NOUN **crucifixions** nailing someone's hands and feet to a large wooden cross and leaving them to die. Crucifixion was often used as a punishment by the ancient Romans and Christ was killed in this way

crude ADJECTIVE **cruder, crudest 1** made or done in a rough or simple way: *a crude map drawn on the back of an envelope* **2** crude oil is as it was when it came out of the ground. It has not been refined **3** rude or vulgar: *a crude joke*

▶ **crudely** ADVERB **1** roughly or simply: *a crudely made table* **2** in a rude or vulgar way

Aa
Bb
Cc
Dd
Ee
Ff
Gg
Hh
Ii
Jj
Kk
Ll
Mm
Nn
Oo
Pp
Qq
Rr
Ss
Tt
Uu
Vv
Ww
Xx
Yy
Zz

cruel ADJECTIVE **crueller, cruellest** someone who is cruel causes pain or suffering to other people without showing any pity
▶ **cruelly** ADVERB in an unkind way, without any pity
▶ **cruelty** NOUN being cruel and having no pity

cruise VERB **cruises, cruising, cruised** to cruise is to travel by ship, plane or car at a steady speed
NOUN **cruises** a holiday spent on a ship, travelling from one port to another
▶ **cruiser** NOUN **cruisers** a kind of fast warship

crumb NOUN **crumbs 1** crumbs are small pieces of bread, cake or biscuit **2** a crumb of something is a tiny piece of it: *a crumb of comfort*

crumble VERB **crumbles, crumbling, crumbled** to crumble is to break down into small pieces: *The walls of the old house were crumbling.*
▶ **crumbly** ADJECTIVE **crumblier, crumbliest** breaking down easily into small pieces the size of crumbs: *dry crumbly soil*

crumpet NOUN **crumpets** a type of small thick pancake with holes in the top

crumple VERB **crumples, crumpling, crumpled** to crumple something is to crush it or squeeze it so that lots of wrinkles or folds are made in it: *He crumpled the piece of paper and threw it in the bin.*

crunch VERB **crunches, crunching, crunched 1** if you crunch food, you make a crushing noise as you break it up with your teeth **2** to crunch is to make a crushing or grinding noise: *The snow crunched under our feet.*
NOUN **crunches** a crushing or grinding noise: *the crunch of feet on the gravel path*
• **come to the crunch** to reach the point when you must make a decision
▶ **crunchy** ADJECTIVE **crunchier, crunchiest** crunchy food is hard and brittle

crusade NOUN **crusades** a campaign, often over a long period of time, in which people try to achieve something that they feel strongly about
▶ **crusader** NOUN **crusaders** someone who goes on a crusade

crush VERB **crushes, crushing, crushed 1** to crush something is to press it or squash it so that it is broken or damaged: *His leg was crushed by a falling rock.* **2** to crush something is to grind it or press it into a pulp or powder: *crush two cloves of garlic*
NOUN **crushes 1** a crush is a crowd of people squeezed tightly together **2** to have a crush on someone older is to feel love for them, usually only for a short time

crust NOUN **crusts 1** a crisp top or surface that forms on something, for example on bread or pastry as it bakes in the oven **2** the Earth's crust is its outside
▶ **crusty** ADJECTIVE **crustier, crustiest** having a crisp baked crust: *a delicious crusty pie*

crustacean NOUN **crustaceans** a sea animal with a hard outer shell, such as a crab, lobster or shrimp

crutch NOUN **crutches** a stick that you put under your arm to help you walk if you have injured your leg or foot

cry VERB **cries, crying, cried 1** to cry is to shout: *He cried out in pain.* **2** you cry when tears fall from your eyes, and often make a sobbing or wailing sound at the same time
NOUN **cries** a shout
• **a far cry** if people say that one thing is a far cry from another, they mean it comes nowhere near or is nothing like that other thing

crypt NOUN **crypts** an underground room beneath a church

cryptic ADJECTIVE having a hidden meaning or answer that is difficult to work out: *a cryptic crossword clue*

crystal NOUN **crystals 1** a crystal is a small, shaped part of a solid material that is formed naturally, for example in salt, ice or a mineral **2** crystal is a kind of high-quality glass

Aa Bb Cc Dd Ee Ff Gg Hh Ii Jj Kk Ll Mm Nn Oo Pp Qq Rr Ss Tt Uu Vv Ww Xx Yy Zz

▶ **crystalline** ADJECTIVE with regularly shaped parts, as in a mineral

▶ **crystallization** *or* **crystallisation** NOUN the process of forming crystals

▶ **crystallize** *or* **crystallise** VERB **crystallizes, crystallizing, crystallized** a substance crystallizes when it forms crystals

cub NOUN **cubs** 1 a baby lion, tiger, bear or wolf 2 a member of the Cub Scouts, the junior branch of the Scout Association

cube NOUN **cubes** 1 a solid shape with six equally sized square sides 2 (*maths*) the cube of a number is the number you get when you multiply the number by itself twice. For example, the cube of 2 is 2 × 2 × 2, which is 8. Look up and compare **square**

cubic ADJECTIVE 1 shaped like a cube 2 (*maths*) a cubic measurement is one used to measure volume. For example, a cubic metre is a space one metre long, one metre wide and one metre high 3 (*maths*) a cubic number is a number that has been multiplied by itself twice, for example 2 × 2 × 2. Look up and compare **square**

cubicle NOUN **cubicles** a small enclosed area that has enough space for one person to stand in, for example when they are changing their clothes

cuboid NOUN **cuboids** a solid shape with six faces that are all rectangular

cuckoo NOUN **cuckoos** a bird that gets its name from the call it makes. The female cuckoo lays her eggs in other birds' nests

cucumber NOUN **cucumbers** a long green vegetable that is usually sliced and eaten raw in salads

cud NOUN a cow, goat or deer chews the cud when it brings partly digested food back up from its stomach to chew again

cuddle VERB **cuddles, cuddling, cuddled** to cuddle someone is to hold them in your arms to show you love them

NOUN **cuddles** if you give someone a cuddle, you put your arms around them and hold them closely

▶ **cuddly** ADJECTIVE **cuddlier, cuddliest** a cuddly person or thing makes you want to cuddle them

cue[1] NOUN **cues** a signal to a performer to start doing something

• **on cue** if something happens on cue, it happens at exactly the right moment

cue[2] NOUN **cues** a long tapered stick used to play snooker and billiards

cuff NOUN **cuffs** a cuff is the end of a sleeve where it fits tightly around the wrist

VERB **cuffs, cuffing, cuffed** to cuff someone is to hit them with your hand

cul-de-sac NOUN **cul-de-sacs** a street that is blocked at one end

culminate VERB **culminates, culminating, culminated** to end with a particular thing, especially something big or important: *The celebrations culminated in a firework display.*

▶ **culmination** NOUN the end of something

culprit NOUN **culprits** someone who is responsible for doing something bad

cult NOUN **cults** 1 a religion, especially one with secret or strange beliefs and rituals 2 a person or thing that becomes a cult becomes very popular

cultivate VERB **cultivates, cultivating, cultivated** 1 to cultivate land is to prepare it so that you can grow things on it 2 to cultivate a crop is to grow it and look after it 3 to cultivate something is to work at it so that it grows or develops: *cultivate a friendship*

▶ **cultivation** NOUN preparing land to grow crops, or growing and looking after crops

cultural ADJECTIVE to do with culture, especially art, music and literature

culture NOUN **cultures** 1 a culture is a society with its own customs and beliefs that set them apart from other people or societies 2 culture is things like music, literature and painting that you learn about to develop your mind

▶ **cultured** ADJECTIVE a cultured person is well educated in things like art, music and literature

cunning NOUN someone who has

Aa
Bb
Cc
Dd
Ee
Ff
Gg
Hh
Ii
Jj
Kk
Ll
Mm
Nn
Oo
Pp
Qq
Rr
Ss
Tt
Uu
Vv
Ww
Xx
Yy
Zz

cunning has the ability to get what they want by secret and clever planning
ADJECTIVE sly and clever: *I have a cunning plan.*

cup NOUN **cups 1** a small container with a handle that you drink out of: *cups and saucers* **2** a decorated metal object or container used as a prize in a competition: *the World Cup*
VERB **cups, cupping, cupped** to cup your hands is to put them together and bend them into a bowl shape

cupboard (pronounced **kub**-erd) NOUN **cupboards** a piece of furniture with doors on it and sometimes shelves inside it, used for storing things in

cupful NOUN **cupfuls** the amount a cup will hold

curate NOUN **curates** a priest whose job is to help a parish priest

curator NOUN **curators** a person in charge of a museum or gallery

curb VERB **curbs, curbing, curbed** to curb something is to control it or hold it back: *He tried hard to curb his spending.*

curd NOUN **curds 1** curd is milk that has been thickened by adding acid to it **2** curds are the slightly solid lumps separated out from milk and used to make cheese. The liquid left over is called whey

curdle VERB **curdles, curdling, curdled 1** milk curdles when it thickens because it has gone bad **2** if something makes your blood curdle, it terrifies you

cure VERB **cures, curing, cured 1** to cure a disease or illness is to make it go away **2** to cure a problem is to solve it and make it go away **3** to cure meat is to put salt on it or dry it to make it last longer
NOUN **cures** something that makes a disease or illness go away: *a cure for cancer*

curfew NOUN **curfews** an official order that people must stay inside their houses after a certain time or between certain hours

curious ADJECTIVE **1** if you are curious about something, you want to know about it **2** if something is curious, it is

strange or difficult to understand
▸ **curiosity** NOUN **curiosities 1** curiosity is being curious **2** a curiosity is something strange and interesting

curl NOUN **curls** a soft twist or ring of hair: *blonde curls*
VERB **curls, curling, curled 1** to curl hair is to form soft twists or rings in it **2** smoke curls when it moves upwards in twisted or curving shapes
• **curl up** to tuck your legs and arms in close to your body and bend your back in a curve
▸ **curler** NOUN **curlers 1** a tube of plastic or sponge that hair is wound around to make it curly **2** someone who plays the game of curling

curlew NOUN **curlews** a type of wild bird with a very long curved bill and long legs

curling NOUN a game played by sliding heavy round stones over ice towards a target stone

curly ADJECTIVE **curlier, curliest** having a curl or curls: *a curly tail* • *curly hair*

currant NOUN **currants** a small dried grape

✦ The words **currant** and **current** sound the same but remember that they have different spellings.

currency NOUN **currencies** the money used in a particular country: *The euro is the Dutch currency.*

current ADJECTIVE something is current if it exists or is happening now: *the current situation*
NOUN **currents 1** a current is a flow of water or air going in one direction **2** an electric current is a flow of electricity through a wire or circuit

✦ The words **current** and **currant** sound the same but remember that they have different spellings. A **currant** is a dried grape.

curriculum NOUN **curriculums** or **curricula** a curriculum is a course of study or all the courses of study at a school or college

curry NOUN **curries** a type of food cooked with spices

curse NOUN **curses** 1 a swear-word 2 if someone puts a curse on you, they say a magic spell that will cause you to have bad luck 3 something you have to put up with even though it is hard
VERB **curses, cursing, cursed** 1 to curse is to use swear-words 2 to curse someone or something is to complain angrily about them

cursor NOUN **cursors** (*ICT*) a flashing mark on a computer screen that shows you where to start keying in information

curt ADJECTIVE short and sounding unfriendly: *a curt reply*

curtain NOUN **curtains** a long piece of material that can be drawn or dropped across a window, stage or cinema screen

curtsy *or* **curtsey** VERB **curtsies, curtsying** *or* **curtseying, curtsied** a woman or girl curtsies when she bends her knees with one leg behind the other: *All the girls curtsied to the princess.*
NOUN **curtsies** *or* **curtseys** a curtsy is this movement made to show respect to someone important

curve NOUN **curves** a curve is a line that bends
VERB **curves, curving, curved** to curve is to bend
▶ **curvy** ADJECTIVE **curvier, curviest** having lots of curves: *a curvy pattern*

cushion NOUN **cushions** 1 a soft plump pad of material that you sit on, rest against or kneel on 2 something that gives protection or keeps something off a hard surface
VERB **cushions, cushioning, cushioned** to cushion a blow is to make it less painful

custard NOUN a thick sauce made from eggs, milk or cream, and sugar

custody NOUN 1 someone who is in custody is being kept in a cell until they can be charged with a crime 2 to have custody of children is to have the right to keep them

custom NOUN **customs** 1 a custom is something that people usually or traditionally do: *Japanese customs* • *It is my custom to walk to the station each morning.* 2 you give a shop your custom when you buy things from it
▶ **customary** ADJECTIVE something that is customary is usual or is done by custom

customer NOUN **customers** a person who buys things or services from a shop or business

customize *or* **customise** VERB **customizes, customizing, customized** to customize something is to make changes to it so that it suits an individual person

customs NOUN customs is the place where you have your luggage inspected when you travel to and from a foreign country

cut VERB **cuts, cutting, cut** 1 to cut something is to divide it, separate it, make a hole in it or shape it, using scissors, a knife or some other sharp instrument 2 to make something less: *My mother cut my pocket money.* 3 (*ICT*) to take something from a file on the computer so you can put it into another file, or to take a whole file out of one place so you can put it into another
• **cut it out** if someone tells you to cut it out, they are telling you to stop doing something
• **cut off something** to cut off something such as gas or electricity is to stop it being supplied to a home
NOUN **cuts** a split or small wound made by something sharp 2 a share of something

cut and paste NOUN (*ICT*) to cut something from one file on the computer and put it into another, or to cut a whole file from one place and put it into another

cute ADJECTIVE **cuter, cutest** 1 attractive or pretty: *a cute little puppy* 2 smart or clever: *Don't try to be cute with me.*

cutlass NOUN **cutlasses** a curved sword that is sharp along only one edge

cutlery NOUN cutlery is knives, forks and spoons

cutlet NOUN **cutlets** a thick piece of

Aa Bb Cc Dd Ee Ff Gg Hh Ii Jj Kk Ll Mm Nn Oo Pp Qq Rr Ss Tt Uu Vv Ww Xx Yy Zz

141

meat that is served with the bone still joined to it

cutting NOUN **cuttings 1** an article cut out of a newspaper or magazine **2** a piece cut off a plant from which a new plant will grow

cycle VERB **cycles, cycling, cycled** to cycle is to ride a bicycle

NOUN **cycles 1** a bicycle **2** a series of things that happen one after the other and then start again: *the cycle of the seasons*

▸ **cyclist** NOUN **cyclists** someone riding a bicycle

cyclepath *or* **cycleway** NOUN **cyclepaths** *or* **cycleways** a path for people to ride bicycles on

cyclone NOUN **cyclones** a large storm that happens in tropical countries, with high winds circling round a calm centre called the eye of the storm

cygnet NOUN **cygnets** a baby swan

cylinder NOUN **cylinders** a solid shape with a round top and bottom and straight sides

▸ **cylindrical** ADJECTIVE shaped like a cylinder

cymbals PLURAL NOUN two circles of brass that are banged together to make a musical sound

cynic (pronounced **sin**-ik) NOUN **cynics** someone who sees something bad in everyone and everything no matter how good they may be

▸ **cynical** ADJECTIVE a cynical person believes the worst about everyone and everything

▸ **cynicism** NOUN the belief that something bad can be found in everything, no matter how good it may seem

Dd

dab VERB **dabs, dabbing, dabbed** to touch something lightly with your fingers or something soft: *Dab your eyes with a tissue.*
NOUN **dabs** a light touch of something: *a dab of blusher on each cheek*

dabble VERB **dabbles, dabbling, dabbled** to dabble in an activity is to do it for fun but not very seriously: *He was a rich man who dabbled in many hobbies.*

dachshund NOUN **dachshunds** a type of dog with short legs and a long body

dad or **daddy** NOUN **dads** or **daddies** a word that people use for **father**, especially when speaking: *Thanks to all the mums and dads who have helped.*

daddy-long-legs NOUN **daddy-long-legs** a crane fly

daffodil NOUN **daffodils** a yellow flower that grows from a bulb and blooms in spring

daft ADJECTIVE **dafter, daftest** silly: *a daft thing to do*

dagger NOUN **daggers** a knife like a small sword

daily ADJECTIVE happening or done every day: *a daily newspaper*
ADVERB every day: *We met daily for a month.*
NOUN **dailies** a newspaper that is published every weekday

dainty ADJECTIVE **daintier, daintiest** small and neat

dairy NOUN **dairies** a place where products like butter and cheese are made from milk

daisy NOUN **daisies** a type of small white flower with a yellow centre. Daisies often grow wild in grass

✦ The word **daisy** has been changed from **day's eye**. It was called this because the flower opens during the day.

dale NOUN **dales** a valley

Dalmatian NOUN **Dalmatians** a type of large dog that has a white coat with dark spots

dam NOUN **dams** a wall across a river that holds a lot of the water back
VERB **dams, damming, dammed** to build a wall across a river to stop it from flowing naturally

damage NOUN harm, hurt or injury : *No lasting damage has been found.*
VERB **damages, damaging, damaged** to hurt, spoil or break something
▸ **damages** PLURAL NOUN an amount of money that someone gets to make up for a loss or injury

dame NOUN **dames 1** in Britain, a title that can be given to a woman who has done something remarkable **2** a woman's part in pantomime that is usually played by a man

damn INTERJECTION an impolite word that someone who is very irritated might use
VERB **damns, damning, damned** to blame someone or say that they are very bad

damp ADJECTIVE **damper, dampest** a bit wet: *Wipe with a damp cloth.*
NOUN slight wetness: *a patch of damp on the wall*
▸ **dampen** VERB **dampens, dampening, dampened** to make something a bit wet: *Dampen the brush before using it.*

damson NOUN **damsons** a small type of plum

dance VERB **dances, dancing, danced** to move your body in time to music
NOUN **dances 1** a set of steps that you do to some kind of music **2** a party for dancing
▸ **dancer** NOUN **dancers** someone who dances

Aa
Bb
Cc
Dd
Ee
Ff
Gg
Hh
Ii
Jj
Kk
Ll
Mm
Nn
Oo
Pp
Qq
Rr
Ss
Tt
Uu
Vv
Ww
Xx
Yy
Zz

dandelion NOUN **dandelions** a yellow flower that is a common weed in people's gardens

✦**Dandelion** comes from the French phrase **dent de lion**, which means *lion's tooth*. This describes what the long thin petals look like.

dandruff NOUN tiny dry flakes of dead skin that can collect near the roots of hair: *an anti-dandruff shampoo*

danger NOUN **dangers** something that may harm or injure you: *the dangers of skiing*

▸ **dangerous** ADJECTIVE **1** likely to hurt someone: *a dangerous substance* **2** risky: *It's dangerous to play near the railway.*

▸ **dangerously** ADVERB in a way that could be harmful: *driving dangerously close to the edge*

dangle VERB **dangles, dangling, dangled** to hang down loosely: *Her hair dangled in her eyes.*

dank ADJECTIVE **danker, dankest** wet and cold

dappled ADJECTIVE covered with patches of light or colour: *a dappled horse*

dare VERB **dares, daring, dared 1** to dare someone to do something is to challenge them to do it: *I dare you to do that again!* **2** to dare to do something is to be brave enough to do it: *I wouldn't dare to argue with the headmaster.*

daredevil NOUN **daredevils** a person who enjoys danger and taking risks
ADJECTIVE dangerous or risky: *a daredevil project*

dark ADJECTIVE **darker, darkest 1** without light: *a dark room* **2** strong or deep in colour: *dark blue* **3** gloomy, sad or miserable
NOUN **1** where there is no light: *I'm not afraid of the dark.* **2** nightfall: *Don't go out after dark without a torch.*
• **in the dark** if you are in the dark about something, you know nothing about it

▸ **darken** VERB **darkens, darkening, darkened** to get or make darker: *The sky darkened as the rain moved nearer.*

▸ **darkness** NOUN where there is no light: *a tiny point of light in the darkness*

darling ADJECTIVE very dear
NOUN **darlings 1** someone you care very much about: *My darling, what's the matter?* **2** someone's favourite: *The child had been her darling since his first day in the class.*

darn VERB **darns, darning, darned** to mend a hole by sewing it up

dart VERB **darts, darting, darted** to move fast in a straight line: *A child darted out of the door as I entered.*
NOUN **darts** a little arrow that can be fired as a weapon or thrown in a game

▸ **darts** NOUN a game where you throw small arrow-shaped objects at a round board called a **dartboard** that has scores on it

dash VERB **dashes, dashing, dashed** to hurry somewhere: *I've got to dash to the shops.*
NOUN **dashes 1** a rush to get somewhere: *a mad dash to the airport* **2** a small amount of something that you add to food or drink: *Add a dash of vinegar.* **3** a punctuation mark that looks like a short line. You use it to interrupt a sentence with a new idea, for example *I'm going out – are you coming?*

dashboard NOUN **dashboards** the panel in front of the driver of a car, containing dials or gauges for things like speed, petrol and oil

data NOUN information or facts

database NOUN **databases** information that is stored on a computer in lists or tables

date¹ NOUN **dates 1** the number of a day of a month or a year: *The date today is 30 July.* **2** a particular day of a particular month and year: *It was on that date that I left home.* **3** an arrangement to go out with someone
VERB **dates, dating, dated 1** to decide how old something is: *The ring's very old but I couldn't date it exactly.* **2** to belong to a certain time: *Our house dates from the nineteenth century.* **3** to look

old-fashioned: *Shoes always date very quickly.*

date² NOUN **dates** a small, dark fruit with a stone that grows on some palm trees

daub VERB **daubs, daubing, daubed** to put something like paint on a surface untidily

daughter NOUN **daughters** someone's female child: *She was the daughter of a poet.*

daughter-in-law NOUN **daughters-in-law** your son's wife

daunt VERB **daunts, daunting, daunted** you are daunted by something if it puts you off doing something: *He was daunted by the amount of homework he had to do.*

▶ **daunting** ADJECTIVE something that is daunting makes you feel slightly nervous because it is big, dangerous or difficult: *the daunting height of the next jump*

dawdle VERB **dawdles, dawdling, dawdled** to walk or do something slowly

dawn NOUN **dawns** the beginning of the day, when it starts to get light

VERB **dawns, dawning, dawned** to start: *A new age has dawned.*

• **dawn on** if something dawns on you, you suddenly start to realize it: *It's beginning to dawn on me that I'm never going to be a star.*

day NOUN **days 1** the time of light between sunrise and sunset **2** the twenty-four hours between one midnight and another: *There are 365 days in a year.* **3** a time or period: *in my grandfather's day*

daydream VERB **daydreams, daydreaming, daydreamed** to think about things you would like to happen instead of concentrating on what you are meant to be doing

daylight NOUN natural light during the day

daze VERB **dazes, dazing, dazed** to make someone feel confused and unable to see or think straight

NOUN to be in a daze is to be confused or unable to think clearly: *I stood there not knowing what to do, staring after her in a daze.*

dazzle VERB **dazzles, dazzling, dazzled** a light dazzles you when it shines so brightly that you cannot see properly

de- PREFIX if a word starts with **de-**, it means 'reverse' or 'take away'. For example, to *decode* something is to take it back out of code

dead ADJECTIVE **1** no longer living: *a dead body* **2** no longer working or active: *The telephone line's dead.*

ADVERB **1** completely: *He just stopped dead in front of me.* **2** exactly: *standing dead in the centre of the circle*

NOUN **1** the dead are all the people who have died **2** the dead of night is the quietest part of it

dead end NOUN **dead ends** a road or path that does not lead anywhere

dead heat NOUN **dead heats** a race that two people finish at exactly the same time

deadline NOUN **deadlines** the time when something, such as a piece of work, must be finished

deadly ADJECTIVE **deadlier, deadliest** able to kill: *a deadly poison*

deaf ADJECTIVE **deafer, deafest** not able to hear properly: *Grandma grew deafer as she got older.*

▶ **deafen** VERB **deafens, deafening, deafened** to make a person deaf or feel deaf: *The explosion deafened us for a moment.*

▶ **deafening** ADJECTIVE unpleasantly loud: *The music was deafening and we had to leave.*

▶ **deafness** NOUN being unable to hear properly

deal NOUN **deals 1** an agreement, especially in business: *I think that's a fair deal.* **2** an amount of something: *a great deal of money* **3** the action of giving out playing cards at the beginning of a game: *It's your deal.*

VERB **deals, dealing, dealt 1** if you deal something, or deal it out, you give it out to a number of people **2** to give

Aa
Bb
Cc
Dd
Ee
Ff
Gg
Hh
Ii
Jj
Kk
Ll
Mm
Nn
Oo
Pp
Qq
Rr
Ss
Tt
Uu
Vv
Ww
Xx
Yy
Zz

out playing cards at the beginning of a game

• **deal in something** to buy and sell something: *They deal in luxury fabrics.*

• **deal with someone** or **something** to do something about a person, situation or problem: *The headteacher deals with any problems that pupils have.*

• **deal with something** a text or speech that deals with something is about that subject: *a book dealing with birds*

▶ **dealer** NOUN **dealers** someone who buys and sells things: *an antiques dealer*

▶ **dealings** PLURAL NOUN someone's dealings are the business arrangements they make

dear ADJECTIVE **dearer, dearest 1** a thing or person that is dear to you is important because you love them: *my dear old teddy* **2** expensive: *too dear for me to buy* **3** the word you use with the name of a person at the beginning of a letter: *Dear Mary*

NOUN **dears** a person that is very lovable: *Nancy is such a dear.*

▶ **dearly** ADVERB very much: *Of course she loves him dearly.*

death NOUN **deaths** the time when a person or animal stops living: *written just before the poet's death*

▶ **deathly** ADJECTIVE like a thing or person that is dead: *a deathly hush*

debate NOUN **debates** a public discussion or argument, for example on television or in parliament

VERB **debates, debating, debated** to discuss a lot of different aspects of something

debris (pronounced **deb**-ree) NOUN the bits of something that has broken up: *the debris of a wrecked ship*

debt (pronounced **det**) NOUN **debts** something, especially money, that a person owes someone

• **in debt** if you are in debt, you owe someone money

debut (pronounced **day**-byoo) NOUN **debuts** the first time a performer

appears in public: *The actor made his debut at the King's Theatre in 1999.*

dec- or **deca-** PREFIX if a word starts with **dec-** or **deca-**, it often has something to do with the number ten. For example, a *decagon* is a shape with ten sides

✦ This comes from the Greek word for *ten*, which is **deka**.

decade NOUN **decades** a period of ten years: *the third decade of the twentieth century*

decagon NOUN **decagons** a flat shape with ten straight sides

decathlon NOUN **decathlons** an athletics competition that has ten different kinds of sporting contest

decay VERB **decays, decaying, decayed** to go rotten

NOUN going bad or rotting: *tooth decay*

deceased ADJECTIVE (*formal*) dead

NOUN the deceased is a particular dead person

deceit NOUN **deceits** lies and trickery

▶ **deceitful** ADJECTIVE not telling the truth

deceive VERB **deceives, deceiving, deceived** to fool or trick someone by telling lies or suggesting something is true: *The sun deceived me into thinking it was warm outside.*

▶ **deceiver** NOUN **deceivers** someone who deceives another person

December NOUN the twelfth month of the year, after November and before January

✦ December was the tenth month of the Roman year and the name comes from the word **decem**, which means *ten* in Latin.
Other words in English where you can work out that **dec** means *ten* are **decimal** and **decade**.

decency NOUN **decencies** respectable and reasonable behaviour

▶ **decent** ADJECTIVE **1** good, honest and respectable: *a decent family* **2** acceptable or good enough: *a decent meal*

Aa
Bb
Cc
Dd
Ee
Ff
Gg
Hh
Ii
Jj
Kk
Ll
Mm
Nn
Oo
Pp
Qq
Rr
Ss
Tt
Uu
Vv
Ww
Xx
Yy
Zz

deception NOUN **deceptions 1** deception is not telling the truth **2** a deception is a trick or lie

▸ **deceptive** ADJECTIVE not showing the true situation: *The photo's deceptive – I'm actually much older than I look there.*

decibel NOUN **decibels** a unit that is used for measuring how loud a sound is

decide VERB **decides, deciding, decided 1** to make up your mind to do something: *Greg decided to work harder at school.* **2** to choose: *I can't decide between the blue and the green one.* **3** to bring about a result: *That mistake decided the match.*

▸ **decided** ADJECTIVE definite: *a decided improvement*

▸ **decidedly** ADVERB very much: *You will feel decidedly better after a rest.*

deciduous ADJECTIVE a deciduous plant does not have leaves in the winter. Look up and compare **evergreen**

decimal ADJECTIVE based on a system of tens or tenths: *decimal fractions*

NOUN **decimals** a fraction shown as a number of tenths and hundredths: *A half, written as a decimal, is 0.5.*

decimalize or **decimalise** VERB **decimalizes, decimalizing, decimalized** to decimalize something such as measurements is to convert them into a system that uses tens or tenths

▸ **decimalization** or **decimalisation** NOUN changing to a decimal system

decimal place NOUN **decimal places** (*maths*) a figure that comes after the decimal point: *Can you round off this number to two decimal places?*

decimal point NOUN **decimal points** (*maths*) the dot after the whole units and before the tenths in a decimal: *To multiply by ten, just move the decimal point to the right.*

decipher VERB **deciphers, deciphering, deciphered** to decipher a code or writing is to work out what it means: *Philip's handwriting has always been difficult to decipher.*

decision NOUN **decisions** something that you have decided: *It was a very difficult decision to make, and I had to think hard before making a choice.*

▸ **decisive** ADJECTIVE **1** a decisive person is good at making up their mind quickly and firmly **2** a decisive action is firm and makes a difference to a result: *a decisive attack by the team*

deck NOUN **decks 1** a deck of a boat is one of its levels or the part you can walk on outside **2** a pack of playing cards: *your turn to shuffle the deck* **3** the part of a computer or tape recorder that plays tapes

deckchair NOUN **deckchairs** a folding chair for sitting outside and relaxing in

declare VERB **declares, declaring, declared** to announce something firmly: *She suddenly declared that she was leaving.*

▸ **declaration** NOUN **declarations** a clear or official announcement: *a declaration of war*

decline VERB **declines, declining, declined 1** to refuse an offer **2** to get weaker, worse or less: *The president's popularity has sharply declined.*

decode VERB **decodes, decoding, decoded** to decode a coded message is to work out its meaning

decompose VERB **decomposes, decomposing, decomposed** to rot

decorate VERB **decorates, decorating, decorated 1** to add something fancy to something to make it look nicer: *We'll decorate the cake with roses made of sugar.* **2** to paint or paper the inside of a room **3** to give someone a medal or an award for doing something special: *He was decorated for bravery in the war.*

▸ **decoration** NOUN **decorations 1** decoration is adding things to improve the look of something **2** an ornament that makes something look pretty: *Christmas decorations*

▸ **decorative** ADJECTIVE meant to make something look pretty: *decorative ribbon round the curtain*

▸ **decorator** NOUN **decorators** a person whose job is to paint and paper rooms

Aa
Bb
Cc
Dd
Ee
Ff
Gg
Hh
Ii
Jj
Kk
Ll
Mm
Nn
Oo
Pp
Qq
Rr
Ss
Tt
Uu
Vv
Ww
Xx
Yy
Zz

Aa
Bb
Cc
Dd
Ee
Ff
Gg
Hh
Ii
Jj
Kk
Ll
Mm
Nn
Oo
Pp
Qq
Rr
Ss
Tt
Uu
Vv
Ww
Xx
Yy
Zz

decorum NOUN proper and dignified behaviour

decoy NOUN **decoys** a thing or person that leads someone into a trap

decrease VERB (pronounced di-**krees**) **decreases, decreasing, decreased 1** to decrease is to become smaller in amount or size: *Jordan's interest in football has decreased as he's got older.* **2** to decrease something is to make it smaller in amount or size

NOUN (pronounced **dee**-krees) **decreases** the amount by which something gets smaller: *a decrease in the number of school students*

▸ **decreasing** ADJECTIVE getting smaller in amount or size

decree VERB **decrees, decreeing, decreed** to announce publicly that something should happen

NOUN **decrees** an official order or statement that something should happen

dedicate VERB **dedicates, dedicating, dedicated 1** to dedicate time to something is to spend time doing only that: *She dedicated her whole life to music.* **2** to mention someone's name right at the beginning of a work you have written, because they are important to you: *The author dedicated his play to his daughter.*

deduce VERB **deduces, deducing, deduced** to work something out from a lot of bits of information

deduct VERB **deducts, deducting, deducted** to deduct something such as money or points is to take them away from a larger amount: *The teacher deducted five points from my test result because I cheated.*

deduction NOUN **deductions 1** an amount that you take away from a bigger figure **2** something that you work out from all the information you have

deed NOUN **deeds 1** something that someone has done: *my good deed for the day* **2** an official document that shows who owns something

deep ADJECTIVE **deeper, deepest 1** going a long way down: *Is the river very deep?* **2** very low in tone: *a deep voice* **3** reaching a long way back: *a deep border of roses* **4** very strong: *deep blue* • *deep dislike*

ADVERB **deeper, deepest 1** in a downward direction: *a hole a metre deep* **2** from front to back: *rows of soldiers standing four deep*

▸ **deepen** VERB **deepens, deepening, deepened 1** to go further down or back: *The river deepens here to more than 2 metres.* **2** to get stronger: *a deepening gloom*

▸ **deeply** ADVERB very much: *deeply in love*

deer NOUN **deer** an animal with four thin legs that runs very fast and gracefully. A male deer has antlers like branches that grow on its head

---

✦ The singular and plural forms of **deer** are the same: *a deer in the woods* • *two deer in the park.*

---

deface VERB **defaces, defacing, defaced** to spoil the way something looks

defeat VERB **defeats, defeating, defeated** to beat someone in a competition or war

NOUN **defeats 1** a defeat is a game or a battle that you have lost **2** defeat is being beaten at something

defect[1] (pronounced **dee**-fekt) NOUN **defects** a fault that stops something from working properly: *a heart defect*

▸ **defective** ADJECTIVE having something wrong with it: *a defective computer program*

defect[2] (pronounced di-**fekt**) VERB **defects, defecting, defected** to go over to the other side, for example to a different political party or an enemy country: *The spy defected to the United States.*

▸ **defection** NOUN **defections** going over to the other side

▸ **defector** NOUN **defectors** someone who defects

defence NOUN **defences 1** protection against attack: *The wall was the city's main defence.* **2** protecting yourself against attack or criticism: *In my defence, I was only doing what I was told.* **3** in a court case, the side that tries to help a person who is accused of doing something wrong

defenceless ADJECTIVE defenceless people, animals or places have no way of protecting themselves: *a defenceless baby seal*

defend VERB **defends, defending, defended** to protect someone or something from being attacked: *Kim always defends his little brother if people say he's too quiet.*

▶ **defendant** NOUN **defendants** the person in court who is accused of committing a crime

▶ **defensive** ADJECTIVE **1** designed to protect: *defensive weapons* **2** worried about being criticized: *a defensive look*

defer VERB **defers, deferring, deferred** to put something off until later: *The meeting has been deferred until more people can come.*

defiance NOUN openly going against someone or something they have said: *Pamela went out, in defiance of her parents' instructions.*

▶ **defiant** ADJECTIVE refusing to obey: *a defiant child*

▶ **defiantly** ADVERB purposely not obeying: *John defiantly refused to go.*

deficiency NOUN **deficiencies** an amount that is less than it should be: *a deficiency of B vitamins*

▶ **deficient** ADJECTIVE without enough of something: *The team is deficient in communication skills.*

deficit (pronounced **def**-i-sit) NOUN **deficits** how much less money you really have than you expected to have: *The accounts show a deficit of several pounds.*

define VERB **defines, defining, defined 1** to give the exact meaning of something like a word or phrase **2** to show the exact outline of something: *The edges of the car park are clearly*

defined by white lines.

definite ADJECTIVE certain: *It's not definite, but the wedding will probably be in August.*

▶ **definitely** ADVERB certainly, without a doubt: *We'll definitely be back by 10 o'clock.*

definite article NOUN **definite articles** (grammar) the name used for the word **the**

✦ There are two kinds of article in English grammar: **the** is called the *definite article* and **a**, or **an**, is called the *indefinite article.*

definition NOUN **definitions** the meaning of a word or phrase

deflate VERB **deflates, deflating, deflated 1** to let the air out of something that has been blown up, like a tyre or balloon **2** to make someone feel less confident or enthusiastic: *Feeling deflated, the team clapped the winners and tried to smile.*

deflect VERB **deflects, deflecting, deflected** to deflect something that is moving is to change its direction: *He deflected the blow with his arm.*

▶ **deflection** NOUN **deflections** a change of direction

deforestation NOUN cutting down large numbers of trees in an area

deform VERB **deforms, deforming, deformed** to spoil the shape of something

▶ **deformed** ADJECTIVE not shaped normally

▶ **deformity** NOUN **deformities** when something is not shaped normally

defrost VERB **defrosts, defrosting, defrosted 1** to defrost frozen food is to make it ready to cook or eat **2** to defrost a fridge or freezer is to remove the ice from it

deft ADJECTIVE **defter, deftest 1** a deft movement is quick and clever **2** a deft person moves neatly and skilfully

▶ **deftly** ADVERB quickly and skilfully

defy VERB **defies, defying, defied 1** to defy someone to do something is to challenge them to do it: *I defy*

Aa
Bb
Cc
Dd
Ee
Ff
Gg
Hh
Ii
Jj
Kk
Ll
Mm
Nn
Oo
Pp
Qq
Rr
Ss
Tt
Uu
Vv
Ww
Xx
Yy
Zz

you to do that again! **2** to defy a person or something like a rule is to openly disobey them **3** if something defies description or explanation, it is impossible to describe or explain: *a scene that defies description*

degenerate VERB **degenerates, degenerating, degenerated** to get worse: *Jonathan's work has degenerated since he moved schools.*

degrade VERB **degrades, degrading, degraded** to make someone feel that they are not important or not worth anything

▶ **degrading** ADJECTIVE making a person feel worthless

degree NOUN **degrees**
1 a unit for measuring temperature, shown by the symbol °: *It's 30° (degrees) here today.*
2 (*maths*) a unit for measuring angles, shown by the symbol °: *An angle of 90° (degrees) is a right angle.*
3 a very small amount: *improving slowly by degrees*
4 a qualification that students can study for at a university or college

dehydrate VERB **dehydrates, dehydrating, dehydrated 1** to dehydrate something is to dry it out by removing all the water from it **2** to dehydrate is to lose so much water from your body that you become weak or ill

▶ **dehydrated** ADJECTIVE **1** if you are dehydrated, you are weak or ill because you have not had enough water to drink **2** dehydrated food has had the water removed from it to make it last longer

▶ **dehydration** NOUN someone who is suffering from dehydration has not had enough water to drink

dejected ADJECTIVE feeling very fed up

▶ **dejection** NOUN a very depressed feeling

delay NOUN **delays** the extra time you have to wait if something happens later than expected: *There was a delay of half an hour before take-off.*

VERB **delays, delaying, delayed 1** to put something off until later: *Don't*

delay – apply now! **2** to make someone or something late: *I was delayed by the arrival of an unexpected visitor.*

delegate VERB (pronounced **del**-i-gait) **delegates, delegating, delegated** to give someone a job to do, especially one that is your responsibility

NOUN (pronounced **del**-i-git) **delegates** a person who represents someone else at a meeting

▶ **delegation** NOUN **delegations** a group of representatives at a meeting or conference

delete VERB **deletes, deleting, deleted** to cross out or remove something

▶ **deletion** NOUN **deletions** a deletion is something that has been removed, for example from a text

deliberate ADJECTIVE (pronounced di-**lib**-rit) not accidental, but done on purpose: *a deliberate lie*

VERB (pronounced di-**lib**-ir-ait) **deliberates, deliberating, deliberated** to think seriously about something for a while: *We're still deliberating about what to do next.*

▶ **deliberately** ADVERB on purpose, not by accident: *They deliberately left the door open so that the mice could escape.*

▶ **deliberation** NOUN careful consideration of a matter: *After much deliberation, they reached a decision.*

delicacy NOUN **delicacies** something delicious and unusual to eat: *These eggs are regarded as a great delicacy in some countries.*

delicate ADJECTIVE
1 a delicate object can easily be broken
2 a delicate pattern is fine and dainty
3 a delicate person is often ill
4 a delicate situation needs careful attention to avoid a problem arising

delicatessen NOUN **delicatessens** a shop that sells cooked meat, cheese and other prepared foods

delicious ADJECTIVE very good to eat, drink or smell: *a delicious meal*

delight NOUN **delights** great pleasure:

Felicity squealed with delight when she saw us.

VERB **delights, delighting, delighted** to please someone very much

▸ **delighted** ADJECTIVE very pleased: *We'd be delighted to come to the party.*

▸ **delightful** ADJECTIVE very pleasing

delinquent NOUN **delinquents** a person who behaves badly in the community, especially by breaking the law

▸ **delinquency** NOUN bad behaviour or law-breaking

delirious ADJECTIVE **1** confused and unable to think normally because you have a very high temperature **2** extremely happy or excited: *Martha was delirious when she found she'd passed her exam.*

▸ **delirium** NOUN a confused state of mind that occurs when you have a very high temperature

deliver VERB **delivers, delivering, delivered 1** to deliver something is to take it to the door of someone's home or workplace: *We're delivering leaflets to all the houses in this area.* **2** to deliver a speech is to say it out loud **3** to deliver a baby is to help with its birth

▸ **delivery** NOUN **deliveries** when or how something is delivered

delta NOUN **deltas** (*geography*) the area like a triangle that is formed if a river splits into separate branches where it flows into the sea

delude VERB **deludes, deluding, deluded** to delude someone is to make them believe something that is not true

deluge NOUN **deluges 1** a downpour or flood **2** a large amount of anything

VERB **deluges, deluging, deluged** to be deluged with something is to receive lots and lots of it: *We have been deluged with entries for our competition.*

delusion NOUN **delusions** something that a person believes even though it is not true

delve VERB **delves, delving, delved** to look for something as if you are digging

for it: *Nan was delving into her handbag for something.*

demand VERB **demands, demanding, demanded 1** to ask for something as if you are giving an order: *I demand to know where you've been!* **2** to need: *This work demanded all our skills.*

NOUN **demands 1** a request that is almost an order **2** a need: *There is not much demand for sun cream at this time of year.*

▸ **demanding** ADJECTIVE needing a lot of time or effort: *a very demanding job*

demeanour NOUN the way you behave: *Something in his demeanour made me suspicious.*

democracy NOUN **democracies 1** a form of government where people elect representatives to lead them **2** a country that has an elected government

▸ **democrat** NOUN **democrats** a person who believes that people should be allowed to vote for their government

▸ **democratic** ADJECTIVE involving a system where people elect the government

demolish VERB **demolishes, demolishing, demolished** to demolish a building is to knock it down: *The flats will be demolished immediately.*

▸ **demolition** NOUN knocking a building down

demon NOUN **demons** an evil spirit

demonstrate VERB **demonstrates, demonstrating, demonstrated 1** to show someone how to do something or how something works: *Can you demonstrate how to turn the machine on?* **2** to let people know how you feel about something, especially by marching or waving signs in public

▸ **demonstration** NOUN **demonstrations 1** an explanation of how to do something or how something works: *a cookery demonstration* **2** an expression of how someone feels about something, especially by marching in public to

Aa Bb Cc Dd Ee Ff Gg Hh Ii Jj Kk Ll Mm Nn Oo Pp Qq Rr Ss Tt Uu Vv Ww Xx Yy Zz

protest about it: *a demonstration against nuclear weapons*

▶ **demonstrative** ADJECTIVE a demonstrative person often or easily shows how they are feeling

▶ **demonstrator** NOUN **demonstrators 1** a person who protests about something in public **2** a person who shows how something is done

demoralize or **demoralise** VERB **demoralizes, demoralizing, demoralized** if something demoralizes you, it takes away your confidence or hope

den NOUN **dens 1** the home of a wild animal: *a lion's den* **2** a person's private place where they can get away from other people

denial NOUN **denials** saying that something is not true

denim NOUN a tough cotton fabric that jeans and other clothes are made out of

denominator NOUN **denominators** (*maths*) the number below the line in a fraction

denounce VERB **denounces, denouncing, denounced** to denounce someone or something is to criticize them publicly

dense ADJECTIVE **denser, densest 1** thick or very closely packed together: *dense fog* • *a dense forest* **2** slow to understand something

▶ **density** NOUN **densities 1** how thick or closely packed something is **2** how heavy something is for its size

dent NOUN **dents** a hollow in a surface, caused by something hitting it: *a dent in the side of the car*

VERB **dents, denting, dented** to hit something and make a hollow shape in it

dental ADJECTIVE to do with teeth: *dental hygiene*

dentist NOUN **dentists** a doctor for people's teeth

▶ **dentistry** NOUN the work of a dentist

dentures PLURAL NOUN a set of false teeth

deny VERB **denies, denying, denied 1** to deny something is to say that it is not true: *Nina denied that she had stolen anything.* **2** to deny a request is to say 'no' to it **3** to deny yourself something is to do without something you want or need

deodorant NOUN **deodorants** a product, such as a spray, that people put on their bodies to stop unpleasant smells

depart VERB **departs, departing, departed** to leave: *The train departs at 9.15.*

department NOUN **departments** a section of a school, shop, business or government: *the new head of the English department*

departure NOUN **departures** a time when a thing or person leaves a place: *All departures are shown on the left of the timetable.*

depend VERB **depends, depending, depended 1** to depend on someone or something is to rely on them: *Young children depend on their parents for everything.* **2** to depend on something is to be decided by it: *The price of our fruit depends on the weather.*

▶ **dependable** ADJECTIVE if someone is dependable, you can rely on them

dependant NOUN **dependants** a person's dependants are the people they look after by giving them a home, food, and money

dependent ADJECTIVE relying on something or someone: *She became dependent on her aunt.*

▶ **dependence** NOUN not being able to do without something

depict VERB **depicts, depicting, depicted** (*formal*) to show something or someone in a picture or describe them in writing: *The sketch depicts a railway station.*

deplete VERB **depletes, depleting, depleted** to become depleted is to get smaller or less: *The food stores were being depleted.*

deplore VERB **deplores, deploring, deplored** to deplore something is to think it is very bad

depopulate → deride

depopulate VERB **depopulates, depopulating, depopulated** to depopulate a place is to reduce the number of people who live there: *A war depopulated this region in the last century.*

▶ **depopulation** NOUN the process where fewer and fewer people live in an area

deport VERB **deports, deporting, deported** to be deported is to be sent out of a country

▶ **deportation** NOUN **deportations** sending someone out of a country

depose VERB **deposes, deposing, deposed** to be deposed is to be removed from an important position: *The president has been deposed.*

deposit NOUN **deposits 1** part of the price of something that you pay in advance: *Pay a deposit now and we won't sell this to anyone else.* **2** an amount of money that you pay into a bank or building society account **3** a layer of something that is left behind or that forms over a long time: *A deposit of dust was everywhere when the builders left.* VERB **deposits, depositing, deposited 1** to put money in a bank account **2** to put or leave something somewhere: *Deposit your luggage here and pick it up later.*

deposition NOUN (*geography*) deposition takes place when running water slows down and leaves mud and stones behind

depot (pronounced **dep**-oh) NOUN **depots 1** a place where vehicles like buses or trains are kept when they are not in use **2** a store: *a weapons depot*

depress VERB **depresses, depressing, depressed** to depress someone is to make them feel unhappy or fed up

▶ **depressed** ADJECTIVE unhappy or fed up

▶ **depressing** ADJECTIVE making a person feel unhappy or fed up: *depressing weather*

▶ **depression** NOUN **depressions 1** feeling unhappy or fed up **2** a time when the industry and business

in a country is not doing well, and many people do not have jobs **3** a hollow or dip in a surface: *a depression left where he'd been sitting in the sand* **4** (*geography*) a patch of low air pressure that often brings bad weather

deprive VERB **deprives, depriving, deprived** to deprive somebody of something is to take it away from them: *She's been deprived of sleep since the noisy neighbours moved in.*

▶ **deprivation** NOUN not having the basic things that people need

▶ **deprived** ADJECTIVE not having all the things that are necessary for a basically good life: *a deprived area of the inner city*

depth NOUN **depths 1** how deep something is: *measure the depth of the water* **2** a deep place: *the depths of the ocean* **3** how strong something is: *the depth of the colour*

• **in depth** in great detail

• **out of your depth** involved in things too difficult for you to understand

deputy NOUN **deputies 1** someone who takes over when the person in charge is not there: *the deputy head teacher* **2** someone's assistant: *the sheriff and all his deputies*

derail VERB **derails, derailing, derailed** to force a train to leave the track

▶ **derailment** NOUN **derailments** a derailment happens when a train comes off the track

derby NOUN **derbies 1** a race, especially for horses **2** a sports match between two teams from the same area

derelict ADJECTIVE a derelict building or derelict land is not being used and is in very bad condition

deride VERB **derides, deriding, derided** to deride someone or something is to laugh at them because you think they are ridiculous

▶ **derision** NOUN unkind laughter when you think someone or something is ridiculous

Aa Bb Cc **Dd** Ee Ff Gg Hh Ii Jj Kk Ll Mm Nn Oo Pp Qq Rr Ss Tt Uu Vv Ww Xx Yy Zz

153

derivation NOUN **derivations** where something, especially a word, comes from

▶ **derivative** NOUN **derivatives** a word that is formed from another word. For example, *derision* is a derivative of the verb *deride*

descend VERB **descends, descending, descended** to go or climb downwards

▶ **descendant** NOUN **descendants** someone's descendants are the people who live at a later time in the same family

▶ **descended** ADJECTIVE to be descended from someone is to come after them in the same family

▶ **descent** NOUN **descents 1** going or climbing downwards: *Our descent of the mountain was as hard as the upward climb.* **2** a downward slope

describe VERB **describes, describing, described** to tell someone what something or someone is like: *Can you describe what you saw?*

▶ **description** NOUN **descriptions 1** explaining what someone or something is like: *an author who's good at description* **2** the way someone describes a thing, person or event: *a very funny description of what happened* **3** a sort, type or kind: *people of all descriptions*

▶ **descriptive** ADJECTIVE describing someone or something: *a descriptive poem*

desert¹ (pronounced di-**zurt**) VERB **deserts, deserting, deserted** to go away and leave someone or something, especially the army

desert² (pronounced **dez**-ert) NOUN **deserts** an area of land where it does not rain much, so the earth is very dry and not many plants will grow

desert island NOUN **desert islands** a tropical island where nobody lives

deserve VERB **deserves, deserving, deserved** to deserve something is to have earned it because of the way you are or something you have done

▶ **deservedly** ADVERB rightly

▶ **deserving** ADJECTIVE a deserving person or cause is good and should be helped

design VERB **designs, designing, designed 1** to plan a building or product before it is built or made **2** if something is designed for someone or for a particular purpose, it is intended for them: *This dictionary is designed to be used by school pupils.*

NOUN **designs 1** design is planning new shapes and ideas: *studying craft and design* **2** a design is a plan or diagram of something that could be made: *a design for a new racing car* **3** a pattern: *a geometric design*

designate VERB **designates, designating, designated** to choose someone or something to do a particular job

desirable ADJECTIVE worth having and wanted very much: *a desirable house by the sea*

desire VERB **desires, desiring, desired** to desire something is to want it very much: *all the riches you could desire*

NOUN **desires** a longing or something you want very much: *a secret desire*

desk NOUN **desks** a table for writing at

desolate ADJECTIVE **1** a desolate place is empty of people **2** a desolate person is lonely and very unhappy

▶ **desolation** NOUN a feeling of unhappiness and emptiness

despair NOUN no hope: *a feeling of despair*

VERB **despairs, despairing, despaired** to give up hope

▶ **despairing** ADJECTIVE feeling that there is no hope

despatch VERB **despatches, despatching, despatched** another spelling of **dispatch**

desperate ADJECTIVE **1** extremely bad or serious: *a desperate situation* **2** needing something very much: *desperate for food*

▶ **desperately** ADVERB extremely or very much: *desperately in need*

▶ **desperation** NOUN a feeling that you will do anything to make things better

despicable ADJECTIVE very bad or evil: *a despicable crime*

despise VERB **despises, despising, despised** to despise someone or something is to hate them very much

despite PREPOSITION despite someone or something means without taking any notice of them: *Despite the rain, we had a great picnic.*

despondency NOUN feeling fed up
▶ **despondent** ADJECTIVE fed up or depressed

dessert (pronounced diz-**urt**) NOUN **desserts** a pudding or sweet at the end of a meal

destination NOUN **destinations** the place someone is on the way to

destined ADJECTIVE if something is destined, it will happen anyway: *destined to become a star*

destiny NOUN **destinies** what will happen in the future: *I believe you can change your own destiny.*

destitute ADJECTIVE without money, food or anywhere to live

destroy VERB **destroys, destroying, destroyed 1** to destroy something is to ruin it completely: *a city destroyed in the war* **2** to destroy an animal is to kill it deliberately because it is ill or not wanted

▶ **destroyer** NOUN **destroyers 1** someone who destroys something **2** a fast warship

▶ **destruction** NOUN completely destroying something

▶ **destructive** ADJECTIVE doing a lot of damage: *the destructive effects of a bad diet*

detach VERB **detaches, detaching, detached** to separate things from each other: *You can detach the hood from the jacket.*

▶ **detached** ADJECTIVE **1** a detached house is not joined to another house **2** not caring or interested in either side of an argument

▶ **detachment** NOUN **detachments 1** not feeling involved in what other people have strong opinions about **2** a group of people, especially soldiers, chosen for a special job

detail NOUN **details** a small part, fact or item: *Draw the outline and then fill in the details.*
• **in detail** with nothing left out

▶ **detailed** ADJECTIVE including all the small facts or the smallest parts of something: *a detailed drawing*

detain VERB **detains, detaining, detained 1** to make someone stay somewhere: *detained by the police for 24 hours* **2** to delay someone: *I'm sorry to have detained you.*

detect VERB **detects, detecting, detected 1** to discover something that is not obvious **2** to notice: *I detected a hint of annoyance in his voice.*

▶ **detection** NOUN finding out or noticing things: *Early detection of this illness is very important.*

▶ **detective** NOUN **detectives** someone who tries to find out information, especially to solve crimes

detention NOUN **detentions** making a person stay in a place, especially in prison or in school after everyone else has left, as a punishment

deter VERB **deters, deterring, deterred** to put someone off doing something

detergent NOUN **detergents** a chemical for cleaning things: *washing-up detergent*

deteriorate VERB **deteriorates, deteriorating, deteriorated** to get worse: *deteriorating health*

▶ **deterioration** NOUN growing worse: *a deterioration in her condition*

determination NOUN a fixed idea that you will do something, however difficult it may be: *a determination to win*

▶ **determine** VERB **determines, determining, determined 1** to control or influence what happens: *The weather will determine how long the event lasts.* **2** to decide to do something: *William determined to do something about this.*

▶ **determined** ADJECTIVE with a fixed idea that you are going to do something: *The team was determined to finish first if they possibly could.*

Aa
Bb
Cc
Dd
Ee
Ff
Gg
Hh
Ii
Jj
Kk
Ll
Mm
Nn
Oo
Pp
Qq
Rr
Ss
Tt
Uu
Vv
Ww
Xx
Yy
Zz

Aa
Bb
Cc
Dd
Ee
Ff
Gg
Hh
Ii
Jj
Kk
Ll
Mm
Nn
Oo
Pp
Qq
Rr
Ss
Tt
Uu
Vv
Ww
Xx
Yy
Zz

deterrent NOUN **deterrents** something that puts people off doing something

detest VERB **detests, detesting, detested** to detest someone or something is to hate them very much

detonate VERB **detonates, detonating, detonated** to explode or make something explode: *The bomb could detonate at any moment.* • *They planted explosives in the building, then detonated them.*

▸ **detonator** NOUN **detonators** something that sets off an explosive like a bomb

detour NOUN **detours** a different and longer way of getting somewhere

detract VERB **detracts, detracting, detracted** to make something seem less good or enjoyable: *The rain detracted from the fun of the picnic.*

devastate VERB **devastates, devastating, devastated** to devastate a place is to ruin it completely

▸ **devastated** ADJECTIVE **1** completely ruined **2** very shocked and upset

▸ **devastation** NOUN **1** ruin and destruction: *scenes of devastation after the explosion* **2** a feeling of being very badly shocked

develop VERB **develops, developing, developed 1** to grow or make something grow bigger, better or more complicated: *The young animals develop very quickly.* • *The story soon developed into an interesting mystery.* **2** to develop a camera film is to make photographs from it **3** to develop an area is to put up new buildings there: *plans to develop this land*

▸ **development** NOUN **developments 1** there is development or a development when something grows bigger, better or more advanced or more complicated **2** a new event in a story **3** an area of land with new buildings on it

deviate VERB **deviates, deviating, deviated** to do something different or go in a different direction from what you might expect or predict

▸ **deviation** NOUN **deviations** something that is different from what is normal

device NOUN **devices** a tool, instrument or piece of equipment: *a device for cleaning keyboards*

devil NOUN **devils 1** an evil spirit **2** a wicked person

▸ **devilish** ADJECTIVE very wicked

devious ADJECTIVE clever in a sly way

devise VERB **devises, devising, devised** to think up a plan or way of doing something

devolution NOUN giving some government power to smaller areas

devote VERB **devotes, devoting, devoted 1** to devote time to a thing or person is to spend that time with them **2** to devote yourself to a thing or person is to be interested and involved only with them

▸ **devoted** ADJECTIVE extremely loving: *a devoted daughter*

▸ **devotion** NOUN great love

devour VERB **devours, devouring, devoured** to devour food is to eat it all very quickly

devout ADJECTIVE a devout person takes the beliefs of a religion very seriously

dew NOUN tiny drops of water that form, especially on the ground, at night

▸ **dewy** ADJECTIVE wet, especially with moisture from the cool night air

di- PREFIX if a word starts with **di-**, it usually has something to do with two, twice or double. For example, a *dioxide* has two atoms of oxygen

✦ This comes from **dis**, a Greek word which means *twice*.

diabetes (pronounced die-i-**bee**-teez) NOUN a disease that causes a person to have too much sugar in their blood

▸ **diabetic** ADJECTIVE a person who is diabetic has diabetes

NOUN a diabetic is someone who has diabetes

diabolical ADJECTIVE very bad or evil

diagnose VERB **diagnoses, diagnosing, diagnosed** to decide what is wrong with a thing or person
► **diagnosis** NOUN **diagnoses** a decision about what is wrong: *The doctor made a diagnosis from one look at the patient.*

diagonal ADJECTIVE going from one corner and across the middle to the opposite corner

diagram NOUN **diagrams** a drawing that explains something

dial NOUN **dials** a circle of numbers that often has a central pointer that moves around it to show a measurement
VERB **dials, dialling, dialled** to dial a telephone number is to call it

dialect NOUN **dialects** the language used by people who live in a particular area

✦ People who speak different **dialects** use different words from each other. People who have different **accents** pronounce the same words differently.

dialogue NOUN **dialogues 1** dialogue is talk between people **2** a dialogue is a conversation

diameter NOUN **diameters** a straight line from one side of a circle to the other that passes through its centre

diamond NOUN **diamonds 1** a very hard, clear gem that is a form of carbon **2** a four-sided pointed shape (◇) **3** diamonds is one of the four suits of playing cards, which have the symbol ♦ printed on them

diaphragm (pronounced **die**-a-fram) NOUN **diaphragms** a layer of muscle that separates the stomach from the chest and that moves up and down when you breathe

diarrhoea (pronounced die-a-**ree**-a) NOUN if you have diarrhoea, you go to the toilet very often and the solid waste from your body is too watery

diary NOUN **diaries** a book listing the dates of the year and the arrangements you make for the future or the things you did in the past

dice NOUN **dice** a small cube with

different numbers of dots on each face. You throw a dice and use the number of dots as a score when it's your turn in a game

✦ **Dice** is the plural of **die**. The singular, **die**, is not often used.
In fact, **dice** is now used as a singular or a plural noun: *Where are the dice?* • *The dice is on the floor.*

dictate VERB **dictates, dictating, dictated 1** to dictate something is to say words for someone to write down: *He has to type the letters that his boss dictates.* **2** to dictate to someone is to order them to do things
► **dictation** NOUN **dictations** a piece of text that someone speaks and another person writes down
► **dictator** NOUN **dictators** a person who has complete power over everyone else

dictionary NOUN **dictionaries** a book that gives words in alphabetical order and their meanings: *a French dictionary* • *a dictionary of medical words*

did VERB a way of changing the verb **do** to make a past tense: *I did the dishes yesterday, it's your turn today.*

didn't a short way to say and write **did not**

die[1] VERB **dies, dying, died** to stop living
• **die away** to die away is to fade away
• **die down** to die down is to get less: *wait for the fuss to die down*
• **die out** to die out is to disappear gradually: *More and more species of animal are dying out.*

die[2] NOUN **dies** a type of mould, used to shape metals and plastics

diesel NOUN a type of oil that is used as fuel for engines and boilers

diet NOUN **diets 1** the food that a person eats: *Do you have a healthy diet?* **2** a special course of foods for a person who, for example, has an illness or wants to lose weight: *Maybe you need to go on a diet.*

Aa
Bb
Cc
Dd
Ee
Ff
Gg
Hh
Ii
Jj
Kk
Ll
Mm
Nn
Oo
Pp
Qq
Rr
Ss
Tt
Uu
Vv
Ww
Xx
Yy
Zz

VERB **diets, dieting, dieted** to eat only certain foods, especially when trying to lose weight

differ VERB **differs, differing, differed** 1 to differ from something is not to be the same as it 2 to differ is to disagree with someone: *They differ over just about everything.*

different ADJECTIVE a thing or person is different from another if they are not the same

▸ **difference** NOUN **differences** 1 the way that something is not the same as something else 2 (*maths*) the amount between two numbers: *The difference between 6 and 10 is 4.*

✦Many people think it is wrong if you say **different to**, so you should say **different from**: *This pencil is different from that one.*

difficult ADJECTIVE 1 not easy 2 hard to please: *a difficult customer*

▸ **difficulty** NOUN **difficulties** 1 difficulty is not being easy: *You should be able to do this without difficulty.* 2 a difficulty is something that causes a problem: *We had a few difficulties at the beginning of the day.*

diffuse VERB **diffuses, diffusing, diffused** to spread something, especially light, widely and evenly

dig VERB **digs, digging, dug** 1 to lift up and turn over earth with a spade 2 to make a hole, especially in the ground 3 to poke someone

NOUN **digs** 1 a poke: *a dig in the ribs* 2 a remark that you make to irritate someone deliberately: *I pretended not to hear her dig about my clothes.* 3 a place where archaeologists remove earth to look for ancient remains

digest VERB **digests, digesting, digested** to digest food is to break it down in the stomach so that your body can use it

▸ **digestion** NOUN the way your body treats what you eat

digger NOUN **diggers** a machine that can move or break up large amounts of earth

digit NOUN **digits** a number from 0 to 9

digital ADJECTIVE 1 based on the use of numbers 2 a digital clock or watch shows the time as a row of numbers, rather than on a round face. Look up and compare **analogue** 3 digital recording stores sound as sets of numbers

digital television NOUN a method of broadcasting that uses digital technology

dignified ADJECTIVE calm and serious

dignity NOUN 1 a calm manner: *He told them to be quiet, to behave with some dignity.* 2 pride and self-respect: *It takes all the dignity out of a horse to make him do tricks.*

dike NOUN **dikes** 1 a wall that holds water back 2 a ditch that water runs along

dilapidated ADJECTIVE falling to pieces

dilate VERB **dilates, dilating, dilated** to make or get larger or wider: *The pupils of your eyes dilate in the dark.*

dilemma NOUN **dilemmas** a problem situation when you have to make a difficult choice between two options

diligence NOUN a serious and careful attitude to work

▸ **diligent** ADJECTIVE hard-working

dilute VERB **dilutes, diluting, diluted** to add water to a liquid so that it is not as strong: *Try diluting the juice with fizzy water.*

▸ **diluted** ADJECTIVE a diluted liquid is weaker because water has been added to it

▸ **dilution** NOUN adding water to a strong liquid to make it weaker

dim ADJECTIVE **dimmer, dimmest** 1 a dim light or colour is not bright or clear 2 a dim person is not very quick at understanding

VERB **dims, dimming, dimmed** to get or make darker or more difficult to see

▸ **dimly** ADVERB not very brightly or clearly: *I can only see you very dimly through the lens.*

dimension NOUN **dimensions** a measurement such as the length, width or area of something: *Please give the dimensions of the doorway.*

Aa
Bb
Cc
Dd
Ee
Ff
Gg
Hh
Ii
Jj
Kk
Ll
Mm
Nn
Oo
Pp
Qq
Rr
Ss
Tt
Uu
Vv
Ww
Xx
Yy
Zz

diminish VERB **diminishes, diminishing, diminished** to get or make less or smaller

dimple NOUN **dimples** a small hollow like a dent in the skin of your chin or cheek: *He has dimples when he smiles.*

din NOUN a very loud noise

dine VERB **dines, dining, dined** to have dinner

▸ **diner** NOUN **diners 1** someone who is eating dinner, especially in a restaurant **2** in the US, a restaurant like a motorway service station

dinghy NOUN **dinghies** a small boat for rowing or sailing

dinner NOUN **dinners** a main meal in the evening or in the middle of the day

dinosaur NOUN **dinosaurs** an extinct prehistoric giant reptile

✦**Dinosaur** comes from the Greek for 'terrible lizard'.

dip VERB **dips, dipping, dipped 1** to put something in and out of a liquid quickly: *Dip the clothes in the dye.* **2** to slope downwards: *The field dips down towards the bottom of the valley.* **3** to dip a vehicle's headlights is to lower them so that they are not dazzling to other drivers
NOUN **dips**
1 a liquid that something can be put into for a short time
2 a slope downwards in the land
3 a quick swim
4 a soft food that you eat by dipping things in it

diploma NOUN **diplomas** a qualification that someone can study for in a particular subject

diplomacy NOUN **1** communication between countries **2** managing to deal with people without offending them

▸ **diplomat** NOUN **diplomats** a person whose job is to keep good relationships and communications between countries

▸ **diplomatic** ADJECTIVE **1** to do with the relationships between countries: *the diplomatic service* **2** if you are

diplomatic, you are careful not to say things which will offend or upset someone

dire ADJECTIVE dreadful: *in dire need*

direct ADJECTIVE **1** straight, or as straight as possible: *a direct route to the airport* **2** frank and honest
VERB **directs, directing, directed 1** to aim or make something go a particular way: *Their weapons were directed at us.* **2** to tell someone how to get somewhere: *Could you please direct me to the post office?* **3** to control or guide something: *The police direct the traffic when it's busy.*

▸ **directly** ADVERB **1** straight away: *The manager will see you directly.* **2** straight: *looking directly at me*

▸ **directness** NOUN being frank and honest with people: *Geraldine's directness sometimes seems like rudeness.*

direction NOUN **directions**
1 direction is controlling or organizing
2 a direction is the place or point a thing or person goes towards or faces: *Which direction is the library?*
3 a direction is an order or instruction: *a list of directions on the side of the packet*
4 directions are instructions for getting somewhere: *Try to follow my directions to the hidden treasure.*

director NOUN **directors 1** the manager of a business **2** a person who makes a film or organizes a stage show

directory NOUN **directories 1** a book that tells you people's names, addresses and telephone numbers **2** (*ICT*) a group of computer files with a particular name: *Put this file in the 'letters' directory.*

direct speech NOUN (*grammar*) in a story or report, direct speech tells you the actual words that a person said. Look up and compare **indirect speech**

dirt NOUN any substance that is not clean or makes something unclean, such as mud or dust

dirty ADJECTIVE **dirtier, dirtiest 1** not clean: *dirty floors* **2** not polite: *dirty*

Aa
Bb
Cc
Dd
Ee
Ff
Gg
Hh
Ii
Jj
Kk
Ll
Mm
Nn
Oo
Pp
Qq
Rr
Ss
Tt
Uu
Vv
Ww
Xx
Yy
Zz

language **3** unfair or dishonest: *a dirty trick*

dis- PREFIX **1** if a word starts with **dis-**, it can have something to do with separation and moving apart. For example, *disjointed* means 'not connected properly' **2** if a word starts with **dis-**, it may also mean 'not' something. For example, *dislike* means 'not like'

disabled ADJECTIVE having a physical or mental problem that makes some aspects of life difficult

▸ **disability** NOUN **disabilities** a physical or mental problem that makes some aspects of life difficult

disadvantage NOUN **disadvantages** something that makes things difficult or not desirable: *It's a great idea – the only disadvantage is that it's expensive.*

disagree VERB **disagrees, disagreeing, disagreed 1** if people disagree, they have a different opinion about something: *I completely disagree with you about that.* **2** if something, such as food, disagrees with you it makes you feel ill

▸ **disagreeable** ADJECTIVE unpleasant

▸ **disagreement** NOUN **disagreements 1** disagreement is having different opinions **2** a disagreement is an argument

disappear VERB **disappears, disappearing, disappeared** to vanish or go out of sight

▸ **disappearance** NOUN **disappearances** when something or someone vanishes: *The police are investigating the disappearance of the necklace.*

disappoint VERB **disappoints, disappointing, disappointed** to let someone down: *I'm sorry to disappoint you, but I can't come to your party.*

▸ **disappointed** ADJECTIVE feeling let down

▸ **disappointment** NOUN **disappointments** a feeling of being let down because something does not happen or turns out worse than expected: *It was a disappointment to*

find that all the tickets had already been sold.

disapprove VERB **disapproves, disapproving, disapproved** to disapprove of someone or something is to think that they are bad, wrong or unsuitable: *My parents disapproved of my new friend.*

▸ **disapproval** NOUN thinking something is not good

disarm VERB **disarms, disarming, disarmed 1** to disarm someone is to take a weapon away from them: *A security guard managed to disarm the man.* **2** to give up weapons that you have

▸ **disarmament** NOUN getting rid of war weapons

disaster NOUN **disasters** a terrible happening, especially if there is great damage or injury

▸ **disastrous** ADJECTIVE causing great damage, injury or loss

disbelief NOUN not believing something: *an expression of complete disbelief*

▸ **disbelieve** VERB **disbelieves, disbelieving, disbelieved** to think someone is lying or something is untrue

disc NOUN **discs 1** something flat and round **2** a CD

discard VERB **discards, discarding, discarded** to throw something away: *a discarded wrapper on the pavement*

discern VERB **discerns, discerning, discerned** to see or understand something

discharge VERB **discharges, discharging, discharged 1** to discharge a prisoner is to let them go **2** to discharge a substance like a polluting liquid or gas is to give it off or let it out: *a factory that discharges dangerous products into the environment*

NOUN **discharges 1** carrying out an order or duty: *injured in the discharge of his duty* **2** letting someone go: *an honourable discharge from the army* **3** a substance that comes or leaks out of something

disciple (pronounced dis-**ie**-pil) NOUN **disciples 1** a person who follows and believes in someone else's ideas **2** one of the original followers of Jesus Christ

disciplinarian NOUN **disciplinarians** a person who is very strict

disciplinary ADJECTIVE to do with rules for how to behave and with punishment for breaking rules

discipline NOUN strict training or rules that are supposed to lead to good behaviour

disclose VERB **discloses, disclosing, disclosed 1** if you disclose a secret or private information, you tell it to someone **2** (formal) to disclose something is to uncover it

disco NOUN **discos** a place or party where people dance to recorded music

discolour VERB **discolours, discolouring, discoloured** to go or make something a strange or unpleasant colour

discomfort NOUN feeling uncomfortable: The doctor asked if I had felt any discomfort.

disconnect VERB **disconnects, disconnecting, disconnected** to separate things that were joined together

discontent NOUN a feeling of not being happy or satisfied with a situation

▶ **discontented** ADJECTIVE not satisfied and wanting to change a situation

discount NOUN **discounts** some money taken off a price to make it cheaper: a 10% discount on all goods

discourage VERB **discourages, discouraging, discouraged** to put someone off doing something: I was discouraged by all the people I knew who had failed.

▶ **discouragement** NOUN **1** a disappointment that puts you off doing something **2** an effort to put you off something that you want to do

▶ **discouraging** ADJECTIVE making you feel less hopeful or confident about something: discouraging news

discover VERB **discovers, discovering, discovered** to find information, a place or an object, especially for the first time: The settlers discovered gold in the mountains. • We discovered that the paint wouldn't mix with water.

▶ **discoverer** NOUN **discoverers** a person who finds something for the first time

▶ **discovery** NOUN **discoveries** finding something, especially by accident: the discovery of America

discreet ADJECTIVE quiet and not attracting people's attention

discriminate VERB **discriminates, discriminating, discriminated 1** to see differences between things and prefer one to another **2** to treat different people or groups differently in the same situation, often because of their colour, religion or sex

▶ **discrimination** NOUN **1** being able to see differences in things and decide if they are good or bad **2** treating people differently for no good reason

discus NOUN **discuses** a heavy disc that athletes throw as far as they can in a competition

discuss VERB **discusses, discussing, discussed** to talk about something in detail

▶ **discussion** NOUN **discussions 1** discussion is talk between people: discussion between world leaders **2** a discussion is a conversation **3** a piece of writing in which you look at a subject from every point of view, and present reasons for and against each one

disdain NOUN not liking a thing or person because you do not think they are good or interesting enough

disease NOUN **diseases** an illness

▶ **diseased** ADJECTIVE not healthy, especially because of an illness: diseased leaves on the roses

disgrace NOUN **1** something that makes you feel ashamed: It's no disgrace to come last if you tried hard. **2** if you are in disgrace, other people do not approve of

Aa
Bb
Cc
Dd
Ee
Ff
Gg
Hh
Ii
Jj
Kk
Ll
Mm
Nn
Oo
Pp
Qq
Rr
Ss
Tt
Uu
Vv
Ww
Xx
Yy
Zz

what you have done: *Debbie's in disgrace for telling us all Jane's secrets.*

► **disgraceful** ADJECTIVE shameful or very bad

disguise VERB **disguises, disguising, disguised** if you disguise yourself, you wear clothes you would not normally wear or things like make-up or a wig, to hide who you really are

NOUN **disguises 1** a disguise is something you wear to hide who you really are **2** if you are in disguise, you are wearing things like clothes or make-up to hide who you really are

disgust NOUN a strong feeling that you do not like or approve of something: *The sight of the worms filled Lottie with disgust.*

► **disgusted** ADJECTIVE sickened by something bad, wrong or unpleasant

► **disgusting** ADJECTIVE extremely unpleasant: *a disgusting drink*

dish NOUN **dishes 1** a plate or bowl for food **2** food that has been prepared for eating: *a fish dish* **3** a large disc that is an aerial for receiving satellite signals, especially for television broadcasts

VERB **dishes, dishing, dished**
• **dish something out** to give something to a lot of people or in large amounts

dishevelled ADJECTIVE with messed-up hair and untidy clothes

dishonest ADJECTIVE not telling the truth and cheating people: *a dishonest way of doing business*

► **dishonesty** NOUN cheating or not being honest

disinfect VERB **disinfects, disinfecting, disinfected** to disinfect something is to destroy germs on it that might cause disease

► **disinfectant** NOUN **disinfectants** a product that kills germs

disintegrate VERB **disintegrates, disintegrating, disintegrated** to fall to pieces

► **disintegration** NOUN falling apart

disinterested ADJECTIVE not having personal feelings for or against

someone or something: *A disinterested judge will make a fair decision.*

disk NOUN **disks** (*ICT*) a round flat object that computers use to store information on: *Save the file on a floppy disk.* • *The virus could infect your hard disk.*

disk drive NOUN **disk drives** (*ICT*) the part of a computer that holds and operates the disks that store information

dislike VERB **dislikes, disliking, disliked** if you dislike someone or something, you do not like them: *I dislike having to get up early, but I have to do it.*

dislocate VERB **dislocates, dislocating, dislocated** to dislocate a joint is to put a bone out of its correct position: *Tom dislocated his shoulder in a rugby match.*

► **dislocation** NOUN when something, especially a bone, gets moved from its correct position

dislodge VERB **dislodges, dislodging, dislodged** to move something, especially when it is stuck, from its place

disloyal ADJECTIVE not loyal or faithful to someone you should be supporting

► **disloyalty** NOUN not being loyal or faithful

dismal ADJECTIVE gloomy and not at all bright or attractive

dismantle VERB **dismantles, dismantling, dismantled** to dismantle something is to take it apart

dismay NOUN an unpleasant feeling of surprise and worry: *We watched in dismay as Tom fell into the water.*

dismiss VERB **dismisses, dismissing, dismissed 1** to dismiss someone is to send them away: *The class were dismissed by the teacher early today.* **2** to dismiss a subject is to decide not to consider it any longer: *They dismissed my excuses and gave me a punishment anyway.*

► **dismissal** NOUN **dismissals** when someone gets sent away especially from their job: *an unfair dismissal*

dismount VERB **dismounts, dismounting, dismounted** to get off a bicycle or horse

disobedience NOUN when someone does not do as they are told

▶ **disobedient** ADJECTIVE not doing as you are told

disobey VERB **disobeys, disobeying, disobeyed** not to do what you are told to do: *Do not disobey me!*

disorder NOUN **disorders 1** disorder is a state of confusion or a disturbance **2** a disorder is an illness

▶ **disorderly** ADJECTIVE behaving badly: *a disorderly crowd*

dispatch VERB **dispatches, dispatching, dispatched** to dispatch something or someone is to send them somewhere: *a parcel dispatched on the 29th*

dispel VERB **dispels, dispelling, dispelled** to dispel a thought or feeling is to make it go away: *The teacher tried to dispel our fears about the maths test.*

dispense VERB **dispenses, dispensing, dispensed 1** to give something out, especially medicine **2** to dispense with something is to decide to do without it

▶ **dispenser** NOUN **dispensers** a machine or container that you can get measured amounts of something from: *a cash dispenser*

disperse VERB **disperses, dispersing, dispersed** to scatter or send things or people off in different directions: *The crowd is now beginning to disperse.*

▶ **dispersal** NOUN things or people going in different directions

displace VERB **displaces, displacing, displaced** to put or take something or someone out of the place they seemed to be fixed in: *I think she's going to displace the champion.* • *Thousands of people were displaced during the war.*

▶ **displacement** NOUN movement out of the usual place

display NOUN **displays 1** a show or exhibition: *a display of the children's work* **2** (*ICT*) the way you see things on a computer screen: *You can change the display so that it's bigger.*

• **on display** something that is on display is arranged for people to see

VERB **displays, displaying, displayed** to set things out for an exhibition or to show something off for people to see: *The treasure will be displayed in the museum for two months.*

displease VERB **displeases, displeasing, displeased** to displease someone is to annoy them

▶ **displeasure** NOUN annoyance

disposable ADJECTIVE a disposable product is meant to be used and then thrown away

disposal NOUN getting rid of something: *a waste-disposal unit in the kitchen*

• **at your disposal** a thing or person that is at your disposal is ready for you to use: *There will be a car at your disposal.*

dispose VERB **disposes, disposing, disposed** to dispose of something is to get rid of it: *People dispose of their rubbish in the yard.*

▶ **disposed** ADJECTIVE to be disposed to do something is to be willing to do it: *I don't like her and I'm not disposed to help her.*

disprove VERB **disproves, disproving, disproved** to disprove something is to prove that it is not true

dispute NOUN **disputes** an argument, especially about work or between countries

VERB **disputes, disputing, disputed** to argue about something: *They dispute that they have been treated fairly.*

disqualify VERB **disqualifies, disqualifying, disqualified** to disqualify someone is to prevent them from taking part in a competition because they have done something wrong: *Three contestants have been disqualified for wearing the wrong kind of shoes.*

▶ **disqualification** NOUN stopping someone from taking part in a competition because they have done something wrong

Aa
Bb
Cc
Dd
Ee
Ff
Gg
Hh
Ii
Jj
Kk
Ll
Mm
Nn
Oo
Pp
Qq
Rr
Ss
Tt
Uu
Vv
Ww
Xx
Yy
Zz

disrespect NOUN being rude and behaving without respect towards someone

▸ **disrespectful** ADJECTIVE not polite towards someone: *disrespectful language*

disrupt VERB **disrupts, disrupting, disrupted** to disrupt something is to disturb the normal way that it happens: *Power cuts have disrupted two days of school.*

▸ **disruption** NOUN **disruptions** disturbance of the smooth running of something: *disruption in the town centre caused by a burst water pipe*

▸ **disruptive** ADJECTIVE causing disturbance and disorder: *Disruptive pupils will be sent out of the room.*

dissatisfaction NOUN irritation or not being pleased about something

▸ **dissatisfied** ADJECTIVE to be dissatisfied with something is not to be pleased about it

dissect VERB **dissects, dissecting, dissected** to cut something up so that you can examine it

▸ **dissection** NOUN cutting something up so that you can see all its parts in detail

dissolve VERB **dissolves, dissolving, dissolved** to melt or be melted in liquid: *Keep stirring and the sugar will dissolve completely.*

distance NOUN **distances** the space between things: *Measure the distance between the lines accurately.*

• **in the distance** a long way off: *the sound of a train in the distance*

▸ **distant** ADJECTIVE **1** far off, not close: *a distant shout* • *a distant cousin* **2** cold and unfriendly: *behaving in a distant manner*

distil VERB **distils, distilling, distilled** (*science*) to make a liquid pure by boiling it and cooling the vapour that is produced

▸ **distillation** NOUN (*science*) the process of making a liquid pure by boiling it and cooling the vapour that is produced

▸ **distillery** NOUN **distilleries** a factory that makes strong alcoholic drinks like whisky and brandy

distinct ADJECTIVE **1** clear and definite: *a distinct improvement* **2** different: *two languages that are quite distinct*

▸ **distinction** NOUN **distinctions** **1** a difference: *We have to make a distinction between pupils who don't care and pupils who don't try.* **2** an honour: *She had the distinction of being the first woman airline pilot.* **3** a high mark in an examination: *Sandy always got distinctions in his piano exams.*

▸ **distinctive** ADJECTIVE different and easy to recognize: *a distinctive singing voice*

distinguish VERB **distinguishes, distinguishing, distinguished 1** to see a difference between things: *Jamie can't distinguish green from red because he's colour blind.* **2** to distinguish something is to make it out, either by seeing or hearing it

▸ **distinguished** ADJECTIVE famous and respected: *a distinguished scientist*

distort VERB **distorts, distorting, distorted 1** to distort something is to twist it out of shape: *Her face was distorted with the pain.* **2** to distort information or facts is to change them so that they are no longer correct or true: *a newspaper report that distorts the truth* **3** to distort a sound is to change it and make it sound strange and unclear: *A microphone can distort your voice.*

▸ **distortion** NOUN changing something so that it is noticeably different

distract VERB **distracts, distracting, distracted** to take your attention away: *Gerry distracted the teacher while the others swopped answers.*

▸ **distraction** NOUN **distractions** something that takes your attention away from what you are doing: *I haven't finished because I've had so many distractions.*

distraught ADJECTIVE extremely worried or upset

distress NOUN pain, sadness or worry VERB **distresses, distressing, distressed** to upset someone

distribute → divisor

distribute VERB **distributes, distributing, distributed** to give something out to lots of people: *Please distribute the books around the class.* • *a company that distributes products to shops*
▸ **distribution** NOUN when something goes or is taken out to different places

district NOUN **districts** one part of a country or town: *the district council*

distrust VERB **distrusts, distrusting, distrusted** not to trust someone or something
NOUN suspecting, or not trusting someone or something: *a look of distrust*
▸ **distrustful** ADJECTIVE full of suspicion

disturb VERB **disturbs, disturbing, disturbed 1** to interrupt something that is going on, or someone who is doing something: *I'm sorry to disturb you, but I need to ask you a question.* **2** to disturb something is to change the way it has been arranged: *I knew that someone had been at my desk because the papers had been disturbed.* **3** something that disturbs you upsets or worries you
▸ **disturbance** NOUN **disturbances** an outbreak of noise or noisy behaviour: *disturbances in the street at night*

disused ADJECTIVE not used any more: *a disused railway station*

ditch NOUN **ditches** a long narrow hole in the ground, especially one that has water in it
VERB **ditches, ditching, ditched** (*slang*) to ditch something is to get rid of it

dither VERB **dithers, dithering, dithered** to hesitate and be unable to make a decision

ditto NOUN the same again
▸ **ditto mark** NOUN a symbol (˝) in a list that means that the word above it should be repeated

divan NOUN **divans** a couch or bed that has no back, headboard or sides

dive VERB **dives, diving, dived 1** to go into water headfirst **2** to go down steeply and quickly: *an eagle diving down into a field*
NOUN **dives** a downwards movement, especially headfirst into water

diverse ADJECTIVE different or varied: *a diverse selection of cheeses*
▸ **diversity** NOUN variety

diversion NOUN **diversions 1** an alternative route to the usual one: *There was a diversion because the bridge was closed.* **2** something that takes your attention away, especially an amusement: *The little boys created a diversion while the big ones stole our bikes.* • *The puppet show was a welcome diversion.*

divert VERB **diverts, diverting, diverted** to make something, especially traffic, go a different way

divide VERB **divides, dividing, divided 1** to separate into parts: *divide the class into small groups* • *a single cell that divides and becomes two cells* **2** (*maths*) to find how many times one number contains another. For example, if you divide 12 by 3 you get 4, which can be written as $12 \div 3 = 4$

dividend NOUN **dividends 1** (*maths*) an amount to be divided **2** part of the profits that a company makes, which is paid to people who own shares in the company

divine ADJECTIVE **1** belonging to a god or like a god **2** wonderful
VERB **divines, divining, divined** to search for underground water or minerals by holding a special Y-shaped stick that moves when it is near them

divisible ADJECTIVE able to be divided exactly: *12 is divisible by 2, 3, 4 and 6.*

division NOUN **divisions 1** division is dividing things, numbers or people: *We're learning a different way of doing division sums.* • *the fair division of the money between everyone* **2** a division is a gap or barrier that separates things: *The curtain is a division between the two rooms.* **3** a division is a section of something: *There are eight teams in our division.*

divisor NOUN **divisors** (*maths*) a number that you divide into another

Aa Bb Cc Dd Ee Ff Gg Hh Ii Jj Kk Ll Mm Nn Oo Pp Qq Rr Ss Tt Uu Vv Ww Xx Yy Zz

165

Aa
Bb
Cc
Dd
Ee
Ff
Gg
Hh
Ii
Jj
Kk
Ll
Mm
Nn
Oo
Pp
Qq
Rr
Ss
Tt
Uu
Vv
Ww
Xx
Yy
Zz

number. For example, 10 is the divisor in 100 ÷ 10

divorce NOUN **divorces** the official end of a marriage

VERB **divorces, divorcing, divorced** to end a marriage with someone

Diwali (pronounced di-**wa**-li) NOUN the Hindu or Sikh religious festival of lights, which takes place in October or November

DIY ABBREVIATION short for **do-it-yourself**

dizzy ADJECTIVE **dizzier, dizziest** giddy: *Spinning round will make you dizzy.*

DJ ABBREVIATION a person who plays pieces of music on the radio or at a disco. **DJ** is short for **disc jockey**

DNA ABBREVIATION short for **deoxyribonucleic acid**, the substance in living things that carries information about your individual genes

do VERB **does, doing, did, done** **1** to carry out an action or deal with a task: *do your homework* **2** to get along or manage: *How are you doing?* **3** to be enough: *Will a pound do?*

• **do away with** to do away with something or someone is to get rid of them or kill them

• **do something up** **1** to do something up is to fasten it: *Do your jacket up – it's cold out there.* **2** to do something up is to decorate it: *We're doing up our hall.*

NOUN **dos** (*informal*) a party or celebration

+ The verb **do** is very important in making English sentences.

You use it so you do not repeat a verb: *We rarely have a picnic, but when we do, it always rains.*

You often use it with a more important verb: ***Do** you understand?* • *I **do** not care.* • *I **do** like chocolate.*

docile ADJECTIVE a docile person or animal is quiet and easy to control

dock¹ NOUN **docks** part of a harbour where ships can load and unload their cargo

VERB **docks, docking, docked** **1** to go

into, or put a ship into a dock: *When we've docked, a crane will unload the containers.* **2** a spacecraft docks when it joins another craft during a flight

▸ **docker** NOUN **dockers** someone who works at the docks, loading and unloading ships

dock² VERB **docks, docking, docked** **1** to dock someone's pay is to make it less **2** to dock an animal's tail is to cut it short

doctor NOUN **doctors** someone who has been trained in medicine and treats people who are ill

+ **Doctor** is the Latin word for *teacher*, but the meaning has changed in English.

document NOUN **documents** a paper with official information on it: *Keep this document for your records.*

documentary NOUN **documentaries** a film, or a television or radio programme, that shows real people and real situations

dodge VERB **dodges, dodging, dodged** to avoid something by a quick or clever movement: *Graeme managed to dodge out of the way before the ball hit him.*

NOUN **dodges** a trick to avoid something

dodo NOUN **dodoes** or **dodos** a type of large bird that is extinct

doe NOUN **does** the female of certain animals like deer, rabbits or hares

does VERB the form of the verb **do** that is used with **he, she** and **it**

doesn't a short way to say and write **does not**

dog NOUN **dogs** a four-footed animal that barks and that people often keep as a pet

dog-eared ADJECTIVE a dog-eared page has a curled or bent corner

dogged (pronounced **dog**-id) ADJECTIVE determined or stubborn

dogsbody NOUN **dogsbodies** someone who gets all the small, uninteresting jobs to do

do-it-yourself ADJECTIVE designed to

be built by anyone at home, rather than by someone specially trained

doldrums PLURAL NOUN
• **in the doldrums** someone who is in the doldrums is fed up

dole NOUN someone who is on the dole has no job and is getting payments from the government

doll NOUN **dolls** a toy model of a person

dollar NOUN **dollars** the main unit of money in many countries including the United States, Canada, Australia and New Zealand

dolphin NOUN **dolphins** a very intelligent sea mammal of the whale family that has a long pointed mouth

domain NOUN **domains** the area that one person or government rules over

dome NOUN **domes** the roof of a building in the shape of the top half of a ball

domestic ADJECTIVE **1** to do with homes and houses: *domestic tasks like cleaning and cooking* **2** a domestic animal is not wild, but kept as a pet or on a farm
▸ **domesticated** ADJECTIVE **1** a domesticated animal is one that lives in contact with humans, either as a pet or on a farm **2** a domesticated person likes looking after their home and family

dominant ADJECTIVE stronger or more noticeable than others: *The dominant feature of this illness is a rash.*

dominate VERB **dominates, dominating, dominated** to control others by being strongest or most powerful: *He dominates every conversation.*
▸ **domination** NOUN when a powerful person controls everyone else

dominoes NOUN a game played with small rectangular blocks that have different numbers of dots on them

donate VERB **donates, donating, donated** to give something, especially money, as a gift: *Would you donate something to our charity?*
▸ **donation** NOUN **donations** something that someone gives without getting anything back

done VERB a form of the verb **do** that is used with a helping verb to make a past tense: *I've done my homework and now I'm going out on my bike.*

donkey NOUN **donkeys** a type of animal that looks like a small horse with long ears. A donkey may also be called an **ass**

donor NOUN **donors** someone who gives something that someone else can use: *Blood donors are urgently needed.*

don't a short way to say and write **do not**

doom NOUN an unpleasant end like ruin or death
▸ **doomed** ADJECTIVE bound to fail: *The project was doomed from the start.*

door NOUN **doors** a panel, often on a hinge, that you can open and close. It usually covers the entrance to a building, room or cupboard

doorstep NOUN **doorsteps** the step in front of the door of a house

doorway NOUN **doorways** an opening in a wall for a door

dope NOUN **dopes** an idiot
VERB **dopes, doping, doped** to dope someone is to drug them

dormant ADJECTIVE not active at the moment: *a dormant volcano*

dormitory NOUN **dormitories** a bedroom for several people, especially in a school

---

✦ **Dormitory** comes from the Latin word **dormire**, which means *to sleep*. The words **dormant** and **dormouse** are also linked to the word **dormire**.

---

dormouse NOUN **dormice** a small animal like a mouse that has a long furry tail, lives in forests and hibernates

dose NOUN **doses** an amount of medicine that you take at one time
▸ **dosage** NOUN **dosages** the amount of a medicine that you should take

dot NOUN **dots** a small round mark
• **on the dot** exactly on time: *Belinda arrived at three o'clock on the dot, just as she'd promised.*

Aa
Bb
Cc
Dd
Ee
Ff
Gg
Hh
Ii
Jj
Kk
Ll
Mm
Nn
Oo
Pp
Qq
Rr
Ss
Tt
Uu
Vv
Ww
Xx
Yy
Zz

Aa
Bb
Cc
Dd
Ee
Ff
Gg
Hh
Ii
Jj
Kk
Ll
Mm
Nn
Oo
Pp
Qq
Rr
Ss
Tt
Uu
Vv
Ww
Xx
Yy
Zz

VERB **dots, dotting, dotted 1** to dot something is to put a dot or dots on it: *Remember to dot the letter 'i'.* • *Dot the cake with cherries.* **2** if people or things are dotted somewhere, they are spread over an area: *Cushions were dotted around the floor.*

dote VERB **dotes, doting, doted**
• **dote on someone** to dote on someone is to be extremely fond of them

double ADJECTIVE **1** containing twice as much: *a double dose of medicine* **2** made up of two of the same sort: *double doors* **3** suitable for two people: *a double cabin*
NOUN **doubles 1** twice as much: *Jan gets double the pocket money I get.* **2** a thing or person that looks exactly like another one: *I saw your double in the street yesterday.* **3** in games like tennis and badminton, you play doubles when two of you play against two other people
• **at the double** very quickly
VERB **doubles, doubling, doubled** to multiply something by two
• **double up** to bend over in laughter or pain

double bass NOUN **double basses** the largest instrument in the violin family, which plays very low notes

double-cross VERB **double-crosses, double-crossing, double-crossed** to cheat someone

double-decker NOUN **double-deckers** a bus with an upper floor

doubly ADVERB more than usual: *Make doubly sure that the door's locked.*

doubt NOUN **doubts** a feeling of not being sure about something: *I have doubts about this plan.* • *I have no doubt you are quite right.*
VERB **doubts, doubting, doubted** to be unsure about something: *I doubt that you will understand.*

doubtful ADJECTIVE **1** to be doubtful about something is to be unsure about it **2** something that is doubtful is not likely: *It was doubtful that they would ever be found now.*

dough (rhymes with **no**) NOUN a mixture of flour and water for making bread

doughnut NOUN **doughnuts** a round cake that is deep-fried. It may have a hole in the middle or be filled with something like jam or chocolate

dour ADJECTIVE **dourer, dourest** stern and unhappy: *a dour expression*

dove NOUN **doves** a kind of pigeon that is usually white

dowdy ADJECTIVE **dowdier, dowdiest** looking dull, uninteresting and unfashionable

dowel NOUN **dowels** a wooden or metal peg that fastens two things together by fitting into a hole in each one

down¹ ADVERB **1** towards or in a lower position: *get down* • *sit down* **2** to a smaller size: *cut the picture down to fit the frame* **3** along: *go down to the post office*
• **go down with** to become ill with something: *She's gone down with flu.*
PREPOSITION **1** towards or in a lower part: *tears running down his face* **2** along: *walking down the road*

down² NOUN light, soft feathers

downcast ADJECTIVE feeling sad

downfall NOUN **downfalls** ruin or defeat: *the downfall of a powerful leader*

download VERB **downloads, downloading, downloaded** (*ICT*) to download information from the Internet is to get it from there and put it on your computer
NOUN **downloads** something that you have downloaded from the Internet

downpour NOUN **downpours** a heavy fall of rain

downs PLURAL NOUN low grassy hills

downstairs ADVERB to a lower floor of a building: *go downstairs*
ADJECTIVE on a lower floor: *the downstairs bathroom*

downstream ADVERB further down a river in the direction that it flows, usually towards the sea

downward ADJECTIVE moving or leading to a lower place or position: *a downward slope*
ADVERB downwards

downwards ADVERB to a lower place or position: *The path winds downwards to the lakeside.*

dowry NOUN **dowries** money and property that a woman brings to a marriage from her family

doze VERB **dozes, dozing, dozed** to sleep lightly
• **doze off** to fall into a light sleep
NOUN **dozes** a light sleep: *I had a doze after lunch.*

dozen NOUN **dozens** twelve: *a dozen eggs*

Dr ABBREVIATION short for **Doctor**

drab ADJECTIVE **drabber, drabbest** uninteresting and without any bright colours

draft NOUN **drafts** a rough piece of writing which contains the basic ideas but is not finished yet: *This is just the first draft of my essay.*
VERB **drafts, drafting, drafted** to make a rough plan of something

drag VERB **drags, dragging, dragged** 1 to drag something or someone is to pull them along roughly: *Thomas came out dragging his schoolbag behind him.* 2 if time or an event drags it seems to pass very slowly: *The play seemed to drag on for hours.* 3 to drag a river or lake is to search it with a net
NOUN a boring task or event: *Choir practice was always such a drag.*

dragon NOUN **dragons** an imaginary, fire-breathing reptile with wings

dragonfly NOUN **dragonflies** a long thin insect with double wings

drain VERB **drains, draining, drained** 1 to drain something is to let the water run out of it: *They must drain the reservoir to repair the dam.* • *Drain the washed cabbage well before cutting it up.*
2 to drain is to flow away: *watching the liquid drain down the sink*
3 to drain a container of drink is to drink it all

4 to drain a person is to make them very tired
NOUN **drains** 1 a pipe or ditch for waste water to flow away in 2 something that uses up your energy or money

▶ **drainage** NOUN removing waste water by systems of pipes and rivers

▶ **drained** ADJECTIVE if you are drained, you have no strength left: *After running in the race, I felt completely drained.*

drake NOUN **drakes** a male duck

drama NOUN **dramas** 1 drama is acting, directing and producing plays 2 a drama is a play for the theatre or television 3 drama is something exciting happening

▶ **dramatic** ADJECTIVE 1 to do with plays and the theatre: *a dramatic production* 2 exciting 3 sudden and unexpected: *a dramatic rise in exam passes*

▶ **dramatist** NOUN **dramatists** a person who writes plays

▶ **dramatization** or **dramatisation** NOUN **dramatizations** or **dramatisations** a dramatization is a play based on an existing story or book

▶ **dramatize** or **dramatise** VERB **dramatizes, dramatizing, dramatized** 1 to turn something into a play for the theatre or television: *This story has been dramatized several times.* 2 to make a story or report more exciting than the actual event

drank VERB a way of changing the verb **drink** to make a past tense: *We drank our tea and left as quickly as possible.*

drape VERB **drapes, draping, draped** to arrange cloth so that it hangs gracefully: *She draped the scarf over her head.*

▶ **drapes** PLURAL NOUN in American English, drapes are long heavy curtains

drastic ADJECTIVE a drastic action has an extreme effect: *We need to do something drastic here.*

▶ **drastically** ADVERB in a sudden and extreme way: *Nora has changed drastically in the last few months.*

draught NOUN **draughts** a current of air

▶ **draughty** ADJECTIVE **draughtier, draughtiest** a draughty room or

Aa
Bb
Cc
Dd
Ee
Ff
Gg
Hh
Ii
Jj
Kk
Ll
Mm
Nn
Oo
Pp
Qq
Rr
Ss
Tt
Uu
Vv
Ww
Xx
Yy
Zz

building is cold and full of moving air currents

draughts NOUN a game for two people who move round black or white pieces on a squared board

draughtsman or **draughtswoman** NOUN **draughtsmen** or **draughtswomen** someone whose job is to draw plans

draw VERB **draws, drawing, drew, drawn**

1 to make a picture with a pencil or pen

2 to draw a vehicle is to pull it along behind: *Horses drew the carriage.*

3 if something draws people it attracts them: *The circus always draws huge audiences.*

4 to draw someone or something to a place is to move them there by pulling them gently: *Draw your chair up to the table.*

5 to score equal points in a game: *This pair have drawn every match they've played so far.*

NOUN **draws 1** an equal score: *The game ended in a draw.* **2** a lottery or raffle

drawback NOUN **drawbacks** a disadvantage: *The main drawback of the plan is that it's expensive.*

drawbridge NOUN **drawbridges** a bridge at the entrance of a castle that can be raised or lowered

drawer NOUN **drawers** a sliding box in a table, chest or cupboard

drawing NOUN **drawings** a picture drawn with a pencil or pen

drawing pin NOUN **drawing pins** a short pin with a large flat head that you use to fix paper to an upright surface like a board

drawl VERB **drawls, drawling, drawled** to speak slowly and lazily

NOUN a slow, lazy way of speaking

drawn VERB a form of the verb **draw** that is used with a helping verb to make a past tense: *I've drawn several styles for you to choose from.*

dread VERB **dreads, dreading, dreaded** to be very afraid and worried about something: *We're all dreading the exams.*

NOUN a feeling of great fear: *The thought of flying fills me with dread.*

dreadful ADJECTIVE terrible: *dreadful news* • *a dreadful film*

▶ **dreadfully** ADVERB **1** very badly: *The children have been behaving dreadfully all day.* **2** very much: *I'm dreadfully sorry.*

dreadlocks PLURAL NOUN hair that is worn in long twisted strands

dream NOUN **dreams 1** the things you think while you are asleep: *I had a very strange dream last night.* **2** if you are in a dream, you are concentrating on your thoughts and not on what is going on around you **3** a hope or ambition: *It was always her dream to go to Hollywood.*

VERB **dreams, dreaming, dreamt** or **dreamed** to imagine something, especially while you are asleep: *Last night I dreamt that my Mum was having another baby.* • *Did you say that or did I dream it?*

dreary ADJECTIVE **drearier, dreariest** dull and boring

dredge VERB **dredges, dredging, dredged** to scrape mud or waste off the bottom of a lake or river

▶ **dredger** NOUN **dredgers** a ship that digs a channel in a river or seabed

drench VERB **drenches, drenching, drenched** to be drenched is to be completely wet

dress NOUN **dresses 1** a dress is a piece of clothing for girls or women like a top and skirt joined together **2** dress is clothing: *dancers in traditional dress*

VERB **dresses, dressing, dressed 1** to put clothes on: *The doorbell rang while I was dressing.* • *Mum still has to dress my little brother.* **2** to dress a wound is to put a plaster or bandage on it

• **dress up** to put on special clothes: *Colin always loved to dress up as a pirate.*

▶ **dressing** NOUN **dressings 1** a light sauce for food, especially salad **2** a bandage or plaster for a wound

dresser NOUN **dressers** a kitchen cupboard with open shelves at the top

dressmaker NOUN **dressmakers** a person who makes clothes for women

dress rehearsal NOUN **dress rehearsals** the final rehearsal for a stage show when the actors wear their costumes

drew VERB a way of changing the verb **draw** to make a past tense: *Who drew this face on the board?*

dribble VERB **dribbles, dribbling, dribbled 1** to let liquid leak out of your mouth **2** in football, to kick the ball gently along in front of you as you run

dried VERB a way of changing the verb **dry** to make a past tense. It can be used with or without a helping verb: *Julia dried the glasses with a soft cloth.* • *After the fruit has been dried, it will keep for ages.*

drift VERB **drifts, drifting, drifted 1** to move with the tide or current of flowing water: *The boat drifted for days before being found.* **2** to wander about or live with no clear purpose

NOUN **drifts 1** a pile of snow or sand that has been blown by the wind **2** the general meaning of what someone says: *I think I get your drift.*

driftwood NOUN wood that the sea washes up on to beaches

drill VERB **drills, drilling, drilled** to drill a hole is to make a hole with a drill in something hard

NOUN **drills 1** a tool for making holes in hard materials like wood or stone **2** an exercise that is repeated frequently: *a fire drill*

drink VERB **drinks, drinking, drank, drunk 1** to swallow a liquid **2** to drink alcohol: *My Dad refused the wine because he doesn't drink.*

NOUN **drinks 1** a drink is a liquid that you swallow when you are thirsty **2** drink is alcoholic liquids: *Please do not bring drink into the hOostel.*

drip NOUN **drips 1** a drop of liquid: *We're trying to catch the drips in a bucket.* **2** a series of falling drops of liquid: *I could hear the drip of the bathroom tap all night.* **3** a piece of equipment for slowly giving a hospital patient a liquid that their body needs

VERB **drips, dripping, dripped 1** to fall in drops: *water dripping from the trees* **2** to let a liquid fall in drops: *I can hear a tap dripping somewhere.*

dripping NOUN the fat that comes out of roasting meat

drive VERB **drives, driving, drove, driven 1** to control a vehicle such as a car **2** to hit a ball very hard, especially in golf **3** to force someone into a certain state: *That tune's driving me crazy.*

NOUN **drives 1** a journey in a car: *Let's go for a drive.* **2** a private road up to a house: *a car parked in the drive* **3** drive is energy and enthusiasm: *someone with a lot of drive*

driven VERB a form of the verb **drive** that is used with a helping verb to make a past tense: *Have you ever driven a car like this before?*

driver NOUN **drivers** a person who drives a vehicle such as a car

drizzle NOUN light rain

VERB **drizzles, drizzling, drizzled** to rain gently

drone VERB **drones, droning, droned 1** to speak in a dull, boring voice: *The man seemed to drone on and on.* **2** to make a low humming sound

NOUN **drones 1** a low humming sound **2** a male bee

drool VERB **drools, drooling, drooled** to dribble

droop VERB **droops, drooping, drooped** to bend weakly or hang down: *The flowers are drooping.*

drop NOUN **drops 1** a small blob of liquid: *drops of water on the window* **2** a small quantity: *only a drop of milk left in the bottle* **3** a fall or decrease: *Kevin's new job will mean a drop in pay.*

VERB **drops, dropping, dropped 1** to fall or to let something fall: *Drop the gun now!* • *An apple dropped from the tree.* **2** to become lower or less: *The temperature drops a lot in the evening.*

drought (pronounced drowt) NOUN **droughts** a time when very little rain falls

drove VERB a way of changing the verb

Aa
Bb
Cc
Dd
Ee
Ff
Gg
Hh
Ii
Jj
Kk
Ll
Mm
Nn
Oo
Pp
Qq
Rr
Ss
Tt
Uu
Vv
Ww
Xx
Yy
Zz

Aa
Bb
Cc
Dd
Ee
Ff
Gg
Hh
Ii
Jj
Kk
Ll
Mm
Nn
Oo
Pp
Qq
Rr
Ss
Tt
Uu
Vv
Ww
Xx
Yy
Zz

drive to make a past tense: *We drove to London down the M1.*

drown VERB **drowns, drowning, drowned** 1 to die from not being able to breathe under water 2 to drown someone is to kill them by keeping them under water so that they cannot breathe 3 to drown or drown out a sound is to block it out with a louder one: *The music in the club drowned out our conversation.*

drowsy ADJECTIVE **drowsier, drowsiest** sleepy

drudgery NOUN boring, hard work

drug NOUN **drugs** 1 a medicine: *a new drug for curing colds* 2 an illegal substance that people take to make them feel or think differently, or because they cannot stop using it
VERB **drugs, drugging, drugged** to give someone a drug that will make them unconscious

drum NOUN **drums** 1 an instrument that is round and has a skin stretched over it that you hit to make a rhythm 2 a container in the shape of a cylinder: *an oil drum*
VERB **drums, drumming, drummed** 1 to beat a drum 2 to tap your fingers repeatedly
▶ **drummer** NOUN **drummers** a person who plays the drums

drunk VERB a form of the verb **drink** that is used with a helping verb to make a past tense: *Haven't you drunk your cup of tea yet?*
ADJECTIVE **drunker, drunkest** someone who is drunk has drunk so much alcohol that they behave differently from normal
NOUN **drunks** someone who is always drinking too much alcohol

dry ADJECTIVE **drier, driest** 1 not wet or damp 2 not lively or interesting: *a dry book* 3 dry humour is funny in a way that is not obvious
VERB **dries, drying, dried** to remove or lose all the liquid from something
▶ **dryly** or **drily** ADVERB if you say something dryly, you say it in a way that is funny but seems to be serious
▶ **dryness** NOUN being dry

dry cleaning NOUN a way of cleaning clothes with special chemicals instead of water

dual ADJECTIVE made up of two of something: *Our plan has a dual purpose.*

dual carriageway NOUN **dual carriageways** a road where the traffic going in each direction is separated by some kind of barrier

dub VERB **dubs, dubbing, dubbed** 1 to add new sound to a film: *We watched Robin Hood, dubbed into Italian.* 2 to give someone another name, especially a nickname

dubious ADJECTIVE 1 feeling doubtful about something: *I'm a bit dubious about this new timetable.* 2 probably dishonest: *a dubious character*

duchess NOUN **duchesses** 1 the title of a woman who has the same rank as a duke 2 the wife of a duke

duck NOUN **ducks** a water bird with webbed feet, short legs and a wide, flat beak
VERB **ducks, ducking, ducked** 1 to duck is to lower your head quickly, as if you were avoiding being hit 2 to duck someone is to push them under water

duckling NOUN **ducklings** a baby duck

duct NOUN **ducts** a tube or pipe

dud NOUN **duds** something that is faulty or does not work properly

due ADJECTIVE 1 expected to arrive: *Their plane is due in ten minutes.* 2 needing to be paid: *The rent is due at the beginning of the month.*
• **due to** because of: *The delay was due to roadworks on the motorway.*
ADVERB directly: *due south of here*

duel NOUN **duels** a fight between two people in past times to settle an argument
VERB **duels, duelling, duelled** to fight another person to decide an argument

duet NOUN **duets** a piece of music for two singers or players

dug VERB a way of changing the verb **dig** to make a past tense. It can be used with or without a helping verb: *The children dug a hole under the apple tree.* • *A huge hole had been dug.*

duke NOUN **dukes** a nobleman of high rank

dull ADJECTIVE **duller, dullest 1** not bright: *a dull day • a dull blue colour* **2** not lively: *a dreadfully dull party* **3** not clear or ringing: *a dull thump on the door*
▸ **dullness** NOUN being dull
▸ **dully** ADVERB **1** in a boring and uninteresting way **2** not brightly: *lights shining dully in the distance*

duly ADVERB as expected: *We duly handed over our gifts to the birthday girl.*

dumb ADJECTIVE **dumber, dumbest 1** not able to speak **2** stupid: *That's the dumbest idea you've ever had.*

dumbfounded ADJECTIVE if you are dumbfounded, you are unable to speak because you are so surprised

dummy NOUN **dummies 1** a model of a person, especially for displaying clothes in a shop **2** a plastic object that a baby sucks for comfort **3** an imitation of anything

dump VERB **dumps, dumping, dumped 1** to dump rubbish is to leave it somewhere because you do not want it **2** to dump something is to put it down in a careless way: *We dumped our schoolbags in the hall.*
NOUN **dumps 1** a place for leaving rubbish **2** (*informal*) a messy or dirty place

dumpling NOUN **dumplings** a cooked ball of dough that may be served with meat dishes

dumpy ADJECTIVE **dumpier, dumpiest** short and thick or fat

dun NOUN a greyish brown colour

dunce NOUN **dunces** a person who finds learning difficult

dune NOUN **dunes** a low hill of sand

dung NOUN the solid waste of animals

dungarees PLURAL NOUN a pair of trousers with a bib and braces attached

dungeon NOUN **dungeons** a dark underground prison

duo NOUN **duos** two people, especially a pair of musicians

dupe VERB **dupes, duping, duped** to trick or cheat someone: *The tourists were duped into handing over their money.*

duplicate (pronounced **dyoo**-pli-kait) VERB **duplicates, duplicating, duplicated** to make a copy or copies of something
NOUN (pronounced **dyoo**-pli-kat) **duplicates** an exact copy
▸ **duplication** NOUN copying something exactly

durable ADJECTIVE lasting a long time and not easily damaged: *a durable fabric for working clothes*
▸ **durability** NOUN how long-lasting something is: *We do tests on the products for durability.*

duration NOUN how long something lasts or continues: *a play of two hours' duration*

during PREPOSITION while something else is happening: *We left during the interval.*

dusk NOUN the time in the evening when it is starting to get dark

dust NOUN a fine powder of something, especially household dirt
VERB **dusts, dusting, dusted 1** to clean dry dirt from surfaces: *The books have to be dusted regularly.* **2** to cover something with a fine powder: *Dust the cake with icing sugar.*

dustbin NOUN **dustbins** a large container for household rubbish

duster NOUN **dusters** a cloth for removing dust from surfaces

dustman NOUN **dustmen** a person whose job is to collect household rubbish

dusty ADJECTIVE **dustier, dustiest** covered in dust

dutiful ADJECTIVE obedient: *He was always a dutiful son.*

duty NOUN **duties 1** something a person should do, especially as part of their job: *It's your duty to check the doors are locked.* **2** a tax: *raising the duty on imports*

duvet (pronounced **doo**-vay) NOUN **duvets** a quilt stuffed with feathers or artificial fibres and used on a bed

Aa
Bb
Cc
Dd
Ee
Ff
Gg
Hh
Ii
Jj
Kk
Ll
Mm
Nn
Oo
Pp
Qq
Rr
Ss
Tt
Uu
Vv
Ww
Xx
Yy
Zz

Aa
Bb
Cc
Dd
Ee
Ff
Gg
Hh
Ii
Jj
Kk
Ll
Mm
Nn
Oo
Pp
Qq
Rr
Ss
Tt
Uu
Vv
Ww
Xx
Yy
Zz

DVD ABBREVIATION short for **digital versatile disk** or **digital video disk**, a type of disk that pictures and sounds can be recorded on, and which can hold more information than a CD

dwarf NOUN **dwarfs** or **dwarves** a person or thing that is much smaller than normal
VERB **dwarfs, dwarfing, dwarfed** to make something else look small: *The new hotel dwarfs the old shops that surround it.*

dwell VERB **dwells, dwelling, dwelt** (*formal*) to live somewhere

• **dwell on something** to think or speak about something for a long time: *There's no point in dwelling on your mistakes now.*

dwindle VERB **dwindles, dwindling, dwindled** to grow less and less: *our dwindling supplies*

dye NOUN **dyes** a powder or liquid that you use to change the colour of fabric
VERB **dyes, dyeing, dyed** to dye

something such as fabric is to make it a different colour: *I dyed my white shirt black.*

dying VERB a form of the verb **die** that is used with another verb to make different tenses: *I'm dying to see that film.* • *No one realized he was dying.*

dyke NOUN **dykes** another spelling of **dike**

dynamic ADJECTIVE full of energy and very active

dynamite NOUN a type of powerful explosive

dynamo NOUN **dynamos** a machine that converts the energy of movement into electricity

dynasty NOUN **dynasties** a series of rulers or leaders from the same family

dyslexia NOUN difficulty in learning to read and in spelling

▶ **dyslexic** ADJECTIVE a dyslexic person has difficulty in learning to recognize and form written words correctly

Ee

E ABBREVIATION short for **east**

each ADJECTIVE each person or thing in a group or pair is every one as an individual: *He had a heavy suitcase in each hand.*
PRONOUN every one individually: *Each of the girls had a different costume.*
• **each other** to, or for, the other: *The team hugged each other.* • *The cat and dog don't like each other much.*

eager ADJECTIVE very keen to do or have something: *He seems eager to learn.*
▶ **eagerly** ADVERB keenly, enthusiastically: *All her fans were eagerly waiting for the next book.*
▶ **eagerness** NOUN being enthusiastic and keen: *In his eagerness to be first, he kept on running.*

eagle NOUN **eagles** a large bird with a hooked beak and sharp claws called talons

ear¹ NOUN **ears** your ears are the two parts of your body at each side of your head that you hear with. See the picture on the next page

ear² NOUN **ears** an ear of corn or wheat is the part at the top of the plant's stem where the grains or seeds grow

earache NOUN pain inside your ear

eardrum NOUN **eardrums** the part inside your ear that vibrates when sound hits it

earl NOUN **earls** a British nobleman

earlobe NOUN **earlobes** the soft rounded part that hangs down at the bottom of your ear

early ADJECTIVE AND ADVERB **earlier, earliest 1** happening or arriving before others or before the expected or normal time: *He'd taken an earlier train.* • *I'm tired so I'm going to bed early tonight.* **2** near the beginning of something: *He likes getting up in the early morning.* • *She showed musical talent early in life.*

earmark VERB **earmarks, earmarking, earmarked** to earmark something is to select it to be used for a special purpose or to be given special attention

earn VERB **earns, earning, earned 1** to earn is to get money in return for work: *My brother earns a bit of money from his Saturday job.* **2** to earn something good, such as praise, is to get it because you have done something well

earnest ADJECTIVE serious about, or really meaning, what you do or say
• **in earnest** if someone is in earnest they are serious or sincere about something

earnings PLURAL NOUN your earnings are all the money that you get from working or by investing money

earring NOUN **earrings** a piece of jewellery worn on the ear

earshot NOUN if a sound is in earshot it is within the range of your hearing: *I couldn't hear what they were saying because they were just out of earshot.*

earth NOUN **earths 1** the Earth is the planet we live on **2** earth is the ground or soil: *digging in the earth* **3** the earth is the wire in an electrical circuit or piece of equipment that channels the electric current into the ground and makes it safe to use
▶ **earthly** ADJECTIVE to do with the Earth, rather than the sky or heaven

earthquake NOUN **earthquakes** an event when the ground shakes because of pressure that has built up in the rocks of the Earth's crust

earthworm NOUN **earthworms** a common type of worm found in soil

earthy ADJECTIVE **earthier, earthiest 1** like soil: *an earthy smell* **2** earthy humour is rather rude or vulgar

earwig NOUN **earwigs** a common garden insect with pincers at its tail

the ear

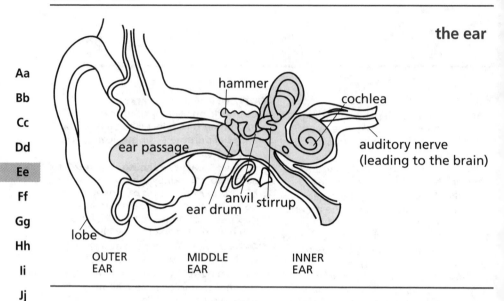

hammer
cochlea
ear passage
auditory nerve
(leading to the brain)
anvil stirrup
ear drum
lobe

OUTER EAR MIDDLE EAR INNER EAR

ease VERB **eases, easing, eased 1** to ease is to make or become less difficult or painful: *The doctor gave him some painkillers to ease the pain.* **2** to ease something into or out of a place is to put it there or take it out gently: *They eased the last big block into position.*
NOUN **1** to do something with ease is to do it without any effort or difficulty: *He won the race with ease.* **2** ease is rest: *He was taking his ease in a hammock in the garden.*
• **at ease** if you are at ease with something you feel comfortable about it: *He sounded more at ease with her than he really was.*

easel NOUN **easels** a frame used by an artist to support the picture he or she is working on

♦This word comes from the Dutch word **ezel**, which means a *donkey*, because of its shape and its job of carrying things.

easily ADVERB **1** without a lot of effort or difficulty: *He won easily.* **2** by a long way: *She's easily the most successful female pop singer today.* **3** very possibly: *It could easily be two weeks before you get a replacement.*

east NOUN **1** the direction where you see the sun rising in the morning, opposite to west **2** the East and the Far East are the countries in Asia
ADJECTIVE in, from, or towards the east: *an east wind* • *East London*
ADVERB to the east: *We headed east.*

Easter NOUN a Christian festival commemorating Christ's rising from the dead, celebrated in spring

easterly ADJECTIVE coming from, or going towards, the east: *an easterly breeze* • *They headed off in an easterly direction.*
NOUN **easterlies** a wind that comes from the east

eastern ADJECTIVE belonging to or coming from the east: *an eastern custom*

eastward or **eastwards** ADVERB to or towards the east: *sailing eastwards towards the rising sun*

easy ADJECTIVE **easier, easiest** not difficult or hard to do: *an easy sum*
• **take it easy** you take it easy when you relax or don't work too hard

eat VERB **eats, eating, ate, eaten 1** to eat food is to chew and swallow it **2** to eat is to have a meal: *What time would you like to eat?*

• eat something away to eat something away is to destroy it gradually: *The cliffs were being eaten away by the sea.*

• eat something up to eat something up is to eat it all or to use it all up: *Eat up your greens.* • *Buying a computer game had eaten up all my pocket money.*

eaves PLURAL NOUN the eaves of a building are the parts where the roof hangs over the walls

eavesdrop VERB **eavesdrops, eavesdropping, eavesdropped** to listen to other people's conversations without them knowing

ebb VERB **ebbs, ebbing, ebbed** the tide ebbs when the water in the sea moves away from the land. Look up and compare **flow**

• ebb away something ebbs away when it gradually gets less and less until it disappears

NOUN the ebb is when the water in the sea moves away from the land

• at a low ebb if something is at a low ebb it is at a low level: *Her confidence was at a low ebb.*

ebony NOUN a very hard black wood from an African tree

eccentric ADJECTIVE an eccentric person behaves very oddly

▶ **eccentricity** NOUN **eccentricities** odd behaviour

echo NOUN **echoes** an echo happens when a sound travelling away from you bounces off a surface and comes back towards you, so you hear it for a second time

VERB **echoes, echoing, echoed 1** a sound echoes when it is comes back and you hear it again **2** to echo what someone has said is to repeat it

✦ **Echo** is the Greek word for *sound*.

éclair NOUN **éclairs** a long thin cake made of light pastry, filled with cream and with chocolate on top

eclipse NOUN **eclipses 1** an eclipse of the sun happens when the sun disappears behind the moon and the sky goes dark for a few minutes **2** an eclipse of the moon happens when the Earth comes between the moon and the sun, and the Earth's shadow falls on the moon

eco- PREFIX if a word starts with **eco-**, it has something to do with the environment. For example, *eco-friendly* means not damaging to the environment

ecology NOUN **1** ecology is the study of how plants and animals exist together in their environment and how they are affected by their environment **2** the ecology of a particular area is all the plants and animals in that area and how they depend on each other and on the special conditions in that area to exist

▶ **ecological** ADJECTIVE to do with ecology or the ecology of a particular area

▶ **ecologist** NOUN **ecologists** someone who studies ecology

economics NOUN economics is the study of how money is created and spent

▶ **economist** NOUN **economists** someone who studies economics

economy NOUN **economies 1** a country's economy is all the wealth it creates through producing and selling goods, and the way that wealth is used **2** economy is using something, especially money, carefully to avoid waste **3** to make economies is to make savings

▶ **economic** ADJECTIVE **1** to do with an economy: *an economic forecast* **2** making money or profit: *The business was no longer economic and closed down.*

▶ **economical** ADJECTIVE not wasting money: *an economical car that doesn't use a lot of fuel*

▶ **economize** or **economise** VERB **economizes, economizing, economized** to economize is to be careful about spending money

ecosystem NOUN **ecosystems** a system in which plants and animals exist together, depending on each other and on the surrounding conditions for survival

Aa
Bb
Cc
Dd
Ee
Ff
Gg
Hh
Ii
Jj
Kk
Ll
Mm
Nn
Oo
Pp
Qq
Rr
Ss
Tt
Uu
Vv
Ww
Xx
Yy
Zz

Aa
Bb
Cc
Dd
Ee
Ff
Gg
Hh
Ii
Jj
Kk
Ll
Mm
Nn
Oo
Pp
Qq
Rr
Ss
Tt
Uu
Vv
Ww
Xx
Yy
Zz

eczema NOUN a disease in which itchy red patches appear on the skin

edge NOUN **edges 1** the side or end of something: *the edge of the cliff* • *A rectancle has four edges.* **2** a side of something that is sharp enough to cut: *The knives have sharp edges.*

• **on edge** nervous and easily irritated: *He's a bit on edge because he's waiting for his exam results.*

VERB **edges, edging, edged 1** to edge something is to border it: *pillowcases edged with lace* **2** to move slowly and carefully: *Harry edged along the narrow ledge.*

▸ **edgy** ADJECTIVE **edgier, edgiest** to be edgy is to feel nervous and a bit bad-tempered

edible ADJECTIVE if something is edible, it can be eaten: *edible mushrooms*

edit VERB **edits, editing, edited 1** to edit a book, magazine or newspaper is to prepare it to be published or printed by correcting the text or putting all its parts together in order **2** to edit a film or tape recording is to cut it or alter it so that it is ready to be broadcast

▸ **edition** NOUN **editions** an edition of a book, magazine or newspaper is all the copies that are printed at the same time

▸ **editor** NOUN **editors 1** someone who corrects or brings together all the parts of a book, magazine, newspaper or film **2** someone in charge of what goes into a newspaper, or part of a newspaper

educate VERB **educates, educating, educated** to educate people is to teach them and to give them knowledge

▸ **education** NOUN education is teaching, especially in schools or colleges

▸ **educational** ADJECTIVE to do with teaching and learning

eel NOUN **eels** a type of fish that has a long thin body like a snake

eerie ADJECTIVE if something is eerie, it is strange in a frightening way: *a dark and eerie old house*

▸ **eerily** ADVERB strangely or weirdly: *The forest suddenly became eerily silent.*

✦**Eerie** comes from an old Scots word which means *afraid* or *cowardly*.

effect NOUN **effects 1** if one thing has an effect on another, it influences it or causes something to happen to it: *His asthma has no effect on his brilliance as a footballer.* **2** the effect of something is the result it has: *He was suffering from the effects of a long plane journey.*

▸ **effective** ADJECTIVE working well or giving the results you want: *an effective treatment for the common cold*

✦Be careful not to confuse **effect**, which is a noun, with **affect**, which is a verb.
*One thing has an **effect** on another.*
*One thing **affects** another.*

effervescent ADJECTIVE **1** an effervescent liquid bubbles or fizzes because it is full of gas: *an effervescent drink* **2** someone with an effervescent personality seems to bubble with enthusiasm and energy

efficient ADJECTIVE doing something well and quickly, without wasting money, energy etc: *the efficient use of energy* • *The hotel staff were very polite and efficient.*

▸ **efficiency** NOUN efficiency is doing something well and quickly, without wasting money, energy etc

effort NOUN **efforts 1** effort is hard work: *It needs a lot of effort to be an athlete.* **2** an effort is a try: *It was a really good effort.*

▸ **effortless** ADJECTIVE not needing, or seeming not to need, a lot of hard work or energy

eg or **e.g.** ABBREVIATION short for **exempli gratia**, which is Latin for 'for example': *animals found in Africa, eg the lion and the giraffe*

egg NOUN **eggs 1** an egg is a shell or case with a developing baby bird, reptile or fish inside **2** an egg is one of these laid by a hen or other bird that we eat as food: *a hard-boiled egg* **3** an egg is a special cell stored inside the body of a female mammal which can grow into a baby

• put all your eggs in one basket if you put all your eggs in one basket, you put all your money or effort into one thing and if it fails, you will lose everything

VERB **eggs, egging, egged**
• egg someone on to egg someone on is to encourage them, usually to do something bad

ego NOUN **egos** your ego is the opinion you have of your own importance: *All the attention and praise was good for her ego.*

eiderdown NOUN **eiderdowns** a warm top covering for a bed, filled with feathers or some other light material

Eid-ul-Adha (pronounced eed-ul-**ad**-ha) NOUN a Muslim festival held to celebrate how the prophet Abraham was willing to sacrifice his son

Eid-ul-Fitr (pronounced eed-ul-**fee**-tir) NOUN a Muslim festival held to celebrate the end of **Ramadan**

✦**Eid** is an Arabic word meaning *festival.*

eight NOUN **eights** the number 8
eighteen NOUN the number 18
eighteenth ADJECTIVE AND ADVERB after seventeenth and before nineteenth: *my cousin's eighteenth birthday party*
eighth ADJECTIVE AND ADVERB after seventh and before ninth: *the eighth book in the series* • *I came eighth in the sack race.*
NOUN **eighths** the fraction ⅛, which means one of eight equal parts of something: *an eighth of a mile*
eightieth ADJECTIVE AND ADVERB after seventy-ninth and before eighty-first: *the eightieth day of the year*
eighty NOUN **eighties** the number 80
either ADJECTIVE **1** the one or the other: *She can write with either hand.* **2** both: *There are goalposts at either end of the pitch.*
PRONOUN the one or the other of two: *He can't afford either of them.*
ADVERB as well: *If you don't go, I won't go either.*

CONJUNCTION **either** is used with **or** to show a choice or alternative: *You can have either a video game or a CD.*

eject VERB **ejects, ejecting, ejected**
1 to eject something is to throw it out with sudden force: *The octopus ejected a cloud of black ink.* **2** if a pilot ejects from an aircraft in an emergency, he or she operates a special seat which is fired out of the cockpit

elaborate (pronounced i-**lab**-or-it) ADJECTIVE involving complicated detail or decoration: *an elaborate plan* • *an elaborate costume*
VERB (i-**lab**-or-ait) **elaborates, elaborating, elaborated**
• elaborate on something to elaborate on something is to explain it by give more details about it

elastic ADJECTIVE able to stretch and then spring back
NOUN elastic is a strip of fabric with rubber woven into it to make it stretchy
▸ **elasticity** NOUN (pronounced el-is-**tis**-i-ti) the quality of being stretchy or springy

elated ADJECTIVE very pleased and excited: *They were elated at the thought of the holidays.*

elbow NOUN **elbows** the joint in the middle of your arm that bends
VERB **elbows, elbowing, elbowed** to elbow someone is to poke or push them with your elbow

elder ADJECTIVE older: *elder brothers and sisters*
NOUN **elders** your elders are people who are older than you
▸ **elderly** ADJECTIVE an elderly person is old
▸ **eldest** ADJECTIVE oldest: *his eldest child*

elect VERB **elects, electing, elected** to elect someone is to choose them by voting: *elect a president*
▸ **election** NOUN **elections** the choosing of someone by voting: *standing for election* • *a presidential election*
▸ **elector** NOUN **electors** someone who votes in an election

Aa
Bb
Cc
Dd
Ee
Ff
Gg
Hh
Ii
Jj
Kk
Ll
Mm
Nn
Oo
Pp
Qq
Rr
Ss
Tt
Uu
Vv
Ww
Xx
Yy
Zz

Aa
Bb
Cc
Dd
Ee
Ff
Gg
Hh
Ii
Jj
Kk
Ll
Mm
Nn
Oo
Pp
Qq
Rr
Ss
Tt
Uu
Vv
Ww
Xx
Yy
Zz

▶ **electorate** NOUN **electorates** all the people who can vote in an election

electric ADJECTIVE made or worked by electricity: *an electric spark* • *an electric light*

▶ **electrical** ADJECTIVE carrying or producing electricity: *an electrical circuit* • *an electrical storm*

electrician NOUN **electricians** someone whose job is to fit or repair electric lights and other electrical equipment

electricity NOUN a form of energy used to make light and heat and to give power to machinery

✦ **Electric** comes from the Greek word **elektron**, which means *amber*. This is because amber makes electricity when it is rubbed.

electrify VERB **electrifies, electrifying, electrified 1** to electrify machinery or equipment is to make it work on electric power **2** if something electrifies you, it excites you a lot: *The concert electrified the huge audience.*

electro- PREFIX if a word starts with **electro-** it has something to do with electricity. For example, an *electromagnet* is a magnet that is worked by an electric current

electrocute VERB **electrocutes, electrocuting, electrocuted** to be electrocuted is to be killed by a strong electric current which passes through the body: *He was electrocuted while he was trying to fix the lights.*

▶ **electrocution** NOUN killing someone or being killed by a strong electric current

electrode NOUN **electrodes** (*science*) a small metal device that allows an electric current to pass from a source of power, such as a battery, to a piece of equipment

electromagnet NOUN **electromagnets** a magnet that works when electricity passes through it

electron NOUN **electrons** (*science*) a particle with a negative electric charge that orbits the nucleus of an atom

electronic ADJECTIVE **1** electronic equipment uses very small electrical circuits such as silicon chips and transistors **2** to do with electronics: *an electronics lab*

▶ **electronics** NOUN electronics is a branch of physics that studies electrons and the way they can be used in machinery

electroplating NOUN using electricity to coat one metal with another metal

elegance NOUN being graceful and tastefully dressed

▶ **elegant** ADJECTIVE stylish and smart: *an elegant lady*

element NOUN **elements**
1 (*science*) a chemical element is a substance which cannot be split into separate or simpler substances. Hydrogen, oxygen, nitrogen and carbon are examples of elements
2 the elements of something are the basic parts that make it up: *the elements of mathematics*
3 the elements are things like rain and wind that make the weather, especially bad weather: *They were stuck on a bare hillside, completely exposed to the elements.*
4 a small part or bit of something: *There is an element of truth in what he said.*
5 a bent piece of metal containing an electric wire that heats an electric kettle or oven
• **in your element** if you are in your element you are doing the thing that you are best at or that you enjoy the most

elementary ADJECTIVE at the simplest or most basic level: *an elementary particle* • *an elementary school*

elephant NOUN **elephants** a very large grey animal with a long trunk, large flapping ears, and tusks made of ivory

elevate VERB **elevates, elevating, elevated** to elevate something is to raise it

▶ **elevator** NOUN **elevators** an elevator is a lift for carrying people between the floors in a building

eleven NOUN **elevens** the number 11

eleventh ADJECTIVE after tenth and before twelfth: *the eleventh day of the eleventh month*

elf NOUN **elves** in stories, a tiny fairy that gets up to mischief. An elf is often described as having a thin face with pointed ears

▶ **elfin** ADJECTIVE like an elf: *a small elfin face*

eligible ADJECTIVE an eligible person is suitable for or allowed to do something: *In Britain, you're not elegible to vote until you're eighteen.*

▶ **eligibility** NOUN being suitable or qualifying for something

eliminate VERB **eliminates, eliminating, eliminated** to eliminate something is to get rid of it completely: *eliminate poverty*

▶ **elimination** NOUN getting rid of something completely

elite NOUN **elites** the elite in a society or group are the best or most important people in it: *the sporting elite*
ADJECTIVE belonging to an elite

elk NOUN **elk** *or* **elks** a type of very large deer with large horns that is found in northern Europe and Asia

ellipse NOUN **ellipses** an oval shape

▶ **elliptical** ADJECTIVE shaped like an oval: *a planet with an elliptical orbit*

elm NOUN **elms** a type of tall tree with broad round leaves

elocution NOUN elocution is the art of speaking correctly and clearly

elongate VERB **elongates, elongating, elongated** to elongate is to get or make longer

eloquent ADJECTIVE able to talk and express yourself well

else ADVERB other than or besides the thing or person already talked about: *They didn't have anywhere else to go.*
• **or else** otherwise: *Put on a jumper or else you'll catch cold.*

elsewhere ADVERB in another place: *Luckily, he'd been elsewhere when his house was destroyed.*

elude VERB **eludes, eluding, eluded**
1 to elude someone who is looking for you is to get away from them without being seen or caught **2** if something eludes you, you can't get hold of it or remember it: *The phrase he wanted eluded him.*

▶ **elusive** ADJECTIVE difficult to see or find

email *or* **e-mail** NOUN **emails** *or* **e-mails** short for **electronic mail**, a message or messages that are sent between computers: *They keep in touch by email.* • *He sent me an email.*
VERB **emails, emailing, emailed** *or* **e-mails, e-mailing, e-mailed** to email someone is to send them an email

embankment NOUN **embankments** a steep bank of earth or rock built up along the sides of a railway, canal or motorway

embark VERB **embarks, embarking, embarked** to embark is to get on a ship at the beginning of a journey
• **embark on** to embark on something is to begin it: *They had embarked on an exciting new project.*

embarrass VERB **embarrasses, embarrassing, embarrassed** to embarrass someone is to make them feel uncomfortable or ashamed

▶ **embarrassed** ADJECTIVE looking or feeling ashamed or self-conscious

▶ **embarrassing** ADJECTIVE causing embarrassment: *an embarrassing mistake*

▶ **embarrassment** NOUN a feeling of discomfort and shame

embassy NOUN **embassies** a building where an ambassador lives and works

embellish VERB **embellishes, embellishing, embellished** to embellish something is to add details to it to make it more fancy or more interesting

▶ **embellishment** NOUN **embellishments** an embellishment is something added as decoration or to make something more interesting

embers PLURAL NOUN the small hot pieces left when coal or wood is burnt in a fire

emblem NOUN **emblems** an object or image that is used as a symbol

Aa
Bb
Cc
Dd
Ee
Ff
Gg
Hh
Ii
Jj
Kk
Ll
Mm
Nn
Oo
Pp
Qq
Rr
Ss
Tt
Uu
Vv
Ww
Xx
Yy
Zz

Aa
Bb
Cc
Dd
Ee
Ff
Gg
Hh
Ii
Jj
Kk
Ll
Mm
Nn
Oo
Pp
Qq
Rr
Ss
Tt
Uu
Vv
Ww
Xx
Yy
Zz

for something else: *The thistle is the emblem of Scotland.*

embrace VERB **embraces, embracing, embraced 1** to embrace someone is to put your arms round them and hold them tight **2** to embrace something, such as an idea or belief, is to accept it or adopt it **3** to embrace something is to include it: *a subject that embraces both maths and science*
NOUN **embraces** a hug

embroider VERB **embroiders, embroidering, embroidered** to embroider is to stitch patterns with coloured threads
▶ **embroidery** NOUN decorative stitching

embryo NOUN **embryos** (*science*) a baby animal or bird at the very earliest stages of its development when it starts growing inside its mother's womb or inside an egg

emerald NOUN **emeralds 1** a green precious stone **2** a bright green colour

emerge VERB **emerges, emerging, emerged** to emerge is to come out: *The baby crocodiles emerge from the eggs.*

emergency NOUN **emergencies** an emergency is a sudden, unexpected event, often one that puts people's lives or property in danger

emigrant NOUN **emigrants** someone who leaves one country to go and live in another

emigrate VERB **emigrates, emigrating, emigrated** to emigrate is to leave your country to go and live in another country

✦ Do not confuse this with the word **immigrate**. You **immigrate** when you come to a new country and live there but you **emigrate** when you leave your country.

eminent ADJECTIVE an eminent person is famous and well-respected: *an eminent lawyer*

emission NOUN **emissions 1** emission is emitting something **2** an emission is something that is given out, such as the fumes from a car's exhaust or smoke from a factory chimney

emit VERB **emits, emitting, emitted** to emit something, such as light, heat, gas or a sound, is to give it out: *The machine emitted a high-pitched screech.*

emotion NOUN **emotions** emotions are strong feelings, such as love, hate, fear, jealousy or anger: *He showed no emotion as he was sentenced to jail.* • *She tried to control her emotions.*
▶ **emotional** ADJECTIVE showing or having strong feelings: *an emotional farewell*

empathize or **empathise** VERB **empathizes, empathizing, empathized** to empathize with someone is to feel close to them because you have experienced the same things they have
▶ **empathy** NOUN empathy is feeling close to someone because you know how they feel

emperor NOUN **emperors** the ruler of an empire

emphasis NOUN **emphases** emphasis is special importance given to something or extra stress put on something to make it stand out: *Say the line with a bit more emphasis.*
▶ **emphasize** or **emphasise** VERB **emphasizes, emphasizing, emphasized** to emphasize something is to make it stand out: *I want to emphasize the importance of road safety.*
▶ **emphatic** ADJECTIVE an emphatic statement is made strongly or firmly

empire NOUN **empires 1** an empire is a group of countries governed by a single ruler **2** a business empire is a group of companies controlled by one person or organization

employ VERB **employs, employing, employed** if you employ someone, they work for you, and you pay them: *The company employs skilled workers.*
▶ **employee** NOUN **employees** someone who works for a company or another person
▶ **employer** NOUN **employers** a company or person who employs people

▶ **employment** NOUN employment is work, especially for pay

empress NOUN **empresses** a female ruler of an empire

empty ADJECTIVE **emptier, emptiest** having nothing or no one inside: *an empty glass* • *an empty classroom*
VERB **empties, emptying, emptied**
1 to empty is to make or become empty: *Empty your pockets.* **2** to empty something is to tip or pour it out of a container: *The dustmen were emptying the rubbish out of the bins.*

▶ **emptiness** NOUN being empty

emu (pronounced ee-myoo) NOUN **emus** a large Australian bird that cannot fly and looks similar to, but is smaller than, an ostrich

emulate VERB **emulates, emulating, emulated** to emulate someone is to copy them because you admire them

en- PREFIX if a word starts with **en-**, it means 'to cause to be'. For example, to *enable* someone to do something is to cause them to be able to do it

enable VERB **enables, enabling, enabled** if something enables you to do something, it makes it possible for you to do it: *Sponsorship would enable more young athletes to develop.*

enamel NOUN **enamels 1** a hard shiny coating that is baked on to metal in a very hot oven to protect or decorate it **2** the hard white coating on teeth
ADJECTIVE made of or covered with enamel: *an enamel plate*

enchant VERB **enchants, enchanting, enchanted 1** if something enchants you, it delights or charms you **2** fairies and witches in stories enchant people when they put a magic spell or charm on them

▶ **enchanted** ADJECTIVE magical or under a magic spell: *an enchanted forest*

▶ **enchanting** ADJECTIVE delightful or charming: *an enchanting smile*

▶ **enchantment** NOUN **enchantments** a feeling of delight or wonder

enclose VERB **encloses, enclosing, enclosed 1** to enclose something is to surround it with a fence or wall **2** to

enclose something in an envelope or package is to put it inside

▶ **enclosure** NOUN **enclosures 1** an area of land with a wall or fence around it **2** something you put in an envelope or package with a letter

encore (pronounced ong-**kor**) NOUN **encores** an extra song or dance performed at the end of a stage show because the audience has shown that they want more

encounter VERB **encounters, encountering, encountered 1** to encounter something is to come up against it: *They encountered many difficulties on their journey.* **2** to encounter someone is to meet them by chance
NOUN **encounters** a meeting: *an encounter with enemy troops*

encourage VERB **encourages, encouraging, encouraged 1** to encourage someone is to support them and make them feel confident about what they are doing or are planning to do **2** to encourage something is to do something that will make it more likely to happen

▶ **encouragement** NOUN supporting or giving confidence to someone or something: *The crowd was shouting encouragement to the team.*

▶ **encouraging** ADJECTIVE giving confidence or hope: *an encouraging sign*

encyclopedia *or* **encyclopaedia** NOUN **encyclopedias** *or* **encyclopaedias** a book with information about many subjects or on a particular subject

▶ **encyclopedic** *or* **encyclopaedic** ADJECTIVE giving or having a lot of facts and information about many things

✦ The word **encyclopedia** comes from the Greek word **enkyklios**, which means *everyday*, and **paideia**, which means *education*.
An encyclopedia is thought to give you a general education because it tells you about lots of different subjects.

end NOUN **ends 1** the end of something is its last part or the place where it

Aa
Bb
Cc
Dd
Ee
Ff
Gg
Hh
Ii
Jj
Kk
Ll
Mm
Nn
Oo
Pp
Qq
Rr
Ss
Tt
Uu
Vv
Ww
Xx
Yy
Zz

finishes: *the end of the day • I read the book from beginning to end.* **2** the ends of something are the parts farthest away from the middle: *He was running from one end of the pitch to the other.* **3** an end is a result that you aim for or a purpose that you have: *They used their power for their own private ends.*

• **make ends meet** to make ends meet is to have enough money to buy what you need

• **on end** without a stop: *The rain continued for days and weeks on end.*

VERB **ends, ending, ended** to finish: *Our holiday ends tomorrow. • He ended his speech with a joke.*

• **end up** to be in a particular place or situation that you were not expecting: *The illness got worse and he ended up in hospital. • My Mum and Dad were out so I ended up going to Jack's house.*

endanger VERB **endangers, endangering, endangered** to endanger something is to put it in danger or at risk

endangered species NOUN **endangered species** an endangered species is a type of animal or plant that is in danger of dying out

endeavour VERB **endeavours, endeavouring, endeavoured** to endeavour to do something is to try to do it, especially in a serious or determined way

NOUN **endeavours 1** endeavour is the effort or energy people put into doing things: *human endeavour* **2** an endeavour is an attempt to do something which needs effort or energy: *I wish you luck in all your endeavours.*

ending NOUN **endings** the last part: *The story had a happy ending.*

endorse VERB **endorses, endorsing, endorsed** to endorse something is to give it your support

▸ **endorsement** NOUN **endorsements** something that supports or confirms another thing: *an endorsement of the new plan*

endure VERB **endures, enduring, endured 1** to endure something is to put up with it over a long period of time: *He didn't know if he could endure the loneliness any more.* **2** to endure is to last: *These trees have endured for decades.*

▸ **endurance** NOUN the ability to last or to survive long periods of strain

enemy NOUN **enemies 1** someone or something that is against you or wants to do you harm **2** in a war, the enemy is the people or country you are fighting against

energetic ADJECTIVE very active and lively: *an energetic dance*

energy NOUN **energies 1** the strength or power to work or be active: *He's got bags of energy.* **2** a form of power, such as heat or electricity: *trying to save energy • nuclear energy*

enforce VERB **enforces, enforcing, enforced** to enforce a rule or law is to use it and make sure people obey it

engage VERB **engages, engaging, engaged 1** to engage someone is to start to employ them **2** to engage in an activity is to do it or keep busy doing it

▸ **engaged** ADJECTIVE **1** if two people are engaged they have promised to marry each other **2** a telephone or toilet is engaged when someone is using it

▸ **engagement** NOUN **engagements 1** a promise that you will marry someone **2** an appointment to meet someone or to do something for a certain period of time

engine NOUN **engines 1** a machine that turns energy into movement by burning fuel **2** the vehicle at the front of a train that pulls the coaches

engineer NOUN **engineers 1** someone who works with or designs engines and machines **2** someone who designs and makes things like bridges and roads

VERB **engineers, engineering, engineered** to engineer something is to make it happen by clever planning: *He tried to engineer a meeting between the two sides.*

▸ **engineering** NOUN engineering is the science or work of designing and making machinery, or of designing roads and bridges

engrave VERB **engraves, engraving, engraved** to engrave a design or lettering is to carve it into a hard surface, such as metal or glass

► **engraving** NOUN **engravings** the process or skill of carving designs or lettering into metal or glass

engrossed ADJECTIVE if you are engrossed in something, it takes your whole attention or interest

enhance VERB **enhances, enhancing, enhanced** to enhance something is to make it better or greater

enjoy VERB **enjoys, enjoying, enjoyed** **1** to enjoy something is to get a feeling of pleasure from it: *They seemed to enjoy the concert.* **2** to enjoy yourself is to have a good time: *We enjoyed ourselves at the party.*

► **enjoyable** ADJECTIVE giving a feeling of pleasure

► **enjoyment** NOUN pleasure

enlarge VERB **enlarges, enlarging, enlarged** to enlarge something is to make it bigger

► **enlargement** NOUN **enlargements** **1** increasing in size **2** a larger photograph made from a smaller one

enlist VERB **enlists, enlisting, enlisted** **1** to enlist is to join the army, navy or air force **2** if you enlist the help or support of someone, you get it

enormous ADJECTIVE very big: *an enormous tree*

► **enormously** ADVERB **1** very greatly: *They all enjoyed themselves enormously.* **2** extremely: *enormously grateful*

✦ This word comes from the Latin word **enormis**, which means *unusual* or *not normal.*

enough ADJECTIVE as much or as many as you need, want or can put up with: *I've got enough problems without this!* PRONOUN as much as you need, want or can put up with: *Have you all had enough to eat and drink?* ADVERB as much as is needed or wanted: *You've gone far enough.*

enquire VERB **enquires, enquiring, enquired** to ask a question or questions in order to get information

► **enquiry** NOUN **enquiries** a question that you ask to find something out

enrage VERB **enrages, enraging, enraged** if something enrages you, it makes you very angry

enrich VERB **enriches, enriching, enriched** to enrich something is to improve it by adding something to it: *Art enriches people's lives.*

enrol VERB **enrols, enrolling, enrolled** to enrol is to put your name on a register or list: *Jackie enrolled at a stage school.*

► **enrolment** NOUN enrolling or the number of people enrolled

ensure VERB **ensures, ensuring, ensured** to ensure is to make certain: *Please ensure you have all your belongings with you.*

✦ The words **ensure** and **insure** sound the same, but they have different meanings and spellings. To **insure** something is to pay money to a company who will pay the cost if it is damaged.

entail VERB **entails, entailing, entailed** **1** one thing entails another when it makes that other thing necessary: *Learning the piano entails hours of practice.* **2** what something entails is what is involved in doing it: *Can you tell me what the job will entail?*

entangled ADJECTIVE if things are entangled, they are wound around each other so that it is difficult to separate them

enter VERB **enters, entering, entered** **1** to enter, or enter a place, is to go in, or to go into it **2** to enter a competition is to take part in it **3** to enter something in a book or list is to write it in the book or list **4** to enter data into a computer is to key it in

enterprise NOUN **enterprises** **1** if someone shows enterprise they have

Aa
Bb
Cc
Dd
Ee
Ff
Gg
Hh
Ii
Jj
Kk
Ll
Mm
Nn
Oo
Pp
Qq
Rr
Ss
Tt
Uu
Vv
Ww
Xx
Yy
Zz

the ability to think of and try out new ideas and find ways to carry them out **2** an enterprise is something that involves planning and risk, such as a business

▸ **enterprising** ADJECTIVE an enterprising person is adventurous and able to think of new ways of doing things

entertain VERB **entertains, entertaining, entertained 1** to entertain people is to amuse them: *Emily entertained us by telling jokes.* **2** to entertain people is to invite them as your guests for a meal or a drink

▸ **entertainer** NOUN **entertainers** someone who does an act on stage, radio or TV to entertain people

▸ **entertaining** ADJECTIVE amusing

▸ **entertainment** NOUN **entertainments** something that amuses people or gives them pleasure

enthral VERB **enthrals, enthralling, enthralled** if something enthrals you, it fascinates you and holds your attention completely

enthusiasm NOUN if someone has enthusiasm, they are very keen to do or try things or they show a great deal of interest in something

▸ **enthusiast** NOUN **enthusiasts** someone who is very interested or involved in a particular thing: *James is a great cycling enthusiast.*

▸ **enthusiastic** ADJECTIVE eager and showing keenness: *enthusiastic applause*

entire ADJECTIVE an entire thing is the whole of it: *He spent the entire day paddling in the sea.*

▸ **entirely** ADVERB totally or completely: *It was my fault entirely.*

entitle VERB **entitles, entitling, entitled** if something entitles you to something, it gives you the right to have it or do it: *Children are not entitled to vote.*

▸ **entitlement** NOUN something you are entitled to: *holiday entitlement*

entrance NOUN **entrances 1** a place where you can go in or out: *He left by a side entrance.* **2** to make an entrance is to come into a room or come on to a stage

entrant NOUN **entrants** someone who enters a competition

entry NOUN **entries 1** going in or entering: *his entry into politics* • *There was a high iron gate barring our entry.* **2** an entry in a diary or book is one of the items written or printed in it

envelop VERB **envelops, enveloping, enveloped** if one thing envelops another, it surrounds it and covers it completely: *A thick fog enveloped the hills.*

envelope NOUN **envelopes** a folded paper covering for a letter or other document, especially one that is to be sent by post

envious ADJECTIVE if you are envious of someone, you want something that they have

environment NOUN **environments 1** a person's or animal's environment is their surroundings where they live **2** the environment is all the things, such as air, land, sea, animals and plants, that make up the natural world around us

▸ **environmental** ADJECTIVE to do with the environment

envy NOUN if you feel envy, you want what someone else has

VERB **envies, envying, envied** to envy someone is to want what they have: *We envied him, because he did not have to go to school.*

enzyme NOUN **enzymes** (*science*) one of a group of chemical substances made in both animals and plants. These substances cause certain chemical changes to begin or which control the speed of chemical changes

eon NOUN **eons** a very long time

epic NOUN **epics** a long story, poem or film about great events or exciting and heroic adventures

epicentre NOUN **epicentres** (*geography*) the epicentre of an earthquake is the point on the ground just above where the earthquake starts and where it is strongest

epidemic NOUN **epidemics** an illness which spreads widely and many people catch: *a flu epidemic*

epilepsy NOUN epilepsy is an illness that affects the brain and which causes short spells of unconsciousness and uncontrolled movements of the body called convulsions

▶ **epileptic** ADJECTIVE caused by epilepsy: *an epileptic fit* NOUN **epileptics** someone who suffers from epilepsy

episode NOUN **episodes 1** one of the parts of a story or one of the programmes in a radio or TV series **2** an event: *It was one of the most embarrassing episodes of his life.*

epitaph NOUN **epitaphs** a dead person's epitaph is what is written about them on their gravestone

equal ADJECTIVE **1** two or more things are equal when they are of the same size, value or amount **2** if you are equal to a task, you are fit or able to do it

VERB **equals, equalling, equalled** one thing equals another when they are the same in size, value or amount

NOUN **equals** a person's equal is someone who is as good as they are

▶ **equality** NOUN being the same size, value or amount

▶ **equally** ADVERB evenly or in the same way: *The two drivers were equally to blame for the accident.*

equalize or **equalise** VERB **equalizes, equalizing, equalized** to equalize things is to make them equal

▶ **equalizer** or **equaliser** NOUN **equalizers** or **equalisers** something that makes things equal, especially a goal that makes two teams' scores equal

equation NOUN **equations** (*maths*) a statement that two things are equal with the two parts written on either side of an equals sign, for example *15 + 4 = 25 − 6*

equator NOUN (*geography*) the equator is the line drawn on maps that goes around the Earth halfway between the North Pole and the South Pole

equestrian ADJECTIVE to do with horse riding

equilateral triangle NOUN **equilateral triangles** (*maths*) an equilateral triangle has sides that are equal in length

equilibrium NOUN equal balance between two things

equinox NOUN **equinoxes** either of two times of year, in March and September, when day and night are equal in length

equip VERB **equips, equipping, equipped** to equip someone is to provide them with all the things that they will need to do a particular activity: *They equipped themselves with ropes and ice axes for climbing the mountain.*

▶ **equipment** NOUN equipment is a set of tools and special clothing needed to do a particular activity or job: *a shop selling camping equipment*

equivalent ADJECTIVE if two or more things are equivalent, they have the same value, use, meaning or effect

NOUN **equivalents** something that is equivalent to something else: *Two sixes are the equivalent of three fours.*

era NOUN **eras** a particular period in history: *the era of the dinosaurs*

erase VERB **erases, erasing, erased** to erase something is to rub it out or make it disappear

▶ **eraser** NOUN **erasers** a piece of rubber used to remove writing or marks made in pencil or ink

erect ADJECTIVE upright: *an erect posture* VERB **erects, erecting, erected** to erect something is to put it up: *They erected their tents.*

▶ **erection** NOUN **erections** something that stands up or is built

erode VERB **erodes, eroding, eroded** if something erodes or is eroded, it is slowly worn away

▶ **erosion** NOUN the gradual wearing away of something, such as stone or soil

errand NOUN **errands** if you go on an errand for someone, you go somewhere to do something for them

error NOUN **errors** a mistake: *There's an error in this column of figures.*

erupt VERB **erupts, erupting, erupted 1** if a volcano erupts, hot lava, ash and dust are thrown out of it **2** something erupts when it suddenly starts, especially

Aa
Bb
Cc
Dd
Ee
Ff
Gg
Hh
Ii
Jj
Kk
Ll
Mm
Nn
Oo
Pp
Qq
Rr
Ss
Tt
Uu
Vv
Ww
Xx
Yy
Zz

Aa
Bb
Cc
Dd
Ee
Ff
Gg
Hh
Ii
Jj
Kk
Ll
Mm
Nn
Oo
Pp
Qq
Rr
Ss
Tt
Uu
Vv
Ww
Xx
Yy
Zz

in a violent or noisy way: *Violence erupted at the demonstration.*

► **eruption** NOUN **eruptions** an eruption is when a volcano throws out lava, ash and dust

escalate VERB **escalates, escalating, escalated** if something escalates, it increases or gets more intense

escalator NOUN **escalators** a moving stair for carrying people between the floors of a building

escapade NOUN **escapades** an adventure, often one where rules or laws are broken

escape VERB **escapes, escaping, escaped 1** to escape is to get out or away to safety or freedom: *The lion had escaped from its cage.* **2** to escape something is to avoid it: *You're lucky to have escaped punishment.* **3** if something escapes you, it slips from your memory

NOUN **escapes 1** getting free: *a failed escape from prison* **2** a way to get free or get away to safety: *I only had thirty minutes to plan my escape.*

escort VERB **escorts, escorting, escorted** to escort someone is to go somewhere with them: *The thief was escorted from the building by police.*

NOUN **escorts** someone who escorts another person, especially to look after them

Eskimo NOUN **Eskimos** Eskimos are the Inuit people, who live in cold places such as Greenland, Canada and Alaska

✦ Nowadays, the Inuit prefer not to be called Eskimos.

especially ADVERB particularly: *It was especially cold that morning.*

✦ Remember the difference between **especially** and **specially**. **Especially** means 'particularly': *I like all of the characters, especially Harry.* **Specially** means 'for a special purpose': *I cooked this meal specially for you.*

espionage NOUN spying to find out another country's or company's secrets

esplanade NOUN **esplanades** a long

level road, especially along the seaside in a town

essay NOUN **essays** a long piece of writing about a particular subject

essence NOUN **essences 1** the essence of something is its most important part or its true character **2** essence is a concentrated liquid, especially taken from a plant and containing its flavour or scent

essential ADJECTIVE if something is essential, it is absolutely necessary and you must have it or do it

NOUN **essentials** an essential is something that you must have

establish VERB **establishes, establishing, established 1** to establish something is to set it up: *He established a small bakery business.* **2** to establish something is to find it out and prove it: *establishing the truth*

► **establishment** NOUN **establishments 1** the establishment of something is setting it up or proving it **2** an establishment is a place where a business is set up and is operating

estate NOUN **estates 1** a large piece of land belonging to one person or one family **2** a large area with lots of houses or factories and businesses built on it: *a housing estate • an industrial estate* **3** a person's estate is all the things they have or own, such as property and money

estate agent NOUN **estate agents** someone whose job is to sell people's houses

esteem NOUN esteem is thinking well of someone: *He was held in high esteem by his team mates.*

estimate VERB **estimates, estimating, estimated** to estimate something is to try to judge what its size, amount or value is without measuring it accurately

NOUN **estimates** a rough judgement of the size, amount or value of something

► **estimation** NOUN estimating or rough judgement made without accurate measurements or all the facts

estuary NOUN **estuaries** the wide part of a river where it meets the sea

etc or **etc.** ABBREVIATION short for **et cetera**, which is Latin for 'and the rest'. Etc is used after a list to show that there are other things that have not been named: *An art shop selling paints, canvases, brushes, etc.*

etch VERB **etches, etching, etched** to draw lines and patterns on metal and glass by letting acid eat away the places where you want the lines to be

▸ **etching** NOUN **etchings** (*art*) an etching is a print made from a metal plate that has the picture etched on to it

eternal ADJECTIVE lasting for ever or seeming to last for ever: *the eternal cycle of the seasons*

▸ **eternally** ADVERB for ever

eternity NOUN eternity is time that never ends

ethic NOUN **ethics 1** an ethic is a rule or principle by which someone lives: *the work ethic* **2** ethics are rules or principles about what is right and wrong

▸ **ethical** ADJECTIVE to do with ethics or what is morally right

ethnic ADJECTIVE ethnic is used to refer to the particular race or culture that someone belongs to: *an ethnic group*

eucalyptus NOUN **eucalyptuses** or **eucalypti** a type of Australian tree that is evergreen and whose leaves contain a strong-smelling oil that is used as a flavouring

euphemism NOUN **euphemisms** a word or phrase that you use instead of one that might offend or shock people. For example, euphemisms such as *to pass on*, or *to slip away* are used when people want to avoid mentioning death or dying

euro NOUN **euros** the currency used in many countries that are in the European Union

European ADJECTIVE to do with or belonging to the continent of Europe

NOUN **Europeans** someone who comes from Europe

euthanasia NOUN euthanasia is

helping someone who is suffering from an incurable disease to die

evacuate VERB **evacuates, evacuating, evacuated 1** if people evacuate a place, they leave it because it has become dangerous **2** to evacuate people from a place is to help or order them to leave because it has become dangerous

▸ **evacuation** NOUN **evacuations** leaving or emptying a place, especially because it has become dangerous

▸ **evacuee** NOUN **evacuees** someone who has been evacuated from a place, especially during a war

evade VERB **evades, evading, evaded** to evade something is to avoid it or avoid dealing with it directly

evaluate VERB **evaluates, evaluating, evaluated** to evaluate something is to decide how good or useful it is

evaporate VERB **evaporates, evaporating, evaporated** if liquid evaporates, it turns into a gas or vapour and disappears

▸ **evaporation** NOUN turning into a vapour or gas

evasion NOUN **evasions** evasion is purposely avoiding something

eve NOUN **eves** the eve of a particular day is the day or evening before

even ADJECTIVE

1 an even surface is level and smooth

2 things are even when they are equal: *The scores were even.*

3 an even number is one that can be divided by 2 without a remainder, for example 12, 104 and 6000. Look up and compare **odd**

4 someone who has an even temper is calm and doesn't suddenly change their mood

• **get even with someone** to get even with someone who has done something to harm you is to get your revenge on them

ADVERB even is used to emphasize another word: *It was even colder the next morning.*

• **even so** though that may be true: *It looks like the right one, but even so, I'd like to check.*

Aa
Bb
Cc
Dd
Ee
Ff
Gg
Hh
Ii
Jj
Kk
Ll
Mm
Nn
Oo
Pp
Qq
Rr
Ss
Tt
Uu
Vv
Ww
Xx
Yy
Zz

VERB **evens, evening, evened**
• **even out 1** if something evens out, it becomes level **2** if two or more things even out, they become equal or balanced

evening NOUN **evenings** evening is the last part of the day and the early part of the night

evenly ADVERB **1** levelly or smoothly: *Spread the icing evenly over the top of the cake.* **2** equally: *evenly balanced*

event NOUN **events 1** a happening that stands out or is important for some reason: *events in history* **2** one of the items in a programme of sports or entertainment: *The next event is the sack race.*
▸ **eventful** ADJECTIVE full of action, excitement and important events: *She's led an eventful life.*

eventual ADJECTIVE happening at the end of a period of time or as a result of some process: *the eventual winner*
▸ **eventually** ADVERB finally

ever ADVERB **1** at any time or at all: *Have you ever been to France?* **2** always: *ever ready to help* **3** of all time or on record: *the biggest pizza ever*
• **ever after** from that time onwards and for always: *They got married and lived happily ever after.*
• **ever so** extremely: *It's ever so kind of you.*

evergreen ADJECTIVE evergreen plants do not lose their leaves in the winter. Look up and compare **deciduous**
NOUN **evergreens** an evergreen tree or shrub

everlasting ADJECTIVE going on or lasting for ever

every ADJECTIVE all the people or things of a particular kind without leaving any out: *Every runner will get a medal for taking part.* • *Every day, he does 200 press-ups.*
• **every so often** something happens or is done every so often when it happens or is done occasionally but not regularly or all the time

everybody PRONOUN all people or every person: *I thought everybody liked ice cream.*

everyday ADJECTIVE not special or unusual: *an everyday occurrence*

everyone PRONOUN every person or all people: *Everyone looks happy today.*

everything PRONOUN all things: *Everything in the room was covered in dust.*

everywhere ADVERB in every place: *We looked for him everywhere.*

evict VERB **evicts, evicting, evicted** to evict someone from a house or land is to force them to leave it
▸ **eviction** NOUN **evictions** evicting someone from their home or land

evidence NOUN **1** evidence is anything that makes people believe that something is true or has happened **2** someone gives evidence in court when they tell the jury or judge what they know about the case
▸ **evident** ADJECTIVE obvious or easily understood: *It was evident that he was not going to speak.*
▸ **evidently** ADVERB seemingly: *Evidently, there was some sort of argument.*

evil ADJECTIVE an evil person or an evil act is wicked and causes great harm
NOUN **evils 1** wickedness **2** something that causes great harm or destruction

evolution NOUN evolution is the long slow process by which animals and plants change over hundreds and thousands of years to adapt better to their environment

evolve VERB **evolves, evolving, evolved** to evolve is to change very gradually

ewe NOUN **ewes** an adult female sheep

ex- PREFIX if **ex-** comes at the beginning of a word, it adds the meaning 'outside' or 'former' to the rest of the word. For example, the *exterior* of something is its outside surface and an *ex-president* is someone who used to be president but isn't any longer

exact ADJECTIVE **1** precise and absolutely correct : *the exact spot where the accident happened* **2** an exact description or picture has a lot of detail and is very accurate

exaggerate ➜ exclaim

▶ **exactly** ADVERB correctly or in an exact way

exaggerate VERB **exaggerates, exaggerating, exaggerated** to exaggerate is to make something seem better, bigger or more important than it really is

▶ **exaggeration** NOUN **exaggerations** exaggerating or a statement that exaggerates

exam NOUN **exams** an examination

examination NOUN **examinations 1** an examination is a formal test of someone's knowledge or ability **2** examination is looking carefully at something

examine VERB **examines, examining, examined 1** to examine something is to look at it carefully **2** to examine pupils or students is to test their knowledge by asking them questions

example NOUN **examples 1** an example of something is a thing of that kind **2** if someone is or sets a good example, they behave in a way that others should copy

exasperate VERB **exasperates, exasperating, exasperated** something exasperates you when it makes you feel very annoyed and frustrated

▶ **exasperated** ADJECTIVE extremely annoyed

▶ **exasperating** ADJECTIVE extremely annoying

▶ **exasperation** NOUN a feeling of frustrated anger

excavate VERB **excavates, excavating, excavated** to dig in the ground or dig something out of the ground: *They'd excavated tons of rock to build the foundations.*

▶ **excavation** NOUN **excavations 1** a hole made by digging in the ground **2** something dug out of the ground

▶ **excavator** NOUN **excavators** a machine that is used for digging

exceed VERB **exceeds, exceeding, exceeded** to exceed something is to go beyond or above it: *His exam results exceeded his teacher's expectations.*

▶ **exceedingly** ADVERB very: *an exceedingly boring journey*

excel VERB **excels, excelling, excelled** to excel at something is to be extremely good at it and better than most other people

excellent ADJECTIVE extremely good or of a very high standard

▶ **excellence** NOUN excellence is very high quality or great ability

except PREPOSITION AND CONJUNCTION other than, apart from, or not including: *He works every day except Sunday.*

exception NOUN **exceptions** something that is not the same as the others in a group or something that a statement does not apply to: *an exception to the rule*

▶ **exceptional** ADJECTIVE unusual or outstanding: *Gail has an exceptional gift for writing.*

▶ **exceptionally** ADVERB very: *exceptionally fine weather*

excerpt NOUN **excerpts** a short piece of writing, music or film that has been taken from a larger complete work

excess NOUN **excesses** an excess of something is too much of it

▶ **excessive** ADJECTIVE too much or too great

exchange VERB **exchanges, exchanging, exchanged** to exchange things is to swap them or to give one and take the other instead NOUN **exchanges** a swap

excite VERB **excites, exciting, excited** to excite someone is to make them feel very eager or to give them a pleasant feeling of danger

▶ **excited** ADJECTIVE not calm because you are looking forward very much to something

▶ **excitement** NOUN a pleasant feeling of looking forward to something

▶ **exciting** ADJECTIVE thrilling or full of lively action

exclaim VERB **exclaims, exclaiming, exclaimed** to exclaim is to say something suddenly or loudly: *'What a wonderful surprise!' she exclaimed, clapping her hands in delight.*

▶ **exclamation** NOUN **exclamations** an exclamation is a word, phrase or

Aa Bb Cc Dd **Ee** Ff Gg Hh Ii Jj Kk Ll Mm Nn Oo Pp Qq Rr Ss Tt Uu Vv Ww Xx Yy Zz sentence spoken suddenly or loudly and expressing strong feelings and emotions, such as surprise, anger, pain, admiration, frustration or desperation

exclamation mark NOUN **exclamation marks** the punctuation mark that you use instead of a full stop after an exclamation, for example *Stop talking now!*

exclude VERB **excludes, excluding, excluded** to exclude someone or something is to not include them or to prevent them from taking part: *He was excluded from school for a week as a punishment.*

exclusive ADJECTIVE **1** an exclusive place is meant for or used by only a certain special group of people, such as the rich **2** if something is exclusive, it is found in only one place, and you can't get it anywhere else: *an exclusive offer* **3** if one thing is exclusive of another it does not include that other thing: *It costs £20, exclusive of postage.*

▶ **exclusively** ADVERB only: *The stadium is used exclusively for big international events.*

excrement NOUN the solid waste that comes out of the bodies of humans and animals

excrete VERB **excretes, excreting, excreted** to send waste or some other substance out of the body or a body part

▶ **excretion** NOUN sending out waste from the body

excruciating ADJECTIVE excruciating pain is very very severe

excursion NOUN **excursions** a trip somewhere for pleasure

excuse VERB (pronounced eks-**kyooz**) **excuses, excusing, excused 1** to excuse someone is to forgive them for doing something, especially if they had a good reason for doing it: *Such behaviour cannot be excused.* **2** to be excused from doing something is to be let off doing it

NOUN (pronounced eks-**kyoos**) **excuses** something you say to explain something you have done wrong

execute VERB **executes, executing, executed 1** to execute someone is to

kill them as an official punishment **2** to execute something is to carry it out

▶ **execution** NOUN **executions** killing someone by order of the law

▶ **executioner** NOUN **executioners** someone who executes people who have been condemned to death

executive NOUN **executives** a senior manager in a business or organization

exemplary ADJECTIVE exemplary behaviour is so good it should be followed as an example

exemplify VERB **exemplifies, exemplifying, exemplified** to exemplify something is to be an example of it or to show what it is by giving an example

exempt ADJECTIVE if you are exempt from something, such as a law or a test, it does not apply to you or you do not have to do it

▶ **exemption** NOUN **exemptions** being exempt from doing something

exercise NOUN **exercises 1** exercise is movements or games done to keep your body fit and healthy **2** an exercise is something you do to practise something

VERB **exercises, exercising, exercised** to exercise is to move around and be active so that you use your muscles and keep fit and healthy

exert VERB **exerts, exerting, exerted** to exert yourself is to make an effort

▶ **exertion** NOUN **exertions** exertion is hard physical work or effort

exhale VERB **exhales, exhaling, exhaled** to breath air out of your lungs through your nose and mouth. Look up and compare **inhale**

▶ **exhalation** NOUN breathing out

exhaust VERB **exhausts, exhausting, exhausted 1** if something exhausts you, it uses up all your strength or energy **2** to exhaust a supply of something is to use it all up

NOUN **exhausts** a device which carries the fumes out of a vehicle's engine through a pipe

▶ **exhausted** ADJECTIVE very tired or worn out

▶ **exhaustion** NOUN a feeling of great tiredness

exhibit NOUN **exhibits** something that is put on display in a gallery or museum VERB **exhibits, exhibiting, exhibited** to exhibit something is to show it: *She exhibits her paintings at a small local gallery.*

▶ **exhibition** NOUN **exhibitions** a public show or open display

▶ **exhibitor** NOUN **exhibitors** someone who exhibits their work or produce at a public gallery or show

exile VERB **exiles, exiling, exiled** to exile someone from their country is to force them to leave
NOUN **exiles 1** an exile is someone who has been forced to leave their country **2** exile is being forced to live in a country that is not your own: *For half his life he lived in exile in Europe.*

exist VERB **exists, existing, existed 1** to exist is to be or to have life: *Do fairies really exist, do you think?* **2** to exist is to stay alive: *How do they exist on such a low wage?*

▶ **existence** NOUN **1** being or being alive **2** a way of living: *a solitary existence*

exit VERB **exits, exiting, exited** to exit is to go out: *They exited the stadium by the west gate.*
NOUN **exits 1** a way out of somewhere: *Leave the motorway by the next exit.* **2** to make an exit is to leave: *He made a hasty exit.*

exorcism NOUN **exorcisms** a spell or ritual to drive out an evil spirit from a place or a person

▶ **exorcist** NOUN **exorcists** someone who performs exorcism

▶ **exorcize** or **exorcise** VERB **exorcizes, exorcizing, exorcizing** to exorcize a demon or other evil spirit is to drive it out

exotic ADJECTIVE something exotic is interesting, colourful or strange, usually because it comes from a foreign country that is very different from your own

expand VERB **expands, expanding, expanded** something expands when it grows bigger or wider or opens out to become bigger or wider

expanse NOUN **expanses** an area of land, sea or sky that stretches over a big distance: *a wide expanse of desert*

expansion NOUN getting bigger or wider: *the expansion of metal when it is heated*

expect VERB **expects, expecting, expected 1** to expect something is to believe that it will happen or it will be the case: *I expect it will be warm in Portugal.* **2** if you are expecting something, you are waiting for it to happen or arrive: *I'm expecting a parcel.* **3** to expect something is to think that it ought to happen or that you have a right to it: *I expected a bit more gratitude.*

▶ **expectant** ADJECTIVE **1** to be expectant is to be hopeful that something good will happen **2** an expectant mother is a pregnant woman

▶ **expectation** NOUN **expectations** something you expect to happen at some time in the future

▶ **expecting** ADJECTIVE a woman who is expecting is pregnant

expedition NOUN **expeditions** a journey made for a purpose, especially one made by a group of people: *an expedition to the South Pole*

expel VERB **expels, expelling, expelled 1** to expel something is to force it out **2** to expel a pupil from school is to make them leave the school because they have behaved so badly

expense NOUN **expenses 1** expense is the cost of something in money **2** your expenses are the sums of money you have to spend in order to live or do your job

▶ **expensive** ADJECTIVE costing a lot of money

experience NOUN **experiences 1** experience is knowledge that a person gains by doing something or doing it for a long time **2** an experience is an event that you are involved in

▶ **experienced** ADJECTIVE having knowledge gained from practice

Aa
Bb
Cc
Dd
Ee
Ff
Gg
Hh
Ii
Jj
Kk
Ll
Mm
Nn
Oo
Pp
Qq
Rr
Ss
Tt
Uu
Vv
Ww
Xx
Yy
Zz

Aa
Bb
Cc
Dd
Ee
Ff
Gg
Hh
Ii
Jj
Kk
Ll
Mm
Nn
Oo
Pp
Qq
Rr
Ss
Tt
Uu
Vv
Ww
Xx
Yy
Zz

experiment NOUN **experiments 1** a scientific test to discover something unknown or to check that an idea is true **2** something done to find out what will happen or what its effect will be

VERB **experiments, experimenting, experimented 1** to experiment is to carry out scientific experiments **2** to try something to find out what the result will be

▸ **experimental** ADJECTIVE as a test or trial

expert NOUN **experts** someone who knows a lot about a particular subject

ADJECTIVE very knowledgeable or skilled at something

▸ **expertise** NOUN skill or knowledge

expire VERB **expires, expiring, expired** something expires when it runs out or becomes out of date: *Your passport expired last week.*

▸ **expiry** NOUN running out or becoming out of date

explain VERB **explains, explaining, explained 1** to explain something is to give more or simpler information or instructions so that it is easier to understand or do **2** to explain yourself is to give someone reasons for your behaviour

▸ **explanation** NOUN **explanations 1** something that explains **2** a piece of writing that tells you how something works or how it happens

▸ **explanatory** ADJECTIVE intended to explain

explode VERB **explodes, exploding, exploded 1** to explode is to blow up like a bomb with a loud noise **2** if someone explodes they suddenly lose their temper

exploit VERB (pronounced iks-**ploit**) **exploits, exploiting, exploited** to exploit someone or a situation is to use them to get some benefit for yourself

NOUN (pronounced **eks**-ploit) **exploits** a daring action or adventure

▸ **exploitation** NOUN exploiting someone or something

explore VERB **explores, exploring, explored 1** to explore a place is to look around it and find out what it is like **2** to explore something is to study it to discover things about it or find out how good it might be

▸ **exploration** NOUN **explorations** exploration is exploring a place or thing

▸ **explorer** NOUN **explorers** someone who travels to a remote or unknown place to find out what it is like

explosion NOUN **explosions** a very loud noise made, for example, when a bomb goes off or something is blown up

explosive NOUN **explosives** explosives are substances that can explode and that are used to blow things up

ADJECTIVE likely to explode: *a highly explosive gas*

export VERB (pronounced eks-**port**) **exports, exporting, exported 1** to export goods is to send them out of your country to be sold abroad **2** (*ICT*) to export data on a computer is to send it from one file to another, or one computer to another

NOUN (pronounced **eks**-port) **exports** exports are goods that are sent and sold abroad

expose VERB **exposes, exposing, exposed 1** to expose something is to uncover it so that it is seen **2** to expose someone is to show people what or who they really are **3** to expose someone to something is to let them experience it or suffer it

▸ **exposure** NOUN **exposures 1** exposing **2** a piece of film that has been exposed to light and will become a photograph when it is developed

express VERB **expresses, expressing, expressed** to express a thought or feeling is to put it into words or show it by your actions

ADJECTIVE travelling fast from one place to another: *an express train*

▸ **expression** NOUN **expressions 1** expressing things by words or actions **2** a group of words that have a particular meaning

▸ **expressive** ADJECTIVE having the ability to express meaning or feelings clearly

expulsion NOUN **expulsions** expulsion, or an expulsion, is when someone or something is forced out or expelled

exquisite ADJECTIVE very beautiful

extend VERB **extends, extending, extended 1** to extend a part of your body is to hold it out **2** to extend something is to make it longer

▸ **extension** NOUN **extensions 1** extending **2** something that adds length or more time to something **3** a part added on to a building

▸ **extensive** ADJECTIVE covering a large space or wide area

▸ **extent** NOUN **1** the space something covers **2** an amount or degree: *It was, to a great extent, his own fault.*

exterior ADJECTIVE at, on or for the outside: *exterior walls*

NOUN **exteriors** the exterior of something is its outside: *The exterior of the house was painted bright blue.*

exterminate VERB **exterminates, exterminating, exterminated** to exterminate living things, especially pests, is to kill them all

external ADJECTIVE outside or on the outside: *an external wall*

extinct ADJECTIVE **1** extinct animals or plants have died out completely and no longer exist **2** an extinct volcano stopped erupting a long time ago

▸ **extinction** NOUN being destroyed completely or dying out completely

extinguish VERB **extinguishes, extinguishing, extinguished** to extinguish a light or flame is to put it out

▸ **extinguisher** NOUN **extinguishers** a device used to spray foam or chemicals on to a fire to put it out

extortionate ADJECTIVE far too expensive: *an extortionate price*

extra ADJECTIVE an extra thing or amount is more than usual or necessary

ADVERB very: *extra large*

NOUN **extras 1** something extra, especially a charge that is not included in the original price **2** an actor who appears for a short time in a film as one of a crowd in the background

extra- PREFIX if a word starts with extra-, it means 'beyond' or 'more'. For example, something *extraordinary* is beyond ordinary, and is very unusual

extract VERB (pronounced eks-**tract**) **extracts, extracting, extracted** to extract something is to take it out: *extract a tooth*

NOUN (pronounced **eks**-tract) **extracts 1** a substance that has been extracted **2** a short piece from a book or film

▸ **extraction** NOUN **extractions 1** extraction is taking something out: *a tooth extraction* • *the extraction of oil from the sea bed* **2** your extraction is where your family comes from: *She is of Italian extraction.*

extraordinary ADJECTIVE very special or unusual: *an extraordinary child*

▸ **extraordinarily** ADVERB very unusually or surprisingly

extraterrestrial ADJECTIVE from a planet or place other than the Earth

NOUN **extraterrestrials** a being from another planet

extravagant ADJECTIVE **1** spending too much money **2** using too much of something

extravaganza NOUN **extravaganzas** a spectacular public show

extreme ADJECTIVE **1** far from being ordinary or usual: *His reaction to the news was a bit extreme.* **2** far away from the centre or middle: *The boy on the extreme right of the picture.* **3** very great: *extreme cold*

NOUN **extremes 1** something that is extreme: *extremes of temperature* **2** if you go to extremes, you do or say extraordinary things

▸ **extremely** ADVERB very: *extremely naughty*

extrovert NOUN **extroverts** someone who is confident and enjoys being with other people. Look up and compare **introvert**

exuberant ADJECTIVE to be exuberant is to be in very high spirits: *The players were exuberant when they won.*

Aa
Bb
Cc
Dd
Ee
Ff
Gg
Hh
Ii
Jj
Kk
Ll
Mm
Nn
Oo
Pp
Qq
Rr
Ss
Tt
Uu
Vv
Ww
Xx
Yy
Zz

the eye

nerves

cornea

pupil

lens

iris

optic nerve
(leading to the brain)

retina

Aa

Bb

Cc

Dd

Ee

Ff

Gg

Hh

Ii

Jj

Kk

Ll

Mm

Nn

Oo

Pp

Qq

Rr

Ss

Tt

Uu

Vv

Ww

Xx

Yy

Zz

eye NOUN **eyes** your eyes are the two parts of your body at the front of your head that you see with. See the picture above

VERB **eyes, eyeing, eyed** to eye someone or something is to look at them, especially because you are interested in them

eyeball NOUN **eyeballs** the round part that makes up your whole eye

eyebrow NOUN **eyebrows** your eyebrows are the lines of hair above your eyes

eyelash NOUN **eyelashes** your eyelashes are the hairs round the edges of your eyes

eyelid NOUN **eyelids** your eyelids are the pieces of skin that cover your eyes when your eyes are closed

eyesight NOUN the ability to see: *Her eyesight is poor and she has to wear contact lenses.*

eyesore NOUN **eyesores** something ugly that spoils a view or scene

eyewitness NOUN **eyewitnesses** someone who has seen something happen, for example a crime being committed

Ff

F ABBREVIATION short for **Fahrenheit**

fable NOUN **fables** a story, usually about animals, that teaches a lesson

fabric NOUN **fabrics** cloth: *Wool is a natural fabric.*

fabulous ADJECTIVE extremely good: *The weather was fabulous.*

face NOUN **faces**
1 the front of your head where your eyes, nose and mouth are
2 the part of a clock or watch where the numbers are
3 the steep side of a mountain or cliff
4 one of the flat outside surfaces of a shape
VERB **faces, facing, faced 1** to be opposite someone or something: *My house faces the park.* **2** to look or turn in the direction of someone or something: *They turned and faced each other.* **3** to have to deal with a difficult situation: *She faced many difficulties.*

facial ADJECTIVE relating to your face: *a facial expression*

facility NOUN **facilities** a building or piece of equipment that you can use for doing something: *sports facilities*

fact NOUN **facts** something that you know is true
• **in fact** you say 'in fact' when you are going to give more exact information: *They know each other well; in fact, they went to school together.*

factor NOUN **factors 1** something that causes or influences a situation: *The weather is often one of the main factors in choosing where to go for a holiday.* **2** (*maths*) a number that you can divide another by and not have a remainder. For example, 3 is a factor of 6

factory NOUN **factories** a building where something is made in large amounts: *a chocolate factory*

factual ADJECTIVE based on facts: *factual information*

fad NOUN **fads** something that is popular for a short time only

fade VERB **fades, fading, faded 1** to disappear gradually: *Our hope of winning the match was starting to fade.* **2** to lose colour and brightness: *The jeans had faded.*

faeces PLURAL NOUN solid waste from people's or animal's bodies

Fahrenheit (pronounced **fa**-ren-hite) NOUN a system for measuring temperature in which water freezes at 32 degrees and boils at 212 degrees

fail VERB **fails, failing, failed 1** to not pass an exam or test: *My brother failed his driving test.* **2** to be unsuccessful in what you are trying to do: *They failed in their attempt to sail round the world.* **3** to not do what is expected or needed: *The parcel failed to arrive.* • *The brakes failed.*
▸ **failing** NOUN **failings** a fault
▸ **failure** NOUN **failures 1** someone or something that is not successful: *She felt like a failure.* **2** the act of failing: *Their first attempt ended in failure.*

faint ADJECTIVE **fainter, faintest 1** difficult to see, hear or smell: *There's a faint mark on the carpet.* • *the faint sound of footsteps* **2** if you feel faint, you feel as though you might become unconscious
VERB **faints, fainting, fainted** to suddenly become unconscious and fall to the ground: *Richard fainted when he saw the blood.*
▸ **faintly** ADVERB **1** in a way that is difficult to see, hear or smell: '*Yes,*' she said faintly. **2** slightly: *He looked faintly ridiculous.*

fair[1] ADJECTIVE **fairer, fairest**
1 treating everyone equally: *It's not fair that my brother can stay up later than me.*
2 fair skin or hair is very light in colour

Aa
Bb
Cc
Dd
Ee
Ff
Gg
Hh
Ii
Jj
Kk
Ll
Mm
Nn
Oo
Pp
Qq
Rr
Ss
Tt
Uu
Vv
Ww
Xx
Yy
Zz

3 fair weather is very pleasant, with no rain **4** quite good but not very good: *a fair attempt* **5** quite large in size or amount: *He lives a fair distance away from here.*

▸ **fairly** ADVERB **1** quite: *I was fairly nervous about the test.* **2** in a way that is reasonable: *We were treated fairly.*

▸ **fairness** NOUN being fair

fair² NOUN **fairs 1** an event with lots of stalls where you can buy things **2** a collection of rides that you can go on for entertainment, which moves from town to town

fairy NOUN **fairies** an imaginary creature that has magical powers and looks like a small person

fairy lights PLURAL NOUN coloured lights for decoration, especially on a Christmas tree

fairy story or **fairy tale** NOUN **fairy stories** or **fairy tales** a traditional story in which magic things happen

faith NOUN **faiths 1** great trust: *I have a lot of faith in him.* **2** religious belief: *people of different faiths*

faithful ADJECTIVE loyal and keeping your promises: *a faithful friend*

▸ **faithfully** ADVERB in a loyal way

fake ADJECTIVE not real, but copying something else: *fake diamonds*
NOUN **fakes** a copy of something rather than the real thing
VERB **fakes, faking, faked 1** to pretend something: *John faked a cough so he could miss school.* **2** to make a copy of something and pretend it is real

falcon NOUN **falcons** a type of bird that kills other birds and small animals for food

fall VERB **falls, falling, fell, fallen 1** to drop down to the ground: *The apples fell from the tree.* **2** if you fall, you have an accident and hit the ground: *Ben fell downstairs.* **3** if an amount, price or temperature falls, it goes down
• **fall out** to fall out is to stop being friends with someone
NOUN **falls 1** an accident in which you hit the ground: *My grandmother had*

a fall last week. **2** a drop in a price, amount or temperature: *a fall in prices* **3** the American English word for **autumn**

fallout NOUN radioactive dust from a nuclear explosion

fallow ADJECTIVE fallow land has been left without crops on it so the soil can improve

false ADJECTIVE **1** if something you say or believe is false, it is not true or correct: *He made a false statement to the police.* **2** an object that is false is not real or natural: *false teeth*

▸ **falsely** ADVERB incorrectly: *I was falsely accused of theft.*

▸ **falseness** NOUN being untrue or unreal

falter VERB **falters, faltering, faltered 1** to speak in an uncertain way and keep stopping **2** to move in an unsteady way

fame NOUN the quality of being famous: *young actors who look for fame*

▸ **famed** ADJECTIVE famous for a particular reason: *Venice is a city famed for its canals.*

familiar ADJECTIVE **1** if someone or something is familiar, you know them very well: *His voice sounded familiar.* **2** if you are familiar with something, you have seen it or used it before: *I'm not familiar with this software.*

▸ **familiarize** or **familiarise** VERB **familiarizes, familiarizing, familiarized** to familiarize yourself is to make sure you know something: *Try to familiarize yourself with the rules.*

family NOUN **families 1** a group of people who are related to each other: *Most people in my family have brown hair.* **2** a group of animals, plants or languages that are related to each other

famine NOUN **famines** a situation in which many people do not have enough food and may die

famished ADJECTIVE extremely hungry

famous ADJECTIVE known by many people: *a famous actor*

fan¹ NOUN **fans** someone who likes a person or thing very much: *football fans*

fan² NOUN **fans 1** a machine with thin blades that spin round and make the air cooler **2** something that you hold and wave in front of your face to make you feel cooler

VERB **fans, fanning, fanned** to fan yourself is to use a fan to cool yourself down

fanatic NOUN **fanatics** someone who likes someone or something in an extreme way: *a cycling fanatic*

▸ **fanatical** ADJECTIVE extremely enthusiastic about something

fanciful ADJECTIVE imagined and not realistic: *fanciful ideas about moving to Spain*

fancy VERB **fancies, fancying, fancied 1** to like the idea of having or doing something: *Do you fancy going swimming?* **2** (*informal*) to be attracted to someone: *My friend fancies you.*

ADJECTIVE **fancier, fanciest** decorated and not plain: *fancy cakes*

fancy dress NOUN clothes that you wear to a party to make you look like another person or thing

fanfare NOUN **fanfares** a short, loud piece of music played on a trumpet

fang NOUN **fangs** a long, sharp tooth of a fierce animal

✦ This word comes from an Old English word **fang**, which means 'something caught', because animals seize things in their teeth.

fantastic ADJECTIVE extremely good: *We had a fantastic time at the zoo.*

fantasy NOUN **fantasies** something good that you imagine will happen but that probably will not happen: *He has a fantasy about being rich and famous.*

far ADVERB **farther** or **further, farthest** or **furthest 1** a long distance: *We have walked quite far.* **2** much: *She's a far better swimmer than I am.* **3** a lot of progress: *I haven't got very far with my maths homework.*

• **so far** until now: *I've only read ten pages so far.*

ADJECTIVE the far part of something is the greatest distance from you: *a house on the far side of the lake*

farce NOUN **farces 1** a situation that is funny or stupid **2** a play in which funny and stupid things happen

fare NOUN **fares** the price of a journey by bus, train or aeroplane: *The train fare to London is £33.*

farewell INTERJECTION an old-fashioned word for **goodbye**

far-fetched ADJECTIVE extremely unlikely to be true

farm NOUN **farms** an area of land where crops are grown and animals are kept

▸ **farmer** NOUN **farmers** someone who owns and works on a farm

farmhouse NOUN **farmhouses** a house on a farm where the farmer lives

farmyard NOUN **farmyards** an area surrounded by buildings on a farm

fascinate VERB **fascinates, fascinating, fascinated** to interest someone very much

▸ **fascinating** ADJECTIVE extremely interesting: *a fascinating story*

▸ **fascination** NOUN a great interest in something: *I've always had a fascination for unusual animals.*

Fascism (pronounced **fash**-izm) NOUN a type of government in which the leaders are very powerful and strict

▸ **Fascist** NOUN **Fascists** someone who believes in Fascism

ADJECTIVE believing in or to do with Fascism

fashion NOUN **fashions** something that is very popular at a particular time: *a fashion for tight jeans*

• **in fashion** fashionable: *Short skirts were in fashion then.*

• **out of fashion** not fashionable

▸ **fashionable** ADJECTIVE liked by many people at a particular time

fast ADJECTIVE **faster, fastest 1** quick: *a fast car* **2** if a clock or watch is fast, it shows a time that is later than the correct time

ADVERB **faster, fastest** quickly: *She can run very fast.*

fasten VERB **fastens, fastening, fastened** to join or tie two things together

▸ **fastener** NOUN **fasteners**

Aa
Bb
Cc
Dd
Ee
Ff
Gg
Hh
Ii
Jj
Kk
Ll
Mm
Nn
Oo
Pp
Qq
Rr
Ss
Tt
Uu
Vv
Ww
Xx
Yy
Zz

something that is used to join two things together

fat ADJECTIVE **fatter, fattest** a fat person has a wide round body

NOUN **fats 1** an oily substance that forms a layer under your skin which keeps you warm **2** an oily substance in food that gives you energy but can be unhealthy if you eat too much: *foods with a high fat content* **3** oil from animals or plants that is used for frying food: *You need more fat in the pan.*

fatal ADJECTIVE **1** causing someone to die: *a fatal accident* **2** causing serious problems: *a fatal mistake*

▶ **fatality** NOUN **fatalities** a death in an accident

▶ **fatally** ADVERB in a way which causes death: *He was fatally wounded.*

fate NOUN **1** a power that seems to control what happens **2** the things that will happen to someone, especially unpleasant things: *It was his fate to be captured again after his escape.*

father NOUN **fathers** your male parent

▶ **fatherhood** NOUN being a father

father-in-law NOUN **father-in-laws** *or* **fathers-in-law** the father of someone's wife or husband

fatherly ADJECTIVE kindly and protective: *a fatherly hug*

fathom VERB **fathoms, fathoming, fathomed** to understand something after thinking about it: *I still can't fathom why he didn't tell me.*

fatigue NOUN extreme tiredness

fatten VERB **fattens, fattening, fattened** to make an animal fatter so it can be eaten

▶ **fattening** ADJECTIVE making you fat: *Chocolate is quite fattening.*

fatty ADJECTIVE **fattier, fattiest** fatty food contains a lot of fat

fault NOUN **faults 1** a mistake or something that is wrong: *There's a fault in the engine.* **2** if something bad is your fault, you are responsible for it: *Whose fault is it that we lost the keys?* **3** (*geography*) a long crack in the Earth's surface that causes an earthquake if it moves

▶ **faultless** ADJECTIVE perfect

▶ **faulty** ADJECTIVE **faultier, faultiest** something that is faulty has something wrong with it: *a faulty computer*

fauna NOUN animals: *the fauna and flora of the area*

favour NOUN **favours** something you do for someone to help them: *Could you do me a favour and check my homework?*

• **be in favour of something** if you are in favour of something, you think that it is a good idea: *Hands up all those in favour of going to the beach.*

▶ **favourable** ADJECTIVE good and suitable: *favourable weather conditions*

▶ **favourably** ADVERB in a way that makes something seem good: *This computer compares favourably with others.*

favourite ADJECTIVE your favourite person or thing is the one you like best: *My favourite colour is purple.* • *Who's your favourite teacher?*

▶ **favouritism** NOUN favouritism is unfairly treating one person or group better than others

fawn NOUN **fawns** a young deer

fax NOUN **faxes 1** a message that is sent and printed by a special machine attached to a telephone line **2** a machine used for sending a message like this

VERB **faxes, faxing, faxed** to send someone a fax

fear NOUN **fears 1** a feeling of being very frightened: *She was shaking with fear.* **2** a frightened feeling that you have about something: *John has a fear of spiders.*

VERB **fears, fearing, feared** to be afraid of someone or something

fearful ADJECTIVE feeling frightened about something

▶ **fearfully** ADVERB in a frightened way

fearless ADJECTIVE not frightened by anything

▶ **fearlessly** ADVERB in a way that shows you are not frightened: *She fearlessly climbed the tree.*

feast NOUN **feasts** a large meal for a special occasion

feat → felt

feat NOUN **feats** something someone does that impresses you because it needs a lot of skill, strength or courage

feather NOUN **feathers** one of the long light things that cover a bird's body
▸ **feathery** ADJECTIVE soft and light like a feather

feature NOUN **features** 1 a part or quality of something: *a house with many interesting features* 2 a part of your face, such as your eyes or nose
VERB if something features a particular thing or person, it includes them: *The new film features Johnny Depp.*

February NOUN the second month of the year, after January and before March

fed VERB a way of changing the verb **feed** to make a past tense. It can be used with or without a helping verb: *Anna fed the dog.* • *Have you fed the cat?*

federal ADJECTIVE 1 in a federal system, a country is divided into states and each state has its own government but there is still a national government that deals with important things 2 the federal government in a system like this is the national government
▸ **federation** NOUN **federations** a group of states or organizations which have joined together

fed up ADJECTIVE slightly annoyed or bored: *I'm fed up doing homework.*

fee NOUN **fees** an amount of money that you must pay for a service

feeble ADJECTIVE **feebler, feeblest** 1 physically very weak 2 not very good: *a feeble attempt to be funny*
▸ **feebly** ADVERB in a weak way

feed VERB **feeds, feeding, fed** 1 to give food to a person or animal: *Dad was feeding the baby.* 2 animals feed when they eat food: *Don't disturb the dog when he's feeding.* • *Rabbits feed on grass.*

feel VERB **feels, feeling, felt**
1 to have a particular feeling: *I feel tired.* • *Do you feel better today?*
2 to touch something with your fingers to see what it is like
3 to experience something touching you or happening to you: *Suddenly, she felt a hand on her shoulder.* • *He could feel himself falling.*
4 if something feels hot, smooth, dry etc, that is how it seems when you touch it: *Your forehead feels hot.*
5 to think or believe something: *I feel he should have asked my opinion first.*
6 if you feel like something, you want it or want to do it: *I feel like going for a swim.*
▸ **feeler** NOUN **feelers** one of the two long things on an insect's head, which it uses to sense things
▸ **feeling** NOUN **feelings** something that you experience in your mind or body: *a feeling of excitement*

feet NOUN the plural of **foot**

feline ADJECTIVE to do with cats

fell[1] VERB a way of changing the verb **fall** to make a past tense: *Suddenly, she fell off the chair.*

fell[2] VERB **fells, felling, felled** to cut a tree down

fellow ADJECTIVE your fellow students or players are the people in your class or school, or in your team
NOUN **fellows** (*informal*) an old-fashioned word for a boy or man: *He's an unusual fellow.*
▸ **fellowship** NOUN 1 a feeling of friendliness between people who have similar interests 2 a club or organization

felt[1] NOUN a type of cloth made of rolled and pressed wool

felt[2] VERB a way of changing the verb **feel** to make a past tense. It can be used with or without a helping verb: *He felt very tired.* • *Have you felt how soft this fur is?*

Aa Bb Cc Dd Ee **Ff** Gg Hh Ii Jj Kk Ll Mm Nn Oo Pp Qq Rr Ss Tt Uu Vv Ww Xx Yy Zz

Aa
Bb
Cc
Dd
Ee
Ff
Gg
Hh
Ii
Jj
Kk
Ll
Mm
Nn
Oo
Pp
Qq
Rr
Ss
Tt
Uu
Vv
Ww
Xx
Yy
Zz

female ADJECTIVE belonging to the sex that can give birth or lay eggs: *A female lion is called a lioness.*
NOUN **females** a female animal or person

feminine ADJECTIVE **1** to do with women, or having qualities that are typical of a woman **2** (*grammar*) feminine forms of words refer to females. For example, *she* is a feminine pronoun
▶ **femininity** NOUN being like a woman

feminism NOUN the belief that women should have the same rights and opportunities as men
▶ **feminist** NOUN **feminists** someone who has this belief

fen NOUN **fens** an area of flat, wet land

fence NOUN **fences** a wooden or metal barrier

fencing NOUN a sport in which people fight with swords

fend VERB **fends, fending, fended**
• **fend for yourself** to look after yourself, without help or protection from other people

ferment VERB **ferments, fermented, fermenting** when beer or wine ferments, it is changed chemically because of the effect of yeast or bacteria

fern NOUN **ferns** a plant with long leaves like feathers

ferocious ADJECTIVE extremely fierce: *a ferocious dog*
▶ **ferociously** ADVERB in a very fierce way
▶ **ferocity** NOUN being fierce

ferret NOUN **ferrets** a small animal with a long body, used to hunt rabbits

ferry NOUN **ferries** a boat that carries people and vehicles

fertile ADJECTIVE **1** fertile land is good for growing crops on **2** a fertile woman or female animal is able to have babies
▶ **fertility** NOUN the state of being fertile

fertilize or **fertilise** VERB **fertilizes, fertilizing, fertilized 1** to put male

and female cells together so that a baby or a young plant or animal is produced **2** to add a substance to soil so that plants grow better
▶ **fertilization** or **fertilisation** NOUN the act of fertilizing something
▶ **fertilizer** or **fertiliser** NOUN **fertilizers** or **fertilisers** a substance you put on soil to make plants grow better

fervent ADJECTIVE extremely enthusiastic: *a fervent belief* • *a fervent football fan*

festival NOUN **festivals 1** a special time when people have a holiday to celebrate something: *a religious festival* **2** a time when there are a lot of special events of a particular type: *a film festival*
▶ **festive** ADJECTIVE relating to happy celebrations
▶ **festivities** PLURAL NOUN the things you do to celebrate a special event

festoon VERB **festoons, festooning, festooned** to decorate a place with lots of ribbons, balloons or flowers

fetch VERB **fetches, fetching, fetched** to go somewhere and bring something or someone back with you: *Could you fetch the newspaper for me, please?*

fete or **fête** NOUN **fetes** or **fêtes** a special event with stalls and games, to raise money for a school, church etc

fetlock NOUN **fetlocks** the part of a horse's leg above its hoof

feud (pronounced **fyood**) NOUN **feuds** an argument between two people or groups that goes on for a very long time

fever NOUN **fevers** if you have a fever, your body temperature is higher than normal because you are ill
▶ **feverish** ADJECTIVE feeling very hot because you are ill

few ADJECTIVE **fewer, fewest** not many: *She has few friends.*
NOUN a small number: *'Did you take any photos?' 'Only a few.'*

fiancé NOUN **fiancés** a woman's fiancé is the man she is engaged to

fiancée NOUN **fiancées** a man's fiancée is the woman he is engaged to

fib NOUN **fibs** a lie that is not about anything important: *He's telling fibs again.*
VERB **fibs, fibbing, fibbed** to tell a harmless lie

▸ **fibber** NOUN **fibbers** someone who tells unimportant lies

fibre NOUN **fibres** 1 a thin thread of something 2 a cloth made up of thin threads 3 a substance in food, which humans cannot digest and which helps your bowels work properly

fibreglass NOUN a strong material made from tiny pieces of glass and plastic

fickle ADJECTIVE 1 often changing unexpectedly: *the fickle British weather* 2 someone who is fickle often changes their opinions or their friends

fiction NOUN books that describe imaginary people and situations rather than real ones

▸ **fictional** ADJECTIVE existing only in a book, not in real life: *fictional detective, Sherlock Holmes*

▸ **fictitious** ADJECTIVE imaginary and not true

fiddle NOUN **fiddles** a violin
VERB **fiddles, fiddling, fiddled** 1 to play or interfere with something in an annoying way: *Stop fiddling with your hair.* 2 to play the fiddle

▸ **fiddly** ADJECTIVE something that is fiddly is difficult to do or use because it is so small

fidget to keep moving because you are nervous or bored

▸ **fidgety** ADJECTIVE uncomfortable and fidgeting a lot

field NOUN **fields** 1 an area of ground used for growing crops or keeping animals on 2 an area of grass used for playing sport on
VERB **fields, fielding, fielded** in games like cricket and baseball, to be the person or team that throws the ball back after someone has hit it

fieldwork NOUN research that is done outside and not in a classroom or laboratory

fiend NOUN **fiends** 1 an evil spirit 2 someone who is very keen on something: *a computer games fiend*

fierce ADJECTIVE **fiercer, fiercest** 1 violent and angry: *a fierce animal* 2 strong or intense: *a fierce storm*

▸ **fiercely** ADVERB in a violent or angry way

fiery ADJECTIVE 1 like fire 2 becoming angry very easily

fifteen NOUN the number 15

fifteenth ADJECTIVE AND ADVERB after fourteenth and before sixteenth: *my brother's fifteenth birthday*

fifth ADJECTIVE AND ADVERB after fourth and before sixth: *the fifth day of my holiday*
NOUN **fifths** the fraction ⅕, which means one of five equal parts of something: *A fifth of the money is mine.*

fiftieth ADJECTIVE AND ADVERB after forty-ninth and before fifty-first: *It's my grandfather's fiftieth birthday tomorrow.*

fifty NOUN **fifties** the number 50

fig NOUN **figs** a fruit with a lot of seeds in it, which can be dried

fight VERB **fights, fighting, fought** 1 to use your body or weapons to try to hurt someone who is doing the same to you 2 to argue with someone
NOUN **fights** the act of fighting with someone: *They had a fight in the playground.*

▸ **fighter** NOUN **fighters** 1 someone who is fighting 2 a fast military plane used for attacking

figment NOUN **figments** a figment of your imagination is something you have imagined that does not really exist

figurative ADJECTIVE figurative language is words used in a different way from the usual way, to show a likeness or create a particular image. For example, if you say someone is a *mouse*, you mean that they are as timid as a mouse

figure NOUN **figures** 1 a number 2 the shape of a person: *There was a dark figure in the doorway.*

figure of speech NOUN **figures of speech** a word or phrase used in a

Aa Bb Cc Dd Ee **Ff** Gg Hh Ii Jj Kk Ll Mm Nn Oo Pp Qq Rr Ss Tt Uu Vv Ww Xx Yy Zz

different way from usual to create a particular image. For example, if you say someone is a *lion*, you do not mean that they are really a lion, but they are as brave or fierce as a lion

file¹ NOUN **files 1** a folder for keeping papers in **2** (*ICT*) a place for storing information together in a computer

• **in single file** if people walk in single file, they walk one behind another

file² NOUN **files** a tool with a rough edge, used for making things smooth

VERB **files, filing, filed** to shape something and make it smooth using a file

fill VERB **fills, filling, filled 1** to make a container full: *He filled our glasses with water.* **2** to become full: *The concert hall quickly filled with people.*

• **fill in** to fill in a form is to write information on it

fillet NOUN **fillets** a piece of meat or fish with no bones in it

filling NOUN **fillings 1** something used for filling a hole in your tooth: *Ben hasn't got any fillings.* **2** something used for filling something else: *pancakes with a chocolate filling*

filling station NOUN **filling stations** a place where you buy petrol

filly NOUN **fillies** a young female horse

film NOUN **films 1** a story that you watch in a cinema or on television **2** something you put inside a camera so you can take photographs

VERB **films, filming, filmed** to make a film of something

filter NOUN **filters** something that traps solid material and lets liquid or gas pass through

VERB **filters, filtered, filtering** to put a liquid or gas through a filter to remove solid material

filth NOUN **1** dirt **2** rude words or behaviour

▶ **filthy** ADJECTIVE **1** very dirty **2** very rude: *filthy language*

fin NOUN **fins** one of the parts on a fish that help it to swim

final ADJECTIVE coming at the end: *the final chapter of a book*

NOUN **finals** the last game in a competition, which decides who will win

finale (pronounced fi-na-li) NOUN **finales** the last part of a show or piece of music

finalize or **finalise** VERB **finalizes, finalizing, finalized** to arrange the last details of something such as a plan

finally ADVERB **1** after a long time: *When he finally arrived, it was after midnight.* **2** used to introduce the last in a list of things: *Finally, I would like to thank everyone who has helped.*

finance NOUN **finances 1** affairs to do with money: *John is an expert in finance.* **2** the money needed for something: *The school doesn't have the finance for a new gym.*

VERB **finances, financing, financed** to give the money that pays for a plan or business

▶ **financial** ADJECTIVE relating to money

finch NOUN **finches** a small bird with a short beak

find VERB **finds, finding, found 1** to get or see something accidentally, or after you have been looking for it: *I can't find my pencil case.* • *I found a £10 note in the street.* **2** to discover something: *Have you found the answer yet?* **3** to have a particular opinion about someone or something: *I found him very rude.*

• **find and replace** (*ICT*) a feature on a computer that can find all the places in a file where a particular letter, number or word appears, and replace it with something else

• **find something out** to find something out is to discover information about it: *I'll try and find out the train times.*

fine¹ NOUN **fines** money that someone must pay as a punishment

VERB **fines, fined, fining** to make someone pay a fine: *He was fined £100 for parking illegally.*

fine² ADJECTIVE **finer, finest 1** if you are fine, you are healthy and well: *'How are you?' 'Fine, thanks.'* **2** good or acceptable: *'Shall we meet at 4 o'clock?'*

Aa
Bb
Cc
Dd
Ee
Ff
Gg
Hh
Ii
Jj
Kk
Ll
Mm
Nn
Oo
Pp
Qq
Rr
Ss
Tt
Uu
Vv
Ww
Xx
Yy
Zz

'Yes, that's fine.' • *fine weather* **3** very thin or delicate: *fine lines*
▶ **finely** ADVERB **1** in very thin small pieces: *Chop the onion finely.* **2** in a beautiful or impressive way: *a finely decorated room*

finger NOUN **fingers** one of the long parts at the end of your hand

fingerprint NOUN **fingerprints** the mark that your finger makes when you touch something

finish VERB **finishes, finishing, finished 1** to end: *What time did the film finish?* **2** to stop doing something or complete it: *Have you finished your homework?* • *I'll just finish my drink.*

fir NOUN **firs** a type of tree that keeps its leaves in winter

fire NOUN **fires 1** flames and heat that burn and destroy something: *The building was destroyed by fire.* • *There was a fire at the school last night.* **2** a pile of wood or coal that is burning to give heat: *Dad put another log on the fire.* **3** a device that heats a room using gas or electricity
• **on fire** burning and producing flames: *The house was on fire.*
VERB **fires, firing, fired 1** to fire a gun is to shoot a bullet from it **2** to fire someone from their job is to dismiss them from it so they no longer have it

fire alarm NOUN **fire alarms** a bell that rings to warn you of a fire

firearm NOUN **firearms** (*formal*) a gun

fire brigade NOUN **fire brigades** the group of people whose job is to put out fires

fire engine NOUN **fire engines** a vehicle that carries firefighters and equipment to put out a fire

firefighter NOUN **firefighters** someone whose job is to put out a fire

firefly NOUN **fireflies** a fly with a tail that shines in the dark

fireman NOUN **firemen** a man whose job is to put out a fire

fireplace NOUN **fireplaces** the space for a fire in the wall of a room

firewood NOUN wood for burning as fuel

firework NOUN **fireworks** a device that can be lit so that it flies into the sky and explodes, making bright lights

firm¹ ADJECTIVE **firmer, firmest 1** not soft: *a firm bed* **2** strict and not changing your mind: *a very firm teacher*

firm² NOUN **firms** a company: *My mum works for an electronics firm.*

first ADJECTIVE coming before everything else: *the first name on the list*
ADVERB **1** before anyone or anything else, sometimes written as 1st: *I finished the exam first.* • *Finish your dinner first.* **2** doing better than everyone else: *Philip came first in the cookery competition.*
PRONOUN the person or thing that comes before all others: *Who is first in the queue?*
• **at first** at the start of a period of time: *At first, I hated school, but I like it now.*
▶ **firstly** ADVERB used for introducing the first of several points or items: *Firstly, I'd like to welcome everybody.*

first aid NOUN simple treatment that you give to someone who is injured or ill

first-class ADJECTIVE AND ADVERB something that is first class is the best or most expensive type: *a first-class compartment on the train*

first-hand ADJECTIVE learned through personal experience or involvement and not from being told by other people

first-rate ADJECTIVE excellent: *a first-rate doctor*

fish NOUN **fish** *or* **fishes** a creature that lives and swims in water. People often eat fish as food. See the picture on the next page
VERB **fishes, fishing, fished** to catch fish

fisherman NOUN **fishermen** someone who catches fish as a job or sport

fishing NOUN the sport of catching fish

fishmonger NOUN **fishmongers 1** someone who sells fish **2** a fishmonger's is a shop that sells fish

fishy ADJECTIVE **fishier, fishiest 1** like a fish **2** something that is fishy is not quite right and makes people suspicious: *He sensed something fishy was going on.*

Aa Bb Cc Dd Ee **Ff** Gg Hh Ii Jj Kk Ll Mm Nn Oo Pp Qq Rr Ss Tt Uu Vv Ww Xx Yy Zz

a fish

mouth scales lateral line

eye

dorsal fin

gill cover
gill

pectoral fin

pelvic fin

caudal (or tail) fin

fission NOUN (*science*) splitting up the nucleus of an atom so that energy is given out

fist NOUN **fists** your hand when it is closed tightly

fit[1] ADJECTIVE **fitter, fittest 1** healthy and active because you do exercise: *I'm trying to get fit.* **2** good enough: *This food isn't fit to eat.*

VERB **fits, fitting, fitted**

1 to be the right size for someone or something: *The dress fits you perfectly.* • *The cupboard will fit in the corner.*

2 to fix something in a place: *We're having new kitchen units fitted next week.*

3 to have space to put people or things: *I can't fit any more into the suitcase.*

4 if something is fitted with particular equipment, it has that equipment: *Most bikes are fitted with front and back brakes.*

▶ **fitness** NOUN how healthy and well someone is: *exercises to improve fitness*

▶ **fitting** ADJECTIVE suitable: *a fitting end to the day*

fit[2] NOUN **fits** if someone has a fit, they suddenly become unconscious and may make uncontrolled movements

five NOUN **fives** the number 5

fix VERB **fixes, fixing, fixed 1** to attach something to something else: *She fixed the shelves to the wall.* **2** to mend something: *He's trying to fix my computer.* **3** to arrange something: *Have you fixed a time for your friends to come over?*

fizz VERB **fizzes, fizzing, fizzed** if liquid fizzes, it produces a lot of bubbles

▶ **fizzy** ADJECTIVE **fizzier, fizziest** a fizzy drink has bubbles in it

fizzle VERB **fizzles, fizzling, fizzled** to make a hissing, bubbling sound

• **fizzle out** if something fizzles out, it fails, or ends without much good coming of it: *Our plan fizzled out because no one put in much effort.*

fjord (pronounced **fyord**) NOUN **fjords** (*geography*) a narrow area of water surrounded by cliffs, especially in Norway

flabby ADJECTIVE **flabbier, flabbiest** with too much loose flesh on the body

flag NOUN **flags** a piece of cloth with a pattern on it, used as the symbol of a country or organization: *The American flag has stars and stripes on it.*

flagpole NOUN **flagpoles** a tall pole that a flag is hung from

flagstone NOUN **flagstones** a flat piece of stone used for making a path or floor

flake NOUN **flakes** a small thin piece of something

▸ **flaky** ADJECTIVE **flakier, flakiest** likely to break down into small thin pieces: *flaky pastry*

flamboyant ADJECTIVE **1** confident and lively: *a flamboyant actor* **2** bright and colourful: *flamboyant clothes*

flame NOUN **flames** the bright burning gas that you see in a fire

flamingo NOUN **flamingoes** or **flamingos** a large pink bird with long legs

flammable ADJECTIVE something that is flammable burns easily

✦ **Inflammable** and **flammable** mean the same thing.

flan NOUN **flans** a pie that is not covered at the top: *a lemon flan*

flank NOUN **flanks** the side of an animal or an army

flannel NOUN **flannels 1** a soft, light cloth **2** a piece of cloth used for washing yourself

flap VERB **flaps, flapping, flapped** if a bird flaps its wings, it moves them up and down
NOUN **flaps 1** a movement up and down, like that of a bird's wings **2** a piece of something that hangs down over an opening

flare VERB **flares, flared, flaring** to burn with a sudden bright light: *If you poke a fire, it flares more fiercely.*
• **flare up 1** if an illness or injury flares up, it suddenly starts again or becomes worse **2** to flare up is to suddenly become angry

flash NOUN **flashes** a sudden bright light: *a flash of lightning*
VERB **flashes, flashing, flashed** to shine quickly

flashy ADJECTIVE **flashier, flashiest** expensive and meant to impress people: *a flashy car*

flask NOUN **flasks 1** a special container for keeping drinks hot or cold **2** a container for liquid, used in a science laboratory

flat ADJECTIVE **flatter, flattest 1** level and not sloping: *a flat roof* **2** a flat tyre does not have any air in it **3** a flat battery has no more power in it
• **flat out** as quickly as possible: *Mum worked flat out to get the decorating finished.*
NOUN **flats 1** a set of rooms that someone lives in, which are part of a larger building **2** (*music*) in written music, a sign (♭) that makes a note lower by half a tone
▸ **flatly** ADVERB in a definite way: *He flatly refused to do it.*
▸ **flatten** VERB **flattens, flattening, flattened** to make something become flat

flatter VERB **flatters, flattering, flattered** to say nice things about someone, often because you want them to do something for you
▸ **flattery** NOUN nice things you say to someone because you want to please them

flaunt VERB **flaunts, flaunting, flaunted** to display something in an obvious way: *The king liked to flaunt his riches.*

flavour NOUN **flavours** the taste that something has: *Chocolate is my favourite ice-cream flavour.*
▸ **flavouring** NOUN **flavourings** something added to food to give it a particular taste

flaw NOUN **flaws** a fault in someone or something
▸ **flawed** ADJECTIVE not perfect
▸ **flawless** ADJECTIVE perfect, with no faults: *a flawless performance*

flax NOUN a plant tha]t has seeds from which a type of cloth is made

flea NOUN **fleas** a very small insect that jumps and bites people or animals

fleck NOUN **flecks** a very small mark or dot of colour
▸ **flecked** ADJECTIVE marked with flecks

fled VERB a way of changing the verb **flee** to make a past tense. It can be used with or without a helping verb: *The burglar fled through the front*

Aa
Bb
Cc
Dd
Ee
Ff
Gg
Hh
Ii
Jj
Kk
Ll
Mm
Nn
Oo
Pp
Qq
Rr
Ss
Tt
Uu
Vv
Ww
Xx
Yy
Zz

door. • *She had fled when she heard us coming.*

fledgling NOUN **fledglings** a young bird that has just learned to fly

flee VERB **flees, fleeing, fled** to run away or escape: *She turned and fled.*

fleece NOUN **fleeces 1** a jacket or top made from a soft, light, warm material: *If you're going outside, put your fleece on.* **2** a soft, light, warm material used for making jackets and tops **3** the wool on a sheep

▸ **fleecy** ADJECTIVE **fleecier, fleeciest** soft and warm, like wool

fleet NOUN **fleets** a large number of ships or vehicles: *a fleet of boats*

fleeting ADJECTIVE lasting for only a short time: *a fleeting smile*

flesh NOUN **1** the soft part of your body that covers your bones **2** the soft inside part of fruit and vegetables

▸ **fleshy** ADJECTIVE **fleshier, fleshiest** having a lot of flesh

flew VERB a way of changing the verb **fly** to make a past tense: *When I opened the door, the bird flew away.*

flex VERB **flexes, flexing, flexed** to bend

NOUN a piece of wire covered in plastic, which carries electricity to a piece of equipment

flexible ADJECTIVE **1** able to bend without breaking **2** able to change to suit different people or situations: *flexible arrangements*

▸ **flexibility** NOUN the quality of being flexible

flick VERB **flicks, flicking, flicked** to hit something quickly and lightly, for example with the ends of your fingers

flicker VERB **flickers, flickering, flickered** if a light or flame flickers, it does not burn steadily but seems to get darker then lighter

flies NOUN the plural of the noun **fly**

VERB the form of the verb **fly** in the present tense that you use with **he, she** or **it**: *I like watching Superman when he flies through the air.*

flight NOUN **flights 1** a journey in an aeroplane or helicopter **2** the action

of flying: *a flock of geese in flight* **3** a flight of stairs is a set of stairs

flimsy ADJECTIVE **flimsier, flimsiest 1** likely to break or tear: *flimsy material* **2** a flimsy excuse is one that is obviously not true

flinch VERB **flinches, flinching, flinched** to move part of your body suddenly, for example because you are frightened or in pain

fling VERB **flings, flinging, flung** to throw something using a lot of force: *He flung the curtains open.*

flint NOUN **flints** a hard, grey stone that can produce a spark

flip VERB **flips, flipped, flipping** to flick or toss something over

flipper NOUN **flippers 1** one of the large flat feet that seals, turtles and other animals have to help them swim **2** a wide, flat shoe that you wear to help you swim underwater

flirt VERB **flirts, flirting, flirted** to behave as though you think someone is attractive: *Emma was flirting with her sister's boyfriend.*

flit VERB **flits, flitting, flitted** to move quickly and lightly from one place to another: *His eyes flitted round the room.*

float VERB **floats, floating, floated** to move along or stay on the surface of water and not sink

NOUN **floats 1** something that is designed to float, for example an object you hold when you are learning to swim **2** a decorated platform that is pulled along by a vehicle in a parade **3** an electric van used for delivering milk

flock NOUN **flocks** a group of sheep, goats or birds

flog VERB **flogs, flogging, flogged 1** to hit someone several times, especially with a whip or cane **2** (*informal*) to sell something

flood NOUN **floods 1** a lot of water in a place that is usually dry **2** a large number of people or things: *a flood of complaints about the noise*

VERB **floods, flooding, flooded 1** if water floods a place, it covers it in large amounts **2** if people flood into a place, they arrive there in large numbers

a flower

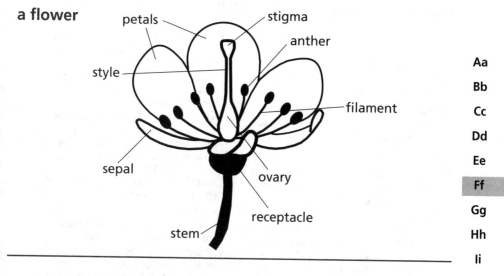

petals
stigma
anther
style
filament
sepal
ovary
receptacle
stem

floodlight NOUN **floodlights** a bright light used at night for lighting a sports field or the outside of a building
▸ **floodlit** ADJECTIVE lit by a floodlight

floor NOUN **floors 1** the surface that you stand on in a room: *There were lots of toys on the bedroom floor.* **2** one of the levels in a building: *Which floor is your apartment on?*

flop VERB **flops, flopping, flopped 1** to fall or sit down suddenly and heavily: *He flopped into the nearest armchair.* **2** to hang in a loose and untidy way: *His hair flopped over his eyes.*
▸ **floppy** ADJECTIVE **floppier, floppiest** soft and able to bend easily

floppy disk NOUN **floppy disks** a piece of plastic that you put in a computer, which can store information

flora NOUN plants: *prehistoric flora and fauna*
▸ **floral** ADJECTIVE **1** made of flowers **2** decorated with pictures of flowers: *floral wallpaper*
▸ **florist** NOUN **florists 1** someone who sells flowers **2** a florist's is a shop selling flowers

floss NOUN **1** floss or dental floss is thread you use for cleaning between your teeth **2** a mass of fine, silky threads: *candy floss*

flotsam NOUN objects from a ship or shipwreck that have been floating in the sea. Look up and compare **jetsam**

flounder VERB **flounders, floundering, floundered** to struggle or move in a clumsy way

flour NOUN powder made from wheat, used for making bread and cakes

✦ The words **flour** and **flower** sound the same, but remember that they have different spellings. A **flower** is a bloom on a plant.

flourish VERB **flourishes, flourishing, flourished** to develop quickly and well

flout VERB **flouts, flouting, flouted** if you flout a rule, you do not obey it

flow VERB **flows, flowing, flowed 1** if a liquid flows, it moves along: *The River Thames flows through London.* **2** the tide flows when the water in the sea moves towards the land. Look up and compare **ebb**
NOUN **flows** a steady movement of something

flow chart NOUN **flow charts** a chart showing the different steps you have to take to make something work, for example a computer program

flower NOUN **flowers** the part of a plant that has coloured petals: *Tulips are my favourite flower.* See the picture on page 209

VERB **flowers, flowering, flowered** to produce flowers: *Bluebells usually flower in May.*

✦ The words **flower** and **flour** sound the same, but remember that they have different spellings. **Flour** is used to make bread and cakes.

flu NOUN an illness like a very bad cold with muscle pains and weakness. Flu is short for **influenza**

flue NOUN **flues** a passage that takes air or smoke away from a fire or heater

fluent ADJECTIVE able to speak a foreign language very well: *Ben is fluent in French.* • *She speaks fluent German.*

fluff NOUN small, soft pieces that come off wool or other material

▸ **fluffy** ADJECTIVE **fluffier, fluffiest** soft like fluff

fluid NOUN **fluids** a liquid

ADJECTIVE able to flow like a liquid: *Blood is a fluid substance.*

fluke NOUN **flukes** (*informal*) a lucky or unusual thing that happens by accident

flume NOUN **flumes** a channel carrying water that you can slide down at a swimming pool

flung VERB a way of changing the verb **fling** to form a past tense. It can be used with or without a helping verb: *He flung his bag down on the floor.* • *She had flung herself on the ground.*

fluorescent ADJECTIVE a fluorescent light is a tube filled with a gas that gives off a bright light when electricity passes through it

fluoride NOUN a chemical added to toothpaste or water to protect your teeth

flurry NOUN **flurries** a small amount of something that happens quickly over a short period of time: *a flurry of snow*

flush VERB **flushes, flushing, flushed** 1 to press or pull a handle to make water go down a toilet 2 to become red in the face

flustered ADJECTIVE feeling nervous and confused

flute NOUN **flutes** an instrument you play by holding it at one side of your mouth and blowing into it

flutter VERB **flutters, fluttering, fluttered** to move lightly and quickly through the air

fly VERB **flies, flying, flew, flown** 1 to move through the air: *The bird flew across the garden.* 2 to travel in an aeroplane: *We're flying to Spain tomorrow.* 3 (*informal*) to move very quickly: *Tom came flying down the street on his bike.*

NOUN **flies** a small insect that flies

flyer NOUN **flyers** a small piece of paper that advertises something

flyover NOUN **flyovers** a road that goes up and crosses another road

flywheel NOUN **flywheels** a heavy wheel in a machine or engine

foal NOUN **foals** a young horse

foam NOUN 1 a mass of small bubbles on top of a liquid 2 a soft material that is full of small holes and used in mattresses and chairs

focus VERB **focuses, focusing, focused** 1 to concentrate on one particular thing: *Focus your attention on your homework.* 2 to adjust something such as a camera or telescope so that you can see an object clearly

fodder NOUN food for horses or farm animals

foe NOUN **foes** (*old-fashioned or formal*) an enemy

foetus (pronounced **fee**-tis) NOUN **foetuses** a baby before it is born

fog NOUN thick cloud near the ground that makes it difficult to see

▸ **foggy** ADJECTIVE **foggier, foggiest** having a lot of fog: *a foggy day*

foghorn NOUN **foghorns** something that makes a loud noise to warn of danger at sea when it is foggy

foil NOUN metal in very thin sheets, used for wrapping food

fold VERB **folds, folding, folded** 1 to bend one part of something so that it covers another part: *Dan folded the letter and put it in the envelope.* **2** if something such as furniture folds, you can make it smaller to put it away by bending some parts: *Do these garden chairs fold?*

• **fold your arms** to cross your arms over your chest

folder NOUN **folders 1** a cardboard cover for holding papers **2** (*ICT*) a place where you keep documents on a computer

foliage NOUN (*formal*) the leaves on a tree or plant

folk NOUN **1** (*informal*) people: *Paul's parents seem like nice folk.* **2** traditional in a particular country or area: *folk music* • *folk tales*

follow VERB **follows, following, followed**

1 to go after someone or something: *He followed her down the street*

2 to happen after something: *The meal was followed by a dance.*

3 if you follow a road, you go in the same direction as it: *Follow the path to the end and turn right.*

4 to understand what someone is saying: *Do you follow me?*

5 to obey instructions or advice: *I followed his advice.*

▸ **follower** NOUN **followers** someone who supports or admires someone or something

▸ **following** ADJECTIVE the following day, week etc is the next one: *School finished on Friday and we went on holiday the following Wednesday.*

fond ADJECTIVE **fonder, fondest** if you are fond of someone or something, you like them very much

▸ **fondly** ADVERB in a way that shows you like someone or something

▸ **fondness** NOUN a liking of someone or something

font[1] NOUN **fonts** in a church, a large stone bowl for holding water during a baptism ceremony

font[2] NOUN **fonts** a style of letters and figures that you can use when typing or printing something

food NOUN things that you eat to stay alive: *What's your favourite food?*

food chain NOUN (*science*) a system in which one creature is eaten by a bigger one, which itself is eaten by a creature that is even bigger, and so on

food group NOUN **food groups** a food group is one of the different types of food that we eat. One group contains bread, cereals and potatoes; one contains fruit and vegetables; another contains milk and dairy foods; another contains meat, fish and other sources of protein, and the final group is food containing fat and sugar

fool NOUN **fools** a stupid person
VERB **fools, fooling, fooled** to fool someone is to trick them

• **fool about** or **fool around** to fool about or fool around is to behave in a silly way

▸ **foolish** ADJECTIVE silly or stupid

foot NOUN **feet 1** your feet are the parts of your body that you stand on **2** the bottom of something: *the foot of a mountain* **3** an imperial unit for measuring length, equal to 12 inches or about 30 centimetres

football NOUN **footballs 1** a game played by two teams who try to kick a ball into a goal, especially **association football 2** a ball used for playing football

foothill NOUN **foothills** (*geography*) a hill at the bottom of a higher mountain

foothold NOUN **footholds** a place where you can put your foot when you are climbing

footing NOUN **1** your balance on your feet: *I lost my footing and fell.* **2** the relationship between two people or groups: *two groups on an equal footing*

footpath NOUN **footpaths** a path you can walk on, especially in the countryside

footprint NOUN **footprints** a mark that your foot leaves: *footprints in the snow*

footstep NOUN **footsteps** the sound of someone walking: *I could hear footsteps.*

for PREPOSITION
1 intended to be received by someone: *There's a letter for you.*
2 intended to do something: *What's this switch for?*
3 used to show a certain amount: *I've lived here for eight years.* • *We walked for two miles.* • *I got these trainers for £30.*
4 showing who a feeling is about: *I felt very sorry for him.*
5 used to show a reason: *He was told off for running in the corridor.*
6 meaning: *What's the word for 'girl' in French?*
7 in favour of something: *Are you for or against the new plan?*

forbid VERB **forbids, forbidding, forbade, forbidden** to tell someone that they must not do something
▶ **forbidden** ADJECTIVE not allowed

force VERB **forces, forcing, forced 1** to make someone do something: *The rain forced us to abandon the picnic.* **2** to make something move by using your strength: *She forced the door open.*
NOUN **1** power or strength: *The force of the explosion damaged many buildings.* **2** (*science*) force is something that makes an object move, or changes its speed or direction **3** a group of police, soldiers etc who are trained to work together: *a peacekeeping force*
▶ **forceful** ADJECTIVE powerful: *a forceful argument*
▶ **forcefully** ADVERB in a powerful way

ford NOUN **fords** a shallow part of a river that you can drive across

fore- PREFIX if a word starts with **fore-**, it adds the meaning 'before' or 'at the front of'. For example, your *forehead* is at the front of your head

forecast NOUN **forecasts** a statement about what is going to happen, especially with the weather

forefather NOUN **forefathers** someone in your family who lived a long time ago

forefinger NOUN **forefingers** the finger that is next to your thumb

foregone ADJECTIVE
• **a foregone conclusion** something that is certain to happen

foreground NOUN the part of a view or picture that is nearest to you

forehand NOUN in games like tennis and squash, a way of hitting the ball by holding the racket at the side of the body with your hand facing towards the ball

forehead NOUN **foreheads** the top front part of your head

foreign ADJECTIVE from a country that is not your country: *foreign languages*
▶ **foreigner** NOUN **foreigners** someone who comes from a country that is not your country

foreman NOUN **foremen** the person who is in charge of a group of factory workers or builders

foremost ADJECTIVE the most famous or important

foresee VERB **foresees, foreseeing, foresaw, foreseen** to know about something before it happens
▶ **foresight** NOUN the ability to know what will happen in the future

forest NOUN **forests** a place where a lot of trees are growing together
▶ **forestry** NOUN planting and looking after trees and forests

forever NOUN always: *You can't stay in your room forever.*

foreword NOUN **forewords** a short introduction at the start of a book

forfeit (pronounced for-fit) VERB **forfeits, forfeiting, forfeited** to have something taken away from you because you have done something wrong

forge VERB **forges, forging, forged 1** to make an illegal copy of something: *He was sent to prison for forging passports.* **2** to forge hot metal is to hammer it into a shape
NOUN **forges** a place where metal is heated to be shaped, for example a blacksmith's
▶ **forgery** NOUN **forgeries 1** the crime of copying something and trying to make it look real **2** an illegal copy of something

Aa Bb Cc Dd Ee **Ff** Gg Hh Ii Jj Kk Ll Mm Nn Oo Pp Qq Rr Ss Tt Uu Vv Ww Xx Yy Zz

forget VERB **forgets, forgetting, forgot, forgotten** not to remember something: *I forgot to get a birthday card for Dad.*

▶ **forgetful** ADJECTIVE often forgetting things

forgive VERB **forgives, forgiving, forgave, forgiven** to stop being angry with someone: *Have you forgiven him for breaking your skateboard?*

▶ **forgiveness** NOUN forgiving someone

forgot VERB a way of changing the verb **forget** to make a past tense: *I forgot to ask what time the party is.*

▶ **forgotten** VERB a form of the verb **forget** that is used with a helping verb to show that something happened in the past: *He has forgotten to lock the door.* ADJECTIVE not remembered by anyone: *forgotten heroes of the war*

fork NOUN **forks 1** something with a handle and points that you use for lifting food to your mouth **2** a point where a road or river divides and goes off in two different directions

fork-lift truck NOUN **fork-lift trucks** a vehicle with equipment on the front for lifting and moving heavy things

forlorn ADJECTIVE looking lonely and unhappy

form NOUN **forms**

1 a type of something: *trains, planes and other forms of transport*

2 a piece of paper with questions and spaces to write your answers: *You have to fill in a form to get a passport.*

3 a shape something has or makes: *The chairs had been arranged in the form of a circle.*

4 the year someone is in at school: *My sister's in the sixth form.*

VERB **forms, forming, formed 1** to start, or make something start, to appear or exist: *How was the Earth formed?* **2** to make a particular shape: *The children held hands and formed a circle.* **3** to start an organization or club

formal ADJECTIVE **1** suitable for an official or important situation: *a formal letter* **2** formal language and words

follow rules strictly and are suitable for writing

▶ **formality** NOUN **formalities** something that must be done but does not have much meaning

format NOUN **formats 1** the way something is designed or arranged: *The information is available in CD format.* **2** (*ICT*) the way a computer document is arranged, for example how big the letters are and how wide the margins are on the page

▶ **format** VERB **formats, formatting, formatted** (*ICT*) to format something such as a disk or a flash drive is to make it ready to have computer information copied onto it

formation NOUN **formations 1** the making or shaping of something: *the formation of fossils over time* **2** a formation is a shape made by the way people or things are arranged

former ADJECTIVE before but not now: *the former President • In former times, people did not travel so much.* NOUN the former is the first of two people or things you are mentioning. The second one is the **latter**: *We visited America and Canada but stayed longer in the former.*

▶ **formerly** ADVERB once, in the past: *Their house was formerly a shop.*

formidable ADJECTIVE difficult or frightening: *a formidable task*

formula NOUN **formulas** or **formulae 1** in maths or chemistry, a set of letters, numbers or symbols that stand for an idea or chemical compound: *What's the formula for calculating the area of a circle?* **2** the way to make something and the substances used in it

▶ **formulate** VERB **formulates, formulating, formulated** to invent and develop a plan or idea

forsake VERB **forsakes, forsaking, forsook, forsaken** (*formal*) to leave someone or something for ever

fort NOUN **forts** a building that has been strengthened to protect it against attack

forth ADVERB (*formal*) an old-fashioned

Aa
Bb
Cc
Dd
Ee
Ff
Gg
Hh
Ii
Jj
Kk
Ll
Mm
Nn
Oo
Pp
Qq
Rr
Ss
Tt
Uu
Vv
Ww
Xx
Yy
Zz

word that means forwards or onwards: *They went forth into the desert.*

fortieth ADJECTIVE AND ADVERB after thirty-ninth and before forty-first: *It's Mum's fortieth birthday tomorrow.*

fortification NOUN **fortifications** something that is built to defend a place against attack

fortify VERB **fortifies, fortifying, fortified 1** to make a place such as a castle difficult to attack **2** to make someone feel very healthy or full of energy

fortnight NOUN a period of two weeks: *We're going to Greece for a fortnight.*

▸ **fortnightly** ADVERB happening every two weeks

fortress NOUN **fortresses** a place that has been protected against attack

fortunate ADJECTIVE lucky: *We arrived at the station late but were fortunate to catch the train.*

▸ **fortunately** ADVERB luckily: *Fortunately, nobody was injured.*

fortune NOUN **fortunes 1** a fortune is a lot of money: *His uncle died and left him a fortune.* **2** fortune is luck: *She had the good fortune to win first prize.*

forty NOUN **forties** the number 40

forward ADJECTIVE in the direction that is in front of you: *a forward movement*

VERB **forward, forwarding, forwarded** to send a letter or email you have received to someone else

NOUN **forwards** in football and hockey, a forward is a player who mostly plays in the front line of a team and tries to score goals. In rugby, a forward is one of the players that makes up a scrum

ADVERB forwards: *Holly leaned forward to look at the picture.*

forwards ADVERB **1** in the direction that is in front of you: *The car moved slowly forwards.* **2** towards the front: *Move forward so you can see properly.*

fossil NOUN **fossils** the remains of an animal or plant that have hardened into rock after a very long time

▸ **fossilize** or **fossilise** VERB **fossilizes, fossilizing, fossilized** to become a fossil

fossil fuel NOUN **fossil fuels** fuels that are made from the remains of animals and plants. Coal, crude oil and natural gas are fossil fuels

foster VERB **fosters, fostering, fostered 1** if an adult fosters a child who is not theirs, they let the child live in their house and look after him or her **2** to encourage something to develop

foster child NOUN **foster children** a child who is being looked after by adults who are not his or her parents

foster parent NOUN **foster parents** an adult who is looking after children who are not their own

fought VERB a way of changing the verb **fight** to make a past tense. It can be used with or without a helping verb: *He fought with his brother.* • *They had fought for freedom and lost.*

foul ADJECTIVE **fouler, foulest** extremely unpleasant: *a foul smell*

NOUN **fouls** in sport, a foul is an action that is against the rules

> ✦ Be careful not to confuse the spellings of **foul** and **fowl**. **Fowl** are birds such as chickens and turkeys.

found VERB **founds, founding, founded** to start an organization: *The college was founded in 1950.*

foundations PLURAL NOUN the foundations of a building are its solid base under the ground

founder NOUN **founders** the person who starts an organization

fountain NOUN **fountains** a jet of water used for decoration in a garden or park

fountain pen NOUN **fountain pens** a pen full of ink that flows out through a nib

four NOUN **fours** the number 4

fourteen NOUN the number 14

fourteenth ADJECTIVE AND ADVERB after thirteenth and before fifteenth: *It's my sister's fourteenth birthday tomorrow.*

fourth ADJECTIVE AND ADVERB after third and before fifth: *He finished fourth in the race.*

Aa Bb Cc Dd Ee **Ff** Gg Hh Ii Jj Kk Ll Mm Nn Oo Pp Qq Rr Ss Tt Uu Vv Ww Xx Yy Zz

fowl NOUN **fowl** or **fowls** a bird that is kept for its meat and eggs, for example a chicken

✦ This word has developed from the Old English word for *bird*, which is **fugel**.

fox NOUN **foxes** a wild animal that looks like a dog, and that has red fur and a thick tail

foxglove NOUN **foxgloves** a tall flower with purple bell-shaped flowers

foyer (pronounced **foi**-ay) NOUN **foyers** the entrance hall in a theatre, office building etc

fraction NOUN **fractions** (*maths*) an amount, such as ½ or ⅜, that is part of a whole number

fracture VERB **fractures, fracturing, fractured** to crack or break something, especially a bone in your body: *Emma's fractured her arm.*
NOUN **fractures** a crack or break in something, especially a bone in your body

fragile (pronounced **fra**-jile) ADJECTIVE not very strong and likely to break
▸ **fragility** (pronounced fra-**jil**-i-ti) NOUN the state of being delicate and easy to break

fragment NOUN **fragments** a fragment of something is a small piece that has broken off

fragrance NOUN **fragrances** a pleasant smell
▸ **fragrant** ADJECTIVE something that is fragrant smells very pleasant

frail ADJECTIVE **frailer, frailest** weak
▸ **frailty** NOUN weakness

frame NOUN **frames 1** a piece of wood or metal around the edge of a picture, mirror etc **2** the part that holds the lenses in a pair of glasses **3** the structure around which something is built or made: *the frame of a house*

framework NOUN **frameworks** the structure on which something is planned or built

franchise NOUN **franchises** a right to sell the goods of a particular company

frank ADJECTIVE **franker, frankest**
saying honestly what you think, even if this upsets people
▸ **frankly** ADVERB as an honest opinion: *Frankly, I don't think Sam's good enough for the team.*

frantic ADJECTIVE mad or wild because of worry or panic: *a frantic search for the missing dog*
▸ **frantically** ADVERB in a wild, worried way

fraud NOUN **frauds 1** the crime of deceiving people to get money **2** someone who deceives other people by pretending

fraught ADJECTIVE **1** if you are fraught, you are anxious and tense **2** if something such as a situation is fraught, it makes people worried **3** if a situation is fraught with danger, it is full of danger and problems

frayed ADJECTIVE frayed material is starting to come apart at the edges

freak NOUN **freaks 1** a keen fan of something: *a football freak* **2** a strange person
ADJECTIVE extremely unusual: *a freak accident*

freckle NOUN **freckles** a small brown mark on your skin, especially your face
▸ **freckled** ADJECTIVE covered in freckles

free ADJECTIVE **1** not costing any money: *It's free to get into the museum.* **2** not taken by someone, or not busy: *Is this seat free?* • *Are you free this evening?* **3** if you are free to do something, you are allowed to do it: *You are free to go anywhere you like.*
VERB **frees, freeing, freed** to get someone out of a prison or a place where they are trapped: *Firefighters managed to free the driver from the wreckage.*
▸ **freedom** NOUN the right to do what you want
▸ **freely** ADVERB without being limited or blocked: *You can speak freely to me.*

free-range ADJECTIVE **1** free-range animals are allowed to move freely around a farm **2** free-range eggs come from chickens that are allowed to move around freely

Aa
Bb
Cc
Dd
Ee
Ff
Gg
Hh
Ii
Jj
Kk
Ll
Mm
Nn
Oo
Pp
Qq
Rr
Ss
Tt
Uu
Vv
Ww
Xx
Yy
Zz

Aa
Bb
Cc
Dd
Ee
Ff
Gg
Hh
Ii
Jj
Kk
Ll
Mm
Nn
Oo
Pp
Qq
Rr
Ss
Tt
Uu
Vv
Ww
Xx
Yy
Zz

freewheel VERB **freewheels, freewheeling, freewheeled** to ride a bicycle without turning the pedals

freeze VERB **freezes, freezing, froze, frozen**
1 to turn into ice or become solid
2 to store food at a very cold temperature so it keeps for a long time
3 to stop moving suddenly: *He froze when he saw the big dog.*
4 (*ICT*) if a computer or other piece of electronic equipment freezes, everything on the screen becomes still because it is not working properly
▸ **freezer** NOUN **freezers** a machine for keeping food very cold

freezing point NOUN (*science*) the temperature at which a liquid becomes solid

freight (pronounced **frait**) NOUN goods that are being carried by a lorry, ship or plane
▸ **freighter** NOUN **freighters** a large ship or plane for carrying goods

frenzy NOUN a state of great excitement, activity and emotion

frequency NOUN **frequencies 1** (*technology*) the frequency of sound or radio waves is the number of waves that pass the same point over one second. Human beings cannot hear sounds that have extremely high frequencies **2** the number of times that something happens

frequent ADJECTIVE happening often: *Dan makes frequent visits to his grandmother.*
▸ **frequently** ADVERB often: *He is frequently late for school.*

fresh ADJECTIVE **fresher, freshest 1** just made or collected: *fresh orange juice* **2** clean: *He put fresh sheets on the bed.*
▸ **freshen** VERB **freshens, freshening, freshened** to make something cleaner
▸ **freshly** ADVERB only just made or done: *freshly made bread*

freshwater ADJECTIVE a freshwater fish lives in rivers and lakes, rather than in the sea

fret VERB **frets, fretting, fretted** to feel worried, unhappy and unable to relax

friar NOUN **friars** a Roman Catholic monk

friction NOUN the rubbing of one surface against another surface

Friday NOUN **Fridays** the day of the week after Thursday and before Saturday: *It's my birthday on Friday.*

✦**Friday** comes from the Old English word **Frigedaeg**, which means *Freya's Day*. Freya is the Norse goddess of love.

fridge NOUN **fridges** a machine for keeping food cool. Fridge is short for **refrigerator**

fried VERB a way of changing the verb **fry** to make a past tense. It can be used with or without a helping verb: *Dad fried the fish in butter.* • *Mum has fried chicken for dinner.*

friend NOUN **friends** someone who you know and like: *Lindsay is my best friend.*
▸ **friendly** ADJECTIVE kind and welcoming: *She's very friendly to everyone.*
▸ **friendship** NOUN **friendships** the relationship you have with a friend

fries PLURAL NOUN long thin pieces of potato that are fried in deep fat
VERB the form of the verb **fry** in the present tense that you use with **he, she,** or **it**

frieze NOUN **friezes** a horizontal strip of decorated paper that you put on a wall

frigate NOUN **frigates** a small warship

fright NOUN a sudden feeling of fear: *You gave me a fright, jumping out like that!*
▸ **frighten** VERB **frightens, frightening, frightened** to frighten someone is to make them feel scared
▸ **frightened** ADJECTIVE scared: *He's frightened of snakes.*
▸ **frightening** ADJECTIVE something that is frightening makes you feel scared: *a frightening experience*

frightful ADJECTIVE very bad: *frightful weather*

▸ **frightfully** ADVERB an old-fashioned word for **very**: *I'm frightfully sorry.*

frill NOUN **frills** folds of cloth used as a decoration around the edge of something

▸ **frilly** ADJECTIVE **fillier, frilliest** decorated with frills

fringe NOUN **fringes** hair that hangs down over your forehead

frisky ADJECTIVE **friskier, friskiest** lively and full of energy: *a frisky puppy*

fritter[1] NOUN **fritters** a piece of food that is covered in batter and fried

fritter[2] VERB **fritters, frittering, frittered**

• **fritter away** if you fritter away money or time, you waste it

frivolous ADJECTIVE a frivolous person behaves in a slightly silly way when they should be serious

frizzy ADJECTIVE **frizzier, frizziest** frizzy hair has very tight curls in it

frock NOUN **frocks** an old-fashioned word for a dress

frog NOUN **frogs** a small brown or green animal that can jump and lives near water

frogman NOUN **frogmen** someone whose job is to swim underwater wearing a rubber suit and using special breathing equipment

frolic VERB **frolics, frolicking, frolicked** to play in a lively and happy way

from PREPOSITION

1 showing where something started: *She's driving up from London.* • *Read the poem from the beginning.*

2 showing what has made something happen: *Yogurt is made from milk.* • *He was shivering from the cold.*

3 showing where someone was born or where they live: *my cousin from Canada* • *Ryan's friend from the next street*

4 out of a place or away: *He took a notebook from the drawer.* • *Take those sweets from her before she eats them all!*

front NOUN **fronts**

1 the front of something is the part of it that faces forwards: *The front of the house is painted red.*

2 the part of something that is closest to where you are, or closest to the direction it faces or moves in: *The teacher asked Amy to come out to the front of the class.*

3 a seashore or a road or path beside it

4 an area where fighting takes place during a war

5 (*geography*) a weather front is the warm or cold edge of a mass of air

ADJECTIVE at the front of something: *the front door*

• **in front** at the front of something

frontier NOUN **frontiers** a dividing line between two countries

frost NOUN a very thin layer of white ice crystals that forms on surfaces outside when the weather is cold

▸ **frosted** ADJECTIVE frosted glass has been specially treated so you cannot see through it

▸ **frosty** ADJECTIVE **frostier, frostiest**
1 when it is frosty, everything is covered in frost **2** not very friendly: *a frosty welcome*

froth NOUN foam on top of a liquid

▸ **frothy** ADJECTIVE **frothier, frothiest** a frothy liquid has foam on top

frown VERB **frowns, frowning, frowned** to wrinkle your forehead because you are thinking very hard or because you are worried or angry

NOUN **frowns** an expression in which your forehead is wrinkled

frozen VERB the form of the verb **freeze** that is used with a helping verb to show that something happened in the past: *It's so cold that the lake has frozen.*

ADJECTIVE frozen food is stored at a very cold temperature to make it stay fresh for a long time: *a packet of frozen peas*

fruit NOUN the fleshy part of a plant, which you can sometimes eat, that holds seeds: *Grapes are my favourite fruit.*

▸ **fruity** ADJECTIVE **fruitier, fruitiest** having the taste of fruit: *a fruity soft drink*

Aa
Bb
Cc
Dd
Ee
Ff
Gg
Hh
Ii
Jj
Kk
Ll
Mm
Nn
Oo
Pp
Qq
Rr
Ss
Tt
Uu
Vv
Ww
Xx
Yy
Zz

fruitful ADJECTIVE something that is fruitful has good results: *a fruitful meeting of world leaders*

fruitless ADJECTIVE not producing the result you wanted: *a fruitless search*

frustrate VERB **frustrates, frustrating, frustrated** if something frustrates you, it makes you feel annoyed because you cannot do or achieve what you want

▸ **frustration** NOUN **frustrations** a feeling of being annoyed because you cannot do or achieve what you want

fry VERB **fries, frying, fried** to cook something in hot oil or fat

fudge NOUN a soft sweet made from butter and sugar

fuel NOUN **fuels** a substance such as gas, wood or coal that burns to give heat, light, or power

fugitive NOUN **fugitives** someone who has escaped from the police

fulfil VERB **fulfils, fulfilling, fulfilled** to do what you wanted to do or what you are expected to do: *He fulfilled his promise to help.*

▸ **fulfilment** NOUN a feeling of having achieved something successfully

full ADJECTIVE **fuller, fullest 1** containing as much as possible: *The train was full.* • *a full bottle of milk* • *The room was full of children.* **2** if you are full or full up, you cannot eat any more **3** if something is full, it is complete and has nothing missed out: *He told me the full story.* • *I got full marks in the spelling test.*

• **full up** with no space for anyone or anything else

full moon NOUN **full moons** the moon when it is a full circle

full stop NOUN **full stops** the punctuation mark that looks like a small dot. You use it to show where a sentence ends

full-time ADJECTIVE AND ADVERB if someone works full-time or has a full-time job, they work for all the hours of a normal job

fully ADVERB completely: *He hasn't fully recovered from the accident.*

fumble VERB **fumbles, fumbling, fumbled** to use your hands in an awkward way: *Raj fumbled in his pocket for the key.*

fume VERB **fumes, fuming, fumed** to be very angry

fumes PLURAL NOUN smoke or gas that is unpleasant to breathe in

fun NOUN enjoyment and pleasure: *Skateboarding is good fun.* • *We had a lot of fun at the party.*

• **make fun of someone** to tease someone or make other people laugh at them

function NOUN **functions 1** the purpose of someone or something: *The function of an iron is to press the creases out of clothes.* **2** (*maths*) in mathematics, a function is what you do to change one set of numbers into another set

VERB **functions, functioning, functioned** to work in the correct way

▸ **functional** ADJECTIVE practical and useful

fund NOUN **funds** an amount of money for a particular purpose

VERB **funds, funding, funded** to provide money for a particular purpose

fundamental ADJECTIVE important and necessary: *the fundamental rules of football*

funeral NOUN **funerals** a ceremony that people have when someone dies

funfair NOUN **funfairs** a collection of rides that you can go on for entertainment

fungus NOUN **fungi** a plant with no leaves or flowers, for example a mushroom

funnel NOUN **funnels 1** something that is wide at the top and narrow at the bottom, used for pouring liquids or powder into a narrow opening **2** a chimney through which smoke leaves a ship

funny ADJECTIVE **funnier, funniest 1** a funny person or thing makes you laugh: *a funny story* **2** strange or unusual: *There was a funny noise coming from the engine.*

▸ **funnily** ADVERB in a way that is odd: *Funnily enough, we were born at the same time on the same day.*

Aa
Bb
Cc
Dd
Ee
Ff
Gg
Hh
Ii
Jj
Kk
Ll
Mm
Nn
Oo
Pp
Qq
Rr
Ss
Tt
Uu
Vv
Ww
Xx
Yy
Zz

funny bone NOUN **funny bones** a part of your elbow that tingles when you bang it

fur NOUN the soft hair on some animals

furious ADJECTIVE extremely angry

furnace NOUN **furnaces** a large oven for melting metal or glass

furnish VERB **furnishes, furnishing, furnished** to put furniture in a house or room

furniture NOUN objects such as beds, tables and chairs that you put in a room

furrow NOUN **furrows** a long narrow cut made in the ground by a plough

furry ADJECTIVE **furrier, furriest** covered in fur

further ADJECTIVE **1** a greater distance: *Which is further from here, London or Aberdeen?* **2** more: *If you need further information, please ask.*
ADVERB for a greater distance: *Let's walk a bit further before we stop for a rest.*

furthermore ADVERB (*formal*) a word that is used when you are adding something to what you have just said: *I don't want to go, and furthermore, I won't go.*

furthest ADVERB to the greatest distance or degree: *Who can throw the ball the furthest?*

furtive ADJECTIVE an action that is furtive is done secretly: *a furtive glance*
▶ **furtively** ADVERB in a secret way

fury NOUN extreme anger

fuse NOUN **fuses** a wire inside a plug or piece of electrical equipment that protects the equipment if there is too much electricity. If this happens, the wire

melts, which breaks the flow of electricity
VERB **fuses, fusing, fused 1** to join together, or to join two things together **2** if a piece of electrical equipment fuses, it stops working because the fuse has melted

fuselage (pronounced **fyoo**-zi-laj) NOUN **fuselages** the main body of an aeroplane

fusion NOUN (*technology*) joining things together, such as the nuclei of atoms

fuss NOUN unnecessary worry or excitement about something: *I don't know what all the fuss is about.*
• **make a fuss of someone** to give someone a lot of attention
VERB **fusses, fussing, fussed** to worry too much about something or give it too much attention: *She fusses over her pet dog.*
▶ **fussy** ADJECTIVE **fussier, fussiest** someone who is fussy worries too much about small details that are not important

futile (pronounced **fyoo**-tile) ADJECTIVE useless and having no effect
▶ **futility** (pronounced fyoo-**til**-it-i) NOUN being useless

future NOUN the future is the time that will come: *You can't know what will happen to you in the future.*
• **in future** from now: *In future, please be more careful.*

future tense NOUN the form of a verb that you use when you are talking about what will happen in the future

fuzz NOUN fine, light hair or feathers
▶ **fuzzy** ADJECTIVE **fuzzier, fuzziest 1** a fuzzy picture is unclear **2** fuzzy hair is soft and curly

Aa
Bb
Cc
Dd
Ee
Ff
Gg
Hh
Ii
Jj
Kk
Ll
Mm
Nn
Oo
Pp
Qq
Rr
Ss
Tt
Uu
Vv
Ww
Xx
Yy
Zz

Gg

g ABBREVIATION short for **gram** or **grams**

gabble VERB **gabbles, gabbling, gabbled** to gabble is to talk so quickly it is difficult for other people to understand what you are saying

gable NOUN **gables** an end of a house or building where the wall and the roof form a triangular shape

gadget NOUN **gadgets** a tool or small piece of equipment

Gaelic NOUN a language spoken in Ireland and parts of Scotland

gag NOUN **gags 1** something put round, in or over someone's mouth to stop them speaking **2** a joke or funny story told by a comedian

VERB **gags, gagging, gagged** to gag someone is to stop them speaking

gaggle NOUN **gaggles** a group of geese

gaiety NOUN being lively and having fun

gaily ADJECTIVE if you do something gaily, you do it in a lively happy way

gain VERB **gains, gaining, gained 1** to gain something is to win it, get it or earn it: *You gain twenty extra points for that move.* • *There's nothing to gain from telling lies.* **2** if a clock or watch gains, it goes faster than it should and shows a later time than the real time

• **gain on someone** to get closer to someone who is ahead of you, for example in a race or competition

NOUN **gains** gain, or a gain, is something that you get that is more than you had before

gait NOUN **gaits** your gait is the way you walk

gala NOUN **galas** a special public event or entertainment: *a swimming gala*

galaxy NOUN **galaxies** a galaxy is a huge group of stars in the universe. Our galaxy is the Milky Way

gale NOUN **gales** a very strong wind

gall VERB **galls, galling, galled** if something galls you, it annoys you

NOUN cheek or courage: *He wouldn't have the gall to call me that to my face.*

gallant ADJECTIVE **1** gallant behaviour shows courage and honour: *a gallant effort* **2** very polite and considerate: *a gallant young man*

▸ **gallantry** NOUN **gallantries** gallant behaviour or a gallant act

galleon NOUN **galleons** (*history*) a large Spanish sailing ship used in the sixteenth and seventeenth centuries for making long sea journeys

gallery NOUN **galleries 1** a large building or a shop where works of art are displayed to the public **2** a high open balcony at the back or side of a church, theatre or law court

galley NOUN **galleys 1** (*history*) a type of ship used in ancient times that was moved through the water by lots of large oars **2** a room or area on a boat or aeroplane where cooking is done

gallon NOUN **gallons** an imperial unit for measuring the volume of a liquid, equal to 8 pints or about 4.55 litres

gallop NOUN **gallops** a running pace

VERB **gallops, galloping, galloped** a horse gallops when it runs at its fastest pace with all four feet off the ground at the same time

gallows NOUN a high wooden frame where criminals used to be hanged

galore ADJECTIVE in large numbers: *There were presents galore.*

✦ **Galore** is always placed after the noun it is describing.

galvanize *or* **galvanise** VERB **galvanizes, galvanizing, galvanized** to galvanize iron or steel is to coat it with zinc to stop it rusting

gamble VERB **gambles, gambling, gambled 1** to bet money on the result

of something, for example a card game or horse race **2** to take a risk or chance
NOUN **gambles** something you decide to do that may not turn out the way you want

▸ **gambler** NOUN **gamblers** someone who gambles money on the result of a race or game

game NOUN **games**
1 a game is any activity or contest with a set of rules in which players try to do better than others or try to get points: *a computer game • card games*
2 games are all the sports children are taught in school
3 in some sports, a game is one of the parts of a complete match: *He won the first set 7 games to 5.*
4 game is wild animals and birds that are hunted for sport
• **give the game away** to give the game away is to let other people know about something you have been trying to hide or keep secret
ADJECTIVE someone who is game is ready to do things, especially things that involve risk

gamekeeper NOUN **gamekeepers** someone whose job is to look after wild animals and birds on private land in the countryside

gammon NOUN gammon is the salted and smoked meat from the leg of a pig

gander NOUN **ganders** a male goose

gang NOUN **gangs 1** a group of friends who meet regularly or go around together **2** a group of criminals or other troublemakers
VERB **gangs, ganging, ganged**
• **gang up on someone** if people gang up on another person they act together against that person

gangster NOUN **gangsters** a member of a gang of criminals

gangway NOUN **gangways 1** a narrow passage, for example where people can walk between rows of seats **2** a narrow platform or bridge used to get on and off a ship, which can be moved away when the ship sails

gap NOUN **gaps 1** an opening or space

in the middle of something or between things: *a gap in the wall • a gap between his front teeth* **2** something missing: *a gap in his memory* **3** a difference between two things: *the gap between rich and poor*

gape VERB **gapes, gaping, gaped 1** to gape is to stare with your mouth open, usually because you are very surprised or impressed **2** something that gapes is wide open

garage NOUN **garages 1** a building, often a small one beside a house, for storing a car or other vehicle **2** a place where vehicles are repaired, or a shop selling petrol and often other items for vehicles or road journeys

✦ This word comes from the French word **garer**, which means *to shelter*. The word **guard** is also linked to **garer**.

garbage NOUN rubbish

garbled ADJECTIVE a garbled message or piece of information is difficult to understand because the words seem mixed up

garden NOUN **gardens** an area of land where flowers, trees and vegetables are grown

▸ **gardener** NOUN **gardeners** someone who does gardening

▸ **gardening** NOUN working in and taking care of a garden

gargle VERB **gargles, gargling, gargled** to rinse your mouth and throat with a liquid by holding it in your mouth and letting air from your throat bubble through it

gargoyle NOUN **gargoyles** a stone carving of an ugly creature's head, with an open mouth forming a spout, used to carry rainwater that comes off the roof of a building

garish ADJECTIVE garish colours or patterns are too bright

garland NOUN **garlands** flowers or leaves woven together into a circle

garlic NOUN a plant related to the onion with bulbs that divide into sections called cloves, used in cooking to add flavour

Aa
Bb
Cc
Dd
Ee
Ff
Gg
Hh
Ii
Jj
Kk
Ll
Mm
Nn
Oo
Pp
Qq
Rr
Ss
Tt
Uu
Vv
Ww
Xx
Yy
Zz

garment NOUN **garments** a piece of clothing

garnet NOUN **garnets** a hard red precious stone

garnish VERB **garnishes, garnishing, garnished** to garnish food is to decorate it

NOUN **garnishes** something used to decorate food, for example herbs or nuts

garrison NOUN **garrisons** a group of soldiers guarding a town or fortress, or the building they live in

garter NOUN **garters** a broad band of elastic used to keep a stocking or sock up

gas NOUN **gases** or **gasses** 1 (*science*) a substance that is not liquid or solid and that moves about like air: *Oxygen and carbon dioxide are two of the gases that make up air.* 2 any natural or manufactured gas that burns easily and is used as fuel: *natural gas • coal gas* 3 gas is short for gasoline, the name used in North America for petrol

▸ **gaseous** ADJECTIVE in the form of a gas

gash NOUN **gashes** a deep open cut

VERB **gashes, gashing, gashed** to gash something is to cut deeply into it

gas mask NOUN **gas masks** a mask worn over the face so that poisonous gas is not inhaled

gasoline NOUN the American English word for petrol

gasometer NOUN **gasometers** a large tank used for storing gas

gasp VERB **gasps, gasping, gasped** 1 to gasp is to take a short sudden breath in through your open mouth making a sound as you do so: *They all gasped in horror.* 2 to gasp for air is to take sudden short breaths because you need to get oxygen into your lungs quickly

NOUN **gasps** the sound of a sudden short breath

gastric ADJECTIVE to do with the stomach: *gastric flu*

gate NOUN **gates** 1 a movable structure with hinges that is used to close an opening in a wall or fence 2 the numbered area where passengers wait

before getting on an aeroplane 3 all the people attending a sports match or the total amount of money they pay to get into the match

gateau (pronounced **gat**-oe) NOUN **gateaus** or **gateaux** a light cake made in layers, usually with cream or chocolate filling

gatecrash VERB **gatecrashes, gatecrashing, gatecrashed** if someone gatecrashes a party or other event, they go to it although they haven't been invited

gateway NOUN **gateways** 1 an opening with a gate across it 2 anything that is an entrance or like an entrance: *a gateway to the future*

gather VERB **gathers, gathering, gathered**

1 to meet or come together in a group

2 to gather things is to collect them or bring them together

3 to gather speed is to get faster and faster

4 to gather something is to hear or read about it: *I gather he's lived here for more than fifty years.*

▸ **gathering** NOUN **gatherings** a meeting of people

gaudy ADJECTIVE **gaudier, gaudiest** gaudy colours are very strong and bright

gauge (pronounced **gaij**) NOUN **gauges** 1 a device for measuring things, such as temperature, depth or height 2 the width or thickness of something, for example the width of a railway line or the thickness of wire

VERB **gauges, gauging, gauged** 1 to gauge something is to measure it 2 to gauge something is to make a guess at it: *I can never gauge what his reaction will be.*

gaunt ADJECTIVE if someone is gaunt, they look very thin and tired or unhealthy

gauntlet NOUN **gauntlets** a type of thick glove with a part that covers the wrist and lower part of the arm

• **throw down the gauntlet** to throw down the gauntlet is to challenge someone

gauze NOUN a very thin material that you can see through. Gauze is sometimes used to cover cuts and scratches
▶ **gauzy** ADJECTIVE **gauzier, gauziest** transparent

gave VERB a way of changing the verb **give** to make a past tense: *Jodie gave Robbie some of her sweets.*

gay ADJECTIVE **gayer, gayest 1** an old-fashioned word meaning lively and full of fun: *happy and gay* **2** an old-fashioned word meaning brightly coloured: *gay banners*

gaze VERB **gazes, gazing, gazed** to look at something steadily
NOUN **gazes** a long steady look

gazelle NOUN **gazelles** a type of African or Asian animal that looks like a small deer and that can move quickly and gracefully

gear NOUN **gears 1** gear is the clothes and equipment you need or use for a particular sport or job: *tennis gear* **2** the gears in a vehicle are the parts that connect the speed of the engine to the speed of the vehicle

geese NOUN the plural of **goose**

gel NOUN **gels** gel is a thick substance that looks like jelly and is used to hold your hair in a certain style

gelatine NOUN a clear substance used in cooking that sets to form jelly

gem NOUN **gems** a valuable stone or mineral, for example a diamond or emerald, that can be cut and polished and used in jewellery

gender NOUN **genders 1** gender is being male or female **2** (*grammar*) the gender of a word tells you if it is masculine, feminine or neuter

gene (pronounced **jeen**) NOUN **genes** (*science*) a part of a living cell of an animal or plant which contains information inherited from its parents and which affects things like hair or skin colour

genealogy NOUN **genealogies** the history of how people in a family are linked from one generation to the next

genera NOUN the plural of **genus**

general ADJECTIVE **1** involving everyone or most things: *a general feeling of gloom* • *general knowledge* **2** broad and not detailed: *Can you give me a general idea of what it will cost?*
NOUN **generals** an important army officer
• **in general** to do with most people or things: *Schools in general are achieving better results.*
▶ **generalize** or **generalise** VERB **generalizes, generalizing, generalized** to make a statement that does not go into any detail
▶ **generally** ADVERB usually: *Children generally start school at about age five.*

general election NOUN **general elections** an election to choose the leaders of a whole country

general practitioner NOUN **general practitioners** a doctor who sees ill people from a particular area at a local clinic or surgery, or visits them at home

✦ **General practitioner** is often shortened to **GP**.

generate VERB **generates, generating, generated** to generate something is to create it: *His work generated a lot of interest.*
▶ **generation** NOUN **generations 1** a generation is a single step in a family tree. For example, your grandparents are from one generation and your parents are from the next generation **2** generation is creating something: *electricity generation*
▶ **generator** NOUN **generators** a machine that makes power, especially electricity

generosity NOUN being kind and giving

generous ADJECTIVE **1** a generous person is kind and gives to others in an unselfish way **2** a generous gift is bigger or more than expected
▶ **generously** ADVERB in a generous way: *Please give generously.*

genetic ADJECTIVE (*science*) to do with genes, or inherited through the genes: *a genetic disorder*

Aa
Bb
Cc
Dd
Ee
Ff
Gg
Hh
Ii
Jj
Kk
Ll
Mm
Nn
Oo
Pp
Qq
Rr
Ss
Tt
Uu
Vv
Ww
Xx
Yy
Zz

Aa
Bb
Cc
Dd
Ee
Ff
Gg
Hh
Ii
Jj
Kk
Ll
Mm
Nn
Oo
Pp
Qq
Rr
Ss
Tt
Uu
Vv
Ww
Xx
Yy
Zz

genetically modified ADJECTIVE genetically modified plants or animals have had one or more of their genes changed artificially so that their natural characteristics are changed or improved

♦ **Genetically modified** is often shortened to **GM**, as in *GM foods*.

genetics NOUN (*science*) the science of finding out about genes, and how they work

genial ADJECTIVE a genial person is friendly and pleasant to be with
▸ **genially** ADVERB in a friendly and pleasant way

genie NOUN **genies** or **genii** in Arabian and Persian stories, a magical spirit who watches over and grants the wishes of the person who controls it

genitals PLURAL NOUN a person's genitals are their sexual organs

genius NOUN **geniuses** 1 a genius is someone who is unusually clever or skilful 2 genius is extraordinary cleverness or skill

genre (pronounced **jong**-ri) NOUN **genres** the particular type of writing, music, film or television programme something is. For example, biography is a genre of writing, and soap opera is a genre of television programme

genteel ADJECTIVE if someone is genteel they behave in a very polite, good-mannered way, often because they think this makes them seem more high-class

gentle ADJECTIVE **gentler, gentlest** 1 a gentle person is kind and calm: *a gentle giant* 2 soft and light: *a gentle breeze • a gentle tap on his shoulder*
▸ **gentleness** NOUN being gentle
▸ **gently** ADVERB in a gentle way

♦ The word **gentle** comes from the French word **gentil**, which means well-bred and polite.

gentleman NOUN **gentlemen** 1 a word used to refer politely to a man: *Good morning, gentlemen.* 2 a man who is very polite and good-mannered: *He's a real gentleman.*

gentlemanly ADJECTIVE gentlemanly behaviour is polite and good-mannered

gentry NOUN an old-fashioned word for people from one of the higher classes of society

genuine ADJECTIVE 1 real, not fake: *a genuine work of art* 2 honest and not pretending: *a genuine person*
▸ **genuinely** ADVERB really or honestly: *I was genuinely impressed.*

genus NOUN **genera** a genus is a class of animals or plants which usually includes several different species

geography NOUN geography is the study of the Earth's surface and the people on it
▸ **geographer** NOUN **geographers** someone who studies geography
▸ **geographic** ADJECTIVE to do with geography and where things are placed on the Earth's surface

♦ **Ge** is the Greek word for *the Earth*. If a word starts with **geo**, you can guess that it has something to do with the Earth.
Another example is **geology**.

geology NOUN the study of the Earth's rocks, minerals and soil, what they are made up of and how they were created
▸ **geologist** NOUN **geologists** someone who studies geology

geometry NOUN (*maths*) a type of mathematics that deals with the study of angles, lines, curves and shapes
▸ **geometric** or **geometrical** ADJECTIVE a geometric shape or design is made up of straight lines and angles

geranium NOUN **geraniums** a kind of bushy garden plant that has red, pink, purple or white flowers

gerbil NOUN **gerbils** a small animal similar to a rat, but with long back legs

germ NOUN **germs** a tiny living thing that can cause disease

germinate VERB **germinates, germinating, germinated** a seed germinates when it begins to sprout or grow
▸ **germination** NOUN germinating

gesture NOUN **gestures** a movement made with part of your body which expresses a meaning or feeling, for example pointing at something, nodding or winking

VERB **gestures, gesturing, gestured** to make a gesture with part of your body, especially your hand, arm or head

get VERB **gets, getting, got**
1 you get something when someone gives it to you or you fetch it: *Kiera got lots of birthday presents.*
2 you have got something when you have it or own it: *Have you got a rubber I could borrow?* • *They haven't got a TV.*
3 you get someone to do something for you when you ask or persuade them to do it: *Get Rory to help you lift that big box.*
4 you get somewhere when you arrive there: *We got to New York at 5 o'clock in the morning.*
5 you get a bus or some other form of transport when you travel on it: *Mum gets the train to work.*
6 if you get a disease or illness, you catch it: *I hope your sister doesn't get the measles.*
7 to be in a particular state, or to put something in a particular state: *I'm getting tired – can we go home now?* • *Try not to get your new shoes dirty.*
• **get away with** to get away with something is to manage to do something wrong or illegal without being caught or punished
• **get by** to get by is to manage, especially with the money you have
• **get on 1** to make progress or to do well: *You have to study hard if you want to get on.* • *I've got to get on with my homework.* **2** if people get on, or get on with each other, they like each other and are friendly to each other: *Jake and Mikey seem to get on really well.*
• **get out of** to get out of something is to avoid doing it
• **get over** to get over something is to

recover from it: *It took her a long time to get over the shock.*

geyser NOUN **geysers** (*geography*) a rush of hot water that comes out of the ground like a fountain

ghastly ADJECTIVE **ghastlier, ghastliest** horrible or very ugly: *a ghastly smell*

gherkin NOUN **gherkins** a kind of pickled vegetable that looks like a small cucumber

ghetto NOUN **ghettos** an area in a town or city where a certain group of people live, especially poor people

ghost NOUN **ghosts** a spirit of a dead person
▸ **ghostly** ADJECTIVE **ghostlier, ghostliest 1** like a ghost **2** very pale

ghoul (pronounced **gool**) NOUN **ghouls**
1 in Muslim stories, an evil spirit that steals and eats dead bodies **2** someone who is very interested in death and disaster
▸ **ghoulish** ADJECTIVE unnaturally interested in death and disaster

giant NOUN **giants 1** in stories, an imaginary being like a huge person that is often evil or frightening **2** a very large thing: *an industrial giant*
ADJECTIVE huge or bigger than normal: *a giant crane* • *a giant tortoise*

gibbon NOUN **gibbons** a type of ape with long thin arms and legs

giddy ADJECTIVE **giddier, giddiest** if you feel giddy you feel dizzy
▸ **giddiness** NOUN a feeling of dizziness

gift NOUN **gifts** a present
▸ **gifted** ADJECTIVE a gifted person is extremely good at something or extremely clever

gigantic ADJECTIVE huge, like a giant

giggle VERB **giggles, giggling, giggled** to giggle is to laugh in a silly or nervous way
NOUN **giggles** a silly or nervous laugh

gild VERB **gilds, gilding, gilded** to gild something is to cover it with gold

gills PLURAL NOUN a fish's gills are the openings at each side of its body just

Aa
Bb
Cc
Dd
Ee
Ff
Gg
Hh
Ii
Jj
Kk
Ll
Mm
Nn
Oo
Pp
Qq
Rr
Ss
Tt
Uu
Vv
Ww
Xx
Yy
Zz

Aa
Bb
Cc
Dd
Ee
Ff
Gg
Hh
Ii
Jj
Kk
Ll
Mm
Nn
Oo
Pp
Qq
Rr
Ss
Tt
Uu
Vv
Ww
Xx
Yy
Zz

behind its head, which allow it to breathe

gimmick NOUN **gimmicks** something that is meant to attract people's attention, but has no other value

gin NOUN an alcoholic drink made with grain and flavoured with juniper berries

ginger NOUN **1** the knobbly root of a tropical plant which has a spicy taste and is used in cooking **2** a reddish-orange colour

gingerbread NOUN a kind of cake flavoured with powdered ginger

gingerly ADVERB if you do something gingerly, you do it very slowly and carefully because you are nervous: *He stepped gingerly on the wobbly bridge.*

Gipsy NOUN **Gipsies** another spelling of **Gypsy**

giraffe NOUN **giraffes** an African animal with a spotted coat, long legs and a very long neck

girder NOUN **girders** a beam made of iron, steel or wood, used as a support in bridges and buildings

girdle NOUN **girdles** a tight piece of underwear that women wear to make them look slimmer

girl NOUN **girls** a female child or young woman

girlfriend NOUN **girlfriends 1** a girl or woman that a boy or man is having a special relationship with or is in love with **2** a female friend

girlish ADJECTIVE like a girl, usually used to describe an older woman's behaviour or appearance: *a girlish laugh*

girth NOUN **girths** something's girth is the distance it measures around the middle

gist (pronounced *jist*) NOUN the gist of a story or argument is its basic meaning or its main point

give VERB **gives, giving, gave, given**
1 to give something to someone is to let them have it or to pass it on to them: *My brother gave me his old bike.*
2 to make someone feel or believe something: *The sudden explosion gave us all a shock.* • *John gave me the impression he didn't want to come.*

3 to allow someone to have something: *Mum has given us another ten minutes to watch TV.*
4 if someone gives a party or performance, they hold a party or they perform in front of other people
5 to give a cry, shout or laugh is to make that sound out loud: *He gave a whoop of joy.*
6 if something gives, it bends or collapses when too much weight is put on top of it: *The rotten floorboard gave under him and his foot went through.*
• **give something away** to give away something, such as a secret, is to tell it to someone without meaning to
• **give in** to give in is to admit defeat
• **give out** if a machine or a part of your body gives out, it stops working
• **give up** to give up is to stop trying to do something because it has become too difficult
• **give way 1** something gives way when it breaks or collapses **2** drivers give way when they stop at a junction or roundabout and allow other traffic to pass in front of them
▶ **given** ADJECTIVE decided or selected: *On any given day, there are several dozen accidents.*
▶ **giver** NOUN **givers** someone who gives something

glacial ADJECTIVE to do with ice or glaciers: *a glacial period*

glacier NOUN **glaciers** (*geography*) a huge mass of ice moving slowly down a valley

glad ADJECTIVE **gladder, gladdest** pleased or happy: *We're very glad you could make it to the party.*
▶ **gladden** VERB **gladdens, gladdening, gladdened** to make someone glad
▶ **gladly** ADVERB happily or with pleasure: *I'll gladly do what you ask.*
▶ **gladness** NOUN a feeling of pleasure or happiness

glade NOUN **glades** an open space in a wood or forest

gladiator NOUN **gladiators** (*history*) in ancient Rome, a man trained to fight with other men or with wild animals to amuse spectators

glamorous ADJECTIVE attractive, fashionable and exciting

glamour NOUN the excitement of being rich, fashionable or famous

glance VERB **glances, glancing, glanced 1** to look quickly at something and then look away again **2** if something moving glances off another thing, it hits that thing then flies off sideways

NOUN **glances** a short quick look

gland NOUN **glands** a part of the body which stores substances from the body to be used later or to be got rid of

▸ **glandular** ADJECTIVE to do with a gland or glands: *glandular fever*

glare VERB **glares, glaring, glared 1** to look at someone or something angrily **2** to shine with a very bright light that hurts your eyes

NOUN **glares 1** a fierce or angry look **2** very strong bright light that dazzles you

▸ **glaring** ADJECTIVE standing out in a very obvious way: *a glaring mistake*

glass NOUN **glasses 1** glass is a hard breakable material that lets light through **2** a glass is a container for drinks made of this material, or the amount it will hold: *a tall glass • She drank three glasses of milk.*

ADJECTIVE made of glass: *a glass bowl*

▸ **glasses** PLURAL NOUN glasses are a pair of clear lenses inside a frame that you wear over your eyes to help you see more clearly

▸ **glassy** ADJECTIVE **glassier, glassiest 1** shiny like glass, or transparent like glass **2** if someone's eyes are glassy, they have no expression in them

glaze VERB **glazes, glazing, glazed 1** to glaze a window is to fit a sheet or sheets of glass into it **2** to glaze pots is to bake a hard shiny covering on their surface

• **glaze over** if someone's eyes glaze over, they become expressionless

NOUN **glazes** a shiny covering

▸ **glazier** NOUN **glaziers** someone whose job is to put glass in windows

gleam VERB **gleams, gleaming, gleamed** to shine or glow brightly: *The children's eyes gleamed with excitement.*

NOUN **gleams 1** a beam or flash of light: *the gleam of headlights in the distance* **2** brightness or shininess: *the gleam of newly polished furniture*

glee NOUN joyful excitement or pleasure

▸ **gleeful** ADJECTIVE feeling or showing glee

▸ **gleefully** ADVERB happily or joyfully

glen NOUN **glens** a valley in Scotland

glide VERB **glides, gliding, glided 1** to move smoothly, especially over a surface **2** to fly in a glider

▸ **glider** NOUN **gliders** a kind of aeroplane with no engine that is towed into the air by another aeroplane, where it flies on air currents

glimmer VERB **glimmers, glimmering, glimmered** to burn or shine weakly or faintly

NOUN **glimmers 1** a faint light **2** a glimmer of something such as hope is a faint sign of it

glimpse NOUN **glimpses** a brief look at something

VERB **glimpses, glimpsing, glimpsed** to glimpse something is to see it for a very short time

glint VERB **glints, glinting, glinted** to reflect flashes of light

NOUN **glints** a light reflected off a surface, especially a metal one

glisten VERB **glistens, glistening, glistened** if a surface glistens, light reflects off it, because it has a shiny surface or is wet

glitter VERB **glitters, glittering, glittered** to shine or sparkle with small flashes of light

NOUN glitter is tiny pieces of shiny material used to decorate your skin, hair or clothes or for making pictures

gloat VERB **gloats, gloating, gloated** to show too much pleasure at your own success or at someone else's failure

global ADJECTIVE **1** to do with or involving the whole world: *global*

Aa
Bb
Cc
Dd
Ee
Ff
Gg
Hh
Ii
Jj
Kk
Ll
Mm
Nn
Oo
Pp
Qq
Rr
Ss
Tt
Uu
Vv
Ww
Xx
Yy
Zz

businesses **2** involving everyone or everything: *a global increase in pay*

▶ **globally** ADVERB world-wide or generally

global warming NOUN (*geography*) the gradual warming of the Earth's surface and atmosphere as a result of the greenhouse effect, causing rises in sea temperature and weather changes around the world

globe NOUN **globes 1** the globe is the Earth: *people from around the globe* **2** a large ball with a map of the Earth printed on it that can be turned on a stand **3** anything shaped like a ball or sphere

glockenspiel NOUN **glockenspiels** a musical instrument made up of a row of metal bars that you hit with sticks to make different notes

gloom NOUN **1** darkness or near-darkness: *A shape appeared out of the gloom.* **2** sadness or depression: *the feeling of gloom in the dressing room of the losing team*

▶ **gloominess** NOUN **1** being dark, nearly dark or dull: *the gloominess of a winter's morning* **2** being sad or depressed: *Her gloominess made us all feel bad.*

▶ **gloomy** ADJECTIVE **gloomier, gloomiest 1** dark or nearly dark: *a gloomy passageway* **2** sad or depressing: *a gloomy picture of the future*

glorify VERB **glorifies, glorifying, glorified** to glorify someone or something is to praise them very highly, in a way that makes them seem impressive: *glorify God* • *The book glorifies war.*

glorious ADJECTIVE **1** beautiful in a very impressive way: *glorious singing* **2** deserving or having glory: *a glorious victory*

glory NOUN **glories 1** honour and praise **2** something that is beautiful and very impressive: *the glories of medieval architecture*

gloss NOUN gloss is surface brightness

glossary NOUN **glossaries** a list of words, with explanations of their meanings

glossy ADJECTIVE **glossier, glossiest** smooth and shiny: *a glossy surface* • *glossy hair*

glove NOUN **gloves** gloves are two matching pieces of clothing that you wear on your hands

glow VERB **glows, glowing, glowed** to burn or shine with a warm or soft light
NOUN warm or soft light: *the glow of the fire*

glower VERB **glowers, glowering, glowered** to stare at something or somebody in an angry way

glow-worm NOUN **glow-worms** a kind of beetle that glows in the dark

glucose NOUN (*science*) a kind of sugar that is found in certain foods, like fruit, and which gives you energy

glue NOUN **glues** a substance used for sticking things together
VERB **glues, gluing** or **glueing, glued** to glue something is to stick it with glue

▶ **gluey** ADJECTIVE covered with glue or sticky like glue

glum ADJECTIVE **glummer, glummest** looking or feeling sad and depressed

gluten NOUN a sticky protein found in wheat and some other cereals

glutton NOUN **gluttons 1** someone who is very greedy and eats too much **2** someone who is very eager for something, especially something that does them no good: *a glutton for punishment*

▶ **gluttony** NOUN eating too much

gnarled ADJECTIVE twisted and knobbly

gnash VERB **gnashes, gnashing, gnashed** if someone gnashes their teeth, they grind them or snap them together, especially because they are angry

gnat NOUN **gnats** a small flying insect that bites and sucks blood

gnaw VERB **gnaws, gnawing, gnawed** to chew something hard or scrape at it with the teeth

gnome (pronounced **noam**) NOUN **gnomes 1** in stories, a small fairy creature that looks like a little old man wearing a soft pointed hat **2** a figure

Aa
Bb
Cc
Dd
Ee
Ff
Gg
Hh
Ii
Jj
Kk
Ll
Mm
Nn
Oo
Pp
Qq
Rr
Ss
Tt
Uu
Vv
Ww
Xx
Yy
Zz

like this that some people put in their gardens as a decoration

gnu (pronounced **noo** or **nyoo**) NOUN **gnu** or **gnus** a type of antelope found in Africa

go VERB **goes, going, went, gone**
1 to go somewhere is to travel or move there: *I'm going home now.*
2 to go somewhere is to lead to that place: *Does this road go to Inverness?*
3 to leave: *It's six o'clock. I'll have to go soon.*
4 the place where something goes is the place where it fits or is kept: *That piece of the jigsaw goes at the top.*
5 to become: *Her face went pale. • Your soup's gone cold.*
• **go in for** to go in for something is to take part in it
• **go off** food goes off when it becomes bad
• **go on** to go on is to continue: *Go on with your work • The baby went on crying.*
• **going to** about to: *What were you going to say?*
NOUN **goes** a go is a try or a turn
• **on the go** if someone is on the go, they are busy or active

goal NOUN **goals 1** in games like football and hockey, the goal is the area where you have to put the ball to score a point **2** a goal is a point scored when a ball goes into this area **3** an aim that you want to achieve

goat NOUN **goats** an animal with horns and long rough hair

gobble VERB **gobbles, gobbling, gobbled 1** if someone gobbles their food, they eat it very quickly **2** a turkey gobbles when it makes a series of loud sounds

goblet NOUN **goblets** a drinking cup with a stem and a rounded bowl

goblin NOUN **goblins** in stories, an evil ugly fairy creature

god NOUN **gods 1** a god is one of several beings that some people believe have the power to change or affect nature, or what happens to individuals **2** God is the being that Christians, Muslims, Jews and members of other religions worship

godchild NOUN **godchildren** a god-daughter or godson

goddess NOUN **goddesses** a female god

godparent NOUN **godparents** a godfather or godmother

goggles PLURAL NOUN people wear goggles over their eyes to protect them, for example when they are swimming underwater or working with materials that might damage their eyes

go-kart NOUN **go-karts** a small low vehicle that is used for racing, but which has a much less powerful engine than a real racing car

gold NOUN **1** a pale yellow precious metal **2** a yellow colour
▶ **golden** ADJECTIVE gold-coloured or made of gold: *golden hair*
▶ **goldish** ADJECTIVE like gold in colour

golden wedding NOUN **golden weddings** the 50th anniversary of a couple's marriage

goldfish NOUN **goldfish** a small fish with golden or orange scales that is kept as a pet

gold medal NOUN **gold medals** a medal made of gold awarded to the person who comes first in a sporting event

golf NOUN a game played on a large area of specially designed land. The players hit a small ball with long clubs into a series of small holes
▶ **golfer** NOUN **golfers** someone who plays golf

gondola NOUN **gondolas 1** a type of open boat used on the canals and waterways of Venice and rowed by a single oar at the back **2** the part of a cable car that people sit or travel in **3** the part underneath a hot-air balloon that people travel in
▶ **gondolier** NOUN **gondoliers** someone who rows a gondola

gone VERB the form of the verb **go** that is used with a helping verb to show that something happened in the past: *I tried to catch him before he left, but he had gone.*

Aa
Bb
Cc
Dd
Ee
Ff
Gg
Hh
Ii
Jj
Kk
Ll
Mm
Nn
Oo
Pp
Qq
Rr
Ss
Tt
Uu
Vv
Ww
Xx
Yy
Zz

Aa
Bb
Cc
Dd
Ee
Ff
Gg
Hh
Ii
Jj
Kk
Ll
Mm
Nn
Oo
Pp
Qq
Rr
Ss
Tt
Uu
Vv
Ww
Xx
Yy
Zz

gong NOUN **gongs** a large round piece of metal that is hit with a stick to make a loud noise as a signal

good ADJECTIVE **better, best**
1 something good is enjoyable or pleasant, or is of a high standard: *Did you have a good holiday?*
2 a good person is kind and thoughtful: *My grandparents are very good to me.*
3 good behaviour is correct or proper: *He has very good manners.*
4 to be good at something is to be able to do it well: *Sam's very good at drawing horses.*
5 giving you the result you want: *a good way to make Mum happy*
6 something is good for you when it benefits you in some way, especially by keeping you healthy
NOUN good is rightness: *the difference between good and evil*
• **for good** for ever: *He won't be coming back; he's gone for good.*

goodbye INTERJECTION you say 'goodbye' to people you are leaving or who are leaving you

goodness NOUN **1** being good and kind **2** the goodness in food is the things in it that will make you healthy when you eat it

goods PLURAL NOUN goods are things for sale: *goods from other countries*

goodwill NOUN goodwill is kind wishes: *The King and Queen sent him a message of goodwill.*

goose NOUN **geese** a bird with a long neck and webbed feet

gooseberry NOUN **gooseberries** a small round pale green fruit with a hairy skin that grows on a low bush

goosepimples *or* **goosebumps** PLURAL NOUN if you get goosepimples or goosebumps, tiny lumps appear on your skin, usually because you are cold or have had a fright

gore VERB **gores, goring, gored** if a bull or other animal gores someone, it injures them with its horns or tusks
NOUN gore is lots of blood

gorge NOUN **gorges** (*geography*) a deep narrow valley between hills

gorgeous ADJECTIVE beautiful: *The baby's absolutely gorgeous.* • *lots of gorgeous food*

gorilla NOUN **gorillas** a very large ape with a large head, long arms and a strong heavy body

✦ Be careful not to confuse the spellings of **gorilla** and **guerilla**. A **guerilla** is a type of fighter.

gorse NOUN gorse is a type of wild shrub with yellow flowers and sharp spines on its stems

gory ADJECTIVE **gorier, goriest** with lots of blood: *a gory film*

gosling NOUN **goslings** a baby goose

gospel NOUN **gospels 1** the gospel is the teachings of Christ **2** the Gospels are the parts of the Christian Bible describing the teachings of Christ **3** the truth: *He swore that what he had told me was gospel.*

gossip VERB **gossips, gossiping, gossiped** to gossip is to have a conversation with someone about what other people are doing
NOUN **gossips 1** gossip is informal talk, often about what other people are doing **2** a gossip is someone who gossips a lot

✦ This word comes from the Old English word **godsipp**, which means *godparent*. This is because your godparent is thought of as someone you can talk to.

got VERB a way of changing the verb **get** to make a past tense. It can be used with or without a helping verb: *Katy got a bike for her birthday.* • *Your brother has already got into the car.*

gouge VERB **gouges, gouging, gouged** to gouge something out is to dig it out using your fingernails or a sharp tool

govern VERB **governs, governing, governed** to govern a country is to control it and decide its rules

▶ **governess** NOUN **governesses** especially in the past, a woman employed by parents to teach their children at home

▸ **government** NOUN **governments** a government is the group of people who put the laws of a country into effect

▸ **governor** NOUN **governors** **1** school governors are the group of people who manage a particular school's business **2** someone who is the head of government in a state

GP ABBREVIATION **GPs** short for **general practitioner**, a doctor who sees patients at a local surgery

grab VERB **grabs, grabbing, grabbed** **1** to grab something is to grasp or take it suddenly or roughly: *He grabbed my bag and ran away.* **2** to grab something is to take it eagerly or in a hurry: *Let's stop and grab a bite to eat.*

grace NOUN **graces** **1** grace is a beautiful way of walking or moving **2** if someone behaves with grace, they are gentle, pleasant and thoughtful **3** approval or favour: *with the grace of God*

graceful ADJECTIVE graceful movements are elegant and attractive

▸ **gracefully** ADVERB with grace

gracious ADJECTIVE behaving in a polite and kind way: *a gracious lady • It was very gracious of you to apologize.*

▸ **graciously** ADVERB politely and kindly

grade NOUN **grades** a grade is a level of quality

VERB **grades, grading, graded** to grade things is to sort them according to their size or quality, or to mark them according to how good they are

gradient NOUN **gradients** a measure of how steep a slope is, which is shown as a percentage or a number out of ten

gradual ADJECTIVE going or changing slowly and steadily: *a gradual increase*

▸ **gradually** ADVERB slowly and steadily: *The weather gradually got colder.*

graduate VERB **graduates, graduating, graduated** to graduate from college or university is to successfully finish your course and get a degree or diploma

NOUN **graduates** someone who has a degree from a university or college

▸ **graduation** NOUN **graduations** the ceremony held when students at a college or university graduate

graffiti NOUN words or pictures painted or drawn on a wall

✦ **Graffiti** is an Italian word that means 'little scribbles'.

graft VERB **grafts, grafting, grafted** to take something, for example a piece of skin or a part of plant, and attach it in a new place so that it can grow there

NOUN **grafts** something such as a piece of skin or the stem of a plant that has been attached in a new place so it can grow there

grain NOUN **grains**
1 a grain is a single seed from a cereal plant like wheat or maize
2 grain is the seeds of cereal plants
3 a tiny piece of something: *a grain of pollen*
4 the grain on wood is the pattern of lines that run along or across its surface

gram or **gramme** NOUN **grams** or **grammes** the basic unit in the metric system for measuring weight. This is often shortened to **g**

grammar NOUN grammar is the correct use of words in speech and writing, and the rules about putting them together: *It's bad grammar to say 'I done'.*

grammar school NOUN **grammar schools** a type of secondary school that you must pass a test to get into

grammatical ADJECTIVE grammatical speech or writing is correct according to the rules of grammar

gramophone NOUN **gramophones** an old-fashioned word for a record-player

gran NOUN **grans** (*informal*) a grandmother

grand ADJECTIVE **grander, grandest** **1** great or fine: *a grand house* **2** noble: *She's a very grand old lady.*

grandchild NOUN **grandchildren** a child of someone's child

grand-daughter NOUN **grand-daughters** the daughter of someone's son or daughter

Aa
Bb
Cc
Dd
Ee
Ff
Gg
Hh
Ii
Jj
Kk
Ll
Mm
Nn
Oo
Pp
Qq
Rr
Ss
Tt
Uu
Vv
Ww
Xx
Yy
Zz

Aa
Bb
Cc
Dd
Ee
Ff
Gg
Hh
Ii
Jj
Kk
Ll
Mm
Nn
Oo
Pp
Qq
Rr
Ss
Tt
Uu
Vv
Ww
Xx
Yy
Zz

grandfather NOUN **grandfathers** the father of your father or mother

grandmother NOUN **grandmothers** the mother of your father or mother

grandparent NOUN **grandparents** a parent of your father or mother

grandson NOUN **grandsons** the son of someone's son or daughter

grandstand NOUN **grandstands** a place for spectators at a sports stadium or racetrack, with rows of seats built one above the other

granite NOUN a very hard greyish or reddish rock

granny NOUN **grannies** (*informal*) a grandmother

grant VERB **grants, granting, granted 1** to grant something that someone has asked for is to allow it or give it: *grant permission* **2** to admit that something is true: *It's very difficult, I grant you.*
NOUN **grants** a sum of money that has been given or awarded for a special purpose: *a repair grant*

Granthi (pronounced **grun**-tee) NOUN **Granthis** the guardian of a Sikh temple and the Guru Granth Sahib, the holy book of the Sikh religion

granule NOUN **granules** a very small grain or part: *sugar granules*

grape NOUN **grapes** a small green or blackish-red berry that grows in bunches and is used to make wine

grapefruit NOUN **grapefruit** or **grapefruits** a large citrus fruit with yellow skin and yellow or pink flesh

graph NOUN **graphs** a diagram with lines drawn between different points on squared paper, used to show how things compare to each other

> ✦ **Graphe** is the Greek word for *writing*. If a word contains **graph**, you can guess that it has something to do with writing or something written as words or pictures.
> Other examples are **graphics** and **autograph**.

graphic ADJECTIVE **1** to do with drawing, painting or writing: *the graphic arts* **2** showing or giving a lot of detail, often too much detail

▶ **graphics** PLURAL NOUN pictures, drawings and decorative lettering, especially those done on a computer or used in computer games or Web pages

graphite NOUN a soft black type of carbon that is used for the lead in pencils

grapple VERB **grapples, grappling, grappled 1** to grapple with a difficult problem is to try hard to deal with it **2** to grapple with someone is to wrestle or struggle with them

grasp VERB **grasps, grasping, grasped 1** to grasp something is to take hold of it or hold it tightly **2** to grasp something is to understand it: *I'm hearing the words more clearly now, but I still can't grasp their meaning.*

grass NOUN **grasses** a plant with long thin leaves called blades, which grows on lawns and in fields

▶ **grassy** ADJECTIVE **grassier, grassiest** covered with grass: *a grassy field*

grasshopper NOUN **grasshoppers** an insect with long back legs that can hop or jump long distances

grassland NOUN **grasslands** (*geography*) a large area covered with grass

grate¹ VERB **grates, grating, grated 1** to grate food is to cut it into fine strands or shreds using a grater **2** something grates when it makes an unpleasant squeaking or scratching noise as it rubs, or is rubbed, against something

grate² NOUN **grates** a framework of metal bars in a fireplace, where the fuel is burned

grateful ADJECTIVE feeling thankful or showing or giving thanks: *I'm very grateful for all your kindness.*

▶ **gratefully** ADVERB thankfully

grater NOUN **graters** a kitchen tool that has lots of small holes with sharp edges on its surface, used for grating things like cheese or vegetables

grating NOUN **gratings** a covering for an outside drain with holes in it so that water and air can pass through

gratitude NOUN if you feel gratitude towards someone, you want to repay them for something kind that they have done

grave¹ NOUN **graves** a place where a dead body is buried

grave² ADJECTIVE **graver, gravest** very serious: *a grave mistake*

gravel NOUN small stones used to cover roads, paths and driveways

gravestone NOUN **gravestones** a piece of stone with writing on it which says who is buried in a grave

graveyard NOUN **graveyards** a place where dead people are buried

gravity NOUN **1** (*science*) gravity is the force that pulls things towards the earth and causes them to fall to the ground **2** gravity is seriousness: *the gravity of the crime*

✦ This word comes from the Latin word **gravitas**, which means *heaviness*. The force of gravity makes things seem heavier by pulling them down.

gravy NOUN a sauce made from the juices that come out of meat while it is cooking

graze VERB **grazes, grazing, grazed 1** animals graze when they move around eating grass and other plants **2** to graze your skin is to scratch it by dragging it against something hard **3** if something grazes you it touches you lightly as it goes past

NOUN **grazes** a graze is a scratch or scratches on your skin made by something hard and rough

grease NOUN thick fat or oil, or any oily substance

VERB **greases, greasing, greased** to grease something is to rub grease on it

▶ **greasy** ADJECTIVE **greasier, greasiest** oily or fatty

great ADJECTIVE **greater, greatest**
1 very important or special: *a great day for the school*
2 very talented or distinguished: *one of the greatest scientists of all time*
3 very large: *The elephant lifted one of its great feet.*

4 very enjoyable or very good: *It was a great film.*
5 you use the word 'great' to show that a family member is another generation above or below. For example, your *great-grandmother* is the mother of your grandmother or grandfather, and your *great-grandson* is the son of your grandson or granddaughter

NOUN **greats** an extremely famous, special or important person or thing: *one of Hollywood's greats*

▶ **greatly** ADVERB very much: *She wasn't greatly pleased.*

▶ **greatness** NOUN being very impressive, important or talented

greed NOUN great or selfish desire for more of something than you need, especially food or money

▶ **greedily** ADVERB in a way that shows greed for food or money: *My brother ate his lunch greedily.*

▶ **greediness** NOUN a selfish wish to have or eat more than you need

▶ **greedy** ADJECTIVE **greedier, greediest** wanting more of something than you actually need

green NOUN the colour of grass and the leaves of most plants

▶ **greenery** NOUN green leaves

▶ **greenish** ADJECTIVE quite green, but not completely green in colour

green fingers PLURAL NOUN someone who has green fingers is good at gardening and making plants grow

greengrocer NOUN **greengrocers 1** someone who sells fruit and vegetables in a shop **2** a greengrocer's is a shop selling fruit and vegetables

greenhouse NOUN **greenhouses** a shed made of glass, used for growing plants in

greenhouse effect NOUN (*geography*) the greenhouse effect is the heating of the Earth's surface caused by gases (**greenhouse gases**) in the atmosphere which trap the heat from the sun

greens PLURAL NOUN green vegetables such as cabbage: *Be sure to eat all your greens.*

Aa
Bb
Cc
Dd
Ee
Ff
Gg
Hh
Ii
Jj
Kk
Ll
Mm
Nn
Oo
Pp
Qq
Rr
Ss
Tt
Uu
Vv
Ww
Xx
Yy
Zz

Aa
Bb
Cc
Dd
Ee
Ff
Gg
Hh
Ii
Jj
Kk
Ll
Mm
Nn
Oo
Pp
Qq
Rr
Ss
Tt
Uu
Vv
Ww
Xx
Yy
Zz

greet VERB **greets, greeting, greeted**
1 to greet someone is to say something to them when they arrive or when you meet them **2** if something is greeted in a certain way, people react to it in that way: *The announcement was greeted with howls of protest.*
▸ **greeting** NOUN **greetings** something said when you meet someone, such as 'hello' or 'hi' or 'good morning'

grenade NOUN **grenades** a weapon like a small bomb that soldiers throw

grew VERB a way of changing the verb **grow** to make a past tense: *Stephen grew three centimetres last summer.*

grey NOUN a colour between black and white
▸ **greyish** ADJECTIVE quite grey, but not completely grey in colour

greyhound NOUN **greyhounds** a type of slim dog that can run very fast over short distances and is used for racing

grid NOUN **grids**
1 a pattern of lines that cross each other horizontally and vertically and form squares in between
2 (*geography*) a map or chart with a set of numbered lines
3 a grating made up of bars that cross each other like a grid
4 a network of electricity lines that covers a large area

grid reference NOUN **grid references** (*geography*) a set of two numbers or letters used to show a place on a grid

grief NOUN great sorrow, especially when someone has died
• **come to grief** if you come to grief you fail or have an accident

grievance NOUN **grievances** something that you think is wrong and that you complain about

grieve VERB **grieves, grieving, grieved** to grieve is to feel very sad for a while, especially because someone has died or because you miss something that you have lost

grievous ADJECTIVE **1** a grievous wound or injury is very serious **2** something grievous causes sorrow or sadness

grill VERB **grills, grilling, grilled 1** to grill food is to cook it by putting it close to something hot **2** to grill someone is to ask them lots of questions
NOUN **grills** the part of a cooker where food can be grilled

grille NOUN **grilles** a metal grating covering a door, window or other space in a wall

grim ADJECTIVE **grimmer, grimmest**
1 if someone looks grim, they have a serious and slightly fierce expression on their face **2** something grim is dreadful, upsetting or shocking

grimace VERB **grimaces, grimacing, grimaced** to twist your face in an ugly way, because you are in pain or you are disgusted at something
NOUN **grimaces** an ugly twisted expression

grime NOUN dirt that has been on a surface for a long time and is difficult to get off
▸ **grimy** ADJECTIVE **grimier, grimiest** covered with grime

grin VERB **grins, grinning, grinned** to grin is to smile broadly showing your teeth
NOUN **grins** a wide smile

grind VERB **grinds, grinding, ground**
1 to grind something solid is to crush it into a powder between two hard surfaces **2** to grind something is to sharpen or polish it against a hard or rough surface **3** to grind your teeth is to rub them together sideways
NOUN something that is difficult and boring to do: *the daily grind of work*
▸ **grinder** NOUN **grinders** a machine that grinds things, such as coffee beans

grindstone NOUN **grindstones** a circular stone that turns on top of another stone and is used in mills to grind corn
• **have your nose to the grindstone** to be working very hard, usually for long periods of time

grip VERB **grips, gripping, gripped 1** if you grip something, you hold it tightly **2** if something grips you, it holds your attention completely
NOUN **grips 1** a hold or grasp: *a tight*

grip • in the grip of winter 2 a small U-shaped wire used to keep hair in place

▶ **gripping** ADJECTIVE holding your attention completely: *the climax of a gripping film*

grisly ADJECTIVE something that is grisly is frightening because it involves death or violence

gristle NOUN a kind of tough stretchy tissue that is sometimes found in meat

grit NOUN **1** grit is tiny sharp pieces of stone or sand **2** if someone has grit, they have courage and determination

▶ **gritty** ADJECTIVE **grittier, grittiest** **1** having a rough texture like grit **2** courageous or determined **3** showing the harsher side of life as it really is

grizzly ADJECTIVE grey
NOUN **grizzlies** a grizzly bear

grizzly bear NOUN **grizzly bears** a type of large brown bear found in parts of the United States and Canada

groan VERB **groans, groaning, groaned** **1** to make a long deep sound because you are in pain or you think something is bad **2** to make a sound like a groan: *The trees creaked and groaned.*
NOUN **groans** a deep moan made in the back of your throat

grocer NOUN **grocers** **1** someone who runs a shop or supermarket selling groceries **2** a grocer's is a shop selling groceries

▶ **groceries** PLURAL NOUN groceries are foods and other household goods that you buy in a shop or supermarket

groggy ADJECTIVE **groggier, groggiest** if you feel groggy, you can't think clearly, for example because you are weak after an illness

groin NOUN **groins** your groin is the part of your body between your legs where they join your body

groom VERB **grooms, grooming, groomed** **1** to groom an animal is to look after it, especially by brushing or combing its coat **2** animals groom each other when they clean each other's coats by licking or picking through the hair
NOUN **grooms** **1** someone who looks after horses **2** a bridegroom

groove NOUN **grooves** a long narrow channel cut into a surface

grope VERB **gropes, groping, groped** **1** to grope for something you can't see is to feel about with your hand to try to find it **2** to grope for an answer, or for the right word, is to try to find it without being sure how to do so

gross ADJECTIVE **grosser, grossest** **1** coarse, vulgar and bad-mannered **2** very bad: *gross ignorance* **3** (*informal*) disgusting **4** very fat **5** a gross amount is the total amount without anything being taken away: *The gross weight of the parcel includes all the packaging.*
NOUN **gross** or **grosses** a gross is 12 dozen or 144

▶ **grossly** ADVERB hugely

grotesque ADJECTIVE very strange and ugly-looking: *grotesque masks*

ground[1] NOUN **grounds** **1** the ground is the Earth's surface: *fall to the ground • on higher ground* **2** ground is earth or soil: *stony ground* **3** a ground is a sports field, especially one belonging to a particular club: *What's the name of Tottenham Hotspur's ground?*

▶ **grounded** ADJECTIVE **1** a child is grounded when they aren't allowed out, as a punishment **2** a pilot or plane is grounded when they aren't allowed to fly

▶ **grounds** PLURAL NOUN **1** the grounds of a large house or building are the areas of land that surround it and are part of the same property **2** to have grounds for doing something is to have reasons for doing it **3** grounds are tiny pieces or powder made by grinding: *coffee grounds*

ground[2] VERB a way of changing the verb **grind** to make a past tense. It can be used with or without a helping verb: *Then we ground the wheat to make flour. • The coffee has been ground too finely.*

group NOUN **groups** a number of people or things that are together or that belong together
VERB **groups, grouping, grouped** to

Aa
Bb
Cc
Dd
Ee
Ff
Gg
Hh
Ii
Jj
Kk
Ll
Mm
Nn
Oo
Pp
Qq
Rr
Ss
Tt
Uu
Vv
Ww
Xx
Yy
Zz

bring people or things together in a group or groups

grouse¹ NOUN **grouse** a type of plump speckled bird that lives on moorland and is hunted for sport

grouse² NOUN **grouses** a complaint VERB **grouses, grousing, groused** to grouse about something is to complain about it

grove NOUN **groves** a small group of trees growing close together

grovel VERB **grovels, grovelling, grovelled** to obey someone in a very eager way that shows you do not respect yourself enough

grow VERB **grows, growing, grew, grown 1** to grow is to get bigger, taller, wider or stronger: *He's grown as tall as his father.* • *The club has grown into a big business.* **2** to grow plants is to look after them while they grow: *We grow vegetables in our garden.* **3** to become: *It was growing dark.*

• **grow out of something** to grow out of something you used to do or wear when you were younger is to become too old or big for it

growl VERB **growls, growling, growled 1** an animal such as a dog or lion growls when it makes a deep threatening noise in its throat **2** a person growls when they talk in a deep voice, often because they are angry NOUN **growls** a deep threatening sound: *The dog let out a low growl.*

growth NOUN **growths 1** growing or getting bigger: *the rapid growth of computer technology* **2** the process by which things grow: *Warm weather will speed up the plant's growth.* **3** a lump that grows on the body: *A growth developed on his hand.*

grub NOUN **grubs 1** a grub is the soft-bodied form of an insect just after it has hatched from the egg **2** (*informal*) food

grubby ADJECTIVE **grubbier, grubbiest** dirty: *Go and wash those grubby hands!*

grudge VERB **grudges, grudging, grudged** if you grudge giving something to someone, you feel annoyed because you think they don't

deserve it: *I don't grudge him his good luck, because he deserves it.*
NOUN **grudges** if you have a grudge against someone, they have done something to you that you are angry about and haven't forgiven

gruel NOUN gruel is a kind of thin porridge that poor people used to eat

gruelling ADJECTIVE very difficult and tiring: *a gruelling climb to the summit of the mountain*

gruesome ADJECTIVE something that is gruesome is upsetting because it involves very violent injuries

gruff ADJECTIVE **gruffer, gruffest** a gruff voice is deep and harsh-sounding

grumble VERB **grumbles, grumbling, grumbled** to grumble is to complain in a bad-tempered way

grumpy ADJECTIVE **grumpier, grumpiest** bad-tempered: *He's grumpy if he has to get up early.*

grunt VERB **grunts, grunting, grunted** to make a deep snorting noise like a pig NOUN **grunts** a deep snorting noise

guarantee NOUN **guarantees** a promise that something will definitely be done or that something will be replaced free of charge if it goes wrong VERB **guarantees, guaranteeing, guaranteed** to guarantee something is to make a promise that it will happen or be done

guard NOUN **guards 1** someone whose job is to protect a person or place, or to make sure that prisoners don't escape **2** something that protects from damage or accidents: *a gum guard* • *a fire guard* **3** someone who is in charge of a railway train or coach

• **keep guard** or **stand guard** to watch over someone or something VERB **guards, guarding, guarded** to guard a person or place is to watch over them

• **guard against** to guard against something is to take care not to let it happen

▶ **guardian** NOUN **guardians 1** a child's or young person's guardian is someone with the legal right and duty to take care of them **2** someone who protects something

guerrilla NOUN **guerrillas** someone fighting as part of a secret army trying to defeat the people controlling their country

guess VERB **guesses, guessing, guessed** to guess is to give an answer or opinion without knowing or being sure of all or any of the facts

NOUN **guesses** an answer or opinion made by guessing

guest NOUN **guests 1** someone you invite to your house or to a party **2** someone staying in a hotel

guidance NOUN if someone gives you guidance, they give you advice about how you should do something

guide VERB **guides, guiding, guided 1** to guide someone is to show them the way or how to do something **2** to guide something is to make it go in a certain direction

NOUN **guides 1** someone who shows tourists around or who leads travellers **2** a book that gives information about a place **3** a Guide is a girl who is a member of the Guide Association, an international organization for girls

guide dog NOUN **guide dogs** a specially trained dog used by a blind person to help them get around

guidelines PLURAL NOUN rules that tell you what you should do, or pieces of information about how to do something

guild NOUN **guilds 1** a society of craftsmen or tradesmen **2** a society or social club

guile NOUN guile is being clever in a secret or sneaky way

guillotine NOUN **guillotines 1** (*history*) a simple machine used in the past for cutting people's heads off, with a blade that falls from the top of a wooden frame **2** a machine with a very sharp blade used for cutting paper

guilt NOUN **1** an uneasy feeling you get when you know you have done something wrong: *She felt no guilt at what she had done.* **2** the fact that

you have done something wrong: *He admitted his guilt and accepted the punishment.*

▶ **guilty** ADJECTIVE **guiltier, guiltiest 1** you feel guilty when you feel that you have done something wrong **2** if someone is guilty of something, other people think that something they do is wrong: *He's guilty of neglecting his school work to play sport.* **3** someone is found guilty of a crime when a jury or judge decides that they did it

guinea NOUN **guineas** a British gold coin used in the past

guinea pig NOUN **guinea pigs 1** a small animal with long soft hair that is kept as a pet **2** someone who is asked to try something new that nobody else has tried yet

guise NOUN **guises** a disguise or appearance

guitar NOUN **guitars** an instrument with a rounded body shaped like a figure of eight, a long neck and strings that you play with your fingers

▶ **guitarist** NOUN **guitarists** someone who plays the guitar

gulf NOUN **gulfs 1** (*geography*) a large bay filled by the sea **2** if there is a gulf between people or things, they are very far apart or very different from each other

gull NOUN **gulls** a common sea bird

gullet NOUN **gullets** your gullet is the tube that food goes down into your stomach

gullible ADJECTIVE a gullible person believes what they are told and is easily tricked

gully NOUN **gullies** (*geography*) a deep channel worn away by a river or stream

gulp VERB **gulps, gulping, gulped** to gulp is to swallow air or liquid quickly in large mouthfuls: *He gulped down his tea.*

NOUN **gulps 1** the sound made when you gulp **2** a large mouthful

gum NOUN **gums**
1 a type of glue used to stick paper or card
2 your gums are the parts inside your

Aa
Bb
Cc
Dd
Ee
Ff
Gg
Hh
Ii
Jj
Kk
Ll
Mm
Nn
Oo
Pp
Qq
Rr
Ss
Tt
Uu
Vv
Ww
Xx
Yy
Zz

mouth just above your top teeth and below your bottom teeth **3** chewing gum **4** a sticky jelly-like sweet: *fruit gums* VERB **gums, gumming, gummed** to stick something with gum

▸ **gummy** ADJECTIVE **gummier, gummiest** sticky like gum

gum tree NOUN **gum trees** a tree that produces gum, especially the eucalyptus tree

gun NOUN **guns** a weapon that fires bullets or shells from a metal tube

gunfire NOUN **1** the firing of guns **2** the sound of bullets being fired from a gun

gunpowder NOUN a powder that explodes when it is lit

gurdwara (pronounced **goor**-dwar-a) NOUN **gurdwaras** a building where Sikhs go to worship

gurgle VERB **gurgles, gurgling, gurgled 1** water gurgles when it makes a pleasant bubbling sound as it flows **2** to make small bubbling sounds in your throat with saliva or some other liquid

guru (pronounced **goo**-roo) NOUN **gurus 1** a Hindu or Sikh religious leader and teacher **2** any greatly respected teacher or leader

Guru Granth Sahib (pronounced **goo**-roo grunt **sa**-ib) NOUN the holy book of the Sikh religion. It is also called the **Adi-Granth**

gush VERB **gushes, gushing, gushed 1** water or other liquid gushes when it flows out suddenly and strongly **2** to gush is to talk with exaggerated feeling or emotion

gust NOUN **gusts** a sudden strong rush of wind

▸ **gusty** ADJECTIVE **gustier, gustiest** gusty weather has sudden rushes of wind between calmer periods

gut NOUN **guts** your gut is your stomach and intestines VERB **guts, gutting, gutted 1** to gut a dead fish or animal is to remove the organs from inside its body **2** to gut a place is to destroy or remove everything inside it

▸ **guts** PLURAL NOUN **1** guts are intestines **2** someone who has guts has courage

gutter NOUN **gutters** a channel for carrying water, especially one fixed to the edge of a roof or by the side of the road for carrying away rainwater into the underground drains

guy NOUN **guys 1** (*informal*) a man or boy **2** a figure burnt on a bonfire on 5 November, to remember a man called Guy Fawkes who tried to blow up the Houses of Parliament in 1605

guzzle VERB **guzzles, guzzling, guzzled** to guzzle food or drink is to eat or drink it quickly and greedily

gym NOUN **gyms 1** a gym is a large room with special equipment for doing exercises **2** a gym is a hall in a school where you do PE **3** gym is the exercises and games that you do in a school gym

gymkhana NOUN **gymkhanas** a horse-riding event which includes races and jumping competitions

gymnasium NOUN **gymnasiums** or **gymnasia** (*formal*) a gym

gymnast NOUN **gymnasts** someone trained to do gymnastics

▸ **gymnastics** NOUN exercises done indoors in a gym using special equipment like bars, ropes and beams

Gypsy NOUN **Gypsies** a member of a group of people who travel from place to place and have no fixed home

Hh

habit NOUN **habits** a habit is something that you do regularly: *Tommy has a bad habit of grinding his teeth.*

habitat NOUN **habitats** an animal's or plant's habitat is the place where it lives or grows

habitual ADJECTIVE **1** doing something again and again: *a habitual criminal* **2** done regularly, as a habit: *a habitual morning cup of coffee*

hack VERB **hacks, hacking, hacked 1** to chop something roughly: *They hacked their way through the thick jungle.* **2** to hack into a computer is to get access to the information in it without permission
▸ **hacker** NOUN **hackers** someone who uses their computer skills to get access to information in other people's computers illegally or without permission

hacksaw NOUN **hacksaws** a saw with a thin blade used to cut metal

had VERB **1** a way of changing the verb **have** to make a past tense: *I had a cold last week.* **2 had** is also used as a helping verb along with a main verb: *I had enjoyed my stay in France.* • *He had had enough.*

haddock NOUN **haddock** or **haddocks** a type of sea fish with firm white flaky flesh

Hadith NOUN in Islam, the traditions based on what Mohammed and his followers did in their lives, which give Muslims guidance on how to live

hadn't a short way to say and write **had not**: *He hadn't expected to win.*

haemorrhage (pronounced hem-o-rij) NOUN **haemorrhages** very serious bleeding that is difficult to stop

hag NOUN **hags** an ugly old woman

haggard ADJECTIVE tired and ill-looking

haggis NOUN **haggises** a Scottish food made with minced sheep's heart mixed with oatmeal and spices

haggle VERB **haggles, haggling, haggled** to bargain over something you want to buy, and try to make the seller lower the price

haiku (pronounced hie-koo) NOUN **haikus** or **haiku** a type of short Japanese poem with 17 syllables

hail[1] VERB **hails, hailing, hailed 1** to hail a taxi or a person is to shout or wave to get their attention **2** if you hail someone or something as another thing, you say that they are that thing: *He was hailed as a hero when he rescued the child.*

hail[2] NOUN hailstones falling from the sky
VERB **hails, hailing, hailed** it hails when hailstones fall

hailstones PLURAL NOUN small white balls of frozen water that fall in showers from the sky

hair NOUN **hairs 1** a hair is one of the thread-like things that grow on the surface of the skin of animals and humans **2** your hair is the mass of hairs that grow on your head

hairdresser NOUN **hairdressers** someone who cuts, styles and colours people's hair
▸ **hairdressing** NOUN the art, skill or work of a hairdresser

hair-raising ADJECTIVE terrifying or dangerous: *a hair-raising ride on the Big Dipper*

hairstyle NOUN **hairstyles** a way of cutting or wearing your hair

hairy ADJECTIVE **hairier, hairiest 1** covered with hair: *Most men have hairy legs.* **2** terrifying or dangerous: *If it is stormy, the ferry crossing can get a bit hairy.*
▸ **hairiness** NOUN being covered with hair

hajj NOUN the journey or pilgrimage to Mecca that all Muslims should try to make at least once in their lifetime

► **hajji** NOUN **hajjis** a Muslim who has made a pilgrimage to Mecca

halal ADJECTIVE halal meat is from animals killed and prepared according to the laws of Islam

half NOUN **halves** 1 a half is one of two equal parts that together make up the whole of something: *He ate half and I ate the other half.* 2 the fraction ½, equivalent to the decimal fraction 0.5 and equal to one divided by two ADJECTIVE 1 being one of two equal parts: *a half brick* 2 not full or complete: *a half smile* ADVERB 1 to the level or extent of a half: *This glass is only half full.* 2 partly or almost: *a half-open door* 3 nearly: *It wasn't half as scary as I expected it to be.*

• **by half** if you say that someone is too clever by half, you mean that their cleverness is annoying and will end up causing trouble for them

• **not half** people say 'not half' when they want to emphasize that they agree completely with what someone else has just said: *'That was a great goal, wasn't it?' 'Not half.'*

half-baked ADJECTIVE a half-baked idea is one that is silly because someone has not thought about it properly

half-brother NOUN **half-brothers** your half-brother has either the same father or the same mother as you do

half day NOUN **half days** a holiday for half the working or school day, either for the morning or the afternoon

half-hearted ADJECTIVE without much enthusiasm

► **half-heartedly** ADVERB not very enthusiastically: *Thomas started his homework half-heartedly.*

half-mast NOUN if a flag is at half-mast it is flown from a position halfway up the flagpole, usually as a sign of mourning for someone who has died

half moon NOUN **half moons** the moon when it looks like a semicircle

half-sister NOUN **half-sisters** your half-sister has either the same father or the same mother as you do

half-term NOUN **half-terms** a short holiday from school about halfway through the school term

half-time NOUN in games like football, hockey and rugby, half-time is a break from play in the middle of the match

halfway ADVERB AND ADJECTIVE in the middle between two points, or between the beginning and the end: *Halfway through the lesson I started to feel ill.*

hall NOUN **halls** 1 an area just inside the entrance to a house from which you can get to other rooms or to the stairs 2 a large building or room where meetings, concerts and other events are held

hallelujah INTERJECTION a shout or exclamation of praise to God

hallmark NOUN **hallmarks** 1 a mark stamped on things made of gold or silver to show their quality 2 the hallmark of something is its main feature: *The hallmark of a good writer is the ability to hold your attention.*

hallo INTERJECTION another spelling of **hello**

Hallowe'en NOUN October 31, the time when ghosts and witches are traditionally supposed to wander about, and when people get dressed up in costumes and masks

✦ This word comes from the old word **All-Hallow-Even**, which means 'the eve of All Saints' Day'.

hallucinate VERB **hallucinates, hallucinating, hallucinated** to see things that aren't really there

► **hallucination** NOUN **hallucinations** a vision someone has of something that doesn't really exist

hallway NOUN **hallways** an entrance hall in a house or building

halo NOUN **haloes** a ring of light round the head of an angel or saint in pictures and paintings, showing that they are holy

halt VERB **halts, halting, halted** to stop moving and stand still NOUN **halts** a stop: *The train came to a halt and we got off.*

halter NOUN **halters** a rope or strap

Aa
Bb
Cc
Dd
Ee
Ff
Gg
Hh
Ii
Jj
Kk
Ll
Mm
Nn
Oo
Pp
Qq
Rr
Ss
Tt
Uu
Vv
Ww
Xx
Yy
Zz

put over a horse's head so that it can be held or led

halve VERB **halves, halving, halved 1** to halve something is to divide or cut it into two equal parts **2** if something is halved, it is reduced to half its original size or amount

halves NOUN the plural of **half**

ham¹ NOUN **hams** ham is smoked and salted meat from the leg of a pig

ham² NOUN **hams 1** an actor who is bad because their acting does not seem natural **2** a radio ham is someone who operates a radio transmitter and receiver as a hobby

hamburger NOUN **hamburgers** a round flat cake of minced meat that is fried and usually eaten in a bun

✦ Hamburgers were named after the city of **Hamburg** in Germany. The meat used to be called Hamburg steak.

hamlet NOUN **hamlets** a small village

hammer NOUN **hammers** a tool with a heavy metal or wooden head at the end of a handle, used for knocking nails in or for breaking up hard material like stones and concrete
VERB **hammers, hammering, hammered 1** to hit something with a hammer: *hammering the nails in one by one* **2** to hit something several times, making a lot of noise: *hammering on the door with his fists* **3** to hammer someone in a game or competition is to beat them by a lot of points: *We hammered the other team 10-0.*
• **hammer something out** to hammer something out is to discuss it until everyone is satisfied: *hammer out an agreement*

hammock NOUN **hammocks** a kind of bed made up of a long piece of heavy fabric which is hung from ropes at either end so that it swings above the ground

hamper¹ NOUN **hampers** a large basket with a lid used for carrying food, plates and cutlery, especially for picnics

hamper² VERB **hampers, hampering, hampered** to hamper someone or

something is to stop them making progress

hamster NOUN **hamsters** a small animal with soft fur and a short tail, often kept as a pet

hand NOUN **hands**
1 your hand is the part of your body at the end of your arm just below your wrist
2 a narrow pointer on a clock or watch that moves round and shows the time
3 if you give someone a hand, you give them your help
4 a unit, equal to 4 inches or about 10 centimetres, used for measuring the height of horses: *a huge horse of almost 16 hands*
5 the cards that a player has been dealt in a card game
6 a worker on a farm, in a factory or on a ship
• **at hand** something that is at hand is available quickly: *Help is at hand.*
• **by hand** you do or make something by hand when you use your hands to do or make it
• **in hand** something is in hand when it is being dealt with
• **on hand** if someone or something is on hand, they are ready and available to help or be used
• **out of hand** if things get out of hand, they get out of control
• **to hand** if something is to hand, it is near you and you are able to reach it or use it easily
VERB **hands, handing, handed** to hand something to someone is to pass it to them

handbag NOUN **handbags** a small bag for carrying personal belongings like your purse and keys

handbook NOUN **handbooks** a book of instructions on how to do something: *an illustrated handbook on first aid*

handcuffs PLURAL NOUN a pair of metal rings joined by a chain which are used by the police to lock around the wrists of someone they have arrested

handful NOUN **handfuls 1** an amount

Aa
Bb
Cc
Dd
Ee
Ff
Gg
Hh
Ii
Jj
Kk
Ll
Mm
Nn
Oo
Pp
Qq
Rr
Ss
Tt
Uu
Vv
Ww
Xx
Yy
Zz

that you can hold in your hand: *a handful of rice* **2** a small number: *Only a handful of people turned up.* **3** a person or animal whose behaviour makes them difficult to deal with

handicap NOUN **handicaps** a physical or mental disability that makes some aspects of life difficult
VERB **handicaps, handicapping, handicapped** to handicap someone is to make them unable to do something properly
▸ **handicapped** ADJECTIVE disabled, either mentally or physically

handicraft NOUN **handicrafts** a craft done using the hands, such as sewing, knitting or pottery

handiwork NOUN someone's handiwork is something that they have made or done

handkerchief NOUN **handkerchiefs** a small piece of cloth or tissue paper used for wiping your nose

handle NOUN **handles 1** a part of an object that you use to pick it up and hold it: *a brush with a long handle* **2** a lever or knob on a door that you hold when you open and close the door
• **fly off the handle** if someone flies off the handle, they lose their temper
VERB **handles, handling, handled 1** to handle something is to touch or hold it with your hands: *Try not to handle the fruit too much.* **2** to handle something is to deal with or cope with it: *Mr Peters is handling all the arrangements for the trip.*

handlebars PLURAL NOUN the part of a bicycle that you hold in your hands and use for steering the bicycle

handrail NOUN **handrails** a narrow rail that people can hold on to for safety

handsome ADJECTIVE **handsomer, handsomest 1** a handsome boy or man is good looking **2** a handsome amount of money is large: *They made a handsome profit.*

hands-on ADJECTIVE done or experienced by yourself in a practical way, rather than watching others do it

handstand NOUN **handstands** a gymnastic movement in which you balance your body upside down carrying your weight on your hands and holding your legs straight up in the air

handwriting NOUN writing done with a pen or pencil
▸ **handwritten** ADJECTIVE written with a pen or pencil, not typed or printed

handy ADJECTIVE **handier, handiest 1** useful and easy to use: *a handy size for carrying in your pocket* **2** nearby and easily reached: *The house is handy for the station.*

handyman NOUN **handymen** someone who does small building and repair jobs

hang VERB **hangs, hanging, hung** or **hanged 1** to hang something is to attach it or support it at the top so that it is held above the ground: *Hang your jackets up on the pegs.* **2** something hangs when it is supported near the top and is held above the ground: *A picture was hanging on the wall.* **3** to hang someone is to kill them by tying a rope around their neck and removing a support from under their feet
• **hang about** or **hang around** to stay in one place doing nothing: *Don't let's hang about any more. Let's get started.*
NOUN
• **get the hang of something** to learn how to do something after a bit of practice

✦ **Hung** is the usual past tense of the verb **hang**. However, you use **hanged** instead of **hung** about someone who dies by hanging.

hangar NOUN **hangars** a big shed that aeroplanes are kept in

hanger NOUN **hangers** a shaped piece of metal, wood or plastic with a hook, used to hang clothes

hang-glider NOUN **hang-gliders** a type of vehicle that flies using air currents with the pilot strapped in a harness that hangs beneath a large kite-like frame
▸ **hang-gliding** NOUN the sport or pastime of flying in hang-gliders

Aa Bb Cc Dd Ee Ff Gg **Hh** Ii Jj Kk Ll Mm Nn Oo Pp Qq Rr Ss Tt Uu Vv Ww Xx Yy Zz

hangman NOUN **hangmen** someone whose job is to hang people who have been given death as a punishment

hangover NOUN **hangovers 1** a sick feeling, often with an aching head, that people sometimes get after they have drunk too much alcohol **2** something that remains after an event or period of time is over: *a hangover from the 1960's*

hank NOUN **hanks** a small loose bundle made up of strands of hair, wool or thread

hanker VERB **hankers, hankering, hankered** to hanker for or after something is to want to have it very much

hankie *or* **hanky** NOUN **hankies** (*informal*) a short form of the word **handkerchief**

Hanukkah (pronounced **ha**-nu-ka) NOUN Hanukkah is a Jewish festival lasting for eight days in December. It is also called the Feast of Dedication or the Festival of Lights because a candle is lit on each of the eight days

haphazard ADJECTIVE with no planning or system

hapless ADJECTIVE unlucky: *the hapless victims of the shipwreck*

happen VERB **happens, happening, happened 1** something happens when it takes place or occurs: *When did this happen?* • *I pressed the button but nothing happened.* **2** if something happens to a person or thing, an event or situation affects or involves them: *Do you know what's happened to the front door key?* **3** if you happen to do or see something, you do or see it by chance: *She just happened to be there and saw the whole thing.*

▶ **happening** NOUN **happenings** an event

happy ADJECTIVE **happier, happiest 1** joyful: *the happiest day of her life* **2** pleased or contented: *I'd be happy to help.* **3** lucky: *a happy coincidence*

▶ **happily** ADVERB joyfully, contentedly or luckily: *smiling happily* • *Happily, it all turned out well.*

▶ **happiness** NOUN being happy

happy-go-lucky ADJECTIVE a happy-go-lucky person is cheerful, enjoying anything good that happens and not worrying about the future

harass VERB **harasses, harassing, harassed** to harass someone is to keep annoying them, pestering them or interfering with their life

▶ **harassed** ADJECTIVE feeling worried and anxious because you have too much to do

▶ **harassment** NOUN harassing someone or being harassed

harbour NOUN **harbours** a place protected from wind and rough seas where ships and boats can shelter and dock

VERB **harbours, harbouring, harboured 1** to harbour a criminal is to protect them from being found or arrested by the police **2** to harbour a feeling is to keep it in your mind: *She'd harboured a grudge against them.*

✦This word comes from the Old English words **here**, which means *army*, and **beorg**, which means *protection*. A harbour was thought to be a safe place for troops.

hard ADJECTIVE **harder, hardest**
1 feeling firm and solid when touched and not easily broken or bent out of shape: *hard as rock* • *a hard bed*
2 difficult: *a very hard sum* • *He's had a hard life.*
3 needing a lot of effort: *hard work*
4 tough or not easy to deal with: *hard luck* • *They drive a hard bargain.*
ADVERB **harder, hardest 1** strongly or violently: *It was raining hard when we got there.* **2** with more effort: *You must work harder.*
• **hard of hearing** someone who is hard of hearing is nearly deaf

hardback NOUN **hardbacks** a book that has a stiff hard cover. Look up and compare **paperback**

hardboard NOUN thin strong board made from wood pulp that has been softened and pressed together

Aa
Bb
Cc
Dd
Ee
Ff
Gg
Hh
Ii
Jj
Kk
Ll
Mm
Nn
Oo
Pp
Qq
Rr
Ss
Tt
Uu
Vv
Ww
Xx
Yy
Zz

hard disk NOUN **hard disks** (*ICT*) a disk inside a computer where a lot of information is stored

harden VERB **hardens, hardening, hardened 1** to become firm or solid: *The molten lava hardens to form rock.* **2** to become tougher or less sympathetic: *His attitude had hardened and he wouldn't put up with bad behaviour any longer.*

hard-hearted ADJECTIVE tough and unsympathetic to other people's feelings or problems

hardline ADJECTIVE people with hardline attitudes or opinions stick to what they believe and refuse to change or compromise

hardly ADVERB **1** only just or almost not: *I hardly know him.* • *She'd hardly put the key in the door when down came the rain.* **2** hardly is used for emphasis to mean 'not at all': *She's hardly likely to want him at the party after the way he insulted her.*

hardness NOUN **hardnesses** the state of being hard or how hard something is in comparison to other things

hardship NOUN **hardships** something that is very difficult to cope with: *financial hardship*

hard shoulder NOUN the hard shoulder is the strip at either side of a motorway for use in an emergency, for example if your car has broken down

hard up ADJECTIVE poor: *He's too hard up to be able to afford the fees.*

hardware NOUN **1** hardware is tools and equipment used, for example, in the house and garden **2** (*ICT*) computer hardware is pieces of equipment like the central processing unit and disk drives. Look up and compare **software**

hardy ADJECTIVE **hardier, hardiest** hardy plants, animals or people are strong and tough and able to cope with difficult conditions

hare NOUN **hares** an animal similar to a rabbit, but larger and with longer back legs and bigger ears

hark VERB **harks, harking, harked** an old-fashioned word meaning

listen: *Hark, the herald angels sing.* • *Hark at him!*
• **hark back** to hark back to some event in the past is to talk about it

harm VERB **harms, harming, harmed** to harm someone or something is to hurt or damage them: *You might harm your eyes if you sit too close to the TV.* NOUN damage or injury: *No harm will come to you.* • *It would do no harm to ask.*

▶ **harmful** ADJECTIVE causing damage or injury: *protecting your skin from the sun's harmful rays*

▶ **harmless** ADJECTIVE not dangerous or not causing any damage or annoyance: *a harmless little insect*

harmonica NOUN **harmonicas** an instrument that you hold to your mouth and play by blowing and sucking air through it

harmonious ADJECTIVE **1** harmonious sound or music is pleasant to listen to **2** harmonious colours or designs go well together and don't clash **3** people who have a harmonious relationship cooperate with each other and don't have disagreements

▶ **harmoniously** ADVERB in a pleasant or peaceful way

harmonize or **harmonise** VERB **harmonizes, harmonizing, harmonized 1** (*music*) singers or musicians harmonize when they sing or play together using notes that combine pleasantly with the main tune **2** things harmonize when they fit or combine well together

harmony NOUN **harmonies 1** harmony is combining notes or colours in a way that sounds or looks pleasant **2** (*music*) a harmony is a musical part that combines pleasantly with the main melody **3** harmony is when people exist together without fighting or arguing: *living in harmony with our neighbours*

harp NOUN **harps** an instrument with strings stretched across an open triangular frame. A harp stands upright and is played by plucking the strings with your fingers
VERB **harps, harping, harped**

Aa
Bb
Cc
Dd
Ee
Ff
Gg
Hh
Ii
Jj
Kk
Ll
Mm
Nn
Oo
Pp
Qq
Rr
Ss
Tt
Uu
Vv
Ww
Xx
Yy
Zz

• **harp on** or **harp on about something** to harp on or harp on about something is to keep on talking about it in an annoying way

▶ **harpist** NOUN **harpists** someone who plays the harp

harpoon NOUN **harpoons** a spear with a rope attached at one end and used to kill fish and whales

harrowing ADJECTIVE very upsetting or disturbing: *a harrowing experience*

harry VERB **harries, harrying, harried** to harry someone is to harass or worry them

harsh ADJECTIVE **harsher, harshest 1** very uncomfortable: *a harsh climate* **2** unpleasantly strong or loud: *harsh light* • *the harsh cry of a raven* **3** cruel and unkind: *a harsh punishment*

▶ **harshly** ADVERB roughly, severely or cruelly

▶ **harshness** NOUN being harsh

harvest NOUN **harvests 1** harvest is the time of year when ripe crops are gathered **2** a harvest is the amount of a crop that is gathered: *This year's coffee harvest was very poor.*

VERB **harvests, harvesting, harvested** to gather a crop when it is ripe: *harvesting grapes*

▶ **harvester** NOUN **harvesters 1** a piece of machinery that gathers in a crop **2** a worker who helps to pick, cut or gather in a crop

has VERB **1** the form of the verb **have** that is used with *he, she* and *it* to make a present tense: *He has large and dreamy eyes.* **2 has** is also used as a helping verb along with a main verb: *He has gone home.*

hash NOUN **hashes 1** a dish made with cooked meat and vegetables that have been chopped up and recooked **2** to make a hash of something is to make a mess of it

hasn't a short way to say and write **has not**: *Hasn't it been a lovely day?*

hassle VERB **hassles, hassling, hassled** to hassle someone is to put pressure on them or cause them problems

NOUN **hassles** hassle, or a hassle, is something that causes you problems or inconvenience

haste NOUN **1** haste is hurry or speed: *In her haste she forgot to lock the door.* **2** to make haste is to hurry

▶ **hasten** VERB **hastens, hastening, hastened 1** to hasten something is to make it happen faster or sooner **2** (*formal*) to hasten somewhere is to hurry there

▶ **hastily** ADVERB in a hurried way: *Hastily, he hid the sweets he had stolen.*

▶ **hasty** ADJECTIVE **hastier, hastiest** a hasty action is one that is done too quickly without enough thought

hat NOUN **hats** a covering for your head

hatch¹ VERB **hatches, hatching, hatched 1** baby birds and reptiles hatch when they break out of their eggs: *The eggs should hatch in six to eight days.* **2** to hatch a plot is to think of it and develop its details, especially in secret

hatch² NOUN **hatches** a door or covering over an opening in a floor, wall or ship's deck

hatchback NOUN **hatchbacks** a car with a sloping door at the back that opens upwards

hatchet NOUN **hatchets** a small axe

• **bury the hatchet** people who have been fighting or quarrelling bury the hatchet when they make up

hate VERB **hates, hating, hated** to hate something or someone is to dislike them very much: *He hates tidying his bedroom.*

NOUN **1** hate is very strong dislike: *Her eyes were full of hate and disappointment.* **2** your hates are the things that you dislike very much: *It's one of his pet hates.*

▶ **hatred** NOUN hatred is a very strong feeling of dislike

hateful ADJECTIVE very nasty or very bad: *a hateful thing to say*

hat-trick NOUN **hat-tricks 1** in games like football and hockey, a hat-trick is three goals scored by one player in a single match **2** in cricket, a bowler gets a hat-trick when they get three batsmen out with three balls bowled one after the other

haughty ADJECTIVE **haughtier, haughtiest** a haughty person is proud and thinks they are better or more important than other people

haul VERB **hauls, hauling, hauled** to haul something heavy is to pull it using a lot of effort: *He managed to haul himself up on to a narrow ledge.*

NOUN **hauls 1** a quantity of something, gathered or caught at one time: *a huge haul of cod and haddock* **2** a strong tug or pull: *Give the rope one more good haul.*

haulage NOUN the business of taking goods from one place to another by road or railway

haunch NOUN **haunches 1** your haunches are your bottom and the upper part of your thighs: *He squatted down on his haunches in the dust.* **2** a haunch of meat comes from the upper part of the animal's leg

haunt VERB **haunts, haunting, haunted 1** a ghost is believed to haunt a place when it is present there or appears there **2** someone haunts a place when they go there again and again: *He haunts the football ground, trying to get a glimpse of his heroes.* **3** a bad feeling or memory haunts you when you can't stop thinking about it

NOUN **haunts** a place where you go again and again: *The deer had vanished, gone to their secret haunts.*

▶ **haunted** ADJECTIVE a haunted place is somewhere where ghosts are believed to be

have VERB **has, having, had**

1 to have something is to own or possess it, or to include it: *I'll look at your essay when I have a free moment.* • *He has a limp.*

2 to have an illness is to suffer from it: *Carol's had chickenpox.* • *Mum has a terrible headache.*

3 to have something is to get or receive it: *I had a phone call from him last week.*

4 to have a baby is to give birth to it: *The cat had kittens.*

5 to have food or drink is to eat it or drink it: *I have lunch at school.*

6 you have something done when you get it done: *He's having a tooth out.*

7 if you have to do something, you must do it: *You have to tell me what was said.*

8 have is also used as a helping verb along with a main verb: *I have left some money for you.*

• **have someone on** to tell someone something is true when it isn't

• **have it out** to have it out with someone is to talk to them to try to settle a disagreement

haven NOUN **havens** a place that people go to for safety or peace

haven't a short way to say and write **have not**: *I haven't seen the film.*

haversack NOUN **haversacks** a canvas bag with shoulder straps that you use to carry things on your back when you are walking

havoc NOUN to cause havoc is to cause damage, destruction or confusion

hawk NOUN **hawks** a bird of prey with a short, strong hooked beak and very good eyesight

hawthorn NOUN **hawthorns** a small tree with thorny stems, white flowers and small red berries

hay NOUN grass that has been cut and dried and is used to feed animals

hay fever NOUN an allergy to pollen that some people have, which causes them to sneeze and have watery or itchy eyes and a runny nose

haystack NOUN **haystacks** a large pile of cut hay stacked up in layers and stored until it is needed

haywire ADJECTIVE if something goes haywire it goes out of control

hazard NOUN **hazards** a risk of harm or danger

VERB **hazards, hazarding, hazarded 1** to hazard something is to risk it **2** to hazard a guess is to make a guess that is quite likely to be wrong

▶ **hazardous** ADJECTIVE dangerous or risky

haze NOUN **hazes** thin mist: *a heat haze*

Aa
Bb
Cc
Dd
Ee
Ff
Gg
Hh
Ii
Jj
Kk
Ll
Mm
Nn
Oo
Pp
Qq
Rr
Ss
Tt
Uu
Vv
Ww
Xx
Yy
Zz

hazel NOUN **hazels** 1 a small tree on which round reddish-brown nuts grow 2 hazel eyes are a greenish-brown colour

hazelnut NOUN **hazelnuts** an edible nut that grows on a hazel tree

hazy ADJECTIVE **hazier, haziest** 1 with a thin mist: *hazy sunshine* 2 vague and unclear: *I only have hazy memories of my grandparents.*

he PRONOUN a word you use to talk about a man, boy, or male animal that has already been mentioned or pointed out: *I like Tommy. He is very friendly.*

head NOUN **heads**

1 the part of a human's or animal's body that contains the brain, eyes and mouth

2 your mind or intelligence: *The idea just popped into my head.*

3 the head of a group or organization is the person in charge

4 the top of something: *the title at the head of the page*

VERB **heads, heading, headed** 1 if you head a group of people, you lead them or are in charge of them 2 to head somewhere is to go towards that place 3 to head a ball is to hit it with your head

• **head someone** *or* **something off** to get in front of someone or something to stop them going any further

headache NOUN **headaches** a pain in the head

headboard NOUN **headboards** the upright part at the top of a bed

headdress NOUN **headdresses** a decoration worn on the head, for example as part of a costume

header NOUN **headers** a header is when you hit the ball in football with your head

headfirst ADVERB you jump or fall headfirst when you jump or fall forwards with your head in front of the rest of your body

heading NOUN **headings** a title at the top or beginning of a page or a section of writing

headland NOUN **headlands** a piece of land that sticks out into the sea

headlight NOUN **headlights** one of a pair of lights at the front of a car, van or lorry

headline NOUN **headlines** a line printed in large letters at the top of a newspaper page or article

headlong ADVERB AND ADJECTIVE 1 headfirst or in an uncontrolled way: *He dived headlong into the muddy stream.* • *a headlong dash towards the finish line* 2 without giving yourself enough time to think: *They were all rushing headlong into silly actions.*

headmaster NOUN **headmasters** a male teacher in charge of a school

headmistress NOUN **headmistresses** a female teacher in charge of a school

head-on ADJECTIVE AND ADVERB 1 when the front part of one car or lorry hits the front part of another car or lorry: *The other car hit us head-on.* • *a head-on collision* 2 directly, without trying to avoid what may be unpleasant: *tackling their problems head-on*

headphones PLURAL NOUN a device for listening to music or radio broadcasts with two receivers that you wear over your ears

headquarters PLURAL NOUN 1 a place from which an army, navy, air force or police force is controlled 2 the central office from which a large business or organization is controlled

heads PLURAL NOUN the side of a coin that has a person's head stamped on it: *Call heads or tails when I toss the coin.*

headstart NOUN if you get a headstart, you get an advantage by starting or beginning before other people

headstrong ADJECTIVE a headstrong person is determined to do what they want to do and won't take advice from other people

head teacher NOUN **head teachers** a teacher in charge of a school

heal VERB **heals, healing, healed** 1 a wound or injury heals when it gets better 2 if you are sick and someone heals you, they make you better or healthy again

▶ **healer** NOUN **healers** someone or

Aa
Bb
Cc
Dd
Ee
Ff
Gg
Hh
Ii
Jj
Kk
Ll
Mm
Nn
Oo
Pp
Qq
Rr
Ss
Tt
Uu
Vv
Ww
Xx
Yy
Zz

something that heals people who are sick

health NOUN **1** your health is the condition of your body or mind, and how well you are: *His health is not good.* • *mental health* **2** the health of something is how good or bad its condition is: *the health of the economy*

health centre NOUN **health centres** a place where doctors and nurses see people from a particular area and hold clinics

healthy ADJECTIVE **healthier, healthiest 1** fit and well: *a healthy baby* **2** good for you: *lots of healthy exercise* **3** in a good state or condition: *a healthy bank balance*

▸ **healthily** ADVERB in a way that is good for you: *You can live healthily by eating well and getting plenty of sleep.*

▸ **healthiness** NOUN being healthy

heap NOUN **heaps 1** an untidy pile of things: *a heap of dirty clothes* **2** a lot or lots: *There's heaps of time before the match starts.*

VERB **heaps, heaping, heaped** to heap things is to pile them up: *His plate was heaped with food.*

hear VERB **hears, hearing, heard**

1 to hear sounds is to be aware of them through your ears: *Can you hear that clicking noise?*

2 to hear news is to be told it: *I heard that she had got into the next round of the competition.*

3 to have heard of someone or something is to know that they exist: *I'd never heard of him before.*

4 you hear from someone when they get in touch with you: *We haven't heard from him for over a month.*

▸ **hearer** NOUN **hearers** your hearers are the people who are listening to you when you are speaking

▸ **hearing** NOUN **hearings 1** your hearing is your ability to hear **2** if something is said in your hearing, you can hear it **3** a hearing is a court trial

hearing aid NOUN **hearing aids** a small device that is fitted into or at the back of the ear to help a deaf person hear

hearsay NOUN hearsay is things other people have told you, which may or may not be true: *Someone told me Jason had run away but I think it's only hearsay.*

hearse NOUN **hearses** a specially designed car or carriage used to carry the coffin at a funeral

heart NOUN **hearts**

1 your heart is the hollow muscular organ inside your chest that pumps blood around your body

2 someone's heart is their feelings and emotions: *She captured the hearts of the audience.* • *He has a kind heart.*

3 a heart is a shape, ♥, that represents the human heart and human love

4 hearts is one of the four suits of playing cards, which have the symbol ♥ printed on them

5 the heart of something is its central or most important part: *getting to the heart of the problem*

• **by heart** if you learn something by heart, you learn it so that you can repeat it exactly

heart attack NOUN **heart attacks** if someone has a heart attack, their heart suddenly stops working properly and they feel very ill and may die

heartbeat NOUN **heartbeats** the regular sound that the heart makes as it pumps blood round the body

hearten VERB **heartens, heartening, heartened** something heartens you when it makes you feel happier or more hopeful

heartfelt ADJECTIVE heartfelt feelings or words are completely sincere: *my heartfelt thanks*

hearth NOUN **hearths** the floor of a fireplace or the area surrounding it

heartless ADJECTIVE unkind and cruel

hearty ADJECTIVE **heartier, heartiest 1** strong and healthy **2** cheerful, loud and friendly: *a hearty welcome* **3** a hearty meal is a large and satisfying meal

▸ **heartily** ADVERB **1** loudly and enthusiastically: *They laughed heartily at all his jokes.* **2** sincerely or completely: *I'm heartily sick of their complaints.*

heat NOUN **heats 1** heat is high

temperature or the warmth that something hot gives out: *the heat from the sun* **2** heat is anger or strong feelings: *She tried to calm them down and take the heat out of the situation.* **3** a heat is a round in a competition or race: *Ian won his heat and went through to the semi-final.*

VERB **heats, heating, heated 1** to heat something, or heat it up, is to raise its temperature or make it warm or hot **2** if something heats up, it becomes warmer or hotter

▸ **heated** ADJECTIVE full of anger or strong feelings: *a heated discussion*

▸ **heater** NOUN **heaters** a device used to heat a room or the inside of a car

▸ **heating** NOUN the system or machinery used to heat a building

heath NOUN **heaths** a high wild area of land covered with grass and low bushes

heathen NOUN **heathens** someone who doesn't believe in God and is not a member of one of the main world religions

heather NOUN **heathers** a small shrub that grows close to the ground on hills and moors and has tiny purple or white flowers

heatwave NOUN **heatwaves** a spell of unusually hot weather, usually lasting for several days or weeks

heave VERB **heaves, heaving, heaved 1** to heave something heavy is to lift, pull, push or throw it using a lot of effort: *The men heaved the bags of coal on to their shoulders.* • *Both teams heaved at the rope.* **2** you heave a sigh when you sigh deeply making your shoulders and chest rise up

heaven NOUN **heavens 1** the place where good people are supposed to go when they die and where God and the angels are believed to live **2** the sky is sometimes called the heavens: *The heavens opened and the rain came lashing down.* **3** a very pleasant place or thing: *This chocolate cake is just heaven.*

▸ **heavenly** ADJECTIVE **1** to do with heaven: *the heavenly choir of angels* **2**

very pleasant: *It's heavenly being able to relax in the sunshine.*

heavy ADJECTIVE **heavier, heaviest 1** something that is heavy weighs a lot **2** the amount that something weighs is how heavy it is **3** heavy rain or a heavy blow has a lot of force **4** a heavy smoker smokes a lot and a heavy drinker drinks a lot of alcohol **5** if your heart is heavy, you feel sad

▸ **heavily** ADVERB with a lot of force or weight

▸ **heaviness** NOUN the state of being heavy or the weight of something

Hebrew NOUN Hebrew is the ancient language of the Jewish race, which was revived and is used in a modern form in Israel

ADJECTIVE in, or to do with, ancient or modern Hebrew

heckle VERB **heckles, heckling, heckled** to interrupt a speaker or performer with loud comments or questions

▸ **heckler** NOUN **hecklers** a member of an audience who heckles a speaker or performer

hectare NOUN **hectares** a unit of area equal to 10,000 square metres or approximately 2½ acres

hectic ADJECTIVE full of very busy activity: *Today has been absolutely hectic.*

he'd a short way to say and write **he had** or **he would**: *He'd never been there before.* • *He'd never have guessed.*

hedge NOUN **hedges** a line of bushes or small trees that are growing close together and form a boundary

VERB **hedges, hedging, hedged** to avoid answering a question

hedgehog NOUN **hedgehogs** a small wild mammal with prickles all over its body

hedgerow NOUN **hedgerows** a line of shrubs and small trees growing close together along the side of a road or field

Aa
Bb
Cc
Dd
Ee
Ff
Gg
Hh
Ii
Jj
Kk
Ll
Mm
Nn
Oo
Pp
Qq
Rr
Ss
Tt
Uu
Vv
Ww
Xx
Yy
Zz

heed VERB **heeds, heeding, heeded** to heed someone's warning or advice is to take notice of it and do as they suggest NOUN if you pay heed to a warning or some advice, or take heed of it, you pay attention to it

▸ **heedless** ADJECTIVE if you are heedless of something you take no notice of it

heel NOUN **heels 1** your heels are the back parts of your feet **2** the heel of a shoe or boot is the part under the back of your foot **3** the heel of a sock or stocking is the part that covers your heel

• **take to your heels** if you take to your heels, you start running

hefty ADJECTIVE **heftier, heftiest 1** big and heavy: *a hefty wrestler* **2** done with a lot of power: *a hefty blow* **3** a hefty amount of money is a large amount

Hegira (pronounced **hej**-i-ra or hi-**jie**-ra) NOUN the beginning of the Islamic era, which dates from the migration of the prophet Mohammed from Mecca to Medina in 622AD

height NOUN **heights 1** how tall or high someone or something is: *What height is Mount Everest?* **2** the height of something is the time or level when it is at its greatest or strongest: *It is the height of stupidity to throw a lighted firework.* **3** a high place: *looking down from the heights*

▸ **heighten** VERB **heightens, heightening, heightened 1** to heighten something is to make it higher: *We'll have to heighten the seat of the bike a little.* **2** something heightens, or is heightened, when it increases or is increased: *The music heightens the tension of the film.*

heir (pronounced **air**) NOUN **heirs** someone who is entitled by law to get money, property or a title from someone when they die

heiress (pronounced **ay**-res) NOUN **heiresses** a girl or woman who receives property or money from someone who has died

heirloom (pronounced **air**-loom) NOUN **heirlooms** something valuable that has been handed down in a family from parents or grandparents to their children or grandchildren

held VERB a way of changing the verb **hold** to make a past tense. It can be used with or without a helping verb: *I held my breath and waited.* • *He had held the job for ten years.*

helicopter NOUN **helicopters** a flying machine without wings that is lifted into the air by large propellers on top which spin round very fast

helium NOUN a very light gas that is sometimes used in balloons to make them stay in the air

helix NOUN **helixes** or **helices** a screw-shaped coil or spiral

hell NOUN **1** hell is the place where people who have sinned are supposed to go when they die and where the Devil and demons are believed to live **2** an evil or very unpleasant place

he'll a short way to say and write **he will** or **he shall**: *He'll be here soon.*

hello INTERJECTION you say 'hello' as a greeting when you meet someone or begin talking to them

NOUN **hellos** or **helloes** a greeting: *We said our hellos.*

helm NOUN **helms** the wheel or handle used to steer a ship or boat

helmet NOUN **helmets** a hard hat worn to protect the head, for example by cyclists or firefighters

help VERB **helps, helping, helped 1** to do something useful for someone: *My Mum helped me with my homework.* • *a rhyme that helps you to remember the colours of the rainbow* **2** if you cannot help something, you cannot stop yourself from doing it, or you cannot stop it happening

• **help yourself** if you help yourself, you take something without waiting for someone to give it to you

NOUN **helps 1** you give someone help when you do something useful for them: *He gave some help with the gardening.* **2** a help is someone or something that helps: *Thanks for the tip. It was a great help.*

INTERJECTION people shout 'Help!' when

they are in danger and want someone to come and help them

▶ **helper** NOUN **helpers** someone who helps another person: *one of Santa's helpers*

helpful ADJECTIVE willing to help, or giving help

▶ **helpfully** ADVERB in a way that gives help: *The woman helpfully showed us the way to the car park.*

helping NOUN **helpings** a portion or serving of food: *He always has second helpings.*

helping verb NOUN **helping verbs** (*grammar*) a short verb like *should*, *will* or *can* that you use with a main verb to make slight differences of meaning, for example a past tense in *Have you finished?* The helping verbs are also called **auxiliary verbs**

helpless ADJECTIVE not able to protect yourself or look after yourself

▶ **helplessly** ADVERB in a helpless way: *I stared helplessly as the dog ran towards me.*

helter-skelter NOUN **helter-skelters** a tall spiral slide

ADVERB to go helter-skelter is to go very fast in an uncontrolled way

hem NOUN **hems** the edge of a piece of material that has been folded over and sewn down

VERB **hems, hemming, hemmed** to hem a piece of cloth is to sew a hem on its edge

• **hem someone in** if people or things hem you in, they surround you and stop you moving in any direction

hemisphere NOUN **hemispheres 1** a shape, which is half a sphere or ball **2** half the Earth, either divided around the equator or from the north to the south pole: *the northern hemisphere*

hemp NOUN a plant grown for the fibres it produces, which are used to make ropes and rough cloth for sacks

hen NOUN **hens** a female chicken

hence ADVERB **1** from this time or from this place: *five years hence* **2** for this reason: *He's just got some bad news, hence his glum expression.*

heptagon NOUN **heptagons** (*maths*) a flat shape with seven straight sides

▶ **heptagonal** ADJECTIVE having seven sides

her PRONOUN a word you use to talk about a woman, a girl, a female animal or a vehicle or ship that has already been mentioned or pointed out: *I'm looking for Mrs Peters. Have you seen her?*

ADJECTIVE belonging to her: *Her hair is blonde.*

herald NOUN **heralds 1** in the past, someone who made important announcements or carried important messages for a king or queen **2** something that is a sign of something that is going to happen or come soon: *snowdrops, the herald of spring*

VERB **heralds, heralding, heralded** to herald something is to announce it or show that it will come soon

heraldry NOUN heraldry is the study of coats of arms and family crests

herb NOUN **herbs** a plant, such as parsley, rosemary or thyme, that is used for making medicines or for flavouring food: *herbs and spices*

▶ **herbal** ADJECTIVE using herbs or to do with herbs: *herbal medicines* • *herbal tea*

herbivore NOUN **herbivores** an animal that eats only grass and plants. Look up and compare **carnivore** and **omnivore**

▶ **herbivorous** ADJECTIVE eating only grass and plants: *Deer are herbivorous.*

herd NOUN **herds** a large group of animals of one type: *a herd of buffalo*

VERB **herds, herding, herded** to herd animals or people is to gather them together and make them go somewhere in a group: *We were herded into a small room at the back.*

here ADVERB at, in or to this place or time: *I like it here.*

• **here and there** things that are here and there are in several different places

INTERJECTION **1** people say 'Here!' to express surprise or anger at something someone is doing: *Here! You aren't supposed to do that!* **2** you say 'here' when you are offering something to someone: *Here, take this one. It's better than the one you have.*

hereafter ADVERB (*formal*) after this or from this time on

NOUN the hereafter is life after death

hereby ADVERB (*formal*) hereby is used in a statement to announce what you are going to do and how it will be done: *We hereby pledge our loyalty to the king.*

hereditary ADJECTIVE a hereditary disease or quality is passed down from one generation to the next through the genes

heredity NOUN the passing on of qualities and characteristics from parents to children through the genes

heritage NOUN things that are passed down from previous generations, or things that have been, or should be, preserved because they provide a link with the past

hermit NOUN **hermits** someone who lives all alone and doesn't have contact with other people

▶ **hermitage** NOUN **hermitages** a place where a hermit lives or a place where someone can go to get away from the world for a while

hero NOUN **heroes** 1 a man or boy who many people admire for his courage and bravery 2 the most important male character in a story or film

▶ **heroic** ADJECTIVE 1 very brave 2 to do with heroes or heroines

▶ **heroine** NOUN **heroines** 1 a woman or girl who many people admire for her courage and bravery 2 the most important female character in a story or film

▶ **heroism** NOUN great bravery and courage that many people admire

heron NOUN **herons** a bird with long legs and a long neck that lives near water and catches fish in its long sharp beak

herring NOUN **herring** *or* **herrings** an edible sea fish with silvery-grey scales that swims in large groups called shoals

hers PRONOUN a word you use to talk about something belonging to a woman, girl, female animal or a vehicle or ship that has already been mentioned or pointed out: *I gave Sandra my phone number and she gave me hers.*

✦ Remember there is no apostrophe between the *r* and the *s* in **hers**.

herself PRONOUN 1 you use **herself** after a verb or preposition when the woman or girl who performs the action is affected by it: *Did Barbara hurt herself when she fell down?* 2 **herself** is also used to show that a girl or woman does something without any help from other people: *She always answers every fan letter herself.* 3 you can use **herself** to show more clearly who you mean: *I wanted to ask Moira herself, but I couldn't get in touch with her.*

he's a short way to say and write **he is** or **he has**: *He's my brother.* • *He's done all the work.*

hesitant ADJECTIVE if someone is hesitant, they aren't very willing to do something or they keep pausing while they are doing it: *He talked in a shy hesitant way.*

hesitate VERB **hesitates, hesitating, hesitated** 1 to pause for a short time while you are doing something 2 to hesitate to do something is to be slightly unwilling to do it

▶ **hesitation** NOUN **hesitations** 1 hesitating: *He did it without hesitation.* 2 a pause: *After a slight hesitation, he said he would do it.*

hew VERB **hews, hewing, hewed, hewn** to hew something hard such as wood or rock is to cut it with a large heavy tool

hexagon NOUN **hexagons** (*maths*) a flat shape with six straight sides

▶ **hexagonal** ADJECTIVE having six sides

hey INTERJECTION an exclamation used to get someone's attention: *Hey, stop that!*

hi INTERJECTION a word you use to greet someone: *Hi, how are you?*

hibernate VERB **hibernates, hibernating, hibernated** an animal that hibernates goes into a kind of sleep

Aa
Bb
Cc
Dd
Ee
Ff
Gg
Hh
Ii
Jj
Kk
Ll
Mm
Nn
Oo
Pp
Qq
Rr
Ss
Tt
Uu
Vv
Ww
Xx
Yy
Zz

for long periods during the winter when food is difficult to find

▶ **hibernation** NOUN hibernating

hiccup NOUN **hiccups 1** if you have hiccups, you make loud gasping noises in your throat **2** a hiccup is a small problem that causes a delay

VERB **hiccups, hiccupping, hiccupped** to hiccup is to make loud gasping noises that you can't control

hide¹ VERB **hides, hiding, hid, hidden** to put or keep someone or something in a place where they can't be seen or found easily: *You hide, and I'll come and look for you.* • *He hid behind a tree.*

hide² NOUN **hides** the skin of an animal

hide-and-seek NOUN a game in which one person hides and the other players look for him or her

hideous ADJECTIVE ugly or horrible to look at

hideout NOUN **hideouts** a hiding place: *The gang had a secret hideout in the mountains.*

hiding¹ NOUN if someone who is being hunted or searched for goes into hiding, they hide themselves in a secret place

hiding² NOUN **hidings** a beating or defeat: *The other team was far better and gave us a terrible hiding.*

hieroglyphics PLURAL NOUN a form of writing in which little pictures are used instead of letters and words. Hieroglyphics were used in ancient Egypt

hi-fi NOUN **hi-fis** a hi-fi is a piece of equipment for playing or recording high-quality sound

ADJECTIVE short for **high fidelity**, which means reproducing very high-quality sound

high ADJECTIVE AND ADVERB **higher, highest**

1 extending far upwards, or a long way off the ground: *a high building* • *diving from the highest board*

2 having a certain height: *10 metres high* • *How high is Snowdon?*

3 near the top of a scale of measurement or list: *high marks* • *a high temperature*

4 a high sound or musical note is near the top of the range of pitch or musical notes: *high voices of the children* • *the highest note you can sing*

5 great or large in amount or importance: *a high number*

ADVERB **higher, highest 1** far above in the air or a long way off the ground: *satellites orbiting high above the Earth.* **2** far up a scale or ranking: *The temperature rose higher and higher.*

NOUN **highs 1** a peak or maximum: *Confidence was at an all-time high.* **2** if someone is on a high, they are feeling very excited and pleased

high chair NOUN **high chairs** a chair with long legs for a baby or young child to sit in while they are eating

high jump NOUN the high jump is an athletic competition in which competitors try to jump over a horizontal pole supported on upright stands

• **for the high jump** if someone is for the high jump, they are going to get into serious trouble

highland ADJECTIVE to do with the highlands: *a highland cottage*

▶ **highlands** PLURAL NOUN the highlands are areas of a country that are high and have a lot of hills or mountains: *the Scottish Highlands*

highlight VERB **highlights, highlighting, highlighted** to highlight something is to make it stand out or draw attention to it

NOUN **highlights 1** the highlight is the best part of an event or period of time: *His singing was the highlight of the concert.* **2** highlights in your hair are streaks or parts that are a lighter colour than the rest of your hair

▶ **highlighter** NOUN **highlighters** a pen with a special type of brightly coloured ink which you use to mark writing or printing to make it stand out and which allows you to see what is written or printed underneath

highly ADVERB **1** very: *a highly infectious disease* **2** to or at a high level: *highly paid computer experts* **3** if you

Aa Bb Cc Dd Ee Ff Gg Hh Ii Jj Kk Ll Mm Nn Oo Pp Qq Rr Ss Tt Uu Vv Ww Xx Yy Zz

think highly of someone or something, you think they are excellent

highly strung ADJECTIVE very nervous and easily upset

Highness NOUN **Highnesses** a title you use when you are speaking about or to a prince or princess

high-rise ADJECTIVE high-rise buildings are modern buildings which are very tall

NOUN **high-rises** a very tall building, especially a tall block of flats

high school NOUN **high schools** a secondary school

highway NOUN **highways** 1 in Britain, the highway is the public road or the main road 2 in the United States and other countries, a highway is a road that links towns and cities

highwayman NOUN **highwaymen** in historical times, a robber who attacked people travelling on the road

hijack VERB **hijacks, hijacking, hijacked** people hijack an aeroplane or other vehicle when they take control of it by force and make it go where they want it to go

▶ **hijacker** NOUN **hijackers** someone who hijacks an aeroplane or other vehicle

hike VERB **hikes, hiking, hiked** 1 to go for long walks in the countryside 2 to hike something such as a price or amount, or hike it up, is to increase it

NOUN **hikes** a long walk in the countryside

▶ **hiker** NOUN **hikers** someone who goes for long walks in the countryside

▶ **hiking** NOUN the pastime of taking long walks in the countryside

hilarious ADJECTIVE very funny

▶ **hilarity** NOUN loud laughter: *His antics caused much hilarity.*

hill NOUN **hills** 1 a high area of land, smaller than a mountain 2 a mound or heap: *a molehill*

• **over the hill** a person who is over the hill is old

▶ **hilly** ADJECTIVE **hillier, hilliest** a hilly area has lots of hills

hilt NOUN **hilts** the handle of a sword or dagger

him PRONOUN a word you use to talk about a man, boy or male animal that has already been mentioned or pointed out: *I'm looking for Mr Peters. Have you seen him anywhere?*

✦Try not to confuse the spellings of **him** and **hymn**.
A **hymn** is a song of praise.

himself PRONOUN 1 you use **himself** after a verb or preposition when the man or boy who performs the action is affected by it: *He poked himself in the eye by mistake.* 2 **himself** is also used to show that a boy or man does something without any help from other people: *He can tie his shoelaces himself.* 3 you can use **himself** to show more clearly who you mean: *I was surprised when Mr Blair himself answered the telephone.*

hind ADJECTIVE an animal's hind parts are the back parts of its body

hinder VERB **hinders, hindering, hindered** to hinder someone or something is to delay them or stop them making progress

▶ **hindrance** NOUN **hindrances** something that stops you making progress

hindsight NOUN knowledge you have after some event, when you know how it has turned out and therefore how it could be done better

Hindu NOUN **Hindus** a person whose religion is Hinduism

ADJECTIVE to do with Hinduism: *The main Hindu gods are Brahma, Vishnu and Shiva.*

▶ **Hinduism** NOUN a religion of India and parts of South East Asia, which teaches that by a cycle of birth and rebirth, life continues forever or until the soul can be released from the cycle

hinge NOUN **hinges** a piece of metal or plastic attaching a door to its frame, so that it can be opened and closed

VERB **hinges, hinging, hinged**

• **hinge on something** if one thing hinges on another thing, it depends on it

hint NOUN **hints** 1 something that is said in a roundabout way without making the

meaning absolutely clear: *She gave me a hint that something exciting was about to happen.* **2** a helpful piece of advice: *Can you give me any hints on the best way of studying for an exam?* **3** a small amount of something: *fizzy water with a hint of lemon*
VERB **hints, hinting, hinted** to say something in a way that suggests something is true but does not say it directly: *Laura hinted that she might be going to get engaged.*

hip NOUN **hips** your hips are the parts at each side of your body, between your waist and the tops of your legs

hippo NOUN **hippos** a hippopotamus

hippopotamus NOUN **hippopotamuses** *or* **hippopotami** a large African animal with a heavy body, a large head, small rounded ears and thick legs. Hippopotamuses live near or in rivers

✦ This word comes from Greek words that mean *river horse*.

hire VERB **hires, hiring, hired 1** you hire something when you pay to use it for a certain period of time and then return it: *On holiday, we hired bikes and cycled for miles.* **2** to hire someone is to pay them to do work
NOUN
• **for hire** something is for hire when you can hire it

his PRONOUN a word you use to talk about something belonging to a man, boy or male animal that has already been mentioned or pointed out: *I didn't have an umbrella so Grandad lent me his.*
ADJECTIVE belonging to him: *He has left his coat behind.* • *The peacock spread his magnificent tail.*

hiss VERB **hisses, hissing, hissed 1** to make a noise like a long 's' sound: *The snake hissed.* **2** if someone hisses, they say something through their teeth without moving their lips: *'Quiet, everyone,' he hissed, crouching down.*
NOUN **hisses** a sound like that made by a snake

historian NOUN **historians** someone who studies history

historic ADJECTIVE important and likely to be remembered for a long time
▶ **historical** ADJECTIVE to do with history

history NOUN **histories 1** history is all the things that happened in the past, or the study of things that happened in the past: *local history* • *My brother is doing history at university.* **2** the history of something is where it came from and what has happened to it before now: *What's the history of this old toy?* **3** a person's history is their past life

hit VERB **hits, hitting, hit 1** to strike someone or something with a blow: *The lorry hit the car head-on.* **2** an idea or feeling hits you when you realize it or feel it: *It suddenly hit me that I was quite alone.*
• **hit it off** if two people hit it off, they get on well together
• **hit on something** to suddenly have a good idea: *By sheer accident, he'd hit on the perfect solution to the problem.*
NOUN **hits 1** a blow or stroke: *That was a great hit by the golfer.* **2** a shot that strikes a target **3** a success with the public: *The show was an instant hit.*
ADJECTIVE successful: *a hit song*

hitch NOUN **hitches** a problem that holds you up
VERB **hitches, hitching, hitched 1** to hitch one thing to another thing is to fasten them together: *He hitched the caravan to the back of the car.* **2** to hitch a lift in someone's car is to signal to the driver to stop and give you a lift to the place where you want to go
• **hitch something up** to hitch up a piece of your clothing is to pull it up: *She hitched up her skirt and climbed over the wall.*

hitchhike VERB **hitchhikes, hitchhiking, hitchhiked** to travel around by getting lifts in other people's cars
▶ **hitchhiker** NOUN **hitchhikers** someone who hitchhikes

Aa
Bb
Cc
Dd
Ee
Ff
Gg
Hh
Ii
Jj
Kk
Ll
Mm
Nn
Oo
Pp
Qq
Rr
Ss
Tt
Uu
Vv
Ww
Xx
Yy
Zz

HIV ABBREVIATION short for **human immunodeficiency virus**, the virus that causes the disease AIDS

HMS ABBREVIATION short for **His** or **Her Majesty's Ship**, used in the names of British Royal Navy ships: *HMS Victory*

hoard VERB **hoards, hoarding, hoarded** to gather things and store them up in large quantities

NOUN **hoards** a large store of things that you have gathered and kept

▸ **hoarder** NOUN **hoarders** someone who likes saving and keeping lots of things

hoarding NOUN **hoardings** a large board in the street for displaying advertisements

hoarse ADJECTIVE **hoarser, hoarsest 1** a hoarse sound is rough and harsh **2** if you are hoarse your voice sounds rough because your throat is sore

hoax NOUN **hoaxes** a kind of trick in which someone says that something has happened or warns that it will happen, but they are not telling the truth

VERB **hoaxes, hoaxing, hoaxed** to trick people into thinking something has happened or will happen

hob NOUN **hobs** a set of rings or plates for cooking on, either on top of a cooker or as a separate unit

hobble VERB **hobbles, hobbling, hobbled** to walk with short unsteady steps because your feet or legs are injured or sore

hobby NOUN **hobbies** something you enjoy doing in your spare time

hobgoblin NOUN **hobgoblins** a type of wicked fairy

hockey NOUN **1** a game for two teams of eleven players, played with curved sticks and a ball on a field with a goal at either end **2** ice hockey

hoe NOUN **hoes** a garden tool with a metal blade at one end, used for digging out weeds

VERB **hoes, hoeing, hoed** to use a hoe to dig out weeds from the soil

hog VERB **hogs, hogging, hogged** to hog something is to keep it for yourself and not share it with others

NOUN **hogs** another word for a pig

• **go the whole hog** to leave nothing out, especially to do something in the most expensive or luxurious way possible

Hogmanay NOUN the name used in Scotland for December 31, or New Year's Eve, and the celebrations held that night

hoist VERB **hoists, hoisting, hoisted** to hoist something is to lift it up

NOUN **hoists** a machine for lifting things

hold VERB **holds, holding, held**
1 to hold something is to have it in your hand or hands: *He was holding a lovely little puppy.*
2 to keep something in a certain position for a while: *Raise your legs up and hold them there for a count of three.*
3 to contain something: *This rack holds my CDs.*
4 a container that holds a certain amount can have that amount put into it: *It can hold 50 CDs.*
5 a place or vehicle that holds a certain number of people has enough room or seats for that number: *The stadium holds about 70,000 spectators.*
6 to hold an event or celebration, such as a party, is to organize it: *Where are the next Olympic Games going to be held?*

• **hold on** to hold on is to wait for a while: *Can you hold on while I get my coat?*

• **hold someone** or **something up 1** to hold someone or something up is to delay them or it **2** a robber holds up a person or place when they threaten that person, or the people in that place, with a weapon

• **hold something up** if one thing holds up another thing, it supports it: *The walls hold the roof up.*

NOUN **holds 1** the place in a ship or plane where its cargo is stored **2** a grip: *Take a hold of the railing.*

holdall NOUN **holdalls** a large soft bag that you use to carry your clothes and belongings when you are travelling

holder NOUN **holders 1** a container for putting or keeping something in **2** the holder of a job, title, qualification or ticket is the person who has it

Hold-up NOUN **hold-ups 1** a robbery in which guns or other weapons are used to threaten the people being robbed **2** a delay

hole NOUN **holes 1** an opening, tear or gap in something: *a hole in my sock* **2** a pit or burrow in the ground: *They dug a deep hole to plant the tree in.* • *a rabbit hole*

▶ **holey** ADJECTIVE full of holes: *holey socks*

Holi NOUN a Hindu festival held near the end of February

holiday NOUN **holidays 1** a day or period of time when you don't have to work or go to school **2** a period of time spent in a place other than where you live, in order to relax or enjoy yourself

✦ This word comes from the Old English words **halig**, which means *holy*, and **dæg**, which means *day*. A holiday used to be a day when you did not work because it was a religious festival.

holiness NOUN **1** being holy **2** a title used for the Pope: *His Holiness, Pope Benedict*

hollow ADJECTIVE **hollower, hollowest** something hollow has an empty space inside it

holly NOUN **hollies** an evergreen tree with sharp spiky leaves and red berries

holocaust NOUN **holocausts 1** a huge fire or other disaster that causes death and destruction **2** (*history*) the Holocaust was the murder of millions of Jewish people by the Nazis in the 1930's and 1940's

hologram NOUN **holograms** a photograph made using laser beams that seems to be three-dimensional when it is looked at from certain angles

holster NOUN **holsters** a leather holder for a gun, usually worn on a belt

holy ADJECTIVE **holier, holiest 1** to do with God or religion **2** pure and good and having strong religious feelings

homage NOUN to pay homage to someone is to honour them and show or express your respect for them

home NOUN **homes 1** your home is the place where you live or where you were born and brought up **2** the home of something is the place where it began or was invented: *Mumbai, the home of the Indian film industry* **3** a home is a place where people or animals with no one to look after them live and are cared for

VERB **homes, homing, homed**
• **home in on something** to focus very closely on something or move directly towards it

home page NOUN **home pages** (*ICT*) on the Internet, the home page of a website is the page that you start from and which gives you links to all the other parts of the site

homesick ADJECTIVE when people who are away from their home feel homesick, they feel unhappy and want to be back at home

▶ **homesickness** NOUN the feeling of being unhappy because you are away from home

homestead NOUN **homesteads** a farmhouse, especially with land and smaller buildings around it

homewards or **homeward** ADVERB towards home: *trudging homewards after a hard day's work*

homework NOUN school work that you do while you are at home, especially in the evenings or at weekends

homing ADJECTIVE a homing pigeon can find its way back home from a very long way away

homonym NOUN **homonyms** (*grammar*) a word spelt the same way as another word, but with a different meaning and sometimes a different sound. For example, *calf* meaning 'a young cow' and *calf* meaning 'the muscle at the back of your leg' are homonyms

✦ Homonyms in this dictionary are given separate entries with a small number following the word, for example **calf¹** and **calf²**.

homophone NOUN **homophones** (*grammar*) a word that sounds the same

Aa Bb Cc Dd Ee Ff Gg Hh Ii Jj Kk Ll Mm Nn Oo Pp Qq Rr Ss Tt Uu Vv Ww Xx Yy Zz

as another word, but has a different meaning and sometimes a different spelling. For example, *bare* and *bear*, *sea* and *see*, and *hour* and *our* are homophones

honest ADJECTIVE an honest person tells the truth and does not cheat or steal

▸ **honestly** ADVERB **1** truthfully: *He told me honestly what he thought.* • *Honestly, I didn't realize the door should have been kept locked.* **2** without cheating, stealing or breaking the law **3** you say 'honestly' to show that you are annoyed or angry: *Honestly, it just makes me sick!*

▸ **honesty** NOUN being honest, truthful or trustworthy

honey NOUN a sweet thick liquid you can eat that bees make from the nectar of flowers and which they store in their hives

honeycomb NOUN **honeycombs** a structure made by bees with special wax, with lots of compartments or cells in which honey is stored

honeymoon NOUN **honeymoons** a holiday that a husband and wife take together immediately after they get married

honeysuckle NOUN a climbing plant with sweet-smelling yellow or pinkish flowers

honk NOUN **honks** a loud short sound made by a goose or a car horn

VERB **honks, honking, honked** to honk is to make this sound

honorary ADJECTIVE someone who is given an honorary title, or honorary membership of a club or organization, is given it as a mark of respect or honour

honour NOUN **honours**
1 a person's honesty and ability to be trusted: *You are all on your honour to behave like young gentlemen.*
2 the respect or good reputation someone or something deserves: *You'll be doing it for the honour of the school.*
3 something that makes you proud: *the honour of meeting the king*
4 an award given to someone for good work or long service

• **in honour of someone** or **something** to do something in honour of a person or event is to do it as a way of remembering that person or celebrating that event

VERB **honours, honouring, honoured**
1 to honour someone is to make them proud, pay them respect or give them an honour or award for good work **2** to honour a promise or agreement is to keep it

honourable ADJECTIVE trustworthy or deserving respect

▸ **honourably** ADVERB in a decent way that deserves respect: *He behaved very honourably by giving back the money he found.*

hood NOUN **hoods 1** a part attached to the back of a coat or jacket that you can pull up to cover the top and back of your head **2** a folding cover for something

hoodwink VERB **hoodwinks, hoodwinking, hoodwinked** to hoodwink someone is to deceive them

hoof NOUN **hooves** the hard part of the foot of some animals, such as horses, cows or sheep

hook NOUN **hooks 1** a bent piece of metal or plastic that you hang things on **2** a bent piece of metal with a very sharp end used for catching fish

• **off the hook** if you are off the hook, you do not have to do something difficult or unpleasant that you thought you would have to do

VERB **hooks, hooking, hooked 1** to catch a fish using a hook **2** to attach something using a hook or hooks

▸ **hooked** ADJECTIVE a hooked nose curves like a hook

hooligan NOUN **hooligans** someone who behaves in a wild or violent way

▸ **hooliganism** NOUN the behaviour of hooligans

hoop NOUN **hoops** a thin ring of metal or wood

hooray INTERJECTION an exclamation of approval or joy: *Hooray! No more school for three whole days!*

hoot NOUN **hoots 1** the sound made by

an owl or a car horn **2** a loud, sudden burst of laughter, or something that you find very amusing

VERB **hoots, hooting, hooted 1** to hoot is to make the sound of an owl or a car horn **2** to hoot with laughter is to laugh very loudly in sudden bursts

hoover NOUN **hoovers** (*trademark*) a machine for cleaning carpets and floors, which sucks dirt into a bag or container inside

VERB **hoovers, hoovering, hoovered** to clean a carpet or floor using a hoover or vacuum cleaner

hop¹ VERB **hops, hopping, hopped 1** to jump on one leg **2** to jump: *Hop in and I'll give you a lift to the station.*

NOUN **hops** a jump

hop² NOUN **hops** a climbing plant with fruits that are used to flavour beer

hope VERB **hopes, hoping, hoped** to hope for something is to think that it is possible or wish that it would happen

NOUN **hopes 1** hope is the feeling that what you want may happen: *We're not giving up hope, are we?* **2** your hopes are the things that you want to happen

hopeful ADJECTIVE having or feeling hope: *He's very hopeful that things will turn out well.*

▸ **hopefully** ADVERB with a feeling of hope, or in a way that shows you have hope

hopeless ADJECTIVE **1** without any hope of succeeding: *a hopeless dream* **2** very bad: *He was hopeless in goal.*

▸ **hopelessly** ADVERB in a hopeless way

hopscotch NOUN a game played on a grid of squares marked on the ground. You throw a stone and hop from one square to another and back again avoiding the square with the stone in it

horde NOUN **hordes** a large moving crowd

horizon NOUN **horizons** the horizon is the line where the land and sky seem to meet

▸ **horizontal** ADJECTIVE lying level or flat and not upright

hormone NOUN **hormones** a chemical made in your body that controls

things like your body's growth and development

horn NOUN **horns 1** horns are the hard pointed objects that grow out of some animals' heads, such as sheep, goats and cows **2** a device in a vehicle that makes a loud noise as a warning to others **3** a musical instrument that you blow into

▸ **horned** ADJECTIVE having horns

hornet NOUN **hornets** a type of large wasp

horoscope NOUN **horoscopes** your horoscope is information about what some people believe is going to happen to you in the future depending on your zodiac sign

horrendous ADJECTIVE terrible and shocking: *a horrendous crime*

horrible ADJECTIVE very nasty, ugly or unpleasant

▸ **horribly** ADVERB in a way that is very nasty

horrid ADJECTIVE nasty: *a horrid cold • a horrid man*

horrific ADJECTIVE awful, terrifying or upsetting: *a horrific car crash*

▸ **horrifically** ADVERB in an upsetting and awful way

horrify VERB **horrifies, horrifying, horrified** if something horrifies, you it shocks you or upsets you a lot

horror NOUN **horrors 1** horror is a feeling of great shock or alarm: *She threw up her hands in horror.* **2** you have a horror of something if you are very afraid of it: *She has a horror of any creeping, slimy thing.* **3** horrors are very frightening, shocking or terrible experiences: *the horrors of war*

ADJECTIVE meant to frighten you: *horror movies*

horse NOUN **horses** a large animal with long hair on its neck and tail. Horses are used by people to ride on and to pull carts or ploughs

horseback NOUN

• **on horseback** riding a horse

horse-chestnut NOUN **horse-chestnuts** a type of tree on which large reddish-brown nuts called conkers grow

Aa
Bb
Cc
Dd
Ee
Ff
Gg
Hh
Ii
Jj
Kk
Ll
Mm
Nn
Oo
Pp
Qq
Rr
Ss
Tt
Uu
Vv
Ww
Xx
Yy
Zz

horseplay NOUN rough games

horsepower NOUN a unit for measuring the power of engines, equal to about 746 watts

horseradish NOUN a type of plant whose root is used to make a very hot-tasting sauce

horseshoe NOUN **horseshoes** a curved piece of iron nailed on to a horse's hoof to stop the hoof from being worn down

horticulture NOUN the science or study of growing fruit, vegetables and flowers in gardens and greenhouses

hose NOUN **hoses** a tube made from bendy material used for carrying liquids and gases

hosiery NOUN hosiery is socks and stockings

hospice NOUN **hospices** a special type of hospital where sick people who can't be cured are cared for

hospitable ADJECTIVE welcoming to guests and strangers

hospital NOUN **hospitals** a building where people who are sick or have been injured can go to be treated

✦This word comes from the Latin word **hospes**, which means *guest*. A hospital used to be a place where guests could stay.

hospitality NOUN hospitality is being welcoming and friendly to people, giving them food, entertainment or accommodation

host¹ NOUN **hosts**
1 the person who has invited people to a meal, party or to stay at his or her house
2 a country, city or organization that arranges and holds an event
3 the host of a radio or TV show is the person who introduces it and talks to guests
4 (*science*) a parasite's host is the plant or animal it lives or feeds on

host² NOUN a host of things is a very large number of them

hostage NOUN **hostages** someone who is held prisoner until their captors get what they want

hostel NOUN **hostels** a building with rooms that students or travellers can stay in

hostess NOUN **hostesses** a female host

hostile ADJECTIVE **1** unfriendly or showing strong dislike **2** hostile forces in a war are enemy forces
▸ **hostility** NOUN unfriendliness or strong dislike

hot ADJECTIVE **hotter, hottest 1** feeling very warm: *Don't touch the oven. It's very hot.* **2** spicy: *hot curries*

hotdog NOUN **hotdogs** a hot sausage served in a long thin roll

hotel NOUN **hotels** a building with rooms that people pay to stay in when they are away from home

hotheaded ADJECTIVE someone who is hotheaded is quick to get angry, or is too quick to act

hothouse NOUN **hothouses** a heated greenhouse for growing plants that come from hot climates

hotline NOUN **hotlines** a direct telephone line by which people can get or give information quickly in an emergency

hotly ADVERB to discuss, argue or deny something hotly is to do it in an angry or lively way

hound NOUN **hounds** a type of dog used for hunting
VERB **hounds, hounding, hounded** to hound someone is to keep bothering or annoying them for a long time

hour NOUN **hours** a period of time that lasts 60 minutes. There are 24 hours in one day

hourglass NOUN **hourglasses** an instrument used to measure time with two glass containers joined by a thin glass tube through which sand trickles slowly

hourly ADJECTIVE happening once every hour, or calculated by the hour: *an hourly service • an hourly rate of pay*
ADVERB **1** happening once every hour: *Buses to London leave hourly.* **2** if you are paid hourly, you earn a certain

amount of money for each hour that you work

house NOUN (pronounced **hows**) **houses** **1** a building in which people, especially one family, live **2** the part of a theatre or cinema where the audience sits **3** one of the groups into which the pupils of a school are sometimes divided so they, for instance, can compete against each other in sports
VERB (pronounced **howz**) **houses, housing, housed 1** to house people is to provide them with houses to live in **2** if a room or building houses something, that thing is kept there or operates from there: *The extension will house a new bookshop and restaurant.*

houseboat NOUN **houseboats** a boat on a river which people live in

housebreaking NOUN the crime of breaking into people's houses

household NOUN **households** all the people who live in the same house
▸ **householder** NOUN **householders** someone who owns or rents a house

housekeeper NOUN **housekeepers** someone who organizes all the work needed to run a house

house-proud ADJECTIVE someone who is house-proud always keeps their home clean and tidy

house-trained ADJECTIVE a house-trained pet has learnt to be clean inside the house

housewarming NOUN **housewarmings** a party held in someone's new home

housewife NOUN **housewives** a woman who stays at home to look after her family and do the housework, instead of going out to work

housework NOUN housework is all the work you need to do to keep a house clean and tidy

housing NOUN **1** housing is houses of various kinds for people to live in **2** the housing for a machine is the box or structure that the machine fits into

hover VERB **hovers, hovering, hovered 1** if something hovers, it stays still in the air **2** if someone hovers, they stand close to you, usually because they are watching you

hovercraft NOUN **hovercrafts** a vehicle that travels on land or water supported on a cushion of air

how ADVERB
1 how something is done is the way it is done or the means used to do it: *I'll show you how to tie a reef knot.* • *How will we get there?*
2 how is used in questions about measurement, extent, distance, time and age: *I don't know how old Granny is exactly.* • *How far is your school?*
3 how you are is how well or ill you feel: *Hello, how are you today?*
4 how you feel about someone or something is the feelings you have for them
5 you use how to show anger or for emphasis: *How dare you!* • *How sad is that?*

however ADVERB **1** no matter how: *Do it however you like.* **2** in spite of what has just been said: *He thinks it is a great movie. However, no one else thinks so.*

howl NOUN **howls 1** a long, loud, sad sound made by a wolf or dog **2** a loud shout of pain or laughter
VERB **howls, howling, howled 1** a dog or wolf howls when it makes a long, loud, sad-sounding noise **2** to shout or cry loudly: *He was howling with pain.*

HQ ABBREVIATION short for **headquarters**

hub NOUN **hubs 1** the centre part of a wheel where the axle passes through **2** the part of a place where most of the activity is: *the hub of the town*

hubbub NOUN **hubbubs** the noise made by many people talking at the same time

huddle VERB **huddles, huddling, huddled** people or animals huddle, or huddle together, when they move very close to each other and form a tightly packed group
NOUN **huddles** a group of people standing or sitting very close to each other

hue NOUN **hues** a colour or shade

Aa
Bb
Cc
Dd
Ee
Ff
Gg
Hh
Ii
Jj
Kk
Ll
Mm
Nn
Oo
Pp
Qq
Rr
Ss
Tt
Uu
Vv
Ww
Xx
Yy
Zz

human bones

skull

jawbone

collarbone

breastbone

shoulderblade

humerus (upper arm bone)

ribs

ulna (main forearm bone)

backbone (spine)

vertebra

radius (small forearm bone)

pelvis

wrist bones

hand bones

finger bones

femur (thigh bone)

fibula (small shin bone)

kneecap

tibia (large shin bone)

ankle <u>bone</u>

foot bones

toe bones

Aa
Bb
Cc
Dd
Ee
Ff
Gg
Hh
Ii
Jj
Kk
Ll
Mm
Nn
Oo
Pp
Qq
Rr
Ss
Tt
Uu
Vv
Ww
Xx
Yy
Zz

huff NOUN **huffs**
• **in a huff** if someone is in a huff, they are sulking
▶ **huffy** ADJECTIVE **huffier, huffiest** sulky
hug VERB **hugs, hugging, hugged** two people hug when they put their arms around each other's bodies in an affectionate way
NOUN **hugs** the affectionate action of putting your arms around someone
huge ADJECTIVE very big
▶ **hugely** ADVERB very, extremely
hula-hoop NOUN **hula-hoops** a large circle of plastic that you step inside and swing round and round your body by moving your hips

hulk NOUN **hulks 1** a very large and clumsy person or thing **2** an old ship that is not being used
▶ **hulking** ADJECTIVE very large and clumsy
hull NOUN **hulls** the part of a ship or boat that sits in the water
hullabaloo NOUN **hullabaloos** a noisy fuss
hullo INTERJECTION another spelling of **hello**
hum VERB **hums, humming, hummed** you hum when you make musical noises in your throat with your mouth closed
human NOUN **humans** a human or a **human being** is a person

ADJECTIVE typical of human beings: *a very human emotion*

humane ADJECTIVE kind and causing as little suffering as possible

▶ **humanely** ADVERB in a way that causes the least pain possible: *The dog was destroyed humanely.*

humanity NOUN **1** humanity is all human beings **2** someone who shows humanity is kind and understanding towards other people

human rights PLURAL NOUN the rights that every human being has, for example not to be forced to do dangerous work or not to be punished for your beliefs

humble ADJECTIVE **humbler, humblest** a humble person believes they are no better than other people

• **eat humble pie** if someone eats humble pie, they show that they are very sorry for a mistake they have made by admitting it and being humble

humbug NOUN **humbugs 1** humbug is an old-fashioned word for nonsense **2** humbugs are hard sweets made from boiled sugar that you suck

humdrum ADJECTIVE a humdrum existence is boring because things always stay the same and nothing exciting ever happens

humid ADJECTIVE the air or atmosphere is humid when it has a lot of moisture in it

▶ **humidity** NOUN humidity is the amount of moisture that is in the air

humiliate VERB **humiliates, humiliating, humiliated** to humiliate someone is to make them feel silly or ashamed, especially in front of other people

▶ **humiliation** NOUN **humiliations 1** humiliation is being humiliated **2** a humiliation is something that makes you feel disgraced or embarrassed

humility NOUN being humble

hummingbird NOUN **hummingbirds** a tiny bird with a long beak that feeds on nectar from flowers and beats its wings so fast they make a humming sound

humorous ADJECTIVE funny or amusing

humour NOUN **1** the ability someone has to be funny or amusing, or to find things funny or amusing **2** (*formal*) the mood someone is in

VERB **humours, humouring, humoured** to humour someone is to agree with them just to please them

hump NOUN **humps 1** a rounded lump on an animal's back **2** a rounded raised part on a road or other surface

hunch NOUN **hunches** an idea you have about someone or something, which you believe but cannot prove

VERB **hunches, hunching, hunched** to hunch your shoulders or your back is to bring your shoulders up towards your ears so that your body is bent over at the top

hunchback NOUN **hunchbacks** someone whose spine is bent so that there is a lump on their back

▶ **hunchbacked** ADJECTIVE having a crooked back with a lump

hundred NOUN **hundreds** the number 100

▶ **hundredth** ADJECTIVE AND ADVERB coming last in a series of one hundred things: *This is my hundredth visit here.* NOUN **hundredths** one of a hundred equal parts of something: *A centimetre is a hundredth of a metre.*

hung VERB a way of changing the verb **hang** to make a past tense. It can be used with or without a helping verb: *I hung the picture on my bedroom wall.* • *He had hung the washing out before it started raining.*

hunger NOUN the feeling you get when you need to eat

VERB **hungers, hungering, hungered** to hunger for something is to long for it

hungry ADJECTIVE **hungrier, hungriest** having an empty feeling in your stomach and wanting food

▶ **hungrily** ADVERB in a keen way that shows you are hungry: *The dog devoured his food hungrily.*

hunk NOUN **hunks** a big piece of something: *a hunk of rock*

hunt VERB **hunts, hunting, hunted 1** to chase and kill animals for food or

Aa
Bb
Cc
Dd
Ee
Ff
Gg
Hh
Ii
Jj
Kk
Ll
Mm
Nn
Oo
Pp
Qq
Rr
Ss
Tt
Uu
Vv
Ww
Xx
Yy
Zz

sport **2** to hunt for something is to look hard for it everywhere

NOUN **hunts 1** a search for something or someone: *a police hunt for the criminal* **2** an event where people search for or chase animals in order to kill them

▶ **hunter** NOUN **hunters** a person or animal that hunts

▶ **hunting** NOUN chasing and killing animals

hurdle NOUN **hurdles 1** one of several jumps placed round a race track that athletes or horses have to jump over **2** a problem that you have to overcome

VERB **hurdles, hurdling, hurdled** to compete in hurdle races

▶ **hurdler** NOUN **hurdlers** a competitor in a race with hurdles

▶ **hurdling** NOUN jumping over hurdles in a race

hurl VERB **hurls, hurling, hurled** to hurl something is to throw it with a lot of force

hurrah INTERJECTION an exclamation of approval or joy: *Hurrah! No more school for three whole days!*

hurricane NOUN **hurricanes** a fierce storm with very high winds that cause damage

hurried ADJECTIVE something that is hurried is done quickly

▶ **hurriedly** ADVERB quickly

hurry VERB **hurries, hurrying, hurried** to move or go quickly

• **hurry up** to move faster or do something more quickly

NOUN hurry is trying or needing to get somewhere or get something done quickly: *in a hurry to catch the bus* • *There's no hurry.*

hurt VERB **hurts, hurting, hurt 1** to hurt someone or something is to injure or damage them: *She hurt her ankle playing hockey.* • *Try not to hurt anyone's feelings.* **2** if something hurts, or hurts you, it injures you or makes you feel pain

ADJECTIVE injured or showing pain

NOUN pain, injury or distress

hurtful ADJECTIVE causing pain or distress: *a hurtful remark*

hurtle VERB **hurtles, hurtling, hurtled** to move very fast, often in a dangerous or uncontrolled way: *The sledge came hurtling down the bank and crashed into a tree.*

husband NOUN **husbands** a woman's husband is the man she has married

hush INTERJECTION if someone says 'hush!', they want you to be quiet

VERB **hushes, hushing, hushed**

• **hush something up** to stop people getting to know about something

NOUN silence after there has been noise

husk NOUN **husks** the husk of a seed is its dry outer covering

husky[1] ADJECTIVE sounding deep and rough: *a low husky voice*

husky[2] NOUN **huskies** a type of large dog with a thick warm coat, used to pull sledges over snow in the Arctic and Antarctic

hustle VERB **hustles, hustling, hustled** to hustle someone is to push them somewhere or to hurry them along

hut NOUN **huts** a small building or shed made of wood, mud or metal

hutch NOUN **hutches** a box, usually with an open front covered with wire, where pet rabbits are kept

hyacinth NOUN **hyacinths** a plant that grows from a large bulb and has lots of small sweet-smelling flowers growing on one stem

hybrid NOUN **hybrids** a hybrid animal or plant has been bred from two different types or species

hydrant NOUN **hydrants** a pipe connected to the main water supply to which a hose can be attached to get water to put out fires

hydraulic ADJECTIVE to do with or powered by the movement of liquid: *hydraulic brakes*

hydrocarbon NOUN **hydrocarbons** (science) hydrocarbons are various chemical substances containing only carbon and hydrogen. They are found in coal and oil

hydroelectric ADJECTIVE using or to do with electricity made by water power

✦ Hydros is the Greek word for *water*. If a word starts with **hydro**, you can guess that it has something to do with water. Other examples are **hydrofoil** and **hydrogen**.

hydrofoil NOUN **hydrofoils** a fast type of boat that can skim over the water on long structures shaped like an aeroplane's wings

hydrogen NOUN hydrogen is the lightest gas, which combines with oxygen to make water

hyena NOUN **hyenas** a wild animal of the dog family that makes a howling noise that sounds like mad laughter

hygiene NOUN keeping yourself and your surroundings clean so that you stay healthy

▶ **hygienic** ADJECTIVE without any dirt or germs

hymn (pronounced **him**) NOUN **hymns** a religious song praising God

hype NOUN hype is publicity or advertising, especially when it makes something seem better than it is

hyper- PREFIX if **hyper-** comes at the beginning of a word, it adds the meaning 'much bigger', 'much more' or 'too much'. For example, a *hypermarket* is much bigger than a supermarket

✦ Hyper is a Greek word that means *over*.

hyperactive ADJECTIVE more active than normal

hyperlink NOUN **hyperlinks** (*ICT*) a piece of writing on screen that you can click on to take you to a website or another file. It is often called a **link** for short

hypertext NOUN (*ICT*) in computers, hypertext is a special electronic text with cross-reference links called hyperlinks, which let you go to information elsewhere by clicking on a symbol or word

hyphen NOUN **hyphens 1** a punctuation mark that looks like a very short line. You use it to join words or parts of words

together, for example *half-term* **2** a very short line that is used at the end of a line of text to show that a word is split and part of it is on the next line

▶ **hyphenate** VERB **hyphenates, hyphenating, hyphenated** to put a hyphen in a word, or to join words or parts of words with a hyphen

hypnosis NOUN if someone is under hypnosis, they have been put into a state that is similar to a deep sleep but in which they can still obey someone's instructions

▶ **hypnotic** ADJECTIVE having a hypnotizing effect

▶ **hypnotism** NOUN using hypnosis to put someone into a sleep-like state

▶ **hypnotist** NOUN **hypnotists** someone who hypnotizes people, often as a public entertainment

▶ **hypnotize** or **hypnotise** VERB **hypnotizes, hypnotizing, hypnotized** to hypnotize someone is to put them into a sleep-like state

hypocrisy (pronounced hi-**pok**-ri-si) NOUN the behaviour of someone who is not as sincere or honest as they pretend to be

▶ **hypocrite** (pronounced **hip**-i-krit) NOUN **hypocrites** someone who pretends to be sincere and concerned for other people

▶ **hypocritical** ADJECTIVE not having the feelings or beliefs that you pretend to have

hypotenuse (pronounced hie-**pot**-en-yooz) NOUN **hypotenuses** (*maths*) the side of a right-angled triangle that is opposite the right angle

hypothermia NOUN a dangerous lowering of someone's body temperature caused by extreme cold

hypothesis (pronounced hie-**poth**-i-sis) NOUN **hypotheses** a theory or idea that has been worked out as a possible explanation for something but which hasn't been proved to be correct

▶ **hypothetical** ADJECTIVE a hypothetical situation or example is one that is based on what might be possible, rather than fact

hysteria NOUN if someone is suffering

Aa
Bb
Cc
Dd
Ee
Ff
Gg
Hh
Ii
Jj
Kk
Ll
Mm
Nn
Oo
Pp
Qq
Rr
Ss
Tt
Uu
Vv
Ww
Xx
Yy
Zz

hysterical → hysterics

from hysteria, they become very emotional and cry or scream in a wild way

hysterical ADJECTIVE **1** suffering from hysteria **2** if you find something hysterical, you think it is very funny

▶ **hysterically** ADVERB in a hysterical way

hysterics NOUN if someone has hysterics, they cry, scream or laugh in a wild and uncontrolled way

Ii

I PRONOUN a word you use when talking about yourself: *I like ice cream.*

ice NOUN frozen water

ice age NOUN the period of time when the Earth was mostly covered with ice

iceberg NOUN **icebergs** a large piece of ice floating in the sea

ice cap NOUN **ice caps** a permanent covering of ice, for example at the North and South Poles

ice cream NOUN **ice creams** a sweet frozen food made from milk or cream: *strawberry ice cream • Would you like an ice cream?*

ice hockey NOUN a sport played on ice in which two teams try to hit an object called a puck into a net

ice lolly NOUN **ice lollies** a lump of frozen fruit-flavoured juice on a stick

ice skate NOUN **ice skates** ice skates are boots with blades on the bottom, used for moving across ice
▸ **ice-skating** NOUN the sport or pastime of moving across ice wearing ice-skates

icicle NOUN **icicles** a long thin piece of ice that is hanging from something

icing NOUN a mixture of sugar and water, used for decorating cakes

icon NOUN **icons 1** (*ICT*) a small symbol on a computer screen that represents a program or file **2** a statue or painting of a holy person

ICT ABBREVIATION short for **Information and Communications Technology**

icy ADJECTIVE **icier, iciest 1** covered with ice **2** extremely cold: *an icy wind*

ID NOUN **IDs** an official document that proves who you are: *The police officer showed Mum his ID.*

I'd a short way to say and write **I would** or **I had**: *I'd like another drink, please. • I'd seen the film before.*

idea NOUN **ideas** a thought or plan that you have: *That's a good idea.*

• **have no idea** not to know something: *I've no idea where he is.*

ideal ADJECTIVE perfect, especially for a particular purpose: *It's an ideal day for a picnic.*
▸ **idealize** or **idealise** VERB **idealizes, idealizing, idealized** to idealize something is to think that it is perfect when it really is not
▸ **ideally** ADVERB in a perfect situation: *Ideally, I'd like to finish this by tomorrow.*

identical ADJECTIVE if two things are identical, they are exactly the same

identification NOUN **1** an official document that proves who you are **2** the process of finding out who someone is or what something is

identify VERB **identifies, identifying, identified** to say who someone is or what something is: *Can you identify this flower?*
• **identify with someone** if you identify with someone, you feel that you understand them and share their feelings

identity NOUN **identities** who someone is or what something is: *Police are trying to discover the identity of the thief.*

idiom NOUN **idioms** a phrase that has a special meaning. For example, 'let the cat out of the bag' is an idiom that means 'to tell someone a secret'

idiot NOUN **idiots** a stupid person
▸ **idiotic** ADJECTIVE extremely stupid

idle ADJECTIVE **1** someone who is idle is lazy or not doing anything useful **2** a machine or other piece of equipment that is idle is not being used
▸ **idly** ADVERB in a lazy way

✦ Be careful not to confuse the spellings and meanings of **idle** and **idol**.

idol NOUN **idols 1** a famous person who is admired by a lot of people **2**

Bb Cc Dd Ee Ff Gg Hh **Ii** Jj Kk Ll Mm Nn Oo Pp Qq Rr Ss Tt Uu Vv Ww Xx Yy Zz

267

something which people worship as a god

▶ **idolize** or **idolise** VERB **idolizes, idolizing, idolized** to admire someone or something very much: *He idolizes his football heroes.*

ie or **i.e.** ABBREVIATION short for **id est**, which is Latin for 'that is'. You use **ie** when you are giving more information to show what you mean: *The whole trip, ie food, travel and hotel, cost £500.*

if CONJUNCTION **1** whether: *I don't know if I can come on Thursday.* **2** used when talking about possibilities: *Drink some water if you get thirsty.* **3** whenever: *I always call in at his house if I'm passing.*

igloo NOUN **igloos** a hut made from blocks of snow

ignite VERB **ignites, igniting, ignited 1** to catch fire: *The paper suddenly ignited.* **2** to set something on fire: *Flames had ignited the curtains.*

▶ **ignition** NOUN the part of a car that ignites the petrol when you turn the key to start the engine

ignorant ADJECTIVE not knowing about something: *Many people are ignorant about the dangers.*

▶ **ignorance** NOUN being ignorant

ignore VERB **ignores, ignoring, ignored** to pay no attention to someone or something: *He ignored all my advice.* • *I said hello, but she just ignored me.*

iguana NOUN **iguanas** a large lizard that lives in trees

il- PREFIX if a word starts with **il-**, it means 'not'. For example, *illegal* means 'not legal'

ill ADJECTIVE not well: *I was ill yesterday and had the day off school.*

I'll a short way to say and write **I will**: *I'll see you tomorrow.*

illegal ADJECTIVE not allowed by the law: *It's illegal to park here.*

▶ **illegally** ADVERB in a way that is against the law

illegible ADJECTIVE illegible writing is so bad you cannot read it

▶ **illegibly** ADVERB in a way that is impossible to read

illiterate ADJECTIVE not able to read or write

illness NOUN **illnesses 1** an illness is a disease: *childhood illnesses* **2** illness is bad health

illogical ADJECTIVE not based on good reason or logic

illuminate VERB **illuminates, illuminating, illuminated** to make something brighter using lights: *Lights illuminate the castle at night.*

▶ **illuminated** ADJECTIVE **1** lit by lights **2** an illuminated book, especially a very old one, is decorated with coloured letters or pictures

▶ **illumination** NOUN lighting something with lights

illusion NOUN **illusions 1** an idea or belief you have that is false: *He's under the illusion that the teacher can't see him.* **2** something that seems to exist but does not really exist

illustrate VERB **illustrates, illustrating, illustrated** to provide pictures and photographs for a book or magazine: *a book illustrated with colour photographs*

▶ **illustration** NOUN **illustrations** a picture or photograph in a book or magazine

▶ **illustrator** NOUN **illustrators** someone who draws pictures for a book or magazine

ill-will NOUN bad feelings towards someone

im- PREFIX if a word starts with **im-**, it means 'not'. For example, *impossible* means 'not possible'

I'm a short way to say and write **I am**: *I'm hungry.*

image NOUN **images 1** a picture that you have in your mind **2** the impression that someone or something gives to other people: *He needs to improve his image.*

• **be the image of someone** to look exactly like someone: *She's the image of her mother.*

▶ **imagery** NOUN words that produce pictures in your mind when you are reading something or listening to something

Aa
Bb
Cc
Dd
Ee
Ff
Gg
Hh
Ii
Jj
Kk
Ll
Mm
Nn
Oo
Pp
Qq
Rr
Ss
Tt
Uu
Vv
Ww
Xx
Yy
Zz

imaginary ADJECTIVE existing in your mind but not real: *Dragons are imaginary creatures.*

imagination NOUN **imaginations** your ability to form pictures and ideas in your mind: *Most children have a good imagination.*

▶ **imaginative** ADJECTIVE using new and interesting ideas: *He's very imaginative.* • *an imaginative design*

imagine VERB **imagines, imagining, imagined 1** to form a picture of someone or something in your mind: *I tried to imagine what he would look like.* **2** to think or believe something, especially something that is not true: *You must be imagining things.*

imam NOUN **imams** a man who leads the prayers in a mosque

imitate VERB **imitates, imitating, imitated** to copy someone or something

▶ **imitation** NOUN **imitations 1** imitation is copying someone or something **2** an imitation is a copy of something

immaculate ADJECTIVE spotlessly clean

immature ADJECTIVE behaving in a silly and childish way

▶ **immaturity** NOUN silly and childish behaviour

immediate ADJECTIVE happening now without any delay: *I can't give you an immediate answer.*

▶ **immediately** ADVERB now and without any delay: *Come here immediately!*

immense ADJECTIVE very big: *an immense distance*

▶ **immensely** ADVERB extremely: *He's immensely popular.*

immerse VERB **immerses, immersing, immersed 1** to put something in a liquid so it is completely covered **2** if you immerse yourself in something, you give it all of your attention

▶ **immersion** NOUN putting something in liquid

immigrant NOUN **immigrants** someone from another country who has come to live in your country

immigrate VERB **immigrates, immigrating, immigrated** to come and live in a foreign country

▶ **immigration** NOUN coming to live in a foreign country

✦ Do not confuse this with the word **emigrate**. You **immigrate** when you come to a new country and live there but you **emigrate** when you leave your country.

imminent ADJECTIVE something that is imminent will happen very soon

immobile ADJECTIVE not moving or not able to move

▶ **immobilize** or **immobilise** VERB **immobilizes, immobilizing, immobilized** to prevent someone or something from moving normally

immoral ADJECTIVE wrong or bad: *immoral behaviour*

▶ **immorality** NOUN behaviour that is not good or honest

immortal ADJECTIVE living for ever

▶ **immortality** NOUN being immortal

immune ADJECTIVE if you are immune to an illness, you cannot get it

▶ **immunity** NOUN your ability to avoid getting an illness

▶ **immunization** or **immunisation** NOUN putting a substance into someone's body, usually by an injection, to prevent them from getting an illness

▶ **immunize** or **immunise** VERB **immunizes, immunizing, immunized** to put a substance into someone's body to prevent them from getting an illness

imp NOUN **imps 1** an imaginary creature in stories that looks like a small man and behaves badly **2** a naughty child

impact NOUN **impacts 1** the strong effect that something has: *The changes will have a big impact on schools.* **2** the force of one thing hitting another thing: *The front of the car was crushed by the impact.*

impair VERB **impairs, impairing, impaired** to damage something or make it worse: *His hearing was impaired by the constant noise.*

Aa
Bb
Cc
Dd
Ee
Ff
Gg
Hh
Ii
Jj
Kk
Ll
Mm
Nn
Oo
Pp
Qq
Rr
Ss
Tt
Uu
Vv
Ww
Xx
Yy
Zz

Aa
Bb
Cc
Dd
Ee
Ff
Gg
Hh
Ii
Jj
Kk
Ll
Mm
Nn
Oo
Pp
Qq
Rr
Ss
Tt
Uu
Vv
Ww
Xx
Yy
Zz

▸ **impairment** NOUN **impairments** a condition that stops part of your body from working correctly

impale VERB **impales, impaling, impaled** to push a sharp object through something

impartial ADJECTIVE fair and not supporting one person more than another: *an impartial referee*

▸ **impartiality** NOUN being impartial: *A judge must show impartiality.*

impatience NOUN the feeling that you want something to happen now and that you cannot wait

▸ **impatient** ADJECTIVE having or showing impatience

▸ **impatiently** ADVERB in a way that shows you are impatient: *'Hurry up!' she said impatiently.*

impede VERB **impedes, impeding, impeded** to delay the progress of someone or something

impending ADJECTIVE going to happen very soon: *an impending disaster*

imperative ADJECTIVE extremely important or necessary: *It is imperative that you wash your hands before dinner.*
NOUN **imperatives** (*grammar*) a form of a verb which tells you to do something. For example, *go* in the phrase *Go away!* is imperative

imperfect ADJECTIVE not perfect
NOUN the imperfect is the form of the verb that expresses an action in the past that is not complete. For example, *The sun was shining* is in the imperfect

▸ **imperfection** NOUN **imperfections** a fault

imperial ADJECTIVE **1** relating to an empire: *an imperial ruler* **2** imperial units of measurement are units such as gallons and ounces. They come from a system of measurement that is older than the metric system

impersonal ADJECTIVE not very friendly or welcoming: *The hotel building was cold and impersonal.*

impersonate VERB **impersonates, impersonating, impersonated** to copy the way someone talks and behaves, especially to entertain people

▸ **impersonation** NOUN **impersonations** an act in which you impersonate someone: *Ben can do a brilliant impersonation of our teacher.*

▸ **impersonator** NOUN **impersonators** someone who impersonates people

impertinence NOUN rude behaviour that shows you do not respect someone

▸ **impertinent** ADJECTIVE behaving in a rude way and not showing respect: *an impertinent child*

▸ **impertinently** ADVERB in a cheeky way

implement NOUN **implements** a tool
VERB **implements, implementing, implemented** to start using a new plan or system: *The new rules will be implemented next year.*

▸ **implementation** NOUN implementing something: *the implementation of new laws*

implication NOUN **implications 1** a possible effect or result: *What are the implications of the President's announcement?* **2** something that is suggested and not said directly

implore VERB **implores, imploring, implored** to ask in a desperate way for someone to do something

imply VERB **implies, implying, implied** to suggest that something is true without saying it directly: *Are you implying that he lied?*

impolite ADJECTIVE bad mannered and rude to others: *an impolite boy* • *an impolite way to talk*

▸ **impolitely** ADVERB in a rude way

▸ **impoliteness** NOUN rude behaviour and bad manners

import VERB **imports, importing, imported 1** to bring goods into a country from another country in order to sell them: *Many electrical goods are imported from Japan.* **2** (*ICT*) to import data on a computer is to bring it into a file from another one, or to your computer from another place
NOUN **imports** something that has been imported

important ADJECTIVE **1** something

is important if it matters a lot: *an important meeting* **2** an important person has a lot of power

▶ **importance** NOUN being important: *the importance of education*

▶ **importantly** ADVERB seriously or crucially: *You must go to school and, more importantly, you must listen.*

impose VERB **imposes, imposing, imposed 1** to bring in a new rule or law, especially one that is not wanted: *The government imposes taxes on most people.* **2** if you impose on someone, you expect someone to do something for you that may not be convenient for them

▶ **imposing** ADJECTIVE looking very impressive: *an imposing building*

impossibility NOUN **impossibilities** something that is not possible

impossible ADJECTIVE not possible: *an impossible task*

impostor NOUN **impostors** someone who pretends to be someone else in order to deceive people

impractical ADJECTIVE not sensible or reasonable: *an impractical suggestion*

impress VERB **impresses, impressing, impressed** to make someone feel admiration: *His drawings really impressed me.*

▶ **impression** NOUN **impressions** a feeling that you get about someone or something: *I got the impression that he wasn't happy.*

▶ **impressive** ADJECTIVE making you feel admiration: *an impressive performance*

▶ **impressively** ADVERB in a way that makes you feel admiration

imprison VERB **imprisons, imprisoning, imprisoned** to put someone in prison or a place they cannot escape from

improbable ADJECTIVE not likely to happen or be true: *an improbable story*

improper ADJECTIVE improper behaviour is not suitable or right

improper fraction NOUN **improper fractions** a fraction in which the number above the line (the **numerator**)

is greater than the number below the line (the **denominator**)

improve VERB **improves, improving, improved 1** to improve is to get better: *I hope the weather improves soon.* **2** to improve something is to make it better: *I want to improve my French.*

▶ **improvement** NOUN **improvements 1** an improvement is a change that makes something better **2** improvement is making something better

improvise VERB **improvises, improvising, improvised 1** (*music*) to improvise when you are playing music is to play something you have not prepared **2** to improvise when you are dancing is to make movements you have not rehearsed **3** to use whatever is available because you do not have what you need: *They improvised a shelter from branches and blankets.*

impudence NOUN cheeky behaviour or remarks

▶ **impudent** ADJECTIVE rude and not showing respect

impulse NOUN **impulses** a sudden feeling you have that makes you do something

▶ **impulsive** ADJECTIVE doing something suddenly without thinking about the possible results

impure ADJECTIVE not pure

▶ **impurity** NOUN **impurities** something in a substance that makes it dirty or not pure: *impurities in water*

in PREPOSITION

1 inside something: *He keeps his keys in the drawer.* • *The books are in my bedroom.*

2 at a place: *They live in Nottingham.*

3 at a particular time: *It's my birthday in May.*

4 after a period of time: *I'll be back in a few minutes.*

5 using a particular thing: *They were speaking in Japanese.* • *Read the word printed in red.*

6 wearing particular clothes: *Who's the boy in the football shirt?*

ADVERB **1** at your home or place of

work: *I'm sorry, Dad's not in. Can I take a message?* **2** at or into a place: *What time does your train get in?* • *Come in!*

in- PREFIX if a word starts with **in-**, it means 'in' or 'not'. For example, *income* means money that comes in, and *invisible* means 'not visible'

inability NOUN the fact of not being able to do something: *She gets annoyed about her inability to sing.*

inaccuracy NOUN **inaccuracies 1** an inaccuracy is something that is not exact or correct: *an essay full of inaccuracies* **2** inaccuracy is being not precise or correct: *the inaccuracy of the striker's shots at goal*

inaccurate ADJECTIVE not exact or correct: *inaccurate information*

inactive ADJECTIVE **1** not doing anything **2** not working or not being used

‣ **inactivity** NOUN the state of not doing anything

inadequate ADJECTIVE if something is inadequate, there is not enough of it or it is not good enough: *Some villages have inadequate water supplies.*

‣ **inadequacy** NOUN **inadequacies** the fact that someone or something is not good enough

inadvertent ADJECTIVE (*formal*) done by mistake or by accident

‣ **inadvertently** ADVERB (*formal*) by accident: *I had inadvertently left the door unlocked.*

inanimate ADJECTIVE not alive: *inanimate objects like chairs and books*

inappropriate ADJECTIVE not suitable for a particular situation or occasion: *inappropriate behaviour*

‣ **inappropriateness** NOUN being unsuitable for a particular situation

incapable ADJECTIVE not able to do something: *He seemed incapable of understanding me.*

‣ **incapability** NOUN being unable to do something

incense NOUN a substance that smells sweet when you burn it, often used in religious ceremonies

incentive NOUN **incentives** something

that encourages you to do something

inch NOUN **inches** an imperial unit for measuring length, equal to about 2.5 centimetres

incident NOUN **incidents** something unusual or bad that happens: *There was an unpleasant incident in the playground.*

‣ **incidental** ADJECTIVE if something is incidental, it happens with something else but is not very important: *The story of the boy's escape is incidental to the main story.*

‣ **incidentally** ADVERB you say incidentally when you are starting to talk about a new subject, or adding some more information about something: *Incidentally, I saw your brother at the cinema.*

incinerate VERB **incinerates, incinerating, incinerated** to burn something until it becomes ashes

‣ **incinerator** NOUN **incinerators** a container for burning waste

incisor NOUN **incisors** one of the teeth at the front of your mouth that you use to cut food

incite VERB **incites, inciting, incited** to encourage people to cause trouble or fight

‣ **incitement** NOUN encouraging people to cause trouble or fight

inclination NOUN **inclinations** a feeling that you want to do something: *He had no inclination to go to the party.*

incline NOUN **inclines** a slope
VERB **inclines, inclining, inclined 1** if you are inclined to do something, you feel like doing it or have a tendency to do it: *I was inclined to tell him exactly what I thought.* **2** to slope or lean: *He inclined his head towards mine.*

include VERB **includes, including, included** to include a person or thing is to make them part of a larger group or amount: *Did you remember to include Andy?* • *The price of the meal includes a drink.*

‣ **including** PREPOSITION a word used to show that a person or thing is part of a larger group: *We went to all the*

Aa
Bb
Cc
Dd
Ee
Ff
Gg
Hh
Ii
Jj
Kk
Ll
Mm
Nn
Oo
Pp
Qq
Rr
Ss
Tt
Uu
Vv
Ww
Xx
Yy
Zz

museums, including the new one.

▶ **inclusion** NOUN the act of including someone or something or the fact they are included

▶ **inclusive** ADJECTIVE including everything: *From Tuesday to Thursday inclusive is three days.*

income NOUN **incomes** the amount of money you earn

incompatible ADJECTIVE **1** if people are incompatible, they are so different that they cannot have a good relationship **2** too different to exist or be used together: *The software is incompatible with the operating system.*

▶ **incompatibility** NOUN being too different from each other

incompetence NOUN lack of skill

▶ **incompetent** ADJECTIVE not having the skill to do something properly

incomplete ADJECTIVE not finished or not having all the parts it should: *an incomplete painting*

incomprehensible ADJECTIVE impossible to understand

inconsiderate ADJECTIVE not thinking about other people's feelings

inconsistency NOUN **inconsistencies** **1** inconsistency is behaving or doing something differently each time **2** an inconsistency is something that cannot be true if other information is true

▶ **inconsistent** ADJECTIVE doing something in a different way each time

▶ **inconsistently** ADVERB in an inconsistent way

inconvenience NOUN **inconveniences 1** inconvenience is difficulty or problems: *We apologize for any inconvenience caused.* **2** an inconvenience is something that causes problems for you

VERB **inconveniences, inconveniencing, inconvenienced** to cause problems for someone

▶ **inconvenient** ADJECTIVE causing problems: *Have I called at an inconvenient time?*

incorporate VERB **incorporates, incorporating, incorporated** to include something: *a television that*

incorporates all the latest features

incorrect ADJECTIVE wrong: *an incorrect answer*

▶ **incorrectly** ADVERB in a way that is wrong: *You answered incorrectly.*

increase VERB (pronounced in-**krees**) **increases, increasing, increased 1** to increase is to become larger in size or amount: *By midday, the temperature had increased to thirty degrees.* **2** to increase something is to make it larger in size or amount: *My parents have increased my pocket money.*

NOUN (pronounced **in**-krees) **increases** the amount by which something gets bigger: *There's been a big increase in the number of students in the school.*

incredible ADJECTIVE difficult to believe: *an incredible story*

▶ **incredibly** ADVERB used for saying that something is difficult to believe: *Incredibly, no one was injured.*

incubate VERB **incubates, incubating, incubated** to hatch eggs by sitting on them

▶ **incubation** NOUN incubating eggs

▶ **incubator** NOUN **incubators 1** a piece of hospital equipment that keeps a very small baby alive **2** a piece of equipment that keeps eggs warm until they hatch

incurable ADJECTIVE an incurable illness cannot be cured

indeed ADVERB **indeed** is used to emphasize what you have just said: *He was driving very fast indeed.*

indefinite ADJECTIVE **1** not clear or not decided yet: *an indefinite date* **2** without a fixed limit: *an indefinite amount of time*

indefinite article NOUN **indefinite articles** (*grammar*) the name used for the words *a* and *an*

✦ There are two kinds of article in English grammar: **a**, or **an**, is called the *indefinite article* and **the** is called the *definite article.*

indefinitely ADVERB for a period of time with no fixed limits: *The match was postponed indefinitely.*

Aa
Bb
Cc
Dd
Ee
Ff
Gg
Hh
Ii
Jj
Kk
Ll
Mm
Nn
Oo
Pp
Qq
Rr
Ss
Tt
Uu
Vv
Ww
Xx
Yy
Zz

indent VERB **indents, indenting, indented** to start a line of writing further from the edge of the page than other lines
▸ **indentation** NOUN **indentations** a hollow or dent

independent ADJECTIVE **1** an independent country is not controlled by another country **2** not relying on other people for help and support
▸ **independence** NOUN being independent

indestructible ADJECTIVE impossible to destroy

index NOUN **indexes** or **indices** a list in a book that tells you what page you can find information on

✦ This is a Latin word which means both *forefinger* and *informer*. An index *informs* you where you can find something in a book.

index finger NOUN **index fingers** the finger that is next to your thumb

indicate VERB **indicates, indicating, indicated** to show: *an arrow indicating where to go*
▸ **indication** NOUN **indications** a sign: *The teacher gave them no indication of when the test would be marked.*
▸ **indicative** ADJECTIVE if something is indicative of something else, it shows that it is likely to be true: *The footprints are indicative of life on the planet.*
▸ **indicator** NOUN **indicators** **1** a flashing light on a car that shows which way the car is going to turn **2** something that is a sign of something else

indifference NOUN a lack of interest in something
▸ **indifferent** ADJECTIVE **1** not good but not bad either **2** if you are indifferent to something, you show no interest in it or do not have any opinions on it

indigestion NOUN an uncomfortable feeling in your stomach after you have eaten

indignant ADJECTIVE angry because you think you have been treated unfairly: *'Move on, please,' said an indignant voice.*

▸ **indignantly** ADVERB in an indignant way
▸ **indignation** NOUN anger at being treated unfairly

indigo NOUN a dark purplish-blue colour

indirect ADJECTIVE **1** not leading straight to a place: *an indirect route* **2** not directly caused by something or related to something
▸ **indirectly** ADVERB in an indirect way

indirect speech NOUN (*grammar*) in a story or report, indirect speech tells you what someone said without repeating their actual words. Look up and compare **direct speech**

indistinct ADJECTIVE not easy to see, hear or remember

individual ADJECTIVE **1** for one person only, or for one particular person: *an individual apple pie • Each child has an individual peg for their coat.* **2** considered separately from other things: *Put a price ticket on each individual item.*
NOUN **individuals** one person rather than a group
▸ **individuality** NOUN a quality that makes someone or something different from others
▸ **individually** ADVERB separately from other things: *Wrap each cake individually.*

indoor ADJECTIVE inside a building: *an indoor swimming pool*
▸ **indoors** ADVERB inside a building: *Come indoors if it starts to rain.*

indulge VERB **indulges, indulging, indulged** **1** to indulge someone is to let them have or do what they want, especially something that is bad for them **2** to indulge in something good is to allow yourself to do or have it: *My sister was indulging in another cake.*
▸ **indulgence** NOUN indulging yourself or someone else
▸ **indulgent** ADJECTIVE letting someone do what they want even if it is not good for them

industrial ADJECTIVE relating to industry and factories: *an industrial area of town*

Aa
Bb
Cc
Dd
Ee
Ff
Gg
Hh
Ii
Jj
Kk
Ll
Mm
Nn
Oo
Pp
Qq
Rr
Ss
Tt
Uu
Vv
Ww
Xx
Yy
Zz

industrialize *or* **industrialise** VERB **industrializes, industrializing, industrialized** to industrialize a place is to develop a lot of industry there
► **industrialization** *or* **industrialisation** NOUN the development of industry

industrious ADJECTIVE working very hard: *an industrious pupil*

industry NOUN **industries 1** an industry is a particular type of trade or production: *the steel industry* **2** industry is the production of goods, especially in a factory

ineffective ADJECTIVE not achieving anything useful

inefficient ADJECTIVE not working well and wasting time or money: *an inefficient use of school funds*
► **inefficiency** NOUN **inefficiencies** being inefficient, or something that is inefficient: *the inefficiency of oil production* • *inefficiencies in the way we work*
► **inefficiently** ADVERB in a way that wastes time or money

inept ADJECTIVE having or showing no skill: *an inept performance*

inequality NOUN **inequalities** a lack of equality

inevitable ADJECTIVE certain to happen: *It is inevitable that it will rain on sports day.*

inexcusable ADJECTIVE too bad to be excused

inexpensive ADJECTIVE cheap in price

inexperience NOUN a lack of experience or knowledge
► **inexperienced** ADJECTIVE not having much experience or knowledge

inexplicable ADJECTIVE impossible to explain: *She's angry with me for some inexplicable reason.*

infamous ADJECTIVE well-known for something bad: *Dick Turpin was an infamous highwayman.*
► **infamy** NOUN being well-known for something bad

infancy NOUN the time when someone is a baby or very young child

infant NOUN **infants** a baby or very young child
► **infantile** ADJECTIVE **1** infantile behaviour is very silly **2** to do with babies or very young children

> ✦ **Infant** came into English from the French word **enfant**, which means *child*. This in turn came from the Latin word **infans**, which means 'not able to speak'.

infantry NOUN soldiers who fight on foot

infect VERB **infects, infecting, infected** to give someone or something an illness or germs: *Once you have been infected, the virus stays in your body.*
► **infection** NOUN **infections 1** an infection is an illness: *an ear infection* **2** infection is becoming affected by germs
► **infectious** ADJECTIVE **1** an infectious illness can be spread from person to person **2** an infectious feeling or action is one that other people cannot help doing: *infectious laughter*

infer VERB **infers, inferring, inferred** to form an opinion from information you already know

inferior ADJECTIVE not as good as someone or something else: *Amy often felt inferior to the other children in her class.*
► **inferiority** NOUN being inferior to someone or something else

inferno NOUN **infernos** a large and dangerous fire

infested ADJECTIVE full of insects or other pests: *The whole house was infested with mice.*

infinite ADJECTIVE without any limits or end: *The universe is infinite.*
► **infinitely** ADVERB very much: *This computer is infinitely better than the last one.*

infinitive NOUN **infinitives** the basic form of a verb that can be used to make all the other forms, for example *to play* or *to eat*

infinity NOUN space or time without an end or limit

Aa
Bb
Cc
Dd
Ee
Ff
Gg
Hh
Ii
Jj
Kk
Ll
Mm
Nn
Oo
Pp
Qq
Rr
Ss
Tt
Uu
Vv
Ww
Xx
Yy
Zz

infirm ADJECTIVE weak, especially because of old age or illness
▸ **infirmary** NOUN **infirmaries** a hospital
▸ **infirmity** NOUN **infirmities** a weakness

inflamed ADJECTIVE red and swollen because of an infection

inflammable ADJECTIVE easy to set on fire: *Paper is highly inflammable.*

inflammation NOUN swelling, pain and redness in part of your body

inflate VERB **inflates, inflating, inflated** to fill something with air: *The tyres need to be inflated.*
▸ **inflation** NOUN **1** a rise in prices and wages in a country **2** filling something with air

inflect VERB **inflects, inflecting, inflected 1** when a word inflects, it changes its ending **2** to change the tone of your voice
▸ **inflection** NOUN **inflections 1** a change in the form of a word to show its tense or number **2** a word that has been changed in this way. For example, *finds*, *finding* and *found* are inflections of the verb *find* **3** changing the tone of your voice

inflexible ADJECTIVE **1** stiff and unable to bend: *inflexible plastic* **2** impossible or unwilling to change

inflict VERB **inflicts, inflicting, inflicted** to make someone suffer something unpleasant or painful: *The home team inflicted a heavy defeat on the visitors.*

influence NOUN **influences 1** influence is the power to affect other people or things: *a teacher who has a lot of influence over his pupils* **2** an influence is someone or something that has an effect on other people or things: *Anna is a good influence on the other children.*
VERB **influences, influencing, influenced** to have an effect on someone or something: *His advice influenced my decision.*
▸ **influential** ADJECTIVE having a lot of influence

influenza NOUN a formal word for **flu**

info NOUN an informal short form of the word **information**

inform VERB **informs, informing, informed** to tell someone about something: *Have you informed the police?*

informal ADJECTIVE **1** relaxed and friendly, or suitable for relaxed occasions **2** informal words are words that you might use when you are speaking to your friends, but not when you are writing or speaking to adults you do not know well

information NOUN knowledge, facts or details: *We asked for information on things to do in the area.*
▸ **informative** ADJECTIVE giving you a lot of useful information: *an informative book*
▸ **informer** NOUN **informers** someone who gives information to the police in return for money

information technology NOUN the study or use of computers for dealing with information

✦ The abbreviation of information technology is **IT**.

infra-red ADJECTIVE infra-red light cannot be seen but gives out heat

infrequent ADJECTIVE (*formal*) not happening very often
▸ **infrequently** ADVERB (*formal*) not often

infuriate VERB **infuriates, infuriating, infuriated** to make someone very angry
▸ **infuriating** ADJECTIVE something that is infuriating makes you extremely angry

ingenious ADJECTIVE clever and having new ideas: *an ingenious idea* • *He's very ingenious.*
▸ **ingenuity** NOUN being full of good ideas

ingot NOUN **ingots** a block of metal, especially gold or silver

ingratitude NOUN being ungrateful

ingredient NOUN **ingredients** one of the things you use to make a particular food

ingrown or **ingrowing** ADJECTIVE an ingrown nail is growing into your skin

inhabit VERB **inhabits, inhabiting, inhabited** to live in a particular place: *the creatures that inhabit our world*

▶ **inhabitant** NOUN **inhabitants** someone who lives in a place: *the island's inhabitants*

▶ **inhabited** ADJECTIVE with people living there: *The old cottage was no longer inhabited.*

inhale VERB **inhales, inhaling, inhaled** to breathe air into your lungs through your nose and mouth. Look up and compare **exhale**

▶ **inhalation** NOUN breathing in

▶ **inhaler** NOUN **inhalers** a piece of equipment for breathing in medicine or steam

inherit VERB **inherits, inheriting, inherited 1** to get money or other things from someone who has died **2** to get a particular characteristic from one of your parents: *I inherited my fair hair from my mother.*

▶ **inheritance** NOUN money or things that you get from someone who has died

inhibit VERB **inhibits, inhibiting, inhibited** to prevent someone or something from doing something: *His shyness inhibits him from speaking out.*

▶ **inhibited** ADJECTIVE not feeling relaxed or confident enough to do or say what you want

▶ **inhibition** NOUN **inhibitions** a feeling of worry or shyness that stops you doing or saying what you want

inhuman ADJECTIVE extremely cruel

▶ **inhumanity** NOUN cruel behaviour

initial ADJECTIVE at the beginning: *initial difficulties*
NOUN **initials** the first letter of someone's name

▶ **initially** ADVERB at first: *Initially, things were very difficult.*

inject VERB **injects, injecting, injected 1** to put a substance into someone's body using a needle **2** to improve something by adding a particular quality to it: *The teacher* tried to inject some enthusiasm into her students.

▶ **injection** NOUN **injections** putting a substance into someone's body using a needle

injure VERB **injures, injuring, injured** to hurt someone or something: *He injured his knee in a skiing accident.*

▶ **injured** ADJECTIVE hurt: *an injured knee*

▶ **injury** NOUN **injuries** a wound or damage to part of your body: *head injuries*

injustice NOUN **injustices 1** an injustice is an action that is unfair **2** injustice is when people are treated unfairly

ink NOUN **inks** a black or coloured liquid used for writing or printing

▶ **inky** ADJECTIVE covered in ink

inland ADJECTIVE not by the sea
ADVERB in a direction away from the sea

in-laws PLURAL NOUN (*informal*) someone's in-laws are the relatives of their husband or wife, for example a *mother-in-law* or *brother-in-law*

inlet NOUN **inlets** a small area of water that comes into the land

inn NOUN **inns** a small hotel in the country

inner ADJECTIVE **1** on the inside of something: *your inner ear* **2** close to the centre of something : *the inner city* **3** inner feelings are ones that you keep secret

innermost ADJECTIVE your innermost thoughts and feelings are ones that you keep secret

innings NOUN one team's turn at batting in cricket

innocence NOUN **1** when someone is not guilty of a crime: *This new evidence will prove the man's innocence.* **2** when someone does not have much experience of life and how cruel people can be: *The bully took advantage of Sam's innocence.*

▶ **innocent** ADJECTIVE **1** not guilty of a crime **2** not having much experience of life and how cruel people can be

▶ **innocently** ADVERB in an innocent way

an insect

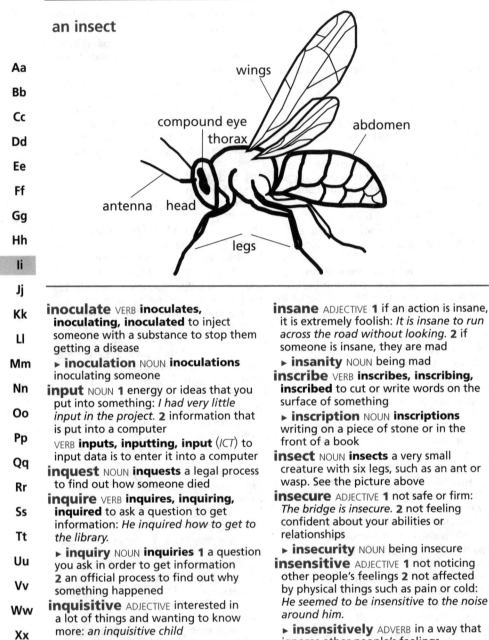

wings

compound eye
thorax

abdomen

antenna   head

legs

Aa
Bb
Cc
Dd
Ee
Ff
Gg
Hh
Ii
Jj
Kk
Ll
Mm
Nn
Oo
Pp
Qq
Rr
Ss
Tt
Uu
Vv
Ww
Xx
Yy
Zz

inoculate VERB **inoculates, inoculating, inoculated** to inject someone with a substance to stop them getting a disease

▸ **inoculation** NOUN **inoculations** inoculating someone

input NOUN **1** energy or ideas that you put into something: *I had very little input in the project.* **2** information that is put into a computer
VERB **inputs, inputting, input** (*ICT*) to input data is to enter it into a computer

inquest NOUN **inquests** a legal process to find out how someone died

inquire VERB **inquires, inquiring, inquired** to ask a question to get information: *He inquired how to get to the library.*

▸ **inquiry** NOUN **inquiries 1** a question you ask in order to get information **2** an official process to find out why something happened

inquisitive ADJECTIVE interested in a lot of things and wanting to know more: *an inquisitive child*

▸ **inquisitively** ADVERB in a way that shows you want to know more: *Our neighbours looked out inquisitively when the police arrived.*

insane ADJECTIVE **1** if an action is insane, it is extremely foolish: *It is insane to run across the road without looking.* **2** if someone is insane, they are mad

▸ **insanity** NOUN being mad

inscribe VERB **inscribes, inscribing, inscribed** to cut or write words on the surface of something

▸ **inscription** NOUN **inscriptions** writing on a piece of stone or in the front of a book

insect NOUN **insects** a very small creature with six legs, such as an ant or wasp. See the picture above

insecure ADJECTIVE **1** not safe or firm: *The bridge is insecure.* **2** not feeling confident about your abilities or relationships

▸ **insecurity** NOUN being insecure

insensitive ADJECTIVE **1** not noticing other people's feelings **2** not affected by physical things such as pain or cold: *He seemed to be insensitive to the noise around him.*

▸ **insensitively** ADVERB in a way that ignores other people's feelings

▸ **insensitivity** NOUN being insensitive

inseparable ADJECTIVE **1** not able to be separated: *A traditional dance is an*

inseparable part of the tribe's celebration.
2 friends who are inseparable spend most of their time together

insert VERB **inserts, inserting, inserted** to put something into something else: *Insert a coin in the meter.*

inside PREPOSITION in or into something: *She put the book inside her bag.*
ADVERB into a building from outdoors: *Come inside, it's raining.*
ADJECTIVE on the inner side, not the outer side: *the inside walls of the house*
NOUN **insides** the inside of something is the part that is in the middle and not on the outside: *The inside of his jacket was torn.*

insight NOUN **insights** an ability to understand something clearly

insignificant ADJECTIVE not at all important

insincere ADJECTIVE pretending to have a feeling that you do not really have: *insincere laughter*
▸ **insincerely** ADVERB in an insincere way
▸ **insincerity** NOUN being insincere

insist VERB **insists, insisting, insisted 1** to say that something must happen or be done: *He insisted on paying.* **2** to keep saying in a firm way that you think something is true: *Mark insists that he hasn't done anything wrong.*
▸ **insistent** ADJECTIVE saying that something must happen or be done: *She was insistent that we visit her.*

insolence NOUN speaking without politeness or respect
▸ **insolent** ADJECTIVE impolite and showing no respect

insoluble ADJECTIVE **1** an insoluble substance cannot dissolve **2** impossible to solve

insomnia NOUN not being able to sleep

inspect VERB **inspects, inspecting, inspected 1** to look very carefully at something or someone **2** to inspect a place is to officially visit it to make sure that it is being run properly

▸ **inspection** NOUN **inspections 1** inspection is looking very carefully at someone or something **2** an inspection is an examination or a visit by an inspector to check something

▸ **inspector** NOUN **inspectors 1** someone whose job is to inspect a place such as a school or restaurant to make sure it is run properly **2** a rank of police officer above a sergeant

inspiration NOUN **inspirations** someone or something that encourages someone and gives them new ideas
▸ **inspirational** ADJECTIVE encouraging someone and giving them new ideas

inspire VERB **inspires, inspiring, inspired** to encourage someone by giving them confidence and new ideas: *My mother inspired me to write stories.*
▸ **inspired** ADJECTIVE having a lot of special qualities: *an inspired performance*

install or **instal** VERB **installs** or **instals, installing, installed** if you install a piece of equipment, you put it in place and make it ready to use: *We're installing a new computer system.*
▸ **installation** NOUN installing equipment

instalment NOUN **instalments 1** one of several payments that you make to pay for something **2** one part of a long story that is told in a magazine or on television

instance NOUN **instances** an example of a situation: *an instance of John's quick thinking*
• **for instance** for example: *Some birds, penguins for instance, cannot fly at all.*

instant ADJECTIVE **1** happening at once: *The film was an instant success.* **2** able to be prepared very quickly: *instant coffee*
▸ **instantaneous** ADJECTIVE done or happening immediately or very quickly
▸ **instantly** ADVERB immediately

instead ADVERB in place of someone or something else: *Ben was ill so John went instead.* • *You could use a pencil instead of a pen.*

Aa Bb Cc Dd Ee Ff Gg Hh Ii Jj Kk Ll Mm Nn Oo Pp Qq Rr Ss Tt Uu Vv Ww Xx Yy Zz

instep NOUN **insteps** the bottom of your foot where it curves upwards

instinct NOUN **instincts** a natural feeling or ability that you have without being taught

▸ **instinctive** ADJECTIVE happening because of instinct: *Parents have an instinctive urge to protect their children.*

▸ **instinctively** ADVERB in an instinctive way: *I knew instinctively that something was wrong.*

institute NOUN **institutes** an organization of people who want to study something, or the building they use

▸ **institution** NOUN **institutions** a large organization: *banks and other financial institutions*

instruct VERB **instructs, instructing, instructed** to instruct someone is to tell them what to do

▸ **instruction** NOUN **instructions** a piece of information that tells you how to do something: *Read the instructions before you begin.*

▸ **instructive** ADJECTIVE providing a lot of useful information

instrument NOUN **instruments 1** something used for making music **2** a tool for doing something

▸ **instrumental** ADJECTIVE **1** instrumental music is written for musical instruments rather than singers **2** helpful in making something happen

insufficient ADJECTIVE (*formal*) not enough: *insufficient food supplies*

insulate VERB **insulates, insulating, insulated** to cover something with a material that does not let electricity, heat or frost through

▸ **insulation** NOUN insulating something, or the material used to do this

▸ **insulator** NOUN **insulators** (*science*) an object or a material that does not let electricity through

insult VERB (pronounced in-**sult**) **insults, insulting, insulted** to insult someone is to say something rude to them

NOUN (pronounced **in**-sult) **insults** a rude remark

▸ **insulting** ADJECTIVE very rude to someone

insurance NOUN an arrangement in which you pay a company money each year and they pay the costs if something you own is damaged or stolen: *car insurance*

insure VERB **insures, insuring, insured** to pay money to a company who will pay the costs if you are injured or if things you own are damaged or stolen

✦ The words **insure** and **ensure** sound the same, but they have different meanings and spellings. **Ensure** means 'to make sure'.

intact ADJECTIVE not broken or damaged

intake NOUN **intakes** the amount of people or things taken in: *this year's intake of students at the school*

integer NOUN **integers** a whole number, not a fraction. An integer can also be 0 or a negative number such as -1 or -2

integral ADJECTIVE forming an essential part of something: *Games are an integral part of life at school.*

integrate VERB **integrates, integrating, integrated 1** to combine two or more things together to make a system **2** to mix with other groups of people

▸ **integration** NOUN integrating people or things

integrity NOUN being honest and having high moral standards

intellect NOUN **intellects** your ability to think about things and understand them

▸ **intellectual** ADJECTIVE relating to your intellect NOUN **intellectuals** someone who is intelligent and likes thinking about serious issues

intelligence NOUN **1** your ability to learn and understand things **2** secret information about other countries

▸ **intelligent** ADJECTIVE clever and able to understand things quickly

intend VERB **intends, intending, intended** to plan or mean to do something: *I didn't intend to upset you.*

Aa
Bb
Cc
Dd
Ee
Ff
Gg
Hh
Ii
Jj
Kk
Ll
Mm
Nn
Oo
Pp
Qq
Rr
Ss
Tt
Uu
Vv
Ww
Xx
Yy
Zz

intense ADJECTIVE very great: *intense heat*

▸ **intensify** VERB **intensifies, intensifying, intensified 1** to intensify is to increase and become greater: *The darkness intensified.* **2** to intensify something is to make it increase and become greater: *The police are intensifying their efforts to catch the criminals.*

▸ **intensity** NOUN the strength of something, such as a feeling or colour

intensive ADJECTIVE involving a lot of effort or activity: *an intensive search of the area*

▸ **intensively** ADVERB in a way that involves a lot of effort

intent ADJECTIVE **1** if you are intent on doing something, you are determined to do it **2** showing a lot of attention and concentration: *an intent stare*

NOUN purpose or intention: *He went to the house with the intent to commit a crime.*

▸ **intently** ADVERB with a lot of attention and concentration

intention NOUN **intentions** the thing you plan to do: *I have no intention of apologising.*

▸ **intentional** ADJECTIVE done deliberately

▸ **intentionally** ADVERB deliberately: *You tripped me up intentionally!*

inter- PREFIX if a word starts with **inter-**, it means 'among' or 'between' different things. For example, *international* means 'between countries'

interact VERB **interacts, interacting, interacted 1** to talk to other people and do things with them **2** if two things interact, they have an effect on each other

▸ **interactive** ADJECTIVE involving communication between two people or things, for example a person and a computer

intercept VERB **intercepts, intercepting, intercepted** to stop something that is going from one place to another

intercom NOUN **intercoms** a system

that allows you to talk to people who are in a different part of a building

interest NOUN **interests 1** the feeling that you like something and want to know more about it: *I have no interest in cricket.* **2** something that you enjoy doing: *My main interests are sport and reading.* **3** extra money that you have to pay back when you have borrowed money, or that a bank puts into your account regularly

VERB **interests, interesting, interested** if something interests you, you like it and want to know more about it

▸ **interested** ADJECTIVE having or showing interest: *Dan is very interested in old cars.*

▸ **interesting** ADJECTIVE making you feel interested: *an interesting story*

interface NOUN **interfaces** something that helps a computer program work with another program

interfere VERB **interferes, interfering, interfered** to get involved in a situation where you are not wanted

• **interfere with** if something interferes with another thing, it prevents it from happening: *Football practice was interfering with his homework.*

▸ **interference** NOUN **1** interfering with something **2** unwanted radio signals that spoil the sound from a radio or spoil the picture on a television

interior NOUN **interiors** the interior of something is the inside of it: *the interior of a house*

ADJECTIVE on the inside of something

interjection WORD CLASS **interjections** (*grammar*) a word or phrase used to express a strong feeling like surprise, shock or anger. For example, *Oh!* and *Hooray!* are interjections

interlude NOUN **interludes** a short pause or interval

intermediate ADJECTIVE if something is intermediate, it is or takes place between two other stages or levels

intermission NOUN **intermissions** a short break in the middle of a play or concert

intermittent ADJECTIVE starting and stopping again and again: *intermittent rain showers*

internal ADJECTIVE **1** on the inside of something, especially your body: *internal injuries* **2** within an organization or country

international ADJECTIVE involving two or more countries: *an international match*

Internet NOUN the Internet is a computer network that allows people around the world to share information

interpret VERB **interprets, interpreting, interpreted 1** to translate what somebody is saying from one language to another **2** to think that something has a particular meaning: *I interpreted his quietness as shyness.*

▶ **interpretation** NOUN **interpretations** interpreting or a way of interpreting something: *What is your interpretation of the poem?*

▶ **interpreter** NOUN **interpreters** someone whose job is to translate what someone says into another language

interrogate VERB **interrogates, interrogating, interrogated** to ask someone a lot of questions in order to get information

▶ **interrogation** NOUN **interrogations** asking someone a lot of questions

interrupt VERB **interrupts, interrupting, interrupted 1** to stop someone in the middle of saying or doing something: *I'm sorry to interrupt, but what time do we have to leave?* **2** to stop a process or activity for a short time: *The headteacher interrupted our class to make an announcement.*

▶ **interruption** NOUN **interruptions** interrupting someone or something: *Interruptions when you're trying to study are annoying.*

intersect VERB **intersects, intersecting, intersected** if lines or roads intersect, they cross each other

▶ **intersection** NOUN **intersections** a place where lines or roads cross each other

interval NOUN **intervals 1** a short break in the middle of a play, concert or school day **2** a period of time between two things

intervene VERB **intervenes, intervening, intervened** to do something to try to stop an argument or fight between other people or countries

▶ **intervention** NOUN intervening in something

interview NOUN **interviews 1** a meeting when someone asks you questions to see if you are suitable for a job **2** a meeting when someone asks a famous person questions

VERB **interviews, interviewing, interviewed** to ask someone questions at an interview

▶ **interviewer** NOUN **interviewers** the person who asks the questions at an interview

intestines PLURAL NOUN the long tubes that take food from your stomach out of your body

intimate ADJECTIVE **1** having a very close relationship with someone: *intimate friends* **2** relating to private and personal things: *intimate details* **3** an intimate knowledge of something is a very good and detailed knowledge

intimidate VERB **intimidates, intimidating, intimidated** to frighten someone, especially by threatening them

▶ **intimidating** ADJECTIVE making you feel worried, frightened or less confident: *His loud voice was intimidating.*

▶ **intimidation** NOUN intimidating someone

into PREPOSITION **1** to the inside of something: *We went into the house.* **2** used for saying how something changes: *She cut the cake into four pieces.* • *The caterpillar changed into a butterfly.* **3** used when talking about dividing one number by another: *2 into 4 goes twice.*

intolerable ADJECTIVE so bad that you cannot put up with it: *Her rudeness is intolerable.*

▶ **intolerably** ADVERB in a way that is too bad to put up with: *It is intolerably hot in here.*

intolerant ADJECTIVE not willing to accept behaviour and ideas that are different from your own

▶ **intolerance** NOUN being intolerant: *the problem of religious intolerance*

intonation NOUN the way that your voice rises and falls when you speak

intricate ADJECTIVE containing a lot of small parts or details: *an intricate pattern*

intrigue VERB (pronounced in-**treeg**) **intrigues, intriguing, intrigued** to make someone feel very interested or curious NOUN (pronounced **in**-treeg) **intrigues** a secret plan or the process of planning this

▶ **intriguing** ADJECTIVE very interesting and unusual

introduce VERB **introduces, introducing, introduced 1** if you introduce two people who do not know each other, you tell each of them the other person's name **2** to make something start to happen or be used: *The new law was introduced in 1999.*

▶ **introduction** NOUN **introductions 1** bringing in something new for the first time **2** an introduction is a piece of writing at the front of a book that tells you what the book is about

▶ **introductory** ADJECTIVE **1** coming at the beginning **2** giving basic information about something: *an introductory course in science*

introvert NOUN **introverts** someone who is quiet and thoughtful and does not enjoy being with other people. Look up and compare **extrovert**

intrude VERB **intrudes, intruding, intruded 1** to become involved in a situation where you are not wanted **2** to enter a place where you should not be

▶ **intruder** NOUN **intruders** someone who enters a place where they should not be

▶ **intrusion** NOUN **intrusions** someone or something that is not wanted in a situation

▶ **intrusive** ADJECTIVE affecting or interrupting you in a way you do not want: *intrusive questions*

intuition NOUN **intuitions 1** intuition is an ability to understand or know something without thinking or being told about it **2** an intuition is an idea that something is true based on your feelings rather than on facts

invade VERB **invades, invading, invaded** to enter a country with an army to attack it or take it over

▶ **invader** NOUN **invaders** someone who invades another country

invalid[1] (pronounced in-**va**-lid) ADJECTIVE not able to be used: *an invalid bus pass • invalid reasons for being late*

invalid[2] (pronounced **in**-va-lid) NOUN **invalids** someone who is ill or unable to look after themselves

invaluable ADJECTIVE extremely useful: *an invaluable piece of advice*

invasion NOUN **invasions** an attack on a country by an army entering it

invent VERB **invents, inventing, invented 1** to design or make something that no one else has ever made: *Thomas Edison invented the electric light bulb.* **2** to think of a story or excuse that is not true

▶ **invention** NOUN **inventions** something someone has invented

▶ **inventive** ADJECTIVE good at thinking of new and interesting ideas

▶ **inventor** NOUN **inventors** someone who has invented something new

inverse NOUN **inverses** the inverse of something is its opposite ADJECTIVE opposite

▶ **inversely** ADVERB in the opposite way

▶ **invert** VERB **inverts, inverting, inverted** to turn something upside down

▶ **inverted** ADJECTIVE turned upside down

invertebrate NOUN **invertebrates** an animal that does not have a backbone, for example an insect or worm

inverted commas PLURAL NOUN the punctuation marks ' ' or " ", which you

Aa
Bb
Cc
Dd
Ee
Ff
Gg
Hh
Ii
Jj
Kk
Ll
Mm
Nn
Oo
Pp
Qq
Rr
Ss
Tt
Uu
Vv
Ww
Xx
Yy
Zz

use in writing to show what someone says, for example *"I'm going home,"* Joe said. They are sometimes called **quotation marks**

invest VERB **invests, investing, invested** to put money in a bank or business in order to make more money: *Don't invest all your money with one bank.*

▸ **investment** NOUN **investments** 1 investing money 2 an investment is something you buy because you think it will be useful or make a profit for you: *A warm coat is a good investment.*

▸ **investor** NOUN **investors** someone who invests money in something

investigate VERB **investigates, investigating, investigated** to try to find out the truth about something: *Police are investigating the crime.*

▸ **investigation** NOUN **investigations** a search for information about something: *a police investigation into the murder*

▸ **investigator** NOUN **investigators** someone who is investigating something

invincible ADJECTIVE impossible to defeat

invisible ADJECTIVE impossible to see

▸ **invisibility** NOUN being impossible to see

invitation NOUN **invitations** an offer that asks if you would like to do something or go somewhere: *I've had an invitation to Helen's birthday party.*

invite VERB **invites, inviting, invited** to invite someone is to ask them if they would like to do something or go somewhere: *Clare's invited me for tea at her house.*

▸ **inviting** ADJECTIVE very attractive and making you want to do something

invoice NOUN **invoices** a piece of paper sent with things you have bought, to tell you how much you must pay

VERB **invoices, invoicing, invoiced** to send someone an invoice

involuntary ADJECTIVE happening without your control: *Sneezing is an involuntary action.*

involve VERB **involves, involving,**

involved 1 to have something as a necessary part: *The college course involves a lot of hard work.* 2 if you are involved in something, you take part in it: *I don't want to get involved in your argument.*

▸ **involvement** NOUN being involved in something

inward ADJECTIVE 1 inside or towards the inside of something 2 inward feelings are ones in your mind that you do not tell other people about

ADVERB **inwards**

▸ **inwardly** ADVERB in your own mind but not told or shown to other people: *Inwardly, she felt very scared.*

inwards ADVERB towards the inside of something

ion NOUN **ions** (science) an atom with an electrical charge

IOU ABBREVIATION short for **I owe you**. An IOU is a note that you sign to say that you owe someone money

IQ ABBREVIATION short for **intelligence quotient**. Someone's IQ is a measure of how intelligent they are

ir- PREFIX if a word starts with **ir-**, it means 'not'. For example, *irregular* means 'not regular'

irate ADJECTIVE extremely angry

iris NOUN **irises** 1 the coloured part of your eye 2 a tall flower

iron NOUN **irons** 1 a hard metal used for making tools 2 a piece of electrical equipment that you use for pressing the creases out of clothes

VERB **irons, ironing, ironed** to make clothes smooth using an iron

ironic ADJECTIVE 1 an ironic situation is funny in a strange way: *It's ironic that we're moving to Edinburgh just as they're leaving.* 2 saying the opposite of what you really mean, as a way of being funny: *My sister was being ironic when she said she loves football.*

▸ **ironically** ADVERB in a way that is ironic: *Molly ironically saluted her bossy sister.*

ironmonger NOUN **ironmongers** 1 someone who sells items such as tools and garden equipment 2 an

Aa
Bb
Cc
Dd
Ee
Ff
Gg
Hh
Ii
Jj
Kk
Ll
Mm
Nn
Oo
Pp
Qq
Rr
Ss
Tt
Uu
Vv
Ww
Xx
Yy
Zz

ironmonger's is a shop selling items such as tools and garden equipment

irony NOUN **ironies 1** irony is using words that are the opposite of what you really mean in order to be funny **2** an irony is a situation that is strange or funny

irregular ADJECTIVE **1** having a shape that is not straight, even or smooth: *irregular teeth* **2** happening at different times so there is no pattern: *an irregular train service* **3** (*formal*) not obeying the usual rules: *irregular behaviour*

▸ **irregularity** NOUN **irregularities 1** being irregular **2** (*formal*) an irregularity is something that breaks a rule: *irregularities in John's behaviour*

▸ **irregularly** ADVERB in an irregular way

irrelevance NOUN **irrelevances 1** irrelevance is when something is not important in a situation **2** an irrelevance is someone or something that is not important in a situation: *His recent injury seemed an irrelevance when he won the race.*

▸ **irrelevant** ADJECTIVE not important in a situation: *Your comments are irrelevant to this discussion.*

irresistible ADJECTIVE too strong or attractive to resist: *The chocolate cake looked irresistible.*

irresponsible ADJECTIVE behaving in a silly way without thinking about bad things that might happen

▸ **irresponsibility** NOUN irresponsible behaviour

▸ **irresponsibly** ADVERB in an irresponsible way

irreversible ADJECTIVE **1** a decision or process that is irreversible cannot be changed back **2** (*science*) if a change is irreversible, then you cannot change it back to the way it was before

irrigate VERB **irrigates, irrigating, irrigated** to supply land or crops with water

▸ **irrigation** NOUN supplying land or crops with water

irritable ADJECTIVE becoming annoyed very easily

▸ **irritability** NOUN being irritable

▸ **irritably** ADVERB in an annoyed way

irritate VERB **irritates, irritating, irritated 1** to make someone feel annoyed **2** to make something such as your skin or eyes sore or itchy: *Some sun creams can irritate your skin.*

▸ **irritation** NOUN **irritations 1** irritation is feeling annoyed about something **2** an irritation is something that annoys you: *His constant complaints are an irritation.* **3** a sore feeling on your skin or in your eyes

is VERB **1** the form of the verb **be** in the present tense that you use with **he, she** or **it**: *He is a fool.* • *It is raining.* **2 is** is also used as a helping verb along with a main verb: *Lisa's mother is going away for a month.*

Islam NOUN the Muslim religion that was started by Mohammed

▸ **Islamic** ADJECTIVE relating to the religion of Islam

island NOUN **islands** an area of land surrounded by sea

isle NOUN **isles** an island. **Isle** is used in poems or in the names of islands: *the Scilly Isles*

isn't a short way to say and write **is not**: *It isn't raining.*

isolate VERB **isolates, isolating, isolated** to isolate something is to keep it separate from other things: *Farmers have to isolate infected animals.*

▸ **isolated** ADJECTIVE **1** feeling alone and unable to meet other people **2** a long way from anywhere else: *an isolated farmhouse* **3** happening only once and not related to other events: *This theft was an isolated incident.*

▸ **isolation** NOUN being separate from other things

isosceles triangle (pronounced ie-sos-i-leez) NOUN **isosceles triangles** a triangle that has two sides of the same length

issue NOUN **issues 1** a subject that people discuss: *a discussion on the issue of education* **2** a newspaper or magazine that is one of a number printed and sold at the same time:

Aa
Bb
Cc
Dd
Ee
Ff
Gg
Hh
Ii
Jj
Kk
Ll
Mm
Nn
Oo
Pp
Qq
Rr
Ss
Tt
Uu
Vv
Ww
Xx
Yy
Zz

Have you seen this week's issue of the magazine?

VERB **issues, issuing, issued** to supply someone with something: *We were all issued with pens.*

it PRONOUN **1** a word you use to talk about a thing that has already been mentioned or pointed out: *I've lost the book. Have you seen it?* **2** used for talking about the weather, time and dates: *It rained yesterday.* • *It's 3 o'clock.* **3** used for talking about a fact or opinion: *It's expensive to travel by train.* • *It's very quiet here, isn't it?*

IT ABBREVIATION short for **information technology**

italic ADJECTIVE using a style of writing in which the letters slope to the right. The examples given in this book are in *italic*

itch VERB **itches, itching, itched** if part of your body itches, you want to scratch it

NOUN **itches** a feeling that you want to scratch part of your body: *I've got an itch on my back.*

▶ **itchy** ADJECTIVE **itchier, itchiest** an itchy part of your body makes you feel as though you want to scratch it

it'd a short way to say and write **it would** or **it had**: *It'd work! I know it would!* • *If you have an excuse, it'd better be good.* **item** NOUN **items** one of a number of things: *There were several items on the list.*

itinerary NOUN **itineraries** a list of places you plan to visit on a journey

it'll a short way to say and write **it will**: *I hope it'll be sunny tomorrow.*

its ADJECTIVE belonging to it: *Keep the watch in its box.*

✦ Be careful not to confuse the spellings of **its** and **it's**.
Its tells you something belongs to **it**: *The bird built **its** nest.*
It's is a short way to write **it is**: *I think **it's** going to rain.*

it's a short way to say and write **it is** or **it has**: *It's raining.* • *It's been a long time since I saw you.*

itself PRONOUN **1** you use **itself** after a verb or preposition when the thing that performs the action is affected by it: *The cat lay in the sun and licked itself.* **2** you use **itself** to show that **it** has done something without any help from others: *The dog managed to get free all by itself.* **3** you can use **itself** to show more clearly the thing you mean: *The garden is big but the house itself is quite small.*

I've a short way to say and write **I have**: *I've finished my homework.*

ivory NOUN the hard white substance that forms the tusks of an elephant

ivy NOUN a plant that has leaves all year and can grow up walls

Jj

jab VERB **jabs, jabbing, jabbed** to jab someone or something is to poke or prod them roughly or sharply: *Jack jabbed me with his finger.*
NOUN **jabs 1** a quick prod or punch **2** an injection, especially one given to prevent an infectious disease: *a flu jab*

jack NOUN **jacks 1** a tool used to raise something heavy off the ground, especially a car or other vehicle **2** a playing card with a picture of a young man, also called a knave. The jack or knave comes between the queen and the ten in value
VERB **jacks, jacking, jacked**
• **jack something up** to lift something using a jack

jackal NOUN **jackals** a wild animal that looks like a dog or fox and is found in Africa and Asia

jackdaw NOUN **jackdaws** a type of small black crow with a greyish head

jacket NOUN **jackets 1** a short coat, usually with long sleeves, that reaches down to your waist or hips **2** a loose paper covering wrapped around a hardback book

jack-knife VERB **jack-knifes, jack-knifing, jack-knifed** if a lorry jack-knifes, it skids out of control and the trailer swings round against the cab

jackpot NOUN **jackpots** the jackpot in a game or lottery is the top prize made up of the money everyone else has bet and which increases until someone wins it

jade NOUN a type of hard green stone used in jewellery and for making ornaments

jagged (pronounced **jag**-id) ADJECTIVE with sharp or uneven edges or angles: *jagged rocks • a jagged tear in the tent*

jaguar NOUN **jaguars** a large South American spotted cat, similar to a leopard, that lives in the jungle

jail NOUN **jails** a prison
VERB **jails, jailing, jailed** to jail someone is to put them in prison
▶ **jailer** NOUN **jailers** someone whose job is to watch over prisoners in a jail

jam NOUN **jams 1** jam is a thick sticky food made by boiling fruit with sugar **2** a jam happens when lots of vehicles or people are packed close together so that they become stuck and can't move
VERB **jams, jamming, jammed 1** to jam something into a space is to push it there so that it fits very tightly or is difficult to get out again **2** something like a door or window jams when it becomes stuck and can't be moved **3** people or vehicles jam a place when they crowd it so that it is difficult for any of them to move

jamb NOUN **jambs** the jamb of a door or window is the upright piece of wood or metal at either side of the frame

jamboree NOUN **jamborees** a large organized event where people from many different places gather, especially a gathering of Scouts

jammy ADJECTIVE **jammier, jammiest 1** filled or covered with jam **2** (*informal*) lucky

jangle VERB **jangles, jangling, jangled** metal objects jangle when they make a noise as they bang against each other

janitor NOUN **janitors** someone whose job is to look after a building, especially a school

January NOUN the first month of the year, after December and before February

✦ **January** comes from the name of the Roman god **Ianus**, who had two faces. One face was looking into the new year, the other looking back to the old year.

jape NOUN **japes** a slightly old-fashioned word for a trick or joke

jar NOUN **jars 1** a cylindrical container that is made of glass and has a lid **2** the amount a jar will hold: *She made six big jars of marmalade from the oranges.* **3** a bump or blow that causes an unpleasant or painful vibration

VERB **jars, jarring, jarred 1** if you jar a part of your body, you hurt it by suddenly shaking it or moving it violently: *He fell awkwardly, jarring his spine.* **2** if something jars or it jars on you, it has an unpleasant effect on you: *The bird's screeching jarred on my ears.*

jargon NOUN **jargons** the special words used by people working in a particular trade or profession, which are difficult for other people to understand: *legal jargon*

jaundice NOUN an illness that makes the skin and the whites of the eyes turn yellow, usually caused by the liver not working properly

▶ **jaundiced** ADJECTIVE **1** having jaundice **2** feeling unhappy and bitter about life in general

jaunt NOUN **jaunts** a trip made for pleasure: *Dad's on one of his fishing jaunts.*

▶ **jaunty** ADJECTIVE **jauntier, jauntiest** cheerful, confident and lively: *a jaunty manner*

javelin NOUN **javelins** a long light spear used in ancient times as a weapon and nowadays thrown in a sporting competition

jaw NOUN **jaws 1** your jaw is the lower part of your face around your mouth and chin, made up of two bones that your teeth grow in **2** an animal's jaws are its mouth and teeth: *The crocodile snapped its jaws shut.*

jay NOUN **jays** a bird with pink, grey, blue, white and black feathers

jazz NOUN a type of music in which the musicians often change the notes or add to the music as they play

VERB **jazzes, jazzing, jazzed**

• **jazz something up** to make something brighter or more colourful

▶ **jazzy** ADJECTIVE **jazzier, jazziest** bright and colourful: *That's a very jazzy tie you have on.*

JCB NOUN **JCBs** a large machine used for digging and moving earth and stones

✦ The **JCB** gets its name from the initials of its manufacturer, *J C Bamford*.

jealous ADJECTIVE feeling that you don't like someone because they have something that you want or because you are afraid that they will take something away from you: *He's jealous of his brother's success.* • *She made me jealous by going out with her other friends.*

▶ **jealousy** NOUN **jealousies** a feeling of being jealous

jeans PLURAL NOUN jeans are casual trousers made of denim with pockets at the front and back

Jeep NOUN **Jeeps** (*trademark*) a type of four-wheeled vehicle that can travel over rough ground

jeer VERB **jeers, jeering, jeered** to jeer at someone is to shout insults at them and make fun of them

NOUN **jeers** an unkind shout or laugh intended to make fun of someone

jelly NOUN **jellies 1** a wobbly food made with gelatine and fruit juice **2** any wobbly substance

jellyfish NOUN **jellyfish** or **jellyfishes** a sea animal with a soft see-through body

jerk VERB **jerks, jerking, jerked 1** to jerk something is to pull it with a sudden rough movement: *He jerked his hand away.* **2** to jerk is to make a short sudden movement: *The driver started the engine and the old bus jerked forward.*

NOUN **jerks** a short sudden movement

jerky ADJECTIVE **jerkier, jerkiest** jerky movements are short and quick, and are often awkward-looking or uncomfortable

jersey NOUN **jerseys 1** a jersey is a warm piece of clothing for the top part of your body **2** jersey is a fine knitted material

Aa Bb Cc Dd Ee Ff Gg Hh Ii Jj Kk Ll Mm Nn Oo Pp Qq Rr Ss Tt Uu Vv Ww Xx Yy Zz

jest VERB **jests, jesting, jested** to joke NOUN **jests** a joke

▶ **jester** NOUN **jesters** in the past, a man who was employed by a king or queen to tell jokes and amuse the court

jet[1] NOUN **jets 1** a powerful stream of liquid or gas forced through a narrow opening **2** a fast aeroplane with powerful engines that drive the plane forward by sucking air in at the front and forcing it out behind

VERB **jets, jetting, jetted** to jet somewhere is to travel there on a jet plane: *jetting off to sunny holiday destinations*

jet[2] NOUN jet is a black mineral that is polished and used to make jewellery

jetsam NOUN objects thrown from a boat or ship and washed ashore. Look up and compare **flotsam**

jetty NOUN **jetties** a platform built at the edge of a lake or the sea for small boats to tie up at

Jew NOUN **Jews** someone who belongs to the Hebrew race of people or who practises the religion of Judaism

jewel NOUN **jewels** a precious stone, used for decoration or display

▶ **jeweller** NOUN **jewellers** someone who makes or sells jewellery

▶ **jewellery** NOUN things that you wear to decorate your body and clothing, such as rings, earrings, bracelets, necklaces and brooches

Jewish ADJECTIVE to do with the Hebrew people or Judaism

jib NOUN **jibs 1** the arm that sticks out from the upright part of a crane **2** a triangular sail at the front of some sailing boats

jiffy NOUN (*informal*)

• **in a jiffy** in a very short time: *I'll be down in a jiffy.*

jig NOUN **jigs** a lively dance in which people jump about

jigsaw NOUN **jigsaws 1** a puzzle made up of lots of different-shaped pieces that fit together to make a picture **2** a type of electric saw with a very thin blade that can cut curved and rounded shapes

jingle VERB **jingles, jingling, jingled** pieces of metal jingle when they make a pleasant ringing sound as they hit each other: *coins jingling in his trouser pocket*

NOUN **jingles 1** a ringing sound made when small or light pieces of metal knock against each other **2** a short catchy song used in an advertisement

jinx NOUN **jinxes** an evil spell or a person or thing that brings bad luck

▶ **jinxed** ADJECTIVE to be jinxed is always to have bad luck

✦ This word comes from the name of a bird called a **jinx**, which was used in spells and charms.

job NOUN **jobs 1** someone's job is the work they do regularly for pay **2** a job is a task or a piece of work: *There are plenty of jobs to do about the house.*

jockey NOUN **jockeys** someone who rides a horse, especially in races

jodhpurs (pronounced **jod**-perz) PLURAL NOUN trousers that are tight around the bottom part of the leg and wider near the top, worn by jockeys and other horse riders

joey NOUN **joeys** a baby kangaroo, especially one that is still in its mother's pouch

jog VERB **jogs, jogging, jogged 1** to jog is to run at quite a slow pace for exercise **2** to jog someone or something is to nudge them or knock against them gently: *You jogged my elbow and made me splash the paint everywhere!* **3** to jog someone's memory is to help them remember

▶ **jogger** NOUN **joggers** someone who jogs for exercise

▶ **jogging** NOUN running at a slowish pace for exercise

join VERB **joins, joining, joined 1** to join two or more things is to put them together or connect them **2** one thing joins another when they come together or meet: *The track joins the main road just around this corner.* **3** you join a club or other organization when you become a member

NOUN **joins** a place where two things are joined

Aa
Bb
Cc
Dd
Ee
Ff
Gg
Hh
Ii
Jj
Kk
Ll
Mm
Nn
Oo
Pp
Qq
Rr
Ss
Tt
Uu
Vv
Ww
Xx
Yy
Zz

joiner NOUN **joiners** someone who works with wood, especially fitting together the wooden parts of houses

joint NOUN **joints** 1 a place where two or more things join 2 your joints are the parts of your body where two or more bones meet 3 a joint of meat is a large piece of meat
ADJECTIVE done together or shared: *a joint effort* • *joint responsibility*
▸ **jointly** ADVERB together

joke NOUN **jokes** something that is said or done to make people laugh
VERB **jokes, joking, joked** to make a joke
▸ **joker** NOUN **jokers** 1 someone who likes telling jokes or doing things to make people laugh 2 one of two cards in a pack of playing cards that have a picture of a clown. The jokers are extra cards and are only used in certain card games

jolly ADJECTIVE **jollier, jolliest** cheerful and happy
ADVERB very: *That was jolly unfair of you!*

jolt NOUN **jolts** 1 a sudden sharp uncomfortable movement: *The train stopped with a jolt.* 2 an unpleasant shock: *The news gave Liam a bit of a jolt.*
VERB **jolts, jolting, jolted** to make a sudden sharp movement

jostle VERB **jostles, jostling, jostled** to push roughly against someone in a crowd: *The prime minister was jostled by an angry crowd.*

jot VERB **jots, jotting, jotted**
• **jot something down** to write something down quickly
NOUN **jots** a small amount: *They don't care a jot what happens.*
▸ **jotter** NOUN **jotters** a book of blank pages used for taking down notes or for doing school exercises

joule NOUN **joules** (*science*) a unit of energy

journal NOUN **journals** 1 someone's journal is a book in which they write down what they have done each day 2 a magazine or newspaper

▸ **journalism** NOUN the work of journalists
▸ **journalist** NOUN **journalists** someone who writes for a newspaper or magazine or for radio or TV

journey NOUN **journeys** 1 you go on a journey when you travel from one place to another 2 a journey is the distance you travel from one place to another: *a long and difficult journey*
VERB **journeys, journeying, journeyed** (*formal*) to journey somewhere is to travel there

joust NOUN **jousts** (*history*) in medieval times, a joust was a fight between two knights on horseback who charged at each other with long lances
VERB **jousts, jousting, jousted** to fight, especially on horseback

jovial ADJECTIVE cheerful and jolly

joy NOUN **joys** 1 joy is a feeling of great happiness 2 a joy is something that gives you this feeling: *full of the joys of spring*

joyful ADJECTIVE filled with or showing great happiness
▸ **joyfully** ADVERB in a way that shows great happiness

joyous ADJECTIVE (*formal*) showing or causing great happiness: *a joyous occasion*

joyride NOUN **joyrides** a fast or dangerous ride in a stolen car
▸ **joyrider** NOUN **joyriders** someone who rides in a stolen car for amusement

joystick NOUN **joysticks** a lever used to control an aircraft or a computer game

jubilant ADJECTIVE full of triumph and happiness at a success
▸ **jubilation** NOUN rejoicing at success

jubilee NOUN **jubilees** a celebration of a special anniversary, for example the anniversary of a coronation

✦ **Jubilee** comes from a Hebrew word meaning *ram's horn*. This is because a ram's horn used to be blown to mark the beginning of a Jewish year of celebration.

Judaism NOUN the Jewish religion,

which follows the teachings of the Old Testament of the Bible

▶ **Judaic** ADJECTIVE to do with the Jewish religion or way of life

judge VERB **judges, judging, judged**
1 to judge something is to form an idea or opinion about it **2** to judge a competition is to decide which of the competitors is best **3** to judge a case in a court of law is to hear the evidence and decide on what is to be done or how someone should be punished

NOUN **judges 1** someone who hears cases in a law court and decides what is to be done **2** someone who judges a competition **3** someone who can decide whether something is good or bad: *a good judge of character*

▶ **judgement** or **judgment** NOUN **judgements** or **judgments 1** the ability to make decisions, especially good or sensible decisions **2** the decision made by a judge in a law court **3** an opinion about something: *In my judgement, it wouldn't be a very sensible thing to do.*

judicial ADJECTIVE to do with judges, judgement or a court of justice

judicious ADJECTIVE wise and showing good judgement

judo NOUN a form of wrestling that came originally from Japan

jug NOUN **jugs** a container for pouring liquids, with a handle and a shaped part at its top edge

juggernaut NOUN **juggernauts** a very long or large lorry

juggle VERB **juggles, juggling, juggled** to keep several things in the air by continuously throwing them up and catching them

▶ **juggler** NOUN **jugglers** someone who entertains people by juggling

juice NOUN **juices 1** juice is the liquid in fruits or vegetables **2** the juices from meat are the liquids that flow out of it while it is being cooked

▶ **juicy** ADJECTIVE **juicier, juiciest** full of juice

jukebox NOUN **jukeboxes** a coin-operated machine that automatically plays records that you select by pressing buttons

July NOUN the seventh month of the year, after June and before August

✦**July** comes from the Latin word for this month, **Julius**, which was named after the Roman emperor *Julius Caesar.*

jumble VERB **jumbles, jumbling, jumbled** to jumble things up is to mix them up so that they are out of order or in an untidy mess

NOUN a jumble is lots of things that have been mixed up in a confused or untidy mess

jumble sale NOUN **jumble sales** a sale where second-hand or unwanted things are sold to raise money

jumbo ADJECTIVE very big: *a jumbo crossword*

NOUN **jumbos 1** a jumbo jet **2** an informal name for an elephant

jumbo jet NOUN **jumbo jets** a very big jet aeroplane that can carry a lot of passengers

jump VERB **jumps, jumping, jumped**
1 to leap into the air: *He jumped off the wall.*
2 to jump something is to leap over it
3 to make a sudden movement because you are surprised or frightened: *I jumped as something crawled out from under the stone.*
4 if you jump to do something or jump at something, you eagerly accept an opportunity: *I thought you would jump at the chance.*
5 if you jump a queue, you join it in front of other people already in the queue

NOUN **jumps 1** a leap **2** something to be jumped over, or a distance that has to be jumped **3** a sudden movement because of surprise or fear

jumper NOUN **jumpers** a warm piece of clothing for the top part of your body, which you pull on over your head

jumpsuit NOUN **jumpsuits** an all-in-one piece of clothing made up of trousers and top

Aa
Bb
Cc
Dd
Ee
Ff
Gg
Hh
Ii
Jj
Kk
Ll
Mm
Nn
Oo
Pp
Qq
Rr
Ss
Tt
Uu
Vv
Ww
Xx
Yy
Zz

jumpy ADJECTIVE **jumpier, jumpiest** nervous and anxious

junction NOUN **junctions** a place where roads or railway lines meet and cross

June NOUN the sixth month of the year, after May and before July

+ **June** comes from the name of the Roman queen of the gods, **Juno**.

jungle NOUN **jungles** trees and plants growing thickly together, especially in tropical areas of the world

junior ADJECTIVE **1** younger: *junior members of the tennis club* **2** meant for younger people: *junior classes* **3** lower in rank: *junior staff*
NOUN **juniors 1** a younger pupil in a school **2** someone who is your junior is younger than you are **3** someone who is lower in rank: *an office junior*

juniper NOUN **junipers** an evergreen bush with small purple berries used to flavour drinks and in cooking

junk NOUN useless or unwanted things: *What will we do with all this old junk?*

junk food NOUN food that is easy to make but is not good for your health

juror NOUN **jurors** one of the members of a jury

jury NOUN **juries** a group of people in a court of law who consider the evidence and decide whether someone is guilty of a crime or not

just¹ ADJECTIVE **1** fair or showing justice: *a just decision* **2** deserved: *It was a just reward for all his efforts.*
▸ **justly** ADVERB fairly

just² ADVERB
1 exactly: *A cold drink was just what I needed.*
2 barely: *I could only just see him.*
3 a very short time ago: *The clock's just struck five.*
4 simply: *I just want to go home.*
• **just about** more or less: *I've just about finished here.*

justice NOUN **justices 1** justice is fairness in dealing with people and their problems **2** justice is being treated properly and fairly by the law **3** a justice is a judge in a court of law

justify VERB **justifies, justifying, justified** to justify something is to give good reasons for it or to show that it is worthwhile or necessary: *She could justify her decision to leave.*
▸ **justifiable** ADJECTIVE able to be justified
▸ **justifiably** ADVERB in a justifiable way
▸ **justification** NOUN **justifications** a good reason or reasons that someone gives for doing something, which show that it is worthwhile or necessary

jut VERB **juts, jutting, jutted** to jut, or to jut out, is to stick out

juvenile ADJECTIVE **1** to do with young people, especially when they are too young to be treated as adults: *a juvenile court* **2** childish: *a juvenile sense of humour*
NOUN **juveniles** (*formal*) a young person

Aa
Bb
Cc
Dd
Ee
Ff
Gg
Hh
Ii
Jj
Kk
Ll
Mm
Nn
Oo
Pp
Qq
Rr
Ss
Tt
Uu
Vv
Ww
Xx
Yy
Zz

kaleidoscope NOUN **kaleidoscopes** a long tube that you look down, with mirrors and pieces of coloured glass at the bottom that form different patterns when you turn the tube

kangaroo NOUN **kangaroos** an Australian animal that jumps, and that carries its babies in a pouch at the front of its body

karaoke (pronounced ka-ri-**oh**-ki) NOUN entertainment in which someone sings a pop song while a machine plays the music

karate (pronounced ka-ra-ti) NOUN a Japanese type of fighting in which you use your hands and feet

> ✦ **Karate** is a Japanese word that means *empty hand*, because you do not hold or use any weapons in this type of fighting.

kayak (pronounced **kie**-ak) NOUN **kayaks** a type of canoe for one person

KB ABBREVIATION short for **kilobyte**

kebab NOUN **kebabs** small pieces of meat and vegetables cooked on a wooden or metal stick

keel NOUN **keels** a long piece of wood or steel at the bottom of a ship
VERB **keels, keeling, keeled**
• **keel over** to keel over is to fall over

keen ADJECTIVE **keener, keenest**
1 enthusiastic and wanting to do something or wanting something to happen: *Jim's a keen swimmer.* • *Everyone seemed very keen to help.* **2** if you have keen eyesight, you see things very clearly
▶ **keenly** ADVERB in an enthusiastic way: *The contest was keenly fought by two experienced players.*
▶ **keenness** NOUN being keen

keep VERB **keeps, keeping, kept**
1 to continue to have something and not give it to anyone else: *You can keep the book. I don't want it back.*
2 to put something in a particular place when you are not using it: *I keep my toys under the bed.*
3 to make someone or something stay a particular way: *Keep the door closed.* • *Keep off the grass.*
4 if food keeps, it stays fresh: *Milk doesn't keep for very long.*
5 if you keep animals, you have them and look after them
6 if you keep doing something, you do it a lot or you do it without stopping: *I keep forgetting to bring my homework.* • *Keep running until you get to the bridge.*
• **keep up** to keep up with someone or something is to move or do something as fast as they do: *He was running so fast that I couldn't keep up.*
▶ **keeper** NOUN **keepers** the person who looks after something, especially animals in a zoo

keepsake NOUN **keepsakes** something that someone gives you so that you will remember them or an occasion

keg NOUN **kegs** a small barrel

kennel NOUN **kennels** a hut for a dog

kept VERB a way of changing the verb **keep** to make a past tense. It can be used with or without a helping verb: *He kept all the letters his grandad sent him.* • *I have kept the receipt.*

kerb NOUN **kerbs** the edge of a pavement

kernel NOUN **kernels** the inside part of a nut, which you eat

kestrel NOUN **kestrels** a bird of the falcon family that kills other creatures for food

ketchup NOUN thick sauce made from tomatoes, which you eat cold

kettle NOUN **kettles** a container for boiling water in

Aa
Bb
Cc
Dd
Ee
Ff
Gg
Hh
Ii
Jj
Kk
Ll
Mm
Nn
Oo
Pp
Qq
Rr
Ss
Tt
Uu
Vv
Ww
Xx
Yy
Zz

kettledrum NOUN **kettledrums** a large drum made of a metal bowl covered with skin

key NOUN **keys**
1 something you use for locking and unlocking something such as a door
2 (*ICT*) a button on a computer keyboard or typewriter
3 (*music*) one of the white or black parts you press on a piano to make a sound
4 (*music*) a set of musical notes: *in the key of D minor*
5 something that makes you able to understand or achieve something: *Hard work is the key to success.* • *The key to the map is over the page.*
ADJECTIVE most important: *Dean is one of the team's key players.*

keyboard NOUN **keyboards 1** (*ICT*) the set of keys on a computer or typewriter **2** (*music*) the set of keys on a musical instrument such as a piano **3** (*music*) an electronic musical instrument that has keys like a piano

keyhole NOUN **keyholes** the part of a lock that you put a key into

keynote NOUN the basic note of a musical key, for example *D in D minor*
ADJECTIVE more important than all others: *the keynote speech*

key word NOUN **key words 1** an important word in a piece of writing that tells you what the piece is about **2** (*ICT*) a word that you key into a computer to help you find the information you are looking for

kg ABBREVIATION short for **kilogram** or **kilograms**

khaki NOUN a greenish-brown colour

✦**Khaki** comes from a word in the Urdu language of Pakistan and India. It means *dusty*, which describes the dull colour.

kick VERB **kicks, kicking, kicked 1** to hit someone or something with your foot: *Jane kicked the ball over the fence.* **2** to move your legs strongly, for example when swimming
NOUN **kicks 1** a strong movement of your leg or foot **2** (*informal*) a feeling of pleasure or excitement: *He gets a kick out of annoying other people.*

kick-off NOUN the start of a football game

kid NOUN **kids 1** (*informal*) a child **2** a young goat
• **with kid gloves** if you treat someone with kid gloves, you are very careful not to upset them
VERB **kids, kidding, kidded** to kid, or kid someone, is to trick them for fun

kidnap VERB **kidnaps, kidnapping, kidnapped** to take someone away using force, and ask for money to return them safely
▶ **kidnapper** NOUN **kidnappers** someone who kidnaps someone else

kidney NOUN **kidneys** one of the two organs in your body that remove waste from your blood and produce urine

kill VERB **kills, killing, killed** to make a person or animal die: *People were killed in the crash.*
▶ **killer** NOUN **killers** a person who kills someone

kiln NOUN **kilns** a large oven for baking pottery or bricks, or for drying grain

kilo NOUN **kilos** a kilogram

kilo- PREFIX if a word starts with **kilo-**, it adds the meaning *one thousand*. For example, a *kilogram* is equal to 1000 *grams*

✦**Kilo** comes from the Greek word for one thousand.

kilobyte NOUN **kilobytes** (*ICT*) a unit used to measure computer memory or data, equal to 1024 bytes. This is often shortened to **KB**

kilogram or **kilogramme** NOUN **kilograms** or **kilogrammes** a metric unit for measuring weight, equal to 1000 grams. This is shortened to **kg**

kilometre NOUN **kilometres** a metric unit for measuring distance, equal to 1000 metres. This is shortened to **km**

kilowatt NOUN **kilowatts** a unit for measuring electrical power, equal to 1000 watts

kilt NOUN **kilts** a pleated tartan skirt that is part of a traditional Scottish way of dressing for both men and women

kimono NOUN **kimonos** a traditional Japanese piece of clothing that looks like a long dress, tied round the middle

kin NOUN your kin are your relatives
• **next of kin** your closest relative

kind¹ NOUN **kinds** a type of something: *What kind of dog have you got?*

kind² ADJECTIVE **kinder, kindest** nice, generous and wanting to make other people happy

kindergarten NOUN **kindergartens** a school for very young children

kindhearted ADJECTIVE kind and generous

kindle VERB **kindles, kindling, kindled 1** to light a fire **2** to start burning
▸ **kindling** NOUN pieces of wood used to start a fire

kindly ADVERB **1** in a way that shows kindness: *The teacher spoke to us kindly.* **2** you can say 'kindly' to mean 'please' when you are rather angry: *Would you kindly be quiet!*
ADJECTIVE kind and caring

kindness NOUN helpfulness and generosity: *an act of kindness*

kinetic ADJECTIVE (*technology*) relating to or produced by movement

king NOUN **kings 1** a man who rules a country: *the King of Norway* **2** in the game of chess, a king is a piece that has a crown and has to be captured to win the game
▸ **kingdom** NOUN **kingdoms 1** a country ruled by a king **2** one of the three divisions of the natural world, which are the animal, vegetable and mineral kingdoms

kingfisher NOUN **kingfishers** a brightly coloured bird that eats fish

king-size ADJECTIVE larger than the usual size: *a king-size bed*

kink NOUN **kinks** a bend or twist in something

kiosk NOUN **kiosks** a small stall selling items such as newspapers and sweets

kipper NOUN **kippers** a smoked fish

kirk NOUN **kirks** a Scottish word for a church

kiss VERB **kisses, kissing, kissed** to touch someone with your lips as a sign of love: *Ellie kissed her mother.*
NOUN **kisses** the act of kissing someone: *He gave her a kiss.*

kiss of life NOUN the kiss of life is a way of helping an ill or injured person to start breathing again by blowing air into their mouth

kit NOUN **kits 1** the clothes or tools that you need for a particular activity or job: *I forgot to bring my football kit.* **2** a set of parts that you can put together to make something: *a model boat kit*

kitchen NOUN **kitchens** a room for preparing and cooking food

kite NOUN **kites 1** a toy that you fly in the air when it is windy **2** a bird from the hawk family

kitten NOUN **kittens** a young cat

kitty¹ NOUN **kitties** a collection of money that a group of people regularly add money to, and use for a particular purpose

kitty² NOUN **kitties** (*informal*) a cat or kitten

kiwi NOUN **kiwis** a bird from New Zealand that can run but not fly

kiwi fruit NOUN **kiwi fruit** a fruit with bright green flesh, black seeds and a hairy skin

km ABBREVIATION short for **kilometre** or **kilometres**

kmph ABBREVIATION short for **kilometres per hour**, a measure of speed

knack NOUN **knacks** a special talent: *Dad has a knack for baking perfect cakes.*

knapsack NOUN **knapsacks** a bag that you carry on your back

knave NOUN **knaves** the jack in a pack of playing cards

knead VERB **kneads, kneading, kneaded** to press dough or clay with your hands to make it ready to use

knee NOUN **knees** the joint in the middle of your leg where it bends

Aa
Bb
Cc
Dd
Ee
Ff
Gg
Hh
Ii
Jj
Kk
Ll
Mm
Nn
Oo
Pp
Qq
Rr
Ss
Tt
Uu
Vv
Ww
Xx
Yy
Zz

Aa
Bb
Cc
Dd
Ee
Ff
Gg
Hh
Ii
Jj
Kk
Ll
Mm
Nn
Oo
Pp
Qq
Rr
Ss
Tt
Uu
Vv
Ww
Xx
Yy
Zz

kneecap NOUN **kneecaps** the bone at the front of your knee

kneel VERB **kneels, kneeling, knelt** to move down so you are resting on your knees

knew VERB a way of changing the verb **know** to make a past tense: *Lucy knew exactly what to do.*

knickers PLURAL NOUN a piece of underwear for women or girls, which covers their bottom

knife NOUN **knives** a tool used for cutting something, which has a handle and a blade

VERB **knifes, knifing, knifed** to stab someone with a knife

knight NOUN **knights 1** in history, a man of a high social rank who was trained to fight **2** a man who has been given an honour by a king or queen that lets him use the title *Sir* **3** in the game of chess, a knight is a piece which is shaped like a horse

knighthood NOUN **knighthoods** the rank or title of a knight

knit VERB **knits, knitting, knitted** to make something using two long needles and wool: *Sandy was knitting a scarf.* • *Do you know how to knit?*

▶ **knitting** NOUN **1** the activity of making things by knitting **2** something that has been or is being knitted

knives NOUN the plural of **knife**

knob NOUN **knobs 1** a round handle on a door or drawer **2** a round button used for controlling a machine **3** a lump: *a knob of butter*

knock VERB **knocks, knocking, knocked 1** to hit something so that it moves or falls: *The cat knocked the vase off the table.* **2** to hit a door or window several times with your knuckles or a knocker in order to attract attention: *Knock before you come in.* **3** to bump into something: *I knocked my elbow on the edge of the door.*

• **knock someone out** to knock someone out is to make someone become unconscious, especially by hitting them

NOUN **knocks 1** the sound of someone knocking on a door or window: *There was a knock at the door.* **2** a blow or injury caused by hitting something: *He's had a nasty knock on the head.*

▶ **knocker** NOUN **knockers** a metal object on a door, which you knock with

knockout NOUN **knockouts** a hit that makes someone unconscious

knoll NOUN **knolls** (*geography*) a small hill

knot NOUN **knots 1** a join made by tying two ends of string or rope together **2** a hard lump in a piece of wood where there used to be a branch **3** a unit for measuring how fast a ship is travelling

VERB **knots, knotting, knotted** to tie something with a knot

know VERB **knows, knowing, knew, known 1** to have information about something or be aware of something: *Do you know where he lives?* • *I didn't know you were Alan's cousin!* **2** to have learnt about something: *I don't know much German.* **3** to be familiar with a person or place: *I didn't know anyone at the party.*

▶ **knowing** ADJECTIVE showing that you know something that is supposed to be secret: *He gave me a knowing look.*

knowledge NOUN **1** the information and understanding that you have about something: *She has a good knowledge of sport.* **2** the fact that you are aware of something: *His parents had no knowledge that he hadn't gone to school.*

▶ **knowledgeable** ADJECTIVE knowing a lot about something

knuckle NOUN **knuckles** one of the parts on your hands where your fingers bend

koala NOUN **koalas** an Australian animal that looks like a small bear, climbs trees and eats eucalyptus leaves

Koran NOUN the Koran is the holy book of the Islamic religion

kosher ADJECTIVE kosher food is prepared according to Jewish law

kung-fu NOUN a Chinese type of fighting using your hands and feet

kW ABBREVIATION short for **kilowatt** or **kilowatts**

Ll

l ABBREVIATION short for **litre** or **litres**

label NOUN **labels 1** a small note that is fixed on to something and gives information about it: *The washing instructions are on the label.* **2** a make or brand of something, for example clothes: *He wanted trainers with a more expensive label.*

VERB **labels, labelling, labelled** to fix a small note to something: *All the boxes have been carefully labelled.*

laboratory NOUN **laboratories** a room filled with special equipment where a scientist works

labour NOUN **1** hard work **2** the process of giving birth to a baby **3** people who work: *the rising cost of labour*

VERB **labours, labouring, laboured** to work hard: *workers labouring in the fields*

▶ **labourer** NOUN **labourers** a person who does hard physical work

labrador NOUN **labradors** a large black or fawn-coloured dog

labyrinth NOUN **labyrinths** a maze that is difficult to find your way through

lace NOUN **laces 1** a cord for doing up shoes or other clothing: *learn to tie your shoe laces* **2** fabric that is made in open patterns in fine thread: *a collar trimmed with lace*

VERB **laces, lacing, laced 1** to lace your shoes is to put laces in them or tie the laces in a knot or bow **2** to lace a drink is to add alcohol to it

lack VERB **lacks, lacking, lacked** to be completely without something or not to have enough of it: *Amy lacks a sense of humour.*

NOUN something that you do not have: *Lack of sleep was making us grumpy.*

lacquer NOUN **lacquers** a kind of varnish

VERB **lacquers, lacquering, lacquered** to cover something with varnish to protect or decorate it

lacrosse NOUN a game for two teams of twelve players who throw and catch the ball with a stick that has a shallow net on the end

lad NOUN **lads** (*informal*) a boy or young man

ladder NOUN **ladders 1** a set of steps that you can move around to climb up to places that you cannot normally reach **2** a long tear that has started from a hole or broken stitch in a stocking or tights

laden ADJECTIVE carrying heavy things: *laden with shopping*

ladle NOUN **ladles** a large spoon for liquids, especially soup

VERB **ladles, ladling, ladled** to lift or serve liquid with a large spoon: *Mrs Moore was busy ladling soup into bowls.*

lady NOUN **ladies 1** a polite word for a woman: *Ask that lady if the seat by her is free.* **2** a woman with good manners: *Mrs Kingsley was a real lady.* **3** the title for the wife of a lord or knight or for a woman with a high social rank

ladybird NOUN **ladybirds** a small beetle that is usually red with black spots

lag VERB **lags, lagging, lagged 1** to move slowly and fall behind other people **2** to cover something such as pipes with a warm covering

lager NOUN **lagers** a light-coloured beer

lagoon NOUN **lagoons** (*geography*) a large shallow pool of seawater separated from the rest of the sea by an area of sand

laid VERB the form of the verb **lay** that is used with a helping verb to show that something happened in the past: *Have you laid the table yet?*

lain VERB the form of the verb **lie** that is used with a helping verb to show that something happened in the past: *I had*

297

lain down for a moment and fallen fast asleep.

lair NOUN **lairs** the den of a wild animal

lake NOUN **lakes** a large stretch of water that has land all around it

lama NOUN **lamas** a Buddhist priest in Tibet

lamb NOUN **lambs 1** a young sheep **2** meat from a young sheep

lame NOUN **lamer, lamest 1** not able to walk properly: *One of the sheep looked a bit lame.* **2** a lame excuse is weak and not very convincing

▸ **lamely** ADVERB weakly: *'This is too hard,' she said lamely.*

lament NOUN **laments** a sad song or poem, especially about someone's death VERB **laments, lamenting, lamented** if you lament something, you say or show how sad you are about not having it any more

laminated ADJECTIVE **1** covered with thin, see-through plastic **2** made by sticking layers together: *laminated glass windows*

lamp NOUN **lamps** a piece of equipment that has a light in it: *a table lamp*

lamppost NOUN **lampposts** a tall pole in the street with a light at the top

lance NOUN **lances** a weapon like a long spear

lance-corporal NOUN **lance-corporals** a soldier ranking above a private and below a corporal

land NOUN **lands 1** the solid parts of the earth's surface: *the land and the sea* **2** land is ground: *good land for growing plants • The farmer bought another piece of land.* **3** a land is a country: *tales from faraway lands*
VERB **lands, landing, landed 1** to come down to the ground: *He fell from the tree and landed on the grass.* **2** to arrive on land or on the shore: *We landed in Spain at about midnight.* **3** to land an aircraft is to bring it down to the ground

landform NOUN **landforms** (*geography*) a natural feature of the surface of the Earth: *valleys and other landforms*

landing NOUN **landings 1** an aircraft or boat returning to land: *an emergency landing* **2** the level floor between flights of steps on a staircase

landlady NOUN **landladies 1** a woman who owns a house that someone else pays to live in **2** a woman who runs a pub

landlocked ADJECTIVE (*geography*) almost or completely surrounded by land

landlord NOUN **landlords 1** a man who owns a house that someone else pays to live in **2** a man who runs a pub

landmark NOUN **landmarks** a place, especially a building, that helps you know where you are because you can see it from all around

landscape NOUN **landscapes** a view of a large area of land, especially a painting or photograph: *a rocky landscape • a landscape artist*

landslide NOUN **landslides** (*geography*) a large amount of the ground slipping down the side of a hill

lane NOUN **lanes 1** a narrow road **2** a strip of a road, the air or the sea that certain vehicles should travel in: *Cyclists are allowed in the bus lanes.*

language NOUN **languages 1** communication in speaking and writing **2** the words that one particular group uses, such as the people that live in one country: *learn a foreign language* **3** a system of symbols or signs that give information, for example in computers

lanky ADJECTIVE **lankier, lankiest** tall and thin

lantern NOUN **lanterns** a case holding a light

lap NOUN **laps 1** the top part of a person's legs when they are sitting down **2** a single turn round a race track
VERB **laps, lapping, lapped 1** to lap something is to lick it up: *a cat lapping milk from a saucer* **2** water laps when it splashes gently against rocks or on a beach **3** to lap someone is to pass them more than once as you go round a race track

• **lap something up** (*informal*) to lap

something up is to enjoy it very much: *She was lapping up all the attention the boys paid her.*

lapel NOUN **lapels** the front part of a coat or jacket collar: *a flower pinned to his lapel*

lapse NOUN **lapses** 1 a space of time: *After a lapse of ten years, Jones started to play football again.* 2 a failure to work properly for a short time: *a memory lapse*

VERB **lapses, lapsing, lapsed** 1 to lapse into a certain condition is to gradually go into it: *The patient has lapsed into unconsciousness.* 2 an agreement or contract lapses when it stops being valid

laptop NOUN **laptops** (*ICT*) a small, portable computer that you can use, for example, when you are travelling

lard NOUN fat that can be used in cooking and that comes from a pig

larder NOUN **larders** a small room or large cupboard for storing food in the past

large ADJECTIVE **larger, largest** big or bigger than normal: *a large man* • *a large house*

• **at large** 1 free, not in captivity: *There is a wild cat at large in the area.* 2 in general: *The public at large do not like the idea.*

▶ **largely** ADVERB mainly: *The church has been largely rebuilt.*

lark NOUN **larks** a singing bird that flies high in the sky

larva NOUN **larvae** an insect in its first stage after coming out of the egg

lasagne NOUN **lasagnes** 1 flat sheets of pasta 2 an Italian dish made up of layers of pasta, meat sauce and cheese

laser NOUN **lasers** a very narrow, powerful beam of light

lash NOUN **lashes** 1 an eyelash 2 a whipping movement: *a lash of the whip*

VERB **lashes, lashing, lashed** 1 to hit something with a whipping movement: *rain that lashed against the windows* 2 to tie something up with rope or string: *The banners were lashed to the walls of the buildings.*

lass NOUN **lasses** (*informal*) a girl

lasso (pronounced la-**soo**) NOUN **lassoes** or **lassos** a long rope with a loop that tightens when the rope is pulled, used especially for catching wild horses

VERB **lassoes, lassoing, lassoed** to throw a rope around something to catch it

last ADJECTIVE 1 coming after all the others: *the last bus of the day* 2 the final one remaining: *my last toffee* 3 most recent: *on my last birthday*

ADVERB 1 after all the others: *Who came last in the relay?* 2 after everything else: *I'll do my maths homework last.* 3 most recently: *When did you see Anna last?*

VERB **lasts, lasting, lasted** 1 to continue or go on: *The lesson seemed to last for ever.* 2 to remain in good condition: *These boots should last for years.*

NOUN the final person or thing: *You are always the last to finish.*

• **at last** in the end: *At last we saw the sea.*

▶ **lastly** ADVERB finally: *Lastly, I want to thank my teacher, Mr Nimmo.*

latch NOUN **latches** a piece of wood or metal that rises and falls to open or fasten a door

late ADJECTIVE **later, latest** 1 coming after the expected time: *a late arrival* 2 far on in time or in a particular period: *a late movie* • *the late 19th century* • *My dad's in his late thirties.* 3 recently dead: *our late uncle*

ADVERB **later, latest** 1 coming after the expected time: *The train arrives later every day.* 2 far on in time: *It's getting late.*

▶ **lately** ADVERB recently: *I haven't been to any parties lately.*

▶ **lateness** NOUN being late

lateral ADJECTIVE at the side, or to or from the side

lateral thinking NOUN trying to solve problems in new ways by thinking about them differently

lathe NOUN **lathes** (*technology*) a machine that turns and cuts wood or metal

lather NOUN foam that you get when you mix soap in water

VERB **lathers, lathering, lathered** to form a froth

Aa
Bb
Cc
Dd
Ee
Ff
Gg
Hh
Ii
Jj
Kk
Ll
Mm
Nn
Oo
Pp
Qq
Rr
Ss
Tt
Uu
Vv
Ww
Xx
Yy
Zz

Latin NOUN the language of the ancient Romans

latitude NOUN (*geography*) the position of a place along an imaginary line north and south of the equator. Look up and compare **longitude**

latter ADJECTIVE the latter is the second one of two people or things you are mentioning. The first one is the **former**: *If I am offered orange juice or milk, I'll always choose the latter.*

lattice NOUN **lattices** a pattern of strips that cross over one another

laugh VERB **laughs, laughing, laughed** to make a sound of enjoyment when you think something is funny

NOUN **laughs** the sound a person makes when they think something is funny

laughing stock NOUN **laughing stocks** a person who people laugh at in an unkind way because they seem ridiculous

laughter NOUN laughing: *the sound of laughter • roaring with laughter*

launch VERB **launches, launching, launched 1** to put a boat or ship in the water for the first time **2** to fire a rocket into the air **3** to start something like a project or start to sell a new product: *The company are launching a new chocolate bar.*

NOUN **launches 1** the act of launching something: *We'll be able to watch the shuttle launch on the TV.* **2** a large motorboat

launch pad NOUN **launch pads** a platform that a spacecraft is launched from

launder VERB **launders, laundering, laundered** to launder clothes is to wash or clean them so that they are ready to wear again

▸ **launderette** NOUN **launderettes** a shop full of washing machines that you can pay to use

▸ **laundry** NOUN **laundries 1** clothes that are going to be washed, or have just been washed **2** a business where you can send washing to be done

lava NOUN the hot liquid rock that comes out of an erupting volcano and becomes solid as it cools down

lavatory NOUN **lavatories** a toilet

lavender NOUN a plant with purple flowers that smell strong and sweet

lavish ADJECTIVE very generous, with more than enough of everything: *a lavish dinner • lavish praise*

VERB **lavishes, lavishing, lavished**

• **lavish something on someone** to lavish something on someone is to give them a lot, or too much of it: *Her parents had always lavished gifts on her.*

law NOUN **laws 1** a rule or set of rules for everyone in a country or state: *Driving at the age of 13 is against the law.* • *You could study law at university.* **2** a scientific rule that explains what always happens in certain circumstances: *The law of gravity means that the apple will fall downwards.*

lawful ADJECTIVE allowed by the law

▸ **lawfully** ADVERB according to the law

lawn NOUN **lawns** an area of smooth grass in a garden

lawnmower NOUN **lawnmowers** a machine for cutting large areas of grass

lawyer NOUN **lawyers** someone whose job is to advise people about the law

lax ADJECTIVE **laxer, laxest** not strict: *Discipline has been too lax recently.*

lay VERB **lays, laying, laid 1** to put something down: *lay the book on the table* **2** to arrange something: *lay the table • lay a trap* **3** when a bird or female animal lays an egg, the egg comes out of its body

✦ Try not to confuse **lay** and **lie**. You **lay** something somewhere, whereas you **lie** somewhere: *Lay your pencils on your desks.* • *I am going to **lie** in bed for a while.*

The past tenses can be confusing too. **Lay** is also a past tense of **lie**: *The cat lay on the mat.*

layer NOUN **layers** a covering that lies over something, or a thickness under something: *grass covered with a layer of snow • a layer of jam in the cake*

layout NOUN **layouts** the way things are set out or arranged: *The layout of the rooms is different.*

laze VERB **lazes, lazing, lazed** to be lazy and do very little: *I just like to laze around in the holidays.*

lazily ADVERB in a slow, unhurried way

lazy ADJECTIVE **lazier, laziest** not wanting to do anything much, especially work: *You must be the laziest pupil in this school.*
▸ **lazily** ADVERB in a slow, unhurried way
▸ **laziness** NOUN being lazy and not willing to work

lb ABBREVIATION short for **pound** or **pounds** in weight: *2lbs of sugar*

lead¹ (pronounced **leed**) VERB **leads, leading, led**
1 to be winning or be more successful: *Coe led the race from the beginning. • Germany is leading, with France in second place.*
2 to show someone the way by going first: *You lead and I'll follow on my bike.*
3 to direct or control a group of people: *Kim was leading a discussion about homework.*
4 if you lead a busy life, you are always busy
5 a road that leads somewhere goes to that place
NOUN **leads**
1 the first or front place: *Jenkins has been in the lead for most of the race.*
2 an electrical wire or cable: *Someone had cut the lead to the alarm.*
3 help or guidance: *Follow my lead and just do what I do. • The police are following up several new leads.*
4 a strap or chain attached to a dog's collar that you can hold when you walk with it: *Please keep your dog on its lead.*

lead² (pronounced **led**) NOUN **leads 1** a soft, dark grey metal **2** the inside part of a pencil that writes, made of graphite

leader NOUN **leaders** a person who leads: *the leader of the expedition*

▸ **leadership** NOUN **1** being a leader: *The team's done well under Sam's leadership.* **2** the ability to lead: *If you want to be a prefect, you'll have to show good leadership.*

leaf NOUN **leaves 1** a part of a plant that grows out from the side of the stem and is usually green **2** a page of a book
• **turn over a new leaf** to make a new start and do better

leaflet NOUN **leaflets** a small printed sheet of paper

leafy ADJECTIVE **leafier, leafiest 1** a leafy plant or tree has a lot of leaves **2** a leafy place has a lot of plants or trees

league NOUN **leagues 1** a group of teams that play sports matches against each other **2** a group of people or nations who agree to work together
• **in league with someone** working together with someone, especially secretly to do something bad

leak NOUN **leaks 1** a hole that liquid or gas can escape or enter through **2** an escape of gas or liquid **3** there is a leak when someone lets out secret information
VERB **leaks, leaking, leaked 1** to escape: *Gas was leaking from somewhere under the floor.* **2** to let liquid or gas in or out through a hole: *My boots leak.* **3** to give secret information away: *This news was leaked to a newspaper yesterday.*
▸ **leakage** NOUN **leakages** an escape of gas, a liquid or information: *We lost a lot of oil through leakage.*

lean VERB **leans, leaning, leant 1** to rest against something: *a boy leaning on the wall* **2** to slope over to one side: *Lean over and get the salt for me would you?* **3** to rely on someone: *You know you can always lean on me.*
ADJECTIVE **leaner, leanest** without any or much fat: *Models have to look lean these days. • I'll only buy lean meat.*

leap VERB **leaps, leaping, leapt** to jump high or long: *dolphins leaping out of the water*
NOUN **leaps** a big jump: *a leap over the river*

Aa Bb Cc Dd Ee Ff Gg Hh Ii Jj Kk Ll Mm Nn Oo Pp Qq Rr Ss Tt Uu Vv Ww Xx Yy Zz

leap year NOUN **leap years** a year that occurs every four years and has 366 days. The extra day is February 29

learn VERB **learns, learning, learnt** or **learned** to get to know something or how to do something: *learn your lines for the play* • *learning how to swim*

▸ **learner** NOUN **learners** a person who is being taught something

▸ **learning** NOUN knowledge: *a man of great learning*

lease NOUN **leases** an agreement to rent something like a flat or house to someone

VERB **leases, leasing, leased** to rent something to someone

leash NOUN **leashes** a lead for taking a dog for a walk

least ADJECTIVE the smallest amount of anything: *The person who had the least difficulty was the tallest.*

ADVERB the lowest amount: *Which trousers cost least?*

• **at least 1** not less than: *She must be at least forty years old.* **2** at any rate: *John has finished, at least he should have.*

leather NOUN **leathers** a material for making shoes, bags and clothes that is made from the skin of an animal

leave VERB **leaves, leaving, left**

1 to go away from someone, something or somewhere: *I left school early.*

2 to not take something with you when you go away: *Mum always leaves her umbrella on the bus.*

3 to put something somewhere: *Leave your shoes in the hall.*

4 to not do something: *I think I'll leave my French homework until tomorrow.*

5 to make someone have a particular feeling or thought: *The poor test result left Josh feeling disappointed.*

6 to give something to someone in a will: *Granny left Jodie all her jewellery.*

NOUN holiday time from work, especially work in the armed forces: *a week's leave*

leaves NOUN the plural of **leaf**

lecture NOUN **lectures 1** a talk by someone to an audience or a group of students **2** a long telling-off

VERB **lectures, lecturing, lectured 1** to give a talk on a particular subject to a class or audience **2** to give someone a good telling-off: *'This is not good for your children,'* he lectured. *'You are letting them get away with too much.'*

led VERB a way of changing the verb **lead** to make a past tense. It can be used with or without a helping verb: *Connor led the boys into the wood.* • *Where have you led us?*

ledge NOUN **ledges** a shelf or something that sticks out like a shelf: *a ledge of rock* • *a window ledge*

lee NOUN the sheltered side of something, away from the wind

leek NOUN **leeks** a long green and white vegetable of the onion family

left¹ ADJECTIVE on the other side from the right side. For example, on the side of a page you usually start reading

ADVERB on or towards the other side from the right: *Now turn left.*

NOUN the left is the other side from the right side: *Can we stop just here on the left?*

left² VERB a way of changing the verb **leave** to make a past tense. It can be used with or without a helping verb: *I have left my book at home.* • *We all thanked them when they left.*

left-handed ADJECTIVE **1** preferring to use your left hand to do things, rather than your right **2** meant to be used by the left hand rather than the right: *a left-handed pair of scissors*

leftovers PLURAL NOUN food that has not been eaten up at a meal: *Shall I put the leftovers in the fridge?*

leg NOUN **legs**

1 one of the parts of the body that animals and humans stand and walk on

2 one half of a pair of trousers

3 one of the upright supports of a piece of furniture like a table or chair

4 one stage in a journey or a contest: *This is the second leg of the race across Europe.*

legacy NOUN **legacies** something that someone leaves in their will

legal ADJECTIVE **1** allowed by the law:

Aa
Bb
Cc
Dd
Ee
Ff
Gg
Hh
Ii
Jj
Kk
Ll
Mm
Nn
Oo
Pp
Qq
Rr
Ss
Tt
Uu
Vv
Ww
Xx
Yy
Zz

legend → leprosy

Is it legal to ride your bike on the pavement? **2** to do with the law: *legal studies*

▶ **legalize** *or* **legalise** VERB **legalizes, legalizing, legalized** to legalize something is to make it allowed by law: *Some American states still haven't legalized gambling.*

legend NOUN **legends** a traditional story that is handed down through generations

▶ **legendary** ADJECTIVE **1** very famous: *his legendary talent for scoring goals* **2** belonging to legends: *legendary monsters*

legible ADJECTIVE easy to read: *The letter became less legible towards the end.*

▶ **legibility** NOUN how easy something is to read

▶ **legibly** ADVERB in a way that is easy to read: *Could you write your name more legibly please?*

legion NOUN **legions 1** (*history*) a group of several thousand Roman soldiers **2** a huge crowd of people: *legions of tourists*

legislation NOUN a law or set of laws

legitimate ADJECTIVE **1** allowed by the law, or set up according to the law : *the legitimate government* **2** reasonable: *a legitimate complaint*

▶ **legitimately** ADVERB according to the law: *not legitimately married*

leisure NOUN your leisure is your spare time

▶ **leisurely** ADJECTIVE not rushed or hurried: *walking at a leisurely pace*

lemon NOUN **lemons 1** an oval fruit with a hard, yellow skin and very sour juice **2** a pale yellow colour

lemonade NOUN a soft drink that has a lemon flavour

lend VERB **lends, lending, lent** to let someone borrow something for a time

• **lend a hand** to help someone

length NOUN **lengths 1** how long something is, or how much time something lasts: *We measured the length of the table.* • *twice the length of a normal lesson* **2** a piece

of something long: *a length of plastic piping*

• **at length** in detail: *The doctor explained the treatment at length.*

▶ **lengthen** VERB **lengthens, lengthening, lengthened 1** to lengthen something is to make it longer: *Mum's going to lengthen my skirt.* **2** to lengthen is to grow longer: *a lengthening queue*

▶ **lengthy** ADJECTIVE **lengthier, lengthiest** taking a long time: *a lengthy delay*

lenient ADJECTIVE not very strict in giving punishments

lens NOUN **lenses 1** a piece of glass that is curved on one or both sides and is used in equipment like glasses, cameras and telescopes **2** (*science*) a part of your eye behind your pupil

✦ **Lens** comes from the Latin word for *lentil*. This is because it was believed that the lens in your eye is shaped like a lentil.

lent VERB a way of changing the verb **lend** to make a past tense. It can be used with or without a helping verb: *Here's the book you lent me yesterday.* • *You haven't lent him money, have you?*

Lent NOUN in the Christian church, the forty days before Easter when, for religious reasons, people give up something they enjoy

lentil NOUN **lentils** a small seed that is often cooked in soups and other dishes

leopard (pronounced **lep**-ard) NOUN **leopards** an animal of the cat family with a spotted skin

leotard NOUN **leotards** a tight-fitting, stretchy piece of clothing that you wear for doing exercises or dancing

leper NOUN **lepers** someone who suffers from leprosy

leprechaun (pronounced **lep**-ri-kon) NOUN **leprechauns** a small, magical creature in Irish folk tales that likes to cause mischief

leprosy NOUN a serious, infectious skin disease that can cause damage to parts of the body

Aa
Bb
Cc
Dd
Ee
Ff
Gg
Hh
Ii
Jj
Kk
Ll
Mm
Nn
Oo
Pp
Qq
Rr
Ss
Tt
Uu
Vv
Ww
Xx
Yy
Zz

less ADJECTIVE AND ADVERB not as much: *We'll have to spend less money.* • *If you complain less, you enjoy life more.*

NOUN a smaller amount: *I've got less than he has.*

PREPOSITION minus: *That leaves £10, less the money I need for sweets.*

▶ **lessen** VERB **lessens, lessening, lessened** to make or become smaller: *The pain in my arm had lessened.*

▶ **lesser** ADJECTIVE smaller or less serious

lesson NOUN **lessons 1** a period of teaching: *When's our next lesson?* **2** something that you learn or that someone teaches you: *one of the most important lessons about history* **3** a reading from the Bible in a church service

let VERB **lets, letting, let 1** to let someone do something is to allow them to do it: *Please let me go!* **2** to let a house or office is to rent it out

• **let someone down** to let someone down is to disappoint them: *If she promises me something, she won't let me down.*

• **let someone off** to let someone off is to not punish them even though they have done something wrong

• **let up** if something lets up, it becomes less: *It seemed as if the rain would never let up.*

lethal ADJECTIVE able to kill: *a lethal weapon*

let's VERB another way of saying 'shall we?': *Let's have a game of cards.*

letter NOUN **letters 1** a message that you write and send to another person **2** one of the written shapes that you combine to write words, like *a*, *b* or *c*

▶ **lettering** NOUN writing, especially when it is for decoration: *The title is on the picture frame in gold lettering.*

lettuce NOUN **lettuces** a green vegetable whose leaves are used in salads

leukaemia NOUN a kind of cancer that affects the body's white blood cells

level ADJECTIVE **1** flat or horizontal: *a piece of level ground* **2** as high as something else or in line with it: *The picture needs to be level with the mirror next to it.*

NOUN **levels 1** a particular position: *Pin the notice up at eye level.* **2** a particular standard or grade: *It's best to start at beginners' level.* **3** a tool that shows if a surface is horizontal or vertical

VERB **levels, levelling, levelled 1** to level something is to make it flat, smooth or horizontal: *The ground will have to be levelled before they can build on it.* **2** to level things is to make them equal: *Grey scored again to level the scores.*

• **level off** or **level out** to level off or level out is to become horizontal: *The plane levelled out at 2000 feet.*

level crossing NOUN **level crossings** a place where a road crosses a railway track

lever NOUN **levers 1** a strong bar for pushing against or pulling on in order to move something heavy **2** a handle that operates a machine

VERB **levers, levering, levered** to move something by forcing a bar under or behind it: *It should be possible to lever the door open.*

lexical ADJECTIVE to do with words

liability NOUN **liabilities 1** responsibility for something **2** a person or thing that is likely to cause a problem for you

liable ADJECTIVE **1** very likely to: *She's liable to lose her temper very suddenly.* **2** responsible for something: *You are liable to pay for any damage.*

liar NOUN **liars** someone who tells lies

liberal ADJECTIVE **1** willing to accept different opinions and different ways of living **2** a liberal amount of something is a lot of it: *a very liberal helping of chocolate pudding*

▶ **liberally** ADVERB in large amounts: *Pour the sauce liberally over the ice cream.*

liberate VERB **liberates, liberating, liberated 1** to set someone free **2** to give someone freedom to do something, or make them feel free

Aa
Bb
Cc
Dd
Ee
Ff
Gg
Hh
Ii
Jj
Kk
Ll
Mm
Nn
Oo
Pp
Qq
Rr
Ss
Tt
Uu
Vv
Ww
Xx
Yy
Zz

liberty → lifestyle

▶ **liberation** NOUN being set free from someone else's control

liberty NOUN **liberties** freedom, especially to do or say what you want: *You are at liberty to walk around the grounds.*

librarian NOUN **librarians** a person whose job is to look after a library

library NOUN **libraries** a building or room that has a collection of books or recordings

lice NOUN the plural form of the word **louse**

licence NOUN **licences** an official document that gives someone permission to do or have something: *a driving licence • a licence to fish*

✦Remember that **licence** with a **c** is a noun: *a driving licence*
License with an **s** is a verb: *You are not licensed to fish here.*

license VERB **licenses, licensing, licensed** to officially allow someone to do something

lichen (pronounced lie-ken) NOUN **lichens** a kind of mossy plant that grows on surfaces like rocks and tree trunks

lick VERB **licks, licking, licked** to move your tongue over something
NOUN **licks 1** a movement of your tongue over something: *Give the spoon one last lick.* **2** a small amount of something: *This room needs a lick of paint.*

licorice NOUN another spelling of **liquorice**

lid NOUN **lids 1** a cover that fits a container like a box or a pot **2** an eyelid

lie¹ VERB **lies, lying, lied** to say something that is not true: *We know Auntie May lies about her age.*
NOUN **lies** a statement that is not true: *The boy's story is a pack of lies.*

lie² VERB **lies, lying, lay, laid 1** to rest in a flat position: *Lie flat on your back.* **2** to be or remain a certain way: *The buildings lay in ruins.*

✦The past tense of **lie** when it means 'to tell an untruth' is **lied**: *I lied about passing the test.*
The past tense of **lie** when it means 'to rest flat' is **lay**: *I lay in bed all day.*

lieutenant (pronounced lef-ten-int) NOUN **lieutenants** a low-ranking officer in the army or navy

life NOUN **lives**
1 a life is the time between being born and dying
2 life is the state of being alive: *feeling her pulse for any sign of life*
3 life is energy and liveliness: *Try to put a bit more life into your singing.*
4 your life is the way you live: *Life on a boat is great fun.*
5 life is all living things: *a book about pond life*

lifebelt NOUN **lifebelts** a large ring that will float and that someone can hold to stop them sinking under water

lifeboat NOUN **lifeboats** a boat for rescuing people at sea

life cycle NOUN **life cycles** (*science*) the different stages that a living thing goes through from its birth to its death

lifeguard NOUN **lifeguards** someone who works at a swimming pool or on a beach to rescue people who are in danger of drowning

life jacket NOUN **life jackets** a jacket filled with air or other light material that will float and stop someone from sinking

lifeless ADJECTIVE **1** dead **2** unconscious or without any signs of life **3** dull and boring: *a lifeless performance*

lifelike ADJECTIVE very like a real living thing or person

lifeline NOUN **lifelines 1** a way of communicating or getting help if you need it: *The telephone is our lifeline.* **2** a rope used to rescue a person who has fallen in water

life-size ADJECTIVE a life-size picture or statue is the same size as the real person

lifestyle NOUN **lifestyles** the way that someone lives: *We try to have a healthy lifestyle.*

Aa Bb Cc Dd Ee Ff Gg Hh Ii Jj Kk **Ll** Mm Nn Oo Pp Qq Rr Ss Tt Uu Vv Ww Xx Yy Zz

305

Aa
Bb
Cc
Dd
Ee
Ff
Gg
Hh
Ii
Jj
Kk
Ll
Mm
Nn
Oo
Pp
Qq
Rr
Ss
Tt
Uu
Vv
Ww
Xx
Yy
Zz

lifetime NOUN **lifetimes** the time that a certain person is alive: *Gran's seen a lot of changes in her lifetime.*

lift VERB **lifts, lifting, lifted 1** to lift something is to pick it up or raise it: *She lifted her hand to her forehead.* **2** if something such as fog lifts, it gradually disappears
NOUN **lifts 1** a moving platform that can take things or people between the floors of a building **2** a ride in someone's car: *Do you want a lift home?* **3** a movement upwards: *ten lifts with each leg*

lift-off NOUN **lift-offs** the time when a spacecraft leaves the ground

light[1] NOUN **lights 1** light is what allows you to see things. Otherwise, it would be dark: *The light in this room is good for painting.* **2** a light is something that gives light, such as a lamp or a candle: *Don't forget to switch off the light.*
• **come to light** if information comes to light, people find out about something
ADJECTIVE **lighter, lightest 1** not dark: *Mike got up as soon as it began to get light.* **2** pale in colour: *light blue*
VERB **lights, lighting, lit 1** to light something is to make it burn with a flame: *Let's light the fire.* **2** to light is to start burning: *Why won't the cooker light?* **3** to light a place is to make it brighter: *In the past, they lit the stage with candles.*

light[2] ADJECTIVE **lighter, lightest 1** not heavy: *a light suitcase* **2** easy, or not too serious: *light work* • *light music* **3** not large or strong: *a light shower*

lighten[1] VERB **lightens, lightening, lightened** to make something less heavy: *We threw two boxes overboard to lighten the boat.*

lighten[2] VERB **lightens, lightening, lightened 1** to make something brighter: *Add more white paint to lighten the colour.* **2** to lighten is to become lighter: *The clouds blew away and the sky lightened.*

lighter NOUN **lighters** a device with a flame or spark that can make something burn, especially a cigarette

light-hearted ADJECTIVE **1** a light-hearted person is cheerful **2** something that is light-hearted is not very serious: *a light-hearted quiz*

lighthouse NOUN **lighthouses** a building like a tower that has a flashing light at the top to warn or guide ships

lighting NOUN equipment for giving light

lightly ADVERB **1** gently: *Mum touched me lightly on the arm and smiled.* **2** not in a very serious way: *They treated the problem too lightly.*

lightning NOUN an electric flash in the sky that often happens just before a clap of thunder

lightweight ADJECTIVE **1** not very heavy: *a lightweight raincoat* **2** not very important or serious

light-year NOUN **light-years** (*science*) the distance that light travels in a year, which is 6 billion miles

like[1] PREPOSITION **1** similar to: *Marnie looks just like her mother.* **2** in a similar way to: *She dances like a professional.* **3** typical of: *It's not like you to be late.*
CONJUNCTION as if: *You look like you've seen a ghost.*

like[2] VERB **likes, liking, liked** to think that something or someone is nice or good: *I like pizza.* • *The teacher likes us to work quietly.*

likeable or **likable** ADJECTIVE a likeable person is attractive and pleasant

likelihood NOUN if there is a likelihood of something happening, it might or will probably happen

likely ADJECTIVE probable or expected: *It's likely they'll be home before us.*

liken VERB **likens, likening, likened** to say that two things are like each other: *Her books have been likened to the old Enid Blyton stories.*

likeness NOUN **likenesses 1** something similar: *I do see a likeness between the girls.* **2** a good likeness is something that looks very similar to the real thing or person: *The portrait is an excellent likeness of Katy.*

likewise ADVERB used for saying that something else is the same, or that you should do the same with something else: *Put the paints away. Likewise any pastels or chalks you have used.*

lilac NOUN **lilacs** a bush or tree with hanging clusters of sweet-smelling white or purple flowers

ADJECTIVE pale purple

lilt NOUN **lilts** a light, swinging rhythm: *speaking with a lilt*

lily NOUN **lilies** a tall plant with large white or coloured flowers

limb NOUN **limbs** 1 a leg or arm 2 a branch of a tree

limber VERB **limbers, limbering, limbered**

• **limber up** to limber up is to stretch and warm your muscles up before doing harder exercise

lime NOUN **limes** 1 a small fruit like a green lemon 2 a large tree with yellow blossom 3 a white substance that is used for making cement and fertilizers 4 a bright yellowish-green colour

limelight NOUN

• **in the limelight** getting a lot of attention, especially from the public

limerick NOUN **limericks** a funny five-line poem

✦ This word comes from the place-name **Limerick** in Ireland. This name was repeated in a nonsense song in a game played in past times.

limestone NOUN a type of rock that is used in building and making cement

limit NOUN **limits** 1 a level or point that you cannot pass: *There's a time limit for this test.* 2 a boundary: *the city limits*

VERB **limits, limiting, limited** to keep someone or something within certain amounts: *I shall have to limit you to one cake each.*

▶ **limitation** NOUN **limitations** a weakness, or something that makes another thing imperfect: *Living in a city has its limitations.*

▶ **limited** ADJECTIVE consisting of only a small number of things: *a limited choice*

limp VERB **limps, limping, limped** to walk unevenly because of a problem with one leg or foot

NOUN **limps** an uneven walk

ADJECTIVE **limper, limpest** not stiff or firm: *a limp lettuce • a limp handshake*

limpet NOUN **limpets** a small cone-shaped shellfish that clings to rocks

line¹ NOUN **lines**
1 a long thin mark or stripe: *a white line in the middle of the road*
2 a row of things or people: *lines of marching soldiers • the third line down on the next page*
3 a length of rope, wire or string: *hanging the washing on the line*
4 a wrinkle, especially on someone's face
5 a railway: *the east coast line*
6 a telephone connection: *There's a strange noise on this line.*
7 a short letter: *I'll drop you a line to let you know how we get on.*

VERB **lines, lining, lined** to line something like a street is to be along both sides of it: *Police officers will line the route of the procession.*

• **line up** to line up is to stand in a row: *Line up for your dinner.*

line² VERB **lines, lining, lined** to cover something with a layer on the inside: *a jacket lined with silk*

linear (pronounced lin-i-er) ADJECTIVE in a line: *a linear sequence of instructions*

line graph NOUN **line graphs** (*maths*) a chart that shows different amounts or quantities by using lines of different lengths next to each other

linen NOUN 1 a kind of cloth that is made from flax 2 things such as sheets or table cloths that used to be made from linen but are now often made from other fabrics

line of symmetry NOUN **lines of symmetry** a line that divides a shape into two parts that are exactly the same

liner¹ NOUN **liners** a large passenger ship

Aa
Bb
Cc
Dd
Ee
Ff
Gg
Hh
Ii
Jj
Kk
Ll
Mm
Nn
Oo
Pp
Qq
Rr
Ss
Tt
Uu
Vv
Ww
Xx
Yy
Zz

liner² NOUN **liners** something that forms a layer inside a container and can be taken out: *a bin liner*

linesman or **lineswoman** NOUN **linesmen** or **lineswomen** someone who judges whether a ball has crossed a line during a game such as tennis

linger VERB **lingers, lingering, lingered** to be slow to leave: *members of the audience lingering in the hall*

linguist NOUN **linguists** someone who knows a lot about languages

lining NOUN **linings** a layer on the inside of something: *a silver box with a velvet lining*

link NOUN **links** 1 one of the rings of a chain 2 someone or something that connects two things: *a rail link between the airport and the station*
VERB **links, linking, linked** 1 to connect objects: *The two buildings are linked by a footbridge.* 2 to say or show that subjects or people are connected

linoleum or **lino** NOUN a smooth, tough covering for floors

lint NOUN a soft material for putting on wounds

lion NOUN **lions** a powerful animal of the cat family. A male lion has a big shaggy mane

✦ This word comes from the Latin word for a lion, which is **leo**.

lioness NOUN **lionesses** a female lion

lip NOUN **lips** 1 either the upper or the lower outside edge of your mouth 2 the shaped part of the outside edge of a container such as a jug: *a saucepan with a lip for pouring*

lip-read VERB **lip-reads, lip-reading, lip-read** to understand what someone is saying by watching the way their lips are moving, rather than by listening to them

lipstick NOUN **lipsticks** a stick of creamy colour that you can put on your lips

liquid NOUN **liquids** a substance that can flow, for example oil or water

liquidize or **liquidise** VERB **liquidizes, liquidizing, liquidized** to make something into a liquid, especially a thick liquid: *Add some cream and liquidize the soup.*

▶ **liquidizer** or **liquidiser** NOUN **liquidizers** or **liquidisers** a machine for making solid or lumpy foods into smooth liquid or paste

liquorice NOUN a black, sticky sweet that is flavoured with the root of the liquorice plant

lisp NOUN **lisps** a speech problem that makes a person say *s* and *z* like *th*

list NOUN **lists** a series of things like names, numbers or prices, one after another: *a shopping list*
VERB **lists, listing, listed** to say or write a lot of words, such as names, one after another: *She listed all the books she has.*

listen VERB **listens, listening, listened** to pay attention to something that you can hear: *Listen to me.* • *I'm listening for the postman.* • *She's not listening.*

listless ADJECTIVE without energy or interest: *feeling listless all day*

lit VERB a way of changing the verb **light** to make a past tense. It can be used with or without a helping verb: *Her face lit up at the idea.* • *I haven't lit the candles yet.*

literacy NOUN being able to read and write

literal ADJECTIVE meaning exactly what it says, not using a special meaning of the words

▶ **literally** ADVERB with that exact meaning: *When she told you to pull your socks up, she didn't mean it literally.*

literary ADJECTIVE to do with books, authors and literature

literate ADJECTIVE able to read and write

literature NOUN 1 novels, poetry and plays: *19th-century literature* 2 all the written information about a subject

litmus paper NOUN (*science*) special paper that changes colour when it is dipped into an acid or alkaline

litre NOUN **litres** the basic unit in the metric system for measuring the volume of a liquid. This is often shortened to **l**

little ADJECTIVE **littler, littlest 1** small: *a little child* • *in a little while* **2** (*formal*) not much: *There's little hope that we'll win.*
• **a little 1** a small amount of: *You'll feel better if you drink a little water.* **2** a bit: *Jump up and down a little to keep warm.* • *Dad seems a little tired today.*

live[1] VERB **lives, living, lived 1** to have your home in a certain place: *How long have you lived in Bradford?* **2** to pass your life in a certain way: *She's used to living alone.* **3** to be alive: *Lord Voldemort lives!*

live[2] ADJECTIVE **1** real, not a model: *The children were handling live snakes.* **2** connected to an electricity supply: *a live socket* **3** a live broadcast or concert actually happens as you watch or listen to it

livelihood NOUN **livelihoods** the way someone earns enough money to live properly

lively ADJECTIVE **livelier, liveliest** cheerful and full of energy: *lively music* • *His little sister's very lively!*

liver NOUN **livers** a large organ in the body that is very important for cleaning the blood

livestock NOUN farm animals: *All the livestock is kept indoors here.*

livid ADJECTIVE extremely angry: *He was livid when she broke his camera.*

living NOUN **livings** a way of earning money: *What does Sam's dad do for a living?*

living room NOUN **living rooms** a room for sitting and relaxing in

lizard NOUN **lizards** a four-footed reptile with a long body and tail and a scaly skin

llama NOUN **llamas** a South American animal like a shaggy camel without a hump

load VERB **loads, loading, loaded 1** to fill a vehicle, such as a car or ship, with what it is going to carry **2** to load a gun is to put bullets in it **3** to load a machine is to put something in it: *load the camera with film*
NOUN **loads 1** a cargo that a vehicle carries **2** as much as a thing or person can carry at one time: *take another load upstairs* **3** a large amount: *a load of rubbish*

loaf NOUN **loaves** a loaf of bread has been shaped and baked in one piece
VERB **loafs, loafing, loafed**
• **loaf about** to loaf about is to spend your time being lazy

loan VERB **loans, loaning, loaned** to lend something to someone: *Mira loaned me the money for the bus.*
NOUN **loans** an amount of money that someone borrows

loathe VERB **loathes, loathing, loathed** to hate something: *My sister loathes shopping.*

lob VERB **lobs, lobbing, lobbed** to throw or hit a ball high into the air
NOUN **lobs** a hit or throw that curves high up into the air

lobby NOUN **lobbies** an entrance hall

lobe NOUN **lobes 1** the soft round part at the bottom of your ear **2** one part of the brain

lobster NOUN **lobsters** a large sea animal with a hard shell, two large claws and eight legs

local ADJECTIVE belonging to and around a certain area: *our local library*
NOUN **locals 1** a person who lives within a certain area: *If you want to know the way, you'd better ask a local.* **2** someone's local is the pub nearest their home

locality NOUN **localities** a certain place and the area round about

locate VERB **locates, locating, located 1** to find an exact position: *trying to locate the school on the map* **2** to be located in a place is to be situated there: *a cottage located in the Highlands*
▶ **location** NOUN **locations** a position or situation: *the exact location of the buried treasure*
• **on location** a film is shot on location when it is not filmed in a studio, but in the real world

loch NOUN **lochs** the word used for **lake** in Scotland

Aa
Bb
Cc
Dd
Ee
Ff
Gg
Hh
Ii
Jj
Kk
Ll
Mm
Nn
Oo
Pp
Qq
Rr
Ss
Tt
Uu
Vv
Ww
Xx
Yy
Zz

lock¹ NOUN **locks 1** a device that you work with a key to fasten things such as doors and drawers **2** a small section of a canal or river with gates at each end. The level of the water in the lock can be changed so that boats can pass to higher or lower sections of the canal or river
VERB **locks, locking, locked 1** to lock something like a door is to fasten it with a key **2** something like a door locks if it is possible to fasten it with a key: *Don't leave valuables in this room because the door doesn't lock.*
• **lock something up** or **away** to lock something up or away is to put it somewhere that can be locked with a key: *Mum locks all her jewellery away in a box.*

lock² NOUN **locks** a lock of hair is a piece of it

locker NOUN **lockers** a small cupboard, especially one that can be locked

locket NOUN **lockets** a little case, usually of silver or gold, on a necklace chain

locomotion NOUN the power of moving from place to place
▸ **locomotive** NOUN **locomotives** a railway engine that pulls trains

locust NOUN **locusts** a large insect like a grasshopper that flies in large groups and often eats and destroys plants

lodge VERB **lodges, lodging, lodged 1** to get stuck somewhere: *A piece of apple had lodged between his front teeth.* **2** to lodge a complaint is to make it officially **3** to live in a room in someone else's house and pay them rent
NOUN **lodges 1** a small house, often at the gate of a larger property **2** a house in the country that is used by hunters
▸ **lodger** NOUN **lodgers** a person who lives in rooms that they rent in someone else's house
▸ **lodging** NOUN **lodgings** a place to stay, especially for a short time

loft NOUN **lofts** the space between the roof of a house and the rooms: *suitcases stored in the loft*

lofty ADJECTIVE **loftier, loftiest** high or tall: *lofty ceilings*

log NOUN **logs 1** a section of a branch or tree trunk that has been cut up **2** an official record of what happens on a journey, especially of a ship or aeroplane

logic NOUN a way of thinking that involves correct reasoning
▸ **logical** ADJECTIVE following reasonably and sensibly from facts or events: *the logical thing to do next*

logo NOUN **logos** a small design that is the symbol of a company or product

loiter VERB **loiters, loitering, loitered** to stand around doing nothing: *Her friends loitered at the door.*

loll VERB **lolls, lolling, lolled 1** to lie or sit about lazily: *Pete's been lolling about, watching football all afternoon.* **2** your head or tongue lolls when it hangs loosely

lollipop NOUN **lollipops** a hard sticky sweet on a stick

lollipop man or **lollipop woman** NOUN **lollipop men** or **lollipop women** a person whose job is to help schoolchildren to cross the road, stopping the traffic by holding up a tall stick with a round sign on it

lolly NOUN **lollies 1** a lollipop **2** an ice lolly

lone ADJECTIVE **1** a lone person or thing is all alone **2** a lone parent is bringing up children on his or her own, without a partner

lonely ADJECTIVE **lonelier, loneliest 1** a lonely person feels sad because they are alone, with no friends around them **2** a lonely place has very few people living in it or visiting it: *a lonely cottage on the hillside*
▸ **loneliness** NOUN **1** being unhappy because you are alone **2** being a long way from anything or anyone else

long¹ ADJECTIVE **longer, longest 1** big from one end to the other: *a long supermarket queue* • *a long way home* **2** lasting or taking a lot of time: *a long delay* • *the long summer holidays*
ADVERB **longer, longest 1** for a long time: *Have you been waiting long?* • *It won't be long till she starts school.* **2** through the whole time: *I've been looking forward to this all day long.*

long² VERB **longs, longing, longed**
to want something very much: *I was longing to see my friends again.* • *Mum was longing for a rest.*

➤ **longing** NOUN **longings** a very strong wish for something: *looking at the food with longing*

longboat NOUN **longboats** (*history*) a type of long sailing boat that was used by Vikings

long division NOUN (*maths*) a dividing sum where you write all the working out in full

longitude NOUN (*geography*) the position of a place east or west of an imaginary line that passes from north to south through Greenwich, London. Look up and compare **latitude**

long jump NOUN the long jump is an athletics contest where you run and then jump as far as possible along the ground

long-range ADJECTIVE **1** able to reach a great distance: *long-range missiles* **2** looking a long way into the future: *a long-range weather forecast*

longship NOUN **longships** another word for a **longboat**

long-sighted ADJECTIVE a long-sighted person sees objects that are far away more clearly than they see things that are closer to them

long-term ADJECTIVE lasting or taking place for a long time: *the long-term effects of this medicine*

loo NOUN **loos** (*informal*) a toilet

look VERB **looks, looking, looked**
1 to turn your eyes to see something: *I looked at my brother.*
2 to appear or seem: *You look tired.* • *Dan's sister looks about sixteen.*
3 to try to find something: *I've looked everywhere but I can't find my calculator.* • *What are you looking for?*
4 to face a certain direction: *The window looks south.*

• **look after someone or something** to look after something or someone is to take care of them: *Dad looks after my baby sister during the day.* • *Will you look after my bag while I go to the toilet?*

• **look down on someone** to think that someone is less important than you or not as good as you: *She looks down on people who are not as rich as her.*

• **look forward to something** to feel happy because you know you're going to enjoy something: *I'm looking forward to the holidays.*

• **look something up** to try to find information about something, for example by looking in a book

NOUN **looks 1** a glance at something or an examination of it: *Take a look at this.*
2 a certain expression on your face: *The teacher has an angry look on her face.*
3 the appearance of a thing or person: *I don't like the look of those black clouds.*

lookalike NOUN **lookalikes** a person who looks very like someone else: *a Prince Charles lookalike*

looking-glass NOUN **looking-glasses** a mirror

lookout NOUN **lookouts 1** a person who watches for danger: *The lookout spotted a boat on the horizon.* **2** a place where someone can keep watch

• **keep a lookout** to keep a lookout is to watch carefully for something

• **your lookout** something that is your lookout is your problem or concern and nobody else's: *If you don't study for the exam, that's your own lookout.*

loom¹ NOUN **looms** a weaving machine for making cloth

loom² VERB **looms, looming, loomed**
1 to appear over or in front of you, especially in a frightening way: *A shadowy figure loomed towards us.*
2 to wait in the future, especially in a worrying way: *A big decision is looming before us.*

loop NOUN **loops 1** the shape of something like a thread or piece of string when it curves around and crosses over itself: *Make a loop and pull one end through it.* **2** (*music*) the repeating of a section of music, for example by using a computer **3** (*ICT*) a command in a computer program to repeat a part of the program
VERB **loops, looping, looped 1** to

loophole → loudspeaker

Aa
Bb
Cc
Dd
Ee
Ff
Gg
Hh
Ii
Jj
Kk
Ll
Mm
Nn
Oo
Pp
Qq
Rr
Ss
Tt
Uu
Vv
Ww
Xx
Yy
Zz

twist something around loosely: *a scarf looped around her neck* **2** to create a loop, for example of a section of music or part of a computer program

loophole NOUN **loopholes 1** a narrow opening in a wall **2** a way you can avoid a rule but not actually break it

loose ADJECTIVE **looser, loosest 1** not tight or firmly fixed: *a loose knot* **2** not tied up or shut in: *hair hanging loose* • *Let the dogs run around loose.*

• **on the loose** free, especially after escaping: *a dangerous criminal on the loose*

▸ **loosen** VERB **loosens, loosening, loosened** to make something less firm, fixed or tight: *I had to loosen my belt.*

loot NOUN stolen goods or money

VERB **loots, looting, looted** to steal things quickly from shops, businesses or homes, especially during a riot or a war

lopsided ADJECTIVE uneven, with one side higher or lower than the other: *a lopsided smile*

lord NOUN **lords 1** the title of men with high social rank, of judges and of bishops: *Lord Asquith* • *the Lord Mayor of London* **2** a master or ruler: *He was lord of all he could see.*

lore NOUN all the knowledge, stories and beliefs that get handed down through the generations

lorry NOUN **lorries** a large motor vehicle for taking heavy loads by road

lose VERB **loses, losing, lost**
1 to forget where you put something: *I've lost my keys.*
2 to have something taken away from you: *Fifty people have lost their jobs.*
3 to have less of something than you had before: *The teacher was losing patience with them.*
4 to be beaten in a contest: *I lost by 4 games to 6.*
5 a clock or watch loses time when it goes too slowly: *My watch is losing about a minute a day.*

▸ **loser** NOUN **losers 1** the person who does not win an argument, contest or battle: *Even the loser will win a huge*

amount of money. **2** someone who never seems to succeed at anything

loss NOUN **losses 1** when you cannot find something or have had something taken away: *the loss of his home in a fire* **2** having less of something than you had before: *a loss of nearly a million pounds* **3** a disadvantage: *It'll be your loss if you don't study for your test.*

lost ADJECTIVE
1 something that is lost is missing: *The painting has been lost for centuries.*
2 someone who is lost does not know where they are: *How did you get lost when you had a map?*
3 you are lost when you are confused: *I'm lost – can you explain that last bit again?*
4 a person is lost if they are killed: *soldiers lost in battle*

lot NOUN **lots 1** a group of things or people: *Another lot of visitors will arrive tomorrow.* **2** an area of land: *a parking lot*
• **a lot** a large number or amount: *a lot of people* • *I like you a lot.*
• **draw lots** to draw lots is to decide who should do something by drawing a different card, stick or piece of paper from several that look the same
• **lots** (*informal*) a large number or amount: *Lots of people love the programme.* • *She puts lots of sugar on her cereal.*
• **the lot** (*informal*) everything: *Alice only wanted one but decided to take the lot.*

lotion NOUN **lotions** a liquid for putting on your skin or hair

lottery NOUN **lotteries** an event where people win money or prizes when their number or ticket is chosen by chance from many others

loud ADJECTIVE **louder, loudest 1** making a lot of sound: *a loud noise* **2** very bright in an unpleasant way: *a loud shirt*

ADVERB **louder, loudest** making a lot of sound: *Could you speak a little louder please?*

▸ **loudly** ADVERB making a lot of sound or noise: *crying loudly*

loudspeaker NOUN **loudspeakers**

the part of a sound system that the sound actually comes out of

lounge NOUN **lounges** a sitting room VERB **lounges, lounging, lounged** to sit or lie around lazily: *students lounging around the common room*

louse NOUN **lice** a small insect that lives on a person or animal

lout NOUN **louts** a young man who behaves in a rough and unpleasant way

lovable ADJECTIVE easy to love or like a lot: *a lovable child*

love NOUN **loves 1** a deep feeling of liking something or someone very much: *my love for my parents* **2** something or someone that you like very much: *Her great love is music.* **3** in a game such as tennis, a score of nothing: *The score was now forty-love.*

VERB **loves, loving, loved** to like someone or something very much: *Greg had always loved cricket.*

▸ **lover** NOUN **lovers** someone who loves something: *an art lover*

lovely ADJECTIVE **lovelier, loveliest 1** beautiful or attractive: *lovely eyes* **2** enjoyable or pleasing: *It was lovely to see you again.*

▸ **loveliness** NOUN how lovely a thing or person is: *gazing at her loveliness*

loving ADJECTIVE full of love: *a loving look*

low¹ ADJECTIVE AND ADVERB **lower, lowest 1** near to the ground: *a low hedge • clouds getting lower and lower* **2** near the bottom of something such as a list or a scale of measurement: *Your name's quite low on the list.* **3** a low sound or musical note is near the bottom of the range of pitch or musical notes: *She spoke in a low voice. • the lowest note you can sing* **4** less than usual in amount or importance: *low prices • Soon their supplies began to run low.* **5** sad or fed up: *Are you feeling a bit low?*

low² VERB **lows, lowing, lowed** to make the noise that a cow makes

lower VERB **lowers, lowering, lowered**

to move something to a position nearer the bottom of something or nearer the ground: *At the end of the session, the scouts lower the flag.*

lower case NOUN upper case letters are letters that are not capitals

lowland ADJECTIVE to do with land that is quite flat and near sea level: *lowland farms*

▸ **lowlands** PLURAL NOUN areas of land without mountains

lowly ADJECTIVE **lowlier, lowliest** having a low, unimportant position

loyal ADJECTIVE always giving support, even in bad times: *a loyal fan*

▸ **loyally** ADVERB in a faithful way: *I loyally voted for him every time.*

▸ **loyalty** NOUN faithful support for your friends

lozenge NOUN **lozenges 1** a sweet that you suck, especially to help a sore throat **2** a diamond shape

Ltd ABBREVIATION short for the word **Limited** in the names of companies: *Joe Bloggs Shoes Ltd*

lubricate VERB **lubricates, lubricating, lubricated** to put oil or grease on something like an engine or machine, to make it run smoothly

▸ **lubrication** NOUN **1** making something move more easily by adding oil or grease **2** a substance like oil or grease that will help moving parts to work more smoothly

luck NOUN **1** the way things happen by chance: *What bad luck that it rained all that day!* **2** something good that happens by chance: *It was a piece of luck that I found the money.*

▸ **luckily** ADVERB by a good chance: *The car hit us but, luckily, nobody was badly hurt.*

▸ **lucky** ADJECTIVE **luckier, luckiest** a lucky person has good things happen to them by chance: *You're lucky to live so near the school.*

ludicrous ADJECTIVE completely ridiculous or silly: *a ludicrous idea*

ludo NOUN a board game with counters that the players move according to the numbers they throw on the dice

Aa
Bb
Cc
Dd
Ee
Ff
Gg
Hh
Ii
Jj
Kk
Ll
Mm
Nn
Oo
Pp
Qq
Rr
Ss
Tt
Uu
Vv
Ww
Xx
Yy
Zz

lug VERB **lugs, lugging, lugged** to pull or drag something with difficulty: *lugging the suitcases up the stairs*

luggage NOUN a traveller's suitcases and bags: *Make sure all your luggage is labelled.*

lukewarm ADJECTIVE **1** less hot than it should be: *The water in the shower was only lukewarm.* **2** not very interested or enthusiastic: *We got a lukewarm welcome when we arrived.*

lull VERB **lulls, lulling, lulled** to make someone feel calm and relaxed: *lulling the baby to sleep*
NOUN **lulls** a time when something noisy or busy stops for a while: *a lull in the fighting*

lullaby NOUN **lullabies** a gentle song to lull a child to sleep

lumber VERB **lumbers, lumbering, lumbered** to move heavily, slowly and clumsily: *We saw a bear lumbering through the forest.*
• **lumbered with something** to be lumbered with something is to be given something that you do not want: *I got lumbered with the washing up.*

lumberjack NOUN **lumberjacks** a person whose job is to cut down and chop up trees

luminous ADJECTIVE glowing in the dark: *luminous stars that you can stick on your ceiling*

lump NOUN **lumps 1** a small, shapeless piece of something: *a lump of coal* • *This custard's got lumps in it.* **2** a hard swelling on your body
▶ **lumpy** ADJECTIVE **lumpier, lumpiest** full of lumps

lunacy NOUN madness

lunar ADJECTIVE to do with the moon

lunatic NOUN **lunatics** someone who is mad: *driving like a lunatic*

✦ This word comes from the Latin word **luna**, which means *moon*. In Latin, **lunaticus** meant 'made mad by the moon'.

lunch NOUN **lunches** the meal that you eat in the middle of the day between breakfast and dinner

lung NOUN **lungs** the two bag-like organs inside your chest that you use for breathing

lunge VERB **lunges, lunging, lunged** to make a sudden strong or violent move forwards
NOUN **lunges** a sudden violent move forwards: *An angry customer made a lunge at the manager.*

lurch VERB **lurches, lurching, lurched** to move along unevenly, especially suddenly rolling to one side: *The boat lurched and we fell over.*
NOUN **lurches** a sudden roll to one side

lure VERB **lures, luring, lured** to tempt a person or animal with some kind of reward: *Scraps of food are used to lure the animals out of their burrows.*

lurk VERB **lurks, lurking, lurked** to wait secretly where you cannot be seen: *Was there someone lurking over there in the shadows?*

luscious ADJECTIVE sweet, delicious and juicy

lush ADJECTIVE **lusher, lushest** lush plants are healthy and growing well

lustre NOUN a shiny appearance
▶ **lustrous** ADJECTIVE shining or glossy

luxury NOUN **luxuries 1** extremely comfortable, expensive surroundings and possessions: *living in luxury* **2** something very pleasant but not necessary: *We can't afford many luxuries.*
▶**luxuriant** ADJECTIVE growing richly and thickly: *luxuriant forest*
▶**luxurious** ADJECTIVE very comfortable and expensive

lying NOUN a form of the verb **lie** that is used with another verb to make different tenses: *Please stop lying to me.* • *She has been lying all along.*

lyric NOUN **lyrics 1** the lyrics of a song are its words **2** a lyric is a short poem about feelings and emotions
▶ **lyrical** ADJECTIVE sounding like poetry or music: *a lyrical description of the scenery*

Mm

m ABBREVIATION short for **metre** or **metres,** or **million**

mac ABBREVIATION **macs** short for **mackintosh,** a type of raincoat: *a plastic mac*

macabre ADJECTIVE something that is macabre is strange and horrible, because it involves evil or death: *a macabre painting of skulls and bones*

macaroni NOUN tubes of pasta cut into short lengths

macaroon NOUN **macaroons** a sweet biscuit made with ground almonds or coconut

machine NOUN **machines** a device with moving parts that is operated by some form of power and is designed to do a particular job: *a washing machine* VERB **machines, machining, machined** to machine something is to sew it, shape it or cut it using a machine or a machine tool

machine-gun NOUN **machine-guns** a type of automatic gun that fires bullets quickly one after the other

machinery NOUN machines: *combine harvesters and other farming machinery*

mackerel NOUN **mackerels** or **mackerel** a small edible sea fish with a narrow striped body

mackintosh NOUN **mackintoshes** a waterproof coat, usually reaching down to the knees or below

mad ADJECTIVE **madder, maddest**

1 mentally ill: *The poor woman went mad with grief.*

2 foolish or reckless: *Swimming in shark-infested waters is a mad thing to do.*

3 very angry: *Mum will be mad when she sees the state of your clothes.*

4 to be mad about someone or something is to like them or it very much: *mad about football*

• **like mad** desperately or using a lot of energy: *She was pedalling like mad to keep up with the rest.*

madam NOUN **madams** a formal and polite way of addressing a woman, especially at the beginning of a letter or when serving her in a shop

mad cow disease NOUN the common name for **BSE,** a disease that affects the brains and nervous systems of cattle

madden VERB **maddens, maddening, maddened** if something maddens you, it annoys you a lot or makes you very angry

made VERB a way of changing the verb **make** to form a past tense. It can be used with or without a helping verb: *When he was on the beach, he made a sandcastle.* • *I think you have made a mistake.*

madly ADVERB desperately, or in a great hurry: *We were rushing about madly trying to get ready in time.*

madness NOUN mental illness, or great foolishness

magazine NOUN **magazines 1** a paper published regularly, for example once a week or once a month, and which has articles and features by various writers and usually lots of photographs or pictures: *a football magazine* • *women's magazines* **2** a place where military equipment is stored

> ✦ The meaning of magazine as 'a paper' came from the meaning of magazine as 'a military storehouse'. The idea is that a magazine is a storehouse of useful items and information.

maggot NOUN **maggots** a fly in the worm-like stage after it has hatched out of its egg and before it develops wings

magic NOUN **1** a strange power that causes things to happen that cannot be explained **2** tricks, such as making things disappear, which seem to people watching to be impossible **3** something beautiful or wonderful: *the island's special magic*

Aa
Bb
Cc
Dd
Ee
Ff
Gg
Hh
Ii
Jj
Kk
Ll
Mm
Nn
Oo
Pp
Qq
Rr
Ss
Tt
Uu
Vv
Ww
Xx
Yy
Zz

▸ **magical** ADJECTIVE wonderful or charming: *a magical atmosphere*

▸ **magically** ADVERB using magic or as if by magic

▸ **magician** NOUN **magicians 1** a man or boy who has magic powers, especially in stories: *Harry Potter and Gandalf are magicians.* **2** someone who does magic tricks to entertain people

magistrate NOUN **magistrates** a person who judges cases of minor crime where there is no jury

magma NOUN **magmas** *or* **magmata** (*geography*) hot melted rock beneath the Earth's crust, which is sometimes forced up to the surface, for example when a volcano erupts

magnet NOUN **magnets** a piece of iron or other metal, which has the power to attract other pieces of metal to it and which points north to south when it hangs free

▸ **magnetic** ADJECTIVE **1** something that is magnetic has the power to attract iron and some other metals towards it **2** someone with a magnetic personality is very popular with other people

▸ **magnetically** ADVERB using magnetism

▸ **magnetism** NOUN **1** the power that a magnet has to attract metals **2** the power some people have to attract or influence other people

▸ **magnetize** *or* **magnetise** VERB **magnetizes, magnetizing, magnetized** to magnetize a metal is to make it magnetic

magnification NOUN **magnifications 1** making things seem larger or closer, or making things more important than they are **2** the amount by which an instrument like a microscope or telescope makes things seem larger. For example, a magnification of 20 makes something look 20 times larger than it really is

magnificent ADJECTIVE very impressive or splendid: *a magnificent lion • a magnificent achievement*

▸ **magnificence** NOUN being magnificent: *the magnificence of the palace*

▸ **magnificently** ADVERB in an impressive way: *He coped magnificently with the crisis.*

magnify VERB **magnifies, magnifying, magnified 1** to make something seem bigger or closer than it really is **2** to make something seem more important or serious than it really is

▸ **magnifier** NOUN **magnifiers** an instrument or lens that makes things look bigger than they really are

magnifying glass NOUN **magnifying glasses** a hand-held lens that you use to look at a small object or very small writing so that you can see it more clearly

magnitude NOUN **magnitudes** a situation's or problem's magnitude is its great size, extent or importance

magnolia NOUN **magnolias** a tree or shrub with large white, pink or purplish flowers that have a sweet scent

magpie NOUN **magpies** a black and white bird of the crow family that likes to collect shiny objects

mahogany NOUN a hard reddish wood used to make furniture, which comes from a tree that grows in tropical parts of Central and South America

maid NOUN **maids** a girl or woman whose job is to keep the rooms clean and tidy in a hotel or house

maiden NOUN **maidens** an old-fashioned word for a young unmarried woman

ADJECTIVE **1** first: *a ship's maiden voyage* **2** in cricket, a maiden over is when no runs are scored by the batting side after six balls

maiden name NOUN **maiden names** the surname or last name that a woman had before she was married

mail[1] NOUN letters or parcels carried by post

VERB **mails, mailing, mailed** to mail a letter or parcel is to send it by post

mail[2] NOUN mail, or chain mail, is armour worn on the body, which is made up of lots of small connected steel rings or plates

maim VERB **maims, maiming, maimed** to maim a person or animal is to injure them very seriously, causing permanent damage to their body

main ADJECTIVE most important or principal: *a main road* • *The main thing is to stay calm.*

NOUN **mains** a pipe that carries water or gas into houses or buildings: *a burst gas main*

▶ **mains** PLURAL NOUN the mains are the pipes or cables that carry water or electricity to houses and buildings: *Plug this into the mains.*

mainland NOUN the mainland of a country is its biggest single area of land rather than any islands that form part of the same country

mainly ADVERB mostly or in most cases: *This week we've mainly been revising for exams.*

maintain VERB **maintains, maintaining, maintained 1** to maintain something is to keep it at the same amount, or to keep it going: *The rally drivers have to maintain high speeds on dangerous and twisty roads.* **2** to maintain a house or piece of equipment is to keep it in good condition and working well **3** to maintain someone is to give them the money they need to live on

▶ **maintenance** NOUN **1** regular cleaning or repair done to keep something in good condition or good working order **2** money paid to someone for them to live on

maisonette NOUN **maisonettes** a flat or apartment on two floors within a building

maize NOUN a tall cereal plant that has large seedheads called cobs. The yellow seeds, called sweetcorn, are packed tightly together on the cob

majestic ADJECTIVE very impressive, or behaving in a very dignified or impressive way, as a king or queen might do

▶ **majestically** ADVERB impressively or regally

majesty NOUN **majesties 1** (*formal*) majesty is greatness: *the majesty of the mountains* **2** a title used when speaking to or about a king or queen: *Their Majesties will be attending a thanksgiving service next week.*

major ADJECTIVE **1** something major is very big, very serious or very important: *a major catastrophe* • *a major route into the city* **2** (*music*) a major scale has a semitone between the first and the third notes and between the seventh and eighth notes. A major key or chord is based on this scale

NOUN **majors** an army officer above the rank of captain

majority NOUN **majorities 1** the largest number of people or things in a group **2** the number of votes by which the winner of an election beats the person who comes second

make VERB **makes, making, made**

1 to create, produce or prepare something: *She makes all her own clothes.* • *I'm making a cup of coffee.* • *Let's make the bedclothes into a tent.*

2 something makes something else happen when it causes or forces that other thing to happen: *The explosion made the house shake.* • *He made the dog sit and stay.* • *Hay always makes me sneeze.*

3 to make a point, suggestion or promise is to give it

4 you make the answer to a sum a particular amount when that is the amount you calculate it to be: *I make that £1.20 you owe me.* • *What time do you make it?*

5 two or more quantities make a certain amount when they add up to that amount: *Six and six makes twelve.*

6 to make a particular place or point is to reach that place or point: *We climbed part of the way but we didn't make the summit.* • *If we hurry, we might just make the earlier train.*

7 to make money is to earn it

• **make do** to try to manage on what you have

• **make for something** to make for a

Aa
Bb
Cc
Dd
Ee
Ff
Gg
Hh
Ii
Jj
Kk
Ll
Mm
Nn
Oo
Pp
Qq
Rr
Ss
Tt
Uu
Vv
Ww
Xx
Yy
Zz

place is to go in that direction

• **make it** to succeed in getting to a place in time: *The train leaves in ten minutes – we'll never make it.*

• **make off** to run away or escape

• **make something out 1** to be able to see something or see what it is **2** to make something out is to understand it **3** to make out a cheque or application is to complete it by writing in the details needed

• **make up** people who have been quarrelling make up when they agree to become friends again

• **make something up** to invent something such as a story or excuse

• **make up for something** to make up for something that you have done wrong is to balance it by doing something good

• **make up your mind** to decide

make-believe NOUN pretending or fantasy

• **make believe** if you make believe, you pretend something is real when it isn't: *Let's make believe it's winter and we have to hibernate until the snow goes away.*

maker NOUN **makers** a person, business or machine that makes a particular type of thing: *a film maker* • *a coffee maker*

makeshift ADJECTIVE made from whatever is available and used instead of the real thing or something better: *We used the blankets as makeshift tents.*

make-up NOUN **1** things like lipstick and mascara which people put on their faces to improve their looks **2** a person's or thing's make-up is their character or what they or it consists of

makings PLURAL NOUN if someone or something has the makings of a particular thing, they have all the qualities needed to become that thing: *Olivia has the makings of a successful singer.*

malaria NOUN a serious disease passed to humans by the bite of a type of mosquito, which causes very high fever

male ADJECTIVE **1** a male animal is of the sex that fathers children but does not give birth: *A male swan is called a cob.* **2** to do with men or boys or the things that involve them: *It's mostly a male hobby.*

NOUN **males** a male animal

malfunction VERB **malfunctions, malfunctioning, malfunctioned** a machine malfunctions when it stops working properly or breaks down

NOUN **malfunctions** a fault that causes a machine to stop working properly

malice NOUN malice is a feeling of spite and wanting to harm someone else

➤ **malicious** ADJECTIVE spiteful

➤ **maliciously** ADVERB deliberately causing harm or hurt to someone else

mall NOUN **malls** a shopping centre

mallet NOUN **mallets** a heavy wooden hammer

malnutrition NOUN someone suffering from malnutrition is ill because they have not had enough to eat for a long time

malt NOUN a substance in barley and other grains that is used to flavour beer

mama *or* **mamma** NOUN **mamas** *or* **mammas** a name some people use for their mother

mammal NOUN **mammals** a warm-blooded animal that is not a reptile, fish or bird. Female mammals give birth to their babies, instead of laying eggs, and feed them on milk made in their own bodies

mammoth NOUN **mammoths** a huge hairy type of elephant that lived in prehistoric times

ADJECTIVE huge: *a mammoth task*

man NOUN **men 1** an adult male human being **2** man is a word sometimes used for human beings generally: *Man is closely related to the apes.*

VERB **mans, manning, manned** to man something is to be the person that runs it or operates it

manage VERB **manages, managing, managed 1** to manage to do something is to succeed in doing it **2** to manage something like a shop or business is to be in charge of running it **3** to survive on very little money: *I don't* *know how he manages on his student grant.*

manageable ADJECTIVE something is manageable if you can control it or deal with it fairly easily

management NOUN **1** controlling a business or other activity: *He always wanted to go into football management.* **2** the management of a company are the people who work as its managers

manager NOUN **managers** someone who is responsible for managing a shop or other business, or an organization

manageress NOUN **manageresses** a woman who runs a shop, restaurant or other business

mandarin NOUN **mandarins 1** a high-ranking official in China when it was ruled by an emperor **2** a mandarin, or mandarin orange, is a small fruit rather like an orange but easier to peel because it has a looser skin

mandir NOUN **mandirs** a building where Hindus go to worship

mane NOUN **manes** a horse's or lion's mane is the long hair that grows on its neck

manger (pronounced **mainj**-er) NOUN **mangers** a box for holding hay or other food for animals in a stable

mangle VERB **mangles, mangling, mangled** to mangle something is to crush or twist it out of shape
NOUN **mangles** an old-fashioned machine with two heavy rollers, used for squeezing water out of washed clothes

mango NOUN **mangos** or **mangoes** a large pear-shaped fruit with orange sweet-smelling flesh and a large stone in the middle

mangy (pronounced **mainj**-i) ADJECTIVE **mangier, mangiest 1** suffering from mange, a skin disease of dogs and other hairy animals, which causes scabs on the skin and makes the hair fall out in patches **2** dirty and worn thin: *a mangy old rug*

manhole NOUN **manholes** a covered hole in a road big enough for a person to go down to inspect or repair underground drains

manhood NOUN being a man: *the age when a boy reaches manhood*

mania NOUN **manias 1** a person suffering from mania has a type of madness in which they become very excited and often violent **2** a mania is a very strong enthusiasm for something
▶ **maniac** NOUN **maniacs** a mad or dangerous person
▶ **manic** ADJECTIVE **1** suffering from mania **2** manic actions are done at a very fast and wild pace: *a manic dash round the shops*

manicure VERB **manicures, manicuring, manicured** to manicure your fingernails is to cut and polish them so that they are neat and well-shaped
NOUN **manicures** you have a manicure when someone cuts and polishes your fingernails

manifest VERB **manifests, manifesting, manifested** to be revealed or displayed: *The codes manifest as symbols when you print out the file.*
▶ **manifestation** NOUN **manifestations** something that displays or reveals a characteristic: *a manifestation of evil*

manifesto NOUN **manifestos** or **manifestoes** a written statement of a political party's policies

manipulate VERB **manipulates, manipulating, manipulated 1** to manipulate something is to control or use it in a skilful way **2** to manipulate someone is to influence them cleverly by making them do what you want without them realizing it
▶ **manipulation** NOUN manipulating something or someone

mankind NOUN all human beings

manly ADJECTIVE **manlier, manliest** having the qualities many people expect a man to have, such as strength and courage
▶ **manliness** NOUN being manly

manner NOUN **manners 1** a way in which something is done: *They had been scattered around in a haphazard*

Aa
Bb
Cc
Dd
Ee
Ff
Gg
Hh
Ii
Jj
Kk
Ll
Mm
Nn
Oo
Pp
Qq
Rr
Ss
Tt
Uu
Vv
Ww
Xx
Yy
Zz

manner. **2** the way in which a person behaves towards other people: *I thought his manner was a bit offhand.*

• **all manner of** all kinds of: *all manner of exciting opportunities*

▸ **mannerism** NOUN **mannerisms** a person's mannerisms are their special ways of speaking or behaving that are different from other people

▸ **manners** PLURAL NOUN to have good manners is to behave politely towards other people and to have bad manners, or no manners, is to behave rudely towards others

manoeuvre (pronounced ma-**noo**-ver) NOUN **manoeuvres 1** a difficult movement that needs skill and planning **2** something that you do in a clever or skilful way that affects how a situation will develop **3** military manoeuvres are planned movements of large numbers of troops and equipment

VERB **manoeuvres, manoeuvring, manoeuvred 1** to manoeuvre is to move skilfully **2** to manoeuvre something somewhere is to move it there carefully and accurately: *The prams were impossible to manoeuvre round the corner.*

manor NOUN **manors** a name given to some large old houses, originally built for noblemen

mansion NOUN **mansions** a large grand house

manslaughter NOUN the crime of killing someone without intending to kill them

mantelpiece NOUN **mantelpieces** a frame around a fireplace, especially the top part that forms a shelf

mantle NOUN **mantles** a protective covering: *The garden looked magical under its mantle of crisp white snow.*

manual NOUN **manuals** a book containing information about something, for example the parts of a machine and how to operate it

ADJECTIVE **1** working or operated by a person rather than being automatic: *an old manual loom* **2** involving the hands

or physical strength and skills: *manual labour*

▸ **manually** ADVERB by hand: *manually operated machines*

manufacture VERB **manufactures, manufacturing, manufactured 1** to manufacture things is to make a lot of them, often in a factory **2** to manufacture something, such as an excuse or evidence, is to invent it

▸ **manufacturer** NOUN **manufacturers** a person or business which manufactures things

▸ **manufacturing** NOUN the part of industry involved in making things

---

✦ **Manufacture** comes from the Latin words **manu**, which means *by hand*, and **facere**, which means *to make*, so together it means 'to make by hand'.

---

manure NOUN a mixture containing animal dung, spread on soil to grow better flowers and crops

manuscript NOUN **manuscripts 1** a book or document written by hand **2** an author's manuscript is his or her handwritten or typed version of a book before it is edited and printed

Manx ADJECTIVE coming from the Isle of Man, an island between England and Ireland: *A Manx cat has no tail.*

many PRONOUN **1** a lot or a large number: *I've got lots of CD's. Do you have many?* **2** **how many** means 'what quantity or number': *If you take three chairs away how many will be left?*

ADJECTIVE **more, most** a lot or a large number: *He has many friends.* • *Many people in the world don't have enough to eat.*

Maori NOUN **Maoris** a member of the race of people who lived in New Zealand before anyone arrived from other countries

map NOUN **maps** a diagram of an area of land showing the position of things like hills, rivers and roads as if you are looking at them from above

VERB **maps, mapping, mapped 1** to map an area is to make a map of it **2** to map something is to make a detailed diagram or chart of it to show the position of each of its parts: *mapping DNA*

maple NOUN **maples** a tree with broad leaves that turn red, brown, orange and yellow in the autumn

mar VERB **mars, marring, marred** to mar something is to spoil it in some way

maracas PLURAL NOUN a musical instrument made up of two hollow containers filled with small stones, which are shaken so that the stones rattle

marathon NOUN **marathons 1** a race in which runners cover a distance of 26.2 miles or 42 kilometres **2** a long and difficult task or activity

ADJECTIVE very long and difficult: *a marathon session at the dentist*

✦ This word comes from the place name **Marathon** in Greece. There is a story that in 490 BC a messenger ran from Marathon to Athens after the Greeks won a war against the Persians. The distance he ran is about the same as that in the marathon race.

marauder NOUN **marauders** someone who roams about, stealing or destroying things and attacking people

marble NOUN **marbles 1** marble is a type of rock, which can be black, dark green, pink or white, and usually has veins of other colours through it. It is used for sculpture and for making fireplaces and work tops **2** marbles are small coloured glass balls used for playing a children's game

ADJECTIVE made of marble: *a marble table top*

march VERB **marches, marching, marched 1** soldiers march when they walk together at the same regular pace **2** people march when they walk in a large group through the streets, usually because they are protesting about something **3** to march someone somewhere is to force them to go there by holding them or walking beside them so that they do not escape

NOUN **marches 1** a steady walking pace

or a distance covered by marching: *a slow march* • *a long march* **2** a piece of music for marching to

March NOUN the third month of the year, after February and before April

✦ **March** comes from the name of the Roman god **Mars**. He was god of war and was also connected with the growing of new crops in Spring.

mare NOUN **mares** a female horse or zebra

margarine NOUN a substance made from vegetable oils or animal fats used for cooking or for spreading on bread like butter

margin NOUN **margins 1** a blank area at the top, bottom or either side of a written or printed page **2** an edge or border: *reeds growing on the margins of the lake* **3** an extra amount of something: *We allowed ourselves a margin of several hours, in case we got held up anywhere.*

▶ **marginal** ADJECTIVE if something is of marginal importance, it is not very important because it is not the central or main part of something

▶ **marginally** ADVERB slightly

marigold NOUN **marigolds** a yellow or orange flower

marina NOUN **marinas** a harbour for private boats

marine ADJECTIVE to do with the sea or belonging to the sea: *marine life*

mariner NOUN **mariners** someone who sails boats or ships on the sea

mark NOUN **marks 1** a spot or stain: *There's a dirty mark on the sofa.* **2** a written or printed sign or symbol that stands for something: *a punctuation mark* **3** a point or grade given as a reward for good or accurate work: *He could get much higher marks if he made a bit more effort.*

VERB **marks, marking, marked 1** to mark something is to put a mark, scratch or stain on it **2** to mark someone's work is to look at it and give it points or a grade to show how good or accurate it is **3** in games like football and hockey,

Aa
Bb
Cc
Dd
Ee
Ff
Gg
Hh
Ii
Jj
Kk
Ll
Mm
Nn
Oo
Pp
Qq
Rr
Ss
Tt
Uu
Vv
Ww
Xx
Yy
Zz

you mark a player on the other team when you stay close to them to stop them from getting or passing the ball

▶ **marked** ADJECTIVE noticeable or obvious: *There has been a marked improvement in her work.*

▶ **marker** NOUN **markers 1** something that you use to mark the position of something **2** a pen with a thick point

market NOUN **markets 1** a place where people gather to buy and sell things: *a street market • a fruit market* **2** there is a market for something when people will buy it

• **on the market** for sale

VERB **markets, marketing, marketed** to market something is to use advertising to try and encourage people to buy it

marksman NOUN **marksmen** someone who can shoot very accurately

marmalade NOUN jam made from oranges or other citrus fruit and usually eaten on toast at breakfast time

maroon¹ VERB **maroons, marooning, marooned** if someone is marooned somewhere, they have been left in a place that they cannot get away from, especially a lonely island

maroon² NOUN a dark brownish red colour

marquee (pronounced mar-**kee**) NOUN **marquees** a very large tent used for circuses, weddings or parties

marriage NOUN **marriages 1** the ceremony in which a man and woman become husband and wife **2** the period of time when two people are married to each other: *a long and happy marriage*

marrow NOUN **marrows 1** marrow is the spongy tissue inside long bones such as the ones in your leg **2** a marrow is a long rounded vegetable that grows on the ground

marry VERB **marries, marrying, married** to make someone your husband or wife in a special ceremony, or to perform the ceremony making two people into husband and wife

marsh NOUN **marshes** an area of land that is soft and wet all the time

▶ **marshy** ADJECTIVE marshy ground is very wet and soft

marshal NOUN **marshals 1** an official who controls the crowds at big public events like pop concerts **2** a high-ranking officer in the army, air force or navy **3** in the United States, the chief police officer or fire officer in a city or area

VERB **marshals, marshalling, marshalled** to marshal people or things is to gather them together in an organized way

marshmallow NOUN **marshmallows** a very soft, spongy, pink or white sweet

marsupial NOUN **marsupials** an animal, such as the kangaroo, that gives birth to partly developed babies, which then crawl into a pouch on their mother's belly where they are fed and protected until they grow bigger

martial art NOUN **martial arts** martial arts are fighting sports or techniques of self-defence, such as karate and judo

Martian NOUN **Martians** in science fiction stories, a creature from the planet Mars

martyr NOUN **martyrs** someone who is killed or tortured because they refuse to give up their beliefs

VERB **martyrs, martyring, martyred** when someone is martyred they are killed or tortured because of their beliefs

▶ **martyrdom** NOUN **martyrdoms** being martyred

marvel NOUN **marvels** an astonishing or wonderful person or thing

VERB **marvels, marvelling, marvelled** you marvel at something when you are very surprised or impressed by it

▶ **marvellous** ADJECTIVE wonderful or astonishing: *She was always telling marvellous stories about dragons and sorcerers.*

marzipan NOUN a thick paste made with sugar and crushed almonds and used to make sweets and to decorate cakes

mascara NOUN make-up that is brushed on to the eyelashes to make them thicker and darker

Aa
Bb
Cc
Dd
Ee
Ff
Gg
Hh
Ii
Jj
Kk
Ll
Mm
Nn
Oo
Pp
Qq
Rr
Ss
Tt
Uu
Vv
Ww
Xx
Yy
Zz

mascot NOUN **mascots** a person, animal or object that a group of people keep to bring them luck

masculine ADJECTIVE **1** to do with men, typical of men, or suitable for men **2** (*grammar*) masculine forms of words refer to males. For example, *he* is a masculine pronoun

▶ **masculinity** NOUN being like a man

mash VERB **mashes, mashing, mashed** to mash food is to crush it into a soft mass: *Mash the potatoes.*

NOUN mashed potatoes

mask NOUN **masks** a covering that you wear over your face to protect it or as a disguise

VERB **masks, masking, masked** to mask something is to cover, hide or disguise it: *She sprayed air freshener to mask the cooking smells.*

mason NOUN **masons** a craftsman who cuts and carves stone

▶ **masonry** NOUN the parts of a building that are made of stone

mass NOUN **masses 1** a large lump or heap of something, or a large quantity gathered together: *a mass of tangled metal* • *a mass of blonde curls* **2** a big quantity or number: *He's got masses of toys.* **3** (*science*) mass is a measure of the quantity of matter in an object: *A solid rubber ball has greater mass than a hollow one of the same size.*

ADJECTIVE affecting or involving a lot of people or things: *a mass meeting*

VERB **masses, massing, massed** people or things mass, or mass together, when they gather in large numbers: *soldiers massing on the border*

▶ **Mass** NOUN one of several kinds of service held in the Roman Catholic Church and some other Christian churches

massacre NOUN **massacres** the killing of large numbers of people or animals

VERB **massacres, massacring, massacred** to massacre people or animals is to kill large numbers of them in a cruel and violent way

massage VERB **massages, massaging, massaged** to rub parts of the body

gently but firmly to relax the muscles or treat pain and stiffness

NOUN **massages** treatment by massaging

massive ADJECTIVE **1** very big: *a massive amount* • *Hyenas have massive jaws for tearing flesh and crunching bones.*

▶ **massively** ADVERB extremely: *a TV programme which is massively popular with children*

mass production NOUN making goods in very large quantities, usually in a factory using machines

mast NOUN **masts** a wooden or metal pole for holding up the sails of a boat or ship, or a radio or television aerial

master NOUN **masters 1** a man who owns or is in charge of something: *a dog and its master* • *the master of the house* **2** a male teacher: *Mr Green, the science master* **3** if someone is a master of some activity, they are very good at it: *a master of disguise*

ADJECTIVE fully qualified and experienced: *a master craftsman*

VERB **masters, mastering, mastered 1** to master a subject or skill is to learn enough about it to be able to use it or do it successfully: *Juggling needs quite a lot of practice before you master it.* **2** to master a feeling, such as fear, is to overcome it

▶ **Master** NOUN in the past, a title used for a boy: *young Master Copperfield*

▶ **masterly** ADJECTIVE very clever or skilful: *a masterly performance*

mastermind NOUN **masterminds** the mastermind of a clever scheme or crime is the person who thinks of it and organizes the people who carry it out

VERB **masterminds, masterminding, masterminded** to mastermind a scheme or crime is to think of it and do the planning or organization needed to carry it out

masterpiece NOUN **masterpieces 1** a book, painting, piece of music or other work of art that is one of the greatest of its kind **2** someone's masterpiece is the greatest piece of work they have done

Aa
Bb
Cc
Dd
Ee
Ff
Gg
Hh
Ii
Jj
Kk
Ll
Mm
Nn
Oo
Pp
Qq
Rr
Ss
Tt
Uu
Vv
Ww
Xx
Yy
Zz

mastery NOUN **1** great skill at something: *We were amazed at his mastery of chess at such a young age.* **2** control of something: *mastery of the seas*

mat NOUN **mats 1** a flat piece of material for covering or protecting part of a floor **2** a small piece of material for protecting a table's surface or for resting something on: *a table mat • a mouse mat*

matador NOUN **matadors** the man who kills the bull in a bullfight

match¹ NOUN **matches** a short piece of wood or other material tipped with a substance that catches fire when it is rubbed against a rough surface

match² NOUN **matches 1** a contest or game between two players or two teams **2** something that is similar to, or the same as, another thing, especially in its colour or pattern: *This isn't the same make of paint but it's a very good match.* **3** a person or animal who is able to equal another: *I could beat him over a mile but I was no match for him when it came to the 100 metres.*
VERB **matches, matching, matched 1** two things match when they are similar to or the same as each other **2** to match, or match up to, another person or thing is to be as good as them

matchbox NOUN **matchboxes** a small cardboard box for holding matches

mate NOUN **mates 1** a friend or companion **2** an officer on a ship **3** an animal's mate is the male or female it mates with
VERB **mates, mating, mated** animals mate when a male and a female come together so that they can produce young

material NOUN **materials 1** cloth or fabric: *I need some material to make a costume for the school play.* **2** anything used for making something else: *a shop selling artist's materials*

maternal ADJECTIVE **1** to do with, or typical of, a mother: *strong maternal feelings* **2** from your mother's side of your family: *your maternal grandmother*

maternity ADJECTIVE to do with pregnancy and giving birth: *a maternity dress • a maternity hospital*

math NOUN a short form of the word **mathematics** that is used mainly in the United States and Canada

mathematical ADJECTIVE to do with or using mathematics: *a mathematical genius • a mathematical calculation*

mathematician NOUN **mathematicians** someone who studies mathematics or is an expert in mathematics

mathematics NOUN the study of measurements, numbers, quantities and shapes

maths NOUN a short form of the word **mathematics**

matinée NOUN **matinées** a performance at a theatre or cinema in the afternoon or morning

matrimony NOUN (*formal*) the state of being married

matrix NOUN **matrices** (*maths*) a rectangular table of numbers in rows and columns

matron NOUN **matrons 1** a senior nurse in charge of a hospital **2** a woman in charge of housekeeping or nursing at a hostel or boarding school

matt or **mat** ADJECTIVE a matt surface or matt finish is dull, without any shine or gloss

matted ADJECTIVE tangled and stuck together in a thick mass: *matted hair*

matter NOUN **matters 1** matter is any substance that takes up space and is part of the physical universe **2** a subject, situation or issue: *He wants to see you to discuss a personal matter.* **3** if something is the matter, something is wrong or someone is ill or has a problem: *What's the matter with Rachel? She's very quiet.*
• **as a matter of fact** in fact
VERB **matters, mattering, mattered** to matter is to be important: *Winning matters to him more than it should.*
▶ **matter-of-fact** ADJECTIVE a matter-of-fact person deals with or talks about an unusual or upsetting situation in a calm way, as if it was something that

Aa
Bb
Cc
Dd
Ee
Ff
Gg
Hh
Ii
Jj
Kk
Ll
Mm
Nn
Oo
Pp
Qq
Rr
Ss
Tt
Uu
Vv
Ww
Xx
Yy
Zz

happened every day: *She tried hard to be matter-of-fact about it all.*

▸ **matters** PLURAL NOUN the situation being discussed or dealt with now: *It won't help matters if you start to cry.*

matting NOUN stiff material used to make mats

mattress NOUN **mattresses** a thick firm layer of padding for lying on, usually as part of a bed

mature ADJECTIVE **1** fully grown or developed: *A mature male elephant can weigh several tons.* **2** grown-up: *He's not very mature for his age.*
VERB **matures, maturing, matured** to become mature

▸ **maturity** NOUN being grown-up or adult

maul VERB **mauls, mauling, mauled** to maul a person or animal is to hurt them badly in a rough and savage attack: *The zookeeper was mauled by one of the lions.*

mauve NOUN a pale purple colour

maximum NOUN AND ADJECTIVE the greatest number or quantity, or the highest point: *The maximum I'm prepared to pay is £20.*

may VERB **might 1** you may do something if there is a possibility you will do it: *I may go to college to study art.* **2** you may do something when you have someone's permission to do it: *You may leave the table now.* • *May I ask what you're doing in my room?*

May NOUN the fifth month of the year, after April and before June

✦ **May** comes from the name of the Roman earth goddess **Maia**.

maybe ADVERB perhaps or possibly: *Maybe you'd like to come to lunch one day?*

mayday NOUN **maydays** a word used over the radio by ships or aeroplanes that are in trouble

✦ This comes from the French phrase 'venez **m'aider**', which means 'come and help me'.

mayhem NOUN great confusion and noise

mayonnaise NOUN a smooth creamy sauce made from oil, egg yolks and vinegar, often eaten with salad or in sandwiches

mayor NOUN **mayors** a man or woman elected as the official leader of a town or city

mayoress NOUN **mayoresses** a mayor's wife

maypole NOUN **maypoles** a tall decorated pole with long ribbons attached at the top. People hold the ribbons as they dance round the pole in a traditional celebration of the first day of May

maze NOUN **mazes** a confusing network of paths, each with a high wall or hedge on either side, designed as a puzzle to see how well you can find your way

MB ABBREVIATION (*ICT*) short for **megabyte**

me PRONOUN a word you use to talk about yourself: *Would you get me a drink, please.* • *Lots of cakes for tea, all for you and me.*

✦ In a sentence in which you are doing the action, you use **I** before the verb. You use **me** after the verb:
✓ *The teacher gave the best mark to **me**.*
✓ *The teacher gave the best marks to Emily, Rory and **me**.*

mead NOUN an alcoholic drink made from honey

meadow NOUN **meadows** a field of grass

meagre ADJECTIVE a meagre amount is a very small amount: *They can't possibly survive the winter on such meagre supplies.*

meal NOUN **meals** a meal is food that you eat at one time, for example breakfast, lunch or dinner

mean¹ VERB **means, meaning, meant 1** a word or action means something when it shows something or you understand something from it: *The definitions in this dictionary tell you what the words mean.* • *Dark clouds usually mean rain.*

2 you mean to do something when you intend to do it: *I'm sorry. I didn't mean to stand on your foot.*

3 you mean what you say when you aren't joking or telling lies

4 something that means something to you is important to you: *That puppy means an awful lot to her.*

mean² ADJECTIVE **meaner, meanest 1** a mean person won't spend money or share what they have with others **2** if someone is mean to you, they are nasty and unkind

mean³ ADJECTIVE (*maths*) **1** a mean point or quantity is halfway between two other points or quantities **2** average: *The mean rainfall is worked out by taking a measurement every day, adding all the measurements together and dividing by the number of days.*

meander (pronounced mee-**an**-der) VERB **meanders, meandering, meandered** if a river meanders, it has several bends in it

✦ This word comes from a river in Turkey called **Maeander**, which winds in this way.

meaning NOUN **meanings** what a word or action means

meaningful ADJECTIVE **1** a meaningful expression or gesture is intended to show something: *a meaningful look* **2** something meaningful is useful or important: *meaningful discussions*

meaningless ADJECTIVE **1** having no meaning: *It's just all meaningless waffle.* **2** having no purpose or importance: *He felt as if his life was meaningless.*

meanness NOUN **1** selfishness or lack of generosity **2** nastiness

means NOUN **1** a means of doing something is a way or method of doing it: *Traffic jams are so frequent, many people are looking for a different means of transport.* **2** a person's means is the money they have or earn: *Living beyond your means is spending more than you have or can earn.*

• **by all means** yes, of course: *'Can I have a look at your magazine?' 'By all means.'*

• **by no means** in no way: *It is by no means the best film I've ever seen.*

meant VERB a way of changing the verb **mean** to form a past tense. It can be used with or without a helping verb: *I meant every word I said.* • *She had meant to tell him the news, but had forgotten.*

meantime ADVERB meantime is used to refer to the time between now and some event in the future

• **in the meantime** means for now: *If you have lost your pencil, you can use mine in the meantime.*

meanwhile ADVERB meanwhile is used to refer to something that is happening during this time or at the same time as something else is happening: *I went out to play football; meanwhile, my sister stayed in and played computer games.*

measles NOUN an infectious disease mainly affecting children, which causes red spots on the skin and a fever

measly ADJECTIVE **measlier, measliest** small in value or amount: *All I had to eat was one measly little biscuit.*

measure VERB **measures, measuring, measured 1** to measure something is to find its width, height, length, weight or amount: *Stand straight against the wall so that I can measure your height.* **2** if something measures a certain number of units, its size or amount is given in that number of units: *The room measures 3.5 metres from the door to the window.*

NOUN **measures** a unit used in measuring: *A kilogram is a measure of weight, while a kilometre is a measure of distance or length.*

▶ **measurement** NOUN **measurements** a size or amount found by measuring

▶ **measures** PLURAL NOUN actions taken to achieve a particular aim: *strict measures to reduce crime*

meat NOUN **meats** the flesh of animals used as food, such as pork, lamb or beef

▶ **meaty** ADJECTIVE **meatier, meatiest**

Aa
Bb
Cc
Dd
Ee
Ff
Gg
Hh
Ii
Jj
Kk
Ll
Mm
Nn
Oo
Pp
Qq
Rr
Ss
Tt
Uu
Vv
Ww
Xx
Yy
Zz

full of meat or tasting of meat: *a nice meaty pie with a crisp crust*

mechanic NOUN **mechanics** someone whose job is to keep machinery working and repair it when it breaks down, especially someone who repairs vehicle engines

mechanical ADJECTIVE **1** to do with machines, or worked by machinery: *mechanical engineering • a mechanical toy* **2** mechanical behaviour or actions are done without thinking or concentrating

mechanics NOUN **1** mechanics is the study and art of building machinery: *car mechanics* **2** the mechanics of something are the details or processes involved in making it work: *the mechanics of their campaign*

mechanism NOUN **mechanisms** a working part of a machine, or its system of working parts: *the cogs and springs that are part of the clock's mechanism*

medal NOUN **medals** a metal disc, usually with a design or writing stamped on it, given as a prize in a competition

medallion NOUN **medallions** a piece of jewellery with a disc like a medal hanging on a long chain that is worn around the neck

medallist NOUN **medallists** someone who has won a medal in a competition

meddle VERB **meddles, meddling, meddled** to interfere in someone else's business or in something that you do not understand properly

media PLURAL NOUN the media are newspapers, television and radio or any other means of communicating information to the public

mediaeval ADJECTIVE another spelling of **medieval**

median NOUN **medians** (*maths*) **1** the middle number or point in a series. For example, the median of *2, 4, 6, 8, 10* is 6 **2** a straight line from an angle of a triangle to the opposite side of the triangle

medical ADJECTIVE to do with healing and medicine or doctors and their work NOUN **medicals** a general examination

done by a doctor to find out the state of a person's health

▶ **medically** ADVERB by or using medicine

medicinal ADJECTIVE to do with medicine or having an effect like medicine

medicine NOUN **medicines 1** the science of the treatment of illness and disease: *studying medicine* **2** any substance used to treat or prevent diseases and illnesses: *cough medicine*

medieval ADJECTIVE to do with or in the Middle Ages, the period of history from about the beginning of the 12th century to the end of the 15th century

mediocre ADJECTIVE dull and ordinary, with no special or exciting qualities

▶ **mediocrity** NOUN being dull and ordinary

meditate VERB **meditates, meditating, meditated 1** to spend time being quiet, still and relaxed, especially for spiritual or religious reasons: *He was sitting cross-legged, meditating.* **2** to think about something deeply and carefully: *She was meditating about the future.*

▶ **meditation** NOUN **meditations** meditating, or deep thought

medium ADJECTIVE at the middle point between two ends in a range, for example between small and large, low and high, or light and dark: *a man of medium height with medium brown hair*

NOUN **mediums** or **media 1** a means or substance by which something is expressed, communicated or produced: *The World Wide Web is a new medium for advertising.* **2** someone who believes they can communicate with dead people

✦ You can use the plural **mediums** or **media** for the first meaning, but only **mediums** for the second meaning.

meek ADJECTIVE **meeker, meekest** a meek person is gentle and not likely to complain or argue with other people

▶ **meekly** ADVERB without complaining or arguing: *'Sorry', said Lily meekly.*

Aa
Bb
Cc
Dd
Ee
Ff
Gg
Hh
Ii
Jj
Kk
Ll
Mm
Nn
Oo
Pp
Qq
Rr
Ss
Tt
Uu
Vv
Ww
Xx
Yy
Zz

▸ **meekness** NOUN being gentle and unlikely to complain-

meet VERB **meets, meeting, met**
1 to come face to face with someone by chance: *I met a puppy as I was walking. We got talking, puppy and I.*
2 to come together with one other person, or a group of other people, at the same time and in the same place: *Let's meet outside the cinema.*
3 to be introduced to someone and get to know them for the first time: *Have you met my big sister, Jane?*
4 two things meet when they come together or touch: *I've got so fat, my waistband doesn't meet round my middle.*
5 to meet a challenge, or a certain attitude or response, is to face it or be faced with it
6 to meet the cost of something is to pay for it
7 to meet a need is to provide what is needed

▸ **meeting** NOUN **meetings** a gathering of people, usually to discuss something

mega- PREFIX **1** when **mega-** comes at the beginning of some words it means *a million.* For example, a *megabyte* is a million bytes of computer memory and a *megaton* is a million tons **2** when **mega-** comes at the beginning of other words it means *huge* or *great.* For example, if someone is called a *megastar,* they are a very big star

✦ This comes from the Greek word **mega,** which means *big.*

megabyte NOUN **megabytes** (*ICT*) a unit used to measure computer memory or data, equal to approximately a million bytes. This is often shortened to **MB**

megaphone NOUN **megaphones** a device shaped like an open-ended cone that someone speaks through to make their voice sound louder

melancholy (pronounced **mel**-an-kol-i) NOUN sadness
ADJECTIVE sad and lonely, or making you feel sad: *The dog gave a melancholy howl.*

mellow ADJECTIVE **mellower, mellowest** soft, not strong or unpleasant: *the mellow sound of the clarinet*
VERB **mellows, mellowing, mellowed**
1 fruit or wine mellows when it becomes ripe or mature, and soft **2** a person mellows with age when they become more tolerant and pleasant as they get older

melodic ADJECTIVE having a melody

melodious ADJECTIVE a melodious sound or voice is tuneful and pleasant to listen to

melodrama NOUN **melodramas** a style of drama with lots of exciting action that is more extreme than in real life, or a play or film in this style

▸ **melodramatic** ADJECTIVE someone behaves in a melodramatic way when they exaggerate to make things seem more sensational or exciting than they really are

melody NOUN **melodies** a tune, especially a pleasant-sounding one

melon NOUN **melons** a large rounded fruit with a green or yellow skin, yellow or orange sweet-tasting flesh and lots of seeds in the middle

melt VERB **melts, melting, melted** something melts when it becomes soft and runny as it is heated

melting point NOUN **melting points** (*science*) the temperature at which a particular substance melts when it is heated

member NOUN **members** a person who belongs to a group, club or society

▸ **membership** NOUN **memberships**
1 being a member: *He has membership of many clubs.* **2** the membership of a group, club or society is all the people who are its members

membrane NOUN **membranes 1** a thin layer of skin that covers or connects the organs inside the body **2** any thin layer or covering

memento NOUN **mementos** a memento is something that you buy or keep to remind you of something you have done or a place you have visited

memoirs PLURAL NOUN someone's memoirs are a book that they write about their life's experiences

memorable ADJECTIVE a memorable event is one that you can, or will, remember because it is special or important

▶ **memorably** ADVERB in a way that will not be forgotten

memorial NOUN **memorials** a statue or monument put up as a way of remembering and honouring a person or event: *the Prince Albert Memorial* • *a war memorial*

ADJECTIVE acting as a memorial: *the John Andrews memorial trophy*

memorize or **memorise** VERB **memorizes, memorizing, memorized** to memorize something is to learn it thoroughly so that you can remember it later

memory NOUN **memories 1** memory is the power of your mind to remember things **2** a memory is something you remember: *happy memories of his school days*

• **in living memory** from a time that people who are alive now can still remember

• **in memory of** as a way of remembering a dead person: *a minute's silence in memory of the accident victims*

men NOUN the plural of **man**

menace NOUN **menaces 1** something that causes trouble or danger: *These biting flies are a real menace.* **2** threatening trouble, harm or violence: *His voice was full of menace.*

VERB **menaces, menacing, menaced** to threaten someone or something with trouble, harm or violence

▶ **menacing** ADJECTIVE threatening or evil-looking

mend VERB **mends, mending, mended** to mend something is to repair or fix it

NOUN

• **on the mend** if someone who has

been ill or injured is on the mend, they are starting to get better

menstruation NOUN menstruation is the regular flow of blood that a woman has from her womb each month

mental ADJECTIVE **1** to do with or using the brain or intelligence: *mental ability* • *mental arithmetic* **2** an informal word for mad or suffering from an illness of the mind

▶ **mentality** NOUN **mentalities** someone's mentality is the attitudes and opinions they have

▶ **mentally** ADVERB in or with the mind: *You must commit yourself mentally and physically when you practice yoga.*

mention VERB **mentions, mentioning, mentioned** to mention something is to say it to someone

menu NOUN **menus 1** a list of the food available in a restaurant **2** (*ICT*) on a computer, a list of options that you can choose from by clicking with the mouse or scrolling down the list

MEP ABBREVIATION **MEPs** short for **Member of the European Parliament**, someone who has been elected to the parliament of the European Union

mercenary NOUN **mercenaries** a soldier who hires himself out to any army or country that will pay him to fight

merchandise NOUN goods that are bought and sold

merchant NOUN **merchants** someone who carries on a business buying and selling goods

merchant navy NOUN **merchant navies** a country's merchant navy is its fleet of ships that are used to transport goods and passengers, not its fighting ships

merciful ADJECTIVE kind and forgiving

▶ **mercifully** ADVERB people say 'mercifully' to show that they are glad or grateful for something: *After the heat outside, the room was mercifully cool.*

merciless ADJECTIVE cruel and without

Aa
Bb
Cc
Dd
Ee
Ff
Gg
Hh
Ii
Jj
Kk
Ll
Mm
Nn
Oo
Pp
Qq
Rr
Ss
Tt
Uu
Vv
Ww
Xx
Yy
Zz

showing any mercy: *The heat was merciless.*

mercury NOUN a silvery chemical element mostly used in liquid form in things like thermometers and barometers

mercy NOUN **mercies** someone who has or shows mercy is kind and willing to forgive someone they could punish if they wanted to

• **at the mercy of** if you are at the mercy of someone or something, you are in their power: *The defeated Armada was at the mercy of the winds.*

mere ADJECTIVE **merest** nothing more than or only: *The flight from London to Madrid cost a mere £25.*

▸ **merely** ADVERB only or simply: *I asked him again but he merely shrugged his shoulders.*

merge VERB **merges, merging, merged** two or more things merge when they combine with each other or they become mixed together: *The highway merged with several others to form a new road.*

▸ **merger** NOUN **mergers** the joining of two businesses to form a single large company

meridian NOUN **meridians** (*geography*) an imaginary line around the Earth passing through the north and south pole

meringue (pronounced ma-**rang**) NOUN **meringues** a mixture of whipped egg-whites and sugar cooked slowly in the oven until it is dry and crisp

merit NOUN **merits 1** merit is value or importance **2** the merits of something are the things that make it good or valuable

VERB **merits, meriting, merited** to merit something is to deserve it

mermaid NOUN **mermaids** in stories, a beautiful creature who lives in the sea and is half woman, half fish

merry ADJECTIVE **merrier, merriest** happy and cheerful

▸ **merrily** ADVERB happily and cheerfully

merry-go-round NOUN **merry-go-rounds** a ride at a funfair with wooden animals and vehicles that you sit on as the ride goes round and round

mesh NOUN **meshes** mesh is lengths of wire or thread formed into a net

mess NOUN **messes 1** an untidy or dirty state or sight **2** something that is in a confused state or that involves lots of problems

VERB **messes, messing, messed**

• **mess about** or **mess around** to do silly or annoying things

• **mess something up** to spoil something or damage it

message NOUN **messages** a piece of news or information sent from one person to another

VERB **messages, messaging, messaged** to message someone is to send them a message using a mobile phone or computer

▸ **messaging** NOUN sending and receiving messages using mobile phones or computers

messenger NOUN **messengers** someone who carries messages or letters from one person to another

messiah NOUN **messiahs** someone who comes to save or deliver people from misery or evil

messy ADJECTIVE **messier, messiest** untidy or dirty

▸ **messily** ADVERB sloppily or untidily

met VERB a way of changing the verb **meet** to form a past tense. It can be used with or without a helping verb: *We met yesterday.* • *I thought you two had met before.*

metal NOUN **metals** a hard shiny material that melts when it is heated, for example iron, steel, gold, silver and tin

▸ **metallic** ADJECTIVE hard and shiny like metal, or sounding like metal when it is hit

metallurgy NOUN the study of metals

metamorphose VERB **metamorphoses, metamorphosing, metamorphosed** something metamorphoses when it changes its appearance or form completely and becomes something else

metamorphosis NOUN **metamorphoses** a complete change made in something's appearance or form, such as happens with some living creatures, like frogs and butterflies, as they grow and develop

metaphor NOUN **metaphors** a way of describing something in a powerful and expressive way by comparing it to something else. For example, it is a metaphor to say that someone who is very eager to do something is *straining at the leash* suggesting they are like a dog that wants to be let off the lead so that it can run free

▶ **metaphorical** ADJECTIVE using a metaphor or metaphors

meteor NOUN **meteors** a mass of rock travelling through space very fast, sometimes seen in the night sky as a shooting star

meteoric ADJECTIVE very fast, like a meteor travelling through space

meteorite NOUN **meteorites** a meteor that has fallen to Earth

meteorology NOUN the study of weather

▶ **meteorologist** NOUN **meteorologists** someone who studies the weather and makes weather forecasts

meter NOUN **meters** an instrument that measures and records something, such as the amount of gas or electricity used in a house

✦ The words **meter** and **metre** sound the same but remember that they have different spellings. A **metre** is a measure of length.

methane NOUN a gas found in coal mines and marshes and produced when plant material rots

method NOUN **methods 1** a way of doing something: *What's the best method of revising for a test?* **2** if something you do has method, you do it in a well-planned or organized way

▶ **methodical** ADJECTIVE well-ordered and efficient: *Let us be methodical and take one thing at a time.*

methodically ADVERB orderly and efficiently

meticulous ADJECTIVE paying careful attention to every detail

▶ **meticulously** ADVERB very carefully

metre NOUN **metres 1** the basic unit in the metric system for measuring length. This is often shortened to **m 2** the regular rhythm of poetry or music

▶ **metrical** ADJECTIVE having the regular rhythm of poetry or music

✦ The words **metre** and **meter** sound the same but remember that they have different spellings. A **meter** is a device for measuring something.

metric ADJECTIVE using the metric system: *a metric unit of measurement*

metric system NOUN a system of measuring and weighing that uses units such as litres and grams. It is based on counting in tens and multiples of ten

metronome NOUN **metronomes** (*music*) a piece of equipment that makes a regular sound like a clock, which musicians use to help them keep the correct beat when they are practising music

mettle NOUN **1** if something tests your mettle, it tests your courage or ability **2** if you are on your mettle, you are ready and prepared to do your best

mew VERB **mews, mewing, mewed** to make a sound like a cat

NOUN **mews** the sound a cat makes

▶ **mews** PLURAL NOUN buildings built around a yard or lane. Mews were originally stables

mg ABBREVIATION short for **milligram** or **milligrams**

miaow NOUN **miaows** the call or sound that a cat makes

VERB **miaows, miaowing, miaowed** a cat miaows when it makes this sound

mice NOUN the plural of **mouse**

micro- PREFIX if **micro-** comes at the beginning of a word, it adds the meaning *very small*. For example, a *microchip* is a very small silicon chip used to make computer circuits

Aa
Bb
Cc
Dd
Ee
Ff
Gg
Hh
Ii
Jj
Kk
Ll
Mm
Nn
Oo
Pp
Qq
Rr
Ss
Tt
Uu
Vv
Ww
Xx
Yy
Zz

microbe → midwife

✦ This comes from the Greek word mikros, which means *little*.

microbe NOUN **microbes** (*science*) a tiny living creature that can only be seen under a microscope

microchip NOUN **microchips** a very small part used in computers that has several tiny electrical circuits on it

microcomputer NOUN **microcomputers** (*ICT*) a small computer containing microchips or a microprocessor

micro-organism NOUN **micro-organisms** (*science*) a tiny living thing, such as a germ, that can only be seen under a microscope

microphone NOUN **microphones** a piece of equipment that can record sounds or that can make your voice sound louder when you speak or sing into it

microprocessor NOUN **microprocessors** (*ICT*) a set of microchips that make up a computer's central processing unit

microscope NOUN **microscopes** an instrument with lenses that make very tiny objects look much larger so that you can study them closely
> **microscopic** ADJECTIVE microscopic objects are so small they can only be seen using a microscope

microwave NOUN **microwaves 1** a very short radio wave **2** a microwave oven

microwave oven NOUN **microwave ovens** an oven that cooks food very quickly using electrical and magnetic waves rather than heat

mid- PREFIX if **mid-** comes at the beginning of a word, it has something to do with the middle of something. For example, *midwinter* is the middle of the winter

midday NOUN noon, or the middle of the day

midden NOUN **middens** a rubbish heap or dung heap

middle NOUN **middles 1** the point, position or part furthest from the sides or edges: *an island in the middle of the ocean* • *Let me sit in the middle.* **2** the point in a period of time that is halfway through that period of time: *Autumn half-term comes in the middle of October.* • *The teacher fainted in the middle of our history lesson.* **3** your middle is your waist
ADJECTIVE between two things or at the halfway point: *He's the middle child of a family of five boys.* • *the middle section of the book*

middle-aged ADJECTIVE between the ages of 40 and 60

middle class NOUN **middle classes** the middle class is the social class between the working class and the upper class, and consists of educated, professional or skilled people
ADJECTIVE coming from, or to do with, the middle class

middle school NOUN **middle schools** a school for children between the ages of 8 or 9 and 12 or 13

midge NOUN **midges** a type of tiny biting insect

midget NOUN **midgets** a person who is fully developed but has not grown to normal size
ADJECTIVE very small: *a midget submarine*

midland ADJECTIVE coming from or in the midlands
> **midlander** NOUN **midlanders** someone who is born in or lives in the midlands
> **midlands** PLURAL NOUN the midlands of a country are the areas in the middle of the country

midnight NOUN twelve o'clock at night

midst NOUN **1** to be in the midst of several people or things is to be surrounded by them **2** if you are in the midst of something, you are in the middle of doing it

midsummer NOUN the middle of the summer

midway ADVERB at the middle point between two places

midwife NOUN **midwives** a nurse who is specially trained to help women when they are having their babies

✦ This word comes from the Old English words **mid**, which means *with*, and **wif**, which means *woman*, because a **midwife** is with a woman who is having a baby.

might¹ VERB **1 might** is used as a past tense of **may**: *John asked if he might come with us.* **2 might** is also used if there is a possibility of something: *He might stay.* • *It might rain.*

might² NOUN power or strength: *He pulled with all his might.*

mighty ADJECTIVE **mightier, mightiest 1** powerful: *Atlas took the weight of the sky on his mighty shoulders.* **2** very great: *a mighty effort*

▶ **mightily** ADVERB **1** extremely: *He was mightily grateful for his warm snowsuit when the blizzard came.* **2** with great power or strength: *The wind blew mightily and shook the windows and doors.*

▶ **mightiness** NOUN great power or strength

migrant NOUN **migrants** migrants are people who move from place to place, usually looking for work

ADJECTIVE moving from place to place

migrate VERB **migrates, migrating, migrated** birds, and sometimes animals, migrate when they travel from one region or country to another at certain times of the year

▶ **migration** NOUN **migrations** a movement of a large number of people, animals or birds from one place to another: *the migration of millions of animals across the African plains*

mike NOUN **mikes** (*informal*) a short form of the word **microphone**

mild ADJECTIVE **milder, mildest 1** mild weather is quite warm **2** mild things don't have a strong or powerful effect: *Use a mild soap on baby's skin.* **3** a mild person is gentle and quiet

mildew NOUN a disease of plants in which a spongy white fungus covers their leaves and stems

mildly ADVERB **1** in a calm and gentle way **2** slightly: *I was mildly amused at his antics.*

• **to put it mildly** used to show that you are not expressing yourself as strongly as you could in the circumstances: *It was a bit of a shock, to put it mildly.*

mile NOUN **miles** an imperial unit for measuring distance, equal to 1760 yards or 1.6 kilometres

▶ **mileage** NOUN the total number of miles that a vehicle has travelled, or the number of miles a vehicle can travel on a certain amount of fuel

milestone NOUN **milestones 1** an upright stone or post beside a road that marks the number of miles from a place **2** an important point, especially in your life or career

militant ADJECTIVE taking strong, sometimes violent action

NOUN **militants** someone who takes strong, sometimes violent action to change the political or social system

military ADJECTIVE to do with the army, navy or air force

NOUN the military is a country's armed forces, especially its officers

milk NOUN **1** a white liquid that female mammals make in their bodies to feed their young **2** this liquid that we get from cows, goats and sheep and use to drink or to make butter and cheese

VERB **milks, milking, milked 1** to milk an animal is to take milk from it **2** to milk a person or a situation is to get as much as possible from them or it, in a clever or selfish way

milkman NOUN **milkmen** someone whose job is to deliver milk to people's houses

milkshake NOUN **milkshakes** a drink made by blending milk, ice cream and a flavouring

milk tooth NOUN **milk teeth** the first set of teeth that grows in a child's mouth. They fall out and are replaced by larger adult teeth at about the age of 7 or 8

milky ADJECTIVE **milkier, milkiest 1** pale and cloudy, like milk: *a milky liquid* **2** containing a lot of milk: *a hot milky drink*

Aa
Bb
Cc
Dd
Ee
Ff
Gg
Hh
Ii
Jj
Kk
Ll
Mm
Nn
Oo
Pp
Qq
Rr
Ss
Tt
Uu
Vv
Ww
Xx
Yy
Zz

Aa
Bb
Cc
Dd
Ee
Ff
Gg
Hh
Ii
Jj
Kk
Ll
Mm
Nn
Oo
Pp
Qq
Rr
Ss
Tt
Uu
Vv
Ww
Xx
Yy
Zz

Milky Way NOUN the light band that can be seen in the night sky made up of thousands of millions of stars. The Milky Way is the galaxy to which our sun belongs

mill NOUN **mills 1** a building with machinery for grinding corn and other grain **2** a factory where goods of a particular type are made, by crushing, grinding or rolling a natural material: *a paper mill* • *a steel mill* **3** a machine for grinding things like coffee or pepper by crushing it between hard surfaces
VERB **mills, milling, milled** to mill something is to crush it or roll it between hard or heavy surfaces

millennium NOUN **millennia** a period of a thousand years

✦ This word comes from the Latin words **mille**, which means *a thousand*, and **annus**, which means *year*. The word **annual** also comes from the word **annus**.

miller NOUN **millers** someone who grinds corn and other grain in a mill

milligram *or* **milligramme** NOUN **milligrams** *or* **milligrammes** a metric unit for measuring weight, equal to one thousandth of a gram. This is often shortened to **mg**

millilitre NOUN **millilitres** a metric unit for measuring the volume of a liquid, equal to one thousandth of a litre. This is often shortened to **ml**

millimetre NOUN **millimetres** a metric unit for measuring length, equal to one thousandth of a metre. This is often shortened to **mm**

million NOUN **millions** the number 1000000, a thousand thousand

millionaire NOUN **millionaires** a rich person who has at least a million pounds or a million dollars

millstone NOUN **millstones** a heavy round stone used to grind grain
• **a millstone round your neck** a problem or duty that prevents you from doing what you want

mime NOUN **mimes** mime is acting using movements and gestures, but no words
VERB **mimes, miming, mimed 1** to express something by making movements or gestures rather than using words **2** a singer mimes when they move their mouth as if they were singing, but without making a sound

mimic VERB **mimics, mimicking, mimicked** to mimic someone or something is to copy their actions, the way they talk or their appearance
NOUN **mimics** a mimic is someone who copies the way other people speak or behave, usually for fun
▶ **mimicry** NOUN copying someone

min ABBREVIATION **mins** a short form of the word **minute** used in writing: *Fry for 10-15 mins until golden brown.*

mince NOUN meat that has been cut up into very small pieces
VERB **minces, mincing, minced** to mince meat or some other food is to cut it into very small pieces
• **mince your words** you don't mince your words when you say exactly what you think of something

mincemeat NOUN a mixture of chopped dried fruits and nuts, with suet and spices, used to fill pies
• **make mincemeat of someone** to beat someone very easily in a fight, argument or competition

mince pie NOUN **mince pies** a pie filled with mincemeat, usually eaten at Christmas time

mind NOUN **minds** your mind is your brain, or your ability to think, understand or remember
• **in two minds** to be in two minds is not to be able to decide between two alternatives
• **make up your mind** to decide
• **speak your mind** to say what you really think
VERB **minds, minding, minded**
1 you mind something when it upsets or annoys you: *I don't mind cold weather.*
2 you ask someone if they would mind doing something, or if they would mind

if you did something, when you are asking them politely to do it, or if they object to you doing it: *Would you mind opening the window?*
3 to mind someone or something is to look after them
4 you tell someone to mind something when you are telling them to watch out for some hazard or danger: *Mind your head on that branch.*
▸ **minder** NOUN **minders** someone who looks after another person and protects them from harm

mindless ADJECTIVE **1** a mindless task is boring and does not need any thought or imagination **2** mindless violence or destruction is stupid and done for no purpose

mine[1] PRONOUN a word you use to talk about something belonging to **me**: *Is this book yours or mine?* • *a friend of mine*

mine[2] NOUN **mines 1** a place where things are dug out of the ground, for example coal, metals and minerals, or precious stones **2** a type of bomb that is hidden in the ground or in the sea and which explodes when someone stands on it or a ship hits it
VERB **mines, mining, mined 1** to mine something like coal or gold is to dig it out of the ground **2** to mine an area of land or sea is to place explosive mines in it

minefield NOUN **minefields 1** an area of land with explosive mines in it **2** a situation that is full of hidden dangers or problems

miner NOUN **miners** someone who works in a mine

mineral NOUN **minerals** any of various substances found in the ground, such as coal, or dissolved in water, such as salt

mingle VERB **mingles, mingling, mingled** people or things mingle when they are mixed together or move about amongst each other

mini- PREFIX if **mini-** comes at the beginning of a word, it means it is a small or short type of something. For example, a *minibus* is a small bus

miniature ADJECTIVE very small
NOUN **miniatures** a very small copy or model of a larger thing, or a very small portrait of someone

minibeast NOUN **minibeasts** a small creature such as an insect or a spider

minibus NOUN **minibuses** a small bus for around 12 to 15 passengers

minim NOUN **minims** (*music*) a musical note equal in length to two crotchets, or half a semibreve or whole note. The symbol for a minim is ♩

minimal ADJECTIVE something minimal is very small or the least amount possible: *The storm caused minimal damage to the school.*

minimize or **minimise** VERB **minimizes, minimizing, minimized** to minimize something is to reduce it to the smallest size or extent possible

minimum NOUN AND ADJECTIVE the smallest number or quantity, or the lowest point: *The minimum contribution is £5.*

minister NOUN **ministers 1** the name given to a priest in some branches of the Christian church **2** a government minister is a politician in charge of a government department: *the Minister for Education*
VERB **ministers, ministering, ministered** to minister to someone is to provide them with some sort of help, usually because they are sick
▸ **ministry** NOUN **ministries 1** the profession of a priest or minister **2** a government department

mink NOUN **mink 1** a small slim animal with a pointed face, short legs and very soft fur **2** the dark-brown fur of the mink
ADJECTIVE made from the fur of the mink: *a mink coat*

minnow NOUN **minnows** a type of small fish that lives in fresh water

minor ADJECTIVE **1** something minor is not very big, not very serious or not very important: *a minor problem* • *a minor road* **2** (*music*) a minor scale has a semitone between the second and third notes. A minor key or chord is based on this scale

NOUN **minors** someone who is under the age when people legally become adults

minority NOUN **minorities 1** a small group of people that is part of a much larger group **2** a group of people in a society that are a different race or have a different religion than most other people in the society

mint¹ NOUN **mints 1** mint is a plant with strong-smelling leaves used as a flavouring in cooking **2** a mint is a sweet flavoured with the mint plant

mint² NOUN **1** a place, controlled by the government, where new coins are made **2** (informal) a very large amount of money: *That fancy house must have cost a mint.*

• **in mint condition** something is in mint condition when it looks as if it has just been newly made

minus PREPOSITION **1** (maths) taking away or subtracting: *8 minus 2 is 6* **2** without: *He came back home covered in mud and minus one shoe.*

ADJECTIVE **1** less than zero: *minus ten degrees* **2** minus is used after a letter to show that a mark or grade is slightly less than by the letter alone: *I got an A minus for my essay.*

NOUN **minuses** (maths) a minus, or minus sign (–), is a mathematical symbol showing that a number is to be taken away from another, or that a number is less than zero

minuscule ADJECTIVE tiny: *a minuscule spot on her blouse*

minute¹ NOUN **minutes**

1 sixty seconds or a sixtieth part of an hour

2 (maths) in measuring an angle, the sixtieth part of a degree

3 a moment or very short time: *Wait a minute while I go back for my schoolbag.*

4 the minutes of a meeting are notes taken while the meeting is going on describing what has been discussed or agreed

ADJECTIVE showing the number of minutes: *the minute hand of your watch*

minute² (pronounced mine-**yoot**)

ADJECTIVE tiny: *You only need to use a minute amount of the ointment.*

miracle NOUN **miracles 1** a wonderful act or event that cannot be explained **2** a piece of great good luck: *It's a miracle that you weren't killed running across that busy road.*

▸ **miraculous** ADJECTIVE wonderful and amazing, like a miracle

▸ **miraculously** ADVERB amazingly: *Miraculously, he got out of the wrecked car without a scratch.*

mirage NOUN **mirages** in deserts and hot countries, you see a mirage when you see something that is not really there, usually a false image of a large area of water in the distance caused by currents of hot air rising

mire NOUN deep mud or dirt

mirror NOUN **mirrors** a piece of glass with a reflective backing that you can look at yourself in

VERB **mirrors, mirroring, mirrored** one thing mirrors another when it looks or behaves exactly like that other thing or like a reflection of it

mirth NOUN mirth is a fairly formal word for laughter or fun

mis- PREFIX if **mis-** comes at the beginning of a word, it adds the meaning *bad* or *badly*, or *wrong* or *wrongly*. For example, to *mistreat* something is to treat it badly

misbehave VERB **misbehaves, misbehaving, misbehaved** to behave badly

miscarriage NOUN **miscarriages 1** if a pregnant woman has a miscarriage, the baby comes out of her womb too early and does not survive **2** a miscarriage of justice happens when someone is wrongly punished for a crime they did not commit

miscellaneous ADJECTIVE a miscellaneous collection or group is one that contains many different kinds of things

mischief NOUN naughty behaviour that does not cause any serious harm: *I hope you children haven't been getting up to mischief.*

▶ **mischievous** ADJECTIVE full of mischief

miser NOUN **misers** someone who hates spending money, and saves as much as they can

▶ **miserly** ADJECTIVE very unwilling to spend money

miserable ADJECTIVE

1 very unhappy: *She's miserable because all her friends are away.*

2 making you feel unhappy or depressed: *What a miserable wet day it's been!*

3 sad and grumpy: *Smile! Don't be such a miserable old so-and-so!*

4 mean: *I got a miserable 20p pocket money this week!*

misery NOUN **miseries 1** great unhappiness, or something that causes great unhappiness **2** a depressing person, who spoils other people's fun

misfit NOUN **misfits** someone whose behaviour or attitudes is very different from most other people, and who does not fit in with any group well

misfortune NOUN **misfortunes** bad luck

mishap NOUN **mishaps** an unlucky accident

mislay VERB **mislays, mislaying, mislaid** to mislay something is to lose it, usually because you can't remember where you put it

mislead VERB **misleads, misleading, misled** to mislead someone is to give them wrong information so that they believe something is true when it isn't

▶ **misleading** ADJECTIVE giving the wrong impression or information

misprint NOUN **misprints** a mistake in printing: *That's definitely a misprint. It should be 10, not 1000.*

miss VERB **misses, missing, missed**

1 to fail to hit or catch something you are aiming at: *The arrow missed the target.*

2 to miss an event is to be unable to attend it or watch it: *Granny never misses this programme.*

3 to miss a train, bus or plane is to not arrive in time to catch it

4 to miss a person or place is to be sad because that person is not with you or you are not at that place

5 to miss something is to realize that you do not have it or that it is lost: *When did you first miss your purse?*

• **miss something out** to not include something, either by mistake or on purpose

• **miss out on something** if you miss out on something good, you do not get any of it, or you do not take part in it: *He arrived late and missed out on all the games.*

NOUN **misses 1** a failure to hit a target: *He scored two hits and a miss.* **2** to give something a miss is to not do it

Miss NOUN **Misses 1** a title used for girls and unmarried women **2** a word used by schoolchildren when they are talking to a female teacher, whether she is married or not

missile NOUN **missiles** a weapon or other object that is thrown or fired

missing ADJECTIVE lost: *two missing front teeth*

mission NOUN **missions 1** a task or purpose: *astronauts on a mission to Mars* **2** a group of people representing a country or religion who are sent to another country: *a diplomatic mission*

▶ **missionary** NOUN **missionaries** a person who goes to another country to convert the people there to a particular religion

misspell VERB **misspells, misspelling, misspelt** or **misspelled** to spell something in the wrong way

▶ **misspelling** NOUN **misspellings** a word that is spelt the wrong way

mist NOUN **mists** a thin fog, made up of tiny water droplets in the air

VERB **mists, misting, misted** something mists up, or mists over, when it becomes covered with tiny droplets of water or mist

mistake NOUN **mistakes** something wrong that you do or say and which you did not mean to do or say

VERB **mistakes, mistaking, mistook, mistaken** to mistake one person or

Aa
Bb
Cc
Dd
Ee
Ff
Gg
Hh
Ii
Jj
Kk
Ll
Mm
Nn
Oo
Pp
Qq
Rr
Ss
Tt
Uu
Vv
Ww
Xx
Yy
Zz

thing for another person or thing is to think wrongly they are that other person or thing

▶ **mistaken** ADJECTIVE you are mistaken if you are wrong about something

▶ **mistakenly** ADVERB wrongly

Mister NOUN **Misters** a title used for men and boys. It is usually shortened to **Mr**

mistletoe NOUN a plant with green leaves and small white berries that grows on the branches of trees. Traditionally, at Christmas time, people kiss each other under a piece of mistletoe hung up somewhere in a room

mistook VERB a way of changing the verb **mistake** to make a past tense: *I mistook him for someone else.*

mistreat VERB **mistreats, mistreating, mistreated** to mistreat someone or something is to treat them badly or cruelly

▶ **mistreatment** NOUN bad or cruel treatment

mistress NOUN **mistresses 1** a woman who owns or is in charge of something: *Are you the mistress of the house?* • a dog and his mistress **2** a female teacher: *a games mistress*

mistrust VERB **mistrusts, mistrusting, mistrusted** to mistrust a person or thing is to be suspicious of them or it

NOUN mistrust is a feeling of doubt or suspicion that people who do not trust each other have

misty ADJECTIVE **mistier, mistiest 1** the weather is misty when there is mist in the air **2** your eyes are misty when you cannot see very clearly, usually because your eyes are filled with tears

▶ **mistiness** NOUN being misty

misunderstand VERB **misunderstands, misunderstanding, misunderstood** to think you have understood what someone has said or done, when in fact you have not understood it correctly: *I misunderstood the teacher's instructions and got my homework all wrong.*

▶ **misunderstanding** NOUN **misunderstandings 1** a mistake you make about what someone else means **2** a slight disagreement or argument

misuse VERB (pronounced mis-**yooz**) **misuses, misusing, misused** to misuse something is to use it in the wrong way or to treat it badly

NOUN (pronounced mis-**yoos**) misuse of something is using it in the wrong way

mite NOUN **mites** a tiny creature belonging to the same family as spiders

mitt or **mitten** NOUN **mitts** or **mittens** a type of glove without separate parts for the four fingers

mix VERB **mixes, mixing, mixed**

1 to mix something is to put two or more things together so that they combine or form a mass: *Mixing a little black paint into the white will give you a light grey.* • *We each took a turn to mix the Christmas cake.*

2 things mix when they combine: *Oil and water don't mix.*

3 you mix with other people when you talk to them or get to know them socially

4 if you mix things up, you confuse them and think one is the other: *He said he might have got me mixed up with Jim.*

NOUN **mixes** a mixture: *an odd mix of comedy and horror*

▶ **mixed** ADJECTIVE containing several different things or types of people: *a mixed grill*

▶ **mixer** NOUN **mixers** any machine used for mixing things: *a cement mixer*

▶ **mixture** NOUN **mixtures** a combination of several things: *cough mixture* • *a mixture of joy and sadness*

mixed number NOUN **mixed numbers** a number that is made up of a whole number and a fraction, for example 2½

ml ABBREVIATION short for **millilitre** or **millilitres**

mm ABBREVIATION short for **millimetre** or **millimetres**

mnemonic NOUN **mnemonics** a word, phrase or poem that helps you remember something. For example, the phrase *i before e, except after c* is

Aa Bb Cc Dd Ee Ff Gg Hh Ii Jj Kk Ll **Mm** Nn Oo Pp Qq Rr Ss Tt Uu Vv Ww Xx Yy Zz a mnemonic that many people use to remind them if *e* or *i* comes first in words like *relief* and *receive*

moan VERB **moans, moaning, moaned 1** to make a deep noise in your throat because you are in pain or distress **2** to complain

NOUN **moans 1** a deep noise of pain or distress that someone makes in their throat **2** something you say that shows your dissatisfaction with something

moat NOUN **moats** a deep ditch dug round a castle and filled with water to stop attackers being able to get to the castle walls easily

mob NOUN **mobs** a mob is an angry crowd of people

VERB **mobs, mobbing, mobbed** people mob someone they want to see or meet when they crowd round that person

▶ **mobbed** ADJECTIVE if a place is mobbed, it is very crowded

mobile ADJECTIVE something is mobile when it moves or can move around

NOUN **mobiles 1** a mobile phone, a telephone that you can carry around with you **2** a hanging decoration that moves in air currents

▶ **mobility** NOUN being able to move around

mobilize *or* **mobilise** VERB **mobilizes, mobilizing, mobilized** to mobilize people is to make them move or take action

moccasin NOUN **moccasins** moccasins are shoes made from pieces of soft leather stitched together with thin strips of leather, worn originally by Native American people

mock VERB **mocks, mocking, mocked** to mock someone is to make fun of them in a cruel way, by making jokes about them or copying what they say or do

ADJECTIVE not real or genuine: *a mock leather sofa*

▶ **mockery** NOUN making fun of someone cruelly

mock-up NOUN **mock-ups** (*design*) a rough model of something you are going to make later, which shows you how it will look or work

mode NOUN **modes 1** a way or method of doing something: *a mode of transport* **2** (*maths*) in a range of numbers, the mode is the number that occurs most frequently. For example, the mode of *2, 4, 5, 2, 7* is *2*

model NOUN **models 1** a copy of something made on a much smaller scale: *a model of the Crystal Palace* **2** a particular type or design of something that is made in large numbers: *This is our latest model of washing machine.* **3** a person who wears new clothes or fashions to show them off to possible buyers

VERB **models, modelling, modelled 1** to model something in clay is to form the clay into the shape of that thing **2** to model for an artist is to sit or stand while the artist draws or paints you **3** to model a piece of clothing or jewellery is to wear it to show it off to possible buyers

modem NOUN **modems** (*ICT*) a device used for connecting a computer to a telephone line and for sending information from one computer to other computers

moderate ADJECTIVE (pronounced **mod**-i-rit) **1** not going to extremes: *The doctor told him to take a moderate amount of exercise every day.* **2** of medium or average quality or ability: *People of moderate intelligence find the quiz quite easy.*

VERB **moderates, moderating, moderated** (pronounced **mod**-i-rait) to moderate something is to make it less extreme or less strong

▶ **moderately** ADVERB slightly, quite or fairly: *moderately cheap accommodation*

▶ **moderation** NOUN behaviour that is not too extreme

modern ADJECTIVE modern things belong to the present or recent times rather than the past

▶ **modernity** NOUN being modern

modernize *or* **modernise** VERB **modernizes, modernizing, modernized** to modernize something is

Aa
Bb
Cc
Dd
Ee
Ff
Gg
Hh
Ii
Jj
Kk
Ll
Mm
Nn
Oo
Pp
Qq
Rr
Ss
Tt
Uu
Vv
Ww
Xx
Yy
Zz

to make it more up-to-date

▶ **modernization** *or*
modernisation NOUN adding new
parts or equipment to something to
make it more modern

modest ADJECTIVE **1** a modest person
does not like boasting or talking about
their achievements **2** a modest amount
is a small amount

modification NOUN **modifications**
a change made in something to make it
work better or more efficiently

modify VERB **modifies, modifying,
modified 1** to modify something is to
make a small change or changes in it
to improve it **2** to modify your views or
opinions is to change them so that they
are less extreme

module NOUN **modules 1** a separate
unit that is part of a larger unit or
structure: *the space station's escape
module* **2** a unit of work that forms one
part of an educational course

moist ADJECTIVE **moister, moistest**
slightly wet

▶ **moisten** VERB **moistens,
moistening, moistened** to moisten
something is to make it moist: *He licked
his lips to moisten them.*

moisture NOUN wetness, especially tiny
drops of water in the air or condensed
on a surface

molar NOUN **molars** one of the large
square teeth at the back of your mouth
that you use for chewing food

mole¹ NOUN **moles** a small black or
dark brown furry animal that lives
underground in tunnels that it digs
with its strong claws. Moles have poor
eyesight but very good hearing

mole² NOUN **moles** a small dark-
coloured permanent mark or lump on
someone's skin

molecule NOUN **molecules** (*science*)
the smallest unit that a chemical
element or compound can be divided
into and still remain what it is.
Molecules are made up of two or more
atoms

▶ **molecular** ADJECTIVE (*science*) to do
with molecules: *molecular structure*

molehill NOUN **molehills** a pile of
earth that a mole pushes up to the
surface while it is digging its tunnels
underground

molest VERB **molests, molesting,
molested** to molest someone is to
attack or annoy them

mollusc NOUN **molluscs** any of a large
group of animals with no bones inside
their bodies, but protected by an outer
shell. Shellfish and snails are molluscs

molten ADJECTIVE molten rock or metal
is in a liquid state, having been melted

moment NOUN **moments 1** a short
period of time: *Stop what you're doing
for a moment.* **2** a particular point in
time: *Just at that moment, she heard a
door slam.*

▶ **momentarily** ADVERB for a short
period of time: *He was momentarily
suspended in the air.*

▶ **momentary** ADJECTIVE lasting for
only a moment: *There was a momentary
pause and then everyone started talking.*

momentous ADJECTIVE very important
or significant: *a momentous occasion*

momentum NOUN **1** (*science*) the
force that makes a moving object
continue moving **2** something gains
momentum when it begins to move or
develop faster and faster

monarch NOUN **monarchs** a royal ruler
of a country, especially a king or queen

▶ **monarchy** NOUN **monarchies** a
system of government in which the
official head of state is a monarch, or a
country with this system

monastery NOUN **monasteries**
a building or other place where a
community of monks lives

▶ **monastic** ADJECTIVE to do with
monks or monasteries

Monday NOUN **Mondays** the day
of the week after Sunday and before
Tuesday

✦**Monday** is from the Old English word
Monandæg, which means *day of the
moon.*

money NOUN **1** money is coins or
banknotes used to buy things: *I don't have*

enough money to buy the jacket I want. **2** money is wealth: *Only people with money can afford yachts and personal jets.*

mongoose NOUN **mongooses** a small animal related to the weasel, found in South East Asia and Africa, which kills and eats snakes

mongrel NOUN **mongrels** a dog whose parents are of different breeds

monitor VERB **monitors, monitoring, monitored** to monitor something is to keep a careful check on it

NOUN **monitors 1** an instrument used to keep a constant check on something: *a heart monitor* **2** (*ICT*) a screen attached to a computer which displays or shows the file or program being worked on **3** a school pupil who helps to see that school rules are kept

monk NOUN **monks** a member of a community of men who spend their lives in religious worship in a monastery

monkey NOUN **monkeys** an animal with a long tail that walks on four legs and lives in trees

• **make a monkey out of someone** to make someone look foolish

VERB **monkeys, monkeying, monkeyed**

• **monkey about** or **monkey around** to behave in a silly or mischievous way

mono- PREFIX if **mono-** comes at the beginning of a word, it adds the meaning *one* or *single*. For example, a *monologue* is a long speech made by one person

monochrome ADJECTIVE (*art*) in one colour

monopolize or **monopolise** VERB **monopolizes, monopolizing, monopolized** to monopolize something is to keep it all for yourself, and to exclude others: *He monopolized the conversation and no one had the chance to speak.*

monopoly NOUN **monopolies** a business company or organization has a monopoly when it is the only company selling a particular product or providing a particular service

monorail NOUN **monorails** a railway on which the trains run on a single rail, rather than two rails

monotone NOUN **monotones** if you say something in a monotone, you do not vary the tone of your voice while you are speaking

monotonous ADJECTIVE something is monotonous when it is boring because it never varies

▶ **monotony** NOUN dullness and lack of variety

monsoon NOUN **monsoons** the monsoon is a season in some hot countries when heavy rain falls

monster NOUN **monsters 1** in stories, a huge or frightening creature **2** a cruel or evil person

ADJECTIVE enormous: *a monster truck*

monstrosity NOUN **monstrosities** a very large and very ugly thing

monstrous ADJECTIVE **1** extremely large: *a monstrous crocodile* **2** monstrous behaviour is very unfair and cruel

month NOUN **months 1** one of twelve periods that a year is divided into: *In Britain, the winter months are December, January and February.* **2** any period of approximately four weeks or 30 days: *We had to wait for months for an appointment.*

▶ **monthly** ADJECTIVE AND ADVERB happening once a month or each month: *a monthly salary* • *He is paid monthly.*

monument NOUN **monuments 1** something that has been built in memory of a person or event: *a monument to Sir Walter Scott* **2** any building or structure that is historically important: *The Parthenon is one of Greece's ancient monuments.*

▶ **monumental** ADJECTIVE **1** like a monument, or used on a monument: *monumental sculpture* **2** enormous: *I felt like a monumental idiot when I realized what I had done.*

moo VERB **moos, mooing, mooed** a cow moos when it makes a long low sound

NOUN **moos** the long low sound a cow makes

mood NOUN **moods** your mood is

Aa
Bb
Cc
Dd
Ee
Ff
Gg
Hh
Ii
Jj
Kk
Ll
Mm
Nn
Oo
Pp
Qq
Rr
Ss
Tt
Uu
Vv
Ww
Xx
Yy
Zz

your feelings or temper at a particular time: *I woke up in a bad mood this morning.*

moody ADJECTIVE **moodier, moodiest** a moody person changes their mood often or suddenly, from cheerful to grumpy and impatient
▸ **moodily** ADVERB in a bad-tempered way
▸ **moodiness** NOUN being moody

moon NOUN **moons 1** the large sphere that orbits the Earth once a month and which you can see in the night sky as a full circle or a partial circle depending on the time of month **2** a similar body going round certain other planets, such as Saturn

moonlight NOUN the light that seems to come from the moon, but which is really light from the sun reflected off the surface of the moon
▸ **moonlit** ADJECTIVE lit by the moon: *a clear moonlit night*

moor¹ NOUN **moors** a large stretch of open land with poor soil and very few, or no, trees

moor² VERB **moors, mooring, moored** to moor a boat is to tie it up using a rope, cable or anchor

mooring NOUN **moorings** a place where you can tie a boat up

moorland NOUN **moorlands** an area where there are a lot of moors

moose NOUN **moose** a type of large deer with large, flat, rounded horns

mop NOUN **mops 1** a tool for washing floors made up of a pad or mass of thick threads attached to a long handle **2** a mop of hair is a thick, often untidy, mass of hair
VERB **mops, mopping, mopped 1** to mop a floor is to wash it with a mop **2** to mop up is to wipe liquid off a surface

mope VERB **mopes, moping, moped** someone mopes when they are in a bored and depressed mood and do not want to do anything

moped NOUN **mopeds** a light motorcycle with a small engine that you can also pedal like a bicycle

moral NOUN **morals** a story or event

has a moral if a lesson about how to behave is learned from it
ADJECTIVE **1** having to do with character or principles, especially right and wrong, or good and evil **2** a moral person behaves in a way that is right, good or proper

morale NOUN the morale of a person or group of people is how confident they are, or how successful they think they will be

morality NOUN **1** the morality of something is whether it is right or wrong according to standards of good or bad behaviour **2** a person's morality is their standard of behaviour and the beliefs they have about what is right and wrong

morally ADVERB to behave morally is to behave in a good or proper way

morals PLURAL NOUN someone's morals are the beliefs they have about what is right and wrong

morbid ADJECTIVE having or showing an unhealthy interest in death or sad and unpleasant things
▸ **morbidity** NOUN being morbid
▸ **morbidly** ADVERB in a morbid way

more ADJECTIVE a greater quantity or amount: *He has more toys than anyone else I know.* • *Could you get me three more mugs from the cupboard?*
PRONOUN **1** a greater quantity or amount: *More than forty people turned up.* **2** an additional quantity or amount: *Is there any more jelly?*
ADVERB **1 more** is used to make comparative forms of adjectives and adverbs: *He's more patient than I am.* **2 more** is the comparative form of **much** and means 'to a greater degree': *At first I didn't like her much but I'm beginning to like her more and more.*
▸ **moreish** ADJECTIVE something is moreish if it makes you want more

moreover ADVERB you use **moreover** to mean 'besides' when you are adding information to a statement you have just made: *We came home early because it started to rain. Moreover, the children were getting tired.*

morning NOUN **mornings** the part of the day from midnight to midday

morse code

A	•—	N	—•	
B	—•••	O	———	
C	—•—•	P	•——•	**Aa**
D	—••	Q	——•—	**Bb**
E	•	R	•—•	**Cc**
F	••—•	S	•••	**Dd**
G	——•	T	—	**Ee**
H	••••	U	••—	**Ff**
I	••	V	•••—	**Gg**
J	•———	W	•——	**Hh**
K	—•—	X	—••—	**Ii**
L	•—••	Y	—•——	**Jj**
M	——	Z	——••	**Kk**
				Ll

Mm

morphine NOUN a drug used to make someone sleep or to relieve pain

morse code NOUN a code used in signalling and telegraphy, made up of long and short signals called dots and dashes. In the picture above, you can see the dots and dashes used for different letters

morsel NOUN **morsels** a small piece of food: *a tasty morsel*

mortal ADJECTIVE **1** being mortal is being certain to die at some time and unable to live forever **2** a mortal wound causes death **3** people who are mortal enemies hate each other so much they want to kill each other

NOUN **mortals** a human being

▶ **mortality** NOUN being mortal and certain to die one day

▶ **mortally** ADJECTIVE causing, or resulting in, death: *The soldier was mortally wounded.*

mortar NOUN **1** a mixture of cement, sand and water used in building to hold bricks in place **2** a type of heavy gun that fires shells

mortgage (pronounced **mor**-gij) NOUN **mortgages** a type of loan made by a bank or building society to people who want to buy a house or land

mortified ADJECTIVE extremely embarrassed

mortuary NOUN **mortuaries** a place where dead bodies are kept before they are buried or cremated

mosaic NOUN **mosaics** a design formed by fitting together small pieces of coloured marble or glass

mosque NOUN **mosques** a building where Muslims go to worship

mosquito NOUN **mosquitoes** an insect found in many parts of the world, which feeds by biting and sucking blood

moss NOUN **mosses** a small plant found in damp places and forming a soft green mat over the ground

▶ **mossy** ADJECTIVE **mossier, mossiest** covered with moss

most ADJECTIVE **most** is the superlative form of **many** and **much**. It means 'more than other people or things': *Who scored most goals last season?*

PRONOUN **1** nearly all, or the majority: *Most of my friends are allowed to walk to school.* **2** the largest amount: *They both had a lot but who had the most?*

ADVERB **most** is the superlative form of **much** and means 'to the greatest degree': *What kind of music do you like most?*

▶ **mostly** ADVERB in most cases or in

Nn

Oo

Pp

Qq

Rr

Ss

Tt

Uu

Vv

Ww

Xx

Yy

Zz

Aa
Bb
Cc
Dd
Ee
Ff
Gg
Hh
Ii
Jj
Kk
Ll
Mm
Nn
Oo
Pp
Qq
Rr
Ss
Tt
Uu
Vv
Ww
Xx
Yy
Zz

most parts: *They mostly play indoors.*

MOT NOUN **MOTs** a test done in the United Kingdom by qualified mechanics on cars over a certain age to find out if they are safe to be driven

motel NOUN **motels** a type of hotel near a motorway or highway, where travellers can get rooms for the night

moth NOUN **moths** a creature similar to a butterfly, but usually active at night, rather than during the day

mother NOUN **mothers** your female parent

VERB **mothers, mothering, mothered** to mother someone is to treat them with protective kindness, like a mother does

▶ **motherhood** NOUN being a mother

mother-in-law NOUN **mothers-in-law** the mother of your husband or wife

motherly ADJECTIVE kind and protective

motif NOUN **motifs 1** (*art*) a shape or design that may be repeated to form a pattern **2** (*music*) a short piece of music that is repeated in different places in a longer piece of music **3** a movement that is repeated at different points in a dance

motion NOUN **motions 1** motion is moving or movement: *The motion of the waves made him sleepy.* **2** a motion is a single movement or gesture: *He flicked the fly away with a quick motion of his wrist.*

• **go through the motions** to pretend to do something or to do it without any enthusiasm

VERB **motions, motioning, motioned** you motion to someone when you signal to them using your hand or some other part of your body

▶ **motionless** ADJECTIVE not moving at all

motivate VERB **motivates, motivating, motivated 1** you are motivated by particular feelings or desires when they cause you to act in a certain way **2** to motivate someone is to make them feel interested and enthusiastic enough to do something

▶ **motivation** NOUN something that

motivates a person

motive NOUN **motives** the reason someone has for doing something

motor NOUN **motors** a machine, usually a petrol engine or electrical device, that provides power

ADJECTIVE driven by an engine: *a motor mower*

motorbike NOUN **motorbikes** a two-wheeled vehicle with a powerful engine that you sit astride like a bicycle

motorboat NOUN **motorboats** a boat driven by a motor

motor car NOUN **motor cars** a car

motorcycle NOUN **motorcycles** a motorbike, motor scooter or moped

▶ **motorcyclist** NOUN **motorcyclists** someone who rides a motorbike, motor scooter or moped

motorist NOUN **motorists** someone who drives a car

motorway NOUN **motorways** a wide road with several lanes going in both directions

mottled ADJECTIVE covered with patches of different colours or shades

motto NOUN **mottoes** a short sentence or phrase used by a person or organization as a principle to guide their behaviour: *The motto of the Scouts is 'Be prepared'.*

mould[1] NOUN **moulds** a shaped container that you pour a substance into so that the substance has the shape of the container when it cools and hardens: *a jelly mould*

VERB **moulds, moulding, moulded 1** to form something in a mould: *The gold is moulded into ingots.* **2** to shape something using your hands: *Mum moulded the icing into pretty flower shapes.*

mould[2] NOUN **moulds** mould is a fungus that forms green or black patches on stale food or on damp walls and ceilings

▶ **mouldy** ADJECTIVE **mouldier, mouldiest** covered with mould: *a mouldy old loaf*

moult VERB **moults, moulting, moulted** birds and animals moult when they shed their feathers or hair, or their skin

mound NOUN **mounds** a small hill or heap of earth or some other material

mount VERB **mounts, mounting, mounted**
1 to mount stairs is to go up them
2 to mount a horse is to get up on its back
3 the level of something mounts when it rises: *Fear and panic were mounting as the seconds ticked away.*
4 to mount a picture or object is to put it in a frame or to stick it on card to display it
NOUN **mounts 1** a mountain: *Mount Everest* **2** an animal you ride on, such as a horse or a camel

mountain NOUN **mountains** a very high hill
▸ **mountaineer** NOUN **mountaineers** someone who climbs mountains using ropes and other special equipment
▸ **mountaineering** NOUN the sport or pastime of climbing mountains
▸ **mountainous** ADJECTIVE a mountainous area has a lot of mountains

mounted ADJECTIVE on horseback: *a mounted policeman*

mourn VERB **mourns, mourning, mourned** to mourn is to be very sad because someone has died
▸ **mournful** ADJECTIVE full of sadness
▸ **mourning** NOUN someone who is in mourning is grieving for someone who has died

mouse NOUN **mice 1** a small animal with a long tail, bright eyes and grey or brown fur **2** (*ICT*) a device that you move with your hand over a flat surface to move the cursor on a computer screen. It has buttons that you press to tell the computer to do something

mousse NOUN **mousses 1** a light fluffy dessert made with whipped cream and eggs: *chocolate mousse* **2** a white fluffy substance used for styling hair

moustache NOUN **moustaches** a line of hair that some men grow above their top lip

mousy ADJECTIVE **mousier, mousiest 1** a mousy person is shy and timid **2** mousy hair is a light brown colour

mouth NOUN **mouths 1** your mouth is the part of your face that you use to speak and eat and which contains your tongue and teeth **2** (*geography*) the mouth of a river is the place where it flows into the sea
• **down in the mouth** someone who is down in the mouth looks unhappy
VERB **mouths, mouthing, mouthed** to mouth words is to make the shapes of the words with your mouth without making the sounds
▸ **mouthful** NOUN **mouthfuls** an amount you put or hold in your mouth at one time: *He took a mouthful of water and spat it out again.*

mouth organ NOUN **mouth organs** an instrument that you hold to your mouth and play by blowing and sucking through the rows of reeds inside it

mouthpiece NOUN **mouthpieces** the part of a musical instrument or telephone that you put in or close to your mouth

movable ADJECTIVE able to be moved

move VERB **moves, moving, moved**
1 you move something when you take it from one place and put it in another: *Please move your toys off the kitchen table.*
2 if something moves, it changes its position: *I'm sure I saw that curtain move.*
3 to move is to change from one house or place of work to another
4 if something moves you, it has a strong effect on your feelings and emotions
NOUN **moves 1** a change of position: *They made no move to help.* **2** the moving of a piece in a game such as ludo or chess: *Come on, it's your move.* **3** a change to another home or another place of work
▸ **movement** NOUN **movements**
1 changing position or a change of position **2** a division in a long piece of classical music **3** an organization or association with a common purpose or

Aa
Bb
Cc
Dd
Ee
Ff
Gg
Hh
Ii
Jj
Kk
Ll
Mm
Nn
Oo
Pp
Qq
Rr
Ss
Tt
Uu
Vv
Ww
Xx
Yy
Zz

Aa
Bb
Cc
Dd
Ee
Ff
Gg
Hh
Ii
Jj
Kk
Ll
Mm
Nn
Oo
Pp
Qq
Rr
Ss
Tt
Uu
Vv
Ww
Xx
Yy
Zz

aim: *the Scout movement*

movie NOUN **movies** a film

moving ADJECTIVE having a strong effect on your feelings and emotions: *She made a moving speech.*

mow VERB **mows, mowing, mowed, mown** or **mowed** to mow grass is to cut it with a mower

MP ABBREVIATION **MPs** short for **Member of Parliament**, someone who has been elected to the British parliament

MP3 NOUN MP3 is a way of making sound files smaller so that you can download them easily from the Internet. The files can be played on an MP3 player

Mr NOUN **Messrs** short for **Mister**, a title used before a man's name, for example when writing his name on an envelope or at the beginning of a letter

Mrs NOUN **Mrs** short for **Mistress**, a title used before a married woman's name, for example, when writing her name on an envelope or at the beginning of a letter

Ms NOUN a title sometimes used before a woman's name, whether she is married or unmarried, for example when writing her name on an envelope or at the beginning of a letter

much ADJECTIVE **1** a lot or a large amount: *There was much laughter coming from the girls' room.* **2 much** is used in questions about quantities or amounts: *How much fruit do you eat each day?*
PRONOUN a lot or a large amount: *I usually don't have much to eat at lunchtime.*
ADVERB **1** about: *Both books are much the same.* **2** greatly or a lot: *Do you miss your old school much?*

muck NOUN **1** dirt or filth: *The floor is covered in muck from your muddy boots.* **2** animal dung: *The farmer was spreading muck on the fields.*
VERB **mucks, mucking, mucked**
• **muck about** or **muck around** to behave in a silly way
• **muck out something** to muck out horses or other farm animals is to clean their stalls or pens

• **muck something up** to spoil or ruin something
▶ **mucky** ADJECTIVE **muckier, muckiest** dirty: *Don't leave those mucky boots in the hall, please.*

mucus NOUN a thick slimy liquid that protects the delicate tissues that line certain parts of your body, for example inside your nose

mud NOUN soft wet soil that sticks to your clothes and shoes

muddle NOUN **muddles** a muddle is a confused or disorganized state
VERB **muddles, muddling, muddled** if something muddles you, it confuses you
• **muddle things up** to mix things up so that you do not know which is which or where they are

muddy ADJECTIVE **muddier, muddiest** covered or filled with mud

mudguard NOUN **mudguards** a flap over the back wheel of a car, lorry or bicycle, which stops mud from the road being splashed upwards

muesli NOUN a food eaten for breakfast, consisting of a mixture of grains, nuts and dried fruit

muffin NOUN **muffins 1** a round, flat, savoury cake eaten toasted or hot with butter **2** a type of sweet, cup-shaped sponge cake

muffle VERB **muffles, muffling, muffled** to muffle a sound is to make it quieter by putting a cover over the source of the sound
▶ **muffled** ADJECTIVE muffled sounds or voices are low and indistinct because they are heard through something that blocks out most of the sound
▶ **muffler** NOUN **mufflers** a type of long scarf worn wrapped around the neck and the bottom of the face

mug[1] NOUN **mugs** a cup with straight sides and a handle

mug[2] VERB **mugs, mugging, mugged** to mug someone is to attack and rob them in the street
▶ **mugger** NOUN **muggers** a criminal who attacks and robs people in the street

muggy ADJECTIVE **muggier, muggiest** muggy weather is hot and humid

mule¹ NOUN **mules** an animal bred from a male donkey and a female horse

mule² NOUN **mules** mules are slippers with no backs

multi- PREFIX if **multi-** comes at the beginning of a word, it adds the meaning *many* to the word. For example, *multicultural* means 'involving many cultures'

✦ This comes from the Latin word **multus**, which means *much*.

multimedia ADJECTIVE (*ICT*) a multimedia computer can run sound and images as well as ordinary programs

multiple ADJECTIVE involving many things of the same sort: *multiple injuries* NOUN **multiples** a number or quantity that contains another amount an exact number of times: *9 and 12 are multiples of 3*

multiplication NOUN **multiplications** multiplying numbers or things

multiplier NOUN **multipliers** (*maths*) the number by which a number is multiplied. For example, 10 is the multiplier in 150 × 10

multiply VERB **multiplies, multiplying, multiplied 1** (*maths*) to increase a number by adding it to itself a certain number of times. For example, 10 multiplied by 3 is 30, which can be written 10 × 3 = 30 **2** things multiply when they increase in number

multitude NOUN **multitudes** a huge number: *I've got a multitude of things to do before I go.*

mum¹ NOUN **mums** an informal word for **mother**

mum² ADJECTIVE to keep mum is to keep quiet and not speak to anyone about something that should remain a secret

mumble VERB **mumbles, mumbling, mumbled** to speak without opening your mouth wide enough so that what you say is not clear

mummify VERB **mummifies, mummifying, mummified** to mummify a dead body is to make it into a mummy

mummy¹ NOUN **mummies** a child's word for **mother**

mummy² NOUN **mummies** a mummy is a dead body that has been preserved and wrapped in bandages

mumps NOUN an infectious disease, mainly affecting children, in which glands in the neck become very swollen and sore

munch VERB **munches, munching, munched** to munch something is to chew it with regular movements of your jaws and your mouth closed

mundane ADJECTIVE something that is mundane is dull because it is so ordinary or familiar

municipal ADJECTIVE to do with a city or town, especially the local government of that city or town: *municipal elections*

mural NOUN **murals** a picture that is painted directly on to a wall

murder NOUN **murders** murder is the crime of killing someone deliberately VERB **murders, murdering, murdered** to murder someone is to kill them deliberately
▶ **murderer** NOUN **murderers** someone who has murdered another person
▶ **murderous** ADJECTIVE **1** very angry and threatening: *a murderous look* **2** likely to kill you: *We had to escape from the murderous heat.*

murky ADJECTIVE **murkier, murkiest 1** dark and difficult to see through: *murky water* **2** not clearly known about, and possibly dishonest or illegal: *a man with a murky past*

murmur VERB **murmurs, murmuring, murmured** to speak so quietly that people can hardly hear you NOUN **murmurs 1** a low weak voice **2** a low continuous humming noise made by voices or sounds in the distance

muscle NOUN **muscles** the parts of your body that move your limbs and organs, which you can make bigger and stronger by exercising VERB **muscles, muscling, muscled**
• **muscle in** someone muscles in when they involve themselves in something that is not their business

Aa
Bb
Cc
Dd
Ee
Ff
Gg
Hh
Ii
Jj
Kk
Ll
Mm
Nn
Oo
Pp
Qq
Rr
Ss
Tt
Uu
Vv
Ww
Xx
Yy
Zz

Aa
Bb
Cc
Dd
Ee
Ff
Gg
Hh
Ii
Jj
Kk
Ll
Mm
Nn
Oo
Pp
Qq
Rr
Ss
Tt
Uu
Vv
Ww
Xx
Yy
Zz

▶ **muscular** ADJECTIVE to do with the muscles

museum NOUN **museums** a place where collections of interesting things are displayed for people to see

mush NOUN mush is a soft wet mass of something: *The fruit turns into a mush as it boils.*

mushroom NOUN **mushrooms** a type of fungus that you can eat, with a round top

VERB **mushrooms, mushrooming, mushroomed** something mushrooms when it increases its size very quickly

mushy ADJECTIVE **mushier, mushiest** 1 in a soft wet mass: *mushy peas* 2 involving or making you feel too much emotion: *The film got all mushy and I stopped watching.*

music NOUN sounds arranged or combined in patterns, sung or played by instruments

• **face the music** to face someone who is angry with you and will tell you off or punish you

▶ **musical** ADJECTIVE 1 to do with music: *musical training* 2 a musical sound is pleasant to listen to NOUN **musicals** a play or film in which there is lots of singing and dancing

▶ **musician** NOUN **musicians** someone who plays music on an instrument

musket NOUN **muskets** a type of old fashioned gun with a long barrel

▶ **musketeer** NOUN **musketeers** a soldier who carried a musket

Muslim NOUN **Muslims** a person who is a follower of Islam

ADJECTIVE to do with Islam: *Friday is the Muslim holy day.*

mussel NOUN **mussels** a type of shellfish with two hinged black oval shells

must VERB **must** is used with another verb to show that you have to do something or that something is certain or very likely: *You must finish your homework before you go out.* • *I saw it on the telly so it must be true.*

mustard NOUN crushed seeds of the mustard plant made into a paste and used to give food a hot taste

muster VERB **musters, mustering, mustered** 1 to muster troops is to gather them together in a group for inspection 2 to muster something like courage is to try to find as much of it as possible

mustn't a short way to say and write **must not**: *You mustn't tease the cat.*

musty ADJECTIVE **mustier, mustiest** having a damp unpleasant smell

mute ADJECTIVE not speaking or not able to speak

▶ **muted** ADJECTIVE 1 muted colours are soft and not harsh or bright 2 muted voices or sounds are low or made quieter

mutilate VERB **mutilates, mutilating, mutilated** to mutilate something is to damage it by breaking a part off or cutting pieces off it

▶ **mutilation** NOUN being damaged

mutiny NOUN **mutinies** rebelling against someone in authority, especially sailors on a ship rebelling against their captain and officers

▶ **mutinous** ADJECTIVE likely to rebel, or wanting to rebel against someone in authority

mutter VERB **mutters, muttering, muttered** to speak quietly under your breath: *Katy sighed and muttered but did as she was told.*

mutton NOUN meat from a sheep

mutual ADJECTIVE 1 given or done by people to one another: *mutual admiration* 2 shared by two people: *Peter and Ahmed have a mutual friend who works at the library.*

▶ **mutually** ADVERB in a way that involves two people: *We were mutually involved in the plan.*

muzzle NOUN **muzzles** 1 a dog's muzzle is the part, including its nose and mouth, that sticks out from its face 2 a muzzle is a set of straps put over a dog's nose and mouth to stop it biting people 3 the muzzle of a gun is the open end of its barrel where the bullet or shell comes out

VERB **muzzles, muzzling, muzzled** 1 to

muzzle a dog is to put a muzzle on it **2** to muzzle someone is to do something to stop them talking

my ADJECTIVE belonging to me: *There's my Mum and Dad.* • *Have you seen my boots anywhere?*

myrrh (pronounced **mer**) NOUN a brown strong-smelling resin that comes from an African or Asian tree and is used in medicines and perfumes

myself PRONOUN **1** you use **myself** after a verb or preposition when **I** is the subject of the action and is also affected by it: *I've washed myself all over, even behind my ears.* • *I felt rather proud of myself.* **2** you also use **myself** to show that you do something without any help from anyone else: *I suppose I'll have to do it myself if no one else can be bothered.* **3** you can use the word

myself to show more clearly who you mean: *I have not seen the film myself.*

mysterious ADJECTIVE **1** difficult to understand or explain **2** if someone is being mysterious about something, they avoid talking about it, making you even more curious to know about it

▸ **mysteriously** ADVERB in a mysterious way: *It disappeared mysteriously in a little puff of smoke.*

mystery NOUN **mysteries** something that you do not understand and which cannot be, or has not been, explained

mystic NOUN **mystics** someone who tries to gain knowledge about sacred or spiritual things, usually by meditating or going into a trance

▸ **mystical** ADJECTIVE to do with the spiritual world, or beyond ordinary human understanding

Aa
Bb
Cc
Dd
Ee
Ff
Gg
Hh
Ii
Jj
Kk
Ll
Mm
Nn
Oo
Pp
Qq
Rr
Ss
Tt
Uu
Vv
Ww
Xx
Yy
Zz

Nn

N ABBREVIATION short for **north**

nab VERB **nabs, nabbing, nabbed** (*informal*) **1** to nab something is to grab or take it: *Someone's nabbed all the best sandwiches already.* **2** to nab someone is to catch or arrest them: *The police nabbed a man climbing out of the back window.*

nag VERB **nags, nagging, nagged** to remind someone again and again about something they have not done: *Mum has to nag me every night to do my homework.*
NOUN **nags** (*informal*) a horse

nail NOUN **nails 1** a thin pointed piece of metal that you hit into a surface with a hammer **2** the hard covering on top of the ends of your fingers and toes
VERB **nails, nailing, nailed** to attach or join something by hammering it with nails: *Nail the number on the door.*

naive (pronounced nie-**eev**) ADJECTIVE believing things are simple and people are good when in fact life is more difficult: *She had a naive belief that he never lied to her.*

naked (pronounced **nay**-kid) ADJECTIVE **1** not wearing any clothes **2** not covered or protected: *a naked flame*

name NOUN **names 1** the word or words that you always call a certain person, place or thing: *What's your name?* • *I can't remember the name of the street.* **2** if someone has a good name, a lot of people think they are good and if someone has a bad name, a lot of people think they are bad: *This is how football fans get a bad name.*
VERB **names, naming, named** to name a person, place or thing is to decide on a certain word to call them: *They've named their son Samuel.*

nameless ADJECTIVE without a name or with a name that is not known: *The writer of the letter wants to remain nameless.*

namely ADVERB that is to say: *Two of our members, namely the Grimes brothers, have won medals this term.*

nanny NOUN **nannies 1** a person whose job is to look after a child in its own home **2** a word that some children use for their grandmother

nanny-goat NOUN **nanny-goats** a female goat

nap NOUN **naps** a short sleep during the day: *Dad sometimes has a nap in the afternoon.*
VERB **naps, napping, napped** to have a short sleep

nape NOUN the nape of your neck is the back of your neck

napkin NOUN **napkins** a piece of cloth or paper that you can use during a meal to wipe your mouth or fingers

nappy NOUN **nappies** a pad for fastening around a baby's bottom

narrate VERB **narrates, narrating, narrated** to tell a story: *Freddie narrated the events that led up to the explosion.*
▸ **narration** NOUN **narrations** the telling of a story: *a documentary about the war with a narration by some of the soldiers*
▸ **narrative** NOUN **narratives 1** a story that someone tells **2** a piece of writing that tells a story or tells you what happened
ADJECTIVE telling a story
▸ **narrator** NOUN **narrators** the narrator of a story is the person who tells it

narrow ADJECTIVE **narrower, narrowest 1** not very wide: *a narrow gateway* • *The road was too narrow for overtaking.* **2** only just happening, with hardly any room or time to spare: *a narrow escape*
▸ **narrowly** ADVERB closely: *We were narrowly defeated by 6 goals to 5.*

narrow-minded ADJECTIVE not willing to consider anybody else's beliefs or ideas

nasal ADJECTIVE **1** to do with the nose: *the nasal passages* **2** a nasal voice or sound comes mainly through your nose

✦ This word comes from the Latin word **nasus**, which means *nose*.

nasty ADJECTIVE **nastier, nastiest 1** very unpleasant or unkind: *a nasty taste in my mouth* • *saying nasty things about her family* **2** serious: *a nasty injury*

nation NOUN **nations 1** a country with its own government **2** the people of a country: *Today the nation is voting for a new government.*

▶ **national** ADJECTIVE to do with a whole country: *the local, national and international news*

nationalism NOUN **1** the belief that the people of a country should have their own government **2** a great love for your own country

▶ **nationalist** NOUN **nationalists 1** someone who wants their country to have its own government **2** someone with a great love for their own country

nationality NOUN **nationalities** your nationality is your membership of a nation: *Louis has dual nationality because his mother is French and his father is American.*

nationalize *or* **nationalise** VERB **nationalizes, nationalizing, nationalized** to nationalize an industry is to bring it under the control of the government

nationwide ADJECTIVE in every area throughout a country: *a nationwide search for the robbers*

native ADJECTIVE **1** your native country is the one you were born in **2** your native language is the first one you learnt

NOUN **natives** a native of a country is someone who was born there

Native American NOUN **Native Americans** a person from the race of people who lived in North or South America before the Europeans arrived there

Nativity NOUN the birth of Jesus Christ

natural ADJECTIVE **1** to do with or made by nature, not by people or machines: *the natural world* • *An earthquake is an example of a natural disaster.* **2** natural behaviour is what you do normally without thinking: *It's only natural to be a little nervous before a test.*

natural gas NOUN gas that comes from under the sea or underground and can be used as fuel

naturalist NOUN **naturalists** a person who studies plants or animals

naturalize *or* **naturalise** VERB **naturalizes, naturalizing, naturalized** a person is naturalized when they become a legal citizen of a country they were not born in

naturally ADVERB **1** you say 'naturally' to mean 'of course': *'Will you take me with you?' 'Naturally.'* **2** in a way that is normal: *Joe began to relax and behave a bit more naturally.* **3** without help from anything artificial: *Let the skin heal naturally.*

nature NOUN **natures 1** everything in the world that was not made or changed by people: *I love those nature programmes about animals.* **2** what something is basically like: *questions of a difficult nature* **3** the kind of person someone is: *It's not in her nature to be unkind.*

nature reserve NOUN **nature reserves** an area of land that is kept separate to protect the plants and animals that live there

nature trail NOUN **nature trails** a path through the countryside where you can see particularly interesting plants and wildlife

naughty ADJECTIVE **naughtier, naughtiest** a naughty child does things they should not do

▶ **naughtiness** NOUN bad behaviour or not doing as you are told

nausea NOUN the feeling that you are about to be sick

▶ **nauseating** ADJECTIVE making you feel sick: *a nauseating smell*

Aa
Bb
Cc
Dd
Ee
Ff
Gg
Hh
Ii
Jj
Kk
Ll
Mm
Nn
Oo
Pp
Qq
Rr
Ss
Tt
Uu
Vv
Ww
Xx
Yy
Zz

nautical ADJECTIVE to do with ships and the sea

naval ADJECTIVE to do with the navy

✦ This word comes from the Latin word **navis**, which means *ship*. The word **navigate** is also linked to **navis**. It comes from a Latin word that meant 'to drive a ship'.

navel NOUN **navels** the small hollow in the centre of your stomach where the cord connected you to your mother before you were born

navigate VERB **navigates, navigating, navigated** to decide which way you should go in a vehicle such as a car, boat or plane: *Mum usually drives and Dad navigates.*

▸ **navigation** NOUN deciding which way to go in a vehicle such as a car, plane or boat

▸ **navigator** NOUN **navigators** a person who decides which direction a vehicle should go in

navy NOUN **navies** the part of a country's armed forces that works at sea

navy blue NOUN a dark blue colour

Nazi (pronounced **nat**-si) NOUN **Nazis** a member of the political party led by Adolf Hitler in Germany during World War II

▸ **Nazism** NOUN the beliefs of the Nazis

NB ABBREVIATION short for the Latin phrase **nota bene**, which means *note well*. You can write this to make someone pay particular attention to something in a piece of writing

near PREPOSITION not far away: *the shop near our house*

ADVERB **nearer, nearest** close by a thing or person: *Stand a little nearer and you'll be able to see better.*

ADJECTIVE **nearer, nearest** not far away: *the near future* • *a near neighbour*

VERB **nears, nearing, neared** to approach or get close: *As we neared the building, the faces at the window became clearer.*

nearby ADJECTIVE AND ADVERB quite close to where you are or the place you are talking about: *We went to a nearby restaurant for dinner.* • *Do you live nearby?*

nearly ADVERB almost but not completely: *We're nearly there.* • *Nearly everyone had a good time.*

neat ADJECTIVE **neater, neatest 1** clean and tidy: *a neat bedroom* **2** done skilfully: *a neat shot into the corner of the goal* **3** a liquid, especially a drink, is neat when it is not mixed with anything

nebula NOUN **nebulae** (*science*) a cloud of dust or gas that shines in the night sky

necessarily ADVERB for certain: *Men aren't necessarily stronger than women.*

necessary ADJECTIVE needed in order to get a result: *Is it necessary for everyone to fill in their own form?* • *We can stay a bit longer if necessary.*

necessity NOUN **necessities** something that is needed or that must happen: *A warm coat is a necessity in this weather.*

neck NOUN **necks 1** the part of the body between the head and the shoulders **2** the opening in a piece of clothing that you put your head through **3** the narrow part of a bottle near its opening

• **neck and neck** almost level with each other in a race or competition

necklace NOUN **necklaces** a piece of jewellery for wearing around your neck, such as a string of beads or jewels, or a chain

nectar NOUN the sweet liquid that bees collect from flowers to make honey

nectarine NOUN **nectarines** a fruit very similar to a peach but with a smooth skin

need VERB **needs, needing, needed 1** to have to do something: *We all need to eat and drink.* **2** to be without something that would be helpful or useful: *What I need here is a sharp knife.*

NOUN **needs 1** you have a need for something when you want it but do not have it: *If you feel the need of some company, just give me a call.* **2** if there is no need to do something, it is not necessary: *There's no need to shout.* **3** your needs are the things that it is necessary for you to have

needle NOUN **needles**
1 a small pointed piece of metal for sewing
2 a long thin piece of wood, metal or plastic that is used for knitting
3 a sharp instrument for giving injections of medicine
4 a moving pointer, especially on a dial, for example on a compass

needless ADJECTIVE not necessary: *a needless waste of money*

needy ADJECTIVE **needier, neediest** poor: *help for needy families who have lost their homes*

negative ADJECTIVE
1 a negative answer or response says or means *no*: *We got a very negative reaction.*
2 to have a negative attitude is to feel uncertain and not very hopeful
3 (*maths*) a negative number is one that is less than zero, for example −5
4 (*science*) a negative electric charge carries electrons
NOUN **negatives** a film before it is printed, where light objects appear dark and dark objects appear light

neglect VERB **neglects, neglecting, neglected 1** if you neglect someone or something, you don't give them proper care and attention: *I've been neglecting my homework because I've been so busy.* **2** if you neglect to do something, you forget to do it: *I neglected to lock the door and found it wide open when I got home.*
NOUN lack of proper care: *All the houseplants had died from neglect.*

negligence NOUN not doing the things you should do or not doing them carefully enough
▶ **negligent** ADJECTIVE careless about the things you should do carefully

negotiate (pronounced ni-**goh**-shi-ait) VERB **negotiates, negotiating, negotiated 1** to try to reach an agreement with someone by having

discussions with them: *I've negotiated with dad to stay out till 11 o'clock.* **2** to negotiate a difficult place on a path or road is to get past it successfully: *We managed to negotiate the last corner and finished the race in third place.*
▶ **negotiation** NOUN **negotiations** discussion of a subject in order to reach an agreement on it
▶ **negotiator** NOUN **negotiators** a person who tries to make people come to an agreement by having discussions

neigh VERB **neighs, neighing, neighed** to make the noise that a horse makes
NOUN **neighs** the noise that a horse makes

neighbour NOUN **neighbours** the people who live near you
▶ **neighbourhood** NOUN **neighbourhoods** an area of a town or city: *This is a pretty neighbourhood with a lot of trees and parks.*
▶ **neighbouring** ADJECTIVE next or nearby: *the mayors of all the neighbouring towns*

✦ **Neighbour** comes from the Old English words **neach**, which means *near*, and **gebure**, which means 'a person living in (a place)'. **Neachgebur** means 'someone living nearby'.

neither ADJECTIVE AND PRONOUN not either: *Neither woman seemed to understand English.* • *Neither of us can go.*
CONJUNCTION neither is often used with **nor** to show negative possibilities: *I neither know, nor care, where he is.*

neon NOUN a kind of gas that shines very brightly when electricity passes through it: *your name in neon lights*

nephew NOUN **nephews** your nephew is the son of your brother or sister

nerve NOUN **nerves 1** a nerve is one of the tiny thread-like connections that carry messages about feelings and movements between your brain and other parts of your body **2** nerve is a kind of boldness or courage: *I didn't have the nerve to jump.*

Aa
Bb
Cc
Dd
Ee
Ff
Gg
Hh
Ii
Jj
Kk
Ll
Mm
Nn
Oo
Pp
Qq
Rr
Ss
Tt
Uu
Vv
Ww
Xx
Yy
Zz

nets

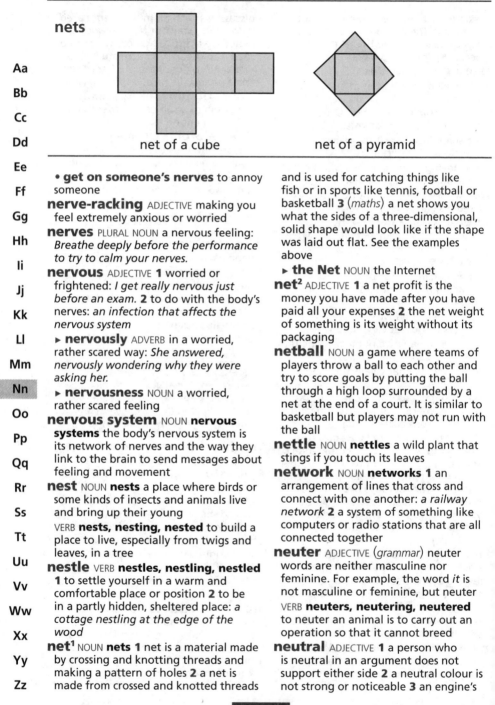

net of a cube   net of a pyramid

• **get on someone's nerves** to annoy someone

nerve-racking ADJECTIVE making you feel extremely anxious or worried

nerves PLURAL NOUN a nervous feeling: *Breathe deeply before the performance to try to calm your nerves.*

nervous ADJECTIVE **1** worried or frightened: *I get really nervous just before an exam.* **2** to do with the body's nerves: *an infection that affects the nervous system*

▸ **nervously** ADVERB in a worried, rather scared way: *She answered, nervously wondering why they were asking her.*

▸ **nervousness** NOUN a worried, rather scared feeling

nervous system NOUN **nervous systems** the body's nervous system is its network of nerves and the way they link to the brain to send messages about feeling and movement

nest NOUN **nests** a place where birds or some kinds of insects and animals live and bring up their young
VERB **nests, nesting, nested** to build a place to live, especially from twigs and leaves, in a tree

nestle VERB **nestles, nestling, nestled** **1** to settle yourself in a warm and comfortable place or position **2** to be in a partly hidden, sheltered place: *a cottage nestling at the edge of the wood*

net¹ NOUN **nets** **1** net is a material made by crossing and knotting threads and making a pattern of holes **2** a net is made from crossed and knotted threads

and is used for catching things like fish or in sports like tennis, football or basketball **3** (*maths*) a net shows you what the sides of a three-dimensional, solid shape would look like if the shape was laid out flat. See the examples above

▸ **the Net** NOUN the Internet

net² ADJECTIVE **1** a net profit is the money you have made after you have paid all your expenses **2** the net weight of something is its weight without its packaging

netball NOUN a game where teams of players throw a ball to each other and try to score goals by putting the ball through a high loop surrounded by a net at the end of a court. It is similar to basketball but players may not run with the ball

nettle NOUN **nettles** a wild plant that stings if you touch its leaves

network NOUN **networks** **1** an arrangement of lines that cross and connect with one another: *a railway network* **2** a system of something like computers or radio stations that are all connected together

neuter ADJECTIVE (*grammar*) neuter words are neither masculine nor feminine. For example, the word *it* is not masculine or feminine, but neuter
VERB **neuters, neutering, neutered** to neuter an animal is to carry out an operation so that it cannot breed

neutral ADJECTIVE **1** a person who is neutral in an argument does not support either side **2** a neutral colour is not strong or noticeable **3** an engine's neutral gear is not connected to its forward or backward driving parts

▶ **neutralize** or **neutralise** VERB **neutralizes, neutralizing, neutralized** to neutralize something is to prevent it from having any effect

neutron NOUN **neutrons** (*science*) a particle with no electrical charge that joins with **protons** to make up the nucleus of an atom

never ADVERB not ever, or not at any time: *I've never been abroad.* • *It's never too late to learn.*

nevertheless ADVERB however or anyway: *I couldn't swim; nevertheless, I jumped in to try to save him.*

new ADJECTIVE **newer, newest 1** not existing or known about before: *a new discovery* **2** just bought, made or received: *a new jacket* **3** different: *Take this book back and get a new one from the library.*

newly ADVERB only recently: *a newly-painted room*

new moon NOUN the moon when it is shaped like a thin curve or crescent

news PLURAL NOUN **1** information about something that has just happened **2** a radio or television report about recent events: *listening to the news at 9 o'clock*

newsagent NOUN **newsagents 1** someone who sells newspapers and magazines **2** a newsagent's is a shop that sells newspapers and magazines and usually other things like sweets and stationery: *She bought some envelopes at the newsagent's.*

newspaper NOUN **newspapers** a collection of reports and pictures about recent events that is published daily or weekly on a set of folded sheets of paper

newt NOUN **newts** a small animal like a lizard that lives both in water and on land

New Testament NOUN the second part of the Bible, about the teachings of Jesus Christ

newton NOUN **newtons** (*science*) a unit for measuring how strong a force is

next ADJECTIVE the one that follows immediately after: *What's the next name on the list?* • *Let's meet next week.* ADVERB after the present thing, person or time: *Who's next?* • *What will happen next?*

nib NOUN **nibs** the point of a pen

nibble VERB **nibbles, nibbling, nibbled** to take little bites of something: *A mouse had nibbled right through the wires.*

nice ADJECTIVE **nicer, nicest 1** pleasant, good or attractive: *We'll find somewhere nice to sit, out in the fresh air.* **2** kind or friendly: *James is quite nice really, once you get used to him.*

▶ **nicely** ADVERB **1** in a pleasant way: *Ask the lady nicely, dear.* **2** well: *They've settled in nicely at their new school.*

▶ **niceness** NOUN being pleasant or attractive

nick NOUN **nicks 1** a small cut **2** (*informal*) a police station VERB **nicks, nicking, nicked 1** to nick something is to make a very small cut in it **2** (*informal*) to nick something is to steal it: *Who's nicked my pen?* **3** (*informal*) to nick someone is to arrest them

nickel NOUN **nickels 1** nickel is a greyish-white metal that is often mixed with other metals **2** a nickel is an American or Canadian coin worth five cents

nickname NOUN **nicknames** a name that you use for someone that is not their real name

nicotine NOUN the poisonous substance that is the drug contained in tobacco

niece NOUN **nieces** your niece is the daughter of your brother or sister

niggle VERB **niggles, niggling, niggled** if something niggles you, it worries or annoys you slightly, but continually

night NOUN **nights** the time of darkness between the sun going down in the evening and rising again in the morning

nightdress NOUN **nightdresses** a loose dress for sleeping in

nightfall NOUN the time when it gets dark in the evening: *We arranged to meet at nightfall.*

Aa
Bb
Cc
Dd
Ee
Ff
Gg
Hh
Ii
Jj
Kk
Ll
Mm
Nn
Oo
Pp
Qq
Rr
Ss
Tt
Uu
Vv
Ww
Xx
Yy
Zz

nightgown NOUN **nightgowns** a loose gown for sleeping in

nightingale NOUN **nightingales** a small bird that sings beautifully

nightly ADJECTIVE AND ADVERB every night: *nightly visits to the cinema* • *adverts that you see at least twice nightly*

nightmare NOUN **nightmares 1** a frightening dream **2** a very unpleasant experience: *The journey turned out to be a complete nightmare.*

✦ The ending of this word comes from the Old English word **mare**, which means *evil spirit*. It used to be believed that bad dreams at night were caused by evil spirits.

nightshirt NOUN **nightshirts** a long loose shirt for sleeping in

nil NOUN nothing: *The score was eight-nil.*

nimble ADJECTIVE **nimbler, nimblest 1** a nimble movement is quick, quiet and easy **2** a nimble person moves quickly and neatly

▶ **nimbly** ADVERB in a quick neat way: *He jumped nimbly aside.*

nimbus NOUN (*geography*) dark grey cloud that usually brings rain or snow

nine NOUN **nines** the number 9

nineteen NOUN the number 19

nineteenth ADJECTIVE AND ADVERB after eighteenth and before twentieth: *the nineteenth day of the month*

ninetieth ADJECTIVE AND ADVERB after eighty-ninth and before ninety-first: *It's my great-grandfather's ninetieth birthday tomorrow.*

ninety NOUN **nineties** the number 90

ninth ADJECTIVE AND ADVERB after eighth and before tenth: *I came ninth out of ten – it could have been worse!*

NOUN **ninths** the fraction ⅑, which means one of nine equal parts of something: *There are nine of us so divide the cake into ninths.*

nip VERB **nips, nipping, nipped 1** to pinch, squeeze sharply or bite **2** to nip somewhere is to go there quickly or for a short time: *I must just nip to the shops.*

NOUN **nips 1** a small bite or pinch **2** a cold feeling: *a nip in the air that feels like winter*

nipple NOUN **nipples** the pointed part of a breast that a baby sucks milk from

nippy ADJECTIVE **nippier, nippiest 1** cold or frosty: *It's a bit nippy out today.* **2** a nippy car is easy to turn and move quickly

nit NOUN **nits** the egg of a louse or other small insect

nitrogen NOUN a colourless gas that makes up about four-fifths of the air we breathe

no INTERJECTION a word that you use to express things like refusing, denying or disagreeing: *'Are you alright?' 'No, my leg's hurting.'*

ADJECTIVE not any: *They have no money.*

ADVERB not at all: *She's no better.*

nobility NOUN **1** people in the highest classes of society, for example royalty **2** being noble

noble ADJECTIVE **nobler, noblest 1** brave, fine and good: *making a noble effort to be nice* **2** belonging to a high social class or royalty: *coming from a noble family*

NOUN **nobles** a member of the upper classes of a society

nobleman or **noblewoman** NOUN **noblemen** or **nobelwomen** a man or woman of high rank in society

nobody PRONOUN not any person: *Nobody tells me what to do!* • *There was nobody at home.*

NOUN **nobodies** a person who is not at all important: *He's just a nobody who thinks he's somebody.*

nocturnal ADJECTIVE happening or active at night: *Nocturnal animals do not usually hunt during the day.*

nod VERB **nods, nodding, nodded** to move your head up and down as if you were agreeing or saying 'yes'

NOUN **nods** an up-and-down movement of your head

noise NOUN **noises 1** a noise is a sound: *Did you hear a noise outside?* **2** noise is sound that you do not like: *Could you please make a little less noise?*

Aa
Bb
Cc
Dd
Ee
Ff
Gg
Hh
Ii
Jj
Kk
Ll
Mm
Nn
Oo
Pp
Qq
Rr
Ss
Tt
Uu
Vv
Ww
Xx
Yy
Zz

▸ **noisy** ADJECTIVE **noisier, noisiest**
making a lot of sound that you do not
like: *a noisy party*

✦ This word comes an old French word
that means an *uproar.*

nomad NOUN **nomads** a person who
wanders from place to place, rather
than living in the same place all the time

nominate VERB **nominates,
nominating, nominated** to nominate
someone to do something is to
suggest that they should do it: *Charles
nominated Peter as leader of the group.*

▸ **nomination** NOUN **nominations** a
suggestion that a certain thing or person
should be chosen for something: *We've
had several nominations so we'll have to
have a vote. • There are five nominations
for Best Picture.*

non- PREFIX you can add **non-** to the
beginning of many words to make them
mean the opposite, or *not.* For example,
non-smokers are people who do not
smoke

none PRONOUN not one: *None of
them are going to admit to being
wrong. • We looked for more biscuits
but there were none left.*

ADVERB not at all: *I heard the answer but
I'm none the wiser.*

non-existent ADJECTIVE not existing:
*Many types of butterfly are almost non-
existent in this area.*

non-fiction NON-FICTION non-fiction
is books and writing that tell you
about real people and situations, not
imaginary ones

nonsense NOUN **1** something that does
not make sense: *His theory is a load of
nonsense.* **2** silly behaviour: *Stop your
nonsense now please.*

non-stop ADJECTIVE AND ADVERB without
a break or a pause: *There was non-stop
hammering from the room above. • It's
rained non-stop for three days.*

noodle NOUN **noodles** noodles are
long thin pieces of pasta

nook NOUN **nooks** a corner or a space,
especially where someone or something
can be hidden

noon NOUN twelve o'clock in the day:
We'll have our lunch at noon.

no one or **no-one** PRONOUN not any
person: *No one's in at the moment.*

noose NOUN **nooses** a loop of rope
that tightens when the end is pulled

nor CONJUNCTION a word that is used
with **neither** before a second negative
possibility: *Neither Jack nor Jenny is at
home.*

✦ You use **or** when you start with
either: *Either he goes or I do.*

You use **nor** when you start with
neither: *Neither you nor I will ever
understand this.*

normal ADJECTIVE usual and expected:
It's normal to feel hungry at lunchtime.

▸ **normality** NOUN the state of
things as they usually are: *After all the
excitement it was good to return to
normality.*

▸ **normally** ADVERB **1** usually: *We
normally go to bed pretty early.* **2** in
the usual way: *This plant has developed
normally but this one is diseased.*

Norse ADJECTIVE to do with countries
in Scandinavia, for example Sweden,
Denmark and Norway, a long time
ago: *Norse gods • the Norse languages*

north NOUN **1** the direction a compass
needle points, opposite to south **2** the
part of a country or the world that is in
the north

ADJECTIVE in, from, or towards the
north: *the cold North wind • the north
wall of the building*

ADVERB to the north: *travelling north on
the motorway*

north-east NOUN the area midway
between north and east: *the north-east
of Scotland*

northerly ADJECTIVE coming from,
or going towards, the north: *a
northerly breeze • going in a northerly
direction • the island's most northerly
point*

NOUN **northerlies** a wind that comes
from the north

northern ADJECTIVE belonging to

Aa
Bb
Cc
Dd
Ee
Ff
Gg
Hh
Ii
Jj
Kk
Ll
Mm
Nn
Oo
Pp
Qq
Rr
Ss
Tt
Uu
Vv
Ww
Xx
Yy
Zz

or coming from the north: *the cold northern climate* • *Northern districts will have some rain.*

northward or **northwards** ADVERB to or towards the north: *We cycled northwards for several miles.*

north-west NOUN the area midway between north and west: *the north-west of England*

nose NOUN **noses 1** the part of your face that you breathe and smell through **2** the front part of something that sticks out, for example the front of an aircraft

nosedive NOUN **nosedives** a dive straight downwards
VERB **nosedives, nosediving, nosedived** to dive down headfirst: *The rocket flew straight up and then nosedived straight down again.*

nosey or **nosy** ADJECTIVE **nosier, nosiest** always wanting to find out about other people and what they are doing

nostalgia NOUN a feeling of sadness when you remember happy times in the past
▸ **nostalgic** ADJECTIVE thinking of, or reminding you of happy times in the past: *a nostalgic evening of black and white movies*

nostril NOUN **nostrils** your nostrils are the two openings in your nose that you breathe and smell through

✦ This word comes from the Old English words **nosu**, which means *nose*, and **thyrel**, which means *hole*, so together they mean 'a hole in the nose'.

not ADVERB a word that is used to express negatives and opposites. It often becomes **n't** when it is added to verbs: *It isn't fair.* • *I can't hear you.*

notable ADJECTIVE important and worth remembering: *The most notable part of the evening was the music.*
▸ **notably** ADVERB particularly: *I loved the old buildings, notably the palace.*

notch NOUN **notches** a small, V-shaped mark that has been cut into something

note NOUN **notes**

1 a word or sentence to tell or remind someone of something: *They've left a note to say that dinner's in the oven.*
2 a short letter: *This is just a quick note to let you know we're well.*
3 a written comment: *a note at the bottom of the page*
4 a piece of paper money: *a five pound note*
5 (*music*) a single musical sound or the sign that stands for it
VERB **notes, noting, noted** to note something is to notice and remember it

notebook NOUN **notebooks 1** a small book that you write things down in **2** (*ICT*) a laptop computer

nothing PRONOUN not anything: *There was nothing in the cupboard.* • *Nothing's the matter with me.*

notice VERB **notices, noticing, noticed** to realize something because you see, hear, feel, smell or taste it: *I noticed a funny smell in the hall.* • *Did you notice the way George was looking at Emily?*
NOUN **notices 1** a notice is a written or printed announcement: *a notice pinned on the board* **2** (*formal*) something comes to your notice when you realize it: *It's come to our notice that you are always late.* **3** you give someone notice of something when you tell or warn them that it is going to happen: *Please give me notice if you plan to visit.* • *I need more notice next time.*

noticeable ADJECTIVE obvious or easy to see: *a noticeable difference in his appearance*
▸ **noticeably** ADVERB that you can easily see: *We were all noticeably more relaxed after dinner.*

notify VERB **notifies, notifying, notified** to notify someone is to tell them about something in an official way: *Please notify the headteacher if you are not able to attend this meeting.*

notion NOUN **notions** an idea, a belief or an understanding: *I had a notion that this wouldn't really matter to you.*

notorious ADJECTIVE famous for something bad

▶ **notoriously** ADVERB well known to be (something bad): *That model is notoriously unreliable.*

nougat (pronounced **noo**-ga) NOUN a sticky kind of sweet that contains nuts

nought NOUN **noughts 1** nothing **2** the figure 0: *Write twenty as a two and a nought.*

noun WORD CLASS **nouns** (*grammar*) a word that refers to a person or a thing. For example *tree*, *Sue* and *idea* are nouns

nourish VERB **nourishes, nourishing, nourished** to nourish people, animals or plants is to give them the food they need to keep them healthy

▶ **nourishment** NOUN healthy food and drink

novel NOUN **novels** a book that tells a story that is not true: *a romantic novel* ADJECTIVE completely new and original: *What a novel idea!*

▶ **novelty** NOUN **novelties 1** something new and original **2** a small, cheap toy

November NOUN the eleventh month of the year, after October and before December

✦ **November** was the ninth month of the Roman year and the name comes from the word **novem**, which means *nine* in Latin.

novice NOUN **novices** a beginner

now ADVERB **1** at the present time: *It is now five o'clock.* **2** immediately: *I'll do it now.*

• **now and again** *or* **now and then** from time to time

nowadays ADVERB these days: *Nowadays, women usually have their babies in hospital.*

nowhere ADVERB not anywhere: *We've got nowhere to go.*

nozzle NOUN **nozzles** a part at the end of a pipe that controls how fast a liquid comes out of it

nuclear ADJECTIVE **1** to do with the reaction that occurs when atoms are split apart or forced together: *A nuclear* submarine is powered by nuclear energy. **2** (*science*) to do with the nucleus of an atom

nuclear energy NOUN the energy that is created when atoms are split apart or forced together

nucleus NOUN **nuclei** (*science*) the central part of an atom, made up of **protons** and **neutrons**

nude ADJECTIVE not wearing any clothes NOUN **nudes** a nude is a picture or statue of someone without clothes on

nudge VERB **nudges, nudging, nudged** to give someone a gentle push, especially with your elbow

nudity NOUN not having any clothes on

nugget NOUN **nuggets** a small lump of something, especially gold or chicken

nuisance NOUN a thing or person that annoys you

numb (pronounced **num**) ADJECTIVE **number, numbest** a part of your body is numb when you cannot feel it properly: *I was so cold my hands had gone completely numb.*

▶ **numbness** NOUN when you lose the feeling in a part of your body

number NOUN **numbers 1** a word or figure showing how many or a position in a series: *the number four* • *Please write down any three figure number.* **2** a group or collection of people or things: *a large number of animals* **3** a popular song or piece of music: *a catchy number*
VERB **numbers, numbering, numbered 1** to number a group of things or people is to give them all a number: *The boxes are all clearly numbered.* **2** a group that numbers a certain quantity is made up of that many: *The crowd numbered many thousands.*

numeracy NOUN being able to count and do sums

numeral NOUN **numerals** a symbol that stands for a number: *a Roman numeral*

numerate ADJECTIVE a numerate person knows how to use numbers to do calculations

Aa
Bb
Cc
Dd
Ee
Ff
Gg
Hh
Ii
Jj
Kk
Ll
Mm
Nn
Oo
Pp
Qq
Rr
Ss
Tt
Uu
Vv
Ww
Xx
Yy
Zz

numerator NOUN **numerators** (*maths*) the number above the line in a fraction, for example 3 in ¾

numerical ADJECTIVE to do with numbers: *Put the cards into numerical order.*

numerous ADJECTIVE many: *Numerous people have had the same experience.*

nun NOUN **nuns** a member of a religious group of women who live in a convent

nurse NOUN **nurses** a person whose job is to look after people when they are ill or injured, especially in a hospital
VERB **nurses, nursing, nursed** to nurse someone is to look after them when they are ill or injured: *He had nursed her back to health over several weeks.*

nursery NOUN **nurseries 1** a place where parents can take their children to be looked after while they are at work **2** a room for young children **3** a place where plants are grown and sold

nursery school NOUN **nursery schools** a school for children between three and five years old

nursing home NOUN **nursing homes** a small private hospital or home, especially for old people

nurture VERB **nurtures, nurturing, nurtured** to nurture a person, animal, or plant is to look after them so that they grow healthily

nut NOUN **nuts 1** a fruit from certain trees that has a hard shell and a firm inside that you can eat **2** a small piece of metal with a hole in the middle of it for screwing onto the end of a bolt

nutmeg NOUN **nutmegs** a hard seed that is grated or used as a brown powder to flavour food

nutrient NOUN **nutrients 1** a substance in food that gives you energy and makes you healthy **2** a substance in the soil that helps plants to grow healthily

nutrition NOUN eating healthy food: *Good nutrition is necessary for a quick recovery.*
▸ **nutritious** ADJECTIVE good for you to eat or drink

nutshell NOUN
• **put something in a nutshell** to say something using as few words as possible: *To put it in a nutshell, if you don't work, you won't pass your exam.*

nutty ADJECTIVE **nuttier, nuttiest 1** containing nuts or tasting of nuts **2** silly or crazy

nuzzle VERB **nuzzles, nuzzling, nuzzled** an animal nuzzles you when it rubs its nose gently against you

nylon NOUN **nylons** a strong fabric made from chemicals

Aa
Bb
Cc
Dd
Ee
Ff
Gg
Hh
Ii
Jj
Kk
Ll
Mm
Nn
Oo
Pp
Qq
Rr
Ss
Tt
Uu
Vv
Ww
Xx
Yy
Zz

Oo

oak NOUN **oaks** a large tree with hard wood and seeds called acorns

OAP ABBREVIATION short for **old age pensioner**

oar NOUN **oars** a long piece of wood with a flat end, used for rowing a boat

oasis NOUN **oases** a place in a desert where there is water and where trees grow

oath NOUN **oaths 1** a solemn promise: *He swore an oath to support the king.* **2** a swear word: *curses and oaths*

oatmeal NOUN oats that have been ground to a powder

oats PLURAL NOUN a type of grassy plant or its grain, used as food: *Horses eat oats.*

obedience NOUN being willing to do what you are told: *Teachers expect obedience from their pupils.*

▶ **obedient** ADJECTIVE ready to do what you are told: *an obedient child*

obese (pronounced oh-**bees**) ADJECTIVE very fat

▶ **obesity** NOUN being very fat

obey VERB **obeys, obeying, obeyed** to do what you are told to do: *I obeyed the order.*

obituary NOUN **obituaries** an announcement in a newspaper that someone has died, often with a short account of their life

object NOUN **objects** (pronounced ob-jikt) **1** something that you can see and touch: *There were various objects on the table.* **2** an aim or purpose: *His main object in life was to become rich.* **3** (*grammar*) the word or words in a sentence that stand for the person or thing that the verb affects, for example *me* in *He hit me*

VERB **objects, objecting, objected** (pronounced ob-**jekt**) to object to someone or something is to say that you do not like them or do not agree with

them: *I object to her rudeness.* • *Jack objected to going to bed so early.*

▶ **objection** NOUN **objections 1** objecting to something: *His view is open to objection.* **2** a reason for objecting: *My objection is that he is too young.*

objective NOUN **objectives** an aim or purpose: *His objective was to score more than one goal.*

ADJECTIVE if you are objective, you are fair and try to look at things from different points of view

obligation NOUN **obligations** a promise or duty: *You are under no obligation to buy this.*

obligatory ADJECTIVE if something is obligatory, you must do it because of a law or rule: *It is obligatory to attend school.*

oblige VERB **obliges, obliging, obliged 1** (*formal*) to oblige someone is to do something to help them: *Could you oblige me by carrying this, please?* **2** if you are obliged to do something, you have to do it: *I was obliged to invite him to my party.*

▶ **obliged** ADJECTIVE (*formal*) grateful: *I am obliged to you for all your help.*

▶ **obliging** ADJECTIVE ready to help other people: *a most obliging gentleman*

oblique (pronounced oh-**bleek**) ADJECTIVE **1** sloping: *an oblique line* **2** not saying something in a direct way, or not saying exactly what you mean: *an oblique reply*

oblong NOUN **oblongs** a rectangle that is longer than it is wide

ADJECTIVE shaped like an oblong: *an oblong table*

oboe NOUN **oboes** a woodwind musical instrument

obscene ADJECTIVE not decent and likely to offend people: *obscene photographs*

▶ **obscenity** NOUN **obscenities**

obscenity is words or acts that are not decent and offend people

obscure ADJECTIVE **1** not easy to see or understand: *an obscure outline* • *He writes obscure poems.* **2** not famous or well-known: *an obscure actor*
VERB **obscures, obscuring, obscured** to obscure something is to hide it: *Thick clouds obscured the sun.*
▶ **obscurity** NOUN being obscure

observant ADJECTIVE good at noticing things

observation NOUN **observations**
1 observation is noticing or watching: *He has been kept in hospital for observation.* **2** an observation is a remark or comment: *She made a couple of observations about the weather.*

observatory NOUN **observatories** a place with large telescopes for studying the stars or weather

observe VERB **observes, observing, observed**
1 to observe something is to notice it: *I observed her smiling face.*
2 to observe something is to watch it carefully: *She continued to observe his actions with interest.*
3 to observe something is to obey or keep it: *observe the rules* • *observe a tradition*
4 to observe is to remark: '*It's a lovely day,*' *he observed.*
▶ **observer** NOUN **observers** someone who observes

obsess VERB **obsesses, obsessing, obsessed** if something obsesses you, it fills your mind completely: *Tom is obsessed by football.*
▶ **obsession** NOUN **obsessions 1** an obsession is a feeling or idea that you cannot stop thinking about: *an obsession with motorbikes* **2** obsession is being unable to stop doing something or thinking about something: *David's tidiness borders on obsession.*

obsolete ADJECTIVE out of date or no longer in use: *The steam locomotive has become obsolete.*

obstacle NOUN **obstacles** something that stands in your way and stops you from doing something

obstinate ADJECTIVE refusing to give in to someone or something: *She won't change her mind – she's very obstinate.*
▶ **obstinacy** NOUN being stubborn and obstinate
▶ **obstinately** ADVERB in an obstinate, stubborn way: *Anil obstinately refused to speak to me.*

obstruct VERB **obstructs, obstructing, obstructed 1** to obstruct something is to block it: *The road was obstructed by a fallen tree.* **2** to obstruct someone or something is to stop them from getting past or to hold them back: *The crashed lorry obstructed the traffic.*
▶ **obstruction** NOUN **obstructions** blocking or preventing something: *an obstruction in the pipe* • *the obstruction of justice*

obtain VERB **obtains, obtaining, obtained** to get: *He obtained a large sum of money by selling houses.*

obtuse ADJECTIVE stupid and slow to understand: *Are you being deliberately obtuse?*

obtuse angle NOUN **obtuse angles** (*maths*) an angle that is more than 90 degrees and less than 180 degrees

obvious ADJECTIVE easy to see or understand: *It was obvious that she was ill.* • *an obvious reason*
▶ **obviously** ADVERB clearly: *Obviously, I'll need some help.*

occasion NOUN **occasions 1** a particular time when something happens: *I've met him on several occasions.* **2** a special event: *The Queen's birthday was a great occasion.*
▶ **occasional** ADJECTIVE happening now and then: *occasional outings to the seaside*
▶ **occasionally** ADVERB now and then: *I occasionally go to the theatre.*

occupant NOUN **occupants** someone who lives or works in a house or building: *the occupants of the flat*

occupation NOUN **occupations 1** a person's occupation is their job **2** an occupation is something that you do in your free time: *Reading is his favourite occupation.* **3** occupation is the occupying of territory: *the Roman occupation of Britain*

occupier NOUN **occupiers** the person who lives in a particular house or flat

occupy VERB **occupies, occupying, occupied**
1 to occupy a space is to fill it: *A table occupied the centre of the room.*
2 to occupy a house or building is to live or work there: *The family used to occupy a small flat.*
3 to occupy yourself or your time is to keep busy: *He occupied himself with the garden.*
4 to occupy territory is to capture it: *Soldiers were occupying the town.*

occur VERB **occurs, occurring, occurred 1** to happen: *The accident must have occurred last night.* **2** to exist or be found: *Giants occur in fairy tales.* **3** if something occurs to you, it comes into your mind: *That never occurred to me.*
▸ **occurrence** NOUN **occurrences** something that happens

ocean NOUN **oceans 1** the ocean is the salt water that covers most of the Earth's surface **2** an ocean is one of the five large areas of sea in the world, for example the Atlantic Ocean

octagon NOUN **octagons** a flat shape with eight sides
▸ **octagonal** ADJECTIVE having eight sides: *an octagonal coin*

octave NOUN **octaves** (*music*) a range of eight musical notes, for example from one C to the next C above or below it

October NOUN the tenth month of the year, after September and before November

✦ **October** was the eighth month of the Roman year and the name comes from the word **octo**, which means *eight* in Latin.
Another word in English where you can work out that **octo** means *eight* is **octopus**.

octopus NOUN **octopuses** a sea creature with eight arms that are called tentacles

✦ This word comes from the Greek words **octo**, which means *eight*, and **pous**, which means *feet*.

odd ADJECTIVE **odder, oddest**
1 unusual or strange: *He's wearing very odd clothes.*
2 an odd number is one that cannot be divided exactly by 2: *5 and 7 are odd numbers.*
3 not one of a matching pair or group: *an odd shoe*
4 left over: *Have you got any odd bits of wood I could use?*
5 not regular: *She makes the odd mistake when she speaks English.*
▸ **oddity** NOUN **oddities** a strange or unusual person or thing: *He's always been a bit of an oddity.*
▸ **oddly** ADVERB strangely: *You're behaving very oddly.*
▸ **oddness** NOUN being strange or unusual

oddments PLURAL NOUN scraps or pieces left over from something else: *She made the jacket from oddments of material.*

odds PLURAL NOUN **1** the chances of something happening: *The odds are that he will win.* **2** difference: *It makes no odds.*
• **odds and ends** small objects of different kinds

ode NOUN **odes** a type of poem, often written to someone or something: *ode to autumn*

odour NOUN **odours** a smell, especially an unpleasant one

of PREPOSITION
1 belonging to: *a friend of mine* • *Where is the lid of this box?*
2 away from: *within two miles of his home*
3 from among: *one of my friends*
4 made from or out of: *a house of bricks*
5 used to show an amount or measurement of something: *a gallon of petrol*
6 about: *the story of his adventures*
7 containing: *a box of chocolates*

Aa
Bb
Cc
Dd
Ee
Ff
Gg
Hh
Ii
Jj
Kk
Ll
Mm
Nn
Oo
Pp
Qq
Rr
Ss
Tt
Uu
Vv
Ww
Xx
Yy
Zz

off → offside

8 used to show the cause of something: *She died of hunger.*

9 used to show a removal or taking away: *robbed of her jewels*

off ADVERB **1** away from a place or position: *He marched off down the road.* • *Take your shoes off.* **2** not working or in use: *Switch off the light.* **3** completely: *Finish off your work.*

ADJECTIVE **1** cancelled: *The holiday is off.* **2** gone sour or rotten: *This milk is off.* **3** not switched on: *The radio was off.*

PREPOSITION

1 away from or down from: *a mile off the coast* • *It fell off the table.*

2 out of a vehicle: *We got off the bus.*

3 taken away from: *There is £10 off the usual price.*

4 not wanting something: *Jane is not well and is off her food.*

• **badly off** if you are badly off, you are poor

• **well off** if you are well off, you are rich

offence NOUN **offences 1** an offence is a crime: *The police charged him with several offences.* **2** offence is a feeling of hurt, anger or annoyance: *His rudeness caused offence.*

• **take offence at something** to feel hurt or angry at something

offend VERB **offends, offending, offended 1** to offend someone is to make them feel upset or angry: *She will be offended if you don't go to her party.* **2** to offend is to commit a crime

▸ **offender** NOUN **offenders** a person who has committed a crime

▸ **offensive** ADJECTIVE **1** rude or insulting: *offensive remarks* **2** disgusting: *an offensive smell* **3** used for attacking: *offensive weapons*

NOUN **offensives** an attack: *a military offensive*

offer VERB **offers, offering, offered 1** to offer someone something is to ask if they would like it: *She offered me more tea.* **2** to offer to do something is to say that you will do it: *No one offered to help me carry the bags.* **3** to offer an amount of money is to say how much

you are willing to pay for something: *He offered me £20 for my bike.*

NOUN **offers 1** an act of offering: *an offer of help* **2** an amount of money offered: *They made an offer of £100,000 for the house.*

▸ **offering** NOUN **offerings 1** a gift: *a birthday offering* **2** money that people give during a church service: *The offering will now be collected.*

offhand ADJECTIVE rude or impolite: *You were a bit offhand with her this morning.*

ADVERB without taking time to think carefully: *Can you tell me offhand how much it might cost?*

office NOUN **offices**

1 a building or set of rooms in which the business of a company is done: *Our head offices are in London.*

2 the room in which a particular person works: *the bank manager's office*

3 a room or building used for a particular purpose: *lost property office*

4 an important job or position: *the office of President*

officer NOUN **officers 1** a person in the army, navy or air force who is in charge of ordinary soldiers **2** a policeman or policewoman

official ADJECTIVE **1** done or given out by people in power: *an official announcement* **2** making up part of the tasks of a job or office: *official engagements*

NOUN **officials** a person who holds a job with authority: *government officials*

▸ **officially** ADVERB **1** as an official: *He attended the ceremony officially.* **2** formally: *The new library is now officially open.*

offset VERB **offsets, offsetting, offset** one thing offsets another when it balances it out or makes up for it

offshore ADJECTIVE **1** in or on the sea, not far from the coast: *offshore oilrigs* **2** blowing away from the coast, out to sea: *offshore breezes*

offside ADJECTIVE in a position not allowed by the rules of a game such as football: *The goal was disallowed because the player was offside.*

offspring NOUN **offspring** a person or animal's offspring is their child or baby animal: *How many offspring does a cat usually have at one time?*

often ADVERB many times: *I often go to the cinema.*

ogre NOUN **ogres 1** a frightening cruel giant in fairy tales **2** a frightening person

oh INTERJECTION a cry of surprise, admiration, pain or annoyance: *Oh, what a lovely present!* • *Oh no, I've forgotten my homework.*

oil NOUN **oils 1** a greasy liquid that will not mix with water: *olive oil* • *vegetable oil* **2** a substance made from the remains of dead animals and plants. It can be taken out of the ground and used as fuel

VERB **oils, oiling, oiled** to oil something is to put oil on or into it: *The machine will work better if it's oiled.*

oilfield NOUN **oilfields** a place where oil is found in the ground or under the sea: *the oilfields of the North Sea*

oil paint NOUN **oil paints** paint made with oil

▸ **oil painting** NOUN **oil paintings** a picture painted with oil paints

oil rig NOUN **oil rigs** a structure set up for drilling an oil well

oilskin NOUN **oilskins 1** cloth made waterproof with oil **2** a piece of clothing made of this

oil well NOUN **oil wells** a hole that is drilled into the ground or seabed in order to get oil

oily ADJECTIVE **oilier, oiliest 1** like, or covered with, oil: *an oily liquid* • *an oily rag* **2** too friendly or flattering: *his oily manner*

oink NOUN **oinks** the sound made by a pig

ointment NOUN **ointments** a cream that you rub on your skin to soothe or heal it

OK *or* **okay** INTERJECTION, ADJECTIVE AND ADVERB an informal way of saying 'all right': *OK! I'll do it!* • *an okay song* • *Do I look OK?*

✦ **OK** probably comes from an American advertisement from the past, in which 'all correct' was spelt *oll korrect* as a joke.

old ADJECTIVE **older, oldest**
1 having lived or existed a long time: *an old man* • *an old building*
2 having a particular age: *nine years old*
3 belonging to times long ago: *the good old days*
4 worn-out, or no longer used: *She threw away her old clothes.*
5 former or previous: *I preferred my old school to this one.*

old age NOUN the later part of a person's life: *He wrote poems in his old age.*

Old English NOUN the English language before about 1150

old-fashioned ADJECTIVE not modern or fashionable: *old-fashioned clothes*

Old Testament NOUN the first part of the Bible

olive NOUN **olives 1** a small oval fruit with a hard stone, which is used to make cooking oil **2** the tree on which it grows **3** a yellowish-green colour

Olympic games *or* **Olympics** PLURAL NOUN a sports competition held once every four years for sportsmen and sportswomen from all over the world

omelette NOUN **omelettes** a dish made of eggs beaten and fried, sometimes with a filling: *a cheese omelette*

omen NOUN **omens** a sign of future events: *The storm was a bad omen.*

▸ **ominous** ADJECTIVE giving a warning about something bad that is going to happen: *ominous clouds*

omission NOUN **omissions 1** omission is the leaving out of something: *the omission of his name from the list* **2** an omission is something that has been left out: *There are omissions in his report.*

omit VERB **omits, omitting, omitted 1** to omit something is to leave it out: *You can omit the last chapter of the book.* **2** (*formal*) to omit to do something is to

Aa
Bb
Cc
Dd
Ee
Ff
Gg
Hh
Ii
Jj
Kk
Ll
Mm
Nn
Oo
Pp
Qq
Rr
Ss
Tt
Uu
Vv
Ww
Xx
Yy
Zz

not do it: *He omitted to tell his Mum where he was going.*

omnivore NOUN **omnivores** an animal that eats all kinds of food, plants as well as meat. Look up and compare **carnivore** and **herbivore**

▸ **omnivorous** ADJECTIVE eating all kinds of food: *Human beings are omnivorous.*

on PREPOSITION

1 touching, fixed to or covering the upper or outer side of something: *on the table*

2 supported by: *standing on one leg*

3 during a certain day: *on Friday*

4 about: *a book on Scottish history*

5 with: *Do you have a pen on you?*

6 near or beside: *a shop on the main road*

7 taking part in: *He is on the committee.*

ADVERB **1** so as to be touching, fixed to or covering the upper or outer side of something: *Put your coat on.* **2** forwards or onwards: *They moved on.* **3** working or being used: *Switch the light on.*

ADJECTIVE **1** working or being used: *The television is on.* **2** planned: *Do you have anything on this evening?* **3** not cancelled: *Is the party still on?*

once ADVERB **1** a single time: *He did it once.* **2** at a time in the past: *People once lived in caves.*

CONJUNCTION when or as soon as: *Once you've finished, you can go.*

one NOUN **ones** the number 1: *One and one is two.*

PRONOUN **1** a single person or thing: *One of my friends called round.* **2** a rather formal word for **anyone** or **you**: *One can see the sea from here.*

ADJECTIVE a single: *We had only one reply.*

• **one another** used when an action takes place between two or more people: *They looked at one another.*

oneself PRONOUN **1** you use **oneself** after a verb or preposition when the subject is **one**: *One should wash oneself every day.* **2** you also use the word **oneself** for emphasis: *One always has to do these things oneself.*

one-sided ADJECTIVE **1** with one person or side having a big advantage over the other: *a one-sided contest* **2** showing only one view of a subject: *a one-sided discussion*

one-way ADJECTIVE a one-way street is one in which traffic can move in one direction only

ongoing ADJECTIVE continuing: *ongoing talks*

onion NOUN **onions** a round vegetable that has a strong taste and smell

onlooker NOUN **onlookers** someone who watches something happening: *A crowd of onlookers had gathered.*

only ADVERB **1** not more than: *There are only two weeks until the holiday.* **2** alone: *Only you can do it.* **3** not longer ago than: *I saw her only yesterday.*

ADJECTIVE without any others of the same type: *the only book of its kind*

CONJUNCTION but or however: *I'd like to come, only I have to do my homework.*

onset NOUN **onsets** the onset of something is the beginning of it: *the onset of a cold*

onto PREPOSITION to a place or position on: *The fans ran onto the pitch.*

onward ADJECTIVE going forward in place or time: *their onward journey* • *the onward march of science*

ADVERB onwards: *He led them onward through the night.*

onwards ADVERB forward in place or time: *from nine o'clock onwards*

ooze VERB **oozes, oozing, oozed** to flow slowly: *The glue oozed out of the tube.*

✦ **Ooze** comes from an Old English word, **wos**, which means *juice* or *sap*.

opal NOUN **opals** a precious stone that is milky in colour, with streaks of other colours

opaque ADJECTIVE impossible to see through: *an opaque liquid*

open ADJECTIVE

1 not shut: *The door is wide open.*

2 allowing the inside to be seen: *an open book*

3 not enclosed: *open countryside*
4 honest: *He was very open with me about his work.*
5 not yet decided: *The matter is still open for discussion.*
VERB **opens, opening, opened 1** to open something is to make it open: *He opened the door.* **2** to open is to become open: *The door opened.* **3** to open something is to begin it: *He opened the meeting with a speech of welcome.*

▶ **opener** NOUN **openers** something that opens something else: *a tin opener*

▶ **opening** NOUN **openings 1** a hole or space: *an opening in the fence* **2** a beginning: *the opening of the film* **3** a chance, especially for a job: *There are few openings for ex-footballers.*

▶ **openly** ADVERB without trying to hide anything: *She talked openly about her illness.*

open-minded ADJECTIVE ready to take up new ideas

opera NOUN **operas** a musical play in which the words are sung: *an opera by Verdi*

operate VERB **operates, operating, operated 1** to operate is to work: *The printer doesn't seem to be operating properly.* **2** to operate a machine is to make it work: *How do you operate this computer?* **3** to operate on someone is to perform a surgical operation on them: *The surgeon operated on the man's heart.*

▶ **operation** NOUN **operations 1** a carefully planned action involving several people: *a rescue operation* **2** the process of working: *Our plan is now in operation.* **3** an occasion when a surgeon cuts into someone's body in order to remove part of it or to treat a disease: *an operation for appendicitis*

▶ **operator** NOUN **operators 1** someone who works a machine: *a lift operator* **2** someone who connects telephone calls: *Ask the operator to put you through to that number.*

opinion NOUN **opinions** what you think or believe: *My opinions about education have changed.*

opponent NOUN **opponents** someone who is against you, for example in a war or competition: *He beat his opponent by four points.*

opportunity NOUN **opportunities** a chance to do something: *I had the opportunity to go to Paris.*

oppose VERB **opposing, opposes, opposed** to oppose someone or something is to be against them: *people who opposed the school's decision* • *Who is opposing him in the election?*

opposite ADJECTIVE **1** on the other side of something: *on the opposite side of town* **2** completely different: *They walked off in opposite directions.*
PREPOSITION AND ADVERB facing: *the house opposite mine* • *Who lives in the house opposite?*
NOUN **opposites** one thing is the opposite of another if it is completely different from it: *Hot is the opposite of cold.*

opposition NOUN **1** opposition is resisting or fighting against someone or something: *There is a lot of opposition to his new ideas.* **2** opposition can also be the people you are fighting or competing against: *a strong opposition* **3** the Opposition is the main political party that opposes the party in government

oppress VERB **oppresses, oppressing, oppressed 1** to oppress someone is to govern or treat them cruelly: *The king oppressed his people.* **2** if something oppresses you, it worries or distresses you: *The heat oppressed her.*

▶ **oppression** NOUN **1** cruel treatment **2** worry or distress

▶ **oppressive** ADJECTIVE **1** cruel and harsh: *oppressive government* **2** causing worry: *an oppressive situation* **3** unpleasantly hot: *the oppressive heat of the desert*

opt VERB **opts, opting, opted**
• **opt for something** to choose something: *I opted for the strawberry gateau.*
• **opt out** to decide not to do something: *I opted out of the exam.*

Aa
Bb
Cc
Dd
Ee
Ff
Gg
Hh
Ii
Jj
Kk
Ll
Mm
Nn
Oo
Pp
Qq
Rr
Ss
Tt
Uu
Vv
Ww
Xx
Yy
Zz

- **opt to do something** to choose to do something: *She opted to stay on at school.*

optic *or* **optical** ADJECTIVE to do with the eyes or sight: *optic nerve* • *an optical aid*

optical illusion NOUN **optical illusions** something which deceives the eye, often making you think you can see something that is not actually there

optician NOUN **opticians** someone who tests your eyesight and makes and sells spectacles

optics NOUN the science of light

optimism NOUN the belief that good things will happen: *full of optimism*

▸ **optimist** NOUN **optimists** someone who usually expects or hopes that something good will happen

▸ **optimistic** ADJECTIVE hoping or believing that something good will happen: *an optimistic person*

▸ **optimistically** ADVERB in an optimistic way: *'She might still come,' he said optimistically.*

option NOUN **options 1** choice: *You have no option.* **2** a thing that you choose or that may be chosen: *There are several options open to me.*

▸ **optional** ADJECTIVE if something is optional, you can choose it but you do not have to do or have it: *Music is optional at my school.*

opulent ADJECTIVE showing wealth: *She lived in opulent surroundings.*

or CONJUNCTION **1** used to show choices or alternatives: *Would you prefer tea or coffee?* **2** because if not: *You'd better go or you'll miss your bus.*

oral ADJECTIVE **1** spoken, not written: *an oral examination* **2** to do with the mouth: *oral hygiene*

▸ **orally** ADVERB **1** by speaking: *I prefer to communicate orally rather than by email.* **2** by mouth: *medicine to be taken orally*

orange NOUN **oranges 1** an orange is a juicy citrus fruit with a thick skin of a colour between red and yellow **2** orange is the colour of this fruit

▸ **orangey** ADJECTIVE quite orange but not completely orange in colour

orang-utan NOUN **orang-utans** a large man-like ape

✦ **Orang-utan** comes from a language called Malay that is spoken in Singapore and Malaysia. It means *wild man* or *forest man*.

oration NOUN **orations** a formal speech: *a funeral oration*

▸ **orator** NOUN **orators** someone who makes formal speeches

orb NOUN **orbs** a sphere or anything in the shape of a ball

orbit NOUN **orbits** the path along which something moves around a planet or other body in space: *The spaceship is in orbit round the moon.*
VERB **orbits, orbiting, orbited** to go round something in space: *The spacecraft is orbiting Earth.*

orchard NOUN **orchards** an area where fruit trees are grown: *a cherry orchard*

orchestra NOUN **orchestras** a large group of musicians playing together: *Jo plays violin in the school orchestra.*

orchid NOUN **orchids** a plant with brightly-coloured flowers

ordain VERB **ordains, ordaining, ordained** to ordain someone is to make them a priest or minister

ordeal NOUN **ordeals** a difficult or painful experience

order NOUN **orders**
1 an instruction to do something: *The soldier was given the order to shoot.*
2 an instruction to supply something: *The waiter came to take our order.*
3 the way things are arranged: *alphabetical order*
4 peaceful conditions and behaviour: *law and order*
5 an organized state when things are in their proper places: *It was time to bring some order into my life.*
VERB **orders, ordering, ordered 1** to order someone to do something is to tell them to do it: *The doctor ordered her to rest for a few days.* **2** to order something is to ask for it to be supplied: *I ordered some magazines from the newsagent.*

Aa Bb Cc Dd Ee Ff Gg Hh Ii Jj Kk Ll Mm Nn Oo Pp Qq Rr Ss Tt Uu Vv Ww Xx Yy Zz

orderly ADJECTIVE **1** well-behaved, quiet: *Please form an orderly queue.* **2** in proper order: *an orderly arrangement of objects*

ordinal number NOUN **ordinal numbers** (*maths*) an ordinal number is any number which shows where something comes in a series, for example *first, second, third*

ordinary ADJECTIVE normal and not very special: *an ordinary Monday morning*

ore NOUN **ores** rock or earth from which a metal is obtained: *iron ore*

organ NOUN **organs 1** a part of your body that has a special purpose: *Eyes are the organs that we use to see.* **2** a musical instrument with keys like a piano

organic ADJECTIVE **1** found in or made by living things: *organic fertilizers* **2** organic food is produced without using chemicals: *organic vegetables*

organism NOUN **organisms** any living thing

organist NOUN **organists** someone who plays the organ

organization *or* **organisation** NOUN **organizations** *or* **organisations 1** an organization is a group of people who work together for a purpose: *a business organization* **2** organization is the organizing of something: *The success of the project depends on good organization.*

organize *or* **organise** VERB **organizes, organizing, organized 1** to organize something is to plan and arrange it: *We've organized a surprise party for his birthday.* **2** to organize something is to sort things into a particular order: *He organized all the papers on his desk.*

▸ **organizer** *or* **organiser** NOUN **organizers** *or* **organisers** someone who organizes something

oriental ADJECTIVE in or from the east: *oriental art*

orienteering NOUN a sport in which you run across country, finding your way with a map and a compass

origami NOUN the Japanese art of paper-folding

✦ **Origami** comes from the Japanese words **ori**, which means *fold*, and **kami**, which means *paper*.

origin NOUN **origins 1** the place from which someone or something comes: *the origins of the English language* **2** the cause: *the origin of his fear of flying*

▸ **original** ADJECTIVE **1** existing from the start, first: *The original story had been changed down through the centuries.* **2** not copied, new: *an original design • original ideas* **3** an original work of art is one that the artist did, and not a copy NOUN **originals** the earliest version: *This is the original – all the others are copies.*

▸ **originally** ADVERB **1** in or from the beginning: *His family comes from Scotland originally.* **2** in a new and different way: *She dresses very originally.*

originate VERB **originates, originating, originated 1** to originate is to start or come into being: *This style of painting originated in China.* **2** to originate something is to create it: *She is responsible for originating the word.*

ornament NOUN **ornaments** an object used to decorate something: *china ornaments on the mantelpiece* VERB **ornaments, ornamenting, ornamented** to ornament something is to add decorations to make it look beautiful: *The ceiling was richly ornamented.*

▸ **ornamental** ADJECTIVE for decoration: *an ornamental pond*

▸ **ornamentation** NOUN things added to something to decorate it

ornate ADJECTIVE decorated with a complicated design: *an ornate doorway*

orphan NOUN **orphans** a child whose parents are both dead

▸ **orphanage** NOUN **orphanages** a home for orphans

orthodox ADJECTIVE traditional in beliefs or methods: *orthodox Jews • orthodox medical treatment*

Aa
Bb
Cc
Dd
Ee
Ff
Gg
Hh
Ii
Jj
Kk
Ll
Mm
Nn
Oo
Pp
Qq
Rr
Ss
Tt
Uu
Vv
Ww
Xx
Yy
Zz

Aa
Bb
Cc
Dd
Ee
Ff
Gg
Hh
Ii
Jj
Kk
Ll
Mm
Nn
Oo
Pp
Qq
Rr
Ss
Tt
Uu
Vv
Ww
Xx
Yy
Zz

Orthodox Church NOUN a group of Christian churches in eastern Europe

ostrich NOUN **ostriches** a large bird which cannot fly but runs very fast

other ADJECTIVE

1 the second of two: *Where is the other glove?*

2 the rest: *Jack is here and the other children are at school.*

3 different or extra: *There must be some other reason.*

4 recently past: *just the other day*

PRONOUN **1** the second of two: *Here's one sock but where is the other?* **2** the rest: *Joe is here but where are the others?*

• **other than** except: *There was no one there other than an old woman.*

otherwise ADVERB **1** or else: *You'd better go now otherwise you'll be late for school.* **2** except for what you have mentioned: *The new boy raised his hand. Otherwise, no one moved.* **3** in a different way: *John, otherwise known as 'Ginger' because of his red hair*

otter NOUN **otters** a small furry river animal that feeds on fish

ought VERB **1** **ought** is used to show what you should do: *You ought to help them.* **2** **ought** is also used to show what is likely to happen: *The weather ought to be fine.*

ounce NOUN **ounces** an imperial unit for measuring weight, equal to $\frac{1}{16}$ of a pound or 28.35 grams: *You need five ounces of flour to make this cake.*

our ADJECTIVE belonging to us: *That is our car.*

ours PRONOUN a word you use to talk about something belonging to us: *That car is ours.* • *These books are ours.*

ourselves PRONOUN **1** you use **ourselves** after a verb or preposition when **we** is the subject of the action and is also affected by it: *We saw ourselves in the mirror.* **2** **ourselves** is also used to show that you have done something without any help from other people: *We painted the room ourselves.* **3** you can use **ourselves** to show more clearly who you mean: *We ourselves played no part in this.*

out ADVERB

1 into or towards the open air: *go out for a walk*

2 from inside something: *She opened her bag and took out an umbrella.*

3 away from a place, such as home or from the office: *I'm afraid he's out at the moment.*

4 loudly: *shout out the answer*

5 completely: *tired out*

6 no longer hidden or secret: *The secret is out.*

7 dismissed from a game: *The batsman is out.*

• **out of** to be out of something is to have no more of it left: *We're out of biscuits.*

• **out of date** old or old-fashioned: *This telephone directory is out of date.*

out-and-out ADJECTIVE complete: *an out-and-out liar*

outback NOUN the remote parts in the middle of Australia where few people live

outbreak NOUN **outbreaks** a sudden beginning, usually of something unpleasant: *the outbreak of war*

outburst NOUN **outbursts** a sudden forceful expression of an emotion, especially anger: *a sudden outburst of rage*

outcast NOUN **outcasts** someone who people do not want to accept as part of their group

outcome NOUN **outcomes** a result: *What was the outcome of your discussion?*

outcry NOUN **outcries** a strong reaction or protest by a large number of people: *The decision caused a public outcry.*

outdo VERB **outdoes, outdoing, outdid, outdone** to outdo someone is to do better than them: *The girls tried to outdo each other in their kindness.*

outdoor ADJECTIVE outside or for use outside: *an outdoor swimming pool* • *outdoor shoes*

▶ **outdoors** ADVERB outside: *She sat outdoors in the sun.* • *Don't go outdoors if it's raining.*

outer ADJECTIVE nearer the outside: *outer space* • *outer layers*

outfit NOUN **outfits** a set of clothes worn together: *a wedding outfit*

outgrow VERB **outgrows, outgrowing, outgrew, outgrown** to outgrow something is to grow too big or too old for it: *She has outgrown all her clothes.* • *Babies quickly outgrow their toys.*

outhouse NOUN **outhouses** a small building, such as a shed, which is attached to or close to a larger building

outing NOUN **outings** a short trip, made for pleasure: *an outing to the seaside*

outlaw NOUN **outlaws** someone who is given no protection by the law in their country because they are a criminal
VERB **outlaws, outlawing, outlawed** to outlaw something is to make it illegal: *The sale of alcohol was outlawed.*

outlet NOUN **outlets 1** a way of letting something out: *an outlet from the main tank* • *an outlet for his energy* **2** a place to sell goods: *one of the company's main outlets*

outline NOUN **outlines 1** the line forming the outside of something: *First he drew the outline of the face, then added the features.* **2** a short description of something: *Don't tell me the whole story – just give me the outline.*
VERB **outlines, outlining, outlined 1** to outline something is to draw the line forming the outside of it **2** to outline a plan or story is to give a short description of it

outlook NOUN **outlooks 1** a view: *Their house has a wonderful outlook.* **2** the way that a person thinks about things: *He has a strange outlook on life.* **3** what seems likely to happen: *the weather outlook*

outnumber VERB **outnumbers, outnumbering, outnumbered** to outnumber something is to be more in number than it: *The boys in the class outnumber the girls.*

out-patient NOUN **out-patients** someone who comes to hospital for treatment but does not stay overnight

outpost NOUN **outposts 1** a small military camp far away from the main army, especially to protect it from a surprise attack **2** a settlement far from where most people live

output NOUN **outputs 1** a quantity of goods produced or an amount of work done: *The output of this factory increased last year.* **2** (*ICT*) the information produced by a computer
VERB **outputs, outputting, output** (*ICT*) a computer outputs data when it produces it

outrage NOUN **outrages** a shocking or cruel action: *The decision to close the hospital is an outrage.*
VERB **outrages, outraging, outraged** to outrage someone is to hurt, shock or insult them: *Fay was outraged by his remarks.*
▸ **outrageous** ADJECTIVE shocking, terrible: *outrageous behaviour*

outright ADVERB **1** immediately: *He was killed outright.* **2** completely: *We won outright.*
ADJECTIVE **1** complete: *an outright fool* **2** without any doubt: *She is the outright winner.*

outset NOUN the beginning: *Joe hated school from the outset.*

outside NOUN **outsides** the outer surface of something: *The outside of the house was painted white.*
ADJECTIVE **1** of, on or near the outer part of anything: *the outside edge* **2** an outside chance is a slight chance: *an outside chance of winning*
ADVERB on or to the outside, outdoors: *Let's eat outside.*
PREPOSITION on the outer side of, not inside: *He was standing outside the gate.*
▸ **outsider** NOUN **outsiders 1** someone not included in a particular group: *The new boy in the class felt like an outsider.* **2** a horse or person not expected to win a race or contest

outskirts PLURAL NOUN the outer parts of a town or city: *He lives on the outskirts of Edinburgh.*

Aa
Bb
Cc
Dd
Ee
Ff
Gg
Hh
Ii
Jj
Kk
Ll
Mm
Nn
Oo
Pp
Qq
Rr
Ss
Tt
Uu
Vv
Ww
Xx
Yy
Zz

outspoken ADJECTIVE saying exactly what you mean, even if it upsets people

outstanding ADJECTIVE **1** excellent: *an outstanding student* **2** not yet paid or done: *You must pay all outstanding bills.*

outward ADJECTIVE outside or towards the outside of something **2** your outward behaviour is what other people see, even if it is not what you really mean or feel
ADVERB outwards

▸ **outwardly** ADVERB shown to other people, but not your true feelings : *Outwardly, they looked happy.*

outwards ADVERB towards the outside of something

outweigh VERB **outweighs, outweighing, outweighed** to outweigh something is to be more important than it: *The advantages outweigh the disadvantages.*

outwit VERB **outwits, outwitting, outwitted** to outwit someone is to defeat them by being cleverer than they are: *She outwitted the police and managed to escape.*

oval ADJECTIVE shaped like an egg but flat: *an oval table*
NOUN **ovals** an oval shape

✦ This word comes from the Latin word **ovalis**, which means *like an egg*.

ovary NOUN **ovaries** **1** part of a woman's body where eggs are formed **2** (*science*) the part of a flower where seeds are formed

oven NOUN **ovens** an enclosed space, usually part of a cooker, for cooking and heating food

over PREPOSITION

1 higher than, above: *Hang that picture over the fireplace.*

2 more than: *He's over 90 years old.*

3 across: *We ran over the bridge.*

4 about: *They quarrelled over the children.*

5 by means of: *We often talk over the telephone.*

ADVERB

1 across: *He walked over to speak to them.*

2 downwards: *The baby's fallen over.*

3 above in number: *children aged seven and over*

4 left or remaining: *two cakes each, and two over*

5 through: *read the passage over*
ADJECTIVE finished: *The match is already over.*
NOUN **overs** in cricket, a series of six balls bowled by the same bowler from the same end of the pitch

over- PREFIX **over-** at the start of a word means *too* or *too much*. For example, to *overeat* is to eat too much and *overcareful* means too careful

overall NOUN **overalls** a piece of clothing worn over ordinary clothes to protect them
ADJECTIVE including everything: *the overall cost*

overalls PLURAL NOUN trousers or a suit made of hardwearing material worn by workmen to protect their clothes

overarm ADJECTIVE AND ADVERB with your hand and arm raised above the level of your shoulder, moving down in front of your body: *an overarm throw*

overbearing ADJECTIVE bossy and too confident

overboard ADVERB over the side of a ship or boat into the water: *He jumped overboard.*

overcast ADJECTIVE dark with clouds: *It became overcast but it didn't rain.*

overcoat NOUN **overcoats** a heavy coat worn over all other clothes

overcome VERB **overcomes, overcoming, overcame, overcome** **1** to overcome someone or something is to defeat them eventually: *She overcame her fear of the dark.* **2** to be overcome by something is to become helpless because of it: *overcome with grief • overcome by fumes*

overdo VERB **overdoes, overdoing, overdid, overdone** **1** to overdo something is to do it too much: *It's good to work hard but don't overdo it.* **2** to overdo food is to cook it for too long: *The meat was rather overdone.*

overdose NOUN **overdoses** more of

Aa
Bb
Cc
Dd
Ee
Ff
Gg
Hh
Ii
Jj
Kk
Ll
Mm
Nn
Oo
Pp
Qq
Rr
Ss
Tt
Uu
Vv
Ww
Xx
Yy
Zz

a drug or medicine than is safe: *Her daughter took an overdose.*

overdue ADJECTIVE **1** not yet paid, done or delivered although the time for doing this has passed: *overdue library books* **2** late: *The train is overdue.*

overflow VERB **overflows, overflowing, overflowed 1** liquid overflows when it reaches the top of a container and starts to spill over the sides: *The river overflowed its banks.* **2** a container overflows when it is so full that its contents spill out: *boxes overflowing with toys*

overgrown ADJECTIVE full of plants that have grown too large and thick: *The back garden is completely overgrown with weeds.*

overhang VERB **overhangs, overhanging, overhung** to overhang something is to stick out or hang over it

overhaul VERB **overhauls, overhauling, overhauled** to overhaul something is to examine it carefully and repair any faults

overhead ADJECTIVE AND ADVERB above your head, or high up in the sky: *A plane was flying overhead.* • *overhead cables*

overheads PLURAL NOUN the money that a business has to spend regularly on things like rent and electricity

overhear VERB **overhears, overhearing, overheard** to hear something when you were not meant to: *I overheard them talking about me.*

overjoyed ADJECTIVE very happy

overlap VERB **overlaps, overlapping, overlapped 1** to overlap something is to cover a part of it: *Each roof-tile overlaps the one below it.* **2** if things overlap, they lie partly over each other: *The curtains should be wide enough to overlap.*

overleaf ADVERB on the other side of the page: *See the comments overleaf.*

overlook VERB **overlooks, overlooking, overlooked 1** if a room, building or window overlooks something, you can see that thing from the room, building or window: *The house overlooks the river.* **2** to

overlook something is to fail to see or notice it: *You have overlooked one important detail.* **3** to overlook something such as a fault is to take no notice of it: *I shall overlook your lateness this time.*

overnight ADJECTIVE AND ADVERB **1** for the night: *an overnight bag* • *We stayed in London overnight.* **2** sudden or suddenly: *an overnight success* • *He became a hero overnight.*

overpower VERB **overpowers, overpowering, overpowered** to overpower someone is to defeat them through being stronger: *He was overpowered by two policemen.*

▶ **overpowering** ADJECTIVE very strong: *an overpowering smell* • *overpowering sadness*

overrun VERB **overruns, overrunning, overran, overrun 1** to overrun a place is to spread quickly all over it: *The house is overrun with mice.* **2** if something overruns, it goes on for longer than it should: *The programme overran by half an hour.*

overseas ADJECTIVE AND ADVERB abroad: *an overseas job* • *They went overseas.*

overshadow VERB **overshadows, overshadowing, overshadowed** to overshadow someone or something is to seem much more successful or important than them or it: *Clare was always overshadowed by her brilliant sister.*

oversight NOUN **oversights** a mistake, especially one that you make because you have not noticed something

overtake VERB **overtakes, overtaking, overtook, overtaken** to overtake a vehicle is to catch up with and pass it

overthrow VERB **overthrows, overthrowing, overthrew, overthrown** to overthrow someone is to force them out of power: *The government has been overthrown.*

overtime NOUN time spent working outside your normal hours

overture NOUN **overtures 1** (*music*) a piece of music played at the start of an opera or ballet **2** a friendly attempt

Aa
Bb
Cc
Dd
Ee
Ff
Gg
Hh
Ii
Jj
Kk
Ll
Mm
Nn
Oo
Pp
Qq
Rr
Ss
Tt
Uu
Vv
Ww
Xx
Yy
Zz

to start a discussion or relationship: *overtures of peace*

overweight ADJECTIVE too heavy: *My Dad's half a stone overweight.*

overwhelm VERB **overwhelms, overwhelming, overwhelmed 1** to overwhelm someone is to defeat them completely: *Our soldiers were overwhelmed by the enemy.* **2** to overwhelm someone is to load them with too great an amount of something: *overwhelmed with work* **3** if a feeling overwhelms someone, it has a strong and sudden effect on them: *overwhelmed with joy*

▶ **overwhelming** ADJECTIVE very great or strong: *an overwhelming victory* • *overwhelming relief*

overwork VERB **overworks, overworking, overworked 1** to overwork is to work too hard **2** to overwork someone is to make them work too hard

NOUN the act of working too hard: *Overwork made him ill.*

▶ **overworked** ADJECTIVE made to work too hard: *The staff are overworked.*

ovum NOUN **ova** (*science*) an egg from which a young animal or person develops

owe VERB **owes, owing, owed 1** to owe someone something is to be in debt to them: *I owe Val £10.* **2** to owe something to someone is to have them to thank for it: *He owes his success to his family.*

• **owing to** because of: *Owing to the rain, the football has been cancelled.*

owl NOUN **owls** a bird that hunts at night and feeds on small birds and animals

own VERB **owns, owning, owned** you own something if it belongs to you: *I own a bicycle.*

• **own up** to admit that you did something: *No one owned up to breaking the window.*

ADJECTIVE belonging to the person mentioned: *all his own work*

PRONOUN own is used for something belonging to another person: *I lent him a pencil because he forgot to bring his own.*

• **get your own back** to have revenge

• **on your own 1** without help: *Did he do it all on his own?* **2** alone: *Please don't leave me on my own.*

owner NOUN **owners** a person who owns something

▶ **ownership** NOUN owning something

own goal NOUN **own goals** a goal someone scores by mistake against their own side in a game

ox NOUN **oxen** a bull or cow used for pulling loads

oxide NOUN **oxides** a compound of oxygen and another element

oxidize *or* **oxidise** VERB **oxidizes, oxidizing, oxidized** (*science*) **1** to oxidize something is to cause it to combine with oxygen **2** to oxidize is to be combined with oxygen

oxygen NOUN a gas that has no taste, colour or smell, and forms part of the air

oyster NOUN **oysters** a type of shellfish that can be eaten

oz ABBREVIATION short for **ounce** or **ounces**

ozone NOUN a form of oxygen with a strong smell

ozone layer NOUN the layer of ozone that is part of the Earth's atmosphere and that protects the planet from the radiation of the sun

Aa
Bb
Cc
Dd
Ee
Ff
Gg
Hh
Ii
Jj
Kk
Ll
Mm
Nn
Oo
Pp
Qq
Rr
Ss
Tt
Uu
Vv
Ww
Xx
Yy
Zz

p ABBREVIATION short for **page** or **pence**

pace VERB **paces, pacing, paced** to walk backwards and forwards, especially because you are worried or impatient: *He paced up and down the hospital corridor, waiting for news.* • *She was pacing the floor nervously.*

NOUN **paces 1** a step, or a speed of walking or running: *Take four paces forward.* • *a slow pace* **2** a rate at which something happens or moves forward: *the pace of change*

pacemaker NOUN **pacemakers** a small device, fitted by a surgeon, that keeps someone's heart beating at the correct rhythm

pacifist (pronounced **pas**-i-fist) NOUN **pacifists** someone who believes war is wrong and should be avoided

pacify (pronounced **pas**-i-fie) VERB **pacifies, pacifying, pacified** to pacify someone is to calm them down

pack NOUN **packs**
1 things that are wrapped together or put in a bag so that you can carry them
2 a packet: *a pack of baby wipes*
3 a set of 52 playing cards
4 a group of certain animals, especially animals of the dog family: *a pack of wolves*

VERB **packs, packing, packed 1** to pack or to pack a bag is to put your belongings into a bag or suitcase for a journey: *She packed hurriedly and caught the next train.* **2** if people pack a place, they fill it so that there is very little, or no, space left
• **pack something in** (*informal*) to stop doing something

package NOUN **packages 1** a parcel that has been wrapped up for sending by post **2** a number of things that are sold or used together: *a software package*

VERB **packages, packaging, packaged** to package something, or package it up, is to put it in a parcel, wrapping or bundle

packet NOUN **packets** a container made of paper or cardboard, or the container with its contents: *a packet of biscuits*

pact NOUN **pacts** an agreement or treaty between two people, groups or countries: *They made a pact always to look out for each other.*

pad NOUN **pads**
1 a cushion-like object made of a soft material
2 a soft cushion-like part on the paw of some animals, such as dogs
3 a book of several sheets of paper fixed together at one edge and used for writing on
4 a platform for launching rockets

VERB **pads, padding, padded 1** to pad something is to stuff or protect it with soft material **2** to pad is to walk softly making little or no sound
• **pad out something** to pad out an essay or speech is to add extra and unnecessary words to it to make it longer
▶ **padding** NOUN **1** material used for stuffing chairs or cushions **2** extra and unnecessary words added to an essay or speech

paddle VERB **paddles, paddling, paddled 1** you paddle when you walk about in shallow water **2** to paddle a boat or canoe is to move it through the water using a paddle

NOUN **paddles** a short oar, often with a wide part at one or both ends, used for paddling a small boat or canoe

paddock NOUN **paddocks** a grassy field with a fence around it where horses and other animals are kept

paddy field NOUN **paddy fields** a field used to grow rice

padlock NOUN **padlocks** a lock with a U-shaped bar which hinges to one side and can be passed through a ring or chain and locked in position

pagan NOUN **pagans** someone who is not a member of any of the world's main religions, but who does practise some sort of religion
▸ **paganism** NOUN pagan beliefs and practices

page[1] NOUN **pages** one side of a sheet of paper in a book, newspaper or magazine, or one of the sheets of paper that make up a book, newspaper or magazine: *Turn to page 135 in your history books.*

page[2] NOUN **pages** 1 a small boy who helps a bride at her wedding 2 in historical times, a boy who worked as an attendant to a knight

pageant (pronounced **paj**-ent) NOUN **pageants** 1 a type of outdoor entertainment or parade with people dressed up in colourful costumes and often acting out scenes from history 2 any splendid and colourful show or display
▸ **pageantry** NOUN splendid and colourful display that forms part of a grand ceremony or parade

pagoda NOUN **pagodas** a Chinese temple, with several storeys or levels and overhanging roofs

pail NOUN **pails** a bucket, or its contents: *a milk pail • a pail of water*

pain NOUN **pains** an unpleasant uncomfortable feeling in your body or mind, because you have been hurt: *He's broken his leg in three places and is in great pain. • the pain of leaving loved ones behind*
▸ **pained** ADJECTIVE if someone has a pained expression, their face shows that they are upset or offended

painful ADJECTIVE 1 sore, or causing pain or distress: *Is your knee still painful? • Will the treatment be painful?* 2 involving a lot of hard work or effort: *Their progress up the steep mountain was slow and painful.*
▸ **painfully** ADVERB in a painful or

distressing way: *The poor little dog was painfully thin.*

painkiller NOUN **painkillers** a drug that takes away pain

painless ADJECTIVE causing no pain

painstaking ADJECTIVE paying careful attention to every detail, or needing a lot of careful attention to detail: *It's painstaking work building a model out of matchsticks.*

paint NOUN **paints** a colouring substance to be put on surfaces in the form of liquid or paste
VERB **paints, painting, painted** 1 to put paint on walls and other parts of a building 2 to make a picture, or pictures, using paint
▸ **painter** NOUN **painters** 1 a person whose job is to put paint on walls and other parts of buildings 2 an artist who makes pictures using paint
▸ **painting** NOUN **paintings** 1 painting is the activity of painting walls or pictures 2 a painting is a picture made using paints

pair NOUN **pairs** 1 two things of the same kind used or kept together: *a pair of socks • a pair of china dogs* 2 a single thing made up of two parts: *a pair of shears*
VERB **pairs, pairing, paired** to pair things is to form them into pairs or sets of two
• **pair off** people pair off when they form pairs or couples

✦ The words **pair** and **pear** sound the same but remember that they have different spellings. A **pear** is a fruit.

pal NOUN **pals** your pals are your friends

palace NOUN **palaces** a large and magnificent house, especially one for a king, queen or emperor

palate NOUN **palates** 1 your palate is the top part of the inside of your mouth. The front part feels hard and bony and the part further back is soft 2 a person's palate is their particular taste or liking, especially for certain kinds of food: *dishes to suit every palate*

pale ADJECTIVE **paler, palest** 1 light in

colour: *pale blue* • *the pale light of dawn* **2** someone who is pale has less colour in their skin than normal, often because they are ill or have had a shock: *What's the matter? You've gone pale all of a sudden.*

palette NOUN **palettes** a small flat piece of wood on which artists mix their colours

pall NOUN **palls** a pall of smoke is a cloud of smoke that hangs over something

VERB **palls, palling, palled** if something palls, it begins to bore you, usually because you have done or seen it too often

pallid ADJECTIVE unnaturally or unhealthily pale in colour: *There were tears running down his pallid cheeks.*

palm NOUN **palms 1** the inner surface of your hand between your wrist and fingers **2** a tree with very large leaves which spread out from the top of the trunk. Palms usually grow in warm countries

VERB **palms, palming, palmed**
• **palm something off** to palm an unwanted thing off on someone is to get rid of it by giving it to them

pamper VERB **pampers, pampering, pampered** to pamper someone is to spoil them by doing too much for them

pamphlet NOUN **pamphlets** a thin book with a paper cover

pan NOUN **pans 1** a metal container with a handle or handles, used for cooking food **2** a toilet bowl

VERB **pans, panning, panned** if a film, television or video camera pans somewhere, it moves in that direction to follow something or give a wider view of a scene

pancake NOUN **pancakes** a thin cake made by frying a mixture of milk, flour and eggs in a pan

panda NOUN **pandas** a large and rare black and white bear-like animal that lives in the mountains of China and eats bamboo

pandemonium NOUN wild and noisy confusion

pane NOUN **panes** a flat piece of glass used in a window

panel NOUN **panels 1** a flat rectangular piece of wood or other material, often set into a door or wall **2** a group of people who are chosen to judge a competition or take part in a discussion **3** a separate section on the page of a book, that gives information about a particular subject
▸ **panelling** NOUN wood or other material used for panels in walls and doors

pang NOUN **pangs** a sudden sharp or painful feeling: *pangs of hunger*

panic NOUN panic is sudden great fear, especially the kind that spreads through a crowd and causes people to scream or rush about not knowing what to do

VERB **panics, panicking, panicked** to become so frightened that you lose the power to think clearly
▸ **panicky** ADJECTIVE tending to panic

✦ This word comes from the Greek word **panikon**, which means *fear of Pan*. Pan was a Greek god who was said to scare people and animals.

panorama NOUN **panoramas** a wide view in all directions, usually of a large area of land or of a city and the surrounding landscape

pansy NOUN **pansies** a small garden flower with large flat rounded petals, usually white, yellow or shades of purple

pant VERB **pants, panting, panted 1** to gasp for breath **2** to say something while gasping for breath: *'I've just sprinted two miles to catch this train,'* he panted.

panther NOUN **panthers** a leopard, especially one that is black rather than having a spotted coat

pantomime NOUN **pantomimes** a show put on at Christmas time, often based on a popular fairy tale, and including singing, dancing and comedy acts

pantry NOUN **pantries** a small room near a kitchen, used for storing food

pants PLURAL NOUN **1** a piece of underwear that covers your bottom **2** the American English word for trousers

Aa
Bb
Cc
Dd
Ee
Ff
Gg
Hh
Ii
Jj
Kk
Ll
Mm
Nn
Oo
Pp
Qq
Rr
Ss
Tt
Uu
Vv
Ww
Xx
Yy
Zz

Aa
Bb
Cc
Dd
Ee
Ff
Gg
Hh
Ii
Jj
Kk
Ll
Mm
Nn
Oo
Pp
Qq
Rr
Ss
Tt
Uu
Vv
Ww
Xx
Yy
Zz

papa NOUN **papas** a name some people use for their father

papal ADJECTIVE to do with the pope: *a papal visit*

papaya NOUN **papayas** a large yellow fruit with sweet orange flesh, which grows on a tropical tree

paper NOUN **papers** 1 paper is a material made from wood pulp or rags and is used for writing, printing and wrapping things in: *a piece of paper* 2 a newspaper: *Have you read today's paper?* 3 a piece of paper with things written or printed on it: *an examination paper • identity papers*
VERB **papers, papering, papered** to paper a wall or room is to put wallpaper on it

paperback NOUN **paperbacks** a book with a cover that can bend easily, made of very thin card. Look up and compare **hardback**

papier-mâché NOUN a mixture of shredded paper and glue, which is used to make models, bowls and boxes and which hardens as it dries

papyrus NOUN **papyri** or **papyruses** 1 papyrus is a type of paper made from the reed-like stems of a tall water plant that grows in North Africa. Papyrus was used by the ancient Egyptians, Romans and Greeks 2 a papyrus is an ancient manuscript written on this paper

par NOUN in golf, par is the number of strokes that a good golfer should take to complete a hole, or all the holes, on the golf course
• **below par** something that is below par does not reach a certain standard required
• **on a par** equal in size or importance

parable NOUN **parables** a story, especially in the Bible, that is told to teach people something, especially a moral or religious lesson

parachute NOUN **parachutes** an umbrella-shaped piece of light material attached to a person or object so that, when they are dropped from a plane, they fall slowly to the ground
VERB **parachutes, parachuting,**

parachuted to jump from a plane and fall slowly to the ground supported by a parachute
▸ **parachutist** NOUN **parachutists** someone who parachutes

parade NOUN **parades** 1 a line of people or vehicles moving forward in a procession, often as a celebration of some event 2 soldiers are on parade when they are standing together in formal rows or ranks for marching or to be inspected
VERB **parades, parading, paraded** to march in line or move forward in a procession

paradise NOUN 1 paradise is heaven: *eternal paradise* 2 any place that has everything you want can be called a paradise: *The island is a paradise for bird watchers.*

paradox NOUN **paradoxes** a statement or situation in which two things that seem to contradict each other are combined, but the statement or situation is true or real despite this
▸ **paradoxical** ADJECTIVE combining two things that seem to contradict each other

paraffin NOUN a type of oil that is made from coal or petroleum and is used as a fuel in heaters and camping stoves

paragraph NOUN **paragraphs** (*grammar*) a section of a piece of writing, which has its first sentence starting on a new line

parallel ADJECTIVE parallel lines go in the same direction and are always the same distance apart along their length

parallelogram NOUN **parallelograms** (*maths*) a flat shape with four sides, and opposite sides that are parallel to each other

paralyse VERB **paralyses, paralysing, paralysed** 1 something paralyses a person or animal when it stops the normal movement in their body or part of their body: *The scorpion paralyses its prey with its sting.* 2 to make something come to a complete stop where no movement is possible: *Heavy* *snow falls paralysed the road and rail network.*

▶ **paralysis** NOUN paralysis is loss of the power of movement in a part of the body, or loss of the ability to move or work

paramedic NOUN **paramedics** a person who is not a doctor, but who is trained to give emergency medical treatment

paramount ADJECTIVE more important than anything else: *The children's safety is paramount.*

paranoia NOUN **1** paranoia is a form of mental illness in which someone imagines they are very important or that they have been badly treated by others **2** paranoia is a tendency some people have to be sensitive and suspicious because they imagine other people want to harm them or are making fun of them

▶ **paranoid** ADJECTIVE suffering from paranoia: *He was paranoid about getting caught.*

parapet NOUN **parapets** a low wall along the edge of a bridge, balcony or roof

paraphernalia NOUN paraphernalia is a large number of different objects and pieces of equipment: *Kevin packed all his fishing paraphernalia into the back of the car.*

paraphrase NOUN **paraphrases** a paraphrase of something is a different way of saying or writing it

VERB **paraphrases, paraphrasing, paraphrased** to paraphrase something is to express it in a different way

parasite NOUN **parasites** an animal or plant that lives on, and gets its food from, another animal or plant

parasol NOUN **parasols** an umbrella used to give shade from the sun

paratrooper NOUN **paratroopers** a soldier trained to drop by parachute into enemy country

▶ **paratroops** PLURAL NOUN a group of these soldiers

parcel NOUN **parcels** something wrapped in paper or cardboard and tied with string or sticky tape

parched ADJECTIVE **1** if you are parched, you are very thirsty **2** parched land has been dried by the sun so that there is no moisture for plants to grow

parchment NOUN **parchments 1** parchment is a material made from animal skin, used long ago for writing on **2** a parchment is a piece of this with writing on

pardon VERB **pardons, pardoning, pardoned 1** to forgive or excuse someone for a fault they have or a crime they have committed **2** some people say 'pardon' or 'pardon me', either because they haven't heard what has been said or they want to apologize for something they have done

NOUN **pardons** someone who has been sentenced to be punished for a crime receives a pardon when their punishment is cancelled

pare VERB **pares, paring, pared** to pare something is to cut or trim it, layer by layer

parent NOUN **parents** your parents are your mother and father

▶ **parentage** NOUN a person or animal's parentage is who or what each of their parents are

▶ **parental** ADJECTIVE to do with a parent or parents

parenthesis NOUN **parentheses** (*grammar*) parentheses are curved brackets put round information that adds to the main point but is not an essential part of a sentence

parenthood NOUN the condition of being or becoming a parent: *the responsibilities of parenthood*

parish NOUN **parishes** a district or area with its own church and priest or minister

▶ **parishioner** NOUN **parishioners** someone who lives in a parish, especially someone who goes to services in the parish church

park NOUN **parks** a piece of land in a town or city that has grass and trees and where people can go for fresh air or leisure

VERB **parks, parking, parked** to park a vehicle is to stop it somewhere, for

Aa Bb Cc Dd Ee Ff Gg Hh Ii Jj Kk Ll Mm Nn Oo **Pp** Qq Rr Ss Tt Uu Vv Ww Xx Yy Zz

Aa
Bb
Cc
Dd
Ee
Ff
Gg
Hh
Ii
Jj
Kk
Ll
Mm
Nn
Oo
Pp
Qq
Rr
Ss
Tt
Uu
Vv
Ww
Xx
Yy
Zz

example by the side of the road or in a drive or car park

parka NOUN **parkas** a type of long warm jacket with a hood

parking meter NOUN **parking meters** a metal box on a pole that has a slot where you can put coins to pay for parking your car in the space next to the meter

parliament NOUN **parliaments** a group of people, usually politicians, who meet to discuss and make a particular country's laws: *the parliament of Scotland*
  ▸ **parliamentary** ADJECTIVE to do with a parliament: *a parliamentary debate*

parlour NOUN **parlours 1** an old-fashioned word for a living room in a house **2** a shop selling a particular product or service: *an ice-cream parlour* • *a beauty parlour*

parody NOUN **parodies** a parody is an imitation of an author's, artist's or musician's work or style, done to make fun of them
  VERB **parodies, parodying, parodied** to parody someone or their work is to imitate them or their style in an amusing way

parole NOUN a criminal on parole has been allowed out of prison before their sentence is finished on condition that they behave well

> ✦**Parole** is French for *word*. A prisoner gives his *word* of honour he will not break the law when he is released.

parrot NOUN **parrots** a bird with a strong curved beak, beady eyes and brightly-coloured or grey feathers. Parrots can be taught to imitate human speech and are often kept as pets
  • **parrot fashion** to learn something parrot fashion is to learn it and be able to repeat it exactly

parsley NOUN a type of herb with curly or flat green leaves, used to add flavour in cooking

parsnip NOUN **parsnips** a vegetable, similar in shape to a carrot, and which is a pale cream colour and grows underground

parson NOUN **parsons** any Christian priest, especially one belonging to the Church of England
  ▸ **parsonage** NOUN **parsonages** a parson's house

part NOUN **parts 1** a division or piece of something: *The pizza is cut into six equal parts.* • *a part for the engine* **2** a character in a play or film, or the words or actions that a character has to say or do in a play or film: *a leading part in the musical* • *He's learned his part well.*
  VERB **parts, parting, parted** people or things part when they separate and move away from each other or out of each other's company
  • **part with something** to give something away, sell it or let it be taken away from you

partial ADJECTIVE **1** not complete: *a partial success* **2** to be partial to something is to be fond of it: *Wallace is partial to a little piece of cheese.* **3** to be partial is to prefer or favour one person or side over another in an unfair way: *She's too partial to be a good judge.*
  ▸ **partiality** NOUN preferring one side over another, for example in a competition or trial
  ▸ **partially** ADVERB partly: *a partially eaten biscuit*

participant NOUN **participants** someone who takes part in something with other people

participate VERB **participates, participating, participated** to participate in something is to take part in it: *I was among the girls asked to participate in the school sports day.*
  ▸ **participation** NOUN taking part

participle NOUN **participles** (*grammar*) a participle is a word formed from a verb and used as an adjective or to form different tenses of the verb. For example, *spending*, *looking* and *passing* are called **present participles** and *canned*, *stolen* and *dealt* are called **past participles**

particle NOUN **particles** a very small piece that you can hardly see: *a particle of dust*

particular ADJECTIVE a particular person or thing is a special or separate one that is not to be confused with any other
• **in particular** especially

NOUN **particulars** your particulars, or the particulars of a situation, are your personal details, or the details of that situation

parting NOUN **partings 1** leaving someone or saying goodbye to them **2** you have a parting in your hair when it has been brushed or combed in opposite directions on either side of a line across your head

partition NOUN **partitions 1** a kind of thin wall, used to divide up a room, but not usually reaching up as far as the ceiling **2** dividing something in parts

partly ADVERB in some ways or to a certain extent: *I was partly to blame for the mix-up.*

partner NOUN **partners 1** one of two people who do something together, like dance or play in a game **2** people who are business partners share the ownership of a business **3** someone's partner is the person they are married to or live with

▶ **partnership** NOUN **partnerships** a connection between two or more people who are partners

part of speech NOUN **parts of speech** (*grammar*) the parts of speech are the various groups that words belong to depending on the job they do. The parts of speech you will find in this dictionary are noun, pronoun, verb, adjective, adverb, preposition, conjunction and interjection

✦ A part of speech is the same as a **word class**.

partridge NOUN **partridges** a small plump grey and brown wild bird that nests on the ground and is hunted for sport and food

part-time ADJECTIVE AND ADVERB if you work part-time or have a part-time job, you work for only part of a full working day or week

party NOUN **parties 1** a party is an event where people gather to celebrate something or to enjoy each other's company **2** a political party is an organized group of people who share the same political beliefs **3** a party of people is a group of people travelling or doing something together

pass VERB **passes, passing, passed**
1 to move towards and then go beyond something: *The procession passed in front of the town hall.* • *The lorry passed us on a bend.*
2 to pass something to someone is to hand it to them: *Pass me the butter, please.*
3 to pass a test or exam is to be successful in it
4 something passes when it ends or goes away: *The storm passed and the sun came out again.*
5 to pass a law is to make it
• **pass away** if someone passes away, they die
• **pass out** to faint or become unconscious

NOUN **passes**
1 a ticket or card that allows you to get into a place or to travel somewhere
2 in games like football, hockey and rugby, a pass is a kick, hit or throw that sends the ball from one player to another in the same team
3 a successful result in an exam
4 a narrow gap between mountains

passable ADJECTIVE **1** if something is passable, it is of quite a good standard but is not the best **2** a road is passable if it is not completely blocked

passage NOUN **passages**
1 a narrow corridor
2 a tube from an opening in the body: *Your nasal passages are connected to your nose.*
3 a part or section in a piece of writing or music: *Read the next passage aloud.*
4 a journey in a ship
5 passing: *the passage of time*

passageway NOUN **passageways** a way through between walls or other barriers

Aa
Bb
Cc
Dd
Ee
Ff
Gg
Hh
Ii
Jj
Kk
Ll
Mm
Nn
Oo
Pp
Qq
Rr
Ss
Tt
Uu
Vv
Ww
Xx
Yy
Zz

passenger NOUN **passengers** someone travelling in a car, bus, ship or plane who is not the driver or one of the crew

passer-by NOUN **passers-by** someone who is passing in the street when something happens

passion NOUN **passions** very strong feeling or emotion, especially anger or love

▸ **passionate** ADJECTIVE showing strong emotions

passive ADJECTIVE **1** someone who is passive accepts what is happening without trying to change or oppose it **2** (*grammar*) a passive verb is the form of a verb used when the person or thing that is the subject of the verb has something done to them, rather than doing it. For example: *The leaves are being eaten by caterpillars.*

▸ **passively** ADVERB in a passive way, without resisting

Passover NOUN a Jewish festival held in March or April celebrating the freeing of the Jews from slavery in Egypt

passport NOUN **passports** a document with your photograph and personal details that you must carry when you are travelling abroad

password NOUN **passwords** a secret word or phrase that you have to know before you are allowed into a place, or which you must type into a computer before you can see the information in it

past NOUN **1** the past is the time before the present **2** someone's past is what they have done in their life before the present time

ADJECTIVE over or ended: *in the past year* • *Summer is nearly past and autumn is on the way.*

PREPOSITION **1** up to and beyond: *She dashed past me, gasping as she ran.* **2** later than: *Are the children in their beds? It's past eight o'clock.*

pasta NOUN a food made from a special type of flour, water and eggs and formed into lots of different shapes, all of which have special names, such as spaghetti, macaroni or lasagne

paste NOUN **pastes 1** a soft moist mixture **2** a type of glue for sticking paper together or to fix wallpaper to walls

VERB **pastes, pasting, pasted 1** to paste something is to stick it with glue **2** (*ICT*) to paste a piece of information or a file on the computer is to put it somewhere, after you have copied or cut it from another place

pastel ADJECTIVE pastel colours are pale and contain a lot of white: *pastel blue*

NOUN **pastels** pastels are chalky crayons used to draw and colour with

pasteurize or **pasteurise** VERB **pasteurizes, pasteurizing, pasteurized** to pasteurize milk is to heat it so that all the bacteria in it are killed

▸ **pasteurization** or **pasteurisation** NOUN a process which involves heating milk to kill all the bacteria in it

✦ This is named after Louis **Pasteur**, a French chemist who invented the process in the 19th century.

pastille NOUN **pastilles** a small sugary sweet, often sucked as a medicine for sore throats or coughs

pastime NOUN **pastimes** something you enjoy spending your time doing

pastor NOUN **pastors** a religious minister or priest

pastoral ADJECTIVE **1** to do with the countryside or country life: *a pastoral scene* **2** concerned with people's general needs rather than their religion or education

past participle NOUN **past participles** (*grammar*) the form of a verb used after a helping verb such as *has* or *was* to show that something happened in the past. For example, *fought* in *I have fought with my brother* is a past participle

pastry NOUN **pastries 1** pastry is a mixture of flour and fat used to make pies and cakes **2** a pastry is a cake made with pastry

past tense NOUN (*grammar*) the past

tense of a verb is used to refer to things that happened or existed before the present. For example: *The race was over so I relaxed and put my feet up.*

pasture NOUN **pastures** a field with grass for cattle and other animals to eat

pasty[1] (pronounced **pais**-ti) ADJECTIVE **pastier, pastiest** having unhealthily pale skin, especially on the face

pasty[2] (pronounced **pas**-ti) NOUN **pasties** a small pie made with pastry filled with chopped meat and vegetables

pat VERB **pats, patting, patted** to pat someone or something is to hit them or it gently with your hand, usually as a sign of affection
NOUN **pats** a light, gentle blow or touch, usually with the palm of your hand

patch NOUN **patches 1** a piece of material sewn on to a piece of clothing to cover a hole or tear **2** a piece of material worn over a damaged or blind eye **3** a small area of something: *a patch of grass*
• **not a patch on someone** or **something** not nearly as good as someone or something else: *He's a good player, but not a patch on Wayne Rooney.*
VERB **patches, patching, patched** to patch something is to repair a tear or hole in it by sewing a piece of material over it
• **patch up** to patch up a quarrel is to end it and be friendly again
• **patch something up** to patch something up is to mend it

patchwork NOUN small pieces of fabric sewn together in a decorative pattern

patchy ADJECTIVE **patchier, patchiest** not evenly spread, or good only in parts: *patchy fog* • *The standard of cooking can be a bit patchy.*

pâté NOUN **pâtés** a smooth or lumpy paste made by chopping and blending meat, fish or vegetables with flavourings

patent NOUN **patents** (pronounced **pay**-tent or **pat**-int) a licence from the government that gives one person or company the right to make and sell

a product and to stop others from copying it
VERB **patents, patenting, patented** (pronounced **pay**-tent or **pat**-int) to patent something you have invented or developed is to get a licence for it from the government
ADJECTIVE (pronounced **pay**-tent) obvious: *his patent lack of enthusiasm*
▶ **patently** ADVERB very clearly: *It's patently obvious he had no intention of doing it.*

paternal ADJECTIVE **1** to do with, or behaving like, a father: *He showed off his daughter's trophy with paternal pride.* **2** from your father's side of the family: *my paternal grandparents*

path NOUN **paths 1** a track across a piece of land made or used by people or animals walking **2** the line along which something travels **3** a particular course of action or way of doing something

pathetic ADJECTIVE **1** something pathetic causes you to feel pity or sadness: *the pathetic cries of a lost kitten* **2** if you say a person or thing is pathetic you think they are useless or hopeless: *This knife is pathetic. It won't even cut butter!*

pathway NOUN **pathways** a route from one place to another that people or things travel along

patience NOUN **1** the ability or willingness to stay calm: *Mr Green lost patience with him, which he seldom did with any of the pupils.* **2** a card game played by one person

patient ADJECTIVE a patient person is able to stay calm and self-controlled, especially when they have to wait a long time for something or tolerate something
NOUN **patients** someone being seen or treated by a doctor, or being treated for a particular illness: *The nurse called, 'Next patient, please.'* • *kidney patients*
▶ **patiently** ADVERB in a patient way: *waiting patiently for a bus*

patio NOUN **patios** a paved area beside or at the back of a house, used for sitting outdoors in good weather

Aa
Bb
Cc
Dd
Ee
Ff
Gg
Hh
Ii
Jj
Kk
Ll
Mm
Nn
Oo
Pp
Qq
Rr
Ss
Tt
Uu
Vv
Ww
Xx
Yy
Zz

Aa

Bb

Cc

Dd

Ee

Ff

Gg

Hh

Ii

Jj

Kk

Ll

Mm

Nn

Oo

Pp

Qq

Rr

Ss

Tt

Uu

Vv

Ww

Xx

Yy

Zz

patriot NOUN **patriots** someone who loves and is loyal to his or her country
▶ **patriotic** ADJECTIVE loving, and loyal to, your country
▶ **patriotism** NOUN loyalty to and pride in your country

patrol VERB **patrols, patrolling, patrolled** to patrol an area is to go around it looking out for trouble or making sure no one is there who should not be
NOUN **patrols 1** a police or army patrol is the group of soldiers or policemen who patrol an area **2** someone on patrol is walking around a building or area making sure there is no trouble or no one is trying to get in without permission

patron NOUN **patrons 1** if an artist or musician has a patron, they have someone who supports them and buys their work **2** a patron of a charity is someone, usually someone well-known, who gives it their public support **3** a shop's or business's patrons are its customers
▶ **patronage** NOUN support or money given by a patron to the arts or a charity

patter[1] VERB **patters, pattering, pattered** to make quick, light, tapping sounds: *rain pattering on the windows*
NOUN a series of quick, light, tapping sounds: *the patter of mice as they scurried around in the attic*

patter[2] NOUN patter is fast talk, such as when someone is trying to sell you something

pattern NOUN **patterns 1** a guide used for making something: *a sewing pattern* **2** a design that is repeated over and over again, for example on a piece of fabric or on wallpaper **3** the way in which something happens or is organized: *the pattern of the seasons*
▶ **patterned** ADJECTIVE having a pattern

patty NOUN **patties** a small flat cake made with chopped meat or vegetables and usually fried

pause VERB **pauses, pausing, paused** to stop what you are doing for a short time
NOUN **pauses** a short stop

pave VERB **paves, paving, paved** to pave an area is to lay paving stones or some other hard material on it

pavement NOUN **pavements** a raised path beside a road, for pedestrians to walk on

pavilion NOUN **pavilions 1** a building at a sports ground where players change their clothes and keep their equipment **2** a large building or tent

paw NOUN **paws** an animal's foot
VERB **paws, pawing, pawed** an animal paws something when it feels or touches it with its paw

pawn VERB **pawns, pawning, pawned** to pawn something valuable is to give it to someone in exchange for a loan. If the loan is repaid, the article is given back to the person who has pawned it
NOUN **pawns** in the game of chess, a pawn is one of the small, least important pieces
▶ **pawnbroker** NOUN **pawnbrokers** someone who runs a shop where people can pawn valuable things

pay VERB **pays, paying, paid**
1 to pay for something is to give money in exchange for it
2 to pay someone is to give them money for something or for doing something for you
3 it pays to do something if it brings you a benefit of some sort: *Crime does not pay.*
4 to pay for something you have done is to suffer because of it: *I paid for my laziness when I failed the test.*
5 to pay attention or a compliment is to give it
• **pay someone back** if someone has done something bad to you and you pay them back, you do something bad to them in return
NOUN someone's pay is the amount of money they get for doing their job
▶ **payment** NOUN **payments 1** an amount of money paid for something **2** paying money or being paid

PC ABBREVIATION **PCs 1** short for **personal computer 2** short for **police**

constable, used before a police officer's name: *PC Evans*

PE ABBREVIATION short for **physical education**

pea NOUN **peas** a small, round, green vegetable that grows in pods on a climbing plant

peace NOUN there is peace when there is no war, or everything is quiet and calm: *The two countries have been at peace for 50 years.* • *I want a little peace to get on with my homework.*

▶ **peaceful** ADJECTIVE **1** a peaceful place is quiet and calm **2** a peaceful nation does not try to go to war with other countries

▶ **peacefully** ADVERB quietly and calmly

✦ The words **peace** and **piece** sound the same but remember that they have different spellings. A **piece** is a bit of something.

peach NOUN **peaches** a soft round fruit with a velvety skin, pale orange flesh and a large stone inside

peacock NOUN **peacocks** a large bird belonging to the same family as pheasants. The male bird's tail, which he can raise and spread out like a fan, has long blue and green feathers with round black markings at the ends

peak NOUN **peaks 1** a peak is the pointed top of a mountain or hill, or anything that looks like this: *snow-covered peaks* • *Beat the egg whites until they form soft peaks.* **2** the peak of something is its highest, greatest or busiest point or time: *the peak of perfection* **3** the peak of a cap is the front part that sticks out

VERB **peaks, peaking, peaked** something peaks when it reaches its highest, greatest or busiest point or time: *Traffic usually peaks about 5 or 6 o'clock.*

✦ The words **peak** and **peek** sound the same but remember that they have different spellings. A **peek** is a quick look.

peal NOUN **peals 1** a sound made by one or more large bells ringing together **2** a loud rolling noise, such as thunder makes

VERB **peals, pealing, pealed 1** bells peal when they ring loudly together **2** thunder peals when it makes a loud continuous noise

peanut NOUN **peanuts** a kind of nut that grows underground in a shell similar to a pea pod

peanut butter NOUN a thick paste made with crushed peanuts which you spread on bread

pear NOUN **pears** a fruit which is round at the bottom and narrows towards the stem at the top

✦ The words **pear** and **pair** sound the same but remember that they have different spellings. A **pair** is a set of two things.

pearl NOUN **pearls** a valuable, white, rounded stone formed by oysters and some other shellfish inside their shells

peasant NOUN **peasants** someone who lives and works on the land, especially a farmer who owns a small piece of land that he works on himself

peat NOUN **peats** material formed in the ground over many years as layers of dead plants rot down, and used for gardening and as a fuel for burning

pebble NOUN **pebbles** a small stone that has been worn smooth by water

peck VERB **pecks, pecking, pecked** a bird pecks when it taps or hits something, or picks something up, with its beak

NOUN **pecks 1** a tap or bite with the beak **2** a quick light kiss: *a peck on the cheek*

peckish ADJECTIVE if you feel peckish, you feel a little bit hungry

peculiar ADJECTIVE **1** strange or odd: *a very peculiar smell* **2** something that is peculiar to a person, place or thing, belongs to, or is found in, that particular person, place or thing, and no other

▶ **peculiarity** NOUN **peculiarities 1** an odd or strange thing, or the quality

Aa
Bb
Cc
Dd
Ee
Ff
Gg
Hh
Ii
Jj
Kk
Ll
Mm
Nn
Oo
Pp
Qq
Rr
Ss
Tt
Uu
Vv
Ww
Xx
Yy
Zz

Aa
Bb
Cc
Dd
Ee
Ff
Gg
Hh
Ii
Jj
Kk
Ll
Mm
Nn
Oo
Pp
Qq
Rr
Ss
Tt
Uu
Vv
Ww
Xx
Yy
Zz

of being odd or strange **2** a distinctive feature or characteristic
▸ **peculiarly** ADVERB **1** strangely: *behaving very peculiarly* **2** in a distinctive way: *a peculiarly British habit*

pedal NOUN **pedals** a lever worked by the foot, such as on a bicycle or piano
VERB **pedals, pedalling, pedalled** to pedal a bike or toy car is to make it move forward by pressing down on the pedals

peddle VERB **peddles, peddling, peddled** to peddle goods or wares is to go from place to place or house to house selling them

pedestal NOUN **pedestals** the base that something stands on, for example a statue or wash hand basin

pedestrian NOUN **pedestrians** someone who is walking on a pavement or road

pedigree NOUN **pedigrees** **1** if an animal has a pedigree, there is a record showing that its parents and other ancestors were all of the same breed **2** your pedigree is your background or the people you are descended from
ADJECTIVE having a pedigree: *a pedigree cow*

pedlar NOUN **pedlars** a person who travels round selling small objects, usually from door to door

peek VERB **peeks, peeking, peeked** to look, especially when you should not be looking
NOUN **peeks** a quick look

✦ The words **peek** and **peak** sound the same but remember that they have different spellings. A **peak** is the top of something.

peel VERB **peels, peeling, peeled 1** to peel a fruit or vegetable is to take off its skin or outer covering **2** paint or skin peels when it comes off in small pieces
NOUN peel is the skin of certain fruits and vegetables

peep VERB **peeps, peeping, peeped** to look through a narrow opening or from behind something
NOUN **peeps** a quick look at something

peer VERB **peers, peering, peered** to peer at something is to look at it with your eyes narrowed because you cannot see very clearly
NOUN **peers 1** your peers are the people who are the same age, class or status as you **2** in Britain, peers are members of the nobility or people who have been awarded a title

peg NOUN **pegs 1** a wooden, plastic or metal clip used for hanging clothes on a washing line **2** a hook for hanging coats, hats or jackets on **3** a piece of wood or metal driven into the ground to secure a tent, or as a marker

Pekinese *or* **Pekingese** NOUN **Pekineses** *or* **Pekingeses** a type of small dog with long silky hair, large eyes and a small wrinkled nose

pelican NOUN **pelicans** a large white bird found in tropical parts of the world, which dives for fish and stores the ones it catches in a pouch under its beak

pelican crossing NOUN **pelican crossings** a road crossing for pedestrians with lights that are operated by the people waiting to cross

pellet NOUN **pellets** a small hard round object formed by pressing and rolling material into a tightly-packed ball

pelt VERB **pelts, pelting, pelted 1** to pelt someone with things is to throw things at them one after the other **2** rain pelts down when it falls fast and heavily **3** to pelt is to run or move very fast: *He came pelting down the road on his bike.*
NOUN **pelts** the skin from an animal: *beaver pelts*

pelvis NOUN **pelvises** your pelvis is the bowl-shaped bone at your hips

pen¹ NOUN **pens** an instrument for writing or drawing in ink

pen² NOUN **pens** a small area of land surrounded by a fence and used for keeping animals in

pen³ NOUN **pens** a female swan

penalize *or* **penalise** VERB **penalizes, penalizing, penalized** to penalize someone is to punish them for doing something that is against the rules

penalty NOUN **penalties 1** a punishment for doing wrong **2** in games like football, rugby and hockey, a penalty is a free shot at goal given because a player in the other team has broken a rule of the game

penance NOUN if someone does penance they suffer a punishment willingly to make up for doing something wrong

pence NOUN the plural of **penny**

pencil NOUN **pencils** something you use for writing or drawing, which has a stick of graphite or a coloured stick through the middle of it

pendant NOUN **pendants** an ornament that hangs from a chain or necklace

pendulum NOUN **pendulums** a weight that swings from side to side and operates the mechanism of a clock

penetrate VERB **penetrates, penetrating, penetrated** to get into or through something: *Rain could not penetrate those thick trees.*
▸ **penetration** NOUN going into or through something

pen friend NOUN **pen friends** a **pen pal**

penguin NOUN **penguins** a bird that cannot fly but which uses its wings like flippers to swim underwater. Penguins are found in the Antarctic

penicillin NOUN a drug used to treat diseases and illnesses caused by bacteria

peninsula NOUN **peninsulas** (*geography*) a piece of land surrounded by water on every side except the end where it joins a larger land mass
▸ **peninsular** ADJECTIVE to do with, or formed like, a peninsula

penis NOUN **penises** the organ male animals use to urinate and reproduce

penknife NOUN **penknives** a small knife with blades that fold into the handle and which you can carry in your pocket

pennant NOUN **pennants** a small narrow flag that tapers to a point at one end

penniless ADJECTIVE if someone is penniless, they have no money

penny NOUN **pennies** a small bronze British coin worth one hundredth of £1

pen pal NOUN **pen pals** a friend you exchange letters with, but do not meet

pension NOUN **pensions** a sum of money paid regularly to a person who has retired from work
▸ **pensioner** NOUN **pensioners** a retired person who is receiving a pension

pentagon NOUN **pentagons** (*maths*) a flat shape with five straight sides and five angles
▸ **pentagonal** ADJECTIVE having five sides: *a pentagonal dish*

pentathlon NOUN **pentathlons** an athletics competition that has five different kinds of sporting contest: swimming, cross-country riding, running, fencing and pistol-shooting

pentecost NOUN **1** a Jewish festival held fifty days after Passover **2** a Christian festival held seven weeks after Easter

penultimate ADJECTIVE the penultimate thing is the last but one in a series

people NOUN **peoples 1** people are men, women and children **2** a people is one of the races of human beings: *all the peoples of the world* **3** the plural of **person**: *one person or many people*
VERB **peoples, peopling, peopled** a place is peopled by a certain group if they are the people who live there

pepper NOUN **peppers 1** pepper is a hot-tasting powder made by grinding dried seeds called peppercorns **2** a pepper is a red, yellow, orange or green hollow fruit used as a vegetable
▸ **peppery** ADJECTIVE hot-tasting, like pepper

peppermint NOUN **peppermints 1** peppermint is a strong flavouring obtained from a type of mint plant, used in sweets and toothpaste **2** a sweet flavoured with peppermint
ADJECTIVE flavoured with peppermint: *peppermint toothpaste*

per PREPOSITION **1** for every or for each:

Aa
Bb
Cc
Dd
Ee
Ff
Gg
Hh
Ii
Jj
Kk
Ll
Mm
Nn
Oo
Pp
Qq
Rr
Ss
Tt
Uu
Vv
Ww
Xx
Yy
Zz

Aa
Bb
Cc
Dd
Ee
Ff
Gg
Hh
Ii
Jj
Kk
Ll
Mm
Nn
Oo
Pp
Qq
Rr
Ss
Tt
Uu
Vv
Ww
Xx
Yy
Zz

The meal will cost £15 per person. **2** in every or in each: *sixty kilometres per hour*

perceive VERB **perceives, perceiving, perceived** to perceive something is to notice it with one of your senses: *the way that humans perceive colour*

percent ADVERB in or for every 100: *forty per cent*

▸ **percentage** NOUN **percentages 1** a number or amount in each hundred, written as a fraction with that number over a hundred, for example ³⁵⁄₁₀₀. It can also be written with a percentage sign, for example 35% **2** a part or proportion of something: *A high percentage of pupils get top grades.*

perception NOUN **perceptions 1** the ability to see, hear or understand **2** your perception of something is the way you see or understand it

perceptive ADJECTIVE a perceptive person is good at noticing or understanding things

perch VERB **perches, perching, perched 1** a bird perches when it sits or stands on a branch or some other place above the ground **2** to perch somewhere high or narrow is to sit there

NOUN **perches** a branch or other place above the ground that a bird sits or stands on

percussion NOUN (*music*) musical instruments that you play by hitting them with your hands or with sticks, or by shaking them. Drums, cymbals, tambourines and triangles are percussion instruments

perfect ADJECTIVE (pronounced per-**fikt**) **1** without any mistakes or faults: *a perfect score* **2** exact: *a perfect circle* **3** complete: *a perfect stranger*

VERB **perfects, perfecting, perfected** (pronounced per-**fekt**) to perfect something is to make it perfect, without any faults

▸ **perfection** NOUN making perfect or being perfect

▸ **perfectly** ADVERB **1** without any mistakes or faults: *She did the pirouette perfectly.* **2** exactly: *perfectly square* **3** completely: *perfectly ridiculous*

perfect number NOUN **perfect numbers** (*maths*) a number that is the sum of all the numbers (including 1 but excluding the number itself) that can be multiplied to give that number as a result. For example, 6 is a perfect number because $1+2+3=6$, and 28 is also a perfect number because $1+2+4+7+14=28$

perforate VERB **perforates, perforating, perforated** to perforate something is to pierce it and make a small hole in it

▸ **perforation** NOUN **perforations** a small hole made in something, especially the series of small holes made around the edges of stamps so that they can be torn from the sheet

perform VERB **performs, performing, performed 1** to perform something, such as a play, piece of music or a dance is to do it in front of an audience **2** to perform something is to do it or carry it out: *Surgeons perform operations.*

▸ **performance** NOUN **performances 1** something performed in front of an audience **2** a level of success achieved in doing something: *a brilliant performance*

▸ **performer** NOUN **performers** someone who does an act in front of an audience

perfume NOUN **perfumes 1** a perfume is a smell, especially a pleasant one **2** perfume is a pleasant smelling liquid or cream that you put on your body to make it smell nice

VERB **perfumes, perfuming, perfumed** to perfume something is to put perfume on it or fill it with a pleasant smell

perhaps ADVERB possibly or maybe: *The bus is late – perhaps it has broken down again.*

peril NOUN **perils** danger: *the perils of sailing round the world alone* • *The business's future was in peril.*

▸ **perilous** ADJECTIVE very dangerous or full of danger: *a perilous journey on foot across miles of desert*

perimeter NOUN **perimeters 1** the perimeter of an area is its outer edge or boundary **2** (*maths*) the perimeter of a flat shape is the length around its outside edge

period NOUN **periods 1** a period of time is a length of time: *a period of several weeks* **2** a stage or phase in history: *the Regency period* **3** a woman's or girl's period is the time each month when blood flows from her womb

ADJECTIVE from or in the style of a period in history: *period costumes*

▶ **periodic** ADJECTIVE for a certain length of time and at regular intervals: *He gets periodic bouts of asthma.*

▶ **periodical** NOUN **periodicals** a magazine that is published regularly, for example once a week or once a month

periscope NOUN **periscopes** an instrument consisting of a special arrangement of angled mirrors in a tube, which makes it possible for you to look at things over the top of a barrier in front of you. Periscopes are used in submarines

perish VERB **perishes, perishing, perished** to die, especially in a war or from extreme cold

perk VERB **perks, perking, perked**

• **perk up** if you perk up, you feel more lively and cheerful

NOUN **perks** a perk is an extra benefit or advantage that someone gets from their job

perm NOUN **perms** a chemical treatment for hair that gives a long-lasting curly hairstyle

VERB **perms, perming, permed** to perm hair is to treat it with chemicals so that it stays in a curly style for a long time

permafrost NOUN (*geography*) ground that is permanently frozen in cold areas of the world

permanent ADJECTIVE **1** lasting for ever, or for a long time: *Will the scar be permanent?* **2** a permanent job is one that is expected to last for a long time, rather than being temporary **3** never changing: *a permanent state of chaos*

▶ **permanently** ADVERB for ever

permeable ADJECTIVE if rock or soil is permeable, it allows water through it

permissible ADJECTIVE something that is permissible is allowed

permission NOUN you get or are given permission to do something when someone says you are allowed to do it

permit VERB (pronounced per-**mit**) **permits, permitting, permitted** to permit something is to allow it to happen

NOUN (pronounced **per**-mit) **permits** an official document allowing a person to do something: *a fishing permit*

perpendicular ADJECTIVE **1** standing straight upwards: *a perpendicular line* **2** (*maths*) touching another line to make a right angle. For example, the touching lines in a rectangle are perpendicular to each other

perpetual ADJECTIVE never ending or continuous: *perpetual darkness*

perplex VERB **perplexes, perplexing, perplexed** if something perplexes you, it puzzles or baffles you

▶ **perplexed** ADJECTIVE puzzled: *a perplexed expression*

▶ **perplexity** NOUN being puzzled or confused: *'Hum!' said he, scratching his chin in some perplexity.*

persecute VERB **persecutes, persecuting, persecuted** to persecute someone is to make them suffer, especially because of their opinions or beliefs

▶ **persecution** NOUN being persecuted

persevere VERB **perseveres, persevering, persevered** to continue with something even though it is difficult

▶ **perseverance** NOUN getting on with something even if it is difficult

persist VERB **persists, persisting, persisted 1** if something persists, it continues for a long time **2** you persist with something when you keep on doing it and refuse to give up **3** to keep talking about something: *'It was you,' I persisted.*

▶ **persistence** NOUN continuing with something in spite of people saying you should not

Aa
Bb
Cc
Dd
Ee
Ff
Gg
Hh
Ii
Jj
Kk
Ll
Mm
Nn
Oo
Pp
Qq
Rr
Ss
Tt
Uu
Vv
Ww
Xx
Yy
Zz

▶ **persistent** ADJECTIVE **1** refusing to give up: *Even though I said I wasn't interested, the salesman was very persistent.* **2** continuing without a break: *persistent rain*

person NOUN **people** *or* **persons** a human being

• **in person** someone does something in person when they do it themselves, instead of someone else doing it for them

personal ADJECTIVE **1** belonging to, or done by, one particular person and no one else: *a personal opinion* • *a personal appearance* **2** private: *It's personal and none of your business.*

▶ **personality** NOUN **personalities** **1** your personality is your character and the qualities you have **2** someone with personality behaves in a way that makes a strong impression on you **3** a personality is a famous person

▶ **personally** ADVERB **1** you say 'personally' when you are giving your own opinion about something: *'Personally, I would have ignored it.'* **2** done by you and not by anyone else: *He wrote to everyone personally.*

personnel NOUN the personnel in a business or organization are the people employed in it or who are part of it

perspective NOUN **perspectives 1** (*art*) the technique of drawing solid objects on a flat surface so that they appear to have the correct shape and distance from each other **2** if you put something that happens into perspective, you do not make it more important than it is **3** a point of view: *Try to see things from a different perspective.*

perspire VERB **perspires, perspiring, perspired** to sweat

▶ **perspiration** NOUN sweat

persuade VERB **persuades, persuading, persuaded** to persuade someone is to give them good reasons why they should, or should not, do something

▶ **persuasion** NOUN persuading

▶ **persuasive** ADJECTIVE a persuasive person or argument can change

your mind or make you decide to do something

perturb VERB **perturbs, perturbing, perturbed** something perturbs you when it makes you feel uncomfortable and worried

▶ **perturbed** ADJECTIVE worried

pessimism NOUN the habit of expecting things to turn out badly. Look up and compare **optimism**

▶ **pessimist** NOUN **pessimists** someone who usually expects bad things to happen

▶ **pessimistic** ADJECTIVE expecting that things will turn out badly: *a pessimistic outlook*

pest NOUN **pests 1** an insect that eats crops and garden plants, or an animal that destroys things **2** someone who is a pest is a nuisance

pester VERB **pesters, pestering, pestered** to pester someone is to annoy them continually

pesticide NOUN **pesticides** a substance used to kill insects that eat or destroy plants and crops

pet NOUN **pets 1** a tame animal that you keep in your home **2** a person who is given special attention and seems to be the favourite: *He's teacher's pet.*
VERB **pets, petting, petted** to pet an animal is to pat it and stroke it

petal NOUN **petals** one of the coloured parts of a flower

peter VERB **peters, petering, petered**
• **peter out** if something peters out, it gradually comes to an end or stop

petite ADJECTIVE a girl or woman who is petite is attractively small or slim

petition NOUN **petitions** a request for something, especially one signed by many people and sent to a government or someone in authority

petrify VERB **petrifies, petrifying, petrified** if something petrifies you, it frightens you very much

petrochemical NOUN **petrochemicals** a chemical made from petroleum or natural gas

petrol NOUN a fuel for engines, made from oil

petroleum NOUN an oil found underground or under the seabed and used to make petrol

petticoat NOUN **petticoats** a piece of clothing that a girl or woman wears under her skirt

petty ADJECTIVE **pettier, pettiest 1** having very little importance: *petty details* **2** if someone is being petty, they concentrate on or criticize small unimportant details

petulant ADJECTIVE someone who is petulant is bad-tempered, impatient and huffy, like a spoilt child

▸ **petulance** NOUN being huffy and impatient

pew NOUN **pews** a long wooden bench in a church

pewter NOUN a dull grey metal made from a mixture of lead and tin

PG ABBREVIATION short for **parental guidance**, a film classification used in Britain, which means that some parts may not be suitable for a child to see

pH NOUN (*science*) a scale used to measure the acidity or alkalinity of a solution. Acids have a pH value between 0 and 7 and alkalis have a pH value between 7 and 14

phantom NOUN **phantoms** a ghost

pharaoh (pronounced **fay**-roh) NOUN **pharaohs** one of the powerful rulers of ancient Egypt

pharmacist NOUN **pharmacists** someone who prepares and sells medicines

▸ **pharmacy** NOUN **pharmacies** a shop where medicines are prepared and sold

phase NOUN **phases** a stage in something's development or progress
VERB **phases, phasing, phased**
• **phase something in** *or* **out** to phase something in, or to phase it out, is to introduce it, or get rid of it, gradually or in stages

pheasant (pronounced **fez**-int) NOUN **pheasants** a large bird with a long tail, that is hunted for sport and eaten

phenomenal ADJECTIVE extraordinary or amazing

▸ **phenomenally** ADVERB in an extraordinary way: *a phenomenally good show*

phenomenon NOUN **phenomena** something that is seen to happen or exist, especially something that is interesting or unusual

philately (pronounced fil-**at**-i-li) NOUN stamp collecting

▸ **philatelist** NOUN **philatelists** someone who collects postage stamps

philosopher NOUN **philosophers** someone who studies philosophy

philosophical ADJECTIVE **1** to do with philosophy **2** if you are philosophical about something, such as a disappointment, you stay calm and are not upset by it

philosophy NOUN **philosophies 1** philosophy is the search for knowledge and truth about the universe and human beings and their behaviour **2** a philosophy is a set of beliefs

phobia NOUN **phobias** an unreasonable fear or hatred of something

phoenix (pronounced **fee**-niks) NOUN **phoenixes** in stories and myths, a bird that burns itself on a fire and is born again from its own ashes

phone NOUN **phones** a telephone
VERB **phones, phoning, phoned** to phone someone is to call them on the telephone

phoneme (pronounced **foan**-eem) NOUN **phonemes** one of the sounds that you use to say things in your language. For example, the sounds 'ee' and 'f' are phonemes: *There are different ways to spell the same phoneme.*

phoney ADJECTIVE **phonier, phoniest** fake or false: *a phoney French accent*

photo NOUN **photos** a photograph

photocopier NOUN **photocopiers** a machine that copies a document by taking a photograph of it

photograph NOUN **photographs** a picture taken by a camera
VERB **photographs, photographing, photographed** to photograph something is to take a picture of it using a camera

Aa
Bb
Cc
Dd
Ee
Ff
Gg
Hh
Ii
Jj
Kk
Ll
Mm
Nn
Oo
Pp
Qq
Rr
Ss
Tt
Uu
Vv
Ww
Xx
Yy
Zz

photosynthesis

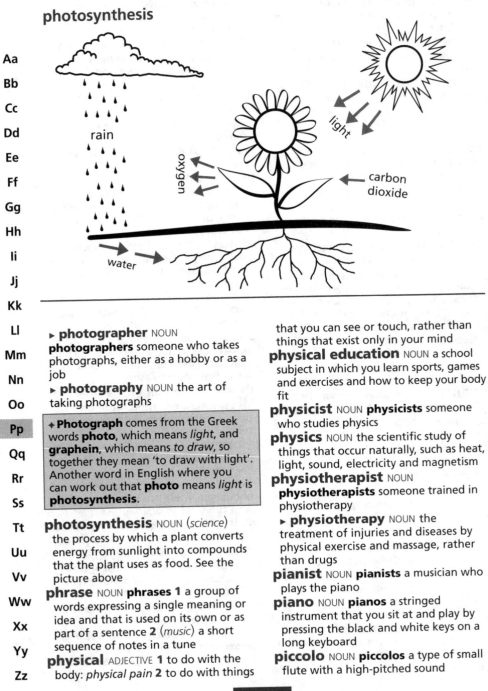

rain

oxygen

light

carbon dioxide

water

Aa
Bb
Cc
Dd
Ee
Ff
Gg
Hh
Ii
Jj
Kk
Ll
Mm
Nn
Oo
Pp
Qq
Rr
Ss
Tt
Uu
Vv
Ww
Xx
Yy
Zz

▶ **photographer** NOUN **photographers** someone who takes photographs, either as a hobby or as a job

▶ **photography** NOUN the art of taking photographs

✦ **Photograph** comes from the Greek words **photo**, which means *light*, and **graphein**, which means *to draw*, so together they mean 'to draw with light'. Another word in English where you can work out that **photo** means *light* is **photosynthesis**.

photosynthesis NOUN (*science*) the process by which a plant converts energy from sunlight into compounds that the plant uses as food. See the picture above

phrase NOUN **phrases 1** a group of words expressing a single meaning or idea and that is used on its own or as part of a sentence **2** (*music*) a short sequence of notes in a tune

physical ADJECTIVE **1** to do with the body: *physical pain* **2** to do with things

that you can see or touch, rather than things that exist only in your mind

physical education NOUN a school subject in which you learn sports, games and exercises and how to keep your body fit

physicist NOUN **physicists** someone who studies physics

physics NOUN the scientific study of things that occur naturally, such as heat, light, sound, electricity and magnetism

physiotherapist NOUN **physiotherapists** someone trained in physiotherapy

▶ **physiotherapy** NOUN the treatment of injuries and diseases by physical exercise and massage, rather than drugs

pianist NOUN **pianists** a musician who plays the piano

piano NOUN **pianos** a stringed instrument that you sit at and play by pressing the black and white keys on a long keyboard

piccolo NOUN **piccolos** a type of small flute with a high-pitched sound

pick VERB **picks, picking, picked**
1 to pick a person or thing is to choose them
2 to pick something, or pick it off, is to lift it off, using your finger and thumb
3 to pick fruit or flowers is to break or pull them off the plant or tree they are growing on
4 to pick a lock is to use a piece of wire to open it
5 to pick a fight or quarrel is to deliberately get someone to fight or quarrel with you
• **pick on someone** to bully someone or treat them unkindly
• **pick someone up** to go and fetch someone from the place where they are waiting to be collected
• **pick something up 1** to lift something using your fingers or hands **2** to learn something by watching or listening rather than being taught in a lesson
NOUN **picks 1** if you have, or take, your pick of things, you choose whichever you like **2** the pick of a group of people or things are the best in that group

picket VERB **pickets, picketing, picketed** to stand outside a factory or other place of work in order to protest about something and to persuade other workers not to go in

pickpocket NOUN **pickpockets** a criminal who steals things from people's pockets

picky ADJECTIVE **pickier, pickiest** fussy

picnic NOUN **picnics** a meal that you have outdoors at a place that you walk or travel to
VERB **picnics, picnicking, picnicked** to have a picnic
▸ **picnicker** NOUN **picnickers** people who are having a picnic

pictogram NOUN **pictograms** a picture or symbol that represents a letter, word or idea, used instead of letters of the alphabet in some writing systems, for example in Chinese

pictorial ADJECTIVE having lots of pictures or using pictures to show something

picture NOUN **pictures 1** a painting, drawing or photograph **2** an image: *He had a picture in his mind of what he wanted to do.* • *television pictures*
VERB **pictures, picturing, pictured** to picture something is to form an image of it in your mind
ADJECTIVE with a picture or pictures: *a picture postcard* • *a picture book*

picturesque ADJECTIVE attractive or interesting to look at: *a picturesque old castle*

pie NOUN **pies** food baked in a covering of pastry

piebald ADJECTIVE having patches of two different colours, especially black and white: *a piebald horse*

piece NOUN **pieces**
1 a part or bit of something: *a jigsaw with 300 pieces* • *a piece of cake*
2 something that has been written or composed: *There's a short piece in the paper about our school.* • *a piece of music*
3 one of the objects you move about the board in games like chess
4 a coin of a particular value: *a 50p piece* • *'Pieces of eight, pieces of eight,'* squawked the parrot.
VERB **pieces, piecing, pieced**
• **piece things together** to fit things together to try to make something that is complete

✦ The words **piece** and **peace** sound the same but remember that they have different spellings. **Peace** is quietness and calmness.

piecemeal ADJECTIVE AND ADVERB to do things piecemeal or in a piecemeal way is to do a little bit at a time and in no particular order

pie chart NOUN **pie charts** a chart in the form of a circle divided into sections, showing the different amounts that something is divided into

pied ADJECTIVE having two colours, like the red and yellow costume of the Pied Piper or the black and white plumage of a magpie

pier NOUN **piers** a platform of stone or

Aa
Bb
Cc
Dd
Ee
Ff
Gg
Hh
Ii
Jj
Kk
Ll
Mm
Nn
Oo
Pp
Qq
Rr
Ss
Tt
Uu
Vv
Ww
Xx
Yy
Zz

wood by a lake or the sea, where boats and ships can tie up

pierce VERB **pierces, piercing, pierced** a sharp object pierces something when it goes in or through it

▶ **piercing** ADJECTIVE a piercing sound is very sharp and seems to travel through solid objects

pig NOUN **pigs** an animal with a broad heavy body, small eyes and a snout

pigeon NOUN **pigeons** a bird with a plump body and a small head, often seen in towns and cities or kept for racing

pigeonhole NOUN **pigeonholes** one of a series of boxes or compartments, each for a different person, used to put their letters or messages in

VERB **pigeonholes, pigeonholing, pigeonholed** to pigeonhole someone is to decide what type of person they are or what they are suitable for

piggyback NOUN **piggybacks** someone gives you a piggyback when they carry you on their back with their arms supporting your legs

pig-headed ADJECTIVE stubborn

piglet NOUN **piglets** a baby pig

pigment NOUN **pigments 1** any substance used for colouring or making paint or dye **2** the substance in your skin that gives it its colour

pigmy NOUN **pigmies** another spelling of **pygmy**

pigsty NOUN **pigsties 1** a pen where pigs are kept **2** a dirty or very untidy place

pigtail NOUN **pigtails** hair that has been plaited and hangs down at the side or back of the head

pike NOUN **pike** or **pikes** a large fish that lives in freshwater lakes

pilchard NOUN **pilchards** a small sea fish, rather like a herring, that you eat fresh or buy packed in tins

pile NOUN **piles 1** a heap or stack of things one on top of the other **2** piles of something means a lot of it: *My little brother has piles of toys.*

VERB **piles, piling, piled** to pile things or pile them up is to put them one on top of the other in a heap or stack

pilfer VERB **pilfers, pilfering, pilfered** to steal small amounts of something or small items, especially from the place where you work

pilgrim NOUN **pilgrims** a person who is travelling to a holy place

▶ **pilgrimage** NOUN **pilgrimages** a journey that someone makes to a holy place

pill NOUN **pills** a small tablet of medicine

pillage VERB **pillages, pillaging, pillaged** when invaders or enemies pillage they steal things from the place they have invaded or conquered

pillar NOUN **pillars** an upright post used in building as a support or decoration

pillarbox NOUN **pillarboxes** a metal container in the street for posting letters in

pillion NOUN **pillions** a seat for a passenger behind the rider or driver of a bicycle or motorbike

pillow NOUN **pillows** a large soft cushion that you lay your head on when you are in bed

pillowcase or **pillowslip** NOUN **pillowcases** or **pillowslips** a cloth covering for a pillow

pilot NOUN **pilots** someone who flies a plane, or who guides a ship into and out of a harbour

VERB **pilots, piloting, piloted** to pilot a plane is to operate its controls

pimple NOUN **pimples** a raised spot on the skin

pin NOUN **pins** a short thin pointed piece of metal for pushing through fabric or paper to hold it in place

VERB **pins, pinning, pinned 1** to pin something is to fasten it with a pin **2** to pin something or someone somewhere is to hold them so that they cannot move from that place: *They pinned me to the ground.*

PIN ABBREVIATION short for **personal identification number**, which is a secret number that every person with a bank card uses when they get money out of a cash machine or when they pay for something using their card

pinafore NOUN **pinafores** a sleeveless dress, worn over a blouse or jumper

pincers PLURAL NOUN **1** a tool for gripping things tightly **2** a lobster's or crab's claws

pinch VERB **pinches, pinching, pinched** **1** to pinch someone is to squeeze their skin or flesh tightly between your thumb and forefinger **2** if a shoe or piece of clothing pinches, it hurts you because it is too small or tight **3** (*informal*) to pinch something is to steal it
NOUN **pinches 1** a small amount that you can pick up between your finger and thumb: *add a pinch of salt* **2** a nip with the thumb and forefinger
▶ **pinched** ADJECTIVE if someone's face is pinched, it looks thin and pale because they are cold or ill

pine[1] NOUN **pines** a tall evergreen tree with cones containing seeds and with leaves like needles

pine[2] VERB **pines, pining, pined**
• **pine away** to become weaker and weaker because you are so sad about a person or thing you have lost
• **pine for someone** *or* **something** to want or miss someone or something very much

pineapple NOUN **pineapples** a large fruit with sweet firm yellow flesh and a tough brown skin divided into small diamond shapes

ping VERB **pings, pinging, pinged 1** to make a noise like a small hard object bouncing off metal **2** to ping something, like a wire or piece of elastic, is to pull it so that it bends or stretches, and then let it go suddenly so that it makes a sharp noise
NOUN **pings** a pinging noise: *electronic pings and bleeps*

ping-pong NOUN another name for the game of table tennis

pink NOUN a pale red colour with a lot of white in it
▶ **pinkish** ADJECTIVE quite pink but not completely pink in colour

pint NOUN **pints** an imperial unit for measuring the volume of a liquid, equal to just over half a litre

pioneer VERB **pioneers, pioneering, pioneered** to pioneer something is to be the first to do or make it
NOUN **pioneers 1** someone who is one of the first people to go to a new country to live and work there **2** a person who is the first to develop a new skill or method

pious ADJECTIVE a pious person takes religious rules and morals very seriously and always thinks and acts in a good and religious way

pip NOUN **pips** a small seed from fruits like apples and oranges

pipe NOUN **pipes 1** a metal or plastic tube through which water or gas can flow **2** a tube with a hollow bowl at one end used for smoking tobacco **3** an instrument that you play by blowing air into one end of a hollow tube
VERB **pipes, piping, piped 1** to pipe liquid or gas is to carry it from one place to another through pipes **2** to play a pipe or bagpipes
• **pipe down** used for telling someone to stop talking or making a noise
• **pipe up** someone pipes up when they suddenly say something after they have been quiet for a while

pipeline NOUN **pipelines** a long pipe that crosses the land or sea and carries oil or gas
• **in the pipeline** if something is in the pipeline, it is being dealt with or is going to happen

piper NOUN **pipers** someone who plays a pipe or bagpipes

piping NOUN **1** the piping in a building is the system of pipes through which water or gas flows **2** piping is playing a pipe or the bagpipes
ADVERB
• **piping hot** boiling or nearly boiling

piracy NOUN **1** robbing ships and boats at sea **2** making copies of records or films without permission, to sell or to pass to someone else

piranha NOUN **piranhas** a small fierce fish that lives in rivers in South America

pirate NOUN **pirates 1** someone who robs ships and boats at sea **2** someone

Aa
Bb
Cc
Dd
Ee
Ff
Gg
Hh
Ii
Jj
Kk
Ll
Mm
Nn
Oo
Pp
Qq
Rr
Ss
Tt
Uu
Vv
Ww
Xx
Yy
Zz

pirouette → place

who makes a copy of a record or film without permission, to sell or to pass to someone else

pirouette (pronounced pir-oo-**et**) NOUN **pirouettes** a dance movement in which you spin round very fast while standing on one leg
VERB **pirouettes, pirouetting, pirouetted** to spin your body in a full circle once or several times

pistol NOUN **pistols** a small gun that is held in the hand

piston NOUN **pistons** a round piece of metal that fits inside a cylinder in an engine and moves up and down or backwards and forwards inside it

pit NOUN **pits** 1 a large hole in the ground 2 a deep mine, especially a coal mine
• **the pits** the place on a motor-racing track where the cars can stop to get fuel or have their tyres changed by the mechanics in their team
VERB **pits, pitting, pitted**
• **pit someone against someone** to make one person fight or compete with another person

pitch¹ NOUN **pitches** 1 an area of ground, often with special lines marked on it, used to play games like football, rugby or cricket 2 a sound's pitch is how high or low it is 3 the level or intensity that something reaches: *The excitement reached fever pitch when Zidane headed the ball into the net.*
VERB **pitches, pitching, pitched**
1 to pitch a tent is to put it up
2 to pitch something at a particular level is to set it or direct it at that level: *She pitched her voice low.* • *The programme is pitched at children under five.*
3 to pitch forward is to fall forward suddenly
4 if a ship pitches, it goes up and down from front to back as it moves forward
5 in baseball, you pitch when you are the player who throws the ball at the batting team
• **pitch in** to join in or make a contribution to something

pitch² NOUN pitch is a black sticky substance made from tar
ADJECTIVE it is pitch dark when it is very dark and you can see nothing

pitched battle NOUN **pitched battles** a fierce fight or argument with two people or groups drawn up against each other like armies

pitcher NOUN **pitchers** a large jug

pitchfork NOUN **pitchforks** a tool with two prongs and a long handle, used to lift hay and straw

pitfall NOUN **pitfalls** a possible danger or difficulty, or a mistake that can be made easily

pith NOUN pith is the white layer between the skin and the flesh of an orange or other citrus fruit

pitiful ADJECTIVE 1 sad and pathetic: *a pitiful sight* 2 of such bad quality that you have no respect for it: *a pitiful excuse*

pittance NOUN a very small sum of money

pity NOUN 1 pity is sorrow you feel for other people's troubles or difficulties 2 you say that something is a pity if you are sorry about it 3 to take pity on someone is to feel so sorry for them that you help them or give them something
VERB **pities, pitying, pitied** to pity someone is to feel sorry for them

pivot NOUN **pivots** a pin or centre on which something balances and turns
VERB **pivots, pivoting, pivoted** to turn or revolve while balancing on a central point

pixel NOUN **pixels** (*ICT*) one of the tiny elements that pictures on a computer or TV screen are made up of, with each pixel occupying a unit of computer memory

pixie NOUN **pixies** in stories, a small good fairy or elf

pizza NOUN **pizzas** a flat round piece of dough topped with cheese, tomatoes and herbs and baked in an oven

placard NOUN **placards** a board with a notice or message on it that is carried by someone in public

place NOUN **places** 1 a particular area

or position: *a place by the sea* • *Put the books back in their proper place on the shelf.* • *I imagine Beijing is a very interesting place.* **2** a seat, or a space at a table for someone to sit and eat: *Please go back to your places and sit down.* **3** a position in an order, series or queue: *She was in first place after the second round.* • *Work out this sum to two decimal places.*

• **in place of** instead of: *Kelly's here in place of John, who is ill.*

• **out of place 1** something is out of place when it is not in its usual position **2** you feel out of place when you feel that you do not fit in with the people or things around you

VERB **places, placing, placed 1** to place something somewhere is to put it there **2** to place someone in a certain position is to put them there: *He had placed me in a very awkward spot by promising that I would go to the party.* **3** to place a bet or an order is to make a bet or an order

placid ADJECTIVE gentle and calm

plague NOUN **plagues 1** a large number of insects or other pests that suddenly appear and cause damage or a nuisance **2** the plague is a disease that spreads rapidly and kills many people

VERB **plagues, plaguing, plagued** something plagues you when it causes you a lot of discomfort or annoyance

plaice NOUN **plaice** a type of flat fish found in the sea

plaid (pronounced **plad**) NOUN **plaids** a long piece of cloth, especially with a tartan pattern, that people in Scottish Highland costume wear over their shoulders

plain ADJECTIVE **plainer, plainest**
1 without any decoration or without a pattern: *a plain white room*
2 simple or ordinary: *good plain cooking*
3 easy to see or understand: *as plain as the nose on your face* • *He made it quite plain that he didn't like me.*
4 straightforward: *That's just plain nonsense.*

NOUN **plains** a large flat area of land

✦ The words **plain** and **plane** sound the same but remember that they have different spellings. A **plane** is an aeroplane or a tool for smoothing wood.

plait (pronounced **plat**) NOUN **plaits** lengths of something such as hair or straw that are twisted over each other in turn

VERB **plaits, plaiting, plaited** to twist strands of hair or straw in this way

plan VERB **plans, planning, planned 1** to plan something is to work out how it may be done or make the arrangements to do it **2** to plan something, such as a building, is to design it **3** to plan to do something is to decide to do it at some time before you actually do it

NOUN **plans 1** an idea of how to do something or a method worked out for doing it **2** a drawing showing the layout of a building or town as if you are looking at it from above

plane[1] NOUN **planes** an aeroplane

plane[2] NOUN **planes 1** a carpenter's tool with a cutting blade set in a frame and used for making a level or smooth surface **2** a flat or level surface: *A cube has six planes.*

VERB **planes, planing, planed** to plane wood is to make it smooth and level using a plane

ADJECTIVE a plane shape is flat and has length and width you can measure, but not height or depth. It might also be called a **two-dimensional** shape

✦ The words **plane** and **plain** sound the same but remember that they have different spellings. **Plain** means ordinary, or is a flat area of land.

planet NOUN **planets** any of the large objects in space that orbit round a sun. The planets that orbit round our sun are Mercury, Venus, Earth, Mars, Jupiter, Saturn, Uranus and Neptune. See the picture on the next page

▶ **planetary** ADJECTIVE to do with the planets, especially those in our own solar system

Aa
Bb
Cc
Dd
Ee
Ff
Gg
Hh
Ii
Jj
Kk
Ll
Mm
Nn
Oo
Pp
Qq
Rr
Ss
Tt
Uu
Vv
Ww
Xx
Yy
Zz

the planets

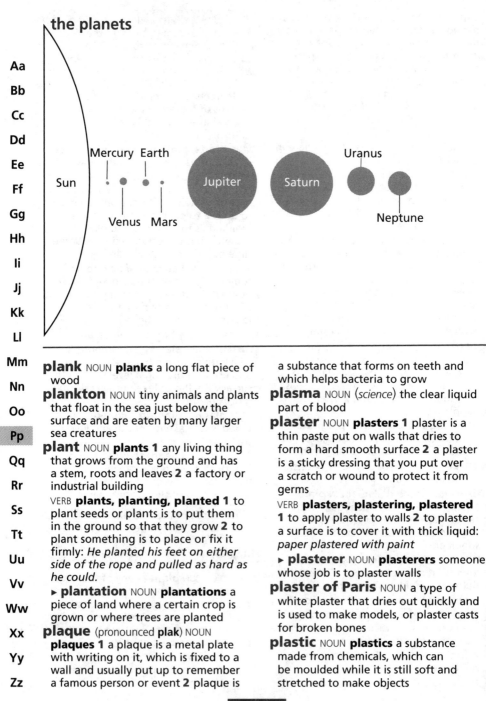

Sun · Mercury · Earth · Venus · Mars · Jupiter · Saturn · Uranus · Neptune

plank NOUN **planks** a long flat piece of wood

plankton NOUN tiny animals and plants that float in the sea just below the surface and are eaten by many larger sea creatures

plant NOUN **plants 1** any living thing that grows from the ground and has a stem, roots and leaves **2** a factory or industrial building

VERB **plants, planting, planted 1** to plant seeds or plants is to put them in the ground so that they grow **2** to plant something is to place or fix it firmly: *He planted his feet on either side of the rope and pulled as hard as he could.*

▶ **plantation** NOUN **plantations** a piece of land where a certain crop is grown or where trees are planted

plaque (pronounced **plak**) NOUN **plaques 1** a plaque is a metal plate with writing on it, which is fixed to a wall and usually put up to remember a famous person or event **2** plaque is a substance that forms on teeth and which helps bacteria to grow

plasma NOUN (*science*) the clear liquid part of blood

plaster NOUN **plasters 1** plaster is a thin paste put on walls that dries to form a hard smooth surface **2** a plaster is a sticky dressing that you put over a scratch or wound to protect it from germs

VERB **plasters, plastering, plastered 1** to apply plaster to walls **2** to plaster a surface is to cover it with thick liquid: *paper plastered with paint*

▶ **plasterer** NOUN **plasterers** someone whose job is to plaster walls

plaster of Paris NOUN a type of white plaster that dries out quickly and is used to make models, or plaster casts for broken bones

plastic NOUN **plastics** a substance made from chemicals, which can be moulded while it is still soft and stretched to make objects

Plasticine NOUN (*trademark*) a soft substance rather like clay which you can mould to make models

plastic surgery NOUN an operation to improve a patient's appearance or to repair scars

plate NOUN **plates**
1 a shallow dish for holding food
2 a thin flat sheet of metal or some other hard substance
3 a large picture or photograph in a book
4 (*geography*) one of the large areas of rock that make up the Earth's surface and that move very slowly under or over each other
VERB **plates, plating, plated** to plate an object is to cover it with a thin layer of metal, such as silver or tin

plateau (pronounced **pla**-toh) NOUN **plateaus** or **plateaux** (*geography*) a broad, fairly flat area of land that is higher than the land around it on at least one side

platform NOUN **platforms 1** a raised floor from which performers or speakers can be seen by an audience **2** a raised area beside the tracks at a railway station, where passengers can get on and off trains **3** a floating structure used as a base for drilling for oil

platinum NOUN a silvery-white precious metal

platoon NOUN **platoons** a group of soldiers

platter NOUN **platters** a large flat dish used for serving food

platypus NOUN **platypuses** a small animal found in Australia. It has a broad flat beak like a duck, webbed feet and a hairy body

play VERB **plays, playing, played**
1 to play is to spend time amusing yourself with games or toys: *Are you coming out to play?*
2 you play a team game when you take part in it: *He plays cricket on Saturdays.*
3 to play a musical instrument is to make music with it
4 to play a DVD, CD or tape is to put it into the player and listen to it or watch it
5 an actor plays a particular part when he or she acts that part
6 to play a part in something is to be one of the people involved in it
• **play down** to play down a success or a problem is to make it seem less impressive or serious
• **play up** a person or animal plays up when they behave badly
NOUN **plays 1** play is having fun with games and toys, or the action that goes on in a team game: *learning through play* • *Rain stopped play.* **2** a play is a story acted out in the theatre or on TV or radio

▶ **player** NOUN **players 1** someone who plays a game **2** a machine for playing DVDs, CDs, tapes or records

playful ADJECTIVE full of fun or wanting to play

▶ **playfully** ADVERB in a playful way

playground NOUN **playgrounds** an area, for example beside a school or in a public park, where children can play

playgroup NOUN **playgroups** a place where very young children go regularly to play and learn together

playing-card NOUN **playing-cards** a card from a set of 52, made up of four suits of 13 cards: hearts, clubs, diamonds and spades

playmate NOUN **playmates** someone you play with

play-off NOUN **play-offs** a match or game played to decide the winner from two players or teams with equal points in a competition

playschool NOUN **playschools** a nursery school or playgroup

playtime NOUN **playtimes** a short break in the morning or afternoon at school, when you can go out to play

playwright NOUN **playwrights** someone who writes plays

plea NOUN **pleas 1** an urgent and emotional request for something **2** someone charged with a crime makes a plea when they state to a court whether they are guilty or not guilty

Aa
Bb
Cc
Dd
Ee
Ff
Gg
Hh
Ii
Jj
Kk
Ll
Mm
Nn
Oo
Pp
Qq
Rr
Ss
Tt
Uu
Vv
Ww
Xx
Yy
Zz

Aa
Bb
Cc
Dd
Ee
Ff
Gg
Hh
Ii
Jj
Kk
Ll
Mm
Nn
Oo
Pp
Qq
Rr
Ss
Tt
Uu
Vv
Ww
Xx
Yy
Zz

plead VERB **pleads, pleading, pleaded** or **pled 1** to try to persuade someone in an urgent and emotional way, because you want something very much **2** to plead in a court is to answer a charge, saying 'guilty' or 'not guilty'

pleasant ADJECTIVE **1** something pleasant gives you a feeling of enjoyment and happiness **2** a pleasant person has a friendly and likeable manner

▸ **pleasantly** ADVERB in a pleasant way: *His laugh was pleasantly like a chuckle.*

please VERB **pleases, pleasing, pleased 1** to please someone is to do what they want or to give them pleasure or satisfaction **2** to do as you please is to do exactly as you want, not thinking what other people may want

ADVERB AND INTERJECTION a polite word you use when you are asking for something or accepting an offer: *Please don't park in front of the drive.* • *'Would you like another biscuit?' 'Yes, please.'*

▸ **pleasing** ADJECTIVE giving pleasure or satisfaction: *a pleasing result*

pleasure NOUN **pleasures 1** a feeling of enjoyment or satisfaction, or something that gives you this feeling **2** pleasure is time spent enjoying yourself rather than working: *Is your trip for work or for pleasure?*

▸ **pleasurable** ADJECTIVE something that is pleasurable gives pleasure or enjoyment

pleat NOUN **pleats** a fold sewn or pressed into a piece of cloth

▸ **pleated** ADJECTIVE having folds or folded lines: *a pleated skirt*

plectrum NOUN **plectrums** (*music*) a small hard piece of plastic or metal used to pick the strings of a guitar

pledge NOUN **pledges** a solemn promise

VERB **pledges, pledging, pledged** to pledge to do something is to promise solemnly to do it

plentiful ADJECTIVE something is plentiful when there is a good supply of it or it exists in large amounts

plenty NOUN **1** as much as you need:

You have plenty of time to complete the test. **2** a large amount or number: *There's plenty more bread in the freezer if we run out.*

pliable ADJECTIVE easy to bend or shape without breaking

pliers PLURAL NOUN pliers are a tool with two flat surfaces that come together to grip things

plight NOUN **plights** a bad condition or situation

plod VERB **plods, plodding, plodded 1** to walk slowly as if your feet and legs are heavy **2** to work slowly but steadily, especially on a job that you find boring

plonk VERB **plonks, plonking, plonked** to plonk something somewhere is to put it down heavily: *He plonked himself down on the sofa and turned on the telly.*

NOUN **plonks** a sound made by something dropping heavily

plop NOUN **plops** the sound of a small or light object dropping into water: *The frog jumped back into the pond with a plop.*

VERB **plops, plopping, plopped** to plop is to fall or drop making this sound

plot NOUN **plots 1** a secret plan, especially for doing something illegal or evil **2** the story of a play, novel or film **3** a small piece of land to be used as a gardening area or for building a house on: *a vegetable plot*

VERB **plots, plotting, plotted 1** to plan to do something illegal or evil **2** to plot things on a graph is to mark them as points on the graph and then make a connecting line between the points

plough (pronounced **plow**) NOUN **ploughs** a farm tool with a heavy blade that is pulled through the top layer of the soil to turn it over or break it up

VERB **ploughs, ploughing, ploughed** to plough is to turn over soil with a plough

• **plough through** to plough through work is to do your work slowly and with difficulty until you reach the end

plover NOUN **plovers** a wading bird that nests on open ground

ploy NOUN **ploys** a carefully thought-out plan or method of achieving something

pluck VERB **plucks, plucking, plucked 1** to pluck something is to take hold of it and pull it sharply so that it comes out or off **2** to pluck a chicken or turkey is to pull its feathers off before cooking it NOUN a rather old-fashioned word for courage
▸ **plucky** ADJECTIVE **pluckier, pluckiest** having courage

plug NOUN **plugs 1** an object attached to an electrical appliance by a wire and which you fit into a socket in the wall to get electricity for the appliance **2** an object that you use for blocking a hole, especially in a bath or sink to stop the water from running away
VERB **plugs, plugging, plugged 1** to plug a hole or gap is to push something into it to block it **2** to plug something new is to mention it so that people know about it: *The author plugged his new book during the interview.*

plum NOUN **plums** a soft red or yellow fruit with a smooth skin and a stone in the centre

plumage NOUN a bird's plumage is its covering of feathers

plumb VERB **plumbs, plumbing, plumbed** to plumb a stretch of water is to measure how deep it is

plumber NOUN **plumbers** someone whose job is to fit and repair water, gas and sewage pipes
▸ **plumbing** NOUN **1** the work of a plumber **2** the plumbing in a building is the system of pipes that carry water and gas

plume NOUN **plumes** a long broad feather, or something that has the shape of a long broad feather: *ostrich plumes* • *a plume of smoke*

plummet VERB **plummets, plummeting, plummeted** to plummet is to fall very fast

plump ADJECTIVE **plumper, plumpest** fat or rounded, in a pleasant way: *plump rosy cheeks*
VERB **plumps, plumping, plumped**

• **plump something up** to plump up cushions or pillows is to squash and shake them so that they become rounded

plunge VERB **plunge, plunging, plunged 1** to plunge is to dive: *He plunged off the high board.* • *She plunged into the crowd, pushing her way through.* **2** to plunge something into water is to push it quickly into the water so that it is covered **3** to plunge something into something else is to push it violently or suddenly into that thing: *The pirate plunged his dagger into the sack, spilling the contents all over the deck.*
NOUN **plunges** a dive or fall from a high place

plural NOUN **plurals** a plural is the form of a noun, pronoun, adjective or verb that you use when there is more than one of something. For example, *feet* is the plural of *foot* and *toes* is the plural of *toe*
ADJECTIVE in the plural form

plus PREPOSITION **1** (*maths*) adding: *8 plus 2 is 10* **2** as well as: *There are six children, plus two adults.*
ADJECTIVE **1** more than zero: *plus ten degrees* **2** plus is used after a letter or number to show that a mark or number is more than the mark or number indicated by the letter or number alone: *He got a B plus for his project.* • *You have to be 60 plus to join the club.*
NOUN **pluses** (*maths*) a plus, or plus sign (+), is a mathematical symbol showing that a number is to be added to another

plush ADJECTIVE **plusher, plushest** plush places are very smart, elegant and expensive

ply NOUN **plies 1** a thickness, layer or strand: *two-ply wool* **2** plywood

plywood NOUN a material made up of thin layers of wood glued together

pm or **p.m.** ABBREVIATION short for **post meridiem** which is Latin for 'after midday'. **pm** is added after the time to show that the time is the afternoon or evening rather than the morning, for example *2pm*. Look up and compare **am**

Aa Bb Cc Dd Ee Ff Gg Hh Ii Jj Kk Ll Mm Nn Oo **Pp** Qq Rr Ss Tt Uu Vv Ww Xx Yy Zz

PM ABBREVIATION short for **prime minister**

pneumatic (pronounced nyoo-**mat**-ik) ADJECTIVE **1** filled with air: *pneumatic tyres* **2** worked by air pressure or compressed air: *a pneumatic drill*

pneumonia (pronounced nyoo-**moh**-nya) NOUN a serious illness of the lungs that makes breathing very difficult and sometimes kills people

poach VERB **poaches, poaching, poached 1** to hunt and kill fish, birds or animals without permission on someone else's land **2** to poach food is to cook it by heating it gently in water or some other liquid

▸ **poacher** NOUN **poachers** someone who hunts and kills fish or game illegally

pocket NOUN **pockets**
1 an extra piece of cloth sewn into a piece of clothing and used for keeping small items in, like money or keys
2 any pouch-like container, for example in a suitcase or at the sides of a pool table
3 the amount of money you have or can afford: *presents to suit every pocket*
4 a small area or group: *pockets of mist*
• **out of pocket** you are out of pocket when you have spent money, usually without getting any benefit
VERB **pockets, pocketing, pocketed** to pocket something is to put it in your pocket, or to take it and keep it for yourself, especially dishonestly

pocket money NOUN an allowance of money that you get or use for buying small personal items or things like sweets and magazines

pod NOUN **pods** a long narrow seed case that grows on plants like peas and beans

podcast VERB **podcasts, podcasting, podcast** to put sound files on the Internet that people can download into digital audio players
NOUN **podcasts** a set of sound files that have been put on the Internet and can be downloaded to an audio player

podgy ADJECTIVE **podgier, podgiest** slightly fat

podium NOUN **podiums** a small platform that someone stands on, for example a speaker at a public meeting

poem NOUN **poems** a piece of writing in imaginative language arranged in patterns of lines and sounds, often, but not always, rhyming

poet NOUN **poets** someone who writes poetry

▸ **poetic** ADJECTIVE written as a poem, or having qualities of beauty and imagination like poetry

▸ **poetry** NOUN poems as a group or as a form of literature. Look up and compare **prose**

poignant (pronounced **poin**-yant) ADJECTIVE something poignant makes you feel great sadness or pity

point NOUN **points**
1 a sharp end: *the point of a needle*
2 (*maths*) a small dot (·) used in decimal fractions
3 a particular place or a particular moment: *the highest point on the British mainland* • *At that point, we all burst out laughing.*
4 a mark used to score a competition, game or test: *Who got the highest number of points?*
5 your good points and bad points are your personal qualities or characteristics
6 a fact, idea or opinion that is a part of an argument or discussion, or the most important part of what is being said: *What's your point?*
7 the point of doing something is its purpose: *What's the point of going home if you just have to go straight back out again?*
VERB **points, pointing, pointed 1** to point is to stretch your finger in the direction of something to show other people what or where you mean **2** to point something is to aim it in a particular direction: *He pointed the camera at me.* **3** to point to something is to show that it is true or to explain it: *All the evidence points to an inside job.*

point-blank ADJECTIVE AND ADVERB **1** in an abrupt or rude way: *She refused*

pointed ➜ polite

point-blank to come. **2** very close: *The gun was fired at point-blank range.*

pointed ADJECTIVE with a sharp end: *a pointed stick*

pointer NOUN **pointers 1** a long instrument used to point at things, for example on a wall map or blackboard **2** the needle on a dial

pointless ADJECTIVE having no purpose or meaning: *a pointless argument*

point of view NOUN **points of view** your point of view is the way you look at things

poise NOUN **1** to have poise is to behave in a confident and dignified way **2** poise is balance

VERB **poises, poising, poised** to be poised somewhere is to be waiting there ready to move: *He was poised on the edge of the diving board.*

poison NOUN **poisons** any substance that causes death or illness when taken into your body

VERB **poisons, poisoning, poisoned 1** to poison someone is to kill or harm them with poison **2** to poison something is to add poison to it

▶ **poisonous** ADJECTIVE **1** a poisonous substance causes illness or death when taken into your body: *This cleaning liquid is poisonous.* **2** producing poison: *a poisonous snake*

poke VERB **pokes, poking, poked 1** to poke is to push something sharp into something: *He poked me in the ribs.* **2** to poke something through a gap or hole is to stick it through: *She poked her head through the hatch.*

NOUN **pokes** a sharp prod

▶ **poker** NOUN **pokers 1** a heavy metal rod used for moving wood or coal about in a fire **2** poker is a card game played for money

poky ADJECTIVE **pokier, pokiest** a poky place is small and uncomfortable

polar ADJECTIVE (*geography*) at or to do with the north or south pole

polar bear NOUN **polar bears** a large white bear that lives in the Arctic

polaroid NOUN **polaroids** (*trademark*)

a type of photograph that is developed inside the camera

pole¹ NOUN **poles** a long thin rounded piece of wood or metal

pole² NOUN **poles 1** (*geography*) the north and south pole are the two points on the Earth at the north and south end of its axis **2** (*science*) either of the opposite ends of a magnet

pole vault NOUN **pole vaults** an athletic event in which competitors try to jump over a high bar by pushing themselves up and over it with a long flexible pole

police NOUN the police are the people whose job is to prevent crime, keep order and see that laws are obeyed

policeman *or* **policewoman** NOUN **policemen** *or* **policewomen** a police officer

police officer NOUN **police officers** a member of the police, both the uniformed officers and detectives in plain clothes

police station NOUN **police stations** a building where the police have their offices and where people are taken when they are arrested

policy NOUN **policies** a planned or agreed course of action: *It is not the school's policy to have a uniform.*

polio NOUN polio is a serious disease that affects the nerves and muscles and can cause paralysis. Nowadays, polio is very rare because most children are vaccinated against it

polish VERB **polishes, polishing, polished** to polish something is to rub it until it shines

• **polish something off** (*informal*) to polish something off is to finish it completely

NOUN **polishes** a substance used to polish wood or metal

polite ADJECTIVE **politer, politest** a polite person has good manners

▶ **politely** ADVERB in a well-mannered way: *'Would you like a seat?' he asked her politely.*

▶ **politeness** NOUN being well-mannered

Aa Bb Cc Dd Ee Ff Gg Hh Ii Jj Kk Ll Mm Nn Oo Pp Qq Rr Ss Tt Uu Vv Ww Xx Yy Zz

403

political ADJECTIVE to do with politics, politicians or government

politician NOUN **politicians** someone involved in politics, especially someone who tries to get elected to a parliament or local council

politics NOUN politics is the study of the ways in which countries are governed, or the work of governing a country

polka NOUN **polkas** a kind of fast lively dance, or music for this dance

poll NOUN **polls 1** a political election in which people vote, or the number of votes cast in an election **2** a poll is a survey of people picked at random to find out what the general public opinion of something is

pollen NOUN the powder, often yellow, that a flower releases and which fertilizes the female part of the plant

pollinate VERB **pollinates, pollinating, pollinated** a plant is pollinated when pollen fertilizes it and its fruit and seeds begin to form

▸ **pollination** NOUN when pollen from a male flower lands on the female part of a plant and fruit and seeds begin to form

pollute VERB **pollutes, polluting, polluted** to pollute the air, the soil or a river is to release harmful substances into it

▸ **pollution** NOUN the release of harmful chemicals and other substances into the air, water or soil

polo NOUN a game played on horseback by two teams of players who hit a ball along the ground using long-handled hammers called mallets

polo neck NOUN **polo necks** a jumper with a high round neck

poltergeist NOUN **poltergeists** a type of ghost that is believed to move or throw solid objects around, or cause strange things to happen in a house

poly- PREFIX if **poly-** comes at the beginning of a word, it adds the meaning *many* to the word. For example, a *polygon* is a figure with many sides and angles

✦ This comes from the Greek word **polys**, which means *much*.

polygon NOUN **polygons** a figure or shape with three or more sides and angles

▸ **polygonal** ADJECTIVE having many sides and many angles

polyhedron NOUN **polyhedrons** (*maths*) a solid shape with many sides

polystyrene NOUN a very light plastic substance like stiff foam, used for packaging and insulation

polythene NOUN a very thin plastic material used for making bags, light containers and protective coverings

pomp NOUN pomp is solemn and splendid display or ceremony

pompous ADJECTIVE a pompous person behaves as if they are very important

poncho NOUN **ponchos** a loose piece of clothing covering the shoulders and top half of the body which has a hole for your head to go through

pond NOUN **ponds** a small area of water, smaller than a lake and larger than a pool

ponder VERB **ponders, pondering, pondered** to think about something carefully and for a long time

pony NOUN **ponies** a type of small horse

ponytail NOUN **ponytails** a hairstyle in which the hair is gathered up at the back of the head and tied so that it hangs down like a tail

pony-trekking NOUN travelling across the countryside, often for quite long distances, on ponies

poodle NOUN **poodles** a breed of dog with curly hair, often clipped in a fancy way

pool[1] NOUN **pools 1** a pond or puddle, or any other small area of still water **2** a swimming pool

pool[2] NOUN **pools 1** a group of people or things shared by several people: *a car pool* **2** the money that people play for in a card game

VERB **pools, pooling, pooled** to pool things is to put them all together into one large group that everyone can use

Aa
Bb
Cc
Dd
Ee
Ff
Gg
Hh
Ii
Jj
Kk
Ll
Mm
Nn
Oo
Pp
Qq
Rr
Ss
Tt
Uu
Vv
Ww
Xx
Yy
Zz

poor ADJECTIVE **poorer, poorest 1** a poor person has very little money or property **2** of a low standard: *a poor imitation* **3** you call a person or animal 'poor' when you think they deserve pity or sympathy: *The poor little thing is all wet.*
▸ **poorly** ADVERB **1** badly: *a poorly lit passage* **2** ill: *Gran's feeling a bit poorly.*

pop¹ NOUN **pops 1** a sudden sound like a small explosion **2** fizzy drink
VERB **pops, popping, popped 1** to pop is to make a sudden sound like a small explosion **2** something pops out when it comes out suddenly

pop² NOUN modern music that is popular at the current time

popcorn NOUN the seeds of maize that burst open into crisp fluffy balls when they are heated

pope NOUN **popes** the head of the Catholic Church

poppy NOUN **poppies** a tall flower that grows wild in fields and has broad, flat, red petals

popular ADJECTIVE something that is popular is liked by a lot of people
▸ **popularity** NOUN the popularity of something is how many people like it
▸ **popularize** *or* **popularise** VERB **popularizes, popularizing, popularized** to popularize something is to make it popular

populate VERB **populates, populating, populated** people or animals populate an area when they live there
▸ **populated** ADJECTIVE a populated area has a lot of people living in it
▸ **population** NOUN **populations** the population of an area is the number or type of people living in it

porcelain NOUN AND ADJECTIVE a type of fine china, used to make crockery and ornaments: *a porcelain doll*

porch NOUN **porches** a small roofed entrance to a building

porcupine NOUN **porcupines** an animal that has lots of long sharp spines called quills growing on its back

pore¹ NOUN **pores** one of the tiny openings in your skin that sweat comes out of

pore² VERB **pores, poring, pored**
• **pore over** to pore over books or documents is to read them very carefully, giving them your full attention

pork NOUN meat from a pig

porous ADJECTIVE a porous material lets liquids and gases pass through it

porpoise NOUN **porpoises** a large sea mammal, similar to a dolphin but with a shorter and rounder nose

porridge NOUN a food made by boiling oats in water, usually eaten for breakfast

port NOUN **ports 1** a place where ships stop to pick up passengers or goods **2** a town or city that has harbours
ADJECTIVE the port side of a ship or aircraft is the left side when you are facing the front. Look up and compare **starboard**

portable ADJECTIVE something portable can be carried around

portcullis NOUN **portcullises** a kind of spiked gate, found in some old castles, that slides downwards from above

porter NOUN **porters 1** someone whose job is to carry baggage for people at railway stations or on long treks **2** a person who looks after the entrance of a college, office or factory

portfolio NOUN **portfolios** pieces of writing or art you have done, gathered into a folder

porthole NOUN **portholes** a round window in a ship's or boat's side

portion NOUN **portions** a portion of something is one of several pieces or parts it can be or is divided into: *a portion of land*

portly ADJECTIVE **portlier, portliest** a portly person is rather fat, especially round their middle

portrait NOUN **portraits 1** (*art*) a painting, drawing or photograph of a person **2** a description in words of a person, place or thing

portray VERB **portrays, portraying, portrayed 1** to portray a person or thing is to make a picture or written description of them or it **2** an actor portrays a person or an emotion when they act the part of that person or act out that emotion

Aa
Bb
Cc
Dd
Ee
Ff
Gg
Hh
Ii
Jj
Kk
Ll
Mm
Nn
Oo
Pp
Qq
Rr
Ss
Tt
Uu
Vv
Ww
Xx
Yy
Zz

▶ **portrayal** NOUN **portrayals** a description or representation of something, especially in words

pose VERB **poses, posing, posed 1** to pose for a photo or portrait is to stay in a particular position so that the photographer or artist can take or paint your picture **2** to pose as something is to pretend to be that person or thing: *a thief posing as a gas repair man* **3** if something poses a problem, risk or threat, it causes that problem, risk or threat to exist NOUN **poses 1** a particular position into which you put your body **2** pretended behaviour that is intended to impress people: *He's not tough at all. It's all just a pose.*

▶ **poser** NOUN **posers 1** someone who pretends to be something they are not, just to impress other people **2** a poser is a question or problem that is difficult to answer or solve

posh ADJECTIVE **posher, poshest 1** a posh place is very smart and expensive **2** a posh person is from a high social class

position NOUN **positions 1** a place or situation: *Tom could see the whole garden from his position in the tree.* • *This puts me in a very difficult position.* **2** a way of standing, sitting or lying: *sleeping in an awkward position* **3** a job: *Uncle Frank has applied for a position as a security guard.*
VERB **positions, positioning, positioned** if you position something somewhere, you put it there: *The council had positioned the sign where no one could see it.* • *Detectives positioned themselves across the road from the house.*

positive ADJECTIVE
1 you are positive about something when you are very sure about it
2 a positive answer or response means or says 'yes'
3 to have a positive attitude is to feel hopeful and confident
4 (*maths*) a positive number is one that is greater than zero
5 (*science*) a positive electric charge does not carry electrons

▶ **positively** ADVERB completely or absolutely: *You look positively exhausted.*

posse (pronounced **pos**-i) NOUN **posses** a group of people, usually including an officer of the law, who chase a criminal who is on the run

possess VERB **possesses, possessing, possessed** to possess something is to have it or own it

▶ **possessed** ADJECTIVE someone who is possessed is being controlled by an emotion or an evil spirit

▶ **possession** NOUN **possessions 1** possession is having or owning something **2** your possessions are the things you have or own

▶ **possessive** ADJECTIVE **1** a possessive person is not willing to share the things they have with other people **2** (*grammar*) in grammar, a possessive is a word that shows who or what a person or thing belongs to. For example, *my*, *yours* and *theirs*, and nouns with *'s* added at the end, are possessives

possibility NOUN **possibilities** something that is possible

possible ADJECTIVE **1** something that is possible can happen, or may happen: *It isn't possible for human beings to travel to the planets yet.* **2** something that is possible may be true: *It's possible I made a mistake.*

▶ **possibly** ADVERB perhaps: *Possibly I was wrong.*

post- PREFIX if **post-** comes at the beginning of a word, it adds the meaning *after* to the word. For example, *postwar* means 'after a war'

post¹ NOUN **posts** a long piece of wood or metal fixed upright in the ground

post² NOUN the postal service, which collects and delivers letters and parcels, or the letters and parcels sent or delivered by this service: *I sent it by post, not by fax.* • *Has the morning post arrived yet?*
VERB **posts, posting, posted** to post a letter or parcel is to send it by the postal service, for example by taking it to the post office or putting it in a postbox

post³ NOUN **posts 1** a job: *He was dismissed from his post.* **2** a place where someone, such as a soldier or security guard, is on duty
VERB **posts, posting, posted** if someone is posted somewhere, they are sent there for a while to work

postage NOUN the amount of money you have to pay to send a letter or parcel through the post

postal ADJECTIVE to do with the service that collects and delivers letters and parcels

postbox NOUN **postboxes** a box in a public place where letters can be posted

postcard NOUN **postcards** a card for writing messages on that you can send through the post without an envelope

post code NOUN **post codes** a special series of letters and numbers at the end of an address that helps the postal service to sort letters and parcels

poster NOUN **posters** a large notice in a public place advertising something or giving information

posterior ADJECTIVE at the back or rear: *in a posterior position*
NOUN **posteriors 1** the back of something **2** your posterior is your bottom

postman NOUN **postmen** someone who delivers letters and parcels to people's houses or businesses

postmark NOUN **postmarks** a mark that a post office stamps on a letter to show when and where it was posted

post office NOUN **post offices** a place where you can post letters and parcels, buy stamps and use various other postal services

postpone VERB **postpones, postponing, postponed** to postpone something is to put it off until a later time

▸ **postponement** NOUN **postponements** putting something off until a later time

postscript NOUN **postscripts** if a letter has a postscript, it has an extra message under the writer's signature, usually with the abbreviation **PS** before it

posture NOUN **postures** your posture is the way you usually stand, sit or walk

posy NOUN **posies** a small bunch of flowers

pot NOUN **pots** a deep container, often with a lid, used for cooking, holding liquids, storing things like jam, or for growing plants in

potassium NOUN (*science*) potassium is a soft, silvery-white metallic element

potato NOUN **potatoes** a round white or yellowish vegetable that grows underground

potency NOUN power or strength

potent ADJECTIVE powerful or strong: *a potent drug*

potential ADJECTIVE capable of developing into a particular thing: *He's a potential prime minister.*
NOUN your potential is the qualities you have that can be developed successfully

pothole NOUN **potholes** a hole in the road

potion NOUN **potions** a drink containing medicine or poison, or having a magic effect

potter VERB **potters, pottering, pottered** to wander about doing small jobs or nothing very important

pottery NOUN **potteries 1** pottery is things such as plates, bowls and ornaments made out of baked clay **2** a pottery is a workshop or factory where things are made out of baked clay
▸ **potter** NOUN **potters** someone who makes pottery and articles out of clay

potty¹ NOUN **potties** a container that a small child uses as a toilet

potty² ADJECTIVE **pottier, pottiest** (*informal*) someone who is potty is mad

pouch NOUN **pouches 1** a small bag **2** the fold of skin that a female kangaroo carries her baby in

poultry NOUN birds such as chickens and turkeys that are bred for people to eat

pounce VERB **pounces, pouncing, pounced** to jump forward suddenly to attack or catch hold of something: *The cat pounced on the mouse.*

Aa Bb Cc Dd Ee Ff Gg Hh Ii Jj Kk Ll Mm Nn Oo Pp Qq Rr Ss Tt Uu Vv Ww Xx Yy Zz

Aa
Bb
Cc
Dd
Ee
Ff
Gg
Hh
Ii
Jj
Kk
Ll
Mm
Nn
Oo
Pp
Qq
Rr
Ss
Tt
Uu
Vv
Ww
Xx
Yy
Zz

pound NOUN **pounds 1** the main unit of money in Britain, made up of 100 pence and usually written £ **2** an imperial unit for measuring weight, equal to 0.454 kilograms

VERB **pounds, pounding, pounded** to pound something is to hit it hard: *Someone was pounding at the door trying to get in.*

pour VERB **pours, pouring, poured**
1 to pour a liquid is to make it flow out of a container in a stream
2 to pour is to flow out fast and in large quantities
3 people or things pour in when they arrive in large numbers
4 if it is pouring, it is raining heavily

pout VERB **pouts, pouting, pouted** if someone pouts, they push out their lips, or only their lower lip, because they are annoyed

poverty NOUN being very poor

powder NOUN **powders 1** a substance in the form of a fine dry dust **2** powder is a cosmetic that some women pat on their skin to make it look smooth
▸ **powdered** ADJECTIVE dried and made into a powder: *powdered milk*
▸ **powdery** ADJECTIVE made up of very small pieces or particles, like powder: *powdery snow*

power NOUN **powers**
1 power is strength or force
2 to have power is to have the ability or authority to control people or things: *political power*
3 to have the power to do something is to have the ability to do it: *He's lost the power of speech.*
4 power is any form of energy used to drive machines: *wind power*
5 (*maths*) the power of a number is the result you get by multiplying the number by itself a certain number of times, for example 2 × 2 × 2 or 2^3 is the third power of 2, or 2 to the power of 3
VERB **powers, powering, powered** (*technology*) to power something is to provide it with the energy to work: *a machine powered by steam*

powerful ADJECTIVE strong or having the ability to control other people
▸ **powerfully** ADVERB in a strong, powerful way

powerless ADJECTIVE unable to control or affect things

power station NOUN **power stations** a building where electricity is made from coal, oil, gas or nuclear power

practical ADJECTIVE **1** something that is practical is useful or efficient: *a very practical solution to the problem* **2** a practical person is good at doing things rather than thinking about them
NOUN **practicals** an examination that tests practical ability and skill rather than theory

practical joke NOUN **practical jokes** a trick played on someone by doing something rather than using words

practically ADVERB almost: *The theatre was practically full.*

practice NOUN **practices 1** practice is doing something often so that you get better at it: *He'll soon get the hang of the violin with a bit more practice.* **2** to put a theory, plan or idea into practice is to do it **3** a doctor's or lawyer's practice is the place where they work

✦ Remember that **practice** with a **c** is a noun: *I need some **practice**.*
Practise with an **s** is a verb: *You must **practise** often.*

practise VERB **practises, practising, practised 1** to practise something is to do it again and again so that you get better at it **2** to practise something is to make it a habit or to do it: *He practises yoga.* **3** a doctor or lawyer practises when they do their professional work

prairie NOUN **prairies** (*geography*) a large area of flat grassy land in North America

praise VERB **praises, praising, praised** to praise someone or something is to say how well they have done
NOUN **praises** praise is saying how good someone is or how well they have done

pram NOUN **prams** a small wheeled

vehicle that a baby sits or lies in and which is pushed about by someone walking

prance VERB **prances, prancing, pranced** to prance is to dance or jump about, often in a silly way

prank NOUN **pranks** a trick or practical joke

prawn NOUN **prawns** a shellfish that looks like a large shrimp

pray VERB **prays, praying, prayed 1** to speak to God **2** to pray for something is to hope and beg for it: *We were praying for a nice sunny day.* • *Mum prayed that the train wouldn't be late.*
▸ **prayer** NOUN **prayers 1** a prayer is the words that you use when you pray **2** prayer is praying: *They knelt in prayer.*

✦ The words **pray** and **prey** sound the same, but remember that they have different spellings. **Prey** is the creatures an animal hunts.

pre- PREFIX if **pre-** is added at the beginning of a word, it adds the meaning *before* to the word. For example, *prehistoric* times are the times before history was written down

preach VERB **preaches, preaching, preached 1** to talk about right and wrong, often as part of a religious service **2** to preach a particular way of behaving is to advise people to behave in that way: *He preached patience and understanding.*
▸ **preacher** NOUN **preachers** someone who preaches or gives sermons

precarious ADJECTIVE not safe: *They had pitched the tent on the side of a hill in a precarious position.*

precaution NOUN **precautions** something you do to avoid an accident or problem happening

precede VERB **precedes, preceding, preceded** one thing precedes another when it comes before that other thing

precinct NOUN **precincts 1** an area of shops in the centre of a town or city where no cars or motor vehicles are allowed **2** the precincts of a building are the areas within its boundaries or inside

its walls: *the cathedral precincts*

precious ADJECTIVE **1** valuable or highly valued by someone: *precious stones* • *His books are very precious to him.* **2** precious little or precious few means very little or very few

precipice NOUN **precipices** a very steep cliff

precise ADJECTIVE **1** exact: *At that precise moment, the bell rang.* **2** careful and accurate: *Her work is very precise.*
▸ **precisely** ADVERB exactly: *Precisely when did he give you the letter?*
▸ **precision** NOUN being exact and accurate: *He hit the target again and again with precision.*

predator NOUN **predators** an animal that hunts and eats other animals
▸ **predatory** ADJECTIVE hunting, killing and eating other animals

predecessor NOUN **predecessors** someone's predecessor in a job is the person who had the job before them

predicament NOUN **predicaments** if someone is in a predicament, they are in a difficult situation

predict VERB **predicts, predicting, predicted** to predict something is to say that it will happen before it actually does happen
▸ **predictable** ADJECTIVE if you say that something was predictable, you knew it would happen
▸ **prediction** NOUN **predictions** predicting, or something that is predicted

predominant ADJECTIVE the predominant person or thing in a group is the one that stands out most: *The predominant colour in his paintings is blue.*
▸ **predominantly** ADJECTIVE mostly or mainly: *The trains are predominantly old, out-of-date models.*

preen VERB **preens, preening, preened 1** a bird preens when it smoothes and cleans its feathers **2** you preen yourself when you make yourself look nice, for example by combing your hair or adjusting your clothes

preface NOUN **prefaces** the preface

Aa
Bb
Cc
Dd
Ee
Ff
Gg
Hh
Ii
Jj
Kk
Ll
Mm
Nn
Oo
Pp
Qq
Rr
Ss
Tt
Uu
Vv
Ww
Xx
Yy
Zz

to a book is a short section at the beginning that introduces the rest of the book or the story

prefect NOUN **prefects** a senior pupil in a school who has been given some powers to help in the running of the school

prefer VERB **prefers, preferring, preferred** to prefer one thing to another is to like the first one better

▸ **preferable** ADJECTIVE if one thing is preferable to another, you like it, or would like it, better than the other thing

▸ **preference** NOUN **preferences** your preferences are the things you like or prefer

prefix NOUN **prefixes** a letter, or a group of letters, that is added to the beginning of a word to make another word

pregnant ADJECTIVE a woman or female animal is pregnant when she is carrying an unborn baby in her womb

▸ **pregnancy** NOUN **pregnancies** being pregnant, or the time when a woman or female animal is pregnant

prehistoric ADJECTIVE belonging to the time before history was written down: *prehistoric cave paintings*

prejudice NOUN **prejudices** an unfair opinion or dislike of a person or thing

VERB **prejudices, prejudicing, prejudiced** one thing prejudices another when it harms it or puts it in danger

▸ **prejudiced** ADJECTIVE disliking someone or something for reasons that are not fair

preliminary ADJECTIVE preliminary things are said or done to prepare for a main event or what is to come next

premature ADJECTIVE **1** a premature baby is born before the time it should have been born **2** an action is premature when it is done too early

premier ADJECTIVE leading or most important: *France's premier resort*

NOUN **premiers** a prime minister

première NOUN **premières** the première of a film or play is its first public showing or performance

premises PLURAL NOUN the premises of

a company or business are the buildings and land it uses

premium NOUN **premiums** a premium is a regular amount paid to an insurance company for insurance cover

• **at a premium** if something is at a premium it is difficult to get and so is more expensive

premonition NOUN **premonitions** a strange feeling that something is going to happen before it actually does happen

preoccupation NOUN **preoccupations** something you think about all or most of the time

▸ **preoccupied** ADJECTIVE thinking so much about one thing that you do not pay enough attention to other things

▸ **preoccupy** VERB **preoccupies, preoccupying, preoccupied** something preoccupies you when you think about it a lot

prep NOUN (*informal*) homework

ADJECTIVE short for **preparatory**, as in *prep school*

preparation NOUN **preparations 1** preparing for something **2** something done to prepare for something: *preparations for the wedding*

preparatory ADJECTIVE preparing for something that comes later

prepare VERB **prepares, preparing, prepared 1** to prepare is to get ready to deal with something or do it: *The children are preparing for their end-of-term test.* **2** to prepare someone or something for something is to get them ready to deal with it or do it: *The coach's job is to prepare the team for every match.* **3** to prepare food is to do whatever is needed to make it ready for eating

▸ **prepared** ADJECTIVE **1** made ready in advance **2** you are prepared for something, or prepared to do something, when you are ready for it, or are willing to do it

preposition WORD CLASS **prepositions** (*grammar*) a word put before a noun or pronoun to show how it is related or connected to another word or phrase in the same clause or sentence. For example, in the sentence *I put my schoolbooks in my bag*, the word *in* is a preposition

preposterous ADJECTIVE ridiculous: *What a preposterous suggestion!*

prep school NOUN **prep schools** a prep school is a private school for children, especially boys, between the ages of 7 and 13

prescribe VERB **prescribes, prescribing, prescribed** a doctor prescribes a drug for a patient when he or she tells the patient which drug to take

▸ **prescription** NOUN **prescriptions** an instruction from a doctor to a pharmacist stating what medicine should be prepared for a particular patient

presence NOUN **1** your presence somewhere is your being there **2** to do something in someone's presence is to do it while they are there

present[1] NOUN **presents** something given as a gift

VERB **presents, presenting, presented** **1** to present someone with something is to give it to them, usually as an award for good work or high achievement **2** someone presents a radio or TV show when they introduce it **3** you present information when you communicate it to other people **4** something presents a problem when it becomes difficult to deal with **5** you present yourself somewhere when you go there and let someone know you have arrived **6** you present one person to another when you introduce them

present[2] NOUN the present is the time now

ADJECTIVE **1** someone is present somewhere when they are there **2** to do with the time now: *the present day • pupils past and present*

presentation NOUN **presentations** the presenting of something such as a gift or a talk

presently ADVERB (*formal*) **1** soon: *The bus should be here presently.* **2** just

now: *Are you presently a member of the tennis club?*

present participle NOUN (*grammar*) the form of a verb used after a helping verb such as *is* or *was* to show that something is or was taking place at that time. For example, *going* in *I am going to the shops* is a present participle

present tense NOUN (*grammar*) the present tense of a verb is the form used to show that the action of the verb is happening here and now. For example, *throw* and *throws* in *I throw the ball* and *he throws it back* are present tense forms of the verb to *throw*

preservation NOUN preserving: *preservation of the rainforest*

preserve VERB **preserves, preserving, preserved** to preserve something is to keep it as it is and stop it being lost or destroyed

NOUN **preserves** a food, such as jam or bottled fruit, that has been boiled with sugar to stop it going bad

preside VERB **presides, presiding, presided** to preside over a meeting or formal event is to be in overall charge of it

presidency NOUN **presidencies** the position of being a president, or the time when someone is a president

president NOUN **presidents 1** a president is the elected head of state in a republic **2** the president of a company or organization is the person with the top job in that company or organization

press VERB **presses, pressing, pressed** **1** to press something is to push it or squeeze it **2** you press clothes when you iron them **3** to press for something is to be forceful in trying to get someone to agree to it

NOUN **presses 1** newspapers and journalists are the press **2** a press is a printing machine **3** a pressing action

pressgang NOUN **pressgangs** (*history*) a group of tough men who went around ports and seaside towns forcing men to join the navy

VERB **pressgangs, pressganging, pressganged** if you are pressganged into doing something, a group of people force you to do it

pressing ADJECTIVE a pressing problem is one that needs to be dealt with now or very soon

press-up NOUN **press-ups** a floor exercise in which you push the top half of your body up off the floor by pressing down with your hands and arms

pressure NOUN **pressures** 1 the force on or against a surface by something pressing on it: *air pressure* 2 pressure is strong persuasion: *He put me under pressure to agree.* 3 pressures are the stresses and strains of life

▶ **pressurize** or **pressurise** VERB **pressurizes, pressurizing, pressurized** 1 to pressurize someone into doing something is to force them to do it 2 to pressurize something, for example an aeroplane, is to keep the air pressure inside it the same as the air pressure outside

prestige NOUN someone has prestige when other people have a very good opinion of them, especially because of their rank or success

presumably ADVERB you say 'presumably' when you suppose something is true: *If you're going out to play, presumably you've done your homework.*

presume VERB **presumes, presuming, presumed** to presume something is to believe that it is true without having any proof

▶ **presumption** NOUN **presumptions** presuming, or something presumed

▶ **presumptuous** ADJECTIVE a presumptuous person behaves in a confident way that shows a lack of respect for other people

pretence NOUN pretending something

pretend VERB **pretends, pretending, pretended** 1 to make believe that something is true as part of play: *Let's pretend we're submarine captains.* 2 to try to make people believe something that is not true: *She's only pretending to like me.*

▶ **pretender** NOUN **pretenders** 1 someone who pretends 2 someone who

claims the right to be king or queen of a country

pretty ADJECTIVE **prettier, prettiest** attractive to look at: *pretty flowers • a pretty little girl*

ADVERB quite: *a pretty good mark*
• **pretty much, pretty nearly, pretty well** almost: *My homework is pretty much finished.*

▶ **prettiness** NOUN being attractive to look at

prevail VERB **prevails, prevailing, prevailed** to prevail is to win a contest or battle

▶ **prevailing** ADJECTIVE (*geography*) the prevailing winds are winds that blow most frequently in a part of the world

prevalence NOUN how prevalent something is

▶ **prevalent** ADJECTIVE common and widespread

prevent VERB **prevents, preventing, prevented** to prevent something happening is to stop it happening

▶ **prevention** NOUN preventing something

▶ **preventive** ADJECTIVE a preventive medicine stops you getting a disease or illness

preview NOUN **previews** a viewing of something before it is released or shown to the general public

previous ADJECTIVE happening earlier or at some time in the past

▶ **previously** ADVERB before or earlier

prey NOUN the creatures a predator hunts, kills and eats are its prey: *Small birds are the usual prey of the sparrow hawk.*

VERB **preys, preying, preyed** 1 to prey on something is to hunt it and kill it: *Lions prey on the vast herds of wildebeest and antelope in the Serengeti.* 2 if something preys on your mind, you cannot stop thinking or worrying about it

price NOUN **prices** the price of something is the amount of money it costs: *What price are your apples today? • Prices in the shops were rising.*

VERB **prices, pricing, priced** to price

Aa Bb Cc Dd Ee Ff Gg Hh Ii Jj Kk Ll Mm Nn Oo Pp Qq Rr Ss Tt Uu Vv Ww Xx Yy Zz

things is to find out how much they cost or to mark a price on them

▶ **priceless** ADJECTIVE **1** a priceless item is so valuable that it is not possible to put a price on it **2** very funny: *The surprised expression on his face was priceless.*

▶ **pricey** ADJECTIVE **pricier, priciest** expensive: *Petrol is getting very pricey.*

prick VERB **pricks, pricking, pricked** if something sharp pricks you, it sticks into your skin, hurting you

prickle NOUN **prickles** a short sharp spine, like the ones on a hedgehog's back or on a bramble bush

VERB **prickles, prickling, prickled** if something prickles, it makes your skin feel as if it is being pricked by lots of sharp little points

▶ **prickly** ADJECTIVE **pricklier, prickliest** covered in prickles, or feeling like lots of sharp little spines

pride NOUN **prides 1** pride is the good feeling you get when you know you have done something well, or when someone you are connected with has done something well: *His heart swelled with pride.* **2** pride is self-respect: *You should take pride in your appearance.* **3** a pride of lions is a family group of lions

priest NOUN **priests 1** a person who is qualified to conduct services in one of the Christian churches **2** a person with official duties of various kinds in other religions

▶ **priestess** NOUN **priestesses** a female priest in certain ancient or non-Christian religions

▶ **priesthood** NOUN the position of being a priest, or priests as a group

prig NOUN **prigs** a rather old-fashioned word for someone who always behaves correctly and tends to find fault with other people's behaviour

▶ **priggish** ADJECTIVE behaving like a prig

prim ADJECTIVE **primmer, primmest** very formal and correct and easily shocked by rudeness

primary ADJECTIVE first or most important: *the primary route into the city*

primary colour NOUN **primary**

colours (*art*) the primary colours are the colours red, blue and yellow. Most other colours can be made by mixing two or more of the primary colours

primary school NOUN **primary schools** a school for children between the ages of 4 and 12

primate NOUN **primates 1** primates are animals that belong to the group that includes monkeys, apes and humans **2** an archbishop

prime ADJECTIVE greatest, or of the best quality: *a matter of prime importance* • *a prime cut of beef*
NOUN someone is in their prime when they are at the time of their life when they are at their best because they are experienced and wise and are still physically fit
VERB **primes, priming, primed** to prime something is to make it ready for the next stage: *Prime the wood before painting.*

prime minister NOUN **prime ministers** the leader of the government in Britain, and many other countries of the world

prime number NOUN **prime numbers** (*maths*) a number that cannot be divided equally by any number except itself and 1. For example, 3, 5, 7 and 11 are prime numbers, but 9 is not a prime number because it can be divided equally by 3

primitive ADJECTIVE **1** belonging to the earliest stages of development: *primitive societies* • *a primitive kind of computer* **2** rough and unsophisticated: *The hotel was pretty primitive.*

primrose NOUN **primroses** a wild plant with groups of small pale yellow flowers growing from the centre of a cluster of long rounded leaves

prince NOUN **princes** the son or grandson of a king or queen

princess NOUN **princesses** the daughter or granddaughter of a king or queen, or the wife of a prince

principal ADJECTIVE most important: *Steel-making was the principal industry in the area.*

Aa
Bb
Cc
Dd
Ee
Ff
Gg
Hh
Ii
Jj
Kk
Ll
Mm
Nn
Oo
Pp
Qq
Rr
Ss
Tt
Uu
Vv
Ww
Xx
Yy
Zz

NOUN **principals** the head of a school, college or university

▶ **principally** ADVERB mainly or mostly: *She collects old toys, principally dolls.*

principle NOUN **principles 1** a principle is a general rule that something is based on: *We follow the principle of first come, first served.* **2** your principles are the rules of behaviour that you live by: *It was against his principles to borrow money.*

• **in principle** to agree to something in principle is to agree with it in a general way, though you may not agree with all its details

• **on principle** if you do something on principle, you do it because you believe it is right

▶ **principled** ADJECTIVE a principled person always does things that they believe are morally right

print VERB **prints, printing, printed 1** to print something from a computer is to make a copy of it using a computer printer: *Print five copies of the letter.* **2** to print a book or newspaper is to publish it: *These comics are printed in Dundee.* **3** you print when you write words with each letter separate from the one next to it, not joined up: *Print your name at the top of the form.*

NOUN **prints 1** print is the words in a book or newspaper **2** a print is a mark, picture or design made by something pressing down on a surface

▶ **printer** NOUN **printers 1** a machine that prints words and pictures **2** a person or company whose business is printing documents, books and newspapers

prior ADJECTIVE earlier or previous: *I couldn't go because I had a prior engagement.*

priority NOUN **priorities 1** something that has to be dealt with before other things: *Your priority should be to do the work correctly, not quickly.* **2** the right to do something before other people: *Drivers on your right have priority at a roundabout.*

prise VERB **prises, prising, prised** to prise something is to force it open, off or out, often using a flat tool as a lever: *He prised open the lid with a knife.*

prism NOUN **prisms 1** (*science*) a piece of glass with many different planes and angles that split light into its rainbow colours **2** (*maths*) a solid shape with parallel sides and two ends that are the same shape and size

prison NOUN **prisons** a building where criminals are kept

▶ **prisoner** NOUN **prisoners 1** someone who is kept in prison as a punishment **2** someone who is locked up or kept from moving about freely, against their will

privacy NOUN being private, and not having other people see you or know about you: *A higher fence will give us a bit more privacy.*

private ADJECTIVE **1** belonging to and used by only one person, or a small group of people: *a private beach* **2** kept secret or away from people in general: *Our discussions must be strictly private.* **3** owned and run by individual people or companies, not the government: *private industry*

NOUN **privates** an ordinary soldier in the army

▶ **privately** ADVERB **1** secretly: *Privately, he thought the teacher was wrong.* **2** away from other people: *Can we talk privately?*

privatization *or* **privatisation** NOUN the process by which a business owned and controlled by the government is sold to private individuals and companies

privatize *or* **privatise** VERB **privatizes, privatizing, privatized** to privatize a government-owned business is to sell it to private individuals and companies

privet NOUN a plant used in hedges

privilege NOUN **privileges** a special right or advantage given to only one person, or to only a few people

▶ **privileged** ADJECTIVE having advantages or privileges that other people do not have

Aa
Bb
Cc
Dd
Ee
Ff
Gg
Hh
Ii
Jj
Kk
Ll
Mm
Nn
Oo
Pp
Qq
Rr
Ss
Tt
Uu
Vv
Ww
Xx
Yy
Zz

prize NOUN **prizes** something won in a competition or given as a reward for good work

VERB **prizes, prizing, prized** to prize something is to value it very much

pro NOUN **pros** short for **professional**: *a golf pro*

pro- PREFIX **1** if **pro-** comes at the beginning of a word, it adds the meaning *before* or *forward*. For example, a *prologue* is the part before a play and to *proceed* is to go forward **2** if **pro-** comes at the beginning of a word, it adds the meaning *in favour of* or *supporting*. For example, to be *pro-Europe* is to support the European Union

probability NOUN **probabilities** the probability of something happening is how likely it is to happen: *What's the probability of seeing the eclipse clearly?*

probable ADJECTIVE likely: *A candle was the probable cause of the fire.*

▶ **probably** ADVERB likely to be the case, or likely to happen: *It's probably just a cold, rather than flu.* • *The weather forecast said we'd probably get rain in the afternoon.*

probation NOUN if someone is on probation, they are being watched to see if they behave or do a job well

probe NOUN **probes 1** an investigation **2** a spacecraft with no people aboard that is sent into space to investigate things

VERB **probes, probing, probed** to investigate a matter thoroughly by asking questions and examining evidence

problem NOUN **problems 1** a situation, matter or person that causes difficulties, or is difficult to deal with: *There's a problem with the car. It won't start.* **2** a puzzle or question that has to be solved: *The teacher set us the problem of calculating how much water the tank would hold.*

▶ **problematic** ADJECTIVE causing problems

procedure NOUN **procedures 1** a way of doing something or the order in which things are done: *What's*

the procedure for logging on to the database? **2** a piece of writing that tells you how to do something

proceed VERB **proceed, proceeding, proceeded** to proceed is to go on or go forward: *Let's proceed to the next chapter.*

▶ **proceedings** PLURAL NOUN things done or said: *A power cut interrupted proceedings.*

▶ **proceeds** PLURAL NOUN the proceeds from a sale or fund-raising event are all the money made from it

process NOUN **processes 1** a series of things that have to be done in order to achieve something: *Learning to play a musical instrument is a long process.* **2** to be in the process of doing something is to be in the middle of doing it: *I was in the process of cleaning my room when the phone rang.*

VERB **processes, processing, processed** to process something is to deal with it in a number of stages

▶ **procession** NOUN **processions** a line of people or vehicles moving along one behind the other

proclaim VERB **proclaims, proclaiming, proclaimed** to proclaim something is to announce it publicly

▶ **proclamation** NOUN **proclamations** a public announcement of something important

prod VERB **prods, prodding, prodded** to prod something is to poke at it roughly

prodigal ADJECTIVE to be prodigal is to spend or waste money

prodigy NOUN **prodigies** a wonderfully clever or talented person, especially a young person

produce VERB **produces, producing, produced** (pronounced pro-**dyoos**) **1** to produce something is to make, grow or create it: *factories producing goods for export* • *Will the tree produce fruit this year?* • *The sun produces both light and heat.* **2** to produce something is to bring it out so that people can see it: *The magician produced a rabbit from a hat.* **3** to produce a film or play is to

Aa
Bb
Cc
Dd
Ee
Ff
Gg
Hh
Ii
Jj
Kk
Ll
Mm
Nn
Oo
Pp
Qq
Rr
Ss
Tt
Uu
Vv
Ww
Xx
Yy
Zz

product → progress

arrange for it to be made and shown to the public

NOUN (pronounced **prod**-yoos) produce is things grown or produced on farms

▸ **producer** NOUN **producers 1** someone who arranges for a film, television programme or play to be made, by organizing all the equipment, sets and actors, and the money to pay for them **2** someone who makes products or grows produce to be sold: *meat producers*

product NOUN **products 1** something that is produced, either by manufacturing it or growing it on a farm **2** one thing is the product of another when it is the result of that other thing: *Accidents like this are the product of carelessness.* **3** (*maths*) the product is the result you get when you multiply two numbers: *144 is the product of 12 multiplied by 12, or 4 multiplied by 36.*

▸ **production** NOUN **productions 1** making, growing or producing something, or the amount that is produced **2** a version of a play, opera or ballet

productive ADJECTIVE **1** producing a lot: *a productive piece of land* **2** giving good or useful results: *a productive meeting*

▸ **productivity** NOUN the rate at which goods are made or produced, or the rate at which one person works to produce something

profession NOUN **professions** a profession is a job or occupation that needs special qualifications and training, such as medicine, law, teaching and engineering

▸ **professional** ADJECTIVE **1** to do with a profession: *professional training* **2** doing something for money rather than as a hobby or as an amateur: *a professional footballer* **3** someone who is professional does their job with skill and care: *She is always very calm and professional.*

▸ **professionally** ADVERB in a professional way, or for money rather than as an amateur: *a professionally*

qualified accountant • *He used to play football professionally.*

professor NOUN **professors 1** the head of a university department **2** in the United States, a professor is a teacher in a university or college

proficiency NOUN the level of skill you have reached in doing something

▸ **proficient** ADJECTIVE good at something that needs skill or practice: *He's proficient in several languages.*

profile NOUN **profiles 1** a person's profile is the shape of their face seen from the side **2** a profile of someone is a short description of their life

profit NOUN **profits** to make a profit is to make money by selling something for more than you paid for it

VERB **profits, profiting, profited** to profit from something is to benefit from it

▸ **profitable** ADJECTIVE making a good profit

profound ADJECTIVE **1** very great: *profound respect* **2** something said or written is profound if it shows great knowledge and deep thought

▸ **profoundly** ADVERB very: *I was profoundly shocked by what she said.*

program NOUN **programs** (*ICT*) a set of coded instructions put into a computer that allows the computer to perform a task

VERB **programs, programming, programmed** (*ICT*) to program a computer is to put a program into it, which will control how it works or what it does with data

programme NOUN **programmes 1** a show on TV or radio **2** a leaflet or thin book that gives information and details about an event **3** a list of planned events or actions: *a programme of exercise*

progress NOUN **1** progress is improvement: *Freya has made a lot of progress in maths this year.* **2** progress is forward movement: *The bus made very slow progress on the wet and winding roads.*

VERB **progresses, progressing, progressed 1** to develop or improve:

Things are progressing nicely. **2** to go forward: *They progressed slowly up the icy ridge.*

▶ **progression** NOUN going forward, or forward movement

▶ **progressive** ADJECTIVE **1** using the most modern ideas and styles: *progressive dance* **2** gradually improving or getting worse: *a progressive illness*

prohibit VERB **prohibits, prohibiting, prohibited** to prohibit something is to say officially that people cannot do it

▶ **prohibition** NOUN **prohibitions** a law or order preventing people from doing something

▶ **prohibitive** ADJECTIVE the cost of something is prohibitive if it is so expensive you cannot buy it

project NOUN **projects 1** a piece of work done by a pupil or student, often involving study and research **2** a plan: *What's his next project going to be?*

VERB **projects, projecting, projected 1** to stick or jut out **2** to project a film is to show it by running it through a projector **3** to project your voice is to make it carry over a long distance, especially to the back of a theatre

▶ **projection** NOUN **projections 1** a projection is something that sticks or juts out **2** projection is projecting something, especially films

projectionist NOUN **projectionists** someone who operates a film projector in a cinema

projector NOUN **projectors** a machine used to project films on to a screen by focussing a beam of light behind the film through a lens

prologue NOUN **prologues** a short introductory part at the beginning of a play, story or poem

prolong VERB **prolongs, prolonging, prolonged** to prolong something is to make it go on for longer

prom NOUN **proms** a promenade

promenade (pronounced prom-i-nad) NOUN **promenades** a long wide pavement by the sea

prominent ADJECTIVE **1** standing out or easily seen: *prominent teeth* • *a*

prominent landmark **2** a prominent person is famous: *a prominent writer*

▶ **prominence** NOUN being prominent, or something that is prominent

promise VERB **promises, promising, promised 1** you promise when you say that you will, or will not, do something: *I promise to be good.* **2** you promise something to someone when you say that you will give them something or help them in some way: *Sorry, you can't have this seat. I promised it to Vishal.* **3** something promises something good when it shows signs of being good or successful: *It promises to be another lovely day tomorrow.*

NOUN **promises 1** something promised: *Make me a promise that you won't be late.* **2** if someone or something shows promise, they show signs of future success

▶ **promising** ADJECTIVE seeming likely to be good or nice in the future: *a promising student* • *This clear sky looks promising for this afternoon's match.*

promote VERB **promotes, promoting, promoted 1** to promote someone is to move them to a higher ranking job **2** to promote something is to work to spread and encourage it, or to make it popular: *His aim was to promote peace amongst nations.* • *This month, we're promoting a new range of make-up.*

▶ **promotion** NOUN **promotions 1** if someone gets a promotion, they are given a higher ranking job **2** special advertising, designed to make a product popular

prompt ADJECTIVE someone is prompt when they do something without delay

VERB **prompts, prompting, prompted 1** to prompt someone to do something is to cause or encourage them to do it **2** to prompt an actor is to tell them the line that they have to say next

▶ **promptly** ADVERB immediately, without waiting or hesitating

▶ **promptness** NOUN being quick to do something

prone ADJECTIVE **1** you are prone to something if you are likely to suffer from it: *He's prone to headaches.* **2**

Aa
Bb
Cc
Dd
Ee
Ff
Gg
Hh
Ii
Jj
Kk
Ll
Mm
Nn
Oo
Pp
Qq
Rr
Ss
Tt
Uu
Vv
Ww
Xx
Yy
Zz

someone who is prone is lying flat, especially face down

prong NOUN **prongs** a spike of a fork

pronoun WORD CLASS **pronouns** (*grammar*) a word that can be used in place of a noun or a noun phrase. For example, in the sentence *Gary ate the ice cream cone*, *Gary* and *the ice cream cone* could be changed to pronouns and the sentence would be *He ate it*

pronounce VERB **pronounces, pronouncing, pronounced 1** to pronounce words or letters is to say them: *The two 'z's in pizza are pronounced 'tz'.* **2** (*formal*) to pronounce something is to declare it formally and publicly: *The court pronounced him guilty of all charges.*

▶ **pronounced** ADJECTIVE noticeable: *He had a pronounced limp.*

pronunciation NOUN **pronunciations** pronouncing words, or the way a word is pronounced

proof NOUN **proofs** evidence that shows definitely that something is true

prop NOUN **props 1** a heavy piece of wood or metal used to hold a building or other structure up **2** props are the pieces of furniture and other objects used on a stage or on a film set to help make a scene look real

VERB **props, propping, propped** to prop something against an upright surface is to lean it there: *An old bicycle was propped against the wall.*

• **prop something up** to prop something up is to use a prop or props to stop it falling down

propaganda NOUN propaganda is ideas, news or opinions that are spread by a political group or by one side in a war, in order to influence people

propel VERB **propels, propelling, propelled** to propel something is to drive it forward, often using an engine or some other source of power

▶ **propeller** NOUN **propellers** a shaft with revolving blades that drives a ship or aeroplane forward

proper ADJECTIVE **1** right or correct: *Is this the proper way to put up a tent?* **2**

complete or thorough: *Shona gave her room a proper clean.* **3** right according to rules about what is sensible or polite: *It's only proper that you should thank the teacher for her help.*

▶ **properly** ADVERB correctly: *Sit up properly in your chair.*

proper fraction NOUN **proper fractions** (*maths*) a fraction in which the number above the line (the **numerator**) is less than the number below the line (the **denominator**)

proper noun NOUN **proper nouns** (*grammar*) a noun that names a particular person, place or thing. Proper nouns usually begin with a capital letter, for example *Marianne*, *Mauritius*, *Mississippi* and *March*

property NOUN **properties 1** your property is something that belongs to you **2** a property is a house or other building **3** a quality: *the health-giving properties of sea air*

prophecy NOUN **prophecies** if someone makes a prophecy, they say that something will happen at some time in the future

prophesy VERB **prophesies, prophesying, prophesied** to say what will happen in the future

prophet NOUN **prophets 1** someone who claims to be able to predict what will happen in the future **2** prophets are believed by some to be people chosen by God to communicate God's will to the people on Earth

proportion NOUN **proportions 1** a proportion of an amount or total is part of it **2** the proportion of one thing to another is how much there is of one compared with the other **3** something's proportions are its size and measurements

▶ **proportional** ADJECTIVE one thing is proportional to another when it is not too big or small compared to the other thing

proposal NOUN **proposals 1** a plan or suggestion **2** when someone asks another person to marry them

propose VERB **proposes, proposing, proposed 1** to propose something is to suggest it: *Dad proposed that we spend a long weekend in the country.* **2** (*formal*) if you propose to do something, you intend to do it: *He doesn't propose to dance with any girls at the party.* **3** to propose to someone is to ask them to marry you

proprietor NOUN **proprietors** the proprietor of a shop or business is its owner

prose NOUN writing that is not poetry

prosecute VERB **prosecutes, prosecuting, prosecuted** to prosecute someone is to accuse them of a crime and take them to court
▸ **prosecution** NOUN **prosecutions 1** the process of taking someone to court **2** the lawyer or team of lawyers who try to prove that someone is guilty in a court of law

prospect NOUN **prospects 1** how likely it is that something good will happen: *There is little prospect of the weather improving.* **2** the feeling you have about something that is going to happen: *Having to make a speech to the whole school was a terrifying prospect.* **3** prospects means how successful something is likely to be in the future: *What are the team's prospects this season?*
VERB **prospects, prospecting, prospected** to prospect for gold and other precious metals is to search for it in the earth

prosper VERB **prospers, prospering, prospered** to do well, especially by making money
▸ **prosperity** NOUN success, especially having plenty of money
▸ **prosperous** ADJECTIVE a prosperous person has done well, especially by making a lot of money in business

prostrate ADJECTIVE lying flat

protect VERB **protects, protecting, protected** to protect someone or something is to guard them from harm and keep them safe: *Protect the young plants from frost.*
▸ **protection** NOUN **1** protecting **2** safety or shelter: *The boats were heading for the protection of the harbour.*

▸ **protective** ADJECTIVE providing protection
▸ **protector** NOUN **protectors** someone who protects another person

protein NOUN **proteins** a substance found in foods like eggs, meat and milk, which your body needs to stay healthy

protest VERB **protests, protesting, protested** to protest about something is to say publicly that you think it is wrong
NOUN **protests** a strong statement saying that something is wrong or an organized demonstration against something

Protestant NOUN **Protestants** a member of one of the Christian churches that broke away from the Catholic Church at the time of the Reformation

proton NOUN **protons** (*science*) a particle with a positive electric charge that along with **neutrons** makes up the nucleus of an atom

prototype NOUN **prototypes** the first built version of a new design, for example for a new model of car, used to test how well it works before it is manufactured in large numbers

protractor NOUN **protractors** an object, shaped like a half circle, used to draw and measure angles on paper

protrude VERB **protrudes, protruding, protruded** to protrude is to stick out from something
▸ **protrusion** NOUN **protrusions** something that sticks or is pushed out

proud ADJECTIVE **prouder, proudest 1** feeling pride **2** behaving in a way that shows you think you are more important than other people
▸ **proudly** ADVERB in a proud way: *The head teacher spoke proudly about the school.*

prove VERB **proves, proving, proved** to prove something is to show that it is true by providing evidence

proverb NOUN **proverbs** a wise saying that gives advice or makes a statement about something that is true
▸ **proverbial** ADJECTIVE well-known, like a proverb

Aa
Bb
Cc
Dd
Ee
Ff
Gg
Hh
Ii
Jj
Kk
Ll
Mm
Nn
Oo
Pp
Qq
Rr
Ss
Tt
Uu
Vv
Ww
Xx
Yy
Zz

Aa
Bb
Cc
Dd
Ee
Ff
Gg
Hh
Ii
Jj
Kk
Ll
Mm
Nn
Oo
Pp
Qq
Rr
Ss
Tt
Uu
Vv
Ww
Xx
Yy
Zz

provide VERB **provides, providing, provided 1** to provide something is to give or supply it **2** to provide for someone is to supply the money and other things they need to live

province NOUN **provinces 1** a division of a country, usually with its own local government **2** the provinces are the parts of a country away from the capital
▸ **provincial** ADJECTIVE belonging to the provinces or typical of the provinces

provision NOUN **provisions 1** providing something **2** to make provision for something is to prepare for it
▸ **provisions** PLURAL NOUN food and other items you need, for example if you go on a long journey

provocation NOUN **provocations** something someone does deliberately to make someone else angry

provoke VERB **provokes, provoking, provoked** to provoke someone is to deliberately make them angry

prow NOUN **prows** the prow of a boat is the raised part at the front or bows

prowl VERB **prowls, prowling, prowled** to move quietly and in a secretive way, usually intending to do something bad
▸ **prowler** NOUN **prowlers** someone who prowls, for example someone who is intending to burgle a house

proximity NOUN nearness: *People living in such proximity can get on each other's nerves.*

prudent ADJECTIVE careful and wise, and not taking any risks, especially with money
▸ **prudence** NOUN being careful and cautious

prune[1] VERB **prunes, pruning, pruned** to prune a plant or tree is to cut bits off it to make it smaller

prune[2] NOUN **prunes** a dried plum

pry VERB **pries, prying, pried** to try to find out things that people would rather you didn't know

PS ABBREVIATION short for **postscript**. PS is written before an extra bit that you add to the end of a letter after your signature

psalm (pronounced **sam**) NOUN **psalms** a holy song, especially one from the Bible

pseudonym (pronounced **soo-doh-nim**) NOUN **pseudonyms** a name that someone, especially a writer, uses instead of their real name

PSHE ABBREVIATION short for **personal, social and health education**

psychiatry (pronounced sy-**ky**-a-tri) NOUN the branch of medicine that studies and treats mental illness
▸ **psychiatric** ADJECTIVE to do with psychiatry or mental illness
▸ **psychiatrist** NOUN **psychiatrists** a doctor who treats mentally ill people

psychology (pronounced sy-**kol**-i-ji) NOUN the study of the mind and how it affects the way humans and animals act
▸ **psychological** ADJECTIVE to do with the mind
▸ **psychologist** NOUN **psychologists** someone who has studied psychology and human behaviour

pub NOUN **pubs** a place where people buy and drink alcoholic drinks

puberty NOUN the time when a child's body begins to change into an adult's

public NOUN **1** the public are people generally **2** to do something in public is to do it where anyone can see it or can take part
ADJECTIVE
1 to do with all the people of a country or community: *public opinion*
2 for anyone to use: *a public park*
3 known by everyone: *The government is making the information public.*
4 a public figure is someone who is well known and appears in newspapers or on television a lot

publication NOUN **publications**
1 something, such as a magazine or newspaper, that is printed and sold **2** publishing something: *the publication of the last Harry Potter book*

publicity NOUN **1** advertising or anything done to make the public aware of something **2** public interest or attention

publicize *or* **publicise** VERB
publicizes, publicizing, publicized to publicize something is to advertise it or make it known publicly

publish VERB **publishes, publishing, published** to publish something is to print it in a book, newspaper or magazine
> **publisher** NOUN **publishers** a person or company that publishes books, newspapers or magazines
> **publishing** NOUN the work or business of printing books, newspapers and magazines

puck NOUN **pucks** the hard disc hit by the players in ice hockey

pucker VERB **puckers, puckering, puckered** to squeeze or push something together to form creases or wrinkles

pudding NOUN **puddings** a sweet dish that you eat as the last course at dinner

puddle NOUN **puddles** water filling a shallow hole in the ground

puff VERB **puffs, puffing, puffed 1** to puff smoke or steam is to blow it out **2** you puff when you breathe quickly because you have been exercising **3** to puff something out, or puff it up, is to make it swell or become larger
NOUN **puffs** a small amount of breath, wind, air or smoke

puffin NOUN **puffins** a small black-and-white sea bird with a large coloured beak that makes it look a bit like a parrot

puffy ADJECTIVE **puffier, puffiest** swollen: *puffy eyes*

pull VERB **pulls, pulling, pulled 1** to pull something is to take hold of it and bring it towards you **2** if you pull a muscle, you stretch it or strain it so that it is painful
• **pull a face** to twist your face into an ugly or funny shape
• **pull in** a driver pulls in when they move to the side of the road and stop
• **pull something off** to pull something off is to manage to do it successfully
• **pull out 1** a driver pulls out when they move out of a side road on to a main road or they move to an outer lane to overtake another vehicle **2** to pull out of an arrangement is to stop taking part in it
• **pull through** someone who has been dangerously ill pulls through when they recover
• **pull up** a driver pulls up when they slow down and stop
• **pull yourself together** to get control of your emotions
NOUN **pulls** a pulling movement

pulley NOUN **pulleys** a device for lifting heavy things, consisting of a wheel with a rope going over the top of it

pullover NOUN **pullovers** a knitted piece of clothing for the top half of your body that you pull on over your head

pulp NOUN **pulps 1** the soft fleshy part of a fruit **2** a soft mass, especially a soft mass of wood that is used to make paper
VERB **pulps, pulping, pulped** to make something into a soft mass

pulpit NOUN **pulpits** a high platform in a church that the minister stands on to give a sermon

pulsate VERB **pulsates, pulsating, pulsated** to vibrate or move with a regular rhythm

pulse[1] NOUN **pulses** your pulse is the regular beat that you feel on your wrist or neck caused by the heart pumping blood through your arteries
VERB **pulses, pulsing, pulsed** something that pulses vibrates or moves with a regular rhythm

pulse[2] NOUN **pulses** pulses are seeds you can eat, such as peas, beans and lentils

pulverize *or* **pulverise** VERB **pulverizes, pulverizing, pulverized** to pulverize something is to crush it to dust or powder

puma NOUN **pumas** a large wild animal of the cat family that lives in North America

pumice NOUN a light, soft kind of stone that can be used to smooth or clean something

pummel VERB **pummels, pummelling, pummelled** to pummel

Aa
Bb
Cc
Dd
Ee
Ff
Gg
Hh
Ii
Jj
Kk
Ll
Mm
Nn
Oo
Pp
Qq
Rr
Ss
Tt
Uu
Vv
Ww
Xx
Yy
Zz

someone or something is to beat them or it hard and repeatedly with your fists

pump NOUN **pumps** a device or machine used to force or drive liquids or gases in, through or out of something: *a bicycle pump*
VERB **pumps, pumping, pumped** to pump liquid or gas is to force it up, through or out of something using a pump

pumpkin NOUN **pumpkins** a very large round vegetable with thick yellow skin and soft orange flesh

pun NOUN **puns** a joke using words that have more than one meaning, or words that sound the same but have different meanings. For example: *Two pears make a pair*

punch VERB **punches, punching, punched** to hit someone or something with your fist
NOUN **punches 1** a blow with the fist **2** a machine for making holes

punchline NOUN **punchlines** the punchline of a joke or funny story is the part at the end that makes you laugh

punctual ADJECTIVE arriving exactly on time, not early or late
▶ **punctuality** NOUN being on time
▶ **punctually** ADVERB on time

punctuate VERB **punctuates, punctuating, punctuated 1** (*grammar*) to punctuate written work is to put commas, full stops and other punctuation marks in it **2** if something is punctuated with things, these things happen or are done all through it or during it: *Her story was punctuated by giggles.*
▶ **punctuation** NOUN (*grammar*) the process of putting commas, full stops and other punctuation marks in writing

punctuation mark NOUN **punctuation marks** (*grammar*) any of the special marks, such as full stops and commas, used in writing to mark off pauses or breaks in what has been written

puncture NOUN **punctures** a hole made right through the outer surface of something
VERB **punctures, puncturing, punctured** to puncture something is to

make a hole in its outer skin or covering

pungent ADJECTIVE a pungent smell is very strong and noticeable

punish VERB **punishes, punishing, punished** to punish someone is to make them suffer for something they have done wrong
▶ **punishable** ADJECTIVE having a particular punishment: *The crime of murder is punishable by death in many countries.*
▶ **punishment** NOUN **punishments 1** punishing someone, or being punished **2** a particular method of making someone suffer for something they have done wrong

punk NOUN **punks 1** rock music played in a very loud and aggressive way **2** a young person with a style of dressing and behaving that is meant to shock people, such as having spiky coloured hair and wearing ripped clothes with chains and pins on them

punt NOUN **punts** a boat with a flat bottom that is moved along on rivers by someone standing upright and pushing with a long pole
VERB **punts, punting, punted** to punt is to travel on a river in a punt

puny ADJECTIVE **punier, puniest** weak and small

pup NOUN **pups** a young dog or a young seal

pupa NOUN **pupae** (*science*) the form of an insect's body when it is changing from a larva to its adult form, for example the form a caterpillar has inside a chrysalis before it changes into a butterfly or moth

pupil NOUN **pupils 1** a child or adult who is being taught **2** the pupil of your eye is the round opening in the middle of your eye through which light passes

puppet NOUN **puppets** a doll that can be moved by wires or strings, or fitted over your hand and moved by your fingers
▶ **puppeteer** NOUN **puppeteers** someone who operates puppets

puppy NOUN **puppies** a baby dog

purchase VERB **purchases,**

purchasing, purchased to purchase something is to buy it

NOUN **purchases** something you have bought

▸ **purchaser** NOUN **purchasers** a buyer

pure ADJECTIVE **purer, purest 1** not mixed with anything else: *pure gold* • *pure greed* **2** clean: *pure water* **3** a pure person is innocent and does not do any wrong things

▸ **purely** ADVERB only or simply: *Our meeting was purely accidental.*

purge VERB **purges, purging, purged** to purge people or things is to get rid of them because they are not wanted

NOUN **purges** the act of getting rid of people or things that are not wanted

purify VERB **purifies, purifying, purified** to purify something is to make it clean or pure

purity NOUN being pure

purple NOUN a dark reddish-blue colour

▸ **purplish** ADJECTIVE quite purple but not completely purple in colour

purpose NOUN **purposes 1** you have a purpose when you are intending to do or achieve a particular thing **2** something's purpose is the job or role it is intended for

• **on purpose** to do something on purpose is to do it intentionally

▸ **purposely** ADVERB on purpose

purposeful ADJECTIVE showing you are intending to do a particular thing: *a purposeful walk to the shops*

▸ **purposefully** ADVERB in a way that shows you are intending to do a particular thing: *Sarah began to walk purposefully towards the house.*

purr VERB **purrs, purring, purred** a cat purrs when it makes a low vibrating noise because it is contented

purse NOUN **purses** a small container for money, for carrying in a handbag or pocket

VERB **purses, pursing, pursed** you purse your lips when you draw them together into a round shape with your mouth tightly shut

pursue VERB **pursues, pursuing, pursued 1** to pursue someone is to follow or chase them, usually in order to catch them **2** to pursue an activity or aim is to be involved in it or work hard at it

▸ **pursuer** NOUN **pursuers** someone who tries to catch the person or thing in front

▸ **pursuit** NOUN **pursuits 1** pursuing someone or something: *a pack of dogs in pursuit of a hare* **2** trying to achieve an aim or goal **3** an activity that interests you or that you do as a hobby: *My favourite pursuits are football and reading.*

pus NOUN a thick yellowish liquid that forms in infected wounds

push VERB **pushes, pushing, pushed 1** to push something is to press against it with your hands or body so that it moves **2** to push someone is to try hard to make them do something: *He wouldn't do any work if he wasn't pushed.*

• **push someone around** to push someone around is to bully them

• **push off** (*informal*) to push off is to go away

NOUN **pushes** a pushing movement

pushchair NOUN **pushchairs** a small folding chair on wheels used for pushing a young child around

pushy ADJECTIVE **pushier, pushiest** a pushy person behaves in a forceful way, determined to get their own way or to get attention

puss or **pussy** NOUN **pusses** or **pussies** a name people often call their pet cat

put VERB **puts, putting, put 1** to put something somewhere is to move it or place it there: *Put the shopping over there.* • *He put his hand over his eyes.* **2** to put something is to say or to write it: *I wouldn't put it like that.* • *I had to write a message in the card but I didn't know what to put.* **3** to cause someone or something to be in a particular situation or mood: *You've put me in a difficult position.* • *The news put Dad in a bit of a bad mood.*

Aa
Bb
Cc
Dd
Ee
Ff
Gg
Hh
Ii
Jj
Kk
Ll
Mm
Nn
Oo
Pp
Qq
Rr
Ss
Tt
Uu
Vv
Ww
Xx
Yy
Zz

putrid → python

Aa
Bb
Cc
Dd
Ee
Ff
Gg
Hh
Ii
Jj
Kk
Ll
Mm
Nn
Oo
Pp
Qq
Rr
Ss
Tt
Uu
Vv
Ww
Xx
Yy
Zz

• **put someone down** to put someone down is to criticize them or make them feel silly

• **put someone off** if something puts you off something, it makes you not want to do it or have it

• **put something off** to put something off is to delay it until a later time

• **put someone out** if someone or something puts you out, they cause you inconvenience or trouble

• **put up with** to put up with someone or something that is annoying or unpleasant is to accept them or it without complaining

putrid ADJECTIVE rotten and smelling bad

putt NOUN **putts** in golf, a gentle hit of the ball that you make so that it will go into the hole

VERB **putts, putting, putted** in golf to hit a ball gently so that it rolls forward on the green towards the hole

▸ **putter** NOUN **putters** a golf club used for putting

putty NOUN an oily grey or white paste used for fixing glass in window frames

puzzle NOUN **puzzles 1** a game or toy that gives you a problem to solve **2** something that is a puzzle is hard to understand

VERB **puzzles, puzzling, puzzled** something puzzles you if you do not understand it or you cannot decide what it means

PVC ABBREVIATION short for **polyvinyl chloride**, which is a type of plastic

pygmy NOUN **pygmies** a member of an African tribe of very small people
ADJECTIVE of a kind that is much smaller than the normal kind: *a pygmy hippopotamus*

pyjamas PLURAL NOUN a suit with a top and matching trousers that you wear in bed

✦ **Pyjamas** comes from the Persian and Hindi word **payjamah**, which means 'clothing for the leg', because pyjamas have trousers.

pylon NOUN **pylons** a tall metal tower that supports electric power cables

pyramid NOUN **pyramids 1** a solid shape, with flat triangular sides, that comes to a point at the top **2** a tomb with this shape built for one of the ancient Egyptian pharaohs

python NOUN **pythons** a large snake that kills its prey by winding itself around it and crushing it in its powerful coils

Qq

quack NOUN **quacks** the sound made by a duck
VERB **quacks, quacking, quacked** a duck quacks when it makes this sound

quad NOUN **quads** short for **quadrangle** or **quadruplet**

quadrangle NOUN **quadrangles 1** (*maths*) a square, rectangle or other figure with four sides **2** a four-sided courtyard surrounded by buildings, usually in a school or college

quadrant NOUN **quadrants** (*maths*) a quarter of a circle

quadrilateral NOUN **quadrilaterals** (*maths*) a shape with four straight sides
ADJECTIVE having four sides

quadruped NOUN **quadrupeds** an animal that has four feet: *Cows, goats and sheep are all quadrupeds.*

quadruple ADJECTIVE **1** four times as much or as many **2** made up of four parts
VERB **quadruples, quadrupling, quadrupled 1** to quadruple something is to make it four times greater: *The shopkeeper had quadrupled the price.* **2** to quadruple is to become four times greater: *The river quadrupled in size during the rainy season.*

quadruplet NOUN **quadruplets** one of four children born at one time to the same mother

quagmire NOUN **quagmires** wet boggy ground: *Heavy rain had turned the garden into a quagmire.*

quail NOUN **quails** a type of small bird like a partridge

quaint ADJECTIVE **quainter, quaintest** pleasant, especially in an old-fashioned way: *quaint customs*

quake VERB **quakes, quaking, quaked** to tremble or shake: *The ground quaked under their feet.*
NOUN **quakes** (*informal*) an earthquake

Quaker NOUN **Quakers** a member of a religious group founded in the 17th century, which disagrees with violence and war

qualification NOUN **qualifications** an exam you have passed or a skill that you have that makes you suitable for a job or type of work: *What qualifications do you need for this job?*

qualify VERB **qualifies, qualifying, qualified 1** to qualify for something, such as a job, is to be suitable for it: *He is too young to qualify for a place in the team.* **2** to qualify as something, such as a doctor or a lawyer, is to pass all the exams that are needed to do the job **3** to qualify something, such as a statement or a remark, is to make it less strong by adding or changing words

quality NOUN **qualities 1** how good or bad something is: *cloth of poor quality* **2** a part of someone's character that makes them behave in a certain way: *Her best qualities are her kindness and honesty.*

quantity NOUN **quantities** amount or number: *a small quantity of paper • large quantities of tinned food*

quarantine NOUN if a person or animal is in quarantine, they are kept away from other people or animals because they have or might have a disease that they could pass on

quarrel VERB **quarrels, quarrelling, quarrelled** to quarrel with someone is to argue angrily with them: *I've quarrelled with my brother. • We often hear them quarrelling next door.*
NOUN **quarrels** an angry argument: *I've had a quarrel with my brother.*
▶ **quarrelsome** ADJECTIVE quarrelling a lot: *quarrelsome children*

quarry NOUN **quarries 1** a place where stone is dug out of the ground **2** an animal that is being hunted

quart NOUN **quarts** an imperial unit for measuring the volume of a liquid, equal to 1.136 litres or 2 pints

quarter NOUN **quarters 1** a quarter is one of four equal parts that together make up the whole of something: *We cut the cake into quarters.* **2** (*maths*) the fraction ¼, equivalent to the decimal fraction 0.25, and equal to one divided by four **3** one fourth of a year, three months
VERB **quarters, quartering, quartered** to quarter something is to divide it into four equal parts

quarter-final NOUN **quarter-finals** the third-last round in a competition, immediately before the semi-final

quarters PLURAL NOUN a place to stay, especially for soldiers

quartet NOUN **quartets** (*music*) **1** a group of four musicians or singers **2** a piece of music written for four musicians or singers

quartz NOUN a hard substance found in rocks in the form of crystals that can be used in electronic clocks and watches

quaver VERB **quavers, quavering, quavered** to shake or tremble: *Her voice quavered with fright as she spoke.*
NOUN **quavers 1** a trembling: *He tried to sound brave but there was a quaver in his voice.* **2** (*music*) a musical note equal to half a crotchet. The symbol for a quaver is ♪

quay (pronounced **kee**) NOUN **quays** the edge of a harbour where ships are loaded or unloaded

queasy ADJECTIVE **queasier, queasiest** feeling sick: *The motion of the boat made her queasy.*

queen NOUN **queens**
1 a woman who rules a country: *Queen Elizabeth II*
2 the wife of a king: *the king and his queen*
3 in the game of chess, the queen is a piece that has a crown and can move in any direction
4 a playing card with a picture of a queen: *the queen of hearts*
5 a female bee, ant or wasp that lays eggs

queer ADJECTIVE **queerer, queerest** odd or strange: *queer behaviour*

quench VERB **quenches, quenching, quenched 1** to quench your thirst is to drink until you no longer feel thirsty **2** to quench a fire is to put it out

query NOUN **queries 1** a question: *Please phone me if you have any queries.* **2** a question mark
VERB **queries, querying, queried** to query something is to question whether it is correct or true: *My Dad rang the gas company to query the bill.*

quest NOUN **quests** a search, especially a long one: *his quest for the truth*

question NOUN **questions**
1 what you ask when you want to know something: *After the talk, some people asked questions.*
2 one of the things you have to answer or write about in an exam: *I didn't have time to answer all the questions*
3 a subject for discussion: *There is the question of how much to pay him.*
4 a suggestion or possibility: *There's no question of him leaving.*

questionable ADJECTIVE something that is questionable does not seem to be completely good, correct, or honest: *Her reasons seem questionable.*

question mark NOUN **question marks** the punctuation mark (?) that you write after a question, for example *Are you coming out to play?*

questionnaire NOUN **questionnaires** a list of questions to be answered by several people to get information for a survey

queue NOUN **queues** a line of people waiting for something: *There was a long queue outside the cinema.*
VERB **queues, queueing, queued** to stand in a line waiting for something: *We had to queue for three hours to get the tickets.*

quibble VERB **quibbles, quibbling, quibbled** to argue or complain about details that are not important
NOUN **quibbles** an argument or complaint about unimportant details

quiche (pronounced **keesh**) NOUN **quiches** an open tart filled with beaten eggs, cheese and other savoury fillings

Aa
Bb
Cc
Dd
Ee
Ff
Gg
Hh
Ii
Jj
Kk
Ll
Mm
Nn
Oo
Pp
Qq
Rr
Ss
Tt
Uu
Vv
Ww
Xx
Yy
Zz

quick ADJECTIVE **quicker, quickest 1** fast: *a quick walker* **2** done in a short time: *a quick trip into town* **3** doing something without delay: *She's always quick to help.*

▸ **quickly** ADVERB if someone does something quickly, they do it rapidly or at great speed: *Come quickly! Someone's fallen in the river!*

quicksand NOUN **quicksands** loose wet sand that sucks in anything that lands on it

quick-tempered ADJECTIVE if someone is quick-tempered, they are easily made angry

quid NOUN **quid** (*slang*) a pound (£1): *He paid fifty quid for the jacket.*

quiet ADJECTIVE **quieter, quietest 1** not loud: *a quiet voice* **2** calm and peaceful: *a quiet life*
NOUN a quiet state or time: *in the quiet of the night*

▸ **quieten** VERB **quietens, quietening, quietened 1** to quieten something or someone is to make them quiet: *Her mother was trying to quieten her.* **2** to quieten, or quieten down, is to become quiet: *Things seem to have quietened down.*

▸ **quietly** ADVERB with little or no sound: *She slipped quietly from the room.*

▸ **quietness** NOUN being quiet: *the quietness of early morning*

quill NOUN **quills** a large feather of a goose or other bird made into a pen

quilt NOUN **quilts** a warm cover for a bed, filled with feathers or some other material

quintet NOUN **quintets** (*music*) **1** a group of five musicians or singers **2** a piece of music written for five musicians or singers

quit VERB **quits, quitting, quit** or **quitted 1** to quit doing something is to stop it: *My Mum's trying to quit smoking.* **2** to quit something is to leave it: *He's quit his job.*

▸ **quitter** NOUN **quitters** someone who gives up too easily

quite ADVERB **1** rather: *I'm quite hungry*

but *I don't mind waiting.* **2** completely: *I'm afraid I'm not quite ready.*

quiver¹ VERB **quivers, quivering, quivered** to tremble or shake: *Her lip quivered and her eyes filled with tears.*

quiver² NOUN **quivers** a case for carrying arrows

quiz NOUN **quizzes** a competition in which you have to answer questions on different subjects: *a TV quiz show*
VERB **quizzes, quizzing, quizzed** to quiz someone is to ask them lots of questions

quoits NOUN a game in which heavy flat rings called quoits are thrown onto small pegs

quota NOUN **quotas** the part or share given to each member of a group: *Each school has received its quota of funds.*

quotation NOUN **quotations 1** quotation is the act of repeating something that someone else has said or written **2** a quotation is a set of words taken from a speech or piece of writing: *a quotation from Shakespeare* **3** a quotation is the price that someone says they will charge you for doing a job: *We got a quotation for fixing the roof.*

quotation marks PLURAL NOUN (*grammar*) the punctuation marks ' ' or " ", which you use in writing to show that someone's words are being repeated exactly. They are sometimes called **inverted commas**

quote VERB **quotes, quoting, quoted 1** to quote someone is to repeat their words exactly as they said or wrote them **2** to quote words is to use them in a quotation **3** to quote a price is to tell someone how much you will charge them for doing a job: *He quoted a price for repairing the bicycle.*

quotient NOUN **quotients** (*maths*) the result you get when you divide one number by another. For example, 4 is the quotient when 12 is divided by 3

Qur'an (pronounced koo-**ran**) NOUN the Qur'an is the Koran, the holy book of the Islamic religion

Aa
Bb
Cc
Dd
Ee
Ff
Gg
Hh
Ii
Jj
Kk
Ll
Mm
Nn
Oo
Pp
Qq
Rr
Ss
Tt
Uu
Vv
Ww
Xx
Yy
Zz

Rr

rabbi NOUN **rabbis** a Jewish religious minister

✦ This is a Hebrew word that means *my master*.

rabbit NOUN **rabbits** a long-eared furry animal that lives in holes in the ground that are called burrows

rabble NOUN a noisy, uncontrolled crowd of people

rabid ADJECTIVE affected with rabies

rabies NOUN a disease that causes madness and then death. Humans catch rabies if they are bitten by an animal that has it

raccoon NOUN **raccoons** a small furry animal from North America that has a bushy striped tail

race[1] NOUN **races** a competition to be first at something: *a two-mile horse race* • *the race to put the first man on the moon*
VERB **races, racing, raced 1** to try to do something first, before anyone else: *I'll race you to the postbox.* **2** to go very fast: *The car raced along the narrow lanes.* • *I could feel my heart racing with excitement.*

race[2] NOUN **races** a large group of people who have the same ancestors and look the same in some ways, for example in the colour of their skin or their hair

racecourse NOUN **racecourses** the track that racehorses run on

racetrack NOUN **racetracks** a piece of ground on which races are run

racial ADJECTIVE to do with a person's race or different races of people: *efforts to stop racial prejudice*

racism NOUN disliking people, or treating them badly or unfairly, simply because they belong to a different race

▸ **racist** NOUN **racists** someone who dislikes people who belong to

a different race from them ADJECTIVE showing racism: *racist taunts*

rack NOUN **racks 1** a framework with rails, shelves or hooks, for holding or storing things: *a mug rack* **2** a device for torturing people by stretching them
VERB **racks, racking, racked** to rack your brains is to try as hard as you can to think of something

racket[1] NOUN **rackets** an oval frame with strings stretched across it that you use for hitting the ball in games like tennis and squash

racket[2] NOUN **rackets 1** a loud and disturbing noise: *Will you turn that racket down?* **2** an illegal scheme for making money

racoon NOUN **racoons** another spelling of **raccoon**

radar NOUN a system that uses radio waves that bounce off solid objects to find the position of aeroplanes or ships

radiance NOUN happiness that shows on your face

▸ **radiant** ADJECTIVE showing a lot of happiness: *a picture of the radiant bride*

radiate VERB **radiates, radiating, radiated 1** to radiate heat or light is to send it out **2** things radiate from a central point when they form a pattern of lines like spokes in a wheel

▸ **radiation** NOUN radioactive energy that can harm or kill people if they are exposed to it

▸ **radiator** NOUN **radiators 1** part of a central heating system that releases heat into a room **2** part of an engine that keeps it cool

radical ADJECTIVE a radical idea is one that involves big, important changes

radio NOUN **radios 1** a system of broadcasting that uses sound waves instead of wires to send messages **2** an electrical device that receives or sends messages as sound waves

the radius
of a circle

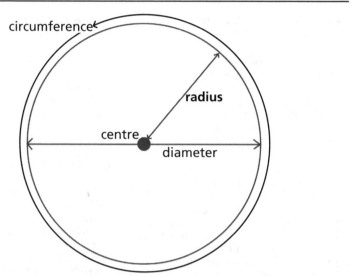

VERB **radios, radioing, radioed** to communicate with someone by radio: *Tell them to radio for help.*

radioactive ADJECTIVE giving off rays that can be dangerous, even in very small amounts

▶ **radioactivity** NOUN the energy that is produced by the atoms of some substances, such as uranium, and which may be harmful

radish NOUN **radishes** a small round vegetable with a red skin that is eaten raw in salads

radius NOUN **radii** (*maths*) the distance from the centre of a circle to its outside edge. See the picture above

✦ A **radius** is so called because it is the Latin word for 'the spoke of a wheel', which goes from the centre to the outside edge.

raffle NOUN **raffles** a lottery to win a prize: *a book of raffle tickets*
VERB **raffles, raffling, raffled** to raffle something is to offer it as a prize in a lottery

raft NOUN **rafts** a simple boat made from pieces of wood tied together to form a platform to sit on

rafter NOUN **rafters** one of the sloping pieces of wood that form the framework inside a roof

rag NOUN **rags** an old piece of cloth: *dressed in rags* • *Polish the wood with a soft rag.*

rage NOUN violent anger: *I've never seen him fly into a rage like that before.*
• **all the rage** very fashionable: *Flares are all the rage again.*

ragged (pronounced rag-id) ADJECTIVE torn and untidy: *ragged clothes*

raid NOUN **raids** 1 a sudden unexpected attack by soldiers or military planes: *a bombing raid* 2 a sudden unexpected visit from the police, who force their way into a building and search it
VERB **raids, raiding, raided** 1 to raid a place is to attack it suddenly, without warning 2 to raid a place is to use force to get into it, in order to search for something

▶ **raider** NOUN **raiders** a person who attacks, searches for something and removes it

rail NOUN **rails** 1 a bar for hanging things on: *a towel rail* 2 a long steel bar that is one of the tracks that a train runs on 3 rail travel or travel by rail is travelling by train

Aa
Bb
Cc
Dd
Ee
Ff
Gg
Hh
Ii
Jj
Kk
Ll
Mm
Nn
Oo
Pp
Qq
Rr
Ss
Tt
Uu
Vv
Ww
Xx
Yy
Zz

▶ **railing** NOUN **railings** one of the vertical bars that make up a fence: *He was leaning on the railings.*

railway NOUN **railways** a track for trains to travel on: *a house by the railway* • *a short railway journey*

rain NOUN drops of water falling from the clouds: *a heavy shower of rain*
VERB **rains, raining, rained** it is raining when drops of water fall from the clouds

• **be rained off** an event such as a sports match is rained off if rain stops it from happening

rainbow NOUN **rainbows** an arch of different colours that you can see in the sky when it is raining and the sun is shining at the same time

raincoat NOUN **raincoats** a light waterproof coat

rainfall NOUN the amount of rain that falls in a certain place over a certain period of time

rainforest NOUN **rainforests** an area of thick tropical forest with very tall trees and a high rainfall

rain gauge NOUN **rain gauges** an instrument for measuring how much rain has fallen

rainy ADJECTIVE **rainier, rainiest** a rainy day is one when it rains a lot

raise VERB **raises, raising, raised**
1 to raise something is to lift it up: *Raise your hand if you know the answer.* • *The wreck was slowly raised from the seabed.*
2 to raise an amount or number is to increase it: *They've raised prices again.*
3 to raise a subject is to mention it in a discussion: *I want to raise a matter that we all care very much about.*
4 to raise money is to get money together for a certain reason: *We're raising money for the school.*
5 to raise children is to look after them until they are grown up
6 to raise crops is to grow them

raisin NOUN **raisins** a dried grape

rake NOUN **rakes** a gardening tool like a large comb with a long handle

VERB **rakes, raking, raked** to use a rake, usually to collect leaves or smooth the soil

• **rake in** (*informal*) to rake in money is to get a lot of it easily: *We were raking the money in from everyone at the sale.*

rally NOUN **rallies** **1** a large meeting of people, especially for an outdoor meeting **2** a car race on a course that includes ordinary roads and forest tracks **3** in sports like tennis, a rally is a series of strokes and returns that make up one point
VERB **rallies, rallying, rallied** **1** to feel better and improve after being ill or suffering a setback: *The team have rallied now and will probably win.* **2** to rally or rally round is when people join together to support or help someone: *Everyone rallied round to help when Mum was ill.*

ram NOUN **rams** a male sheep
VERB **rams, ramming, rammed** **1** if a vehicle rams something, it hits it very hard: *The boat was clearly going to ram the pier.* **2** to push something into something else with a lot of force: *He rammed the cake into his mouth.*

RAM NOUN (*ICT*) short for **Random Access Memory**, which is a type of computer memory

Ramadan NOUN the ninth month of the Islamic calendar, when Muslims fast during the day

ramble VERB **rambles, rambling, rambled** **1** to walk about the countryside for pleasure **2** to ramble, or ramble on, is to speak or write a lot without keeping to the subject
NOUN **rambles** a long walk in the countryside

▶ **rambler** NOUN **ramblers** a person who enjoys walking in the countryside

ramp NOUN **ramps** a sloping surface: *We should be able to get the wheelchair up the ramp quite easily.*

rampage VERB **rampages, rampaging, rampaged** people or animals rampage when they rush about wildly or violently
NOUN

• on the rampage to go on the rampage is to seem to go mad, causing damage and trouble

rampart NOUN **ramparts** a mound or wall that is built around a castle or town to defend it

ramshackle ADJECTIVE a ramshackle building is in very bad condition and falling apart

ran VERB a way of changing the verb **run** to make a past tense: *I ran all the way here.*

ranch NOUN **ranches** a large farm, especially one in North America, where they keep cattle and horses

rancid ADJECTIVE tasting or smelling sour: *When we came home we found the rancid butter in the fridge.*

random ADJECTIVE done without a plan or a system: *a random selection*

range NOUN **ranges**
1 a number of different things that are of the same type: *a huge range of evening wear*
2 the distance that something can travel: *Spectators have to stand well out of range of the arrows.*
3 (*music*) the distance between the top and bottom notes of a voice or musical instrument
4 an area where you can practise hitting golf balls or shooting: *a firing-range*
5 a group of hills or mountains: *a mountain range in the distance*
6 an old-fashioned kitchen stove
VERB **ranges, ranging, ranged 1** to range between two things is to include those things and several other things too: *holidays ranging from hostels to luxury hotels* **2** to wander around or over a place: *We ranged over the hills for days.*
▶ ranger NOUN **rangers** a person whose job is to look after a forest or park

rank NOUN **ranks** someone's position, grade or level in an organization or in society: *A private is the lowest rank in the British army.* • *A duchess has a very high social rank.*
VERB **ranks, ranking, ranked** to have a certain position amongst other things: *He ranks as one of the world's best actors.*

ransack VERB **ransacks, ransacking, ransacked** to ransack a place is to search through it and steal or damage things: *The Inspector came home to find his flat had been ransacked.*

ransom NOUN **ransoms** a ransom is the money that kidnappers demand before they will give back someone they have taken hostage

rant VERB **rants, ranting, ranted** to speak in a loud, angry, uncontrolled way

rap VERB **raps, rapping, rapped 1** to hit something quickly and sharply: *Mother's piano teacher used to rap her over the knuckles when she played a wrong note.* **2** to perform a song by speaking the words in rhythm
NOUN **raps 1** a quick sharp tap or hit: *a rap at the door* **2** a pop song in which someone speaks the words in a rhythm

rapid ADJECTIVE moving, acting or happening very quickly: *a rapid response to the emergency situation*
▶ rapidly ADVERB very quickly: *moving rapidly on to the next question*
▶ rapids PLURAL NOUN parts of a river where the water flows very quickly, usually over dangerous rocks

rare ADJECTIVE **rarer, rarest 1** not often done or found, or not occurring often: *a rare example of a blue diamond* • *It's rare to find a vase like this in perfect condition.* **2** rare meat is not cooked all the way through
▶ rarely ADVERB not very often: *Grandma rarely goes out.*
▶ rarity NOUN **rarities 1** a rarity is something that is not found very often: *This vase is truly a rarity.* **2** rarity is unusualness: *very expensive because of its rarity*

rascal NOUN **rascals 1** a cheeky or naughty child **2** an old-fashioned word for a dishonest person

rash[1] ADJECTIVE **rasher, rashest** a rash person does foolish things quickly without thinking first

rash[2] NOUN **rashes** an area of redness or red spots on your skin, caused by an

Aa
Bb
Cc
Dd
Ee
Ff
Gg
Hh
Ii
Jj
Kk
Ll
Mm
Nn
Oo
Pp
Qq
Rr
Ss
Tt
Uu
Vv
Ww
Xx
Yy
Zz

illness or allergy

rasher NOUN **rashers** a rasher of bacon is a thin slice of it

rasp VERB **rasps, rasping, rasped** to make a rough grating noise

NOUN **rasps** a rough grating sound: *the loud rasp of the old hinges moving*

raspberry NOUN **raspberries** a red berry that you can eat and that grows on bushes

rat NOUN **rats** a small furry animal like a large mouse with a long tail

rate NOUN **rates** how fast or often something happens: *The rate of progress has been very slow. • The disease is spreading at a tremendous rate.*

• **at any rate** anyway: *He's gone to see his cousin or something – a relative at any rate.*

VERB **rates, rating, rated** to rate someone or something is to decide how good or bad they are: *How do you rate him as a player?*

rather ADVERB

1 a bit or somewhat: *It's rather cold in here, isn't it?*

2 you would rather do something if you would prefer to do it: *I'd rather talk about this later if you don't mind.*

3 more correctly: *I've already agreed; or rather, I haven't said 'no'.*

4 used to answer 'yes' to a question or suggestion: *'Did you enjoy that?''Rather!'*

ratio NOUN **ratios** (*maths*) the relationship between two numbers or amounts. For example, if you say *The child to teacher ratio is five to one* then you mean there are five children to every teacher

ration NOUN **rations** your ration of something is how much of it you are allowed to have: *I ate my ration of biscuits for the day before lunchtime.*

VERB **rations, rationing, rationed** to ration something is to limit the amount of it that people are allowed because there is not a lot available: *My granny is always telling me about when sugar was rationed.*

rational ADJECTIVE reasonable and sensible

▸ **rationally** ADVERB thinking reasonably and sensibly: *After the accident, Gill wasn't behaving rationally.*

rattle VERB **rattles, rattling, rattled 1** to rattle is to make lots of short, sharp, hard sounds: *a closed door rattling in the wind* **2** to rattle something is to shake it so that it makes a noise: *a person rattling a box and asking for money* **3** to rattle a person is to worry them or make them nervous: *A police warning had rattled the gang.*

NOUN **rattles 1** a baby's toy that makes a noise when it is shaken **2** the noise something hard and loose makes when it is shaken: *There's a bad rattle coming from the engine.*

rattlesnake NOUN **rattlesnakes** a poisonous snake that lives in America. Its tail makes a rattling sound when it gets angry

raucous ADJECTIVE a raucous sound is rough and loud: *raucous laughter*

ravage VERB **ravages, ravaging, ravaged** to ravage something is to damage it until it is almost destroyed: *The building was ravaged by fire.*

rave NOUN **raves** a large party held in a large building where people dance to very loud music

VERB **raves, raving, raved 1** to talk about something very enthusiastically: *The newspapers have been raving about this programme.* **2** someone is raving when they talk in an uncontrolled way, as if they were mad

raven NOUN **ravens** a large black bird like a crow

ravenous ADJECTIVE very hungry

ravine NOUN **ravines** a deep narrow valley with steep sides

raw ADJECTIVE **rawer, rawest**

1 raw food is not cooked: *a salad of raw vegetables*

2 a raw substance is in its natural state before it is used for anything or put through any processes: *raw cotton*

3 a raw recruit is someone who has no training or experience

4 a raw wound is sore where the skin has been damaged

Aa
Bb
Cc
Dd
Ee
Ff
Gg
Hh
Ii
Jj
Kk
Ll
Mm
Nn
Oo
Pp
Qq
Rr
Ss
Tt
Uu
Vv
Ww
Xx
Yy
Zz

5 cold and wet and windy: *raw weather conditions*

raw material NOUN **raw materials** a natural substance that other things are made from

ray NOUN **rays** a beam of light: *a few rays of sunshine*

razor NOUN **razors** an instrument with a sharp blade that can be used to shave hair

RE ABBREVIATION short for **religious education**

re- PREFIX **1** if **re-** is put at the beginning of a word, it can add the meaning *again*. For example, to *reappear* is to appear again **2** **re-** can also add the meaning *back*. For example, to *refund* money is to give it back

reach VERB **reaches, reaching, reached 1** to reach a place is to arrive there: *We didn't reach the cottage till long after dark.* **2** to be able to reach something is to be able to touch or get hold of it: *I can't reach the top shelf.* **3** to reach to somewhere is to extend as far as that: *Charlotte's hair reaches right down her back.*
NOUN
• **out of reach** something is out of reach if you cannot touch it or get to it
• **within** something is within reach if you can touch it or get to it

react VERB **reacts, reacting, reacted** to do something as a result of something else happening: *How did Helen react when she heard the news?*
▸ **reaction** NOUN **reactions** behaviour that is a direct result of something else: *Did you see his reaction when he found out?*

read VERB **reads, reading, read 1** to look at something, such as writing, and understand it: *Read a book.* • *I'd like to learn to read music.* **2** to say aloud what is written or printed: *Read me a story please, Mummy.* **3** an instrument reads something when that is what it shows: *The thermometer reads 31 degrees.*
NOUN **reads** something that is a good read is enjoyable to read
▸ **readable** ADJECTIVE easy or enjoyable to read

▸ **reader** NOUN **readers** a person who reads, especially a particular book or newspaper: *Regular readers will recognize this name.*

readily ADVERB **1** something is readily available if it is easy to get **2** you do something readily if you do it willingly: *The whole family readily agreed to help.*

reading NOUN **readings 1** reading is looking at and understanding written words **2** a reading is a part of a book that someone reads to an audience **3** a reading is a measurement on a gauge

ready ADJECTIVE **1** prepared for something: *Are the children ready for bed?* • *Dinner's ready.* **2** willing: *Are you sure you're ready to give up chocolate for a whole week?*
▸ **readiness** NOUN being ready and prepared for something: *The car had been filled with petrol in readiness for the journey.*

real ADJECTIVE **1** actually existing, not invented or imaginary: *real people with real problems* **2** genuine, not a copy: *The seats are made of real leather.*

realism NOUN the style that tries to show things as they really are, especially in art, books and films
▸ **realist** NOUN **realists** a person who deals with situations as they really are, rather than pretending that they are different
▸ **realistic** ADJECTIVE **1** very like real life: *The fight scenes were very realistic.* **2** dealing with the real situation in a sensible way: *a realistic outlook on life*
▸ **realistically** ADVERB **1** in a way that is very like real life: *The grapes were realistically painted.* **2** seeing things as they really are: *Realistically, there was no chance that he could win.*

realize or **realise** VERB **realizes, realizing, realized** to realize something is to know and understand it: *I suddenly realized that he wasn't joking.*
▸ **realization** or **realisation** NOUN when you suddenly realize something: *The realization that they were sinking caused instant panic.*

Aa Bb Cc Dd Ee Ff Gg Hh Ii Jj Kk Ll Mm Nn Oo Pp Qq **Rr** Ss Tt Uu Vv Ww Xx Yy Zz

really ADVERB **1** actually, in fact: *We're in the same class but we're not really friends.* **2** very: *a really lovely day* **3** certainly: *We'll really have to work hard to finish on time.*

realm NOUN **realms 1** an area of activity, study or interest: *the realm of general science* **2** a country that is ruled by a king or queen

reap VERB **reaps, reaping, reaped** to cut and gather a crop such as corn
- ▸ **reaper** NOUN **reapers** a person or machine that brings in the harvest

rear NOUN **1** the back part of something: *seats towards the rear of the plane* **2** your rear is the part of your body that you sit on
VERB **rears, rearing, reared 1** to rear children or animals is to look after them as they grow **2** a horse or other animal rears, or rears up, when it lifts its front legs up into the air

reason NOUN **reasons 1** the reason for something is why it happened or exists: *The reason I'm worried is that I forgot to do my homework.* **2** reason is your ability to think clearly and form opinions: *Will you please listen to reason?*
- ▸ **reasonable** ADJECTIVE **1** sensible and not foolish: *I suppose it's a reasonable decision from your point of view.* • *Any reasonable person would agree with that.* **2** quite good, big, etc: *He has a reasonable chance of success.* **3** fair and not too expensive: *The café serves drinks and snacks at a reasonable price.*

reassure VERB **reassures, reassuring, reassured** to reassure someone is to say something to stop them from feeling worried: *We would like to reassure parents that we will not leave the children alone.*
- ▸ **reassurance** NOUN **reassurances** something that stops someone from feeling worried
- ▸ **reassuring** ADJECTIVE helping to make a person feel confident and happy or safe: *a reassuring look*

rebel VERB **rebels, rebelling, rebelled** (pronounced ri-**bel**) to refuse to obey

someone: *Teenagers often rebel against their parents.*
NOUN **rebels** (pronounced **reb**-il) a person who fights against, or simply does not obey, people in authority, especially their government
- ▸ **rebellion** NOUN **rebellions 1** rebellion is when people refuse to do what they are told **2** a rebellion is a fight against an authority such as a government
- ▸ **rebellious** ADJECTIVE difficult to control and not wanting to obey: *a rebellious child*

reboot VERB **reboots, rebooting, rebooted** (*ICT*) to start a computer up again: *You'll have to reboot to save these changes.*

rebound VERB **rebounds, rebounding, rebounded** to bounce back again: *The ball hammered against the crossbar and rebounded into the net.*

rebuke VERB **rebukes, rebuking, rebuked** (*formal*) to rebuke someone is to tell them off: *Teachers are always rebuking her for being rude.*
NOUN **rebukes** a telling-off

recall VERB **recalls, recalling, recalled 1** to remember: *Do you recall how we used to play here as children?* **2** to recall a product is to ask everyone who has bought it to return it because there is something wrong with it: *The manufacturer has recalled all the cars because of a fault.* **3** to recall a person is to order them to return to their country or the place where they work: *The Swedish government recalled its ambassador.*

recapture VERB **recaptures, recapturing, recaptured 1** to recapture something is to make someone experience or feel it again: *The film perfectly recaptures the atmosphere of Hollywood.* **2** to recapture a prisoner or animal is to catch them again after they have escaped

recede VERB **recedes, receding, receded** to move backwards or into the distance
- ▸ **receding** ADJECTIVE someone's hair

is receding if they are going bald at the front

receipt (pronounced ri-**seet**) NOUN
receipts 1 a receipt is a piece of paper you get when you pay money or hand something over to someone **2** receipt is the fact that you have received something: *On receipt of the card, you must sign it.*

receive VERB **receives, receiving, received 1** to get something that someone gives or sends to you: *Did you receive my last letter?* **2** to receive guests is to greet and welcome them: *The mayor stood near the door and received his guests personally.*
▶ **receiver** NOUN **receivers 1** the part of a telephone that you hear through **2** equipment that picks up radio or television signals

recent ADJECTIVE happening only a short time ago: *a recent rise in prices* • *These changes are all quite recent.*
▶ **recently** ADVERB a short time ago: *I saw Ann quite recently.*

reception NOUN **receptions**
1 a reception is a formal party, for example for a wedding
2 reception is the place where visitors arrive and are welcomed in hotels, office buildings or hospitals: *The people at reception will tell you which room to go to.*
3 how someone reacts to something: *I got a pretty cool reception when I asked the boss for more money.*
4 how clear the sound or picture is that you get on your radio or television: *Our reception up here in the hills is not always very good.*
▶ **receptionist** NOUN **receptionists** a person whose job is to welcome people who arrive in a building and answer enquiries

recess NOUN **recesses 1** a place where a wall is set back a bit to make a small space: *The post office has a recess with a small shelf where you can write a note.*
2 a time when parliament or law courts do not work
▶ **recession** NOUN **recessions**

a country is in recession when its businesses are not doing well and unemployment is increasing

recipe NOUN **recipes** a set of instructions on how to prepare or cook a particular dish and a list of its ingredients: *a recipe for chocolate-chip cookies*

recipient NOUN **recipients** a person who receives something

recite VERB **recites, reciting, recited** to say something, such as a poem, aloud from memory
▶ **recital** NOUN **recitals** a public performance of music, songs or poetry, usually by one person

reckless ADJECTIVE doing things without caring or thinking about the results of your actions: *reckless driving*
▶ **recklessly** ADVERB carelessly and possibly dangerously
▶ **recklessness** NOUN behaving carelessly and possibly causing harm or damage

reckon VERB **reckons, reckoning, reckoned 1** to suppose or believe: *I reckon they're in love.* **2** to calculate: *Do you reckon we'll be finished on time?*

reclaim VERB **reclaims, reclaiming, reclaimed** to reclaim land is to make it suitable for using, especially if it was too wet before: *The new factories by the river are built on reclaimed land.*

recline VERB **reclines, reclining, reclined** to lie or sit leaning back or sideways

recluse NOUN **recluses** a person who lives alone and prefers not to mix with other people

recognize or **recognise** VERB **recognizes, recognizing, recognized**
1 to recognize someone or something is to know who or what you are seeing or hearing because you have seen or heard them before: *I recognized you from your photo.* **2** to accept that something is true: *The teacher recognized that I was not to blame.*
▶ **recognition** NOUN recognizing someone or something: *a smile of recognition*
▶ **recognizable** or **recognisable**

Aa
Bb
Cc
Dd
Ee
Ff
Gg
Hh
Ii
Jj
Kk
Ll
Mm
Nn
Oo
Pp
Qq
Rr
Ss
Tt
Uu
Vv
Ww
Xx
Yy
Zz

Aa
Bb
Cc
Dd
Ee
Ff
Gg
Hh
Ii
Jj
Kk
Ll
Mm
Nn
Oo
Pp
Qq
Rr
Ss
Tt
Uu
Vv
Ww
Xx
Yy
Zz

ADJECTIVE **1** easy to identify because you have seen it before: *He is barely recognizable since he shaved off his beard.* **2** easy to see or notice: *a recognizable difference*

recoil VERB **recoils, recoiling, recoiled** to move back suddenly from a thing or person because you are afraid or disgusted: *Billy recoiled from the hand that tried to catch hold of him.*

recollect VERB **recollects, recollecting, recollected** to remember: *I recollect that it was a cold Tuesday morning.*

▸ **recollection** NOUN **recollections** something that you remember: *I have absolutely no recollection of what happened.*

recommend VERB **recommends, recommending, recommended 1** to advise someone to do something: *The doctor has recommended that the whole family takes a holiday.* **2** to recommend something is to suggest to someone that it would be good or suitable for them: *My friend recommended this book to me.*

▸ **recommendation** NOUN **recommendations** something that a person suggests would be good or suitable for someone else: *a list of recommendations from the tourist board*

reconcile VERB **reconciles, reconciling, reconciled 1** to accept that you will have to do, or deal with, something unpleasant: *He isn't reconciled to the idea of spending six weeks in hospital.* **2** you are reconciled with someone when you are friendly with them again after an argument

▸ **reconciliation** NOUN being friendly with someone again after an argument or disagreement

reconstruction NOUN **reconstructions** a reconstruction of something, such as a crime, is when people try to act out how it happened

record VERB **records, recording, recorded** (pronounced ri-**kord**) **1** to record something, such as music or a television programme, is to copy it on to a tape or disc so that it can be played again later: *The band recorded their first album in 1982.* **2** to record a piece of information is to write it down

NOUN **records** (pronounced **rek**-ord) **1** a piece of information that has been written down and stored: *We have a record of all the names of the past members.* **2** a round flat piece of plastic that music was stored on in the past: *a pile of old jazz records* **3** the highest, lowest, best or worst level or performance: *Denise is determined to beat her own record on this jump.*

▸ **recorder** NOUN **recorders 1** a machine that copies sounds or pictures, such as a tape recorder or video recorder **2** a wind instrument with holes that you cover with your fingers as you blow

▸ **recording** NOUN **recordings** a tape or video of sounds or pictures

recount VERB **recounts, recounting, recounted** to recount something that has happened is to tell someone about it in detail

NOUN **recounts** a piece of writing that tells someone about events and the order in which they happened

recover VERB **recovers, recovering, recovered 1** to get better after being ill, injured or upset: *My aunt is recovering from a short illness.* • *The patient has not yet recovered consciousness.* **2** to get something back that has been lost, stolen or used up: *The wreck has been recovered from the seabed.*

▸ **recovery** NOUN **recoveries 1** when someone gets better: *We expect all our patients to make a full recovery.* **2** getting something back: *the recovery of stolen goods*

recreation NOUN enjoyable things that you do in your spare time: *The park is a pleasant place for outdoor recreation.*

recruit VERB **recruits, recruiting, recruited** to get someone to join your organization: *The company recruits a few school-leavers each year.*

NOUN **recruits** a person who joins an organization: *a line of new recruits*

▶ **recruitment** NOUN getting people to join organizations like clubs, military forces or businesses

rectangle NOUN **rectangles** a four-sided shape with opposite sides that are of equal length and four right angles

▶ **rectangular** ADJECTIVE with two pairs of straight sides and four right angles: *a rectangular table*

recuperate VERB **recuperates, recuperating, recuperated** to get better after being ill

▶ **recuperation** NOUN getting better after being ill

recur VERB **recurs, recurring, recurred** to happen again, either once or several times: *There is a possibility that this situation will recur.*

▶ **recurrence** NOUN **recurrences** when something happens again: *a recurrence of the same problem*

recycle VERB **recycles, recycling, recycled** to save something so that it can be used again: *I keep the bags in this drawer and recycle them.*

▶ **recycled** ADJECTIVE not made from new materials, but from something that has been saved and used again: *cardboard made from recycled paper*

▶ **recycling** NOUN saving things so that they can be used again, either as they are or in another production process

red NOUN **1** the colour of blood, or any similar shade **2** an orangey-brown hair colour

• **see red** to suddenly get very angry: *The way she looked at me just made me see red.*

▶ **reddish** ADJECTIVE quite red but not completely red in colour

redeem VERB **redeems, redeeming, redeemed 1** to redeem something is to get it back by paying some money: *You can redeem your coat from the cloakroom with this ticket.* **2** if something good redeems a person or thing, it makes up for something bad about them **3** to redeem a person is to save them from evil, especially in the Christian religion

▶ **redemption** NOUN **1** when a thing is paid for and returned to its owner

2 when a person is saved from evil, especially in the Christian religion

red-handed ADJECTIVE

• **catch someone red-handed** to catch someone just as they are doing something wrong or illegal

red herring NOUN **red herrings** something designed to make someone believe the wrong thing or to give them the wrong idea about something

red-letter ADJECTIVE

• **red-letter day** a day that is especially happy or important

reduce VERB **reduces, reducing, reduced** to reduce something is to make it smaller or less: *We have reduced the number of classes to four.*

▶ **reduction** NOUN **reductions** when something is made smaller or less: *The shop is offering massive price reductions.*

redundant ADJECTIVE to be made redundant is to be told that you are not needed to do your job any more

▶ **redundancy** NOUN **redundancies** when a person is not needed to do their job any more: *A company losing money often means redundancy for many workers.*

reed NOUN **reeds 1** a tall stiff grass that grows in or near water. Reeds are used to make baskets **2** (*music*) a part of the mouthpiece of some wind instruments

reef NOUN **reefs** a chain of rocks or a bank of sand just above or below the surface of the sea

reek VERB **reeks, reeking, reeked** to smell terrible: *His clothes reeked of fish.*

reel NOUN **reels 1** a cylinder that turns to wind up anything long and untidy, such as thread or film **2** a lively Scottish or Irish dance

VERB **reels, reeling, reeled** to walk unsteadily

• **reel something off** to say a long list of things quickly, without having to think

ref ABBREVIATION **1** short for **reference 2** short for **referee**

refer VERB **refers, referring, referred 1** to refer to something is to mention it: *The teacher referred to the homework*

Aa
Bb
Cc
Dd
Ee
Ff
Gg
Hh
Ii
Jj
Kk
Ll
Mm
Nn
Oo
Pp
Qq
Rr
Ss
Tt
Uu
Vv
Ww
Xx
Yy
Zz

we had done last week. **2** to refer a person to someone else or to a place is to send them there to get more help: *The doctor referred me to the hospital to get an X-ray.*

referee NOUN **referees** in some sports, the person who makes sure the players obey the rules

VERB **referees, refereeing, refereed** to carefully watch the players and make decisions about whether a game is being played correctly

reference NOUN **references 1** a mention of something: *She made no reference to what had happened the day before.* **2** a direction that tells you where else to look for something: *a reference in the dictionary to another entry* **3** a written report on someone's character: *To get a job, you need good references from people who know you.*

referendum NOUN **referenda** or **referendums** a chance for the people of a country to vote on whether they agree with something their government is suggesting

refill VERB **refills, refilling, refilled** to fill something again: *We'll need to refill the tank before we go much further.*

NOUN **refills** a full container to replace one that is empty of something that has been used up: *Can you buy refills for that kind of pen?*

refine VERB **refines, refining, refined** to refine a substance is to make it pure

▸ **refined** ADJECTIVE a refined substance such as oil has been through a process that removes all dirt or other waste material from it

▸ **refinery** NOUN **refineries** a factory where raw materials, such as oil or foods, are purified

reflect VERB **reflects, reflecting, reflected 1** something is reflected when you can see an image of it in a surface like a mirror **2** to be a sign of something happening or existing: *Her face reflected how she felt inside.* **3** to think about something calmly

▸ **reflection** NOUN **reflections 1** an image that you can see in a surface like a mirror **2** a sign of something being

responsible: *Your bad manners are a reflection on your parents.* **3** your reflections are your thoughts: *I wrote my reflections in my diary.*

▸ **reflective** ADJECTIVE a reflective person thinks deeply about things

▸ **reflector** NOUN **reflectors** a piece of shiny metal, especially on a vehicle or bicycle, that throws back light from other vehicles

reflex NOUN **reflexes 1** an automatic uncontrollable movement that you make in a certain situation: *The doctor will check your reflexes by tapping your knee with a small hammer.* **2** you have good reflexes if you can react quickly and well when something unexpected and sudden happens

reflex angle NOUN **reflex angles** (*maths*) an angle that is more than 180 degrees and less than 360 degrees

reflexive ADJECTIVE (*grammar*) to do with words that show that the subject of a verb is the same as its object. For example, in the sentence *He washed himself*, *wash* is a **reflexive verb** and *himself* is a **reflexive pronoun**

reform VERB **reforms, reforming, reformed 1** to reform something is to make big changes to improve it **2** to reform is to stop doing bad things: *David decided to reform and not steal any more.*

NOUN **reforms** big changes that improve something: *reforms in the health service*

▸ **reformation** NOUN **1** change in order to make an improvement **2** (*history*) the Reformation was change in the Christian Church in the 16th century when the Protestant churches were formed

▸ **reformer** NOUN **reformers** a person who makes changes to improve things

refrain VERB **refrains, refraining, refrained** (*formal*) to stop yourself doing something: *Please refrain from talking in the library.*

NOUN **refrains** the chorus of a song

refresh VERB **refreshes, refreshing, refreshed 1** to make you feel like you have new energy: *a rest to refresh you* **2** to make you feel cooler: *a drink that refreshes* **3** to refresh your memory is to

Aa
Bb
Cc
Dd
Ee
Ff
Gg
Hh
Ii
Jj
Kk
Ll
Mm
Nn
Oo
Pp
Qq
Rr
Ss
Tt
Uu
Vv
Ww
Xx
Yy
Zz

remind yourself of something
▸ **refreshing** ADJECTIVE making you feel more energetic again: *a refreshing cup of tea*
▸ **refreshment** NOUN **refreshments** food and drink

refrigerate VERB **refrigerates, refrigerating, refrigerated** to refrigerate food or drink is to make and keep it cold to stop it going off
▸ **refrigeration** NOUN keeping things at a low temperature
▸ **refrigerator** NOUN **refrigerators** a machine that you can store food or drink in to keep it cold and fresh

refuel VERB **refuels, refuelling, refuelled** to fill up with fuel again: *stopping on the motorway to refuel*

refuge NOUN **refuges** a place where someone can feel safe from danger
▸ **refugee** NOUN **refugees** a person who goes to another country to live because they are not safe in their own country any more

refund VERB **refunds, refunding, refunded** to give someone back some money that they have paid: *We'll refund your money if you're not completely satisfied.*
NOUN **refunds** money that you have paid and then get back

refuse[1] (pronounced ri-**fyooz**) VERB **refuses, refusing, refused 1** to decide not to take something that you are offered: *Gerry refused a cup of tea but took a glass of water.* **2** to decide not to do something that you are asked to do: *I simply refuse to go shopping with you again.*
▸ **refusal** NOUN **refusals 1** a decision not to accept something: *three refusals and twenty acceptances for our party invitations* **2** a decision not to do something: *a refusal to shake hands*

refuse[2] (pronounced **ref**-yoos) NOUN rubbish that people throw away

regain VERB **regains, regaining, regained** to regain something is to get it back: *Can the team regain the cup?*

regal ADJECTIVE royal, like a king or queen

regard VERB **regards, regarding, regarded 1** to regard a person or thing as something is to think about them like that: *My grandmother still regards my mother as a child.* **2** (*formal*) to regard a thing or person is to study the way they look: *He regarded me for a moment, smiled, and patted me on the head.*
NOUN regard is consideration: *They went ahead without regard for our opinion.* • *The professor's work is held in high regard.*
▸ **regards** PLURAL NOUN your regards are your best wishes: *Give my regards to Fiona when you see her.*

regarding PREPOSITION about: *I'd like to talk to you regarding next weekend.*

regardless ADVERB without paying any attention to something: *Regardless of the cost, Dad's determined to take this holiday.*

regatta NOUN **regattas** a series of yacht races

regenerate VERB **regenerates, regenerating, regenerated** to make or become new again: *The council is regenerating old housing.*
▸ **regeneration** NOUN making or growing again in good condition: *the regeneration of damaged skin*

reggae NOUN a West Indian style of music that has strong bouncy rhythms

regime NOUN **regimes 1** a system of government: *a communist regime* **2** a routine: *a strict regime of diet and exercise*

regiment NOUN **regiments** a part of an army commanded by a colonel
▸ **regimental** ADJECTIVE to do with an army regiment

region NOUN **regions** a large area of land such as a part of a country: *the wine-making regions of Spain*
▸ **regional** ADJECTIVE to do with or coming from a particular region of a country: *a regional accent*

register VERB **registers, registering, registered**
1 to put your name down for something: *We registered for the new term's swimming class.*

Aa
Bb
Cc
Dd
Ee
Ff
Gg
Hh
Ii
Jj
Kk
Ll
Mm
Nn
Oo
Pp
Qq
Rr
Ss
Tt
Uu
Vv
Ww
Xx
Yy
Zz

2 to have a name added to an official list of records: *You must register your son's birth in the next week.*

3 information registers with someone if they understand it and take it in: *She certainly heard the news but I don't know if it really registered.*

4 an instrument registers a measurement when it shows it: *Earthquakes are measured by what they register on the Richter scale.*

NOUN **registers** a list of names: *the attendance register • a register of births and deaths*

▶ **registrar** NOUN **registrars** a person whose job is to keep a record of births, marriages and deaths

▶ **registration** NOUN **registrations** putting your name down for something: *a registration form*

▶ **registry** NOUN **registries** an office or building where official records are kept

regret VERB **regrets, regretting, regretted** to regret something is to wish it had not happened: *Yes I'm sorry, I regret saying that.*

NOUN **regrets** a sad feeling: *Marion had no regrets about leaving home.*

▶ **regretful** ADJECTIVE feeling sad about something that has happened

▶ **regrettable** ADJECTIVE something is regrettable if you wish it had not happened: *a regrettable accident*

regular ADJECTIVE **1** happening after intervals of the same length of time: *a regular heartbeat • eating regular meals* **2** usual or normal: *our regular teatime* **3** of a standard size: *a regular portion of fries*

▶ **regularity** NOUN when something happens repeatedly after gaps of similar length: *check the regularity of his pulse*

▶ **regularly** ADVERB often: *I visit my Grandma regularly.*

regulate VERB **regulates, regulating, regulated** to regulate something is to control it: *regulate the temperature of the central heating • We may need to regulate the number of cars on the road.*

▶ **regulation** NOUN **regulations** a rule or law: *We can't allow that – it's against the regulations.*

rehearse VERB **rehearses, rehearsing, rehearsed** to practise performing something: *Can we rehearse that last bit again?*

▶ **rehearsal** NOUN **rehearsals 1** a rehearsal is a practice of a performance: *the dress rehearsal* **2** rehearsal is practising: *Regular rehearsal will help you to get it right*

reign VERB **reigns, reigning, reigned** to rule over a country as a king or queen: *Queen Victoria reigned for over sixty years.*

NOUN **reigns** the time when someone is the king or queen of a country

reimburse VERB **reimburses, reimbursing, reimbursed** to reimburse someone is to give them back the money they have paid out: *The theatre will reimburse everyone who had tickets for the cancelled performance.*

reindeer NOUN **reindeer** a large deer with large horns that lives in Arctic regions

reinforce VERB **reinforces, reinforcing, reinforced** to reinforce something is to make it stronger: *reinforced glass*

▶ **reinforcement** NOUN **reinforcements 1** anything that makes something stronger **2** reinforcements are extra military troops

reins PLURAL NOUN straps attached to a horse's head that the rider uses to control it

reject VERB (pronounced ri-**jekt**) **rejects, rejecting, rejected 1** to reject something is to refuse to accept it: *The machine rejected my coin.* **2** you are rejected if you apply for a job and do not get it

NOUN (pronounced **ree**-jekt) **rejects** a product that is not good enough to sell

▶ **rejection** NOUN **rejections** when a thing or person is not accepted: *I didn't apply because I was afraid of rejection.*

rejoice VERB **rejoices, rejoicing,**

rejoiced to feel or show great happiness

relate VERB **relates, relating, related 1** to relate to something to is be connected or linked with it: *Is violent crime related to violence on TV?* **2** to relate a story is to tell it: *They related their strange experience to their friends.* **3** to relate to someone is to understand how they feel

▸ **related** ADJECTIVE **1** to be related to someone is to belong to the same family: *We have the same surname but we're not related.* **2** to be related is to be linked or connected in some way

relation NOUN **relations 1** a relation between things is some kind of connection: *Your essay bears no relation to the title you were given.* **2** a relation is someone in your family: *all our friends and relations*

▸ **relationship** NOUN **relationships 1** the way people feel about each other is their relationship: *Anne felt she had a good relationship with her brother.* **2** the way things are when you consider them together: *What's the relationship between these numbers?*

relative NOUN **relatives** a member of your family

ADJECTIVE compared with other people or things: *She lives in relative luxury.*

▸ **relatively** ADVERB fairly or quite: *That suit's relatively cheap.*

relax VERB **relaxes, relaxing, relaxed 1** to become less worried or stressed: *A short holiday will help you relax.* **2** to rest completely: *The family spent the afternoon relaxing in the garden.* **3** to relax a muscle or another part of your body is to make it less tense **4** to relax something, like a rule, is to make it less strict

▸ **relaxation** NOUN rest from work or worrying things

relay VERB **relays, relaying, relayed** to relay information or a message is to pass it on to someone else

NOUN **relays** a race for teams where a runner or swimmer takes over when the previous team member stops running or swimming

release VERB **releases, releasing, released 1** to release someone or something is to let them go: *Release the handbrake slowly.* • *Three more prisoners have been released.* **2** a film or book is released when the public are allowed to see it

NOUN **releases 1** when someone or something is set free: *the release of the hostages* **2** something like a film or book that has been made available to the public: *the band's latest release*

relegate VERB **relegates, relegating, relegated** to move someone down to a lower grade or level: *My team has been relegated to the Third Division.*

▸ **relegation** NOUN being moved down to a lower position

relent VERB **relents, relenting, relented** to give in a bit when you have been very strict

▸ **relentless** ADJECTIVE never letting up: *the relentless heat of the desert sun*

relevant ADJECTIVE something is relevant if it has something to do with what is happening or being discussed: *Is this answer relevant to the question?*

▸ **relevance** NOUN how much something has to do with anything or anyone else: *What possible relevance can this have to me?*

reliable ADJECTIVE **1** a reliable person is someone you can depend on **2** reliable information is probably true or correct **3** a reliable machine does not often break down

▸ **reliability** NOUN being reliable: *the reliability of the witness* • *the car's reliability*

reliant ADJECTIVE you are reliant on a thing or person when you depend on them and cannot manage without them: *a charity totally reliant on donations from the public*

▸ **reliance** NOUN the way you rely on a thing or person: *Our reliance on cars these days is frightening.*

relic NOUN **relics** an object from the past

relief NOUN **1** a good feeling caused by

religious symbols

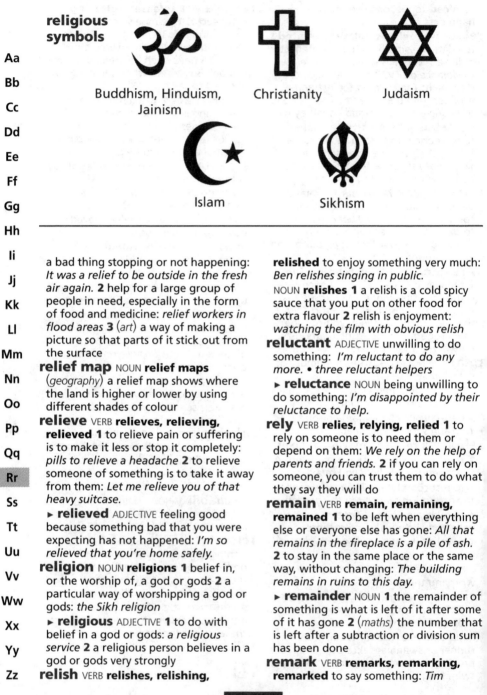

Buddhism, Hinduism, Jainism

Christianity

Judaism

Islam

Sikhism

---

a bad thing stopping or not happening: *It was a relief to be outside in the fresh air again.* **2** help for a large group of people in need, especially in the form of food and medicine: *relief workers in flood areas* **3** (*art*) a way of making a picture so that parts of it stick out from the surface

relief map NOUN **relief maps** (*geography*) a relief map shows where the land is higher or lower by using different shades of colour

relieve VERB **relieves, relieving, relieved 1** to relieve pain or suffering is to make it less or stop it completely: *pills to relieve a headache* **2** to relieve someone of something is to take it away from them: *Let me relieve you of that heavy suitcase.*

▸ **relieved** ADJECTIVE feeling good because something bad that you were expecting has not happened: *I'm so relieved that you're home safely.*

religion NOUN **religions 1** belief in, or the worship of, a god or gods **2** a particular way of worshipping a god or gods: *the Sikh religion*

▸ **religious** ADJECTIVE **1** to do with belief in a god or gods: *a religious service* **2** a religious person believes in a god or gods very strongly

relish VERB **relishes, relishing,**

relished to enjoy something very much: *Ben relishes singing in public.*

NOUN **relishes 1** a relish is a cold spicy sauce that you put on other food for extra flavour **2** relish is enjoyment: *watching the film with obvious relish*

reluctant ADJECTIVE unwilling to do something: *I'm reluctant to do any more.* • *three reluctant helpers*

▸ **reluctance** NOUN being unwilling to do something: *I'm disappointed by their reluctance to help.*

rely VERB **relies, relying, relied 1** to rely on someone is to need them or depend on them: *We rely on the help of parents and friends.* **2** if you can rely on someone, you can trust them to do what they say they will do

remain VERB **remain, remaining, remained 1** to be left when everything else or everyone else has gone: *All that remains in the fireplace is a pile of ash.* **2** to stay in the same place or the same way, without changing: *The building remains in ruins to this day.*

▸ **remainder** NOUN **1** the remainder of something is what is left of it after some of it has gone **2** (*maths*) the number that is left after a subtraction or division sum has been done

remark VERB **remarks, remarking, remarked** to say something: *Tim* remarked that he liked Di's hat.

NOUN **remarks** something someone says, such as an opinion or a thought: *He made a nasty remark about my writing.*

remarkable ADJECTIVE surprising, interesting or impressive: *It's remarkable how often you can see the same film and not get bored.*

remedy NOUN **remedies** something that gets rid of a problem or minor illness: *a remedy for spots*

VERB **remedies, remedying, remedied** to remedy a bad situation is to put it right

remember VERB **remembers, remembering, remembered 1** to have something in your mind from the past: *How much of what you saw can you remember?* • *Can you remember the colour of his jacket?* **2** not to forget to do something: *Remember to take your key with you.*

▸ **remembrance** NOUN

• **in remembrance** if you do something in remembrance of a person who is dead, you do it to show that you have not forgotten them

remind VERB **reminds, reminding, reminded** to make someone remember something: *Remind me to close the window before I go out.* • *That picture reminds me of our holiday last year.*

▸ **reminder** NOUN **reminders** a note that helps someone remember to do something

reminisce (pronounced rem-in-**iss**) VERB **reminisces, reminiscing, reminisced** to think about things that you remember from the past

remnant NOUN **remnants** a small piece of something that is left after the rest has been used, lost or destroyed: *We can use the remnants of the curtains to make cushion covers.*

remorse NOUN a deep feeling of guilt about something bad or wrong that you have done: *a confession full of remorse*

remorseful ADJECTIVE feeling very guilty and sorry

▸ **remorsefully** ADVERB in a way that shows that you feel very guilty about

having done something bad or wrong

remorseless ADJECTIVE **1** a remorseless person does not feel sorry or guilty at all **2** without stopping or ending: *the remorseless crash of the waves*

▸ **remorselessly** ADVERB **1** without showing pity or guilt **2** without stopping

remote ADJECTIVE **remoter, remotest 1** a remote place is very far away from other places: *a remote Highland village* **2** a remote chance is very slight: *There's not even a remote possibility that we'll win.*

▸ **remotely** ADVERB at all: *I'm not even remotely interested.*

remote control NOUN **remote controls 1** remote control is controlling something from a distance by using an electronic device **2** a remote control is a device for controlling something, for example a television set, from a distance

remove VERB **removes, removing, removed 1** to remove something is to take it away or get rid of it: *The police have removed the car that was dumped here.* **2** to remove clothes is to take them off: *Please remove your shoes at the door.*

▸ **removal** NOUN **removals** taking something away: *the removal of rubbish*

render VERB **renders, rendering, rendered** to put a thing or person into a certain state or condition: *His behaviour rendered me speechless.*

rendezvous (pronounced **ron**-day-voo) NOUN **rendezvous** an arranged meeting, especially a secret one

renew VERB **renews, renewing, renewed 1** to renew something like a licence is to pay for it to be valid again after it runs out: *You can renew your bus pass at the office.* **2** to start something or do something again: *We'll renew our attempt to get the rules changed.*

renovate VERB **renovates, renovating, renovated** to renovate a building is to do it up so that it is in good condition again

▸ **renovation** NOUN **renovations** repairs to a building that restore it to good condition

Aa
Bb
Cc
Dd
Ee
Ff
Gg
Hh
Ii
Jj
Kk
Ll
Mm
Nn
Oo
Pp
Qq
Rr
Ss
Tt
Uu
Vv
Ww
Xx
Yy
Zz

Aa
Bb
Cc
Dd
Ee
Ff
Gg
Hh
Ii
Jj
Kk
Ll
Mm
Nn
Oo
Pp
Qq
Rr
Ss
Tt
Uu
Vv
Ww
Xx
Yy
Zz

renown NOUN fame: *a man of great renown*

▶ **renowned** ADJECTIVE famous: *The island is renowned for its beauty.*

rent VERB **rents, renting, rented 1** to rent something, for example a house, flat or car, is to pay the owner money so that you can live there or use it: *a rented flat* **2** to rent something, or rent something out, is to let other people use it if they pay you: *We rented the house to students while we were away.*

NOUN **rents** money you pay to the owner of a house or other building so that you can live in it or use it

▶ **rental** NOUN **rentals 1** renting things out to people: *a car rental business* **2** the amount of rent you pay

repair VERB **repairs, repairing, repaired** to repair something that is damaged or not working is to fix it: *Can the washing-machine be repaired?*

NOUN **repairs** something you do to fix something that is damaged or not working

• **good** or **bad repair** good, or bad, repair is good, or bad, condition: *The car is in remarkably good repair for its age.*

repay VERB **repays, repaying, repaid 1** to give back money that you have borrowed **2** to do something for somebody in return for something they did for you: *How can we ever repay this kindness?*

▶ **repayment** NOUN **repayments** amounts of money that you pay back until you have paid back all the money you borrowed

repeat VERB **repeats, repeating, repeated 1** to say something again: *Could you repeat your name please?* • *Don't you dare repeat this to your friends.* **2** to do something again: *I hope this mistake will never be repeated.*

NOUN **repeats** something that happens again, especially a broadcast: *watching repeats of old comedy shows*

▶ **repeatedly** ADVERB again and again

repel VERB **repels, repelling, repelled 1** to force a thing or person away: *This material repels water and is used for*

rainwear. **2** things repel each other when they move apart without any help **3** to be repelled by something is to be disgusted by it

▶ **repellent** NOUN **repellents** a chemical that you use to keep something away: *an insect repellent*

ADJECTIVE disgusting or very unpleasant: *a repellent sight*

repent VERB **repents, repenting, repented** to be sorry for something that you have done

▶ **repentance** NOUN being sorry for what you have done

▶ **repentant** ADJECTIVE sorry

repetition NOUN **repetitions 1** repetition is saying or doing things again: *learning by repetition* **2** a repetition of something is when it is said or done again: *We don't want a repetition of yesterday's argument.*

▶ **repetitive** ADJECTIVE boring because the same thing is repeated many times

replace VERB **replaces, replacing, replaced 1** to replace something is to put it back in its previous or proper position: *Make sure you replace the books in exactly the right order.* **2** to take the place of another thing or person: *The company is about to replace all the old computers.*

▶ **replacement** NOUN **replacements** a person or thing that is in the place of a previous one: *This is broken so I'd like a replacement please.*

replay VERB **replays, replaying, replayed** a sports match is replayed when it is played again, usually because there was no clear winner the first time

NOUN **replays 1** a sports match that is played a second time: *He scored in the second-round replay.* **2** an incident in a sports match that is shown again during a broadcast: *an instant action replay*

replica NOUN **replicas** a model of something, usually much smaller than the original

reply VERB **replies, replying, replied** to answer: *You haven't replied to my question yet.*

NOUN **replies** an answer: *We've*

had a number of replies to our advertisement. • In reply, Phoebe gave a nod.

report NOUN **reports 1** an account of something that has happened: *Reports of an accident are just coming in.* **2** a piece of writing that gives you information about someone or something, or about something that has taken place **3** a description of someone's progress: *a school report*

VERB **reports, reporting, reported 1** to tell people about what has happened: *Did you report the incident to the police?* • *The whole story was reported in the papers.* **2** to report someone is to make an official complaint about what they have done: *I reported the bus driver for not stopping for me.* **3** to report to a place is to go there and say that you have arrived: *Please report to reception when you enter the building.*

reported speech NOUN (*grammar*) another name for **indirect speech**, where you report what someone has said without using their exact words

reporter NOUN **reporters** a person who writes articles and reports for newspapers, or television or radio news programmes

represent VERB **represents, representing, represented 1** to represent people is to speak or act on their behalf: *Our MPs represent us in our government.* **2** to represent a thing is to be a symbol of it: *The crown represents the king or queen.* **3** to represent something in a certain way is to describe it that way: *The children in the picture were all represented as angels.*

▸ **representative** NOUN **representatives 1** a person who acts or speaks on behalf of other people **2** a person whose job is to sell the products of the company they work for: *a sales representative*

repress VERB **represses, repressing, repressed** to repress people is to control them by force

▸ **repression** NOUN very strict

controlling of people, not allowing them to do things such as vote in elections

▸ **repressive** ADJECTIVE a repressive government controls the people of a country very strictly

reprieve NOUN **reprieves** an order to cancel or delay a punishment or other unpleasant event

VERB **reprieves, reprieving, reprieved** when someone is reprieved, something unpleasant that was due to happen to them is cancelled or delayed

reprimand VERB **reprimands, reprimanding, reprimanded** (*formal*) to reprimand someone is to scold them

NOUN **reprimands** a telling-off

reprint NOUN **reprints** a new copy of something like a photograph or a book

VERB **reprints, reprinting, reprinted** to print more copies of a book

reprisal NOUN **reprisals** something that is done against a person or group of people because of what they had done previously: *The country will suffer reprisals for their attacks.*

reproach VERB **reproaches, reproaching, reproached** (*formal*) to reproach someone is to tell them that you think they have behaved or are behaving badly: *The teacher reproached the pupils for their noisiness.*

NOUN criticism: *a look of reproach*

reproduce VERB **reproduces, reproducing, reproduced 1** to reproduce something is to make or produce it again or copy it: *The child had reproduced his father's signature.* **2** to reproduce is to have babies

▸ **reproduction** NOUN **reproductions 1** copying things, especially works of art: *reproduction furniture* **2** the process in which people, animals and plants produce babies or young animals and plants

reptile NOUN **reptiles** a cold-blooded animal, such as a snake or lizard

republic NOUN **republics** a country with no king or queen, that is ruled by an elected government and usually has a president

Aa
Bb
Cc
Dd
Ee
Ff
Gg
Hh
Ii
Jj
Kk
Ll
Mm
Nn
Oo
Pp
Qq
Rr
Ss
Tt
Uu
Vv
Ww
Xx
Yy
Zz

Aa

Bb

Cc

Dd

Ee

Ff

Gg

Hh

Ii

Jj

Kk

Ll

Mm

Nn

Oo

Pp

Qq

Rr

Ss

Tt

Uu

Vv

Ww

Xx

Yy

Zz

▶ **republican** ADJECTIVE belonging to a republic or wanting your own country to be a republic

repulsion NOUN **1** (*science*) repulsion is the way some things move apart without any help **2** disgust

repulsive ADJECTIVE disgusting

reputation NOUN **reputations** the opinion that most people have of a thing or person: *a restaurant with a very good reputation* • *He has a reputation for being a very tough player.*

request VERB **requests, requesting, requested** to ask for something: *Can I request a taxi for eight o'clock?*

NOUN **requests 1** something that someone asks: *I've got a request to make.* • *hundreds of requests for information* **2** something that someone asks for, especially a piece of music on the radio: *Tell me the title of your request.*

require VERB **requires, requiring, required 1** to require something is to need it: *Do you require any further information?* **2** to be required to do something is to have to do it: *All pupils are required to study at least one modern language.*

▶ **requirement** NOUN **requirements** something that is needed: *Write a list of your requirements and we'll design the kitchen for you.*

rescue VERB **rescues, rescuing, rescued** to save someone from danger: *Firefighters rescued the people from the burning house.*

NOUN **rescues** when someone is saved from danger: *stranded on an island with no hope of rescue*

▶ **rescuer** NOUN **rescuers** a person who saves someone from a dangerous situation

research NOUN **researches** to do or carry out research is to study a subject in a lot of detail, in order to find out new information: *money for research into the causes of cancer*

VERB **researches, researching, researched** to research something is to study it in a lot of detail, in order to find out new information

▶ **researcher** NOUN **researchers** a person who finds out and studies information about a subject

resemble VERB **resembles, resembling, resembled** to be similar in some way, especially in looks: *Tom resembles his father in his laid-back attitude to life.*

▶ **resemblance** NOUN **resemblances** something similar about things or people, especially in the way they look: *Can you see the resemblance between the brothers?*

resent VERB **resents, resenting, resented** to resent someone or something is to be irritated, angry or bitter about them: *I resent the way nobody asked me how I felt.*

▶ **resentful** ADJECTIVE feeling irritated, angry or bitter: *a resentful look*

▶ **resentment** NOUN a feeling of bitterness about something: *There was resentment amongst the other pupils when Julia was made class captain.*

reservation NOUN **reservations 1** a reservation is a booking for something like a table in a restaurant, a hotel room, a theatre ticket or a ticket to travel somewhere: *I'd like to make reservations for two rooms please.* **2** to have reservations about something is to be unsure about how good or sensible it is: *Peter had reservations about moving abroad.* **3** a reservation is an area of land that is set aside for a particular purpose, for example for Native Americans in the USA

reserve VERB **reserves, reserving, reserved 1** to reserve something, like a table in a restaurant or a theatre ticket, is to arrange to have it: *Dad phoned the restaurant to reserve a table.* **2** to reserve something is to keep it to use later: *Mix in half the sugar, reserving the rest for the icing.*

▶ **reserved** ADJECTIVE **1** something like a table in a restaurant is reserved when it is being kept for someone in particular **2** a reserved person does not talk very much about how they feel

reservoir NOUN **reservoirs** a large lake, often man-made, where water is collected and stored

reside VERB **resides, residing, resided** (*formal*) to live in a place

▸ **residence** NOUN **residences** a residence, or a place of residence, is where someone lives: *one of the queen's official residences* • *What is your country of residence?*

▸ **resident** NOUN **residents** a resident of a place is someone who lives there: *a letter to all the residents in the street*

▸ **residential** ADJECTIVE **1** a residential area is mostly made up of housing, not offices or factories **2** a residential activity is one where you live and work in the same place: *a residential course for teachers*

residue NOUN **residues** an amount left after the rest has gone or been used up

resign VERB **resigns, resigning, resigned** to give up your job: *Harry resigned after a row with the manager.*
• **resigned to** to be resigned to an unpleasant fact is to accept it and decide to put up with it: *I'm resigned to not being a musical genius but I can still enjoy playing.*

▸ **resignation** NOUN **resignations 1** to hand in your resignation is to give up your job **2** resignation is accepting something unpleasant and putting up with it: *a look of resignation*

resilience NOUN resilience is a quality that things or people can have that means they are not easily damaged or hurt

▸ **resilient** ADJECTIVE resilient things or people are able to survive hard treatment without being badly affected

resin NOUN a sticky substance produced by certain trees

resist VERB **1** to resist something, like change, is to try to stop it happening **2** to resist someone is to try to stop them doing something **3** you resist a temptation when you do not give in to it

▸ **resistance** NOUN **1** an attempt to stop someone or something: *the body's*

resistance to disease **2** (*science*) the ability of a substance to slow down the way that electricity flows through it

▸ **resistant** ADJECTIVE not willing or likely to be changed by something: *a water-resistant watch*

resize VERB **resizes, resizing, resized** to resize something, for example an image on a computer screen, is to make it bigger or smaller

resolute ADJECTIVE very determined not to give up or change your mind

▸ **resolutely** ADVERB very firmly: *We have resolutely refused to do extra work.*

▸ **resolution** NOUN **resolutions 1** a resolution is a firm decision to do something: *a New Year's resolution* **2** resolution is the solving of a problem

resolve VERB **resolves, resolving, resolved 1** to resolve to do something is to make a firm decision to do it: *We have resolved to try harder next time.* **2** to resolve a problem is to solve it or deal successfully with it
NOUN great determination: *I have always admired his resolve.*

resort VERB **resorts, resorting, resorted** you resort to doing something when everything else you have tried has failed: *The worst thing would be to resort to violence.*
NOUN **resorts** a place where people go for their holidays: *a popular seaside resort*
• **a last resort** something you would prefer not to do, but you do because everything else has failed: *As a last resort I suppose we could try asking someone to give us some money.*

resound VERB **resounds, resounding, resounded** to echo around

resource NOUN **resources** resources are substances or qualities that you have and are able to use: *natural mineral resources like coal* • *We'll need all our resources of patience to put up with this.*

▸ **resourceful** ADJECTIVE good at finding ways of doing things, especially of solving problems

respect NOUN **respects 1** a feeling

Aa
Bb
Cc
Dd
Ee
Ff
Gg
Hh
Ii
Jj
Kk
Ll
Mm
Nn
Oo
Pp
Qq
Rr
Ss
Tt
Uu
Vv
Ww
Xx
Yy
Zz

that a thing or person deserves your attention, admiration or consideration **2** a way of looking at things: *The plan was good in every respect.*

VERB **respects, respecting, respected** to respect someone is to treat them with kindness and attention

respectable ADJECTIVE **1** decent and honest: *Simon comes from a perfectly respectable family.* **2** fairly good or, at least, not bad: *Now he's beginning to earn a respectable amount of money.*
▸ **respectability** NOUN being good, honest and decent
▸ **respectably** ADVERB decently

respectful ADJECTIVE showing respect: *a respectful attitude*
▸ **respectfully** ADVERB in a way that shows respect: *Everyone respectfully bowed their heads as the coffin went past.*

respective ADJECTIVE to do with each thing that has been mentioned: *David and Diane are each good at their respective jobs.*
▸ **respectively** ADVERB according to the order of things already mentioned: *Colin, Jane and Ian were given £5, £3 and £1 respectively.*

respiration NOUN breathing
▸ **respirator** NOUN **respirators** a machine that helps a person to breathe when they are too ill to do it naturally

resplendent ADJECTIVE very bright and splendid-looking

respond VERB **responds, responding, responded** to answer or react: *If someone hits you, you tend to respond by hitting back.*
▸ **response** NOUN **responses** an answer or reaction: *His response was a shake of his head.*

responsibility NOUN **responsibilities** **1** responsibility for something is a duty that you must do or deal with properly: *The manager has responsibility for all the business.* **2** a responsibility is a job or duty that you are trusted to do: *It's my responsibility to make sure all the doors are locked.* **3** responsibility is being able to sensibly

do things that you are trusted with: *My sister wasn't ready for the responsibility of having children.*

responsible ADJECTIVE
1 to be responsible for something is to be the person whose job or duty that thing is: *Who is responsible for keeping the money?*
2 to be responsible for something like a mistake is to be the person whose fault it is
3 a responsible job is one that includes important duties and decisions
4 a responsible person is someone you can trust

rest VERB **rests, resting, rested 1** to spend time doing very little, or nothing, in order to relax: *You should rest every few minutes when you're lifting such heavy weights.* **2** to rest against something is to lean against it: *a spade resting against a wall* **3** to rest one thing on something else is to put it there gently: *Mo rested her hands on the piano keys for a moment.*
NOUN **rests 1** a time when you relax or sleep: *I need a rest before I can work any more.* **2** something that is used as a support: *an adjustable headrest* **3** the rest of something is what is left or remaining: *I don't want to spend the rest of my life here.* • *The rest of the country will have showers.*

restaurant NOUN **restaurants** a place where you can buy and eat a meal

✦ This is a French word that comes from the word **restaurer**, which means *to restore*, because the food was thought to refresh you and make you feel better.

restful ADJECTIVE making you feel calm and relaxed: *restful music* • *a restful afternoon*

restless ADJECTIVE not able to stay still or quiet because you are nervous and worried or bored: *The audience began to get restless after about an hour.*
▸ **restlessly** ADVERB in an uncomfortable, fidgety way: *standing and waiting restlessly by the door*

▶ **restlessness** NOUN an uncomfortable feeling that makes you want to move about or do something active

restore VERB **restores, restoring, restored** to put something back the way it was before: *In just a few minutes, Mr Cox had restored order in the classroom.*

▶ **restoration** NOUN putting something back the way it was before: *After the fire, the restoration of the church took three years.*

restrain VERB **restrains, restraining, restrained** to hold tightly to control a thing or person: *One of the children got very excited and had to be restrained by a parent. • We had to restrain ourselves from laughing.*

▶ **restraint** NOUN **restraints 1** a restraint is something that prevents you from doing something **2** restraint is self-control: *She behaved with amazing restraint considering how insulting Lara was being.*

restrict VERB **restricts, restricting, restricted** to limit or control something: *We are restricting people to one ticket each.*

▶ **restriction** NOUN **restrictions** a limit or control: *Are there any parking restrictions on this road?*

▶ **restrictive** ADJECTIVE preventing normal behaviour: *restrictive laws*

result NOUN **results 1** the result of something is what happens because of it: *Stuart failed all his exams, as a result of never doing any work.* **2** the result of a contest is the number of points each team or contestant won **3** a student's exam results are the marks or grades they got

VERB **results, resulting, resulted** to happen because of something else: *The fire apparently resulted from a cigarette not being put out properly.*

resume VERB **resumes, resuming, resumed** to start again: *Normal services will resume next week.*

▶ **resumption** NOUN when something starts again: *the resumption of peace talks*

resurrect VERB **resurrects, resurrecting, resurrected** to bring back to life or back into use: *We've resurrected the old custom of gathering the family together for dinner.*

▶ **resurrection** NOUN **1** bringing back to life or use **2** the Resurrection is the Christian belief that Jesus Christ rose again three days after his death

resuscitate VERB **resuscitates, resuscitating, resuscitated** to resuscitate an unconscious person is to make them start breathing again

▶ **resuscitation** NOUN helping an unconscious person start breathing again

retail NOUN selling goods to members of the public

▶ **retailer** NOUN **retailers** a person who sells goods to the public, usually in a shop

retain VERB **retains, retaining, retained** to keep something: *A smaller house would retain heat better in the winter.*

▶ **retention** NOUN keeping something and not letting it go

retina NOUN **retinas** or **retinae** the back of the eyeball, where images that you see are picked up by the brain

retire VERB **retires, retiring, retired** to stop working because you are old enough to receive a pension: *Our third contestant is a retired teacher.*

▶ **retirement** NOUN the time when you stop working and receive a pension instead of earning a living: *I hope you enjoy your retirement.*

retiring ADJECTIVE quiet and shy

retort VERB **retorts, retorting, retorted** to make a quick reply

NOUN **retorts** a sharp answer: *an angry retort*

retrace VERB **retraces, retracing, retraced**

• **retrace your steps** to go over the same route that you took earlier

retreat NOUN **retreats** a movement backwards

VERB **retreats, retreating, retreated** to move back or move away because you do not want to fight

Aa
Bb
Cc
Dd
Ee
Ff
Gg
Hh
Ii
Jj
Kk
Ll
Mm
Nn
Oo
Pp
Qq
Rr
Ss
Tt
Uu
Vv
Ww
Xx
Yy
Zz

Aa
Bb
Cc
Dd
Ee
Ff
Gg
Hh
Ii
Jj
Kk
Ll
Mm
Nn
Oo
Pp
Qq
Rr
Ss
Tt
Uu
Vv
Ww
Xx
Yy
Zz

retrieve VERB **retrieves, retrieving, retrieved** to get something back after leaving it somewhere: *Can you help me retrieve my pen from the back of the sofa?*

▶ **retriever** NOUN **retriever** a kind of large light brown or black dog that hunters use to fetch birds or animals that have been shot

return VERB **returns, returning, returned 1** to return is to go back to a place: *We fly out on Friday and return the following Wednesday.* • *The search will continue as soon as daylight returns.* **2** to return something is to give it, put it or send it back: *Please return your books by Friday.* **3** to return something like a look or a smile is to do it to someone who does it to you: *I hope I can return the favour one day.*

NOUN **returns**

1 a time when you come or go back again: *On my return to the house, I found the door wide open.*

2 a **return ticket**: *Do you want a single or a return?*

3 something that is given or sent back **4** a shot that someone hits back in tennis or a similar game: *a wonderful return of service*

return match NOUN **return matches** a second match between the same teams

return ticket NOUN **return tickets** a ticket that allows you to travel to a place and back again

reunion NOUN **reunions** a meeting of people such as friends or family members who have not seen each other for a long time:

▶ **reunite** VERB **reunites, reuniting, reunited** people are reunited when they meet again after not seeing each other for a long time

rev NOUN **revs** a revolution of an engine, which is one turn of its pistons

VERB **revs, revving, revved** to press the accelerator of a car to make the engine go faster.

Rev ABBREVIATION short for **Reverend** when it is written down: *the vicar, Rev Green*

reveal VERB **reveals, revealing, revealed 1** to reveal something is to allow it to be seen **2** to reveal information is to tell it to someone: *The newspaper is claiming that it can reveal all the details.*

revel VERB **revels, revelling, revelled 1** to celebrate in a jolly way: *friends revelling the night away* **2** to revel in something is to enjoy it very much: *Maxine revelled in all the attention she got at her birthday party.*

revelation NOUN **revelations** a surprising piece of information that you did not know before: *an article full of revelations about his private life*

revenge NOUN to get revenge on someone who has harmed you is to harm them in return

revenue NOUN money that is given as payment to a business or organization: *Most of the government's revenue comes from taxes.*

reverberate VERB **reverberates, reverberating, reverberated** to produce several loud echoes: *the sounds of gunfire reverberating along the valley*

▶ **reverberation** NOUN **reverberations** a repeated echo

revere VERB **reveres, revering, revered** to revere someone is to respect and admire them very much

▶ **reverence** NOUN great respect

Reverend NOUN the title that comes before the name of a Christian minister: *Have you met Reverend Cook before?*

reverse VERB **reverses, reversing, reversed 1** to reverse is to move backwards **2** to reverse a vehicle is to drive it backwards **3** to reverse a decision is to cancel it

▶ **reversal** NOUN **reversals** a reversal is when a change or decision that has been made is undone

▶ **reversible** ADJECTIVE **1** a decision or process that is reversible can be cancelled **2** (*science*) if a change is reversible, then you can change it back to the way it was before **3** a reversible garment can be worn with either side in or out

revert VERB **reverts, reverting, reverted** to go back to the way something was before: *When the TV broke, we reverted to the radio.*

review VERB **reviews, reviewing, reviewed 1** to review something, such as a system or process, is to look at the way it works to see if any changes need to be made **2** to review something, like a book, film or performance, is to write something saying what you thought of it

NOUN **reviews 1** a check on the way something such as a process works, to see if it needs changing: *a review of the education system* **2** a critic's opinion of something such as a book, film or performance: *The play received some good reviews.*

▶ **reviewer** NOUN **reviewers** a person who gives their opinion about something such as a book, film or performance

revise VERB **revises, revising, revised 1** to revise a piece of written work is to make changes to improve it: *The revised dictionary has hundreds of new words in it.* **2** to study for an exam by looking again at the work you have done

▶ **revision** NOUN **revisions 1** a new version of an old text, with improvements made **2** work that you do to learn your work before an exam

revive VERB **revives, reviving, revived 1** to revive someone is to bring them back to consciousness again **2** to revive something is to become interested in it again or make it popular again: *reviving some of the traditional customs of the countryside*

▶ **revival** NOUN **revivals** when something becomes active or popular again: *a revival of an old children's TV programme*

revolt NOUN **revolts** an attempt by the people to take power in a country by violence and force

VERB **revolts, revolting, revolted 1** to rise up and try to seize power in a country **2** to disgust someone: *The very idea revolted me.*

▶ **revolting** ADJECTIVE disgusting

revolution NOUN **revolutions 1** when people use force and violence to overturn a government and take power **2** a complete change in anything: *the industrial revolution of the nineteenth century* **3** a complete turn of something such as a wheel

▶ **revolutionary** ADJECTIVE completely new and different, and so bringing about a complete change: *revolutionary computerized machines in our factories*

NOUN **revolutionaries** a person who is involved in or who is in favour of overturning a government

▶ **revolutionize** *or* **revolutionise** VERB **revolutionizes, revolutionizing, revolutionized** to introduce a lot of new and different methods or ideas so that something changes completely: *The silicon chip has revolutionized computers.*

revolve VERB **revolves, revolving, revolved** to turn round and round a central point: *a revolving door* • *The Earth revolves around the Sun.*

▶ **revolver** NOUN **revolvers** a pistol that has a cylinder of bullets in it that turns after each shot

reward NOUN **rewards** something you get for doing something good or useful: *a £300 reward for any information that helps catch the criminal*

VERB **rewards, rewarding, rewarded** to give someone something for being good or useful: *The class was rewarded for its good behaviour.*

rewind VERB **rewinds, rewinding, rewound** to wind a tape or cassette backwards to the beginning or an earlier place

rewrite VERB **rewrites, rewriting, rewrote, rewritten** to write something again: *You'll have to rewrite this because it is full of mistakes.*

rheumatism NOUN a disease that causes painful swelling in a person's joints and muscles

rhino NOUN **rhinos** a short form of the word **rhinoceros**

rhinoceros NOUN **rhinoceroses** a large animal from Africa and Asia that

Aa
Bb
Cc
Dd
Ee
Ff
Gg
Hh
Ii
Jj
Kk
Ll
Mm
Nn
Oo
Pp
Qq
Rr
Ss
Tt
Uu
Vv
Ww
Xx
Yy
Zz

has thick grey skin and one or two horns on its nose

> ✦The word comes from the Greek word **rhinokeros**. This is made up of **rhinos**, which means *nose*, and **keras**, which means *horn*. A **rhinoceros** is so called because of the horn on its snout.

rhododendron NOUN **rhododendrons** a large bush that has evergreen leaves and large flowers

rhombus NOUN **rhombuses** or **rhombi** (*maths*) a flat shape with four straight sides and four angles that are not right angles

rhubarb NOUN a plant that has red stems that are cooked and eaten as a fruit

rhyme VERB **rhymes, rhyming, rhymed** if two words rhyme, they end with the same sound. For example, *ghost* rhymes with *toast*

NOUN **rhymes 1** a rhyme is a word that sounds like another, or a pair of words that have a similar sound: *I don't think there is a rhyme for 'orange'.* **2** poetry, or a poem, that uses similar-sounding words at the end of the lines

rhythm NOUN **rhythms** a repeated pattern of sounds or movements

▸ **rhythmic** ADJECTIVE having a rhythm

▸ **rhythmically** ADVERB with a rhythm

rib NOUN **ribs** one of the curved bones in your chest, around your heart and lungs

ribbon NOUN **ribbons** a long narrow strip of fabric that you can use as a decoration for clothes, hair or parcels

rice NOUN brown or white grains that are cooked and used as food: *a bowl of boiled rice*

rich ADJECTIVE **richer, richest**
1 a rich person has a lot of money or possessions
2 rich food contains a lot of sugar or fat
3 rich soil contains a lot of things that make plants grow well
4 rich colours are strong and bright
5 anything rich is full of a lot of good things: *fruit juices rich in vitamins • the city's rich history*

rickshaw NOUN **rickshaws** a kind of two-wheeled cart for passengers that is pulled by one or more people and used in East Asia

ricochet (pronounced rik-oh-**shay**) VERB **ricochets, ricocheting, ricocheted** to bounce or rebound off a surface

Richter scale (pronounced **rik**-ter) NOUN a way of measuring how strong earthquakes are: *Earthquakes can measure anything between 0 and 8 on the Richter scale.*

rid VERB **rids, ridding, rid** to clear or empty a place of something: *Scientists are working to rid the world of this virus.*

NOUN
• **get rid of** to make something or someone go away: *We got rid of that old sofa and bought a new one.*

▸ **riddance** NOUN **good riddance** is a phrase you can use when you are glad that someone or something has gone

riddle[1] NOUN **riddles 1** a word puzzle **2** a mystery that is difficult to solve: *How the burglar got into the house is a bit of a riddle.*

riddle[2] VERB **riddles, riddling, riddled** something is riddled with holes if it has holes all over it

ride VERB **rides, riding, rode, ridden**
1 to travel on a horse or bicycle: *I never learnt to ride a bike.* **2** to travel in or on a vehicle

NOUN **rides** a journey in or on a vehicle: *a bus ride into town • pony rides*

▸ **rider** NOUN **riders** someone sitting on and controlling a bike or horse

ridge NOUN **ridges 1** a narrow strip of land that is higher than the ground on either side of it, for example along the top of a mountain **2** the top edge of something where two sloping surfaces meet: *the ridge of the roof*

ridicule VERB **ridicules, ridiculing, ridiculed** to ridicule a person or thing is to make fun of them

▸ **ridiculous** ADJECTIVE very silly

rife ADJECTIVE something is rife when it is all over the place: *Rumours about the row were rife.*

rifle NOUN **rifles** a powerful gun with a long barrel that you hold against your shoulder to fire

VERB **rifles, rifling, rifled**
• **rifle through something** to search through something quickly: *I caught him rifling through the papers on my desk.*

rift NOUN **rifts 1** a break in a friendship between people because of a disagreement: *a rift between the two families that lasted for years* **2** a large long crack in the land

rig VERB **rigs, rigging, rigged** to rig something such as an election or competition is to fix it dishonestly so you get the results you want: *Everyone agreed that the election must have been rigged.*
• **rig something up** to make, fix or build something in a hurry: *We rigged up a new aerial using a wire coat hanger.*

NOUN **rigs** a large platform that supports the equipment which gets oil or gas from under the ground or the sea

▶ **rigging** NOUN the system of ropes that support and control the sails of a ship

right ADJECTIVE **1** correct: *I got most of the answers wrong but a couple were right.* **2** good and proper: *It doesn't seem right that so many people in the world are hungry.* **3** on the other side from the left side: *I write with my right hand.*

ADVERB

1 on or towards the other side from the left: *Now turn right.*
2 exactly: *Don't move; stay right there.*
3 immediately: *I'll be right there.*
4 all the way: *This road goes right round the outside of the park.*
5 correctly: *Can't you do anything right?*
• **right away** immediately

NOUN **1** the right is the opposite side to the left side: *There's a chemist over there on the right.* **2** a right is something that you should be allowed: *Everyone has a right to a decent education.*
• **in your own right** not because of anyone else: *His father is very well-known but Michael is also a famous actor in his own right.*

right angle NOUN **right angles** (*maths*) an angle of 90 degrees, like the corner of a square

right-angled triangle NOUN **right-angled triangles** (*maths*) a triangle that has one corner that is 90 degrees

righteous ADJECTIVE a righteous person is a very good person

▶ **righteousness** NOUN being very good and doing the right thing

rightful ADJECTIVE proper and as it should be: *return the stolen goods to their rightful owners*

▶ **rightfully** ADVERB properly and fairly: *She lives in the house which rightfully belongs to her.*

right-handed ADJECTIVE preferring to use your right hand to do things, rather than your left: *It's not fair that most of these gadgets are designed for right-handed people.*

rightly ADVERB correctly or fairly: *Phil has rightly pointed out that we should include Robert.*

rigid ADJECTIVE **1** stiff and impossible to bend: *The kite has a rigid frame.* **2** unable to move because of a strong emotion such as fear: *The girl stood in the doorway, rigid with fear.* **3** rigid rules are very strict and cannot be changed

▶ **rigidity** NOUN being very stiff or strict
▶ **rigidly** ADVERB stiffly or strictly

rigorous ADJECTIVE very careful, strict and thorough: *ready for the rigorous training that you get in the army* • *rigorous checks on all the equipment*

rim NOUN **rims 1** the top edge of a container such as a cup or bowl **2** the outside edge of something like a wheel

rind NOUN **1** the hard outside edge of cheese or bacon **2** the skin or peel of fruit such as lemons

ring[1] NOUN **rings 1** anything in the shape of a circle: *The children sit in a ring around the story-teller.* • *The curtains are attached to rings on a*

Aa
Bb
Cc
Dd
Ee
Ff
Gg
Hh
Ii
Jj
Kk
Ll
Mm
Nn
Oo
Pp
Qq
Rr
Ss
Tt
Uu
Vv
Ww
Xx
Yy
Zz

Aa
Bb
Cc
Dd
Ee
Ff
Gg
Hh
Ii
Jj
Kk
Ll
Mm
Nn
Oo
Pp
Qq
Rr
Ss
Tt
Uu
Vv
Ww
Xx
Yy
Zz

pole. **2** a small circle, usually of some kind of metal, that you wear on your finger: *a wedding ring* **3** the area where a performance takes place: *a boxing ring • a circus ring*

ring² NOUN **rings 1** the sound a bell makes: *Did I hear a ring at the door?* **2** a telephone call: *I'll give you a ring tomorrow.*

VERB **rings, ringing, rang, rung 1** to make a sound like a bell: *I think I heard the doorbell ring.* **2** to telephone someone: *Can I ring you back later?*

ringleader NOUN **ringleaders** the leader of a gang of criminals or troublemakers

ringlet NOUN **ringlets** a long curl of hair

ringmaster NOUN **ringmaster** the person in charge at a circus, who introduces the performers

ring road NOUN **ring roads** a road that goes right around a town or city

rink NOUN **rinks** a large area of ice for skating on

rinse VERB **rinses, rinsing, rinsed** to rinse something is to wash it with clean water

NOUN **rinses** a wash with clean water

riot NOUN **riots** a crowd of people behaving noisily and violently in the streets

VERB **riots, rioting, rioted** to behave noisily and violently with a lot of other people in the street

▸ **rioter** NOUN **rioters** a person who is part of a violent crowd in the street

▸ **riotous** ADJECTIVE noisy and uncontrolled

rip VERB **rips, ripping, ripped 1** to tear something roughly: *ripping sheets into strips for bandages • Steve had ripped his trousers on the barbed wire.* **2** to snatch something from someone: *A reporter ripped the notebook right out of my hand.*

• **rip someone off** (*slang*) to cheat someone out of some money, especially by charging too much for something

NOUN **rips** a rough tear: *There was a rip in my sleeve where the handlebars had caught it.*

RIP ABBREVIATION short for **rest in peace**, a phrase that is often written on gravestones

ripe ADJECTIVE **riper, ripest** ripe fruit or crops are ready to be picked or eaten: *Slightly green bananas will soon be completely ripe.*

▸ **ripen** VERB **ripens, ripening, ripened** when fruit or crops ripen they become ready to pick or eat

▸ **ripeness** NOUN how completely ready a growing food is to pick or eat: *Check the ripeness of the fruit by squeezing it very gently.*

ripple NOUN **ripples** a tiny wave on the surface of water

rise VERB **rises, rising, rose, risen 1** to go upwards: *a column of smoke rising through the air • Ahead, the ground rose steeply. • The sun rises in the east.* **2** to get up: *We all rose when the judge entered. • His habit was to rise early for breakfast.*

• **rise up** if people rise up, they start to rebel and protest against a government

NOUN **rises** an increase: *a pay rise*

• **give rise to** to cause: *The accident has given rise to worries about safety.*

risk NOUN **risks** a possibility that something bad will happen: *There's a risk that the whole project might be called off. • Do we want to take this risk?*

VERB **risks, risking, risked** to take a chance of damaging or losing something: *Soldiers are risking their lives every day.*

▸ **risky** ADJECTIVE **riskier, riskiest** dangerous: *a risky route to the top of the mountain*

rite NOUN **rites** a ceremony, especially one to do with a religion

ritual NOUN **rituals** a set of actions that are part of a ceremony for certain occasions

rival NOUN **rivals** a person or organization that competes with another: *a match between fierce rivals*

VERB **rivals, rivalling, rivalled** to be as good, or nearly as good, as something or someone else: *Shop-bought* vegetables can't rival the ones you grow yourself.

▸ **rivalry** NOUN when people or organizations compete against each other: *There's a lot of rivalry between the twins.*

river NOUN **rivers** a large stream of water that flows across land: *the River Thames*

rivet NOUN **rivets** a short kind of nail that holds pieces of metal together

VERB **rivets, riveting, riveted**

• **be riveted by something** to be very interested in something

▸ **riveting** ADJECTIVE extremely interesting: *The last half hour of the film was simply riveting.*

road NOUN **roads** a hard, level surface for vehicles to travel along: *The British drive on the left-hand side of the road.*

roam VERB **roams, roaming, roamed** to travel or wander around: *There wasn't anything else to do but roam the streets.*

roar VERB **roars, roaring, roared** to make a loud, angry sound like a lion: *traffic roaring past in the street below*

NOUN **roars** a loud noise like the sound a lion makes

roast VERB **roasts, roasting, roasted** to cook or be cooked in an oven or over a fire: *Roast the potatoes at the same time as the turkey.*

NOUN **roasts** a piece of meat that has been cooked in the oven

ADJECTIVE cooked in the oven: *roast potatoes • roast beef*

rob VERB **robs, robbing, robbed** to rob someone is to steal something from them: *I've been robbed! • They stole thousands of pounds when they robbed the bank.*

▸ **robber** NOUN **robbers** a person who steals

▸ **robbery** NOUN **robberies** when something is stolen: *a bank robbery*

robe NOUN **robes** a long loose piece of clothing: *The mayor wears a chain and a robe on special occasions.*

robin NOUN **robins** a small brown bird with a red breast

robot NOUN **robots** a machine that can do things like a person

rock[1] NOUN **rocks** 1 rock is the hard stone substance that the Earth is made of 2 a rock is a large stone 3 rock is a sweet that is sold at tourist attractions. It is usually in the form of a long stick

rock[2] VERB **rocks, rocking, rocked** 1 to rock is to move or swing gently backwards and forwards or from side to side 2 to rock something is to make it move backwards and forwards or from side to side: *She was rocking the baby in her arms.*

NOUN a type of loud music with a deep beat

▸ **rocker** NOUN **rockers** the curved part of a chair or cradle that it can move backwards and forwards on

rockery NOUN **rockeries** a place where people grow small plants among rocks and stones

rocket NOUN **rockets** 1 a spacecraft for travelling from Earth into space 2 a large missile 3 a kind of firework that explodes high in the sky

VERB **rockets, rocketing, rocketed** to go upwards very very quickly: *rocketing prices*

rocky[1] ADJECTIVE **rockier, rockiest** full of, or covered with rocks

rocky[2] ADJECTIVE shaky, unsteady or uncertain: *Their relationship got off to a rocky start when she didn't even recognize him.*

rod NOUN **rods** a long thin pole or bar, especially made of wood or metal: *a fishing rod*

rode VERB a way of changing the verb **ride** to make the past tense: *I rode my bike for hours at a time in those days.*

rodent NOUN **rodents** any kind of small furry animal with sharp teeth, such as a mouse, rat or rabbit

rodeo NOUN **rodeos** a show of riding and other skills by cowboys

rogue NOUN **rogues** a cheating and dishonest person, especially one that likes to play tricks

▸ **roguish** ADJECTIVE mischievous: *a roguish twinkle in his eye*

role NOUN **roles** 1 the part that someone

Aa
Bb
Cc
Dd
Ee
Ff
Gg
Hh
Ii
Jj
Kk
Ll
Mm
Nn
Oo
Pp
Qq
Rr
Ss
Tt
Uu
Vv
Ww
Xx
Yy
Zz

plays in a play or film: *a starring role in a new British film* **2** the purpose or reason for what something or someone does: *A parent's role is to provide a safe background to a child's life.*

roll VERB **rolls, rolling, rolled**

1 to move along, turning over and over: *a ball rolling down a slope*

2 to move along on wheels: *Take the brake off and let the car roll forwards.*

3 to form something into the shape of a ball or cylinder: *Roll the sleeping bag up tightly and tie the string around it.*

4 to roll something is to make it flat by crushing it under a rolling cylinder: *I am going to roll the lawn.* • *rolled metal*

5 to rock from side to side: *In rough weather, the ship rolls a bit.*

• **roll up** (*informal*) to arrive: *Some guests were only just rolling up when the first ones started to leave.*

NOUN **rolls**

1 a very small loaf of bread: *a cheese roll for lunch*

2 a cylinder shape made from a large flat piece of something like carpet or paper: *We'll need 12 rolls of wallpaper for this room.*

3 a list of names **4** a long rumbling sound: *a drum roll* • *a roll of thunder*

rollcall NOUN **rollcalls** when someone calls out the names from a list

roller NOUN **rollers 1** something in the shape of a cylinder that turns like a wheel and is often used to flatten things **2** an object like a cylinder that you can wind hair around when it is wet to make it curl **3** a long heavy wave on the sea

rollerblades PLURAL NOUN boots that have a single row of wheels on the bottom

rollerskates PLURAL NOUN boots with pairs of wheels on the bottom

rolling pin NOUN **rolling pins** a thick round stick or rod that you roll over pastry to flatten it

ROM ABBREVIATION (*ICT*) short for **Read Only Memory**, a type of memory in a computer that allows you to see information but not change it

romance NOUN **romances 1** romance is the exciting emotions people feel when they are falling in love **2** a romance is a love affair: *his first romance* **3** a romance is a love story: *Betty used to read mainly romances.*

▶ **romantic** ADJECTIVE to do with love: *a romantic relationship* • *a romantic dinner for two*

▶ **romantically** ADVERB in a way that suggests love or a love affair: *She's not romantically involved with anyone just now.*

romp VERB **romps, romping, romped** to play in a lively way

NOUN **romps** a fast-moving, lively game

roof NOUN **roofs 1** the part that covers the top of a building or vehicle: *The house has a red tiled roof.* **2** the top inside surface of your mouth

rook NOUN **rooks 1** a large black bird like a crow **2** in the game of chess, a rook is a piece that is shaped like a castle

room NOUN **rooms 1** one of the areas a building is divided into inside: *We have three rooms downstairs and four upstairs.* **2** enough space for something: *Is there room for a grand piano on the stage?*

▶ **roomy** ADJECTIVE **roomier, roomiest** having a lot of space inside it

roost NOUN **roosts** the place where a bird rests at night

VERB **roosts, roosting, roosted** to sit or sleep at night

▶ **rooster** NOUN **roosters** a cockerel

root NOUN **roots**

1 the underground part of a plant

2 the part of a tooth or hair that attaches it to the body

3 the basic cause of a problem: *The root of all our troubles is that we don't have enough money.*

4 your roots are your family connections and where you come from

VERB **roots, rooting, rooted** to grow roots: *The seedlings rooted nicely when I planted them in the compost.*

• **be rooted to the spot** to be unable

to move, for example because you are surprised or afraid

• **root around** to search roughly and untidily for something: *Who's been rooting around in my desk?*

• **root something out** to find something and get rid of it

rope NOUN **ropes** a very thick twisted cord: *an anchor tied on the end of a long piece of rope*

rose¹ NOUN **roses 1** a garden plant with prickly stems and sweet-smelling flowers **2** a pink colour

rose² VERB a way of changing the verb **rise** to make a past tense: *The temperature in the room rose steadily as the day wore on.*

rosemary NOUN an evergreen plant that has sweet-smelling leaves that can be used to flavour food in cooking

rosette NOUN **rosettes** a round decoration or a badge made of gathered ribbon. Rosettes may be given as prizes or worn to show that you support a particular group or party

Rosh Hashanah (pronounced rosh ha-**sha**-na) NOUN a Jewish festival celebrating the new year

rosy ADJECTIVE **rosier, rosiest 1** having a pink colour: *rosy cheeks* **2** hopeful or cheerful: *The future certainly looks rosy for Hugh.*

rot VERB **rots, rotting, rotted** to go rotten and decay: *The leaves fall on the forest floor and gradually rot into the soil.*

NOUN **1** decay where something is going rotten: *They've discovered some rot in the roof timbers.* **2** nonsense: *You do talk such rot!*

rota NOUN **rotas** a list of people who take turns to do a job

rotary ADJECTIVE going round and round like a wheel

rotate VERB **rotates, rotating, rotated 1** to turn or spin like a wheel: *Each wheel rotates on its own axle.* **2** to go through a series of changes and then start again at the beginning: *Rotating the different kinds of vegetables we grow keeps the soil healthy.*

▶ **rotation** NOUN **rotations 1** going around like a wheel: *The rotation of the blades keeps the air moving.* **2** working through a series of changes and then beginning again

rotor NOUN **rotors** a part of a machine that turns round, especially a helicopter blade

rotten ADJECTIVE **1** going bad or decaying: *John stepped on a rotten floorboard and it gave way beneath him.* **2** bad quality: *a rotten meal* **3** unfair or unkind: *That was a rotten thing to say.*

rotter NOUN **rotters** a person who behaves badly towards someone else

rough ADJECTIVE **rougher, roughest 1** not smooth: *a rough track along the side of the field* • *rough skin on the bottom of your feet* **2** violent: *Rugby is such a rough game, some schools refuse to play it.* **3** not exact: *a rough sketch of the building*

▶ **roughen** VERB **roughens, roughening, roughened** to remove the smoothness of something: *Roughen the edges before you apply the glue to them.*

▶ **roughly** ADVERB **1** in a quick way, without being careful or gentle: *If you handle the flowers roughly, you'll damage them.* **2** approximately: *There were roughly a thousand people in the stadium.*

▶ **roughness** NOUN **1** not being gentle **2** not being smooth

roulette NOUN a gambling game in which a ball is dropped on to a spinning wheel that has sections with different numbers on them

round ADJECTIVE **rounder, roundest 1** the same shape as a circle: *a round table* **2** the same shape as part of a circle: *a round archway* **3** the same shape as a ball: *The Earth is round.*

ADVERB AND PREPOSITION **1** around, or on all sides: *I glanced round at the pictures on the walls.* • *The Moon goes round the Earth.* **2** from one person or place to another: *The news got round pretty quickly.*

NOUN **rounds**

1 a burst of something like laughing,

Aa Bb Cc Dd Ee Ff Gg Hh Ii Jj Kk Ll Mm Nn Oo Pp Qq Rr Ss Tt Uu Vv Ww Xx Yy Zz

Aa
Bb
Cc
Dd
Ee
Ff
Gg
Hh
Ii
Jj
Kk
Ll
Mm
Nn
Oo
Pp
Qq
Rr
Ss
Tt
Uu
Vv
Ww
Xx
Yy
Zz

cheering, clapping or firing: *Let's give him a round of applause.*
2 a route of calls that someone makes: *We're always last on the postman's round.*
3 a level in a contest: *a second-round match*
4 a single bullet or shell for a gun
5 a song in which each singer begins the tune a little after the previous one
VERB **rounds, rounding, rounded** to go around a corner: *As I rounded the corner, I came face to face with Sharon.*
• **round on someone** to attack someone suddenly: *She rounded on me as if I'd hit her.*
• **round someone** or **something up** to round up people or animals is to collect them together: *Farmers are rounding the animals up for the winter.*
• **round up** or **down** to round a number up or down is to make it a whole number: *If you round up 3.75 you get 4.*

roundabout NOUN **roundabouts 1** a circular platform in a playground or a funfair that turns while you ride on it **2** a road junction where several roads meet and the traffic must travel around a central island before continuing

rounders NOUN a team game similar to baseball

rouse VERB **rouses, rousing, roused** to wake someone up
▶ **rousing** ADJECTIVE exciting and making people feel enthusiastic: *a rousing march from the brass band*

rout NOUN **routs** a complete defeat

route NOUN **routes** a way of getting somewhere: *Terry's route to school takes him past the swimming pool.*

routine NOUN **routines 1** a fixed order of doing things: *Our daily routine includes three good meals and plenty of exercise.* **2** a dance routine is a fixed set of dance steps
ADJECTIVE a routine job or task is an ordinary one that is done regularly: *a routine inspection*

rove VERB **roves, roving, roved** to wander around: *Harry has been roving about the world.*

▶ **rover** NOUN **rovers** a wanderer or unsettled person

row¹ (rhymes with **low**) NOUN **rows** a number of things arranged beside each other in a line: *the front row of seats* • *Sow the seeds in a straight row.* • *a row of figures*
• **in a row** happening one after another: *They've lost five matches in a row.*

row² (rhymes with **low**) VERB **rows, rowing, rowed** to pull a boat through water using oars

row³ (rhymes with **how**) NOUN **rows 1** a noisy argument or a fight **2** a loud unpleasant noise: *Why are the children making such a row?*
VERB **rows, rowing, rowed** to argue noisily

rowdy ADJECTIVE **rowdier, rowdiest** noisy and rough: *a rowdy party*

rowing boat NOUN **rowing boats** a small boat that you row with oars

royal ADJECTIVE to do with a king or queen or their family: *a royal wedding*
▶ **royalty** NOUN all the members of the king or queen's family

rub VERB **rubs, rubbing, rubbed 1** to move your hand backwards and forwards over a surface, usually pressing down at the same time: *He lowered his head and rubbed his eyes.* **2** to press against something and move backwards and forwards: *My shoes are rubbing and giving me blisters.*
NOUN **rubs** a backwards and forwards movement of your hand while pressing down: *Let me give your neck a rub where it's aching.*

rubber NOUN **rubbers 1** rubber is a strong substance that stretches and can be man-made or made from tree juices: *rubber-soled shoes* **2** a rubber is a small block that you can use to rub on pencil marks to erase them

rubbish NOUN **1** things that have been thrown away or should be thrown away: *a rubbish bin* **2** complete nonsense: *Her new chat show is utter rubbish.*

rubble NOUN the broken pieces that are left when a building falls down

ruby NOUN **rubies** a dark red stone that is used as a jewel

rucksack NOUN **rucksacks** a bag that you carry on your back, especially when you are walking or climbing

✦ This is a German word which comes from **ruck**, which means *back*, and **sack**, which means *bag*.

rudder NOUN **rudders** the flat piece of wood or metal at the back of a boat, under the water, that moves to steer it in a different direction. An aeroplane also has a rudder on its tail

ruddy ADJECTIVE **ruddier, ruddiest** pink and healthy looking: *a ruddy complexion*

rude ADJECTIVE **ruder, rudest 1** not polite: *a rude answer* **2** embarrassing and not proper in a polite situation: *rude jokes* **3** rough and basic: *a rude stable*

▶ **rudely** ADVERB in a bad-mannered way, without being polite: *'Not likely!' he said rudely.*

▶ **rudeness** NOUN bad manners or not being polite: *I apologize for my friend's rudeness.*

ruffian NOUN **ruffians** a person who behaves in a rough violent way

ruffle VERB **ruffles, ruffling, ruffled 1** to disturb something, such as a hairstyle, by making it untidy: *A small bird sat on the fence, ruffling its feathers.* **2** to annoy or upset someone: *She never seems to get ruffled.*

rug NOUN **rugs** a large mat on the floor

rugby NOUN a game played by two teams on a large field with an oval ball that the players must try to take over a line at the end of the pitch

✦ **Rugby** is named after *Rugby* School in Warwickshire, England. The game is supposed to have been invented there.

rugged (pronounced **rug**-id) ADJECTIVE rough or unevenly shaped: *rugged countryside* • *The man had a really rugged face.*

ruin VERB **ruins, ruining, ruined** to ruin something is to destroy it: *The rain ruined my hairstyle.*

NOUN **ruins 1** a ruin is something such as a building that has fallen to pieces: *a Roman ruin* **2** ruin is when someone has lost all the money they had: *If this plan did not work, he would be facing certain ruin.*

• **in ruins** to be in ruins is to be destroyed: *a city in ruins after the earthquake* • *All our plans were in ruins now that Bob had walked out.*

rule NOUN **rules 1** an instruction about what is or what is not allowed: *It's against the rules to move your feet when you're holding the ball.* **2** government, or control by politicians or a king or queen: *a country under the rule of the military* **3** the way things usually happen: *As a rule, more people go to work by car when it's raining.*

VERB **rules, ruling, ruled 1** to rule something, such as a country, is to control it **2** to make an official decision: *The judge has ruled that the prisoner can go free.* **3** to rule a line is to draw a straight line: *a pad of ruled paper*

▶ **ruler** NOUN **ruler 1** a person who controls or governs a country **2** a strip of wood, plastic or metal that can be used to help you to draw a straight line or for measuring short lengths

▶ **ruling** NOUN **rulings** a decision by someone like a judge: *The committee's ruling is that the race was a draw.*

rum NOUN a strong alcoholic drink made from sugar cane

rumble VERB **rumbles, rumbling, rumbled** to make a low continuous sound: *tanks rumbling along the road*

NOUN **rumbles** a long low sound like thunder

rummage VERB **rummages, rummaging, rummaged** to search for something by untidily moving things out of the way: *rummaging in her handbag for a pen*

rummy NOUN a card game where each player has seven cards and tries to

Aa
Bb
Cc
Dd
Ee
Ff
Gg
Hh
Ii
Jj
Kk
Ll
Mm
Nn
Oo
Pp
Qq
Rr
Ss
Tt
Uu
Vv
Ww
Xx
Yy
Zz

collect sets of three cards or more by changing them for different ones

rumour NOUN **rumours** information that people pass to each other, although it may not be true: *There's a rumour going round that our teacher is getting married.*

VERB **rumours, rumouring, rumoured** something is rumoured if people say it is true, although it may not be

rump NOUN **rumps** the area around an animal's tail or above its back legs

run VERB **runs, running, ran, run**

1 to move with very fast steps: *We had to run for the bus.*

2 to follow a certain route: *The number 5 bus runs every 10 minutes. • This road runs over the hill to the next village.*

3 to run someone somewhere is to give them a lift: *Dad runs us to school if it's raining.*

4 a liquid runs when it flows easily: *tears running down my face • Your nose is running.*

5 an engine or other machinery runs, or you run it, when it works or operates: *The engine runs on diesel oil.*

6 a scheme or system runs, or you run it, when it happens or works: *We're running a new course in the spring.*

7 to continue: *The film runs for 2 hours without a break.*

8 to run your hand over something is to pass your hand across its surface: *Grace ran her finger down the list until she came to her name.*

9 to compete to be elected to an official job: *Mr Bush was running for president*

• **run a risk** to take a chance that something bad might happen: *If we don't leave now, we'll run the risk of having to return in the dark.*

• **run away** to leave somewhere in secret

• **run out of something** to have none of something left: *We've run out of vinegar but we could use lemon juice instead.*

NOUN **runs**

1 a fast movement, quicker than a walk: *break into a run and get there faster*

2 a race or period of exercise: *a cross-country run*

3 a trip or journey in a vehicle: *a quick run into town to do the shopping*

4 a point that a player wins in a game, such as cricket, by running a certain distance after hitting the ball

5 a period of time during which something is repeated: *a run of bad luck*

6 a long fenced area where animals are kept: *a chicken run*

runaway NOUN **runaways** someone who has run away from home

ADJECTIVE a runaway vehicle is out of control and moving very fast

run-down ADJECTIVE **1** continually feeling tired and not very healthy: *Mother's feeling run-down after having the flu.* **2** a run-down building is not kept in good condition

rung[1] NOUN **rungs** a step on a ladder

rung[2] VERB the form of the verb **ring** that is used with a helping verb to show that something hapened in the past: *I've rung all my friends and can't get anyone to go with me.*

runner NOUN **runners 1** a person or animal that runs: *a fast runner* **2** the blade of a skate or sledge

runner-up NOUN **runners-up** the person that finishes in second place in a competition

running NOUN organization and management: *You'll be responsible for the running of the shop.*

• **be in** or **out of the running** to have, or not have, the chance of winning something: *The player is still in the running for the championship.*

ADJECTIVE continuing without a break: *a running commentary on the events*

ADVERB one after the other: *for three days running*

runny ADJECTIVE **runnier, runniest**

1 like a liquid: *Heat the jam until it is runny.* **2** if you have a runny nose, you need to blow it frequently

runway NOUN **runways** the long road-like surface at an airport that aircraft take off from and land on

rupture VERB **ruptures, rupturing,**

Aa Bb Cc Dd Ee Ff Gg Hh Ii Jj Kk Ll Mm Nn Oo Pp Qq **Rr** Ss Tt Uu Vv Ww Xx Yy Zz

ruptured to break: *a patient with an appendix that has ruptured*

NOUN **ruptures** a break or tear, especially in a muscle or joint

rural ADJECTIVE to do with the countryside

rush NOUN **rushes** 1 a hurry: *We were just in time but it had been a dreadful rush.* 2 a large number of people trying to get to the same place at the same time: *a rush for the door*

VERB **rushes, rushing, rushed** 1 to rush is to go somewhere in a hurry: *I rushed downstairs as soon as I heard the thump.* • *Fletcher was rushed to the hospital in an ambulance.* 2 to rush is to do something too quickly or in a hurry: *Don't rush it or you'll just make a mistake.* 3 to rush someone is to attack them suddenly, hoping to surprise them

rusk NOUN **rusks** a hard dry biscuit that babies eat

rust NOUN a reddish-brown substance that forms on iron and other metals if they are exposed to air and wetness

VERB **rusts, rusting, rusted** to become rusty

▸ **rusty** ADJECTIVE **rustier, rustiest** rusty metal has a reddish-brown substance on it that makes it weak and brittle

rustle VERB **rustles, rustling, rustled** to make a soft sound like dry leaves rubbing together: *people rustling sweet papers at the cinema*

NOUN **rustles** a soft sound like dry leaves: *the rustle of a silk dress*

rut NOUN **ruts** 1 a deep track made by a wheel 2 a boring routine: *I'm in a rut and the only way out is to change my job.*

ruthless ADJECTIVE a ruthless person does what they think they must do without caring how cruel or kind they are being

▸ **ruthlessly** ADVERB without taking into account how kind or cruel you are being

▸ **ruthlessness** NOUN doing things without thinking about how kind or cruel you are being

rye NOUN a kind of grain that is used for making flour and whisky

Aa
Bb
Cc
Dd
Ee
Ff
Gg
Hh
Ii
Jj
Kk
Ll
Mm
Nn
Oo
Pp
Qq
Rr
Ss
Tt
Uu
Vv
Ww
Xx
Yy
Zz

Ss

S ABBREVIATION short for **south**

Sabbath NOUN the day of the week

set aside for rest and worship in
certain religions. The Jewish Sabbath is

Saturday, for Muslims it is Friday and for
most Christians, it is Sunday

sabotage NOUN deliberate damage
that someone does to buildings or

equipment in secret

VERB **sabotages, sabotaging,**

sabotaged to deliberately damage an
enemy's equipment or plans

sabre NOUN **sabres** a curved sword
that was used in the past by soldiers on

horses

sac NOUN **sacs** any part of a plant or

animal that is like a bag, especially one
that contains liquid

saccharin NOUN a very sweet chemical
that can be used instead of sugar

▶ **saccharine** ADJECTIVE very sweet or
sickly

sachet (pronounced **sa**-shay) NOUN

sachets a small plastic or paper packet
containing a small amount of a liquid or

powder: *a handy sachet of shampoo for
your suitcase*

sack NOUN **sacks** a sack is a very large
bag used for carrying or storing things

• **the sack** the sack is when you are
told to leave your job: *That new boy got*

the sack for stealing coins from the till.

VERB **sacks, sacking, sacked** to sack

someone is to tell them that they no
longer have a job, usually because

they are not good at it: *He was sacked
because he was always late for work.*

sacrament NOUN **sacraments** any of
several important Christian ceremonies

such as baptism and Communion

sacred ADJECTIVE **1** holy, or to do with a
god **2** to do with religion or worship: *a*

CD of sacred music

sacrifice NOUN **sacrifices 1** something

that is killed and offered to a god in the

hope that something good will then
happen: *Ancient peoples killed small and
large animals in this place as sacrifices to
their gods.* **2** giving up something for the
sake of someone or something else: *We
didn't earn much and we had to make a
lot of sacrifices to afford a house.*

VERB **sacrifices, sacrificing, sacrificed**
1 to kill something and offer it to a god
2 to give something up for the sake of
someone or something else: *The boy
bravely sacrificed his life for another.*

sad ADJECTIVE **sadder, saddest 1** feeling
unhappy: *a sad look* **2** making you feel
unhappy: *a sad film*

▶ **sadden** VERB **saddens, saddening,
saddened** you are saddened if
something makes you feel unhappy: *We
were greatly saddened by the news.*

▶ **sadly** ADVERB **1** unfortunately: *Sadly,
we must say goodbye to Mrs Green
today.* **2** unhappily: *She looked up sadly
and tried to smile.*

▶ **sadness** NOUN a feeling of
unhappiness or pity

saddle NOUN **saddles** a seat for a rider
of a horse or a bicycle

VERB **saddles, saddling, saddled** to
saddle a horse is to put a seat on it so
that you can ride it

• **saddle someone with something**
to give someone a job that nobody
wants to do: *They've saddled me with
doing the washing up.*

sadism NOUN enjoying being cruel or
hurting other people

▶ **sadist** NOUN **sadists** a person who
enjoys hurting other people

▶ **sadistic** ADJECTIVE a sadistic person
enjoys hurting other people

sae ABBREVIATION short for **stamped
addressed envelope**

safari NOUN **safaris** an expedition or
tour when people hunt or watch wild
animals, especially in Africa

> ✦ This word comes from the African language Swahili and it means *journey*.

safari park NOUN **safari parks** a large area of land where wild animals are kept for visitors to see

safe ADJECTIVE **safer, safest 1** not harmed: *Thank goodness you're safe!* **2** not involving danger or risk: *the safest way to travel long distances* • *That ladder doesn't look very safe to me.*
NOUN **safes** a strong metal box for keeping valuables in: *The safe had been blown open with dynamite.*

▶ **safely** ADVERB without risk or danger: *getting everyone home safely* • *safely tucked up in bed*

safeguard NOUN **safeguards** something which protects someone or something from harm or danger: *The double lock is a safeguard against theft.*
VERB **safeguards, safeguarding, safeguarded** to protect someone or something from danger: *Vaccinations should safeguard our children from these deadly diseases.*

safety NOUN being safe: *Everyone dived for safety.* • *We must put the safety of our passengers first.*

safety belt NOUN **safety belts** a strap in a car or plane that stops you being thrown out of your seat if there is a crash

safety pin NOUN **safety pins** a pin with a guard that covers the sharp point when it is closed

sag VERB **sags, sagging, sagged** to droop or not to be firm: *a mattress that has begun to sag in the middle*

saga NOUN **sagas** a long story, especially one about several generations of a family

sage NOUN **sages** sage is a herb that is used in cooking to add flavour

said VERB a way of changing the verb **say** to make a past tense. It can be used with or without a helping verb: *They've said I can come back any time.* • *I've told you everything he said.*

sail VERB **sails, sailing, sailed 1** to travel in a ship or a boat: *My ambition is to sail across the Atlantic on an ocean liner.* **2** to start a journey in a ship: *The ferry sails at noon.*
• **sail through something** to do something quickly and easily: *Amy sailed through her exams with no bother.*
NOUN **sails 1** a sheet of canvas attached to a mast on a boat that catches the wind and carries the boat along **2** a broad flat blade that turns on a windmill

▶ **sailor** NOUN **sailors** someone who works on a ship

saint NOUN **saints 1** someone that the Christian church believes was especially holy **2** a particularly good and kind person

▶ **saintly** ADJECTIVE very good or very holy

sake NOUN **sakes**
• **for someone's sake** for someone's sake is for them or for their benefit: *For his mother's sake, he didn't want to make a fuss.* • *Please don't go to any trouble just for my sake.*
• **for the sake of it** to do something for the sake of it is to do it simply because you want to: *I'm sure she argues with me just for the sake of it.*
• **for the sake of something** to do something for the sake of something is to do it because you want to achieve that thing: *I gave in for the sake of peace.*

salaam INTERJECTION a greeting that is used especially by Muslims

salad NOUN **salads** a mixture of mostly raw vegetables that sometimes includes other foods like ham or cheese

salami NOUN a type of spicy sausage that is usually served cold in thin slices

salary NOUN **salaries** an amount of money that a person is paid for doing their job for a year. It is usually divided into twelve monthly payments

salat NOUN the prayers that Muslims say five times each day

sale NOUN **sales 1** when something is sold for money: *a sale of hand-made carpets* • *a house for sale* • *This week's edition is on sale now.* **2** an occasion

Aa
Bb
Cc
Dd
Ee
Ff
Gg
Hh
Ii
Jj
Kk
Ll
Mm
Nn
Oo
Pp
Qq
Rr
Ss
Tt
Uu
Vv
Ww
Xx
Yy
Zz

when goods in a shop are sold at cheaper prices than usual: *the January sales*

salesman, saleswoman *or* **salesperson** NOUN **salesmen, saleswomen** *or* **salespeople** a person whose job is to sell goods to customers

saline ADJECTIVE containing salt

saliva NOUN the watery liquid produced in your mouth

sally VERB **sallies, sallying, sallied** to rush out suddenly

NOUN **sallies** a sudden rush or attack

salmon NOUN **salmon 1** a salmon is a large sea fish with a silvery skin. It swims up rivers to lay its eggs **2** salmon is an orange-pink colour

salon NOUN **salons** a shop where services such as hairdressing or beauty treatments take place

saloon NOUN **saloons 1** a bar where alcoholic drinks are served **2** a car with a hard roof, several seats and a separate space for luggage **3** a dining-room for passengers on a ship

salt NOUN **salts 1** salt is small white crystals that come from the ground (**rock salt**) or the sea (**sea salt**), used for flavouring food **2** (*science*) a salt is a substance formed from a metal and an acid

VERB **salts, salting, salted** to put salt on something, usually on food for flavour or on roads to stop ice forming

▸ **salty** ADJECTIVE **saltier, saltiest** containing salt or tasting very strongly of salt: *I thought the soup was awfully salty.*

salute VERB **salutes, saluting, saluted 1** to greet someone with a formal gesture. Soldiers salute their officers by standing still and raising one hand to their forehead **2** to praise someone or what they have done: *Today we salute the brave people of this town.*

NOUN **salutes** a movement that shows respect to someone you meet, especially a military officer

salvage VERB **salvages, salvaging, salvaged** to rescue what you can after a disaster of some kind, especially the sinking of a ship: *some furniture that*

was salvaged from the building after the fire

salvation NOUN being saved or saving someone or something

same ADJECTIVE exactly alike or very similar: *I was wearing the same jacket as Barbara.* • *The two cases are exactly the same.*

PRONOUN something that is alike or similar: *You know I'd do the same for you.*

• **all the same** anyway, nevertheless, or in spite of something: *The flight might be delayed but you have to check in now all the same.*

sample NOUN **samples** a small part of something that shows what the rest is like

VERB **samples, sampling, sampled** to take or test a small part of something: *Would you like to sample our new product?*

sanctuary NOUN **sanctuaries 1** a holy place, for example in a church, mosque or temple **2** a safe place: *refugees seeking sanctuary* • *a bird sanctuary*

sand NOUN **sands** tiny grains of rock that are found on beaches, on river-beds and in deserts

VERB **sands, sanding, sanded** to make a rough surface smooth by rubbing it with sandpaper: *The wood looked very different after it had been sanded down and varnished.*

sandal NOUN **sandals** sandals are light open shoes with straps for wearing in warm weather

sandbag NOUN **sandbags** a small sack filled with sand. Sandbags are used to build walls to keep out flooding water or bullets

sand dune NOUN **sand dunes** a hill of sand on or near a beach

sandpaper NOUN strong paper with a layer of sand glued to one side, used for smoothing wood or rough metal surfaces

sandpit NOUN **sandpits 1** a hole filled with sand **2** a small area filled with sand for children to play in

sandstone NOUN a type of soft rock that is often used in building

Aa
Bb
Cc
Dd
Ee
Ff
Gg
Hh
Ii
Jj
Kk
Ll
Mm
Nn
Oo
Pp
Qq
Rr
Ss
Tt
Uu
Vv
Ww
Xx
Yy
Zz

sandwich NOUN **sandwiches** two slices of bread with a filling between them: *What's so special about cucumber sandwiches?*

VERB **sandwiches, sandwiching, sandwiched** to be sandwiched between things or people is to be squashed between them: *I was sandwiched between the backs of two huge people.*

✦ This word comes from the name of the Earl of **Sandwich**. It is said that in the 18th century he ate sandwiches so that he would not have to stop playing cards to be served meals.

sandy ADJECTIVE **sandier, sandiest 1** containing or covered with sand: *sandy soil* **2** light reddish-brown: *a sandy-haired child*

sane ADJECTIVE **saner, sanest 1** not mad or mentally ill: *The judge was told that Foster was sane at the time of the murder.* **2** sensible: *She seems like a sane enough person.*

sang VERB a way of changing the verb **sing** to make a past tense: *We sang folk songs all evening to Gerry's guitar.*

sanitary ADJECTIVE to do with keeping clean and healthy: *Diseases spread quickly where sanitary conditions are poor.*

sanitation NOUN ways of protecting people's health by providing clean water and getting dirty water and waste away from buildings

sanity NOUN not being mad or mentally ill

sank VERB a way of changing the verb **sink** to make a past tense: *Many ships sank without trace in those days.*

sap NOUN the juice inside plants and trees

VERB **saps, sapping, sapped** to sap your strength or energy is to gradually make you feel more and more tired: *The terrible heat sapped our energy by lunchtime.*

sapling NOUN **saplings** a young tree

sapphire NOUN **sapphires** a dark blue precious stone that is used in jewellery

sarcasm NOUN saying one thing when you actually mean the opposite. People often use sarcasm when they are trying to be funny

▸ **sarcastic** ADJECTIVE meaning the exact opposite in order to hurt or amuse someone: *When we told Marge we liked her hat, she didn't know if we were being sarcastic or not.*

sardine NOUN **sardines** a type of small sea fish that is either eaten fresh or packed tightly in small tins

sari NOUN **saris** a long piece of fabric that is worn like a dress by Hindu women. It is wound round the waist and the end is draped over one shoulder or over the head

sarong NOUN **sarongs** a wide piece of fabric that covers the lower part of the body. It is wound round the waist or under the arms

sash NOUN **sashes** a strip of cloth worn around the waist or over one shoulder, usually as part of a uniform

sat VERB a way of changing the verb **sit** to make a past tense. It can be used with or without a helping verb: *Class 3 sat quietly, waiting for their teacher.* • *I've sat here for an hour waiting for you!*

satchel NOUN **satchels** a small bag with a shoulder strap that is used to carry schoolbooks

satellite NOUN **satellites** an object in space that moves around a planet or star

satellite television NOUN broadcasts that are sent and received using satellites that are designed for that purpose

satin NOUN a fabric with a shiny surface

satisfaction NOUN a contented feeling after getting or doing what you wanted: *I get a lot of satisfaction out of baking my own bread.*

satisfactory ADJECTIVE **1** good enough but not outstanding: *Gareth's progress in maths has been satisfactory.* **2** right or wanted: *a very satisfactory result*

satisfy VERB **satisfies, satisfying, satisfied 1** to be satisfied is to be

Aa
Bb
Cc
Dd
Ee
Ff
Gg
Hh
Ii
Jj
Kk
Ll
Mm
Nn
Oo
Pp
Qq
Rr
Ss
Tt
Uu
Vv
Ww
Xx
Yy
Zz

happy or contented: *I'm afraid I'm not satisfied with the way we've been treated.* **2** to satisfy someone is to give them what they want or need: *I don't think a biscuit will satisfy a boy who's been playing football all afternoon.*

satsuma NOUN **satsumas** a fruit like a small orange with no pips

saturate VERB **saturates, saturating, saturated** to be saturated is to be soaking wet

Saturday NOUN **Saturdays** the day of the week after Friday and before Sunday

✦ **Saturday** comes from the Old English word **Sæterdæg**, which means *Saturn's day*. Saturn is the Roman god of harvest.

sauce NOUN **sauces** a liquid that food is cooked in or served with: *I like plenty of tomato sauce with my chips.*

saucepan NOUN **saucepans** a deep round cooking pot that usually has a long handle and a lid

saucer NOUN **saucers** a small shallow dish that is used for resting a cup on

saucy ADJECTIVE **saucier, sauciest** cheeky

sauna NOUN **saunas** a steam bath where you sit in a room filled with the steam produced by throwing cold water on hot coals

saunter VERB **saunters, sauntering, sauntered** to walk slowly in a relaxed way: *people sauntering round the park on a warm evening*
NOUN **saunters** a gentle stroll

sausage NOUN **sausages** meat that is minced and stuffed into a skin to make long tube shapes

savage ADJECTIVE fierce and cruel: *a savage attack by a stray dog*
VERB **savages, savaging, savaged** to be savaged by an animal is to be attacked and badly injured by it
NOUN **savages** an uncivilized person
▶ **savagely** ADVERB fiercely and cruelly

savanna *or* **savannah** NOUN **savannas** *or* **savannahs** (*geography*) a

grassy plain without trees, especially in Africa

save VERB **saves, saving, saved**
1 to save someone or something is to rescue them from something unpleasant: *The firefighters saved everyone in the building.* • *We saved our photographs but everything else in the loft was wrecked by the leaking water.*
2 to save someone's life is to prevent them from dying: *There's no doubt that the safety belts saved our lives.*
3 to save something is to store it for later: *Jamie saves half his pocket money every week.* • *Save your computer files on a backup disk if you can.*
4 to save time or money is to use less time or money than you would normally do: *Save 20% on all our products this week.* • *You can save 40 minutes by going along the motorway.*
NOUN **saves** when a goalkeeper prevents the other team from scoring a goal: *a brilliant save, just in front of the goalpost*
▶ **savings** PLURAL NOUN money that you collect and keep to use at some time in the future: *Colin's going to spend all his savings on a drum kit.*
▶ **saviour** NOUN **saviours 1** a person who rescues someone or something from danger **2** the Saviour, in Christian religions, is Jesus Christ

savour VERB **savours, savouring, savoured** to eat or drink something slowly in order to enjoy it for longer: *We ate the cakes slowly, savouring every mouthful.*
▶ **savoury** ADJECTIVE not sweet or not containing sugar

saw¹ NOUN **saws** a tool with a thin notched blade that can cut through wood or metal

saw² VERB a way of changing the verb **see** to make a past tense: *I know you were there because I saw you with my own eyes.*

sawdust NOUN the thick dust that is created when wood is cut with a saw

saxophone NOUN **saxophones** a

wind instrument with a long curved metal body. You play it by blowing it and pressing different keys

say VERB **says, saying, said 1** to speak words out loud: *I was just going to say 'hello'.* **2** to express in written words: *What does the notice say?*

NOUN to have a say or to have your say is to be able to give your opinion: *The others all decided to go and I didn't even have a say in the matter.*

▸ **saying** NOUN **sayings** a phrase or sentence that people often use and which sometimes gives wise advice: *Gran's favourite saying is 'an apple a day keeps the doctor away'.*

scab NOUN **scabs** a crust of dried blood that forms over a wound as it heals

▸ **scabby** ADJECTIVE **scabbier, scabbiest 1** covered in scabs: *a scabby knee* **2** not in good condition or nice-looking: *a scabby old hairbrush*

scabbard NOUN **scabbards** a cover for a sword or dagger, sometimes hanging from a belt around the waist

scaffold NOUN **scaffolds** a platform used in the past to execute criminals on

scaffolding NOUN a framework of poles and planks for workmen to stand on when they are working on the outside of a tall building

scald VERB **scalds, scalding, scalded** to be scalded is to be burnt by very hot liquid or steam

NOUN **scalds** a burn caused by hot liquid or steam

scale NOUN **scales**

1 a series of marks or divisions used for measuring something: *an earthquake that measured 3.2 on the Richter scale*

2 the size of something, such as a model or a map, compared to the actual size of the thing it represents: *A scale of 10:1 means the model is ten times bigger than the real thing.*

3 the general size of something: *steel production on a huge scale*

4 (*music*) a sequence of musical notes, especially between notes that are octaves apart: *the scale of G major*

VERB **scales, scaling, scaled** to scale something high is to climb up it

scales NOUN **1** the small overlapping plates that cover the skin of fish and reptiles **2** an instrument for weighing: *a set of kitchen scales*

scallop NOUN **scallops** a shellfish that you can eat and that lives inside two hinged fan-shaped shells

scalp NOUN **scalps** the skin on top of your head where your hair grows

scalpel NOUN **scalpels** a small knife, used especially by surgeons, with a very sharp thin blade

scaly ADJECTIVE **scalier, scaliest** covered with small, dry particles and flaky

scamp NOUN **scamps** a mischievous child

scamper VERB **scampers, scampering, scampered** to run quickly, taking short steps

scampi PLURAL NOUN large prawns that are usually deep fried in batter or breadcrumbs

scan VERB **scans, scanning, scanned**

1 to scan something such as a page of writing is to read it very quickly: *Lou scanned the jobs section of the paper, looking for anything suitable.*

2 to scan an area is to look all around it from one position

3 to scan something with a scanner is to examine it with a device that uses the information from beams of light or sound to make a picture of it: *You can scan the picture and then send it to me in an email.*

4 a poem scans when it has a rhythmic pattern

NOUN **scans 1** a quick look through a piece of writing or around an area **2** a process that produces an image on a screen by directing beams of light or sound at an object: *The doctor sent Amy for a brain scan.*

scandal NOUN **scandals 1** a scandal is a disgraceful or shocking situation **2** scandal is information about other people that is considered shocking: *Heard any juicy scandal recently?*

▸ **scandalous** ADJECTIVE disgraceful or

Aa
Bb
Cc
Dd
Ee
Ff
Gg
Hh
Ii
Jj
Kk
Ll
Mm
Nn
Oo
Pp
Qq
Rr
Ss
Tt
Uu
Vv
Ww
Xx
Yy
Zz

outrageous: *It's scandalous that we can't do more to help these people.*

scanner NOUN **scanners** a machine that gets information about an object by directing beams of light or sound at it. It uses the information to make an image of the object that can be seen on a screen

scant ADJECTIVE **scanter, scantest** very little or hardly enough: *She had paid scant attention so I wasn't surprised when she looked at me blankly.*

▸ **scanty** ADJECTIVE **scantier, scantiest** very small or hardly big enough: *a scanty nightshirt*

scapegoat NOUN **scapegoats** a person who takes the blame for something that was not all their fault

scar NOUN **scars** a mark that is left on skin after a wound has healed

VERB **scars, scarring, scarred** to be scarred is to have permanent marks where you were injured: *The accident left him scarred for life.*

scarce ADJECTIVE **scarcer, scarcest** difficult to get: *Food was scarce, as it always is in wartime.*

▸ **scarcely** ADVERB hardly, or almost not at all: *Carmen's throat was so sore she could scarcely speak.*

▸ **scarcity** NOUN a shortage of something

scare VERB **scares, scaring, scared** to scare someone is to frighten them

NOUN **scares 1** a scare is a fright: *It gave us all a bit of a scare when Mother fainted.* **2** a scare is a sudden worry that lots of people have about something: *a bomb scare*

▸ **scared** ADJECTIVE frightened: *After the attack she was too scared to go out.*

scarecrow NOUN **scarecrows** a simple model of a person in a field, set up to frighten birds and stop them from eating crops

scarf NOUN **scarves** a long strip or square of cloth that you wear around your neck, shoulders or head to keep warm or for decoration

scarlet NOUN a bright red colour

scary ADJECTIVE **scarier, scariest** making you feel frightened: *It was scary when the doors suddenly blew open.*

scatter VERB **scatters, scattering, scattered 1** to scatter a thing or things is to spread them in lots of places over a wide area: *Scatter the seeds evenly over the prepared soil.* **2** a group of people scatter when they run away in different directions

scavenge VERB **scavenges, scavenging, scavenged** to search amongst rubbish for things that can be used or eaten: *stray dogs scavenging food from the dustbins*

▸ **scavenger** NOUN **scavengers** a wild bird or animal that feeds mainly on the flesh of dead animals and on other waste material

scene NOUN **scenes 1** the setting that an event takes place in: *the scene of the crime* **2** a small section of a play, a book or a film: *We'll have to film the ball scene next.* **3** a place or situation as someone sees it: *Before me was a scene of celebration.* • *The scene in the town square is just the same as yesterday.*

• **make a scene** to make an embarrassing fuss

▸ **scenery** NOUN the countryside around about you: *You get to see some wonderful scenery from the train.*

▸ **scenic** ADJECTIVE with pleasant things to look at: *The ringroad is a more scenic route to the other side of town.*

scent NOUN **scents 1** a perfume: *The scent of lilies can fill a whole room.* **2** the smell of an animal that other animals can follow

VERB **scents, scenting, scented** to discover something by smell: *A hungry animal will scent food long before it sees it.*

sceptic NOUN **sceptics** a person who has doubts about things that other people are sure about: *Of course the sceptics said the photographs of the aliens were fakes.*

▸ **sceptical** ADJECTIVE doubting that something is true: *Ken thinks it'll work, but I'm still sceptical.*

sceptre NOUN **sceptres** a rod that

a king or queen carries at official ceremonies

schedule NOUN **schedules** a plan or timetable that shows when certain things should happen or be done: *a flight schedule*

• **on schedule** on time: *To my surprise, the coach left right on schedule.*

scheme NOUN **schemes** a plan of action: *a new scheme to build a carpark on the old playing field*
VERB **schemes, scheming, schemed** to make secret plans, especially to cause harm or damage

▸ **scheming** ADJECTIVE crafty or cunning

scholar NOUN **scholars** a person who studies and knows a lot about a particular subject: *a scholar of Greek*

▸ **scholarly** ADJECTIVE showing a deep knowledge of a subject: *a scholarly work about Victorian art*

▸ **scholarship** NOUN **scholarships 1** a scholarship is money for a student to study at a school or university: *There are several scholarships available for very bright students.* **2** scholarship is serious study of a subject

school NOUN **schools 1** a place where children and teenagers go to be educated: *You'll go to school when you're five years old.* **2** all the pupils and teachers in a school: *The whole school was in the playground, watching the fire.* **3** a large number of fish or dolphins that swim together in a group
VERB **schools, schooling, schooled** to school someone to do something is to train them to do it: *The boys have been schooled to be polite to visitors.*

▸ **schooling** NOUN your schooling is the education you receive, especially at school

schoolchildren PLURAL NOUN children who go to school

schoolteacher NOUN **schoolteachers** a teacher in a school

schooner NOUN **schooners** a sailing ship with two masts

science NOUN **sciences 1** studying the natural world and the things that happen in it **2** a particular study about

the natural world, especially chemistry, physics or biology

✦The word **science** comes from the Latin word **scientia**, which means *knowledge*.

science fiction NOUN stories and films that are set in the future or other parts of the universe

scientific ADJECTIVE **1** to do with science: *scientific research* **2** based on expert knowledge or a system of rules and tests, like the study of a science: *Jeremy's explanation of why my seeds didn't come up wasn't very scientific – he said it was because they were mine!*

▸ **scientifically** ADVERB according to the rules of science: *a scientifically proven law*

scientist NOUN **scientists** a person who studies science or whose work involves science: *a laboratory where scientists test bacteria found in food*

scissors PLURAL NOUN a cutting tool that has two blades joined in the middle. You use scissors by opening and closing the blades with the fingers and thumb of one hand

scoff VERB **scoffs, scoffing, scoffed 1** to scoff at a thing or person is to think that they do not deserve your serious attention: *The president scoffed at the idea of a revolution in his country.* **2** to scoff something is to eat it very fast

scold VERB **scolds, scolding, scolded** to tell someone off for doing something wrong

▸ **scolding** NOUN **scoldings** a telling-off

scone NOUN **scones** a small, round, plain cake that is often eaten with butter and jam

scoop VERB **scoops, scooping, scooped** to lift something with your hands cupped like a spoon
NOUN **scoops 1** a hollow instrument like a bowl or shovel for lifting liquid or loose substances like sand or sugar **2** a piece of news that nobody else has heard yet: *This story was a wonderful scoop for the Evening Mail.*

Aa
Bb
Cc
Dd
Ee
Ff
Gg
Hh
Ii
Jj
Kk
Ll
Mm
Nn
Oo
Pp
Qq
Rr
Ss
Tt
Uu
Vv
Ww
Xx
Yy
Zz

scooter NOUN **scooters** a vehicle with two wheels at either end of a board and a tall handle. You ride it by standing on the board with one foot and pushing the ground with the other

scope NOUN **1** the whole range of things that a subject deals with: *I'm afraid your question goes outside the scope of this meeting.* **2** freedom or opportunity to do something: *There's plenty of scope for improving these plans.*

scorch VERB **scorches, scorching, scorched** to burn the surface of something by touching it with something hot and leaving a brown mark

▸ **scorching** ADJECTIVE very hot: *It is a scorching day.*

score VERB **scores, scoring, scored** **1** to get a point in a game, test or competition: *Hamilton has scored again for the Rovers.* • *Jenny was first in the maths test because she scored 19 out of 20.* **2** to keep a record of the points that are won in a game or competition: *Who's scoring?* **3** to scratch a surface with something sharp: *Score a straight line across the card and fold it carefully.*
NOUN **scores 1** the number of points that you get in a game, test or competition: *What's the final score?* • *On this test, a score of more than 15 is good.* **2** an old word for twenty

scorn VERB **scorns, scorning, scorned** to look down on someone or something because you think they are bad or worthless: *The family scorned everyone's attempts to help them.*
NOUN a complete lack of respect because you think someone or something is bad or worthless

▸ **scornful** ADJECTIVE full of scorn: *scornful remarks*

▸ **scornfully** ADVERB in a way that shows you do not respect someone or something: *He laughed scornfully.*

scorpion NOUN **scorpions** a small creature like an insect with four pairs of legs and a long tail with a sting on the end

scour VERB **scours, scouring, scoured** **1** to clean a surface by scraping and rubbing hard: *The saucepans needed hours of scouring.* **2** to search a large area thoroughly: *Teams of villagers scoured the hillside for the missing climber.*

scout NOUN **scouts 1** a scout is a person who is sent out to gather information, especially one who is sent ahead of a group on an expedition **2** a Scout is a young person who is a member of the Scout Association
VERB **scouts, scouting, scouted**
• **scout around** to scout around for something is to go looking for it: *I'll scout around for a chair that matches the others.*

scowl VERB **scowls, scowling, scowled** to lower your eyebrows in an angry or puzzled way: *What are you scowling at?*
NOUN **scowls** an angry or puzzled look

scramble VERB **scrambles, scrambling, scrambled**
1 to climb using your hands and feet: *scrambling up the hillside*
2 to push and shove with other people to get to something: *people scrambling to get to the bargains before anyone else*
3 to scramble eggs is to mix them together and cook them
4 to scramble a broadcast or message is to code it so that it cannot be understood easily
NOUN **scrambles 1** a difficult climb over rough ground **2** a struggle to get to something before other people **3** a motorbike race over rough ground

scrap NOUN **scraps 1** a scrap is a small piece of something bigger: *a scrap of paper to write your address on* • *There isn't a scrap of evidence against us.* **2** scrap is rubbish, especially waste metal that could be used again **3** a scrap is a fight: *a bit of a scrap going on in the playground*
VERB **scraps, scrapping, scrapped** to throw something away because it is useless: *Let's just scrap the whole idea now.*

scrapbook NOUN **scrapbooks** a book with blank pages that you can fill up with cuttings or pictures that you want to keep together

scrape VERB **scrapes, scraping, scraped 1** to remove something from a surface, using something such as a knife or a stick: *I'll have to scrape the mud off this window before I clean it.* **2** to damage or hurt something by rubbing it against a rough surface: *Lydia had scraped her elbow when she fell off her bike.*

• **scrape through** to scrape through an exam is to pass it, but only just

• **scrape together** to scrape together money is to just manage to collect enough money from different people or places

NOUN **scrapes 1** when something hard or rough is rubbed or scratched against a surface **2** a difficult or embarrassing situation: *You expect boys to get into scrapes when they're young.*

scrappy ADJECTIVE **scrappier, scrappiest** not well put together or organized: *a scrappy essay*

scratch VERB **scratches, scratching, scratched 1** to make a mark on a surface with something sharp or pointed: *Mick scratched the car when he brushed the wall.* • *Generations of students had scratched their names on these desks.* **2** to rub your nails on your skin, usually because you feel itchy: *Try not to scratch the spots.*

NOUN **scratches** a mark left on a surface by something sharp

• **from scratch** from the very beginning, often for the second time: *Let's just start again from scratch.*

• **up to scratch** good enough: *David's work has not been up to scratch this term.*

▶ **scratchy** ADJECTIVE **scratchier, scratchiest** rough: *scratchy sandpaper* • *a scratchy woollen jersey*

scrawl VERB **scrawls, scrawling, scrawled** to write in a very untidy way
NOUN very untidy handwriting

scrawny ADJECTIVE **scrawnier, scrawniest** very thin and bony

scream VERB **screams, screaming, screamed** to make a long high-pitched cry because you are frightened, angry or in pain: *Everyone screamed on the roller coaster.*

NOUN **screams** a loud and high-pitched cry: *The neighbours came running when they heard the screams.*

screech NOUN **screeches** a sudden, harsh, high-pitched sound: *the screech of an owl in the night* • *a screech of tyres as the car sped away*

VERB **screeches, screeching, screeched** to make a sudden, harsh, high-pitched sound

screen NOUN **screens 1** the part of a computer, television or cinema that you look at to see images: *You should be sitting at least two metres away from the screen.* **2** an upright frame or panel that protects people from something or makes a more private area in a room: *You have to go behind the screen to be examined.*

VERB **screens, screening, screened 1** to show a television programme or film: *They are screening the whole series for the third time.* **2** to hide something from view or shelter it: *This part of the garden is screened by a high fence.* **3** to test lots of people for a particular illness: *All the workers here should be screened for the virus.*

screw NOUN **screws** an object like a nail with a slot in its head and a spiral ridge all the way down it

VERB **screws, screwing, screwed 1** to fix a screw into something: *Screw the bits of wood together.* **2** to fit something with a turning movement: *Screw the lid on tightly.*

screwdriver NOUN **screwdrivers** a tool with a metal stick that fits into the head of a screw so that when you turn it, the screw also turns

scribble VERB **scribbles, scribbling, scribbled 1** to write very quickly and untidily: *I scribbled his name down before I forgot it.* **2** to draw meaningless lines in an untidy way: *The baby had a pen and was scribbling on the wall.*

NOUN **scribbles 1** handwriting that is

Aa
Bb
Cc
Dd
Ee
Ff
Gg
Hh
Ii
Jj
Kk
Ll
Mm
Nn
Oo
Pp
Qq
Rr
Ss
Tt
Uu
Vv
Ww
Xx
Yy
Zz

very untidy **2** meaningless untidy lines that someone has drawn

scrimp VERB **scrimps, scrimping, scrimped** to spend as little money as possible by living cheaply: *After scrimping and saving for a year, we had enough money for a short holiday.*

script NOUN **scripts 1** the words of a film or play: *The actors were reading from their scripts at rehearsal.* **2** a way of writing down language: *The Russian language is written in a different script.*

scripture NOUN **scriptures** the holy writings of a religion, for example the Bible

scroll NOUN **scrolls** a long roll of paper with writing on it

VERB **scrolls, scrolling, scrolled** (*ICT*) to move text up or down on a computer screen so that you can see other parts of a file

scrounge VERB **scrounges, scrounging, scrounged** (*informal*) to get the things you want by asking other people for them instead of buying them yourself: *You should buy your own sweets instead of scrounging off me all the time.*

▸ **scrounger** NOUN **scroungers** (*informal*) a person who gets what they want by asking other people instead of buying their own things

scrub VERB **scrubs, scrubbing, scrubbed** to rub something hard to get it clean: *We'll need to scrub these stains off the floor.*

scruff NOUN **scruffs** a scruff is a person who looks very untidy

• **by the scruff of the neck** by the collar or the back of a person's or animal's neck: *The mother cat lifts her kittens in her mouth by the scruff of the neck.*

▸ **scruffy** ADJECTIVE **scruffier, scruffiest** untidy and dirty

scrum NOUN **scrums** the part of a rugby game where groups of players from both teams form a circle by joining arms with their heads down and try to win the ball by pushing against the players of the other team

scrumptious ADJECTIVE delicious

scuba diving NOUN swimming underwater while breathing air through a pipe and mouthpiece connected to tanks fixed on your back

scuffle NOUN **scuffles** a fight involving a small number of people

scull VERB **sculls, sculling, sculled 1** to row a boat using small paddles **2** to move in water paddling with your hands, but with your arms by your sides

scullery NOUN **sculleries** a small room by a kitchen, especially in a big old house, where the washing-up is done and food is cleaned before being used

sculpt VERB **sculpts, sculpting, sculpted** to carve or make models of objects or figures using materials such as clay or stone

▸ **sculptor** NOUN **sculptors** an artist who makes models of objects or figures

▸ **sculpture** NOUN **sculptures 1** a sculpture is a model of an object or figure that an artist carves or makes out of a material like stone, wood or clay **2** sculpture is the work of an artist who creates models: *go to art college to study sculpture*

scum NOUN **1** a layer of dirt or dust floating on the surface of a liquid **2** (*slang*) a very impolite word for a person or people that you find disgusting

scurry VERB **scurries, scurrying, scurried** to move in a hurry with a lot of short steps

scurvy NOUN a disease caused by not eating enough fresh fruit and vegetables

scuttle VERB **scuttles, scuttling, scuttled 1** to move along with lots of short fast steps: *a beetle scuttling away* **2** to scuttle a boat is to purposely make a hole in it to sink it

scythe NOUN **scythes** a tool with a handle and a long curved blade that is used for cutting long grass or harvesting crops

sea NOUN **seas 1** the salt water that covers most of the Earth's surface: *Australia is completely surrounded by sea.* **2** a large lake of salt water: *the Dead Sea*

seabed NOUN the floor of the sea: *a wreck on the seabed*

seafarer NOUN **seafarers** a sailor or a person who travels by sea

▶ **seafaring** ADJECTIVE used to travelling by or working at sea: *a seafaring nation*

seagull NOUN **seagulls** a sea bird with webbed feet, short legs and long wings with grey, black or white feathers

seahorse NOUN **seahorses** a type of small fish that swims upright and has a horse-like head and neck

seal¹ VERB **seals, sealing, sealed** to close something firmly: *Don't seal the envelope yet.*

NOUN **seals 1** anything that keeps something firmly closed: *Break the seal with scissors before opening the box.* • *We need a new seal on the washing-machine door.* **2** an official mark stamped on a piece of wax and attached to a document to show that it is genuine

seal² NOUN **seals** an animal with a small head and a shiny coat that lives mainly in the sea

sea level NOUN the average level of the surface of the sea, when it is between high and low tide

sea lion NOUN **sea lions** a type of large seal

seam NOUN **seams 1** a join between two edges: *the trousers have split down the back seam* **2** a seam of coal is a band or layer of it in the ground

seaman NOUN **seamen** a sailor who is not an officer

seaplane NOUN **seaplanes** an aircraft that is designed to take off from and land on water

sear VERB **sears, searing, seared** to hurt or burn

search VERB **searches, searching, searched** to look carefully for a thing or person: *I've searched everywhere for my keys.*

NOUN **searches 1** an attempt to find something or someone: *They made a thorough search of the countryside.* **2** (*ICT*) you do a search on the Internet

when you type words into a search engine to find information

search engine NOUN **search engines** (*ICT*) a program that searches pages on the Internet for the words you have keyed in, to find the information you want

searchlight NOUN **searchlights** a strong beam of light that can pick out distant objects at night: *A figure running across the field was caught in the searchlight.*

seashore NOUN the land next to the sea, especially the rocky or sandy parts that the sea covers when the tide is high

seasick ADJECTIVE feeling ill or being sick when you are on a boat, because of its movement on the sea: *Some lucky people have never been seasick.*

seaside NOUN the seaside is a place beside the sea where people go on holiday

season NOUN **seasons 1** one of the four main periods that the year is divided into: *Spring is my favourite season.* **2** the particular period of the year that a certain activity takes place: *the football season*

VERB **seasons, seasoning, seasoned** to season food is to flavour it by putting salt, pepper or other herbs and spices into it

▶ **seasonal** ADJECTIVE happening only at certain times of the year

▶ **seasoning** NOUN **seasonings** salt, pepper and other herbs and spices that you can use to flavour food

season ticket NOUN **season tickets** a ticket that you can use as often as you want for a certain period of time

seat NOUN **seats 1** a piece of furniture for sitting on: *a garden seat* • *a theatre seat* **2** the part of a piece of clothing that covers your bottom: *There's a rip in the seat of my trousers.* **3** a position in parliament or on a committee: *The party lost three seats in the election.*

VERB **seats, seating, seated 1** to seat a person is to give them somewhere to sit: *The host and hostess were seated at opposite ends of the table.* **2** to seat

Aa
Bb
Cc
Dd
Ee
Ff
Gg
Hh
Ii
Jj
Kk
Ll
Mm
Nn
Oo
Pp
Qq
Rr
Ss
Tt
Uu
Vv
Ww
Xx
Yy
Zz

a certain number of people is to have enough room for them all to sit down: *The new theatre seats twice as many people as the old one did.*

seat belt NOUN **seat belts** a strap in a car, plane or bus that stops you being thrown out of your seat in a crash: *Please fasten your seat belts now.*

seaweed NOUN a type of plant that grows in the sea

secluded ADJECTIVE quiet, private and hidden from view: *a secluded corner of the garden*

▶ **seclusion** NOUN peacefulness and privacy

second ADJECTIVE AND ADVERB next after the first: *Julia is their second daughter.* • *Craig came second in the final exam.*

NOUN **seconds 1** a thing or person that is number two in a series: *This programme is the second in a series of three.* **2** one sixtieth of a minute or a very short time: *one minute and thirty seconds* • *Just wait a second.* **3** a product that has been made with a fault and so is not perfect: *The factory shop sells seconds at very cheap prices.*

VERB **seconds, seconding, seconded 1** to second an idea or plan is to support it and agree when someone suggests it **2** to second a fighter is to be an attendant and support them

ADJECTIVE developing from something that came first or before: *Freddie had measles and then developed a secondary infection.*

▶ **secondary** ADJECTIVE **1** coming after the thing that is first **2** not essential or not as important

▶ **secondly** ADVERB a word that you use to introduce the second thing in a list: *And secondly, I'd like to thank Mrs Ambrose for all her help.*

secondary school NOUN **secondary schools** a school for pupils between the ages of 11 and 18 that children go to after primary school

second-hand ADJECTIVE AND ADVERB not new because of being owned before by someone else: *Our car was second-*

hand when we bought it. • *Kathryn buys all her clothes second-hand.*

second nature NOUN a firmly fixed habit that you do not think about: *Driving is difficult at first but it soon becomes second nature.*

secrecy NOUN being secret: *The mission must be carried out in total secrecy.*

secret NOUN **secrets 1** a piece of information that must not be told to anyone else: *The birthday party was a well-kept secret.* **2** something that nobody knows or understands: *looking for the secret of eternal youth*

ADJECTIVE not to be told or shown to other people: *a secret passage* • *secret government files*

secretary NOUN **secretaries 1** a person whose job is to type letters, keep files and take notes at business meetings for another person or a group of people: *Please leave a message with my secretary if I'm out.* **2** a person who is in charge of a government department

▶ **secretarial** ADJECTIVE to do with the job of a secretary

secrete VERB **secretes, secreting, secreted** to make and release a substance: *The plant secretes a sticky liquid that attracts flies.*

▶ **secretion** NOUN **secretions** a substance that a part of a plant or animal makes and releases

secretive ADJECTIVE liking to keep secrets from people: *Logan was very secretive about his past.*

▶ **secretively** ADVERB so that nobody else knows or finds out

secret service NOUN **secret services** a government department that deals with spying: *a secret service agent*

sect NOUN **sects** a small group of people within a larger group, who have certain different opinions about things, especially about their religion

sectarian ADJECTIVE to do with there being different small groups within a larger one, each with different opinions and beliefs, especially about religion

section NOUN **sections 1** a part or a division of something: *The table has three* sections that fit together. • *The novels will be in the fiction section of the library.* **2** the side view of something when it is cut right through or across: *a section showing the inside of a plant stem*

sector NOUN **sectors 1** a part of any kind of area: *the American sector of the city* • *the business sector of the community* **2** (*maths*) a part of a circle formed by two radii and the part of the circumference between them

secure ADJECTIVE **securer, securest 1** safe, happy and not worried about any danger: *a secure family background* **2** safe against attack or harm: *Locks will keep your house secure against burglars.* **3** firmly fixed or fastened: *Check that the ropes are secure.*

VERB **secures, securing, secured 1** to fix or fasten something firmly: *The tent was secured with ropes and pegs.* **2** to get something important: *Sheila has secured a place at the best college in the country.*

▶ **security** NOUN being protected from harm or any danger: *matters of national security* • *the security of a loving family*

sedate VERB **sedates, sedating, sedated** to give someone a drug to make them feel calmer and less nervous or excited

ADJECTIVE quiet, calm and dignified

▶ **sedation** NOUN giving someone a drug to make them feel calmer

▶ **sedative** NOUN **sedatives** a medicine that helps you feel calm

sediment NOUN the solid grains that settle at the bottom of a liquid

see VERB **sees, seeing, saw, seen**
1 to look at something and notice it: *The dog goes mad whenever he sees a cat.* • *We're going to London to see the sights.*
2 to meet someone or spend time with them: *Have you seen Peter much lately?*
3 to understand something: *Now I see what you mean.*
4 to see someone as something is to imagine them like it: *Can you see me as an astronaut?*

5 to see someone somewhere is to go there with them: *I'll see you to the door.*
6 to see that something happens is to make sure that it happens
• **see through someone** or **something** to realize what someone is up to or that something is not true, and not be tricked by them or it
• **see to something** to deal with something: *Don't you worry about the travel arrangements – I'll see to them.*

seed NOUN **seeds** a thing that a plant produces and that new plants grow from: *Sow the seeds about two inches deep in the soil.*

▶ **seedling** NOUN **seedlings** a very young plant

seek VERB **seeks, seeking, sought 1** to search for something: *We sought him high and low but never found him.* **2** to try to get or achieve something: *She's seeking fame and fortune.* **3** to ask for something: *You should seek the teacher's advice.*

seem VERB **seems, seeming, seemed** to appear to be something or to give the impression of being something: *You didn't seem to be interested.* • *Things seem calm at the moment.*

▶ **seemingly** ADVERB apparently: *The queue to get in was seemingly endless.*

▶ **seemly** ADJECTIVE **seemlier, seemliest** (*formal*) decent or suitable: *That's not very seemly behaviour for a little girl.*

seen VERB a form of the verb **see** that is used with a helping verb to show that something happened in the past: *I haven't seen you for ages.* • *I wouldn't have seen that if you hadn't pointed it out.*

seep VERB **seeps, seeping, seeped** to leak or flow slowly through something: *Water was seeping through the ceiling.*

seesaw NOUN **seesaws** a playground toy that children sit on either end of, pushing off the ground with their feet and alternately swinging up and down

seethe VERB **seethes, seething, seethed** to be extremely angry

see-through ADJECTIVE so thin that

Aa
Bb
Cc
Dd
Ee
Ff
Gg
Hh
Ii
Jj
Kk
Ll
Mm
Nn
Oo
Pp
Qq
Rr
Ss
Tt
Uu
Vv
Ww
Xx
Yy
Zz

Aa
Bb
Cc
Dd
Ee
Ff
Gg
Hh
Ii
Jj
Kk
Ll
Mm
Nn
Oo
Pp
Qq
Rr
Ss
Tt
Uu
Vv
Ww
Xx
Yy
Zz

you can see what is on the other side: *a blouse with see-through sleeves*

segment NOUN **segments** a section or a division of something: *Divide the orange into segments.*

segregate VERB **segregates, segregating, segregated** to keep one kind of person or animal separate from another kind: *The young bulls are segregated from the cows.*

▶ **segregation** NOUN separating different kinds of animals or people from each other

seismic ADJECTIVE to do with earthquakes

seize VERB **seizes, seizing, seized** to seize something is to grab it: *Joel seized my hand and shook it.* • *I saw the open goal and seized my chance.*

• **seize up** to stop moving easily: *I knelt on the floor so long that my knees seized up.*

▶ **seizure** NOUN **seizures** a sudden attack of an illness, for example a heart attack

seldom ADVERB rarely or not often: *Gran seldom goes out in the evenings any more.*

select VERB **selects, selecting, selected** to choose from several things that are available: *Gail has been selected for the school hockey team.*

▶ **selection** NOUN **selections 1** a range of things that you can choose from: *a wide selection of boots and shoes* **2** something that has been chosen from amongst others: *Bring your selection to the cash desk at the door.*

self NOUN **selves** the real you: *Actors try to forget their true selves.*

self-centred ADJECTIVE thinking only about yourself and not other people

self-confident ADJECTIVE believing in your own power and sure that you will succeed

self-conscious ADJECTIVE feeling nervous and uncomfortable when you are with other people because you feel they are looking at you and criticizing you

self-defence NOUN trying to defend

yourself from someone who is attacking you: *classes in self-defence* • *He said he fired the gun in self-defence.*

self-esteem NOUN thinking well of yourself: *Robert lacks self-esteem.*

self-importance NOUN thinking too well of yourself and that you are more important than other people

selfish ADJECTIVE thinking only about yourself and not what other people might want or need: *It would be selfish not to offer one of your sweets to your friend.*

▶ **selfishly** ADVERB thinking only about yourself: *He selfishly finished the food before we'd taken any.*

▶ **selfishness** NOUN thinking only about yourself

selfless ADJECTIVE thinking about other people's wants or needs before your own

self-portrait NOUN **self-portraits** a drawing or painting that an artist makes of himself or herself

self-raising flour NOUN flour that is used in baking and that includes an ingredient that makes the mixture rise when it is cooked

self-reliance NOUN the ability to manage alone, without asking for help from other people

▶ **self-reliant** ADJECTIVE not needing the help of other people because you can manage by yourself

self-respect NOUN your respect for yourself and care that you behave correctly

self-righteous ADJECTIVE thinking that you are a very good person because you do not do bad things

self-service NOUN a system in a shop or restaurant where customers serve themselves and, usually, pay at a checkout

self-sufficient ADJECTIVE able to provide everything you need for yourself: *If we were a self-sufficient country, we would never need to import any food at all.*

sell VERB **sells, selling, sold** to give somebody something in exchange for money: *Nigel sold his car and bought a motorbike.*

▶ **seller** NOUN **sellers** a person who has something for sale

Sellotape NOUN (*trademark*) a type of see-through sticky tape that is used especially for sticking pieces of paper together

semaphore NOUN a way of signalling using your arms in different positions to signal different letters

semi- PREFIX if a word starts with **semi**, it adds the meaning *half* or *partly*. For example, *semi-conscious* means partly conscious

✦ This comes from the Latin word part **semi-**, which means *half*.

semibreve NOUN **semibreves** (*music*) a musical note that is the same length as four crotchets. The symbol for a semibreve is **o**

semicircle NOUN **semicircles** half a circle: *The class sits around the teacher in a semicircle.*

semicolon NOUN **semicolons** (*grammar*) a punctuation mark (;) that separates items in a list or different parts of a sentence: *Several things need to be done: the menu; a seating plan; tickets.*

semi-detached ADJECTIVE a semi-detached house is joined to another house on one side

semi-final NOUN **semi-finals** one of the two matches in a competition just before the final, which is a match for the winners of the two semi-finals: *Sweden reached the semi-final of the 1994 World Cup.*

semitone NOUN **semitones** (*music*) the difference between two notes that are next to each other on the piano

semolina NOUN grains of wheat that are used for making pasta and milky puddings

senate NOUN **senates** the highest-ranking part of parliament in some countries, for example the United States and France

▶ **senator** NOUN **senators** a member of a senate

send VERB **sends, sending, sent 1** to make something go to a place or person: *I'll send you an email.* • *Our luggage was sent on the next flight.* **2** to tell someone to go somewhere: *Graham was feeling sick so the school sent him home.*

▶ **sender** NOUN **senders** the person that a letter or parcel comes from: *If this letter is undelivered, please return it to the sender.*

senile ADJECTIVE someone who is senile is confused because they are old

senior ADJECTIVE **1** higher in rank or more powerful: *You must salute when you meet a more senior officer.* **2** older: *We expect senior pupils to protect the younger children.*

▶ **seniority** NOUN how old or powerful a person is: *We sat along the table in order of seniority.*

senior citizen NOUN **senior citizens** a person who has passed the usual retiring age: *Senior citizens can travel free with a bus pass.*

sensation NOUN **sensations 1** a feeling, especially one coming from your sense of touch: *a burning sensation in his chest* **2** a state of excitement or shock: *The announcement caused quite a sensation.*

▶ **sensational** ADJECTIVE **1** wonderful and impressive: *Kate looked sensational in her new dress.* **2** causing a lot of excitement, shock or horror: *sensational news*

sense NOUN **senses**

1 one of the five powers of sight, touch, taste, hearing and smell: *Janet lost her sense of smell after an illness.*

2 an ability to understand or appreciate something: *I don't think he has much of a sense of humour.*

3 a feeling: *People need work that gives them a sense of achievement.*

4 sense is the ability to make sensible decisions: *Someone had the sense to call an ambulance.*

5 a meaning: *A single English word can have lots of different senses.* • *You only have to understand the general sense of the passage.*

Aa
Bb
Cc
Dd
Ee
Ff
Gg
Hh
Ii
Jj
Kk
Ll
Mm
Nn
Oo
Pp
Qq
Rr
Ss
Tt
Uu
Vv
Ww
Xx
Yy
Zz

VERB **senses, sensing, sensed** to become aware of something although it is not very obvious: *I sensed that not many people agreed with what I was saying.*

▶ **senseless** ADJECTIVE **1** unconscious or stunned: *A firemen was knocked senseless by a falling lamp post.* **2** foolish and with no purpose: *a senseless battle over a piece of useless ground*

sensible ADJECTIVE not foolish but showing common sense: *the most sensible thing to do* • *It would be sensible to get that promise in writing.*

▶ **sensibly** ADVERB using your common sense: *Jeff very sensibly pulled the curtains before putting the light on.*

sensitive ADJECTIVE **1** very quickly and easily affected by anything: *skin that is very sensitive to the sun* • *The alarm is very sensitive and is sometimes set off by birds or cats.* **2** very easily hurt or upset: *Brian's very sensitive about being bald.*

▶ **sensitively** ADJECTIVE in a way that carefully considers how people are feeling: *The matter has been dealt with very sensitively.*

▶ **sensitivity** NOUN how easily something or someone is affected by something

sensor NOUN **sensors** a device that notices things such as heat, light or movement: *A sensor on the front of the camera measures how much light is available.*

sent VERB a way of changing the verb **send** to make a past tense. It can be used with or without a helping verb: *I've sent ten email messages this morning.* • *Jenkins was sent to prison for ten years.*

sentence NOUN **sentences 1** (*grammar*) a sequence of words that usually includes a verb and expresses a statement, a question or a command **2** the punishment that a judge gives a person who has been found guilty of a crime: *Floyd received a five year prison sentence.*

VERB **sentences, sentencing, sentenced** to tell a person who has been found guilty of a crime what their punishment will be: *The whole gang was sentenced to life imprisonment.*

sentiment NOUN **sentiments** a view or feeling about a subject: *Several other people share these sentiments.*

▶ **sentimental** ADJECTIVE **1** feeling or making you feel too much emotion: *a sentimental love story* **2** to do with emotions: *I know the ring is not valuable but I love it for sentimental reasons.*

sentry NOUN **sentries** a soldier who guards an entrance

sepal NOUN **sepals** one of the green leaves under the petals of a flower

separate ADJECTIVE (pronounced **sep**-i-rit or **sep**-rit) different and not joined or connected: *This is a completely separate matter.* • *The farm is separate from the rest of the estate.*

VERB **separates, separating, separated** (pronounced **sep**-i-rait) **1** to split up the people in a group or the parts of something that can be divided: *Could we please separate the boys from the girls for this exercise?* • *The north and the south are separated by a range of high mountains.* **2** to decide to live apart: *They are not divorced but they separated some time ago.*

▶ **separately** ADVERB not together: *Each of the suspects was interviewed separately by the police.*

▶ **separation** NOUN **separations 1** when people are apart from each other: *Lily found the separation from her family very difficult while she was working abroad.* **2** keeping things apart: *I firmly believe in the separation of work from family life.*

September NOUN the ninth month of the year, after August and before October

✦ **September** was the seventh month of the Roman year and the name comes from the word **septem**, which means *seven* in Latin.

Aa Bb Cc Dd Ee Ff Gg Hh Ii Jj Kk Ll Mm Nn Oo Pp Qq Rr Ss Tt Uu Vv Ww Xx Yy Zz

septic ADJECTIVE full of poisonous germs: *If the cut goes septic, you will have to take a course of antibiotics.*

sequel NOUN **sequels** a book, play or film that continues an earlier story

sequence NOUN **sequences 1** a series of things that follow each other: *a remarkable sequence of events* **2** a short section of something like a dance or a film: *an opening sequence that involves the whole cast* **3** a series of things that follow each other in a particular order: *Can you fill in the next three figures in the sequence that starts 1,4,9?*

sequin NOUN **sequins** a small shiny disc that can be sewn on clothes to catch the light

✦ A **sequin** was the name of an old Turkish and Italian gold coin. The name was used for the discs on clothes because they look like shiny coins.

serenade NOUN **serenades** a song or other piece of music that, according to tradition, is performed at night beneath a woman's window
VERB **serenades, serenading, serenaded** to sing or play music for someone

serene ADJECTIVE calm and peaceful: *a serene smile*

sergeant NOUN **sergeants 1** a soldier who has a higher rank than a private or a corporal **2** a police officer who has the rank between constable and inspector

sergeant-major NOUN **sergeant-majors** an army rank above sergeant

serial NOUN **serials** a story in parts that you read, see or listen to at different times

✦ The words **serial** and **cereal** sound the same but remember that they have different spellings. A **cereal** is a grain used as food.

series NOUN **series 1** a number of similar things that happen one after the other: *a series of accidents* **2** a set of television or radio programmes with the same subject and characters: *a nature series* • *an old series of 'Cheers'*

serious ADJECTIVE **1** important and needing proper attention: *a more serious matter* **2** very bad: *a serious accident* **3** not joking: *I can never tell when he's joking and when he's being serious.*

sermon NOUN **sermons** a talk such as the ones preachers give in church

serpent NOUN **serpents** an old word for a snake

servant NOUN **servants** a person whose job is to do things for someone else

serve VERB **serves, serving, served**
1 to work for someone: *Brown had served the family for fifty years.* • *Johnson served his country in two world wars.*
2 to hand people things they want to buy in a shop or what they want to eat: *Are you being served?* • *I'll serve the soup and you can give out the spoons.*
3 to have a certain purpose or use: *The cave served as a shelter for the night.*
4 to serve time or a prison sentence is to stay in prison as a punishment for committing a crime
5 to serve in tennis or some other games is to start play by throwing the ball up and hitting it
• **it serves you right** used for saying that someone deserves something bad that happens to them: *If you're sick, it serves you right for eating too much chocolate.*
NOUN **serves** in tennis, a serve is throwing the ball up and hitting it to start playing a point: *a very fast serve*
▶ **server** NOUN **servers 1** (*ICT*) a central computer that gives out information to other computers and stores information from them **2** the person who starts playing a point in tennis

service NOUN **services**
1 working for someone or something: *resigning after 25 years' service to the company* • *He received an award for his services to the community.*
2 an industry that does things for people rather than producing goods: *the health service* • *Postal services are more frequent now.*

3 the help that the people who work in a shop or restaurant give to their customers: *I loved the things they sell but the service in that shop is awful.*

4 an examination and repair of a machine or car to make sure it is working well: *Your car should have a regular service.*

5 the services are a country's army, navy and air force

6 a religious ceremony, especially in a church: *a service of remembrance*

7 a set of matching plates and bowls or cups and saucers: *a dinner service • a china tea service*

8 throwing the ball up and hitting it to start playing a point in tennis: *a terrible first service*

• **in service** or **out of service** a machine or vehicle that is in service or out of service is available for use or not available for use: *These aircraft are very old and have now been taken out of service.*

VERB **services, servicing, serviced** to service a vehicle or machine is to check it to make sure it is working properly and to make any necessary small repairs

service station NOUN **service stations** a place where you can buy petrol

serviette NOUN **serviettes** a piece of paper or cloth that you can use during a meal to wipe your mouth or fingers

session NOUN **sessions 1** a period of time that you do something for: *Next session we'll be able to decorate the work you've done today.* **2** a meeting or a series of meetings: *the next session of Parliament* **3** a term of a school or college

set VERB **sets, setting, set**

1 to place something somewhere: *Set the tray down on the table.* • *a house that was set back from the road*

2 to adjust a clock or control so that it is ready to work: *Don't forget to set the video to record.*

3 to become hard or firm: *Wait an hour or so for the jelly to set.*

4 the sun sets when it goes down: *watching the setting sun*

5 to set words to music is to compose music to go with them

6 to set someone doing something is to start them doing it: *His comment set me thinking.*

7 to set someone something to do is to give it to them to do: *The teacher didn't set us any homework.*

• **set about** to set about doing something is to start to do it: *It's time we set about learning our lines for the play.*

• **set in** if something unpleasant sets in, it starts: *It looks like winter has set in.*

ADJECTIVE **1** fixed or compulsory, not something you can choose: *a set piece for this year's music exam* • *Each person had set jobs to do.* **2** ready or prepared: *Are we all set to go?*

NOUN **sets**

1 a number of things or people that have something in common or are used together: *a set of chairs* • *a chess set* • *the set of odd numbers* •*I'm in the top set for maths.*

2 a radio or television: *We have a technical problem; please do not adjust your set.*

3 the scenery and furniture where actors perform in a play or film, on a stage or in a studio

4 a series of games that form part of a tennis match

setback NOUN **setbacks** a problem that stops you making progress for a while

set square NOUN **set squares** a hard flat triangle with one right angle that you can use to help you draw angles and straight lines

settee NOUN **settees** a sofa

setting NOUN **settings 1** the position of the controls of a machine or instrument: *What setting did you have the oven on?* **2** the background for something such as a building or some sort of action, either in real life or in a story: *a beautiful setting for a hotel* • *Edinburgh is the setting for his latest film.* **3** a place setting or a table setting is the cutlery and crockery for one person at a meal

settle VERB **settles, settling, settled**
1 to decide or agree on something: *Can you settle this argument for us?* • *Have you settled a date for the wedding yet?*
2 to become relaxed and comfortable in a certain situation or position: *We settled into army life very easily.* • *Harry settled into his armchair and fell asleep.*
3 to go somewhere and make your home there: *The family settled in New South Wales.*
4 to land and rest somewhere: *A fly settled on the picture frame for a moment.* • *Shake the bottle, then wait while the flakes inside settle.*
5 to settle a bill or debt is to pay it: *The bill can be settled in cash or with a cheque.*
▶ **settlement** NOUN **settlements 1** an agreement: *a new peace settlement* **2** a place where people arrived and set up their homes: *an ancient riverside settlement*
▶ **settler** NOUN **settlers** a person who goes to live in a new country or an area that has few or no people living in it
seven NOUN **sevens** the number 7
seventeen NOUN the number 17
seventeenth ADJECTIVE AND ADVERB after sixteenth and before eighteenth: *my sister's seventeenth birthday*
seventh ADJECTIVE AND ADVERB after sixth and before eighth: *the seventh day of the week*
NOUN **sevenths** the fraction $\frac{1}{7}$, which means one of seven equal parts of something: *There are seven of us so divide the pie into sevenths.*
seventieth ADJECTIVE AND ADVERB after the sixty-ninth and before the seventy-first
seventy NOUN **seventies** the number 70
sever VERB **severs, severing, severed** to cut through something or cut something off: *The phone cables were severed in the high winds.*
several ADJECTIVE more than two but not very many: *Several people stopped to look in the window.* • *I've asked him several times but he hasn't repaid the money.*

severe ADJECTIVE **1** extremely bad: *severe weather conditions* • *a severe punishment* **2** stern and not gentle or kind: *a severe expression as she concentrated*
▶ **severity** NOUN extreme seriousness: *I don't think you understand the severity of the situation.*
sew VERB **sews, sewing, sewed, sewn** to use a needle and thread or a sewing machine to join fabric with stitches: *Could you teach me to sew?* • *I'll need some red thread to sew that button back on.*
sewage NOUN waste matter that is carried away from toilets in buildings
▶ **sewer** NOUN **sewers** a large pipe or underground channel for carrying away waste matter from drains in and near buildings
sex NOUN **sexes 1** either of two groups that humans are divided into: males and females **2** sex is an act that a man and a woman perform to make a baby or for enjoyment
▶ **sexual** ADJECTIVE to do with sex: *the body's sexual organs*
sexism NOUN the belief that one sex, particularly your own, is better than the other, and therefore the unfair treatment of the other sex
▶ **sexist** NOUN **sexists** a person who believes that their own sex is better than the other ADJECTIVE unfair to one particular sex: *sexist remarks*
shabby ADJECTIVE **shabbier, shabbiest** old and worn: *a shabby house full of shabby furniture*
shack NOUN **shacks** a roughly-built hut or shed
shackle NOUN **shackles** shackles are a pair of metal rings, joined by a chain, that are locked around a prisoner's wrists or ankles
shade NOUN **shades**
1 shade is an area of slight darkness caused by blocking sunlight: *sitting in the shade of a tree* • *plants that grow in shade*
2 a shade is an object that prevents a light being too bright: *a lampshade*

Aa
Bb
Cc
Dd
Ee
Ff
Gg
Hh
Ii
Jj
Kk
Ll
Mm
Nn
Oo
Pp
Qq
Rr
Ss
Tt
Uu
Vv
Ww
Xx
Yy
Zz

3 a colour that is a bit lighter or darker than a similar colour: *a darker shade of lipstick*

4 a very small amount or difference: *Can you make it a shade looser?*

VERB **shades, shading, shaded 1** to block bright light from an area: *a row of trees shading the path* **2** (*art*) to draw or paint an area of a picture to make it look darker

shadow NOUN **shadows 1** a shadow is a dark shape on a surface caused when an object is between the surface and a bright light: *children trying to jump on each other's shadow* **2** shadow is an area darkened by the blocking out of light: *I couldn't see his face because it was in shadow.*

▸ **shadowy** ADJECTIVE like a shadow, not easy to see clearly: *The shadowy figures moved in and out of the trees.*

shady ADJECTIVE **shadier, shadiest 1** a shady place is out of bright sunlight **2** slightly dishonest or illegal: *shady deals*

shaft NOUN **shafts**

1 the long straight part of a tool or weapon

2 a bar or rod in a machine that turns round to make other parts of the machine move: *The engine's drive shaft is twisted.*

3 a long narrow passage that goes down into the ground or down through a building: *a lift shaft • a mine shaft*

4 a shaft of light is a ray or beam of light

shaggy ADJECTIVE **shaggier, shaggiest** shaggy hair is thick and untidy

shake VERB **shakes, shaking, shook, shaken 1** to shake is to move quickly or unsteadily with very small movements: *The earth shook when the bomb landed. • Mina was shaking with fear.* **2** to shake something is to move it quickly from side to side or backwards and forwards: *The wind shook the trees and rattled the windows.* **3** to shake someone is to shock or upset them: *We were terribly shaken by the news of his death.*

NOUN **shakes 1** a quick movement from side to side or backwards and forwards: *Give the bottle a quick shake.* **2** a very quick moment: *I'll be there in two*

shakes. **3** a drink of milk and some sort of flavouring

▸ **shakily** ADVERB in an unsteady way: *a new lamb walking shakily round its mother*

▸ **shaky** ADJECTIVE **shakier, shakiest** trembling: *Her voice was shaky as she tried to explain how she fell.*

shale NOUN a soft grey type of rock that breaks easily into flaky layers

shall VERB **should** a helping verb that is used along with a main verb to make future tenses when the subject of the verb is **I** or **we**: *I shall never forget this moment.*

shallow ADJECTIVE **shallower, shallowest** not deep: *a shallow lake*

sham NOUN a person or thing is a sham if they are not what they pretend to be or seem to be: *Her niceness was just a sham; she was really cruel.*

shamble VERB **shambles, shambling, shambled** if someone shambles, or shambles along, they walk slowly and awkwardly without lifting their feet properly: *The old man shambled along, leaning on his stick.*

shambles NOUN if something is a shambles, it is completely disorganized or in a terrible mess: *The attic was a shambles, full of broken furniture.*

shame NOUN **1** shame is an embarrassing feeling of guilt or foolishness, especially because you have done something wrong **2** if something brings shame on or to people, it brings them disgrace because it is bad or morally wrong **3** if you say something is a shame, you mean it is a pity: *What a shame that you can't come to the party.*

VERB **shames, shaming, shamed** to shame someone is to make them feel ashamed or embarrassed

shameful ADJECTIVE disgraceful: *shameful behaviour*

▸ **shamefully** ADVERB disgracefully

shameless ADJECTIVE someone who is shameless feels no shame, although they have done something that other people think is wrong or immoral

▸ **shamelessly** ADVERB without feeling shame: *He lied shamelessly.*

shampoo NOUN **shampoos** a soapy

shapes

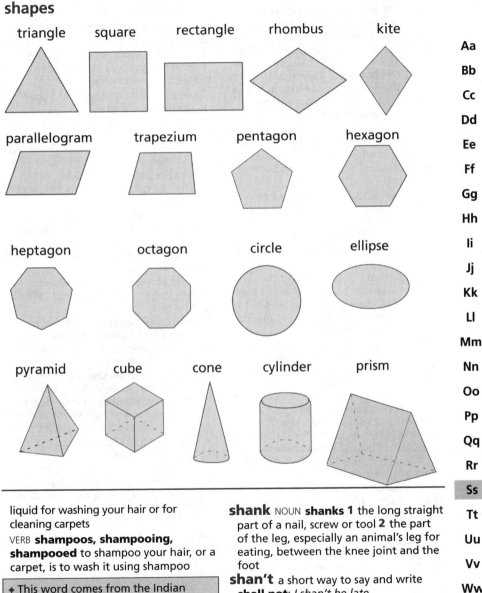

triangle square rectangle rhombus kite

parallelogram trapezium pentagon hexagon

heptagon octagon circle ellipse

pyramid cube cone cylinder prism

Aa
Bb
Cc
Dd
Ee
Ff
Gg
Hh
Ii
Jj
Kk
Ll
Mm
Nn
Oo
Pp
Qq
Rr
Ss
Tt
Uu
Vv
Ww
Xx
Yy
Zz

liquid for washing your hair or for cleaning carpets

VERB **shampoos, shampooing, shampooed** to shampoo your hair, or a carpet, is to wash it using shampoo

> ✦ This word comes from the Indian language Hindi, from the word **champu**, which means *squeeze*. You use a squeezing action to wash with it.

shamrock NOUN **shamrocks** a plant like clover with rounded leaves in three parts

shank NOUN **shanks 1** the long straight part of a nail, screw or tool **2** the part of the leg, especially an animal's leg for eating, between the knee joint and the foot

shan't a short way to say and write **shall not**: *I shan't be late.*

shanty NOUN **shanties** a roughly-built hut or shack

shape NOUN **shapes 1** something's shape is its outline or form: *a mountain in the shape of a crown* **2** shapes are things like squares, circles, rectangles, diamonds and triangles. See the examples on the previous page **3** the shape that a person or thing is in is their condition: *The team is in good shape for Saturday's match.*

• **out of shape 1** if a piece of clothing is out of shape, it has been stretched so that it is no longer the shape it should be **2** if a person is out of shape, they are not as fit as they once were

• **take shape** things take shape when they start to develop a form that you can recognize, or they start to become organized

VERB **shapes, shaping, shaped** to shape something is to form it or model it into a certain shape: *He shapes the clay pots on the potter's wheel.*

• **shape up** to develop in a satisfactory way

▸ **shapeless** ADJECTIVE having no particular shape: *a shapeless old cardigan*

share VERB **shares, sharing, shared 1** to share something is to divide it among a number of people so that each person gets some: *Are you going to eat that whole pizza yourself or are you going to share it?* **2** to share something with other people is to give some of it to them or allow them to use it too: *There aren't enough books to go round so some of you will have to share.* **3** to share experiences or interests with other people is to have the same experiences or interests as they have: *They shared an obsession with golf.*

NOUN **shares 1** a share is one of the parts of something that has been, or is to be, divided among several people **2** someone's share in an activity or project, which involves several people, is the part they play in it

shark NOUN **sharks** a large fish whose mouth is full of rows of very sharp teeth

sharp ADJECTIVE **sharper, sharpest**

1 a sharp object has a thin edge that can cut or a point that can pierce: *a sharp knife*

2 a sharp fall or increase is sudden and steep: *a sharp rise in crime*

3 sharp images are clear and distinct with no blurred edges

4 a sharp pain is sudden and stabbing

5 a person or animal with sharp hearing or eyesight is good at hearing or seeing

6 something that tastes sharp tastes bitter, like lemon juice

7 someone who is sharp is very quick to understand or react

ADVERB **1** punctually: *He was to be there at 5 o'clock sharp.* **2** with a sudden or abrupt change of direction: *Turn sharp left at the next set of traffic lights.*

NOUN **sharps** in written music, a sign (#) that makes a note higher by another half tone

▸ **sharpen** VERB **sharpens, sharpening, sharpened** to sharpen something is to make it sharp or sharper: *The leopard was sharpening its claws on a tree.*

▸ **sharpener** NOUN **sharpeners** a device that you use to sharpen pencils or knives

shatter VERB **shatters, shattering, shattered 1** to break into lots of tiny pieces **2** if something shatters you, it upsets you a lot or makes you very tired

shave VERB **shaves, shaving, shaved 1** people shave when they use a razor to cut away hair growing on their faces or bodies **2** to shave something is to cut or scrape thin layers off it with a sharp blade

▸ **shaver** NOUN **shavers** an electrical tool for shaving hair

▸ **shavings** PLURAL NOUN very thin strips of wood or metal that have been cut off a surface with a plane or other sharp tool

shawl NOUN **shawls** a large rectangular piece of cloth for covering your shoulders

she PRONOUN a word you use to talk about a woman, girl, female animal or boat that has already been mentioned or pointed out for the first time: *Madeleine is funny. She tells jokes and imitates people.* • *This boat is great for racing and she steers very easily.*

sheaf NOUN **sheaves** a bundle, especially a bundle of ripe corn that has been cut and tied together

Aa
Bb
Cc
Dd
Ee
Ff
Gg
Hh
Ii
Jj
Kk
Ll
Mm
Nn
Oo
Pp
Qq
Rr
Ss
Tt
Uu
Vv
Ww
Xx
Yy
Zz

shear VERB **shears, shearing, sheared, sheared** or **shorn** to clip or cut wool from a sheep using shears
• **shear off** if a piece of metal, such as a bolt, shears off, it breaks off
▸ **shears** PLURAL NOUN a tool with two large sharp-edged blades which move over each other, used for cutting sheep's wool or hair, or for trimming hedges

sheath NOUN **sheathes** a long narrow case for holding or carrying a sword or dagger
▸ **sheathe** VERB **sheathes, sheathing, sheathed** to sheathe a sword is to put it into a sheath

she'd a short way to say and write **she had** or **she would**: *She'd forgotten her umbrella.* • *She'd rather not say.*

shed NOUN **sheds** a simple wooden or metal building used for working in or for storing things
VERB **sheds, shedding, shed 1** people shed their clothes, reptiles shed their skins and birds shed their feathers when they take or cast them off and get rid of them **2** a tree sheds its leaves when they drop off in the autumn **3** to shed tears or blood is to have tears flowing from your eyes or blood flowing from a wound

sheen NOUN a soft shine or glossiness on a surface

sheep NOUN **sheep** a medium-sized farm animal with a thick wool fleece

✦The singular and plural forms of **sheep** are the same: *a sheep in the field* •*two sheep in the pen.*

sheepdog NOUN **sheepdogs** a dog bred or trained to round up and drive sheep

sheepish ADJECTIVE if someone looks sheepish, they look embarrassed

sheer ADJECTIVE **1** a sheer cliff or rock face is vertical **2** a sheer fabric is so thin you can see through it **3** pure or complete: *He ate four bags of crisps. It was just sheer greed.*

sheet NOUN **sheets**
1 a large piece of cloth that you put on

a bed: *I'll just change the sheets on your bed.*
2 a single piece of paper used for writing or printing on
3 a flat piece of metal or glass
4 a continuous layer of ice

sheikh (pronounced **shaik**) NOUN **sheikhs** an Arab chief or ruler

shelf NOUN **shelves 1** a board fixed horizontally to a wall or as part of a cupboard, used for putting things on **2** a part of the landscape or seabed that is formed like a shelf, with a flat top

shell NOUN **shells 1** a hard covering on an egg or a nut, or protecting the soft bodies of creatures like snails, crabs, shellfish and tortoises **2** an explosive missile or cartridge fired from a large gun **3** the framework of a building or other structure

she'll a short way to say and write **she will** or **she shall**

shellfish NOUN **shellfish** shellfish are creatures with a hard outer shell that live in fresh water or the sea

shelter NOUN **shelters 1** a shelter is a building or other structure that provides protection from harm or bad weather **2** to take shelter is to go somewhere that gives protection from danger or bad weather
VERB **shelters, sheltering, sheltered 1** to shelter somewhere is to stay in a place where you are protected from harm or bad weather **2** to shelter someone or something is to protect them

shelve VERB **shelves, shelving, shelved** to shelve a plan is to decide not to do it now, but you might do it in the future

shepherd NOUN **shepherds** someone who looks after sheep
VERB **shepherds, shepherding, shepherded** to shepherd people somewhere is to keep them in a group and direct them in or into a place

sherbet NOUN **sherbets** sherbet is a sharp-tasting powder with a fruit flavour

sheriff NOUN **sheriffs 1** in the United States, a sheriff is the head of police in

Aa
Bb
Cc
Dd
Ee
Ff
Gg
Hh
Ii
Jj
Kk
Ll
Mm
Nn
Oo
Pp
Qq
Rr
Ss
Tt
Uu
Vv
Ww
Xx
Yy
Zz

a particular county **2** in England and Wales, a sheriff is the representative of the king or queen in a particular county, who has mostly ceremonial duties **3** in Scotland, a sheriff is a county judge who tries cases in local courts

sherry NOUN sherry is a type of strong wine that has had brandy added to it

she's a short way to say and write **she is** or **she has**: *She's my friend.* • *She's always been my friend.*

shield NOUN **shields 1** a piece of armour that is used to block an attack by a sword or other weapon **2** a competition trophy in the shape of this piece of armour **3** a protection from harm or danger: *The spacecraft has a heat shield for when it re-enters the Earth's atmosphere.*

VERB **shields, shielding, shielded** to shield someone or something is to protect them from harm or danger: *He had his hand over his eyes, shielding them from the strong sun.*

shift VERB **shifts, shifting, shifted** if you shift something, or it shifts, you move it, or it changes its position

NOUN **shifts**

1 a move or change to another position: *a slight shift in speed*

2 the period of time a worker does his or her job: *on the early shift*

3 a loose dress

4 a key on a computer keyboard or typewriter that changes what you type to a different set of letters, for example capitals

shilling NOUN **shillings** an old British coin worth five pence

shimmer VERB **shimmers, shimmering, shimmered** to shine with a quivering light

shin NOUN **shins** the front of your leg below the knee

shine VERB **shines, shining, shone**

1 something shines when it gives off or reflects light

2 you shine a light on something when you point the light in its direction

3 you shine something when you polish it

4 if you shine at something, you are so good at it you stand out from everyone else

▶ **shining** ADJECTIVE **1** having a shine **2** a shining example of something is one that stands out because it is so good

shingle NOUN shingle is a mass of small pebbles on a seashore or river bank

shiny ADJECTIVE **shinier, shiniest** reflecting light or polished so as to reflect light

ship NOUN **ships** a large boat that carries passengers or cargo, or both, on long sea journeys

VERB **ships, shipping, shipped** to ship something somewhere is to have it carried on a ship

shipping NOUN the business of carrying goods, especially by ship, or ships travelling from place to place

shipwreck NOUN **shipwrecks** a ship that has been destroyed or sunk, especially by hitting rocks

shipyard NOUN **shipyards** a place where ships are built

shirk VERB **shirks, shirking, shirked** to shirk something is to avoid doing something that you should be doing

▶ **shirker** NOUN **shirkers** someone who avoids work, a responsibility or a duty

shirt NOUN **shirts** a piece of clothing for the top half of your body, with long or short sleeves, a collar, and buttons down the front

shiver VERB **shivers, shivering, shivered** to tremble or quiver because you are cold or frightened

NOUN **shivers** a quivering or trembling feeling that goes through your body when you get cold or get a fright

▶ **shivery** ADJECTIVE having shivers

shoal NOUN **shoals** a shoal of fish is a large group of them swimming together

shock NOUN **shocks 1** shock, or a shock, is a strong and unpleasant reaction you get when you have had a fright or a bad injury **2** a sudden bump or jolt that comes with great force: *The shock of the impact threw us all forward.* **3** if you get an electric shock, a current of electricity passes through your body

VERB **shocks, shocking, shocked** if something shocks you, it upsets or horrifies you

▶ **shocking** ADJECTIVE upsetting or horrifying

shoddy ADJECTIVE **shoddier, shoddiest** not very well made or made with poor quality materials

shoe NOUN **shoes** shoes are the things you wear on your feet over your socks, which usually cover the area between your toes and your ankles

shoelace NOUN **shoelaces** a thin piece of cord or leather threaded through the holes of a lace-up shoe to fasten it

shoestring NOUN

• **on a shoestring** to do something on a shoestring is to do it for very little money

shone VERB a way of changing the verb **shine** to make a past tense. It can be used with or without a helping verb: *The sun shone all day.* • *It had shone all week.*

shoo INTERJECTION you say 'shoo!' when you want to chase a person or animal away

shook VERB a way of changing the verb **shake** to make a past tense: *He shook his head sadly.*

shoot VERB **shoots, shooting, shot**

1 to shoot a gun or other weapon is to fire it: *I shot an arrow in the air.*

2 to shoot someone or something with a gun or other weapon is to kill or wound them with it

3 a person or thing shoots somewhere when they travel there very fast: *He shot past me in his new red sports car.* • *Pain shot through his body.* • *Prices shot up overnight.*

4 in games like football and hockey, a player shoots when they kick or hit the ball at the goal

5 to shoot a scene for a film is to record it on film

✦ The words **shoot** and **chute** sound the same but remember that they have different spellings. A **chute** is a sloped channel.

shooting star NOUN **shooting star** a meteor that burns up in the Earth's atmosphere, making a trail of bright light in the night sky

shop NOUN **shops 1** a place which sells things **2** a place where work of a particular kind is done, for example in a factory

VERB **shops, shopping, shopped** to buy things in shops

shopkeeper NOUN **shopkeepers** someone who owns a shop

shoplifter NOUN **shoplifters** someone who steals things from shops

▶ **shoplifting** NOUN the crime of stealing things from shops

shopper NOUN **shoppers** someone who shops or is shopping: *crowds of Saturday shoppers*

shopping NOUN **1** the activity of going round shops to buy things: *Let's go shopping for new clothes.* **2** the things you buy at the shops: *She carried all the shopping in to the kitchen.*

shore NOUN **shores** the area of land beside the sea or beside a lake

shorn VERB a way of changing the verb **shear** to make a past tense. It is used with a helping verb: *The farmer had shorn the sheep.*

short ADJECTIVE **shorter, shortest**

1 not very long: *a short skirt* • *a short speech*

2 small, not tall: *a short man*

3 if something is short, or in short supply, there is less than there should be, or there is not enough of it to go round: *We are two players short.*

4 if someone is short with you, they are rude and abrupt in the way they talk to you

• **for short** as a shortened form: *I'm Alisdair, you can call me Al for short.*

• **short of something** to be short of something is to not have enough of it

ADVERB

• **fall short** if something falls short, it is not as good or as big as it should be

• **stop short** to stop suddenly just before reaching a particular point: *My*

Aa
Bb
Cc
Dd
Ee
Ff
Gg
Hh
Ii
Jj
Kk
Ll
Mm
Nn
Oo
Pp
Qq
Rr
Ss
Tt
Uu
Vv
Ww
Xx
Yy
Zz

ball stopped slightly short of the last hole.

▸ **shortage** NOUN **shortages** a lack of something: *food shortages*

shortbread NOUN a rich sweet biscuit made from flour, sugar and butter

short-circuit VERB **short-circuits, short-circuiting, short-circuited** a piece of electrical equipment short-circuits when the electric current is carried away from its normal path by something breaking the normal electrical circuit

shortcoming NOUN **shortcomings** a fault or weakness a person has

shortcut NOUN **shortcuts** a quicker route between two places, or a quicker way of doing something

shorten VERB **shortens, shortening, shortened** to shorten something is to make it shorter: *I couldn't bring myself to shorten such a lovely name.*

shorthand NOUN shorthand is a fast way of writing what someone is saying

short list NOUN **short lists** a list of the best people for a job

short-lived ADJECTIVE lasting only for a short time

shortly ADVERB **1** soon: *We'll be arriving at Waverley Station shortly.* **2** not long: *Shortly before midday, the headmaster asked everyone to go to the assembly hall.*

shorts PLURAL NOUN shorts are a piece of clothing for the bottom half of your body, with short legs that reach down to the tops of your thighs or as far down as your knees

short-sighted ADJECTIVE **1** a short-sighted person cannot see things clearly unless the object is very close **2** an idea that is short-sighted does not take into account what is likely to happen in the future

short-tempered ADJECTIVE a short-tempered person loses their temper easily

short-term ADJECTIVE lasting or taking place for only a short time

shot VERB a way of changing the verb **shoot** to make a past tense. It can be

used with or without a helping verb: *The ships shot at each other using large cannons.* • *Nelson's battleships had shot the rigging from most of the enemy ships.*

shotgun NOUN **shotguns** a type of long gun with one or two barrels, which fires little metal pellets

should VERB

1 should is used as a past tense of the verb **shall**: *He said that we should all go home.*

2 ought to: *I wonder whether or not I should go.*

3 used to say what is likely to happen: *The train should be arriving in a couple of minutes.*

4 sometimes used with *I* or *we* to express a wish: *I should love to come to your party.*

5 should is also used to refer to an event that is rather surprising: *There was a little tap on the door, and who should pop his head round but Uncle George.*

shoulder NOUN **shoulders** one of the top parts of your body between your neck and the tops of your arms

VERB **shoulders, shouldering, shouldered 1** to shoulder something is to carry it on your shoulder or shoulders **2** to shoulder a responsibility is to accept it as something you must do

shoulderblade NOUN **shoulderblades** one of the two flat bones at the top of your back on either side of your spine

shouldn't a short way to say and write **should not**: *You shouldn't have waited out in the rain.*

shout VERB **shouts, shouting, shouted** to say something very loudly NOUN **shouts** a loud cry or call

shove VERB **shoves, shoving, shoved** to shove something is to push it hard or roughly

• **shove off** if someone tells another person to shove off, they are telling that person rudely to go away

NOUN **shoves** a hard or rough push

shovel NOUN **shovels** a tool like a spade that can be small with a short handle or large with a long handle

VERB **shovels, shovelling, shovelled** to shovel things is to scoop them up and move them using a shovel

show VERB **shows, showing, showed, shown**
1 to show something is to allow it or cause it to be seen: *Show me your new bike.* • *There's a cartoon showing at the local cinema.*
2 something shows if it can be seen: *The scar hardly shows.*
3 to show someone something is to point it out to them or demonstrate it to them: *Can you show me how to tie a reef knot?*
4 to show someone somewhere is to guide them in that direction: *The steward showed us to our seats.*
5 something shows something, such as a particular quality, when it makes it clear or proves that it is true: *His actions showed great courage.* • *The evidence shows that he couldn't have committed the crime.*
• **show off** to behave in a way that attracts attention
• **show up** to arrive
• **show someone up** if someone shows you up, they embarrass you in front of other people
NOUN **shows**
1 an entertainment in the theatre or on radio or TV
2 an event where people or businesses can show things to the public: *a fashion show*
3 a show of something is a sign of it or a demonstration of it: *There was no show of support for Tom's idea.* 4 if people do things for show, they do them to impress other people

show business NOUN show business is the entertainment industry, including films, theatre, radio and television

+ **Show business** is often shortened to **showbiz**.

shower NOUN **showers 1** a short fall of rain, snow or sleet: *sunshine and showers* **2** a sudden burst or fall of things: *a shower of sparks* **3** a device that sends out water in a stream or spray and that you stand under to wash your body
VERB **showers, showering, showered**
1 to wash your body under a shower
2 someone is showered with gifts or compliments when they are given lots of them at the same time
▸ **showery** ADJECTIVE showery weather is when showers of rain fall between periods when it is dry

shown VERB a form of the verb **show** that is used with a helping verb to show that something happened in the past: *Niall had shown us how well he could act.*

showroom NOUN **showrooms** a place where goods are displayed for people to see: *a car showroom*

showy ADJECTIVE **showier, showiest** showy things attract attention because they are big and bright, although they may not be beautiful or in good taste

shrank VERB a way of changing the verb **shrink** to make a past tense: *The hot wash shrank my jersey.*

shrapnel NOUN shrapnel is pieces of metal from the case of an exploding bomb or shell that fly out in all directions

shred NOUN **shreds 1** a long thin strip: *His shirt was torn to shreds.* **2** a shred of something is a very small amount of it: *They didn't have a shred of evidence to link him to the crime.*
VERB **shreds, shredding, shredded** to shred something is to tear it into long thin strips

shrew NOUN **shrews** a tiny animal, similar to a mouse but with a long pointed nose

shrewd ADJECTIVE **shrewder, shrewdest** wise and showing good judgement: *a shrewd politician* • *a shrewd guess*

shriek VERB **shrieks, shrieking, shrieked** to give a piercing scream or to speak in a loud shrill voice
NOUN **shrieks** a piercing scream

shrill ADJECTIVE high-pitched, clear and piercing

Aa
Bb
Cc
Dd
Ee
Ff
Gg
Hh
Ii
Jj
Kk
Ll
Mm
Nn
Oo
Pp
Qq
Rr
Ss
Tt
Uu
Vv
Ww
Xx
Yy
Zz

shrimp → shy

shrilly ADVERB with a shrill sound or voice: *A child was calling shrilly for its mother.*

shrimp NOUN **shrimps** *or* **shrimp** a small shellfish with a long tail that turns pink when it is cooked and is similar to, but smaller than, a prawn

shrine NOUN **shrines** a sacred place where people go to worship, often because it has something to do with a holy person

shrink VERB **shrinks, shrinking, shrank, shrunk 1** to get smaller **2** you shrink from something when you move away from it in horror or disgust, or when you want to avoid it

shrivel VERB **shrivels, shrivelling, shrivelled** to become smaller and wrinkled

shroud NOUN **shrouds** a cloth wrapped around a dead body
VERB **shrouds, shrouding, shrouded** to shroud something is to cover it completely: *hills shrouded in mist*

shrub NOUN **shrubs** a small bush
▶ **shrubbery** NOUN **shrubberies** an area in a garden where shrubs are grown

shrug VERB **shrugs, shrugging, shrugged** to raise and lower your shoulders in a movement that shows you do not know something or that you do not care about it
• **shrug something off** if you shrug something off, it does not bother you very much: *He's fit enough to shrug off colds.*
NOUN **shrugs** a quick raising and lowering movement of the shoulders

shrunk VERB a way of changing the verb **shrink** to make a past tense. It is used with a helping verb: *The hot water had shrunk my jersey.*
▶ **shrunken** ADJECTIVE having been shrunk: *a small, shrunken old man*

shudder VERB **shudders, shuddering, shuddered** you shudder when your whole body shakes for a moment because you have seen or heard something shocking or disgusting
NOUN **shudders** a sudden shaking movement of your body

shuffle VERB **shuffles, shuffling, shuffled 1** to slide your feet along the ground without lifting them **2** to shuffle things, such as playing-cards, is to mix them up so that they are in random order

shun VERB **shuns, shunning, shunned** to shun someone is to deliberately ignore them because they have done something wrong

shunt VERB **shunts, shunting, shunted 1** to shunt railway engines or carriages is to move them from one track to another **2** to shunt people or things about or around is to move them from place to place

shut VERB **shuts, shutting, shut 1** to close something: *Shut the door.* • *He shut his eyes and went to sleep.* **2** a shop or other business shuts when it stops being open or the staff stop working and go home
• **shut down** if a shop or other business shuts down, it closes and does not open again
• **shut up** to shut up is to be quiet or stop talking
ADJECTIVE closed: *All the shops are shut after 6 o'clock.*
▶ **shutter** NOUN **shutters 1** a wooden cover for a window that hinges from the side **2** the moving cover over the lens of a camera, which opens when a photograph is taken

shuttle NOUN **shuttles 1** in weaving, the shuttle is the part that carries the thread backwards and forwards across the loom **2** a shuttle is an air, train or other transport service that operates backwards and forwards between two places
VERB **shuttles, shuttling, shuttled** to shuttle between places is to travel to and fro between them

shuttlecock NOUN **shuttlecocks** an object made up of a cone of cork or plastic with feathers stuck around its rim, used in the game of badminton

shy ADJECTIVE **shyer, shyest** a shy person feels very uncomfortable when they have to speak or do something

Aa Bb Cc Dd Ee Ff Gg Hh Ii Jj Kk Ll Mm Nn Oo Pp Qq Rr Ss Tt Uu Vv Ww Xx Yy Zz

in front of other people, or when they meet new people

VERB **shies, shying, shied** if a horse shies, it turns to the side suddenly because it has been frightened

Siamese cat NOUN **Siamese cats** a breed of cat with a slim body, blue eyes and greyish brown fur

Siamese twins PLURAL NOUN an old-fashioned name for **conjoined twins**

sibling NOUN **siblings** a person's siblings are their brothers and sisters

sick ADJECTIVE **sicker, sickest**

1 if you feel sick, you feel as if you are going to vomit

2 you are sick when you vomit

3 sick people or animals are ill

4 if you are sick of something, you are very tired of it

▸ **sicken** VERB **sickens, sickening, sickened 1** if something sickens you, it disgusts you or makes you feel like vomiting **2** an old-fashioned word meaning to become ill

▸ **sickening** ADJECTIVE disgusting

▸ **sickly** ADJECTIVE **sicklier, sickliest 1** someone who is sickly is often ill or gets ill easily: *a sickly child* **2** something sickly is unhealthy looking or makes you want to vomit: *a sickly green colour*

▸ **sickness** NOUN **sicknesses** an illness or disease

side NOUN **sides**

1 the side of something is the part at or near its edge: *a house by the side of the river • at the side of the garden*

2 one of two or more surfaces of a figure, shape or structure, especially one of the surfaces that is not the top, bottom, front or back: *A cube has six sides. • Put the label on the side of the box.*

3 your sides are the left and right parts of your body: *I've got a pain in my left side.*

4 one of the two teams playing in a match, or one of the two groups of people involved in an argument or battle

• **side by side** next to each other

• **take sides** to agree with or support one person, or group of people, in an argument or fight they are having with someone else

VERB **sides, siding, sided**

• **side with someone** to support a person or group in an argument they are having with someone else

sideboard NOUN **sideboards** a piece of furniture with cupboards and drawers

sidecar NOUN **sidecars** a small vehicle that is attached to the side of a motorbike for a passenger

side effect NOUN **side effects** if something has side effects, it has effects that are additional to the effect it is supposed to have

sideline NOUN **sidelines 1** an extra job apart from your normal work **2** on a sports pitch, the sidelines are the lines along both sides of the pitch marking the outer edges of the playing area

sideshow NOUN **sideshows** a small show that is part of a larger more important show

sideways ADVERB something that goes sideways goes towards the side, or with its side facing the direction it is moving

siding NOUN **sidings** a short stretch of track where trains and coaches are shunted off the main track when they are not being used

siege NOUN **sieges** a situation in which a town or fort is completely surrounded by an enemy army that prevents supplies from getting in

sieve (pronounced **siv**) NOUN **sieves** a bowl with a bottom made of fine mesh, used to separate liquids from solids, or small fine pieces from larger ones

sift VERB **sifts, sifting, sifted 1** to sift a substance is to pass it through a sieve to separate out lumps or larger pieces **2** to sift things is to go through them, examining each one carefully

sigh VERB **sighs, sighing, sighed** to take a long, deep breath and breathe out noisily because you feel tired, relieved or unhappy

NOUN **sighs** a noisy breath out because you feel tired, relieved or unhappy

Aa
Bb
Cc
Dd
Ee
Ff
Gg
Hh
Ii
Jj
Kk
Ll
Mm
Nn
Oo
Pp
Qq
Rr
Ss
Tt
Uu
Vv
Ww
Xx
Yy
Zz

sight NOUN **sights**
1 sight is the power of seeing things: *A very young kitten's sight is not very good.*
2 a sight is something that you see or something that is worth seeing: *It was a sight I'll never forget.* • *We are going out today to look at the sights of London.*
3 something that is in sight can be seen and something that is out of sight cannot be seen
4 a person or thing that looks ridiculous, unusual or shocking: *What a sight she is with that bright blue hair!*

• **a sight for sore eyes** a person or thing that you are very glad to see

✦ The words **sight** and **site** sound the same but remember that they have different spellings. A **site** is the place where something is.

sightseeing NOUN sightseeing is travelling around looking at interesting things and places
▸ **sightseer** NOUN **sightseers** someone who travels round looking at interesting things

sign NOUN **signs** 1 a mark or gesture with a special meaning: *He gave the sign to join him.* 2 a notice that gives information to the public: *The sign said 'No parking'.* 3 one thing is a sign of another thing when it shows what is happening or what will happen: *Leaves falling are a sign of autumn.*
VERB **signs, signing, signed** 1 you sign something or sign your name on something when you write your signature on it 2 to sign someone, especially a professional player in certain sports, is to sign a contract with them making them part of your team 3 to sign to someone is to make a sign or gesture to them: *He signed to me to come in.*

• **sign up** to sign up for something is to join in with that thing

signal NOUN **signals** 1 a sign, a gesture, a light or a sound giving a command, warning or other message 2 a radio or

TV signal is the wave of sound or light received by a radio or TV
VERB **signals, signalling, signalled**
1 to send information by signals 2 to signal to someone is to make a signal or signals to them

signalman *or* **signaller** NOUN **signalmen** *or* **signallers** someone whose job is to control railway signals

signature NOUN **signatures** your name, written by you in a way that you and other people can recognize

signature tune NOUN **signature tunes** a tune that is used to identify a TV or radio series, usually played at the beginning and end of the programme

significant ADJECTIVE important or meaning something: *a very significant remark*
▸ **significance** NOUN meaning or importance: *a matter of great significance*
▸ **significantly** ADVERB in a significant way

signify VERB **signifies, signifying, signified** to have a certain meaning: *A symbol of a skull and crossbones signifies a poison.*

sign language NOUN a system of gestures made with the hands and fingers used to communicate with deaf people

signpost NOUN **signposts** a post by a road showing which direction to go to get to a particular place

Sikh NOUN **Sikhs** someone whose religion is Sikhism
ADJECTIVE to do with Sikhs or Sikhism: *the Sikh temple at Amritsar*
▸ **Sikhism** NOUN a religion believing in one God, founded by Guru Nanak in Punjab in North India

silence NOUN **silences** 1 silence is complete quietness when no sound can be heard 2 a silence is a time when there is no sound or no one speaks
VERB **silences, silencing, silenced**
1 to silence someone is to stop them speaking 2 to silence something is to stop it making a noise
▸ **silencer** NOUN **silencers** 1 a device

on a car exhaust that reduces noise **2** a device used on a gun to lessen the sound made when it is fired

▸ **silent** ADJECTIVE completely quiet

▸ **silently** ADVERB without making any sound

silhouette NOUN **silhouettes** the shape of a person or thing seen against a light background with just an outline filled with shadow

silicon NOUN a substance in the form of grey crystals or brown powder, used in electronic devices

silk NOUN **silks** very soft fine fibres made by silkworms, or a soft smooth fabric with a slight sheen that is made from these ADJECTIVE made of silk: *a silk kimono*

▸ **silken** ADJECTIVE soft, fine and slightly shiny

▸ **silky** ADJECTIVE **silkier, silkiest** soft and smooth like silk: *silky hair*

silkworm NOUN **silkworms** a type of moth whose caterpillar spins fine silk threads which are used to make silk

sill NOUN **sills** a horizontal piece of wood or stone at the bottom part of the opening of a window or door

silly ADJECTIVE **sillier, silliest** foolish or stupid

▸ **silliness** NOUN silly behaviour

silt NOUN fine sand and mud that is carried along and left behind by flowing water

silver NOUN **1** a shiny grey precious metal **2** a whitish grey colour **3** things made of silver or a silvery grey metal, such as cutlery and coins

ADJECTIVE silver-coloured or made of silver: *a silver cup • silver hair*

▸ **silvery** ADJECTIVE like silver in colour: *Birch trees have silvery bark.*

silver medal NOUN **silver medals** a medal made of silver awarded to the person who comes second in sporting events

silver wedding NOUN **silver weddings** a couple who celebrate their silver wedding have been married for 25 years

similar ADJECTIVE two things are similar when they are quite like each other but not exactly the same: *An alligator is similar to a crocodile, but smaller.*

▸ **similarity** NOUN **similarities** the way one thing is like another thing

▸ **similarly** ADVERB in the same or a similar way

simile (pronounced sim-i-li) NOUN **similes** a sentence or phrase in which one thing is described by being compared with another, usually by using *as* or *like*. For example, *Its fleece was white as snow* and *He ran like a hare* are similes

simmer VERB **simmers, simmering, simmered** to simmer food is to cook it slowly over a low heat or to boil it very gently

• **simmer down** to become calm again after you have been angry

simper VERB **simpers, simpering, simpered** to smile or speak in a silly unnatural way

simple ADJECTIVE **simpler, simplest 1** straightforward or very easy to do: *simple instructions • a simple sum* **2** plain or basic: *a simple design*

▸ **simplicity** NOUN being simple and uncomplicated

▸ **simply** ADVERB **1** in a straightforward, uncomplicated way: *I'll explain it simply so that you all understand.* **2** only: *Now, it's simply a question of waiting until something happens.* **3** completely or absolutely: *The concert was simply fantastic.*

simplify VERB **simplifies, simplifying, simplified** to simplify something is to make it simpler and therefore easier to do or understand

▸ **simplification** NOUN making something less complicated and therefore easier to do or understand

simulate VERB **simulates, simulating, simulated** to simulate a real thing is to create another thing that looks or seems like the real one

▸ **simulation** NOUN **simulations** simulating something, or something that simulates the real one

▸ **simulator** NOUN **simulators** a machine that creates the conditions of a

Aa
Bb
Cc
Dd
Ee
Ff
Gg
Hh
Ii
Jj
Kk
Ll
Mm
Nn
Oo
Pp
Qq
Rr
Ss
Tt
Uu
Vv
Ww
Xx
Yy
Zz

real situation, especially the flight of an aeroplane

simultaneous ADJECTIVE happening or done at exactly the same time: *a simultaneous broadcast on radio and TV*

▶ **simultaneously** ADVERB at exactly the same time

sin NOUN **sins** a wicked act, especially one that breaks a religious law

since CONJUNCTION **1 since** is used when you are giving a reason for something and has more or less the same meaning as **because**: *I decided to go shopping, since it was Saturday and I'd just got my pocket money.* **2** after a particular event or time: *He's getting on very well since he moved to the new school.* • *He's grown a lot since you saw him last.*

PREPOSITION from the time of something in the past until the present time: *Theresa has been dancing since she was three.* • *I've grown three inches since last year.*

ADVERB **1** from the time that has already been mentioned onwards: *She joined the choir last month and has been going to practice regularly since.* **2** at a later time than the time first mentioned: *They were enemies for years but they have since become friends.*

sincere ADJECTIVE **1** a sincere person is honest and means what they say **2** a sincere feeling is real and not faked

▶ **sincerely** ADVERB honestly and truly

▶ **sincerity** NOUN being honest or real

sinew NOUN **sinews** a type of strong body tissue like cord that joins your muscles to your bones

sinful ADJECTIVE **1** sinful behaviour is bad or wicked, especially because it breaks a religious law **2** a sinful person has committed a sin or sins

▶ **sinfulness** NOUN being bad or wicked

sing VERB **sings, singing, sang, sung**
1 people sing when they make musical sounds with their voices **2** birds and some other animals sing when they make musical calls

▶ **singer** NOUN **singers** a person who sings

▶ **singing** NOUN singing is making musical sounds with your voice

singe VERB **singes, singeing, singed** to singe something is to burn its surface or edge slightly by touching it with something hot: *The cat singed its whiskers on the electric fire.*

single ADJECTIVE **1** a single thing is only one and no more **2** someone who is single is not married **3** for use by one person: *a single room*

NOUN **singles 1** a ticket for a journey you make in one direction but not back again **2** a recording of a song that is released on its own, and not as part of an album **3** in games like tennis and badminton, you play singles when you play against only one other person

VERB **singles, singling, singled**

• **single someone or something out** to pick someone or something in particular from a group of people or things

single-handed ADJECTIVE without anyone else's help

single-minded ADJECTIVE a single-minded person sticks to one aim or purpose in a determined way

singly ADVERB one at a time or one by one: *You usually see tigers singly but sometimes you will see a small family group.*

singular ADJECTIVE **1** (*grammar*) a singular form of a word is the form used to refer to one person, thing or group, rather than two or more **2** very noticeable or out of the ordinary: *a poem of singular beauty*

NOUN (*grammar*) the form of a noun, pronoun, adjective or verb that you use when it expresses the idea of one person, thing or group, rather than two or more: *The singular is 'sheep' and the plural is also 'sheep'.*

▶ **singularly** ADVERB remarkably: *He was singularly unprepared for life in the outback.*

sinister ADJECTIVE threatening evil or harm: *a sinister black figure with a large hood covering the face*

Aa Bb Cc Dd Ee Ff Gg Hh Ii Jj Kk Ll Mm Nn Oo Pp Qq Rr **Ss** Tt Uu Vv Ww Xx Yy Zz

✦ **Sinister** is a Latin word which means *left*. The ancient Romans believed that the left side was unlucky.

sink VERB **sinks, sinking, sank, sunk**
1 to drop below the surface of water and go on moving downwards to the bottom: *The boat sank in a storm.* **2** to go down or get lower: *The sun was sinking towards the horizon.* • *He sank to his knees.* **3** to sink into something is to push or go deeply into it, or to pass through its surface: *The rainwater sank into the soil.* • *The dog sank its teeth into the postman's leg.*
• **sink in** if information you are given sinks in, you understand it properly
NOUN **sinks** in a kitchen or bathroom, a large fixed container with taps and a drain, used for washing

sinner NOUN **sinners** someone who has committed a sin

sinus NOUN **sinuses** an air-filled hollow in the bones of your skull that connects with your nose

sip VERB **sips, sipping, sipped** to sip a drink is to drink it slowly taking only a little mouthful at a time

siphon NOUN **siphons** a bent pipe or tube through which a liquid is drawn from one container into a second container placed at a lower level

sir NOUN **sirs 1** a polite way of addressing a man, for example at the beginning of a letter or when serving him in a shop **2** a title used before the name of a knight: *Sir Galahad*

sire NOUN **sires 1** the father of an animal, especially an animal bred on a farm **2** a title that was sometimes used in the past when talking to a king

siren NOUN **sirens** a device that makes a very loud hooting or wailing noise to warn people of something: *The ambulance came hurtling along the road with its siren on.*

sister NOUN **sisters** your sister is a girl or woman who has the same parents as you do
▶ **sisterhood** NOUN **sisterhoods 1** sisterhood is a feeling of friendship among women and girls **2** a sisterhood is a group of women, especially nuns

sister-in-law NOUN **sisters-in-law** your brother's wife, or your husband or wife's sister

sit VERB **sits, sitting, sat**
1 you sit or sit down when you have your weight supported on your bottom rather than your feet
2 you sit or sit down when you lower yourself into this position so that your bottom is resting on a surface
3 something sits in the place where it is resting or lying: *There was a big parcel sitting on the kitchen table.*
4 you sit an exam when you do the exam

sitcom NOUN **sitcoms** short for **situation comedy**, a television comedy series that is set in the same place and includes the same characters in each episode

site NOUN **sites** a place where something was, is, or is to be situated or located, or a place used for a certain purpose: *the site of a battle* • *a good site to build a house*

sitting-room NOUN **sitting-rooms** a room where people can sit down and relax

situate VERB **situates, situating, situated** something is situated in a certain place or position when it has been placed or built there
▶ **situation** NOUN **situations 1** a place where anything stands or is located: *Plant the sunflowers in a sunny situation.* **2** a set of circumstances or a state of affairs: *The situation in the areas affected by the drought is getting more and more difficult every day.*

six NOUN **sixes** the number 6

sixteen NOUN the number 16

sixteenth ADJECTIVE AND ADVERB after fifteenth and before seventeenth

sixth ADJECTIVE AND ADVERB after fifth and before seventh
NOUN **sixths** the fraction ⅙, which means one of six equal parts of something

sixtieth ADJECTIVE AND ADVERB after fifty-ninth and before sixty-first: *Grandmother's sixtieth birthday*

Aa
Bb
Cc
Dd
Ee
Ff
Gg
Hh
Ii
Jj
Kk
Ll
Mm
Nn
Oo
Pp
Qq
Rr
Ss
Tt
Uu
Vv
Ww
Xx
Yy
Zz

sixty NOUN **sixties** the number 60

size NOUN **sizes** 1 how big or small something is, or how long, wide, high, and deep it is 2 a shoe or clothes size is one that is made to fit a certain size of feet or body

VERB **sizes, sizing, sized**

• **size someone** or **something up** to look carefully at someone or something to find out what they are like

▸ **sizeable** or **sizable** ADJECTIVE fairly big

sizzle VERB **sizzles, sizzling, sizzled** to make a hissing noise like the sound of food frying

skate NOUN **skates** 1 a boot with a blade fitted to the bottom, used for gliding smoothly over ice 2 a **rollerskate**

VERB **skates, skating, skated** to move over ice wearing skates on your feet, or to move over the ground with rollerskates on your feet

▸ **skater** NOUN **skaters** someone who skates or rides a skateboard

▸ **skating** NOUN 1 the sport or pastime of moving over the surface of ice wearing skates 2 skateboarding

skateboard NOUN **skateboards** a long narrow board with wheels fitted to the bottom, for riding on in a standing or crouching position

▸ **skateboarder** NOUN **skateboarders** someone who rides a skateboard

▸ **skateboarding** NOUN riding on skateboards

skeleton NOUN **skeletons** the frame of bones inside your body that supports all your muscles and organs

sketch NOUN **sketches** 1 a drawing that is done quickly, often as a guide for a more detailed picture or plan 2 a very short funny play

VERB **sketches, sketching, sketched** to sketch something is to draw it quickly

skew VERB **skews, skewing, skewed** something is skewed when it lies at an angle

skewer NOUN **skewers** a long thin pointed piece of metal or wood that is pushed through small pieces of food so

that they can be cooked under a grill or on a barbecue

ski NOUN **skis** skis are two long narrow strips of wood or metal used for gliding over snow and which you attach to special boots

VERB **skis, skiing, skied** or **ski'd** to move over snow with a pair of long narrow strips of wood or metal attached to your boots

▸ **skier** NOUN **skiers** a person who skis

▸ **skiing** NOUN the sport of gliding over snow on skis

skid VERB **skids, skidding, skidded** to slide over a surface in an uncontrolled way

skies NOUN the plural of **sky**: *sunny skies*

skilful ADJECTIVE having a lot of skill and ability

▸ **skilfully** ADVERB with skill

▸ **skilfulness** NOUN being skilful

skill NOUN **skills** 1 to have skill is to be clever or expert at doing something 2 a skill is a talent that you develop through training and practice: *football skills*

▸ **skilled** ADJECTIVE 1 a skilled person is expert at what they do: *a skilled pianist* 2 a skilled job needs training and practice

skim VERB **skims, skimming, skimmed** 1 something skims a surface when it travels along just above the surface 2 to skim something floating on the top of a liquid is to remove it

▸ **skimmed** ADJECTIVE skimmed milk has had some of the cream removed

skimpy ADJECTIVE **skimpier, skimpiest** skimpy clothes do not cover much of your body

skin NOUN **skins** 1 the tissue that covers the outer surface of the bodies of humans and animals 2 the thin outer covering on fruit and some vegetables 3 a layer that forms on the top of some liquids

VERB **skins, skinning, skinned** to skin something is to remove its skin

skinny ADJECTIVE **skinnier, skinniest** thin

skint ADJECTIVE (*informal*) a way of

saying you have no money: *I can't afford the ticket. I'm totally skint.*

skip VERB **skips, skipping, skipped**
1 to move forward springing or hopping from one foot to the other as you go
2 to jump over a skipping-rope
3 to skip something is to leave it out and go on to the next thing
4 to skip school or lessons is to not attend them
NOUN **skips** a skipping movement: *Off the rabbit went, with a hop, skip and a jump.*

skipper NOUN **skippers** the captain of a boat or ship, or of an aircraft or spacecraft

skipping rope NOUN **skipping ropes** a rope that you jump over and which is swung round repeatedly by two people holding it at either end, or which you hold and swing over and under your own body

skirmish NOUN **skirmishes** a short battle or fight

skirt NOUN **skirts** a piece of clothing that hangs from the waist
VERB **skirts, skirting, skirted 1** to go around the border or edge of something: *a dense wood that skirted the grounds* **2** you skirt around something when you avoid it by going around it

skirting *or* **skirting board** NOUN **skirtings** *or* **skirting boards** a length of wood fixed to the bottom of an inside wall where it meets the floor

skittle NOUN **skittles** one of several bottle-shaped objects that you try to knock down with a ball in the game of skittles

skulk VERB **skulks, skulking, skulked** to wait somewhere, hidden from view

skull NOUN **skulls** the bony part of your head that contains your brain and forms a framework for your face

skunk NOUN **skunks** a small North American animal with black-and-white fur and a long bushy tail. A skunk defends itself by spraying a stinking liquid at its attacker

sky NOUN **skies** the area of space above the Earth where you can see the sun, moon, stars and clouds

✦ **Sky** is a word from the Old Norse language, which was used long ago in countries such as Norway and Denmark. It means *cloud*.

skylark NOUN **skylarks** a small brown bird that flies upwards and hovers in the sky singing a sweet song

skylight NOUN **skylights** a window set into a roof

skyscraper NOUN **skyscrapers** a tall building with lots of storeys

slab NOUN **slabs** a thick flat slice of something: *an enormous slab of chocolate cake*

slack ADJECTIVE **slacker, slackest**
1 loose and not pulled tight: *These trousers are too slack around the waist.*
2 careless or lazy: *slack discipline • She's slack about her work and doesn't show much interest.*
VERB **slacks, slacking, slacked** to do less work than you should
▶ **slacken** VERB **slackens, slackening, slackened 1** to slacken something is to loosen it **2** the pace or strength of something slackens when it gets slower or weaker
▶ **slackness** NOUN being loose or lazy
▶ **slacks** PLURAL NOUN slacks are smart but loose casual trousers

slam VERB **slams, slamming, slammed**
1 to slam something, such as a door, is to shut it with a bang **2** to slam something is to hit it or put it down hard

slang NOUN very informal words or expressions that you use in everyday speech or to people of your own age, but not in writing or when you are being polite

slant VERB **slants, slanting, slanted** to slope or move diagonally
NOUN **slants 1** a slope or diagonal direction **2** someone's slant on something is their particular point of view

slap NOUN **slaps 1** a hit, done with the palm of the hand or anything flat **2** a sound made by something hitting a flat surface

Aa
Bb
Cc
Dd
Ee
Ff
Gg
Hh
Ii
Jj
Kk
Ll
Mm
Nn
Oo
Pp
Qq
Rr
Ss
Tt
Uu
Vv
Ww
Xx
Yy
Zz

VERB **slaps, slapping, slapped** to slap someone or something is to hit them with the palm of your hand or something flat

slapdash ADJECTIVE careless: *slapdash work*

slapstick NOUN a type of comedy in which actors or comedians get laughs by behaving in a silly way, for example by falling over

slash VERB **slashes, slashing, slashed 1** to slash something is to cut it with a sharp blade swung in a quick swinging movement **2** to slash things like prices is to cut them by a large amount

NOUN **slashes 1** a long cut made by a sharp blade **2** (*ICT*) one of two punctuation marks (/ or \), used especially in computing and in website addresses

slat NOUN **slats** a long strip of plastic or wood put together with others to form something such as a window blind or bench

slate NOUN **slates 1** slate is a type of stone that can be split into thin pieces along natural lines in the stone **2** a slate is a rectangular piece of this rock used for roofing or, in the past, for schoolchildren to write on with chalk

slaughter VERB **slaughters, slaughtering, slaughtered** to slaughter people or animals is to kill them in large numbers

NOUN the killing of large numbers of people or animals

slave NOUN **slaves** a person who is owned by another person and who is usually made to work hard for little or no pay

VERB **slaves, slaving, slaved** to work very hard

▸ **slavery** NOUN **1** buying, selling and using slaves **2** very hard work for very little reward

slay VERB **slays, slaying, slew, slain** to slay a person or animal is to kill them. This is an old-fashioned word that is sometimes used in books: *The dragon was slain by Saint George.*

sledge or **sled** NOUN **sledges** or **sleds 1** a small vehicle with metal runners underneath or with a flat underside that you sit on to slide over snow **2** a vehicle with ski-like runners underneath that is pulled over snow by dogs or horses

sledgehammer NOUN **sledgehammers** a large heavy hammer that you swing with both arms

sleek ADJECTIVE **sleeker, sleekest** smooth, soft and glossy: *A mink has sleek dark-brown fur.*

sleep NOUN **sleeps 1** sleep is rest that you have with your eyes closed and in a natural state of unconsciousness **2** a sleep is a period of time when you rest in this way

VERB **sleeps, sleeping, slept** to rest with your eyes closed and in a state of unconsciousness

• **sleep in** to sleep for too long so that you are late for something

▸ **sleeper** NOUN **sleepers 1** someone who is sleeping **2** a carriage on a train where you can sleep **3** one of the heavy wooden or metal beams that a railway track is laid on

sleeping bag NOUN **sleeping bags** a large sack made of layers of warm fabric and used for sleeping in, especially by someone who is camping

sleepless ADJECTIVE if you have a sleepless night, you are unable to go to sleep at all

sleepwalker NOUN **sleepwalkers** someone who walks about while they are sleeping

▸ **sleepwalking** NOUN walking about in an unconscious state, as if sleeping

sleepy ADJECTIVE **sleepier, sleepiest** feeling tired and wanting to sleep

▸ **sleepily** ADVERB in a tired or sleepy way

▸ **sleepiness** NOUN the feeling of being tired and wanting to sleep

sleet NOUN a mixture of rain and snow

sleeve NOUN **sleeves** the part of a piece of clothing that covers your arm or part of your arm

▸ **sleeveless** ADJECTIVE having no sleeves

sleigh NOUN **sleighs** a large sledge pulled by a horse or horses

slender ADJECTIVE **1** slim or thin, especially in an attractive way: *She had long slender legs.* **2** small or slight: *His chances of winning are extremely slender.*

slept VERB a way of changing the verb **sleep** to make a past tense. It can be used with or without a helping verb: *He slept for ten hours.* • *He had slept all morning and afternoon.*

slice NOUN **slices** a thin or smaller piece cut from a larger piece of food

VERB **slices, slicing, sliced 1** to slice something, or slice it up, is to cut it into slices **2** to slice something is to cut it with a sharp blade or knife: *The knife slipped and sliced my finger.*

slick ADJECTIVE **slicker, slickest 1** a slick performance is done well without seeming to involve much effort **2** a slick talker is clever at persuading people

NOUN **slicks** a layer of oil that has been spilt on the surface of the sea

slide VERB **slides, sliding, slid 1** to slip or move over a surface quickly and smoothly **2** to move downwards or get worse: *She's let standards slide since we were last here.*

NOUN **slides 1** an apparatus with a smooth sloping surface for children to slide down **2** (*science*) a small clear glass or plastic plate on which specimens are put so that they can be looked at under a microscope **3** a small transparent photograph that you put in a projector to be viewed on a screen

slight ADJECTIVE **slighter, slightest 1** small or not great: *a slight increase in temperature* • *a slight problem* • *Lewis has a slight cold.* **2** slim and light: *He has a slight build.*

▸ **slightly** ADVERB by only a small amount

slim ADJECTIVE **slimmer, slimmest 1** thin or slender: *slim fingers* **2** small or slight: *The chances of winning the lottery are very slim.*

slime NOUN a soft, sticky, half-liquid substance that looks a bit like thin jelly

▸ **slimy** ADJECTIVE **slimier, slimiest** covered with, or feeling like, slime

sling VERB **slings, slinging, slung 1** to sling something is to throw it hard **2** to sling something over your shoulder is to throw it over your shoulder so that it hangs down

NOUN **slings 1** a bandage that is hung from someone's neck or shoulder to support an injured arm **2** a strong band of material that is used to support something that is being lifted or to throw stones

slink VERB **slinks, slinking, slunk** to move quietly, trying not to be noticed

slip VERB **slips, slipping, slipped 1** to slide accidentally and lose your balance **2** to slip in or out of a place, or to slip away, is to go in or out, or go away, quietly and without anyone noticing you **3** to slip something somewhere is to slide it there or put it there quickly

• **slip up** to make a mistake or do something wrong

NOUN **slips**

1 an accidental slide

2 a small mistake

3 a small piece of paper: *Fill in the green slip and give it back to me.*

4 a piece of thin underclothing that a girl or woman wears under their dress or skirt

• **give someone the slip** to escape from someone without their noticing

slipper NOUN **slippers** a soft shoe for wearing indoors

slippery ADJECTIVE smooth, wet or shiny and not easy to balance on or hold

slip road NOUN **slip roads** a road used by traffic going on to or leaving a motorway

slipshod ADJECTIVE careless and untidy

slit NOUN **slits** a long cut or narrow opening

VERB **slits, slitting, slit** to slit something is to make a long narrow cut in it

slither VERB **slithers, slithering, slithered** to slide or slip: *The ice-cubes slithered off the table.*

sliver NOUN **slivers** a long thin piece which is cut or broken from something

Aa
Bb
Cc
Dd
Ee
Ff
Gg
Hh
Ii
Jj
Kk
Ll
Mm
Nn
Oo
Pp
Qq
Rr
Ss
Tt
Uu
Vv
Ww
Xx
Yy
Zz

Aa
Bb
Cc
Dd
Ee
Ff
Gg
Hh
Ii
Jj
Kk
Ll
Mm
Nn
Oo
Pp
Qq
Rr
Ss
Tt
Uu
Vv
Ww
Xx
Yy
Zz

slobber VERB **slobbers, slobbering, slobbered** a person or animal slobbers when saliva dribbles out of their mouth

slog VERB **slogs, slogging, slogged** to work very hard

slogan NOUN **slogans** a phrase that is easy to remember and is often repeated, used especially in advertising

slop VERB **slops, slopping, slopped** liquid slops when it moves around or splashes or spills

slope VERB **slopes, sloping, sloped** to go in a direction that is not level or straight but at an upward or downward slant

NOUN **slopes 1** an upward or downward slant **2** the side of a hill

sloppy ADJECTIVE **sloppier, sloppiest 1** careless **2** showing love in a way that is silly and embarrassing

slot NOUN **slots** a small narrow opening, especially one that you put coins into

sloth NOUN **sloths 1** a South American animal that lives mostly in trees and moves very slowly **2** sloth is laziness

slouch VERB **slouches, slouching, slouched** to move, stand or sit with your shoulders rounded and your head hanging forward

slovenly ADJECTIVE dirty or untidy: *slovenly work*

slow ADJECTIVE **slower, slowest 1** not fast or not moving quickly: *a slow march* • *Our progress was slow.* **2** if a clock or watch is slow, it shows a time earlier than the correct time

VERB **slows, slowing, slowed** to slow, or to slow down, is to become slower or to make something slower

▶ **slowly** ADVERB in a slow way: *He walks very slowly.*

slow-motion ADJECTIVE a slow-motion scene in a film has the action slowed down to slower than its real speed

sludge NOUN thick, soft, slimy mud or any substance that is like this

slug NOUN **slugs** a creature with a long soft body like a snail, but with no shell

slum NOUN **slums** a building or part of a town or city where the conditions are dirty and overcrowded

slumber VERB **slumbers, slumbering, slumbered** to sleep

NOUN **slumbers** sleep

slump VERB **slumps, slumping, slumped 1** a price or amount slumps when it becomes less: *Sales have slumped in the last few months.* **2** you slump, or slump down, when your body sinks so that you are lying heavily against something: *He was slumped over his desk, fast asleep.*

NOUN **slumps** a period when businesses are not selling many goods

slung VERB a way of changing the verb **sling** to form a past tense. It can be used with or without a helping verb: *He slung his backpack over his shoulder.* • *They had slung all their coats into a corner without hanging them up.*

slunk VERB a way of changing the verb **slink** to form a past tense. It can be used with or without a helping verb: *The fox slunk away into the bushes.* • *He had slunk up behind me and shouted 'Boo!'.*

slur VERB **slurs, slurring, slurred** to pronounce words unclearly

NOUN **slurs** an insult that is likely to damage someone's reputation

slurp VERB **slurps, slurping, slurped** to drink very noisily

slush NOUN partly melted snow on the ground

▶ **slushy** ADJECTIVE **slushier, slushiest 1** soft and almost liquid, like partly melted snow **2** romantic in a silly way: *a slushy novel*

sly ADJECTIVE **slyer** or **slier, slyest** or **sliest** cunning and good at deceiving others

▶ **slyly** ADVERB in a cunning way

▶ **slyness** NOUN being deceitful and cunning

smack VERB **smacks, smacking, smacked 1** to smack someone is to slap them **2** to smack your lips is to make a loud sucking noise by bringing your lips together tightly and then opening your mouth again quickly

NOUN **smacks** a slap, or the sound made by a slap

small ADJECTIVE **smaller, smallest 1** little: *a small country* • *This coat is too small for you.* • *a small problem* **2** if something makes you feel small, it makes you feel silly and unimportant **3** a small voice is soft and difficult to hear
► **smallness** NOUN how small something is compared to other things

smart ADJECTIVE **smarter, smartest 1** neat: *my smartest clothes* **2** clever and quick **3** fast: *a smart pace*
VERB **smarts, smarting, smarted** if a part of your body smarts, you feel a stinging pain there
► **smarten** VERB **smartens, smartening, smartened** to smarten, or smarten up, is to make a person or place look neater: *Smarten up a bit before you go to school.*
► **smartly** ADVERB **1** neatly and fashionably: *smartly dressed businessmen* **2** quickly or briskly: *You'll have to walk pretty smartly if you want to catch the train.*
► **smartness** NOUN being smart

smash VERB **smashes, smashing, smashed 1** to break, or break something into pieces: *He kicked the ball and it smashed the window.* • *The vase fell off the table and smashed.* **2** to smash something, or smash into it, is to hit or crash into it with great force
NOUN **smashes 1** the sound of something breaking **2** a road accident in which two vehicles hit each other and are damaged
► **smashing** ADJECTIVE great or splendid: *That was a smashing film.*

smear VERB **smears, smearing, smeared** to spread a surface with something sticky or oily

smell NOUN **smells 1** smell is the power or sense of being aware of things through your nose **2** a smell is something you notice using this sense: *a strong smell of garlic* **3** a sniff at something: *Have a smell at this milk and tell me if you think it's off.*
VERB **smells, smelling, smelled** *or* **smelt 1** to smell something is to notice it through your nose **2** something that smells gives off a smell of some kind

smelly ADJECTIVE **smellier, smelliest** giving off a strong or bad smell

smelt VERB **smelts, smelting, smelted** to melt a material that contains metal in order to separate the metal from the rest of the material

smile VERB **smiles, smiling, smiled** to show pleasure or amusement by turning up the corners of your mouth
NOUN **smiles** an expression of pleasure or amusement in which you turn up the corners of your mouth

smirk VERB **smirks, smirking, smirked** to smile in a self-satisfied, cheeky or silly way
NOUN **smirks** a self-satisfied, cheeky or silly smile

smith NOUN **smiths** someone who works with metals: *a blacksmith*

smock NOUN **smocks** a loose piece of clothing worn over other clothes to protect them

smog NOUN smoke from car exhausts and chimneys mixed with fog, which hangs over some cities and towns

smoke NOUN the cloud of gases and bits of soot given off by something that is burning
VERB **smokes, smoking, smoked 1** something smokes when it gives off smoke **2** someone who smokes puts a lit cigarette, cigar or pipe in their mouth and breathes in the smoke
► **smoker** NOUN **smokers** someone who smokes cigarettes, cigars or a pipe
► **smoking** NOUN the habit of smoking cigarettes, cigars or a pipe
► **smoky** ADJECTIVE **smokier, smokiest 1** filled with smoke **2** like smoke: *a smoky grey colour*

smooth ADJECTIVE **smoother, smoothest 1** something smooth has an even surface that is not rough or bumpy **2** a smooth substance has no lumps **3** a smooth ride or smooth progress has no jerks, stops or problems
VERB **smoothes, smoothing, smoothed** to smooth something is to

make it smooth or flat: *She smoothed the bed covers and tidied her bedroom.*
▶ **smoothly** ADVERB in a smooth way
▶ **smoothness** NOUN being smooth
smother VERB **smothers, smothering, smothered 1** if someone is smothered, they die because something is over their nose and mouth and they cannot breathe **2** to smother flames is to cover them so that no oxygen gets to the fire and it goes out
smoulder VERB **smoulders, smouldering, smouldered** to burn slowly, without a flame
smudge NOUN **smudges** a mark made by rubbing something across a surface or pressing something greasy against it
VERB **smudges, smudging, smudged** to smudge something is to rub something across it so that it smears
smug ADJECTIVE **smugger, smuggest** someone who is smug shows by their behaviour that they are very pleased with themselves
▶ **smugly** ADVERB in a self-satisfied way
▶ **smugness** NOUN being pleased with yourself
smuggle VERB **smuggles, smuggling, smuggled 1** to bring things into a country secretly and illegally **2** to smuggle something somewhere is to take it there secretly: *He smuggled the puppy into his room without his parents knowing.*
▶ **smuggler** NOUN **smugglers** someone who smuggles goods into a country
snack NOUN **snacks** a small meal, or something like a biscuit or piece of fruit eaten between meals
snag NOUN **snags** a small problem
VERB **snags, snagging, snagged** to snag your clothing is to catch or tear it on something sharp or rough
snail NOUN **snails** a small creature with a soft body and a shell on its back that it can draw its body into for protection
snake NOUN **snakes** a type of reptile with a long thin body and no legs, which moves along the ground with twisting movements

snap VERB **snaps, snapping, snapped**
1 to break with a sudden sharp noise
2 something snaps shut when it closes with a sudden sharp noise
3 you snap your fingers when you rub your thumb and finger together in a quick movement, making a cracking noise
4 if someone snaps at you, they speak to you in a sharp angry way
5 an animal snaps when it makes a biting movement with its jaws
NOUN **snaps 1** the sound of something breaking or of an animal bringing its teeth together quickly **2** a photograph
▶ **snappily** ADVERB **1** quickly **2** in a bad-tempered way
▶ **snappy** ADJECTIVE **snappier, snappiest** if someone is snappy, they speak to people in a bad-tempered way
• **make it snappy** if someone tells you to make it snappy, they mean you should be quick
snapshot NOUN **snapshots** a photograph taken quickly
snare NOUN **snares** a kind of trap for catching animals
VERB **snares, snaring, snared** to trap an animal
snarl VERB **snarls, snarling, snarled** an animal, such as a dog or wolf, snarls when it growls in a threatening way
NOUN **snarls** an angry-sounding growl
snatch VERB **snatches, snatching, snatched 1** to snatch something is to grab it suddenly **2** to snatch something, like a sleep or a meal, is to take it quickly when you have time or the chance
NOUN **snatches** a short piece of music or conversation
sneak NOUN **sneaks** someone who tells tales or is deceitful
VERB **sneaks, sneaking, sneaked 1** to go somewhere quietly and secretly **2** to tell tales to someone in authority such as a teacher
• **sneak up on someone** to creep up behind someone, to surprise them or give them a fright
▶ **sneakily** ADVERB in a sneaky way

▶ **sneaky** ADJECTIVE **sneakier, sneakiest** deceitful or secretive

sneer VERB **sneers, sneering, sneered 1** to raise your top lip at one side in an unkind smile **2** to sneer at something is to be very unkind about it and show that you have no respect for it: *John sneered at my attempt to write a story.*
NOUN **sneers** a sneering expression or remark

sneeze VERB **sneezes, sneezing, sneezed** to suddenly and uncontrollably blow out air from your nose and mouth
NOUN **sneezes** this action and sound

snide ADJECTIVE spiteful in an almost hidden way: *I made snide little remarks whenever he spoke.*

sniff VERB **sniffs, sniffing, sniffed** to breathe in air through your nose with a small noise, or to draw air into your nose so that you can smell something
NOUN **sniffs** a quick loud breath taken in through your nose

sniffle VERB **sniffles, sniffling, sniffled** to sniff over and over again, especially because you have a cold or are crying

snigger VERB **sniggers, sniggering, sniggered** to laugh quietly in an unpleasant and cruel way
NOUN **sniggers** a quiet unpleasant laugh

snip VERB **snips, snipping, snipped** to snip something is to cut small pieces off it using scissors
NOUN **snips** a quick cutting action made with a pair of scissors

sniper NOUN **snipers** a person armed with a gun who shoots at people from a hiding place

snippet NOUN **snippets** a small piece of news, information or conversation: *a snippet of information*

snivel VERB **snivels, snivelling, snivelled** to cry and sniff weakly and in a way that does not make other people feel sympathy for you

snob NOUN **snobs** a snob is someone who admires people of high social class or things that are of high quality, and despises people who are of a lower class than they are, or does not like the things that ordinary people like

▶ **snobbery** NOUN the behaviour of snobs

▶ **snobbish** ADJECTIVE being a snob

snooker NOUN a game for two players played on a large table with several coloured balls which have to be hit into a pocket at the side of the table using a long stick called a cue

snoop VERB **snoops, snooping, snooped** to try to find out things in a secretive way: *Jane was snooping around to try to find my diary.*

▶ **snooper** NOUN **snoopers** someone who snoops

snooty ADJECTIVE **snootier, snootiest** a snooty person behaves in a rude and unfriendly way to people they think are not as good as they are

snooze NOUN **snoozes** a short light sleep
VERB **snoozes, snoozing, snoozed** to sleep, especially not very deeply or for a short time

snore VERB **snores, snoring, snored** to make a noise like a snort while you are sleeping, when you breathe in

snorkel NOUN **snorkels** a tube that allows an underwater swimmer to breathe, with one end sticking out above the water to let in air
VERB **snorkels, snorkelling, snorkelled** to swim underwater using a snorkel to breathe

snort VERB **snorts, snorting, snorted 1** to make a noise by pushing air out through your nostrils: *The horses snorted, stamping their hooves.* **2** to make this noise because you are angry, disagree or think something is funny: *'Don't be stupid!' she snorted.*
NOUN **snorts** a loud noise made by breathing out through your nose: *a snort of laughter*

snout NOUN **snouts** the mouth and nose of a pig or animal like that

snow NOUN water that has frozen into soft white pieces called flakes that falls from the sky: *The children loved playing in the snow.* • *Thick snow had blocked the road across the mountain.*

Aa
Bb
Cc
Dd
Ee
Ff
Gg
Hh
Ii
Jj
Kk
Ll
Mm
Nn
Oo
Pp
Qq
Rr
Ss
Tt
Uu
Vv
Ww
Xx
Yy
Zz

VERB **snows, snowing, snowed** when it snows, snow fall from the sky: *It's been snowing all night.*

snowball NOUN **snowballs** a ball of snow that children make and throw at each other: *a snowball fight*

snowdrift NOUN **snowdrifts** a lot of snow that the wind has blown into a pile

snowdrop NOUN **snowdrops** a small white flower that grows from a bulb in the early spring

snowman NOUN **snowmen** a figure of a person, made of snow

snowplough NOUN **snowploughs** a large vehicle that clears snow from the roads

snowstorm NOUN **snowstorms** a storm with a heavy fall of snow

snowy ADJECTIVE **snowier, snowiest 1** covered with snow **2** perfectly white: *a fat gentleman with a snowy beard*

snub VERB **snubs, snubbing, snubbed** to snub someone is to insult them by ignoring them or being rude to them: *I tried to speak to him but he just snubbed me and turned away.*
ADJECTIVE a snub nose is small and turns up at the end

snuff or **snuff out** VERB **snuffs, snuffing, snuffed** to put out a candle flame, often with your fingers
NOUN a type of tobacco in the form of a powder

snuffle VERB **snuffles, snuffling, snuffled** to make sniffing noises, especially because you have a cold

snug ADJECTIVE **snugger, snuggest** warm and cosy: *We were all quite snug in our sleeping bags.*

snuggle or **snuggle up** VERB **snuggles, snuggling, snuggled** to curl up and get warm: *Sam snuggled closer to his mother and soon fell asleep.*

so ADVERB
1 to such an extent or to a great extent: *I was so relieved to hear her voice.* • *The box was so heavy he could not lift it.* • *Thank you so much for all your help.*
2 you can use **so** when you are talking about something mentioned, or shown by a gesture: *a little boy about so high* • *'I feel sick after all those sweets.' 'I told you so, didn't I?'* • *'Are you coming to the party?' 'I hope so.'*
3 also: *Jane's ten and so am I.*
4 in this way or that way: *Stretch your leg out so.*
• **so as to** in order to: *We got there early so as to get good seats.*
• **so far** up to now: *Well, I've enjoyed his lessons so far.*
• **so forth** more things that are similar: *pens, pencils and so forth*
• **so that** in order that: *Could you wash my jeans so that I can wear them tomorrow?*
• **so what?** used for saying that something does not matter
CONJUNCTION therefore: *He asked me to come, so I did.* • *So they got married and lived happily ever after.*

soak VERB **soaks, soaking, soaked 1** to soak something is to cover it in liquid and leave it there: *If you soak your blouse, the stain might come out.* **2** to soak someone is to make them very wet
• **soak up something** if a piece of cloth or paper soaks up a liquid, it sucks it up or absorbs it: *Mum used a towel to soak up the spilt milk.*
▶ **soaking** ADJECTIVE very wet

soap NOUN **soaps 1** a substance that you use to wash yourself and other things: *a bar of soap* **2** another word for **soap opera**: *Gran likes to watch all the soaps on TV.*
▶ **soapy** ADJECTIVE **soapier, soapiest** covered in or full of soap bubbles: *soapy water*

soap opera NOUN **soap operas** a television series about a group of families and their daily lives

✦ These shows were given their name because when they first started they were sponsored by soap companies, and so advertisements for soap would have been seen with the show.

soar VERB **soars, soaring, soared 1** to fly high up into the air: *An eagle soared high above their heads.* **2** if prices soar,

Aa
Bb
Cc
Dd
Ee
Ff
Gg
Hh
Ii
Jj
Kk
Ll
Mm
Nn
Oo
Pp
Qq
Rr
Ss
Tt
Uu
Vv
Ww
Xx
Yy
Zz

things become much more expensive very quickly: *The price of petrol has soared over the last ten years.*

sob VERB **sobs, sobbing, sobbed** to cry noisily: *Lisa lay on her bed, sobbing.*
NOUN **sobs** the sound of someone sobbing

sober ADJECTIVE **1** not drunk **2** serious: *a sober man* **3** not bright, or with very little decoration: *sober colours*
▸ **soberly** ADVERB in a serious, solemn way: *soberly dressed*
▸ **soberness** NOUN being sober

so-called ADJECTIVE used when you think that the way someone or something is described is not very suitable: *your so-called friend, Mr Williams*

soccer NOUN another word for **association football**

sociable ADJECTIVE friendly and enjoying being with other people

social ADJECTIVE **1** to do with society or a community: *social problems such as bad housing* **2** social animals live in groups **3** to do with meeting and being friendly with other people: *a social club*

socialism NOUN the belief that a country's main industries and land should be owned by the government and not by individual people
▸ **socialist** NOUN **socialists** someone who believes in socialism ADJECTIVE believing in or to do with socialism: *a socialist state*

social work NOUN work that the government pays for to help people who are poor, ill or have problems
▸ **social worker** NOUN **social workers** someone who is paid by the government whose job is to help people who are poor, ill or have problems

society NOUN **societies**
1 all the people in the world in general: *Drugs are a huge danger to society.*
2 a particular group of people, especially fashionable and wealthy people: *high society*
3 a social club with a particular interest: *the debating society*
4 being with other people: *I've always*

enjoyed the society of people older than myself.

sociology NOUN the study of human behaviour and societies
▸ **sociologist** NOUN **sociologists** someone who studies how human societies are organized and how people behave

sock NOUN **socks** a covering for your foot that you wear inside your shoe: *a pair of socks*
• **pull your socks up** to try harder to do something better than before: *You'll have to pull your socks up if you want to pass this exam.*

socket NOUN **sockets** a shaped hole or hollow that something fits into: *an electric socket*

soda NOUN **sodas 1** (*science*) a word for a substance that contains **sodium 2** another word for **soda water**

soda water NOUN fizzy water that contains carbon dioxide gas

sodden ADJECTIVE very wet: *The ground's sodden after all that rain.*

sodium NOUN (*science*) a silvery white element that is part of many substances, for example sodium chloride (salt)

sofa NOUN **sofas** a long comfortable chair for two or three people

soft ADJECTIVE **softer, softest**
1 not hard or firm: *a nice soft cushion* • *soft silky hair*
2 not strict or tough: *He's far too soft with his children.* • *Ben's too soft to get into a fight.*
3 not loud: *a soft voice*
4 not too bright: *Her bedroom is decorated in soft pastel colours.*
▸ **soften** VERB **softens, softening, softened 1** to soften something is to make it become soft: *Soften the plasticine by working it with your hands.* **2** to soften is to become soft: *Her voice softened as she looked at the baby.*
▸ **softly** ADVERB gently or quietly: *Snow was falling softly in the moonlight.* • *She stroked the cat softly.*
▸ **softness** NOUN being soft, gentle, or quiet: *the softness of the pillows*

Aa
Bb
Cc
Dd
Ee
Ff
Gg
Hh
Ii
Jj
Kk
Ll
Mm
Nn
Oo
Pp
Qq
Rr
Ss
Tt
Uu
Vv
Ww
Xx
Yy
Zz

soft drink NOUN **soft drinks** a drink that does not contain alcohol: *The club serves cola and other soft drinks.*

software NOUN (*ICT*) computer programs. Look up and compare **hardware**

soggy ADJECTIVE **soggier, soggiest** wet and soft: *soggy ground*

soil NOUN the top layer of the ground, which you can grow plants in: *sandy soil*
VERB **soils, soiling, soiled** to soil something is to make it dirty: *soiled linen*

solar ADJECTIVE relating to or powered by energy from the sun: *solar panels*

✦ **Solar** comes from the Latin word **sol**, which means *sun*.

solar power NOUN electricity that is made using the sun's light and heat

solar system NOUN the Sun and the planets that move around it

sold VERB a way of changing the verb **sell** to make a past tense. It can be used with or without a helping verb: *Tom sold me his old bike.* • *Have your parents sold their house yet?*

solder VERB **solders, soldering, soldered** to join two pieces of metal with metal that has been melted
NOUN melted metal used to join pieces of metal together

soldier NOUN **soldiers** someone who is in the army

sole¹ ADJECTIVE **1** only: *Her sole ambition was to be famous.* **2** belonging to one person alone: *He has sole ownership of the company.*
▸ **solely** ADVERB only or alone: *You are solely responsible for your own actions.*

sole² NOUN **soles 1** the underside of your foot **2** the underside of your shoe: *The sole came off my shoe as I was running.*

sole³ NOUN **soles** or **sole** a flat fish that people can eat

solemn ADJECTIVE **1** serious: *a solemn expression* • *a rather solemn little boy* **2** a solemn occasion is celebrated in a dignified way with a lot of ceremony
▸ **solemnity** NOUN when someone or something is solemn

▸ **solemnly** ADVERB in a solemn way

solicitor NOUN **solicitors** someone whose job is giving advice about the law system to people, for example when they buy a house or a business, or if the police arrest them

solid ADJECTIVE
1 (*science*) with a fixed shape, not in the form of a liquid or a gas
2 not hollow: *a solid chocolate teddy*
3 firm and strong: *a solid piece of furniture*
4 (*maths*) a solid shape is flat and has length, height and width you can measure. It might also be called a **three-dimensional** shape: *A cube is a solid figure.*
5 with no pauses in between: *I've been working for six solid hours.*
NOUN **solids 1** (*science*) something that is not a liquid or a gas **2** (*maths*) a shape that has length, width, and height
▸ **solidly** ADVERB **1** strongly or firmly: *a solidly built structure* **2** continuously: *We've been working solidly since nine o'clock this morning.*

solidify VERB **solidifies, solidifying, solidified 1** to solidify is to become solid **2** to solidify something is to make it become solid
▸ **solidification** NOUN becoming solid

solitary ADJECTIVE lonely or alone: *a solitary figure*

solitude NOUN when you are alone

solo NOUN **solos** a piece of music or a song for one person to play or sing: *Emma sang a solo in the Christmas concert.*
ADJECTIVE alone: *a solo flight*
▸ **soloist** NOUN **soloists** someone who is singing or playing a solo

solstice NOUN **solstices** the **summer solstice** is the day of the year when there are most hours of daylight and the **winter solstice** is the day when there are most hours of darkness

soluble ADJECTIVE **1** a soluble substance will dissolve in water: *soluble aspirin* **2** a soluble problem can be solved

solute NOUN **solutes** (*science*) a substance dissolved in a liquid

solution NOUN **solutions 1** an answer to a problem, question or puzzle: *They have been unable to find a solution to the problem.* **2** (*science*) a liquid with a substance dissolved in it: *a salt-water solution*

solve VERB **solves, solving, solved 1** to solve a problem or puzzle is work out the answer: *Solve the riddle to win a prize.* **2** to solve a mystery or crime is to work out what happened

solvent NOUN **solvents** (*science*) something that dissolves another substance

sombre ADJECTIVE **1** dark and gloomy: *sombre colours* **2** serious and sad: *a sombre mood*

sombrero NOUN **sombreros** a Mexican hat with a broad brim

some ADJECTIVE **1** quite a large number or amount: *It's all right; I've got some money.* **2** a small number or amount: *There's some soup left but not enough for everyone.* • *Some people agreed but others didn't.* **3** certain: *You're like your father in some ways.*
PRONOUN part of a number or amount: *I've made a cake – would you like some?*

somebody PRONOUN **1** a person that you do not know or name: *Somebody knocked at the door.* **2** an important person: *He really thinks he's somebody in that big car.*

somehow ADVERB in some way: *Don't worry, we'll manage somehow.*

someone PRONOUN a person that you do not know or name: *Is there someone there?*

somersault NOUN **somersaults** a jump in which you turn over forwards or backwards in the air
VERB **somersaults, somersaulting, somersaulted** to do a somersault: *She somersaulted neatly into the water.*

something PRONOUN **1** a thing that is not known or stated: *Let's have something to eat before we go.* **2** a slight amount or degree: *There is something in what he says.*

sometimes ADVERB at times: *I still see him sometimes.*

somewhat ADVERB rather: *a somewhat lonely man*

somewhere ADVERB **1** in or to some place: *They live somewhere near Oxford.* **2** used when you are not sure of an amount, time or number: *She must be somewhere between 35 and 40.*

son NOUN **sons** someone's male child

sonar NOUN special equipment that uses sound waves to find out where things are under water

song NOUN **songs 1** a piece of music with words that you can sing: *a pop song* **2** the activity of singing: *A blackbird suddenly burst into song.*

songbird NOUN **songbirds** a bird that sings

sonic ADJECTIVE relating to sound: *a sonic boom*

son-in-law NOUN **sons-in-law** your daughter's husband

sonnet NOUN **sonnets** a type of poem that has fourteen lines

soon ADVERB **sooner, soonest 1** in a short time from now: *It will soon be Christmas.* **2** early: *It's too soon to tell whether she'll recover.*
• **as soon** if you would as soon do one thing as another, you are equally willing to do them both: *I'll do the ironing but I'd just as soon do the washing-up.*
• **as soon as** when: *We ate as soon as they arrived.*
▶ **sooner** ADVERB rather or more willingly: *I'd sooner do it myself than ask her to help.*
• **sooner or later** at some time in the future: *You're bound to bump into him sooner or later.*

soot NOUN the black powder that collects in chimneys
▶ **sooty** ADJECTIVE **sootier, sootiest** covered in soot or like soot

soothe VERB **soothes, soothing, soothed 1** to make someone feel calmer or happier: *The little boy was so upset that it took his mother nearly an hour to soothe him.* **2** to make pain less strong: *I bathed to soothe my sore muscles.*
▶ **soothing** ADJECTIVE **1** making you

Aa
Bb
Cc
Dd
Ee
Ff
Gg
Hh
Ii
Jj
Kk
Ll
Mm
Nn
Oo
Pp
Qq
Rr
Ss
Tt
Uu
Vv
Ww
Xx
Yy
Zz

feel calmer or happier **2** making pain less strong

sophisticated ADJECTIVE **1** a sophisticated person knows a lot about the world and about what is fashionable **2** sophisticated ideas, machines and processes are complicated and well-developed

▶ **sophistication** NOUN when someone or something is sophisticated

sopping ADJECTIVE very wet

soppy ADJECTIVE **soppier, soppiest** too sentimental in a way that seems silly: *a soppy love song*

soprano NOUN **sopranos** (*music*) **1** a very high singing voice **2** a woman or young boy with a high singing voice

sorcery NOUN magic or the ability to make magic spells work

▶ **sorcerer** NOUN **sorcerers** a man who can make magic spells work

▶ **sorceress** NOUN **sorceresses** a woman who can make magic spells work

sore ADJECTIVE **sorer, sorest** red and painful: *a sore finger*

NOUN **sores** a red, painful spot on your skin

▶ **sorely** ADVERB very much or a lot: *Mr. Watson will be sorely missed by the school.*

▶ **soreness** NOUN being painful

sorrow NOUN **sorrows** grief or sadness because you are disappointed or someone has died: *I couldn't find the words to comfort her in her sorrow.*

▶ **sorrowful** ADJECTIVE feeling or showing sorrow: *a long, sorrowful face*

sorry ADJECTIVE **sorrier, sorriest 1** sorry is a word you use when you are apologizing or saying you regret something: *I'm sure Tim is sorry he upset you.* • *Sorry, I didn't mean to hurt you.* **2** if you are sorry for someone, you feel pity for them: *I felt so sorry for Lizzie when she failed her exam.* **3** bad or unfortunate: *the sorry plight of the refugees*

sort NOUN **sorts** a type or kind of person or thing: *What sort of books do you read?* • *You meet all sorts of people at school.*

• **sort of** slightly: *It was sort of strange, seeing dad at school.*

VERB **sorts, sorting, sorted** to sort people or things is to separate them into different groups according to their type: *Can you sort the washing into whites and coloureds?*

• **sort something out 1** if you sort out one type of thing from a group of things, you separate it from them: *Sort out the books that have to go back to the library.* **2** if you sort out a problem or difficult situation, you solve it or deal with it: *There are a lot of things to sort out before we go on holiday.*

SOS NOUN a signal that you send to ask for help: *The ship sent an SOS to the coastguard after it hit the rocks.*

so-so ADJECTIVE not particularly good: *Jo's work this term has only been so-so.*

sought VERB a way of changing the verb **seek** to make a past tense. It can be used with or without a helping verb: *He sought his parents' permission.* • *I have sought to solve this problem.*

soul NOUN **souls 1** the part of a person that is not their body but is their spirit, which some people believe lives on after they die **2** a person: *The poor old soul got an awful shock.*

sound NOUN **sounds 1** something that you can hear: *There isn't a sound coming from the children's bedroom.* • *the sound of breaking glass* **2** the way that something such as a description or piece of news seems from what you have heard: *I don't like the sound of your new teacher.*

VERB **sounds, sounding, sounded 1** if something sounds good or bad, it seems that way from what you have heard about it: *Tom's holiday sounds wonderful.* **2** if something sounds like something else the two sounds are very similar: *That sounds like Zoe's voice in the kitchen.* **3** to sound something is to make a noise with it: *Sound your horn before you turn the corner.*

• **sound someone out** to talk to someone to find out their opinion: *Could you sound John out about my suggestion?*

Aa Bb Cc Dd Ee Ff Gg Hh Ii Jj Kk Ll Mm Nn Oo Pp Qq Rr **Ss** Tt Uu Vv Ww Xx Yy Zz

ADJECTIVE **sounder, soundest** 1 strong, firm, or healthy: *The walls of the old church were still sound.* • *a sound heart* 2 a sound sleep is deep and difficult to wake up from 3 thorough and complete: *a sound knowledge of French*

sound barrier NOUN if a plane breaks the sound barrier, there is a loud noise as it begins to go faster than the speed that sound travels at

soundtrack NOUN **soundtracks** a recording of the music from a film or television programme

soup NOUN **soups** a liquid food made from meat, fish, or vegetables

sour ADJECTIVE **sourer, sourest** 1 sour food has a bitter taste like a lemon, sometimes because it is going bad: *sour plums* • *The milk had gone sour in the sun.* 2 a sour person is bad-tempered and unpleasant: *a sour face*

source NOUN **sources** 1 the place where something begins or is naturally present: *a rich source of gas* 2 (*geography*) a spring that is the start of a river

south NOUN 1 the direction on your right when you are facing towards the rising sun 2 the part of a country or the world that is in the south

ADJECTIVE in, from, or towards the south: *the south coast* • *the south wind*

ADVERB to the south: *The river flows south into the sea.*

south-east NOUN the area midway between south and east: *It should be another sunny day in the south-east.*

southerly ADJECTIVE coming from, or going towards, the south

NOUN **southerlies** a wind that comes from the south

southern ADJECTIVE belonging to or coming from the south: *the southern states of the USA*

southward *or* **southwards** ADVERB to or towards the south: *We were soon heading southward down the motorway.*

south-west NOUN the area midway between south and west

souvenir NOUN **souvenirs** something that you buy to remind you of a particular place or occasion: *We brought back some shells as souvenirs of our holiday.*

sovereign NOUN **sovereigns** 1 a king or queen 2 an old gold coin

sow¹ (rhymes with **low**) VERB **sows, sowing, sowed, sown** to sow seeds is to scatter them on or in the ground so that they will grow

sow² (rhymes with **how**) NOUN **sows** a female pig

soya bean *or* **soy bean** NOUN **soya beans** *or* **soy beans** a type of bean that contains a lot of protein

spa NOUN **spas** a place where people go to drink or bathe in water that comes out of the ground at a natural spring

space NOUN **spaces** 1 a gap or empty place: *a parking space* • *Fill in the spaces on your answer sheet.* 2 the area available to use or do something: *There isn't enough space to hold a party here.* • *Can you make space for one more person?* 3 the empty area beyond the Earth's atmosphere, where the planets and stars are: *Another rocket was launched into space yesterday.*

VERB **spaces, spacing, spaced** if you space things or space them out, you leave gaps between them: *Try to space your work out neatly.*

spacecraft NOUN **spacecrafts** a vehicle that can travel into space

spaceman NOUN **spacemen** a man who travels into space

spaceship NOUN **spaceships** a vehicle that can travel into space

space shuttle NOUN **space shuttles** a vehicle like a plane that can travel into space and come back to Earth to be used again

spacious ADJECTIVE with a lot of room inside it: *a spacious apartment*

spade NOUN **spades** 1 a tool with a broad blade that you use for digging 2 spades is one of the four suits of playing cards, which have the symbol ♠ printed on them: *the ace of spades*

spaghetti NOUN a type of pasta that is like long thin string: *a plate of spaghetti with tomato sauce*

Aa
Bb
Cc
Dd
Ee
Ff
Gg
Hh
Ii
Jj
Kk
Ll
Mm
Nn
Oo
Pp
Qq
Rr
Ss
Tt
Uu
Vv
Ww
Xx
Yy
Zz

spam NOUN emails that you do not want, sent to you by companies or by people who do not know you

span NOUN **spans** the length of time that something lasts: *The country had changed completely within the span of twenty years.*

VERB **spans, spanning, spanned** to span something is to stretch across it: *An old wooden bridge spans the river.*

spangle NOUN **spangles** a small sparkling piece of metal used as a decoration on clothes: *The acrobat's costume was covered in spangles.*

spaniel NOUN **spaniels** a type of dog with long ears that hang down

spank VERB **spanks, spanking, spanked** to hit someone on the bottom with your hand flat, especially as a punishment

spanner NOUN **spanners** a tool used for tightening or loosening nuts or screws

spar VERB **spars, sparring, sparred** to fight or argue with someone

spare ADJECTIVE **1** a spare room or thing is extra and is not being used at the moment: *a spare tyre • I've got a spare ticket for Saturday's concert, if you'd like it.* **2** spare time is time when you are free to do what you want

VERB **spares, sparing, spared 1** if you can spare something or someone, you can manage without them: *We can't spare anyone to help out today.* **2** if you can spare the time to do something, you have enough time to do it: *I'm sorry, but I can't spare the time to go out tonight.* **3** to avoid hurting someone or making things difficult for them: *Break the news gently to spare her as much pain as possible.*

• **to spare** if you have time or money to spare, you have more than you need

NOUN **spares** a spare part for a car or piece of equipment

▸ **sparing** ADJECTIVE careful or using very little of something

spark NOUN **sparks 1** a very small burning piece thrown out of a fire or when two hard surfaces are rubbed together: *Sparks were shooting out of the bonfire.* **2** a small amount of something such as enthusiasm or interest: *There seemed to be no spark of life in the old woman.*

VERB **sparks, sparking, sparked 1** to make a spark **2** to spark something or spark off something is to start or cause it: *Her remark sparked off a huge row about football.*

sparkle VERB **sparkles, sparkling, sparkled** to glitter or shine: *Her jewels sparkled in the firelight.*

▸ **sparkling** ADJECTIVE **1** shining or glittering: *sparkling lights* **2** a sparkling drink has bubbles of gas in it: *a sparkling mineral water*

spark plug or **sparking plug** NOUN **spark plugs** or **sparking plugs** a small part in a car engine that produces a spark to light the gases that make it start

sparrow NOUN **sparrows** a small brown bird

sparse ADJECTIVE **sparser, sparsest** if something is sparse, there is not much or not enough of it: *sparse hair*

spasm NOUN **spasms** a sudden movement of your muscles that you cannot control: *The muscles of his leg had gone into spasm.*

spate NOUN a sudden large number or amount: *a spate of burglaries*

spatter VERB **spatters, spattering, spattered** if you spatter something, you splash it with small drops of liquid: *His hair was spattered with paint.*

spawn NOUN the eggs of frogs, toads or fish: *frog spawn*

VERB **spawns, spawning, spawned** if fish or frogs spawn, they lay eggs

speak VERB **speaks, speaking, spoke, spoken 1** to say something: *Could I speak to you for a moment? • She was so tired she could hardly speak.* **2** to be able to talk in a particular language: *Do you speak Greek?* **3** to make a speech: *The headmaster spoke for almost an hour about the school's problems.*

• **speak up** to speak more loudly: *Speak up, we can't hear you at the back.*

▶ **speaker** NOUN **speakers 1** someone who is speaking **2** a piece of equipment that increases the sound coming out of a radio, CD-player or cassette player

spear NOUN **spears** a long thin weapon with a metal point

VERB **spears, spearing, speared** to push a long thin point into something: *He speared a piece of meat with his fork.*

special ADJECTIVE **1** unusual and different from others: *I was allowed to stay up late as it was a special occasion.* • *Andrea's always been my special friend.* **2** meant for or having a specific purpose: *Special trains will take fans to the match.*

▶ **specialist** NOUN **specialists** someone who knows a lot about a particular subject: *a skin specialist*

▶ **speciality** NOUN **specialities** something that someone does particularly well: *Birthday cakes are my speciality.*

specialize or **specialise** VERB **specializes, specializing, specialized** to give all of your attention to studying one particular subject or doing one particular thing in your job: *Jessica's decided to specialize in portrait photography.*

▶ **specialization** or **specialisation** NOUN study of a particular subject or work at a particular job

specially ADVERB with one particular purpose: *Jo's had her costume specially made for the party.*

✦ Remember the difference between **specially** and **especially**. **Specially** means 'for a special purpose': *I cooked this meal specially for you.*

Especially means 'particularly': *I like all of the characters, especially Harry.*

species NOUN **species** a group of animals or plants whose members share most features

specific ADJECTIVE **1** giving all the details about something in a clear way: *Sarah's directions weren't very specific.* **2** exact or particular: *We each have our own specific jobs to do.*

▶ **specifically** ADVERB **1** for one particular purpose and no other: *flats designed specifically for the elderly* **2** clearly and exactly: *I specifically told you not to go out tonight.*

specification NOUN **specifications** a clear description of the details of something such as a plan, contract, or machine: *The car was built to his own specifications.*

specify VERB **specifies, specifying, specified** to specify what you want is to state it clearly: *Please specify the colour and size your require on the order form.*

specimen NOUN **specimens** something that is a sample of a particular group or kind of thing: *The specimens were arranged in cases, clearly labelled.*

speck NOUN **specks 1** a very small piece of something: *a speck of dust* **2** a small spot: *a speck of paint*

speckle NOUN **speckles** a small coloured spot: *The egg was covered with speckles.*

▶ **speckled** ADJECTIVE covered in speckles: *a speckled hen*

spectacle NOUN **spectacles** a wonderful or impressive sight: *The royal wedding was a great spectacle.*

▶ **spectacles** PLURAL NOUN glasses that you wear to help you see properly: *a pair of spectacles*

spectacular ADJECTIVE very impressive: *a spectacular firework display* • *The scenery was absolutely spectacular.*

▶ **spectacularly** ADVERB impressively, or by a very large amount: *a spectacularly successful film*

spectator NOUN **spectators** someone who is watching an event

spectre NOUN **spectres** a ghost

spectrum NOUN **spectra** or **spectrums 1** (*science*) all the different colours produced when light passes through glass or water **2** all the different types or forms of something: *a broad spectrum of opinions*

speculate VERB **speculates, speculating, speculated** to guess: *I*

Aa
Bb
Cc
Dd
Ee
Ff
Gg
Hh
Ii
Jj
Kk
Ll
Mm
Nn
Oo
Pp
Qq
Rr
Ss
Tt
Uu
Vv
Ww
Xx
Yy
Zz

wouldn't like to speculate about what might have happened to him.

▸ **speculation** NOUN **speculations 1** speculation is guessing something **2** a speculation is a guess

sped VERB a way of changing the verb **speed** to make a past tense. It can be used with or without a helping verb: *The holidays have just sped by.* • *A bullet sped past his ear.*

speech NOUN **speeches 1** speech is the ability to speak: *He seemed to have lost the power of speech.* **2** speech is the way that you speak: *She was so tired that her speech was slurred.* **3** a speech is a talk that you give in front of a lot of people: *The bride's father usually makes a speech.*

▸ **speechless** ADJECTIVE if you are speechless, you cannot talk because you are so surprised or shocked: *His remarks left her speechless.*

speed NOUN **speeds 1** the rate at which someone or something is moving: *He was driving at a speed of about 30 miles per hour.* **2** quickness: *Speed is important in this job.*

VERB **speeds, speeding, sped** or **speeded 1** to move quickly or hurry: *I'm going to speed through my homework, then watch TV.* **2** to drive faster than the law says you can: *Dad didn't think he was speeding until he saw the police car.*

speedometer NOUN **speedometers** a piece of equipment in a car that measures how fast you are travelling

speedy ADJECTIVE **speedier, speediest** quick: *Thanks for the speedy reply to my letter.*

spell[1] VERB **spells, spelling, spelt** or **spelled 1** to say or write the letters of a word in the correct order: *Could you spell your name for me?* **2** to make up a word: *L-i-g-h-t spells 'light'.*

spell[2] NOUN **spells** a short period of time: *The weather will be dull with sunny spells.*

spell[3] NOUN **spells** a set of words that are supposed to make something magic happen: *The wicked witch cast a spell on Snow White.*

spellcheck or **spellchecker** NOUN **spellchecks** or **spellcheckers** (*ICT*) a computer program that checks the words in a file have been spelled properly

spelling NOUN **1** the way that a word is spelt: *What's the correct spelling of 'weird'?* **2** the ability to spell well: *Your spelling is terrible.*

spend VERB **spends, spending, spent 1** to use money to buy things: *Adam spends all his pocket money on sweets.* **2** to pass time: *I used to spend hours reading in my room.*

spent VERB a way of changing the verb **spend** to make a past tense. It can be used with or without a helping verb: *Mum spent weeks making that sweater.* • *Have you spent your birthday money yet?*

sperm NOUN a special cell stored inside the body of a male mammal and which can fertilize a female egg

sphere NOUN **spheres** a solid object that is the shape of a ball

▸ **spherical** ADJECTIVE shaped like a ball

spice NOUN **spices** any substance that adds flavour to food: *herbs and spices* • *Ginger is a spice.*

▸ **spicy** ADJECTIVE **spicier, spiciest** tasting hot on your tongue: *spicy chilli tortillas*

spider NOUN **spiders** a small creature with eight legs that spins a web made of very fine threads

spike NOUN **spikes** a hard, thin point: *There were sharp spikes on top of the wall.*

▸ **spiky** ADJECTIVE **spikier, spikiest** with sharp points: *a spiky hairstyle*

spill VERB **spills, spilling, spilt** or **spilled 1** to spill a liquid is to let it run out accidentally: *Careful! You're going to spill your tea.* **2** to spill is to run out accidentally: *The milk spilled all over the floor.*

spin VERB **spins, spinning, spun 1** to turn round and round very quickly: *The ballerina spun round and round on her toes.* **2** to make long, thin threads out of cotton, wool or another material by pulling it and twisting it

spinach NOUN a vegetable with large, flat, green leaves

spinal ADJECTIVE relating to your spine: *a spinal injury*

spindle NOUN **spindles** the pin that something turns on, for example a knob on a radio or a reel of thread

▸ **spindly** ADJECTIVE **spindlier, spindliest** long and thin: *a creature with long, spindly arms*

spine NOUN **spines 1** the line of bones down the back of a person or animal **2** a stiff spike that grows on animals, such as the hedgehog, or on plants: *the spines of a cactus*

spinning wheel NOUN **spinning wheels** a piece of equipment for spinning thread, with a large wheel that turns and makes spindles move

spinster NOUN **spinsters** a woman who is not married

spiral ADJECTIVE coiled or winding round and round: *a spiral staircase*

NOUN **spirals** something with a spiral shape: *The shell formed a perfect spiral.*

VERB **spirals, spiralling, spiralled 1** to move in a spiral **2** to increase very quickly

spire NOUN **spires** a tall pointed roof on a church tower

spirit NOUN **spirits**

1 your soul, which some people believe lives on after you die: *Some villagers thought the graveyard was haunted by evil spirits.*

2 bravery or liveliness: *a horse with spirit*

3 a strong alcoholic drink: *whisky, vodka and other spirits*

4 a general feeling or attitude: *team spirit • a town with a strong community spirit*

▸ **spirited** ADJECTIVE lively and with a lot of personality: *a spirited performance*

▸ **spiritual** ADJECTIVE connected with someone's soul or to ghosts: *a spiritual experience*

spit NOUN **spits 1** the watery liquid inside your mouth **2** a metal bar that you put meat on to roast

VERB **spits, spitting, spat** if you spit, you push liquid or food out of your mouth: *She took one mouthful and then spat it out on to her plate.*

spite NOUN a feeling of wanting to offend or upset someone: *He threw my picture away out of spite.*

• **in spite of** if you do something or something happens in spite of something else, the first thing does not prevent the other: *We decided to go to the seaside in spite of the rain.*

spiteful ADJECTIVE doing or saying something nasty just to hurt someone: *It isn't like Maddy to be spiteful. • a spiteful remark*

▸ **spitefully** ADVERB in a way that aims to hurt people

spitting image NOUN someone who looks exactly like someone else: *Tara's the spitting image of her mother.*

spittle NOUN the watery liquid inside your mouth

splash VERB **splashes, splashing, splashed 1** if you splash someone with a liquid, or splash a liquid over someone, you throw drops of it over them: *Kate quickly splashed her face with water. • The car drove off, splashing mud all over my new coat.* **2** if a liquid splashes somewhere, it flies there in drops: *The water splashed over the edge of the pan.* **3** if you splash or splash a part of your body in water, you move the water around in a noisy way

NOUN **splashes 1** the water sent up when something moves through it, or the noise this makes: *He fell into the pool with a loud splash.* **2** a mark made on something where liquid has fallen on it: *jeans covered in splashes of paint* **3** a splash of colour is a bright patch of it

spleen NOUN **spleens** an organ inside your body near your stomach

splendid ADJECTIVE magnificent, rich, or grand: *The king was a splendid sight in his robes.*

▸ **splendour** NOUN when something looks very grand or magnificent: *the splendour of the royal palaces*

splint NOUN **splints** a piece of wood

Aa
Bb
Cc
Dd
Ee
Ff
Gg
Hh
Ii
Jj
Kk
Ll
Mm
Nn
Oo
Pp
Qq
Rr
Ss
Tt
Uu
Vv
Ww
Xx
Yy
Zz

used to keep a broken arm or leg in the right position

splinter NOUN **splinters** a small piece of wood or glass that breaks off a large piece: *She got a splinter in her hand from the broken fence.*

VERB **splinters, splintering, splintered** if a piece of wood splinters, small thin pieces of it break off

split VERB **splits, splitting, split 1** if something splits, it breaks or tears apart: *Your trousers have split down the back.* **2** if you split something, you break it or tear it apart: *The lightning had split the tree in two.* **3** to divide a group of people into smaller groups: *The teacher split us up into groups of six to do the experiment.*

• **split up** if two people who have a relationship split up, they stop going out together: *Did you know Katy's split up with her boyfriend?*

NOUN **splits** a crack, tear or break in something: *There's a long split in your sleeve.*

• **do the splits** to sit on the floor with one leg stretched straight out in front of you and one behind

splutter VERB **splutters, spluttering, spluttered** to make spitting noises when you talk because you are excited, angry or shocked: *'I don't know what you're talking about!' he spluttered.*

spoil VERB **spoils, spoiling, spoilt** or **spoiled 1** to spoil something is to damage or ruin it: *Tommy scribbled on my picture and spoilt it.* **2** if food spoils, it starts to go bad: *If you don't put it in the fridge, it will spoil.* **3** to spoil someone is to give them too much of what they want so that they do not appreciate it

spoilsport NOUN **spoilsports** someone who refuses to join in other people's fun: *Come on, Barry, don't be such a spoil-sport!*

spoke¹ NOUN **spokes** one of the thin pieces that come out from the centre of the wheel to the edge

spoke² VERB a way of changing the verb **speak** to make a past tense: *He spoke so fast that I couldn't understand him.*

▸ **spoken** VERB a form of the verb **speak** that is used with a helping verb to show that something happened in the past: *I've spoken to your teacher, and everything's fine.*

spokesman, spokeswoman or **spokesperson** NOUN **spokesmen, spokeswomen** or **spokespeople** someone who speaks on behalf of other people

sponge NOUN **sponges 1** a soft object, made from natural or artificial material, that you use to wash your body **2** a light cake or pudding: *a sponge pudding*

VERB **sponges, sponging, sponged 1** to sponge something is to wash it with a sponge **2** (*informal*) to try to get money from someone without making any effort to give anything back

▸ **spongy** ADJECTIVE **spongier, spongiest** feeling soft like a sponge: *a spongy texture*

sponsor VERB **sponsors, sponsoring, sponsored 1** to sponsor something such as an event or project is to pay some or all of its cost as a way of advertising: *A local company sponsors my son's football team.* **2** to sponsor someone is to promise to pay them an amount of money, which they will give to charity, if they do a particular thing

NOUN **sponsors** a person or company that sponsors someone or something *official sponsors of the 2002 World Cup*

▸ **sponsorship** NOUN the money someone pays to sponsor an event or a person

spontaneous ADJECTIVE **1** natural: *a spontaneous laugh* **2** not planned: *a spontaneous offer of help*

▸ **spontaneity** NOUN the quality of being spontaneous

spook NOUN **spooks** a ghost

▸ **spooky** ADJECTIVE **spookier, spookiest** frightening because it makes you think of ghosts: *a spooky ghost story* • *spooky music*

spool NOUN **spools** a cylindrical object that film or thread is wound around: *a spool of cotton*

spoon NOUN **spoons** an object with a

thin handle and a shallow bowl at one end that you use for eating food

VERB **spoons, spooning, spooned** to lift up food on a spoon: *She was slowly spooning the cereal into the baby's mouth.*

▸ **spoonful** NOUN **spoonfuls** the amount a spoon will hold

sport NOUN **sports 1** sport is games and physical activities like football, tennis and swimming: *Adam loves all kinds of sport.* **2** a sport is a particular game or activity: *Alex particularly enjoys winter sports.* **3** a kind and helpful person: *Max will give us a hand – he's a good sport.*

▸ **sporting** ADJECTIVE playing fair: *a very sporting player*

sports car NOUN **sports cars** a fast car that has only two seats and no roof

sportsman or **sportswoman** NOUN **sportsmen** or **sportswomen** a man or woman who takes part in sport

spot NOUN **spots**
1 a small mark or stain on something
2 a round shape that is part of a pattern: *a pink dress with white spots*
3 a red raised mark on your skin: *Teenagers often suffer from spots.*
4 a place: *a lovely spot for a picnic* • *X marks the spot where the treasure is buried.*
VERB **spots, spotting, spotted** to notice something or someone: *I suddenly spotted Ian over by the window.*

spotless ADJECTIVE totally clean: *a spotless white handkerchief*
▸ **spotlessly** ADVERB something that is spotlessly clean is very clean

spotlight NOUN **spotlights** a small bright light, for example on a stage

spotty ADJECTIVE **spottier, spottiest**
1 someone who is spotty has a lot of spots: *a spotty face* **2** covered in round shapes of a different colour: *a spotty scarf*

spout NOUN **spouts 1** the long thin part of a teapot or kettle that you pour the water out of **2** a jet of water
VERB **spouts, spouting, spouted** to come out in a fountain: *The oil came spouting up out of the ground.*

sprain VERB **sprains, spraining, sprained** to sprain a joint, such as your ankle or wrist, is to twist it and hurt yourself: *a sprained ankle*
NOUN **sprains** a painful injury when you twist a joint such as your ankle or wrist: *Her wrist isn't broken; it's just a bad strain.*

sprang VERB a way of changing the verb **spring** to make a past tense: *The cat sprang on to the mouse.*

sprawl VERB **sprawls, sprawling, sprawled 1** to sit, lie or fall with your legs and arms spread out: *Tony lay sprawled at full length on the sofa.* **2** if a town, building, or group of buildings sprawls, it covers a large area in an untidy way: *a large, sprawling old house*

spray NOUN **sprays 1** a fine mist of liquid: *The spray from the waterfall wet their hair.* **2** a device with a lot of little holes that produces a mist of liquid: *a perfume spray* **3** a liquid that you spray on to something: *a hairspray*
VERB **sprays, spraying, sprayed** to cover something with a mist of fine drops of liquid: *A sprinkler was spraying water on to the lawn.*

spread VERB **spreads, spreading, spread**
1 to put a layer of something onto a surface: *She spread her toast thickly with butter.* • *Tom was carefully spreading cream onto the top of the cake.*
2 to spread something or to spread something out is to open something out flat or to make it cover a surface: *Spread the map out so that we can look at it.* • *Ann spread all her shopping out on her bed.*
3 if news spreads, it becomes known by a lot of different people: *Rumours spread very quickly in this little village.*
4 to spread things or spread things out is to space them over a period of time so they do not all happen at once: *Luckily, the exams were spread out over two whole weeks.*
NOUN **spreads 1** the area, time or range

Aa
Bb
Cc
Dd
Ee
Ff
Gg
Hh
Ii
Jj
Kk
Ll
Mm
Nn
Oo
Pp
Qq
Rr
Ss
Tt
Uu
Vv
Ww
Xx
Yy
Zz

that something covers: *the spread of a disease* **2** a type of paste that you spread on bread: *chicken spread*

spree NOUN **sprees** a burst of doing something: *a shopping spree*

sprig NOUN **sprigs** a small branch of a plant: *a sprig of holly*

sprightly ADJECTIVE a sprightly person is lively and moves quickly

spring VERB **springs, springing, sprang, sprung 1** to jump quickly, usually up: *He's the type who just springs out of bed in the morning.* **2** to develop from something else: *His confidence springs from his loving family background.*

NOUN **springs**
1 a coil of wire: *a chair with a broken spring*
2 the season of the year between winter and summer when plants start to grow: *the first day of spring*
3 a jump or quick movement
4 a small stream that flows up out of the ground: *a mountain spring*

springboard NOUN **springboards** a type of board that divers can jump from into the water

spring-cleaning NOUN thorough cleaning of your house, especially in the spring

springy ADJECTIVE **springier, springiest** a springy surface or substance easily springs back into its original shape: *a springy mattress • springy floorboards*

sprinkle VERB **sprinkles, sprinkling, sprinkled** to scatter small drops or pieces of something over a surface: *Mum sprinkled chocolate chips onto the trifle.*

▶ **sprinkler** NOUN **sprinklers** a device that you use to sprinkle something, especially water on to a garden

sprint VERB **sprints, sprinting, sprinted** to run fast for a short distance: *He sprinted down the street after her.*

NOUN **sprints** a short running race: *the 100 metre sprint*

▶ **sprinter** NOUN **sprinters** an athlete who is good at running fast for short distances

sprite NOUN **sprites** a fairy

sprout VERB **sprouts, sprouting, sprouted 1** to produce new leaves and shoots: *Buds were sprouting on the sycamore tree.* **2** to grow: *His hair sprouted out of his head in clumps.*

NOUN **sprouts 1** a new shoot: *bean sprouts* **2** a **Brussels sprout**

spruce[1] NOUN **spruces** a type of fir tree

spruce[2] ADJECTIVE **sprucer, sprucest** neat and smart: *You're looking very spruce in your new suit.*

sprung VERB a form of the verb **spring** that is used with a helping verb to show that something happened in the past: *James had sprung to his feet when she came in.*

spud NOUN **spuds** (*informal*) a potato

spur NOUN **spurs 1** a small pointed object that a rider wears on their heel to stick into the horse to make it go faster **2** anything that makes someone try harder

• **on the spur of the moment** suddenly, without thinking or planning first: *On the spur of the moment, he decided to take a day off work.*

VERB **spurs, spurring, spurred**
• **spur someone on** if something spurs someone on, it encourages them to do something: *Winning the prize spurred her on to try even harder.*

spurt VERB **spurts, spurting, spurted** to pour out in a heavy flow: *Blood was spurting from a wound on his head.*

NOUN **spurts 1** a sudden burst of a liquid: *a spurt of blood* **2** a sudden increase of effort, energy, or feeling: *We'll have to put a spurt on if we want to catch that train.*

spy NOUN **spies** someone who is employed by the government of their country to secretly find out information about another country

VERB **spies, spying, spied 1** to work as a spy **2** to spy someone or something is to see or notice them: *I spy, with my little eye, something beginning with S.*

Aa Bb Cc Dd Ee Ff Gg Hh Ii Jj Kk Ll Mm Nn Oo Pp Qq Rr Ss Tt Uu Vv Ww Xx Yy Zz

squabble VERB **squabbles, squabbling, squabbled** to quarrel
NOUN **squabbles** a quarrel

squad NOUN **squads** a small group of people who are doing a job together: *a squad of bricklayers*

squadron NOUN **squadrons** a group of people in the army, navy or air force

✦ **Squad** and **squadron** both come from the Latin word **exquadra**, which means a *square*. This is because soldiers used to stand in a square formation when they were being attacked.

squalid ADJECTIVE dirty and poor: *a squalid room in a hostel*

squall NOUN **squalls** a sudden bad storm
▶ **squally** ADJECTIVE stormy: *a squally night at sea*

squalor NOUN very dirty living conditions: *The old man had been living alone in squalor.*

squander VERB **squanders, squandering, squandered** to squander money or time is to waste it: *He squandered all his pocket money on chocolate.*

square NOUN **squares 1** a flat shape with four equal sides and four right angles **2** an open space with buildings on all four sides: *a tree-lined square • Trafalgar Square* **3** (*maths*) the square of a number is the number you get when you multiply the number by itself, for example the square of 3 is 3 × 3, which is 9. Look up and compare **cube**
ADJECTIVE
1 shaped like a square: *a square cushion*
2 measuring a particular amount on each side: *The room was about 3 metres square.*
3 (*maths*) a square measurement is one used to measure area. For example, a square metre is a space one metre long and one metre wide
4 (*maths*) a square number is a number that has been multiplied by itself, for example 3 × 3, which is written as 3^2
5 with equal scores or amounts: *The*

two teams were all square at half-time, at 3-3. • *If you pay for the coffee, we'll be square.*
6 straight or level: *Keep the paper square with the edge of the table.*
VERB **squares, squaring, squared 1** to make something have a square shape: *Square off the end of the piece of wood.* **2** (*maths*) to square a number is to multiply it by itself: *Four squared is sixteen.*

square root NOUN **square roots** (*maths*) the square root of a number is the number that gives the first number when it is multiplied by itself: *Three is the square root of nine.*

squash VERB **squashes, squashing, squashed** to press, squeeze or crush someone or something: *We were all squashed into the back of the car.*
NOUN **squashes 1** a squash is a situation when people or things are squashed: *It was a bit of squash fitting everything in his suitcase.* **2** a sweet drink with a fruit flavour: *an orange squash* **3** squash is a game in which you hit a small rubber ball against the walls of a court with a racket

squat VERB **squats, squatting, squatted 1** to crouch down on your heels: *He squatted on the ground to eat his lunch.* **2** to live in a building without having permission to be there
ADJECTIVE **squatter, squattest** short and fat: *a rather squat little man*
▶ **squatter** NOUN **squatters** someone who squats in a building: *The empty house had been taken over by squatters.*

squawk VERB **squawks, squawking, squawked** to make a loud, high-pitched cry
NOUN **squawks** a loud, high-pitched cry: *The hen gave a squawk.*

squeak VERB **squeaks, squeaking, squeaked** to make a small, high-pitched sound: *That door squeaks when you open it.*
NOUN **squeaks** a small, high-pitched sound
▶ **squeaky** ADJECTIVE **squeakier, squeakiest** making a noise like a squeak: *a squeaky floorboard*

Aa
Bb
Cc
Dd
Ee
Ff
Gg
Hh
Ii
Jj
Kk
Ll
Mm
Nn
Oo
Pp
Qq
Rr
Ss
Tt
Uu
Vv
Ww
Xx
Yy
Zz

squeal VERB **squeals, squealing, squealed** to give a loud, shrill cry: *The baby squealed with delight when he saw his mother.*

NOUN **squeals** a loud, shrill cry: *a squeal of pain*

squeamish ADJECTIVE easily shocked or made to feel sick: *I've always been squeamish about injections.*

squeeze VERB **squeezes, squeezing, squeezed 1** to press something tightly: *She squeezed my hand encouragingly.* **2** to force something into or out of a small space or container: *The cat tried to squeeze itself under the sofa.* • *He was trying to squeeze the last of the toothpaste out of the tube.*

NOUN **squeezes 1** the action of squeezing or pressing something **2** a tight fit: *We all got into the car, but it was a tight squeeze.*

squelch NOUN **squelches** the noise you make when you move through something thick and sticky like mud

squid NOUN **squids** a sea creature with tentacles

squiggle NOUN **squiggles** a short, wavy line

squint VERB **squints 1** to half-close your eyes when you are looking at something: *She looked up at him, squinting in the sunlight.* **2** to have eyes that look in different directions

NOUN **squints** a problem with your eyes that makes them look in different directions

squire NOUN **squires** (*history*) a man who used to own land in the country in the past

squirm VERB **squirms, squirming, squirmed** to wriggle or twist your body because you are embarrassed or in pain: *She squirmed when she remembered how rude she had been.*

squirrel NOUN **squirrels** a small reddish-brown or grey animal with a bushy tail that lives in trees and eats nuts

squirt VERB **squirts, squirting, squirted** to shoot out a jet of liquid: *The kids were squirting each other with water.*

St ABBREVIATION short for **Saint** or **Street**

stab VERB **stabs, stabbing, stabbed** to stab someone or something is to push something sharp into them with a lot of force: *The woman was stabbed with a knife.* • *She stabbed the pin into the cushion angrily.*

NOUN **stabs** a sharp feeling: *a stab of pain*

stability NOUN being steady and balanced

stabilize *or* **stabilise** VERB **stabilizes, stabilizing, stabilized 1** to stabilize is to become balanced or steady: *She's been very ill but her condition has stabilized.* **2** to stabilize someone or something is to make them balanced or steady: *Put a book under the table leg to stabilize it.*

stable ADJECTIVE **1** firm and steady: *This bracket will help to keep the shelf stable.* **2** a stable relationship is one that has lasted for some time and will probably continue **3** a stable person is sensible and calm

NOUN **stables 1** a building to keep a horse in **2** a place where you can learn to ride a horse: *a riding stables*

stack NOUN **stacks** a large pile of things: *a stack of books*

VERB **stacks, stacking, stacked** to stack things is to pile them up neatly: *Stack the dishes in the sink and I'll wash them later.*

stadium NOUN **stadiums** or **stadia** a large sports ground with seats: *a football stadium*

staff NOUN **staffs 1** the people who work in a particular place: *The company has a staff of 150.* • *Six new members of staff are joining the school this term.* **2** a stick **3** (*music*) a set of spaced lines for writing music on

stag NOUN **stags** a male deer

stage NOUN **stages 1** the raised platform in a theatre where the actors perform **2** a step in a process or series of developments: *The work is still in its early stages.* • *It's hard to predict what will happen at this stage.*

VERB **stages, staging, staged** to put

a play or other performance on in a theatre: *an opera staged in Verona*

stagecoach NOUN **stagecoaches** a coach pulled by horses that people used in the past to travel around the country

stagger VERB **staggers, staggering, staggered 1** to walk unsteadily, swaying from side to side: *He staggered across the room and fell into a chair.* **2** to amaze someone: *I was staggered when they got married.* **3** to stagger events is to arrange them so that they don't all happen at the same time: *We have to stagger our lunchbreaks at school because the dining hall isn't big enough.*

▶ **staggering** ADJECTIVE very surprising: *The amount of money collected was absolutely staggering.*

stagnant ADJECTIVE stagnant water is dirty and unhealthy because it does not flow: *a stagnant pond*

stain VERB **stains, staining, stained 1** to leave a permanent coloured mark on something: *The coffee you spilt has stained the carpet.* **2** to dye wood a different colour

NOUN **stains** a dirty mark that is hard to remove from something: *overalls covered in oil stains*

stair or **stairs** NOUN **stairs 1** a set of steps that lead to another level in a building: *A flight of stairs led down to the cellar.* **2** one of these steps

staircase NOUN **staircases** a set of stairs: *a marble staircase*

stake NOUN **stakes 1** a strong pointed stick, for example to support a fence **2** an amount of money that you bet on something: *a £5 stake*

• **at stake** if something is at stake, you risk losing it: *She felt that her whole future was at stake in the competition.*

VERB **stakes, staking, staked** to bet an amount of money on something: *I'll stake £10 on Paul winning.*

stalactite NOUN **stalactites** (*geography*) a spike of limestone that hangs from the roof of a cave

stalagmite NOUN **stalagmites** (*geography*) a spike of limestone that rises up from the floor of a cave

stale ADJECTIVE **staler, stalest** not fresh but dry and tasteless: *stale bread* • *The air smelt stale inside the room.*

stalemate NOUN a position in a game of chess or an argument when neither side can make a move or win

stalk NOUN **stalks** the stem of a flower, leaf or fruit: *an apple stalk*

VERB **stalks, stalking, stalked 1** to stalk an animal or person is to follow them quietly, trying to keep hidden: *a tigress stalking her prey* **2** to stalk is to walk proudly and stiffly: *He was stalking angrily up and down.*

stall NOUN **stalls 1** a compartment for one animal in a cowshed or barn **2** a table or open-fronted shop where things are laid out to be sold: *a market stall* **3** the stalls are the lower floor of a theatre, where the audience sits

VERB **stalls, stalling, stalled 1** if a vehicle stalls or someone stalls it, its engine suddenly stops while you are driving **2** to delay doing something: *I wish he'd stop stalling and give me an answer.*

stallion NOUN **stallions** a male horse

stamen NOUN **stamens** (*science*) a spike inside a flower that produces pollen

stamina NOUN the strength to keep doing something for a long time: *exercises to increase your stamina*

stammer VERB **stammers, stammering, stammered 1** to have a speech problem that makes it difficult for you to pronounce the first letters of some words **2** to speak like this because you are frightened or nervous

NOUN **stammers** a speech problem that makes it difficult for you to pronounce the first letters of some words: *He had a bad stammer when he was a child.*

stamp VERB **stamps, stamping, stamped 1** to bring your foot down firmly on the ground: *She stamped her feet to keep them warm.* **2** to stick a stamp on a letter **3** to print letters, numbers or a design on something: *Each letter is stamped with the date we receive it.*

Aa
Bb
Cc
Dd
Ee
Ff
Gg
Hh
Ii
Jj
Kk
Ll
Mm
Nn
Oo
Pp
Qq
Rr
Ss
Tt
Uu
Vv
Ww
Xx
Yy
Zz

• **stamp something out** to try to stop something from happening: *a plan to stamp out crime*

NOUN **stamps**

1 a postage stamp: *first-class stamps*

2 the movement or sound of a foot being brought down hard on the ground

3 an object that you put into ink and press onto a surface to print words, numbers, or a design: *a date stamp*

4 a design or mark that you make with this object: *a manufacturer's stamp*

stampede NOUN **stampedes** a sudden wild rush of animals or people: *a buffalo stampede* • *The bell went and there was a stampede for the door.*

VERB **stampedes, stampeding, stampeded** to rush in a stampede

stance NOUN **stances 1** the way someone stands **2** an attitude or set of opinions: *What is the school's stance on homework?*

stand VERB **stands, standing, stood**

1 to be upright on your feet, not sitting or lying: *The horse was standing on three legs.* • *I was so tired I could barely stand.*

2 to get up onto your feet: *The whole class used to stand when a teacher came into the room.* • *Stand up and let me look at you.*

3 to be or stay in a particular position or way: *The train stood outside Waterloo for nearly an hour.* • *The judge ordered that the sentence should stand.* • *Durham stands on the River Wear.*

4 to bear: *I can't stand her brother, Mark.* • *Marie couldn't stand hearing her parents arguing any more.*

• **stand for something** if particular letters stand for particular words, they are short for them: *UN stands for United Nations.*

• **stand in for someone** to do someone else's job for a short time: *Emma will stand in for Mrs. Harris while she is on holiday.*

• **stand out** if someone or something stands out, you notice them immediately: *The blue colour stands out against the white background.*

• **stand up for someone** to defend or support someone when they are being teased or criticized: *My big sister, Fran, always stood up for me.*

• **stand up to someone** to fight back when someone attacks you or says horrible things to you: *You've got to learn to stand up to bullies.*

NOUN **stands 1** something that an object stands on: *a television stand* • *a large mirror on a stand* **2** rows of seats where people sit to watch a game or event: *Spectators were cheering from the stands.* **3** someone's opinion about something: *a tough stand on crime*

standard NOUN **standards 1** a level that you can judge things against: *a school with high standards of behaviour* **2** an official rule for measuring things: *The kilogram is the international standard of weight.*

ADJECTIVE normal or usual: *the standard charge for postage*

▶ **standardize** or **standardise** VERB **standardizes, standardizing, standardized** to make or keep things all the same shape or size as it is more convenient: *We're trying to standardize the filing system.*

standby NOUN something or someone that is available to be used when they are needed

standstill NOUN a complete stop: *Icy roads brought traffic to a standstill.*

stanza NOUN **stanzas** a verse of a poem

> ✦ This is an Italian word which means *stopping place*, because there is a break at the end of each verse where you stop.

staple¹ NOUN **staples** a type of food or product that you use a lot of: *There's a village shop for staples such as milk and butter.*

ADJECTIVE main: *Their staple diet is rice.*

staple² NOUN **staples** a piece of wire that you force through papers to fasten them together: *a box of staples*

VERB **staples, stapling, stapled** to fasten papers together with a staple

▶ **stapler** NOUN **staplers** a small tool for stapling papers together

star NOUN **stars 1** a mass of burning gas in the sky that you can see at night as a point of light **2** a shape with five or six points **3** a famous actor, singer, or performer: *a film star • a pop star* VERB **stars, starring, starred 1** if an actor stars in something, they play one of the main parts in it: *Tom Cruise is to star in the sequel.* **2** if a film or play stars someone, they have one of the main parts in it: *the new film starring Kate Winslet*

starboard ADJECTIVE the starboard side of a ship or aircraft is the right side when you are facing the front. Look up and compare **port**

starch NOUN **starches 1** a white carbohydrate found in foods such as potatoes, pasta and bread **2** a powder used to make clothes stiff

▶ **starchy** ADJECTIVE containing a lot of starch

stardom NOUN being a famous performer: *She shot to stardom after appearing on a TV talent show.*

stare VERB **stares, staring, stared** to look at someone or something for a long time: *Gemma spends her days staring out of the window.* NOUN **stares** a fixed look

starfish NOUN **starfishes** a sea creature with five points or arms

stark ADJECTIVE **starker, starkest 1** plain and bare: *a stark, barren landscape* **2** complete: *The cool indoors was in stark contrast to the heat outside.*

starling NOUN **starlings** a common bird with dark, shiny feathers

starry ADJECTIVE **starrier, starriest** full of stars or shining like stars: *a starry sky • starry eyes*

start VERB **starts, starting, started 1** to begin: *Suddenly, a bird started to sing. • What time did you start working this morning? • Children may start school when they are four.* **2** to start a machine is to make it begin to work: *Start the car and drive off.* **3** to jump because you are surprised: *The thunder made me start.*

NOUN **starts 1** the beginning: *Right from the start, I knew I'd be happy here. • The runners lined up for the start of the race.* **2** a sudden movement or shock: *Her news gave me quite a start.* **3** in a race or chase, the advantage of starting earlier or further forward than others: *We gave Amy a bit of a start as she's the youngest.*

startle VERB **startles, startling, startled** to give someone a shock or surprise: *Oh, you startled me!*

starve VERB **starves, starving, starved 1** to die or suffer because you have not got enough to eat: *If we don't get food aid into the country, these people are going to starve to death.* **2** to starve someone is to not give them enough to eat: *They were accused of starving their prisoners.*

▶ **starvation** NOUN when you are very hungry and have not got enough to eat: *Thousands are dying of starvation.*

▶ **starving** ADJECTIVE *(informal)* very hungry: *What's for supper? I'm starving.*

state NOUN **states**
1 the condition that someone or something is in: *Look at the state of your bedroom! • She's always complaining about the state of our public transport.*
2 a government or a country: *The state should provide for the sick and elderly.*
3 a part of a country that has its own government: *The law differs from state to state in America.*
4 if someone is in a state, they are upset and worried: *There's no point getting in a state about things.*
5 *(science)* the form of a substance, which can be solid, liquid or gas
VERB **states, stating, stated** to say or write something: *The letter clearly states that you must bring some identification with you.*

stately home NOUN **stately homes** a large country house where a noble family lived

statement NOUN **statements 1** something that you say or write: *The police asked me to make a written* *statement of what I saw.* **2** a piece of paper that the bank sends you that shows how much money you have in your account and what you have spent

statesman NOUN **statesmen** an important political leader

static ADJECTIVE not moving or changing: *Temperatures should stay static for the next few days.*

NOUN tiny sparks of electricity caused by rubbing two surfaces together: *You get static when you comb your hair with a plastic comb.*

station NOUN **stations 1** a building where trains, buses or coaches stop to let people get on or off **2** a place where police officers, fire officers or ambulance drivers work: *The police station is at the top of the High Street.* **3** a radio or television station is a company that makes or broadcasts programmes

VERB **stations, stationing, stationed** to station someone somewhere is to put them in a particular place: *They stationed a guard at each door.*

▸ **stationary** ADJECTIVE not moving: *a stationary vehicle*

stationery NOUN paper, pens, crayons, and other things you use to write or draw with

statistics PLURAL NOUN figures and facts about a particular subject: *Statistics show that more babies were born this year than last year.*

▸ **statistical** ADJECTIVE to do with statistics: *All the statistical evidence supports our case.*

▸ **statistically** ADVERB using statistics

statue NOUN **statues** a figure of a person or animal carved out of stone, metal or wood: *a statue of Napoleon*

status NOUN **statuses** someone's position or rank in a society: *She achieved high status in her work.*

staunch ADJECTIVE **stauncher, staunchest** loyal and faithful: *a staunch supporter of the team*

stave NOUN **staves** (*music*) the set of spaced lines that musical notes are written on

VERB **staves, staving, staved**

• **stave something off** to stop something bad from happening: *We had a packet of crisps to stave off our hunger.*

stay VERB **stays, staying, stayed 1** to remain in a place: *I stayed in Padua for three years.* • *Would you like to stay for dinner?* **2** to continue to be in a particular condition: *She tried to stay calm as they waited.*

NOUN **stays** time spent in a place: *The trip includes an overnight stay in Bangkok.*

steady ADJECTIVE **steadier, steadiest** firm and not moving: *This table isn't very steady.*

VERB **steadies, steadying, steadied 1** to steady something is to make it firm: *I took a deep breath to steady my nerves.* **2** to steady is to stop moving or changing: *House prices have begun to steady.*

▸ **steadily** ADVERB at a gradual, steady pace: *Your work is improving steadily.*

steak NOUN **steaks** a thick slice of meat or fish: *a fillet steak* • *two tuna steaks*

steal VERB **steals, stealing, stole, stolen 1** to take something without the owner's permission: *The thieves stole money and jewellery.* • *It's wrong to steal.* **2** to move quietly: *She stole out to the garden.*

stealth NOUN action or movement that is secret or quiet

▸ **stealthy** ADJECTIVE **stealthier, stealthiest** done secretly or quietly: *stealthy footsteps*

steam NOUN **1** the clouds of tiny drops of liquid that rise from boiling water **2** power produced by steam: *Diesel fuel has replaced steam on the railways.*

VERB **steams, steaming, steamed 1** to give off steam: *A kettle was steaming on the stove.* **2** to move by means of steam: *The ship steamed across the bay.* **3** to steam food is to cook it by steam: *steamed vegetables*

• **steam up** to become covered with steam: *My glasses steamed up and I couldn't see a thing.*

Aa
Bb
Cc
Dd
Ee
Ff
Gg
Hh
Ii
Jj
Kk
Ll
Mm
Nn
Oo
Pp
Qq
Rr
Ss
Tt
Uu
Vv
Ww
Xx
Yy
Zz

steam engine NOUN **steam engines** an engine, especially a railway engine, that is driven by steam

steamer NOUN **steamers** a ship that is driven by steam

steamroller NOUN **steamrollers** a type of vehicle that has large, heavy wheels and is used to flatten the surface of newly-made roads. Steamrollers used to be driven by steam

steed NOUN **steeds** an old word for a horse: *The knight mounted his trusty steed.*

steel NOUN a very hard metal that is a mixture of iron and carbon. Steel is used to make tools, vehicles and many other things

VERB **steels, steeling, steeled**
• **steel yourself** to prepare yourself for something unpleasant: *She steeled herself for the test results.* • *He steeled himself to face his father.*

▶ **steely** ADJECTIVE **steelier, steeliest** hard or cold or strong like steel: *a steely gaze*

steep ADJECTIVE **steeper, steepest** a steep hill or slope rises sharply: *It was a steep climb.* • *The path was too steep for me to cycle up.*

steeple NOUN **steeples** a tall tower that comes to a point, sometimes part of a church

steeplechase NOUN **steeplechases** a race for horses or people in which obstacles must be jumped

✦ It is called a **steeplechase** because in the past these races were run across the country from one village to the next, and the church steeple in the next village marked the end of the race.

steer VERB **steers, steering, steered** to steer a vehicle is to control the direction it is going in: *He steered the car through the narrow streets.* • *The captain steered out of the harbour.*

steering wheel NOUN **steering wheels** the wheel inside a vehicle that the driver uses to control the direction it is moving in

stem NOUN **stems 1** the part of a plant from which the leaves and flowers grow **2** the narrow part of various objects, for example of a wine glass

VERB **stems, stemming, stemmed 1** to stem something is to stop it: *He used his scarf to stem the flow of blood.* **2** to stem from something is to come from it or be caused by it: *Her problems with her schoolwork stem from laziness.*

stench NOUN **stenches** a strong bad smell

stencil NOUN **stencils 1** a piece of paper, metal or plastic with pieces cut out of it, which is coloured or painted over to produce a design on a surface **2** a design produced in this way

step NOUN **steps**
1 the action of lifting your foot off the ground and putting in down again in walking, running or dancing: *He took a step forward.*
2 the sound made by someone's foot coming down on the ground when they walk etc: *I'm sure I heard steps outside.*
3 a particular movement of the feet, for example in dancing: *Try to learn these simple steps.*
4 the flat part of a stair that you put your foot on when going up or down: *The postman left the parcel on the front step.*
5 one of a series of actions involved in doing or achieving something: *the first step to becoming an actor* • *I shall take steps to prevent this happening again.*

VERB **steps, stepping, stepped 1** to take a step: *He opened the door and stepped out.* **2** to walk: *Please step this way.*
• **step something up** to increase something: *Brian stepped up his speed and won the race.*

step- PREFIX if a word starts with **step-**, it shows that people are related not by blood but by another marriage. For example, your *stepfather* is a man who is married to your mother but is not your own father

✦ This comes from the Old English word part **stoep**, which originally meant *orphan*.

Aa
Bb
Cc
Dd
Ee
Ff
Gg
Hh
Ii
Jj
Kk
Ll
Mm
Nn
Oo
Pp
Qq
Rr
Ss
Tt
Uu
Vv
Ww
Xx
Yy
Zz

stepfather NOUN **stepfathers** your stepfather is a man who is married to your mother but is not your own father

stepladder NOUN **stepladders** a small ladder that can be folded in and out, with flat steps

stepmother NOUN **stepmothers** your stepmother is a woman who is married to your father but is not your own mother

steppe NOUN **steppes** (*geography*) a dry grassy area of flat land, usually without trees, especially one found in central Europe and Asia

stepping-stone NOUN **stepping-stones** a stone that rises above the surface of water and can be used for crossing over to the other side of a stream or river

stereo ADJECTIVE short for **stereophonic**: *stereo sound*

NOUN **stereos** a radio or a CD player which plays the sound through two speakers

stereophonic ADJECTIVE a stereophonic system uses two speakers so that the listener feels surrounded by sound

sterile ADJECTIVE **1** not able to produce babies, seeds or crops: *sterile land* **2** completely clean and free from germs: *A surgeon's instruments must be sterile.*

▸ **sterility** NOUN being sterile: *the sterility of the soil*

sterilize or **sterilise** VERB **sterilizes, sterilizing, sterilized 1** to sterilize something is to make it completely free from germs, for example by boiling it in water **2** to sterilize a person or animal is to do an operation on them to make them unable to have babies

▸ **sterilization** or **sterilisation** NOUN **1** the treatment of food or surgical instruments in order to destroy germs **2** an operation that is carried out on people or animals so that they cannot have babies

stern¹ NOUN **sterns** the back part of a ship

stern² ADJECTIVE **sterner, sternest 1** looking or sounding angry, serious or unfriendly: *The teacher looked rather stern.* • *a stern voice* **2** harsh or severe: *a stern prison sentence*

▸ **sternly** ADVERB in a stern way: *The teacher spoke sternly to the class.*

stethoscope NOUN **stethoscopes** an instrument used by a doctor to listen to your heartbeat or breathing

stew VERB **stews, stewing, stewed** to stew something is to cook it by boiling it slowly: *First she stewed the apples to make the tart.*

NOUN **stews** a mixture of vegetables, or meat and vegetables, cooked slowly together in liquid in a pan: *beef stew and dumplings*

steward NOUN **stewards 1** a man whose job is to look after passengers on an aircraft or a ship **2** a person who is an official at events such as races and concerts

stewardess NOUN **stewardesses** an old-fashioned word for a woman whose job is to look after passengers on an aircraft or a ship

stick¹ NOUN **sticks 1** a branch or twig from a tree: *We searched for sticks to make a fire.* **2** a long thin piece of wood shaped for a special purpose: *a walking-stick* • *a hockey-stick* • *a drumstick* **3** a long piece of something: *a stick of rhubarb* • *a stick of rock*

stick² VERB **sticks, sticking, stuck**

1 to stick something in or into something is to push it in: *Stop sticking your elbows into me!* • *Stick the knife in your belt.*

2 to stick something is to fix it with something like glue: *Never mind, we can always stick the pieces back together.*

3 to stick is to become fixed and unable to move: *The car stuck in the mud.*

4 to stick to something is to become attached firmly to it: *These seeds stick to your clothes.*

5 to stick to something such as a decision is to keep it: *We've decided to stick to our original plan.*

• **stick out 1** if something sticks out, it pushes out and stays there: *A nail stuck out from the plank.* **2** if someone or something sticks out, you notice them immediately: *Her bright red hair makes her stick out in a crowd.*

• **stick up for someone** to defend

someone: *Maya sticks up for her best friend even when she is wrong.*

sticker NOUN **stickers** a label or sign with a design or message, for sticking on something

stick insect NOUN **stick insects** an insect with a long thin body and legs that look like twigs

sticky ADJECTIVE **stickier, stickiest 1** designed or likely to stick to another surface: *Mend the book with some sticky tape.* • *sticky fingers* **2** difficult: *a sticky situation*

stiff ADJECTIVE **stiffer, stiffest**
1 difficult to bend or move: *stiff cardboard* • *a stiff neck* • *I can't turn the tap on – it's too stiff.*
2 difficult to do: *a stiff test*
3 strong: *a stiff breeze*
4 not relaxed or friendly: *She replied with stiff politeness.*
▶ **stiffen** VERB **stiffens, stiffening, stiffened 1** to stiffen something is to make it stiff: *stiffen cotton with starch* **2** to stiffen is to become stiff: *She suddenly stiffened in fright.*
▶ **stiffly** ADVERB in a stiff way: *Grandad got up stiffly from his chair.* • *'No thank you,' she replied stiffly.*
▶ **stiffness** NOUN being stiff

stifle VERB **stifles, stifling, stifled 1** to be stifled is to be prevented from breathing: *stifled by the fumes* **2** to stifle something is to keep it back: *She stifled a giggle.*
▶ **stifling** ADJECTIVE very hot and stuffy: *stifling heat*

stile NOUN **stiles** a step or a set of steps for climbing over a wall or fence

still ADJECTIVE **stiller, stillest 1** without movement or noise: *Keep still while I brush your hair!* • *The city seems very still in the early morning.* **2** not fizzy: *still lemonade*
ADVERB **1** up to the present time or the time mentioned: *Are you still working for the same company?* • *By Sunday she still hadn't replied to the invitation.* **2** even so, nevertheless: *It's difficult but we must still try.* **3** even: *Still more people were arriving.*

VERB **stills, stilling, stilled** to still something is to make it calm or quiet: *It was time to still the rumours.*
▶ **stillness** NOUN being still: *the stillness of early morning*

still life NOUN **still lifes** (*art*) a painting or drawing of a still object or objects, rather than a living thing

stilts PLURAL NOUN **1** a pair of poles with supports for the feet, on which you can stand and walk about **2** tall poles to support a house built over water

stimulate VERB **stimulates, stimulated, stimulating 1** to stimulate someone is to encourage or excite them: *After seeing the concert, he was stimulated to take up the violin again.* **2** to stimulate something is to make it more active: *changes designed to stimulate growth*
▶ **stimulant** NOUN **stimulants** something, such as a drug or medicine, that makes you feel more active: *Caffeine and nicotine are stimulants.*
▶ **stimulation** NOUN being stimulated: *stimulation of the senses*

stimulus NOUN **stimuli** something that makes a living thing do something: *Light is the stimulus that causes a flower to open.*

sting NOUN **stings 1** the part of some animals and plants, such as the wasp or nettle, which can prick the skin and cause pain or irritation: *Bees usually leave their stings in the wound.* **2** the wound or pain caused by a sting
VERB **stings, stinging, stung 1** if an insect or plant stings you, they prick your skin and put poison into the wound: *The child was badly stung by nettles.* • *Do these insects sting?* **2** if something stings, it is painful: *The salt water made his eyes sting.*

stingy (pronounced **stin**-ji) ADJECTIVE **stingier, stingiest** mean, not generous: *A very stingy person is sometimes called a Scrooge.*

stink NOUN **stinks** a bad smell: *the stink of rotting fish*
VERB **stinks, stinking, stank** or **stunk,**

Aa
Bb
Cc
Dd
Ee
Ff
Gg
Hh
Ii
Jj
Kk
Ll
Mm
Nn
Oo
Pp
Qq
Rr
Ss
Tt
Uu
Vv
Ww
Xx
Yy
Zz

stunk to have a bad smell: *The house stinks of cats.*

stir VERB **stirs, stirring, stirred 1** to stir something is to mix it with a circular movement: *He put sugar in his tea and stirred it.* **2** to stir is to move: *The baby stirred in its sleep.* • *The breeze stirred her hair.*

• **stir something up** to cause something: *You're always trying to stir up trouble.*

NOUN **stirs 1** an act of stirring: *Now give the paint a stir.* **2** a fuss: *Their arrival caused quite a stir.*

stirrup NOUN **stirrups** a metal loop hanging from a horse's saddle, that you put your foot in when riding

stitch NOUN **stitches 1** the loop you make in thread or wool, using a needle, when you are sewing or knitting: *She sewed the hem with small neat stitches.* **2** a sharp pain in your side, especially when you are running: *He was out of breath and had a stitch.*

VERB **stitches, stitching, stitched** to sew: *I stitched the button on to my coat.*

stoat NOUN **stoats** a small fierce animal similar to a weasel

stock NOUN **stocks**

1 a store of goods, for example in a shop or warehouse: *Buy now while stocks last!*

2 the animals of a farm: *The farmer goes to market to buy more stock.*

3 stocks are shares in companies that people can buy through a stock exchange

4 liquid in which meat or vegetables have been cooked, used for example for making soup: *chicken stock*

5 a type of sweet-smelling garden flower

6 a person's stock is their family origins: *of peasant stock*

VERB **stocks, stocking, stocked 1** to stock something is to keep a supply of it for sale: *Most supermarkets now stock organic products.* **2** to stock a place with something is to fill it or supply it with something: *Dad stocked the fridge with plenty of drinks.*

stock car NOUN **stock cars** a car that has been strengthened to take part in a type of racing where cars deliberately collide with each other

stocking NOUN **stockings** a close-fitting covering for the leg and foot, worn by women

stockpile NOUN **stockpiles** a large store of something: *She keeps a stockpile of flour in her cupboard.*

stocky ADJECTIVE **stockier, stockiest** a stocky person is short and strongly built

stodgy ADJECTIVE **stodgier, stodgiest**
1 stodgy food is heavy and filling: *The rice pudding was stodgy and tasteless.*
2 a stodgy book or person is dull and boring

stoke VERB **stokes, stoking, stoked** to stoke a fire is to put coal, wood or other fuel on it

stole[1] VERB a way of changing the verb **steal** to make a past tense: *How can you be sure that she stole the money?*

stole[2] NOUN **stoles** a length of material, such as fur or silk, worn by women around their shoulders

stomach NOUN **stomachs 1** the bag-like part inside the body where food goes when it is swallowed, and where it is digested **2** courage: *I don't have the stomach for dangerous sports.*

VERB **stomachs, stomaching, stomached** to bear or put up with: *I can't stomach TV programmes that show real operations.*

stomp VERB **stomps, stomping, stomped** to walk heavily and noisily: *He stomped off to his room in a temper.*

stone NOUN **stones** or **stone**

1 stone is the hard material that rocks are made of: *a house built of stone*

2 a stone is a piece of this: *The boys were throwing stones into the water.*

3 a piece of this shaped for a special purpose, for example a tombstone or paving stones

4 a gem or jewel: *diamonds, rubies and other stones*

5 the hard shell around the seed in some fruits, for example peaches and cherries

6 a measure of weight equal to 14 pounds or 6.35 kilograms: *My dad weighs twelve stone.*

VERB **stones, stoning, stoned 1** to stone someone is to throw stones at them **2** to stone fruit is to take the stones out of it

ADJECTIVE made of stone: *stone tools*

▸ **stony** ADJECTIVE **stonier, stoniest 1** hard like stone **2** full of, or covered with, stones: *a stony beach* **3** hard and cold in manner: *a stony stare*

✦ The plural of **stone** is **stones**, except when it means a measure of weight. Then you use the plural **stone**.

stood VERB a way of changing the verb **stand** to make a past tense. It can be used with or without a helping verb: *She stood quietly in the corner.* • *He had stood there all day.*

stool NOUN **stools** a seat without a back

stoop VERB **stoops, stooping, stooped 1** to bend your body forward and downward: *The doorway was so low that she had to stoop to get through it.* **2** to stoop to doing something is to be wicked or bad enough to do it: *Surely he wouldn't stoop to stealing.*

stop VERB **stops, stopping, stopped**

1 to stop is to come to a halt or come to an end: *The car stopped in front of our house.* • *The rain stopped.*

2 to stop something is to bring it to a halt or bring it to an end: *Stop the car now!* • *Please stop this nonsense.*

3 to stop doing something is to finish doing it or not do it any longer: *We stopped talking and listened.*

4 to stop someone doing something is to prevent them from doing it: *Can't you stop her working so hard?*

5 to stop something or stop something up is to block it or close it up: *He stopped his ears with his hands.* • *Stop up the hole with newspaper.*

NOUN **stops 1** the act of stopping: *We made two stops on our journey.* **2** a place where something, such as a bus,

stops **3** a full stop: *All sentences should end with a stop.*

▸ **stoppage** NOUN **stoppages 1** a stopping by workers, a strike: *The company lost millions because of the month-long stoppage.* **2** a blockage in a narrow part of something

▸ **stopper** NOUN **stoppers** something, such as a cork, that is put into the neck of a bottle or jar to close it

stopwatch NOUN **stopwatches** a watch that can be stopped and started, used for timing races

storage NOUN the storing of something: *Our furniture has gone into storage.*

store NOUN **stores 1** a supply of goods from which things are taken as they are needed: *Squirrels keep a store of food.* **2** a place where things are kept: *a store for books* **3** a shop: *the village store* • *a department store*

VERB **stores, storing, stored** to store something is to keep it somewhere for use in the future: *Store the wine in a cool dry place.*

storey NOUN **storeys** one of the floors or levels in a building: *a house with two storeys*

stork NOUN **storks** a wading bird with a long bill, neck and legs

storm NOUN **storms 1** a sudden burst of bad weather with strong winds, rain or snow, and sometimes thunder and lightning **2** a violent outburst: *a storm of protests* • *a storm of applause*

VERB **storms, storming, stormed**

1 to storm is to shout or move in an angry way: *She stormed out of the room.* • *'How dare you!' he stormed.* **2** to storm a place is to attack it suddenly and violently in order to capture it: *Troops stormed the embassy.*

▸ **stormy** ADJECTIVE **stormier, stormiest 1** stormy weather is weather with strong winds, rain or snow, and sometimes thunder and lightning **2** full of anger: *a stormy meeting* • *a stormy relationship*

story NOUN **stories** a description of an event or events, which can be real or invented

Aa
Bb
Cc
Dd
Ee
Ff
Gg
Hh
Ii
Jj
Kk
Ll
Mm
Nn
Oo
Pp
Qq
Rr
Ss
Tt
Uu
Vv
Ww
Xx
Yy
Zz

Aa
Bb
Cc
Dd
Ee
Ff
Gg
Hh
Ii
Jj
Kk
Ll
Mm
Nn
Oo
Pp
Qq
Rr
Ss
Tt
Uu
Vv
Ww
Xx
Yy
Zz

stout ADJECTIVE **stouter, stoutest 1** fat: *a rather stout middle-aged man* **2** brave: *stout resistance* **3** thick and strong: *stout walking-boots*

▶ **stoutly** ADVERB in a stout way

▶ **stoutness** NOUN being stout

stove NOUN **stoves** a device for cooking or for heating a room: *a gas stove*

stow VERB **stows, stowing, stowed** to stow something is to pack it or put it away: *The sailor stowed his belongings in his locker.*

• **stow away** to hide yourself on a vehicle, such as a ship or aeroplane, before its departure so that you can travel without paying

stowaway NOUN **stowaways** a person who hides on a ship or aircraft so that they can travel without paying the fare

straddle VERB **straddles, straddling, straddled** to straddle something is to stand or sit with one leg on each side of it: *Dad turned the chair round and straddled it.*

straggle VERB **straggles, straggling, straggled** to walk too slowly to keep up with others: *Some of the younger children were straggling behind.*

▶ **straggler** NOUN **stragglers** a person who walks too slowly and gets left behind the main group: *Let's stop for a minute and let the stragglers catch up.*

▶ **straggly** ADJECTIVE **stragglier, straggliest** growing untidily: *straggly hair*

straight ADJECTIVE **straighter, straightest**

1 not bent, curved or curly: *a straight line* • *straight hair*

2 honest: *Give me a straight answer!*

3 in the proper position, not crooked: *That picture isn't straight.*

4 tidy, sorted out: *I'll never get this room straight* • *Now let's get the facts straight!*

5 not smiling or laughing: *You should keep a straight face when you tell a joke.*

ADVERB **1** in a straight line, without changing direction: *Turn right, then go straight on.* **2** at once, without any delay: *I came straight here.* **3** honestly: *You're not playing straight.*

• **straight away** immediately: *Could you sign this for me straight away?*

▶ **straighten** VERB **straightens, straightening, straightened** to become or make something straight: *The road curved then straightened.* • *He straightened his tie.*

straightforward ADJECTIVE **1** simple: *a straightforward task* **2** honest: *a nice straightforward boy*

strain VERB **strains, straining, strained**

1 to strain a muscle or other part of the body is to injure it through too much use: *You'll strain your eyes reading in the dark.*

2 to strain to do something is to make a great effort to do it: *He strained to reach the rope.*

3 to strain something is to stretch it or pull it or push it too far: *Your constant demands are straining my patience.*

4 to strain a mixture is to separate the liquid from it by passing it through a sieve: *Now strain the water off the vegetables.*

NOUN **strains 1** an injury to a muscle or other part of the body caused by straining it: *eye-strain* **2** the bad effects on the mind and body of too much work and worry: *suffering from strain* **3** too great a demand on something: *You children are a strain on my patience!*

▶ **strainer** NOUN **strainers** a sieve for separating liquids from solids: *a tea-strainer*

strait NOUN **straits** (*geography*) a narrow strip of sea between two pieces of land: *the Straits of Gibraltar*

strand NOUN **strands** a length of something soft and fine, for example hair or thread

stranded ADJECTIVE **1** a ship is stranded if it is stuck on sand or rocks **2** a person is stranded if they are left helpless: *She was left stranded without money or passport.*

strange ADJECTIVE **stranger, strangest** **1** unusual or odd: *a strange noise coming from the engine* **2** not familiar, not known or seen before: *a strange land*

▶ **strangely** ADVERB in a strange way: *Mum looked at me strangely.*

▶ **strangeness** NOUN being strange: *the strangeness of the situation*

stranger NOUN **strangers 1** a person you do not know: *Children should never talk to strangers.* **2** a person who is in a place they do not know: *I'm afraid I don't know where the station is. I'm a stranger here myself.*

strangle VERB **strangles, strangling, strangled** to strangle someone is to kill them by squeezing their throat tightly: *The victim had been strangled with a scarf.*

strap NOUN **straps** a long narrow piece of leather or cloth used to hold things, fasten things or hang things on: *a watch-strap* • *a bag with a shoulder strap*

VERB **straps, strapping, strapped** to strap something is to fasten it with a strap: *I usually strap my bag to my bike.*

strategy NOUN **strategies** a plan that is designed to achieve something

stratum NOUN **strata** (*geography*) a layer of rock in the Earth's crust

straw NOUN **straws 1** straw is dried stalks of grain: *The cows need fresh straw.* **2** a straw is a thin tube, usually made of plastic, for sucking up a drink

strawberry NOUN **strawberries** a soft red fruit with many tiny seeds on its skin

stray VERB **strays, straying, strayed** to wander or get lost: *Be careful not to stray from the path.* • *The farmer was searching for some sheep that had strayed.*

ADJECTIVE **1** wandering or lost: *stray dogs* **2** happening here and there, scattered: *The sky was clear except for a few stray clouds.*

NOUN **strays** a cat or dog that has no home

streak NOUN **streaks 1** a long thin line or mark: *hair with blonde streaks* • *dirty streaks on the window* • *a streak of lightning* **2** a trace of something that can be seen in a person: *He has a cowardly streak.*

VERB **streaks, streaking, streaked 1** to streak something is to mark it with streaks: *tears streaking her face* **2** to streak is to move very fast: *The runner streaked round the racetrack.*

▶ **streaked** ADJECTIVE having streaks: *a beard streaked with grey*

▶ **streaky** ADJECTIVE **streakier, streakiest** marked with streaks: *Her face was all streaky with crying.*

stream NOUN **streams 1** a small river: *He managed to jump across the stream.* **2** a flow of something: *streams of people* • *a stream of traffic*

VERB **streams, streaming, streamed** to flow: *Tears streamed down her face* • *The workers streamed out of the factory gates.*

▶ **streamer** NOUN **streamers** a long narrow strip of paper or ribbon, used as a decoration

streamline VERB **streamlines, streamlining, streamlined 1** to streamline something, such as a vehicle, is to shape it in such a way that it will cut through air or water as easily as possible **2** to streamline something is also to make it more efficient, especially by making it simpler: *The company streamlined its production methods.*

street NOUN **streets** a road with buildings, such as houses and shops, on one or both sides: *I live at 32 Montgomery Street.* • *the main shopping street*

strength NOUN **strengths 1** strength is being strong: *He didn't have the strength to lift the box.* **2** a person's strengths are the good things about them: *Her greatest strength is her sense of humour.*

▶ **strengthen** VERB **strengthens, strengthening, strengthened 1** to strengthen something is to make it strong or stronger: *He did exercises to strengthen his muscles.* **2** to strengthen is to become strong or stronger: *The wind strengthened.*

strenuous ADJECTIVE needing or using a lot of effort or energy: *Squash is a strenuous game.* • *The plans met strenuous resistance.*

Aa
Bb
Cc
Dd
Ee
Ff
Gg
Hh
Ii
Jj
Kk
Ll
Mm
Nn
Oo
Pp
Qq
Rr
Ss
Tt
Uu
Vv
Ww
Xx
Yy
Zz

Aa
Bb
Cc
Dd
Ee
Ff
Gg
Hh
Ii
Jj
Kk
Ll
Mm
Nn
Oo
Pp
Qq
Rr
Ss
Tt
Uu
Vv
Ww
Xx
Yy
Zz

stress NOUN **stresses**
1 a physical force that may bend or break something: *metal that bends under stress*
2 the effect on the mind or body of working or worrying too much: *headaches caused by stress*
3 special importance that is attached to something: *The General laid particular stress on the need for secrecy.*
4 extra weight that is put on a part of a word: *In the word 'bedroom' the stress is on 'bed'.*
VERB **stresses, stressing, stressed**
1 to stress someone is to make them suffer stress: *Many of the pressures of everyday life can stress us.* **2** to stress something is to place special importance on it: *Her speech stressed the need for change.* **3** to stress part of a word is to place extra weight on it: *When 'object' is a noun you stress the 'ob'.*

stretch VERB **stretches, stretching, stretched 1** to stretch something is to make it longer or wider, especially by pulling: *Stretch this rope between the two posts.* **2** to stretch is to become longer or wider: *This material stretches.* **3** to stretch from one place to another is to cover the distance between them: *The mountains stretch from the north to the south of the country.*
NOUN **stretches 1** the action of stretching: *I always have a good stretch when I get out of bed.* **2** a length in distance or time: *a dangerous stretch of road • a three-year stretch*
▶ **stretchy** ADJECTIVE **stretchier, stretchiest** able to stretch easily: *jeans made of stretchy denim*

stretcher NOUN **stretchers** a light folding bed with handles for carrying a sick or wounded person

strew VERB **strews, strewing, strewed, strewn** to scatter untidily: *The ground was strewn with rubbish.*

strict ADJECTIVE **stricter, strictest 1** someone who is strict expects other people to obey rules: *This class needs a strict teacher.* **2** something that is strict is meant to be obeyed: *strict school*

rules • *under strict orders* **3** exact: *the strict sense of the word*

stride VERB **strides, striding, strode, stridden** to walk with long steps: *He strode up the path.*
NOUN **strides** a long step: *He crossed the road in three strides.*
• **get into your stride** to get the hang of something
• **take something in your stride** to manage to do something easily: *Her parents were worried about her changing school but she took it all in her stride.*

strife NOUN fighting or quarrelling: *There was a lot of strife within the political party.*

strike VERB **strikes, striking, struck**
1 to strike someone or something is to hit them or it: *He struck me in the face with his fist.* • *My head struck the table.*
2 to strike is to attack: *The enemy troops struck at dawn.*
3 to strike a match is to light it
4 when a clock strikes it makes a noise to show the time: *The clock struck three.*
5 something strikes you when it suddenly comes into your mind or when it impresses you: *It suddenly struck me that I was completely wrong.* • *He was struck by her beauty.*
6 workers strike when they stop work as a protest against something or in an attempt to get something: *The men were striking for higher wages.*
7 to strike oil or gold is to discover it
NOUN **strikes 1** the stopping of work as a protest or in an attempt to get something: *The strike lasted for ten days.* **2** a sudden attack, especially a military one: *repeated air strikes* **3** a discovery of oil or gold
▶ **striker** NOUN **strikers 1** a worker who is striking **2** in football, a player whose job is to try to score goals
▶ **striking** ADJECTIVE if you find something striking, you notice it or are impressed by it: *a striking resemblance • striking beauty*

string NOUN **strings 1** thick thread used for tying things: *a ball of string* **2** the strings of a musical instrument, such as a guitar, are the pieces of wire or other material that are stretched across it **3** a string of things is a number of things coming one after the other: *a string of disasters*

VERB **strings, stringing, strung 1** to string something is to tie it and hang it with string: *Coloured lights were strung across the ceiling.* **2** to string something such as beads is to put them on a string: *She took the pearls to a jeweller to be strung.* **3** to string a musical instrument is to put strings on it

▸ **stringy** ADJECTIVE **stringier, stringiest 1** something that is stringy is long and thin and looks like string: *stringy hair* **2** meat that is stringy is full of tough chewy bits

strip[1] NOUN **strips 1** a long narrow piece: *a strip of paper* **2** an outfit worn by a sports team: *a red football strip*

strip[2] VERB **strips, stripping, stripped 1** to strip something is to take the covering off it: *My mum always strips the beds on Mondays.* **2** to strip is to undress: *He stripped and dived into the water.* • *She stripped the baby for its bath.* **3** to strip someone of something is to take it away from them as a punishment: *The officer was stripped of his rank.*

stripe NOUN **stripes** a band of colour: *a blue suit with thin white stripes*

▸ **striped** ADJECTIVE having stripes: *striped wallpaper*

▸ **stripy** ADJECTIVE **stripier, stripiest** having stripes: *a stripy T-shirt*

strive VERB **strives, striving, strove, striven** to try very hard: *He strives to please his teacher.*

strobe NOUN **strobes** a light that flashes rapidly

strode VERB a way of changing the verb **stride** to make a past tense: *He strode up the hill.*

stroke NOUN **strokes**

1 a stroke is a movement or hit made by swinging your arm or arms while holding an oar, a golf club, a tennis racket or a long-handled weapon: *He felled the tree with one stroke of the axe.*

2 a stroke in swimming is one of the ways that you can move your arms and legs to travel through the water: *breast stroke*

3 a stroke is the sound made by a clock when it strikes the hour: *We arrived on the stroke of midnight.*

4 a stroke is also a sudden illness in the brain that can leave a person unable to move or speak

VERB **strokes, stroking, stroked** to stroke someone or something is to rub them gently: *She was stroking the cat.*

stroll VERB **strolls, strolling, strolled** to walk slowly in a relaxed way

NOUN **strolls** a slow, gentle walk

strong ADJECTIVE **stronger, strongest 1** powerful, not weak: *a strong young man* • *a strong wind* • *a strong smell* **2** not easily worn away or broken: *strong cloth* • *fastened with a strong chain* **3** in number: *a workforce 500 strong*

▸ **strongly** ADVERB **1** in a strong way: *The boxer fought back strongly.* **2** very much: *I strongly recommend that you follow the instructions.*

struck VERB a way of changing the verb **strike** to make a past tense. It can be used with or without a helping verb: *Her head struck the wall.* • *Lightning has struck the building.*

structure NOUN **structures 1** the way that the parts of something are arranged: *the structure of the story* **2** something that is built or constructed: *The bridge was a massive steel structure.*

▸ **structural** ADJECTIVE to do with the structure of something: *The fire caused structural damage to the house.*

struggle VERB **struggles, struggling, struggled 1** to turn and twist your body and try to escape: *The child struggled in his arms.* **2** to struggle to do something is to try hard to do it: *She is struggling to finish her homework.* **3** to fight against difficulty: *All his life he has struggled against poverty.* • *struggling through the mud* NOUN **struggles** a fight: *They got their money back after a long struggle.*

Aa
Bb
Cc
Dd
Ee
Ff
Gg
Hh
Ii
Jj
Kk
Ll
Mm
Nn
Oo
Pp
Qq
Rr
Ss
Tt
Uu
Vv
Ww
Xx
Yy
Zz

Aa
Bb
Cc
Dd
Ee
Ff
Gg
Hh
Ii
Jj
Kk
Ll
Mm
Nn
Oo
Pp
Qq
Rr
Ss
Tt
Uu
Vv
Ww
Xx
Yy
Zz

strum VERB **strums, strumming, strummed** to play a musical instrument, such as the guitar, by sweeping movements of the fingers: *He strummed a tune.* • *She was strumming away happily.*

strut VERB **struts, strutting, strutted** to walk in a stiff, proud way: *The cock strutted round the farmyard.*

NOUN **struts 1** a proud way of walking **2** a bar made of wood or metal which supports something

stub NOUN **stubs** a short piece of something, such as a cigarette or pencil, which is left over when the rest has been used up: *The ashtray was overflowing with cigarette stubs.*

VERB **stubs, stubbing, stubbed** to stub your toe is to knock it painfully against something hard

• **stub something out** to stub out a cigarette is to put it out by pressing it against something

stubble NOUN **1** the short stalks of corn left standing in the fields after the crop has been harvested **2** short coarse hairs growing on a man's face when he has not shaved

stubborn ADJECTIVE a stubborn person refuses to do what other people tell them to do, or to follow advice: *a silly, stubborn child*

▸ **stubbornly** ADVERB in a stubborn way: *She stubbornly refused to listen to my advice.*

▸ **stubbornness** NOUN being determined not to do what other people say

stuck VERB a way of changing the verb **stick** to make a past tense. It can be used with or without a helping verb: *He stuck the stamp on the envelope.* • *I've stuck the broken vase together again.*

stud NOUN **studs** a piece of metal with a large head, used as a fastener or decoration on clothes or on the soles of boots or shoes: *jeans with copper studs* • *I need new studs for my football boots.*

student NOUN **students** someone who is studying, especially at a college or university

studio NOUN **studios 1** the room that an artist or photographer works in **2** a place where films are made **3** a room from which radio or television programmes are broadcast

studious ADJECTIVE a studious person spends a lot of time studying: *Sue is a very studious girl.*

study VERB **studies, studying, studied 1** to study is to spend time learning about a subject: *I'm studying French language.* • *She's studying to be a teacher.* **2** to study something is to look at it carefully: *He studied the railway timetable.* • *We must study the problem in detail.*

NOUN **studies 1** study is reading and learning about something: *the study of history* **2** a study is a room used for studying or quiet work

stuff NOUN **1** a substance or material of any kind: *What's that black oily stuff on the beach?* **2** things or objects: *There's far too much stuff in this cupboard.*

VERB **stuffs, stuffing, stuffed 1** to stuff something is to pack it or fill it tightly: *She used feathers to stuff the cushions.* • *We need to stuff the turkey before we cook it.* **2** to stuff something into a place is to push it in carelessly: *He stuffed the papers into his pocket.*

▸ **stuffing** NOUN **stuffings 1** material used for stuffing things such as cushions or soft toys **2** a savoury mixture used to stuff meat such as turkeys and chickens before cooking: *sage and onion stuffing*

stuffy ADJECTIVE **stuffier, stuffiest 1** a place that is stuffy lacks fresh air: *How can you sit in this stuffy office all day?* **2** a person who is stuffy is dull and old-fashioned

stumble VERB **stumbles, stumbling, stumbled 1** to trip and nearly fall: *Granny stumbled over the edge of the carpet.* **2** to walk with difficulty, nearly falling over: *He stumbled along the track in the dark.* **3** to make mistakes or hesitate: *She stumbled over the difficult words when reading to the class.*

• **stumble across something** or **stumble on something** to find something by chance: *I stumbled across this book today.*

stump NOUN **stumps 1** the part of something, such as a tree, limb or tooth, that is left after the main part has been taken away **2** in cricket, one of the three wooden sticks that make up a wicket
VERB **stumps, stumping, stumped 1** to stump the person batting in cricket is to put them out by touching the stumps with the ball **2** if something stumps you, it is too hard for you: *Those exam questions stumped us all.*

stun VERB **stuns, stunning, stunned 1** to stun someone is to make them unconscious, usually by a blow on the head: *The punch stunned him.* **2** to stun someone is also to surprise or shock them greatly: *We were all stunned by the news of the accident.*

stung VERB a way of changing the verb **sting** to make a past tense. It can be used with or without a helping verb: *The wasp stung him on the finger.* • *Ouch! It's stung me.*

stunk VERB a way of changing the verb **stink** to make a past tense. It can be used with or without a helping verb: *The room stunk of cigar smoke.* • *If the dead mouse hadn't stunk so much, I'd never have found it.*

stunt¹ NOUN **stunts** something daring or unusual that is done to attract attention: *He's always doing stunts on his motorbike.* • *The whole event was a big publicity stunt.*

stunt² VERB **stunts, stunting, stunted** to stunt something is to stop its growth or development: *Lack of water stunted the plants.*
▶ **stunted** ADJECTIVE small and badly shaped: *trees with stunted branches*

stupendous ADJECTIVE wonderful, amazing: *a stupendous achievement*

stupid ADJECTIVE **stupider, stupidest** not clever, slow at understanding: *a stupid mistake* • *You stupid boy!*
▶ **stupidity** NOUN being stupid: *His stupidity cost us first prize.*
▶ **stupidly** ADVERB in a stupid way: *Stupidly, I agreed to do it.*

sturdy ADJECTIVE **sturdier, sturdiest** strong, well built: *a sturdy body* • *sturdy furniture*

stutter VERB **stutters, stuttering, stuttered** to keep repeating parts of words, especially the first part
NOUN **stutters** a speech problem that makes you repeat parts of words: *That child has a bad stutter.*

sty¹ NOUN **sties** a place where pigs are kept

sty² or **stye** NOUN **sties** or **styes** a painful swelling on the eyelid

style NOUN **styles 1** a way of doing something such as writing, acting or speaking: *I like the style of her writing.* **2** a style is a fashion: *a new style of shoe* **3** style is being elegant: *She's got style.*
VERB **styles, styling, styled** to style something such as hair or clothes is to give them a certain style: *I'm having my hair cut and styled.* • *clothes styled for comfort*
▶ **stylish** ADJECTIVE smart, elegant, fashionable: *stylish clothes*

sub- PREFIX if a word starts with **sub-**, it has the meaning of *below* or *under*. For example, a *submarine* is a type of ship that is able to travel under water

subconscious NOUN the part of your mind of which you yourself are not aware but which makes you feel certain things and act in certain ways
ADJECTIVE which exist in the subconscious: *subconscious fears*
▶ **subconsciously** ADVERB in a subconscious way: *Subconsciously she wanted to be famous.*

subdue VERB **subdues, subduing, subdued** to subdue someone is to overpower them or bring them under control: *After months of fighting the rebels were subdued.*
▶ **subdued** ADJECTIVE quiet, in low spirits: *subdued voices* • *You seem very subdued today.*

subheading NOUN **subheadings** a heading that is less important than the main heading in a piece of writing

subject NOUN **subjects** (pronounced **sub**-jikt)
1 something that you learn about, for

Aa Bb Cc Dd Ee Ff Gg Hh Ii Jj Kk Ll Mm Nn Oo Pp Qq Rr Ss Tt Uu Vv Ww Xx Yy Zz

Aa
Bb
Cc
Dd
Ee
Ff
Gg
Hh
Ii
Jj
Kk
Ll
Mm
Nn
Oo
Pp
Qq
Rr
Ss
Tt
Uu
Vv
Ww
Xx
Yy
Zz

example science or mathematics: *My favourite subject at school is French.* **2** the subject of something such as a story or conversation is the person or thing that it is about: *Can we change the subject, please?* **3** (*grammar*) the subject of a sentence is the word or words that stand for the person or thing doing the action of the verb, for example *He* in *He hit me* **4** a person who is under the power of someone or something else: *the king's subjects*
VERB **subjects, subjecting, subjected** (pronounced sub-**jekt**) to subject someone to something is to make them suffer it: *He was subjected to cruel treatment.*

subjective ADJECTIVE resulting from your own thoughts and feelings: *a subjective opinion*

submarine NOUN **submarines** a ship that can travel under water

submerge VERB **submerges, submerging, submerged 1** to submerge something is to cover it with water: *Entire villages had been submerged.* **2** to submerge is to go under water: *I watched the whale submerge.*

▸ **submersion** NOUN submerging or being submerged

submission NOUN **submissions 1** submission is the action of submitting: *forced into submission* **2** a submission is something such as an idea or plan that is offered to someone to be considered by them

submissive ADJECTIVE willing to obey: *a submissive servant*

submit VERB **submits, submitting, submitted 1** to submit is to give in: *The rebels were ordered to submit.* • *I refuse to submit to his control.* **2** to submit something such as a plan or idea is to offer it to someone to be considered by them: *All competition entries must be submitted by Friday.*

subordinate ADJECTIVE lower in rank or less important: *his subordinate officers*
NOUN **subordinates** someone who is

lower in rank or less important than someone else: *She always tries to help her subordinates.*

subordinate clause NOUN **subordinate clauses** (*grammar*) a clause that cannot stand on its own as a sentence, for example *that I got for my birthday* in the sentence *The book that I got for my birthday was boring*

subscribe VERB **subscribes, subscribing, subscribed 1** to subscribe to a charity or other cause is to give money to it: *We each subscribed £5 towards the cost of the clock.* **2** to subscribe to something, such as a magazine or TV channel, is to pay money so that you receive it

▸ **subscriber** NOUN **subscribers** someone who subscribes to something

▸ **subscription** NOUN **subscriptions** money you pay to subscribe to something

subsequent ADJECTIVE following or coming after something else: *The story tells of the soldier's capture and subsequent escape.*

▸ **subsequently** ADVERB later: *She ate the shellfish and subsequently became ill.*

subside VERB **subsides, subsiding, subsided 1** if land or a building subsides, it starts to move downwards: *When buildings subside, cracks usually appear in the walls.* **2** to become less or quieter: *Let's stay here until the wind subsides.*

▸ **subsidence** NOUN sinking down, especially into the ground

subsidize or **subsidise** VERB **subsidizes, subsidizing, subsidized 1** to subsidize someone or something is to give them money as a help: *The government subsidizes the mining industry.* **2** to subsidize something is to pay part of the cost so that the customer pays less: *The company subsidizes meals in its canteen.*

subsidy NOUN **subsidies** money given to help someone or something or to keep prices low

substance NOUN **substances 1** a substance is a material that you can touch and see: *Glue is a sticky substance.* **2** the substance of something is its general meaning: *The substance of her argument was that women were more intelligent than men.*

substantial ADJECTIVE **1** solid and strong: *a substantial table* **2** large: *a substantial sum of money*

▸ **substantially** ADVERB **1** a lot: *Profits have increased substantially.* **2** mostly: *These two items are substantially the same.*

substitute VERB **substitutes, substituting, substituted** to substitute something for something else is to use it instead of something else: *I substituted your name for mine on the list.*

NOUN **substitutes** a person or thing used instead of another: *Use lemons as a substitute for limes.*

▸ **substitution** NOUN **substitutions** substituting something or someone else, or being substituted

subtitle NOUN **subtitles 1** a second title of something such as a book or film **2** a translation of a film that is in a foreign language, appearing at the bottom of the screen: *a French film with English subtitles*

subtle (pronounced **sut**-il) ADJECTIVE **subtler, subtlest** slight, difficult to describe or explain: *There is a subtle difference between these two shades of blue.*

▸ **subtlety** NOUN **subtleties** being subtle: *the subtlety of the colours in the painting*

subtract VERB **subtracts, subtracting, subtracted** (*maths*) to take one number away from another: *If you subtract 4 from 6, you get 2.* • *Most children learn to add and subtract in their first year at school.*

▸ **subtraction** NOUN **subtractions** (*maths*) the act of taking one number away from another: *First we learned addition, then we learned subtraction.*

suburb NOUN **suburbs** an area of houses at the edge of a town or city: *They decided to move out to the suburbs.*

▸ **suburban** ADJECTIVE of suburbs: *suburban housing*

succeed VERB **succeeds, succeeding, succeeded 1** to succeed is to manage to do what you have been trying to do: *If you try hard, I'm sure you'll succeed.* • *She succeeded in getting the job.* **2** to succeed someone is to take their place: *He succeeded his father as manager of the company.*

success NOUN **successes 1** success is managing to do something you have been trying to do: *Have you had any success in finding a job?* **2** a success is someone who does well or something that turns out well: *She's a great success as a teacher.* • *The party was a great success.*

▸ **successful** ADJECTIVE **1** a successful person has managed to do something, or has done very well in a particular way: *Were you successful in passing the test?* • *a successful artist* **2** a successful event is one that goes well: *We had a successful meeting with the headmaster.*

▸ **successfully** ADVERB in a successful way

succession NOUN **successions 1** the right to succeed to a throne or title: *He is third in succession to the throne.* **2** a number of things coming one after the other: *a succession of failures*

▸ **successive** ADJECTIVE following one after the other: *The team won three successive matches.*

▸ **successively** ADVERB one after the other

successor NOUN **successor** a person that follows, and takes the place of, another: *Who will be appointed as the headteacher's successor?*

succulent ADJECTIVE juicy and delicious: *succulent peaches*

succumb VERB **succumbs, succumbing, succumbed** to succumb to something is to give in to it: *She succumbed to temptation.*

such ADJECTIVE **1** of a kind already mentioned: *Such things are difficult to find.* **2** of the same kind: *doctors, nurses and such people* **3** so great or so much: *His excitement was such*

Aa
Bb
Cc
Dd
Ee
Ff
Gg
Hh
Ii
Jj
Kk
Ll
Mm
Nn
Oo
Pp
Qq
Rr
Ss
Tt
Uu
Vv
Ww
Xx
Yy
Zz

Aa
Bb
Cc
Dd
Ee
Ff
Gg
Hh
Ii
Jj
Kk
Ll
Mm
Nn
Oo
Pp
Qq
Rr
Ss
Tt
Uu
Vv
Ww
Xx
Yy
Zz

that he shouted out loud. • *It's such a disappointment!*

suck VERB **sucks, sucking, sucked 1** to take something into your mouth by drawing in air: *The baby was sucking milk from its bottle.* • *She was sucking lemonade through a straw.* **2** to hold something in your mouth while making pulling movements with your lips and tongue: *If your throat's sore, try sucking this sweet.*

• **suck something up** or **suck something in** to draw something in: *The vacuum cleaner sucked up the crumbs.* • *She sucked in her cheeks.*

NOUN **sucks** the action of sucking: *She took a suck of her lollipop.*

▸ **sucker** NOUN **suckers 1** a part of an animal's body that it uses to stick to objects **2** a rubber or plastic pad that can be pressed on to a surface and sticks there

suction NOUN (*science*) reducing the air in a place, and so producing a vacuum, which draws in other air or things to fill the space

sudden ADJECTIVE happening quickly without being expected: *a sudden attack*

▸ **suddenly** ADVERB quickly and unexpectedly: *He suddenly woke up.*

▸ **suddenness** NOUN being sudden: *We were shocked by the suddenness of the events.*

sudoku (pronounced soo-**doh**-koo) NOUN a puzzle in which you have to insert numbers from 1 to 9 into different places in a square grid

suds PLURAL NOUN soap bubbles

sue VERB **sues, suing, sued** to sue a person or organization is to start a law case against them, usually to try to get money from them

suede NOUN a kind of leather with a soft, dull surface which feels like velvet
ADJECTIVE made of suede: *a suede jacket*

suet NOUN a kind of hard animal fat used to make pastry and puddings

suffer VERB **suffers, suffering, suffered 1** to feel pain or misery: *She suffered a lot of pain after the accident.*

2 to suffer from an illness or condition is to have it: *She suffers from headaches.*

▸ **suffering** NOUN pain and misery

sufficiency NOUN enough of something: *a sufficiency of food*

▸ **sufficient** ADJECTIVE enough: *We haven't sufficient food for everyone.*

▸ **sufficiently** ADVERB to a sufficient degree: *I have not learned the song sufficiently to sing it in the concert.*

suffix NOUN **suffixes** (*grammar*) a letter or group of letters that is added to the end of a word to make another word. For example, the suffixes *-ly* and *-ness* can be added to the word *kind* to make *kindly* and *kindness*

suffocate VERB **suffocates, suffocating, suffocated 1** to suffocate someone is to kill them through lack of oxygen: *The thick black smoke was suffocating him.* **2** to suffocate is to die through lack of oxygen: *Babies can suffocate if they sleep with a pillow.*

▸ **suffocation** NOUN being killed through lack of oxygen: *The cause of death was suffocation.*

sugar NOUN **1** a sweet substance that is obtained from the plants sugar cane and sugar beet **2** white or brown grains of sugar that you add to food and drink to make them taste sweeter: *Do you take sugar in your coffee?*

▸ **sugary** ADJECTIVE very sweet: *a cup of hot, sugary tea*

suggest VERB **suggests, suggesting, suggested 1** to suggest something is to put it forward as an idea or a possibility: *He suggested a picnic.* • *I suggest that we have lunch now.* **2** to suggest something is to hint at it: *Are you suggesting that I'm too old for the job?*

▸ **suggestion** NOUN **suggestions 1** an idea put forward: *What a clever suggestion!* **2** a suggestion of something is a hint or trace of it: *There was a suggestion of anger in her voice.*

suicide NOUN **suicides** killing yourself: *to commit suicide*

suit NOUN **suits**
1 a set of clothes, for example a

jacket and trousers, made to be worn together: *Our teacher always wears a suit and tie.*
2 a piece of clothing worn for a particular activity: *a bathing-suit*
3 one of the four sets (spades, hearts, diamonds, clubs) of playing-cards
4 a case in a law court: *He won his suit.*
VERB **suits, suiting, suited 1** something such as a colour, hairstyle or piece of clothing suits you when it makes you look nice: *Blue really suits her.*
2 something suits you when you are happy to agree to it: *Would it suit you if I called round this evening?*

suitable ADJECTIVE something is suitable when it is right for a purpose or occasion: *High-heeled shoes aren't suitable for walking in the country.* • *What would be a suitable time for our meeting?*
▸ **suitability** NOUN being right for the purpose or time: *I am not sure of his suitability for the job.*

suitcase NOUN **suitcases** a container with flat sides and a handle, to put your clothes in when you are travelling

suite NOUN **suites** (pronounced **sweet**) **1** a set of rooms: *a hotel suite* **2** a set of furniture: *a three-piece suite* **3** (*music*) a set of short pieces of music to be played one after the other

suitor NOUN **suitors** an old-fashioned word for a man who wants to marry a woman: *The princess had many suitors.*

sulk VERB **sulks, sulking, sulked** to show that you are angry by being silent: *He's sulking because he's not allowed an ice-cream.*
▸ **sulky** ADJECTIVE **sulkier, sulkiest 1** sulking: *She's in a sulky mood.* **2** tending to sulk: *a sulky girl*

sullen ADJECTIVE angry and silent: *a sullen young man*

sulphur NOUN (*science*) a solid yellow substance found in the ground, which burns with a blue flame and an unpleasant smell and is used to make matches and gunpowder

sulphuric acid NOUN (*science*) a strong acid containing sulphur

sultan NOUN **sultans** a ruler in certain Muslim countries: *the Sultan of Brunei*

sultana NOUN **sultanas 1** a light-coloured seedless raisin **2** a sultan's wife

sum NOUN **sums 1** the total made by two or more things or numbers added together: *The sum of 2, 3 and 4 is 9.* **2** a problem in arithmetic: *I'm better at sums than my mum.* **3** an amount of money: *It will cost a huge sum to repair the roof.*
VERB **sums, summing, summed**
• **sum up** to give the main points of something such as a discussion or evidence given in court

summarize or **summarise** VERB **summarizes, summarizing, summarized** to give a shortened version of something: *He summarized the arguments.*

summary NOUN **summaries** a shortened form of something, giving only the main points: *A summary of his speech was printed in the newspaper.*

summer NOUN **summers** the warmest season of the year, between spring and autumn

summit NOUN **summits 1** the top of a hill or mountain **2** a meeting between heads of governments

summon VERB **summons, summoning, summoned** to summon someone is to order them to come: *The headmaster summoned her to his room.*
• **summon up something** to summon up something such as strength or courage is to gather it: *At last I summoned up the courage to tell him.*
▸ **summons** NOUN **summonses** an order to appear in court

sun NOUN **suns 1** the star in the sky that you see as a huge white disc, and which gives light and heat to the Earth: *The Earth goes round the sun.* **2** sunshine: *We sat in the sun.*

sunbathe VERB **sunbathes, sunbathing, sunbathed** to lie or sit in the sun in order to get a suntan

sunbeam NOUN **sunbeams** a ray of light from the sun

sunburn NOUN redness and soreness of

Aa
Bb
Cc
Dd
Ee
Ff
Gg
Hh
Ii
Jj
Kk
Ll
Mm
Nn
Oo
Pp
Qq
Rr
Ss
Tt
Uu
Vv
Ww
Xx
Yy
Zz

the skin caused by being out in the sun for too long

sundae NOUN **sundaes** a portion of ice-cream served with fruit, syrup or cream: *I think I'll have the toffee nut sundae.*

Sunday NOUN **Sundays** the day of the week after Saturday and before Monday: *My parents always go to church on Sundays.*

♦**Sunday** comes from the Old English word **Sunnandaeg**, which means *day of the sun.*

sundial NOUN **sundials** an instrument that uses sunlight to cast a shadow and show the time

sunflower NOUN **sunflowers** a tall yellow flower whose seeds provide oil

sung VERB the form of the verb **sing** that is used with a helping verb to tell you that something happened in the past: *I've sung that song all day.*

sunglasses PLURAL NOUN dark glasses that protect your eyes from bright sunlight

sunk VERB the form of the verb **sink** that is used with a helping verb to tell you that something happened in the past: *The ship had sunk in minutes.*

sunlight NOUN the light of the sun: *Bright sunlight shone in through the window.*

▶ **sunlit** ADJECTIVE lit up by the sun: *a sunlit room*

sunny ADJECTIVE **sunnier, sunniest 1** full of sunshine: *It's a lovely sunny day.* **2** cheerful: *her sunny nature*

sunrise NOUN **sunrises** the rising of the sun in the morning, or the time of this: *a spectacular sunrise • I was up at sunrise.*

sunset NOUN **sunsets** the setting of the sun in the evening, or the time of this: *a beautiful golden sunset • The younger children were in bed by sunset.*

sunshine NOUN the light and heat of the sun: *The cat was enjoying the warm sunshine.*

sunstroke NOUN an illness caused by staying out in hot sun for too long

suntan NOUN **suntans** a brown colour of the skin, caused by the sun

super ADJECTIVE extremely good or excellent: *We had a super time at the funfair.*

super- PREFIX if a word starts with **super-**, it has the meaning of *above* or *beyond*. For example, someone who is *superhuman* has abilities which are beyond those of a normal person

superb ADJECTIVE magnificent or excellent: *The view from our balcony was superb.*

superficial ADJECTIVE **1** affecting the surface only: *The wound is only superficial. • The building suffered superficial damage.* **2** not deep or detailed: *a superficial knowledge of history*

superintendent NOUN **superintendents 1** a senior police officer **2** someone who is in charge of something such as a building or department

superior ADJECTIVE **1** higher in rank, better or greater: *Is a captain superior to a commander in the navy? • With his superior strength, he defeated his opponent.* **2** thinking that you are better than other people: *I can't stand her superior attitude.*

NOUN **superiors** a person who is better than, or has a higher rank than, you: *You should always respect your superiors.*

▶ **superiority** NOUN being superior: *his superiority over others*

superlative NOUN **superlatives** (*grammar*) in grammar, the superlative form of an adjective or adverb is the form that usually ends with *-est* or is used with *most*. For example, *hardest, worst* and *most difficult* are superlative forms

supermarket NOUN **supermarkets** a large self-service shop that sells food and other goods

supernatural ADJECTIVE not natural or normal and impossible to explain: *supernatural happenings*

supersonic ADJECTIVE faster than the speed of sound: *a supersonic aeroplane*

superstition NOUN **superstitions 1** superstition is belief in magic and other strange powers **2** a superstition is an example of this kind of belief: *There is an old superstition that walking under a ladder will bring you bad luck.*
▸ **superstitious** ADJECTIVE a superstitious person believes in superstitions

supervise VERB **supervises, supervising, supervised** to supervise someone or something is to be in charge of them: *Who supervises this department? • His job is to supervise the factory workers.*
▸ **supervision** NOUN the act of supervising: *The prisoner was kept under close supervision.*
▸ **supervisor** NOUN **supervisors** a person whose job is to make sure that other people's work is done properly

supper NOUN **supper** a meal that you eat in the evening

supple ADJECTIVE **suppler, supplest** a supple person is able to bend and stretch easily: *Take exercise if you want to stay supple.*
▸ **suppleness** NOUN being supple

supplement NOUN **supplements 1** something extra that is added to something **2** an extra part of a newspaper or magazine that comes with the main part
▸ **supplementary** ADJECTIVE extra or additional: *a few supplementary questions*

supply VERB **supplies, supplying, supplied** to supply something is to give or provide it: *The shop was unable to supply what she wanted. • The teacher will supply you with more paper.*
NOUN **supplies 1** supply is supplying something: *The company is involved in the supply of weapons to the Middle East.* **2** a supply is a stock or store: *a supply of food*
ADJECTIVE a supply teacher takes another teacher's place for a time

support VERB **supports, supporting, supported**
1 to support something is to carry its weight: *That chair won't support him.*

2 to support someone is to provide the money that they need to live: *He has a wife and two children to support.*
3 to support someone or something is to help and encourage them: *His family supported his decision.*
4 to support a sports team is to want them to win
NOUN **supports 1** support is the action of supporting **2** a support is something, such as a column or pillar, which takes the weight of something else: *One of the supports of the bridge collapsed.*
▸ **supporter** NOUN **supporters** someone who supports something, especially a sports team: *a Liverpool supporter*

suppose VERB **supposes, supposing, supposed 1** to believe that something is probably true: *I suppose you'll be going to the concert.* **2** to consider something as a possibility: *Suppose you had £100 – what would you buy?*
▸ **supposed** ADJECTIVE **1** believed to be so even if it is not true: *her supposed generosity* **2** you are supposed to do something when people expect you to do it: *You were supposed to come straight home after school.*
▸ **supposedly** ADVERB so it is believed: *He is supposedly one of the best doctors in the country.*

suppress VERB **suppresses, suppressing, suppressed 1** to try to stop a feeling or action: *She suppressed a laugh.* **2** to defeat something such as a rebellion
▸ **suppression** NOUN the act of suppressing something: *the suppression of information*

supreme ADJECTIVE **1** most powerful: *the supreme ruler* **2** greatest: *supreme courage*
▸ **supremacy** NOUN being the most powerful: *the supremacy of the president*

sure ADJECTIVE **1** you are sure of something when you have no doubts about it: *I'm sure I gave him the book.* **2** certain to do or get something: *He's sure to win.* **3** able to be trusted: *a sure way to cure hiccups*

ADVERB an informal way of saying 'of course' or 'certainly': *Sure I'll help you!*

▶ **surely** ADVERB **1** certainly, without doubt: *If you go near the pond you will surely fall in.* **2** surely is sometimes used to express a little doubt: *Surely you won't tell him.*

surf NOUN the foam made when waves break on rocks or on the shore

VERB **surfs, surfing, surfed 1** to ride on waves towards the shore, standing or lying on a surfboard **2** to surf the Internet is to browse through it looking at different websites

surface NOUN **surfaces** the outside or top part of something: *This road has a very bumpy surface.*

VERB **surfaces, surfacing, surfaced 1** to surface is to come up to the surface of water: *The submarine surfaced close to the ship.* **2** to surface something such as a road or path is to put a hard top layer on it: *They are surfacing this road with tarmac.*

surfboard NOUN **surfboards** a long narrow board used in surfing

surfer NOUN **surfers** a person who surfs

surfing NOUN the sport of balancing on a surfboard and riding on waves towards the shore

surge VERB **surges, surging, surged** to suddenly move forward or upward: *The crowd surged towards the fire exit.*

NOUN a sudden rush: *He felt a surge of pain.*

surgeon NOUN **surgeons** a doctor who carries out operations

surgery NOUN **surgeries 1** surgery is the work of a surgeon, carrying out operations **2** a surgery is the room where a doctor or dentist examines their patients

surgical ADJECTIVE to do with a surgeon or his work: *surgical techniques*

▶ **surgically** ADVERB by means of an operation: *The lump will have to be surgically removed.*

surname NOUN **surnames** your last name or family name: *Smith is a common British surname.*

surpass VERB **surpasses, surpassing, surpassed** to be or do better than: *His work surpassed my expectations.*

surplus NOUN **surpluses** an amount left over after what is needed has been taken away: *This country produces a surplus of grain.*

surprise NOUN **surprises 1** something sudden or unexpected: *Your letter was a nice surprise.* **2** the feeling caused by something sudden or unexpected: *He stared at her in surprise.*

VERB **surprises, surprising, surprised 1** to surprise someone is to cause them to feel surprise: *The news surprised me.* **2** to surprise someone is also to come upon them suddenly and without warning: *They surprised the enemy from the rear.*

surrender VERB **surrenders, surrendering, surrendered 1** to surrender is to stop fighting because you know you can't win: *They surrendered to the enemy.* **2** to surrender something is to hand it over to someone in authority: *She surrendered her mobile phone to the teacher.*

NOUN an act of surrendering: *the surrender of the fort to the enemy*

surround VERB **surrounds, surrounding, surrounded 1** to surround someone or something is to be or come all round them: *Enemy troops surrounded the town.* **2** to surround something is to enclose it or put something round it: *He surrounded the castle with a high wall.*

▶ **surroundings** PLURAL NOUN the area around a person or place: *The hotel is set in beautiful surroundings.* • *He was glad to be back in his own surroundings.*

survey VERB **surveys, surveying, surveyed** (pronounced ser-**vay**) to survey something is to look at it or inspect it: *She surveyed her garden from the window.*

NOUN **surveys** (pronounced **ser**-vay) **1** an investigation into what people think: *Would you mind answering some questions? I'm doing a survey.* **2** an inspection or examination

survive VERB **survives, surviving, survived** to stay alive: *He didn't survive long after the accident.*

▶ **survival** NOUN staying alive: *His*

Aa Bb Cc Dd Ee Ff Gg Hh Ii Jj Kk Ll Mm Nn Oo Pp Qq Rr **Ss** Tt Uu Vv Ww Xx Yy Zz

survival depended on finding fresh water.

▶ **survivor** NOUN **survivors** someone who stays alive: *the only survivor of the crash*

suspect VERB **suspects, suspecting, suspected** (pronounced sus-**pekt**) **1** to suspect someone is to think that they have done something wrong: *I suspect her of the crime.* **2** to suspect something is to think that it is likely: *I suspect that she is hiding her true feelings.*

NOUN **suspects** (pronounced **sus**-pekt) someone who is thought to have done something wrong: *There are three suspects in this murder case.*

suspend VERB **suspends, suspending, suspended 1** to suspend something is to hang it: *The meat was suspended from a hook.* **2** to suspend something is to stop it for a while: *All business will be suspended until after New Year.* **3** to suspend someone is to stop them doing their job or taking part in an activity for a time because they have done something wrong: *suspended from school for bad behaviour*

suspense NOUN a state of feeling uncertain and anxious: *We waited in suspense for the result.*

suspension NOUN **1** suspending something or someone: *a two-week suspension from school* **2** the system of springs that supports a motor vehicle, making it more comfortable to ride in

suspicion NOUN **suspicions 1** a thought or feeling that something is likely: *I have a suspicion she is not telling the truth.* **2** a feeling of doubting or not trusting: *They looked at each other with suspicion.*

▶ **suspicious** ADJECTIVE **1** feeling or showing suspicion: *She gave him a suspicious glance.* **2** causing suspicion: *He died in suspicious circumstances.*

▶ **suspiciously** ADVERB in a suspicious way: *She looked at him suspiciously.* • *acting suspiciously*

sustain VERB **sustains, sustaining, sustained 1** to sustain someone is to give help and strength to them: *a few sandwiches to sustain you during*

the journey **2** to sustain an injury is to suffer it: *He sustained head injuries in the crash.* **3** to sustain something is to keep it up or keep it going: *It would be difficult to sustain such a fast pace.*

▶ **sustainable** ADJECTIVE **1** able to be kept going **2** if you use resources in a sustainable way, then you do not cause damage to the environment

swagger VERB **swaggers, swaggering, swaggered** to walk as though pleased with yourself, swinging the arms and body: *He swaggered along the street in his new suit.*

swallow[1] VERB **swallows, swallowing, swallowed 1** to swallow food or drink is to make it pass down your throat to your stomach: *Try to swallow the pill.* **2** to swallow something such as a lie or an insult is to accept it without question: *She'll never swallow that story!*

• **swallow something up** to make something disappear: *New housing has swallowed up large areas of the countryside.*

swallow[2] NOUN a small bird with long pointed wings and a forked tail

swamp NOUN **swamps** a piece of wet, marshy ground

VERB **swamps, swamping, swamped 1** to swamp something is to flood it: *A great wave swamped the deck.* **2** to swamp someone is to overload them with something: *I'm swamped with work.*

swan NOUN **swans** a large, usually white, water bird with a long neck

swap VERB **swaps, swapping, swapped** to exchange one thing for another: *They swapped books with each other.* • *She swapped her bike for a scooter.*

swarm NOUN **swarms** a large number of insects flying or moving together: *a swarm of bees*

VERB **swarms, swarming, swarmed 1** to move in great numbers: *The children swarmed out of the school.* **2** to be swarming with something is to be crowded with it: *streets swarming with tourists*

Aa
Bb
Cc
Dd
Ee
Ff
Gg
Hh
Ii
Jj
Kk
Ll
Mm
Nn
Oo
Pp
Qq
Rr
Ss
Tt
Uu
Vv
Ww
Xx
Yy
Zz

swat VERB **swats, swatting, swatted** to swat a fly is to crush it

sway VERB **sways, swaying, swayed** 1 to sway is to move from side to side with a swinging action: *She swayed in time to the music.* 2 to sway someone is to guide or influence them: *She's too easily swayed by her friends' opinions.*

swear VERB **swears, swearing, swore, sworn** 1 to promise: *I swear to tell the truth.* 2 to use words that are offensive or rude: *He swore under his breath.* 3 to swear someone to something is to make them give a promise about it: *The children were sworn to secrecy.*

• **swear by something** to believe that something is very good or useful: *He swears by plenty of sleep.*

swear-word NOUN **swear-words** a word that is very offensive or rude

sweat NOUN the salty liquid that comes out of your skin when you are hot: *He was dripping with sweat after his run.* VERB **sweats, sweating, sweated** to give out sweat: *Exercise makes you sweat.*

▶ **sweaty** ADJECTIVE **sweatier, sweatiest** wet with sweat

sweater NOUN **sweaters** a jersey or pullover

sweatshirt NOUN **sweatshirts** a type of thick jersey

swede NOUN **swedes** a kind of large, round, yellow vegetable like a turnip

sweep VERB **sweeps, sweeping, swept** 1 to sweep something is to clean it using a brush or broom: *He swept the floor.* 2 to sweep is to move quickly or forcefully: *The disease is sweeping through the country.* • *She swept into my room without knocking.* 3 to sweep someone or something is to move them with a sweeping movement: *The wind nearly swept me off my feet.* • *Whole villages were swept away by the flood.*
NOUN **sweeps** 1 the action of sweeping: *She gave the room a sweep.* 2 a sweeping movement: *He indicated the damage with a sweep of his hand.* 3 a person who cleans chimneys

▶ **sweeper** NOUN **sweepers** in

football, a defensive player who stays behind the other defenders

sweet ADJECTIVE **sweeter, sweetest** 1 tasting like sugar: *strong sweet tea* 2 pleasant: *the sweet smell of flowers* • *the sweet song of the nightingale* 3 attractive or nice: *My baby brother is very sweet.*
NOUN **sweets** 1 a small piece of sweet food, for example chocolate or toffee: *a packet of sweets* 2 something sweet served at the end of a meal: *Would you like to see the sweet menu?*

▶ **sweeten** VERB **sweetens, sweetening, sweetened** 1 to sweeten something is to make it sweet: *Sweeten the raspberries with sugar.* 2 to sweeten is to become sweet: *Her smile sweetened.*

▶ **sweetly** ADVERB in a sweet way: *She smiled sweetly.*

▶ **sweetness** NOUN being sweet

sweetcorn NOUN sweetcorn is the yellow grains of a cereal crop called maize, that are eaten as a vegetable

sweetheart NOUN **sweethearts** a boyfriend or girlfriend: *They were childhood sweethearts.*

sweet tooth NOUN a liking for things that taste sweet: *She never refuses chocolate – she has a very sweet tooth.*

swell VERB **swells, swelling, swelled, swollen** 1 to swell is to get bigger: *The wasp sting made her finger swell.* 2 to swell something is to make it bigger: *Heavy rain had swollen the river.*
NOUN swell is the up and down movement of the sea when there are no breaking waves
ADJECTIVE an informal way of saying 'very good' that is used in American English: *What a swell idea!*

▶ **swelling** NOUN **swellings** a swollen part of the body: *She had a swelling on her arm where she had been stung.*

swelter VERB **swelters, sweltering, sweltered** to be too hot: *I'm sweltering in this heat!*

swept VERB a way of changing the verb **sweep** to make a past tense. It can be used with or without a helping verb: *He*

Aa
Bb
Cc
Dd
Ee
Ff
Gg
Hh
Ii
Jj
Kk
Ll
Mm
Nn
Oo
Pp
Qq
Rr
Ss
Tt
Uu
Vv
Ww
Xx
Yy
Zz

swept up the crumbs. • She has swept the floor.

swerve VERB **swerves, swerving, swerved** to turn quickly to one side: The driver had to swerve to miss the dog.
NOUN **swerves** a quick turn to one side: The bus gave a sudden swerve and I fell off my seat.

swift ADJECTIVE **swifter, swiftest** fast or quick: a swift recovery
NOUN **swifts** a small bird rather like a swallow
▶ **swiftly** ADVERB quickly
▶ **swiftness** NOUN being fast

swill VERB **swills, swilling, swilled** to swill something, or to swill something out, is to wash it out: He swilled out the cups.
NOUN leftover food mixed with water, given to pigs to eat

swim VERB **swims, swimming, swam, swum**
1 to swim is to move through water: I learned to swim when I was five.
2 to swim something is to cross it by swimming: Her ambition is to swim the Channel.
3 to be swimming in a liquid is to be covered with it: meat swimming in grease
4 if your head swims, you feel dizzy
NOUN **swims** an act of swimming: I think I'll go for a swim.
▶ **swimmer** NOUN **swimmers** someone or something that swims: Penguins are excellent swimmers.

swimming baths PLURAL NOUN a place with a pool, or pools, of water, where people can go and swim

swimming costume NOUN **swimming costumes** a piece of clothing worn for swimming, usually by women and girls

swimming pool NOUN **swimming pools** an indoor or outdoor pool for swimming in

swimsuit NOUN **swimsuits** a piece of clothing worn for swimming, usually by women and girls

swindle VERB **swindles, swindling, swindled** to swindle someone is to cheat them, especially out of money: That shopkeeper has swindled me out of £2!
NOUN **swindles** an act of swindling: I paid £20 for this watch and it doesn't work. What a swindle!
▶ **swindler** NOUN **swindlers** a person who swindles others

✦ This word comes from the German word **schwindler**, which means a cheat.

swine NOUN **swine 1** an old word for a pig **2** a rude word for someone who treats others badly: He left me to pay the bill, the swine!

swing VERB **swings, swinging, swung 1** to move from side to side, or forwards and backwards, from a fixed point: You swing your arms when you walk. • The children were swinging on a rope hanging from a tree. **2** to turn suddenly: He swung round and stared at us.
NOUN **swings 1** a seat for swinging, hung on ropes or chains from a support: I like playing on the swings in the park. **2** a swinging movement: the swing of a pendulum
• **in full swing** going on busily: The party was in full swing.

swipe VERB **swipes, swiping, swiped 1** to swipe someone or something is to hit them by swinging your arm or an object: She swiped me across the face. **2** to swipe a credit card is to run it through an electronic device that can read the details on it
NOUN **swipes** a heavy sweeping blow: He took a swipe at the ball.

swirl VERB **swirls, swirling, swirled** to move quickly round in circles: Leaves swirled along the ground.
NOUN **swirls** a swirling movement

swish VERB **swishes, swishing, swished** to move with a rustling sound: Her long skirt swished as she danced.
NOUN **swishes** a swishing sound: He opened the curtains with a swish.

Aa Bb Cc Dd Ee Ff Gg Hh Ii Jj Kk Ll Mm Nn Oo Pp Qq Rr Ss Tt Uu Vv Ww Xx Yy Zz

switch NOUN **switches 1** a device for turning power on and off: *I can't find the light-switch.* **2** a change: *After several switches of direction they were at last on the right road.*

VERB **switches, switching, switched 1** to switch something on or off is to turn it on or off using a switch **2** to switch something is to change it: *Jane switched her job to become a driver.*

switchboard NOUN **switchboards** a board with lots of switches for making connections by telephone

swivel VERB **swivels, swivelling, swivelled** to turn round: *She swivelled her chair round to face the desk.* • *I swivelled round to look at him.*

swollen ADJECTIVE bigger than usual because of swelling: *He had a swollen ankle after falling downstairs.*

VERB the form of the verb **swell** that is used with a helping verb to show that something happened in the past: *Her face had swollen up with crying.*

swoon VERB **swoons, swooning, swooned** an old-fashioned word that means to faint: *She nearly swooned when the group appeared on stage.*

NOUN **swoons** an old word for a faint: *She fell into a swoon.*

swoop VERB **swoops, swooping, swooped** to rush or fly downwards: *The owl swooped down on its prey.*

NOUN **swoops** a sudden downward rush

swop VERB **swops, swopping, swopped** another spelling of **swap**

sword NOUN **swords** a weapon with a long blade

swordfish NOUN **swordfish** or **swordfishes** a type of large fish with a long pointed upper jaw like a sword

swore VERB a way of changing the verb **swear** to make a past tense: *She swore to tell the truth.*

sworn VERB the form of the verb **swear** that is used with a helping verb to show that something happened in the past: *He has sworn he will never tell anyone.*

ADJECTIVE promised always to be something: *They are sworn enemies.*

swot VERB **swots, swotting, swotted** to study hard: *She has been swotting for her exams.*

NOUN **swots** a person who studies hard or too hard

sycamore NOUN **sycamores** a type of large tree with winged seeds

syllable NOUN **syllables** (*grammar*) a word or part of a word that is a single sound. For example, *pen* has one syllable, *pen-cil* has two and *com-pu-ter* has three

syllabus NOUN **syllabuses** or **syllabi** a list of things that a class will study

symbol NOUN **symbols 1** a mark or sign that is used as a short form of something, for example + meaning *plus* and O meaning *oxygen* **2** something that stands for something else: *The dove is a symbol of peace.*

▶ **symbolic** ADJECTIVE used as a sign or symbol of something: *The gift was a symbolic gesture of friendship.*

▶ **symbolize** or **symbolise** VERB **symbolizes, symbolizing, symbolized** to symbolize something is to be a symbol of it: *A ring symbolizes everlasting love.*

symmetry NOUN symmetry is where a single thing has two parts or halves that are exactly the same but the opposite way round, as if one were a mirror image of the other. The opposite of symmetry is **asymmetry**

▶ **symmetrical** ADJECTIVE having symmetry: *The two sides of a person's face are never completely symmetrical.*

sympathetic ADJECTIVE feeling or showing sympathy: *a sympathetic smile*

▶ **sympathetically** ADVERB in a sympathetic way: *She patted his hand sympathetically.*

sympathize or **sympathise** VERB **sympathizes, sympathizing, sympathized** to sympathize with someone is to feel or show sympathy for them: *I sympathize with your trouble.* • *I'm afraid I cannot help, I can only sympathize.*

sympathy NOUN **sympathies 1** the feeling of being sorry for someone in trouble: *She received many letters of*

Aa Bb Cc Dd Ee Ff Gg Hh Ii Jj Kk Ll Mm Nn Oo Pp Qq Rr Ss Tt Uu Vv Ww Xx Yy Zz

sympathy when her husband died. **2** the sharing of the thoughts and opinions of others: *Are you in sympathy with the strikers?*

symphony NOUN **symphonies** a long piece of music to be played by an orchestra

symptom NOUN **symptoms** a symptom of an illness is a sign that someone has that illness: *A cold, fever and headache are the usual symptoms of flu.*

synagogue (pronounced **sin**-a-gog) NOUN **synagogues** a place where Jewish people go to worship

synchronize *or* **synchronise** (pronounced **sin**-kron-ize) VERB **synchronizes, synchronizing, synchronized 1** if events or movements synchronize or are synchronized, they happen at the same time **2** to synchronize clocks or watches is to set them so that they show exactly the same time

▸ **synchronization** *or* **synchronisation** NOUN making things synchronize

syncopate (pronounced **sing**-ki-pait) VERB **syncopates, syncopating, syncopated** (*music*) a piece of music is syncopated when its rhythm is changed by putting stress on beats that you do not usually play strongly

▸ **syncopation** NOUN changing the rhythm of a piece of music by changing the stress on the beats

synonym NOUN **synonyms** (*grammar*) a word that means the same, or nearly the same, as another word. For example, *angry* and *cross* are synonyms

syntax NOUN (*grammar*) the grammar rules to do with the position words may have in a sentence and how they relate to each other

synthesis NOUN **syntheses 1** the making of a product by combining different chemical substances: *Plastic is produced by synthesis.* **2** a mixture: *His latest plan is a synthesis of old and new ideas.*

▸ **synthesizer** *or* **synthesiser** NOUN **synthesizers** *or* **synthesisers** an electronic musical instrument that makes the sounds of various other musical instruments

▸ **synthetic** ADJECTIVE not real: *synthetic leather*

syringe NOUN **syringes** a small instrument shaped like a cylinder with a needle attached to it, used for injecting liquids into the body or for taking blood out of the body

syrup NOUN **syrups** a thick sticky liquid made by boiling water or fruit juice with sugar: *hot pancakes covered with syrup*

system NOUN **systems 1** an arrangement of many parts that work together: *the railway system* **2** a way of organizing something: *a system of education*

▸ **systematic** ADJECTIVE well planned and following a system: *a systematic search of the area*

Aa
Bb
Cc
Dd
Ee
Ff
Gg
Hh
Ii
Jj
Kk
Ll
Mm
Nn
Oo
Pp
Qq
Rr
Ss
Tt
Uu
Vv
Ww
Xx
Yy
Zz

Tt

Aa
Bb
Cc
Dd
Ee
Ff
Gg
Hh
Ii
Jj
Kk
Ll
Mm
Nn
Oo
Pp
Qq
Rr
Ss
Tt
Uu
Vv
Ww
Xx
Yy
Zz

ta INTERJECTION (*informal*) thank you

tab NOUN **tabs** a small piece of fabric, metal or paper attached to something and used to hang it up, identify it, open it or hold it by

tabby NOUN **tabbies 1** a cat with grey or brown fur marked with darker stripes **2** a female cat

table NOUN **tables 1** a piece of furniture with a flat top that is supported on legs **2** numbers or words laid out in rows and columns **3** a list of sums and the answers, which you learn by heart: *Do you know the five times table?*

tablecloth NOUN **tablecloths** a cloth for covering a table

tablespoon NOUN **tablespoons** a large size of spoon, often used for measuring cooking ingredients
▸ **tablespoonful** NOUN **tablespoonfuls** the amount that a tablespoon will hold

tablet NOUN **tablets 1** a pill **2** a flat solid piece of something, such as soap or chocolate **3** a flat surface, usually made of stone or wood, with words carved on it

table tennis NOUN an indoor game for two or four players in which you use a small bat to hit a light hollow ball across a net on a table

tabloid NOUN **tabloids** a newspaper printed on small pages, which often has a lot of photographs

taboo NOUN **taboos** a taboo is anything people are not allowed to do, especially for religious or social reasons
ADJECTIVE forbidden: *a taboo subject*

tack NOUN **tacks 1** a short nail with a broad flat head and a sharp point **2** a course of action or way of approaching something: *We aren't getting anywhere, so we need to try a different tack.*
VERB **tacks, tacking, tacked 1** to tack something is to fasten it with tacks **2**

to tack pieces of fabric is to sew them together with large loose temporary stitches

tackle VERB **tackles, tackling, tackled 1** you tackle a job or problem when you try to deal with it **2** you tackle someone when you ask them directly about something they have done wrong or that they should have done **3** in games like football and rugby, you tackle a player in the other team when you try to get the ball from them
NOUN **tackles 1** tackle is equipment: *fishing tackle • lifting tackle* **2** a tackle is the movement a rugby, football or hockey player makes to try to get the ball from a player in the other team

tacky ADJECTIVE **tackier, tackiest 1** if glue or paint is tacky, it is still rather sticky because it hasn't dried completely **2** cheap and badly made or in bad taste

tact NOUN the ability to avoid hurting people's feelings or offending them

tactful ADJECTIVE not hurting people's feelings or offending them
▸ **tactfully** ADVERB in a way that will not upset someone

tactic NOUN **tactics** someone's tactics are the things they do or the methods they use to get what they want or to help them win
▸ **tactical** ADJECTIVE a tactical action or move is cleverly worked out to achieve the best result

tactless ADJECTIVE thoughtless and not considering other people's feelings

tadpole NOUN **tadpoles** a young frog or toad with a rounded head and long tail. The tail eventually disappears as it develops legs

tag¹ NOUN **tags** a label with information, such as someone's name, printed on it
VERB **tags, tagging, tagged** to tag something is to put a tag or label on it

• **tag along** if someone tags along with another person they go with that person somewhere, often without being invited

tag[2] NOUN a children's game in which one player chases the other players and if he or she manages to catch and touch someone, the player who has been touched then has to chase the others

tail NOUN **tails 1** an animal's, bird's or fish's tail is the part of its body that sticks out from the end of its spine or at the end of its body **2** any part that sticks out, or hangs down, at the back of an object: *The aeroplane had a red and black symbol painted on its tail.* • *His shirt tail was hanging out.*

VERB **tails, tailing, tailed** to tail someone is to follow them, usually to watch what they do or where they go

• **tail off** if something tails off, it gets less and less, or smaller and smaller, until it eventually disappears

tailor NOUN **tailors** someone whose job is making suits, coats or other pieces of clothing

VERB **tailors, tailoring, tailored 1** to tailor clothes is to make them so that they fit well **2** to tailor something for a particular purpose is to design it specially for that purpose

tails PLURAL NOUN the side of a coin opposite the side that has the head on it: *Call heads or tails.*

take VERB **takes, taking, took, taken**

1 you take something when you reach out and get it or get it for yourself: *Take my hand.* • *Someone's taken my ruler.*

2 to take someone or something to a place is to bring them or it with you when you go there: *Take me to your leader.* • *I took the parcel to the post office.*

3 you take one number from another when you subtract the first one from the second one: *If you take 5 from 16, you are left with 11.*

4 you take something when you eat it, drink it or swallow it: *You must take your medicine if you want to get better quickly.*

5 to take something is to accept it: *Take my advice. Wear a warm jumper when you go out.* • *He cannot take criticism.*

6 to take something such as a form of transport or a route is to use it: *We usually take the bus rather than the train.* • *Take the next left after the town hall.*

7 you take an exam or test when you do it

8 to take a photograph is to use a camera to record an image

9 something takes a certain length of time if it lasts for that length of time or you need that amount of time to do it: *The journey took hours and hours.*

10 if a space or container takes a certain amount, it has enough room for it: *This jug takes nearly two litres.*

11 take is used with nouns to refer to actions: *Let's take a look at that sore leg of yours.* • *He took a leap.*

• **be taken in** if someone is taken in, they are tricked into believing something that is not true

• **take off** a plane takes off when it leaves the ground at the beginning of a flight

• **take over** to take over from someone is to replace them and do what they had been doing

• **take part** to take part in some activity is to do it or become involved in it

• **take up something** to take up a hobby or other activity is to start doing it

takeaway NOUN **takeaways** a cooked meal that you buy at a shop or restaurant and take away with you to eat somewhere else

take-off NOUN **take-offs** the moment when an aeroplane leaves the ground at the beginning of a flight

takings PLURAL NOUN the amount of money that a shop, concert or other event makes from its customers

talcum powder *or* **talc** NOUN a fine powder, usually with a pleasant scent, that people put on their bodies

tale NOUN **tales** a story: *tales of great adventures*

Aa
Bb
Cc
Dd
Ee
Ff
Gg
Hh
Ii
Jj
Kk
Ll
Mm
Nn
Oo
Pp
Qq
Rr
Ss
Tt
Uu
Vv
Ww
Xx
Yy
Zz

Aa
Bb
Cc
Dd
Ee
Ff
Gg
Hh
Ii
Jj
Kk
Ll
Mm
Nn
Oo
Pp
Qq
Rr
Ss
Tt
Uu
Vv
Ww
Xx
Yy
Zz

talent NOUN **talents** you have talent, or a talent, when you have special skill or natural ability to do something well

▶ **talented** ADJECTIVE having the skill or ability to do something well

talk VERB **talks, talking, talked** 1 to say words out loud 2 to talk to someone is to have a conversation with them

NOUN **talks** 1 talk is speech or conversation 2 if someone gives a talk, they talk about some subject to an audience

▶ **talkative** ADJECTIVE a talkative person talks a lot

tall ADJECTIVE **taller, tallest** 1 big, or bigger than average, in height: *He's tall for his age. • a tall building* 2 how big someone or something is in height: *He's only three feet tall.*

• **a tall story** a story that is difficult to believe

tally NOUN **tallies** a tally of things is a record you keep so that you can work out the total, for example of points scored or money spent

VERB **tallies, tallying, tallied** two or more things tally when they match or are the same: *His answer tallied with mine.*

Talmud NOUN a book of religious laws written by rabbis, used by members of the Jewish faith

talon NOUN **talons** a long hooked claw on an eagle's or other large bird of prey's foot

tambourine NOUN **tambourines** an instrument made up of a circular frame with skin stretched tightly across it and small round pieces of metal set into the frame in pairs

tame ADJECTIVE **tamer, tamest** a tame animal is used to being with humans and is not dangerous

VERB **tames, taming, tamed** to tame a wild animal is to train it so that it is used to living or working with humans

tamper VERB **tampers, tampering, tampered** to tamper with something is to interfere with it, especially in a way that causes it not to work properly

tan NOUN **tans** 1 you get a tan when your skin is turned brown or browner by the sun 2 tan is a yellowish-brown colour

VERB **tans, tanning, tanned** 1 your skin tans when it is turned a darker colour by the sun 2 animal skins are tanned when they are treated with chemicals to make them into leather

tandem NOUN **tandems** a type of long bicycle for two riders that has two seats and two sets of pedals

• **in tandem** people or things work or go in tandem when they work or go along together

tang NOUN **tangs** a strong or sharp taste or flavour

tangent NOUN **tangents** (*maths*) a straight line that touches a curve or circle but does not go through it

tangerine NOUN **tangerines** a type of small orange with skin that is loose and easy to peel

tangle NOUN **tangles** 1 a tangle is an untidy twisted mass of something, such as rope, wire or hair 2 if you get in a tangle, you get into a confused or muddled state

VERB **tangles, tangling, tangled** 1 to tangle is to become entwined 2 to tangle something is to twist it or muddle it

tank NOUN **tanks** 1 a large container for holding liquids 2 a large heavy army vehicle covered with metal plates and with a long gun on the top

tanka NOUN **tankas** a type of Japanese poem with five lines and 31 syllables

tankard NOUN **tankards** a large metal mug, usually with a handle and sometimes a hinged lid, used for drinking beer

tanker NOUN **tankers** a ship or lorry used to carry oil or other liquids

tanner NOUN **tanners** a person whose job or business is to tan leather

tantalize or **tantalise** VERB **tantalizes, tantalizing, tantalized** if something tantalizes you, it makes you feel frustrated because you want it but can't have it

tantrum NOUN **tantrums** if a child has

or throws a tantrum, they suddenly start to shout, scream or kick in a furious and uncontrolled way

tap¹ NOUN **taps** a device fitted to a water or gas pipe used to turn the water or gas on and off and control the flow
• **on tap** if something is on tap, there is a supply of it available when you need it
VERB **taps, tapping, tapped** 1 to tap a source or supply of something is to use it 2 to tap someone's phone is secretly to put a device in their phone that lets you hear their telephone conversations

tap² NOUN **taps** a light quick knock
VERB **taps, tapping, tapped** to knock lightly: *He tapped on the window to get my attention.*

tapdance VERB **tapdances, tapdancing, tapdanced** to dance in special shoes with metal pieces in the toes and heels that make tapping noises as your feet hit the ground

tape NOUN **tapes** 1 tape is a long narrow ribbon or strip of material, used for tying or sticking things 2 the strip of material across a finishing line on a racetrack: *She was the first through the tape at the finish.* 3 a tape is a length of magnetic tape wound on a cassette, for recording sounds or pictures
VERB **tapes, taping, taped** 1 to tape sounds or images is to record them on tape 2 to tape something or to tape something up is to fasten it with sticky tape

tape-measure NOUN **tape-measures** a long thin piece of plastic or fabric marked with units of measurement that you use to find out the length of things

taper VERB **tapers, tapering, tapered** to get gradually thinner or narrower at one end
NOUN **tapers** a long thin candle used for lighting other candles and fires

tape-recorder NOUN **tape-recorders** a machine that records sounds on magnetic tape and plays recordings back

tapestry NOUN **tapestries** a piece of cloth with a design or picture sewn on it in wool or thick thread

tapeworm NOUN **tapeworms** a long flat worm that lives in the guts of animals, including humans, as a parasite

tapioca NOUN a starchy food in the form of white grains that are cooked in milk and eaten as a pudding

tar NOUN a thick, dark, sticky liquid made from coal or wood, which goes hard when it gets cold and is used in making roads

tarantula NOUN **tarantulas** a large hairy spider that has a poisonous bite

target NOUN **targets** 1 a mark or object that people aim at when they are shooting 2 something or someone being aimed at: *My savings target is £100.* • *He was the target of all the other boys' jokes.*
VERB **targets, targeting, targeted** to target someone or something is to aim at them

tarmac NOUN a mixture of small stones and tar, used for making road surfaces. Tarmac is short for **tarmacadam**

tarnish VERB **tarnishes, tarnishing, tarnished** 1 if metal tarnishes, it becomes dull and stained 2 something tarnishes a person's reputation when it spoils or damages it

tarpaulin NOUN **tarpaulins** a tarpaulin is a piece of strong waterproof canvas

tart¹ NOUN **tarts** a pastry case with a sweet filling of custard, jam or fruit

tart² ADJECTIVE **tarter, tartest** sour-tasting: *The fruit was too tart to eat.*

tartan NOUN **tartans** woollen cloth with a check pattern made up of horizontal and vertical stripes of different colours

task NOUN **tasks** a job or duty that you have to do
• **take someone to task** to challenge someone and find fault with something they have done

task force NOUN **task forces** a group of people or soldiers with a special task to do

tassel NOUN **tassels** a bunch of threads tied firmly together at one end and used as decoration

taste NOUN **tastes**
1 taste is the sense by which you

Aa
Bb
Cc
Dd
Ee
Ff
Gg
Hh
Ii
Jj
Kk
Ll
Mm
Nn
Oo
Pp
Qq
Rr
Ss
Tt
Uu
Vv
Ww
Xx
Yy
Zz

Aa
Bb
Cc
Dd
Ee
Ff
Gg
Hh
Ii
Jj
Kk
Ll
Mm
Nn
Oo
Pp
Qq
Rr
Ss
Tt
Uu
Vv
Ww
Xx
Yy
Zz

recognize different flavours or foods when you touch them with your tongue **2** something's taste is the particular flavour it has when it touches your tongue **3** to have a taste of something is to put a little bit of it in your mouth to find out what its flavour is like **4** your taste or tastes are the kinds of things you like
VERB **tastes, tasting, tasted 1** you taste something when you put it in your mouth so that you can find out what sort of flavour it has: *Have you tasted this cheese?* **2** food tastes a certain way if it has that flavour: *This sauce tastes salty.* **3** if you taste something, you experience it briefly: *They'd tasted victory for the first time and wanted more.*

tasteful ADJECTIVE showing good taste and judgement
▶ **tastefully** ADVERB in a tasteful way

tasteless ADJECTIVE **1** having no flavour **2** vulgar or showing lack of taste

tasty ADJECTIVE **tastier, tastiest** having a good flavour

tattered ADJECTIVE tattered clothing is torn and ragged

tatters PLURAL NOUN
• **in tatters 1** clothes that are in tatters are badly torn **2** something that is in tatters is ruined: *Their holiday plans were in tatters.*

tattoo¹ NOUN **tattoos** a pattern or picture marked on someone's skin by making little holes in the surface of the skin and filling the holes with ink
VERB **tattoos, tattooing, tattooed** to tattoo someone is to put a tattoo on their skin

tattoo² NOUN **tattoos** an outdoor military display with music

tatty ADJECTIVE **tattier, tattiest** scruffy, old and worn

taught VERB a way of changing the verb **teach** to make a past tense. It can be used with or without a helping verb: *Who taught you how to do magic tricks?* • *Miss Kennedy had taught all my older brothers and sisters.*

taunt VERB **taunts, taunting, taunted** to taunt someone is to say cruel and hurtful things to them
NOUN **taunts** a cruel or hurtful remark or comment

taut ADJECTIVE **tauter, tautest** pulled or stretched tight

tavern NOUN **taverns** an old-fashioned word for an inn or pub

tawny ADJECTIVE something that is tawny has a yellowish-brown colour: *a tawny owl*

tax NOUN **taxes** money that you have to pay to the government which helps pay for things like schools and hospitals: *If you work, you pay tax on your income.*
VERB **taxes, taxing, taxed 1** to tax income or goods is to charge tax on them **2** if something taxes you, you find it hard work or a strain
▶ **taxation** NOUN the system of taxing income or goods, or the amount of money the government gets by charging taxes

taxi NOUN **taxis** a car with a driver that you can hire to take you from one place to another
VERB **taxis, taxiing, taxied** an aeroplane taxis when it moves slowly forward along the ground, after it has landed or when it is getting into position to take off

tea NOUN **teas**
1 tea is a drink made by pouring boiling water on dried leaves that come from a small tree or shrub that grows in Asia **2** a cup of tea: *Two teas and a coffee, please.* **3** a light meal, with tea and sandwiches, that some people have between lunch and their evening meal **4** the name some people give to the meal that they have in the early evening

teabag NOUN **teabags** a small bag of thin paper containing tea leaves that you put in a pot or cup and pour boiling water over to make tea

teach VERB **teaches, teaching, taught**
1 to teach is to pass the knowledge and experience you have on to other people to help them learn new

things: *Will you teach me how to sail a dinghy?* • *He taught in the local school.* **2** to teach a particular subject is to give people lessons in that subject: *He teaches violin.*

▶ **teacher** NOUN **teachers** someone who teaches, usually as their job

teacup NOUN **teacups** a cup used for drinking tea

teak NOUN a type of hard yellowish-brown wood

team NOUN **teams 1** a side in a game: *the England cricket team* • *Which football team do you support?* **2** a group of people working together: *a team of engineers*

VERB **teams, teaming, teamed**

• **team up** to team up with other people is to join them so that you can do something together

+ The words **team** and **teem** sound the same but remember that they have different spellings. If something **teems**, there is a lot of it.

teapot NOUN **teapots** a pot with a spout and a handle, used for making and pouring tea

tear¹ (pronounced **tair**) VERB **tears, tearing, torn 1** to tear something is to make a hole or split in it: *You've torn your sleeve on that barbed wire.* **2** to tear something is to pull it using force: *The old buildings were torn down and new ones built in their place.* **3** to tear somewhere is to rush there

NOUN **tears** a hole or split made in something

tear² (pronounced **teer**) NOUN **tears 1** a drop of liquid that forms in, and drops from, your eyes when you cry **2** if someone is in tears, they are crying

▶ **tearful** ADJECTIVE crying or almost crying

tear gas NOUN a gas which stings people's eyes and makes them stream with tears

tease VERB **teases, teasing, teased 1** to tease a person or animal is to annoy them or it on purpose: *Stop teasing the dog!* **2** to tease someone is to make

fun of them or joke with them: *I didn't mean what I said. I was only teasing.*

teaspoon NOUN **teaspoons** a small spoon used for stirring tea or for measuring small amounts of ingredients when you are cooking

▶ **teaspoonful** NOUN **teaspoonfuls** the amount a teaspoon will hold

teat NOUN **teats 1** the part of a female animal that its babies suck at to get milk **2** a small rubber device that is fitted to the end of a baby's feeding bottle

technical ADJECTIVE to do with technology or practical skills: *Does he have any technical training?*

▶ **technicality** NOUN **technicalities** a technicality is a detail of the law or any other set of rules

▶ **technically** ADVERB according to the rules, or according to technical or scientific methods

technician NOUN **technicians** someone whose job is to do practical work in a laboratory or deal with technical equipment

technique NOUN **techniques** a particular method of doing something

technology NOUN **technologies** the study of the way things are made and work

▶ **technological** ADJECTIVE involving technology

teddy *or* **teddy bear** NOUN **teddies** *or* **teddy bears** a toy bear with soft fur

tedious ADJECTIVE long and boring

▶ **tedium** NOUN boredom

tee NOUN **tees 1** an area of level ground from which you hit a golf ball at the beginning of a hole **2** a small plastic peg in the ground, used for resting a golf ball on before you hit it

teem VERB **teems, teeming, teemed 1** if a place teems with people or animals, there are crowds or large numbers of them moving around there **2** it is teeming with rain when rain is falling very fast and heavily

teenage ADJECTIVE suitable for or to do with teenagers

▶ **teenager** NOUN **teenagers** someone who is aged between 13 and 19

Aa

Bb

Cc

Dd

Ee

Ff

Gg

Hh

Ii

Jj

Kk

Ll

Mm

Nn

Oo

Pp

Qq

Rr

Ss

Tt

Uu

Vv

Ww

Xx

Yy

Zz

▶ **teens** PLURAL NOUN your teens are the years of your life between the ages of 13 and 19

tee-shirt NOUN **tee-shirts** a loose shirt with short sleeves that you pull on over your head

teeter VERB **teeters, teetering, teetered** to move about unsteadily and be just about to fall over: *The vase was teetering on the edge of the shelf.*

teeth NOUN the plural of **tooth**: *He got fillings in two back teeth.*

teethe VERB **teethes, teething, teethed** a baby teethes when its first teeth start to come through its gums

teetotal ADJECTIVE someone who is teetotal does not drink any alcohol

▶ **teetotaller** NOUN **teetotallers** someone who does not drink alcohol

telecommunications PLURAL NOUN sending information over long distances by telephone, radio or television

telegram NOUN **telegrams** a message sent by telegraph

telegraph NOUN **telegraphs** a system of sending messages over long distances using radio signals or electrical signals sent along wires

▶ **telegraphic** ADJECTIVE using telegraph

▶ **telegraphy** NOUN the system used for sending messages by telegraph

telepathy NOUN communicating by thought alone

▶ **telepathic** ADJECTIVE someone who is telepathic can communicate with another person's mind without speaking, writing or using gestures

telephone NOUN **telephones** a device that allows you to speak to someone at a distance, using electrical wires or radio

VERB **telephones, telephoning, telephoned** to telephone someone is to contact them using the telephone

▶ **telephonist** NOUN **telephonists** someone who operates a telephone switchboard

✦ **Telephone** comes from the Greek words **tele**, which means *far*, and **phone**, which means *a sound*, so together they mean 'sound at a distance'.
Another word in English beginning with **tele** is **television**.

telescope NOUN **telescopes** an instrument with lenses and mirrors inside that make distant objects seem closer or larger

▶ **telescopic** ADJECTIVE **1** to do with telescopes **2** having sliding parts that can be pushed inside each other

teletext NOUN a service that provides news and information that is regularly updated and which can be viewed in written form on a TV screen

televise VERB **televises, televising, televised** to televise something is to film it and show it on television

television NOUN **televisions 1** television is a system for sending images and sounds in the form of radio waves from a transmitter to a receiver, which changes the radio signals back into pictures and sounds **2** a television, or television set, is the equipment that receives these pictures and sounds

tell VERB **tells, telling, told**
1 to tell someone something is to give them information by speaking to them: *Why won't you tell me your name?*
2 to tell someone to do something is to order them to do it: *I won't tell you again to be quiet.*
3 you can tell what something is, or what is happening, if you know what it is, or understand what is happening: *I couldn't tell if it was a boat or a whale.*
4 to tell the truth or a lie is to give true or untrue information to someone
5 someone who tells gives away a secret
• **tell someone off** to speak angrily to someone because they have done something wrong

telltale NOUN **telltales** a person who tells untrue stories about others
ADJECTIVE a telltale sign is a sign that shows where or what something that

was secret or hidden is

telly NOUN **tellies** an informal word for **television**

temper NOUN **tempers** a person's mood: *Don't ask him until he's in a better temper.*

• **lose your temper** to get angry suddenly

temperament NOUN **temperaments** your temperament is your nature, which affects the way you think and behave

▶ **temperamental** ADJECTIVE a temperamental person changes their mood suddenly and gets upset or excited easily

temperate ADJECTIVE (*geography*) a temperate climate never gets very cold or very hot

temperature NOUN **temperatures** **1** something's temperature is how hot or cold it is **2** if someone has a temperature, their body is hotter than it should be, usually because they are ill

tempest NOUN **tempests** a very violent storm, with strong winds

▶ **tempestuous** ADJECTIVE stormy

template NOUN **templates** a pattern that you can use to make the same shape many times

temple¹ NOUN **temples** a building in which the members of some religions worship

temple² NOUN **temples** your temples are the areas on either side of your forehead at the sides of your eyes

tempo NOUN **tempos** or **tempi** (*music*) the tempo of a piece of music is its speed and rhythm

temporary ADJECTIVE lasting or used only for a short or limited time: *The repair was temporary but at least it stopped the rain getting in.*

▶ **temporarily** ADVERB for a short or limited time only: *He'd repaired the roof temporarily with a piece of plastic.*

tempt VERB **tempts, tempting, tempted** to tempt someone is to make them want to do something or have something, especially something that they should not do or have

▶ **temptation** NOUN **temptations** a

feeling that you want to do something that you know is wrong or that might harm you

▶ **tempting** ADJECTIVE something tempting is attractive and makes you want to do it or have it

ten NOUN **tens** the number 10

tenant NOUN **tenants** someone who pays rent to the owner of a house, building or land in return for being able to use the house, building or land

▶ **tenancy** NOUN **tenancies** the time when someone is a tenant or the agreement that makes someone a tenant

tend¹ VERB **tends, tending, tended** to tend someone or something is to look after them: *doctors and nurses tending the sick and injured*

tend² VERB **tends, tending, tended** something tends to happen when it is likely to happen, or often happens: *She tends to be a bit moody.*

▶ **tendency** NOUN **tendencies** if someone or something has a tendency to do something, they are likely to act in that way

tender ADJECTIVE **1** meat that is tender is easy to chew **2** showing gentle love: *a tender smile* **3** sensitive and delicate: *These plants are too tender to be grown outside.*

▶ **tenderly** ADJECTIVE gently and lovingly: *He smiled at her tenderly.*

▶ **tenderness** NOUN being tender

tendon NOUN **tendons** a type of strong body tissue that attaches your muscles to your bones

tendril NOUN **tendrils** **1** a long, thin, curling stem with which a climbing plant fastens itself to something **2** a long curling section of hair

tenner NOUN **tenners** (*informal*) ten pounds or a ten pound note

tennis NOUN a game played on a court that has a net stretched across the middle. Tennis is played by two or four players who use rackets to hit a ball to and fro across the net

tenor NOUN **tenors** (*music*) **1** a high male singing voice **2** a man who has this singing voice

Aa
Bb
Cc
Dd
Ee
Ff
Gg
Hh
Ii
Jj
Kk
Ll
Mm
Nn
Oo
Pp
Qq
Rr
Ss
Tt
Uu
Vv
Ww
Xx
Yy
Zz

tenpin bowling NOUN an indoor game in which a large heavy ball is rolled along a polished wooden track towards ten skittles or tenpins at the end of the track with the aim of knocking them down

tense[1] NOUN **tenses** (*grammar*) a verb's tense is the form of the verb that shows whether the action of the verb happens here and now (the **present tense**), in the past (the **past tense**) or in the future (the **future tense**)

tense[2] ADJECTIVE **tenser, tensest 1** if you feel tense, you feel nervous and unable to relax **2** a tense situation makes people feel nervous and worried **3** your muscles are tense when they are stretched so that they feel tight

▶ **tension** NOUN **tensions 1** tension is nervousness or worry about something unpleasant that might happen **2** the tension of a piece of wire, rope or wool is how tightly it is stretched or twisted

tent NOUN **tents** a temporary shelter made of canvas or nylon supported by a frame

tentacle NOUN **tentacles** tentacles are the long, thin, flexible parts on the body of an octopus and some other sea animals

tenth ADJECTIVE AND ADVERB after ninth and before eleventh: *the tenth month of the year* • *He came tenth out of twenty in the singing competition.*
NOUN **tenths** the fraction $\frac{1}{10}$, which means one of ten equal parts of something: *a tenth of a litre*

tepee (pronounced **tee**-pee) NOUN **tepees** a sort of tent used by Native American people in the past, made by tying poles together in a cone shape and covering them with animal skins

tepid ADJECTIVE tepid liquid is slightly warm

term NOUN **terms**
1 one of the periods of time that the school or college year is divided into: *the autumn term*
2 any limited period of time: *the president's term of office*
3 a word or expression with a particular meaning, or used in a particular subject area: *What is the term for someone who collects old coins?* • *complicated medical terms*
4 the terms of a contract or other agreement are the individual points or conditions it contains
5 people who are on goods terms, or who are on bad terms, have a good, or bad, relationship with each other
VERB **terms, terming, termed** what something is termed is what it is named or called: *Dogs that are used for hunting are often termed 'hounds'.*

terminal NOUN **terminals**
1 a building at an airport where passengers arrive or depart
2 a bus or rail terminus
3 a place or point where a connection is made to an electrical circuit
4 (*ICT*) a computer terminal is one of several visual display units or monitors connected to one large central computer
ADJECTIVE **1** a terminal illness is one that cannot be cured and that causes death **2** of or at the end

terminate VERB **terminates, terminating, terminated** to end or come to a stop
▶ **termination** NOUN the ending of something

terminus NOUN **termini** or **terminuses** a place or building at the end of a railway or bus route

termite NOUN **termites** a small pale-coloured insect that eats wood

terrace NOUN **terraces**
1 a row of houses that are connected to each other
2 a raised level area, usually with paving, beside a house
3 a raised bank of earth with a level top
4 the terraces at a football or rugby ground are the sloping banks or tiers of seats where spectators stand or sit

terrain NOUN terrain is land, especially a particular type of land: *This is wooded terrain.*

terrapin NOUN **terrapins** a type of

small turtle that lives in freshwater ponds and rivers

terrestrial ADJECTIVE from the Earth, rather than from space or another planet

terrible ADJECTIVE very bad: *a terrible smell* • *a terrible shock* • *Your writing is really terrible.*

▶ **terribly** ADVERB extremely: *I'm terribly sorry I broke your vase.*

terrier NOUN **terriers** any of various breeds of small dog

terrific ADJECTIVE **1** excellent: *The party was terrific.* **2** very great or powerful: *a terrific wind*

▶ **terrifically** ADVERB extremely or very greatly: *We were terrifically pleased to get the award.*

terrify VERB **terrifies, terrifying, terrified** if something terrifies you, it frightens you very much

territory NOUN **territories 1** the land that a country or ruler owns or controls: *on British territory* **2** an area or region: *They were travelling on foot across mountainous territory.*

▶ **territorial** ADJECTIVE to do with territory: *a territorial dispute*

terror NOUN great fear

terrorism NOUN the use of violence by small or illegal political organizations with the aim of forcing a government or society to accept their demands

▶ **terrorist** NOUN **terrorists** someone who uses terrorism

▶ **terrorize** *or* **terrorise** VERB **terrorizes, terrorizing, terrorized** to terrorize people is to frighten them by using, or threatening to use, violence

tessellation NOUN **tessellation** putting shapes together so that there are no spaces between them

▶ **tessellated** ADJECTIVE (*maths*) tessellated shapes fit together without any spaces in between them

test NOUN **tests 1** a set of questions or a short examination to find out your ability or knowledge: *a spelling test* **2** something done to find out whether something is in good condition or is working well: *medical tests*

VERB **tests, testing, tested** to test someone or something is to give them a short examination or to carry out tests on them

testament NOUN **testaments 1** a written statement: *It was a testament of her friendship.* **2** the **Old Testament** and the **New Testament** are the two parts of the **Bible**

testicle NOUN **testicles** one of two glands in a male animal's body where sperm is made

testify VERB **testifies, testifying, testified** to give information or evidence, especially in a law court

testimonial NOUN **testimonials 1** a written statement about someone's character, skills and abilities **2** a gift given to someone as a way of thanking them for service they have given in the past

testimony NOUN **testimonies** a witness's testimony is the statement they make in a law court

test match NOUN **test matches** one of a series of matches played between two international teams, especially cricket teams

test tube NOUN **test tubes** a thin glass tube, closed at one end and open at the other, used in chemical experiments

testy ADJECTIVE **testier, testiest** easily irritated or made angry

tetanus NOUN a very serious disease caused by bacteria getting into a cut in your skin

tether VERB **tethers, tethering, tethered** to tether an animal is to tie it with a rope to a post or bar

tetrahedron NOUN **tetrahedrons** (*maths*) a solid shape with four sides or faces

text NOUN **texts 1** the written or printed words in a book **2** a text message

VERB **texts, texting, texted** to send a text message to someone

textbook NOUN **textbooks** a book containing information on a particular subject, used by pupils in schools or students in colleges

Aa
Bb
Cc
Dd
Ee
Ff
Gg
Hh
Ii
Jj
Kk
Ll
Mm
Nn
Oo
Pp
Qq
Rr
Ss
Tt
Uu
Vv
Ww
Xx
Yy
Zz

textile NOUN **textiles** a cloth or fabric made by weaving

text message NOUN **text messages** a short message typed into a mobile phone and sent to another phone

texture NOUN **textures 1** something's texture is the way it feels when you touch it **2** (*music*) the effect of all the different sounds in a piece of music

than CONJUNCTION **than** is used when you are making comparisons: *The test was easier than I thought it would be.* • *He can run faster than his big brother.*

thank VERB **thanks, thanking, thanked** you thank someone when you let them know you are grateful for something they have done for you or have given you

• **thank you** you say 'thank you' to someone to tell them you are grateful for something they have done

▶ **thanks** PLURAL NOUN you say 'thanks' to someone, or express your thanks to them, when you express your gratitude or appreciation

• **thanks to 1** with the help of: *We didn't miss any of the film, thanks to Dad.* **2** owing to: *We were stuck in the airport all day, thanks to the strike.*

thankful ADJECTIVE happy, relieved and grateful

▶ **thankfully** ADVERB happily or gratefully

thankless ADJECTIVE a thankless job or task is one for which you get no thanks or appreciation

that ADJECTIVE **those** the word **that** is used before a noun to refer to a person or thing that is some distance away from you, or that has already been mentioned: *Who is that girl over there?* • *Pass me that towel, please.*

PRONOUN **those** the word **that** is used instead of a noun to refer to a person or thing that is some distance away from you, or that has already been mentioned: *I don't want to know that.* • *Who is that at the door?* • *That's my friend, Gerry.*

ADVERB to the extent or degree mentioned: *I didn't think I'd run that far.* • *The film wasn't that bad.*

CONJUNCTION **that** is used after verbs that have to do with saying, thinking or feeling, and to connect clauses: *He said that he hated sports.* • *I'm afraid that I can't offer you much help.*

thatch NOUN thatch is reeds, rushes or straw used as a roofing material for houses

VERB **thatches, thatching, thatched** to thatch a roof is to cover it with reeds, rushes or straw

that'd a short way to say and write **that had** or **that would**: *That'd better be the pizza delivery. I'm starving!* • *That'd be nice.*

that'll a short way to say and write **that will**: *That'll never happen.*

that's a short way to say and write **that is**: *That's not what I meant.*

• **that's that** if someone says 'That's that', they mean that there is no more to be done or said about something

thaw VERB **thaws, thawing, thawed** something that has been frozen thaws when it starts to melt

the ADJECTIVE **the** is used before nouns to refer to a particular person, thing or group: *The bus arrived late, as usual.* • *Is it on the right or the left side of the road?* • *The men rode on horses and the women rode in carriages.*

theatre NOUN **theatres 1** a theatre is a building where plays, operas or musicals are performed **2** theatre is the acting profession or the dramatic arts **3** a special room in a hospital where operations are done

▶ **theatrical** ADJECTIVE to do with plays or acting

thee PRONOUN an old-fashioned word for **you**: *I tell thee again, eye of my eye, this hunting is ended.*

theft NOUN **thefts** stealing: *car thefts*

their ADJECTIVE belonging to them: *They told me where their house was.*

▶ **theirs** PRONOUN a word you use to talk about something belonging to a group of people or things that have already been mentioned: *They say it* belongs to them but I know it's not theirs.

✦Be careful not to confuse the spellings of **their**, **there** and **they're**.

There points something out: *Put this box over **there**. • **There** is nothing to do here.*

They're is short for **they are**: *They're late.*

them PRONOUN a word you use to talk about two or more people or things that have already been mentioned: *The girls waved to me and I waved back to them. • 'Do you like your new boots?' 'Yes, I like them a lot.'*

theme NOUN **themes** the main idea, subject, or melody in a piece of writing, a talk, or a piece of music

theme park NOUN **theme parks** an amusement park with activities connected to a special subject or theme

themselves PRONOUN **1** you use **themselves** after a verb or preposition when the people who perform the action are affected by it: *They'd made themselves a cosy little shelter.* **2 themselves** is also used to show that a group of people do something without any help from other people: *They'll have to work it out for themselves.* **3** you can use **themselves** to show more clearly who you mean: *They themselves are innocent.*

then ADVERB **1** at that time, in the past or future: *I didn't know you then. • The rest of the kids should be here by then.* **2** after that time, or next: *I went for a swim and then I went home.*
CONJUNCTION as a result, or in that case: *If you have been eating sweets, then you must brush your teeth.*

theology NOUN the study of God and religion

theorem NOUN **theorems** (*maths*) a statement that has to be proved

theoretical ADJECTIVE something that is theoretical is based on theory and ideas rather than practical knowledge or experience

▶ **theoretically** ADVERB possibly but not absolutely certain

theory NOUN **theories 1** a theory is an idea or suggested explanation that has not yet been proved **2** theory is the ideas and principles of an art or science rather than its practice

therapy NOUN **therapies** the treatment of diseases or disorders, usually without surgery or drugs

▶ **therapist** NOUN **therapists** someone who is an expert in therapy of a particular sort: *a speech therapist*

there ADVERB at, in, or to that place: *Don't stop there. I was just beginning to enjoy the story. • My granny lives there. • I'm going there tomorrow.*
PRONOUN you use **there** with *is* or *are* to draw attention to what is going to follow: *There is a mouse somewhere in this house.*

✦Be careful not to confuse the spellings of **there**, **their** and **they're**.

Their shows you someone owns something: *They have brought **their** exercise books.*

They're is short for **they are**: *They're late.*

thereabouts ADVERB approximately: *It will cost £50 or thereabouts.*

thereby ADVERB (*formal*) in that way: *We cut down all the trees, thereby letting more light into the house.*

therefore ADVERB for that reason or because of that: *She had been awake all that night and therefore was very tired the next day.*

therm NOUN **therms** a unit of heat used for measuring gas

thermal ADJECTIVE using heat or to do with heat

thermometer NOUN **thermometers** an instrument for measuring how hot or cold something is

Thermos NOUN **Thermoses** (*trademark*) a type of **vacuum flask**

thermostat NOUN **thermostats** a device that controls the temperature in a room or of a heating system

thesaurus NOUN **thesauri** or **thesauruses** a book that lists groups of

Aa
Bb
Cc
Dd
Ee
Ff
Gg
Hh
Ii
Jj
Kk
Ll
Mm
Nn
Oo
Pp
Qq
Rr
Ss
Tt
Uu
Vv
Ww
Xx
Yy
Zz

words that have similar meanings and can be used instead of each other

these ADJECTIVE **these** is used before a noun to refer to people or things nearby or which are being mentioned: *Both these cups are dirty.* • *On these cold winter days, you have to wrap up warmly.* • *Can you make me a pair of these gloves?*

PRONOUN **these** is used instead of a noun to refer to people or things nearby or which are being mentioned: *Are these the same as the ones you had yesterday?* • *These are difficult times for everyone.*

they PRONOUN you use **they** to talk about two or more people or things that have already been mentioned or pointed out for the first time: *Apes are not monkeys. They don't have tails.* • *What did they think of your idea?*

they'd a short way to say and write **they had** or **they would**: *They'd all had their lunch.* • *They'd be very grateful for your help.*

they'll a short way to say and write **they will** or **they shall**: *They'll not be hungry again until supper time.*

they're a short way to say and write **they are**: *They're going skating after school.*

they've a short way to say and write **they have**: *They've never been skating before.*

thick ADJECTIVE **thicker, thickest**

1 quite wide from one side to the other: *a thick piece of rope*

2 something is a certain measurement thick when it measures that distance between one side and the other: *The ice was two feet thick.*

3 made up of parts that are very close together or densely packed: *thick wool*

4 not having a lot of liquid in it or not flowing easily: *thick gravy*

5 thick smoke or fog is dense and difficult to see through

6 (*informal*) stupid

NOUN

• **in the thick of something** in the middle of something or in the place where all the action is happening

• **through thick and thin** no matter what happens

▸ **thicken** VERB **thickens, thickening, thickened** to make or become thicker

▸ **thickness** NOUN **thicknesses** how thick something is, especially compared with other things

thicket NOUN **thickets** a mass of bushes growing together

thick-skinned ADJECTIVE a thick-skinned person does not get upset when they are insulted or criticized

thief NOUN **thieves** someone who steals

▸ **thieve** VERB **thieves, thieving, thieved** to steal

▸ **thieving** NOUN stealing

thigh NOUN **thighs** your thighs are the top parts of your legs above your knees

thimble NOUN **thimbles** a metal cover for your finger used when you are sewing to help push the needle through the fabric

thin ADJECTIVE **thinner, thinnest 1** not wide from one side to the other **2** a thin person doesn't have much fat on their body **3** not dense or thick: *His hair is getting a bit thin.* • *a thin porridge*

VERB **thins, thinning, thinned** to make something thin or thinner, for example by adding water or liquid to it

thing NOUN **things 1** an object, or something that is not alive: *I bought a few things for the party when I was in town.* • *Where's the thing for opening bottles?* **2** a fact, item, action or event: *We've got lots of things to discuss.* • *I hope I haven't done the wrong thing.*

think VERB **thinks, thinking, thought 1** to think is to have or form ideas in your mind: *Don't disturb him. He's thinking.* **2** what you think about something is the opinion you have of it: *I don't think much of their new album.* **3** if you are thinking of doing something, you are planning to do it

third ADJECTIVE AND ADVERB after second and before fourth: *That's the third time he's fallen off his bike.*

NOUN **thirds** the fraction ⅓, which means one of three equal parts of something: *The bottle holds a third of a litre.*

Third World NOUN the Third World is an old name given to nations of the world that are just developing and are fairly poor

thirst NOUN thirst is the feeling that you must have something to drink
▸ **thirsty** ADJECTIVE **thirstier, thirstiest** feeling you must have something to drink

thirteen NOUN the number 13
▸ **thirteenth** ADJECTIVE AND ADVERB after twelfth and before fourteenth: *You become a teenager on your thirteenth birthday.*

thirtieth ADJECTIVE AND ADVERB after twenty-ninth and before thirty-first: *February does not have a thirtieth day.*

thirty NOUN **thirties** the number 30

this ADJECTIVE **these** the word **this** is used before a noun to refer to a person or thing nearby or which is being mentioned: *This apple is sour.* • *We have got PE this afternoon.*
PRONOUN the word **this** is used instead of a noun to refer to a person or thing nearby or which is being mentioned: *I can't eat this.* • *Where are you going after this?*
ADVERB to the extent or degree mentioned: *It was this long and this wide.* • *We've come this far. Don't let's give up now.*

thistle NOUN **thistles** a plant with prickly leaves and purple flowers

thorn NOUN **thorns** a hard sharp point that sticks out from the stems of some plants
▸ **thorny** ADJECTIVE **thornier, thorniest 1** covered with thorns **2** a thorny problem or question is difficult to solve or deal with

thorough ADJECTIVE **1** you are thorough when you do something carefully, paying attention to every detail: *He made a thorough search.* **2** complete: *It was a thorough nuisance.*
▸ **thoroughly** ADVERB **1** with great care and attention to every detail: *Clean all the kitchen surfaces thoroughly.* **2** completely: *She was feeling thoroughly fed-up with the whole thing.*

thoroughbred NOUN **thoroughbreds** a horse bred from parents that both have pedigrees

those ADJECTIVE **those** is used before a noun to refer to people or things at a distance from you or which are being mentioned: *Who are those two boys?* • *In those days, people didn't have cars.*
PRONOUN **those** is used instead of a noun to refer to people or things at a distance from you or which are being mentioned: *What are those?* • *Those are just some of the coins in his collection.*

thou PRONOUN an old-fashioned word for **you**

though CONJUNCTION in spite of the fact that: *We only waited for half an hour, though it seemed like hours.* • *He went out, though I told him not to.*
ADVERB however: *It's a pity we didn't win. It was an exciting match, though.*
• **as though** as if: *He looks as though he needs a good meal.*

thought VERB a way of changing the verb **think** to make a past tense. It can be used with or without a helping verb: *I thought I heard a noise.* • *He had thought about the problem all day.*
NOUN **thoughts 1** thought is thinking **2** a thought is an idea or something you think

thoughtful ADJECTIVE **1** if someone looks thoughtful, they look as if they are thinking **2** a thoughtful person is kind and thinks of other people
▸ **thoughtfully** ADVERB in a thoughtful way: *'I just can't work this out,' he said, scratching his head thoughtfully.* • *She'd very thoughtfully left drinks and sandwiches on the kitchen table for us.*
▸ **thoughtfulness** NOUN being thoughtful

thoughtless ADJECTIVE a thoughtless person does things without first thinking about how they or other people will be affected by their actions

▸ **thoughtlessness** NOUN not thinking about how your actions will affect other people

thousand NOUN **thousands** the number 1000

▸ **thousandth** ADJECTIVE AND ADVERB coming last in a series of one thousand things: *the thousandth customer in the shop today* NOUN **thousandths** one of a thousand equal parts of something

thrash VERB **thrashes, thrashing, thrashed 1** to thrash someone is to beat them **2** to thrash or thrash about is to make wild violent movements

thread NOUN **threads** a thin strand of cotton, wool or silk used for sewing VERB **threads, threading, threaded** to thread a needle is to push a strand of thread through the hole in the top of a sewing needle

threadbare ADJECTIVE a threadbare carpet or other piece of fabric has been worn thin by use

threat NOUN a warning that someone is going to hurt you or harm you, especially if you don't do what they say

▸ **threaten** VERB **threatens, threatening, threatened** to threaten someone is to say that they will be harmed or hurt if they do not do something

three NOUN **threes** the number 3

three-dimensional ADJECTIVE a three-dimensional shape is solid and has length, breadth and height that you can measure. It might also be called a **solid** shape

thresh VERB **threshes, threshing, threshed** to thresh corn is to beat it so that the grain is separated from the straw

threshold NOUN **thresholds** a piece of wood or stone on the floor at a door

• **on the threshold** to be on the threshold of something is to be just about to start something new and important: *We are on the threshold of a big change.*

threw VERB a way of changing the verb

throw to make a past tense: *He threw the ball hard.*

thrift NOUN being careful about money, saving as much as you can and not wasting any

▸ **thrifty** ADJECTIVE **thriftier, thriftiest** using money and other things carefully, without wasting any

thrill VERB **thrills, thrilling, thrilled** something thrills you when it makes you feel excited and very pleased NOUN **thrills** something that gives you a glowing feeling of excitement and pleasure

▸ **thriller** NOUN **thrillers** a book, film or play with an exciting plot, full of danger and frightening events

▸ **thrilling** ADJECTIVE very exciting

thrive VERB **thrives, thriving, thrived** or **throve, thrived** or **thriven** if a person or thing thrives, they grow strong and healthy, or become successful

throat NOUN **throats 1** your throat is the top part of the tube that goes from your mouth down to your stomach **2** your throat is also the front part of your neck

throb VERB **throbs, throbbing, throbbed 1** something throbs when it beats regularly, as your heart or pulse does **2** an injured part of your body throbs when you feel pains in it that come and go like the regular beat of your pulse

throne NOUN **thrones 1** a special chair that a king or queen, or a bishop, sits on **2** the throne is the position or power of a monarch

throng NOUN **throngs** a large crowd or gathering

throttle NOUN **throttles** the throttle in a car or machine is the part of the engine through which petrol or steam can be turned on or off VERB **throttles, throttling, throttled** to throttle someone is to grip them by the throat and strangle them

through PREPOSITION **1** entering at one side and coming out at the other: *He walked through the door.* **2** from end to end: *She was flicking through a* *magazine.* **3** because of, or by means of: *He ended up in hospital through his own stupidity.* • *I heard about it through a friend.*

ADVERB **1** entering at one side and coming out at the other: *He opened the hatch and stuck his head through.* **2** from end to end: *You're wet through.* • *Take this booklet away and read it through.*

ADJECTIVE **1** a through route is one that gets you from one place to another and is not blocked anywhere along the way **2** a through train does not stop between the place it leaves from and the end of the line

✦ The words **through** and **threw** sound the same but remember that they have different spellings. **Threw** is the past tense of **throw**.

throughout PREPOSITION all the way through, or in every part: *It rained throughout June and July.* • *There will be regular news bulletins throughout the day.*

ADVERB all the way through, or in every part: *The show was a great success, and the children behaved themselves throughout.*

throw VERB **throws, throwing, threw, thrown 1** to throw something is to send it through the air with force: *He threw the ball into the scrum.* • *She threw her schoolbag down and rushed to switch on the TV.* **2** a horse throws its rider when it makes the rider fall off its back **3** if something throws you, it confuses you

NOUN **throws** a throwing movement: *That was a great throw!*

thrush NOUN **thrushes** a wild bird with brown feathers and lighter speckled breast

thrust VERB **thrusts, thrusting, thrust** to thrust something is to push it quickly and violently: *He thrust his hands into his coat pockets.*

NOUN **thrusts** a quick and violent push forward: *With a thrust of his sword, he scored the winning point.*

thud NOUN **thuds** a dull sound made by something heavy hitting the ground

VERB **thuds, thudding, thudded** to thud is to make this sound

thug NOUN **thugs** a violent and brutal man

thumb NOUN **thumbs** the short thick finger that is at a different angle from the other four fingers on your hand

• **be under someone's thumb** to be completely under someone's control

thump VERB **thumps, thumping, thumped 1** to thump someone or something is to hit them hard **2** to make a regular heavy sound by banging against something

thunder NOUN the loud and deep rumbling sound that you hear after a flash of lightning

VERB **thunders, thundering, thundered** to make a loud rumbling sound, or to talk in a very loud, angry voice

▶ **thunderous** ADJECTIVE very loud, like thunder

▶ **thundery** ADJECTIVE the weather is thundery when there are dark clouds and thunder

thunderstorm NOUN **thunderstorms** a storm with thunder and lightning

Thursday NOUN **Thursdays** the day of the week after Wednesday and before Friday

✦ **Thursday** comes from the Old English word **Thursdæg**, which means *Thor's day*. Thor is the Norse god of thunder.

thus ADVERB **1** as a result of that: *The heating has broken down; thus everyone is being sent home early.* **2** in this or that way: *The poem begins thus: 'I must go down to the sea again.'*

thwart VERB **thwarts, thwarting, thwarted** to thwart someone is to stop them from doing what they want to do

thy ADJECTIVE an old-fashioned word for **your**: *thy will be done*

tiara NOUN **tiaras** a piece of jewellery like a small crown

tick¹ NOUN **ticks 1** a small mark (✓) used to show that something is correct

Aa
Bb
Cc
Dd
Ee
Ff
Gg
Hh
Ii
Jj
Kk
Ll
Mm
Nn
Oo
Pp
Qq
Rr
Ss
Tt
Uu
Vv
Ww
Xx
Yy
Zz

or to mark off the things on a list that you have dealt with **2** the soft regular tapping or clicking noise that a clock makes **3** a very short time: *Can you wait a tick while I get my coat?*
VERB **ticks, ticking, ticked 1** to tick something is to mark it with a tick **2** a clock ticks when it makes regular tapping or clicking noises

tick² NOUN **ticks** a small insect that burrows into an animal's skin and sucks its blood

ticket NOUN **tickets** a small piece of printed paper or card that shows you have paid a fare on a bus, train or aeroplane, or that allows you to get into a concert or other event

tickle VERB **tickles, tickling, tickled 1** to tickle someone is to touch part of their body lightly so that they get a tingling or prickly feeling that makes them laugh **2** something tickles when it causes this tingling or prickly feeling on your skin
NOUN **tickles** a tickling movement
▸ **ticklish** ADJECTIVE if you are ticklish, you are sensitive to tickling
▸ **tickly** ADJECTIVE **ticklier, tickliest** causing a tingling or prickly feeling

tidal ADJECTIVE affected by tides or to do with tides

tidal wave NOUN **tidal waves** a huge wave, often caused by a volcano erupting under the sea or by unusually high tides

tiddlywinks NOUN a game played with small round coloured discs, in which you press one disc down on another making it flip upwards and fall into a cup

tide NOUN the regular rise and fall of the level of the sea
VERB **tides, tiding, tided**
• **tide someone over** if you have or get something to tide you over, it helps you get through a difficult time, especially one when you don't have enough money

tidily ADVERB neatly

tidiness NOUN being tidy or neat

tidings PLURAL NOUN a slightly old-fashioned word for news: *glad tidings*

tidy ADJECTIVE **tidier, tidiest 1** a place is tidy when it is neat and everything is in its proper place **2** a tidy person likes to keep things neat and in their proper place
VERB **tidies, tidying, tidied** to put things back in their proper places and make everything neat

tie VERB **ties, tying, tied 1** to tie one thing to another is to join them or fasten them together, using string, rope or wire **2** to tie a knot or bow is to make loops that you twist round each other to form a knot or bow **3** two teams or competitors tie when they each have the same number of points: *They tied for second place.*
NOUN **ties 1** a narrow strip of material that goes round your neck under your shirt collar and is tied in a knot just under your chin **2** a situation in which two teams or competitors each have the same number of points **3** a match between two teams in a competition

tie-breaker NOUN **tie-breakers** an extra question or test that will decide the winner in a contest where two people or teams have the same score

tier NOUN **tiers** a row or layer, with another row or layer above or below it

tiger NOUN **tigers** a large striped animal related to the cat

tight ADJECTIVE **tighter, tightest 1** fitting very closely or too closely: *a tight shirt* • *The top on this jar is very tight.* **2** very firm: *Have you got a tight grip on that rope?* **3** not leaving much room or space for movement: *a tight bend*
▸ **tighten** VERB **tightens, tightening, tightened** to make or become tight or tighter
▸ **tightly** *or* **tight** ADVERB **1** closely: *She held her doll tight.* **2** firmly: *Hold tight. It's going to be a bumpy ride.* **3** fully stretched: *Make sure that rope is pulled tight.*

tightrope NOUN **tightropes** a long piece of rope high in the air, which an acrobat walks along

tights PLURAL NOUN tights are a one-piece covering for your feet, legs and bottom made of thin stretchy material

Aa
Bb
Cc
Dd
Ee
Ff
Gg
Hh
Ii
Jj
Kk
Ll
Mm
Nn
Oo
Pp
Qq
Rr
Ss
Tt
Uu
Vv
Ww
Xx
Yy
Zz

tigress NOUN **tigresses** a female tiger

tile NOUN **tiles** a piece of baked clay of various sizes, used for putting on roofs, walls or floors
VERB **tiles, tiling, tiled** to tile a roof, wall or floor is to put tiles on it

till¹ NOUN **tills** a machine in a shop used for counting up what customers have bought and which has a drawer or box for the money

till² VERB **tills, tilling, tilled** to till soil is to prepare it for crops or other plants by ploughing it or turning the soil over

till³ PREPOSITION AND CONJUNCTION until

tiller NOUN **tillers** a long piece of wood attached to the rudder at the back of a boat and which you use to steer the boat

tilt VERB **tilts, tilting, tilted** 1 to tilt something is to make it lean to one side: *She tilted her head.* 2 if something tilts, it leans to one side: *The floor tilted slightly.*

timber NOUN 1 wood that is used for building things such as houses 2 trees that can be used to provide wood for building

timbre (pronounced **tam**-bir) NOUN **timbres** the timbre of someone's voice or of a musical instrument is the quality of sound it makes

time NOUN **times**
1 time is the passing of days, weeks, months and years
2 the time is the hour of the day: *What's the time?*
3 the time of something is when it happens or is done: *Do you know the times of the trains to Edinburgh?*
4 the number of minutes, hours, days or years that something takes to do or happen: *It takes a long time for water to wear down rocks.*
5 one of several occasions: *They've won the cup four times.*
6 a particular period: *in olden times*
7 a suitable or right moment: *Now is not a good time to ask for more money.*
VERB **times, timing, timed** 1 to time something is to use a clock or watch to find out how long it takes or when it will be ready 2 to time something well is to choose a good time to do it
• **from time to time** things happen or are done from time to time if they happen or are done occasionally, but not all the time
• **in** or **on time** to be in time, or on time, is to arrive or happen at the right time and not be late, or too late
▸ **timely** ADJECTIVE something that is timely happens at just the right time
▸ **timer** NOUN **timers** a device for timing something

times PLURAL NOUN (*maths*) **times** is used in multiplication between the numbers you are multiplying: *Two times four is eight.*

time scale NOUN **time scales** the time during which an event or process happens: *Evolution happens over a time scale of thousands of years.*

timetable NOUN **timetables** a table listing the times when things should or will happen

timid ADJECTIVE nervous, shy and easily frightened: *Pip's a rather timid child.* • *a timid smile*
▸ **timidity** NOUN being nervous and shy
▸ **timidly** ADVERB in a shy, nervous way

timing NOUN choosing just the right moment to do or say something: *All comedians need to learn good timing.* • *The timing of the party is very important.*

timpani PLURAL NOUN the large metal drums that are usually part of a symphony orchestra

tin NOUN **tins** 1 tin is a soft, silvery metal 2 a tin is a metal container for food: *Let's just open a tin of soup for lunch.* • *a biscuit tin*

tinder NOUN dry material, especially small bits of wood, that can be used to light a fire

tinge NOUN **tinges** a slight amount of something, especially a colour or feeling: *white with a tinge of pink* • *a tinge of sadness in her voice*

Aa
Bb
Cc
Dd
Ee
Ff
Gg
Hh
Ii
Jj
Kk
Ll
Mm
Nn
Oo
Pp
Qq
Rr
Ss
Tt
Uu
Vv
Ww
Xx
Yy
Zz

Aa
Bb
Cc
Dd
Ee
Ff
Gg
Hh
Ii
Jj
Kk
Ll
Mm
Nn
Oo
Pp
Qq
Rr
Ss
Tt
Uu
Vv
Ww
Xx
Yy
Zz

tingle VERB **tingles, tingling, tingled** to prickle, tickle or sting slightly: *My face was tingling in the cold night air.*
NOUN **tingles** a prickling, tickling feeling: *I felt a tingle of excitement as the curtain went up.*

tinker VERB **tinkers, tinkering, tinkered** to try to repair or improve a machine by making small changes: *Phil spends hours tinkering with his motorbike.*
NOUN **tinkers** a person who used to travel around mending pots and pans for people

tinkle VERB **tinkles, tinkling, tinkled** to make a sound like small bells ringing
NOUN **tinkles** a small, repeated ringing sound: *the tinkle of the bell on the cat's collar*

tinny ADJECTIVE **tinnier, tinniest 1** a tinny sound is thin, hard and high: *Keith pressed the buzzer and heard a tinny voice telling him to open the door and go upstairs.* **2** a tinny object is made of thin or bad quality metal

tinsel NOUN strands of shiny, glittery material that is used as a Christmas decoration

tint NOUN **tints** a small amount of colour: *a bluish tint in her green eyes*
VERB **tints, tinting, tinted** to colour something slightly

tiny ADJECTIVE **tinier, tiniest** very, very small: *a baby's tiny hands and feet • the tiniest handwriting you ever saw*

tip¹ NOUN **tips** the point at the end or the top of something: *arrows with poison tips • Point to it with the tip of your finger.*

tip² VERB **tips, tipping, tipped 1** to tip something is to tilt it: *Tip the chairs forward against the tables.* **2** if something tips, it tilts: *The seat tips back.* **3** to spill the contents of a container: *They just tip the rubbish over the side of the ship. • Kitty tipped all her toys on to the floor.*
NOUN **tips 1** a rubbish dump: *taking the old carpet to the tip* **2** a very untidy place: *Your bedroom's a tip.*

tip³ NOUN **tips 1** a small extra amount of money for someone who has done a job for you: *They left almost ten dollars tip.*

2 a small piece of helpful advice: *useful tips on studying for an exam*
VERB **tips, tipping, tipped** to give someone a small gift of money when they have done a good job for you: *How much did you tip the taxi-driver?*

tiptoe VERB **tiptoes, tiptoeing, tiptoed** to walk somewhere very quietly or carefully on your toes: *tiptoeing along the corridor, trying not to wake the other guests*
NOUN
• **on tiptoe** standing or walking balanced on your toes: *I can just see the sea if I stand on tiptoe.*

tire VERB **tires, tiring, tired 1** to run out of energy and need a rest: *Auntie tires easily nowadays and has a rest every afternoon.* **2** to tire of something is to get bored of it: *I'm beginning to tire of Nigel's stories.*
▶ **tired** ADJECTIVE **1** needing a rest: *You must be tired after your journey.* **2** if you are tired of something, you are bored with it: *I'm tired of wearing the same clothes every day.*
▶ **tiring** ADJECTIVE making you feel that you need a rest or sleep: *a tiring climb up the hill*

✦ The words **tire** and **tyre** sound the same but remember that they have different spellings. A **tyre** is the covering of a wheel. However, in North America these words are both spelt **tire**.

tireless ADJECTIVE having a lot of energy and never needing a rest: *tireless efforts to raise money for charity*

tiresome ADJECTIVE annoying or boring: *My sister has a tiresome habit of finishing my sentences for me.*

tissue NOUN **tissues 1** a tissue is a paper handkerchief **2** tissue is very thin paper that is used for protecting delicate objects **3** tissue is the substance that animals and plants are made of: *muscle tissue • plant tissue*

tit NOUN **tits** a type of small bird

titbit NOUN **titbits 1** a small tasty bit of food **2** a small but interesting bit of gossip

title NOUN **titles 1** the name of something like a book, song or film: *What's the title of your poem?* **2** a word that you can use before your name: *Her title is 'Doctor', not 'Mrs'.*

titter VERB **titters, tittering, tittered** to laugh in a silly, nervous or embarrassed way

NOUN **titters** a silly, nervous laugh

to PREPOSITION **1** towards: *walking to the shops* **2** as far as: *a mile from the house to the station* **3** compared with: *win by two goals to one*

ADVERB **1** almost closed: *Would you pull the door to?* **2** awake: *He came to in a few moments.*

• **to and fro** backwards and forwards

toad NOUN **toads** an animal like a large frog

toadstool NOUN **toadstools** a fungus like a large mushroom that is often poisonous

toast NOUN **toasts 1** toast is bread that has been made crisp by being sliced and heated: *toast and marmalade for breakfast* **2** a toast is when people drink together to express a good wish for someone: *I'd like to propose a toast to the bride and groom.*

VERB **toasts, toasting, toasted 1** to toast food is to cook it under a grill or at a fire **2** to toast a person is to have a drink and wish them well

▸ **toaster** NOUN **toasters** a machine for heating slices of bread to make them crisp to eat

tobacco NOUN a type of plant whose leaves are dried and used for smoking or chewing

▸ **tobacconist** NOUN **tobacconists** someone who sells cigarettes, cigars and pipes and sometimes sweets and newspapers

toboggan NOUN **toboggans** a sledge

today NOUN this day: *Today is Tuesday.*

ADVERB **1** on this day: *I can't come today.* **2** nowadays, at the present time: *People are taller today than they were a hundred years ago.*

toddler NOUN **toddlers** a very young child who has just learned to walk

toe NOUN **toes 1** one of the five jointed parts at the end of your foot: *reach up high, standing on your toes* **2** the closed end of a shoe or sock: *a hole in the toe of my sock*

toffee NOUN **toffees** a sticky sweet that may be chewy or hard: *a piece of toffee* • *a bag of toffees*

toga NOUN **togas** a long loose piece of clothing worn by men in ancient Rome

together ADVERB with each other: *The two friends always walk to school together.* • *Mix the sugar and eggs together in a bowl.*

toggle NOUN **toggles 1** a small bar of wood or plastic that passes through a loop to fasten a coat or jacket **2** (*technology*) a switch or a key on a computer keyboard that turns a feature on or off

VERB **toggles, toggling, toggled** (*technology*) to switch between different features or files using a toggle switch or a computer key

toil VERB **toils, toiling, toiled** to work hard for a long time

NOUN hard work that takes a long time

toilet NOUN **toilets 1** a large bowl-shaped piece of furniture where human waste can be washed away **2** a room with a toilet in it

▸ **toiletries** PLURAL NOUN products that people use to keep clean and to look and smell nice: *Perfume, toothpaste, shaving cream and hairspray are all toiletries.*

token NOUN **tokens 1** a plastic or metal disc or a coupon or voucher that can be used instead of money: *a book token worth £10* • *You need to buy special tokens to make the machine work.* **2** a sign of something: *I've got a bracelet as a token of our friendship.*

told VERB the way of changing the verb **tell** to make a past tense. It can be used with or without a helping verb: *Every day the teacher told us a story.* • *Has Sarah told you her news yet?*

tolerable ADJECTIVE something is tolerable if you can put up with it

tolerant ADJECTIVE willing to accept

Aa
Bb
Cc
Dd
Ee
Ff
Gg
Hh
Ii
Jj
Kk
Ll
Mm
Nn
Oo
Pp
Qq
Rr
Tt
Uu
Vv
Ww
Xx
Yy
Zz

that other people have different opinions from yours

▶ **tolerance** NOUN patience and willingness to accept other people's ideas and behaviour

tolerate VERB **tolerates, tolerating, tolerated** to put up with something: *I can't tolerate this noise for much longer.*

toll¹ NOUN **tolls 1** a fee you must pay to cross a bridge or use certain roads **2** the number of people killed or injured by something: *The death toll was highest in the city centre.*

toll² VERB **tolls, tolling, tolled** to ring a bell slowly

tomahawk NOUN **tomahawks** a small axe used by Native Americans as a weapon and a tool

tomato NOUN **tomatoes** a juicy red-skinned fruit that is used like a vegetable in salads, sauces and sandwiches

tomb (pronounced **toom**) NOUN **tombs** a place like a room where a dead body is buried

tombola NOUN **tombolas** a kind of lottery where certain numbered tickets win prizes

tomboy NOUN **tomboys** a girl who likes rough, energetic activities

tombstone NOUN **tombstones** a piece of stone with a dead person's name written on it that stands at the end of that person's grave

tomcat NOUN **tomcats** a male cat

tomorrow NOUN the day after today: *Tomorrow is Wednesday.*

ADVERB on the day after today: *We've got PE tomorrow.*

tomtom NOUN **tomtoms** a drum that you beat with your hands

ton NOUN **tons 1** a measure of weight that is about 1016 kilograms or 2240 pounds in Britain or about 907 kilograms or 2000 pounds in America **2** tons of things or people are a lot of them: *She's got tons of clothes to choose from.*

tone NOUN **tones 1** the sound of something: *I could tell she was angry from the tone of her voice.* • a cello

with a soft gentle tone **2** a brighter or darker version of a certain colour: *several tones of blue* **3** (*music*) a musical interval that equals two **semitones**

VERB **tones, toning, toned 1** to tone with something or tone in with something is to match it or look good with it: *The red scarf tones in with the plum-coloured coat.* **2** to tone, or tone up, your body or muscles is to do exercises to become fitter

tongs PLURAL NOUN a tool with two arms that are joined at one end and are squeezed together to pick something up

tongue NOUN **tongues 1** the fleshy part of your mouth that you can move and that you use to lick, speak, eat and taste **2** a language: *speaking in a foreign tongue* **3** the leather flap underneath the opening of a shoe or boot

tongue-tied ADJECTIVE too nervous, shy or embarrassed to speak

tongue-twister NOUN **tongue-twisters** a phrase or sentence that is difficult to say quickly

tonic NOUN **tonics 1** a tonic is something that makes you feel stronger or gives you energy **2** tonic, or tonic water, is a clear, fizzy, bitter-tasting drink

tonight NOUN the night or evening of today: *I'll have to miss tonight's class, I'm afraid.*

ADVERB on the night or evening of today: *I'm going to bed early tonight.*

tonne NOUN **tonnes** a metric unit of weight of 1000 kilograms or about 2205 pounds

tonsil NOUN **tonsils** either of the soft lumps on either side of the back of your throat

▶ **tonsillitis** NOUN an infection that causes the tonsils to swell and hurt

too ADVERB **1** also: *Can I come too?* **2** more than necessary or more than is sensible: *If the water is too hot, add some cold.* • *You're driving much too fast!*

took VERB a way of changing the verb **take** to make a past tense: *Fran took*

Aa
Bb
Cc
Dd
Ee
Ff
Gg
Hh
Ii
Jj
Kk
Ll
Mm
Nn
Oo
Pp
Qq
Rr
Ss
Tt
Uu
Vv
Ww
Xx
Yy
Zz

a tooth

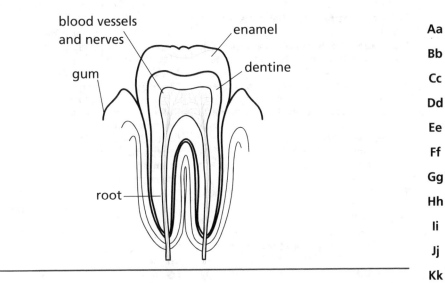

blood vessels and nerves

enamel

gum

dentine

root

me to a concert on my birthday. • *The shopping took all morning.*

tool NOUN **tools 1** a piece of equipment that you hold to do a certain job: *Dad's plumbing tools are in the boot of the car.* **2** (*ICT*) something that a computer program can do: *This program features a drawing tool.*

toolbar NOUN **toolbars** (*ICT*) a bar at the top of computer screen with symbols showing you the different things the program can do. You can select one of the symbols to make the feature work

toot VERB **toots, tooting, tooted** to toot a horn is to make it sound

NOUN **toots** the noise a horn makes: *Mum gave us a toot on the car horn when she arrived.*

tooth NOUN **teeth 1** one of the hard, white, bony parts of the jaw that are used for biting and chewing. See the picture above **2** one of the sharp points of something like a saw or a comb

toothache NOUN a pain in or near a tooth

toothpaste NOUN a cream that you use to clean your teeth

top¹ NOUN **tops**

1 the highest point or part of something: *climbing to the top of the tower • waiting at the top of the steps • distant mountain tops •Start reading at the top of the page.*

2 the upper surface of something: *a vase on the top of the television*

3 the lid or cap of a container: *Screw the top back on tightly.*

4 a piece of clothing for the upper half of your body: *green trousers and a black top*

ADJECTIVE highest or most important: *Our flat is on the top floor. • a top fashion designer*

ADVERB with the highest marks or score: *Elaine comes top in maths every term.*

VERB **tops, topping, topped 1** to top something is to cover its upper surface: *Top the cake with fruit and whipped cream.* **2** to come first in a list: *This album is expected to top the charts next week.*

Aa
Bb
Cc
Dd
Ee
Ff
Gg
Hh
Ii
Jj
Kk
Ll
Mm
Nn
Oo
Pp
Qq
Rr
Ss
Tt
Uu
Vv
Ww
Xx
Yy
Zz

• top something up to fill something up again: *Can I top up your drink for you?*

top² NOUN **tops** a toy that spins around on a point

top hat NOUN **top hats** a tall hat with a flat top that men often wore in the past

topic NOUN **topics** a subject or theme to study, write or talk about: *Choose one of the topics below as the title of your essay.*

topic sentence NOUN **topic sentences** a sentence that tells you what the topic or theme of a paragraph is

topless ADJECTIVE without any clothes on the top half of your body

topmost ADJECTIVE right at the top: *in the topmost branches of the tree*

topple VERB **topples. toppling, toppled** to wobble and fall over

top-secret ADJECTIVE very secret: *a spy passing on information that should have been top-secret*

topsyturvy ADJECTIVE AND ADVERB turned upside down

Torah NOUN the holy book of the Jewish people

torch NOUN **torches 1** a small electric light with batteries in it that you can hold in one hand **2** a big stick with something burning on the end that is carried as a light in a procession

tore VERB a way of changing the verb **tear** to make a past tense: *Heidi tore the parcel open to see what was inside.*

torment VERB **torments, tormenting, tormented** (pronounced tor-**ment**) **1** to torment someone is to treat them cruelly or annoy them in a spiteful way **2** to be tormented by something is to suffer for a long time because of it: *still tormented by bad dreams*

NOUN **torments** (pronounced **tor**-ment) very great pain or worry that goes on for a long time

▶ **tormentor** NOUN **tormentors** a person who makes a person or animal suffer on purpose

torn VERB the form of the verb **tear** that

is used with a helping verb to show that something happened in the past: *The photograph had been torn right down the middle.*

tornado NOUN **tornadoes** a violent storm with a whirling wind that causes a lot of damage

torpedo NOUN **torpedos or torpedoes** a long thin bomb that moves quickly under water and explodes when it hits its target, which is usually a ship or submarine

VERB **torpedoes, torpedoing, torpedoed** to fire a torpedo at something

torrent NOUN **torrents** a lot of water rushing or falling down quickly

▶ **torrential** ADJECTIVE torrential rain is very heavy rain

torso NOUN **torsos** the main part of your body, not including your arms, legs or head

tortoise NOUN **tortoises** a slow-moving animal with a hard shell that covers its body

torture VERB **tortures, torturing, tortured** to torture someone is to hurt them on purpose, usually either as a punishment or to get some information out of them

NOUN **tortures** hurting someone as a punishment or to get information from them: *an instrument of torture*

▶ **torturer** NOUN **torturers** a person who hurts another person on purpose for some reason

toss VERB **tosses, tossing, tossed 1** to toss something is to throw it lightly into the air: *Toss the keys over here, would you?* **2** to toss is to move from side to side again and again when you are lying down: *tossing and turning in her bed all night* **3** to toss, or to toss a coin, is to throw a coin up in the air to see which side it lands on: *We decided to toss for the front seat.*

total NOUN **totals** the number you get when you add everything together: *We've got a total of fifteen cats.* • *thirty people in total*

VERB **totals, totalling, totalled** to

come to a certain amount when added together: *Our collection totalled £320.*

ADJECTIVE complete or absolute: *a total eclipse of the sun* • *The job must be done in total secrecy.*

▶ **totally** ADVERB completely: *Is she totally deaf?* • *I agree with you totally.*

totem pole NOUN **totem poles** a tall wooden pole with carvings and paintings made by Native Americans

totter VERB **totters, tottering, tottered** to walk unsteadily and with small steps as if you are about to fall over

touch VERB **touches, touching, touched**

1 to put your hand or fingers on something: *Please do not touch the items on the shelf.* • *Can you touch the ceiling?*

2 to make contact with a thing or person: *We stood in a long line with our shoulders touching.* • *The car came close, but fortunately didn't actually touch us.*

3 to interfere with something: *Don't let anyone touch my desk while I'm away.*

4 to be touched by something is to be affected emotionally by it: *I was touched by your kind letter.*

• **touch something up** to make small changes to something to improve it: *We decided to touch up the paintwork before we sold the house.*

NOUN **touches**

1 touch is the sense that tells you what things feel like: *The fur was smooth to the touch.*

2 putting a hand or finger on something: *You can start the engine at the touch of a button.*

3 a small thing that you add to improve something: *Fiona was adding the finishing touches to the display.*

4 communication with someone: *Get in touch with me.* • *I have lost touch with Sally.*

touch-and-go ADJECTIVE very uncertain or risky

touching ADJECTIVE making you feel sympathy: *a touching story about a lost puppy*

touchy ADJECTIVE **touchier, touchiest**
1 easily annoyed: *What's she so touchy about today?* **2** a touchy subject is likely to upset or annoy someone: *Pocket money is a touchy subject in this family.*

tough ADJECTIVE **tougher, toughest**
1 strong and not easily worn out: *You'll need a tough pair of shoes for climbing.*
2 strong, fit and not easily beaten: *a tough businesswoman*
3 difficult to deal with: *a tough customer* • *a tough decision*
4 hard to chew: *tough meat*
5 firm or strict: *It's time to get tough with football hooligans.*

▶ **toughen** VERB **toughens, toughening, toughened** to toughen or toughen up a thing or person is to make them stronger

▶ **toughness** NOUN being strong and not easily beaten or worn out

tour NOUN **tours** a visit somewhere, stopping several times at points of interest: *a coach tour of the Lake District* • *a tour of the cathedral*

VERB **tours, touring, toured** to go round a place, stopping at points of interest on the way: *We're going to tour the wine-making regions of France.* • *We've hired a car to tour the city.*

▶ **tourism** NOUN travelling to and visiting places for enjoyment

▶ **tourist** NOUN **tourists** a person who is travelling for enjoyment, or on holiday

tournament NOUN **tournaments** a series of matches that make up a big competition

tousled ADJECTIVE tousled hair is untidy and looks tangled

tout NOUN **touts** a person who tries to sell something, especially very expensive tickets for popular events

tow VERB **tows, towing, towed** to pull something behind you with a rope or chain: *The car broke down and we had to get Dad to tow us home.*

NOUN **tows** pulling something behind you with a rope or chain: *Will you give us a tow home?*

towards *or* **toward** PREPOSITION **1** in a certain direction: *walking towards the gate* • *leaning over towards Bill* **2** in connection with: *Nothing has been done towards organizing the prize-giving.* **3** helping to pay for something: *a donation towards the new roof*

towel NOUN **towels** a piece of thick cloth for drying yourself: *a bath towel*

VERB **towels, towelling, towelled** to dry a thing or person with a towel: *Towel your hair dry before applying the cream.*

▸ **towelling** NOUN thick cotton material that absorbs water well and so is good for drying things: *a bath robe made of towelling*

tower NOUN **towers** a tall narrow building or part of a building: *the clocktower of the church* • *the Eiffel Tower*

VERB **towers, towering, towered**

• **tower over** *or* **above something** *or* **someone** to be much taller than other things or people: *William towers over all his classmates.*

▸ **towering** ADJECTIVE very tall: *towering office blocks in the city centre*

town NOUN **towns** a place where people live and work, which has streets, buildings and a name

> ✦**Town** comes from the Old English word **tun**, which means 'an enclosed area'.

town hall NOUN **town halls** a building that has council offices in it and, usually, a hall for public events

towpath NOUN **towpaths** a path beside a canal or river

toxic ADJECTIVE poisonous: *polluting the rivers with toxic waste*

toy NOUN **toys** an object made for a child to play with

VERB **toys, toying, toyed**

• **toy with something 1** to push something around for no real reason: *toying with her food but not eating it* **2** to toy with an idea is to consider it, but not very seriously

trace VERB **traces, tracing, traced** **1** to find someone or something by following information about where they have been: *The man has been traced to a village in the south of the country.* **2** to make a copy of a picture by covering it with a sheet of thin paper and drawing over the lines you can see through it

NOUN **traces 1** a mark or sign that someone or something leaves behind: *traces of footsteps in the sand* • *He vanished without trace.* **2** a very small amount of something: *traces of gunpowder on his shoes*

tracing paper NOUN very thin paper that you can see the lines of a picture through

track NOUN **tracks**

1 a mark on the ground left by a person, animal or thing that has passed: *following the bear's tracks through the forest*

2 a rough path or road: *a narrow track around the edge of the field*

3 a piece of ground on which races are run

4 a set of rails that a train or tram runs on

5 one of the songs or pieces of music on a CD or tape

• **keep track of someone** *or* **something** to make sure you know where someone or something is and what is happening to them

VERB **tracks, tracking, tracked** to follow the marks that an animal, person or thing leaves as they pass: *It was impossible to track anyone over such stony ground.*

• **track someone** *or* **something down** to find someone or something after a long search: *I'm trying to track down an old schoolfriend.* • *The shop has tracked down the book you ordered.*

tracksuit NOUN **tracksuits** a warm suit with a loose top and trousers that you can wear when exercising or to keep your body warm before or after exercise

tract[1] NOUN **tracts 1** a large area of land **2** a system of tubes and organs in the body: *the digestive tract*

tract² NOUN **tracts** a leaflet or a short essay

traction NOUN pulling or dragging

tractor NOUN **tractors** a slow vehicle with two large rear wheels that is used for pulling heavy loads, for example on a farm

trade NOUN **trades 1** trade is buying, selling or exchanging things or services: *foreign trade* **2** a trade is a job or occupation, especially when it involves skill and training: *a young joiner who is still learning his trade*

VERB **trades, trading, traded** to buy, sell or exchange things or services: *The government wants companies to trade outside Europe.*

• **trade something in** to give something as part of the payment for something new that you are buying: *We traded in our old car for the latest model.*

✦ The word **trade** comes from the Old English word **trada**, which means a *track* or a *path*, because trade is carried out between two places or groups. The word **tread** is also connected to this word.

trademark NOUN **trademarks** a name, word or symbol that a company uses to identify its products

trader NOUN **traders** a person or company that buys and sells things

tradesman NOUN **tradesmen 1** a person who has been trained in a particular skill as their job **2** a shopkeeper

trade union NOUN **trade unions** an organization of workers who are involved in similar work

tradition NOUN **traditions 1** a tradition is a custom that has been passed down from one generation to the next: *Having special birthday meals is a family tradition.* **2** tradition is passing down beliefs and customs from one generation to the next

▶ **traditional** ADJECTIVE existing for a long time and being done by many generations: *traditional Christmas carols*

traffic NOUN **1** travelling vehicles: *air traffic controllers* • *road traffic reports* **2** trade that is illegal

VERB **traffics, trafficking, trafficked** to buy and sell things illegally: *drug trafficking*

traffic lights PLURAL NOUN a set of red, amber and green lights that controls traffic at road junctions

tragedy NOUN **tragedies 1** a very sad event: *The driver avoided a tragedy by his quick reaction.* **2** a story that has a sad ending, especially when the main character dies: *Shakespeare wrote comedies, histories and tragedies.*

tragic ADJECTIVE very sad or to do with suffering: *a tragic mistake*

▶ **tragically** ADVERB very sadly: *The poet died tragically young.*

trail NOUN **trails 1** a series of signs that you follow to find a thing or person: *The children in the story left a trail of paper when they got lost.* **2** a path or track through rough or wild country

VERB **trails, trailing, trailed**

1 to drag or be dragged loosely behind someone: *Her long coat trailed on the floor.* • *Children trailed their boats through the water.*

2 to walk slowly because you are tired: *children trailing along behind their parents*

3 to be behind the winner of a competition: *The English team are trailing by 5 points.*

4 to grow across and down, rather than upwards: *roses trailing over the wall*

▶ **trailer** NOUN **trailers 1** a container on wheels that is pulled behind another vehicle: *a tent in a trailer* **2** a short part of a film or programme that is used as an advertisement for it: *We saw some trailers for new films.*

train¹ NOUN **trains 1** a series of railway carriages or trucks that are pulled by an engine **2** the back part of a long dress that trails on the floor: *The bride's gown had a long train made of lace.*

train² VERB **trains, training, trained**

1 to train a person or animal is to teach them to do something: *Veronica has*

Aa
Bb
Cc
Dd
Ee
Ff
Gg
Hh
Ii
Jj
Kk
Ll
Mm
Nn
Oo
Pp
Qq
Rr
Ss
Tt
Uu
Vv
Ww
Xx
Yy
Zz

Aa
Bb
Cc
Dd
Ee
Ff
Gg
Hh
Ii
Jj
Kk
Ll
Mm
Nn
Oo
Pp
Qq
Rr
Ss
Tt
Uu
Vv
Ww
Xx
Yy
Zz

trained her dog to carry her handbag.
2 to train as something is to learn to do that job: *Andrew trained as a nurse as soon as he left school.*
3 to prepare for a sporting event: *The team trains for three hours every day.*
4 to point a camera or gun in a certain direction: *The enemy's guns are trained on the airport.*
▸ **trainer** NOUN **trainers 1** a person who teaches people or animals to improve their skills **2** trainers are soft shoes that are designed for sports use
▸ **training** NOUN **1** practice and instruction in doing a certain job: *training in computing* **2** preparation for a sports event: *The team will be in training for the next year.*

traitor NOUN **traitors** a person who is not loyal to their friends or country

tram NOUN **trams** a type of electric bus that runs on rails in the street

tramp NOUN **tramps** a person with no home or job who walks from place to place
VERB **tramps, tramping, tramped** to walk with slow, firm, heavy footsteps

trample VERB **tramples, trampling, trampled** to tread on something heavily and roughly: *The sheep have trampled all over the wheat.* • *If you stand there you'll get trampled on.*

trampoline NOUN **trampolines** a piece of canvas that is stretched across a frame for acrobats, gymnasts and children to jump on

trance NOUN **trances** a state like sleep when you are awake, but not aware of what is going on around you

tranquil ADJECTIVE quiet, calm and peaceful
▸ **tranquillity** NOUN calm and peacefulness
▸ **tranquillize** VERB **tranquillizes, tranquillizing, tranquillized** to tranquillize a person or animal is to give them a drug to make them calmer and more relaxed or to help them to sleep
▸ **tranquillizer** NOUN **tranquillizers** a drug that makes people feel calmer and more relaxed

trans- PREFIX if a word starts with **trans-**, it has something to do with moving *across*, *through* or *over* to a different place. For example, *transport* means 'to carry over' to another place

transaction NOUN **transactions** a business deal or one that involves money

transatlantic ADJECTIVE involving crossing the Atlantic Ocean: *a transatlantic flight*

transfer VERB **transfers, transferring, transferred** (pronounced trans-**fer**)
1 to transfer a person or thing is to move it from one place to another: *transferring computer files to a floppy disk* **2** to change to a different vehicle or transport system: *At Kings Cross, transfer to the Central Line.*
NOUN **transfers** (pronounced **trans**-fer)
1 moving a thing or person from one place to another: *The player has asked for a transfer to another club.* **2** a piece of paper with a design on one side that can be ironed or rubbed on to another surface
▸ **transferable** ADJECTIVE a transferable ticket can be used by someone else or can also be used on a different transport system

transform VERB **transforms, transforming, transformed** to transform something is to change it completely: *We could transform this room with a few tins of paint.*
▸ **transformation** NOUN **transformations** a complete change in the way a thing or person looks
▸ **transformer** NOUN **transformers** a device that changes an electric current from one voltage to another

transfusion NOUN **transfusions** a blood transfusion is blood that has been taken from one person and is given to another

transistor NOUN **transistors 1** a small piece of electronic equipment used in radios and televisions to make the sound louder **2** a transistor or a transistor radio is a small radio that you can carry around easily

transition NOUN a change from one state or place to another: *the transition from primary to secondary school*

▶ **transitional** ADJECTIVE to do with changing or developing from one state to another: *a transitional period of a few weeks when the old computer system is replaced*

translate VERB **translates, translating, translated** to put something into a different language: *Can you translate this into French?*

▶ **translation** NOUN **translations 1** writing or speech that has been put into a different language: *a new translation of an old book* **2** changing speech or writing into a different language: *I'm no good at translation although I can understand what's going on.*

▶ **translator** NOUN **translators** a person who puts speech or writing into a different language

translucent ADJECTIVE not transparent, but shiny because light is reflected or can get through

transmission NOUN **transmissions 1** a television or radio broadcast: *a transmission that will be heard by millions all over the world* **2** broadcasting television and radio signals: *a transmission breakdown*

transmit VERB **transmits, transmitting, transmitted** to send out the signals for television or radio programmes

▶ **transmitter** NOUN **transmitters** a piece of equipment that sends and receives signals for television and radio programmes

transparent ADJECTIVE see-through: *The box is made of transparent plastic so that you can see all the wires inside.*

transplant VERB **transplants, transplanting, transplanted 1** to remove a part from one person's body and put it in someone else's **2** to move a plant that is growing in one place to somewhere else: *The seedlings can be transplanted when they have four leaves.*

NOUN **transplants** an operation to put an organ from one person's body into someone else: *a heart transplant*

transport NOUN (pronounced **trans**-port) **1** the vehicles that you travel in, such as cars, trains, aircraft and boats: *travel by public transport* **2** moving people or things from one place to another: *This includes the cost of transport.*

VERB **transports, transporting, transported** (pronounced trans-**port**) to transport something is to move it from one place to another

▶ **transportation** NOUN moving people or things

▶ **transporter** NOUN **transporters** a long vehicle that is usually used for taking a number of large objects, such as cars, to another place

trap NOUN **traps 1** a piece of equipment for catching animals **2** a plan to trick someone into doing or saying something or to catch them doing something wrong: *a speed trap to catch people driving too fast* **3** a small, two-wheeled carriage pulled by a horse

VERB **traps, trapping, trapped 1** to catch an animal in a trap **2** to trick someone into doing or saying something: *The suspect was trapped into admitting that he had been there.* **3** to put someone in a situation that they cannot escape from: *One passenger was trapped in the crashed car until the fire brigade could cut him free.*

trapdoor NOUN **trapdoors** a door in a floor or a ceiling

trapeze NOUN **trapezes** a short bar hanging between two ropes high up from the ground, which gymnasts or acrobats swing on

trapezium NOUN **trapeziums** (*maths*) a flat shape with four sides, but only two parallel sides which are different lengths

✦**Trapezium** is a Latin word, which itself came from the Greek word **trapeza**, which means a *table*.

trapezoid NOUN **trapezoids** (*maths*) a flat shape with four sides, but no parallel sides

Aa
Bb
Cc
Dd
Ee
Ff
Gg
Hh
Ii
Jj
Kk
Ll
Mm
Nn
Oo
Pp
Qq
Rr
Ss
Tt
Uu
Vv
Ww
Xx
Yy
Zz

trash NOUN rubbish: *a lot of trash in the newspapers*
▶ **trashy** ADJECTIVE **trashier, trashiest** of very bad quality: *trashy novels*

trauma NOUN **traumas** a very upsetting, unpleasant experience that has a lasting effect: *suffering the trauma of going to war*
▶ **traumatic** ADJECTIVE very upsetting, unpleasant or frightening: *a traumatic event*

travel VERB **travels, travelling, travelled** to go from one place to another, especially abroad or far from home: *Holly spent the summer travelling in the United States.* • *How fast does sound travel?*
NOUN **travels 1** travel is going from one place to another, especially far from home **2** your travels are the journeys you make: *Did you have good weather on your travels?*
▶ **traveller** NOUN **travellers 1** a person who is on a journey: *a hostel for travellers* **2** a person who lives in a vehicle and does not stay in one place

trawl VERB **trawls, trawling, trawled** to fish by dragging a net along behind a boat
▶ **trawler** NOUN **trawlers** a fishing boat that drags a large net deep in the sea behind it

tray NOUN **trays** a flat piece of something, like wood or plastic, with raised edges, for carrying food and drink

treacherous ADJECTIVE **1** a treacherous person is someone who betrays people they should be loyal to **2** treacherous things or places are very dangerous: *The rain made the road treacherous.*
▶ **treachery** NOUN doing something that might harm your country or someone who trusts you

treacle NOUN a sweet, thick, sticky liquid made from sugar

tread VERB **treads, treading, trod, trodden 1** to tread on something is to walk or step on it: *I accidentally trod on the dog's tail.* • *Don't tread on the flowers.* **2** to walk in a certain way: *We*
trod carefully around the broken glass.
NOUN **treads 1** the sound you make when you walk: *the heavy tread of their boots on the bridge* **2** the tread of a tyre is the raised pattern on its surface that grips the road: *The tread on this tyre is completely worn away in parts.*

treason NOUN the crime of not being loyal to your country and possibly causing it harm, for example, by giving away secret information

treasure NOUN **treasures 1** valuable things, especially if they have been hidden: *looking for where the treasure is buried* **2** a precious thing: *the treasures in our museums*
VERB **treasures, treasuring, treasured** to think that something is very precious: *Mother treasured all the memories of those family outings for the rest of her life.*
▶ **treasurer** NOUN **treasurers** a person who looks after the money of a club or society
▶ **treasury** NOUN **treasuries** the part of a government that is responsible for a country's money

treat VERB **treats, treating, treated**
1 to deal with someone or behave towards them in a certain way: *I think Debbie treated Steve really badly.* • *You should not treat a mistake like this as a joke.*
2 to give a person who is ill some medicine or medical help: *Our doctors use all the latest methods to treat their patients.*
3 to apply some sort of layer or protection to a surface: *The material is treated with a waterproofing spray.*
4 to pay for something special for someone else: *Dad treated us all to a pizza on the way home.*
NOUN **treats 1** an unexpected present for someone that you pay for: *How would you like a treat?* **2** an enjoyable outing that someone organizes for you: *We went to the theatre as a treat.*
▶ **treatment** NOUN **treatments 1** the way you deal with someone or behave towards them: *Will I get special*

treatment if I offer to pay more? **2** the medical care that a patient gets: *My treatment will last for about a month.*

treaty NOUN **treaties** an agreement between countries or governments: *a peace treaty*

treble ADJECTIVE three times bigger or three times as much: *House prices are treble what they were ten years ago.*

VERB **trebles, trebling, trebled 1** to multiply something by three **2** to become or to make something three times as big or as much: *Her pay has trebled over the last year.*

NOUN **trebles** (*music*) **1** the treble is the higher range of notes: *Can you turn up the treble any more?* **2** a musical instrument with a high tone: *a treble recorder* **3** a boy with a high singing voice

treble clef NOUN **treble clefs** (*music*) a sign (𝄞) that is usually written before musical notes that are higher than middle C

tree NOUN **trees** a tall plant with a hard trunk and branches

trek VERB **treks, trekking, trekked** to go on a long and difficult journey on foot: *We'll trek over the mountains to the sea.*

NOUN **treks** a long hard journey, usually on foot

trellis NOUN **trellises** a frame of narrow wooden strips that is used to support climbing plants

tremble VERB **trembles, trembling, trembled 1** to shake because you are cold or frightened: *Joe's hand trembled as he dialled the number.* **2** to sound unsteady: *I heard a trembling voice outside the window.*

tremendous ADJECTIVE **1** very great: *a tremendous amount of work • travelling at a tremendous speed* **2** very good: *That's tremendous news!*

tremor NOUN **tremors 1** a shaking or quivering: *Was there a slight tremor in his voice?* **2** a small earthquake

trench NOUN **trenches** a long narrow hole dug in the ground

trend NOUN **trends 1** a new fashion: *the latest trend in trousers* **2** the way things

are going or developing: *There's a new trend towards healthier eating at school.*

▶ **trendy** ADJECTIVE **trendier, trendiest** fashionable: *trendy people • trendy clothes*

trespass VERB **trespasses, trespassing, trespassed** to enter or go on someone else's land or property without permission: *No trespassing! This is private property.*

▶ **trespasser** NOUN **trespassers** a person who enters someone else's land or property without permission: *Trespassers will be prosecuted.*

trestle NOUN **trestles** a wooden support with legs that is usually used for holding up the end of a table

tri- PREFIX if a word starts with **tri-**, it is usually something to do with the number *three*. For example, a *trio* is a group of three

trial NOUN **trials 1** a test that you do to make sure something works properly or that someone can do something properly: *We're carrying out trials on new products.* **2** a legal process when a jury decides whether or not a person is guilty of a crime: *a fair trial • The suspect will now have to stand trial.*

triangle NOUN **triangles 1** a flat shape with three sides and three angles: *a right-angled triangle.* See the examples on the next page **2** a musical instrument that is a three-sided metal bar that you tap with a short metal stick

▶ **triangular** ADJECTIVE in the shape of a triangle: *a triangular scarf*

tribe NOUN **tribes** a group of families who live together and are ruled by a chief

▶ **tribal** ADJECTIVE belonging to or done by a tribe or tribes: *tribal ceremonies*

tribesman or **tribeswoman** NOUN **tribesmen** or **tribeswomen** a man or woman who belongs to a particular tribe

tribulation NOUN **tribulations** a great sorrow or great suffering

tributary NOUN **tributaries** (*geography*) a stream or river that flows into a larger river or lake

Aa
Bb
Cc
Dd
Ee
Ff
Gg
Hh
Ii
Jj
Kk
Ll
Mm
Nn
Oo
Pp
Qq
Rr
Ss
Tt
Uu
Vv
Ww
Xx
Yy
Zz

triangles

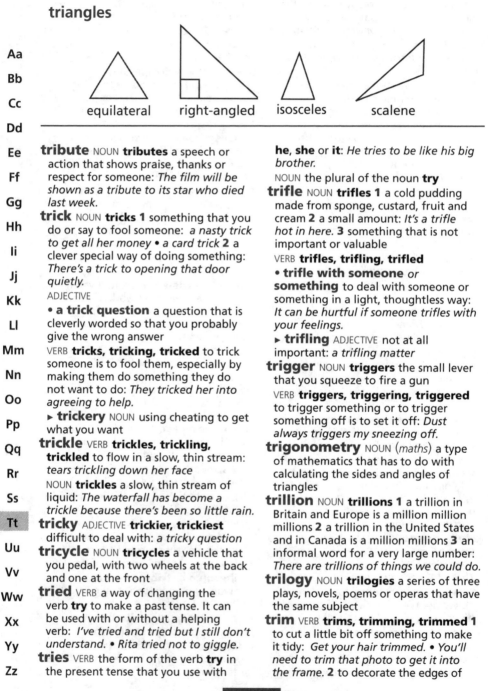

equilateral   right-angled   isosceles   scalene

Aa
Bb
Cc
Dd
Ee
Ff
Gg
Hh
Ii
Jj
Kk
Ll
Mm
Nn
Oo
Pp
Qq
Rr
Ss
Tt
Uu
Vv
Ww
Xx
Yy
Zz

tribute NOUN **tributes** a speech or action that shows praise, thanks or respect for someone: *The film will be shown as a tribute to its star who died last week.*

trick NOUN **tricks 1** something that you do or say to fool someone: *a nasty trick to get all her money* • *a card trick* **2** a clever special way of doing something: *There's a trick to opening that door quietly.*
ADJECTIVE
• **a trick question** a question that is cleverly worded so that you probably give the wrong answer
VERB **tricks, tricking, tricked** to trick someone is to fool them, especially by making them do something they do not want to do: *They tricked her into agreeing to help.*
▸ **trickery** NOUN using cheating to get what you want

trickle VERB **trickles, trickling, trickled** to flow in a slow, thin stream: *tears trickling down her face*
NOUN **trickles** a slow, thin stream of liquid: *The waterfall has become a trickle because there's been so little rain.*

tricky ADJECTIVE **trickier, trickiest** difficult to deal with: *a tricky question*

tricycle NOUN **tricycles** a vehicle that you pedal, with two wheels at the back and one at the front

tried VERB a way of changing the verb **try** to make a past tense. It can be used with or without a helping verb: *I've tried and tried but I still don't understand.* • *Rita tried not to giggle.*

tries VERB the form of the verb **try** in the present tense that you use with

he, she or **it**: *He tries to be like his big brother.*
NOUN the plural of the noun **try**

trifle NOUN **trifles 1** a cold pudding made from sponge, custard, fruit and cream **2** a small amount: *It's a trifle hot in here.* **3** something that is not important or valuable
VERB **trifles, trifling, trifled**
• **trifle with someone** or **something** to deal with someone or something in a light, thoughtless way: *It can be hurtful if someone trifles with your feelings.*
▸ **trifling** ADJECTIVE not at all important: *a trifling matter*

trigger NOUN **triggers** the small lever that you squeeze to fire a gun
VERB **triggers, triggering, triggered** to trigger something or to trigger something off is to set it off: *Dust always triggers my sneezing off.*

trigonometry NOUN (*maths*) a type of mathematics that has to do with calculating the sides and angles of triangles

trillion NOUN **trillions 1** a trillion in Britain and Europe is a million million millions **2** a trillion in the United States and in Canada is a million millions **3** an informal word for a very large number: *There are trillions of things we could do.*

trilogy NOUN **trilogies** a series of three plays, novels, poems or operas that have the same subject

trim VERB **trims, trimming, trimmed 1** to cut a little bit off something to make it tidy: *Get your hair trimmed.* • *You'll need to trim that photo to get it into the frame.* **2** to decorate the edges of something: *a coat trimmed with white fur*

NOUN **trims** cutting a small amount off something: *Ask the hairdresser for a quick trim.*

trinket NOUN **trinkets** a small cheap ornament or piece of jewellery

trio NOUN **trios** 1 a group of three people or things, especially musicians 2 a piece of music for three players or singers

trip NOUN **trips** a short journey to a place and back again: *a shopping trip • a trip to the zoo*

VERB **trips, tripping, tripped** 1 to trip is to catch your foot on something and fall, or nearly fall over: *Caroline tripped over the edge of the carpet. • Mind you don't trip on the step.* 2 to trip someone or trip someone up is to make them fall or stumble: *One of the boys tripped me up.*

tripe NOUN 1 parts of the stomach of a cow or sheep, used as food 2 an informal word for rubbish or nonsense

Tripitaka NOUN a set of three texts containing the teachings of Buddha

✦ **Tripitaka** means *three baskets*. It was said that the teachings were first written on palm leaves and stored in three separate baskets.

triple ADJECTIVE 1 three times as much or as many: *We had triple the number of entries this year.* 2 made up of three parts: *triple-glazed windows • a triple somersault*

VERB **triples, tripling, tripled** to become or to make something three times as big: *The number of students learning Latin has tripled this year.*

triplet NOUN **triplets** one of three children born to the same mother at the same time

tripod NOUN **tripods** a stand with three legs for supporting something like a camera

triumph NOUN **triumphs** a great victory or success: *another triumph for the champions • a shout of triumph*

VERB **triumphs, triumphing, triumphed** to win or succeed: *a man who triumphed over the hardships of a poor background*

▸ **triumphant** ADJECTIVE very happy after winning or succeeding: *the triumphant medal-winners*

trivia NOUN details and small matters that are not important

▸ **trivial** ADJECTIVE small and not important: *You won't lose many marks for a few trivial mistakes.*

trod VERB a way of changing the verb **tread** to make a past tense: *Hey, you trod on my toe just then!*

trodden VERB the form of the verb **tread** that is used with a helping verb to show that something happened in the past: *A lot of feet have trodden on these steps in the past.*

troll NOUN **trolls** an imaginary, ugly, bad-tempered, human-like creature that is either a dwarf or a giant

trolley NOUN **trolleys** 1 a basket on wheels: *a supermarket trolley* 2 a table on wheels

trombone NOUN **trombones** a brass instrument that you blow. You change the notes by pushing a sliding tube in and out

troop NOUN **troops** 1 a troop is a group of people: *a troop of children on a school outing* 2 troops are soldiers: *troops advancing from the west*

VERB **troops, trooping, trooped** to go somewhere in a large group: *tourists trooping around all the art galleries*

trophy NOUN **trophies** a prize, such as a cup or medal, for winning a competition

tropic NOUN **tropics** (*geography*) 1 either of two imaginary circles around the Earth. The **Tropic of Cancer** is 23 degrees north of the equator and the **Tropic of Capricorn** is 23 degrees south 2 either of the hot regions to the north or south of the equator

▸ **tropical** ADJECTIVE to do with, in or from the tropics: *a tropical rainforest*

trot VERB **trots, trotting, trotted** to run fairly fast with small steps

NOUN **trots** a jogging kind of run

• **on the trot** one after another: *three wins on the trot*

▶ **trotters** PLURAL NOUN the feet of pigs or sheep, used as food

trouble NOUN **troubles 1** something that gives you a lot of work or problems: *A washing-machine would save you a lot of trouble.* • *You'd have no trouble finding a better job.* **2** your troubles are your worries and problems
VERB **troubles, troubling, troubled 1** to trouble someone is to bother or disturb them: *I'm sorry to trouble you, but can you help me please?* **2** to trouble to do something is to make an effort or be bothered to do it: *He didn't even trouble to say where he was going.* **3** to be troubled by something is to worry about it or to suffer from it: *What's troubling you?*
▶ **troublesome** ADJECTIVE causing worry or problems

trough NOUN **troughs** a long narrow container that animals eat or drink from

trousers PLURAL NOUN a garment for the lower half of the body that covers each leg separately

trout NOUN **trout** or **trouts** a kind of fish that lives in rivers and lakes

trowel NOUN **trowels** a tool like a small spade, used for gardening, or spreading cement on bricks

truancy NOUN being absent from school without permission
▶ **truant** NOUN **truants** a pupil who stays away from school without permission
• **play truant** to play truant is to stay away from school without permission

truce NOUN **truces** an agreement to stop fighting for a while

truck NOUN **trucks 1** a lorry **2** an open railway wagon for transporting goods or animals

trudge VERB **trudges, trudging, trudged** to walk with tired, heavy, slow steps: *trudging along in the snow*

true ADJECTIVE **truer, truest 1** real and not invented: *a true story* **2** real and not pretend or supposed: *Are these your true feelings?* • *a true friend*

truffle NOUN **truffles 1** a kind of chocolate with a soft creamy centre **2** a rare fungus that grows underground and is used as food

truly ADVERB really: *Tell me what you truly want to do.* • *I'm truly sorry.*

trump NOUN **trumps** trumps are the suit of cards that has been chosen to be worth more than the others in a card game
VERB **trumps, trumping, trumped** to trump a card is to beat it by playing a card that has a higher value in that game

trumpet NOUN **trumpets** a brass musical instrument that you blow into to make a loud, high, clear sound
VERB **trumpets, trumpeting, trumpeted** an elephant trumpets when it makes a loud noise

truncheon NOUN **truncheon** a short, thick, heavy stick carried by police officers

trundle VERB **trundles, trundling, trundled** to move heavily and slowly along on wheels: *lorries trundling through the empty streets* • *Gordon trundled the wheelbarrow round to the back of the house.*

trunk NOUN **trunks**
1 the main stem of a tree, without its branches or roots
2 an elephant's long nose
3 a large box or chest for storing or transporting clothes and other possessions
4 the main part of a person's body, not including their head, arms or legs

trunks PLURAL NOUN trunks are short trousers or pants worn by men or boys for swimming

trust VERB **trusts, trusting, trusted 1** to believe that someone is honest and loyal: *The colonel picked out ten men he knew he could trust.* **2** to rely on someone to do something properly and not cause damage: *I know I can trust you not to make any mistakes.* • *Can I trust you with my new camera?* **3** to expect and believe that something is so: *I trust that all is well with you?*
NOUN **1** the belief that someone is honest and loyal: *It can be difficult to*

---

get a new pet's trust. **2** a responsibility to look after something or do something properly: *The children had been placed in my trust.*

▶ **trustworthy** ADJECTIVE honest

▶ **trusty** ADJECTIVE reliable: *my trusty friend*

truth NOUN **truths 1** what is true and real: *Please try to tell the truth.* • *The truth is that she never really loved him.* **2** being true: *There is no truth in his story.*

▶ **truthful** ADJECTIVE **1** a truthful person tells the truth **2** truthful information is not false

▶ **truthfully** ADVERB without lying: *Answer the questions as truthfully as you can.*

try VERB **tries, trying, tried 1** to make an effort or an attempt to do something: *Please try to understand.* • *I'm trying to call John but he's not answering the phone.* **2** to do or use something to see if you like it or if it is good: *Try this powder for a cleaner wash.* **3** to find out if someone committed a crime by hearing all the evidence in a court: *They will be tried in the European Court of Human Rights.*

NOUN **tries 1** an attempt to do something: *That was a good try. Better luck next time.* **2** in rugby, a successful attempt to put the ball over the other team's goal line

T-shirt NOUN **T-shirts** another spelling of **tee-shirt**

tub NOUN **tubs 1** a round container for liquid or creamy substances: *a tub of ice-cream* • *a tub that will hold 20 litres of water* **2** a bath: *a long soak in the tub*

tuba NOUN **tubas** a large brass musical instrument that you blow. It usually plays very low notes

tubby ADJECTIVE **tubbier, tubbiest** fat and round

tube NOUN **tubes 1** a long, thin, hollow pipe: *a rubber tube that carries the gas into the other bottle* **2** a long hollow container: *a cardboard tube for storing posters* • *a tube of toothpaste* **3** an underground railway system, especially in London: *We can easily get there by tube.*

tuber NOUN **tubers** a swollen plant root that new plants can grow from: *Potatoes are tubers that you can eat or plant again.*

tuck NOUN **tucks 1** a fold in cloth that is fixed, usually with stitching: *a blouse with tucks down the front* • *We can make a small tuck in the waist to make it fit.* **2** snack foods: *Janie takes tuck money to school every day.*

VERB **tucks, tucking, tucked** to hide an edge or loose end inside or under something else to make it firm or tidy: *Tuck your shirt in.* • *Tuck the flap into the envelope and seal it with tape.*

• **tuck in** to eat with enjoyment: *The kids tucked in without waiting for the adults to arrive.*

• **tucked up** to be tucked up in bed is to be snug and comfortable under the bedclothes

tuck shop NOUN **tuck shops** a shop in a school where you can buy snack food

Tuesday NOUN **Tuesdays** the day of the week after Monday and before Wednesday

+ **Tuesday** comes from the Old English word **Tiwesdæg**, which means *Tiw's day*. Tiw is the Norse god of war and of the sky.

tuft NOUN **tufts** a bunch of something, such as grass or hair, that grows from the same place

tug VERB **tugs, tugging, tugged** to pull something suddenly or strongly towards you: *Stop tugging each other's hair.*

NOUN **tugs 1** a sudden hard pull towards you: *I gave Dad's arm a tug and he looked at me crossly.* **2** a short form of the word **tugboat**

tugboat NOUN **tugboats** a small powerful boat that is used for towing ships

tug-of-war NOUN a contest in which two teams pull opposite ends of a rope and try to pull each other over a line on the ground

tuition NOUN teaching or instruction in how to do something: *mathematics tuition*

Aa Bb Cc Dd Ee Ff Gg Hh Ii Jj Kk Ll Mm Nn Oo Pp Qq Rr Ss **Tt** Uu Vv Ww Xx Yy Zz

tulip NOUN **tulips** a type of flower with a straight stem and a cup-shaped flower that grows from a bulb in the spring

✦**Tulip** comes from a Persian word that means *turban*. People thought the shape of the flower was similar to a turban.

tumble VERB **tumbles, tumbling, tumbled** to fall down and over: *The bike skidded and tumbled into a ditch.* NOUN **tumbles** a fall: *Lucy had taken a tumble over the doorstep.*

tumbledown ADJECTIVE a tumbledown building is falling to pieces

tumbler NOUN **tumblers** a large drinking glass with straight sides

tummy NOUN **tummies** a word children use for their stomach: *Mummy, my tummy aches.*

tumour NOUN **tumours** a lump in or on your body that might make you ill

tumult NOUN **tumults** a loud or confused noise made by a crowd
▶ **tumultuous** ADJECTIVE noisy and confused: *a tumultuous welcome*

tuna NOUN **tuna** a large fish that is used as food

tundra NOUN (*geography*) a large plain with no trees in or near the Arctic

tune NOUN **tunes** a series of musical notes that sound nice together
• **in tune 1** a musical note is in tune if it is exactly the right note **2** a musical instrument is in tune if it produces the right notes
VERB **tunes, tuning, tuned 1** to adjust a musical instrument so that it sounds right **2** to adjust a television or radio to a certain channel or station **3** to adjust an engine so that it works smoothly
▶ **tuneful** ADJECTIVE having a pleasant melody

tunic NOUN **tunics 1** a loose piece of clothing with no sleeves **2** the top half of a policeman's or soldier's uniform

tunnel NOUN **tunnels** a long underground passage
VERB **tunnels, tunnelling, tunnelled** to make an underground passage: *Will*

they tunnel under the river or build a bridge over it?

turban NOUN **turbans** a long piece of cloth that is wrapped round and round the head to make a kind of hat

turbine NOUN **turbines** a machine or engine that is driven by a flow of water or gas

turbulence NOUN disturbance in the water or air that makes ships or aircraft shake
▶ **turbulent** ADJECTIVE disturbed or confused: *a turbulent week for the government*

turf NOUN short thick grass

turkey NOUN **turkeys** a large farmyard bird that is used as food

turmoil NOUN a state of worry and confusion: *Her mind was in turmoil but she tried to stay calm.*

turn VERB **turns, turning, turned**
1 to move or to move something to face in another direction: *He turned and walked away.* • *Why have you turned that picture towards the wall?*
2 to spin around or twist: *a turning wheel* • *Turn the handle to the right.*
3 to change: *She took one look and turned pale.* • *The frog turned into a prince.*
• **turn someone** or **something down** to refuse an offer that someone makes
• **turn something down** to reduce the noise or heat that something is making: *Turn the television down. It's too loud.*
• **turn someone in** to hand someone over to the police
• **turn out 1** to turn out a certain way is to finish or end up like that: *Everything turned out well in the end.* **2** to come out to see or do something: *Not many people turned out for the local election.*
• **turn something up** to increase the sound or heat which something is making: *Can you turn the volume up a bit?*
NOUN **turns 1** a curve, bend or change of direction: *Take the first turn on the right.* **2** something that people do one

Aa
Bb
Cc
Dd
Ee
Ff
Gg
Hh
Ii
Jj
Kk
Ll
Mm
Nn
Oo
Pp
Qq
Rr
Ss
Tt
Uu
Vv
Ww
Xx
Yy
Zz

after the other: *It's your turn next.* **3** a short performance in a show: *Jolly Jack will be the star turn at the Christmas show this year.*

• **a good turn** a favour that you do for someone

• **in turn** if you do things in turn, you do them one after the other

turncoat NOUN **turncoats** a person who changes sides in an argument

turnip NOUN **turnips** a hard, round, white vegetable that grows under the ground

turnover NOUN **turnovers 1** a small sweet pie made of a piece of folded pastry with a fruit filling **2** the turnover of a company is the amount of money it makes

turnstile NOUN **turnstiles** a gate that turns, allowing one person to pass at a time

turntable NOUN **turntables** a turning platform

turpentine NOUN an oily liquid used for things like making paint thinner and cleaning paintbrushes

turquoise NOUN **turquoises 1** a greenish-blue precious stone **2** a greenish-blue colour

turtle NOUN **turtles 1** a large reptile, that usually lives in the sea with a hard shell and flippers for swimming **2** (*ICT*) a type of cursor that you can move around to draw pictures on a computer screen

tusk NOUN **tusks** a long curved pointed tooth that sticks out of the mouth of some animals, such as the elephant and walrus

tussle NOUN **tussles** a struggle with someone to get something

VERB **tussles, tussling, tussled** to argue or struggle with someone over something you both want

tutor NOUN **tutors 1** a private teacher who teaches individual pupils at home **2** a university or college teacher who teaches students in small groups or gives them advice

VERB **tutors, tutoring, tutored** to tutor someone is to teach them

tutu NOUN **tutus** a ballet dancer's dress that has a stiff, sticking-out skirt

TV NOUN **TVs 1** a television set: *We've got a new TV.* **2** television broadcasts: *I think the children watch too much TV.*

tweak VERB **tweaks, tweaking, tweaked** to pull something with a small jerk: *He tweaked my hair roughly.*
NOUN **tweaks** a small pull at something to make a small change

tweed NOUN **tweeds** thick, rough, woollen cloth that is often used for making outdoor clothing

tweezers PLURAL NOUN a small tool for gripping very thin things such as hairs

twelfth ADJECTIVE AND ADVERB after the eleventh and before the thirteenth: *the twelfth day of May*

twelve NOUN **twelves** the number 12

twentieth ADJECTIVE AND ADVERB after the nineteenth and before the twenty-first: *the twentieth day of April*

twenty NOUN **twenties** the number 20

twice ADVERB two times: *You've done that twice now so don't do it again.* • *I could eat twice that amount.*

twiddle VERB **twiddles, twiddling, twiddled** to twist or twirl something round and round: *Try twiddling some knobs to try to make it work.*

twig NOUN **twigs** a small thin piece that grows from a branch of a tree or bush: *We need a pile of dry twigs to start the fire.*
VERB **twigs, twigging, twigged** (*informal*) to suddenly realize something: *Then I twigged what he was talking about.*

twilight NOUN the time after the sun sets when it is not quite dark

twin NOUN **twins** one of two children born to the same mother at the same time
ADJECTIVE belonging to a pair of things that are very similar: *twin beds* • *a car with twin exhaust pipes*

twine NOUN strong string: *a ball of garden twine*

twinge NOUN **twinges** a sudden unpleasant feeling: *a twinge of toothache* • *a twinge of guilt*

Aa
Bb
Cc
Dd
Ee
Ff
Gg
Hh
Ii
Jj
Kk
Ll
Mm
Nn
Oo
Pp
Qq
Rr
Ss
Tt
Uu
Vv
Ww
Xx
Yy
Zz

twinkle VERB **twinkles, twinkling, twinkled 1** lights twinkle when they glitter brightly: *lights twinkling along the shoreline* **2** someone's eyes twinkle when they are bright with excitement or humour

NOUN **twinkles** a bright shining light

twirl VERB **twirls, twirling, twirled** to turn or spin round quickly: *girls twirling in long skirts* • *The leaders of the parade twirled their batons.*

NOUN **twirls** a fast turn or spin around

twist VERB **twists, twisting, twisted 1** to wind or turn round: *Her hair was tangled and twisted around the clip.* • *Twist the handle hard and then pull it to open the door.*
2 to turn the top half of your body: *Gregory twisted round in his chair to look at me.*
3 to bend something out of its proper shape: *After twisting my ankle, I developed a bad limp.* • *The front wheel of the bike twisted when it hit the wall.*

NOUN **twists 1** a turn round: *Give the lid a good hard twist.* **2** the shape of something that has been turned or wound around: *a twist of wire* **3** a change in the way something happens: *an unusual twist at the end of the story*

twitch NOUN **twitches** a jerky little movement

VERB **twitches, twitching, twitched 1** to move jerkily: *Her eyelid twitched* **2** to move something sharply or jerkily: *people twitching curtains to see what was going on outside*

twitter VERB **twitters, twittering, twittered** to make a lot of high-pitched noises: *birds twittering in the trees*

two NOUN **twos** the number 2

two-dimensional ADJECTIVE a two-dimensional shape is flat and has length and width you can measure, but not height or depth. It might also be called a **plane** shape

two-faced ADJECTIVE not honest or not acting in the same way with everyone

tying VERB a form of the verb **tie** that is used with another verb to make different tenses: *I was tying my laces and I fell over.* • *We need to start tying up some parcels.*

type NOUN **types 1** a sort or kind of thing or person: *What type of person would write a letter like this?* • *Choose the right type of shampoo for your hair.* **2** letters and figures that are used in printing: *The title should be in bold type.*

VERB **types, typing, typed** to write using a keyboard on a typewriter or computer: *Type your name and then your password.*

typewriter NOUN **typewriters** a machine that you can use to produce printed text

typhoon NOUN **typhoons** a violent storm in the western Pacific Ocean

typical ADJECTIVE **1** having the usual qualities of a certain type of thing or person: *typical holiday weather* **2** just as you expect from a certain thing or person: *That's typical of Nick.*
▸ **typically** ADVERB **1** in most cases: *An insect typically has six legs and two pairs of wings.* **2** as you would expect from a certain person or thing: *Tracy was typically late.*

typist NOUN **typists** a person whose job is to type, especially in an office

tyranny NOUN **tyrannies** a cruel and unjust way of using power
▸ **tyrannical** ADJECTIVE cruel and not fair towards people: *a tyrannical ruler*

tyrant NOUN **tyrants** a ruler who has complete power and who uses it unfairly and cruelly

tyre NOUN **tyres** a thick rubber ring that is filled with air and covers the edge of a wheel: *The car had a flat tyre.*

Aa Bb Cc Dd Ee Ff Gg Hh Ii Jj Kk Ll Mm Nn Oo Pp Qq Rr Ss **Tt** Uu Vv Ww Xx Yy Zz

Uu

udder NOUN **udders** the part like a bag that hangs under a cow and supplies milk

UFO ABBREVIATION **UFOs** short for **unidentified flying object**, which is something seen in the sky and nobody knows what it is

ugly ADJECTIVE **uglier, ugliest** not very nice to look at: *an ugly man* • *an ugly building*
▸ **ugliness** NOUN being ugly

ulcer NOUN **ulcers** a sore on someone's skin or inside the body

ultimate ADJECTIVE happening at the end of a process: *an ultimate aim*
▸ **ultimately** ADVERB finally

ultra- PREFIX if a word starts with **ultra-**, it means 'very' or 'extremely'. For example, *ultra-careful* means 'extremely careful'

ultraviolet ADJECTIVE (*science*) ultraviolet light is light you cannot see

umbilical cord NOUN **umbilical cords** the cord that connects a baby to its mother before it is born

umbrella NOUN **umbrellas** something you put up and shelter under when it rains, which consists of a frame with cloth over it

✦ This word comes from the Italian word **umbrella**, which means *little shadow*. Umbrellas were first used to shade people from the sun.

umpire NOUN **umpires** someone who watches a game such as tennis or cricket and makes sure that the rules are not broken

umpteen ADJECTIVE an informal word for **many**: *I've told you umpteen times to be quiet.*

un- PREFIX if a word starts with **un-**, it means *not*. For example, *untidy* means 'not tidy'

unable ADJECTIVE not having enough time, strength or skill to do something:

The box was so heavy he was unable to lift it.

unaccustomed ADJECTIVE if you are unaccustomed to something, you are not used to it

unanimous ADJECTIVE agreed by everyone: *a unanimous decision*
▸ **unanimously** ADVERB in a way that is agreed by everyone: *He was elected unanimously.*

unarmed ADJECTIVE without weapons: *unarmed combat* • *an unarmed policeman*

unaware ADJECTIVE not knowing about something: *We were unaware of the danger.*
▸ **unawares** ADVERB when not expected: *Their arrival caught me unawares.*

unbearable ADJECTIVE too painful or annoying to deal with
▸ **unbearably** ADVERB in a way that is difficult to bear: *It is unbearably hot outside.*

unbelievable ADJECTIVE **1** difficult to believe: *an unbelievable excuse.* **2** a word used to emphasize how bad, good or big something is: *an unbelievable success*
▸ **unbelievably** ADVERB in a way that is unbelievable: *She's unbelievably rich.*

uncalled ADJECTIVE if an action is **uncalled for**, it is unpleasant and unfair and people are upset by it: *That remark was completely uncalled for.*

uncanny ADJECTIVE strange and difficult to explain

uncertain ADJECTIVE **1** having doubt about something: *I was uncertain about what to do next.* **2** not definitely known: *The future is uncertain.*

uncle NOUN **uncles 1** the brother of one of your parents **2** your aunt's husband

uncomfortable ADJECTIVE **1** having or causing an unpleasant feeling in your

Aa Bb Cc Dd Ee Ff Gg Hh Ii Jj Kk Ll Mm Nn Oo Pp Qq Rr Ss Tt Uu Vv Ww Xx Yy Zz

body: *I was uncomfortable in the hard bed.* • *uncomfortable shoes* **2** feeling slightly embarrassed, or showing that people feel slightly embarrassed: *Adults seem uncomfortable talking about money.* • *an uncomfortable silence*
‣ **uncomfortably** ADVERB in an uncomfortable way: *Tom shifted uncomfortably in his seat.*

uncommon ADJECTIVE unusual or rare
‣ **uncommonly** ADVERB extremely: *uncommonly talented*

unconscious ADJECTIVE **1** in a state like sleep where you are not aware of what is happening around you because you are seriously ill or injured: *A brick fell on his head and he was knocked unconscious.* **2** an unconscious feeling is one that you are not aware of having **3** if you are unconscious of something, you do not notice it: *He was unconscious of the danger.*
‣ **unconsciously** ADVERB in an unconscious way
‣ **unconsciousness** NOUN being unconscious

uncover VERB **uncovers, uncovering, uncovered 1** to remove a cover from something **2** to discover something that had been secret: *uncover the truth*

undecided ADJECTIVE **1** not able to decide about something: *We were undecided what to do.* **2** which people have not made a decision about: *The date for sports day is still undecided.*

undeniable ADJECTIVE true or certain: *It is undeniable that the Earth goes round the sun.*
‣ **undeniably** ADVERB in a way that is true or certain

under PREPOSITION
1 below or beneath: *The bag is under the table.*
2 less than: *All the clothes are under £20.*
3 working for: *a manager with three members of staff under her*
4 in a state of: *The fire is now under control.*
5 in the section called: *To find a dictionary, look in the library under 'reference'.*
• **under way** if something gets under way, it starts
ADVERB in or to a lower place: *We watched the divers go under.*

under- PREFIX **under-** at the start of a word means *not enough*. For example, to *undercook* something is not to cook it enough

underarm ADJECTIVE AND ADVERB with your hand kept below your shoulder, moving up and forward: *an underarm throw*

underdeveloped ADJECTIVE an underdeveloped country is not modern and does not have many industries

underdog NOUN **underdogs** the weaker person or team in a competition

underdone ADJECTIVE not cooked enough

underestimate VERB **underestimates, underestimating, underestimated 1** to guess that a cost or amount is less than it really is **2** to guess that someone is not as good or powerful as they really are

underfoot ADVERB on the ground where you are walking: *The stones underfoot grew slippery in the rain.*

undergo VERB **undergoes, undergoing, underwent, undergone** if you undergo something you experience it: *He underwent an operation to mend his broken leg.*

undergraduate NOUN **undergraduates** someone who is studying for their first degree at a university

underground ADJECTIVE AND ADVERB **1** below the surface of the ground: *Moles live underground.* • *an underground stream* **2** existing or done secretly: *an underground organization*
NOUN **undergrounds** a railway that is under the ground, usually in a large city

undergrowth NOUN bushes and plants that cover the ground

underhand ADJECTIVE secret and not honest: *underhand business deals*

underline VERB **underlines, underlining, underlined 1** to draw a line underneath something **2** to emphasize that something is important or true: *She underlined the need to be careful crossing the road.*

undermine VERB **undermines, undermining, undermined** to undermine someone or their plans is to make them weaker

underneath ADJECTIVE AND PREPOSITION under something: *Look underneath the table!* • *He was wearing a jumper with a shirt underneath.*

underpants PLURAL NOUN underwear that men and boys wear under their trousers

underpass NOUN **underpasses** a road or path under another road

underprivileged ADJECTIVE having less money and opportunities than other people

understand VERB **understands, understanding, understood**
1 to know what something means: *I can't understand the instructions.* • *Do you understand German?*
2 to know about something: *Doctors still don't understand how the disease is spread.*
3 to know why someone behaves and feels the way they do: *I'll never understand him.*
4 to think something is true: *I understood that you weren't coming.*
▶ **understandable** ADJECTIVE reasonable in a particular situation: *His disappointment is understandable.*
▶ **understanding** ADJECTIVE able to understand other people's feelings and treat them in a kind way NOUN **understandings 1** the ability to see the meaning of something: *I have no understanding of chemistry.* **2** an agreement: *We have an understanding that we will stand up for each other.*

understudy NOUN **understudies** someone who learns the part of another actor so they can play that part if the actor is ill

undertake VERB **undertakes, undertaking, undertook, undertaken** (*formal*) to undertake a task is to accept

it and do it: *John and I undertook to put up the tent.*

undertaker NOUN **undertakers** someone whose job is to arrange funerals

underwater ADJECTIVE AND ADVERB under the surface of water: *an underwater creature* • *Can you swim underwater?*

underwear NOUN clothes you wear next to your skin and under your other clothes

underweight ADJECTIVE not heavy enough

underworld NOUN **1** in some old stories, the place where people go when they die **2** the underworld is criminals and the crimes they commit

undesirable ADJECTIVE not wanted

undivided ADJECTIVE **1** not split into separate parts or groups **2** complete: *You must give me your undivided attention.*

undo VERB **undoes, undoing, undid, undone 1** to open something that is fastened: *He undid his jacket.* **2** to cancel out the effect of something: *She's undone all the good work of the previous teacher.* **3** (*ICT*) to undo a command you have given to a computer is to press a key that will reverse the command and change things back

undoubted ADJECTIVE certain: *Ellie has undoubted talent as a singer.*
▶ **undoubtedly** ADVERB a word you use to emphasize that something is true: *You are undoubtedly correct.*

undress VERB **undresses, undressing, undressed** to take your clothes off
▶ **undressed** ADJECTIVE not wearing any clothes: *He was getting undressed.*

undue ADJECTIVE more than is necessary: *We don't want the children to take undue risks.*

unearth VERB **unearths, unearthing, unearthed 1** to find something by digging in the ground **2** to discover something: *Scientists have unearthed some interesting facts about the disease.*

unearthly ADJECTIVE strange and a bit

Aa
Bb
Cc
Dd
Ee
Ff
Gg
Hh
Ii
Jj
Kk
Ll
Mm
Nn
Oo
Pp
Qq
Rr
Ss
Tt
Uu
Vv
Ww
Xx
Yy
Zz

frightening: *an unearthly sound*

uneasy ADJECTIVE slightly worried or unhappy

▶ **uneasily** ADVERB in a way that shows you are worried or uncomfortable: *John looked uneasily at his watch, knowing he was late.*

▶ **uneasiness** NOUN a feeling of slight worry

unemployed ADJECTIVE someone who is unemployed does not have a job

▶ **unemployment** NOUN **1** the number of people who do not have a job: *Unemployment has risen again.* **2** not having a job

unequal ADJECTIVE different in size, amount or position: *an unequal share of money*

uneven ADJECTIVE **1** not level or smooth: *an uneven road* **2** not all of the same quality: *Your work has been uneven this year.*

▶ **unevenly** ADVERB in an uneven way

unexpected ADJECTIVE surprising because you were not expecting it: *an unexpected visitor* • *an unexpected change in the weather*

▶ **unexpectedly** ADVERB in a way that you were not expecting

unfair ADJECTIVE not right or not fair: *an unfair advantage* • *It's unfair to make the children do so much homework.*

▶ **unfairly** ADVERB in a way that is not fair: *We have been very unfairly treated.*

▶ **unfairness** NOUN being unfair

unfaithful ADJECTIVE not loyal or not keeping your promises

unfamiliar ADJECTIVE not known or seen before: *an unfamiliar feeling* • *an unfamiliar face*

unfasten VERB **unfastens, unfastening, unfastened** to open something that was fastened: *She unfastened her coat.*

unfavourable ADJECTIVE (*formal*) not good and likely to cause problems: *They had planned a barbecue but the weather was unfavourable.*

unfit ADJECTIVE **unfitter, unfittest 1** not suitable or not good enough: *water that's unfit to drink* **2** someone who is unfit is not in good physical condition, especially because they do not do enough exercise

unfold VERB **unfolds, unfolding, unfolded 1** to spread out something that was folded **2** to gradually become known or gradually make something known: *The details of what happened began to unfold.*

unforgettable ADJECTIVE impossible to forget

unforgivable ADJECTIVE unforgivable behaviour is so bad that you cannot forgive the person who has done it

unfortunate ADJECTIVE **1** caused by bad luck: *an unfortunate accident* **2** if something is unfortunate, you wish it had not happened: *an unfortunate thing to say*

▶ **unfortunately** ADVERB a word you use to show that you wish something had not happened: *Unfortunately, I lost the ring.*

unfurl VERB **unfurls, unfurling, unfurled** to unfurl a flag is to unfold it

ungainly ADJECTIVE not graceful

ungrateful ADJECTIVE not showing or saying thanks when someone does something for you or gives you something

▶ **ungratefully** ADVERB in a way that is ungrateful

unhappy ADJECTIVE **unhappier, unhappiest 1** sad: *Ben was unhappy for a long time after his dog died.* **2** not pleased or not satisfied: *We were unhappy with our exam results.* **3** unfortunate: *an unhappy coincidence*

▶ **unhappily** ADVERB **1** in a way that is not happy **2** a word you use to show that something makes you sad or disappointed: *Unhappily, things did not work out as I planned.*

▶ **unhappiness** NOUN being unhappy

unhealthy ADJECTIVE **unhealthier, unhealthiest 1** someone who is unhealthy does not have good health **2** something that is unhealthy is bad for your health: *an unhealthy lifestyle*

unicorn NOUN **unicorns** in stories, an animal like a white horse with a horn on its head

> ✦ This word comes from the Latin word **unus**, which means *one*, and **cornu**, which means *horn*, because there is only one horn on the unicorn's head. The words **unique** and **unit** are also linked to the Latin word **unus**.

uniform NOUN **uniforms** a set of clothes that someone must wear for school or for their job

unify VERB **unifies, unifying, unified** to combine things so they become one

unimportant ADJECTIVE not important
▶ **unimportance** NOUN the fact of not being important

uninhabited ADJECTIVE an uninhabited place does not have people living in it

unintentional ADJECTIVE done by accident and not deliberately
▶ **unintentionally** ADVERB in a way that is not deliberate

uninterested ADJECTIVE not interested: *I am uninterested in sport.*
▶ **uninteresting** ADJECTIVE boring

union NOUN **unions 1** another word for a **trade union 2** a group of states or countries that work together
▶ **unionist** NOUN **unionists 1** a member of a trade union **2** someone who believes that their country or a part of it should be joined to another

unique ADJECTIVE if something is unique, it is the only thing like it and it is completely different from anyone or anything else

unisex ADJECTIVE intended for either men or women: *unisex clothes*

unison NOUN
• **in unison** if people do something in unison, they all do it together

unit NOUN **units 1** a single thing, person or group that can be part of a larger thing: *an army unit • The book is divided into ten units.* **2** a fixed quantity that is used for measuring something: *A metre is a unit of length.* **3**

a department in a hospital that provides a particular type of treatment: *a burns unit*

unite VERB **unites, uniting, united 1** if people or things unite, they join together **2** to unite two or more things is to join them together

universal ADJECTIVE something that is universal affects or includes everyone: *English is almost a universal language.*

universe NOUN everything that exists anywhere, including the Earth, the sun and all the other planets and stars in space: *Somewhere in the universe there might be another world like ours.*

university NOUN **universities** a place where you go to study at the highest level after leaving school

unjust ADJECTIVE not fair: *an unjust punishment.*
▶ **unjustly** ADVERB not fairly: *He was unjustly punished.*

unkempt ADJECTIVE not tidy: *unkempt hair*

unkind ADJECTIVE **unkinder, unkindest** cruel and not kind: *It was unkind of you to tease her.*
▶ **unkindly** ADVERB in an unkind way: *They treated me unkindly.*
▶ **unkindness** NOUN being unkind

unknown ADJECTIVE **1** not known: *For some unknown reason, she was angry with me.* **2** not well known: *an unknown actor*

unleaded ADJECTIVE unleaded petrol does not have lead added to it and therefore causes less harm to the environment

unless CONJUNCTION except when or except if: *We always go for a walk on Sundays, unless it's raining. • Don't come unless I phone you.*

unlike PREPOSITION **1** different from: *I never saw twins who were so unlike each other.* **2** not usual for someone: *It's unlike my mum to be so bad-tempered.*

unlikely ADJECTIVE **1** not likely or expected to happen: *It's unlikely that she'll come.* **2** probably not true: *an unlikely tale*

unload VERB **unloads, unloading,**

Aa
Bb
Cc
Dd
Ee
Ff
Gg
Hh
Ii
Jj
Kk
Ll
Mm
Nn
Oo
Pp
Qq
Rr
Ss
Tt
Uu
Vv
Ww
Xx
Yy
Zz

unloaded to unload something, such as a ship or vehicle, is to remove all the things that it is carrying

unlock VERB **unlocks, unlocking, unlocked** to open something that is locked: *Unlock this door now!*

▶ **unlocked** ADJECTIVE not locked

unlucky ADJECTIVE having, or coming from, bad luck: *I never win at cards – I'm very unlucky. • It was an unlucky defeat.*

▶ **unluckily** ADVERB I am sorry to say: *Unluckily, he is injured and can't play football.*

unmask VERB **unmasks, unmasking, unmasked 1** to unmask someone is to show what they are really like: *He was unmasked as a liar and a cheat.* **2** to unmask someone is to take away their mask or disguise

unmistakable ADJECTIVE not able to be mistaken for anything else: *I'm sure it was Josh I saw – his face is unmistakable.*

▶ **unmistakably** ADVERB in an unmistakable way: *It was unmistakably his handwriting.*

unnatural ADJECTIVE not natural or not normal: *an unnatural silence*

▶ **unnaturally** ADVERB in a way that is not natural

unnecessary ADJECTIVE not necessary or not needed: *I don't want to cause you unnecessary trouble.*

▶ **unnecessarily** ADVERB when it is not necessary: *My dad woke me unnecessarily – it was a school holiday!*

unoccupied ADJECTIVE empty and not lived in: *These houses have been unoccupied for years.*

unpack VERB **unpacks, unpacking, unpacked** to take things out of a suitcase or bag: *I've unpacked my case. • Have you unpacked yet? • He still hasn't unpacked his clothes.*

unpleasant ADJECTIVE nasty: *an unpleasant smell*

▶ **unpleasantly** ADVERB in an unpleasant way

▶ **unpleasantness** NOUN being unpleasant

unplug VERB **unplugs, unplugging,**

unplugged 1 to unplug something electrical is to take its plug out of a socket **2** to unplug something is to remove a blockage from it: *It will not be easy to unplug the pipe.*

unpopular ADJECTIVE not popular or not liked: *His bad behaviour makes him very unpopular with his classmates.*

unravel VERB **unravels, unravelling, unravelled 1** to unravel something is to unwind it or take the knots out of it: *He could not unravel the tangled thread.* **2** to unravel something puzzling is to solve it: *She was determined to unravel the mystery.*

unreal ADJECTIVE **1** extremely strange and slightly frightening: *The silence was unreal.* **2** not actually existing

unreasonable ADJECTIVE asking too much and not fair: *It's unreasonable to expect students to do so much homework.*

▶ **unreasonably** ADVERB in an unreasonable way

unrest NOUN angry public protests by a lot of people: *unrest all over the country*

unruly ADJECTIVE badly behaved and difficult to control: *an unruly child • unruly behaviour*

unscathed ADJECTIVE without being harmed: *They escaped from the burning building unscathed.*

unscrew VERB **unscrews, unscrewing, unscrewed 1** to loosen or remove something by taking out a screw or screws: *Dad unscrewed the cupboard door.* **2** to loosen or remove something with a twisting action: *Joe unscrewed the lid from the bottle and took a drink.*

unseemly ADJECTIVE not suitable or not proper: *unseemly behaviour*

unseen ADJECTIVE not seen or not noticed: *He managed to leave the house unseen.*

unselfish ADJECTIVE generous and thinking of others

▶ **unselfishly** ADVERB in an unselfish way: *George unselfishly shared his sweets.*

▶ **unselfishness** NOUN being generous and thinking of others

unsightly ADJECTIVE ugly and not nice to look at: *The new school building is very unsightly.*

unsound ADJECTIVE not safe or not reliable: *The bridge is structurally unsound.* • *Her evidence is unsound.*

unsteady ADJECTIVE likely to fall and not firm: *After the operation she was very unsteady on her feet.*
▸ **unsteadily** ADVERB in an unsteady way

unsuccessful ADJECTIVE not managing to do something you have been trying to do: *She tried to find him but was unsuccessful.*
▸ **unsuccessfully** ADVERB in a way that is not successful: *I tried unsuccessfully to speak to her.*

unsuitable ADJECTIVE not right for a purpose or occasion: *These shoes are unsuitable for school.*

unthinkable ADJECTIVE too bad or too unlikely to be thought about: *It is unthinkable that he would steal from his own parents.*

untidy ADJECTIVE **untidier, untidiest** not neat or not well organized: *His room is always untidy.*
▸ **untidiness** NOUN being untidy

untie VERB **unties, untying, untied** to loosen or unfasten something that is tied: *She untied his shoelaces for him.*

until PREPOSITION up to the time of: *We waited until ten o'clock.*
CONJUNCTION up to the time when: *Keep walking until you come to the station.*

untimely ADJECTIVE happening too soon or at a time that is not suitable: *his untimely death* • *her untimely return*

unto PREPOSITION an old-fashioned word for **to**: *The knight spoke once more unto the king.*

untold ADJECTIVE **1** not yet told: *the untold story* **2** too great to be counted or measured: *untold riches*

untoward ADJECTIVE **1** unlucky or unfortunate: *If nothing untoward happens, I should be there by lunchtime.* **2** not appropriate: *untoward rudeness*

untrue ADJECTIVE **1** false, not true: *His story is completely untrue.* **2** (*formal*) not faithful or not loyal

unused ADJECTIVE **1** that has not been used: *an unused stamp* **2** if you are unused to something, you do not know it very well or have not done it very often: *I'm unused to spicy food.* • *He was unused to having to cook his own meals.*

unusual ADJECTIVE not normal or not ordinary: *It's unusual for him to arrive late.* • *That's an unusual necklace.*
▸ **unusually** ADVERB to an unusual degree: *unusually cold for the time of year*

unveil VERB **unveils, unveiling, unveiled 1** to unveil something is to take a cover away from it as part of a ceremony: *The Prime Minister unveiled the new statue.* **2** to reveal something: *The headmaster has unveiled plans for shorter breaks during the school day.* **3** to unveil someone is to take a veil away from their face

unwell ADJECTIVE not in good health: *I feel slightly unwell this morning.*

unwieldy ADJECTIVE large and awkward to carry or manage: *This suitcase is too unwieldy for me.*

unwilling ADJECTIVE not wanting to do something: *He's unwilling to accept the money.*
▸ **unwillingness** NOUN being unwilling to do something

unwind VERB **unwinds, unwinding, unwound 1** to unwind something is to undo it from a wound position: *He unwound the bandage from his ankle.* **2** to unwind is to come undone from a wound position: *The snake slowly unwound from the branch.* **3** to relax: *Having a bath is a good way to unwind.*

unwrap VERB **unwraps, unwrapping, unwrapped** to open something that is wrapped: *She carefully unwrapped the present.*

unzip VERB **unzips, unzipping, unzipped** to undo the zip of something: *He unzipped his bag and took out a book.*

up ADVERB
1 towards or in a higher position: *Prices*

Aa
Bb
Cc
Dd
Ee
Ff
Gg
Hh
Ii
Jj
Kk
Ll
Mm
Nn
Oo
Pp
Qq
Rr
Ss
Tt
Uu
Vv
Ww
Xx
Yy
Zz

have gone up again. • *Stand up!*

2 completely, so that something is finished: *Drink up your milk.*

3 out of bed: *I got up at five o'clock this morning.*

4 as far as something or someone: *He came up to me and shook my hand.*

PREPOSITION **1** to or at a higher part of: *He climbed up the tree.* • *She's up the ladder.* **2** along: *walking up the road*

ADJECTIVE

1 going up: *the up escalator*

2 out of bed: *He's not up yet.*

3 ahead: *two goals up at the end of the first half*

4 if the sun is up it has risen

5 finished: *Your time is up.*

6 an informal way of saying 'wrong': *What's up with you today?*

• **up to 1** if you are up to something you are doing that thing, especially in a secretive way: *My little brother is up to no good again.* **2** if you are up to a task, then you have the ability to do it: *Do you think you are up to winning the race?* **3** if a choice is up to you, then you have to decide what to do or have: *Whether we go swimming or just go home is up to you.*

• **up to date** with all the information or features available just now: *I want to bring my diary up to date.* • *I need a computer that is more up to date.*

• **ups and downs** good and bad times

upbringing NOUN **upbringings** the process of bringing up a child: *We had a strict upbringing.*

update VERB **updates, updating, updated 1** to update someone is to give them the latest information: *Could someone update me on what's happening here?* **2** to update something is to make it more modern: *I need to update my computer.*

NOUN **updates 1** bringing someone or something up to date: *I need an update on what is happening.* **2** an updated version of something: *an update of the news*

upgrade VERB **upgrades, upgrading, upgraded 1** to upgrade something

such as machinery or a computer is to improve it, especially by adding or replacing parts **2** to upgrade someone is to promote them

NOUN **upgrades** (*ICT*) in computing, a newer version of a software program

upheaval NOUN **upheavals** a great change or disturbance: *the upheaval of moving house*

uphill ADJECTIVE **1** going upwards: *an uphill part of the track* **2** difficult: *This will be an uphill struggle.*

ADVERB up a slope: *We travelled uphill for several hours.*

uphold VERB **upholds, upholding, upheld** to uphold something, such as a decision, is to support it or agree with it: *The court upheld his complaint.*

upholstery NOUN the coverings and cushions of a seat: *car upholstery*

upkeep NOUN **1** the keeping of something, such as a house or car, in good condition **2** the cost of keeping something, such as a house or car, in good condition

upland NOUN high ground

▸ **uplands** PLURAL NOUN a region with hills or mountains

upload VERB **uploads, uploading, uploaded** (*ICT*) to upload information is to send it from one computer to another or to a place where more people can get it

upon PREPOSITION a more formal word for **on**: *a high cliff upon which stood a castle*

upper ADJECTIVE higher: *the upper floors of the building*

NOUN **uppers** the part of a shoe above the sole: *These shoes have leather uppers.*

upper case NOUN upper case letters are capital letters

upper class NOUN **upper classes** the upper class is the highest social class and consists of people such as royalty and people related to royalty

ADJECTIVE coming from, or to do with, the upper class

uppermost ADJECTIVE highest: *the uppermost room of the house*

Aa Bb Cc Dd Ee Ff Gg Hh Ii Jj Kk Ll Mm Nn Oo Pp Qq Rr Ss Tt **Uu** Vv Ww Xx Yy Zz

upright ADJECTIVE **1** standing straight up: *a row of upright posts* **2** fair and honest: *an upright man*
NOUN **uprights** a vertical post or pole, especially one that supports something such as a fence

uprising NOUN **uprisings** an occasion when many people in a country protest against the government or try to change it using force

uproar NOUN **uproars** a noisy disturbance: *The classroom was in an uproar.*

uproot VERB **uproots, uprooting, uprooted 1** to pull a plant out of the ground together with its roots **2** to make people move away from their homes: *Thousands of people were uprooted by the war.* **3** to leave your home and go and live in another place: *They uprooted and moved to the country.*

upset VERB **upsets, upsetting, upset 1** to make someone sad, angry or worried: *His friend's death upset him very much.* **2** to spoil something: *Her illness has upset our holiday plans.* **3** to knock something over: *The dog upset a vase of flowers.*
ADJECTIVE sad, angry or worried: *He's upset about failing his exam.*
NOUN **upsets 1** sadness or worry: *Her sudden departure caused a lot of upset.* **2** something that causes feelings such as unhappiness and worry: *Losing the match to such a poor team was quite an upset.* **3** a slight disturbance: *a stomach upset*

upshot NOUN the final result of something: *The upshot of all of the delays was that we decided not to go at all.*

upside-down ADJECTIVE AND ADVERB **1** with the top part where the bottom should be and the bottom part where the top should be: *I knew he wasn't really reading – he was holding the book upside-down.* **2** in or into confusion: *The burglars turned the house upside-down.*

upstairs ADVERB to or on a higher floor: *I went upstairs to get the book.*
NOUN the higher floor or floors of a building: *The downstairs needs painting, but the upstairs is nice.*
ADJECTIVE on a higher floor: *an upstairs bedroom*

upstream ADVERB further up a river or stream in the opposite direction to the way it flows: *Salmon swim upstream to lay their eggs.*

uptake NOUN
• **quick** or **slow on the uptake** quick or slow to understand or realize something

uptight ADJECTIVE (*informal*) nervous or anxious: *You seem a bit uptight today.*

up-to-date ADJECTIVE **1** new or modern: *up-to-date technology* **2** having the latest information: *an up-to-date news story*

upward ADJECTIVE moving or leading towards a higher place or position: *an upward movement*
ADVERB upwards

upwards ADVERB to a higher place or position: *He looked upwards and saw the sun.*
• **upwards of** more than: *Upwards of 200 people came to the meeting.*

uranium NOUN (*science*) a radioactive metal that is used to make nuclear energy

urban ADJECTIVE to do with a town or city: *urban life* • *urban traffic*
▸ **urbanization** NOUN being urbanized

urbanize or **urbanise** VERB **urbanizes, urbanizing, urbanized** to make an area less like the countryside and more like a town: *Many of these small islands are being urbanized.*
▸ **urbanization** NOUN being urbanized

urchin NOUN **urchins** a mischievous or dirty child

urge VERB **urges, urging, urged** to urge someone to do something is to try to persuade them to do it: *The teacher urged them to work hard for the exam.*
• **urge someone on** to urge someone on is to encourage them to carry on: *He*

Aa Bb Cc Dd Ee Ff Gg Hh Ii Jj Kk Ll Mm Nn Oo Pp Qq Rr Ss Tt **Uu** Vv Ww Xx Yy Zz urged his followers on.

NOUN **urges** a sudden feeling of wanting to do something: *I felt an urge to hit him.*

urgency NOUN being urgent: *I didn't realize the urgency of the situation.*

urgent ADJECTIVE needing attention immediately: *I have an urgent message for the headmaster.*

▸ **urgently** ADVERB immediately or desperately: *Medical supplies are needed urgently.*

urinate VERB **urinates, urinating, urinated** to pass urine out of the body

urine NOUN the waste liquid passed out of the bodies of humans and animals

urn NOUN **urns 1** a sort of vase for holding the ashes of a dead person who has been cremated **2** a large metal container with a tap, used for heating water or for making large amounts of tea or coffee

us PRONOUN a word you use when you are talking about yourself and at least one other person: *His happy face surprised all of us.* • *Do you want to come with us?*

usage NOUN **usages 1** treatment: *These chairs have had a lot of rough usage.* **2** the way that the words of a language are used

use VERB **uses, using, used 1** to use something is to put it to a purpose: *Use a knife to open it.* • *Use your common sense!* **2** to take an amount of something from a supply: *Who's used all the cheese?*

• **use something up** to use something up is to use all of it so that there is none left: *He used up all the milk.*

NOUN **uses 1** the using of something: *We cannot allow the use of guns.* **2** the purpose for which something can be used: *This knife has a lot of uses.* **3** the value or advantage of something: *Is this coat of any use to you?* • *What's the use of crying?*

▸ **used** ADJECTIVE not new: *a used car*

• **used to 1** to be used to something is to know it well, or to have done it lots of times: *She soon got used to her new school.* **2** if you used to do something,

you did it often or regularly in the past: *We used to go to the seaside every summer.*

useful ADJECTIVE helpful or able to do what needs doing: *She made herself useful by washing the dishes.* • *a useful tool*

▸ **usefulness** NOUN being useful

useless ADJECTIVE having no use, or not doing what it is supposed to do: *This knife's useless – it's completely blunt.* • *I tried to stop the baby crying but it was useless.*

user NOUN **users** a person who uses something: *users of public transport*

user-friendly ADJECTIVE easy to use or understand: *user-friendly software*

usher NOUN **ushers** someone who shows people to their seats in a cinema or theatre

VERB **ushers, ushering, ushered** to go with someone and show them the way: *The waiter ushered him to a table.*

usual ADJECTIVE done or happening most often: *I took my usual route to school this morning.* • *He was late as usual.*

▸ **usually** ADVERB normally, on most occasions: *We usually go on holiday in June.*

utensil NOUN **utensils** a tool or container, especially one for everyday use in the home: *knives, pans and other utensils*

uterus NOUN **uteruses** or **uteri** a more technical word for the **womb**, the part of a woman's or female animal's body where babies grow until they are born

utility NOUN **utilities** a company which supplies gas, electricity, water or another service

utilize or **utilise** VERB **utilizes, utilizing, utilized** (*formal*) to make use of: *Old newspapers can be utilized for making recycled paper.*

utmost ADJECTIVE greatest possible: *You must take the utmost care.*

• **do your utmost** to make the biggest possible effort: *She has done her utmost to help him.*

utter[1] VERB **utters, uttering, uttered**

Aa
Bb
Cc
Dd
Ee
Ff
Gg
Hh
Ii
Jj
Kk
Ll
Mm
Nn
Oo
Pp
Qq
Rr
Ss
Tt
Uu
Vv
Ww
Xx
Yy
Zz

to utter a sound is to make it with your voice: *She uttered a sigh of relief.* • *She didn't utter a single word.*

▸ **utterance** NOUN **utterances** something that is said

utter[2] ADJECTIVE complete or total: *utter silence*

▸ **utterly** ADVERB completely or totally: *I feel utterly exhausted.*

U-turn NOUN **U-turns 1** a turn in the shape of a U, made by a driver to go back the way he or she has just come **2** a complete change of plan, opinion or decision

Aa

Bb

Cc

Dd

Ee

Ff

Gg

Hh

Ii

Jj

Kk

Ll

Mm

Nn

Oo

Pp

Qq

Rr

Ss

Tt

Uu

Vv

Ww

Xx

Yy

Zz

Vv

vacancy NOUN **vacancies 1** a room in a hotel that is available: *Sorry, we have no vacancies.* **2** a job that is available

▸ **vacant** ADJECTIVE not being used: *a vacant seat*

vacate VERB **vacates, vacating, vacated** to leave a place empty: *You have to vacate the hotel room by ten o-clock.*

▸ **vacation** NOUN **vacations** an American English word for a holiday: *a two-week vacation*

vaccinate (pronounced vak-sin-ait) VERB **vaccinates, vaccinating, vaccinated** to put a substance into someone's body to protect them from a disease

▸ **vaccination** NOUN **vaccinations** the process of vaccinating someone

▸ **vaccine** NOUN **vaccines** the substance that is used for vaccinating someone

vacuum (pronounced vak-yoo-im) NOUN **vacuums** (*science*) a space with no air in it

VERB **vacuums, vacuuming, vacuumed** to clean something using a vacuum cleaner

◆ **Vacuum** is a Latin word that means *empty.*

vacuum cleaner NOUN **vacuum cleaners** an electrical machine that sucks dust off the floor

vacuum flask NOUN **vacuum flasks** a container that has a vacuum between its inside and outside coverings, and which keeps drinks hot or cold

vagina NOUN **vaginas** the passage that connects a woman's womb to the outside of her body

vague ADJECTIVE **vaguer, vaguest** not very clear or definite: *I have a vague idea where he lives.*

▸ **vaguely** ADVERB not clearly or precisely: *He looked vaguely familiar.*

vain ADJECTIVE **vainer, vainest 1** too proud of yourself and thinking too much about the way you look **2** useless: *The injured dog made a vain attempt to get up.*

• **in vain** without success: *He tried in vain to squeeze through the bars of the cage.*

▸ **vainly** ADVERB without achieving what you want to do: *I tossed about in bed, vainly trying to get comfortable.*

Vaisakhi NOUN another word for **Baisakhi**

valentine NOUN **valentines 1** a card that you send on Saint Valentine's Day (on 14 February) to show that you love someone **2** the person who you send a valentine to

valiant ADJECTIVE brave: *She made a valiant attempt to rescue the cat.*

▸ **valiantly** ADVERB in a brave way

valid ADJECTIVE **1** legally or officially acceptable and able to be used: *a valid passport* **2** reasonable and acceptable: *a valid excuse*

▸ **validity** NOUN being valid

valley NOUN **valleys** (*geography*) a stretch of low land between hills, often with a river running through it

valour NOUN bravery or courage, for example in a battle

valuable ADJECTIVE **1** worth a lot of money: *a valuable diamond* **2** very useful: *She's a valuable member of the team.*

▸ **valuables** PLURAL NOUN things, especially things that you own, that are worth a lot of money

value NOUN **values 1** the amount that something is worth **2** usefulness and importance

VERB **values, valuing, valued 1** to value something is to think it is important or worthwhile: *Dad values the time he spends with us.* **2** to say how much something is worth: *The jewels were valued at three thousand dollars.*

▸ **valuation** NOUN **valuations 1** the act of deciding how much something is worth **2** an estimated price or value

valve NOUN **valves** something that opens and shuts to control the flow of liquid, air or gas through a pipe

vampire NOUN **vampires** in stories, a dead person who comes out at night and sucks people's blood

van NOUN **vans** a road vehicle, smaller than a lorry, for carrying goods

vandal NOUN **vandals** someone who deliberately damages buildings and other things

▸ **vandalism** NOUN the crime of deliberately damaging something such as a public building

▸ **vandalize** or **vandalise** VERB **vandalizes, vandalizing, vandalized** to deliberately damage something

vane NOUN **vanes 1** a blade that is moved by wind or water and is part of a windmill or mill **2** a pointer, often on top of a steeple, that is moved by the wind and shows which direction it is blowing from

vanilla NOUN a flavouring that comes from the pods of a plant: *vanilla ice-cream*

vanish VERB **vanishes, vanishing, vanished** to disappear and leave nothing behind

vanity NOUN too much pride in the way you look

vaporize or **vaporise** VERB **vaporizes, vaporizing, vaporized** (*science*) to become or make something into a gas: *Water vaporizes to become steam.*

▸ **vaporizer** or **vaporiser** NOUN **vaporizers** or **vaporisers** a device that sprays liquid very finely

vapour NOUN **vapours** (*science*) a lot of tiny drops of liquid in the air. Some liquids and solids can be turned to vapour when they are heated

variable ADJECTIVE changing often and never staying the same

variant NOUN **variants** a different form or version of something

▸ **variation** NOUN **variations** a change in the amount or level of something: *variations in temperature*

varied ADJECTIVE of many different types: *He has varied interests, from reading to outdoor sports.*

variety NOUN **varieties**
1 if something has variety, it has many different things in it: *You need a bit of variety in the food you eat.*
2 a type of something that is slightly different from other similar things: *a new variety of rose*
3 a group with different types of the same thing: *The chairs are available in a variety of colours.* **4** a type of entertainment with singing, dancing and comedy

various ADJECTIVE different: *There were various things to choose from.*

varnish NOUN **varnishes** a liquid that gives a shiny surface to wood
VERB **varnishes, varnishing, varnished** to put varnish on to wood

vary VERB **varies, varying, varied 1** to vary is to change: *The weather varies a lot.* **2** to vary something is to change it slightly

vase NOUN **vases** a container for flowers that is often kept as an ornament

vast ADJECTIVE extremely big: *vast desert lands*

▸ **vastly** ADVERB much: *vastly different*

▸ **vastness** NOUN being extremely big

vat NOUN **vats** a large container for liquids

VAT ABBREVIATION short for **value-added tax**, which is a tax you pay on things you buy

vault NOUN **vaults** a room underground for dead bodies or for storing valuable things

VDU ABBREVIATION (*ICT*) short for **visual display unit**, the screen you use with a computer

veal NOUN meat from a calf

Veda NOUN the most ancient holy writings of the Hindu religion

veer VERB **veers, veering, veered**

Aa
Bb
Cc
Dd
Ee
Ff
Gg
Hh
Ii
Jj
Kk
Ll
Mm
Nn
Oo
Pp
Qq
Rr
Ss
Tt
Uu
Vv
Ww
Xx
Yy
Zz

a Venn diagram

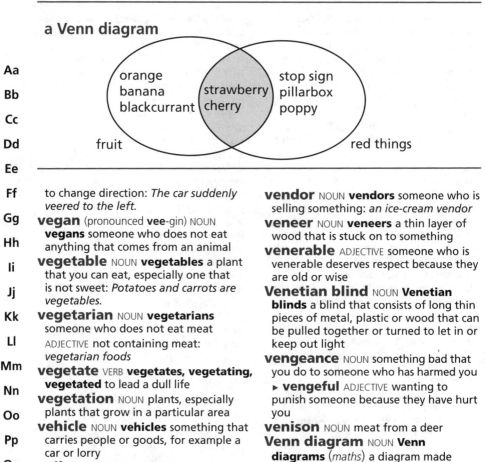

to change direction: *The car suddenly veered to the left.*

vegan (pronounced **vee**-gin) NOUN **vegans** someone who does not eat anything that comes from an animal

vegetable NOUN **vegetables** a plant that you can eat, especially one that is not sweet: *Potatoes and carrots are vegetables.*

vegetarian NOUN **vegetarians** someone who does not eat meat ADJECTIVE not containing meat: *vegetarian foods*

vegetate VERB **vegetates, vegetating, vegetated** to lead a dull life

vegetation NOUN plants, especially plants that grow in a particular area

vehicle NOUN **vehicles** something that carries people or goods, for example a car or lorry

veil NOUN **veils** a piece of material that covers a woman's head and face

vein NOUN **veins** (*science*) **1** one of the very thin tubes inside your body that carry blood to your heart **2** one of the thin lines on a leaf

velocity NOUN **velocities** (*science*) the speed at which something moves

velvet NOUN a type of cloth with a surface that is covered with short hairs and feels very soft

▶ **velvety** ADJECTIVE feeling like velvet

vendetta NOUN **vendettas** an angry disagreement that lasts for a long time

vending machine NOUN **vending machines** a machine that you can buy things from

vendor NOUN **vendors** someone who is selling something: *an ice-cream vendor*

veneer NOUN **veneers** a thin layer of wood that is stuck on to something

venerable ADJECTIVE someone who is venerable deserves respect because they are old or wise

Venetian blind NOUN **Venetian blinds** a blind that consists of long thin pieces of metal, plastic or wood that can be pulled together or turned to let in or keep out light

vengeance NOUN something bad that you do to someone who has harmed you

▶ **vengeful** ADJECTIVE wanting to punish someone because they have hurt you

venison NOUN meat from a deer

Venn diagram NOUN **Venn diagrams** (*maths*) a diagram made up of circles which overlap, used to show which members of one set are also members of another set. See the example above

venom NOUN **1** the poison that some snakes produce **2** deep hatred: *letters full of venom.*

▶ **venomous** ADJECTIVE poisonous

vent NOUN **vents** a small opening to allow air or smoke to pass through

• **give vent to something** to express a feeling, such as anger

ventilate VERB **ventilates, ventilating, ventilated** to let fresh air into a room or building

▶ **ventilation** NOUN letting fresh air into a room or building

▶ **ventilator** NOUN **ventilators 1** a machine that helps someone to breathe by pumping air into and out of their lungs **2** an opening or piece of equipment that lets air into a room or building

ventriloquism NOUN the skill of speaking without moving your lips and making it look as though a puppet is speaking

▶ **ventriloquist** NOUN **ventriloquists** someone who has the skill of ventriloquism

✦These words come from the Latin words **venter**, which means *stomach*, and **loqui**, which means *to speak*. The word used to mean a person who had been taken over by a speaking demon.

venture NOUN **ventures** an activity or project: *a business venture*

VERB **ventures, venturing, ventured** to go somewhere unknown to you, which may be dangerous or unpleasant

venue NOUN **venues** the place where an event takes place

veranda NOUN **verandas** an outdoor terrace with a roof, built on to the side of a house

verb WORD CLASS **verbs** (*grammar*) the word in a sentence that tells you what someone or something does. For example, *eat* and *speak* are verbs

verbal ADJECTIVE spoken rather than written: *a verbal promise*

verdict NOUN **verdicts** a decision whether someone is guilty or not guilty of committing a crime, made in a court of law

verge NOUN **verges** the grassy area at the edge of a road

• **be on the verge of** to be almost happening or almost doing something: *Sanjay was on the verge of tears.*

verify VERB **verifies, verifying, verified** to prove or say for definite that something is true

vermin NOUN animals or insects, such as rats or fleas, which people think are pests

verruca (pronounced vi-**roo**-ka) NOUN **verrucas** a wart on someone's foot

versatile ADJECTIVE **1** useful for many different things: *versatile clothes* **2** able to do many different things: *a versatile actor*

▶ **versatility** NOUN being versatile

verse NOUN **verses 1** a verse is a set of lines that form one part of a song or poem **2** verse is poetry rather than writing

version NOUN **versions 1** a description of events from one person's point of view: *I'd like to hear your version of what happened.* **2** a type of something that is slightly different from the original form: *a techno version of an old pop song*

versus PREPOSITION against. Versus is used when saying who is playing in a sports game: *It's Scotland versus France tonight.*

vertebra NOUN **vertebrae** (*science*) one of the bones that form your backbone

vertebrate NOUN **vertebrates** (*science*) an animal that has a backbone

vertex NOUN **vertices** (*maths*) **1** the point on a cone or pyramid that is opposite the base **2** a point where lines meet in an angle or on a shape

vertical ADJECTIVE standing upright and straight: *vertical lines*

vertigo NOUN feeling dizzy because you are in a very high place

verve NOUN excitement and energy

very ADVERB to a great degree: *I'm very tired.*

ADJECTIVE exact: *At that very moment, the telephone rang.*

Vesak (pronounced **ves**-ak) NOUN an important Buddhist festival that takes place in May

vessel NOUN **vessels 1** a large boat or ship **2** a container for liquids **3** (*science*) a tube that carries blood through your body

vest NOUN **vests 1** a piece of underwear that covers the top part of your body **2** the American English word for a waistcoat

vestment NOUN **vestments** a piece of clothing that a priest or minister wears during religious services

Aa
Bb
Cc
Dd
Ee
Ff
Gg
Hh
Ii
Jj
Kk
Ll
Mm
Nn
Oo
Pp
Qq
Rr
Ss
Tt
Uu
Vv
Ww
Xx
Yy
Zz

Aa
Bb
Cc
Dd
Ee
Ff
Gg
Hh
Ii
Jj
Kk
Ll
Mm
Nn
Oo
Pp
Qq
Rr
Ss
Tt
Uu
Vv
Ww
Xx
Yy
Zz

vestry NOUN **vestries** the room in a church where the priest or minister puts on clothes for a religious service

vet NOUN **vets** someone whose job is to treat animals who are ill or injured. The word is short for **veterinary surgeon**

veteran NOUN **veterans 1** someone who has a lot of experience at something **2** someone who fought in a war

veterinary ADJECTIVE to do with the care of animals that are ill or injured: *veterinary medicine*

veto VERB **vetoes, vetoing, vetoed** to stop something from happening: *The president vetoed the plan to lower taxes.*
NOUN **vetoes 1** the power to stop a law from being passed or a decision from being made **2** an occasion when someone does not let something go ahead

vex VERB **vexes, vexing, vexed** to annoy someone
▸ **vexation** NOUN feeling annoyed

VHF ABBREVIATION (*technology*) short for **very high frequency**

via PREPOSITION travelling through a place: *The train goes to London via Birmingham.*

viaduct NOUN **viaducts** a bridge across a valley, supported by several tall arches

vibrant ADJECTIVE **1** exciting and full of life: *a vibrant city* **2** vibrant colours are very bright

vibrate VERB **vibrates, vibrating, vibrated** to shake very quickly
▸ **vibration** NOUN **vibrations 1** vibration is shaking very quickly **2** a vibration is a quick shaking movement

vicar NOUN **vicars** a priest in the Church of England

vice- PREFIX **vice-** at the start of a word tells you that someone is next in importance. For example, a *vice-president* is someone who is next in rank to a president and takes their place if they are not available

vice[1] NOUN **vices 1** a vice is a bad habit **2** a vice is behaviour that is bad or not decent

vice[2] NOUN **vices** a tool for holding objects firmly while you work on them

vice versa ADVERB the other way around: *I needed his help and vice versa.*

vicinity (pronounced vi-**sin**-i-ti) NOUN the area around a place: *There are no schools in the vicinity.*

vicious ADJECTIVE extremely cruel and wanting to hurt people: *a vicious attack*

victim NOUN **victims** someone who is harmed by a bad situation or bad event: *victims of crime*
▸ **victimize** or **victimise** VERB **victimizes, victimizing, victimized** to treat someone in an unfair way

victor NOUN **victors** the person who has won a game or competition

victory NOUN **victories** winning a battle or competition: *victory in the Cup Final*
▸ **victorious** ADJECTIVE successful in a battle or competition

video NOUN **videos 1** a recording of a film or television programme made on videotape **2** a recording of an event on a cassette that has been made using a video camera **3** a machine for playing videos
VERB **videos, videoing, videoed 1** to record a television programme on to videotape **2** to film an event using a video camera

✦ **Video** was taken from the Latin word **videre**, which means *to see*.

video recorder or **videocassette recorder** NOUN **video recorders** or **videocassette recorders** a machine for recording and playing videos

videotape NOUN **videotapes** magnetic tape that pictures and sounds can be recorded on

view NOUN **views 1** the things you can see from a place: *There's a fantastic view from the top of the hill.* **2** your ability to see things from a place: *The pillar spoilt my view of the concert.* **3** someone's opinion: *What's your view on the new school uniform?*
• **in view of** considering something: *In*

view of the weather, we have cancelled the game.

• **on view** being shown for people to look at: *Several classic cars will be on view.*

• **with a view to** with the intention of: *My grandparents visited apartments in Spain with a view to buying one.*

VERB **views, viewing, viewed 1** to look at something: *Parents can view the plans for the new school buildings.* **2** to think about someone or something in a particular way: *Maths is often viewed as a difficult subject.*

▸ **viewer** NOUN **viewers** someone who watches television: *The programme attracted over ten million viewers.*

viewpoint NOUN **viewpoints 1** a way of thinking about something: *From my viewpoint, the event was a success.* **2** a place from which you look at something: *a good viewpoint at the top of a hill*

vigil (pronounced **vij**-il) NOUN **vigils** a time when people stay awake at night in order to pray, protest or watch someone who is ill

vigilant ADJECTIVE watching things carefully in order to notice any trouble or problems: *Police have urged people to be vigilant after a series of thefts.*

▸ **vigilance** NOUN being careful to notice any trouble or problems

vigorous ADJECTIVE very active or strong: *vigorous defence*

▸ **vigorously** ADVERB in an active or strong way: *We argued vigorously.*

vigour NOUN strength and energy

vile ADJECTIVE **viler, vilest** extremely unpleasant: *a vile taste*

villa NOUN **villas** a large house, especially one used for holidays

village NOUN **villages** a small place in a country area, which is not as big as a town

▸ **villager** NOUN **villagers** someone who lives in a village

villain NOUN **villains** a bad person or a criminal

vindictive ADJECTIVE wanting to harm someone because they have been bad to you

vine NOUN **vines** the plant that grapes grow on

vinegar NOUN a sour liquid used for flavouring food

vineyard NOUN **vineyards** a place where grapes are grown to produce wine

vintage NOUN **vintages 1** the wine that is produced in a particular year or place **2** the time that something is from ADJECTIVE typical of a particular time in the past: *vintage aircraft*

vintage car NOUN **vintage cars** a car made between 1917 and 1930 that is still in very good condition

viola NOUN **violas** (*music*) a musical instrument that looks like a big violin and is played in the same way

violate VERB **violates, violating, violated 1** to violate a law or rule is to break it **2** to violate someone's rights is to not respect them **3** to damage or destroy a special place

▸ **violation** NOUN violating something

violence NOUN behaviour that is rough and intended to hurt someone

violent ADJECTIVE **1** behaving in a rough way that is intended to hurt someone **2** very sudden and strong: *a violent storm*

▸ **violently** ADVERB in a violent way

violet NOUN **violets 1** a small purple flower **2** a purple colour

violin NOUN **violins** (*music*) a musical instrument with four strings, which you hold under your chin and play by drawing a bow across the strings

▸ **violinist** NOUN **violinists** someone who plays the violin

VIP ABBREVIATION **VIPs** short for **very important person**

viper NOUN **vipers** a small poisonous snake

virgin NOUN **virgins** someone who has never had sex

virtual ADJECTIVE **1** almost a particular thing: *He was a virtual prisoner in his own home.* **2** (*ICT*) using computer images that make something seem real: *a virtual tour of the museum*

Aa
Bb
Cc
Dd
Ee
Ff
Gg
Hh
Ii
Jj
Kk
Ll
Mm
Nn
Oo
Pp
Qq
Rr
Ss
Tt
Uu
Vv
Ww
Xx
Yy
Zz

Aa
Bb
Cc
Dd
Ee
Ff
Gg
Hh
Ii
Jj
Kk
Ll
Mm
Nn
Oo
Pp
Qq
Rr
Ss
Tt
Uu
Vv
Ww
Xx
Yy
Zz

▸ **virtually** ADVERB almost: *Virtually all the class can swim now.*

virtual reality NOUN (*ICT*) pictures and sounds that seem real but are actually created by computer software

virtue NOUN **virtues 1** virtue is goodness **2** a virtue is a good quality in a person's character

▸ **virtuous** ADJECTIVE behaving in a very good way

▸ **virtuously** ADVERB in a very good way

virus NOUN **viruses 1** a germ that causes illnesses such as a cold or chickenpox **2** (*ICT*) a computer program that can send itself to many computers, for example by email, and can destroy files on those computers

✦ **Virus** is a Latin word that means *venom*, the poison made by snakes.

visa NOUN **visas** a document that you need to travel to and work in some countries

visibility NOUN **1** how far and well you can see because of conditions such as the weather: *poor visibility* **2** the fact of being easy to see: *Visibility is important for cyclists.*

visible ADJECTIVE able to be seen: *The house is not visible from the road.*

▸ **visibly** ADVERB in a way that is easy to see: *He was visibly upset.*

vision NOUN **visions 1** your ability to see **2** something that you see or imagine might happen: *The bus still hadn't arrived and I had visions of us having to walk.*

visit VERB **visits, visiting, visited** to go and see a place or person

NOUN **visits** the act of visiting a place or person: *I'm going to pay him a visit.*

▸ **visitor** NOUN **visitors** someone who visits a person or place

visor NOUN **visors** the clear part of a helmet that covers someone's face

visual ADJECTIVE to do with seeing: *The blackboard is a visual aid for teaching.*

▸ **visually** ADVERB in a way that involves your ability to see

visual display unit NOUN **visual display units** (*ICT*) a screen that you use with a computer

visualize *or* **visualise** VERB **visualizes, visualizing, visualized** to form a picture of something in your mind: *I remember his name, but I can't visualize him.*

vital ADJECTIVE necessary or extremely important: *vital information*

▸ **vitality** NOUN liveliness and enthusiasm

▸ **vitally** ADVERB extremely: *vitally important*

vitamin NOUN **vitamins** a substance in food that you need to stay healthy: *Oranges contain vitamin C.*

vivid ADJECTIVE **1** producing very clear ideas and pictures in your mind: *vivid memories* **2** very bright: *vivid colours*

▸ **vividly** ADVERB in a very clear way: *I vividly remember meeting him.*

vivisection (pronounced vi-vi-**sek**-shin) NOUN doing experiments on animals that are alive, for medical research

vixen NOUN **vixens** a female fox

vocabulary NOUN **vocabularies 1** the range of words that someone knows and uses: *a child with a good vocabulary* **2** words in a particular language: *We're having a test on French vocabulary.* **3** a list of words and their meanings

vocal ADJECTIVE to do with your voice

▸ **vocalist** NOUN **vocalists** a singer, especially in a band

vocation NOUN **vocations 1** a job or way of life that you feel is very right for you **2** a belief that you should do a particular job or live in a particular way

vodka NOUN a strong clear alcoholic drink

vogue NOUN a fashion at the moment

• **in vogue** fashionable: *Short trousers are in vogue just now.*

voice NOUN **voices 1** the sound you make when you speak or sing: *'Hello!' he said in a loud voice.* **2** your ability to make speaking or singing sounds: *I had a sore throat and lost my voice.*

VERB **voices, voicing, voiced** to express an opinion: *Many people have voiced their concerns.*

volatile ADJECTIVE **1** a volatile person is likely to change their mood very quickly **2** a volatile situation could change very suddenly **3** (*science*) a volatile liquid changes quickly to a gas

volcano NOUN **volcanoes** (*geography*) a mountain with a hole at the top which hot lava sometimes comes out of

▸ **volcanic** ADJECTIVE relating to volcanoes

✦ Volcanoes are named after **Vulcan**, the ancient Roman god of fire.

vole NOUN **voles** a small animal similar to a mouse or rat

volley NOUN **volleys 1** a lot of bullets or weapons that are fired or thrown at the same time **2** in sports like tennis and football, a volley is a shot in which you hit the ball before it hits the ground

VERB **volleys, volleying, volleyed** in some sports, to hit the ball before it hits the ground

volt NOUN **volts** (*science*) a unit for measuring how strong an electric current is

▸ **voltage** NOUN the amount of electrical force something has

volume NOUN **volumes**

1 (*science*) the space that something takes up or the amount of space that a container has

2 the amount of sound that something makes: *Can you turn the volume down on the TV, please?*

3 the amount of something: *The volume of trade has increased.*

4 a book, especially a book that is part of a set

voluntary ADJECTIVE **1** done by choice and not because you have to **2** done without payment: *voluntary work*

volunteer NOUN **volunteers** someone who offers to do something: *Do I have any volunteers to help me tidy up?*

VERB **volunteers, volunteering, volunteered 1** to offer to do something: *Dad volunteered to take us swimming.* **2**

to give information or make a suggestion without being asked for it

vomit VERB **vomits, vomiting, vomited** to bring food back up from your stomach through your mouth

NOUN food that a person or animal has brought back from their stomach through their mouth

vote VERB **votes, voting, voted 1** to choose someone for an official job or choose something by secretly marking a piece of paper or putting your hand up to be counted: *Which party did you vote for?* **2** to decide something by voting: *He was voted best actor.*

NOUN **votes 1** a choice you make by marking a piece of paper or putting your hand up to be counted **2** the right you have to vote in elections

▸ **voter** NOUN **voters** someone who votes in an election

vouch VERB **vouches, vouching, vouched**
• **vouch for someone or something** to say that someone or something is good

voucher NOUN **vouchers 1** a piece of paper that can be used instead of money to pay for something **2** a piece of paper that lets you pay less than usual for something

vow VERB **vows, vowing, vowed** to promise in a very serious way

NOUN **vows** a serious promise

vowel NOUN **vowels 1** one of the letters of the alphabet **a, e, i, o** or **u 2** a speech sound you make that does not use your lips, teeth, or tongue to stop the flow of air

vulgar ADJECTIVE extremely rude and having very bad manners

vulgar fraction NOUN **vulgar fractions** (*maths*) a fraction that is shown with one number above the line and one number below, for example ½ and ¾

vulnerable ADJECTIVE weak and likely to be harmed or damaged: *The disease spreads quickly and old people are especially vulnerable.* • *a place that is vulnerable to attack*

vulture NOUN **vultures** a large bird that eats dead animals

Aa
Bb
Cc
Dd
Ee
Ff
Gg
Hh
Ii
Jj
Kk
Ll
Mm
Nn
Oo
Pp
Qq
Rr
Ss
Tt
Uu
Vv
Ww
Xx
Yy
Zz

Ww

W ABBREVIATION **1** short for **west 2** short for **watt** or **watts**

wad NOUN **wads 1** a pad of loose material, such as cloth or paper, pressed together into one piece: *She cleaned the wound with a wad of cotton wool.* **2** a roll or bundle of bank notes

waddle VERB **waddles, waddling, waddled** to walk moving from side to side, like a duck

wade VERB **wades, wading, waded** to walk through water or mud: *The stream had flooded and we had to wade across.*

• **wade through something** to deal with or read something that is difficult or boring, so it takes you a long time to do: *We've been wading through this old exam paper for weeks.*

▸ **waders** PLURAL NOUN very high waterproof boots that you wear when you are fishing

wafer NOUN **wafers** a very thin flat biscuit, often eaten with ice cream

waffle NOUN **waffles 1** a waffle is a type of pancake with a pattern of squares on it **2** waffle is talk that goes on for a long time but does not say anything interesting

waft VERB **wafts, wafting, wafted** to float through the air: *The smell of freshly baked bread came wafting out of the window.*

wag VERB **wags, wagging, wagged** to move a part of your body or a tail from side to side: *The dog ran backwards and forwards, wagging its tail.* • *Don't you wag your finger at me, boy!*

wage NOUN **wages** a wage or wages are money that you are paid for doing your job: *We collect our wages from the office every Friday afternoon.*
VERB **wages, waging, waged** to wage a war is to start and continue it

wager NOUN **wagers** a bet

VERB **wagers, wagering, wagered** to make a bet

waggle VERB **waggles, waggling, waggled** to move something from side to side or up and down: *Can you waggle your ears?*

wagon *or* **waggon** NOUN **wagons** *or* **waggons 1** a vehicle or cart with four wheels that is used for carrying heavy loads: *a hay wagon* **2** a type of railway truck with no roof, used for carrying things: *a coal wagon*

waif NOUN **waifs** a child who has no home or family and looks poor

wail VERB **wails, wailing, wailed** to cry loudly: *A small child was wailing in the next room.*
NOUN **wails** a loud cry or long noise like a cry: *the wail of a siren*

waist NOUN **waists** the narrow part of your body between your chest and your hips

waistcoat NOUN **waistcoats** a short jacket with no sleeves and usually with buttons up the front

wait VERB **waits, waiting, waited 1** to wait or wait for someone or something is to stay in a place until they arrive: *Several people were already waiting for the bus.* **2** to wait, or wait until something happens, is to not do an action until that thing happens: *I will wait until it stops raining before I leave.*

• **wait on someone** to serve food and drinks to someone: *There are six waitresses to wait on the guests.*
NOUN **waits** a delay or period of waiting: *It seemed like an awfully long wait for the show to start.*

waiter NOUN **waiters** a man who serves people with food in a restaurant

waiting room NOUN **waiting rooms** a room where people can wait, for example in a station or a doctor's surgery

waitress NOUN **waitresses** a woman who serves people with food in a restaurant

waive VERB **waives, waiving, waived** to give up a claim or right to something: *I will waive my right to get a ticket first.*

wake[1] VERB **wakes, waking, woke, woken 1** if you wake or wake up, you stop sleeping: *She suddenly woke up and looked around.* **2** to wake someone is to make them stop sleeping: *Please don't wake the baby!*

wake[2] NOUN **wakes** the strip of disturbed water left behind a moving boat
• **in the wake of something** happening after or because of something: *Many airlines went bankrupt in the wake of the disaster.*

waken VERB **wakens, wakening, wakened 1** to waken is to stop sleeping **2** to waken someone is to make them stop sleeping: *The sound of the doorbell wakened me.*

walk VERB **walks, walking, walked 1** to move on foot fairly slowly: *The door opened and Simon walked in.* • *I think I'll walk to work today.* **2** to travel on foot because you enjoy it: *We usually go walking on the moors every weekend.*
NOUN **walks 1** a journey on foot: *It's just a short walk to the newsagent's.* **2** a way of walking: *I recognised Ann by her walk.* **3** a path that you can walk along for pleasure: *a book of walks in the Lake District*

walkie-talkie NOUN **walkie-talkies** a radio that you can carry with you to send and receive messages

walking stick NOUN **walking sticks** a stick that you can use to help you walk: *Gran needs to use a walking stick since she fell.*

walkover NOUN **walkovers** a game or race that is easy to win: *The score was 3-1 but it was no walkover.*

wall NOUN **walls 1** a structure made of brick or stone that separates or goes around an area: *Hadrian's Wall* • *A high wall surrounds the school.* **2** any of the sides of a room or building: *She hung the new clock on the kitchen wall.*
VERB **walls, walling, walled** to surround or enclose something with a wall

wallaby NOUN **wallabies** an animal like a small kangaroo

wallet NOUN **wallets** a small folding holder for banknotes and cards that you can put in your pocket: *a leather wallet*

wallflower NOUN **wallflowers 1** a spring flower with a sweet smell **2** someone who does not have a partner to dance with

wallop VERB **wallops, walloping, walloped** to hit someone or something hard: *He walloped his head on the door as he came in.*
NOUN **wallops** a hard hit: *She fell off her bike with quite a wallop.*

wallow VERB **wallows, wallowing, wallowed** to roll about in mud or water and enjoy it: *The hippos were wallowing in the mud.*

wallpaper NOUN **wallpapers** paper that you can use to cover and decorate the walls of a room

walnut NOUN **walnuts** a large nut with a hard, round shell

walrus NOUN **walruses** a sea animal like a large seal with very big teeth called tusks

✦ This is a Dutch word that means *whale horse.*

waltz NOUN **waltzes** an old-fashioned dance for couples, to music with three beats in every bar
VERB **waltzes, waltzing, waltzed** to dance a waltz

✦ **Waltz** comes from the German word **waltzen**, which means *to dance.*

wan ADJECTIVE **wanner, wannest** looking pale and sick: *a wan face*

wand NOUN **wands** a long thin stick such as the one a magician or fairy uses when doing magic spells or tricks: *The fairy waved her magic wand and turned a pumpkin into a beautiful coach.*

wander VERB **wanders, wandering, wandered 1** to go from one place to

Aa
Bb
Cc
Dd
Ee
Ff
Gg
Hh
Ii
Jj
Kk
Ll
Mm
Nn
Oo
Pp
Qq
Rr
Ss
Tt
Uu
Vv
Ww
Xx
Yy
Zz

another without any definite plan: *We spent the summer wandering all around southern Italy.* **2** to wander or wander off is to go away from where you should be: *Their little boy had wandered off and could not find them.*

▶ **wanderer** NOUN **wanderers** someone who wanders

wane VERB **wanes, waning, waned** **1** to become less strong: *Support for the government is waning fast.* **2** if the moon wanes, it seems to become smaller. Look up and compare **wax2**

NOUN

• **on the wane** if something is on the wane, it is becoming smaller or less powerful: *I think her interest in pop music is on the wane.*

wangle VERB **wangles, wangling, wangled** to achieve or obtain something by being clever or crafty: *Do you think you could wangle me a couple of free tickets to the concert?*

want VERB **wants, wanting, wanted** **1** to wish for something: *Do you want some cake?* • *Someone wants to speak to you.* • *I'll stay here with you, if you want.* **2** to need or lack something: *Your hands want a good wash.*

NOUN **wants 1** something that you want: *a long list of wants* **2** a lack of something: *He failed the test, but not for want of trying.*

▶ **wanted** ADJECTIVE **1** someone who is wanted is being searched for by the police: *Pictures of the wanted man appeared in all the newspapers.* **2** loved, needed and cared for: *Make your pet feel wanted by giving it plenty of attention.*

▶ **wanting** ADJECTIVE lacking or missing something: *The children were definitely not wanting in enthusiasm.*

war NOUN **wars** armed fighting between two countries or groups: *the war in Afghanistan* • *War broke out between neighbouring tribes.*

VERB **wars, warring, warred** to fight in a war: *The two countries have been warring against each other for centuries.*

warble VERB **warbles, warbling, warbled** to sing like a bird

ward NOUN **wards 1** a room with beds in it in a hospital: *the children's ward* **2** someone who is looked after by an adult who is not their parent, or by a court of law

VERB **wards, warding, warded**

• **ward something off** to do something to stop something from harming you: *He covered his head with his arms to ward off the blows.*

warden NOUN **wardens 1** someone who is in charge of a place, for example an old people's home, hostel or caravan site: *All visitors should report to the warden.* **2** someone who is responsible for looking after or controlling something: *a traffic warden* • *a game warden*

warder NOUN **warders** someone who guards the prisoners in a prison

wardrobe NOUN **wardrobes 1** a tall cupboard that you can hang clothes inside **2** all of the clothes someone owns: *her summer wardrobe*

warehouse NOUN **warehouses** a large building where businesses store things: *a furniture warehouse*

wares PLURAL NOUN things that are for sale: *The large shop windows are used to display our wares.*

warfare NOUN fighting in a war: *modern warfare*

warily ADVERB cautiously: *He eyed the guard dog warily.*

warlike ADJECTIVE a warlike country or person enjoys fighting

warm ADJECTIVE **warmer, warmest** **1** pleasantly hot: *a warm bath* • *As the sun rose we began to feel a little warmer.* **2** warm clothes make you feel warm: *a warm winter coat* **3** kind and friendly: *a warm welcome* • *The school nurse is a warm, kind-hearted person.*

VERB **warms, warming, warmed** to warm someone or something, or warm them up, is to make them warm: *She warmed her hands on the radiator.*

• **warm up 1** to become warm: *I'll put the heating on and the house'll soon warm up.* **2** if you warm up for a sport or activity, you prepare for it by

Aa
Bb
Cc
Dd
Ee
Ff
Gg
Hh
Ii
Jj
Kk
Ll
Mm
Nn
Oo
Pp
Qq
Rr
Ss
Tt
Uu
Vv
Ww
Xx
Yy
Zz

practising or doing gentle exercises: *The football players were on the pitch, warming up.*

▶ **warmly** ADVERB in a warm way: *Make sure you're warmly dressed for the hike.* • *She smiled warmly.*

warm-blooded ADJECTIVE a warm-blooded animal has a temperature that is higher than the air around it

warmth NOUN **1** pleasant heat, or the state of being pleasantly warm: *the warmth of the fire* **2** being kind, friendly and affectionate: *the warmth of her welcome*

warm-up NOUN **warm-ups** a set of gentle exercises that you do before playing a sport, dancing or running

warn VERB **warns, warning, warned** to tell someone that something is dangerous or bad before it happens: *I warned her about the icy roads.*

▶ **warning** NOUN **warnings** an event or something that you say to warn someone: *The volcano erupted without any warning.*

warp VERB **warps, warping, warped** to become or make something twisted and out of shape: *This drawer has warped and is hard to open. The wet weather had warped the back door.*

warrant NOUN **warrants** a document that gives the police the right to arrest someone or search their property

VERB **warrants, warranting, warranted** to be a good reason or excuse for something: *He was naughty, but it did not warrant such a harsh punishment.*

warren NOUN **warrens** a network of tunnels called burrows that rabbits live in

warrior NOUN **warriors** a soldier who fought in battles a long time ago

warship NOUN **warships** a ship with a lot of guns used for fighting at sea

wart NOUN **warts** a small hard lump on the skin

wary ADJECTIVE cautious: *a wary glance* • *I'd be very wary of lending her money.*

was VERB the past tense of the verb **be** that you use with **I**, **he**, **she** or **it**: *I was*

surprised to see Rosie there.* • *Mr Brock was my favourite teacher.*

wash VERB **washes, washing, washed** **1** to wash something is to clean it with water and soap: *Wash your hands and face before we eat.* **2** if water washes against something, it flows against it: *Gentle waves were washing against the boat.*

• **wash something away** if something is washed away, it is carried away by the force of heavy rain or a river: *Whole houses were washed away in the storm.*

• **wash up** to wash the dishes after you have eaten: *It's your turn to wash up, Adam.*

NOUN **washes 1** the act of washing someone or something **2** all the clothes that need to be washed: *Your red shirt is in the wash.* **3** the waves that a boat causes as it moves

▶ **washer** NOUN **washers 1** a flat ring made of metal or rubber that you put under a screw to keep it tightly in place **2** a washing machine

▶ **washing** NOUN all the clothes that need to be washed: *a pile of dirty washing*

washbasin NOUN **washbasins** a small sink for washing your hands and face in

washing machine NOUN **washing machines** a piece of electrical equipment that you wash clothes in

washing-up NOUN **1** all the dishes that need to be washed: *How come there's so much washing-up tonight?* **2** the act of washing dishes: *You sit down and relax while I do the washing-up.*

wasn't a short way to say and write **was not**: *Are you sure Mark wasn't joking?*

wasp NOUN **wasps** an insect with a thin black and yellow striped body that can sting you

waste VERB **wastes, wasting, wasted** **1** to waste something is to use more of it than you need: *I'm trying not to waste any paper.* **2** if you waste time or money, you spend it in a way that is not

Aa
Bb
Cc
Dd
Ee
Ff
Gg
Hh
Ii
Jj
Kk
Ll
Mm
Nn
Oo
Pp
Qq
Rr
Ss
Tt
Uu
Vv
Ww
Xx
Yy
Zz

water cycle

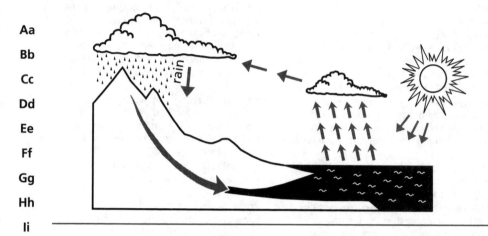

rain

useful: *You're wasting your time trying to fix the television.*

NOUN **wastes 1** waste is rubbish or things that are not needed: *industrial waste* **2** a bad use of something: *The computer turned out to be a waste of money.* **3** a large area of land where there are no people, animals or plants: *the frozen wastes of Siberia*

ADJECTIVE **1** waste products or materials are useless and thrown away: *waste paper* **2** waste land has no buildings or crops on it

▶ **wasteful** ADJECTIVE involving or causing waste: *It's very wasteful, throwing all these apples away.*

watch VERB **watches, watching, watched 1** to look at someone or something: *Roy's watching the football match in the other room.* **2** to be careful about something: *Watch you don't trip over that root.* **3** to look after someone or something: *Could you watch the baby for me while I go to the shop?*

NOUN **watches 1** a small clock that you wear on your wrist **2** a time when someone keeps guard: *Two guards kept watch over the prisoners.*

watchdog NOUN **watchdogs** a dog that is trained to guard a building

watchful ADJECTIVE careful to notice what is happening: *Sue kept a watchful eye on her little sister.*

watchman NOUN **watchmen** a man whose job is to guard a building: *a night watchman*

water NOUN a clear liquid with no taste that falls from the sky as rain

VERB **waters, watering, watered 1** to water a plant is to give water to it **2** if your eyes water, they produce tears: *The thick smoke made her eyes water.* **3** if your mouth waters, it produces saliva because you see something good to eat

watercolour NOUN **watercolours 1** a type of paint that is mixed with water, not oil: *a box of watercolours* **2** a painting done with watercolour paints: *a watercolour of a thatched cottage*

watercress NOUN a plant that grows in water and has rounded leaves that taste peppery

water cycle NOUN (*geography*) the way in which water from the sea evaporates into the air, condenses to form clouds, then falls as rain on to the ground and returns to the sea in rivers and streams. See the picture above

waterfall NOUN **waterfalls** a place where a river or stream falls over a high rock or cliff

waterlogged ADJECTIVE waterlogged ground is so wet that it cannot take in any more water: *The match was cancelled because the pitch was waterlogged.*

watermark NOUN **watermarks** a faint design that you can see in a piece of paper or banknote when you hold it up against the light

watermelon NOUN **watermelons** a large round fruit with a hard green skin and red juicy flesh

waterproof ADJECTIVE waterproof material does not allow water to pass through it

NOUN **waterproofs** a coat or other piece of clothing made of waterproof material: *The fishermen were wearing bright yellow waterproofs.*

watertight ADJECTIVE a watertight join or seal does not let liquid in or out

water vapour NOUN water when it has evaporated to become a lot of tiny drops of liquid in the air

waterway NOUN **waterways** a river or canal that a ship can travel along

waterworks NOUN a waterworks is a place where water is cleaned and stored

watery ADJECTIVE **1** like water: *watery soup* **2** full of water: *watery eyes*

watt NOUN **watts** a unit of electrical power. This is often shortened to **W**: *a 60W bulb*

▶ **wattage** NOUN electric power measured in watts

wave NOUN **waves**

1 a moving ridge of water in the sea: *Surfers were jumping into the waves.*

2 a curving shape in your hair: *Your hair has a natural wave.*

3 a movement of the hand to say hello or goodbye or attract someone's attention: *She gave a cheery wave as the train pulled out of the station.*

4 (*science*) a vibration that travels through the air and carries something such as sound or light: *radio waves*

5 a rush of a feeling or emotion: *The pain seemed to come in waves.*

VERB **waves, waving, waved 1** to move your hand backwards and forwards: *Wave bye-bye to granny.* **2** to move in the wind: *flags waving in the breeze*

wavelength NOUN **wavelengths**
1 (*science*) the distance between one point on a radio wave and the next **2** the length of radio wave that a radio or television station uses to broadcast on. These are marked on radios so that you can find them: *Which wavelength is that station on?*

wavy ADJECTIVE **wavier, waviest 1** a wavy line goes up and down in gentle curves **2** wavy hair has gentle curls in it

wax¹ NOUN
1 the sticky, fatty substance that bees make their cells out of
2 a sticky, yellow substance that forms in your ears
3 a substance used to make candles and crayons, which melts when it is hot
4 a substance used to polish furniture
VERB **waxes, waxing, waxed** to polish wood with wax

wax² VERB **waxes, waxing, waxed** if the moon waxes, it seems to grow bigger. Look up and compare **wane**
▶ **waxy** ADJECTIVE **waxier, waxiest** like wax: *a waxy substance*

waxworks NOUN a waxworks is a place where you can see wax models of famous people

way NOUN **ways**
1 a method or manner of doing something: *She's got a funny way of walking.* • *The best way to make new friends is to join a club.*
2 a road or path: *22 Purley Way*
3 a route or direction: *Could you tell me the way to the cinema?*
4 a distance: *It's quite a long way to the coast.*

• **by the way** you say 'by the way' when you are mentioning another subject: *By the way, I met John in town today.*

• **get your own way** if you get your own way, things happen in the way that

Aa Bb Cc Dd Ee Ff Gg Hh Ii Jj Kk Ll Mm Nn Oo Pp Qq Rr Ss Tt Uu Vv Ww Xx Yy Zz

you want them to: *You should not let children always get their own way.*

• **in the way** if something is in the way, it is blocking your progress or movement: *Am I in the way if I sit here?*

• **no way** you say 'no way' when you disagree strongly with someone or something: *There's no way that that was a penalty!*

WC NOUN a toilet

✦**WC** is short for **water closet**, an old-fashioned word for a toilet.

we PRONOUN a word you use when you are talking about yourself and at least one other person: *We left home at about nine o'clock.*

weak ADJECTIVE **weaker, weakest**

1 feeble and not physically strong: *His illness has left him feeling very weak.* • *a weak heart*

2 not strong in character: *She's too weak to stand up to her boss.* • *a weak excuse*

3 someone who is weak at a subject or activity is not good at it: *I was always weak at maths.*

4 a weak drink or mixture has too much water in it: *a cup of weak tea*

▶ **weaken** VERB **weakens, weakening, weakened 1** to weaken is to become weak: *His determination to leave weakened when Jenny arrived.* **2** to weaken something or someone is to make them weaker: *The bout of flu had weakened her.*

▶ **weakly** ADVERB in a way that is not strong or determined: *She smiled weakly at his joke.*

▶ **weakness** NOUN **weaknesses 1** lack of strength: *the weakness of an argument* **2** a fault or something that you cannot help liking: *Chocolate is my only weakness.*

wealth NOUN **1** riches: *a businessman of great wealth* **2** a wealth of something is a lot of it: *a sports team with a wealth of talent*

▶ **wealthy** ADJECTIVE **wealthier, wealthiest** rich: *a wealthy landowner*

wean VERB **weans, weaning, weaned** to gradually start feeding a baby on food rather than only on its mother's milk

weapon NOUN **weapons** something that you use to fight someone: *weapons of war* • *Our best weapon was surprise.*

wear VERB **wears, wearing, wore, worn**

1 to be dressed in clothes or carrying something on your body: *Ann was wearing her school uniform.* • *How long have you worn glasses?*

2 to arrange your hair in a particular style: *She usually wears her hair in a ponytail.*

3 to have a particular expression on your face: *Ted wore an angry frown.*

4 if a material or surface wears, it gradually becomes thinner because of being used or rubbed: *His sleeves had worn through at the elbows.*

5 if something wears a material or surface, it gradually makes it thinner: *The pressure of the waves slowly wears away the rocks.*

• **wear off** if an effect wears off, it gradually becomes less: *The anaesthetic should soon wear off.*

• **wear on** if time wears on, it passes slowly: *As the day wore on, we got bored.*

• **wear someone out** to make someone very tired: *Walking so far completely wore me out.*

• **wear something out** if you wear something out, it becomes too old or worn for you to use: *Ben seems to wear out a pair of shoes every three months.*

NOUN **1** clothes: *evening wear* **2** damage caused by being used or rubbed: *The carpet was showing signs of wear.*

▶ **wearer** NOUN **wearers** someone who is wearing something

weary ADJECTIVE **wearier, weariest** tired: *He finally got home, weary after a long day.*

▶ **wearily** ADVERB in a tired way: *The old man sighed wearily.*

weasel NOUN **weasels** a small wild animal with a long thin body

weather NOUN how hot, cold, wet

weatherbeaten → weekday

or dry it is outside: *The weather's very warm for October.*
VERB **weathers, weathering, weathered 1** to change gradually because of being exposed to the weather: *buildings weathered by the wind and rain* **2** to survive a bad situation safely: *John weathered the difficulties more easily than his brother.*

weatherbeaten ADJECTIVE rougher and darker because of being outside in all types of weather: *a weatherbeaten face*

weathering NOUN a gradual changing of colour and shape caused by being exposed to all types of weather: *the weathering of the rocks*

weathervane NOUN **weathervanes** a piece of metal that swings in the wind to show which direction the wind is coming from

weave VERB **weaves, weaving, wove, woven 1** to pass threads under and over each other on a frame called a loom to make cloth **2** to move in and out between objects: *a motorbike weaving through the traffic*
▸ **weaver** NOUN **weavers** someone who weaves

✦ The past tense of **weave** when it means 'to make cloth' is **wove**: *She **wove** fine materials.*
The past tense of **weave** when it means 'to move in and out' is **weaved**: *She **weaved** through the crowd.*

web NOUN **webs 1** a spider's web is a type of net it makes to catch insects **2** (*ICT*) the Web is the **World Wide Web**
▸ **webbed** ADJECTIVE webbed feet have skin joining the toes together

weblog NOUN AND VERB (*ICT*) the full form of the word **blog**

web page NOUN **web pages** (*ICT*) a page on a website

website NOUN **websites** (*ICT*) a collection of linked pages on the Web about a subject or an organization

wed VERB **weds, wedding, wedded** to wed someone is to marry them
▸ **wedding**

we'd a short way to say and write **we had** or **we would**: *We'd better hurry up or we'll be late.* • *We'd like to buy the teacher a present.*

wedding NOUN **weddings** a marriage ceremony: *I met her at Lucy and John's wedding.*

wedge NOUN **wedges 1** a piece of hard material that is thick at one end and thin at the other and is used to hold something in place **2** something shaped like a wedge: *He cut himself a thick wedge of chocolate cake.*
VERB **wedges, wedging, wedged** to hold something in place or in a space: *She wedged the door open with a piece of cardboard.* • *Sally found herself wedged in a corner.*

Wednesday NOUN **Wednesdays** the day of the week after Tuesday and before Thursday

✦ **Wednesday** comes from the Old English word **Wodnesdæg**, which means *Woden's day.* Woden is the old German god of war and of wisdom.

wee ADJECTIVE an informal word that some people use to mean very small: *a wee boy*

weed NOUN **weeds** a wild plant that is growing where you do not want it to: *The garden was overgrown with weeds.*
VERB **weeds, weeding, weeded** to remove the weeds from a place: *I offered to weed the garden for my dad.*
▸ **weedy** ADJECTIVE **weedier, weediest 1** full of weeds **2** someone who is weedy is thin and weak

week NOUN **weeks 1** a period of seven days, often from Sunday to Saturday: *I have dance lessons twice a week.* **2** the five days from Monday to Friday when many people go to work: *I don't go out much during the week.*
▸ **weekly** ADJECTIVE happening or produced once a week: *a weekly magazine* ADVERB once a week: *I visit my Grandma weekly.*

weekday NOUN **weekdays** any of the days from Monday to Friday: *The office is only open on weekdays.*

Aa Bb Cc Dd Ee Ff Gg Hh Ii Jj Kk Ll Mm Nn Oo Pp Qq Rr Ss Tt Uu Vv Ww Xx Yy Zz

weekend NOUN **weekends** Saturday and Sunday: *We're going to Oxford for the weekend.*

weep VERB **weeps, weeping, wept** to cry tears: *Mother wept when she heard the terrible news.*

weigh VERB **weighs, weighing, weighed 1** to weigh someone or something is to measure how heavy they are by putting them on some scales: *Brenda weighs herself every day.* **2** to have a particular heaviness: *My suitcase weighed 15 kilograms.*

• **weigh someone down** if something weighs you down, it is heavy or difficult for you to deal with: *I am weighed down with problems.*

weight NOUN **weights 1** the amount that something or someone weighs: *What weight are you?* **2** a piece of solid material that is used to hold things down or weigh things on scales **3** a load or burden: *Getting a job took a weight off his mind.*

weightless ADJECTIVE floating in the air because there is no gravity

▸ **weightlessness** NOUN being weightless

▸ **weighty** ADJECTIVE **weightier, weightiest 1** heavy: *a weighty volume of magic spells* **2** important: *The teachers were discussing weighty problems.*

weir NOUN **weirs** a low dam across a river

weird ADJECTIVE **weirder, weirdest** strange or mysterious: *a weird light in the sky*

▸ **weirdly** ADVERB in a strange way: *weirdly dressed*

▸ **weirdness** NOUN being strange or mysterious

welcome ADJECTIVE **1** if someone or something is welcome, you are happy to accept or receive them: *Joe's parents always make us very welcome.* • *a welcome gift* **2** if someone is welcome to do something, you are happy to let them do it: *You're welcome to borrow my bike when I'm not using it.*

• **you're welcome** something you say after someone has thanked you: *'Thank you for all your help.' 'You're welcome.'*

NOUN **welcomes** the way you receive a visitor: *Her fans gave her a warm welcome.*

VERB **welcomes, welcoming, welcomed 1** to make someone feel that you are happy to see them: *The whole family turned out to welcome us at the airport.* **2** to accept something gladly: *After all that running, he welcomed the chance to sit down.*

weld VERB **welds, welding, welded** to join together pieces of metal by heating them

▸ **welder** NOUN **welders** someone whose job is to weld metals

▸ **welding** NOUN the activity of joining metal by heat

welfare NOUN health, comfort and happiness: *parents concerned for the welfare of their children*

welfare state NOUN a system in which a government provides services such as free health care and money for the unemployed

well¹ ADVERB **better, best 1** in a satisfactory, successful or correct way: *Janet speaks French very well.* **2** thoroughly: *Mix the butter and sugar well before adding the flour.*

• **as well** too: *I'd like an ice cream as well.*

ADJECTIVE **better, best 1** healthy: *I don't feel well today.* **2** good or pleasing: *All is not well at home.*

well² NOUN **wells** a deep hole in the ground where you can get water, oil or gas: *an oil well*

VERB **wells, welling, welled**

• **well up** if tears well up in your eyes, they begin to flow

we'll a short way to say and write **we will**: *I'm sure we'll meet again.*

wellbeing NOUN health and happiness

wellingtons *or* **wellington boots** PLURAL NOUN high rubber boots that cover your lower leg

---

✦ These boots were named after the Duke of **Wellington**, a British army general who wore boots like them.

well-off ADJECTIVE **better-off, best-off 1** rich: *Only the better-off kids had bicycles.* **2** fortunate: *The trouble is, you just don't realize when you're well-off.*

went VERB a way of changing the verb **go** to make a past tense: *Bill went out at about 6 o'clock.*

wept VERB a way of changing the verb **weep** to make a past tense. It can be used with or without a helping verb: *I could have wept when I saw the state of the house.* • *A woman wept openly in the corner.*

were VERB the past tense of the verb **be** that you use with **you, we** or **they**: *We were so relieved to see him.* • *The children were playing in the garden when we arrived.*

✦ Be careful not to confuse the spellings of **were** and **where**. **Where** means to, from or in what place: *Where are you going?*

we're a short way to say and write **we are**: *We're so pleased you could come.*

weren't a short way to say and write **were not**: *Weren't the acrobats amazing?*

werewolf NOUN **werewolves** an imaginary person that changes into a wolf when there is a full moon

west NOUN **1** the direction in which the sun sets, opposite to east: *the west of England* **2** the West is a name for the countries in Europe and North America
ADJECTIVE in, from, or towards the west: *the west coast of America*
ADVERB to the west: *We travelled west as far as the motorway.*

westerly ADJECTIVE coming from, or going towards, the west
NOUN **westerlies** a wind that comes from the west

western ADJECTIVE belonging to, or coming from the west: *Western Europe*
NOUN **westerns** a book or film about cowboys in North America in the past

westward ADVERB to or towards the west: *We travelled westwards.*

wet ADJECTIVE **wetter, wettest 1** full of water or covered with water: *wet clothes* • *It's easy to skid on wet roads.* **2** not dried: *wet paint* **3** rainy: *a wet afternoon*
VERB **wets, wetting, wet** to wet something is to make it wet: *He wet his hair to flatten it down.*

wet suit NOUN **wet suits** a rubber suit that you wear to keep you warm when you swim underwater

we've a short way to say and write **we have**: *We've got something to tell you.*

whack VERB **whacks, whacking, whacked** to hit someone or something hard with a loud noise: *He whacked his brother on the head with a book.*
NOUN **whacks** a hard loud hit: *Jim gave him a whack across the shoulders.*

whale NOUN **whales** a very large mammal that lives in the sea
▸ **whaler** NOUN **whalers** a ship or person that goes out hunting whales
▸ **whaling** NOUN hunting and killing whales

wharf NOUN **wharfs** or **wharves** a platform where ships stop to be loaded and unloaded

what ADJECTIVE AND PRONOUN **1 what** is used to ask questions about things: *What day is it today?* • *What's your brother's name?* **2** you can say **what** in exclamations to emphasize something: *What a beautiful view!* **3** the thing or things: *I hope you find what you're looking for.* • *This bag is just what I wanted.*
• **what if** what will or would happen if: *What if Dad comes back and finds us here?*

whatever ADJECTIVE AND PRONOUN **1** any, anything or any amount: *I can give you whatever money you need.* • *Choose whatever you like from the menu.* **2** no matter what: *You know we'll always love you whatever happens.*

whatsoever ADJECTIVE at all: *Your problems are nothing whatsoever to do with me.*

wheat NOUN a type of grain that is used to make flour

wheel NOUN **wheels 1** one of the round things under a vehicle that turns

Aa
Bb
Cc
Dd
Ee
Ff
Gg
Hh
Ii
Jj
Kk
Ll
Mm
Nn
Oo
Pp
Qq
Rr
Ss
Tt
Uu
Vv
Ww
Xx
Yy
Zz

around as it moves: *The spare wheel is in the boot.* **2** anything that goes around like a wheel: *a potter's wheel*
VERB **wheels, wheeling, wheeled 1** to wheel something is to push it along on wheels: *He got a puncture and had to wheel his bike home.* **2** to move in a wide curve: *Vultures were wheeling overhead.* **3** to turn round quickly: *Kay wheeled around when she heard his voice.*

wheelbarrow NOUN **wheelbarrows** a small cart with only one wheel at the front and with handles that you use to push it

wheelchair NOUN **wheelchairs** a seat with wheels used by people who are ill or cannot walk

wheeze VERB **wheezes, wheezing, wheezed** to breathe with a rough, gasping or whistling sound
NOUN **wheezes** a rough, gasping or whistling breath

whelk NOUN **whelks** a small snail-like sea creature that lives inside a hard shell

when ADVERB at what time: *When did you arrive home?*
CONJUNCTION **1** at the time at which, or during the time at which: *I was just going out when the phone rang.* **2** in spite of the fact that: *How is it that you don't even have 10p when you've only just got your pocket money?*

whenever CONJUNCTION **1** at any time that: *You can borrow my book whenever you want to.* **2** at every time that: *They go swimming whenever they get the chance.*

where ADVERB to, from or in what place: *Where are we going?* • *Where did you get that hat?*
CONJUNCTION to, from or in what place: *I have no idea where we are.*

> ✦ Be careful not to confuse the spellings of **where** and **were**.
> **Were** is the past tense of the verb **be** that you use with **you**, **we** or **they**.
> *Were you sleeping?*

whereabouts NOUN the whereabouts of a person or thing is the place where

they are or it is: *Do you know the whereabouts of your cousin?*
ADVERB near or in what place: *Whereabouts in Texas do you come from?*

whereas CONJUNCTION but: *They thought he was a bit strange, whereas he was simply quiet and shy.* • *He wanted to go to the cinema, whereas I wanted to go swimming.*

where's a short way to say and write **where is** or **where has**: *Where's the cat?* • *Where's he gone?*

whereupon CONJUNCTION at or immediately after which: *His mother told him he couldn't go, whereupon he sat on the floor and started crying.*

wherever ADVERB AND CONJUNCTION to, or in, any place or every place: *He follows me wherever I go.* • *Wherever he is, I am sure he will come back soon.*
ADVERB used instead of 'where' in a question to show that you are surprised: *The cat's disappeared. Wherever can he be?*

whet VERB **whets, whetting, whetted** to whet the blade of a knife is to sharpen it
• **whet your appetite** if something whets your appetite, it makes you want to eat, or it makes you want to do something: *He'd seen a clip of the film, which had whetted his appetite to see more.*

whether CONJUNCTION **whether** is used to show that there is a choice between two possibilities: *Whether we like it or not, we have to get up early.*

whey NOUN whey is the watery part of milk that is left after separating out the solid curds that make cheese

which ADJECTIVE what one or ones: *Which hand do you think the coin is in?*
PRONOUN **1** what one or ones: *Which of these books is yours and which is mine?* **2** you use **which** to talk about the person or thing that has been mentioned in the earlier part of a sentence: *I had eaten four chocolate bars, which made me feel sick.*

whichever ADJECTIVE AND PRONOUN that or any one: *Come on whichever*

Aa
Bb
Cc
Dd
Ee
Ff
Gg
Hh
Ii
Jj
Kk
Ll
Mm
Nn
Oo
Pp
Qq
Rr
Ss
Tt
Uu
Vv
Ww
Xx
Yy
Zz

day suits you. • *You can come round on Monday or Tuesday, whichever suits you.*

whiff NOUN **whiffs** a smell or scent which you notice as it is carried in the air to your nose: *a whiff of garlic*

while CONJUNCTION **1** during the time that: *Will you be going to Disneyland while you are in Florida?* **2** although: *While I understand why you got angry, I think you should try to control your temper.*
NOUN a period of time: *We waited inside for a while but the rain didn't stop.*
VERB **whiles, whiling, whiled**
• **while away something** to while away time is to pass the time doing something: *We whiled away the journey playing 'I spy'.*

whilst CONJUNCTION while: *You could look at these magazines whilst you're waiting.*

whim NOUN **whims** a sudden idea or a sudden desire to do something

whimper VERB **whimpers, whimpering, whimpered** to make a series of low weak crying sounds, showing pain or fear
NOUN **whimpers** a low weak crying or whining sound

whine VERB **whines, whining, whined** **1** a dog or other animal whines when it makes a long high sound **2** a person whines when they talk in a complaining voice
NOUN **whines 1** the sound a dog or animal makes when it whines **2** a complaining voice

whinge VERB **whinges, whingeing, whinged** to complain in a way that other people find annoying

whinny NOUN **whinnies** a gentle series of sounds a horse or pony makes

whip NOUN **whips** a piece of leather or cord fastened to a handle and used to hit animals or people
VERB **whips, whipping, whipped 1** to whip an animal or person is to hit them with a whip **2** to whip liquids like cream or eggs is to beat them so that they form a froth or become thick and stiff
• **whip something out** *or* **whip**

something away to take something out or take it away very quickly
• **whip up something 1** to whip up something to eat is to prepare it quickly **2** to whip up a particular feeling or reaction is to encourage that feeling or reaction in other people

whippet NOUN **whippets** a breed of dog with a slim head and body, like a small greyhound

whirl VERB **whirls, whirling, whirled** to turn or spin very quickly
NOUN **whirls** a very fast turning or spinning movement

whirlpool NOUN **whirlpools** a place in a river or in the sea where a current of water swirls round and round and is sometimes strong enough to drag things down

whirlwind NOUN **whirlwinds** a column of wind that swirls round and round in a spiral as it moves across the land

whirr VERB **whirrs, whirring, whirred** something whirrs when it turns or moves quickly making a buzzing sound
NOUN **whirrs** the buzzing sound made by something turning quickly through the air

whisk NOUN **whisks 1** a piece of kitchen equipment made up of loops of wire and used for mixing things like cream or eggs **2** a fast sweeping movement: *With a whisk of his bushy tail, the squirrel was gone.*
VERB **whisks, whisking, whisked** to whisk foods like cream or eggs is to beat them with a whisk so that they are well mixed or become thick
• **whisk someone** *or* **something away** to take someone or something away very quickly

whisker NOUN **whiskers 1** one of the long stiff hairs that grow on the faces of animals like mice, cats and dogs, and which are sensitive to touch **2** the hair that grows on a man's face is sometimes called his whiskers

whisky NOUN **whiskies** a strong alcoholic drink made from grain or barley, especially in Scotland

Aa
Bb
Cc
Dd
Ee
Ff
Gg
Hh
Ii
Jj
Kk
Ll
Mm
Nn
Oo
Pp
Qq
Rr
Ss
Tt
Uu
Vv
Ww
Xx
Yy
Zz

whisper VERB **whispers, whispering, whispered** to talk very quietly under your breath so that only people near you can hear what you are saying

NOUN **whispers** a very quiet voice: *She hung her head and answered in a whisper.*

whistle VERB **whistles, whistling, whistled 1** to make a high-pitched sound or a musical note by blowing air through your teeth and lips **2** if something whistles, it makes a high-pitched sound

NOUN **whistles 1** a whistling sound **2** a small device that you blow into to make a high-pitched sound: *The referee blew his whistle.* **3** a simple musical instrument that you blow into and which makes high-pitched sounds

white NOUN **1** the very pale colour of milk or snow **2** the white of an egg is the clear substance around the yolk, which turns white if it is cooked

▸ **whiten** VERB **whitens, whitening, whitened** to make something white or whiter

▸ **whitish** ADJECTIVE quite white but not completely white in colour

whiteboard NOUN **whiteboards 1** a board with a white plastic surface that you can write on with marker pens **2** a white plastic board in a classroom that you can write on, or use with a computer to do things such as move words and pictures around

white elephant NOUN **white elephants** something that has cost a lot of money but has no useful purpose

white-hot ADJECTIVE something that is white-hot is so hot it is glowing with white light

whitewash NOUN a thin white liquid, containing lime, used to paint on walls and ceilings to make them white

VERB **whitewashes, whitewashing, whitewashed** to paint whitewash on walls or ceilings

Whitsun NOUN the seventh Sunday after Easter

whizz VERB **whizzes, whizzing, whizzed** to move very fast

NOUN **whizzes** someone who is a whizz at something is an expert at it

who PRONOUN **1** which person or people: *Who is your favourite pop star?* **2** you use **who** when you want to say something else about a person or people you have just mentioned, or to explain which person you mean: *Emily, who lives next door, is 12 years old.* • *It was Malcolm who told me the news.*

who'd a short way to say and write **who had** or **who would**: *It was Dad who'd said I could go to the party.* • *Who'd like another biscuit?*

whoever PRONOUN **1** the person that has done something: *Would whoever it was that left the gate open, please go and close it.* **2** any person: *Bring whoever you like to the party.*

whole ADJECTIVE all of something: *I couldn't eat a whole bar of chocolate.*

NOUN a whole is a complete thing, especially one that is made up of different parts: *Two halves make a whole.*

wholehearted ADJECTIVE wholehearted support or agreement is complete and sincere

wholemeal ADJECTIVE wholemeal bread or biscuits are made from flour that uses whole grains of wheat

whole number NOUN **whole numbers** (*maths*) a number like 4, 27 or 375, which is not a fraction and which has no fractions or decimal places after it

wholesale ADJECTIVE **1** wholesale goods are bought in large amounts by a business which then sells them in smaller amounts to shops or smaller businesses **2** total or complete: *the wholesale destruction of the rain forests.*

wholesome ADJECTIVE healthy and good for you

who'll a short way to say and write **who will** or **who shall**: *Who'll help me to carry this box?*

wholly ADVERB completely: *They were wholly committed to the team.*

whom PRONOUN **whom** is used as the object of a verb or preposition, and

Aa
Bb
Cc
Dd
Ee
Ff
Gg
Hh
Ii
Jj
Kk
Ll
Mm
Nn
Oo
Pp
Qq
Rr
Ss
Tt
Uu
Vv
Ww
Xx
Yy
Zz

means the same as **who**: *He phoned his friend Andrew, whom he hadn't seen for years.* • *To whom should I address the letter?*

✦ Nowadays, people often use **who** instead of **whom**: *He phoned his friend Andrew, **who** he hasn't seen for years.*

whoop VERB **whoops, whooping, whooped** to give a loud shout of joy or excitement

whooping cough NOUN a disease that makes it difficult to breathe and causes a painful cough

who's a short way to say and write **who is** or **who has**: *Who's coming for a walk?* • *Who's got the TV guide?*

✦ Be careful not to confuse the spellings of **who's** and **whose**.
Who's is a short form of **who is** or **who has**: *Who's in the bathroom?*
Whose tells you something belongs to someone: *Whose shoes are these?*

whose ADJECTIVE **1** you use **whose** before a noun when you are asking which person or people something belongs to: *Whose bike is this?* **2** you use **whose** before a noun to mean 'of which' or 'of whom': *the boy whose family owns the castle on the hill*
PRONOUN you use **whose** when you are asking or talking about which person or people something belongs to: *Whose is this?* • *It must be someone's dog but I don't know whose.*

why ADVERB for what reason: *Why did it have to rain today?*

wick NOUN **wicks** the string in a candle or lamp which you light

wicked (pronounced **wik**-id) ADJECTIVE **1** very bad or evil: *a wicked old witch* **2** mischievous: *Don't tip your cup upside-down, you wicked little monkey!* **3** (*slang*) excellent : *That's a wicked new haircut you've got there!*

wicker *or* **wickerwork** NOUN reeds or strips of cane that have been woven together to make things like baskets

wicket NOUN **wickets** in cricket, a set

of three upright wooden rods with two horizontal rods across the top in front of which the batsman stands

wide ADJECTIVE **wider, widest 1** measuring a great distance from side to side: *across the wide Missouri river* **2** having a certain width: *The river is nearly a mile wide at some points.* **3** covering a great range or amount: *a wide knowledge of history*
ADVERB **wider, widest 1** with a great distance from top to bottom or side to side: *The tiger opened his mouth wide, showing his enormous fangs.* **2** if you are wide awake, you are completely awake and alert **3** something that is wide of its target is a long distance away from the target
▶ **widely** ADVERB something that is widely known or widely admired is known or admired by a lot of people
▶ **widen** VERB **widens, widening, widened** to make or cause to be wide or wider

widespread ADJECTIVE found in a lot of places or among a lot of people: *widespread rumours*

widow NOUN **widows** a woman whose husband has died

widower NOUN **widowers** a man whose wife has died

width NOUN **widths** the width of something is how much it measures from side to side: *This curtain material comes in several different widths.*

wield VERB **wields, wielding, wielded 1** to wield a tool or a weapon is to hold it and use it: *pictures of Vikings wielding axes and swords* **2** to wield something, such as power, is to use it

wife NOUN **wives** a man's wife is the woman he has married

wig NOUN **wigs** a covering of false hair that is worn on the head

wiggle VERB **wiggles, wiggling, wiggled** to move from side to side, or backwards and forwards: *Look! I can wiggle my front tooth.*
NOUN **wiggles 1** a movement from side to side or backwards and forwards **2** a line that has lots of bends and curves

wigwam NOUN **wigwams** a cone-shaped tent that Native American people used as shelter in the past

wild ADJECTIVE **wilder, wildest**
1 wild animals or plants live in their natural surroundings and are not kept by human beings: *a wild goat* • *wild rice*
2 a wild area of land is in a natural state and has not been farmed or built on
3 wild behaviour is not controlled and sometimes violent: *The fans went wild with excitement.*
4 wild weather is windy and stormy
5 a wild idea is a bit crazy and isn't very likely to work
6 if you make a wild guess, you guess completely at random
7 if you are wild about something or someone, you are very keen on them
NOUN **wilds** animals that live in the wild live in their natural environment and are not kept as pets or in zoos

wilderness NOUN **wildernesses** a desert or wild area of a country with very few people living in it

wildlife NOUN wild animals, birds and insects

wiles PLURAL NOUN clever tricks used for making people give you what you want

wilful ADJECTIVE **1** a wilful person is determined to do exactly what they want, not what other people think they should do **2** deliberate: *wilful damage*
▶ **wilfully** ADVERB in a determined or deliberate way

will¹ VERB **would 1** will is used to talk about the future: *It will be winter soon.* **2** you use **will** to ask someone to do something, or to tell them to do something, or to ask them what they would like: *Will you hold this for me?* • *Will you please stop making that racket!* • *Will you have tea or coffee?*

will² NOUN **wills 1** your will is the control you have over your own actions and decisions **2** your will is what you want to do and your desire or determination to do it **3** a will is a legal document written by someone saying who they want their property and

money to be given to after their death
VERB **wills, willing, willed** if you will something to happen, you try to make it happen by using the power of your thoughts

willing ADJECTIVE if you are willing, you are ready or happy to do what is asked or needed: *a willing helper* • *He's willing to work hard.*
▶ **willingly** ADVERB if you do something willingly, you do it happily and eagerly
▶ **willingness** NOUN being ready or happy to do what is needed

willow NOUN **willows** a tree with long thin branches that often grows near water

willpower NOUN willpower is the determination and discipline you need to achieve something

wilt VERB **wilts, wilting, wilted 1** if plants wilt, their stems get weak and hang down towards the ground **2** if a person wilts, they become weak or tired

wily ADJECTIVE **wilier, wiliest** clever at getting what you want, especially by tricking people

wimp NOUN **wimps** (*informal*) someone who is not strong or brave

win VERB **wins, winning, won 1** to win is to beat all the others in a competition and get first place or first prize **2** to win something is to get it as a prize
NOUN **wins** a victory

wince VERB **winces, wincing, winced** to make a small, quick, jerking movement with your face or head in pain or embarrassment: *He winced when I reminded him of his mistake.*

winch NOUN **winches** a piece of equipment used for lifting or pulling something heavy by attaching it to a rope which is wound around a cylinder
VERB **winches, winching, winched** to winch something is to lift it or pull it using a winch

wind¹ NOUN **winds**
1 wind, or a wind, is a strong current of air
2 if someone has wind, they have gas

trapped in their stomach, which makes them feel uncomfortable **3** your wind is your breath or your ability to breathe easily **4** (*music*) the wind instruments in an orchestra

wind² (rhymes with **find**) VERB **winds, winding, wound 1** to wind something is to twist it round and round in loops or coils: *A turban is a long piece of cloth that is wound round the head.* **2** to wind or wind up a watch or clock is to turn the screw or key that tightens the spring inside and makes it work **3** a road, path or river winds if it twists and turns

• **wind up** to wind up somewhere is to end up in that place or situation, especially one that is unpleasant or uncomfortable

• **wind someone up** to make someone believe something is true when it isn't, as a joke or to annoy them

• **wind something up** to end something such as a meeting or activity

▶ **winder** NOUN **winders** a key, screw or handle used to wind up a watch, clock or clockwork mechanism

windfall NOUN **windfalls** something, especially money, that you get without expecting it

wind instrument NOUN **wind instruments** (*music*) an instrument in an orchestra that is played by blowing air into it

windmill NOUN **windmills** a building with large sails on the outside, which are turned by the wind and provide power for grinding corn

window NOUN **windows 1** an opening in the wall of a building or in a vehicle, with glass fitted in it so that you can see through it, and which can usually be opened to let in air **2** (*ICT*) an area on a computer screen where you can view or work with information or a computer file

windpipe NOUN **windpipes** the tube that goes from your mouth down your throat and into your lungs

wind power NOUN power that is generated by the wind and which can be turned into electricity or used to make machines work

windscreen NOUN **windscreens** the clear screen at the front of a car or other vehicle

windsurfing NOUN the sport of moving across the surface of water standing on a narrow board with a sail attached to it

windward ADJECTIVE AND ADVERB facing into the wind

windy ADJECTIVE **windier, windiest** if the weather is windy, there is a wind blowing: *a windy day with the white clouds flying*

wine NOUN **wines** an alcoholic drink that is usually made from grapes but which can also be made from the juice of other types of fruit

wing NOUN **wings**

1 a bird's or insect's wings are the parts of its body that it uses to fly with

2 an aeroplane's wings are the two long flat parts that stick out at either side of its body

3 a wing of a building is a part that sticks out from the main building

4 in games like football and hockey, the wings are the two long sides of the pitch, or the players whose position is at either side of the field: *He's dribbling the ball down the wing.* • *She's the best right wing we've ever had in our team.*

5 a wing of a political party or other organization is a group within it that has its own particular role or its own set of ideas and policies: *the right wing of the Labour Party.*

6 in a theatre, the wings are the areas on either side of the stage that are hidden from the audience

▶ **winged** ADJECTIVE having wings: *a winged serpent*

▶ **winger** NOUN **wingers** a player in a sports team whose place is on one of the wings

wink VERB **winks, winking, winked 1** to shut one of your eyes and open it again quickly, as a friendly or secret sign to someone **2** lights wink when they twinkle or go off and on again quickly NOUN **winks** a sign you make by closing and opening one of your eyes quickly

Aa
Bb
Cc
Dd
Ee
Ff
Gg
Hh
Ii
Jj
Kk
Ll
Mm
Nn
Oo
Pp
Qq
Rr
Ss
Tt
Uu
Vv
Ww
Xx
Yy
Zz

Aa
Bb
Cc
Dd
Ee
Ff
Gg
Hh
Ii
Jj
Kk
Ll
Mm
Nn
Oo
Pp
Qq
Rr
Ss
Tt
Uu
Vv
Ww
Xx
Yy
Zz

winkle NOUN **winkles** a small edible sea snail that lives inside a spiral shell
VERB **winkles, winkling, winkled**
• **winkle something out** to get something out with a lot of difficulty and effort

winnings PLURAL NOUN all the money that someone wins from bets or gambling

winter NOUN **winters** the coldest season of the year, between autumn and spring
ADJECTIVE happening or used during winter: *a warm winter coat* • *the winter months*
▶ **wintry** ADJECTIVE cold, like winter

wipe VERB **wipes, wiping, wiped 1** to wipe something is to rub its surface to clean it or dry it **2** (*ICT*) to wipe a computer disk, or a sound or video tape, is to remove all the information, sound or images on it
• **wipe something** *or* **someone out** to destroy someone or something and get rid of them completely
NOUN **wipes 1** an act of wiping: *I need to give my glasses a wipe.* **2** a piece of cloth or tissue used to wipe things with
▶ **wiper** NOUN **wipers** a piece of rubber on a metal support that moves to and fro and clears water from a vehicle's windscreen

wire NOUN **wires 1** metal that has been pulled into a long narrow strand that bends easily **2** a length of wire, or several pieces of it twisted into a cable for carrying electricity or telephone signals
VERB **wires, wiring, wired 1** to wire a house is to fit the cables that are needed to carry electricity to lights and plugs **2** to wire or wire up a piece of equipment is to fit it with electrical cables or a plug so that it can be connected to the power supply

wireless NOUN **wirelesses** an old-fashioned word for a radio

wiry ADJECTIVE **wirier, wiriest 1** someone who is wiry has a slim but strong body **2** wiry hair is strong and curly

wisdom NOUN being able to make sensible decisions about things, based on your knowledge and experience

wisdom tooth NOUN **wisdom teeth** your wisdom teeth are the big teeth at the back of your mouth that grow when you are an adult

✦ Wisdom teeth are so called because they grow when you are an adult, and so have become wiser.

wise ADJECTIVE **wiser, wisest 1** sensible: *a wise decision* • *She was wise enough not to say anything to him.* **2** if you are wise to something, you know about it

wish VERB **wishes, wishing, wished 1** to want something and hope that it will happen: *I wish it would stop raining.* • *What did you wish for when you blew out the candles on your cake?* **2** to want to do something or want it to be done: *Do you wish to pay now or later?* **3** you wish someone something when you say that you hope they will have it: *We all wish you luck.*
NOUN **wishes** something you wish for or want: *Make a wish.*

wishbone NOUN **wishbones** the thin V-shaped bone at the top of a chicken's or other bird's breast. The wishbone is often pulled apart by two people and the person who gets the bigger piece makes a wish

wisp NOUN **wisps** a wisp of smoke or hair is a long, thin, delicate piece or line of it
▶ **wispy** ADJECTIVE **wispier, wispiest** wispy hair or smoke forms wisps

wistful ADJECTIVE if you are wistful, you long sadly for something that you know you cannot have
▶ **wistfully** ADVERB in a wistful way: *He gazed wistfully at the beautiful toy train in the shop window.*

wit NOUN **wits 1** intelligence and common sense **2** a clever humour
• **have your wits about you** if you have your wits about you, you are alert and ready to deal with anything that happens

witch NOUN **witches** a woman or girl

who is supposed to have special magic powers

▶ **witchcraft** NOUN the magic and spells that witches do, especially to make something bad happen

witch doctor NOUN **witch doctors** a man who uses magic to heal people in his tribe

with PREPOSITION

1 in the company of or in the same place as: *Come with me.* • *She keeps her diary on the shelf with her school books.*

2 using: *We stuck it down with glue.*

3 having: *a house with a green door*

4 going in the same direction: *drifting with the tide*

5 as the result of: *He was doubled up with pain.*

6 against: *They've argued with each other since they were small children.*

7 with is used after verbs about covering, filling or mixing: *He covered the table with a sheet.* • *Mix the dry ingredients with the milk in a large bowl.*

8 with is used after verbs about separating or finishing: *I parted with them at the station.* • *Have you finished with this magazine?*

withdraw VERB **withdraws, withdrawing, withdrawn 1** to withdraw is to retreat or move back or away **2** to withdraw something is to remove it or take it back: *I would like to withdraw what I said earlier.* • *He withdrew all his money from his bank account.*

▶ **withdrawal** NOUN **withdrawals 1** withdrawing from something or somewhere **2** a sum of money that you take out of your bank account

wither VERB **withers, withering, withered** a plant withers when it shrinks and dries up

withhold VERB **withholds, withholding, withheld** to withhold something is to refuse to give it to someone

within PREPOSITION **1** inside: *They felt safe within the castle walls.* **2** in no more than, or less than: *We'll be home*

within the hour. **3** not beyond: *A place in the final is within your reach.*

ADVERB inside: *The notice on the restaurant window said: 'Waiters wanted. Apply within.'*

without PREPOSITION not with or not having: *They left without me.* • *Do you take coffee with or without milk?*

withstand VERB **withstands, withstanding, withstood** to withstand something is to bear it successfully: *The buildings are specially designed to withstand earthquakes.*

witness NOUN **witnesses 1** someone who sees an event happening and can tell other people about it: *Were there any witnesses to the accident?* **2** someone who is a witness in a court case gives evidence about the facts of the case

VERB **witnesses, witnessing, witnessed** to witness something is to see it happening

witty ADJECTIVE **wittier, wittiest** a witty person, or a witty comment, is clever and funny

▶ **wittily** ADVERB in a clever and amusing way

wives PLURAL NOUN the plural of **wife**: *Henry the Eighth had six wives.*

wizard NOUN **wizards** a man or boy who is supposed to have special magic powers

▶ **wizardry** NOUN **1** magic performed by a wizard **2** clever or surprising things, especially done using machines: *technical wizardry*

wobble VERB **wobbles, wobbling, wobbled** to rock or move from side to side unsteadily

▶ **wobbly** ADJECTIVE **wobblier, wobbliest** something that is wobbly shakes or moves about unsteadily

woe NOUN **woes 1** woe is sorrow, grief or misery **2** a woe is something that causes grief or misery: *He told me all his woes.*

▶ **woeful** ADJECTIVE **1** miserable or unhappy **2** feeble or useless: *a woeful attempt to be funny*

▶ **woefully** ADVERB miserably or unhappily

Aa Bb Cc Dd Ee Ff Gg Hh Ii Jj Kk Ll Mm Nn Oo Pp Qq Rr Ss Tt Uu Vv **Ww** Xx Yy Zz

wok NOUN **woks** a type of pan shaped like a large bowl, used to cook Chinese-style food

woke VERB a way of changing the verb **wake** to make a past tense: *He woke with a start.*

woken VERB the form of the verb **wake** that is used with a helping verb to show that something happened in the past: *He had woken with a start.*

wolf NOUN **wolves** a wild animal like a dog, which lives in family groups called packs

• **cry wolf** to cry wolf is to give a warning of danger when there is no danger

VERB **wolfs, wolfing, wolfed** to wolf food or wolf it down is to eat it very quickly and greedily

woman NOUN **women** an adult female human being

▶ **womanhood** NOUN being a woman

▶ **womanly** ADJECTIVE like a woman or having the qualities people expect a woman to have

womb (pronounced **woom**) NOUN **wombs** the organ inside a female animal's body where her babies grow until they are ready to be born

won VERB a way of changing the verb **win** to make a past tense. It can be used with or without a helping verb: *We won the cup.* • *We'd won it for four years running.*

wonder VERB **wonders, wondering, wondered 1** you wonder about things when you are curious about them or cannot decide about them: *I wonder what Jack has bought me for Christmas.* **2** you wonder at something when you are surprised by it **3** you use 'I wonder if' when you are asking someone politely about or for something: *I wonder if you could tell me where the post office is?*

NOUN **wonders 1** wonder is the feeling you get when you see something extraordinary or surprising: *The comet filled people who saw it with wonder.* **2** a wonder is something unexpected or extraordinary: *It's a wonder you didn't freeze to death out in that blizzard.*

▶ **wonderful** ADJECTIVE extraordinary or marvellous: *a wonderful view of the mountains*

▶ **wonderfully** ADVERB in a marvellous way: *The concert went wonderfully.*

▶ **wondrous** ADJECTIVE (*formal*) astonishing or impressive: *a wondrous sight*

won't a short way to say and write **will not**: *He won't tell me what he saw.*

wood NOUN **woods 1** wood is the hard material that forms the trunks and branches of trees. It is cut up to make furniture, buildings and paper **2** a wood or the woods is an area of forest or woodland

▶ **wooded** ADJECTIVE a wooded area has a lot of trees growing on it

▶ **wooden** ADJECTIVE **1** made of wood: *wooden toys* **2** a wooden action, expression or behaviour is stiff and unnatural

woodland NOUN **woodlands** land covered with trees

woodlouse NOUN **woodlice** a small creature similar to a beetle, that lives in rotten wood or damp areas

woodpecker NOUN **woodpeckers** a wild bird that uses its strong beak to peck holes in trees to find the insects it eats

woodwind NOUN (*music*) the instruments in an orchestra that are made from wood, such as the oboe, clarinet and bassoon

woodwork NOUN making objects out of wood, using tools like saws, planes and chisels

woodworm NOUN **woodworm** a young form of a type of beetle, which eats wood

woody ADJECTIVE **woodier, woodiest 1** made of wood, or like wood: *a woody smell* **2** full of trees

wool NOUN **1** the soft fibre that grows on the bodies of sheep **2** a thread made from this fibre, used for knitting and making cloth: *a ball of wool.*

▶ **woollen** ADJECTIVE made of wool: *a woollen blanket*

▶ **woollens** PLURAL NOUN jumpers and

Aa
Bb
Cc
Dd
Ee
Ff
Gg
Hh
Ii
Jj
Kk
Ll
Mm
Nn
Oo
Pp
Qq
Rr
Ss
Tt
Uu
Vv
Ww
Xx
Yy
Zz

cardigans made of wool, especially knitted wool

▶ **woolly** ADJECTIVE **woollier, woolliest** covered with wool or with hair that is dense and curly like wool

word NOUN **words 1** a unit of language that is written as a group of letters with spaces on either side **2** to get word about something is to get news about it **3** if you give your word, you give your solemn promise that you will do something

VERB **words, wording, worded** you word something in a certain way when you choose words to express it

▶ **wording** NOUN the wording of something is which words have been used to express it

▶ **wordy** ADJECTIVE **wordier, wordiest** using a lot of words, especially too many words: *a long wordy explanation of what happened*

word class NOUN **word classes** word classes are the various groups that words belong to depending on the job they do. The parts of speech you will find in this dictionary are noun, pronoun, verb, adjective, adverb, preposition, conjunction and interjection

word processing NOUN (*ICT*) using a word processor or a computer to create documents

▶ **word processor** NOUN **word processors** (*ICT*) an electronic machine, with a keyboard and a screen, used to type letters and other documents

wore VERB a way of changing the verb **wear** to make a past tense: *She wore an old pair of jeans.*

work NOUN **works**

1 someone's work is their job or employment: *Dad leaves for work about 8 o'clock in the morning.*

2 work is something you do that needs effort: *It was hard work climbing to the top with heavy packs on our backs.*

3 your work is what you create by working: *The teacher marked my work.*

4 a work is something produced by an artist or composer

5 a works is a factory or workshop

6 the works of a machine or clock are the parts inside it that make it operate

VERB **works, working, worked**

1 you work when you do something that needs effort or energy

2 people who work have a job

3 a machine that works operates properly

4 a plan works when it is successful

5 to work something is to make it operate

6 if something works loose, it slackens or becomes loose slowly

• **work out** something works out a certain way when it turns out that way at the end

• **work something out** you work out something such as a problem when you think about it carefully until you find the answer

▶ **worker** NOUN **workers 1** someone who works for a living, especially in a particular industry: *steel workers* **2** a bee, ant, or termite that does the work in the colony, for example feeding the queen and looking after the eggs

working class NOUN **working classes** the working class is the people in society who do manual or factory work, or similar jobs

workman NOUN **workmen** a man who works with his hands, especially doing building work

workmanship NOUN workmanship is the skill that a craftsman has in making things

worksheet NOUN **worksheets** a sheet listing work that has to be done or that has been done

workshop NOUN **workshops** a place or business where things are built, made or repaired

world NOUN **worlds 1** the Earth or all the people living on it: *The whole world is affected by global warming.* **2** a planet: *a creature from another world* **3** all the people and things that are connected with an activity or subject: *the world of sport*

▶ **worldly** ADJECTIVE **worldlier, worldliest 1** to do with the Earth and life on Earth **2** your worldly goods are all the things that belong to you **3** a worldly person is only interested in things like money and possessions, not in the spirit or the soul

worldwide ADJECTIVE AND ADVERB everywhere in the world

World Wide Web NOUN (ICT) the World Wide Web is a huge network of computers all round the world where you can find information about almost anything

worm NOUN **worms** a small creature with a long, soft body and no legs

VERB **worms, worming, wormed** to worm your way somewhere is to get there by wriggling through small spaces

• **worm something out of someone** to get information from someone gradually and with great difficulty

worn VERB the form of the verb **wear** that is used with a helping verb to show that something happened in the past: *She had worn the dress before.*

ADJECTIVE worn things are damaged by rubbing or wearing: *The carpet is worn and dirty.*

• **worn out** very tired

worry VERB **worries, worrying, worried 1** to worry about a problem is to keep thinking about it in an anxious way because you are not sure how to deal with it or how it will turn out **2** to worry someone is to disturb them and make them anxious or upset

NOUN **worries 1** worry is being anxious **2** a worry is something that makes you anxious

▸ **worried** ADJECTIVE anxious

▸ **worrier** NOUN **worriers** a person who worries, especially all the time

worse ADJECTIVE **worse** is the comparative form of the adjective **bad**, which you use when you are comparing how bad things are: *My brother's room is a worse mess than mine.*

ADVERB more badly, or more severely: *It was raining worse than ever.*

▸ **worsen** VERB **worsens, worsening, worsened 1** something worsens when it becomes worse than it was before

2 to worsen something is to make it worse

worship VERB **worships, worshipping, worshipped 1** to honour a god or gods by praising them and praying to them **2** to love or admire someone or something, especially in a way that stops you seeing their faults

NOUN religious services and other ways of worshipping: *a place of worship*

▸ **worshipper** NOUN **worshippers** someone who worships, especially in a church or temple

worst ADJECTIVE worst is the superlative form of the adjective **bad**, which you use when you are describing something as the most bad: *It was the worst storm we'd ever seen.*

ADVERB badly to the greatest degree: *I did worst in the test.*

worth NOUN **1** something's worth is its value or importance **2** someone's worth is their usefulness or value

ADJECTIVE **1** what something is worth is how much money it is valued at: *The ring is worth £1000.* **2** if something is worth doing or worth considering, it is useful or deserves to be considered

▸ **worthless** ADJECTIVE a worthless person or thing has no value or use

worthwhile ADJECTIVE something that is worthwhile is worth doing or getting involved in because it results in something good

worthy ADJECTIVE **worthier, worthiest 1** to be worthy of something is to deserve it **2** a worthy person, or a worthy cause, deserves to be given respect or support

would VERB **1** a way of changing the verb **will** to make a past tense: *She said she would be in touch later.* **2** you use **would** to ask people if they want something or if they will do something: *Would you like a new bike for your birthday?* • *Would you close the door behind you, please.*

wouldn't a short way to say and write **would not**: *She wouldn't go.*

wound[1] VERB a way of changing the verb **wind** to make a past tense. It can be used with or without a helping verb: *She wound a long, red, knitted scarf around her neck.* • *He had wound the old grandfather clock in the hall.*

wound² (pronounced **woond**) NOUN **wounds** an injury to a person's or animal's body in which the skin has been damaged by a cut or other injury

VERB **wounds, wounding, wounded 1** to wound a person or animal is to cause an injury to their body **2** to wound someone is to hurt their feelings

▸ **wounded** ADJECTIVE a wounded person or animal has been injured

wove VERB a way of changing the verb **weave** to make a past tense: *She wove flowers into her hair.*

woven VERB the form of the verb **weave** that is used with a helping verb to show that something happened in the past: *The scarves were woven from wool.*

wrap VERB **wraps, wrapping, wrapped 1** to wrap something, or to wrap something up, is to put a covering of paper or other material round it **2** to put something like paper or cloth round another thing to cover it: *She wrapped the bandage round my knee.*

▸ **wrapper** NOUN **wrappers** a piece of paper or plastic that something is wrapped in

wrath NOUN (*formal*) great anger

wreak VERB **wreaks, wreaking, wreaked** to wreak something, such as havoc, damage or revenge, is to cause it

wreath NOUN **wreaths** an arrangement of flowers and leaves in the shape of a ring, which is put on a dead person's coffin or grave, or hung up on a door at Christmas time

wreathe VERB **wreathes, wreathing, wreathed** one thing is wreathed in another when it is covered or surrounded by that other thing

wreck VERB **wrecks, wrecking, wrecked 1** to wreck something is to damage it or destroy it **2** a ship is wrecked when it is badly damaged, for example by hitting rocks, and can no longer sail

NOUN **wrecks** a badly damaged ship or an aeroplane or vehicle that has crashed

▸ **wreckage** NOUN the broken or damaged pieces left after something has been wrecked

wren NOUN **wrens** a tiny wild bird with brown feathers and a short tail

wrench VERB **wrenches, wrenching, wrenched** to pull or twist something very hard so that it comes out of its position

NOUN **wrenches 1** a hard pull or twist **2** a tool used to turn things

wrestle VERB **wrestles, wrestling, wrestled 1** to wrestle with someone is to fight with them by gripping them and trying to throw them over or hold them down on the ground **2** to wrestle with a problem is to try very hard to solve it

▸ **wrestler** NOUN **wrestlers** someone who fights by wrestling

▸ **wrestling** NOUN the sport of fighting using special holds and movements to throw your opponent to the ground and to hold them there

wretch NOUN **wretches** a very wicked or very miserable person

▸ **wretched** (pronounced **re**-chid) ADJECTIVE **1** very poor and miserable: *They lived in a wretched little shack in the woods.* **2** very annoying: *Where's that wretched cat?*

wriggle VERB **wriggles, wriggling, wriggled** to twist about: *Stop wriggling about in your chair and sit still!*

▸ **wriggly** ADJECTIVE **wrigglier, wriggliest** a wriggly line has lots of twists and bends in it

wring VERB **wrings, wringing, wrung 1** to twist or squeeze a wet cloth or wet washing so that all or most of the water is forced out **2** to wring something, such as someone's hand, is to twist or squeeze it hard

wrinkle NOUN **wrinkles 1** wrinkles are lines and creases that form in your skin as you get older **2** a wrinkle is a crease or ridge in the surface of something

VERB **wrinkles, wrinkling, wrinkled** you wrinkle your forehead or your nose when you screw it up so that the skin forms into little creases or lines

Aa
Bb
Cc
Dd
Ee
Ff
Gg
Hh
Ii
Jj
Kk
Ll
Mm
Nn
Oo
Pp
Qq
Rr
Ss
Tt
Uu
Vv
Ww
Xx
Yy
Zz

Aa
Bb
Cc
Dd
Ee
Ff
Gg
Hh
Ii
Jj
Kk
Ll
Mm
Nn
Oo
Pp
Qq
Rr
Ss
Tt
Uu
Vv
Ww
Xx
Yy
Zz

▶ **wrinkly** ADJECTIVE **wrinklier, wrinkliest** having lots of wrinkles

wrist NOUN **wrists** one of the two parts of your body where your arms join your hands

write VERB **writes, writing, wrote, written 1** to form letters and words, usually on paper using a pen or pencil **2** you write to someone when you write or type a letter and send it to them **3** to write a story, article, play or music is to create it and write it down

• **write something off** to think of something as being lost or too damaged to be used again

▶ **writer** NOUN **writers** someone who writes books, plays, film scripts or newspaper articles

▶ **writing** NOUN **writings 1** writing is forming letters and words on paper or some other surface so that they can be read **2** your writing is the way you write **3** an author's writings are the things he or she has written

wrong ADJECTIVE **1** not right or not satisfactory: *Is there something wrong with David? He doesn't look happy.* • *Cheating in examinations is wrong.* **2** not correct: *That was the wrong answer.* **3** not suitable: *He has decided he's in the wrong job.*
ADVERB wrongly or incorrectly: *I think I have spelt your name wrong.*

▶ **wrongly** ADVERB not correctly or accurately: *The plug had been fitted wrongly so the machine did not work.*

wrote VERB a way of changing the verb **write** to make a past tense: *He wrote a letter to his pen friend.*

wrung VERB a way of changing the verb **wring** to make a past tense. It can be used with or without a helping verb: *The woman wrung her hands.* • *He had wrung all the water out of the mop.*

wry ADJECTIVE **wryer, wryest** a wry smile, comment or sense of humour is one that shows gentle amusement at something that has gone wrong

WWW or **www** ABBREVIATION (*ICT*) short for **World Wide Web**

Xmas NOUN an informal short spelling of **Christmas**

X-ray NOUN **X-rays** a special kind of photograph that shows the inside of something, especially the inside of someone's body

VERB **X-rays, X-raying, X-rayed** to make an X-ray of something

xylophone NOUN **xylophones** a musical instrument made up of a set of wooden bars that make different notes when you hit them with hammers

> ✦ This word comes from the Greek word **xylon**, which means *wood*, together with the English ending **phone**, which means *sound*, because the instrument has wooden keys.
> Other words in which **phone** means *sound* are **telephone** and **headphones**.

Yy

yacht NOUN **yachts** a sailing boat that you use for racing or for pleasure trips

yachtsman or **yachtswoman** NOUN **yachtsmen** or **yachtswomen** a man or a woman who sails a yacht

yak NOUN **yaks** a type of ox that is found in Central Asia and which has long hair and horns

yam NOUN **yams** a vegetable like a potato that grows in tropical countries

yank VERB **yanks, yanking, yanked** to pull something sharply and roughly: *He yanked the book out of my hand.*
NOUN **yanks** a sudden sharp pull

yap VERB **yaps, yapping, yapped** if a dog yaps, it makes a high-pitched bark
NOUN **yaps** a high-pitched bark

yard[1] NOUN **yards** an imperial unit for measuring length, equal to 91 centimetres or 3 feet

yard[2] NOUN **yards 1** an enclosed area of land used for a particular purpose: *a builders' yard* **2** an American English word for **garden**

yarn NOUN **yarns 1** wool or cotton that has been spun into thread **2** a story that is often long, and might include things that are not true: *The old sailor spun as long a yarn as possible.*

yashmak NOUN **yashmaks** a type of veil that some Muslim women wear

yawn VERB **yawns, yawning, yawned 1** to open your mouth very wide and breathe in, because you are feeling tired or bored **2** if a hole yawns, it is wide open: *The mouth of the cave yawned below them.*
NOUN **yawns** the sound or action of someone yawning

ye PRONOUN an old-fashioned word for **you**

year NOUN **years** a period of 365 days, or 366 days in a leap year, especially the period from 1 January to 31 December. It is based on the length of time it takes for the Earth to go around the sun
▶ **yearly** ADJECTIVE happening every year: *our yearly holiday*

yearn VERB **yearns, yearning, yearned** to yearn for something is to want it very much: *Harry yearned for a guitar of his own.*

yeast NOUN a substance that you add to dough to make bread rise

yell VERB **yells, yelling, yelled** to shout or scream: *'Let me go!' she yelled.*
NOUN **yells** a shout or scream

yellow NOUN the colour of the sun or the middle of an egg
▶ **yellowish** ADJECTIVE quite yellow but not completely yellow in colour

yelp VERB **yelps, yelping, yelped** if a dog yelps, it makes a short, high sound because it is in pain
NOUN **yelps** a short, high sound

yes ADVERB a word you say when you agree with someone or something

yesterday NOUN the day before today
ADVERB on the day before today

yet ADVERB **1** by now, by this time: *Have you read her new book yet?* **2** before something is finished, still: *We might win this game yet.* **3** in addition, besides: *After London, we visited yet more places.*
CONJUCTION however, nevertheless: *He seemed friendly, yet I did not trust him.*
• **as yet** up till now: *I would like to go to Paris but I haven't been as yet.*

Yeti NOUN **Yetis** a hairy creature that looks like a large man and who is supposed to live in the Himalayas

yew NOUN **yews** a tree with very dark green leaves

yield VERB **yields, yielding, yielded 1** to give in or surrender: *The army yielded to the enemy.* **2** to give way to pressure or force: *The door suddenly yielded and he fell into the room.* **3** to yield something is to produce it: *Rich*

626

soil yields good harvests. • *The old book started to yield up its secrets.*

NOUN **yields** the amount of something that is produced: *cows with a high milk yield*

yodel VERB **yodels, yodelling, yodelled** to sing or shout, changing back and forth from your normal voice to a very high voice

yoga NOUN a system of exercise from Hindu beliefs, in which you stretch your muscles, breathe deeply and meditate

yogurt *or* **yoghurt** NOUN **yogurts** *or* **yoghurts 1** a runny food with a slightly sour taste that is made from milk **2** a pot of this food: *a strawberry yogurt*

yoke NOUN **yokes** a wooden frame that you put around the necks of a pair of oxen when they are pulling a cart

VERB **yokes, yoking, yoked** to fasten two things together with a yoke

yolk NOUN **yolks** the yellow part in the middle of an egg

Yom Kippur NOUN a Jewish religious day when people do not eat. It is also called the Day of Atonement

yonder ADVERB an old-fashioned word for 'in that place'

ADJECTIVE over there: *Take my sword and go with it to yonder water side.*

you PRONOUN a word you use to the person or people that you are talking to: *Do you like pizza?* • *Max is taller than you.*

you'd a short way to say or write **you had** or **you would**: *You'd better be careful.* • *You'd be sorry if she left.*

you'll a short way to say and write **you will**: *You'll never guess what happened next!*

young ADJECTIVE **younger, youngest** not old: *a young boy*

NOUN **1** the babies that an animal or bird has: *a sparrow feeding its young* **2** the young are young people

▸ **youngster** NOUN **youngsters** a young person

your ADJECTIVE belonging to the person or people you are talking to: *Can I borrow your ruler?*

> ✦ Be careful not to confuse the spellings of **your** and **you're**.
>
> **Your** means something belongs to the person you are talking to: *I like your shoes.*
>
> **You're** is short for **you are**: *You're my best friend.*

you're a short way to say and write **you are**: *You're a better singer than he is.*

yours PRONOUN a word you use to talk about something belonging to a person or people you are talking to: *Which glass is yours?*

• **Yours faithfully, Yours sincerely** *or* **Yours truly** words that you write before your name at the end of a formal letter

yourself PRONOUN **yourselves 1** you use the words **yourself** or **yourselves** when the person or people you are talking to performs the action of a verb but is also affected by it : *Careful you don't cut yourself on that knife.* • *You'll have to dry yourselves on your T-shirts.* **2** on your own, without any help from anyone else: *Did you really make that skirt yourself?*

youth NOUN **youths 1** the time in your life when you are young: *She spent most of her youth abroad.* **2** a young man aged between about 15 and 20: *a gang of youths* **3** young people as a group: *the youth of today*

▸ **youthful** ADJECTIVE young: *a youthful-looking fifty-year-old.*

you've a short way to say and write **you have**: *You've left the door open again.*

yo-yo NOUN **yo-yos** a toy that is made up of a circular object on a piece of string that you have to try to keep spinning up and down

Aa
Bb
Cc
Dd
Ee
Ff
Gg
Hh
Ii
Jj
Kk
Ll
Mm
Nn
Oo
Pp
Qq
Rr
Ss
Tt
Uu
Vv
Ww
Xx
Yy
Zz

Zz

zany ADJECTIVE **zanier, zaniest** crazy or funny: *a zany sense of humour*

> ✦ This word comes from the name **Zanni**, who was a clown in old Italian comedy plays.

zap VERB **zaps, zapping, zapped** (*slang*) **1** to shoot, kill or destroy something, for example in a computer game **2** to move quickly: *zapping through the TV channels*

zeal NOUN enthusiasm and keenness

> ▸ **zealous** (pronounced **zel**-us) ADJECTIVE very enthusiastic about something: *a zealous supporter of the local team*

zebra NOUN **zebras** an animal like a horse with black and white stripes

zebra crossing NOUN **zebra crossings** a place where you can cross a road, marked in black and white stripes

zenith NOUN the highest point in something: *Scoring those five goals was the zenith of his career.*

zero NOUN **zeros** nothing, or the number 0: *There are six zeros in one million.*

zest NOUN a lot of enjoyment and enthusiasm: *Joe had a great zest for life.*

zigzag ADJECTIVE with lots of sharp bends from left to right: *a zigzag pattern*

VERB **zigzags, zigzagging, zigzagged** to have a lot of sharp bends from left to right: *The path zigzagged up the hillside.*

zimmer NOUN **zimmers** (*trademark*) a metal frame that old people sometimes use to help them walk

zinc NOUN a bluish-white metal

zip NOUN **zips** a fastener on clothes or bags that has two rows of metal or plastic teeth that fit tightly together

when a sliding piece is pulled along them

VERB **zips, zipping, zipped** **1** to fasten something with a zip: *Zip up your jacket, it's cold.* **2** to move somewhere very quickly: *The bullet zipped by his head.* **3** (*ICT*) to make the information on a computer file fit into a much smaller space so that it uses up less memory

zodiac NOUN in astrology, an imaginary strip in the sky that has twelve parts that are named after constellations, for example *Capricorn* and *Aquarius*

zombie NOUN **zombies** **1** a dead body that is supposed to come back to life through witchcraft **2** someone who seems to be very slow or stupid

zone NOUN **zones** an area or part of a place that people set aside and use for a particular purpose: *a no-parking zone*

zoo NOUN **zoos** a place where people keep wild animals to breed them and study them, and where you can go to see these animals

> ✦ The word **zoo** comes from the Greek word **zoion**, which means *animal*.

zoology NOUN the study of animals

> ▸ **zoological** ADJECTIVE to do with animals

> ▸ **zoologist** NOUN **zoologists** a person who studies animals

zoom VERB **zooms, zooming, zoomed** **1** to go somewhere very fast, especially with a loud buzzing noise: *The rocket zoomed up into the air.* **2** if a camera zooms in or out, it makes the thing that is being filmed or photographed look much bigger or smaller

zoom lens NOUN **zoom lenses** a lens on a camera that can make things look bigger or smaller